PRODUCTS LIABILITY

CASES AND MATERIALS

Second Edition

By

David A. Fischer

James Lewis Parks Professor of Law
University of Missouri-Columbia

William Powers, Jr.

Hines H. Baker and Thelma Kelley Baker Chair in Law
University of Texas at Austin

AMERICAN CASEBOOK SERIES®

WEST PUBLISHING CO.
ST. PAUL, MINN., 1994

COPYRIGHT © 1988 WEST PUBLISHING CO.
COPYRIGHT © 1994 By WEST PUBLISHING CO.
                        610 Opperman Drive
                        P.O. Box 64526
                        St. Paul, MN 55164–0526
                        1–800–328–9352
All rights reserved
Printed in the United States of America

Library of Congress Cataloging-in-Publication Data

Fischer, David A., 1943–
    Cases and materials on products liability / by David A. Fischer,
William Powers, Jr. — 2nd ed.
        p.   cm. — (American casebook series)
    Rev. ed. of: Products liability. 1988.
    Includes index.
    ISBN 0–314–03511–7
    1. Products liability—United States—Cases.   I. Powers, William,
1946–   . II. Fischer, David A., 1943–   Products liability.
III. Title. IV. Series.
KF1296.A7F57 1994
346.7303'8—dc20
[347.30638]   94–7714
                                                        CIP

ISBN 0–314–03511–7
        (F. & P.) Prod.Liab. 2d Ed. ACB

To
Matthew D. Fischer and
Christopher G. Fischer

and

Matthew D. Powers, Katherine E. Powers,
Allison K. Powers, Anne O. Powers, and Reid A. Powers

*

Preface

As products liability teachers know, the law in this field has changed dramatically in the last quarter century. It continues to change. The primary focus of this book is to emphasize the major issues confronting courts today. The historical development of the law and the major problems of the past are covered, but they are not its main focus. We have chosen cases not only to introduce students to major doctrinal developments, but also to provide students with examples of courts intelligently grappling with legal issues. We are interested in students both honing legal reasoning skills and learning the basic doctrine of products liability law.

The book is sufficiently flexible to meet widely varying needs. It is appropriate for use in either a two or a three hour course. Some teachers will want to cover some blocks of material in greater depth than other blocks. The structure of the book permits omission of entire chapters or portions of chapters without disrupting the flow of the course. The material may also be taught out of order. To facilitate this, we have divided the material into more chapters in this edition than in the first edition.

After an introduction in chapter 1, chapters 2–4 address the application of negligence, misrepresentation, and warranty law to products cases. Teachers who want to focus on strict tort liability can omit these chapters. Chapters 5 through 10 address various aspects of strict tort liability. Specific topics are broken out into different chapters, again to help teachers easily pick and choose among topics. Chapters 11 through 17—dealing with causation, scope of liability, punitive damages, contribution and indemnity, defenses, and parties and transactions governed by strict liability—cover issues that are relevant to all pertinent theories of recovery.

Most footnotes are omitted from the main cases and other quoted material. We have renumbered the footnotes that are used. Editor's footnotes are indicated by an asterisk. All omissions, other than footnotes, are indicated by asterisks or brackets.

In preparing this book, we have had the help of some very dedicated people. We especially acknowledge the contributions of Cheryl Poelling and Pamela Grisham.

DAVID A. FISCHER
WILLIAM POWERS, Jr.

February, 1994

Acknowledgments

The authors would like to thank the publishers and authors of the following works for allowing them to include excerpts:

American Law Institute, Restatement of Torts, Second §§ 286; 288A; 288B; 288C; 292; 293; 295A and comments b and c; 328D; 395; 402A and comments f, g, h, j, k, and n; 402B and comments i, j, and caveat; 433A and comment 2; 433B; 444; 500; 552 and comment 2; and 908(1). Copyright © 1965, 1977 by The American Law Institute. Reprinted with permission.

American Law Institute and National Conference of Commissioners on Uniform State Laws, Uniform Commercial Code §§ 1–210(10); 2–102; 2–103(a)(4); 2–105; 2–106(1); 2–106(2); 2–201; 2–202; 2–302; 2–313 and comments 3, 5, 6 and 8; 2–314 and comments 2, 7, 9, 12 and 13; 2–315 and comment 5; 2–316 and comments 1, 2, 8 and 9; 2–318; 2–607 and comment 7; 2–711, 2–713, 2–714; 2–715 and comment 5; 2–719; and 2–725. Copyright © 1978 by The American Law Institute and the National Conference of Commissioners on Uniform State Laws. Reprinted with permission.

Ausness, Unavoidably Unsafe Products and Strict Products Liability: What Liability Rule Should be Applied to the Sellers of Pharmaceutical Products? 78 Ky.L.J. 705, 720–23, 745, 747–48, 749–51 (1989/1990). Copyright © 1990 by the Kentucky Law Journal. Reprinted with permission.

Epstein, Product Liability: The Search for the Middle Ground, 56 N.C.L.Rev. 643, 651. Copyright © 1978 by North Carolina Law Review. Reprinted with permission.

Fischer, Proportional Liability: Statistical Evidence and the Probability Paradox, 46 Vand.L.Rev. 1201, 1202 (1993). Copyright © 1993 by Vanderbilt University School of Law. Reprinted with permission.

Fischer, Products Liability—Proximate Cause, Intervening Cause, and Duty, 52 Mo.L.Rev. 547. Copyright © 1987 by David A. Fischer. Reprinted with permission.

Green, Expert Witnesses and Sufficiency of Evidence in Toxic Substances Litigation: The Legacy of *Agent Orange* and Bendectin Litigation, 86 Nw.L.Rev. 643, 668–71, 674 n. 143 (1992). Copyright © 1992 by Northwestern University, School of Law. Reprinted with permission.

Harris, Enhanced Injury Theory: An Analytic Framework, 62 N.C.L.Rev. 640, 649–650. Copyright © 1984 by North Carolina Law Review. Reprinted with permission.

Klemme, The Enterprise Liability Theory of Torts, 47 U.Colo.L.Rev. 153, 158–165 (1976). Copyright © 1976 by the University of Colorado Law Review, Inc. Reprinted with permission.

Landes and Posner, A Positive Economic Analysis of Products Liability, 14 J.Legal Stud. 535, 553–56 (1985). Copyright © 1985 by the University of Chicago. Reprinted with permission.

Noel, Products Defective Because of Inadequate Directions or Warnings, 23 S.W.L.J. 256, 289. Copyright © 1969 by South West Law Journal. Reprinted with permission.

Owen, Problems in Assessing Punitive Damages Against Manufacturers of Defective Products, 49 U.Chi.L.Rev. 1, 15–25. Copyright © 1982 by University of Chicago Law Review. Reprinted with permission.

R. Posner, Economic Analysis of Law, 161 (3d Ed. 1986). Copyright © 1986 by Richard A. Posner. Reprinted with permission of Richard A. Posner and Little, Brown and Company.

Posner, Strict Liability: A Comment, 2 J.Legal Studies 205–212 (1973). Copyright © 1973 by the University of Chicago. Reprinted with permission.

Powers, A Modest Proposal to Abandon Strict Products Liability, 1991 U.Ill.L.Rev. 639, 644–651, 653–654. Copyright © 1991 by the Board of Trustees of the University of Illinois. Reprinted with permission.

Powers, Texas Products Liability Law. Copyright © 1985 by Butterwith Publishers. Reprinted with permission.

Prosser, The Assault Upon the Citadel (Strict Liability to the Consumer), 69 Yale L.J. 1099, 1106. Copyright © 1960 by Yale Law Journal. Reprinted with permission.

Shavell, Strict Liability Versus Negligence, 9 J.Legal Studies 1, 2–9 (1980). Copyright © 1980 by the University of Chicago. Reprinted with permission.

Walkawiak, ed., Uniform Products Liability Law, §§ 104B and 114. Copyright © 1980 by Matthew Bender (New York). Reprinted with permission.

White & Summers, Handbook of the Law Under the Uniform Commercial Code, §§ 12–5, 12–6. Copyright © 1980 by West Publishing Co. Reprinted with permission.

Comment, Criminal Safeguards and the Punitive Damages Defendant, 34 U.Chi.L.Rev. 408, 417. Copyright © 1967 by University of Chicago Law Review. Reprinted with permission.

Comment, Aircraft Crashworthiness: A Return to the Negligence Standard?, 1980 U.Ill.L.F. 1103, 1120–1122. Copyright © 1980 by University of Illinois Law Forum. Reprinted with permission.

Summary of Contents

Manufacturer

Federal preemption

substantial change

Others to sue in addition tomorrow, Fed. gov , FDA

Table of Contents

———

Table of Cases

The principal cases are in bold type. Cases cited or discussed in the text are roman type. References are to pages. Cases cited in principal cases and within other quoted materials are not included.

Table of Statutes

PRODUCTS LIABILITY

CASES AND MATERIALS

Second Edition

*

Chapter 1

INTRODUCTION

"Products liability" refers to civil liability for injuries caused by defective products. It covers several different theories of liability, including negligence, breach of warranty, strict tort liability and misrepresentation.[1] These theories are not mutually exclusive; a plaintiff can rely on two or more of them in the same lawsuit.

Negligence, warranty, and misrepresentation were developed primarily outside of the context of products liability litigation. Negligence applies to products liability litigation pretty much the same way it applies to other personal injury litigation. Warranty law was developed primarily in the context of commercial dealings. Its roots are in contract law. The law of misrepresentation was also developed primarily in the context of commercial dealings. Its roots are in tort law. Unlike the other three theories, strict tort liability was developed as a special theory to deal with injuries caused by defective products. It currently is the most important theory of product liability.

The main advantage of strict liability is that the plaintiff can recover without a showing of fault. The liability of the defendant, however, is far short of that of an insurer. Plaintiff must prove that the product was defective at the time it left defendant's hands, that the product was used in a foreseeable manner, and that the defect was both the cause in fact and proximate cause of the injury. The theory can only be used against certain classes of potential defendants, e.g., those in the business of selling or leasing products. Recovery is generally limited to cases involving personal injury or property damage. Most courts do not recognize an action for pure economic loss, and some do not permit recovery for damage to the product itself.

Breach of warranty is similar to strict liability both in terms of what plaintiff has to prove and the type of conduct that is recognized as a defense. Warranty law, however, imposes three additional obstacles to recovery which arise because of the contractual nature of the remedy.

---

1. Product cases are also governed by the federal Magnuson–Moss Act, 15 U.S.C. § 2301, *et seq.* and in several states by state consumer protection or deceptive trade practices acts.

1

Privity of contract is sometimes required, plaintiff must give a reasonably prompt notice of breach of warranty, and disclaimers are permitted. Another difference is that the four year warranty statute of limitation begins to run at the time of sale. Tort statutes of limitation generally begin to run at the time of the injury.

Strict liability is generally preferable to warranty in personal injury cases because the plaintiff will not have to concern himself with fulfilling the additional requirements of the warranty action. The warranty theory is of primary importance in cases where strict liability does not apply, such as those involving pure economic loss or harm caused by the sale of used goods.

Negligence is harder to establish than strict liability because plaintiff must prove fault in addition to showing causation in fact and proximate cause of damages. In addition, simple contributory negligence in failing to discover a risk is a defense. Sometimes plaintiffs use negligence, at least as an alternate count of liability, on the theory that the jury will be more generous if it believes that defendant was at fault. There are times when plaintiff may have to resort to a negligence theory because strict liability does not apply. This can occur, for example, where the defendant is not in the business of selling the harmful product.

Strict liability is actually very closely related to both negligence and warranty because it grew out of those theories. Knowledge of the roots of strict liability, and its relationship to negligence and warranty, is necessary to understand this theory.

Two landmark cases—*MacPherson v. Buick Motor Co.*[2] and *Greenman v. Yuba Power Products, Inc.*[3]—divide the history of modern products liability law into three eras. Before *MacPherson*, product manufacturers were given special protection: a plaintiff could recover for injuries caused by *negligently* manufactured products only if he was in privity of contract with the defendant. Privity of contract is an appropriate requirement for actions based on contractual obligations, but foreseeability of injury normally defines a defendant's scope of liability in negligence. Nevertheless, before *MacPherson*, American courts usually required a plaintiff to prove that he was in privity of contract with the defendant in order to recover damages from a negligent seller.[4]

Even before *MacPherson*, courts developed an exception to the privity requirement: negligent manufacturers of *inherently dangerous* products could be held liable to remote plaintiffs with whom they were not in privity of contract.[5] In the late nineteenth and early twentieth centuries, courts applied this exception to increasingly innocuous prod-

---

2. 217 N.Y. 382, 111 N.E. 1050 (1916). *See infra* Chapter 2, p. 5.

3. 59 Cal. 2d 57, 27 Cal.Rptr. 697, 377 P.2d 897 (1976). *See infra* Chapter 5, p. 127.

4. The source of the rule was the English case of Winterbottom v. Wright, 10 M. & W. 109, 152 Eng.Rep. 402 (Ex. 1842).

5. *See e.g.* Thomas v. Winchester, 6 N.Y. 397 (1852) (poisonous drug).

ucts.[6] In *MacPherson*, Justice Cardozo applied the exception to an automobile with a defective wheel, holding that the privity rule is not applicable to any product that is dangerous when defective. Since most products that cause injuries are dangerous when defective, *MacPherson* effectively sounded the death knell of the privity rule.

After *MacPherson*, American products liability law entered its second phase. Privity was no longer a hurdle to recovery in products liability cases. During this second phase of American products liability law, product cases were treated like other negligence cases, and a plaintiff was still required to prove that the defendant had failed to use reasonable care. Plaintiffs often faced a difficult burden in proving negligence because the manufacturer's alleged negligent conduct usually occurred prior to the plaintiff's connection with the product or the manufacturer. Moreover, the manufacturer's alleged negligent conduct usually occurred at a location under the manufacturer's control.

During this era a plaintiff could also sue for breach of implied or express warranty. A plaintiff was not required to prove negligence in a suit for breach of warranty, but this theory of recovery posed its own obstacle, since a plaintiff was required to prove privity of contract. *MacPherson* abolished the privity rule in cases based on negligence, not in cases based on breach of warranty. Nevertheless, courts began to whittle away at the privity requirement in warranty cases, first in cases involving implied warranties for food purchased by a member of the plaintiff's family,[7] and then more generally.[8]

Greenman v. Yuba Power Products, Inc.,[9] decided by the California Supreme Court in 1963, ushered in the third stage of modern products liability law by adopting strict tort liability for sellers of defective products. Strict tort liability requires neither privity of contract nor proof of negligence, and it is not subject to disclaimers and the requirement of notice that are applicable to warranties under the Uniform Commercial Code.[10] In 1964, the American Law Institute adopted section 402A of the Restatement (Second) of Torts, which followed *Greenman* and embodied its theory of strict tort liability for sellers of defective products.

See generally Priest, The Invention of Enterprise Liability: A Critical History of the Intellectual Foundations of Modern Tort Law, 14 J.Legal Stud. 461 (1985); Schwartz, The Beginning and the Possible End of the Rise of Modern American Tort Law, 26 Ga.L.Rev. 601 (1992); Spacone, The Emergence of Strict Liability: A Historical Perspective and Other Considerations, Including Senate 100, 8 J.Prod.Liab. 1 (1985).

6. *See e.g.* Devlin v. Smith, 89 N.Y. 470 (1882) (scaffolding); Statler v. George A. Ray Mfg. Co., 195 N.Y. 478, 88 N.E. 1063 (1909) (coffee urn).

7. Greenberg v. Lorenz, 9 N.Y.2d 195, 213 N.Y.S.2d 39, 173 N.E.2d 773 (1961).

8. *See* Henningsen v. Bloomfield Motors, Inc., 32 N.J. 358, 161 A.2d 69 (1960);

Prosser, The Assault Upon the Citadel (Strict Liability to the Consumer), 69 Yale L.J. 1099 (1960).

9. 59 Cal.2d 57, 27 Cal.Rptr. 697, 377 P.2d 897 (1963).

10. *See* Uniform Commercial Code (U.C.C.) §§ 2–316, 2–607.

Chapter 2

NEGLIGENCE

SECTION A. INTRODUCTION

Actionable negligence requires unreasonable conduct that is both a cause in fact and a proximate (or legal cause) of damages. The reasonableness of the conduct is a question for the jury which involves two separate questions. The first is whether a reasonable person in the position of defendant, before the alleged negligent act, would have recognized that the act would create a risk of harm to others. This is purely a question of fact. The second is whether the foreseeable risk is unreasonable, that is, whether the risk is justified by the benefit to be gained by taking it. This requires the jury to exercise judgement about the conduct, and is not a question of fact in the usual sense. Damages are an essential element of the tort of negligence. Thus, the negligent conduct is actionable only if it is both the actual and proximate cause of harm.

Contributory negligence is the most important defense to the negligence action. It is very much like negligence except it requires plaintiff to disregard an unreasonable risk of harm to himself rather than to others. The unreasonable act must be both the actual and proximate cause of plaintiff's harm. Contributory negligence takes two forms. One involves the unreasonable failure to recognize the risk. The other involves the conscious encountering of a known risk.

Contributory negligence is no longer a complete defense in most jurisdictions because of the adoption of comparative negligence. This doctrine reduces plaintiff's recovery in accordance with his relative fault. There are two types of comparative negligence, modified and pure. Under the modified type, plaintiff is completely barred if his negligence exceeds a certain threshold, e.g., more than fifty percent. Under the pure type, plaintiff can always recover something as long as some actionable negligence is attributable to defendant.

Some jurisdictions continue to recognize assumption of risk as a separate defense, while others no longer recognize it except in cases where it happens to also constitute some other defense, such as contributory or comparative negligence. Assumption of risk differs from contrib-

4

utory negligence in several ways. First, it requires that plaintiff be subjectively aware of the risk. Second, the assumption of risk must be voluntary. Third, plaintiff's conduct need not be unreasonable to constitute the defense.

See generally Noel, Manufacturer's Liability for Negligence, 33 Tenn.L.Rev. 444 (1966); Noel, Manufacturer's Negligence of Design or Directions for Use of a Product, 71 Yale L.J. 816 (1962).

SECTION B. DUTY/PRIVITY

In the early days of the law of products liability, manufacturers and sellers of products were given a number of immunities which narrowly restricted the scope of potential liability. One of the most important was the requirement of privity of contract between the plaintiff and defendant as a necessary condition for maintaining a negligence action. The origin of this rule was Winterbottom v. Wright, 10 M. & W. 109, 152 Eng.Rep. 402 (1842). This case held that a person who negligently repaired a stagecoach could not be liable to a passenger injured in an accident resulting from his negligence because the passenger did not have a contract with the defendant. The court stated:

> There is no privity of contract between these parties; and if the plaintiff can sue, every passenger, or even any person passing along the road, who was injured by the upsetting of the coach, might bring a similar action. Unless we confine the operation of such contracts as this to the parties who entered into them, the most absurd and outrageous consequences, to which I can see no limit, would ensue.

Even though *Winterbottom v. Wright* was not a products liability case, courts subsequently applied the rule to negligence actions against sellers of products. Courts gradually began to recognize some exceptions to the privity requirement. The most important was for products that were "imminently" or "inherently" dangerous to human life. In the case of such products, a negligent manufacturer could be liable to a person injured by the product even though there was no privity of contract.

A second immunity that benefited defendants was the rule that product sellers would not be liable for harm caused by products with known or obvious dangers. In other words, dangerous products could give rise to liability only if they possessed latent or unknown dangers.

MacPHERSON v. BUICK MOTOR CO.
Court of Appeals of New York, 1916.
217 N.Y. 382, 111 N.E. 1050.

CARDOZO, J. The defendant is a manufacturer of automobiles. It sold an automobile to a retail dealer. The retail dealer resold to the plaintiff. While the plaintiff was in the car it suddenly collapsed. He was thrown out and injured. One of the wheels was made of defective wood, and its spokes crumbled into fragments. The wheel was not made by the defendant; it was bought from another manufacturer. There is evidence, however, that its defects could have been discovered by reasonable inspection, and that inspection was omitted. There is no claim that the defendant knew of the defect and willfully concealed it. * * * The charge is one, not of fraud, but of negligence. The question to be determined is whether the defendant owed a duty of care and vigilance to any one but the immediate purchaser.

The foundations of this branch of the law, at least in this state, were laid in Thomas v. Winchester, 6 N.Y. 397, 57 Am.Dec. 455. [This case created an exception to the rule that the seller of a product is liable in negligence only to his immediate purchaser.] A poison was falsely labeled. The sale was made to a druggist, who in turn sold to a customer. The customer recovered damages from the seller who affixed the label. "The defendant's negligence," it was said, "put human life in imminent danger." A poison, falsely labeled, is likely to injure any one who gets it. Because the danger is to be foreseen, there is a duty to avoid the injury. Cases were cited by way of illustration in which manufacturers were not subject to any duty irrespective of contract. The distinction was said to be that their conduct, though negligent, was not likely to result in injury to any one except the purchaser.

[The court discusses two of the first cases to apply the rule of Thomas v. Winchester.]

These early cases suggest a narrow construction of the rule. Later cases, however, evince a more liberal spirit. First in importance is Devlin v. Smith, 89 N.Y. 470, 42 Am.Rep. 311. The defendant, a contractor, built a scaffold for a painter. The painter's servants were injured. The contractor was held liable. He knew that the scaffold, if improperly constructed, was a most dangerous trap. He knew that it was to be used by the workmen. He was building it for that very purpose. Building it for their use, he owed them a duty, irrespective of his contract with their master, to build it with care.

From Devlin v. Smith we pass over intermediate cases and turn to the latest case in this court in which Thomas v. Winchester was followed. That case is Statler v. Ray Mfg. Co., 195 N.Y. 478, 480, 88 N.E. 1063. The defendant manufactured a large coffee urn. It was installed in a restaurant. When heated, the urn exploded and injured the plaintiff. We held that the manufacturer was liable. We said that the urn "was of such a character inherently that, when applied to the purposes for which it was designed, it was liable to become a source of great danger to many people if not carefully and properly constructed."

It may be that Devlin v. Smith and Statler v. Ray Mfg. Co. have extended the rule of Thomas v. Winchester. If so, this court is committed to the extension. The defendant argues that things imminently dangerous to life are poisons, explosives, deadly weapons—things whose normal function it is to injure or destroy. But whatever the rule in Thomas v. Winchester may once have been, it has no longer that restricted meaning. A scaffold (Devlin v. Smith, supra) is not inherently a destructive instrument. It becomes destructive only if imperfectly constructed. A large coffee urn (Statler v. Ray Mfg. Co., supra) may have within itself, if negligently made, the potency of danger, yet no one thinks of it as an implement whose normal function is destruction. What is true of the coffee urn is equally true of bottles of aerated water. Torgesen v. Schultz, 192 N.Y. 156, 84 N.E. 956, 18 L.R.A. (N.S.) 726, 127 Am.St.Rep. 894. * * *

We hold, then, that the principle of Thomas v. Winchester is not limited to poisons, explosives, and things of like nature, to things which in their normal operation are implements of destruction. If the nature of a thing is such that it is reasonably certain to place life and limb in peril when negligently made, it is then a thing of danger. Its nature gives warning of the consequences to be expected. If to the element of danger there is added knowledge that the thing will be used by persons other than the purchaser, and used without new tests, then, irrespective of contract, the manufacturer of this thing of danger is under a duty to make it carefully. That is as far as we are required to go for the decision of this case. There must be knowledge of a danger, not merely possible, but probable. It is possible to use almost anything in a way that will make it dangerous if defective. That is not enough to charge the manufacturer with a duty independent of his contract. Whether a given thing is dangerous may be sometimes a question for the court and sometimes a question for the jury. There must also be knowledge that in the usual course of events the danger will be shared by others than the buyer. Such knowledge may often be inferred from the nature of the transaction. But it is possible that even knowledge of the danger and of the use will not always be enough. The proximity or remoteness of the relation is a factor to be considered. We are dealing now with the liability of the manufacturer of the finished product, who puts it on the market to be used without inspection by his customers. If he is negligent, where danger is to be foreseen, a liability will follow.

* * *

There is here no break in the chain of cause and effect. In such circumstances, the presence of a known danger, attendant upon a known use, makes vigilance a duty. We have put aside the notion that the duty to safeguard life and limb, when the consequences of negligence may be foreseen, grows out of contract and nothing else. We have put the source of the obligation where it ought to be. We have put its source in the law.

From this survey of the decisions, there thus emerges a definition of the duty of a manufacturer which enables us to measure this defendant's liability. Beyond all question, the nature of an automobile gives warning of probable danger if its construction is defective. This automobile was designed to go 50 miles an hour. Unless its wheels were sound and strong, injury was almost certain. It was as much a thing of danger as a defective engine for a railroad. The defendant knew the danger. It knew also that the car would be used by persons other than the buyer.

This was apparent from its size; there were seats for three persons. It was apparent also from the fact that the buyer was a dealer in cars, who bought to resell. The maker of this car supplied it for the use of purchasers from the dealer just as plainly as the contractor in Devlin v. Smith supplied the scaffold for use by the servants of the owner. The dealer was indeed the one person of whom it might be said with some approach to certainty that by him the car would not be used. Yet the defendant would have us say that he was the one person whom it was under a legal duty to protect. The law does not lead us to so inconsequent a conclusion. Precedents drawn from the days of travel by stagecoach do not fit the conditions of travel to-day. The principle that the danger must be imminent does not change, but the things subject to the principle do change. They are whatever the needs of life in a developing civilization require them to be.

* * *

In this view of the defendant's liability there is nothing inconsistent with the theory of liability on which the case was tried. It is true that the court told the jury that "an automobile is not an inherently dangerous vehicle." The meaning, however, is made plain by the context. The meaning is that danger is not to be expected when the vehicle is well constructed. The court left it to the jury to say whether the defendant ought to have foreseen that the car, if negligently constructed, would become "imminently dangerous." Subtle distinctions are drawn by the defendant between things inherently dangerous and things imminently dangerous, but the case does not turn upon these verbal niceties. If danger was to be expected as reasonably certain, there was a duty of vigilance, and this whether you call the danger inherent or imminent. In varying forms that thought was put before the jury. We do not say that the court would not have been justified in ruling as a matter of law that the car was a dangerous thing. If there was any error, it was none of which the defendant can complain.

We think the defendant was not absolved from a duty of inspection because it bought the wheels from a reputable manufacturer. It was not merely a dealer in automobiles. It was a manufacturer of automobiles. It was responsible for the finished product. It was not at liberty to put the finished product on the market without subjecting the component parts to ordinary and simple tests. Richmond & Danville R.R. Co. v. Elliott, 149 U.S. 266, 272, 13 Sup.Ct. 837, 37 L.Ed. 728. Under the charge of the trial judge nothing more was required of it. The obligation to inspect must vary with the nature of the thing to be inspected. The more probable the danger the greater the need of caution.

* * *

Other rulings complained of have been considered, but no error has been found in them.

The judgment should be affirmed, with costs.

Notes

1. Was it really necessary for the court to abolish the privity requirement in order to provide Mr. MacPherson with a remedy? Why could he not recover against the dealer who sold him the car?

2. By interpreting the exception to the privity rule so broadly, the court, in effect, eliminated the rule. Any product that is likely to be dangerous if negligently made can now give rise to a cause of action for negligence without a showing of privity. Courts in virtually all states have followed *MacPherson*.

3. Courts also impose strict products liability without requiring privity of contract. In warranty cases, privity can still play a role. *See infra*, pages 86–97.

MICALLEF v. MIEHLE CO., DIV. OF MIEHLE–GOSS DEXTER, INC.

Court of Appeals of New York, 1976.
39 N.Y.2d 376, 384 N.Y.S.2d 115, 348 N.E.2d 571.

COOKE, JUDGE.

The time has come to depart from the patent danger rule enunciated in *Campo v. Scofield*, 301 N.Y. 468, 95 N.E.2d 802.

This action was initiated to recover damages for personal injuries, allegedly resulting from negligent design and breach of an implied warranty. Paul Micallef, plaintiff, was employed by Lincoln Graphic Arts at its Farmingdale plant as a printing-press operator. For eight months he had been assigned to operate a photo-offset press, model RU 1, manufactured and sold by defendant Miehle–Goss Dexter, Inc., to his employer. The machine was 150 feet long, 15 feet high and 5 feet wide and was capable of printing at least 20,000 sheets an hour. Then, while working on January 22, 1969, plaintiff discovered that a foreign object had made its way onto the plate of the unit. Such a substance, known to the trade as a "hickie", causes a blemish or imperfection on the printed pages. Plaintiff informed his superior of the problem and told him he was going to "chase the hickie", whereupon the foreman warned him to be careful. "Chasing a hickie" consisted of applying, very lightly, a piece of plastic about eight inches wide to the printing plate, which is wrapped around a circular plate cylinder which spins at high speed. The revolving action of the plate against the plastic removes the "hickie". Unsuccessful in his first removal attempt, plaintiff started anew but this time the plastic was drawn into the nip point between the plate cylinder and an ink-form roller along with his hand. The machine had no safety guards to prevent such occurrence. Plaintiff testified that while his hand was trapped he reached for a shut-off button but couldn't contact it because of its location.

Plaintiff was aware of the danger of getting caught in the press in "chasing hickies." However, it was the custom and usage in the industry to "chase hickies on the run", because once the machine was stopped, it required at least three hours to resume printing and, in such event, the financial advantage of the high speed machine would be lessened. Although it was possible to have "chased the hickie" from another side of the machine, such approach would have caused plaintiff to be in a leaning position and would have increased the chances of scratching the plate. Through its representatives and engineers, defendant had observed the machine in operation and was cognizant of the manner in which "hickies were chased" by Lincoln's employees.

Samuel Aidlin, a professional engineer, had inspected the machine subsequent to the mishap. In his opinion, based upon the custom in the printing industry, it would have been good custom and practice to have placed guards near the rollers where plaintiff's hand entered the machine, the danger of human contact being well known. Moreover, he testified that at least three different types of guards were available, two for over 30 years, that they would not have impeded the practice of "chasing hickies," and that these guards would have protected an employee from exposure to the risk. Based upon the foregoing, both causes of action, negligence and breach of warranty, were submitted to the jury.

* * *

[The jury found that defendant was negligent, but that plaintiff was barred by contributory negligence. However, it found for the plaintiff on the breach of warranty claim. The trial judge set aside the entire verdict and granted a new trial because of errors in the instructions.]

[T]he Appellate Division, Second Department, in reversing, on the law and relying, *inter alia,* on *Campo v. Scofield,* 301 N.Y. 468, 95 N.E.2d 802, *supra,* reinstated the jury verdict on the negligence cause of action and directed a judgment for defendant on the cause asserting a breach of warranty. It found that the danger of being caught in the machine was well known in the trade and, more importantly, the plaintiff had actual knowledge of the possible consequences in "chasing a hickie".

* * *

[The Court of Appeals first ruled that the trial judge had discretion to grant a new trial because of errors in the instructions.]

We are confronted here with the question as to the continued validity of the patent-danger doctrine of *Campo v. Scofield,* 301 N.Y. 468, 95 N.E.2d 802, *supra.* Plaintiff sought damages by alleging two causes of action, one couched in negligence in the design of the machinery and the other premised upon the breach of an implied warranty. Since the time of trial, a third independent cause of action, one in strict products liability, has been recognized by this court (*Velez v. Craine & Clark Lbr. Corp.,* 33 N.Y.2d 117, 350 N.Y.S.2d 617, 305 N.E.2d 750; *Codling v. Paglia, supra*). The claims constitute separate theories of recovery and the decisions both in this State (e.g., *Velez v. Craine & Clark Lbr. Corp., supra; Rainbow v. Elia Bldg. Co.,* 49 A.D.2d 250, 373 N.Y.S.2d 928;

Jerry v. Borden Co., 45 A.D.2d 344, 358 N.Y.S.2d 426) and beyond (e.g., *Pike v. Hough Co.*, 2 Cal.3d 465, 85 Cal.Rptr. 629, 467 P.2d 229; *Palmer v. Massey–Ferguson*, 3 Wash.App. 508, 476 P.2d 713; Ann., 52 A.L.R.3d 101) have adhered to the distinction (*Victorson v. Bock Laundry Mach. Co.*, 37 N.Y.2d 395, 373 N.Y.S.2d 39, 335 N.E.2d 275).

Directing our attention to the cause of action for negligence in design, defendant asserts, citing *Campo v. Scofield (supra)*, that the action must be dismissed because the danger created by the absence of safeguards on the machine was open and obvious and, therefore, as the manufacturer it was under no duty to protect plaintiff from such a patent defect. *Campo* set forth the following principles (301 N.Y. p. 471, 95 N.E.2d p. 803): "The cases establish that the manufacturer of a machine or any other article, dangerous because of the way in which it functions, and patently so, owes to those who use it a duty merely to make it free from latent defects and concealed dangers. Accordingly, if a remote user sues a manufacturer of an article for injuries suffered, he must allege and prove the existence of a latent defect or a danger not known to plaintiff or other users". It was then declared (p. 472, 95 N.E.2d p. 804): "If a manufacturer does everything necessary to make the machine function properly for the purpose for which it is designed, if the machine is without any latent defect, and if its functioning creates no danger or peril that is not known to the user, then the manufacturer has satisfied the law's demands. We have not yet reached the state where a manufacturer is under the duty of making a machine accident proof or fool-proof. Just as the manufacturer is under no obligation, in order to guard against injury resulting from deterioration, to furnish a machine that will not wear out, see *Auld v. Sears, Roebuck & Co.*, 288 N.Y. 515, 41 N.E.2d 927, affirming 261 App.Div. 918, 25 N.Y.S.2d 491, so he is under no duty to guard against injury from a patent peril or from a source manifestly dangerous."

The requirement that a latent defect be proved, before there could be a recovery against a manufacturer in a negligence action, has retained its vitality [citing cases]. * * * [Critics argue] that the *Campo* doctrine is "a vestigial carryover from pre-*MacPherson* days when deceit was needed for recovery" (2 Harper & James, Torts, § 28.5). * * * As Professors Harper and James succinctly assert: "The bottom does not logically drop out of a negligence case against the maker when it is shown that the purchaser knew of the dangerous condition. Thus if the product is a carrot-topping machine with exposed moving parts, or an electric clothes wringer dangerous to the limbs of the operator, and if it would be feasible for the maker of the product to install a guard or safety release, it should be a question for the jury whether reasonable care demanded such a precaution, though its absence is obvious. Surely reasonable men might find here a great danger, even to one who knew the condition; and since it was so readily avoidable they might find the maker negligent". (2 Harper & James, Torts, § 28.5.)

Other jurisdictions have taken a more liberal position. For example, in *Palmer v. Massey–Ferguson*, 3 Wash.App. 508, 476 P.2d 713, *supra,* the plaintiff brought an action against the manufacturer of a hay baler for injuries sustained while adjusting a drawbar. In response to the defendant's allegations that the patent peril precluded liability, the court said (p. 517, 476 P.2d p. 719): "The manufacturer of the obviously defective product ought not to escape because the product was obviously a bad one. The law, we think, ought to discourage misdesign rather than encouraging it in its obvious form." (See, also, *Pike v. Hough Co.,* 2 Cal.3d 465, 85 Cal.Rptr. 629, 467 P.2d 229, *supra; Byrnes v. Economic Mach. Co.,* 41 Mich.App. 192, 200 N.W.2d 104.) * * * We find the reasoning of these cases persuasive. *Campo* suffers from its rigidity in precluding recovery whenever it is demonstrated that the defect was patent. Its unwavering view produces harsh results in view of the difficulties in our mechanized way of life to fully perceive the scope of danger, which may ultimately be found by a court to be apparent in manufactured goods as a matter of law. * * * Apace with advanced technology, a relaxation of the *Campo* stringency is advisable. A casting of increased responsibility upon the manufacturer, who stands in a superior position to recognize and cure defects, for improper conduct in the placement of finished products into the channels of commerce furthers the public interest. To this end, we hold that a manufacturer is obligated to exercise that degree of care in his plan or design so as to avoid any unreasonable risk of harm to anyone who is likely to be exposed to the danger when the product is used in the manner for which the product was intended (2 Harper & James, Torts, § 28.3; see, also, *Pierce v. Ford Motor Co.,* 190 F.2d 910, 4 Cir.), as well as an unintended yet reasonably foreseeable use [citations].

What constitutes "reasonable care" will, of course, vary with the surrounding circumstances and will involve "a balancing of the likelihood of harm, and the gravity of harm if it happens, against the burden of the precaution which would be effective to avoid the harm" * * * Under this approach, "the plaintiff endeavors to show the jury such facts as that competitors used the safety device which was missing here, or that a 'cotter pin costing a penny' could have prevented the accident. The defendant points to such matters as cost, function, and competition as narrowing the design choices. He stresses 'trade-offs'. If the product would be unworkable when the alleged missing feature was added, or would be so expensive as to be priced out of the market, that would be relevant defensive matter" * * * In this case, there was no evidence submitted at trial to show the cost of guards that could have been attached in relation to the entire cost of the machine.

Also relevant, but by no means exclusive, in determining whether a manufacturer exercised reasonable skill and knowledge concerning the design of the product is whether he kept abreast of recent scientific developments (*Schenebeck v. Sterling Drug,* 423 F.2d 919, 8 Cir.; *La Plant v. DuPont de Nemours & Co.,* 346 S.W.2d 231 [Mo.App.]) and the extent to which any tests were conducted to ascertain the dangers of the product (see Ann., 6 A.L.R.3d 91; 2 Harper & James, Torts, § 28.4). This does not compel a manufacturer to clothe himself in the garb of an insurer in his dealings [citations] nor to supply merchandise which is accident proof (see *Neusus v. Sponholtz*, 369 F.2d 259, 7 Cir.; *Varas v. Barco Mfg. Co.*, 205 Cal.App.2d 246, 22 Cal.Rptr. 737; *Royal v. Black & Decker Mfg. Co.*, 205 So.2d 307 [Fla.App.]). It does require, however, that legal responsibility, if any, for injury caused by machinery which has possible dangers incident to its use should be shouldered by the one in the best position to have eliminated those dangers.

We next examine the duty owing from a plaintiff or, in other words, the conduct on a plaintiff's part which will bar recovery from a manufacturer. As now enunciated, the patent-danger doctrine should not, in and of itself, prevent a plaintiff from establishing his case. That does not mean, however, that the obviousness of the danger as a factor in the ultimate injury is thereby eliminated, for it must be remembered that in actions for negligent design, the ordinary rules of negligence apply (* * * Noel, Manufacturer's Negligence of Design or Directions for Use of a Product, 71 Yale L.J. 816, 818). Rather, the openness and obviousness of the danger should be available to the defendant on the issue of whether plaintiff exercised that degree of reasonable care as was required under the circumstances. * * *

The order of the Appellate Division should be reversed and a new trial granted, with costs to abide the event.

BREITEL, C.J., and JASEN, GABRIELLI, JONES, WACHTLER and FUCHSBERG, JJ., concur.

Order reversed, etc.

Notes

1. A majority of courts are in accord with the principal case in rejecting the open and obvious danger rule. While the obviousness of the danger is no longer controlling in those jurisdictions, it is a relevant consideration. *See, e.g.*, Owens v. Allis–Chalmers Corp., 414 Mich. 413, 425, 326 N.W.2d 372, 377 (1982) which stated:

> [T]he obviousness of the risks that inhere in some simple tools or products is a factor contributing to the conclusion that such products are not unreasonably dangerous. The test, however, is not whether the risks are obvious, but whether the risks were unreasonable in light of the foreseeable injuries.

2. A number of jurisdictions continue to adhere to the rule. *See, e.g.*, Pressley v. Sears–Roebuck and Co., 738 F.2d 1222 (11th Cir.1984) (applying Georgia law; no liability under either negligence or strict liability for failing to equip a riding lawn mower with a deadman switch because the risk of being hit by the moving blade if the operator fell off the mower was obvious). Generally speaking, such jurisdictions apply the rule to all product liability cases, regardless of whether the suit is brought on a negligence, implied warranty, or strict liability theory.

3. When applied in strict liability cases the open and obvious danger rule is often referred to as the "Consumer Expectations" test of defect. This test precludes recovery for harm caused by known or obvious product

risks. In some jurisdictions which reject the blanket immunity for open and obvious dangers, a violation of consumer expectations continues to play a role in determining liability. The role of the open and obvious danger rule in strict liability cases is discussed in Chapter 6. *See* pages 163–77, *infra*.

SECTION C. STANDARD OF CARE

MONING v. ALFONO
Supreme Court of Michigan, 1977.
400 Mich. 425, 254 N.W.2d 759.

LEVIN, JUSTICE.

Royal Moning, when he was 12 years old, lost the sight of an eye which was struck by a pellet fired from a slingshot being used by his 11 year old playmate, Joseph Alfono.

There was evidence that Alfono purchased two 10¢ slingshots from defendant Campbell Discount Jewelry and had given one to Moning, and that the slingshots had been manufactured by defendant Chemtoy Corporation and distributed by defendant King Tobacco and Grocery Company.

Moning claims that it is negligence to market slingshots directly to children, and that the manufacturer, wholesaler and retailer are subject to liability.

The claim against the Alfonos was settled. Upon completion of Moning's proofs, the trial judge directed a verdict for the remaining defendants. The Court of Appeals affirmed.

We remand for a new trial because a manufacturer, wholesaler and retailer of a manufactured product owe a legal obligation of due care to a bystander affected by use of the product, and whether defendants in violation of that obligation created an unreasonable risk of harm in marketing slingshots directly to children is for a jury to decide, reasonable persons being of different minds.

* * *

Negligence is conduct involving an *unreasonable* risk of harm.

Slingshots pose a *risk* of harm. In manufacturing and marketing slingshots the defendants necessarily created such a risk.

The meritorious issues are whether the risk so created was unreasonable because the slingshots were marketed directly to children, and whether this should be decided by the court or by the jury.

* * *

III
REASONABLENESS OF THE RISK OF HARM

Even if a person recognizes that his conduct involves a risk of invading another person's interest, he may nevertheless engage in such conduct unless the risk created by his conduct is unreasonable.

The reasonableness of the risk depends on whether its magnitude is outweighed by its utility. The Restatement provides: "Where an act is one which a reasonable man would recognize as involving a risk of harm to another, the risk is unreasonable and the act is negligent if the risk is of such magnitude as to outweigh what the law regards as the utility of the act or of the particular manner in which it is done." Restatement, *supra*, § 291.

The balancing of the magnitude of the risk and the utility of the actor's conduct requires a consideration by the *court and jury* of the societal interests involved.[1] The issue of negligence may be removed from jury consideration if the court concludes that overriding considerations of public policy require that a particular view be adopted and applied in all cases.

A court would thus refuse to allow a jury to consider whether an automobile manufacturer should be liable for all injuries resulting from manufacturing automobiles on the theory that it is foreseeable that some 50,000 persons may be killed and hundreds of thousands injured every year as a result of manufacturing automobiles. The utility of providing automobile transportation is deemed by society to override the magnitude of the risk created by their manufacture. Similarly, a court might conclude that it would be violative of public policy to hold a manufacturer of slingshots liable for all injuries resulting from their use. The interest of mature persons who wish to purchase and use slingshots might be deemed to supersede the interest of those who may be harmed by their careless or improper use.

The issue in the instant case is not whether slingshots should be manufactured, but the narrower question of whether marketing slingshots directly to children creates an unreasonable risk of harm. In determining that question, the Court must first ask whether the utility of marketing slingshots directly to children so overrides the risk thereby created as to justify the Court in refusing to permit juries to subject persons who engage in such conduct to liability for the resulting harm. If it concludes that the utility does not, as a matter of law, override the risk, then the question of balancing utility and risk is for the jury to decide, again, as part of its consideration of the reasonableness of defendants' conduct, unless the Court concludes that all reasonable persons would be of one mind on that question.

The Restatement suggests a number of factors that should be considered in balancing the utility of the actor's conduct and the magnitude of the risk. First, the magnitude of the risk:

> "In determining the magnitude of the risk for the purpose of determining whether the actor is negligent, the following factors are important:

1. "Conduct is not negligent unless the magnitude of the risk involved therein so outweighs its utility as to make the risk unreasonable. Therefore, one relying upon negligence as a cause of action or defense must convince the *court and jury* that this is the case." Restatement, supra, § 291, Comment b, p. 55 (emphasis supplied).

"(a) the social value which the law attaches to the interests which are imperiled;

"(b) the extent of the chance that the actor's conduct will cause an invasion of any interest of the other or of one of a class of which the other is a member;

"(c) the extent of the harm likely to be caused to the interests imperiled;

"(d) the number of persons whose interests are likely to be invaded if the risk takes effect in harm." Restatement, *supra*, § 293.

a) The law attaches a high social value to the interest of persons in unimpaired eyesight.

b) Slingshots are potentially dangerous. An expert witness, called by Moning, testified that the slingshots Alfono purchased were capable of launching projectiles at speeds exceeding 350 miles per hour. Slingshots cause hundreds of serious injuries each year to school age children. Almost all these injuries are head or eye injuries and occur to children 5 to 14.[2] Experience therefore shows that marketing slingshots to children may with substantial frequency cause an invasion of the interest in unimpaired eyesight of a substantial number of persons.

c) The extent of the harm likely to be caused to the interest so imperiled may be of a most serious nature.

d) The number of persons whose interests are likely to be invaded is difficult to estimate, but it appears that hundreds of injuries, many resulting in serious impairment of vision, occur every year as a result of the use of slingshots by children.

Turning to utility:

"In determining what the law regards as the utility of the actor's conduct for the purpose of determining whether the actor is negligent, the following factors are important:

---

2. Projections from one study indicate that nearly 66,000 school children in the United States during any 9–month school year suffer injuries to the eye. Over 4% of the reported injuries in a study carried out in Louisville were caused by slingshots and other weapons. Such instrumentalities were responsible for 17% of the more serious injuries. Kerby, [Eye Accidents to School Children, 20 Sight–Saving Rev. 2.], pp. 3–4, 11 [(1950)]. Another study shows that "[t]here were an estimated 471 injuries related to slingshots and sling propelled toys during the period July 1, 1974–July 30, 1975, treated in United States hospital emergency rooms, all but 2 of which were head or eye injuries to victims under 15 years of age." U.S. Consumer Product Safety Commission, Bureau of Epidemiology, *Special Report: Injuries Associated with Products Which Have Projectiles* (Draft, October 23, 1975), p. 15. During the same time period, 2, 120 injuries reported to hospital emergency rooms involved projectile products. *Id.*, p. 17. The U.S. Consumer Product Safety Commission states that since "(s)lingshots range from toys to hunting models capable of killing small game * * * it is recommended that high powered slingshots be sold only to persons over 20 years of age." *Id.*, p. 23. The Commission concluded that "(o)verall, projectile products include a diverse array of products which while they share a common hazard are very different in age of users, intended use, and likelihood and consequences of misuse," and that therefore "Commission action would be most effective" "in the area of toy guns and other toy weapons with projectiles and slingshots." *Id.*

"(a) the social value which the law attaches to the interest which is to be advanced or protected by the conduct;

"(b) the extent of the chance that this interest will be advanced or protected by the particular course of conduct;

"(c) the extent of the chance that such interest can be adequately advanced or protected by another and less dangerous course of conduct." Restatement 2d, Torts, § 292.

a) There is a sharp difference of opinion concerning the social value of the child's interest in having direct-market access to slingshots. The view that slingshots should not be sold or used by children is widely held and is reflected in statutes and ordinances prohibiting the sale of slingshots to or their use by minors.

Statutes and other legislative judgments may themselves be a source of common law. "This legislative establishment of policy carries significance beyond the particular scope of each of the statutes involved. The policy thus established has become itself a part of our law, to be given its appropriate weight not only in matters of statutory construction *but also in those of decisional law." Moragne v. States Marine Lines*, 398 U.S. 375, 390–391, 90 S.Ct. 1772, 1782, 26 L.Ed.2d 339 (1970). Similarly, see *Williams v. Polgar*, 391 Mich. 6, 14, 26–28, 215 N.W.2d 149 (1974).

[Discussing numerous statutes in various states regulating possession, sale, and use of slingshots.]

It is apparent from the legislation in other states and innumerable municipalities that all reasonable persons do not agree that marketing slingshots directly to children does not involve an unreasonable risk of harm. The failure of other states and cities to enact like statutes and ordinances, and of the Legislature either to authorize or prohibit the marketing of slingshots directly to children, indicates a variety of opinion, but not a consensus regarding the reasonableness of marketing slingshots directly to children.

b) Children are more likely to obtain slingshots if they are marketed directly to them.

c) Slingshots could be marketed in a manner designed to confine sale to adults and to exclude purchases by children. Instead of manufacturers, wholesalers and retailers effectively determining whether children shall have slingshots, an adult who generally would know the child would decide whether he is of sufficient maturity to have one; the adult would, under the common law, assume responsibility for any negligence on his part in entrusting a slingshot to the child.

Having in mind the parent's interest in protecting the child from potentially dangerous instrumentalities and in avoiding exposure to litigation such as befell the Alfonos, the child's interest in an opportunity to use slingshots cannot be said as a matter of law to be inadequately advanced or protected by allowing a jury to decide that a manufacturer, wholesaler or retailer is negligent in marketing them directly to children.

Balancing the magnitude of the risk and the utility of the conduct in the application of the factors suggested by the Restatement, there is not a sufficient basis for concluding as a matter of law that the utility of the defendants' conduct outweighs the risk of harm thereby created. The sharp difference of opinion regarding the balancing of utility and risk of harm requires submission of these questions for jury assessment as part of its consideration of the reasonableness of the risk of harm and of defendants' conduct.

While "slingshots have a long history of association with the human race" and have been used for hundreds of years by both adults and children, the common law is not immutable, unable to respond to changes in society and technology.

"The customary usage and practice of the industry is relevant evidence to be used in determining whether or not this standard (of reasonably prudent conduct) has been met. Such usage cannot, however, be determinative of the standard. As stated by Justice Holmes:

" 'What usually is done may be evidence of what ought to be done, but what ought to be done is fixed by a standard of reasonable prudence, whether it usually is complied with or not.' *Texas and Pacific R. Co. v. Behymer* (1903), 189 U.S. 468, 470, 23 S.Ct. 622, 47 L.Ed. 905." *Marietta v. Cliffs Ridge, Inc.*, 385 Mich. 364, 369–370, 189 N.W.2d 208, 209 (1971).

As society becomes increasingly urbanized and access to open space decreases, the law responds and develops.

Modern technology may have magnified the risk of ricochet and of injury to persons not in the immediate range or direction in which the slingshot is aimed. Slingshots capable of firing projectiles at 350 miles per hour may be a far cry from those historically made by children from rubber bands and household paraphernalia.

Nor does calling a slingshot a "toy" make it any less dangerous nor immunize its marketing directly to children from the general rules of negligence liability.

There is a qualitative difference between slingshots and other projectile "toys" on the one hand, and baseball equipment and bicycles on the other. The latter are viewed by society essentially as are automobiles in that although children are injured and killed riding bicycles and playing baseball, the utility of such activity is regarded by society and all reasonable persons as outweighing the risk of harm created by their manufacture for and marketing to children. Statutes and ordinances do not prohibit the purchase or use of bicycles or baseball equipment by children. There is no ongoing debate, as there is about slingshots, whether children should have direct market access to bicycles or baseball equipment.

In sum, it cannot be said that there was no "obligation of reasonable conduct for the benefit of the plaintiff",[3] or that all reasonable men would agree that defendants' conduct was not "a substantial factor in producing the result"[4] or regarding "the foreseeability of (the) particular risk"[5] or regarding "the reasonableness of the defendants' conduct with respect to it, or the normal character of (Alfono's conduct)"[6] as an intervening cause.

Since reasonable persons can differ regarding the balance of risk and utility (the reasonableness of the risk of harm) and since there is no overriding policy based on social utility of maintaining absolute access to slingshots by children, we reverse and remand for a new trial.

KAVANAGH, C. J., and WILLIAMS, J., concur.

RYAN and MOODY, JJ., not participating.

[Dissenting opinion of FITZGERALD omitted.]

Notes

1.   Standard principles of negligence now apply fully to people who design, manufacture, and sell products.   Section 395 of the Restatement (Second) of Torts deals with the liability of one who manufacturers chattels. It states:

> A manufacturer who fails to exercise reasonable care in the manufacture of a chattel which, unless carefully made, he should recognize as involving an unreasonable risk of causing physical harm to those who use it for a purpose for which the manufacturer should expect it to be used and to those whom he should expect to be endangered by its probable use, is subject to liability for physical harm caused to them by its lawful use in a manner and for a purpose for which it is supplied.

Comment f to § 395 elaborates:

> *Particulars which require care.* A manufacturer is required to exercise reasonable care in manufacturing any article which, if carelessly manufactured, is likely to cause harm to those who use it in the manner for which it is manufactured. The particulars in which reasonable care is usually necessary for protection of those whose safety depends upon the character of chattels are (1) the adoption of a formula or plan which, if properly followed, will produce an article safe for the use for which it is sold, (2) the selection of material and parts to be incorporated in the finished article, (3) the fabrication of the article by every member of the operative staff no matter how high or low his position, (4) the making of such inspections and tests during the course of manufacture and after the article is completed as the manufacturer should recognize as reasonably necessary to secure the production of a safe article, and (5) the packing of the article so as to be safe for those who must be expected to unpack it.

3. Prosser, *supra*, § 45, pp. 289–290.   5. *Id.*

4. *Id.*   6. *Id.*

2. Defendant sold gasoline to a twelve-year-old child with a lawn mowing business? The child's nine-year-old brother was burned when the purchaser tried to destroy an ant hill in a customer's yard with the gasoline. Was defendant negligent for selling the gasoline to the child?

GARNES v. GULF & WESTERN MFG. CO.

United States Court of Appeals, Eighth Circuit, 1986.
789 F.2d 637.

Ross, Circuit Judge.

This products liability diversity case is controlled by Iowa law. The appellant, Gulf & Western Manufacturing Company (Gulf & Western), appeals from a judgment granting damages to Jerry Garnes for injuries sustained when he fell off of a forging press designed and manufactured by Gulf & Western. Gulf & Western contends that the trial court erred in instructing the jury. We agree and accordingly, reverse the judgment and remand for a new trial.

Facts

On August 29, 1981, Jerry Garnes' employer, Osmundson Manufacturing Company, assigned him the task of performing maintenance work on a forging press. The press had been manufactured in 1952 by Gulf & Western's E.W. Bliss Division and was located in Osmundson's plant in Perry, Iowa.

In order to perform the required maintenance, Garnes was first raised up to the top of the press' back shaft, a height of approximately ten feet, by a fork lift. He then climbed onto the back shaft and inspected the grease hoses inside the press. After removing a broken grease hose and throwing the broken hose and his tools onto the raised fork lift platform, Garnes attempted to step onto the fork lift platform. He missed, fell to the floor, and suffered a fractured vertebra, injury to his nervous system, and multiple abrasions and contusions.

Garnes then initiated this suit against Gulf & Western. * * * Originally, Garnes alleged both negligence and strict liability in tort claims, but the strict liability claim was withdrawn at the end of trial. * * *

At trial, Garnes attempted to show that Gulf & Western was negligent in designing the press without a ladder, handhold, platform, catwalk, or railing. Garnes also contended that Gulf & Western was negligent in failing to provide workers with a warning of the dangers inherent in dismounting the press or with instructions on how to safely dismount the press.

The jury found in favor of Garnes and, by special verdict, announced that his damages totalled $493,000. Because the case had been submitted on a comparative negligence theory, the jury was also asked to apportion the responsibility for Garnes' damages. It did so as follows: Gulf & Western 70%, Garnes 30%, and Garnes' coemployees 0%.

* * *

After judgment was entered, Gulf & Western filed a motion to amend the judgment and a motion for JNOV or a new trial. The trial court denied the motion for JNOV or a new trial * * *.

On appeal, Gulf & Western argues that the trial court committed reversible error in * * * [instructing the jury concerning] the design and warning duties owed by manufacturers * * *.

DISCUSSION

1. Manufacturer's Duties Instruction

The trial court instructed the jury on the design and warning duties owed by manufacturers as follows:

> A manufacturer is held to such reasonable skill, knowledge and diligence as that of experts in its field; that duty extends to the design of the product to protect those who will use the goods from unreasonable risk of harm while the goods are being used for their intended purpose. This duty extends to any person whom the manufacturer had reason to expect would be using the goods, whether or not the person using the goods was the actual purchaser, and the manufacturer is charged with the duty of making the product safe for the foreseeable use to which it might be put.

> You are instructed that it is the law that the manufacturer of a machine has a non-delegable duty to make a machine that includes necessary safety devices.

> You are instructed that it is the law that the manufacturer has a duty to produce a safe product with appropriate warnings and instructions where necessary.

> The use of the Gulf & Western Bliss Forging Press by plaintiff at the time of his injury is to be considered by you as an intended purpose for the use of such product and is a use which a manufacturer should reasonably expect.

Instruction No. 11B. At an instruction conference, Gulf & Western objected to this instruction on the basis that Garnes had not engendered a submissible jury question on the duty to warn element contained in the third paragraph of the instruction. Gulf & Western also objected to the instruction on the basis that it incorrectly stated a manufacturer's duties under Iowa negligence law.

Under Iowa negligence law, manufacturers are required to exercise reasonable care to design a product that is reasonably safe for its intended and foreseeable uses. *See Chown v. USM Corp.,* 297 N.W.2d 218, 220 (Iowa 1980); *Bengford v. Carlem Corp.,* 156 N.W.2d 855, 864 (Iowa 1968). They are also required to exercise reasonable care to warn users of the dangers involved in using the product. *See Nichols v. Westfield Industries, Ltd.,* 380 N.W.2d 392, 400 (Iowa 1985); *Henkel v. R and S Bottling Co.,* 323 N.W.2d 185, 188 (Iowa 1982). But, "[w]here risks are known and obvious, there is no need for a warning under the standards" of care (*see* Restatement (Second) of Torts § 388 (1965)) adopted by the Iowa Supreme Court. *Nichols v. Westfield Industries, Ltd., supra*, 380 N.W.2d at 401 (*citing Strong v. E.I. DuPont de Nemours Co.*, 667 F.2d 682, 687–88 (8th Cir.1981) (plaintiff knew or should have known danger of pull-out in gas pipes); *McIntyre v. Everest & Jennings, Inc.*, 575 F.2d 155, 159–60 (8th Cir.1978) (tipping commode)).

As a matter of law, the danger of falling from the forging press involved in this case was known and obvious. First, the danger of falling from a height in general, and from a slanted surface with no support in particular, is commonly known. Second, Garnes testified that he was familiar with the press (he had inspected or helped others inspect the press approximately twenty-five times within the year prior to the accident) and that he knew he was at a dangerous height while on the back shaft of the press. He further acknowledged that he had always been careful in mounting and dismounting the press because he did not want to slip and fall.

Reviewing the record in the light most favorable to Garnes, we find no evidence upon which a reasonable jury could determine that Gulf & Western had a duty to warn. Because it was wrong to submit the duty to warn element to the jury, the judgment in favor of Garnes must be reversed and the case must be remanded for a new trial.

Gulf & Western's remaining objections to Instruction No. 11B and the other challenged instructions are likely to arise again on retrial. Therefore, we shall address them.

Gulf & Western challenges each paragraph of Instruction No. 11B. With respect to the first paragraph of the instruction, Gulf & Western challenges the statement that "[a] manufacturer is held to such reasonable skill, knowledge and diligence as that of experts in its field." According to Gulf & Western, it was improper to use the term "experts" because Iowa case law requires only that manufacturers exercise reasonable care in designing products.

The trial court concluded that the use of the term "experts" was not clear error because the term is similar to the "state of the art" standard which is often used to determine whether a manufacturer has acted negligently in designing a product. In addition, the court noted that other courts apply an "expert" standard to manufacturers. *See Ross v. Philip Morris & Co.*, 328 F.2d 3, 13–14 n. 13 (8th Cir.1964) ("[e]ven in a negligence case, a manufacturer is held to the skill of an expert, is charged with superior knowledge of the nature and qualities of its products, and is obligated reasonably to keep abreast of scientific information, discoveries, and advances") (applying Missouri law); *Bradbury v. Ford Motor Co.*, 123 Mich.App. 179, 333 N.W.2d 214, 217 (1983) ("manufacturer is held to the knowledge of an expert"); W. Prosser, *Torts* § 96 at 647 n. 63 (4th ed. 1971). We agree with the trial court's conclusion that the use of the term "experts" was not reversibly erroneous, particularly since the term "reasonable" was included in the challenged portion of the instruction.

With respect to the second paragraph of the instruction, Gulf & Western challenges the statement that a manufacturer "has a non-delegable duty to make a machine that includes necessary safety devices." Gulf & Western contends that the term "non-delegable" was misleading, confusing, prejudicial and unnecessary.

The trial court concluded that this instruction was necessary to avoid jury confusion on the issue of who had the duty to place safety devices on the press. Such confusion might arise, the court concluded, because Gulf & Western had attempted to show that Garnes' employer had such a duty.

The concept of non-delegability is legally correct in the context of this case. *See Bilotta v. Kelley Co.,* 346 N.W.2d 616, 624–25 (Minn.1984) ("a manufacturer may not delegate its duty to design a reasonably safe product"). Therefore, we conclude that the trial court did not err in instructing the jury on this concept.

The third paragraph of Instruction No. 11B is challenged on the theory that it overstated Gulf & Western's duty to warn and effectively advised the jury that Gulf & Western had a duty to produce an absolutely safe product. The challenged portion reads: "the manufacturer has a duty to produce a safe product with appropriate warnings and instructions where necessary."

In giving this instruction, the trial court relied heavily upon the fact that it was taken from the following statement: "A manufacturer's *duty to produce a safe product, with appropriate warnings and instructions where necessary,* rests initially on the responsibility each of us bears to exercise care to avoid unreasonable risks of harm to others." *Hall v. E.I. DuPont de Nemours & Co.,* 345 F.Supp. 353, 360 (E.D.N.Y.1972) (emphasis added). The trial court reasoned that the above statement must be an accurate description of the law because it was quoted by the Iowa Supreme Court in *Cooley v. Quick Supply Co.,* 221 N.W.2d 763, 769 (Iowa 1974).

The problem with this reasoning is that the statement does not define the standard of care owed by manufacturers, but rather, defines the source from which a manufacturer's duty of care derives. In fact, in *Hall,* the court specifically stated that the standard of care owed by manufacturers in negligence cases is "reasonable care". *Hall v. E.I. DuPont de Nemours & Co., supra,* 345 F.Supp. at 361. And in *Cooley,* the court specifically stated that a manufacturer's "duty to warn is not absolute" and is governed "by standards of reasonable care." *Cooley v. Quick Supply Co., supra,* 221 N.W.2d at 771. Because the statement in question is not a definition of the duty of care owed by manufacturers, it was not a proper source for a jury instruction on that duty. *See Johnson v. Bryant,* 671 F.2d 1276, 1281 n. 2 (11th Cir.1982) ("a jury may [not] be instructed in the language of an appellate opinion where such would be misleading").

The trial court also concluded that the instruction effectively informed the jury that they were to apply a reasonable care standard to the manufacturer's duty to provide warnings and instructions. This conclusion was premised on the fact that the instruction used the terms "appropriate" and "necessary". According to the court, these terms are synonymous with the term "reasonable".

"A district court 'has broad discretion in framing the form and language of the charge to the jury, and as long as the entire charge fairly and adequately contains the law applicable to the case, the judgment will not be disturbed on appeal.'" *Ferren v. Richards Manufacturing Co.,* 733 F.2d 526, 530 (8th Cir.1984) (*quoting Board of Water Works Trustees v. Alvord, Burdick & Howson,* 706 F.2d 820, 823 (8th Cir.1983)). The instruction at issue, however, fails this standard of review. The problem with the instruction is that it advised the jury that manufacturers have a legal duty to produce a "safe product". Because the instruction omitted a modifying adverb (i.e., "reasonably"), the duty stated is absolute. The terms "appropriate" and "necessary" do not modify the phrase "safe product" but rather, are dependent upon that phrase for their own meaning.[6]

* * *

Finally, Gulf & Western challenges the fourth paragraph of Instruction No. 11B on the basis that it removed a factual issue from the jury's consideration and thereby invaded the jury's province. This portion of the instruction stated: "The use of the Gulf & Western Bliss Forging Press by plaintiff at the time of his injury is to be considered by you as an intended purpose for the use of such product and is a use which a manufacturer should reasonably expect."

The trial court concluded that the instruction was proper because the evidence clearly established that Garnes' use of the press was an intended and foreseeable use. In particular, the court observed that the maintenance work which Garnes was performing at the time of the accident had been recommended by Gulf & Western.

* * *

Here, the trial court failed to leave the factual determination to the jury. However, no reversible error was caused by the instruction because Gulf & Western does not dispute the fact that Garnes' use of the press was an intended and foreseeable use and, in any event, Gulf & Western did not object to this portion of the instruction. *See W.B. Farms v. Fremont National Bank & Trust Co.,* 756 F.2d 663, 667 (8th Cir.1985).

---

6. Gulf & Western argues that the second paragraph of Instruction No. 11B has the same defect as the third paragraph because it uses the phrase "necessary safety devices". The two paragraphs are entirely different, however, because the second paragraph refers to a "machine" where the third paragraph refers to a "safe product".

Similarly, Gulf & Western has argued that the second sentence of the first paragraph of Instruction No. 11B is defective because it states: "the manufacturer is charged with the duty of making the product safe for the foreseeable use to which it might be put." On retrial it would be better to insert the word "reasonably" before the word "safe".

[The court's discussion of the other challenged instructions is omitted.]

The judgment of the district court is reversed and the case is remanded for a new trial.

Notes

1. The court ruled that there is no duty to warn about open and obvious dangers. Would such a duty exist in New York after the decision in *Micallef v. Miehle Co., Div. of Miehle–Goss Dexter, Inc., supra?*

2. *Garnes* imposes on the manufacturer a nondelegable duty to install necessary safety devices. A comparable duty is commonly imposed in strict liability cases. *See* Chapter 9, Section B. 1., *infra.* In negligence cases, courts traditionally have not imposed a nondelegable duty. Rather, they let the jury decide whether a manufacturer acted reasonably in relying on the buyer to install the safety device. *E.g.,* Rhoads v. Service Mach. Co., 329 F.Supp. 367 (E.D.Ark.1971). Which approach is preferable?

3. In products liability cases based on negligence, manufacturers are held to the skill of experts. Therefore, they are charged with superior knowledge of the nature and qualities of their products, and are obligated to keep reasonably informed of the latest scientific information and advances. Reasonable care may also require them to make tests to learn about the dangers posed by their products. *See* 5 F. Harper, F. James, & O. Gray, The Law of Torts § 28.4 (2d Ed.1986).

TAYLOR v. WYETH LABORATORIES, INC.
Court of Appeals of Michigan, 1984.
139 Mich.App. 389, 362 N.W.2d 293.

PER CURIAM.

Plaintiff, Gus Taylor, appeals as of right from a judgment of no cause of action entered following a directed verdict for defendant, Wyeth Laboratories, Inc.

This case arose from the death of plaintiff's wife, Carrie Sue Taylor (decedent). Plaintiff alleged that his wife died from a pulmonary embolism (a blood clot in the lung) which was caused by her consumption of the oral contraceptive Ovral–21, manufactured by defendant Wyeth Laboratories. The medication was prescribed by defendant Dr. Brockington. Defendant Dr. Johnson treated decedent for a broken ankle shortly before her death.

Plaintiff claimed defendant Wyeth had been negligent in two respects: (1) in failing to adequately test Ovral–21 before and after marketing with regard to its use and the occurrence of "thromboembolic disorders" (blood clotting); and (2) in failing to provide physicians with adequate warnings of the specific relationship between Ovral–21 and the occurrence of blood clots, in particular, the increased risk to women with certain blood types. In addition, according to plaintiff, defendant Wyeth failed to advise physicians of available diagnostic tests which should be administered to patients using the substance. Plaintiff alleged that each of these acts or omissions "was a proximate and foreseeable cause" of his wife's death. The defendant physicians reached a settlement with plaintiff during trial.

At trial, plaintiff testified that his wife broke her ankle on January 4, 1979. Dr. Johnson applied a second cast to decedent's leg on January 19, after which decedent continued to complain about pain in her foot and leg. On February 26, 1979, plaintiff took decedent to Dr. Johnson's office for an appointment, at which time decedent collapsed outside the doctor's office and was dead on arrival at the hospital. The medical examiner concluded that she died from a "massive pulmonary embolism or blood clot" which migrated from her leg to the large blood vessel connecting her heart to the lungs. The contraceptive was "a factor in the forming of the clot in this case". Decedent was 34 years old.

At the close of plaintiff's proofs, the trial judge granted defendant's motion for directed verdict. * * *

On appeal, plaintiff raises two issues. First, he contends that the trial judge erred in granting a directed verdict on plaintiff's claim that defendant negligently failed to adequately test for and research the cause of the injurious effects of its product. We agree.

If the evidence, viewed in a light most favorable to plaintiff, establishes a prima facie case, a defense motion for directed verdict should be denied. If material issues of fact remain, upon which reasonable minds might differ, they are for the jury. A plaintiff has the right to ask the jury to believe the case as he presented it, however improbable it may seem. Directed verdicts are particularly disfavored in negligence actions, since the ultimate questions are so often the reasonableness of defendant's conduct and whether that conduct was a proximate cause of the plaintiff's injury.

A manufacturer's duty of reasonable care includes a duty of product inspection and testing during and after the course of manufacture as is reasonably necessary to render the product safe for its users. As in other negligence actions, generally it is a question of fact for the jury whether a manufacturer's failure to test or inspect the product constitutes negligence. Plaintiff must show there was a danger which could have been detected and that the injury was proximately caused by the discoverable defect. In this respect also, such a claim is no different from any negligence claim for which proximate cause is one of the elements of a prima facie case. This issue is one for the jury, provided there is evidence from which reasonable persons could draw a "fair inference" that the injury was caused by the negligent omission.

In this case, plaintiff claimed that defendant should have conducted further testing and research on the relationship between Ovral–21 and blood clotting. Plaintiff submitted expert testimony that a prudent drug manufacturer would have explored the more specific relationship between blood types and the risk of blood clotting. Therefore, we believe that it was error for the trial judge to conclude that there was no evidence that defendant had information indicating such a relationship existed. Defendant's employee, Dr. Lewis, admitted that defendant, along with the other oral contraceptive manufacturers, had such information but did not act upon it because they felt the evidence was insufficient. Plaintiff submitted medical research articles from which the jury could infer what the results of the tests would have been. In addition, Dr. Laird stated that he knew of 13 similar cases in which all of the women concerned had type A blood. Accordingly, reasonable minds could differ as to whether a causal connection existed.

Defendant argued that there is no study which establishes a direct link between blood type and coagulation factors in the blood, a fact which was admitted by plaintiff's expert, Dr. Laird. While the lack of a study is cause for academic interest, it does not dispose of the issue. Plaintiff submitted evidence, in the form of medical research articles and Dr. Laird's testimony, of the heightened danger of thrombosis for women with type A blood. That such women experienced a disproportionate share of the pulmonary embolisms is enough to create a jury question on the "failure to test" claim.

The trial court held that there was no showing of proximate cause, *i.e.,* that defendant Wyeth would have changed its warning as a result of the tests which it failed to perform. However, plaintiff's "failure to test claim", like all those of its kind, requires a certain degree of inferential reasoning. We believe that, on the basis of the evidence submitted, a reasonable jury could properly infer that the failure to test or conduct research on the blood type question was negligence.

Plaintiff also claims on appeal that the trial court erred in granting a directed verdict for defendant on plaintiff's claim that defendant negligently failed to convey adequate warnings and instructions on the dangers associated with the use of Ovral–21.

A manufacturer of a prescription drug has a duty to warn the medical profession of any risks inherent in the use of the drug which the manufacturer "knows or should know" exist. If warnings or instructions are required, the information provided must be adequate, accurate and effective. Determination of whether this duty has been breached in the context of a negligence claim necessitates that the warnings given be examined as to their reasonableness under the circumstances. Whether referred to as "the specific standard of care", or simply as "the reasonableness of the defendant's conduct", the issue is for the jury, unless all reasonable persons would agree or there is some overriding legislative policy to the contrary. This Court has repeatedly held that the adequacy of a warning and the reasonableness of a failure to warn are questions of fact. Moreover, "the duty to warn may exist even where the danger associated with the product is so slight that few have ever been injured by it".

In the within case, plaintiff submitted expert testimony on three alleged inadequacies in the warnings accompanying defendant's product. First, according to the testimony, the warning concerning the danger posed by prolonged immobilization was inadequate, since it was vague and "buried" deep within the printed material. The record does not, therefore, support defendant's argument that there was no evidence of the warning's inadequacy. This was a jury question, to be answered according to the jury's view of the evidence, including the expert testimony and the exhibits at hand.

There was evidence that defendant was aware of the correlation between blood type and blood clotting and chose not to warn about it. In addition to the admission of Dr. Lewis that defendant was aware of this danger, this Court has held that "the manufacturer is held to the knowledge of an expert and is presumed to know of scientific studies and articles concerning the safety of its products". Dr. Laird testified that the patient's blood coagulation factors should be tested and monitored and that two such tests were available at a combined cost of $24 to $40.

When defense counsel impeached Dr. Laird with his testimony in a 1978 trial, in which Laird said the tests should not "be required on a routine basis", and that the tests "are expensive", the witness stated he had changed his opinion since 1978. Further, Dr. Laird stood by his prior statement, explaining that his reference to "the advisability of using the tests" is "different than doing it in every single patient". The trial court held, however, that Dr. Laird's prior testimony, that in 1978 he felt the tests were too expensive to be routinely required, was conclusively favorable to defendant on this point. We believe that this was error.

On a motion for directed verdict, "the trial judge may not select among actual or seeming contradictory statements of a witness given on direct examination and cross-examination what he believes should be applied to that motion". The inconsistency in the expert's testimony presented a question of credibility for the jury. Moreover, the conflict was not an absolute one, given the evidence in the case. Even if Dr. Laird still held the view that a doctor need not give the tests routinely when he prescribes an oral contraceptive, a woman with type A blood would hardly present a "routine" case in which a doctor might reasonably omit these tests, given the information that women of that blood type were at greater risk.

More basically, the question of whether the expense outweighed the risk is precisely the kind of issue which must be decided by the jury. Dr. Laird's personal view is perhaps relevant, but certainly not dispositive. This is a products liability case, not a professional negligence or malpractice case in which expert testimony would be required to demonstrate a breach of the pertinent standard of care. Determination of whether a battery of tests costing $40 is too expensive where a person's life may be at stake does not necessarily call for a strictly professional judgment. The jury had evidence of the risk and the means available to obviate that risk. It was free to reject the expert's opinion.

* * *

For these reasons, we reverse the trial court's judgment. We hold that plaintiff is entitled to a new trial on each of the claims raised against defendant Wyeth Laboratories.

Reversed.

Notes

1. Under the law of negligence the risk must be foreseeable. This requirement represents a major difference between negligence and strict liability, where foreseeability generally is not required.

2. What is foreseeable is a function of several factors. One is the standard of care. The law of negligence requires manufacturers to have the skill of experts, and to keep up with the latest scientific advances. *See* note 3, *supra* page 25. Thus, manufacturers would normally not escape liability because of ignorance of risks which were scientifically knowable at the time of sale.

3. Another consideration affecting foreseeability is the way the risk/utility factors are applied to determine whether the manufacturer's conduct was reasonable. As *Taylor v. Wyeth Laboratories, Inc.* indicates, a manufacturer has a duty to conduct reasonable tests to discover product risks. Obviously, every risk can be discovered if sufficient testing is performed. The same holds true with respect to the manufacturer's ability to discover manufacturing flaws in its products. Virtually every flaw could be discovered if each product were inspected closely enough.

4. In *Taylor v. Wyeth Laboratories, Inc.* the court left the question of reasonableness to the jury. Was this appropriate? Under what circumstances should trial judges decide that a defendant's conduct was reasonable as a matter of law?

5. Contrast the approach that courts use in medical malpractice cases. There, a plaintiff normally cannot get to a jury unless he introduces expert testimony establishing that the defendant deviated from the standards of her profession. In products liability cases, evidence of customary practice is admissible but not controlling. In this regard consider the following case.

OSBORN v. IRWIN MEMORIAL BLOOD BANK

California Court of Appeal, First District, 1992.
5 Cal.App.4th 234, 7 Cal.Rptr.2d 101.

PERLEY, ASSOCIATE JUSTICE.

The trial in this case has been reported as the first in the nation where a blood bank was found liable in connection with transmission of the AIDS virus by a blood transfusion.

In February of 1983, at the age of three weeks, Michael Osborn contracted the AIDS virus from a blood transfusion in the course of surgery on his heart at the University of California at San Francisco Medical Center. The blood used in the operation was supplied by the Irwin Memorial Blood Bank. Michael and his parents, Paul and Mary Osborn, sued Irwin and the University for damages on various theories.

The only causes of action that survived defense motions for nonsuit and directed verdict were claims against Irwin for negligence, and intentional and negligent misrepresentation. After the jury returned a general verdict for plaintiffs, the court granted Irwin's motion for judgment notwithstanding the verdict on the intentional misrepresentation and negligence claims. Irwin was thus held liable only for a negligent misrepresentation.

[The court concluded that a new trial was necessary on the negligent misrepresentation theory because of evidentiary error.]

* * *

The most significant issue on appeal is whether Irwin was entitled to judgment notwithstanding the verdict on the issue of negligence. Qualified experts opined for plaintiffs that Irwin's blood testing and donor screening practices prior to Michael's surgery were negligent in light of concerns about AIDS at the time. On matters such as these that are outside common knowledge, expert opinion is ordinarily sufficient to create a prima facie case. Here, however, there was uncontradicted evidence that Irwin was doing as much if not more in the areas of testing and screening than any other blood bank in the country, and there is no question that it followed accepted practices within the profession. We hold that Irwin cannot be found negligent in these circumstances.

* * *

[Concern about AIDS lead] the Centers for Disease Control (CDC) to convene a meeting on January 4, 1983. According to the invitation, the purpose of the meeting was "to formulate recommendations for the prevention of AIDS with special emphasis on possible transmission through blood and blood products." The meeting was attended by 80 to 100 people, including representatives of all of the major blood banking associations * * *.

* * *

The cause of AIDS was unknown and there was no test for it at the time, but the CDC presented data on the results of various surrogate tests, performed on the blood of a limited population of people who exhibited symptoms of AIDS, which might be used to determine whether a donor was at high risk for the disease. The CDC estimated that only 5 percent of normal controls would be positive in anti-HBc tests for the antibody to the hepatitis B core antigen. However, all 21 of the intravenous drug users in the CDC's test group, and 88.2 percent of the 93 homosexuals or bisexuals in the group, tested positive for this antibody. * * * [A]n "ever recurring" proposal at the meeting was to conduct anti-HBc tests and reject all blood that tested positive. * * * [T]he cost of the test "bothered many but not CDC." * * *

* * *

(2) Irwin's Actions

Plaintiffs' principal theory of negligence is that Irwin should have started anti-HBc surrogate testing for AIDS prior to Michael's operation. Plaintiffs also argue that Irwin's practices with respect to donor questioning were negligent. The evidence of Irwin's actions in these areas was as follows.

* * *

C. *Form of Plaintiffs' Expert Testimony*

The form of their experts' testimony suggests that plaintiffs assumed their case against Irwin was one of ordinary negligence. Plaintiffs' experts did not couch their opinions in terms of the standard of care for blood banks in early 1983. They simply said what Irwin "should" have done, or what a "reasonable person" would have done, in light of what was known about AIDS at the time. We ultimately conclude that this distinction is one of substance as well as form, but the threshold question is whether Irwin should be held to a professional standard of care.

We note that this appears to be a point of first impression in California. The precedents indicating that blood banks are not subject to strict liability for providing contaminated blood (see Health & Saf. Code, § 1606 [distribution of blood is a service rather than a sale]) have observed that blood banks may be sued for negligence but have not undertaken to define the standard of care. * * *

We conclude that the adequacy of a blood bank's actions to prevent the contamination of blood is a question of professional negligence and fulfillment of a professional standard of care. As another court has observed, the "activities of [the blood bank] at issue here—the collection, processing, and testing of blood for transfusion—no doubt require the exercise of professional expertise and professional judgment." (*Doe v. American Red Cross Blood Services, S.C. Region* (D.S.C.1989) 125 F.R.D. 637, 642.)

This conclusion is consistent with most of the cases in other jurisdictions that have considered negligence claims against blood banks. [Citations]; see also Comment (1989) 41 S.C.L.Rev. 107, 114 ["most courts only hold blood banks to a 'professional' rather than a 'reasonable man' standard of care"]. This conclusion is also consistent with California cases that have applied a professional standard to activities involving special training and skill. [Citations]

Irwin was therefore required to exercise with respect to blood testing and donor screening "that reasonable degree of skill, knowledge, and care ordinarily possessed and exercised" by other blood banks "under similar circumstances." [Citations] Although this same standard of care applies generally to "[t]hose undertaking to render expert services in the practice of a profession or trade" [citation], we will refer to authorities in the area of medical malpractice because blood banking has appropriately been treated as a medical service. [Citations]

* * *

E. Sufficiency of Plaintiffs' Expert Opinions

* * *

Looking first at surrogate testing, the undisputed evidence is that no blood bank ran anti-HBc tests for AIDS in January and February of 1983. Although concerns about AIDS and the blood supply had recently surfaced, no recommendations on the subject had been issued by any governmental agency, and the recommendations issued later did not endorse anti-HBc testing. The only published standards at the time were those of the [American Association of Blood Banks], [the American Red Cross] and [the Council of Community Blood Centers], who jointly advised against any routine laboratory screening for AIDS. It is apparent that there were people at the January 4 CDC meeting and at the University who advocated anti-HBc testing. But the professional consensus at the time, reflected in both the joint statement of the blood banking associations and the universal practice among blood banks, was that further study of the test was needed. Plaintiffs' case for anti-HBc testing thus boils down to the proposition that the entire blood banking profession was negligent. We find that proposition to be untenable.

Plaintiffs contend that custom and practice are relevant, but not conclusive, on the standard of care. This is the general rule in cases of ordinary negligence. [Citations] The leading case for this rule is *The T.J. Hooper* (2d Cir.1932) 60 F.2d 737, 740, where Learned Hand wrote that "in most cases reasonable prudence is in fact common prudence; but strictly it is never its measure; a whole calling may have unduly lagged in the adoption of new and available devices. It never may set its own tests, however persuasive be its usages. Courts must in the end say what is required; there are precautions so imperative that even their universal disregard will not excuse their omission." (See also *Texas & Pacific Ry. Co. v. Behymer* (1903) 189 U.S. 468, 470, 23 S.Ct. 622, 623, 47 L.Ed. 905 [Justice Holmes's observation that "what ought to be done is fixed by a standard of reasonable prudence, whether it usually is complied with or not"].) There is no question that California follows this rule in ordinary negligence cases. [Citation]

This is a case of professional negligence, however, and we must assess the role of custom and practice in that context. The question presented here is whether California law permits an expert to second-guess an entire profession. We have found no definitive precedent on this issue and it is not one that is likely to arise.

Custom and practice are not controlling in cases, unlike ours, where a layperson can infer negligence by a professional without any expert testimony. In *Leonard v. Watsonville Community Hosp.* (1956) 47 Cal.2d 509, 305 P.2d 36, for example, where a clamp was left in the plaintiff's body after surgery, the lack of an " 'established practice' " of counting clamps did not preclude a finding of negligence: "[D]efendants seek to avoid liability on the theory that they were required to exercise only that degree of skill employed by other hospitals and nurses in the community. It is a matter of common knowledge, however, that no special skill is required in counting instruments. Although *under such circumstances* proof of practice or custom is some evidence of what should be done and may assist in the determination of what constitutes due care, it does not conclusively establish the standard of care." (*Id.*, at p. 519, 305 P.2d 36 [emphasis added].) Here again California follows the general rule. [Citation]

On the other hand, in cases like ours where experts are needed to show negligence, their testimony sets the standard of care [Citations] and is said to be conclusive. (Citations) "Ordinarily, where a professional person is accused of negligence in failing to adhere to accepted standards within his profession the accepted standards must be established only by qualified expert testimony unless the standard is a matter of common knowledge. However, when the matter in issue is within the knowledge of experts only and not within common knowledge, expert evidence is conclusive and cannot be disregarded." (*Huber, Hunt & Nichols, Inc. v. Moore* (1977) 67 Cal.App.3d 278, 313, 136 Cal.Rptr. 603 [citations omitted]; see also *Lysick v. Walcom, supra*, 258 Cal.App.2d at p. 156, 65 Cal.Rptr. 406.) Qualified expert opinion will thus generally preclude a directed verdict in a professional negligence case.

This case, however, is distinguishable. Experts' testimony ordinarily cannot be "disregarded" because it cannot be said that their opinions about what should have been done do not reflect the custom and practice of the profession. When an expert describes the "standard technique" for a knee operation * * *, or what a reasonable attorney would do to settle a wrongful death action * * *, or how long an architect should take to approve change orders on a construction project * * *, it is impossible to say that no surgeon, lawyer or architect was doing what the expert said was required. Here it is undisputed that no blood bank in the country was doing what the plaintiffs' experts' standard of care would require of Irwin, and we have an unusual situation where we are called upon to address the significance of a universal practice.

* * *

While it may be true that "[a]n increasing number of courts are rejecting the customary practice standard in favor of a reasonable care or reasonably prudent doctor standard" (Prosser & Keeton, The Law of Torts (5th ed., 1988 pocket supp.) p. 30, fn. 53 [citing cases outside California]), numerous commentaries have noted that custom generally sets the standard of care.[7] [Citations]

7. Plaintiffs are thus only partially correct when they assert that the standard of care in medical malpractice cases is "higher" than in cases of ordinary negligence. A medical practitioner is "held to the standard of practice generally accepted by his branch of the profession," but is also "protected by this standard since compliance

Most commentators have urged that a customary or accepted practice standard is preferable to one that allows for the disregard of professional judgment. (Compare Keeton, [Medical Negligence—The Standard of Care (1979) 10 Tex.Tech L.Rev. 351] at pp. 364–365; King, [In Search of a Standard of Care for the Medical Profession: The "Accepted Practice" Formula (1975) 28 Vand.L.Rev. 1213] at p. 1249; and McCoid, *supra*, 12 Vand.L.Rev. at p. 609; with Comment (1970) 23 Vand.L.Rev. 729, 745.) Indeed, the more recent commentaries are not concerned with whether customary practices should be the maximum expected of medical practitioners, but rather with whether those practices should continue to set a minimum standard in a time of increasing economic constraints. (See generally, e.g., Morreim, *Cost Containment and the Standard of Medical Care* (1987) 75 Cal.L.Rev. 1719; Havighurst, *Altering the Applicable Standard of Care* (1986) 49 Law & Contemp. Probs. 265; Note (1985) 98 Harv.L.Rev. 1004.)

The basic reason why professionals are usually held only to a standard of custom and practice is that their informed approach to matters outside common knowledge should not be "evaluated by the ad hoc judgments of a lay judge or lay jurors aided by hindsight." (King, *supra*, 28 Vand.L.Rev. at p. 1249.) In the words of a leading authority, "When it can be said that the collective wisdom of the profession is that a particular course of action is the desirable course, then it would seem that the collective wisdom should be followed by the courts." (Keeton, *supra*, 10 Tex.Tech L.Rev. at pp. 364–365.)

* * *

It follows that Irwin cannot be found negligent for failing to perform tests that no other blood bank in the nation was using. Judgment notwithstanding the verdict was properly granted to Irwin on the issue of anti-HBc testing because there was no substantial evidence that failure to conduct the tests was not accepted *practice* for blood banks in January and February of 1983.

This conclusion is consistent with most of the reported blood bank cases in other jurisdictions. [Citations]

We now turn to the allegations about donor screening.

[Plaintiff's expert] criticized the AIDS-related questions Irwin used in the immediate aftermath of the CDC meeting. However, there were no published standards for such questions at the time, and there was no evidence that any particular questions were generally adopted by blood banks during this period. We find no substantial evidence on the record as a whole that Irwin did not follow accepted practice among blood banks for donor questioning prior to January 19, 1983.

[Discussing the evidence relating to donor screening.]

with accepted practice is generally taken as conclusive evidence of due care." (McCoid, [The Care Required of Medical Practitioners (1959) 12 Vand.L.Rev. 549] at p. 560; see also Comment (1991) 27 Willamette L.Rev. 355, 356 [ordinary negligence standard may be "higher" than professional negligence standard].)

We conclude that plaintiffs did not present a prima facie case of negligence with respect to donor questioning, and that Irwin was entitled to judgment notwithstanding the verdict on negligence.

* * *

V. Disposition

The judgment against Irwin is reversed, and the case is remanded for a new trial of the negligent misrepresentation claim against Irwin. The judgment for Irwin on all other causes of action, and the judgment in favor of the University, are affirmed. * * *

ANDERSON, P.J., and POCHE, J., concur.

Notes

1. The difference between medical malpractice cases and products liability cases, regarding the necessity for expert testimony to show a breach of the pertinent standard of care, can have a profound effect on the way these two classes of cases are decided. *Compare* with *Osborn*, for example, *Taylor v. Wyeth Laboratories, Inc., supra.* If the *Taylor* court had required expert testimony of a violation of customary practice, the defendant would have been entitled to a directed verdict. Thus, a product liability defendant is subject to a greater risk of liability than a malpractice defendant because it gets the worst of both worlds. The product defendant is held to the standard of an expert, but it is not given the benefit of the rule that customary practice among experts is controlling.

2. Not all product liability cases alleging negligence, however, automatically go to the jury without expert testimony. If the alleged negligence involves specialized knowledge or expertise outside the layperson's knowledge, plaintiff must present expert testimony to create a submissible case. In Baltus v. Weaver Div. of Kidde & Co., Inc., 199 Ill.App.3d 821, 145 Ill.Dec. 810, 557 N.E.2d 580 (1990) plaintiff was injured when a transmission slipped off a jack and fell on his right hand. The machine originally had four U-shaped adjustable supports. These supports were attached to a platform on top of the jack and were what the transmissions rested on when they are being repaired. One of the supports was missing at the time of the accident. Plaintiff claimed that the supports should have been permanently affixed to the table of the jack, rather than being removable. The court ruled that plaintiff could not make a submissible case without expert testimony. The court stated:

> The issue is: Does the mere fact that the adjustable supports are removable render the jack *unreasonably* dangerous? Without expert testimony as to the function(s) of the transmission jack, design alternatives that were available to accomplish the same function(s) in a safer manner, or at least some knowledge attributable to [defendant] that its design was unreasonably dangerous, we cannot agree that the jury may simply speculate that it was in fact an unreasonably dangerous machine, due to its design. * * *

> * * * [W]e agree with defendant that product liability cases are analogous to those involving medical malpractice: Both types of cases

involve specialized knowledge that bear directly on the standard of care in the community. While some instances of medical malpractice need no expert opinion that a doctor has fallen below the standard of care (such as a case in which an instrument is left in the patient after surgery), expert opinion usually is required to aid the jury in determining that the pertinent standard of care has been breached. *E.g.*, * * * Smith v. South Shore Hospital (1989), 187 Ill.App.3d 847, 135 Ill.Dec. 300, 543 N.E.2d 868 (testimony by another doctor that he would have done something different is not sufficient to establish a *prima facie* case).

We do not imply that all cases of negligent manufacture or design require expert opinion as to the unreasonably dangerous condition of the product. For example, if a chair is designed to be easily collapsible, for portability, but has the tendency to collapse when someone sits on it, an expert in chair design may not be needed to help the jury decide that the design is unreasonably dangerous; it does not function in the manner expected and is in fact unsafe. * * *

* * * [In this case, in the jack's] normal and intended use the four supports would be in place, as they are an integral part of the jack's assembly. * * * The transmission is held to the [platform] of the jack by the supports, which apparently are adjustable to accommodate different size transmissions. Without expert testimony resting on a foundation of facts regarding this particular design, the jury would be left to speculate that it was unreasonably dangerous *solely* because the supports were removable. (To say that it was "foreseeable" that they would be removed assumes that the removability of the supports *ipso facto* renders the jack unreasonably dangerous as manufactured.) In fact, the record indicates that the jack may have been designed to have other uses, such as a worktable. (See Savage Manufacturing and Sales, Inc. v. Doser (1989), 184 Ill.App.3d 405, 132 Ill.Dec. 662, 540 N.E.2d 402, appeal allowed (1989), 127 Ill.2d 641, 136 Ill.Dec. 607, 545 N.E.2d 131 (Jury verdict in strict liability case against manufacturer reversed on appeal because multi-use press was not unreasonably dangerous for lack of safety guards at point of operation, when plaintiff's own expert admitted that only a unifunctional press could have been equipped with such devices).) We conclude that Baltus cannot establish a breach of the standard of care in this case without expert testimony.

* * *

* * * The standard to which the manufacturer is held is that degree of knowledge and skill of an expert [citation]; therefore, one challenging such design as being unreasonably dangerous should be qualified as an expert also, unless the design is so obviously defective that it is within the common understanding of non-experts. Since we have concluded that the defect alleged in the pending case is not so obvious as to be within the common understanding of non-experts, we also conclude that plaintiff's personal opinion is not sufficient as that of an expert. We cannot presume a breach of duty in negligent manufacture based on the conclusory statement that the supports should not be removed, or removable, for any reason.

3. Normally plaintiff designates the event to which courts apply the test of negligence. He does this by pleading that certain acts or omissions of the defendant were negligent, *e.g.*, improper manufacture or failure to warn. The jury then must determine whether the defendant was negligent in that respect. Plaintiff's choice of theory, of course, is often greatly influenced by available evidence concerning how the accident happened. If, for example, an automobile suspension component collapses because the bolt securing it to the frame came loose, plaintiff's best theory of negligence may be that the bolt was not sufficiently tightened at the factory. *See* Jenkins v. General Motors Corp., 446 F.2d 377 (5th Cir.1971), cert. denied, 405 U.S. 922, 92 S.Ct. 959, 30 L.Ed.2d 793 (1972). The next section deals with the situation where plaintiff may get to the jury without specifying that a particular act or omission was negligent.

SECTION D. RES IPSA LOQUITUR

ESCOLA v. COCA COLA BOTTLING CO. OF FRESNO

Supreme Court of California, 1944.
24 Cal.2d 453, 150 P.2d 436.

GIBSON, CHIEF JUSTICE.

Plaintiff, a waitress in a restaurant, was injured when a bottle of Coca Cola broke in her hand. She alleged that defendant company, which had bottled and delivered the alleged defective bottle to her employer, was negligent in selling "bottles containing said beverage which on account of excessive pressure of gas or by reason of some defect in the bottle was dangerous * * * and likely to explode." This appeal is from a judgment upon a jury verdict in favor of plaintiff.

Defendant's driver delivered several cases of Coca Cola to the restaurant, placing them on the floor, one on top of the other, under and behind the counter, where they remained at least thirty-six hours. Immediately before the accident, plaintiff picked up the top case and set it upon a near-by ice cream cabinet in front of and about three feet from the refrigerator. She then proceeded to take the bottles from the case with her right hand, one at a time, and put them into the refrigerator. Plaintiff testified that after she had placed three bottles in the refrigerator and had moved the fourth bottle about 18 inches from the case "it exploded in my hand." The bottle broke into two jagged pieces and inflicted a deep five-inch cut, severing blood vessels, nerves and muscles of the thumb and palm of the hand. * * * A fellow employee, on the opposite side of the counter, testified that plaintiff "had the bottle, I should judge, waist high, and I know that it didn't bang either the case or the door or another bottle * * * when it popped. It sounded just like a fruit jar would blow up * * *." The witness further testified that the contents of the bottle "flew all over herself and myself and the walls and one thing and another."

The top portion of the bottle, with the cap, remained in plaintiff's hand, and the lower portion fell to the floor but did not break. The broken bottle was not produced at the trial, the pieces having been thrown away by an employee of the restaurant shortly after the accident. Plaintiff, however, described the broken pieces, and a diagram of the bottle was made showing the location of the "fracture line" where the bottle broke in two.

One of defendant's drivers, called as a witness by plaintiff, testified that he had seen other bottles of Coca Cola in the past explode and had found broken bottles in the warehouse when he took the cases out, but that he did not know what made them blow up.

Plaintiff then rested her case, having announced to the court that being unable to show any specific acts of negligence she relied completely on the doctrine of res ipsa loquitur.

Defendant contends that the doctrine of res ipsa loquitur does not apply in this case, and that the evidence is insufficient to support the judgment.

* * *

Res ipsa loquitur does not apply unless (1) defendant had exclusive control of the thing causing the injury and (2) the accident is of such a nature that it ordinarily would not occur in the absence of negligence by the defendant. Honea v. City Dairy, Inc., 22 Cal.2d 614, 616, 617, 140 P.2d 369, and authorities there cited; cf. Hinds v. Wheadon, 19 Cal.2d 458, 461, 121 P.2d 724; Prosser on Torts [1941], 293–301.

Many authorities state that the happening of the accident does not speak for itself where it took place some time after defendant had relinquished control of the instrumentality causing the injury. Under the more logical view, however, the doctrine may be applied upon the theory that defendant had control at the time of the alleged negligent act, although not at the time of the accident, *provided* plaintiff first proves that the condition of the instrumentality had not been changed after it left the defendant's possession. See cases collected in Honea v. City Dairy, Inc., 22 Cal.2d 614, 617, 618, 140 P.2d 369. As said in Dunn v. Hoffman Beverage Co., 126 N.J.L. 556, 20 A.2d 352, 354, "defendant is not charged with the duty of showing affirmatively that something happened to the bottle after it left its control or management; * * * to get to the jury the plaintiff must show that there was due care during that period." Plaintiff must also prove that she handled the bottle carefully. The reason for this prerequisite is set forth in Prosser on Torts, supra, at page 300, where the author states: "Allied to the condition of exclusive control in the defendant is that of absence of any action on the part of the plaintiff contributing to the accident. Its purpose, of course, is to eliminate the possibility that it was the plaintiff who was responsible. If the boiler of a locomotive explodes while the plaintiff engineer is operating it, the inference of his own negligence is at least as great as that of the defendant, and res ipsa loquitur will not apply until he has accounted for his own conduct." See, also, Olson v. Whitthorne & Swan, 203 Cal. 206, 208, 209, 263 P. 518, 58 A.L.R. 129. It is not necessary, of course, that plaintiff eliminate every remote possibility of injury to the bottle after defendant lost control, and the requirement is satisfied if there is evidence permitting a reasonable inference that it was not accessible to extraneous harmful forces and that it was carefully handled by plaintiff or any third person who may have moved or touched it. Cf. Prosser, supra, p. 300. If such evidence is presented, the question becomes one for the trier of fact (see, e.g., MacPherson v. Canada Dry Ginger Ale, Inc., 129 N.J.L. 365, 29 A.2d 868, 869), and, accordingly, the issue should be submitted to the jury under proper instructions.

* * *

Upon an examination of the record, the evidence appears sufficient to support a reasonable inference that the bottle here involved was not damaged by any extraneous force after delivery to the restaurant by defendant. It follows, therefore, that the bottle was in some manner defective at the time defendant relinquished control, because sound and properly prepared bottles of carbonated liquids do not ordinarily explode when carefully handled.

The next question, then, is whether plaintiff may rely upon the doctrine of res ipsa loquitur to supply an inference that defendant's negligence was responsible for the defective condition of the bottle at the time it was delivered to the restaurant. Under the general rules pertaining to the doctrine, as set forth above, it must appear that bottles of carbonated liquid are not ordinarily defective without negligence by the bottling company. In 1 Shearman and Redfield on Negligence (Rev.Ed.1941), page 153, it is stated that: "The doctrine * * * requires evidence which shows at least the probability that a particular accident could not have occurred without legal wrong by the defendant."

An explosion such as took place here might have been caused by an excessive internal pressure in a sound bottle, by a defect in the glass of a bottle containing a safe pressure, or by a combination of these two possible causes. The question is whether under the evidence there was a probability that defendant was negligent in any of these respects. If so, the doctrine of res ipsa loquitur applies.

The bottle was admittedly charged with gas under pressure, and the charging of the bottle was within the exclusive control of defendant. As it is a matter of common knowledge that an overcharge would not ordinarily result without negligence, it follows under the doctrine of res ipsa loquitur that if the bottle was in fact excessively charged an inference of defendant's negligence would arise. If the explosion resulted from a defective bottle containing a safe pressure, the defendant would be liable if it negligently failed to discover such flaw. If the defect were visible, an inference of negligence would arise from the failure of defendant to discover it. Where defects are discoverable, it may be assumed that they will not ordinarily escape detection if a reasonable inspection is made, and if such a defect is overlooked an inference arises that a proper inspection was not made. A difficult problem is presented where the defect is unknown and consequently might have been one not discoverable by a reasonable, practicable inspection. In the Honea case we refused to take judicial notice of the technical practices and information available to the bottling industry for finding defects which cannot be seen. In the present case, however, we are supplied with evidence of the standard methods used for testing bottles.

A chemical engineer for the Owens–Illinois Glass Company and its Pacific Coast subsidiary, maker of Coca Cola bottles, explained how glass is manufactured and the methods used in testing and inspecting bottles. He testified that his company is the largest manufacturer of glass containers in the United States, and that it uses the standard methods for testing bottles recommended by the glass containers association. A pressure test is made by taking a sample from each mold every three hours—approximately one out of every 600 bottles—and subjecting the sample to an internal pressure of 450 pounds per square inch, which is sustained for one minute. (The normal pressure in Coca Cola bottles is less than 50 pounds per square inch.) The sample bottles are also subjected to the standard thermal shock test. The witness stated that these tests are "pretty near" infallible.

It thus appears that there is available to the industry a commonly-used method of testing bottles for defects not apparent to the eye, which is almost infallible. Since Coca Cola bottles are subjected to these tests by the manufacturer, it is not likely that they contain defects when delivered to the bottler which are not discoverable by visual inspection. Both new and used bottles are filled and distributed by defendant. The used bottles are not again subjected to the tests referred to above, and it may be inferred that defects not discoverable by visual inspection do not develop in bottles after they are manufactured. Obviously, if such defects do occur in used bottles there is a duty upon the bottler to make appropriate tests before they are refilled, and if such tests are not commercially practicable the bottles should not be re-used. This would seem to be particularly true where a charged liquid is placed in the bottle. It follows that a defect which would make the bottle unsound could be discovered by reasonable and practicable tests.

Although it is not clear in this case whether the explosion was caused by an excessive charge or a defect in the glass there is a sufficient showing that neither cause would ordinarily have been present if due care had been used. Further, defendant had exclusive control over both the charging and inspection of the bottles. Accordingly, all the requirements necessary to entitle plaintiff to rely on the doctrine of res ipsa loquitur to supply an inference of negligence are present.

It is true that defendant presented evidence tending to show that it exercised considerable precaution by carefully regulating and checking the pressure in the bottles and by making visual inspections for defects in the glass at several stages during the bottling process. It is well settled, however, that when a defendant produces evidence to rebut the inference of negligence which arises upon application of the doctrine of res ipsa loquitur, it is ordinarily a question of fact for the jury to determine whether the inference has been dispelled. Druzanich v. Criley, 19 Cal.2d 439, 444, 122 P.2d 53; Michener v. Hutton, 203 Cal. 604, 610, 265 P. 238, 59 A.L.R. 480.

The judgment is affirmed.

SHENK, CURTIS, CARTER, and SCHAUER, JJ., concurred.

TRAYNOR, JUSTICE.

I concur in the judgment, but I believe the manufacturer's negligence should no longer be singled out as the basis of a plaintiff's right to recover in cases like the present one. In my opinion it should now be recognized that a manufacturer incurs an absolute liability when an article that he has placed on the market, knowing that it is to be used without inspection, proves to have a defect that causes injury to human beings. MacPherson v. Buick Motor Co., 217 N.Y. 382, 111 N.E. 1050, L.R.A.1916F, 696, Ann.Cas.1916C, 440 established the principle, recognized by this court, that irrespective of privity of contract, the manufacturer is responsible for an injury caused by such an article to any person who comes in lawful contact with it. Sheward v. Virtue, 20 Cal.2d 410, 126 P.2d 345; Kalash v. Los Angeles Ladder Co., 1 Cal.2d 229, 34 P.2d 481. In these cases the source of the manufacturer's liability was his negligence in the manufacturing process or in the inspection of component parts supplied by others. Even if there is no negligence, however, public policy demands that responsibility be fixed wherever it will most effectively reduce the hazards to life and health inherent in defective products that reach the market. It is evident that the manufacturer can anticipate some hazards and guard against the recurrence of others, as the public cannot. Those who suffer injury from defective products are unprepared to meet its consequences. The cost of an injury and the loss of time or health may be an overwhelming misfortune to the person injured, and a needless one, for the risk of injury can be insured by the manufacturer and distributed among the public as a cost of doing business. It is to the public interest to discourage the marketing of products having defects that are a menace to the public. If such products nevertheless find their way into the market it is to the public interest to place the responsibility for whatever injury they may cause upon the manufacturer, who, even if he is not negligent in the manufacture of the product, is responsible for its reaching the market. However intermittently such injuries may occur and however haphazardly they may strike, the risk of their occurrence is a constant risk and a general one. Against such a risk there should be general and constant protection and the manufacturer is best situated to afford such protection.

The injury from a defective product does not become a matter of indifference because the defect arises from causes other than the negligence of the manufacturer, such as negligence of a submanufacturer of a component part whose defects could not be revealed by inspection (see

Sheward v. Virtue, 20 Cal.2d 410, 126 P.2d 345; O'Rourke v. Day & Night Water Heater Co., Ltd., 31 Cal.App.2d 364, 88 P.2d 191; Smith v. Peerless Glass Co., 259 N.Y. 292, 181 N.E. 576), or unknown causes that even by the device of res ipsa loquitur cannot be classified as negligence of the manufacturer. The inference of negligence may be dispelled by an affirmative showing of proper care. If the evidence against the fact inferred is "clear, positive, uncontradicted, and of such a nature that it can not rationally be disbelieved, the court must instruct the jury that the nonexistence of the fact has been established as a matter of law." Blank v. Coffin, 20 Cal.2d 457, 461, 126 P.2d 868, 870. An injured person, however, is not ordinarily in a position to refute such evidence or identify the cause of the defect, for he can hardly be familiar with the manufacturing process as the manufacturer himself is. In leaving it to the jury to decide whether the inference has been dispelled, regardless of the evidence against it, the negligence rule approaches the rule of strict liability. It is needlessly circuitous to make negligence the basis of recovery and impose what is in reality liability without negligence. If public policy demands that a manufacturer of goods be responsible for their quality regardless of negligence there is no reason not to fix that responsibility openly.

* * *

It is to the public interest to prevent injury to the public from any defective goods by the imposition of civil liability generally.

* * *

[Justice Traynor points out that strict liability is already imposed on product sellers under the law of warranty. The privity requirement, however, renders the remedy inadequate. Most consumers cannot sue the manufacturer of the harmful product because they are not in privity of contract with him.]

The manufacturer's liability should, of course, be defined in terms of the safety of the product in normal and proper use, and should not extend to injuries that cannot be traced to the product as it reached the market.

Rehearing denied; EDMONDS, J., dissenting.

Notes

1. As used in most jurisdictions, res ipsa loquitur is merely a way of proving negligence with circumstantial evidence. In Zentz v. Coca Cola Bottling Co. of Fresno, 39 Cal.2d 436, 247 P.2d 344 (1952), another exploding bottle case, Chief Justice Gibson elaborated on the nature of the doctrine:

It was stated in Judson v. Giant Powder Co., 107 Cal. 549, 556, 40 P. 1020, 1021, 29 L.R.A. 718, that the doctrine is based on "the experience of the past" and the theory that what "has happened in the past, under the same conditions, will probably happen in the future, and ordinary and probable results will be presumed to take place until the contrary is shown." In another early case it was said: "The bedrock of this principle * * * is that of probabilities * * *." Harrison v. Sutter St. Ry. Co., 134 Cal. 549, 552, 66 P. 787, 788, 55 L.R.A. 608. Since the decision of the Judson case in 1895, the words "probably," "probable," "probability" and "probabilities" have been repeatedly used in this connection, both as part of the rule and as the basic reason, or one of the reasons, for it. [Citations] [In] La Porte v. Houston, 33 Cal.2d 167, 169, 199 P.2d 665 * * * at page 666, we said, after assuming that defendants were in control at the time of the accident, that "the applicability of the doctrine of res ipsa loquitur depends on whether it can be said, in the light of common experience, that the accident was more likely than not the result of their [defendants'] negligence. [Citations.] 'Where no such balance of probabilities in favor of negligence can be found, res ipsa loquitur does not apply.' " In determining whether such a probability exists with regard to a particular occurrence, the courts have relied both upon common knowledge and the testimony of expert witnesses. * * *

All of the cases hold, in effect, that it must appear, either as a matter of common experience or from evidence in the case, that the accident is of a type which probably would not happen unless someone was negligent. In the absence of such a probability there would be no basis for an inference of negligence which would serve to take the place of evidence of some specific negligent act or omission. The defendant, of course, should not be liable unless it appears from all the facts and circumstances that there is a sufficient causal connection between his conduct and the plaintiff's injury, and it has been held that res ipsa loquitur will not apply if it is equally probable that the negligence was that of someone other than the defendant. * * *

2. If the exclusive control requirement were literally applied, res ipsa loquitur would almost never be useful in products liability cases because the seller is usually not in possession of the product at the time of the accident. Some cases have refused to apply the doctrine for this reason. E.g., Cockerham v. Ward, 44 N.C.App. 615, 262 S.E.2d 651 (1980), cert. denied, 300 N.C. 195, 269 S.E.2d 622 (1980) (A rubber strap broke and hit plaintiff in the eye. Res ipsa did not apply in an action against the manufacturer of the strap because he was not in control of the strap when it broke.). Many courts, like the main case, hold that control at the time of the alleged negligent act is sufficient as long as plaintiff proves that the condition of the product had not changed after leaving defendant's hands. The essential thing is to attribute the negligent act to the defendant. Proof of exclusive control at the time of the accident is merely one way to do this.

The Restatement (Second) of Torts § 328D (1965) describes the proof necessary for res ipsa loquitur as follows:

§ 328D. Res Ipsa Loquitur

(1) It may be inferred that harm suffered by the plaintiff is caused by negligence of the defendant when

(a) the event is of a kind which ordinarily does not occur in the absence of negligence;

(b) other responsible causes, including the conduct of the plaintiff and third persons, are sufficiently eliminated by the evidence; and

(c) the indicated negligence is within the scope of the defendant's duty to the plaintiff.

(2) It is the function of the court to determine whether the inference may reasonably be drawn by the jury, or whether it must necessarily be drawn.

(3) It is the function of the jury to determine whether the inference is to be drawn in any case where different conclusions may reasonably be reached.

3. Is there an inference of negligence in the following cases?

A. A tire blew out and caused an accident after six months of normal use.

B. A new tire blew out at the bead while being mounted on a wheel of the proper size. The plaintiff's expert testified that there must have been a defect in the wire bead. Furthermore, it must have been present at the time of manufacture because it is not possible to cause this kind of defect either with a tire iron or with the amount of air pressure that plaintiff had available.

C. A suture needle broke during surgery.

D. A dead worm or moth was found in plug of chewing tobacco.

E. Plaintiff was injured as a result of a premature explosion of dynamite. He sued the separate manufacturers of the dynamite and the blasting cap, claiming that the explosion resulted from the malfunction of one of those products.

4. Res ipsa loquitur creates an inference that the defendant must have been negligent in some way, but the manner is unspecified. Courts sometimes refer to this as general negligence. In cases where all the facts are known, res ipsa loquitur is unnecessary, and most courts do not permit its use. In order to prevail, plaintiff must show that the defendant's conduct was negligent. *See, e.g.*, Elgin Airport Inn, Inc. v. Commonwealth Edison Co., 88 Ill.App.3d 477, 43 Ill.Dec. 620, 410 N.E.2d 620 (1980), affirmed in part and reversed in part on other grounds, 89 Ill.2d 138, 59 Ill.Dec. 675, 432 N.E.2d 259 (1982). Plaintiff's air conditioning equipment was damaged by low voltage electricity caused by a broken casting in defendant's switching mechanism. Defendant tested the switching mechanism on a regular basis, and always found it to be working properly. The only way the defective casting could have been discovered was by disassembling the switching mechanism and examining it. Plaintiff could not rely on res ipsa loquitur to establish that defendant negligently supplied defective electricity since the exact cause of the failure was disclosed. Furthermore, plaintiff's evidence was insufficient to establish specific negligence because it failed to show that defendant could have taken any reasonable precaution that would have prevented the damage.

5. In most jurisdictions res ipsa loquitur creates a permissible inference of negligence which the jury is free to either accept or reject. Ryan v.

Zweck–Wollenberg Co., 266 Wis. 630, 64 N.W.2d 226 (1954). Other jurisdictions give it a greater procedural effect. One approach requires the judge to direct a verdict in favor of plaintiff unless defendant presents evidence sufficient to sustain a finding that defendant either was not negligent or his negligence did not cause the accident. Newing v. Cheatham, 15 Cal.3d 351, 124 Cal.Rptr. 193, 540 P.2d 33 (1975). Another approach shifts the burden of proof to the defendant. Gabriel v. Royal Prods. Div. of Wash. Prods., Inc., 159 So.2d 384 (La.App.1964).

6. A small minority of courts refuse to apply the res ipsa loquitur doctrine unless the defendant has superior knowledge of the cause of the accident. They reason that only then may the defendant justifiably be forced to come forward with evidence explaining what happened. *E.g.*, Ford Motor Co. v. Fish, 232 Ark. 270, 335 S.W.2d 713 (1960) (doctrine not applicable when the product has not been destroyed by the accident).

7. Justice Traynor's concurring opinion proved to be enormously influential in paving the way toward the adoption of strict tort liability. It was not expressly adopted as a separate theory, however, until 1963 in Greenman v. Yuba Power Products, Inc., 59 Cal.2d 57, 27 Cal.Rptr. 697, 377 P.2d 897 (1963), page 127, *infra*. The evolution that led to its adoption took place primarily through the law of warranty.

Chapter 3

MISREPRESENTATION

CROCKER v. WINTHROP LABS., DIV. OF STERLING DRUG, INC.

Supreme Court of Texas, 1974.
514 S.W.2d 429.

REAVLEY, JUSTICE.

Glenn E. Crocker became addicted to a new drug produced by Winthrop Laboratories and known as "talwin" which had been previously thought to be non-addictive. When he was in a weakened condition and his tolerance to drugs very low because of a period of detoxification, Crocker obtained an injection of a narcotic and died soon thereafter. His widow and representative, Clarissa Crocker, brought this action for damages due to his suffering while alive as well as for his wrongful death. She recovered judgment against Winthrop Laboratories in the trial court. The Court of Civil Appeals reversed and rendered judgment for the drug company, holding that while some of the facts found by the jury (including the positive misrepresentation by the drug company that talwin was non-addictive) would warrant the recovery, the additional finding that the drug company could not reasonably have foreseen Crocker's addiction (because of his unusual susceptibility and the state of medical knowledge when the drug was marketed), constituted a complete defense. 502 S.W.2d 850. We hold that the latter finding does not bar the recovery, and we affirm the judgment of the trial court.

In July of 1967 Glenn Crocker suffered a double hernia, as well as frostbite of two fingers, while working as a carpenter in a cold storage vault. He was then 49 years old and was not a user of drugs or alcohol. * * * [T]he several doctors who had treated him had prescribed both demerol (a narcotic) and talwin for relief of pain without observing any cause to believe him to be then addicted to any drug. Crocker told Dr. Palafox that he liked the relief he received from talwin, and Dr. Palafox responded that this was fortunate because talwin had no addicting side effect.

Crocker did develop an addiction to talwin, however, and was able to obtain prescriptions from several doctors as well as to cross the Mexican border to Juarez and acquire the same drug without a prescription under the name of "sosigon." He was hospitalized on June 3, 1968 by a psychiatrist, Dr. J. Edward Stern, for a process of detoxification (to remove the toxic agents in his body) and treatment of his drug dependency. After six days in the hospital being withdrawn from talwin as well as all narcotics, and at a time when his tolerance for potent drugs was very low, Crocker walked out of the hospital and went to his home. Because of his agitated condition and the threats he made against his wife, he was finally successful in having her call Dr. Eugene Engel who, on June 10, 1968, came to the Crocker home and gave Mr. Crocker an injection of demerol. Crocker went to his bed for the last time.

Winthrop Laboratories first put talwin on the market in July of 1967 after extensive testing and approval by the Federal Drug Administration. The descriptive material on the new drug circulated by Winthrop Laboratories in 1967 gives no warning of the possibilities of addiction. There is a heading of a paragraph in the product information of the 1967 edition of Physicians' Desk Reference Book which reads: "Absence of addiction liability." This might be considered misleading, but in view of the evidence of verbal assurances as to the properties of talwin by the drug company's representative, there is no need to deal further with the printed materials. * * * Dr. Palafox testified that the representative of the defendant insisted that talwin could have no addicting effect.

Subsequent experience has proved that talwin is an extremely useful drug for the relief of pain but that it cannot be regarded as non-addictive. * * *

Dr. Palafox was of the opinion that if he had not been assured of the non-addictive character of talwin, he could probably have avoided addiction or dependence by Crocker upon any drug.

* * *

Section 402B applies to those cases of misrepresentation by seller of chattels to the consumer; it reads:

One engaged in the business of selling chattels who, by advertising, labels, or otherwise, makes to the public a misrepresentation of a material fact concerning the character or quality of a chattel sold by him is subject to liability for physical harm to a consumer of the chattel caused by justifiable reliance upon the misrepresentation, even though

    (a) it is not made fraudulently or negligently, and

    (b) the consumer has not bought the chattel from or entered into any contractual relation with the seller.

The carefully written opinion of the Court of Civil Appeals has correctly foreseen that we would apply Section 402B of the Restatement and that the judgment for plaintiff should be affirmed depending upon the effect to be given the findings of the jury in response to special issues 9 and 10. Those findings were as follows:

9. That Crocker's addiction or dependency upon talwin was an abreaction. Abreaction was defined as "an unusual reaction resulting from a person's unusual susceptibility to the product or intended effect of the product in question; that is, such person's reaction is different in the presence of the drug in question from that in the usual person. An abreaction is one in which an unusual result is produced by a known or theoretical mechanism of action. An abreaction is one which could not have been reasonably foreseen in an appreciable class or number of potential users prior to the time Glenn E. Crocker became addicted or dependent on Talwin."

10. That at the time Crocker was taking talwin under doctors' prescriptions, the state of medical knowledge was such that Winthrop Laboratories could not have reasonably foreseen, in the exercise of ordinary care, that talwin would cause an addiction in an appreciable number of persons.

The Court of Civil Appeals held that there should be no liability on the part of the drug manufacturer because the harm to Glenn Crocker could not have been reasonably foreseen in an appreciable number of persons. Since the drug was not unreasonably dangerous to the ordinary user, the Court saw no basis for liability * * *.

Liability of Winthrop Laboratories will be predicated upon the finding of misrepresentation that the drug would not cause physical dependence, a fact conceded by the attorney for the company in his jury argument, and upon the findings of reliance and causation. Whatever the danger and state of medical knowledge, and however rare the susceptibility of the user, when the drug company positively and specifically represents its product to be free and safe from all dangers of addiction, and when the treating physician relies upon that representation, the drug company is liable when the representation proves to be false and harm results. Restatement, Torts, Second, § 402B * * *.

Notes

1. Section 402B states:

One engaged in the business of selling chattels who, by advertising, labels, or otherwise, makes to the public a misrepresentation of a material fact concerning the character or quality of a chattel sold by him is subject to liability for physical harm to a consumer of the chattel caused by justifiable reliance upon the misrepresentation, even though

(a) it is not made fraudulently or negligently, and

(b) the consumer has not bought the chattel from or entered into any contractual relation with the seller.

2. Suppose Winthrop Labs. had stated that "there is absolutely no evidence that talwin is addictive." Would Winthrop Labs. have been liable for misrepresentation under section 402B?

3. Was the representation in *Crocker* public? Does a statement in the Physician's Desk Reference make the representation public?

4. Does the plaintiff in *Crocker* have a claim under section 402A?

5. Section 402B was not cut from whole cloth; it is an outgrowth of the law of intentional misrepresentation (fraud) and negligent misrepresentation, both of which were developed primarily in non-product cases. The law of fraud and negligent misrepresentation is important in products cases for two reasons.

First, the law of fraud and negligent misrepresentation can be relied on directly in a product case. A product seller who fraudulently or negligently misrepresents a product may be liable for resulting damages. A general feature of the law of fraud and negligent misrepresentation is that a plaintiff can recover for purely economic damages. Consequently, a plaintiff who can prove fraud or negligent misrepresentation has an advantage over a plaintiff who can prove only strict tort liability or ordinary negligence, though not over a plaintiff who can prove breach of warranty.

Second, other than the issues specifically addressed by section 402B— such as the defendant's state of mind—many of the rules governing fraud and negligent misrepresentation are applicable to innocent misrepresentation under section 402B.

6. To establish a common law action for fraud, a plaintiff must prove

(a) that the defendant made a false representation of a material fact,

(b) that the defendant knew the statement was false, knew that he had no knowledge of its truth or falsity, or knew that he did not have as strong a basis for his statement as he implied,

(c) that the defendant intended the plaintiff to rely on the statement,

(d) that the plaintiff justifiably relied on the statement, and

(e) that the plaintiff suffered damage.

An action for fraud or negligent misrepresentation differs from an action for breach of contract because the absence of a contract (due to lack of consideration, for example) does not defeat recovery. Moreover, the defendant's mere failure to perform a promise will not support recovery in an action for misrepresentation. To recover for fraud, the plaintiff must prove that the defendant knowingly or recklessly deceived him. To recover for negligent misrepresentation, the plaintiff must prove that the defendant negligently deceived him.

The existence of a special action for negligent misrepresentation, which is distinct from a simple action for negligence, is important in cases involving pure economic harm. Certain types of economic harm are not recoverable in a simple negligence action, but pure economic harm is recoverable in an action for fraud or negligent misrepresentation.

In addition to the different requirements concerning the defendant's state of mind (scienter), most courts also distinguish between fraud and negligent misrepresentation in terms of the defendant's scope of liability.

Most courts have held that a defendant's liability for fraud extends to any person who the defendant had "reason to know" would rely, but that a defendant's liability for negligent misrepresentation extends only to individuals within the class of persons that the defendant actually knew would rely. Most courts also use a different measure of damages depending on the defendant's state of mind. For fraud under section 549 of the Second Restatement of Torts, a plaintiff can choose between out-of-pocket loss or benefit-of-the-bargain damages. A plaintiff can also recover consequential economic loss. For negligent misrepresentation under section 552B, the plaintiff can recover only out-of-pocket loss plus consequential economic damages.

The other elements of a cause of action for misrepresentation—such as the requirement of a false statement of material fact—are the same, irrespective of whether the action is based on fraud, negligent misrepresentation, or innocent misrepresentation under section 402B.

7. Sections 310 and 311 of the Restatement (Second) of Torts provide for liability for "physical harm" caused (respectively) by "conscious representation" and "negligent misrepresentation."

8. Section 402B purports to reflect case law; it is not a statute. Nevertheless, courts tend to "interpret" it like a statute, giving careful attention to the wording and to the comments explaining it.

9. Section 402B applies only to defendants who are "engaged in the business of selling chattels." A single sale, even to the public, is not covered. It is possible that section 402B, like section 402A, applies to all suppliers, including distributors, retailers, lessors, and bailors, whether or not the defendant was the one who actually made the misrepresentation, but courts have not yet applied section 402B to defendants who have not themselves made a misrepresentation or adopted a misrepresentation made by someone else.

It is unclear whether section 402B applies to transactions other than chattel sales, such as hybrid sales-service transactions. Whereas many courts have addressed the applicability of section 402A to these special transactions, few cases have addressed the applicability of section 402B to these transactions. Section 402B itself is addressed to a "seller of chattels," but so is section 402A. Consequently, courts might resolve issues concerning the application of section 402B to special transactions by referring to cases involving section 402A.

10. Most representations are made with words, but a deed—such as masking a defect—can also constitute a representation. Normally, nondisclosures do not constitute representations, but this general rule has several exceptions. A duty to speak and disclose facts exists when a confidential or fiduciary relationship exists between the parties. A duty to disclose also exists when, during the course of negotiations, a party learns that his earlier representations were false, or when a party gives a false impression by revealing some facts while withholding others.

11. To be actionable, a representation must be of a fact rather than of an opinion. Opinions concerning quality or value (or other "sales talk") constitute "puffing" and are not actionable. Predictions of future events

are opinions and therefore are not actionable, although some courts have held otherwise if the speaker purports to have special knowledge. A promise to perform a future act is not a statement of fact, and a failure to perform such a promise is actionable only in contract, unless the defendant made the promise with an intent not to carry it out. Statements of law are opinions rather than facts, except (a) when they are intended to be statements of fact and are understood as such, (b) when a special relationship of trust exists between the parties, or (c) when the defendant represents himself to have special knowledge of the law.

12. To be actionable, a representation of fact must be material. The test of materiality in cases involving common law fraud is whether the statement would be important to a reasonable person. This is an objective test, and it applies unless the defendant actually knows that the plaintiff regards a matter as being important even though a reasonable person would not. The requirement of materiality is designed to prevent a party from using a trivial misrepresentation as an excuse to set aside a bad bargain.

In products liability cases, a statement might be material if it significantly affects the manner in which the plaintiff uses the product, thereby increasing its danger. Most cases addressing the requirement of materiality arise in the context of fraud or negligent misrepresentation. It is possible that slightly different rules will evolve in personal injury cases under section 402B.

13. Section 402B requires that a plaintiff show justifiable reliance on the misrepresentation. According to comment j, liability does not exist "where the misrepresentation is not known, or there is indifference to it, and it does not influence the purchase or subsequent conduct." The representation need not, however, be the "sole inducement to purchase, or to use the chattel, and it is sufficient that it has been a substantial factor in that inducement."

Justifiable reliance is also an element of fraud and negligent misrepresentation, and comment j to section 402B explicitly incorporates the rules concerning reliance developed under those theories. In cases involving fraud or negligent misrepresentation, a plaintiff who is aware of the truth cannot recover. Moreover, some courts have held that if a reasonably prudent person would have been aware of the facts or investigated further, the plaintiff will be deemed to have knowledge of the facts and cannot recover for the misrepresentation.

The injured consumer need not himself be the one to rely on the misrepresentation. It is enough that the purchaser relies on the misrepresentation and then passes the product along to the injured consumer. Note that in *Crocker,* it was the doctor who relied on the representation of non-addictiveness.

14. Section 402B provides for liability only in cases involving "physical harm to a consumer of the chattel." The Tennessee Supreme Court has permitted recovery of pecuniary losses under a theory combining section 402B and a predecessor of section 552C (*see* note 15, *infra*), Ford Motor Co. v. Lonon, 217 Tenn. 400, 398 S.W.2d 240 (1966). Other courts have interpreted section 402B strictly and permitted recovery only for physical harm. *See, e.g.,* Alfred N. Koplin & Co. v. Chrysler Corp., 49 Ill.App.3d 194,

7 Ill.Dec. 113, 364 N.E.2d 100 (1977). In any event, lost wages or profits caused by physical harm are recoverable as normal personal injury damages.

Section 402B itself provides for liability to a "consumer," but a "consumer" need not have actually purchased the product. Comment i provides that an employee or family member of the purchaser who uses the product is also a consumer, as is anyone "who makes use of the chattel in the manner which a purchaser may be expected to use it."

A caveat to section 402B states that "[t]he Institute expresses no opinion as to whether the rule stated in this Section may apply * * * where physical harm is caused to one who is not a consumer of the chattel."

15. Section 552C of the Restatement (Second) of Torts provides:

Misrepresentation in Sale, Rental or Exchange Transaction

(1) One who, in a sale, rental, or exchange transaction with another, makes a misrepresentation of a material fact for the purpose of inducing the other to act or to refrain from acting in reliance upon it, is subject to liability to the other for pecuniary loss caused to him by his justifiable reliance upon the misrepresentation, even though it is not made fraudulently or negligently.

(2) Damages recoverable under the rule stated in this section are limited to the difference between the value of what the other has parted with and the value of what he has received in the transaction.

Note that section 552C is, in its terms, limited to pecuniary damages, measured in subsection (2) by an out-of-pocket measure of damages. One commentator has suggested section 552C can support recovery of more extensive damages. *See* Hill, Damages for Innocent Misrepresentation, 73 Colum.L.Rev. 679 (1973).

Chapter 4

WARRANTY

SECTION A. INTRODUCTION

Warranties have a dual significance for products liability law. First, warranties have historical importance. They provided a basis for liability in product cases before the adoption of strict tort liability, and while strict tort liability has shed most of its warranty heritage, warranty law spawned strict tort liability and influenced its early development.

Second, warranty law still provides an effective remedy for injured consumers. Plaintiffs can join claims of strict tort liability and breach of warranty, and an action for breach of warranty can provide a victim with certain remedies that are not available under strict tort liability, such as recovery of pure economic damages and a variety of remedies available under some states' consumer protection statutes.

Warranty law covers a variety of issues that are not relevant to products liability litigation. Indeed, most of warranty law was developed to regulate commercial dealings. Consequently, the material in this chapter does not offer a systematic survey of warranty law. Instead, it addresses the aspects of warranty law that affect products liability litigation.

Breach of warranty arose in the fourteenth century as a tort cause of action. It was based on the notion that a misrepresentation had been made and was very similar to deceit. It was a form of strict liability because the seller was liable for breach of warranty without regard to intent or negligence. By the late eighteenth century courts recognized the right to sue on the contract for breach of warranty. The tort action, however, continued to remain available as an alternative. Furthermore, the tort history greatly influenced the nature of the action. Because of their tort heritage, warranty obligations can arise as a matter of law without regard to whether the parties intend to create them.

The contractual nature of the remedy also influenced its development. Privity of contract was required between the plaintiff and defendant. Furthermore, the seller was permitted to disclaim the warranty entirely or to limit the remedy available for breach. As a prerequisite to maintaining the action, plaintiff was required to give reasonably prompt notice of breach of warranty.

The common law eventually recognized three types of warranties. They are the implied warranty of merchantability, the implied warranty of fitness for a particular purpose, and the express warranty. These warranties were first codified in the Uniform Sales Act (1906) and later in the Uniform Commercial Code (1951).

Although a product seller was subject to strict liability for breach of warranty, the usefulness of the remedy was very limited because of the requirements of privity and notice of breach and because of the right to disclaim. The move toward strict tort liability began with the relaxation of these impediments to recovery. The privity requirement was first relaxed in cases involving impure food. The first case to do so was decided in 1913, and by 1960 seventeen jurisdictions imposed liability without privity. Courts used a variety of methods to accomplish this result, such as "fictitious agencies or third-party-beneficiary contracts * * * [or warranties] running with the goods from the manufacturer to the consumer, by analogy to a covenant running with the land." Prosser, The Assault Upon the Citadel (Strict Liability to the Consumer), 69 Yale L.J. 1099, 1106 (1960). In the nineteen fifties a few courts began imposing liability without privity in actions against manufacturers of products other than food.

Henningsen v. Bloomfield Motors, Inc., 32 N.J. 358, 161 A.2d 69 (1960), is a landmark case in the development of warranty law. *Henningsen* gave an automobile accident victim a cause of action for breach of implied warranty of merchantability against the automobile manufacturer even though she was not in privity of contract with the defendant. The court also refused to enforce the disclaimer and remedy limitation in the standard form contract. In addition to deciding specific issues and contributing to the development of warranty law, *Henningsen* was important historically because it helped lead to strict liability in tort. Courts recognized that the strict liability they imposed in such cases was really based on tort rather than contract because privity of contract was not required and because normal contract defenses such as disclaimers and remedy limitations were not recognized. *See generally* Ames, The History of Assumpsit, 2 Harv.L.Rev. 1 (1888); Prosser, The Assault Upon the Citadel (Strict Liability to the Consumer), 69 Yale L.J. 1099 (1960); Prosser, The Implied Warranty of Merchantable Quality, 27 Minn.L.Rev. 117 (1943).

Henningsen was decided under the Uniform Sales Act. The basic source of warranty law today is Article 2 of the Uniform Commercial Code, which is now in effect in 49 states. Some warranties are also governed by the federal Magnuson–Moss Act or by state consumer protection or deceptive trade practice legislation. Most states have also developed common law warranties for certain transactions that are not covered by the various statutes.

The warranty provisions of Article 2 apply only to the sale of goods. Section 2–102 provides that Article 2 itself applies to "transactions in goods." Section 2–105 defines "goods" as

> all things (including specifically manufactured goods) which are movable at the time of identification to the contract for sale other than the money in which the price is to be paid, investment securities * * * and things in action. "Goods" also includes the unborn young of animals and growing crops and other identified things attached to realty as described in the section on goods to be severed from realty (Section 2–107).

Consequently, Article 2 is not applicable to services or to real estate transactions.

The specific warranty provisions of Article 2—section 2–313 governing express warranties, section 2–314 governing implied warranties of merchantability, and section 2–315 governing implied warranties of fitness—refer to "sales" or "sellers." A "sale" is defined in subsection 2–106(1) as "the passing of title from the seller to the buyer for a price (Section 2–401)." A "seller" is defined in subsection 2–103(a)(4) as "a person who sells or contracts to sell goods." Section 2–102 expressly excludes from Article 2 any transaction "intended to operate only as a security transaction." Consequently, transactions in "goods" other than sales, such as leases and bailments, are not expressly governed by the Article 2 warranties. They may, however, be governed by common law warranties or by strict tort liability.

Issues concerning the types of transactions governed by the Article 2 warranties can be quite complicated, and various states differ in their interpretation of Article 2. These issues are addressed in more detail in Chapter 17, along with issues concerning the types of transactions governed by strict tort liability. It is important at this point simply to recognize that the Article 2 warranties are applicable to transactions involving a sale of goods.

SECTION B. EXPRESS WARRANTY

Uniform Commercial Code

§ 2–313. Express Warranties by Affirmation, Promise, Description, Sample

(1) Express warranties by the seller are created as follows:

(a) Any affirmation of fact or promise made by the seller to the buyer which relates to the goods and becomes part of the basis of the bargain creates an express warranty that the goods shall conform to the affirmation or promise.

(b) Any description of the goods which is made part of the basis of the bargain creates an express warranty that the goods shall conform to the description.

(c) Any sample or model which is made part of the basis of the bargain creates an express warranty that the whole of the goods shall conform to the sample or model.

(2) It is not necessary to the creation of an express warranty that the seller use formal words such as "warrant" or "guarantee" or that he have a specific intention to make a warranty, but an affirmation merely of the value of the goods or a statement purporting to be merely the seller's opinion or commendation of the goods does not create a warranty.

SALK v. ALPINE SKI SHOP, INC.
Supreme Court of Rhode Island, 1975.
115 R.I. 309, 342 A.2d 622.

DORIS, JUSTICE.

This is a civil action to recover damages for personal injury brought by the plaintiff, Burton Salk, against the defendants, Alpine Ski Shop, Inc. (hereinafter Alpine), a Rhode Island corporation engaged in the sale of ski and other sports equipment, and Cubco, Inc. (hereinafter Cubco), a New Jersey corporation engaged in the manufacture of ski bindings. The case was tried to a justice of the Superior Court sitting with a jury. At the close of the plaintiff's presentation of evidence, the defendants each moved for a directed verdict on all counts of the plaintiff's complaint. The motions were granted, and the plaintiff now appeals from the judgment entered thereon.

It appears from the record that in January of 1967, plaintiff purchased from defendant Alpine various articles of ski equipment including ski bindings manufactured by defendant Cubco. The defendant Alpine installed these ski bindings on plaintiff's skis and allegedly adjusted them according to plaintiff's height, weight, and skiing ability. The plaintiff made use of his new ski equipment on four separate occasions without mishap. On the fifth day, however, plaintiff fell while skiing, his ski bindings did not release, and he broke his leg.

* * *

The plaintiff's second contention is that the trial justice erred when he directed a verdict as to plaintiff's count against defendant Cubco in express warranty. The plaintiff alleges that Cubco, by means of certain advertisements placed in national magazines, expressly warranted to plaintiff that its bindings would release in such a manner as to guarantee freedom from injury. Representative of the advertisements in question is the following language:

"Cubco is the precise binding * * * that releases when it's supposed to. * * * Both heel and toe release at the exact tension you set. And release whichever way you fall."

For the facts of this case to make out a breach of express warranty, plaintiff must first establish that Cubco warranted its bindings would release in every situation presenting a danger to the user's limbs. It is our judgment that Cubco's advertising falls short of this blanket guarantee. During the course of the trial, uncontroverted evidence was presented to the effect that although no binding could be set at a tension sufficiently low to release during a slow fall and still keep the skier on his skis during normal skiing, Cubco bindings had a multi-directional release which could be adjusted to operate at a variety of tensions and once adjusted would release whenever the selected tension was applied. The advertisements brought to our attention do no more than to affirm these uncontroverted facts. In this situation, we cannot say that the trial justice was in error when he directed a verdict on this count, despite his choice of alternative grounds as a basis of his decision.

Notes

1. The *raison d'etre* of express warranties is to permit the parties to a transaction to structure their own deal. Consequently, a lawyer's first task in any case involving an express warranty is to interpret the warranty itself. This issue has been the principal source of litigation about express warranties.

2. In interpreting an express warranty, the entire context of the transaction should be taken into account, including other dealings between the parties and trade practices. Comment 5 to section 2–313 provides that "all descriptions by merchants must be read against the applicable trade usages with the general rules as to merchantability resolving any doubts."

3. In Lane v. C.A. Swanson & Sons, 130 Cal.App.2d 210, 278 P.2d 723 (1955), the plaintiff was injured when a hidden bone from a can of "boned chicken" lodged in his throat. The defendant argued that the term "boned chicken" was merely descriptive of the type of product, not an affirmation that the chicken was absolutely devoid of bone fragments. The court, relying on the word "boned" on the label and on advertisements referring to "No bones," held for the plaintiff.

4. Suppose seller contracts in writing to sell an "automobile" to buyer. Would delivery of a car without an engine constitute a breach of express warranty?

5. Do the problems of interpretation under section 2–313 differ from the problems of interpretation under section 402B of the Restatement (Second) of Torts?

6. Some courts have held that a general assurance of safety constitutes an express warranty that the product will not injure the user. For example, in Drayton v. Jiffee Chem. Corp., 395 F.Supp. 1081 (N.D.Ohio 1975), the court held that an advertisement claiming that a drain cleaner is "safe for household use" constituted an express warranty.

Other courts have interpreted express warranties more strictly. For example, in Whitmer v. Schneble, 29 Ill.App.3d 659, 331 N.E.2d 115 (1975), the seller of a doberman puppy told the buyers that it was "docile." Two years later it bit a child, and the buyers sued for breach of express warranty. The court held that even a docile doberman will bite children under some circumstances, so the express warranty, if any, was not breached. Moreover, the warranty, if any, described the doberman when it was sold and did not warrant that the dog's personality would not change.

7. As section 2–313(1)(c) indicates, an express warranty can be made by sample or model. Comment 6 provides:

> The basic situation as to statements affecting the true essence of the bargain is no different when a sample or model is involved in the transaction. This section includes both a "sample" actually drawn from the bulk of goods which is the subject matter of the sale, and a "model" which is offered for inspection when the subject matter is not at hand and which has not been drawn from the bulk of the goods.

> Although the underlying principles are unchanged, the facts are often ambiguous when something is shown as illustrative, rather than as a straight sample. In general, the presumption is that any sample or model just as any affirmation of fact is intended to become a basis of the bargain. But there is no escape from the question of fact. When the seller exhibits a sample purporting to be drawn from an existing bulk, good faith of course requires that the sample be fairly drawn. But in mercantile experience the mere exhibition of a "sample" does not of itself show whether it is merely intended to "suggest" or to "be" the character of the subject-matter of the contract. The question is whether the seller has so acted with reference to the sample as to make him responsible that the whole shall have at least the values shown by it. The circumstances aid in answering this question. If the sample has been drawn from an existing bulk, it must be regarded as describing values of the goods contracted for unless it is accompanied by an unmistakable denial of such responsibility. If, on the other hand, a model of merchandise not on hand is offered, the mercantile presumption that it has become a literal description of the subject matter is not so strong, and particularly so if modification on the buyer's initiative impairs any feature of the model.

8. An "affirmation of fact or promise" or a "description of goods" can be made by pictures or other forms of communication, as well as by words. For example, in Sylvestri v. Warner & Swasey Co., 398 F.2d 598 (2d Cir.1968), the plaintiff was thrown from a backhoe when a support gave way. The court held that an advertisement with a picture of the backhoe lifting pipe constituted an express warranty that it was suitable for lifting heavy objects, including boulders. The court stated that "[i]t is the 'essential idea' conveyed by the advertising representations which is relevant."

But in Coffer v. Standard Brands, Inc., 30 N.C.App. 134, 226 S.E.2d 534 (1976)—where the plaintiff was injured when he bit down on an unshelled nut sold in a glass jar of otherwise shelled mixed nuts—the court held that the clear glass jar revealing shelled nuts did not constitute an express warranty that the whole jar was devoid of shells. What if the nuts had been sold in a can with a picture of shelled nuts on the label?

9. Express warranties are created under section 2–313(1)(a) only for promises or affirmations of "fact." Section 2–313(2) makes clear that opinions, especially of value, do not constitute express warranties. As in the law of misrepresentation, which is addressed in the previous chapter, it is often difficult to distinguish between "facts" and "opinions."

Comment 8 to section 2–313 provides:

Concerning affirmations of value or a seller's opinion or commendation under subsection (2), the basic question remains the same: What statements of the seller have in the circumstances and in objective judgment become part of the basis of the bargain? As indicated above, all of the statements of the seller do so unless good reason is shown to the contrary. The provisions of subsection (2) are included, however, since common experience discloses that some statements or predictions cannot fairly be viewed as entering into the bargain. Even as to false statements of value, however, the possibility is left open that a remedy may be provided by the law relating to fraud or misrepresentation.

Courts have found that the following statements constitute affirmations of fact and therefore express warranties: that a product will not deteriorate, General Supply and Equip. Co. v. Phillips, 490 S.W.2d 913, 917 (Tex.Civ. App.—Tyler 1972, writ refused n.r.e.); that a product is in "excellent condition," Valley Datsun v. Martinez, 578 S.W.2d 485 (Tex.Civ.App.— Corpus Christi 1979, no writ); and that a product is "adequate" for the job, Burnett v. James, 564 S.W.2d 407, 409 (Tex.Civ.App.—Dallas 1978, writ dismissed).

Conclusions about specific cases depend on the circumstances of the case, and statements that would be interpreted as opinions or puffing in some circumstances may be interpreted to contain implicit factual assertions in other circumstances. Factors that might influence a court's decision include the specificity of a statement, Olin Mathieson Chem. Corp. v. Moushon, 93 Ill.App.2d 280, 235 N.E.2d 263 (1968); Bickett v. W.R. Grace & Co., 12 U.C.C.Rep. 629, 1972 WL 20845 (W.D.Ky.1972), whether the seller hedged, Matlack, Inc. v. Hupp Corp., 57 F.R.D. 151 (E.D.Pa.1972); Swenson v. Chevron Chem. Co., 89 S.D. 497, 234 N.W.2d 38 (1975), and the buyer's expertise and knowledge, Sessa v. Riegle, 427 F.Supp. 760, 766 (E.D.Pa. 1977), affirmed, memorandum decision, 568 F.2d 770 (3d Cir.1978); Weiss v. Rockwell Mfg. Co., 9 Ill.App.3d 906, 915, 293 N.E.2d 375, 381 (1973); Janssen v. Hook, 1 Ill.App.3d 318, 321, 272 N.E.2d 385, 388 (1971).

In Carney v. Sears, Roebuck & Co., 309 F.2d 300 (4th Cir.1962), the court held that a statement that a ladder was "good" quality was an "opinion". In Turner v. Central Hardware Co., 353 Mo. 1182, 186 S.W.2d 603 (1945), the court held that a statement that a ladder was "strong and durable" was a "fact". Neither court was explicitly applying section 2–313.

10. To constitute an express warranty, a promise or affirmation of fact must "relate[ ] to the goods." Promises unrelated to the goods may still create contractual obligations, but they do not constitute warranties. The distinction can be important, because "warranties" are governed by special provisions concerning waiver, privity of contract, and limitations on damages.

11. If a defendant breaches an express warranty, it is irrelevant that he was not at fault or that the goods were nevertheless reasonably safe.

HAUTER v. ZOGARTS

Supreme Court of California, En Banc, 1975.
14 Cal.3d 104, 120 Cal.Rptr. 681, 534 P.2d 377.

TOBRINER, JUSTICE.

* * *

Defendants[1] manufacture and sell the "Golfing Gizmo" (hereinafter Gizmo), a training device designed to aid unskilled golfers improve their games. Defendants' catalogue states that the Gizmo is a "completely equipped backyard driving range." In 1966, Louise Hauter purchased a Gizmo from the catalogue and gave it to Fred Hauter, her 13½-year-old son, as a Christmas present.

The Gizmo is a simple device consisting of two metal pegs, two cords—one elastic, one cotton—and a regulation golf ball. After the pegs are driven into the ground approximately 25 inches apart, the elastic cord is looped over them. The cotton cord, measuring 21 feet in length, ties to the middle of the elastic cord. The ball is attached to the end of the cotton cord. When the cords are extended, the Gizmo resembles the shape of a large letter "T," with the ball resting at the base.

The user stands by the ball in order to hit his practice shots. The instructions state that when hit correctly, the ball will fly out and spring back near the point of impact; if the ball returns to the left, it indicates a right-hander's "slice"; a shot returning to the right indicates a right-hander's "hook." If the ball is "topped," it does not return and must be retrieved by the player. The label on the shipping carton and the cover of the instruction booklet urge players to "drive the ball with full power" and further state: "COMPLETELY SAFE BALL WILL NOT HIT PLAYER."

On July 14, 1967, Fred Hauter was seriously injured while using defendants' product. Thereafter, plaintiffs filed the instant suit on his behalf, claiming false representation, breach of express and implied warranties and strict liability in tort.

Fred Hauter testified at trial that prior to his injury, he had practiced golf 10 to 20 times at driving ranges and had played several rounds of golf. His father instructed him in the correct use of the Gizmo. Fred had read the printed instructions that accompany the product and had used the Gizmo about a dozen times. Before the accident, Fred set up the Gizmo in his front yard according to the printed instructions. The area was free of objects that might have caused the ball to richochet, and no other persons were nearby. Fred then took his normal swing with a seven-iron. The last thing he remembers was extreme pain and dizziness. After a period of uncon-

---

1. Defendants are Rudy C. Zogarts, who does business as House of Zog [manufactur- er] and Miles Kimball Company [seller].

sciousness, he staggered into the house and told his mother that he had been hit on the head by the ball. He suffered brain damage and, in one doctor's opinion, is currently an epileptic.

* * *

We first treat the claim for breach of express warranty, which is governed by California Commercial Code section 2313. The key under this section is that the seller's statements—whether fact or opinion—must become "part of the basis of the bargain." [10] (See Cal.U.Com.Code, § 2313, com. 8; Ezer, *supra*, at p. 287, fn. 39.) The basis of the bargain requirement represents a significant change in the law of warranties. Whereas plaintiffs in the past have had to prove their reliance upon specific promises made by the seller (Grinnell v. Charles Pfizer & Co. (1969) 274 Cal.App.2d 424, 440, 79 Cal.Rptr. 369), the Uniform Commercial Code requires no such proof. According to official comment 3 to the Uniform Commercial Code following section 2313, "no particular reliance * * * need be shown in order to weave [the seller's affirmations of fact] into the fabric of the agreement. Rather, any fact which is to take such affirmations, once made, out of the agreement requires clear affirmative proof."

The commentators have disagreed as to the impact of this new development. (See generally, Note, "Basis of the Bargain"-What Role Reliance? (1972) 34 U.Pitt.L.Rev. 145, 149–150.) Some have said that the basis of the bargain requirement merely shifts the burden of proving non-reliance to the seller. (See 1 Carroll, Cal.Commercial Law, *supra,* § 6.7, p. 210; Boyd, Representing Consumer–The Uniform Commercial Code and Beyond (1968) 9 Ariz.L.Rev. 372, 385.) Indeed, the comments to section 2313 seem to [bear] out this analysis; they declare that "all of the statements of the seller [become part of the basis of the bargain] *unless good reason is shown to the contrary.*" (Cal.U.Com.Code, § 2313, com. 8 (emphasis added).) [11]

Other writers, however, find that the code eliminates the concept of reliance altogether. (See Note, *supra,* 34 U.Pitt.L.Rev. at p. 150; Nordstrom, Sales (1970) §§ 66–68.) Support can be found in the comments to the code for this view also; they declare that "[i]n view of the principle that the whole purpose of the law of warranty is to determine

10. As we explained above, defendants' statement is one of fact and is subject to construction as an express warranty. It is important to note, however, that even statements of opinion can become warranties under the code if they become part of the basis of the bargain. (Cal.U.Com.Code, § 2313, com. 8; Ezer, *supra*, at p. 287, fn. 39.) Thus the California Uniform Commercial Code expands sellers' liability beyond the former Uniform Sales Act (former Civ. Code §§ 1732–1736) and provides greater coverage than Restatement Second of Torts, section 402B, discussed earlier.

11. The code relegates "the metaphysical 'buyer's reliance' requirement to secondary status, where it properly belongs." (Ezer, The Impact of the Uniform Commercial Code on the California Law of Sales Warranties (1961) 8 U.C.L.A.L.Rev. 281, 285.) Ezer also notes: "The Code's implicit premise is that buyer's reliance is prima facie established from the fact that he made the purchase. If the seller can establish that the buyer in fact did not rely on the seller, that the affirmation or promise was not the 'basis of the bargain,' to use the Code language, then there is no express warranty." (*Id.,* at p. 285, fn. 30.)

what it is that the seller *has in essence agreed to sell,* the policy is adopted of those cases which refuse except in unusual circumstances to recognize a material deletion of the seller's obligation. Thus, a contract is normally a contract for a sale of something describable and described." (Cal.U.Com.Code, § 2313, com. 4 (emphasis added).) To these observers, the focus of the warranty shifts from the buyer, who formerly had to rely upon specific statements in order to recover, to the seller, who now must stand behind his words if he has failed adequately to disclaim them. "[T]he seller must show by clear affirmative proof either that the statement was retracted by him before the deal was closed or that the parties understood that the goods would not conform to the affirmation or description. Under such an interpretation, the affirmation, once made, is a part of the agreement, and lack of reliance by the buyer is not a fact which would take the affirmation out of the agreement." (Note, *supra,* 34 U.Pitt.L.Rev. at p. 151.) [12]

We are not called upon in this case to resolve the reliance issue.[13] The parties do not discuss the changes wrought by the Uniform Commercial Code, and plaintiffs are fully able to meet their burden regardless of which test we employ. Fred Hauter's testimony shows that he read and relied upon defendants' representation; he was impressed by "something on the cover dealing with the safety of the item." More importantly, defendants presented no evidence which could remove their assurance of safety from the basis of the bargain. The trial court properly concluded, therefore, that defendants expressly warranted the safety of their product and are liable for Fred Hauter's injuries which resulted from a breach of that warranty.

* * *

Notes

1. Did Fred have a bargain with anyone?

2. Comment 3 to section 2–313 states:

   The present section deals with affirmations of fact by the seller, descriptions of the goods or exhibitions of samples, exactly as any other part of a negotiation which ends in a contract is dealt with. No specific intention to make a warranty is necessary if any of these factors is made part of the basis of the bargain. In actual practice affirmations of fact made by the seller about the goods during a bargain are regarded as part of the description of those goods; hence no particular reliance on

---

12. Thus if a seller agrees to sell a certain quality of product, he cannot avoid liability for selling lower grade goods. No longer can he find solace in the fact that the injured consumer never saw his warranty. (See Lonzrick v. Republic Steel Corp. (1966) 6 Ohio St.2d 227, 237, 218 N.E.2d 185.)

13. Although the code has been the law in California since 1965, we know of no California case which analyzes the basis of the bargain requirement. The scattered cases from other jurisdictions generally have ignored the significance of the new standard and have held that consumer reliance still is a vital ingredient for recovery based on express warranty. (See, e.g., Stang v. Hertz Corp. (1971) 83 N.M. 217, 219, 490 P.2d 475, revd. on other grounds, 83 N.M. 730, 497 P.2d 732; Gillette Dairy, Inc. v. Hydrotex Indus., Inc. (8th Cir.1971) 440 F.2d 969, 974; Capital Equip. Enterprises, Inc. v. North Pier Term. Co. (1969) 117 Ill.App.2d 264, 254 N.E.2d 542, 545; Speed Fastners, Inc. v. Newsom (10th Cir. 1967) 382 F.2d 395, 397.)

such statements need be shown in order to weave them into the fabric of the agreement. Rather, any fact which is to take such affirmations, once made, out of the agreement requires clear affirmative proof. The issue normally is one of fact.

Comment 6 states in part:

> In general, the presumption is that any sample or model just as any affirmation of fact is intended to become a basis of the bargain. But there is no escape from the question of fact.

Section 12 of the Uniform Sales Act provided:

> Any affirmation of fact or any promise by the seller relating to the goods is an express warranty if the natural tendency of such affirmation or promise is to induce the buyer to purchase the goods, and if the buyer purchases the goods relying thereon. No affirmation of the value of the goods, nor any statement purporting to be a statement of the seller's opinion only shall be construed as a warranty.

3. Several courts have continued to require the plaintiff to show some type of reliance to establish an express warranty. *See, e.g.,* Speed Fastners, Inc. v. Newsom, 382 F.2d 395, 397 (10th Cir.1967); Hagenbuch v. Snap–On Tools Corp., 339 F.Supp. 676, 680 (D.N.H.1972); Stang v. Hertz Corp., 83 N.M. 217, 219, 490 P.2d 475, 477 (App.1971), judgment reversed, 83 N.M. 730, 497 P.2d 732 (1972); Terry v. Moore, 448 P.2d 601, 602 (Wyo.1968).

4. Comment 7 to section 2–313 provides that post-sale representations may be considered part of the bargain even if they are not supported by independent consideration. Should a court nevertheless require some form of reliance, such as the purchaser foregoing other safety precautions? *See* Bigelow v. Agway, Inc., 506 F.2d 551 (2d Cir.1974); Terry v. Moore, 448 P.2d 601 (Wyo.1968).

5. Footnote 12 in *Hauter* suggests that an express warranty may be created even though the consumer never even saw it. Obviously, there could be no reliance in such a situation. Are there reasons to enforce a warranty that the consumer has not seen? Do you suppose a court would refuse to enforce a provision of an automobile warranty that the consumer had not read?

An affirmation or promise made to one person who then supplies the product to another person who is unaware of the affirmation or promise can create an express warranty. For example, in Putensen v. Clay Adams, Inc., 12 Cal.App.3d 1062, 91 Cal.Rptr. 319 (1970), the court held that a patient could sue for breach of an express warranty made to his doctor, even though the patient himself was unaware of the warranty. Such cases are appropriately addressed as raising issues concerning the scope of liability for breach of a warranty, not as raising issues concerning the creation of the warranty itself.

6. A product's price presumably reflects the value of a standardized warranty even if the consumer has not read or relied on it. Since a non-relying buyer pays the higher price, should he be given the benefit of the warranty even though he has not relied on it?

7. Does comment 7, which states that post-sale statements can be express warranties, undermine the argument that a consumer must rely on a pre-sale affirmation or promise in order to claim that it is a warranty?

8. Does the difference in language between section 12 of the Uniform Sales Act and section 2–313 of the Uniform Commercial Code require a conclusion that reliance is no longer required? Does the difference affect the underlying standard, or does it merely affect the burden of proof?

9. For a general discussion of the role of reliance in the analysis of express warranties, see Note, "Basis of the Bargain"—What Role Reliance?, 34 U.Pitt.L.Rev. 145 (1972).

10. Section 2–313 does not require express warranties to be in writing. Express warranties are, however, subject to the parol evidence rule of section 2–202:

> Terms with respect to which the confirmatory memoranda of the parties agree or which are otherwise set forth in a writing intended by the parties as a final expression of their agreement with respect to such terms as are included therein may not be contradicted by evidence of any prior agreement or of a contemporaneous oral agreement but may be explained or supplemented
>
> > (a) by course of dealing or usage of trade (Section 1–205) or by course of performance (Section 2–208); and
> >
> > (b) by evidence of consistent additional terms unless the court finds the writing to have been intended also as a complete and exclusive statement of the terms of the agreement.

Section 2–201 provides:

> (1) Except as otherwise provided in this section a contract for the sale of goods for the price of $500 or more is not enforceable by way of action or defense unless there is some writing sufficient to indicate that a contract for sale has been made between the parties and signed by the party against whom enforcement is sought or by his authorized agent or broker. A writing is not insufficient because it omits or incorrectly states a term agreed upon but the contract is not enforceable under this paragraph beyond the quantity of goods shown in such writing.
>
> (2) Between merchants if within a reasonable time a writing in confirmation of the contract and sufficient against the sender is received and the party receiving it has reason to know its contents, it satisfies the requirements of subsection (1) against such party unless written notice of objection to its contents is given within 10 days after it is received.
>
> (3) A contract which does not satisfy the requirements of subsection (1) but which is valid in other respects is enforceable
>
> > (a) if the goods are to be specially manufactured for the buyer and are not suitable for sale to others in the ordinary course of the seller's business and the seller, before notice of repudiation is received and under circumstances which reasonably indicate that the goods are for the buyer, has made either a substantial

beginning of their manufacture or commitments for their procurement; or

(b) if the party against whom enforcement is sought admits in his pleading, testimony or otherwise in court that a contract for sale was made, but the contract is not enforceable under this provision beyond the quantity of goods admitted; or

(c) with respect to goods for which payment has been made and accepted or which have been received and accepted (Sec. 2–606).

SCOVIL v. CHILCOAT
Supreme Court of Oklahoma, 1967.
424 P.2d 87.

* * *

Plaintiff alleged that on October 22, 1960, he took his 1956 model Volkswagen to the place of business of defendant, Scovil Motor Co., Inc., for repairs; that due to the condition of the engine in plaintiff's automobile, the defendants' shop foreman recommended that rather than repairing the old engine, it would be more economical to install a new engine in such automobile; that the plaintiff discussed with the shop foreman the condition of the automobile's fire-wall cover, and that it was agreed such fire-wall cover should be replaced; that from the discussion, an oral contract was entered into with Paul Scovil and Scovil Motor Company, a corporation, for the installing, at a cost of $269.00, of a new engine and a new fire-wall cover in plaintiff's automobile; that, being advised that the repairs on his automobile were completed on October 27, 1960, the plaintiff called for it, paid $300.00 of the bill that was presented to him as charges for the engine installation and other parts and labor, and received the car and a written warranty of the Volkswagen manufacturer on which the name "Scovil Motors, Inc." was stamped in a space provided therein for the selling dealer to be designated. Plaintiff further alleged that although the defendants had specifically agreed to do so, they had failed to remove the old deteriorating firewall cover of his automobile; that, following the instructions of a mechanic in the employ of said defendants, plaintiff obtained and installed a hard-felt fire-wall in the proper place within the engine compartment for the purpose of preventing the engine's air intake from sucking into the engine particles of the worn fire-wall cover and particles of dirt; that plaintiff had inspections made of the engine and fire-wall at 500 miles at Downtown Motor Sales, Inc., (hereafter referred to as "Downtown"), another authorized Volkswagen agency, and was not told of any improper function of the engine or that the method of installation of the fire-wall cover was not a proper one; that shortly following such inspection the engine failed, requiring plaintiff to have the automobile towed in from Stillwater, Oklahoma, to the place of business of Downtown; that Downtown refused to comply with the manufacturer's written warranty and to furnish plaintiff with another motor or to repair the one in plaintiff's automobile. Plaintiff by his action in the trial court sought to recover from defendants, Paul Scovil and Scovil Motor Company, Inc., plaintiffs in error (and Downtown Motor Sales, Inc., technically not a party to the appeal) $269.00 for cost of the engine he had purchased from Scovil Motor Company, a corp., $50.00 expended for towing charges, $1000.00 for loss of use of his automobile, costs and attorney's fees.

* * *

The defendants first contend that the plaintiff's evidence submitted herein was not sufficient to establish that an express warranty, either written or oral, was made by the defendants, Paul Scovil and Scovil Motor Co., Inc., to the plaintiff. We do not agree.

It is true that the written express warranty contained in the service booklet presented to the plaintiff at the time he accepted delivery of the automobile was a manufacturer's warranty, running from such manufacturer to the purchaser (plaintiff). However, according to plaintiff's testimony, defendants stated, prior to plaintiff approving the installation of the new engine, that such engine "would be guaranteed for six thousand miles or six months. * * * "

In the Washington case of Cochran v. McDonald, 23 Wash.2d 348, 161 P.2d 305, 306, the court, quoting 55 C.J., Sales, § 684, stated:

> "A purchaser of personal property with warranty, who is reselling it to another adopts, by his conduct at the resale, the warranty of his seller, thereby assumes a warranty of the same character as that which was expressly accorded to him. The fact of resale does not of itself constitute an adoption of prior warranties so as to render the seller liable for failure of the goods to comply with such warranties; and this is true even though the words of warranty are physically affixed to the goods."

The above stated rule has been recognized in a number of other decisions. See Pemberton v. Dean, 88 Minn. 60, 92 N.W. 478, 60 L.R.A. 311; Orrison v. Ferrante, D.C.Mun.App., 72 A.2d 771; Wallace v. McCampbell, 178 Tenn. 224, 156 S.W.2d 442; 46 Am.Jur.Sales, § 313, p. 495.

In Orrison v. Ferrante, supra, 72 A.2d at p. 773, the Court, although stating that mere resale of an article to which a manufacturer's warranty was affixed did not constitute an adoption of the warranty by the seller, further stated that if "in addition [to such manufacturer's warranty] some affirmation of fact or promise by the seller himself which tends to induce the buyer to purchase the article" was present, such would be sufficient to constitute an adoption. (In this connection, for a discussion concerning adoption of new motor vehicle warranties by retailers see 99 A.L.R.2d 1419 et seq.)

In the instant case, from the plaintiff's testimony standing alone, it is our opinion that a jury could have found that, by their statement, the defendants adopted the written express warranty of the manufacturers. The evidence shows that the defendants said they could not repair the old engine and "guarantee it"; but that if a new engine were installed, it would be guaranteed for a specified number of miles or a specified period of time. Further, it is clear that the plaintiff was interested in having the work warranted. From the evidence, the jury could have found that such statement by defendants was an "affirmation of fact or promise by the seller himself" which tended to induce the plaintiff to purchase the new engine. If so found, defendants' statement would be an adoption by them of the manufacturer's written warranty.

Further, even if the statement made by the defendants relating to the warranty were not found to be an adoption of the manufacturer's warranty, it is our opinion that such statement could have been found to have constituted an express warranty on the part of the defendants.

In Wat Henry Pontiac Co. v. Bradley, 202 Okl. 82, 210 P.2d 348, we held, in paragraph one of the syllabus:

> "To constitute an express warranty no particular form of words is necessary, and any affirmation of the quality or condition of the vehicle, not uttered as a matter of opinion or belief, made by the seller at the time of sale for the purpose of assuring the buyer of the truth of the fact and inducing such buyer to make the purchase, if so received and relied on by the buyer, is an express warranty."

In International Harvester Co. v. Lawyer, 56 Okl. 207, 155 P. 617, 618, we defined a warranty as follows:

> "After a careful examination of the above-cited authorities, we conclude that warranty is a matter of intention. A decisive test is whether the vendor assumes to assert a fact of which the buyer is ignorant, or merely states an opinion, or his judgment, upon a matter of which the vendor has no special knowledge, and on which the buyer may also be expected to have an opinion and to exercise his judgment. In the former case there is a warranty; in the latter case there is not * * *."

We are of the opinion the defendant's statement that the new engine "would be guaranteed for six thousand miles or six months" could have been found by the jury to have been an express warranty under the above quoted decisions. This statement does not appear to be an expression of opinion; rather, it appears to be a definite and unqualified statement that the engine was to be "guaranteed" for the specified time or distance.

Defendants argue that even if plaintiff relied on an oral warranty on the part of such defendants this warranty was merged into and superseded by the manufacturer's written warranty. This argument assumes that such statement relating to the warranty did not constitute an adoption of the written warranty. However, even granting their assumption, arguendo, we are of the opinion that a seller himself may make an express warranty concerning an article although the article is already covered by a written warranty of the manufacturer. See 46 Am.Jur., Sales, § 313, p. 495.

* * *

The trial court did not err in sustaining plaintiff's motion for new trial.

Affirmed.

JACKSON, C.J., IRWIN, V.C.J., and DAVISON, BLACKBIRD, BERRY, HODGES and McINERNEY, JJ., concur.

LAVENDER, J., dissents.

Notes

1. Unlike an implied warranty of merchantability, which is applicable only to sellers who are merchants, an express warranty is applicable to merchants and non-merchants alike. As *Scovil* indicates, unlike an implied warranty of merchantability, which is applicable to all merchants in the chain of distribution, an express warranty is applicable only to a seller who actually makes a representation. Thus, a retailer is not automatically liable under section 2–313 for a manufacturer's express warranties, although a retailer might be liable for breach of an implied warranty of merchantability under section 2–314(2)(f) if the product fails to conform to a manufacturer's promise on the label.

2. A retailer who makes a representation as part of a manufacturer's promotion may create liability for the manufacturer under agency principles, and a retailer who reiterates a manufacturer's promise may be liable for his own express warranty.

SECTION C. IMPLIED WARRANTY OF MERCHANTABILITY

Uniform Commercial Code

§ 2–314. Implied Warranty: Merchantability; Usage of Trade

(1) Unless excluded or modified (Section 2–316), a warranty that the goods shall be merchantable is implied in a contract for their sale if the seller is a merchant with respect to goods of that kind. Under this section the serving for value of food or drink to be consumed either on the premises or elsewhere is a sale.

(2) Goods to be merchantable must be at least such as

(a) pass without objection in the trade under the contract description; and

(b) in the case of fungible goods, are of fair average quality within the description; and

(c) are fit for the ordinary purposes for which such goods are used; and

(d) run, within the variations permitted by the agreement, of even kind, quality and quantity within each unit and among all units involved; and

(e) are adequately contained, packaged, and labeled as the agreement may require; and

(f) conform to the promises or affirmations of fact made on the container or label if any.

(3) Unless excluded or modified (Section 2–316) other implied warranties may arise from course of dealing or usage of trade.

COFFER v. STANDARD BRANDS, INC.
Court of Appeals of North Carolina, 1976.
30 N.C.App. 134, 226 S.E.2d 534.

[Plaintiff was injured when he bit down on an unshelled nut from a bottle of otherwise shelled, mixed nuts. He sued for breach of implied warranty of merchantability, among other grounds.]

BRITT, JUDGE.

* * *

C. IMPLIED WARRANTY

First, we consider plaintiff's claim in the light of the Uniform Commercial Code and defendant's implied warranty of merchantability under G.S. 25–2–314(1). Unless excluded or modified pursuant to G.S. 25–2–316, this warranty arises as a matter of law where the seller is a merchant with respect to the goods in question under G.S. 25–2–104(1). Some basis for determining the merchantability of goods is provided in G.S. 25–2–314(2). This subsection provides as follows:

"(2) Goods to be merchantable must be at least such as

(a) pass without objection in the trade under the contract description; and

(b) in the case of fungible goods, are of fair average quality within the description; and

(c) are fit for the ordinary purposes for which such goods are used; and

(d) run, within the variations permitted by the agreement, of even kind, quality and quantity within each unit and among all units involved; and

(e) are adequately contained, packaged, and labeled as the agreement may require; and

(f) conform to the promises or affirmations of fact made on the container or label if any."

We feel that the goods were impliedly warranted to be nuts, a natural incident of which were the shells. As such they were fit for the ordinary purposes under G.S. 25–2–314(2)(c). The argument could be made that the clear glass jar revealing only shelled nuts was a "promise or affirmation of fact" as provided in G.S. 25–2–314(2)(f). However, we feel that this approach is inconsistent with the nature of the goods at issue and G.S. 25–2–314(2)(c).

In assessing the merchantability of goods under G.S. 25–2–314(2)(a) thru (f), various state and federal regulatory acts are instructive. This is especially pertinent in regard to a determination of merchantability under G.S. 25–2–314(2)(a), (c).

Under G.S. 106–22(9), 106–67.7 and 106–195 the Commissioner of Agriculture and the North Carolina Board of Agriculture are empowered to make and adopt rules and regulations governing the sale of mixed nuts. *See, e.g.,* G.S. 150A–14, effective 1 February 1976. The Board has adopted certain federal standards issued under the Agricultural Marketing Act of 1946, 7 U.S.C. § 1621 et seq. (1970). *See* 2 N.C.A.C. 15K.0217 (1976). These standards govern determination of the quality and merchantability of such nuts. 7 C.F.R. § 51.2(d) (1976). These standards provide that mixed nuts are to contain certain individual varieties within certain percentages. The quality of the mixture is determined by application of the respective standards of quality and merchantability for each variety represented in the mixture, 7 C.F.R. § 51.3520 (1976).

While there appear to be no standards governing the permissible limits for presence of unshelled filberts in a lot of otherwise shelled nuts, such standards do exist for peanuts.

* * *

* * * The range allowable is from 1.00% to 2.50% with an average of 1.82% unshelled peanuts per unit of shelled peanuts. We find these figures highly persuasive in establishing merchantability under G.S. 25–2–314(2)(a). They serve to indicate that in the context of the peanut industry as a regulated trade, there is some tolerance for unshelled nuts in a lot of shelled nuts.

Since mixed nuts are subject to the same standards as individual varieties, it logically follows that as in case of peanuts there is some tolerance in the trade for unshelled filberts as well. Thus the mixed nuts marketed by defendant were merchantable notwithstanding the presence of an unshelled filbert, since the presence of limited quantities of unshelled nuts does not render shelled nuts objectionable in the trade within the meaning of G.S. 25–2–314(2)(a).

G.S. 25–2–314(2)(c) provides that goods are merchantable when they are fit for ordinary purposes. As a food defendant's mixed nuts are subject to various state and federal regulatory acts dealing with the quality of food goods. G.S. 106–129 dealing with adulterated foods is instructive.

" * * * A food shall be deemed to be adulterated:

(1) a. If it bears or contains any poisonous or deleterious substance which may render it injurious to health; *but in case the substance is not an added substance* such food shall not be considered adulterated under this paragraph if the quantity of such

substance in such food does not ordinarily render it injurious to health; * * *." (Emphasis added.)

This language is amplified in regulations promulgated under the Federal Food, Drug and Cosmetic Act, 21 U.S.C. § 342 et seq. (1970). *See, e.g.,* 21 C.F.R. § 122.1(b) (1975). These regulations have been adopted by the State Board of Agriculture pursuant to G.S. 106–128 and are currently in effect in North Carolina. *See* 2 N.C.A.C. 9B.0008 (1976).

Thus, it appears by statute and regulation that a certain limited amount of naturally occurring unshelled filberts is permissible without rendering the food goods adulterated. As such they are fit for ordinary purposes and merchantable under G.S. 25–2–314(2)(c).

Plaintiff can find no comfort in the foreign substance doctrine as the unshelled filbert was not a foreign substance. It is well recognized in this and other jurisdictions passing on the question that the presence of natural impurities is no basis for liability. *Adams v. Great Atl. & Pac. Tea Co.,* 251 N.C. 565, 112 S.E.2d 92 (1960); *Webster v. Blue Ship Tea Room, Inc.,* 347 Mass. 421, 198 N.E.2d 309 (1964).

In *Adams,* the plaintiff alleged that he broke a tooth while eating corn flakes when he bit down on a part of a grain of corn which had crystallized into a state as hard as quartz. Plaintiff sued on the theory of implied warranty and the trial court entered judgment of involuntary nonsuit. The Supreme Court affirmed the judgment on the ground that the crystallized grain of corn was not a foreign substance but was a natural part of the original food not removed in processing, and its presence should have been anticipated by the consumer.

Recovery was denied in numerous cases from other jurisdictions where the impurity was a natural incident of the food. *See: Allen v. Grafton,* 170 Ohio St. 249, 10 Ohio Ops.2d 289, 164 N.E.2d 167 (1960) (oyster shell in oyster stew); *Shapiro v. Hotel Statler Corp.,* 132 F.Supp. 891 (S.D.Cal.1955) (fish bone in fish stew); *Lamb v. Hill,* 112 Cal.App.2d 41, 245 P.2d 316 (1952) (chicken bone in chicken pie); *Silva v. F.W. Woolworth Co.,* 28 Cal.App.2d 649, 83 P.2d 76 (1938) (fragment of turkey bone in roast turkey).

Since the impurity complained of in this case was a natural incident of the goods in question, we feel that there was no breach of the implied warranty of merchantability.

* * *

Conclusion

So long as defendant's goods are merchantable there is no breach of implied warranty. Absent evidence of negligence and express warranty, and given the present posture of strict liability in this jurisdiction, we discern no basis for liability.

For the reasons stated, the judgment appealed from is

Affirmed.

BROCK, C.J., and MORRIS, J., concur.

Notes

1. A landmark case in the development of implied warranties before the adoption of the U.C.C. was Henningsen v. Bloomfield Motors, Inc., 32 N.J. 358, 161 A.2d 69 (1960). Mr. Henningsen bought an automobile from Bloomfield Motors and gave it to his wife as a gift. The automobile was manufactured by Chrysler. Ten days after delivery, Ms. Henningsen was injured in an accident caused by a sudden failure in the steering. The court held that she could recover from Chrysler for breach of an implied warranty of merchantability. The court addressed several issues, including the requirement of privity of contract and the effect of disclaimers. *See* pp. 92–95, 99–102, *infra*. On the law's imposition of an implied warranty of merchantability the court said:

> In the ordinary case of sale of goods by description an implied warranty of merchantability is an integral part of the transaction. R.S. 46:30–20, N.J.S.A. If the buyer, expressly or by implication, makes known to the seller the particular purpose for which the article is required and it appears that he has relied on the seller's skill or judgment, an implied warranty arises of reasonable fitness for that purpose. R.S. 46:30–21(1), N.J.S.A. The former type of warranty simply means that the thing sold is reasonably fit for the general purpose for which it is manufactured and sold. * * * Ryan v. Progressive Grocery Stores, 255 N.Y. 388, 175 N.E. 105, 74 A.L.R. 339 (Ct.App. 1931); 1 Williston on Sales, § 243 (Rev. ed. 1948). As Judge (later Justice) Cardozo remarked in Ryan, supra, the distinction between a warranty of fitness for a particular purpose and of merchantability in many instances is practically meaningless. In the particular case he was concerned with food for human consumption in a sealed container. Perhaps no more apt illustration of the notion can be thought of than the instance of the ordinary purchaser who informs the automobile dealer that he desires a car for the purpose of business and pleasure driving on the public highway.

* * *

> The uniform act codified, extended and liberalized the common law of sales. The motivation in part was to ameliorate the harsh doctrine of *caveat emptor*, and in some measure to impose a reciprocal obligation on the seller to beware. The transcendent value of the legislation, particularly with respect to implied warranties, rests in the fact that obligations on the part of the seller were imposed by operation of law, and did not depend for their existence upon express agreement of the parties. And of tremendous significance in a rapidly expanding commercial society was the recognition of the right to recover damages on account of person injuries arising from a breach of warranty. * * * The particular importance of this advance resides in the fact that under such circumstances strict liability is imposed upon the maker or seller of the product. Recovery of damages does not depend upon proof of negligence or knowledge of the defect. * * *

* * *

Both defendants argue that the proof adduced by plaintiffs as to the happening of the accident was not sufficient to demonstrate a breach of warranty. Consequently, they claim that their motion for judgment should have been granted by the trial court. We cannot agree. In our view, the total effect of the circumstances shown from purchase to accident is adequate to raise an inference that the car was defective and that such condition was causally related to the mishap. See, Yormack v. Farmers' Coop. Ass'n of N.J., 11 N.J.Super. 416, 78 A.2d 421 (App.Div. 1951) * * *. Thus, determination by the jury was required.

The proof adduced by the plaintiffs disclosed that after servicing and delivery of the car, it operated normally during the succeeding ten days, so far as the Henningsens could tell. They had no difficulty or mishap of any kind, and it neither had nor required any servicing. It was driven by them alone. The owner's service certificate provided for return for further servicing at the end of the first 1,000 miles—less than half of which had been covered at the time of Mrs. Henningsen's injury.

The facts, detailed above, show that on the day of the accident, ten days after delivery, Mrs. Henningsen was driving in a normal fashion, on a smooth highway, when unexpectedly the steering wheel and the front wheels of the car went into the bizarre action described. Can it reasonably be said that the circumstances do not warrant an inference of unsuitability for ordinary use against the manufacturer and the dealer? Obviously there is nothing in the proof to indicate in the slightest that the most unusual action of the steering wheel was caused by Mrs. Henningsen's operation of the automobile on this day, or by the use of the car between delivery and the happening of the incident. Nor is there anything to suggest that any external force or condition, unrelated to the manufacturing or servicing of the car operated as an inducing or even concurring factor.

* * *

[T]he question of breach of warranty * * * was properly placed in the hands of the jury. In our judgment, the evidence shown, as a matter of preponderance of probabilities, would justify the conclusion by the ultimate triers of the facts that the accident was caused by a failure of the steering mechanism of the car and that such failure constituted a breach of the warranty of both defendants.

* * *

2. The criteria of subsection 2–314(2) are not exhaustive. Comment 6 provides:

Subsection (2) does not purport to exhaust the meaning of "merchantable" nor to negate any of its attributes not specifically mentioned in the text of the statute, but arising by usage of trade or through case law. The language used is "must be at least such as * * *," and the intention is to leave open other attributes of merchantability.

3. As in the case of strict tort liability, an implied warranty of merchantability does not create true strict liability. A plaintiff must show more than that the product caused injury, and merchantability is not synonymous

with perfection. Like the standard of defectiveness in strict tort liability, merchantability requires only that a product be of reasonable quality. Unlike the standard of defectiveness in strict tort liability, however, the merchantability standard has not been carefully defined by courts.

Some courts have suggested that merchantability should be equated with defectiveness under strict tort liability. *See, e.g.,* Durrett v. Baxter Chrysler–Plymouth, Inc., 198 Neb. 392, 253 N.W.2d 37 (1977); Holloway v. General Motors Corp., 399 Mich. 617, 250 N.W.2d 736 (1977); Vanek v. Kirby, 253 Or. 494, 450 P.2d 778 (1969); Olsen v. Royal Metals Corp., 392 F.2d 116 (5th Cir.1968); Bernard v. Dresser Indus., Inc., 691 S.W.2d 734 (Tex.App.—Beaumont 1985); Dallas Heating Co., Inc. v. Pardee, 561 S.W.2d 16, 21 (Tex.Civ.App.—Dallas 1977, writ refused n.r.e.).

Should a court apply the same rules about whether a risk must be foreseeable under breach of an implied warranty of merchantability as it does under strict tort liability?

4. It is normally not a defense to a claim for breach of an implied warranty of merchantability that the seller (even the retailer) could not have done anything to detect or prevent the defect. In Vlases v. Montgomery Ward Co., 377 F.2d 846 (3d Cir.1967), the plaintiff purchased one-day-old chicks from the defendant's mail order catalogue. After a few weeks, he discovered that the chicks had avian leukosis disease, a form of cancer, and sued defendant. Defendant, the retailer, argued that it is impossible to detect avian leukosis in one-day-old chicks. The court stated:

> The fact that avian leukosis is nondetectable could be an important issue but only as bearing on the charge of negligence, which is no longer in this suit. The Pennsylvania decision in Q. Vandenberg & Sons, N.V. v. Siter, 204 Pa.Super. 392, 204 A.2d 494 (1964) buttresses our conclusion in upholding the implied warranties. There latent defects in certain tulip and hyacinth bulbs went undetected in the face of two inspections and the court, though aware that the imperfections could not be uncovered after growth, limited its concern to the question of whether the seller's express provision that notice of any breach be communicated within a certain time, was reasonable. The entire purpose behind the implied warranty sections of the Code is to hold the seller responsible when inferior goods are passed along to the unsuspecting buyer. What the Code requires is not evidence that the defects should or could have been uncovered by the seller but only that the goods upon delivery were not of a merchantable quality or fit for their particular purpose. If those requisite proofs are established the only exculpatory relief afforded by the Code is a showing that the implied warranties were modified or excluded by specific language under Section 2–316. Lack of skill or foresight on the part of the seller in discovering the product's flaw was never meant to bar liability. The gravamen here is not so much with what precautions were taken by the seller but rather with the quality of the goods contracted for by the buyer.

Vlases involved a flaw. The result might have been different if it had involved a design or warning defect.

5. "Passing without objection in the trade" under subsection 2–314(2)(a) is clarified in comment 2:

The question when the warranty is imposed turns basically on the meaning of the terms of the agreement as recognized in the trade. Goods delivered under an agreement made by a merchant in a given line of trade must be of a quality comparable to that generally acceptable in that line of trade under the description or other designation of the goods used in the agreement. The responsibility imposed rests on any merchant-seller, and the absence of the words "grower or manufacturer or not" which appeared in Section 15(2) of the Uniform Sales Act does not restrict the applicability of this section.

6. "Fair average quality" under subsection 2–314(2)(b) is clarified in comment 7:

Paragraphs (a) and (b) of subsection (2) are to be read together. Both refer, as indicated above, to the standards of that line of the trade which fits the transaction and the seller's business. "Fair average" is a term directly appropriate to agricultural bulk products and means goods centering around the middle belt of quality, not the least or the worst that can be understood in the particular trade by the designation, but such as can pass "without objection." Of course a fair percentage of the least is permissible but the goods are not "fair average" if they are all of the least or worst quality possible under the description. In cases of doubt as to what quality is intended, the price at which a merchant closes a contract is an excellent index of the nature and scope of his obligation under the present section.

7. What if an industry tolerates an occasional bad unit as part of an acceptable multi-unit delivery? Is the implied warranty of merchantability breached for an individual injured by the bad unit? Does it matter whether it is one unshelled nut in a can of shelled nuts or one bad steering mechanism in a shipment of automobiles? Is the problem here one of defining what constitutes the "product"?

8. The most commonly cited subsection under section 2–314 is subsection 2–314(2)(c), which requires that goods be "fit for the ordinary purposes for which such goods are used." As comment 8 states, "[f]itness for the ordinary purposes for which goods of the type are used is a fundamental concept of [subsection 2–314(2)]." Fitness for ordinary purposes is difficult to define, however, because it varies with the purposes for which a particular product is ordinarily used. Once determined, this issue in turn raises the issue of whether a product has been used for its ordinary purpose. If the product has not been used for its ordinary purposes, the product's use is not covered by an implied warranty of merchantability. It may, however, be covered by an implied warranty of fitness. A determination of a product's ordinary purposes depends on the circumstances of each case.

In Hardman v. Helene Curtis Indus., Inc., 48 Ill.App.2d 42, 198 N.E.2d 681 (1964), the plaintiff, a small child, was burned after she sprayed flammable hair spray on her clothing and hair because the hair spray smelled good. The court held it was a jury question whether the hair spray had been used for an "ordinary purpose."

9. Subsection 2–314(2)(d) requires that goods "run, within the variations permitted by the agreement, of even kind, quality and quantity within each unit and among all units involved." Comment 9 to section 2–314 refers

to "the frequent usages of trade which permit substantial variations both with and without an allowance or an obligation to replace the varying units."

10. Subsection 2–314(2)(f) requires that goods "conform to the promises or affirmations of fact made on the container or label if any." Although this requirement is similar to an express warranty under section 2–313, two situations exist in which subsection 2–314(2)(f) might be independently important.

First, a representation made on a package or label might not be a part of the basis of the bargain—because it was not read or relied upon by the buyer—and therefore would not constitute an express warranty. Such a representation might nevertheless be covered by subsection 2–314(2)(f). One goal of subsection 2–314(2)(f) is to police consumer markets by insuring that goods conform to representations on their labels. This goal might be advanced under a "private attorney general" theory by permitting buyers to sue even if they have not themselves read or relied on the representation. This rationale is plausible for express warranties as well, but a court might be more inclined to apply it under subsection 2–314(2)(f), where the seller is a merchant, than under section 2–313, where the seller is not necessarily a merchant. Courts have not actually relied on this rationale, however, and they may in fact require a buyer to show knowledge of or reliance on a representation to trigger subsection 2–314(2)(f).

The second situation in which subsection 2–314(2)(f) might have independent significance is when the defendant is a retailer. Unless a retailer adopts representations a manufacturer has put on a label, the retailer is not responsible for them as express warranties under section 2–313. Section 2–314, however, applies to all sellers in the chain of distribution if they are merchants in the goods in question. Consequently, a retailer might be liable under section 2–314(2)(f), even if he is not liable under subsection 2–313.

11. Even if goods are *not* reasonably fit for their ordinary purpose, they might still be merchantable. If a defect is obvious and the buyer inspects the goods, they are not unmerchantable. *See, e.g.,* Cardwell v. Hackett, 579 S.W.2d 186 (Tenn.App.1978). Similarly, there is no liability for breach of an implied warranty of merchantability if the buyer inspects the goods or accepts them after having been given an opportunity to inspect, if the inspection would reasonably be expected to reveal the product's condition. *See, e.g.,* Calloway v. Manion, 572 F.2d 1033 (5th Cir.1978).

12. Comment 3 to section 2–314 provides that "[a] contract for the sale of secondhand goods * * * involves only such obligation as is appropriate to such goods. * * *"

13. Subsection 2–314(3) provides that "other implied warranties may arise from course of dealing or usage of trade." Comment 12 states that the purpose of "[s]ubsection 3 is to make explicit that usage of trade and course of dealing can create warranties and that they are implied rather than express warranties and thus subject to exclusion or modification under section 2–316."

Subsection 2–314(3) overlaps with section 1–205, which provides generally that course of dealing and usage of trade affect the construction and interpretation of contract provisions. It also overlaps with subsection 2–314(2)(a), which provides that goods are not merchantable if they do not "pass without objection in the trade. * * *" Nevertheless, subsection 2–314(3) may have some independent significance. For example, unlike the obligations created by section 1–205, the obligations created by subsection 2–314(3) are "warranties" that are subject to the special waiver provisions of section 2–316. Even so, subsection 2–314(3) does not create an "implied warranty of merchantability," and thus its warranties may not be subject to the special provisions in section 2–316 directed specifically to implied warranties of merchantability, as opposed to the provisions of section 2–316 directed to warranties generally.

Courts seldom rely on subsection 2–314(3), and its precise relationship to section 1–205 and subsections 2–314(2)(a) and (b) is unclear.

SIEMEN v. ALDEN

Appellate Court of Illinois, 1975.

34 Ill.App.3d 961, 341 N.E.2d 713.

* * *

THOMAS J. MORAN, JUSTICE.

Plaintiff sued defendants to recover for injuries he sustained while operating an automated multi-rip saw. The three-count complaint sought recovery on theories of strict tort liability for sale of a defective product, breach of warranties, and negligence. Plaintiff proceeds on this appeal against defendant Korleski only. He appeals the order of the trial court granting defendant's motion for summary judgment on count one, alleging strict tort liability, and count two, alleging breach of warranties.

Plaintiff had owned and operated a sawmill since 1961. In 1968, he decided to purchase a multi-rip saw to increase his production of decking pallets. Upon the suggestion of a customer, plaintiff contacted Lloyd G. Alden, manufacturer of the saw in question. Alden informed plaintiff that a new saw could not be delivered in less than six months and suggested that plaintiff contact defendant Korleski, who owned two of the Alden saws. Plaintiff contacted defendant, who advised him that he indeed had two saws: the one he was currently using, and an older one purchased in 1962 which had not been used since 1965. Thereafter the parties met on two occasions at defendant's sawmill to discuss plaintiff's possible purchase of the older saw. At the first meeting, defendant demonstrated the newer saw, which operated in the same manner as the one plaintiff was considering purchasing. Plaintiff's son accompanied him to the second meeting, at which time plaintiff was first shown the saw in question. It was sitting, partially dismantled, in a corner and was covered with boards and sawdust. Defendant informed plaintiff that it was in operating condition and that plaintiff would have to supply and install saw blades, motor, shiv, belts, pulleys, and a sawdust removal apparatus in order to use it. Thereafter, the parties agreed on a purchase price of $2900.

Plaintiff's injury, which precipitated the instant suit, occurred in 1970 when a cant of wood exploded while being fed through the saw in question.

On appeal, plaintiff contends that summary judgment in favor of defendant should be reversed because (1) defendant had a sufficient relationship to the saw which injured plaintiff to subject him to strict liability for sale of the defective product, and (2) under the Uniform Commercial Code, Sections 2–314 and 2–315 (Ill.Rev.Stat.1971, ch. 26, §§ 2–314, 2–315), the defendant is liable for implied warranties.

[The court determined that the defendant was not liable under strict tort liability because it was not engaged in the business of selling saws.]

Plaintiff claims that under sections 2–314 and 2–315 of the Uniform Commercial Code (Ill.Rev.Stat. 1971, ch. 26, §§ 2–314, 2–315) a genuine issue of material fact exists as to defendant's liability arising from his saw-related knowledge and skill, and plaintiff's ultimate reliance upon this knowledge in purchasing the saw. Section 2–314 states in pertinent part:

> "Unless excluded or modified * * * a warranty that the goods shall be merchantable is implied in a contract for their sale if the seller is a merchant with respect to goods of that kind."

Section 2–104(1) of the Uniform Commercial Code (Ill.Rev.Stat.1971, ch. 26, § 2–104(1),) defines a merchant as:

> "[A] person who deals in goods of the kind or otherwise by his occupation holds himself out as having knowledge or skill peculiar to the practices or goods involved in the transaction or to whom such knowledge or skill may be attributed by his employment of an agent or broker or other intermediary who by his occupation holds himself out as having such knowledge or skill."

Defendant argues in his reply brief that plaintiff falls within the terms of section 2–104(1) and is therefore a merchant for purposes of section 2–314 by virtue of his "holding himself out as having knowledge or skill." This test, however, is not the standard for determining who is a merchant within the meaning of section 2–314. The Committee Notes to section 2–104 (S.H.A.1971, ch. 26, § 2–104, Committee Notes, ¶ 2, page 97) and to section 2–314 (S.H.A.1971, ch. 26, § 2–314, Committee Comments, ¶ 3, page 232) make it clear that the definition of merchant within 2–314 is a narrow one and that the warranty of merchantability is applicable only to a person who, in a professional status, sells the particular kind of goods giving rise to the warranty.

> "A person making an isolated sale of goods is not a 'merchant' within the meaning of the scope of this section [2–314] and, thus, no warranty of merchantability would apply." S.H.A.1971, ch. 26, § 2–314, Committee Comments, ¶ 3, page 232.

The record is clear that defendant is engaged in the sawmill business. The sale in the instant case was an isolated transaction and therefore did not come within the terms of section 2–314.

* * *

Judgment affirmed.

RECHENMACHER, P.J., and DIXON, J., concur.

Notes

1. In Nelson v. Union Equity Co–Op. Exchange, 548 S.W.2d 352 (Tex.1977), the court was required to decide whether a farmer who sells his crop is a merchant under section 2–104. The ultimate issue in the case was whether a grain futures contract was governed by the statute of frauds in section 2–201; subsection 2–201(a) exempts some contracts "between merchants." Although *Nelson* did not involve an implied warranty of merchantability under section 2–314, the court gave no indication that the definition of merchant under section 2–104 differs depending on whether the case involves the statute of frauds under section 2–201 or an implied warranty of merchantability under section 2–314.

The court held that the farmer was a merchant with respect to his crop:

[A] person is a "merchant" if he (1) deals in goods of the kind, or (2) by his occupation holds himself out as having knowledge or skill peculiar to the *practices* involved in the transaction, or (3) by his occupation holds himself out as having knowledge or skill peculiar to the *goods* involved in the transaction, or (4) employs an intermediary who by his occupation holds himself out as having such knowledge or skill, and that knowledge or skill may be attributed to the person whose status is in question. If the facts show that a person satisfies any of the above criteria, then we are bound to hold that person to be a merchant.

548 S.W.2d at 355. The court held that Nelson, the farmer, satisfied the first three criteria, any one of which made him a "merchant."

Two aspects of the court's reasoning are significant. First, the court held that to be a merchant, a seller need not represent himself as having special skill or knowledge; the fact that he is engaged in an *occupation* that would normally require such skill or knowledge is sufficient. Second, the court observed that the "broad language of section [2–104(1)] and the accompanying text of the Official Comment suggest that the term 'merchant' was intended to apply to all but the most casual or inexperienced sellers." 548 S.W.2d at 357. The court did, however, recite the seller's actual expertise in some detail.

2. Several other courts have held that a farmer is not a merchant with respect to his crop. *See, e.g.,* Loeb and Company, Inc. v. Schreiner, 294 Ala. 722, 321 So.2d 199 (1975); Decatur Cooperative Ass'n v. Urban, 219 Kan. 171, 547 P.2d 323 (1976); Lish v. Compton, 547 P.2d 223 (Utah 1976). *But see* Calloway v. Manion, 572 F.2d 1033 (5th Cir.1978); Prince v. LeVan, 486 P.2d 959, 964 (Alaska 1971).

3. Under the test in *Nelson*, how would the *Siemen* case be decided?

4. Section 2–313 and 2–315 do not refer to "merchants." Consequently, an express warranty and an implied warranty of fitness apply even to sales by non-merchants. Why does the U.C.C. make this distinction?

SECTION D. IMPLIED WARRANTY OF FITNESS FOR PARTICULAR PURPOSE

Uniform Commercial Code

§ 2–315. Implied Warranty: Fitness for Particular Purpose

Where the seller at the time of contracting has reason to know any particular purpose for which the goods are required and that the buyer is relying on the seller's skill or judgment to select or furnish suitable goods, there is unless excluded or modified under the next section an implied warranty that the goods shall be fit for such purpose.

LEWIS v. MOBIL OIL CORP.

United States Court of Appeals, Eighth Circuit, 1971.
438 F.2d 500.

GIBSON, CIRCUIT JUDGE.

In this diversity case the defendant appeals from a judgment entered on a jury verdict in favor of the plaintiff in the amount of $89,250 for damages alleged to be caused by use of defendant's oil.

Plaintiff Lewis has been doing business as a sawmill operator in Cove, Arkansas, since 1956. In 1963, in order to meet competition, Lewis decided to convert his power equipment to hydraulic equipment. He purchased a hydraulic system in May 1963, from a competitor who was installing a new system. The used system was in good operating condition at the time Lewis purchased it. It was stored at his plant until November 1964, while a new mill building was being built, at which time it was installed. Following the installation, Lewis requested from Frank Rowe, a local Mobil oil dealer, the proper hydraulic fluid to operate his machinery. The prior owner of the hydraulic system had used Pacemaker oil supplied by Cities Service, but plaintiff had been a customer of Mobil's for many years and desired to continue with Mobil. Rowe said he didn't know what the proper lubricant for Lewis' machinery was, but would find out. The only information given to Rowe by Lewis was that the machinery was operated by a gear-type pump; Rowe did not request any further information. He apparently contacted a Mobil representative for a recommendation, though this is not entirely clear, and sold plaintiff a product known as Ambrex 810. This is a straight mineral oil with no chemical additives.

Within a few days after operation of the new equipment commenced, plaintiff began experiencing difficulty with its operation. The oil changed color, foamed over, and got hot. The oil was changed a number of times, with no improvement. By late April 1965, approximately six months after operations with the equipment had begun, the system broke down, and a complete new system was installed. The cause of the breakdown was undetermined, but apparently by this time there was some suspicion of the oil being used. Plaintiff Lewis requested Rowe to be sure he was supplying the right kind of oil. Ambrex 810 continued to be supplied.

From April 1965 until April 1967, plaintiff continued to have trouble with the system, principally with the pumps which supplied the pressure. Six new pumps were required during this period, as they continually broke down. During this period, the kind of pump used was a Commercial pump which was specified by the designer of the hydraulic system. The filtration of oil for this pump was by means of a metal strainer, which was cleaned daily by the plaintiff in accordance with the instruction given with the equipment.

In April 1967, the plaintiff changed the brand of pump from a Commercial to a Tyrone pump. The Tyrone pump, instead of using the metal strainer filtration alone, used a disposable filter element in addition. Ambrex 810 oil was also recommended by Mobil and used with this pump, which completely broke down three weeks later. At this point, plaintiff was visited for the first time by a representative of Mobil Oil Corporation, as well as a representative of the Tyrone pump manufacturer.

On the occasion of this visit, May 9, 1967, plaintiff's system was completely flushed and cleaned, a new Tyrone pump installed, and on the pump manufacturer's and Mobil's representative's recommendation, a new oil was used which contained certain chemical additives, principally a "defoamant." Following these changes, plaintiff's system worked satisfactorily up until the time of trial, some two and one-half years later.

Briefly stated, plaintiff's theory of his case is that Mobil supplied him with an oil which was warranted fit for use in his hydraulic system, that the oil was not suitable for such use because it did not contain certain additives, and that it was the improper oil which caused the mechanical breakdowns, with consequent loss to his business. The defendant contends that there was no warranty of fitness, that the breakdowns were caused not by the oil but by improper filtration, and that in any event there can be no recovery of loss of profits in this case.

I. THE EXISTENCE OF WARRANTIES

Defendant maintains that there was no warranty of fitness in this case, that at most there was only a warranty of merchantability and that there was no proof of breach of this warranty, since there was no proof that Ambrex 810 is unfit for use in hydraulic systems generally. We find it unnecessary to consider whether the warranty of merchantability was breached, although there is some proof in the record to that effect, since we conclude that there was a warranty of fitness.

Plaintiff Lewis testified that he had been a longtime customer of Mobil Oil, and that his only source of contact with the company was through Frank Rowe, Mobil's local dealer, with whom he did almost all of his business. It was common knowledge in the community that Lewis was converting his sawmill operation into a hydraulic system. Rowe knew this, and in fact had visited his mill on business matters several times during the course of the changeover. When operations with the new machinery were about to commence, Lewis asked Rowe to get him the proper hydraulic fluid. Rowe asked him what kind of a system he had, and Lewis replied it was a Commercial-pump type. This was all the information asked or given. Neither Lewis nor Rowe knew what the oil requirements for the system were, and Rowe knew that Lewis knew nothing more specific about his requirements. Lewis also testified that after he began having trouble with his operations, while there were several possible sources of the difficulty the oil was one suspected source, and he several times asked Rowe to be sure he was furnishing him with the right kind.

Rowe's testimony for the most part confirmed Lewis'. It may be noted here that Mobil does not contest Rowe's authority to represent it in this transaction, and therefore whatever warranties may be implied because of the dealings between Rowe and Lewis are attributable to Mobil. Rowe admitted knowing Lewis was converting to a hydraulic system and that Lewis asked him to supply the fluid. He testified that he did not know what should be used and relayed the request to a superior in the Mobil organization, who recommended Ambrex 810. This is what was supplied.

When the first Tyrone pump was installed in April 1967, Rowe referred the request for a proper oil recommendation to Ted Klock, a Mobil engineer. Klock recommended Ambrex 810. When this pump failed a few weeks later, Klock visited the Lewis plant to inspect the equipment. The system was flushed out completely and the oil was changed to DTE–23 and Del Vac Special containing several additives. After this, no further trouble was experienced.

This evidence adequately establishes an implied warranty of fitness. Arkansas has adopted the Uniform Commercial Code's provision for an implied warranty of fitness:

> "Where the seller at the time of contracting has reason to know any particular purpose for which the goods are required and that the buyer is relying on the seller's skill or judgment to select or furnish suitable goods, there is unless excluded or modified under the next section an implied warranty that the goods shall be fit for such purpose." 7C Ark.Stat.Ann. § 85–2–315 (1961).

Under this provision of the Code, there are two requirements for an implied warranty of fitness: (1) that the seller have "reason to know" of the use for which the goods are purchased, and (2) that the buyer relies on the seller's expertise in supplying the proper product. Both of these requirements are amply met by the proof in this case. Lewis' testimony, as confirmed by that of Rowe and Klock, shows that the oil was purchased specifically for his hydraulic system, not for just a hydraulic system in general, and that Mobil certainly knew of this specific purpose.

It is also clear that Lewis was relying on Mobil to supply him with the proper oil for the system, since at the time of his purchases, he made clear that he didn't know what kind was necessary.

Mobil contends that there was no warranty of fitness for use in his particular system because he didn't specify that he needed an oil with additives, and alternatively that he didn't give them enough information for them to determine that an additive oil was required. However, it seems that the circumstances of this case come directly within that situation described in the first comment to this provision of the Uniform Commercial Code:

> "1. Whether or not this warranty arises in any individual case is basically a question of fact to be determined by the circumstances of the contracting. Under this section the buyer need not bring home to the seller *actual knowledge of the particular purpose* for which the goods are intended or of his reliance on the seller's skill and judgment, if the circumstances are such that the seller has reason to realize the purpose intended or that the reliance exists."
> 7C Ark.Stat.Ann. § 85–2–315, Comment 1 (1961) (emphasis added).

Here Lewis made it clear that the oil was purchased for his system, that he didn't know what oil should be used, and that he was relying on Mobil to supply the proper product. If any further information was needed, it was incumbent upon Mobil to get it before making its recommendation. That it could have easily gotten the necessary information is evidenced by the fact that after plaintiff's continuing complaints, Mobil's engineer visited the plant, and, upon inspection, changed the recommendation that had previously been made.

Additionally, Mobil contends that even if there were an implied warranty of fitness, it does not cover the circumstances of this case because of the abnormal features which the plaintiff's system contained, namely an inadequate filtration system and a capacity to entrain excessive air. There are several answers to this contention. First of all, the contention goes essentially to the question of causation—i.e., whether the damage was caused by a breach of warranty or by some other cause—and not to the existence of a warranty of fitness in the first place. Secondly, assuming that certain peculiarities in the plaintiff's system did exist, the whole point of an implied warranty of fitness is that a product be suitable for a specific purpose, and that a seller should not supply a product which is not so suited. Thirdly, there is no evidence in the record that the plaintiff's system was unique or abnormal in these respects. It operated satisfactorily under the prior owner, and the new system has operated satisfactorily after it was adequately cleaned and an additive type oil used.

While we will discuss these problems more completely in the question of causation, it may be briefly noted here that the proof shows that plaintiff's filtration system was installed and maintained in strict accordance with the manufacturer's recommendations, that this was a standard system, and that any hydraulic system has a certain unavoidable capacity to entrain air. While a "perfect" system which is run 24 hours a day might not have any air in it, in actual practice there are at least two sources of air. One is from minute leaks in "packing glands." The other source arises from the fact that when the system is shut down, as at night and over the lunch hour, as well as for repairs, the oil drains out of the system and into the reservoir. When the system is started up again, air which has entered the system to replace the drained oil must be dissipated. This dissipation occurs by running the system for a few minutes and is affected by the capacity of the oil to rid itself of air bubbles. It is sufficient to note here that there was no evidence that the plaintiff's system was in any way unique in this respect. Thus, Mobil's defense that there was no warranty of fitness because of an "abnormal use" of the oil is not appropriate here.

* * *

Notes

1. Could the plaintiff in *Lewis* make out a claim under section 2–314 of the U.C.C. or section 402A of the Restatement (Second) of Torts?

2. Does the court do justice to Mobil's argument that the plaintiff's system had certain peculiarities of which Mobil was unaware? If Mobil was unaware of the peculiarities, is it enough to note that "the whole point of an implied warranty of fitness is that a product be suitable for a specific purpose"?

3. Like an express warranty under section 2–313, but unlike an implied warranty of merchantability under section 2–314, an implied warranty of fitness applies to merchants and non-merchants alike. Why should the Code make this distinction?

Again, like an express warranty and unlike an implied warranty of merchantability, an implied warranty of fitness does not automatically apply to all sellers in the chain of distribution. It applies only to sellers whose conduct creates the warranty.

4. Some courts have held that section 2–315 applies only to situations in which the buyer actually has a special purpose for the goods, that is, that section 2–315 does not apply to ordinary purposes, even if the other requirements of section 2–315 are met. *See* Fred's Excavating and Crane Serv., Inc. v. Continental Ins. Co., 340 So.2d 1220 (Fla.App.1976); Ford Motor Co. v. Taylor, 60 Tenn.App. 271, 446 S.W.2d 521 (1969). Other courts have held that both an implied warranty of fitness and an implied warranty of merchantability can apply to goods that are used for their ordinary purpose, as long as the other requirements of sections 2–314 and 2–315 are met. *See* Deffebach v. Lansburgh & Bro., 150 F.2d 591 (D.C.Cir.1945) (seller should have known that lounging robe is likely to come into contact with flames as part of its ordinary purpose) (pre-code, relying upon D.C. code's implied warranty of fitness); ACME Pump Co. v. National Cash Register Co., 32 Conn.Sup. 69, 73, 337 A.2d 672, 675–76 (1974); Scanlon v. Food Crafts, Inc., 2 Conn.Cir. 3, 193 A.2d 610 (1963); Knab v. Alden's Irving Park, Inc., 49 Ill.App.2d 371, 199 N.E.2d 815 (1964) (brought under Illinois version of Uniform Sales Act); Nelson v. Wilkins Dodge, Inc., 256 N.W.2d 472, 476 n. 2

(Minn.1977); Torstenson v. Melcher, 195 Neb. 764, 771–72, 241 N.W.2d 103, 107 (1976); Tennessee Carolina Transp., Inc. v. Strick Corp., 283 N.C. 423, 196 S.E.2d 711 (1973); Jones, Inc. v. W.A. Wiedebusch Plumbing & Heating Co., 157 W.Va. 257, 201 S.E.2d 248, 253–54 (1973).

When would it make a difference whether section 2–315 applied to an ordinary purpose?

Comment 2 to section 2–315 provides that a "contract may of course include both a warranty of merchantability and one of fitness for a particular purpose." Does this resolve the issue?

5. Some courts have required that the buyer prove that the seller actually has skill and expertise. *See* Prince v. LeVan, 486 P.2d 959, 963 (Alaska 1971); Janssen v. Hook, 1 Ill.App.3d 318, 272 N.E.2d 385 (1971). Nothing in section 2–315 or its comments supports this conclusion, however. Even so, a seller's actual skill and expertise might be a factor in determining both whether the buyer actually relied on the seller's judgment and whether the seller had reason to know of the buyer's reliance.

6. Parties to a transaction seldom explicitly agree that the buyer is relying on the seller's skill and judgment in selecting the goods. Consequently, courts must determine whether the buyer has in fact relied by looking at the circumstances of the transaction. One relevant factor is the parties' relative expertise. *See* Brown v. Asgrow Seed Co., 379 S.W.2d 412 (Tex.Civ.App.—San Antonio 1964, writ refused n.r.e.); Texsun Feed Yards, Inc. v. Ralston Purina Co., 447 F.2d 660 (5th Cir.1971); ACME Pump Co., Inc. v. National Cash Register Co., 32 Conn.Sup. 69, 73, 337 A.2d 672, 676 (1974); *but see* Valley Iron & Steel Co. v. Thorin, 278 Or. 103, 109, 562 P.2d 1212, 1216 (1977) (although more familiar with goods than manufacturer, buyer relied upon manufacturer).

Another factor is whether the buyer participated in the selection of the goods. If the buyer or his agent examined the goods, he is less likely to have relied on the seller's judgment, and the seller is less likely to have known of any reliance. *See, e.g.,* Fear Ranches, Inc. v. Berry, 470 F.2d 905, 908 (10th Cir.1972); Sessa v. Riegle, 427 F.Supp. 760, 770 (E.D.Pa.1977) (buyer relying upon his own agent's examination of horse did not rely upon seller); Kopper Glo Fuel, Inc. v. Island Lake Coal Co., 436 F.Supp. 91, 95 (E.D.Tenn. 1977); Donald v. City Nat'l Bank, 295 Ala. 320, 325, 329 So.2d 92, 96 (1976) (no reliance where buyer had boat inspected at his own expense); Valiga v. National Food Co., 58 Wis.2d 232, 257, 206 N.W.2d 377, 390–91 (1973). Subsection 2–316(3)(b), which addresses disclaimers, provides that

> when the buyer before entering into the contract has examined the goods or the sample or model as fully as he desired or has refused to examine the goods there is no implied warranty with regard to defects which an examination ought in the circumstances to have revealed.
> * * *

The specificity with which the buyer ordered the goods is also a factor in determining whether he relied on the seller's expertise. A buyer's claim that he relied on the seller's judgment and that the seller had reason to know of this reliance is weakened if the buyer had control over the good's specifications, *see* Layne Atl. Co. v. Koppers Co., Inc., 214 Va. 467, 473–74,

201 S.E.2d 609, 614–15 (1974); Lewis & Sims, Inc. v. Key Indus., Inc., 16 Wash.App. 619, 557 P.2d 1318 (1976), or if he selected a product by brand name, *see* Siemen v. Alden, 34 Ill.App.3d 961, 965, 341 N.E.2d 713, 716 (1975); Bickett v. W.R. Grace & Co., 12 U.C.C.Rep.Serv. (Callaghan) 629, 1972 WL 20845 (W.D.Ky.1972).

Comment 5 to section 2–315 provides:

Under the present section the existence of a patent or other trade name and the designation of the article by that name, or indeed in any other definite manner, is only one of the facts to be considered on the question of whether the buyer actually relied on the seller, but it is not of itself decisive of the issue. If the buyer himself is insisting on a particular brand he is not relying on the seller's skill and judgment and so no warranty results. But the mere fact that the article purchased has a particular patent or trade name is not sufficient to indicate nonreliance if the article has been recommended by the seller as adequate for the buyer's purposes.

Comment 9 to section 2–316, which addresses disclaimers, provides:

The situation in which the buyer gives precise and complete specifications to the seller is not explicitly covered in this section, but this is a frequent circumstance by which the implied warranties may be excluded. The warranty of fitness for a particular purpose would not normally arise since in such a situation there is usually no reliance on the seller by the buyer.

These factors are neither exhaustive nor conclusive. Whether a buyer relied on a seller's judgment and whether a seller had reason to know of this reliance are usually questions of fact that depend on the totality of a transaction's circumstances, including previous dealings between the parties and trade usage. *See* Dobias v. Western Farmer's Ass'n, 6 Wash.App. 194, 199, 491 P.2d 1346, 1349 (1971); *cf.* Emsco Screen Pipe Co. v. Heights Muffler Co., 420 S.W.2d 179 (Tex.Civ.App.—Houston [14th Dist.] 1967, no writ) (holding that a seller who habitually accepted returned mufflers for credit impliedly warranted to do so).

SECTION E. PERSONS WHO ARE PROTECTED: PRIVITY OF CONTRACT

Unlike strict tort liability, recovery by remote plaintiffs for breach of an Article 2 warranty can still be affected by the concept of privity. The problem of recovery by plaintiffs other than the purchaser is called "horizontal privity." "Vertical privity" refers to the problem of a plaintiff recovering from a defendant further up than the retailer in the chain of distribution.

Historically, the contractual underpinnings of warranty law led courts to enforce warranties only for the benefit of persons who were in privity of contract with the defendant. Even before the adoption of the Uniform Commercial Code, several courts relaxed the privity requirement in cases in which one member of the family purchased a product for other members of the family. For example, in Greenberg v. Lorenz, 9 N.Y.2d 195, 213 N.Y.S.2d 39, 173 N.E.2d 773 (1961), the New York Court of Appeals held that a plaintiff who was injured by adulterated food could recover for breach of implied warranty even though her father had purchased the food. The court presumed that the father had purchased the food as an agent for the other family members. Similarly, in the landmark case of Henningsen v. Bloomfield Motors, Inc., 32 N.J. 358, 161 A.2d 69 (1960), the New Jersey Supreme Court held that a plaintiff who was injured while driving a defective automobile could recover for breach of implied warranty even though her husband had actually purchased the automobile.

Article 2 does not expressly address the problem of vertical privity. The problem of horizontal privity for warranties governed by Article 2 is addressed by section 2–318.

Uniform Commercial Code

§ 2–318. Third Party Beneficiaries of Warranties Express or Implied

Alternative A

A seller's warranty whether express or implied extends to any natural person who is in the family or household of his buyer or who is a guest in his home if it is reasonable to expect that such person may use, consume or be affected by the goods and who is injured in person by breach of the warranty. A seller may not exclude or limit the operation of this section.

Alternative B

A seller's warranty whether express or implied extends to any natural person who may reasonably be expected to use, consume or be affected by the goods and who is injured in person by breach of the warranty. A seller may not exclude or limit the operation of this section.

Alternative C

A seller's warranty whether express or implied extends to any person who may reasonably be expected to use, consume or be affected by the goods and who is injured by breach of the warranty. A seller may not exclude or limit the operation of this section with respect to injury to the person of an individual to whom the warranty extends.

Official Comment

Purposes:

1. The last sentence of this section does not mean that a seller is precluded from excluding or disclaiming a warranty which might otherwise arise in connection with the sale provided such exclusion or modification is permitted by Section 2–316. Nor does that sentence preclude the seller from

limiting the remedies of his own buyer and of any beneficiaries, in any manner provided in Sections 2–718 or 2–719. To the extent that the contract of sale contains provisions under which warranties are excluded or modified, or remedies for breach are limited, such provisions are equally operative against beneficiaries of warranties under this section. What this last sentence forbids is exclusion of liability by the seller to the persons to whom the warranties which he has made to his buyer would extend under this section.

2. The purpose of this section is to give certain beneficiaries the benefit of the same warranty which the buyer received in the contract of sale, thereby freeing any such beneficiaries from any technical rules as to "privity." It seeks to accomplish this purpose without any derogation of any right or remedy resting on negligence. It rests primarily upon the merchant-seller's warranty under this Article that the goods sold are merchantable and fit for the ordinary purposes for which such goods are used rather than the warranty of fitness for a particular purpose. Implicit in the section is that any beneficiary of a warranty may bring a direct action for breach of warranty against the seller whose warranty extends to him [As amended in 1966].

3. The first alternative expressly includes as beneficiaries within its provisions the family, household and guests of the purchaser. Beyond this, the section in this form is neutral and is not intended to enlarge or restrict the developing case law on whether the seller's warranties, given to his buyer who resells, extend to other persons in the distributive chain. The second alternative is designed for states where the case law had already developed further and for those that desire to expand the class of beneficiaries. The third alternative goes further, following the trend of modern decisions as indicated by Restatement of Torts 2d § 402A * * * in extending the rule beyond injuries to the person.

SALVADOR v. ATLANTIC STEEL BOILER CO.

Supreme Court of Pennsylvania, 1974.
457 Pa. 24, 319 A.2d 903.

* * *

Roberts, Justice.

In Kassab v. Central Soya, 432 Pa. 217, 246 A.2d 848 (1968), this Court abolished the requirement of vertical privity in actions for breach of warranty. Today the question is whether the doctrine of horizontal privity should likewise be abandoned.[1] We conclude that the theoretical

1. "Privity of contract is that connection or relationship which exists between two or more contracting parties." Black's Law Dictionary 1362 (4th ed. 1951). See 4 A. Corbin, Contracts § 778 (1951); 8 S. Williston, Contracts § 998A (3d ed. 1964).

If a purchaser is injured by a defective product he may, of course, bring a breach of warranty claim against the seller. As contracting parties they are in privity. If the

injured purchaser wishes to sue the manufacturer or wholesaler he must overcome the privity requirement. Because his contractual relationship is only with the retail seller he cannot establish "vertical" privity with the wholesaler; he is one step further removed from the manufacturer. The "vertical" privity chain begins at the retailer and continues through any number of levels to the manufacturer of the defective foundation which once supported horizontal privity has been undermined; we hold that lack of horizontal privity itself may no longer bar an injured party's suit for breach of warranty.

Allegedly as a result of the explosion of a steam boiler on May 22, 1967, at his place of work, Ahmed Salvador suffered the loss of approximately 77 per cent of his ability to hear. On March 29, 1971, Salvador filed a summons in assumpsit naming as defendants his employer, the retail seller of the boiler, and appellants, the manufacturers of the exploding steam boiler. A complaint was filed on February 3, 1972, and the manufacturers filed preliminary objections in the nature of a demurrer. The trial court sustained the preliminary objections and dismissed the complaint in assumpsit because plaintiff-appellee did not allege a contractual relationship with appellants and thus horizontal privity was lacking.

In an opinion by Judge Cercone, the Superior Court reversed. Salvador v. Atlantic Steel Boiler Co., 224 Pa.Super. 377, 307 A.2d 398 (1973). That court reasoned that the thrust of *Kassab* was the desire to reach the same result in a lawsuit arising from particular facts whether the action is brought in trespass or assumpsit. Id. at 383–384, 307 A.2d at 402. Concluding that the adoption of section 402A of the Restatement (Second) of Torts (1965), eliminates the logical basis for both vertical and horizontal privity, the Superior Court held that the *Kassab* rationale dictated abolition of the horizontal privity requirement in breach of warranty actions. The order sustaining preliminary objections was reversed and the complaint reinstated. We granted the manufacturers' petition for allowance of appeal; we affirm.

In Hochgertel v. Canada Dry Corp., 409 Pa. 610, 187 A.2d 575 (1963), plaintiff, engaged in his duties as a bartender, was injured by flying glass when a bottle of carbonated soda exploded. He sued Canada Dry, the manufacturer, alleging breach of implied warranties. Because Hochgertel was neither the purchaser, a member of the purchaser's family, nor a guest in purchaser's home, this Court held that he could not establish any horizontal privity relationship with the manufacturer. Hence he could not recover.

That decision was based on the Uniform Commercial Code, section 2–318,

> "A seller's warranty whether express or implied extends to any natural person who is in the family or household of his buyer or who is a guest in his home if it is reasonable to expect that such person

product. The question of vertical privity is "who can be sued"?

The question of horizontal privity is "who can sue"? The purchaser can sue the retail seller because they are in privity. When the requirement of vertical privity has been abolished, he may also sue any other entity in the distributive chain. But if the purchaser's wife is injured by a defective product, may she maintain a breach of warranty action? See Uniform Commercial Code § 2–318, 12A P.S. § 2–318 (1970). May the purchaser's injured employee sue successfully? If a bystander is injured is he too entitled to recover for breach of warranty? These are questions of horizontal privity.

may use, consume or be affected by the goods and who is injured in person by breach of the warranty. A seller may not exclude or limit the operation of this section.''

Although this Court determined that Hochgertel as an employee was ''definitely in none of these [§ 2–318] categories,'' it nevertheless recognized that the Code was not dispositive. ''Since the Code was not intended to restrict the case law in this field (see § 2–318, Comment 3 * * *) [8] a study of pertinent Pennsylvania authorities is also necessary for the purposes of this decision.'' After examining the relevant case law, this Court concluded that no Pennsylvania case had extended warranty protection beyond the class of persons enumerated in section 2–318. The *Hochgertel* Court in 1963 declined to do so.

The limitations imposed by *Hochgertel* were quickly challenged. Yentzer v. Taylor Wine Co., 414 Pa. 272, 199 A.2d 463 (1964), decided only one year later on almost identical facts, permitted recovery. There, plaintiff, a hotel employee, purchased a bottle of champagne manufactured by defendant. It was undisputed that Yentzer was acting as an agent of his employer. While preparing to serve the wine to hotel guests, the cork ejected and struck plaintiff in the eye. The trial court concluded that *Hochgertel* controlled, but this Court commented: ''We do not think that the rigid construction we placed on a seller's warranty in *Hochgertel* should be extended to a situation such as this.'' Yentzer v. Taylor Wine Co., supra at 274, 199 A.2d at 464. We held that even though he acted as the agent of his employer, because the employee had actually purchased the champagne himself, he was a ''buyer.'' The dissent properly pointed out that the Court's analysis represented a ''clear departure'' from *Hochgertel*.

Between *Yentzer* and the present case several significant developments occurred in Pennsylvania products liability law. In 1966, Webb v. Zern, 422 Pa. 424, 220 A.3d 853 (1966), adopted section 402A as the law of Pennsylvania. This section imposes liability on the seller or manufacturer of a defective product regardless of the lack of proven negligence or the lack of contractual relation between the seller and the injured party. On the same day, this Court issued its opinion in Miller v. Preitz, 422 Pa. 383, 221 A.2d 320 (1966), reaffirming the requirement of vertical privity in an action for injuries suffered through a breach of warranty.

Only two years later *Miller* was overruled in Kassab v. Central Soya, 432 Pa. 217, 246 A.2d 848 (1968). The Kassabs were purchasers of allegedly defective cattle feed and therefore no question of horizontal privity was presented. The manufacturer of the product, however, argued that it could not be liable because no vertical privity was present,

---

8. Comment 3 provides:

   ''This section expressly includes as beneficiaries within its provisions the family, household, and guests of the purchaser. Beyond this, the section is neutral and is not intended to enlarge or restrict the developing case law on whether the seller's warranties, given to his buyer who resells, extend to other persons in the distributive chain.''

that is, only the retailer and not it, the manufacturer, had a contractual relation with plaintiffs.

We noted that our adoption of section 402A in Webb v. Zern, obliterated any logical basis for retaining the demand for vertical privity.

"Under the Uniform Commercial Code, once a breach of warranty has been shown, the defendant's liability, assuming of course the presence of proximate cause and damages, is absolute. Lack of negligence on the seller's part is no defense. Therefore, prior to the adoption of section 402a, it could be said that to dispense with privity would be to allow recovery in contract without proof of negligence, while requiring a showing of negligence in order to recover for the same wrong against the same defendant if suit were brought in tort. To permit the result of a lawsuit to depend solely on the caption atop plaintiff's complaint is not now, and has never been, a sound resolution of identical controversies."

432 Pa. at 228–229, 246 A.2d at 853. The Court concluded that "on this issue [vertical privity], the code must be co-extensive with Restatement section 402a in the case of product liability." Id. at 231, 246 A.2d at 854 (footnote omitted).

Kassab dealt only with the issue of vertical privity. The Superior Court nevertheless concluded that *Kassab's* rationale likewise required the abolition of the requirement of horizontal privity in breach of warranty cases. We believe the Superior Court is correct.

The basic reason for the *Hochgertel* Court's reticence to impair the horizontal privity requirement was that

"[t]o grant such an extension of the warranty, as urged herein, would in effect render the manufacturer a guarantor of his product and impose liability in all such accident cases even if the utmost degree of care were exercised. This would lead to harsh and unjust results."

409 Pa. at 615–616, 187 A.2d at 578.

Today, as the Superior Court correctly recognized, a manufacturer by virtue of section 402A is effectively the guarantor of his products' safety. See Webb v. Zern, supra; Kassab v. Central Soya, supra. Our courts have determined that a manufacturer by marketing and advertising his product impliedly represents that it is safe for its intended use. We have decided that no current societal interest is served by permitting the manufacturer to place a defective article in the stream of commerce and then to avoid responsibility for damages caused by the defect. He may not preclude an injured plaintiff's recovery by forcing him to prove negligence in the manufacturing process. Webb v. Zern. Neither may the manufacturer defeat the claim by arguing that the purchaser has no contractual relation to him. Kassab v. Central Soya. Why then should the mere fact that the injured party is not himself the purchaser deny recovery?

Because the manufacturer is now a guarantor, the "harsh and unjust result" is worked on the plaintiff who may recover for his injury or loss if his complaint is in trespass, but on identical facts would be denied relief if the pleading is captioned "Complaint in Assumpsit." See *Kassab,* supra at 229, 246 A.2d at 853. This anomalous situation is certainly to be avoided. Thus "[w]ith Pennsylvania's adoption of Restatement 402a, the same demands of legal symmetry which once supported privity now destroy it." Id.

Though we must overrule *Hochgertel,* this is not an occasion when a court reexamines its precedents and finding them in error returns to a "correct" view. On the contrary, as we have said, when *Hochgertel* was decided it was clearly the appropriate accommodation between the law of torts and the law of contracts. Since then Pennsylvania products liability law has progressed, and demands of public policy as well as legal symmetry compel today's decision.

The order of the Superior Court is affirmed.

JONES, C.J., did not participate in the consideration or decision of this case.

Notes

1. As in so much of warranty law, a leading case on the erosion of the privity requirement before the adoption of the U.C.C. was Henningsen v. Bloomfield Motors, Inc., 32 N.J. 358, 161 A.2d 69 (1960). Mr. Henningsen bought an automobile from Bloomfield Motors and gave it to his wife as a gift. Chrysler manufactured the automobile. Ten days after delivery Ms. Henningsen was injured in an accident caused by a sudden failure in the steering. On the issue of privity, the court said:

> As the Sales Act and its liberal interpretation by the courts threw this protective cloak about the buyer, the decisions in various jurisdictions revealed beyond doubt that many manufacturers took steps to avoid these ever increasing warranty obligations. Realizing that the act governed the relationship of buyer and seller, they undertook to withdraw from actual and direct contractual contact with the buyer. They ceased selling products to the consuming public through their own employees and making contracts of sale in their own names. Instead, a system of independent dealers was established; their products were sold to dealers who in turn dealt with the buying public, ostensibly solely in their own personal capacity as sellers. In the past in many instances, manufacturers were able to transfer to the dealers burdens imposed by the act and thus achieved a large measure of immunity for themselves.

* * *

Chrysler points out that an implied warranty of merchantability is an incident of a contract of sale. It concedes, of course, the making of the original sale to Bloomfield Motors, Inc., but maintains that this transaction marked the terminal point of its contractual connection with the car. Then Chrysler urges that since it was not a party to the sale by the dealer to Henningsen, there is no privity of contract between it and the plaintiffs, and the absence of this privity eliminates any such implied warranty.

There is no doubt that under early common-law concepts of contractual liability only those persons who were parties to the bargain could sue for a breach of it. In more recent times a noticeable disposition has appeared in a number of jurisdictions to break through the narrow barrier of privity when dealing with sales of goods in order to give realistic recognition to a universally accepted fact. The fact is that the dealer and the ordinary buyer do not, and are not expected to, buy goods, whether they be foodstuffs or automobiles, exclusively for their own consumption or use. Makers and manufacturers know this and advertise and market their products on that assumption; witness, the "family" car, the baby foods, etc. The limitations of privity in contracts for the sale of goods developed their place in the law when marketing conditions were simple, when maker and buyer frequently met face to face on an equal bargaining plane and when many of the products were relatively uncomplicated and conducive to inspection by a buyer competent to evaluate their quality. * * * With the advent of mass marketing, the manufacturer became remote from the purchaser, sales were accomplished through intermediaries, and the demand for the product was created by advertising media. In such an economy it became obvious that the consumer was the person being cultivated. Manifestly, the connotation of "consumer" was broader than that of "buyer." He signified such a person who, in the reasonable contemplation of the parties to the sale, might be expected to sue the product. Thus, where the commodities sold are such that if defectively manufactured they will be dangerous to life or limb, then society's interests can only be protected by eliminating the requirement of privity between the maker and his dealers and the reasonably expected ultimate consumer. In that way the burden of losses consequent upon use of defective articles is borne by those who are in a position to either control the danger or make an equitable distribution of the losses when they do occur. As Harper & James put it, "The interest in consumer protection calls for warranties by the maker that *do* run with the goods, to reach all who are likely to be hurt by the use of the unfit commodity for a purpose ordinarily to be expected." 2 Harper & James, supra 1571, 1572; also see, 1535; Prosser, supra, 506–511. * * *

Although only a minority of jurisdictions have thus far departed from the requirement of privity, the movement in that direction is most certainly gathering momentum. Liability to the ultimate consumer in the absence of direct contractual connection has been predicated upon a variety of theories. Some courts hold that the warranty runs with the article like a covenant running with land; others recognize a third-party beneficiary thesis; still others rest their decision on the ground that public policy requires recognition of a warranty made directly to the consumer.

* * *

Most of the cases where lack of privity has not been permitted to interfere with recovery have involved food and drugs. [Citations] In fact, the rule as to such products has been characterized as an exception to the general doctrine. But more recently courts, sensing the inequity of such litigation, have moved into broader fields: home permanent wave set, * * * Rogers v. Toni Home Permanent Co., 167 Ohio St. 244, 147 N.E.2d 612 (Sup.Ct.1958); soap detergent, Worley v. Procter & Gamble Mfg. Co., 241 Mo.App. 1114, 253 S.W.2d 532 (1952); inflammable cowboy suit (by clear implication), Blessington v. McCrory Stores Corp., 305 N.Y. 140, 111 N.E.2d 421, 37 A.L.R.2d 698 (Ct.App.1953); exploding bottle, Mahoney v. Shaker Square Beverages, 46 Ohio Op. 250, 102 N.E.2d 281 (C.P.1951); defective emery wheel, DiVello v. Gardner Machine Co., 46 Ohio Op. 161, 102 N.E.2d 289 (C.P.1951); defective wire rope, Mannsz v. Macwhyte Co., 155 F.2d 445 (3 Cir.1946); defective cinder blocks, Spence v. Three Rivers Builders & Masonry Supply, 353 Mich. 120, 90 N.W.2d 873 (Sup.Ct.1958).

We see no rational doctrinal basis for differentiating between a fly in a bottle of beverage and a defective automobile. The unwholesome beverage may bring illness to one person, the defective car, with its great potentiality for harm to the driver, occupants, and others, demands even less adherence to the narrow barrier of privity. 2 Harper & James, supra, 1572; 1 Williston, supra, § 244a, p. 648; Note, 46 Harv.L.Rev. 161 (1932). * * *

Under modern conditions the ordinary layman, on responding to the importuning of colorful advertising, has neither the opportunity nor the capacity to inspect or to determine the fitness of an automobile for use; he must rely on the manufacturer who has control of its construction, and to some degree on the dealer who, to the limited extent called for by the manufacturer's instructions, inspects and services it before delivery. In such a marketing milieu his remedies and those of persons who properly claim through him should not depend "upon the intricacies of the law of sales. The obligation of the manufacturer should not be based alone on privity of contract. It should rest, as was once said, upon 'the demands of social justice.'" Mazetti v. Armour & Co., 75 Wash. 622, 135 P. 633, 635, 48 L.R.A., N.S., 213 (Sup.Ct.1913). "If privity of contract is required," then, under the circumstances of modern merchandising, "privity of contract exists in the consciousness and understanding of all right-thinking persons." Madouros v. Kansas City Coca–Cola Bottling Co., [90 S.W.2d 445, 450 (Mo.App.1936).]

Accordingly, we hold that under modern marketing conditions, when a manufacturer puts a new automobile in the stream of trade and promotes its purchase by the public, an implied warranty that it is reasonably suitable for use as such accompanies it into the hands of the ultimate purchaser. Absence of agency between the manufacturer and the dealer who makes the ultimate sale is immaterial.

* * *

Both defendants contend that since there was no privity of contract between them and Mrs. Henningsen, she cannot recover for breach of any warranty made by either of them. On the facts, as they were developed, we agree that she was not a party to the purchase agreement.

Faber v. Creswick, 31 N.J. 234, 156 A.2d 252 (1959). Her right to maintain the action, therefore, depends upon whether she occupies such legal status thereunder as to permit her to take advantage of a breach of defendants' implied warranties.

For the most part the cases that have been considered dealt with the right of the buyer or consumer to maintain an action against the manufacturer where the contract of sale was with a dealer and the buyer had no contractual relationship with the manufacturer. In the present matter, the basic contractual relationship is between Claus Henningsen, Chrysler, and Bloomfield Motors, Inc. The precise issue presented is whether Mrs. Henningsen, who is not a party to their respective warranties, may claim under them. In our judgment, the principles of those cases and the supporting texts are just as proximately applicable to her situation. We are convinced that the cause of justice in this area of the law can be served only by recognizing that she is such a person who, in the reasonable contemplation of the parties to the warranty, might be expected to become a user of the automobile. Accordingly, her lack of privity does not stand in the way of prosecution of the injury suit against the defendant Chrysler.

* * *

[I]t cannot be overlooked that historically actions on warranties were in tort also, sounding in deceit. * * * Williston on Sales, supra, §§ 195–197. The contract theory gradually emerged, although the tort idea has continued to lurk in the background, making the warranty "a curious hybrid of tort and contract." Prosser, supra, § 83. An awareness of this evolution makes for ready acceptance of the relaxation of rigid concepts of privity when third persons, who in the reasonable contemplation of the parties to the warranty might be expected to use or consume the product sold, are injured by its unwholesome or defective state.

2. Does either the Pennsylvania court's abandonment of the requirement of vertical privity for breach of warranty in *Kassab* or the lack of a privity requirement in actions for strict tort liability require the *Salvador* court's conclusion that horizontal privity is not required in an action for breach of warranty?

3. Should a court expand the scope of liability in a warranty action beyond that which has been designated by the legislature in 2–318?

The court in *Salvador* relies on comment 3 to justify expanding the scope of liability beyond the provisions of section 2–318. Does comment 3 apply to *horizontal* privity?

4. Should the U.C.C. and section 402A have co-extensive requirements in terms of privity?

5. *Salvador* dealt with the problem of *horizontal* privity for an implied warranty of merchantability, but the court did not indicate that its analysis would have been any different if it had been considering an express warranty or an implied warranty fitness, or if it had been considering the problem of vertical privity. Section 2–318 itself lumps the three Article 2 warranties

together. Nevertheless, an express warranty is more "contractual" than an implied warranty of merchantability, and it might be argued that privity limitations make more sense in the context of express warranties—especially if the damages are purely economic and the parties are commercial entities—than in the context of implied warranties of merchantability—especially if the damages are due to personal injury and the plaintiff is a consumer. *But see* J. White & R. Summers, Handbook of the Law Under the Uniform Commercial Code § 11-7 (1980) (privity never required in express warranty case).

6. Many courts require privity in economic loss cases. Some courts permit recovery for *direct* economic loss without privity if plaintiff is a consumer, but do not permit recovery for *consequential* economic loss without privity.

7. In Morrow v. New Moon Homes, Inc., 548 P.2d 279 (Alaska 1976), the court held that lack of vertical privity did not bar recovery in an action for pure economic loss based on breach of an implied warranty of merchantability. The court noted that privity is not required in Alaska in an action for personal injury damages for breach of an implied warranty of merchantability and reasoned that "there is no satisfactory justification for a remedial scheme which extends the warranty action to a consumer suffering personal injury or property damage but denies similar relief to the consumer 'fortunate' enough to suffer only direct economic loss." The court also held that pure economic damage is not recoverable under strict tort liability, which has no privity requirement. Are these two holdings compatible?

8. In terms of privity, should courts distinguish between personal injury cases and those involving pure economic loss? With respect to economic loss cases, should courts distinguish between direct economic loss—such as lost value of the goods—and indirect economic loss—such as lost profits from inability to use the good?

9. Like express warranties, implied warranties of fitness are more "contractual" than implied warranties of merchantability because they depend on actual, albeit often amorphous, representations, and they depend on reliance. Nevertheless, section 2-318 does not distinguish between implied warranties of fitness and implied warranties of merchantability on the issue of horizontal privity.

You should recall that to recover under an implied warranty of fitness, the plaintiff must prove that the *buyer* relied on the seller's judgment in selecting the product for a particular purpose known to the seller. The plaintiff need not have been the buyer, however.

10. Courts in states that have adopted Alternative A to section 2-318 have been required to determine who qualifies as a family member, a household member, or a guest. *See, e.g.,* McNally v. Nicholson Mfg. Co., 313 A.2d 913, 920 (Me.1973) (employees of the purchaser are part of the "business family"); Miles v. Bell Helicopter Co., 385 F.Supp. 1029, 1031 (N.D.Ga.1974) (soldier injured by equipment purchased by the military not part of the "military family"); Miller v. Preitz, 422 Pa. 383, 221 A.2d 320 (1966) (nephew of purchaser held part of family for injury caused by product loaned by aunt who lived next door); Wolfe v. Ford Motor Co., 6 Mass.App. Ct. 346, 376 N.E.2d 143, 149 (1978) (niece who did not live in purchaser's

household held to be part of family); Barry v. Ivarson Inc., 249 So.2d 44 (Fla.App.1971) (tenant of purchaser not within the scope of Alternative A); Stovall & Co. v. Tate, 124 Ga.App. 605, 184 S.E.2d 834 (1971) (student injured by product purchased by school not within the scope of Alternative A).

11. Even in states that have adopted Alternative C or that have by judicial decision extended the scope of liability for breach of warranty to bystanders, liability does not extend to all persons for all injuries caused by the breach of warranty. Only injuries that are proximately caused by the breach are recoverable.

SECTION F.   REMEDIES

Uniform Commercial Code

§ 2–711. Buyer's Remedies in General; Buyer's Security Interest in Rejected Goods

(1) Where the seller fails to make delivery or repudiates or the buyer rightfully rejects or justifiably revokes acceptance then with respect to any goods involved, and with respect to the whole if the breach goes to the whole contract (Section 2–612), the buyer may cancel and whether or not he has done so may in addition to recovering so much of the price as has been paid

   (a) "cover" and have damages under the next section as to all the goods affected whether or not they have been identified to the contract; or

   (b) recover damages for non-delivery as provided in this Article (Section 2–713).

(2) Where the seller fails to deliver or repudiates the buyer may also

   (a) if the goods have been identified recover them as provided in this Article (Section 2–502); or

   (b) in a proper case obtain specific performance or replevy the goods as provided in this Article (Section 2–716).

(3) On rightful rejection or justifiable revocation of acceptance a buyer has a security interest in goods in his possession or control for any payments made on their price and any expenses reasonably incurred in their inspection, receipt, transportation, care and custody and may hold such goods and resell them in like manner as an aggrieved seller (Section 2–706).

§ 2–713. Buyer's Incidental and Consequential Damages

(1) Subject to the provisions of this Article with respect to proof of market price (Section 2–723), the measure of damages for non-delivery or repudiation by the seller is the difference between the market price at the time when the buyer learned of the breach and the contract price together with any incidental and consequential damages provided in this

Article (Section 2–715), but less expenses saved in consequence of the seller's breach.

(2) Market price is to be determined as of the place for tender or, in cases of rejection after arrival or revocation of acceptance, as of the place of arrival.

§ 2–714. Buyer's Damages for Breach in Regard to Accepted Goods

(1) Where the buyer has accepted goods and given notification (subsection (3) of Section 2–607) he may recover as damages for any nonconformity of tender the loss resulting in the ordinary course of events from the seller's breach as determined in any manner which is reasonable.

(2) The measure of damages for breach of warranty is the difference at the time and place of acceptance between the value of the goods accepted and the value they would have had if they had been as warranted, unless special circumstances show proximate damages of a different amount.

(3) In a proper case any incidental and consequential damages under the next section may also be recovered.

§ 2–715. Buyer's Incidental and Consequential Damages

(1) Incidental damages resulting from the seller's breach include expenses reasonably incurred in inspection, receipt, transportation and care and custody of goods rightfully rejected, any commercially reasonable charges, expenses or commissions in connection with effecting cover and any other reasonable expense incident to the delay or other breach.

(2) Consequential damages resulting from the seller's breach include

(a) any loss resulting from general or particular requirements and needs of which the seller at the time of contracting had reason to know and which could not reasonably be prevented by cover or otherwise; and

(b) injury to person or property proximately resulting from any breach of warranty.

SECTION G. LIMITATIONS ON LIABILITY: DISCLAIMERS, DAMAGE LIMITATIONS, TIME LIMITATIONS, AND NOTICE

HENNINGSEN v. BLOOMFIELD MOTORS, INC.

Supreme Court of New Jersey, 1960.
32 N.J. 358, 161 A.2d 69.

[Mr. Henningsen purchased an automobile from defendant Bloomfield Motors and gave it to his wife as a gift. The automobile was manufactured by defendant Chrysler Corporation. Ten days after delivery of the car, Mrs. Henningsen was injured in an accident that resulted when the steering failed suddenly and without warning. Up to this time the car had functioned properly. Mrs. Henningsen sued both defendants for breach of express and implied warranties and for negligence. Her husband joined in the action seeking compensation for his consequential losses. The trial judge dismissed the negligence counts because of insufficient evidence. He gave the case to the jury on the implied warranty theory only. The jury rendered verdicts against both defendants in favor of the plaintiffs. Defendants appealed and plaintiffs cross-appealed, claiming that the negligence count should not have been dismissed.]

[The sales contract signed by Mr. Henningsen was a standard printed form. It contained the following language concerning the warranty. It was in fine print and located on the back of the form:]

"7. It is expressly agreed that there are no warranties, express or implied, *made* by either the dealer or the manufacturer on the motor vehicle, chassis, of parts furnished hereunder except as follows.

" 'The manufacturer warrants each new motor vehicle (including original equipment placed thereon by the manufacturer except tires), chassis or parts manufactured by it to be free from defects in material or workmanship under normal use and service. Its obligation under this warranty being limited to making good at its factory any part or parts thereof which shall, within ninety (90) days after delivery of such vehicle *to the original purchaser* or before such vehicle has been driven 4,000 miles, whichever event shall first occur, be returned to it with transportation charges prepaid and which its examination shall disclose to its satisfaction to have been thus defective; *this warranty being expressly in lieu of all other warranties expressed or implied, and all other obligations or liabilities on its part*, and it neither assumes nor authorizes any other person to assume for it any other liability in connection with the sale of its vehicles. * * * ' " (Emphasis ours.)

* * *

The terms of the warranty are a sad commentary upon the automobile manufacturers' marketing practices. Warranties developed in the law in the interest of and to protect the ordinary consumer who cannot be expected to have the knowledge or capacity or even the opportunity to make adequate inspection of mechanical instrumentalities, like automobiles, and to decide for himself whether they are reasonably fit for the designed purpose. * * * But the ingenuity of the Automobile Manufacturers Association, by means of its standardized form, has metamorphosed the warranty into a device to limit the maker's liability.

* * *

In view of the cases in various jurisdictions suggesting the conclusion which we have now reached with respect to the implied warranty of merchantability, it becomes apparent that manufacturers who enter into promotional activities to stimulate consumer buying may incur warranty obligations of either or both the express or implied character. These developments in the law inevitably suggest the inference that the form of express warranty made part of the Henningsen purchase contract was devised for general use in the automobile industry as a possible means of avoiding the consequences of the growing judicial acceptance of the thesis that the described express or implied warranties run directly to the consumer.

In the light of these matters, what effect should be given to the express warranty in question which seeks to limit the manufacturer's liability to replacement of defective parts, and which disclaims all other warranties, express or implied? In assessing its significance we must keep in mind the general principle that, in the absence of fraud, one who does not choose to read a contract before signing it, cannot later relieve himself of its burdens. * * * And in applying that principle, the basic tenet of freedom of competent parties to contract is a factor of importance. But in the framework of modern commercial life and business practices, such rules cannot be applied on a strict, doctrinal basis. The conflicting interests of the buyer and seller must be evaluated realistically and justly, giving due weight to the social policy evinced by the Uniform Sales Act, the progressive decisions of the courts engaged in administering it, the mass production methods of manufacture and distribution to the public, and the bargaining position occupied by the ordinary consumer in such an economy. This history of the law shows that legal doctrines, as first expounded, often prove to be inadequate under the impact of later experience. In such case, the need for justice has stimulated the necessary qualifications or adjustments. * * *

It is apparent that the public has an interest not only in the safe manufacture of automobiles, but also, as shown by the Sales Act, in protecting the rights and remedies of purchasers, so far as it can be accomplished consistently with our system of free enterprise. In a society such as ours, where the automobile is a common and necessary adjunct of daily life, and where its use is so fraught with danger to the driver, passengers and the public, the manufacturer is under a special obligation in connection with the construction, promotion and sale of his cars. Consequently, the courts must examine purchase agreements closely to see if consumer and public interests are treated fairly.

* * * As we have said, warranties originated in the law to safeguard the buyer and not to limit the liability of the seller or manufacturer. It seems obvious in this instance that the motive was to avoid the warranty obligations which are normally incidental to such sales. The language gave little and withdrew much. In return for the delusive remedy of replacement of defective parts at the factory, the buyer is said to have accepted the exclusion of the maker's liability for personal injuries arising from the breach of warranty, and to have agreed to the elimina-

tion of any other express or implied warranty. An instinctively felt sense of justice cries out against such a sharp bargain. But does the doctrine that a person is bound by his signed agreement, in the absence of fraud, stand in the way of any relief?

In the modern consideration of problems such as this, Corbin suggests that practically all judges are "chancellors" and cannot fail to be influenced by any equitable doctrines that are available. And he opines that "there is sufficient flexibility in the concepts of fraud, duress, misrepresentation and undue influence, not to mention differences in economic bargaining power" to enable the courts to avoid enforcement of unconscionable provisions in long printed standardized contracts. 1 Corbin on Contracts (1950) § 128, p. 188. Freedom of contract is not such an immutable doctrine as to admit of no qualification in the area in which we are concerned. * * *

The traditional contract is the result of free bargaining of parties who are brought together by the play of the market, and who meet each other on a footing of approximate economic equality. In such a society there is no danger that freedom of contract will be a threat to the social order as a whole. But in present-day commercial life the standardized mass contract has appeared. It is used primarily by enterprises with strong bargaining power and position. "The weaker party, in need of the goods or services, is frequently not in a position to shop around for better terms, either because the author of the standard contract has a monopoly (natural or artificial) or because all competitors use the same clauses. His contractual intention is but a subjection more or less voluntary to terms dictated by the stronger party, terms whose consequences are often understood in a vague way, if at all." * * *

The warranty before us is a standardized form designed for mass use. It is imposed upon the automobile consumer. He takes it or leave it, and he must take it to buy an automobile. No bargaining is engaged in with respect to it. In fact, the dealer through whom it comes to the buyer is without authority to alter it; his function is ministerial—simply to deliver it. The form warranty is not only standard with Chrysler but, as mentioned above, it is the uniform warranty of the Automobile Manufacturers Association. * * *

* * *

The task of the judiciary is to administer the spirit as well as the letter of the law. On issues such as the present one, part of that burden is to protect the ordinary man against the loss of important rights through what, in effect, is the unilateral act of the manufacturer. The status of the automobile industry is unique. Manufacturers are few in number and strong in bargaining position. In the matter of warranties on the sale of their products, the Automotive Manufacturers Association has enabled them to present a united front. From the standpoint of the purchaser, there can be no arms length negotiating on the subject. Because his capacity for bargaining is so grossly unequal, the inexorable conclusion which follows is that he is not permitted to bargain at all.

He must take or leave the automobile on the warranty terms dictated by the maker. He cannot turn to a competitor for better security.

* * *

Public policy at a given time finds expression in the Constitution, the statutory law and in judicial decisions. In the area of sale of goods, the legislative will has imposed an implied warranty of merchantability as a general incident of sale of an automobile by description. The warranty does not depend upon the affirmative intention of the parties. It is a child of the law; it annexes itself to the contract because of the very nature of the transaction. Minneapolis Steel & Machinery Co. v. Casey Land Agency, 51 N.D. 832, 201 N.W. 172 (Sup.Ct.1924). The judicial process has recognized a right to recover damages for personal injuries arising from a breach of that warranty. The disclaimer of the implied warranty and exclusion of all obligations except those specifically assumed by the express warranty signify a studied effort to frustrate that protection. True, the Sales Act authorized agreements between buyer and seller qualifying the warranty obligations. But quite obviously the Legislature contemplated lawful stipulations (which are determined by the circumstances of a particular case) arrived at freely by parties of relatively equal bargaining strength. The lawmakers did not authorize the automobile manufacturer to use its grossly disproportionate bargaining power to relieve itself from liability and to impose on the ordinary buyer who in effect has no real freedom of choice, the grave danger of injury to himself and others that attends the sale of such a dangerous instrumentality as a defectively made automobile. In the framework of this case, illuminated as it is by the facts and the many decisions noted, we are of the opinion that Chrysler's attempted disclaimer of an implied warranty of merchantability and of the obligations arising therefrom is so inimical to the public good as to compel an adjudication of its invalidity. * * *

Note

Henningsen was decided under the Uniform Sales Act. How would the disclaimers and remedy limitations fare under sections 2–316 and 2–719 of the U.C.C., which are addressed below?

Uniform Commercial Code
§ 2–316. Exclusion or Modification of Warranties

(1) Words or conduct relevant to the creation of an express warranty and words or conduct tending to negate or limit warranty shall be construed wherever reasonable as consistent with each other; but subject to the provisions of this Article on parol or extrinsic evidence (Section 2–202) negation or limitation is inoperative to the extent that such construction is unreasonable.

(2) Subject to subsection (3), to exclude or modify the implied warranty of merchantability or any part of it the language must mention merchantability and in case of a writing must be conspicuous, and to

exclude or modify any implied warranty of fitness the exclusion must be by a writing and conspicuous. Language to exclude all implied warranties of fitness is sufficient if it states, for example, that "There are no warranties which extend beyond the description on the face hereof."

(3) Notwithstanding subsection (2)

(a) unless the circumstances indicate otherwise, all implied warranties are excluded by expressions like "as is", "with all faults" or other language which in common understanding calls the buyer's attention to the exclusion of warranties and makes plain that there is no implied warranty; and

(b) when the buyer before entering into the contract has examined the goods or the sample or model as fully as he desired or has refused to examine the goods there is no implied warranty with regard to defects which an examination ought in the circumstances to have revealed to him; and

(c) an implied warranty can also be excluded or modified by course of dealing or course of performance or usage of trade.

(4) Remedies for breach of warranty can be limited in accordance with the provisions of this Article on liquidation or limitation of damages and on contractual modification of remedy (Sections 2–718 and 2–719).

TENNESSEE CAROLINA TRANSP., INC. v. STRICK CORP.

Supreme Court of North Carolina, 1973.
283 N.C. 423, 196 S.E.2d 711.

[Plaintiff purchased 150 trailers from defendant. Soon after the trailers were delivered, they began to break in two when used. The plaintiff sued for breach of implied warranty of fitness for particular purpose, stipulating at trial that it was not relying on an implied warranty of merchantability. The defendant argued that any implied warranty of fitness for particular purpose was disclaimed in a security agreement executed several days after the actual sale. After holding that the plaintiff could rely on an implied warranty of fitness even though the trailers were used for their ordinary purpose, the court addressed the disclaimer.]

Each security agreement contains in Paragraph (h) thereof the following language: "There are no promises, understandings, agreements, representations, or warranties * * *, express or implied, respecting the Equipment which are not specified herein." Paragraph (h) is on page 2 of the security agreement, printed in the same color as the other printing and in the smallest print used on that page. On page 3 immediately preceding the signature lines, the words "NOTICE TO BUYER" are printed in block letters. Under these words in small print is this message: "This contract was prepared by Strick Corporation (seller). Do not sign this contract before you read it or if it contains any blank spaces."

Defendant contends the quoted portions of the security agreement exclude all implied warranties, and for this reason the overruling of its motions for directed verdict is assigned as error. Plaintiff contends the attempted exclusion is ineffective under the laws of Pennsylvania, and the trial judge and the Court of Appeals so held.

The Court of Appeals grounded its decision on the conclusion that the disclaimer, not being "conspicuous" within the meaning of Pa.Stat. Ann. tit. 12A, §§ 2–316(2) and 1–201(10) (1970), was therefore ineffective as a matter of law. Many cases have adopted a like approach in applying the Code, refusing to give effect to a disclaimer where it is inconspicuous without further inquiry as to whether the buyer was protected from the surprise of an unexpected and unbargained disclaimer by factors other than the physical conspicuousness of the clause itself. *Eg.* Entron Inc. v. General Cablevision of Palatka, 435 F.2d 995 (5th Cir.1970); Boeing Airplane Co. v. O'Malley, 329 F.2d 585 (8th Cir.1964).

However, the purpose of the "conspicuous" requirement, despite its unqualified language, is, as stated in Comment 1, Pa.Stat.Ann. tit. 12A, § 2–316 (1970), to "protect a buyer from unexpected and unbargained language of disclaimer by * * * permitting the exclusion of implied warranties only by conspicuous language or *other circumstances which protect the buyer from surprise.*" (Emphasis added) Although the emphasized language might refer only to Pa.Stat.Ann. tit. 12A, § 2–316(3) (1970), certainly *actual awareness of the disclaimer* is another circumstance which protects the buyer from the surprise of unexpected and unbargained language of disclaimer. Perhaps an additional circumstance of this sort arises where, as here, the buyer is a non-consumer with bargaining power substantially equivalent to the seller's.

Where both of these circumstances are shown-the buyer is a nonconsumer on substantially equal bargaining terms with the seller and is actually aware of the disclaimer prior to entering the sales contract-possibly the disclaimer should be enforced despite its inconspicuousness, in the absence of a showing of unconscionability, since the purpose of the "conspicuous" requirement has been satisfied.

However, we have found no authoritative Pennsylvania decision applying Pa.Stat.Ann. tit. 12A, § 2–316(2) (1970) in such fashion. Nor have we found an authoritative Pennsylvania decision applying that statute in the rigid fashion employed by the Court of Appeals. In this case, however, it is unnecessary for us to decide whether the "conspicuous" requirement has been satisfied by "other circumstances which protect the buyer from surprise" because the disclaimer here is inoperative by reason of Pa.Stat.Ann. tit. 12A, § 9–206(2) (1970).

That section reads as follows: "When a seller retains a purchase money security interest in goods the Article on Sales (Article 2) governs the sale and any disclaimer * * * of the seller's warranties." Comment (3) says that this section "prevents a buyer from inadvertently abandoning his warranties by a 'no warranties' term in the security agreement when warranties have already been created under the sales arrangement. Where the sales arrangement and the purchase money security transaction are evidenced by only one writing, that writing may disclaim * * * warranties to the extent permitted by Article 2."

Thus, it appears that this section gives no effect to a disclaimer contained in a purchase money security agreement when express or implied warranties have already been created in the written sales arrangement. In such circumstances it is Article 2 of the Uniform Commercial Code, and not the terms of the security agreement, which governs the question of disclaimer.

The Pennsylvania Superior Court has recognized this principle in the form in which it existed in the Original Draft of the Uniform Commercial Code, adopted in Pennsylvania in 1953. See L & N Sales Co. v. Stuski, supra (188 Pa.Super. 117, 146 A.2d 154), where the court, applying Pa.Stat.Ann. tit. 12A, § 9–206(3) (1954), which has since been repealed and its principle incorporated into the present § 9–206(2), said:

> "[T]he conditional sales contract, regardless of language contained therein, under the present circumstances cannot be considered as limiting or releasing plaintiff from liability on any warranty made by the seller at the time the sales contract was executed, since the security agreement was executed subsequent thereto for the purpose of securing the credit extended to the defendant."

Accordingly, the disclaimer, being in the purchase money security agreement, could not as a matter of law disclaim the implied warranties previously created in the written sales arrangement. This assignment of error is overruled.

Defendant also contends that although the issue of "conspicuousness" was properly an issue for the court, Pa.Stat.Ann. tit. 12A, § 1–201(10), still there remained a question for the jury with respect to the validity of the disclaimer. It assigns as error the trial court's failure to submit an issue thereon. Under Pa.Stat.Ann. tit. 12A, § 2–316(3)(c) (1970) an implied warranty can be excluded "by course of dealing or course of performance," and defendant asserts that the jury should have been allowed to determine if such occurred here.

However, there was only slight evidence of any "course of dealing" between the parties. See Pa.Stat.Ann. tit. 12A, § 1–205(1) (1970). And there was no evidence whatsoever showing the exclusion of warranties by the course of such dealing. Nor did the evidence with respect to "course of performance" raise an issue regarding exclusion of implied warranties. Instead, the evidence tends to show that both parties believed there was a warranty throughout the entire course of performance under the contract and acted accordingly. Therefore, no question for the jury existed with respect to the disclaimer; and the failure to submit an issue thereon was not error.

* * *

Notes

1. Is the court's reasoning persuasive that section 9–206(2) prevents the waiver from being effective? If the purpose of section 9–206(2) is to prevent a buyer from inadvertently abandoning his warranties, does it apply to a situation in which the buyer is actually aware of the provision? Or are there special concerns arising from the fact that the disclaimer, although known, appeared in the security agreement rather than the contract of sale?

2. Two commentators have argued that the drafters of section 2–316 intended "a rigid adherence to the conspicuousness requirement in order to avoid arguments concerning what the parties said about warranties at the time of the sale." J. White & R. Summers, Handbook of the Law Under the Uniform Commercial Code, § 12–5 at 444 (1980). Is this argument undermined by the fact that at least for an implied warranty of merchantability, a disclaimer can be oral? How is this issue affected by the parol evidence rule? *See* U.C.C. § 2–202.

3. "Conspicuousness" is defined in section 1–201(10):

A term or clause is conspicuous when it is so written that a reasonable person against whom it is to operate ought to have noticed it. A printed heading in capitals is conspicuous. Language in the body of a form is "conspicuous" if it is in larger or other contrasting type or color. But in a telegram any stated term is "conspicuous". Whether a term or clause is "conspicuous" or not is for decision by the court.

The requirement of conspicuousness has spawned a great deal of litigation. *See, e.g.,* Dorman v. International Harvester Co., 46 Cal.App.3d 11, 120 Cal.Rptr. 516 (1975); Two Rivers Co. v. Curtiss Breeding Serv., 624 F.2d 1242 (5th Cir.1980).

4. A literal reading of section 2–316 suggests that "as is" disclaimers under subsection 2–316(3)(a) are not subject to the requirements in subsection 2–316(2) concerning specific language and conspicuousness. Subsection 2–316(2) explicitly states that its own requirements are "subject to subsection (3)," and subsection (3) explicitly states that its provisions are effective "notwithstanding subsection (2)." Consequently, some courts have read section 2–316 literally to conclude that "as is" disclaimers need not be conspicuous. *See* DeKalb Agresearch, Inc. v. Abbott, 391 F.Supp. 152, 154–55 (N.D.Ala.1974), affirmed, 511 F.2d 1162 (5th Cir.1975); Gilliam v. Indiana Nat'l Bank, 337 So.2d 352 (Ala.Civ.App.1976). Other courts and some commentators, however, have argued that the purposes of section 2–316 require that "as is" disclaimers be conspicuous or that conspicuousness at least be a factor in determining whether an "as is" disclaimer is valid. *See* MacDonald v. Mobley, 555 S.W.2d 916, 919 (Tex.Civ.App.—Austin 1977, writ refused n.r.e.); J. White & R. Summers, Handbook of the Law Under the Uniform Commercial Code § 12–6 at 450; Special Project, Article Two Warranties in Commercial Transactions, 64 Cornell L.Rev. 30, 194–96 (1978).

5. Note that section 2–316(3)(b) provides that a buyer's opportunity to inspect prior to purchase negates an implied warranty with regard to defects that an inspection would reasonably have revealed. Section 2–316(3)(c) provides that course of dealing or usage of trade can also exclude or modify

an implied warranty. Obviously, neither subsection is subject to the "conspicuousness" requirement of subsection 2–316(2).

6. To be effective, a warranty disclaimer must be part of the parties' bargain. Post-sale disclaimers, like other post-sale modifications, are subject to the requirements of section 2–209. Although section 2–209 does not require post-sale modifications to be supported by consideration, it does require that the parties in fact agree to the modification, which may create a difficult obstacle for a seller attempting to enforce a post-sale disclaimer.

7. Some states have statutes that forbid disclaimers altogether in consumer transactions or in consumer transactions involving personal injury. *See, e.g.,* Ala.Code tit. 7, § 2–316(5); Mass.Gen.Laws Ann. ch. 106, § 2–316A (West Cum.Supp.1978–79); Ut.Stat.Ann. tit. 9A, § 2–719(5) (Cum. Supp.1978); Wash.Rev.Code Ann. Tit. 62A, § 2–316(4) (Cum.Supp.1977); Me.Rev.Stat.Ann. tit. 11, § 2–316(5) (Cum.Supp.1978).

8. Given the language of section 2–316(1), it is very difficult for a seller to disclaim an express warranty. Comment 1 to section 2–316 elaborates:

> This section is designed principally to deal with those frequent clauses in sales contracts which seek to exclude "all warranties, express or implied." It seeks to protect a buyer from unexpected and unbargained for language of disclaimer by denying effect to such language when inconsistent with language of express warranty and permitting the exclusion of implied warranties only by conspicuous language or other circumstances which protect the buyer from surprise.

Nevertheless, a disclaimer may affect both the interpretation of an express warranty and the decision whether it is part of the "basis of the bargain." If an express warranty is part of the basis of the bargain and its meaning is unambiguous, however, a contradictory disclaimer is not effective.

9. Disclaimers of oral express warranties raise special problems. The parol evidence rule contained in section 2–202 provides:

> Terms with respect to which the confirmatory memoranda of the parties agree or which are otherwise set forth in a writing intended by the parties as a final expression of their agreement with respect to such terms as are included therein may not be contradicted by evidence of any prior agreement or of a contemporaneous oral agreement but may be explained or supplemented
>
> (1) by course of dealing or usage of trade (Section 1–205) or by course of performance (Section 2–208); and
>
> (2) by evidence of consistent additional terms unless the court finds the writing to have been intended also as a complete and exclusive statement of the terms of the agreement.

Section 2–202 is as applicable to express warranties as it is to other oral provisions. Comment 2 to section 2–316 provides that "[t]he seller is protected under this Article against false allegations of oral warranties by its provisions on parol and extrinsic evidence * * *," and subsection 2–316(1) refers explicitly to section 2–202. Section 2–202(2) requires, however, that "the court [find] the writing to have been intended also as a complete and exclusive statement of the terms of the agreement" in order for the parol evidence rule to exclude consideration of the oral warranty. A written disclaimer under section 2–316 might lead a court to determine that the parties intended the writing to represent their entire agreement concerning warranties, thereby excluding oral warranties under the parol evidence rule.

10. Would a requirement that all warranties are excluded unless the consumer mails in a warranty card pass muster under section 2–316?

Uniform Commercial Code

§ 2–719. Contractual Modification or Limitation of Remedy

(1) Subject to the provisions of subsections (2) and (3) of this section and of the preceding section on liquidation and limitation of damages,

(a) the agreement may provide for remedies in addition to or in substitution for those provided in this Article and may limit or alter the measure of damages recoverable under this Article, as by limiting the buyer's remedies to return of the goods and repayment of the price or to repair and replacement of non-conforming goods or parts; and

(b) resort to a remedy as provided is optional unless the remedy is expressly agreed to be exclusive, in which case it is the sole remedy.

(2) Where circumstances cause an exclusive or limited remedy to fail of its essential purpose, remedy may be had as provided in this Act.

(3) Consequential damages may be limited or excluded unless the limitation or exclusion is unconscionable. Limitation of consequential damages for injury to the person in the case of consumer goods is prima facie unconscionable but limitation of damages where the loss is commercial is not.

McCARTY v. E.J. KORVETTE, INC.

Court of Special Appeals of Maryland, 1975.
28 Md.App. 421, 347 A.2d 253.

DAVIDSON, JUDGE.

On 25 February 1971, Frances McCarty bought four tires manufactured by Denman Rubber Manufacturing Co., at Korvettes Tire & Auto Centers, a retail outlet located on Baltimore National Pike, which was allegedly operated, pursuant to a franchise and lease from E.J. Korvette, Inc., by Tires, Inc. On the back side of the invoice given to Mrs. McCarty, under the title "Korvette Tire Centers All–Road–Hazards Tire Guarantee," the following language appears:

"The tires identified hereon are guaranteed for the number of months (or miles) designated [*36,000 miles*] *against all road hazards* including stone bruises, impact bruises, *blow out,* tread separation, glass cuts and fabric breaks, only when used in normal, noncommercial passenger car service. *If a tire fails to give satisfactory service under the terms of this guarantee,* return it to the nearest

Korvette Tire Center. *We will replace the tire* charging only the proportionate part of the sale price for each month elapsed (or mileage used) from date of purchase, plus the full federal tax.

"The above guarantee does not cover tires run flat, or simply worn out; tires injured by a fire, collision, vandalism, misalignment or mechanical defects of the vehicle. Radial or surface fissures, discoloration or ordinary repairable punctures, do not render tires unfit for service. Punctures will be repaired free.

"Neither the manufacturer nor Korvette Tire Centers shall be liable for any consequential damage and our liability is limited solely to replacement of the product." (Emphasis supplied.)

On 14 June 1971, the appellants, Frances McCarty and her husband, Warren McCarty (consumers) were involved in an automobile accident. As a result of an alleged blowout of the right rear tire, their vehicle swerved off the road and turned over several times causing personal injury to each of them as well as property damage to their car. In the Circuit Court for Baltimore County, the consumers sued E.J. Korvette, Inc., Tires, Inc., and Denman Rubber Manufacturing Co., the appellees, for damages resulting from their alleged breach of express and implied warranties and negligence. At the conclusion of the consumers' case, Judge John Grason Turnbull granted the appellees' motions for directed verdicts. On 4 November 1974, final judgment was entered. It is from that judgment that this appeal is taken.

I

The appellees initially contend that the language contained in the Korvette Tire Centers All–Road–Hazard Tire Guarantee, when read as a whole, does not constitute an express warranty against blowouts, but rather constitutes a guarantee that if a blowout occurs, the tire will be replaced. We do not agree.

* * *

In considering the definition of an express warranty, the Court of Appeals long ago recognized the distinction which exists between an express warranty and an executory promise or contractual undertaking. In *White Automobile Co. v. Dorsey,* 119 Md. 251, 86 A. 617 (1913), * * * [the court] recognized that language relating of [sic] the existing qualities, capabilities and condition of goods constituted an express warranty. Language promising that the seller would repair goods in the event of a breach of the warranty, did not relate to the existing qualities, capabilities or condition of the goods, and, consequently, did not constitute an express warranty, but rather an executory contractual undertaking to be performed in the future.

[In Rittenhouse–Winterson Auto Co. v. Kissner, 129 Md. 102, 98 A. 361 (1916)], the Court of Appeals reasserted its previously drawn distinction between an express warranty and an executory promise. An assurance that a truck would perform in a certain way for a given period of time in the future constituted an express warranty because it had reference to *the existing quality, capacity or condition of the goods*. An assurance that the seller would, at some time in the future, perform certain services in the event that the goods should not conform to the representation, so that the warranty was breached, constituted an executory promise or contractual undertaking because it had reference, not to the existing quality, capacity or condition of the goods, but rather to the assumption of an affirmative contractual duty to be performed in the future.

There is nothing in the language of Comm.L.Art., § 2–313 which requires a departure from these basic principles which were applied under both the common law and the Uniform Sales Act. Applying these principles to the instant case produces a clear result.

Here the language on the invoice given to the buyer to the effect that "the tires identified hereon are guaranteed for 36,000 miles * * * against all road hazards, including * * * blow out * * *'" constitutes an affirmation that the tires are of such existing quality, capacity and condition as to make them capable of rendering service without blowing out before they have been used for 36,000 miles. This assurance of the serviceability of the tires for a given number of miles, because it is a representation as to the existing quality, capacity and condition of the tires, constitutes an express warranty that the tires will not blow out during the first 36,000 miles of use.

Questions remain as to what impact the additional language appearing on the invoice has upon the scope and extent of the express warranty.

* * * The language which not only promises to replace the tire if a blowout occurs, but also attempts to avoid consequential damages and restrict the remedies of the buyer solely to replacement, constitutes a limitation of remedies [that is] governed by the provisions of Comm. L.Art., § 2–719.

* * *

Comm.L.Art., § 2–719 gives the parties considerable latitude in which to fashion their remedies to their particular requirements. It expressly recognizes that parties may limit their remedies to repair and replacement. The parties, however, must accept the legal consequence that there be some fair remedy for breach of the obligations or duties outlined in the contract. Reasonable agreements which limit or modify remedies will be given effect, but the parties are not free to shape their remedies in an unreasonable or unconscionable way. Comm.L.Art., § 2–719(3) recognizes the validity of clauses limiting or excluding consequential damages, otherwise available under Comm.L.Art., § 2–714(3), but expressly states that they may not operate in an unconscionable manner. That subsection also establishes that limitation of consequential damages for injury to the person in the case of consumer goods is *prima facie* unconscionable.

Comm.L.Art., § 2–302(1) sets forth the alternatives available to a court when it finds a limitation of remedy to be unconscionable.[11] That section permits the court in its discretion, after a finding of unconscionability, to refuse to enforce the contract as a whole, if it is permeated by the unconscionability, or *to strike any single clause or group of clauses which are so tainted* or which are contrary to the essential purpose of the agreement, or to simply limit unconscionable clauses so as to avoid unconscionable results. Thus, any clause purporting to modify or limit remedies in an unconscionable manner is subject to deletion and will not be given effect.

* * *

While there is no statutory presumption of unconscionability with respect to a limitation of consequential damages for injury to property in the case of consumer goods, * * * the clause here, which attempts to exclude liability for both personal injury and property damage is so tainted by unconscionability as to warrant deletion in its entirety. If the appellees do not want to be liable for consequential damages, they should not expressly warrant the tires against blowouts.

Under the present circumstances, the clause purporting to restrict remedies solely to replacement is ineffective. It cannot serve to convert the express warranty against blowouts into a guarantee that if a tire blew out, "the tire would be replaced."

* * *

Notes

1. Section 2–302 provides:

(a) If the court as a matter of law finds the contract or any clause of the contract to have been unconscionable at the time it was made the court may refuse to enforce the contract, or it may enforce the remainder of the contract without the unconscionable clause, or it may so limit the application of any unconscionable clause as to avoid any unconscionable result.

(b) When it is claimed or appears to the court that the contract or any clause thereof may be unconscionable the parties shall be afforded a reasonable opportunity to present evidence as to its commercial setting, purpose and effects to aid the court in making the determination.

2. Subsection 2–719(3) provides that limitations of consequential damages for personal injury are "prima facie" unconscionable," not "per se" unconscionable. Can you think of situations in which a seller could overcome the presumption of unconscionability?

---

11. Comm.L.Art., § 2–302(1) provides:

"If the court as a matter of law finds the contract or any clause of the contract to have been unconscionable at the time it was made the court may refuse to enforce the contract, or *it may enforce the remainder of the contract without the unconscionable clause,* or it may so limit the application of any unconscionable clause as to avoid any unconscionable result." (Emphasis added.)

3. Recall that an express warranty usually is not enforced beyond its own terms as interpreted by the court. Is this proposition consistent with section 2–719(3)?

Suppose the seller in *McCarty* had simply promised that "the seller agrees to repair any blowouts." Would this promise create personal injury liability? If not, what policies support the distinction between the example and the result in *McCarty?*

In the same vein, consider the entire category of service contracts. Presumably, an automobile dealer who sells a five-year service contract is not subject to personal injury liability on the basis of the service contract alone. Is this conclusion consistent with *McCarty?*

Midas Muffler routinely advertises that it will replace a muffler for as long as you own the car. How would you advise Midas concerning its potential personal injury liability?

4. Should the language and conspicuous requirements of section 2–316 be applied to section 2–719? Comment 2 to section 2–316 provides:

> This section treats the limitations or avoidance of consequential damages as a matter of limiting remedies for breach, separate from the matter of creation of liability under a warranty. If no warranty exists, there is of course no problem of limiting remedies for breach of warranty. Under subsection (4) the question of limitation of remedy is governed by the sections referred to rather than by this section.

Consequently, most courts have rejected a buyer's claim that remedy limitations must comply with the language and conspicuousness requirements of section 2–316. *See* Orrox Corp. v. Rexnord, Inc., 389 F.Supp. 441, 445–46 (M.D.Ala.1975); Gramling v. Baltz, 253 Ark. 361, 362, 485 S.W.2d 183, 189 (1972), affirmed on rehearing, 253 Ark. 352, 485 S.W.2d 183 (1972); Fargo Mach. & Tool Co. v. Kearney & Trecker Corp., 428 F.Supp. 364, 381 (E.D.Mich.1977); Adams Van Serv., Inc. v. International Harvester Corp., 14 U.C.C.Rep.Serv. (Callaghan) 1142, 1147–49, 1973 WL 21443 (Pa.Com.Pl. 1973) (limitation of remedy upheld although it appears in same clause and same size print as inconspicuous disclaimer).

Should lack of conspicuousness nevertheless be a factor concerning unconscionability under section 2–302? *See generally,* Weintraub, Disclaimer of Warranties and Limitation of Damages for Breach of Warranty Under the U.C.C., 53 Tex.L.Rev. 60 (1974). Should other factors, such as lack of bargaining power or gross unfairness, render a limitation on damages unconscionable under section 2–302 even though the limitation does not violate section 2–316 or 2–719? Does section 2–719(3) exclude these factors from consideration, or does it merely decline to make the presumption of unconscionability rest on these factors?

5. Remedies are normally presumed to be cumulative, and a limitation must be clear and in "most specific terms." Calloway v. Manion, 572 F.2d 1033, 1038 (5th Cir.1978).

SOO LINE RAILROAD CO. v. FRUEHAUF CORP.
United States Court of Appeals, Eighth Circuit, 1977.
547 F.2d 1365.

STEPHENSON, CIRCUIT JUDGE.

This appeal concerns a contract in which Fruehauf Corporation (Magor) agreed to the manufacture, sale and delivery of 500 railroad hopper cars to Soo Line Railroad Company for the approximate price of $9,750,000. Soo Line, in this diversity action initiated against Magor, claims breach of contract and negligence in the manufacture of the railcars, and the district court entered judgment based upon a jury verdict for Soo Line in the amount of $1,238,754.82. Magor appeals contending in general that the trial court erred in failing to construe certain provisions in the contract as barring recovery of damages * * *.

Magor and Soo Line in 1967 created the contract which provided for Magor to manufacture and deliver 500 covered hopper freight railroad cars.

* * *

The agreement was also governed by a document entitled "Terms and Conditions of Sale" which *inter alia* provided that acceptance of the cars was contingent upon inspection by Soo Line and included a warranty provision guaranteeing for one year that the railcars would be free from defects in material and workmanship and in full conformity with the specifications. In general, the warranty provision limited Magor's express obligation to the repair or replacement of any defective parts and provided that the warranty was in lieu of all other express or implied warranties and barred liability for indirect or consequential damages arising from the defects in material or workmanship.

* * *

It is undisputed that, despite an estimated 40–year useful life, the underframes developed serious and widespread cracks in the steel structure and welds within a few months of delivery. Following both unilateral and mutual inspection of the railcars by the parties, Soo Line concluded that the cracks resulted from structural and welding defects and accordingly requested that Magor perform its obligation to repair pursuant to the warranty. However, Magor's management, claiming that the cracking derived from construction specifications required by Soo Line, insisted it had no such responsibility. After Magor refused to repair the cars, Soo Line implemented its own remedial operation. The cost of repairs was $506,862.78, slightly more than $1,000 per car. Soo Line has contended, and the jury verdict reflects, that this expenditure did not fully restore the cars to totally acceptable operating condition.

On July 30, 1971, Soo Line filed its complaint claiming breach of express and implied warranties and negligence based on the structural failure of the railroad cars and Magor's refusal to accept responsibility for repair. Magor in its answer denied liability contending that: the railcars met contract specifications; Soo Line's failure to inspect the cars during manufacture barred recovery; damages were limited by the contract * * *.

Trial commenced on August 13, 1975, and concluded on October 2, 1975, with a jury verdict in favor of Soo Line.

* * *

I.

The most significant issue in this appeal is whether either the disclaimer of liability, inspection clause or remedial limitation contained within the contract bars recovery of any or all damages arising from defective manufacture of the railroad cars. Appellant contends, alternatively, that it is exonerated from liability because the contract: disclaimed liability for implied warranties and negligent manufacture; barred recovery in the event of Soo Line's failure to inspect the railroad cars during manufacture; and in any event limited Magor's damages to the reasonable cost of necessary repairs (an amount not exceeding $506,862.78). In general, appellee asserts that the agreement does not preclude liability for the reasons that: the disclaimer of implied warranties was ineffective because it did not mention the word "merchantability" and is not conspicuous; the inspection clause does not impair any remedy since it related only to acceptance; and the limited remedy is unenforceable because it failed of its essential purpose. * * * We consider initially the remedial limitation upon liability arising from breach of the express warranty.

It is undisputed and the district court found that the document entitled "Terms and Conditions of the Sale" is a part of the contract between Soo Line and Magor. The warranty provision appearing in this document specifically states:

> We will warrant to you (except as to items not manufactured by us) for a period of one year after date of acceptance of each of said cars that they will be free from all defects in material and workmanship under normal use and service, and that the cars will be in full conformity with the specifications referred to herein. Our obligation under this warranty shall be limited to repairing or replacing any part which is found to be defective provided we are notified of the fault or defect when it is first discovered and we are afforded an opportunity for verification, said repairs or replacement to be made at our plant or at such other place as may be mutually agreed upon. This warranty is expressly in lieu of all other warranties expressed or implied, and we shall not be liable for indirect or consequential damages resulting from any such defects in material or workmanship.

The trial court eventually concluded, without articulating a particular reason, that this warranty provision was ineffective to limit Magor's liability.

In this diversity case we are, of course, applying the substantive law of Minnesota. It is clear under Minnesota law that parties to a contract may limit or alter the measure of damages recoverable, as by limiting the buyer's remedies to repair and replacement of nonconforming goods or parts. Minn.Stat.Ann. § 336.2–719(1). * * * A limited remedy to repair or replace goods which are initially defective but are promptly remedied by the seller will normally be enforceable. Minn.Stat.Ann. § 336.2–719, Comment 1.

Nevertheless, limitations on remedies and damages permissible under section 2–719(1) are subject to section 2–719(2), which states:

> Where circumstances cause an exclusive or limited remedy to fail of its essential purpose, remedy may be had as provided in this chapter.

The rationale underlying section 2–719(2) is adequately reflected by the court's statement in *Jones & McKnight v. Birdsboro Corp.*, 320 F.Supp. 39, 43–44 (N.D.Ill.1970):

> This Court would be in an untenable position if it allowed the defendant to shelter itself behind one segment of the warranty when it has allegedly repudiated and ignored its very limited obligations under another segment of the same warranty, which alleged repudiation has caused the very need for relief which the defendant is attempting to avoid.

In applying section 2–719 to the facts in the instant case, we conclude that the remedial limitation contained within the contract failed of its essential purpose and is therefore unenforceable. The record reveals substantial evidence showing that the railroad cars manufactured by Magor were defective with respect to their structure and the welding of certain crucial joints which precipitated serious cracking in the underframes of the cars. * * * Even more significant is the jury's answer to question 6(b) of the special verdict form, which states that Magor did not meet its obligation to repair or replace defective parts on the railcars.[7] The jury also found, as reflected by its answer to question 6(a), that Soo Line had promptly notified Magor, pursuant to the contract, of the defects and afforded Magor the opportunity to verify the defects.

There is adequate evidence in the record supportive of the jury's special verdict response indicating that Magor failed to perform its limited contractual responsibility to repair defects in the railcars. * * *

* * * Based on this evidence, we conclude that the contract's limited remedy of repair failed of its essential purpose, and therefore all available Uniform Commercial Code remedies apply. *See* Minn.Stat.Ann. §§ 336.2–719(2) and 336.2–714.

---

7. A limited remedy fails of its purpose whenever the seller fails to repair goods within a reasonable time. Section 2–719(2) becomes operative when a party is deprived of its contractual remedy and it is unnecessary to prove that failure to repair was willful or negligent. * * *

At this point we must necessarily confront appellant's additional contention that the inspection clause in the contract prohibits recovery of damages. The inspection provision contained within the terms and conditions of sale states:

> All construction is subject to inspection by you or your authorized agent who may have access to any part of our plant where any of this work is in progress. Cars to be satisfactory in every respect before acceptance and final inspection and acceptance to be at our plant. Should you waive inspection, then inspection for the Purchaser will be performed by our regular inspection forces and said inspection will constitute acceptance of the cars at our works by your Company.

> Notwithstanding any other acceptance point herein called out, specified or agreed upon; the buyer agrees that final inspection will be accomplished at our plant and evidenced by a Certificate or Certificates of Inspection to be signed and delivered by your representative inspector to our Company at the time of final inspection, which Certificate will not conflict or abrogate any other terms pertaining to warranty involved herein.

Magor claims that the inspection clause should bar recovery of damages because Soo Line allegedly failed to undertake inspection of the railroad cars during the manufacturing process. We disagree.

It is not readily apparent that Soo Line exercised review of the actual manufacturing process. Nonetheless, the record reflects that Soo Line did conduct inspections of completed cars at Magor's manufacturing plant. On November 8, 1967, D. W. Paul, Soo Line's assistant superintendent of its car department, participated in a joint inspection with representatives of Magor and other companies on the first of the 500 cars to be completed. This joint inspection specified that the quality of workmanship, particularly welding, was to be improved. On December 11, 1967, after visiting the plant, Paul reported that welding in certain plates and bolsters should be improved. During this visit Paul spot-checked approximately 80 cars, found such a significant number of defects that all of the cars were to be recalled for reworking and received assurances that repairs would be performed from Magor's chief engineer, Rolf Mowatt-Larssen, and its general sales manager, W. F. Lowry. Subsequently, Paul received a telephone call from Lowry indicating that Magor's vice president and general manager, R. Van Hassel, had completed plans to avoid any more "system failures" and had stated that all cars already built would be corrected and then reinspected.

Paul returned to Magor's plant in January 1968. His report at this time revealed various structural alignment problems and numerous welding defects. Paul was telephonically guaranteed once again by Van Hassel that all exceptions noted during the visit would be corrected. The trial testimony of D. A. Dominguez, an engineer for Magor, corroborates Paul's inspection reports showing Soo Line had been assured by

Magor that existing defects in the cars would be remedied and that production would be reoriented to avoid problems already discovered.

Review of the language in the inspection clause indicates that a waiver of inspection by the purchaser entitled Magor to perform its own inspection and such inspection would have constituted acceptance of the railcars. In any event, the provision neither expressly provides nor even implies that a failure to exercise the right of inspection constitutes a waiver of any other contractual remedy. * * * When the right to inspect arises *after* the creation of the contract, as in the instant case, acceptance of goods, even with knowledge that they do not conform to the contract, may preclude rejection but it does not impair any other remedy. Minn.Stat.Ann. § 336.2–607(2). *Cf.* Minn.Stat.Ann. § 336.2–316(3)(b) (effect of inspection or refusal of inspection *before* entering into contract). The buyer's right to recover damages for goods that have been accepted but do not conform to the contract is expressly reserved. Minn.Stat.Ann. § 336.2–714(1).

In this case the jury found that Soo Line notified Magor of the faults or defects when they were first discovered and afforded Magor the opportunity to verify and repair or replace the faults or defects at Magor's plant or another place mutually agreeable. The record amply supports the jury's finding in this respect. Accordingly, it is clear that the inspection clause in the contract does not bar liability in the instant case.

Finally, we consider the question whether Magor should be exonerated from liability for consequential damages because the contract contains a specific bar against such damages existing independently of the exclusive remedy to repair. The Minnesota courts have yet to confront this issue. A federal court must, notwithstanding the absence of a controlling state decision, apply the rule it believes the courts of the state would follow. Accordingly, we conclude that the contract does not effectively bar liability for consequential damages. * * * Uniform Commercial Code remedies should be liberally administered, Minn.Stat.Ann. § 336.1–106, and a buyer when entering into a contract does not anticipate that the sole remedy available will be rendered a nullity, thus causing additional damages. In addition, the fundamental intent of section 2–719(2) reflects that a remedial limitation's failure of essential purpose makes available all contractual remedies, including consequential damages authorized pursuant to sections 2–714 and 2–715.

* * *

For the reasons outlined above, we hold that neither the remedial limitation, the inspection provision, nor the disclaimer of consequential damages contained within the Soo Line–Magor contract prohibits liability arising from breach of the express warranty. Without the limiting clauses, the Uniform Commercial Code remedies apply, including those set out in section 2–714 which allows the buyer damages for non-conforming goods. *See* Minn.Stat.Ann. §§ 336.2–719 and 336.2–714.

* * *

Affirmed.

Notes

1. Courts have split on the effect of an independent limitation on consequential damages when a "repair or replacement" clause fails its essential purpose. Some courts have held that a separate and explicit consequential damage exclusion is effective even if the "repair and replacement" clause fails its essential purpose. *See* Lincoln Pulp & Paper Co., Inc. v. Dravo Corp., 436 F.Supp. 262, 278 (D.Me.1977) (under theory that location of exclusion contained in "independent contractual clause" precluded recovery of consequential damages); County Asphalt, Inc. v. Lewis Welding & Eng'g Corp., 323 F.Supp. 1300 (S.D.N.Y.1970), affirmed, 444 F.2d 372 (2d Cir.1971), cert. denied, 404 U.S. 939, 92 S.Ct. 272, 30 L.Ed.2d 252 (1971); Kohlenberger, Inc. v. Tyson's Foods, Inc., 256 Ark. 584, 510 S.W.2d 555 (1974). Other courts have held that a seller's bad faith failure to repair undermines even an explicit, independent limitation of consequential damages. *See* Koehring Co. v. A.P.I., Inc., 369 F.Supp. 882, 890 (E.D.Mich. 1974); United States Fibres, Inc. v. Proctor & Schwartz, Inc., 358 F.Supp. 449, 465 (E.D.Mich.1972), affirmed on other grounds, 509 F.2d 1043 (6th Cir.1975); Jones & McKnight Corp. v. Birdsboro Corp., 320 F.Supp. 39, 43 (N.D.Ill.1970) (buyer entitled to expectation that seller "would not be unreasonably or willfully dilatory" in making repairs under warranty). *See also* Potomac Elec. Power Co. v. Westinghouse Elec. Corp., 385 F.Supp. 572, 578–79 (D.D.C.1974) (seller's conscientious repair efforts preclude liability for consequential damages), reversed memorandum decision, 527 F.2d 853 (D.C.Cir.1975). One commentator has suggested that an independent limitation on consequential damages should fail when the seller's attempt to repair fails, even if the seller has made a good faith effort to repair. *See* Special Project, Article Two Warranties in Commercial Transactions, 64 Cornell L.Rev. 30, 239 (1978).

2. Courts also have split on the issue of whether a "repair or replacement" clause fails its essential purpose when a seller makes a good faith effort to repair or replace goods but is unable to do so. Some courts and commentators have suggested that a seller's motivation is irrelevant. *See* Fargo Mach. & Tool Co. v. Kearney & Trecker Corp., 428 F.Supp. 364 (E.D.Mich.1977); Special Project, Article Two Warranties in Commercial Transactions, 64 Cornell L.Rev. 30, 235–36 (1978). Other courts have held that a seller's good faith attempt is a factor that should be considered. *See* American Elec. Power Co. v. Westinghouse Elec. Corp., 418 F.Supp. 435, 453–54 (S.D.N.Y.1976); Potomac Elec. Power Co. v. Westinghouse Elec. Corp., 385 F.Supp. 572, 578–79 (D.D.C.1974), reversed memorandum decision, 527 F.2d 853 (D.C.Cir.1975); Koehring Co. v. A.P.I., Inc., 369 F.Supp. 882 (D.Mich.1974); Jones & McKnight Corp. v. Birdsboro Corp., 320 F.Supp. 39 (N.D.Ill.1970).

3. In Russo v. Hilltop Lincoln–Mercury, Inc., 479 S.W.2d 211 (Mo.App. 1972), the plaintiff's car was destroyed by an electrical fire caused by a

defective electrical part. The court permitted plaintiff to recover the value of the car. In response to the defendant's argument that a "repair and replacement" provision limited the plaintiff's remedy to replacement of the electrical part, the court stated that this

> provision of the warranty implies the car was repairable. Here it could not be; it was worthless junk. At trial time the defendant had the car, still not repaired. It would be ludicrous to require plaintiff to ask defendant to do the impossible. "Laws governing warranties, express and implied, should be so administered as to be fair to all parties concerned. Such warranties should be meaningful." Jacobson v. Broadway Motors, Inc., Mo.App., 430 S.W.2d 602.

The contract also expressly excluded liability for car rental expense. The court refused to award the plaintiff damages for these expenses. It rejected the plaintiff's argument that the defendant's failure to repair constituted a "failure of purpose" that could be used to trigger the code remedy of incidental damages (here the cost of a rental car). Are these two holdings consistent?

4. The inspection clause in *Soo Line* is an example of the extent to which the parties can structure their own deal. To the extent that the parties' own terms affect remedies, however, courts are likely to scrutinize the terms carefully under section 2–719.

5. *See generally,* Anderson, Failure of Essential Purpose and Essential Failure on Purpose: A Look at Section 2–719 of the Uniform Commercial Code, 31 Sw.L.J. 758 (1977); Eddy, On the "Essential" Purposes of Limited Remedies: The Metaphysics of UCC Section 2–719(2), 65 Calif.L.Rev. 28, 39 (1977); Note, Failure of the Essential Purpose of a Limited Repair Remedy Under Section 2–719 of the Uniform Commercial Code, 32 Baylor L.Rev. 292, 296–98 (1980); Special Project, Article Two Warranties in Commercial Transactions, 64 Cornell L.Rev. 30, 239 (1978).

FORD MOTOR CO. v. MOULTON
Supreme Court of Tennessee, 1974.
511 S.W.2d 690, cert. denied, 419 U.S. 870, 95 S.Ct. 129, 42 L.Ed.2d 109.

CHATTIN, JUSTICE.

This is a personal injury suit brought by Moulton and his wife, Pauline, against Ford Motor Company and a retail Ford dealer, Hull–Dobbs.

* * *

[O]n July 5, 1970, while driving in a westerly direction along Interstate 40, the car suddenly veered to the right, jumped the guard rail and fell twenty-six feet to a street below. It is alleged the car suddenly went out of control because of a defect in the steering mechanism. Moulton was seriously injured.

* * *

The Court of Appeals affirmed the action of the trial judge in dismissing the breach of warranty counts * * *.

The Court of Appeals concluded that Hull–Dobbs had not given Moulton an express warranty. This conclusion is supported by the evidence. That Court found that Ford had given Moulton a one-year or twelve thousand mile express warranty. However, the Court of Appeals held that this warranty had expired, thereby precluding an action for its breach.

Both Hull–Dobbs and Ford had disclaimer clauses in their contracts with Moulton, which purportedly disclaimed all implied warranties. The Court of Appeals found these disclaimer clauses to be valid; and, therefore, sufficient to prevent respondents from having a cause of action for breach of implied warranty.

Respondents make three arguments: First, they insist the disclaimer clauses were not properly drawn in that they failed to comply with the provisions of the Uniform Commercial Code; and are, therefore, invalid. Second, if the disclaimer clauses are properly drawn, they are prima facie unconscionable. * * * Finally, respondents insist that the one-year or twelve thousand mile limitation on the express warranty is prima facie uncons[c]ionable under T.C.A. 47–2–719.

T.C.A. 47–2–316(2) provides that implied warranties of merchantability and fitness may be disclaimed if the disclaimer is conspicuous and mentions merchantability, and if it is in writing with reference to the fitness warranty. The Court of Appeals concluded that the requirement of T.C.A. 47–2–316(2) had been complied with; and, consequently, the disclaimers were validly drawn. We agree with this conclusion.

Respondents insist that even if the disclaimers were drawn in accordance with the provisions of T.C.A. 47–2–316 they are, nevertheless, invalid because they violate T.C.A. 47–2–719.

T.C.A. 47–2–719(3) provides:

> "Consequential damages may be limited or excluded unless the limitation or exclusion is unconscionable. Limitation of consequential damages for injury to the person in the case of consumer goods is prima facie unconscionable but limitation of damages where the loss is commercial is not."

Respondents' argument is that as a result of the accident Moulton sustained personal injuries; that because of the valid disclaimer of warranties, he is unable to bring an action for consequential damages resulting from the accident; and that such an exclusion is violative of T.C.A. 47–2–719(3) since that section "expressly prohibits exclusion of personal injuries by warranty."

In answer to this argument, the Court of Appeals said:

> " * * * Plaintiffs misconstrue[ ] the scope of this Section. (2–719(3)). Subsection (3) thereof provides the limitation of consequential damages for injury to the person in case of consumer goods is prima facie unconscionable, but that Section does not control disclaimer of implied warranties. Official comment 3 to T.C.A. 47–

2–719 states that the seller 'in all cases is free to disclaim warranties in the manner provided in Section 2–316.' "

"The latter Section, which is T.C.A. 47–2–316, provides in subsection (2) that implied warranties of merchantability and fitness may be disclaimed if the disclaimer is conspicuous and mentions merchantability, and if it is in writing with reference to the fitness warranty. The disclaimer here is in writing, and merchantability is explicitly mentioned in the disclaimer of the motor vehicle sales contract."

Most Uniform Commercial Code commentaries agree with the conclusion of the Court of Appeals that disclaimers drawn in accordance with 47–2–316 cannot be considered to violate the provisions of 47–2–719. The following analysis is offered in the one volume treatise of the U.C.C. by White and Summers:

" * * * The proposition enunciated by * * * (a few courts) * * * that a disclaimer that has the effect of modifying or excluding consequential damages may be unconscionable under 2–719(3) * * * is out of line with the scheme of the Code. Comment 3 to 2–719(3) provides: * * * 'Subsection (3) recognizes the validity to clauses limiting or excluding consequential damages but makes it clear that they may not operate in an unconscionable manner. Actually such terms are merely an allocation of unknown or undeterminable risks. The seller in all cases is free to disclaim warranties in a manner provided in Section 2–316.' "

"The last sentence seems to be telling the seller, 'if you really want to limit your liability why don't you disclaim all warranties? Then you wont [sic] have to worry about limiting damages.' Note that the sentence appears after the discussion of remedies limitations and after the discussion of extent to which such clauses are governed by the unconscionability doctrine and that it announces that the seller may disclaim warranties in all cases. These facts strongly indicate that the draftsmen intended for 2–316 to operate independently of 2–719(3)."

"This implication is buttressed by comment to 2–316 * * *: ' * * * If no warranty exists, there is of course no problem of limiting remedies for breach of warranty.' "

"The comment's reasoning is elementary: there can be no consequential damages if there is no breach; there can be no breach of warranty if there is no warranty; there can be no warranty if the seller has disclaimed them pursuant to 2–316. Although a particular disclaimer may be unconscionable under 2–302, it seems clear that the scheme of the Code does not permit a court to disregard that disclaimer on the basis that it operates to exclude the consequential damages that could not be excluded under 2–719(3)."

We think the Court of Appeals correctly determined that the disclaimer clauses did not violate the provisions of 2–719(3).

Respondents did not argue that the Court of Appeals did not consider the question as to whether a warranty disclaimer which meets the provisions of 2–316 can be considered unconscionable within the meaning of the term as used in 2–302. Most commentaries answer this question in the negative. See Leff, Unconscionability and the Code, the Emperor's New Clause, 115 U.Pa.L.Rev., 485 (1967).

Finally, respondents contend that the one-year or twelve thousand mile limitation on the express warranty is prima facie unconscionable under T.C.A. 47–2–719(3). This is essentially the same argument made above. Again, the Court of Appeals rejected respondents' reasoning stating:

"This provision has to do with limitation of remedies, and not with a limitation on the time within which a claim may be asserted. T.C.A. 47–2–607(3)(a) provides for the time within which a claim must be asserted. It states that where goods have been accepted, 'the buyer must within a reasonable time after he discovers or should have discovered a breach notify the seller of the breach or be barred from any remedy.' T.C.A. 47–1–204(1) provides that whenever any provision in the Sales Act requires an action to be taken within a reasonable time 'any time which is not manifestly unreasonable may be fixed by agreement.' "

"Limitation of the period of the express warranty is in effect a limitation of the time within which a claim must be asserted under that warranty. The warranty actually provides for repair or replacement of such parts 'found to be defective' within the limited period, and if such discovery were made presumably a further reasonable period of time would be allowed for giving notice. Here, however, no such discovery within the limited period was made. Thus, plaintiff has no valid claim of breach of express or implied warranty.

"There is no assignment of error that the limited period of express warranty is 'manifestly unreasonable' within the meaning of T.C.A. 47–1–204(1). In the absence of any such assignment, we deem the issue waived by the plaintiffs."

* * *

Notes

1. What policies support a conclusion that a seller can effectively escape liability for personal injury damages by disclaiming a warranty under section 2–316, but cannot do so by limiting damages under section 2–719?

2. Even if a disclaimer is not unconscionable under section 2–719(3), might it be unconscionable under section 2–302? *See* Weintraub, Disclaimer of Warranties and Limitation of Damages for Breach of Warranty Under the U.C.C., 53 Tex.L.Rev. 60, 80–83 (1974). Did the court in *Moulton* do justice to the plaintiff's argument on this point?

3. Subsection 2–607(3)(a) provides that "the buyer must within a reasonable time after he discovers or should have discovered any breach notify the seller of breach or be barred from any remedy. * * *" Is this provision even applicable to the time limitation provision at issue in *Moulton?*

4. The notice requirement of section 2–607(3)(a) can be a pitfall for an unwary plaintiff. Recall that in Greenman v. Yuba Power Products, Inc., 59 Cal.2d 57, 27 Cal.Rptr. 697, 377 P.2d 897 (1963), Justice Traynor referred to this pitfall in his argument that the court should create an action for strict tort liability, rather than force plaintiffs to rely on warranty law.

5. Some courts have held that the notice requirement of section 2–607(3)(a) applies only between a buyer and an immediate seller. Consequently, these courts do not require a buyer to notify a remote seller. *See, e.g.,* Vintage Homes, Inc. v. Coldiron, 585 S.W.2d 886, 888 (Tex.Civ.App.—El Paso 1979, no writ).

One purpose underlying the notice requirement of section 2–607(3)(a) is to give the seller a chance to cure the defect. Is there any reason to apply the requirement to a situation in which the plaintiff's first notice of the defect is an accident that causes personal injury? In such a case, is this an issue that would more appropriately be governed by a statute of limitations?

6. Section 2–725 provides:

(a) An action for breach of any contract for sale must be commenced within four years after the cause of action has accrued. By the original agreement the parties may reduce the period of limitation to not less than one year but may not extend it.

(b) A cause of action accrues when the breach occurs, regardless of the aggrieved party's lack of knowledge of the breach. A breach of warranty occurs when tender of delivery is made, except that where a warranty explicitly extends to future performance of the goods and discovery of the breach must await the time of such performance the cause of action accrues when the breach is or should have been discovered.

* * *

Is this the provision that should have governed the time limitation in *Moulton?*

7. Does section 2–725 justify the mileage limitation in *Moulton?* If not, should the mileage limitation be governed by the conspicuousness and language requirements of section 2–316 or by the unconscionability provision of section 2–719(3)? How would you advise a client who wants to limit liability for automobile repairs to 90 days or 3,000 miles, whichever occurs first?

8. How should a court analyze a time limitation that cuts off the availability of certain remedies, such as personal injury damages, but not others, such as repair and replacement?

9. Notwithstanding the clear language of section 2–725(b), some courts have calculated the statute of limitations from the time of injury in breach of

warranty cases involving personal injury. *See* Cleveland v. Square–D Co., 613 S.W.2d 790 (Tex.Civ.App.—Houston [14th Dist.] 1981, no writ).

If a court calculates the statute of limitation from the time of injury, should it also use the "discovery rule" (which is the normal rule on tort cases), counting only from the time the plaintiff discovered or should have discovered the injury?

10.   Some states have adopted statutes of repose for product injuries, which provide that suit is barred, for example, ten years after the sale, even if the injury did not take place or was not discovered within the time period. *See, e.g.,* Ill.Rev.Stat. ch. 83, § 22.2 (1978). Such statutes are superfluous under the wording of section 2–725, because the four-year provision of section 2–725 runs from the time of sale, unless the warranty specifically refers to future performance.

SECTION H.   MAGNUSON–MOSS ACT

Some warranties are governed by the federal Magnuson–Moss Act as well as by the U.C.C. 15 U.S.C. §§ 2301–12 (1982). In its basic provisions, the Magnuson–Moss Act establishes additional federal requirements for warranties that supplement state law. The Act does not provide a comprehensive scheme of warranties that totally supplants state law. The Act also authorizes the Federal Trade Commission to promulgate appropriate regulations.

The Act applies to contracts for the sale of tangible goods used for "personal, family, or household purposes * * *." 15 U.S.C. § 2301(1). It applies only to transactions in which the buyer is offered a written warranty, 15 U.S.C. § 2301(3) (1982), which is defined in subsection 2301(6) as:

A.   Any written affirmation of fact or written promise made in connection with the sale of a consumer product by a supplier to a buyer which relates to the nature of the material or workmanship and affirms or promises that such material or workmanship is defect free or will meet a specified level of performance over a specified period of time, or

B.   any undertaking in writing in connection with the sale by a supplier of a consumer product to refund, repair, replace, or take other remedial action with respect to such product in the event that such product fails to meet the specification set forth in the undertaking, which written affirmation, promise, or undertaking becomes part of the basis of the bargain between a supplier and a buyer for purposes other than resale of such product.

If a contract clause does not meet the requirements of subsection 2301(6), it is not a written warranty covered by the Act. The Act also applies to service contracts, which are defined in subsection 2301(8) as contracts "in writing to perform, over a fixed period of time or for a specified duration, services relating to the maintenance or repair (or both) of a consumer product."

Subsection 2302(a) authorizes the Federal Trade Commission to promulgate regulations specifying mandatory information that warranties must contain so that they do not "mislead a reasonable, average consumer." The Federal Trade Commission has promulgated regulations that require any written warranties covering goods that cost a consumer at least fifteen dollars to specify (1) the parts and persons covered by the warranty, (2) the time period of the warranty, (3) procedures that must be followed to enforce the warranty, and (4) the remedies that are available under the warranty. This information must be accompanied by a statement explaining that some states do not permit disclaimers and remedy limitations and that the consumer may have other rights provided by law. 16 C.F.R. § 701.3 (1984).

A warrantor must furnish a retailer with a copy of the warranty prior to a sale, and a retailer must in turn make copies of the warranty available to customers for inspection. *Id.* § 702. Mail order firms must advertise that the text of their warranties are available. *Id.* § 702.3. Subsection 2302(c) prohibits a warrantor of a product costing at least fifteen dollars from conditioning the warranty on the consumer's use of a particular product unless the Federal Trade Commission has specifically approved the condition. For example, a warrantor may not condition his warranty on the use of certain maintenance products or authorized service dealers. 16 C.F.R. § 700.10 (1984).

Subsection 2303(a) requires any written warranty covering products sold for more than ten dollars to be labeled as either a "full warranty" or a "limited warranty." Subsection 2304(a) requires a "full warranty" (1) to provide a remedy for any defect within a reasonable time and free of charge, (2) not to limit the duration of any implied warranty, (3) not to limit or exclude consequential damages unless the exclusion appears conspicuously on the face of the warranty, and (4) to permit a plaintiff to elect refund or replacement when a product requires an unreasonable number of repairs. A "full warranty" that does not expressly include these terms is deemed to do so. 15 U.S.C. § 2304(e) (1982). The Federal Trade Commission has promulgated regulations that prohibit a "full warranty" from (1) requiring a consumer to bear any expense of repair, 16 C.F.R. § 700.9 (1984), (2) requiring a consumer to mail in a registration card, *Id.* § 700.7, and (3) restricting the rights of transferees unless the restriction is expressly mentioned in the warranty, Id. § 700.6. Limited warranties are not subject to these provisions. Section 2305 permits a warrantor to give a full warranty on some parts of a product and give a limited warranty on other parts. The distinction must be conspicuously described in the warranty.

Section 2308 provides that a written warranty cannot disclaim any implied warranties that arise under state law. A written warranty may, however, limit the duration of implied warranties arising under state law, as long as the limitation (1) is no shorter than the duration of the express warranty, (2) is not unconscionable, and (3) is set forth in clear language permanently displayed on the face of the warranty. The time limitation provision is significant only for limited warranties because "full warranties" cannot limit the duration of implied warranties at all. 15 U.S.C. § 2303(a) (1982).

Subsection 2310(d) provides that any "consumer who is damaged by the failure of a supplier, warrantor, or service contractor to comply with any obligation under this title or under a written warranty, implied warranty, or service contract" may sue for "damages and other legal and equitable relief." The consumer need not have been the actual purchaser of the product in order to sue for injury; horizontal privity is not required. Subsection 2301(5) provides that an injured consumer can sue any warrantor, including any person who is obligated under an implied warranty under state law. The Act does not itself establish the law governing substantive rights under warranties. Courts must refer to state substantive law. *See* MacKenzie v. Chrysler Corp., 607 F.2d 1162, 1166 (5th Cir.1979); Novosel v. Northway Motor Car Corp., 460 F.Supp. 541, 545 (N.D.N.Y.1978).

To maintain a suit, a consumer must notify the warrantor of a defect within a reasonable time if the warranty so requires. 15 U.S.C. § 2304(b)(4)(1982). Moreover, the consumer must give the warrantor a reasonable opportunity to cure the defect. 15 U.S.C. § 2310(e) (1982). Subsection 2304(c) establishes a defense in cases in which the product has been damaged after leaving the seller's control or has been misused. Sellers also retain defenses that are available under state law.

The Act does not specify a measure of damages; courts must rely on state law. Subsection 2310(d)(2) authorizes courts to award attorney's fees to a consumer but not to a prevailing warrantor. Punitive damages are recoverable only if state law so provides. *See* Saval v. BL Ltd., 710 F.2d 1027, 1033 (4th Cir.1983); Schafer v. Chrysler Corp., 544 F.Supp. 182, 185 (N.D.Ind.1982).

Chapter 5

EMERGENCE OF STRICT
TORT LIABILITY

SECTION A. ADOPTION

GREENMAN v. YUBA POWER PRODUCTS, INC.
Supreme Court of California, 1963.
59 Cal.2d 57, 27 Cal.Rptr. 697, 377 P.2d 897.

TRAYNOR, JUSTICE.

Plaintiff brought this action for damages against the retailer and the manufacturer of a Shopsmith, a combination power tool that could be used as a saw, drill, and wood lathe. He saw a Shopsmith demonstrated by the retailer and studied a brochure prepared by the manufacturer. He decided he wanted a Shopsmith for his home workshop, and his wife bought and gave him one for Christmas in 1955. In 1957 he bought the necessary attachments to use the Shopsmith as a lathe for turning a large piece of wood he wished to make into a chalice. After he had worked on the piece of wood several times without difficulty, it suddenly flew out of the machine and struck him on the forehead, inflicting serious injuries. About ten and a half months later, he gave the retailer and the manufacturer written notice of claimed breaches of warranties and filed a complaint against them alleging such breaches and negligence.

After a trial before a jury, the court ruled that there was no evidence that the retailer was negligent or had breached any express warranty and that the manufacturer was not liable for the breach of any implied warranty. Accordingly, it submitted to the jury only the cause of action alleging breach of implied warranties against the retailer and the causes of action alleging negligence and breach of express warranties against the manufacturer. The jury returned a verdict for the retailer against plaintiff and for plaintiff against the manufacturer in the amount of $65,000. The trial court denied the manufacturer's motion for a new trial and entered judgment on the verdict. The manufacturer and plaintiff appeal. Plaintiff seeks a reversal of the part of the judgment in favor of the retailer, however, only in the event that the part of the judgment against the manufacturer is reversed.

Plaintiff introduced substantial evidence that his injuries were caused by defective design and construction of the Shopsmith. His expert witnesses testified that inadequate set screws were used to hold parts of the machine together so that normal vibration caused the tailstock of the lathe to move away from the piece of wood being turned permitting it to fly out of the lathe. They also testified that there were other more positive ways of fastening the parts of the machine together, the use of which would have prevented the accident. The jury could therefore reasonably have concluded that the manufacturer negligently constructed the Shopsmith. The jury could also reasonably have concluded that statements in the manufacturer's brochure were untrue, that they constituted express warranties,[1] and that plaintiff's injuries were caused by their breach.

The manufacturer contends, however, that plaintiff did not give it notice of breach of warranty within a reasonable time and that therefore his cause of action for breach of warranty is barred by section 1769 of the Civil Code. Since it cannot be determined whether the verdict against it was based on the negligence or warranty cause of action or both, the manufacturer concludes that the error in presenting the warranty cause of action to the jury was prejudicial.

Section 1769 of the Civil Code provides: "In the absence of express or implied agreement of the parties, acceptance of the goods by the buyer shall not discharge the seller from liability in damages or other legal remedy for breach of any promise or warranty in the contract to sell or the sale. But, if, after acceptance of the goods, the buyer fails to give notice to the seller of the breach of any promise or warranty within a reasonable time after the buyer knows, or ought to know of such breach, the seller shall not be liable therefor."

Like other provisions of the uniform sales act (Civ.Code, §§ 1721–1800), section 1769 deals with the rights of the parties to a contract of sale or a sale. It does not provide that notice must be given of the breach of a warranty that arises independently of a contract of sale between the parties. Such warranties are not imposed by the sales act, but are the product of common-law decisions that have recognized them in a variety of situations. * * * It is true that in many of these situations the court has invoked the sales act definitions of warranties (Civ.Code, §§ 1732, 1735) in defining the defendant's liability, but it has done so, not because the statutes so required, but because they provided appropriate standards for the court to adopt under the circumstances presented. * * *

1. In this respect the trial court limited the jury to a consideration of two statements in the manufacturer's brochure. (1) "WHEN SHOPSMITH IS IN HORIZONTAL POSITION—Rugged construction of frame provides rigid support from end to end. Heavy centerless-ground steel tubing insurers [sic] perfect alignment of components." (2) "SHOPSMITH maintains its accuracy because every component has positive locks that hold adjustments through rough or precision work."

The notice requirement of section 1769, however, is not an appropriate one for the court to adopt in actions by injured consumers against manufacturers with whom they have not dealt. (La Hue v. Coca–Cola Bottling, 50 Wash.2d 645, 314 P.2d 421, 422; Chapman v. Brown, D.C., 198 F.Supp. 78, 85, affd. Brown v. Chapman, 9 Cir., 304 F.2d 149.) "As between the immediate parties to the sale [the notice requirement] is a sound commercial rule, designed to protect the seller against unduly delayed claims for damages. As applied to personal injuries, and notice to a remote seller, it becomes a booby-trap for the unwary. The injured consumer is seldom 'steeped in the business practice which justifies the rule,' [James, Product Liability, 34 Texas L.Rev. 44, 192, 197] and at least until he has had legal advice it will not occur to him to give notice to one with whom he has had no dealings." (Prosser, Strict Liability to the Consumer, 69 Yale L.J. 1099, 1130, footnotes omitted.) It is true that in Jones v. Burgermeister Brewing Corp., 198 Cal.App.2d 198, 202–203, 18 Cal.Rptr. 311; Perry v. Thrifty Drug Co., 186 Cal.App.2d 410, 411, 9 Cal.Rptr. 50; Arata v. Tonegato, 152 Cal.App.2d 837, 841, 314 P.2d 130, and Maecherlein v. Sealy Mattress Co., 145 Cal.App.2d 275, 278, 302 P.2d 331, the court assumed that notice of breach of warranty must be given in an action by a consumer against a manufacturer. Since in those cases, however, the court did not consider the question whether a distinction exists between a warranty based on a contract between the parties and one imposed on a manufacturer not in privity with the consumer, the decisions are not authority for rejecting the rule of the La Hue and Chapman cases, supra. (Peterson v. Lamb Rubber Co., 54 Cal.2d 339, 343, 5 Cal.Rptr. 863, 353 P.2d 575; People v. Banks, 53 Cal.2d 370, 389, 1 Cal.Rptr. 669, 348 P.2d 102.) We conclude, therefore, that even if plaintiff did not give timely notice of breach of warranty to the manufacturer, his cause of action based on the representations contained in the brochure was not barred.

Moreover, to impose strict liability on the manufacturer under the circumstances of this case, it was not necessary for plaintiff to establish an express warranty as defined in section 1732 of the Civil Code.[2] A manufacturer is strictly liable in tort when an article he places on the market, knowing that it is to be used without inspection for defects, proves to have a defect that causes injury to a human being. Recognized first in the case of unwholesome food products, such liability has now been extended to a variety of other products that create as great or greater hazards if defective. * * *

Although in these cases strict liability has usually been based on the theory of an express or implied warranty running from the manufacturer to the plaintiff, the abandonment of the requirement of a contract between them, the recognition that the liability is not assumed by

---

2. "Any affirmation of fact or any promise by the seller relating to the goods is an express warranty if the natural tendency of such affirmation or promise is to induce the buyer to purchase the goods, and if the buyer purchases the goods relying thereon. No affirmation of the value of the goods, nor any statement purporting to be a statement of the seller's opinion only shall be construed as a warranty."

agreement but imposed by law * * * and the refusal to permit the manufacturer to define the scope of its own responsibility for defective products * * * make clear that the liability is not one governed by the law of contract warranties but by the law of strict liability in tort. Accordingly, rules defining and governing warranties that were developed to meet the needs of commercial transactions cannot properly be invoked to govern the manufacturer's liability to those injured by their defective products unless those rules also serve the purposes for which such liability is imposed.

We need not recanvass the reasons for imposing strict liability on the manufacturer. They have been fully articulated in the cases cited above. (See also 2 Harper and James, Torts, §§ 28.15–28.16, pp. 1569–1574; Prosser, Strict Liability to the Consumer, 69 Yale L.J. 1099; Escola v. Coca Cola Bottling Co., 24 Cal.2d 453, 461, 150 P.2d 436, concurring opinion.) The purpose of such liability is to insure that the costs of injuries resulting from defective products are borne by the manufacturers that put such products on the market rather than by the injured persons who are powerless to protect themselves. Sales warranties serve this purpose fitfully at best. (See Prosser, Strict Liability to the Consumer, 69 Yale L.J. 1099, 1124–1134.) In the present case, for example, plaintiff was able to plead and prove an express warranty only because he read and relied on the representations of the Shopsmith's ruggedness contained in the manufacturer's brochure. Implicit in the machine's presence on the market, however, was a representation that it would safely do the jobs for which it was built. Under these circumstances, it should not be controlling whether plaintiff selected the machine because of the statements in the brochure, or because of the machine's own appearance of excellence that belied the defect lurking beneath the surface, or because he merely assumed that it would safely do the jobs it was built to do. It should not be controlling whether the details of the sales from manufacturer to retailer and from retailer to plaintiff's wife were such that one or more of the implied warranties of the sales act arose. (Civ.Code, § 1735.) "The remedies of injured consumers ought not to be made to depend upon the intricacies of the law of sales." (Ketterer v. Armour & Co., D.C., 200 F. 322, 323; Klein v. Duchess Sandwich Co., 14 Cal.2d 272, 282, 93 P.2d 799.) To establish the manufacturer's liability it was sufficient that plaintiff proved that he was injured while using the Shopsmith in a way it was intended to be used as a result of a defect in design and manufacture of which plaintiff was not aware that made the Shopsmith unsafe for its intended use.

* * *

The judgment is affirmed.

Gibson, C.J., and Schauer, McComb, Peters, Tobriner and Peek, JJ., concur.

Justice Roger J. Traynor

Notes

1. **Historical note.** Before 1963 plaintiffs in products liability cases had to rely on negligence, breach of warranty, or misrepresentation. These theories were not developed as special causes of action for product cases, and they presented plaintiffs with certain obstacles. Negligence required a plaintiff to prove an act of negligence on the part of the defendant. Warranty law required a plaintiff to contend with privity, notice, and disclaimers.

In 1944, in a famous concurring opinion in *Escola v. Coca Cola Bottling Co. of Fresno, supra* page 37, Justice Roger Traynor of the California

Supreme Court argued that these traditional theories were inadequate and that the court should adopt a special theory for product cases. Nineteen years later, in *Greenman*, Justice Traynor had the opportunity to write for a majority of the court and expressly adopted strict tort liability for manufacturers of defective products.

Two years after that, in 1965, the American Law Institute embraced *Greenman* in section 402A of the Restatement (Second) of Torts. Work on this section was begun prior to the *Greenman* decision. Justice Traynor was a member of the Reporter's Advisory Committee and the Council of the American Law Institute when the section was developed. Wade, On Product "Design Defects" and Their Actionability, 33 Vand.L.Rev. 551, 554 (1980). Early drafts of the section applied only to food and drink. Because of the trend of the recent case law, it was eventually expanded to include all products. The history of the development of the section is traced in Wade, On the Nature of Strict Tort Liability for Products, 44 Miss.L.J. 825, 830–831 (1973). *See also,* Page, Generic Product Risks: The Case Against Comment K and for Strict Tort Liability, 58 N.Y.U.L.Rev. 853, 860–872 (1983).

With the imprimatur of a leading court and the American Law Institute, strict product liability swept the country. Nearly every American jurisdiction adopted it.

A major attraction of strict products liability was that it avoided the contractual strictures of warranty law, such as the rules about privity, notice, and disclaimers. A debate quickly arose about whether it was proper for courts to avoid these statutory limits by adopting a parallel tort theory that did not include them. *Compare* Wade, Tort Liability for Products Causing Physical Injury and Article 2 of the UCC, 48 Mo.L.Rev. 1 (1983), *with,* Franklin, When Worlds Collide: Liability Theories and Disclaimers in Defective Product Cases, 18 Stan.L.Rev. 974 (1966). *See also* Dickerson, Products Liability: Dean Wade and the Constitutionality of Section 402A, 44 Tenn.L.Rev. 205 (1977); Donovan, Recent Developments in Products Liability Litigation in New England: The Emerging Confrontation Between the Expanding Law of Torts and the Uniform Commercial Code, 19 Me.L.Rev. 181 (1967); McNichols, Who Says That Strict Tort Disclaimers Can Never Be Effective? The Courts Cannot Agree, 28 Okla.L.Rev. 494 (1975); Miller, The Crossroads: The Case for the Code in Products Liability, 21 Okla.L.Rev. 411 (1968); Titus, Restatement (Second) of Torts Section 402A and the Uniform Commercial Code, 22 Stan.L.Rev. 713 (1970). The debate, however, was mainly academic. Few courts even mentioned this problem when adopting strict products liability, much less accepted the argument that strict liability is preempted by the UCC.

The history of strict tort liability can be divided roughly into three periods. The first period, roughly the decade or so after *Greenman* was dominated by the question of whether states should even adopt strict tort liability. The answer was almost always "yes," but cases in this era are important not only because they adopted strict products liability, but also because they give us insight into a particular court's views about the rationales underlying this theory of recovery. These rationales are useful in current litigation to help resolve specific issues of implementation. The second period, overlapping with the first and continuing roughly through the 1970s, saw courts spending much time and energy addressing the central question of strict products liability: what constitutes a "defective" product? The third period, which we are still in, is one in which courts are continuing to work out the details of strict products liability, by addressing issues such as defenses, causation, and the applicability of strict products liability to particular products and situations.

2. The Restatement of Torts (Second) § 402A (1965) provides:

§ 402A. Special Liability of Seller of Product for Physical Harm to User or Consumer

(1) One who sells any product in a defective condition unreasonably dangerous to the user or consumer or to his property is subject to liability for physical harm thereby caused to the ultimate user or consumer, or to his property, if

(a) the seller is engaged in the business of selling such a product, and

(b) it is expected to and does reach the user or consumer without substantial change in the condition in which it is sold.

(2) The rule stated in Subsection (1) applies although

(a) the seller has exercised all possible care in the preparation and sale of his product, and

(b) the user or consumer has not bought the product from or entered into any contractual relation with the seller.

3. How would Justice Traynor decide the following cases? How does Justice Traynor's formulation of strict liability differ from the Restatement?

A. A can of spinach contains worms.

B. A spot remover, that does an adequate job of removing spots, causes hepatitis.

C. A camper truck is sold with an inadequate warning concerning the risks of underinflation of tires and overloading of the truck.

D. A riding lawn mower is sold with a blade guard that did not enclose the blade at the rear of the deck housing under the operator's seat. The tip of the blade was 12 to 14 inches from the rear of the mower. The mower was equipped with a bumper on the rear. Below is a photograph of the underside of the mower:

The operators manual cautioned to keep children away from the mower while it was operating. Plaintiff, a two-year-old, was severely injured when the eight-year-old operator of the mower backed it against him, knocked him down, and ran over him.

E. A tobacco product that causes cancer, but it is sold before the risk was scientifically knowable.

4. The *Greenman* decision and the Restatement § 402A provided the intellectual basis for the transition from warranty to strict liability in tort, and represent the beginning of modern products liability law. A great many developments, however, have taken place since 1965. As a result, many courts today depart substantially from the Restatement rule.

5. The basic elements of a strict product liability cause of action are as follows:

1. The defendant was in the business of producing or selling the product.

2. The product was expected to and did reach the purchaser without substantial change in the condition in which it was sold.

3. The product was defective at the time it left the defendant's control.

4. The harm resulted when the product was being used in a reasonably foreseeable manner.

5. The person harmed was foreseeable.

6. The defect was the cause in fact and proximate cause of physical harm to plaintiff's person or property.

The requirement of defect, the third element, represents the most important restriction on liability. This issue is treated in Chapters 6, 7, and 9. Causation in fact (element 6) is addressed in Chapter 11. Proximate cause and foreseeability of the plaintiff (elements 5 and 6) are addressed in Chapter 12. The first element, that the defendant be in the business of selling the product, is covered in Chapter 16.

The fourth element, misuse, will not be treated in a separate section of the book. It is really not a concept that stands on its own. Rather, it is relevant to a variety of issues including defect, proximate cause, and contributory negligence. This book will deal with each of these aspects of misuse in the section of the book dealing with the subjects to which it relates.

The second element, substantial change, is also treated in two places in the book. This is because courts deal with this issue differently, depending on such variables as the type of defect, the type of product, and the time when the change is made. *See* Chapter 9 section B. 1. (Delegability of the Design Process), and Chapter 12 section A. 4. (Product Alteration).

The above represents a very general statement of the elements of a strict liability action. As we shall see, courts vary dramatically in the way they interpret and apply these elements.

SECTION B. POLICIES UNDERLYING STRICT LIABILITY

Courts and scholars have advanced a variety of policy justifications for strict tort liability. Six of them are briefly summarized below.

1. **Compensation (or loss spreading).** Losses inevitably result from the use of complex modern products. These losses can have a disastrous effect on the individual who experiences them. It is humane and fair to shift these losses to all consumers of the product. This can

be accomplished by imposing liability on manufacturers, thus, forcing them to raise prices enough to pay for the losses or insure against them. *See* Holford, The Limits of Strict Liability for Product Design and Manufacture, 52 Tex.L.Rev. 81, 82–84, 87–88 (1973); Wade, On The Nature of Strict Liability for Products, 44 Miss.L.J. 825, 826 (1973).

2. **Deterrence.** Tort liability increases costs, but competition induces manufacturers to minimize them. Imposing liability on manufacturers, therefore, provides them with an incentive to market safer products. In theory, strict liability may create more deterrence than negligence-based liability since negligence imposes liability only if the defendant fails to take measures that a reasonable person would take. Strict liability induces manufacturers to go beyond this if the cost of the added safety measures is less than the potential cost of liability for failing to take them. *See* Holford, The Limits of Strict Liability for Product Design and Manufacture, 52 Tex.L.Rev. 81, 82–84, 87–88 (1973); Wade, On The Nature of Strict Liability for Products, 44 Miss.L.J. 825, 826 (1973).

3. **Encouraging useful conduct.** The first two policies listed, compensation and deterrence, are most commonly cited as the bases for strict tort liability. They are clearly not the only considerations, however, because they almost always point in the direction of imposing liability. Yet, no court has imposed the liability of an insurer on manufacturers by requiring them to pay for all harm caused by their products. This is because of the fear that such absolute liability would place unreasonable burdens on manufacturers and discourage them from producing useful products. The policy of avoiding over-deterrence by balancing the needs of defendants against the needs of plaintiffs is clearly at work, although it is seldom articulated. *See* Epstein, Products Liability: The Search for the Middle Ground, 56 N.C.L.Rev. 643 (1978); Fischer, Products Liability—An Analysis of Market Share Liability, 34 Vand.L.Rev. 1623, 1628–1629 (1981); Klemme, The Enterprise Liability Theory of Torts, 47 U.Colo.L.Rev. 153 (1976).

4. **Proof problems.** Quite often the manufacturer of a defective product is negligent. Modern complexities, however, frequently make it very difficult for plaintiff to establish this. This is particularly so because he is usually at a relative disadvantage because the manufacturer has greater access to expertise, information, and resources. Imposing strict liability relieves plaintiff of the burden of proving fault. *See* Keeton, Product Liability and the Meaning of Defect, 5 St. Mary's L.J. 30, 34–35 (1973); Schwartz, Foreword: Understanding Products Liability, 67 Calif.L.Rev. 435, 459–61 (1979).

The policy of helping plaintiffs avoid proof problems has been quite influential. Throughout these materials you will see instances where courts either eliminate the need to prove a particular element of plaintiff's case, or they shift the burden of proof on the issue to defendant. Examples include proof of causation in warning cases, proof of identity of defendant as the person who manufactured the product, proof that a risk inherent in the product was scientifically unknowable, and proof that the utility of a product's design outweighs its benefits. Indeed, the most significant difference between negligence and strict liability may turn out to be where the burden of proof lies with respect to such issues.

5. **Protection of consumer expectations.** Consumers should be protected from unknown dangers in products. This is particularly true since modern advertising and marketing techniques induce consumers to rely on manufacturers to provide them with safe, high-quality products. Shapo, A Representational Theory of Consumer Protection: Doctrine, Function and Legal Liability for Product Disappointment, 60 Va.L.Rev. 1109 (1974).

6. **Cost internalization.** Forcing manufacturers to raise prices in order to pay for harm caused by their products will lead to a more efficient allocation of resources. The prices of products will then more nearly include all of their true costs, including accident costs. Being aware of the true costs of products, consumers will make more intelligent decisions about which products to purchase. *See* Franklin, Tort Liability for Hepatitis: An Analysis and a Proposal, 24 Stan.L.Rev. 439, 462–463, 465–472 (1972); Katz, The Function of Tort Liability in Technology Assessment, 38 U.Cin.L.Rev. 587, 636, 662 (1969).

Each of these policies has its strengths and weaknesses. None of them, singly or in combination, provides a completely satisfactory basis for strict liability. This may help explain why the doctrine continues to evolve. For a general evaluation of these policies see, Owen, Rethinking the Policies of Strict Products Liability, 33 Vand.L.Rev. 681 (1980); Powers, A Modest Proposal to Abandon Strict Products Liability, 1991 U.Ill.L.Rev. 639; Powers, Distinguishing Between Products and Services in Strict Liability, 62 N.C.L.Rev. 415, 423–428 (1984).

The following readings discuss the major policies in greater detail. As you study strict liability consider whether these policies are valid and whether the courts are effectively implementing them.

KLEMME, THE ENTERPRISE LIABILITY THEORY OF TORTS

47 U.Colo.L.Rev. 153, 158–165 (1976).

II. THE THEORY OF ENTERPRISE LIABILITY STATED GENERALLY

In its broadest terms the theory of enterprise liability in torts is that losses to society created or caused by an enterprise or, more simply, by an activity, ought to be borne by that enterprise or activity. Stated somewhat more precisely, the theory contemplates that losses historically recognized as compensable when caused by an enterprise, or activity, such as producing, distributing and using automobiles, ought to be borne by those persons who have some logical relationship with that enterprise or activity. The underlying justification for this theory, most ably articulated and illustrated by Guido Calabresi some years ago,[26] is a well known ethical premise of classical economics. This postulate is that, recognizing at any one point in time that the total resources available to a society are limited, the "best" way for the members of a community to decide collectively how they want those limited resources to be used and distributed in order to satisfy most efficiently the greatest possible number of the members' individual wants and desires is through an open, competitive market system. The various competing uses to which the community's limited resources might be allocated in order to satisfy the maximum possible individual wants and desires will accordingly be determined through operation of the laws of supply and demand.

To illustrate: at any point in time, the steel available to a society will be limited. Whether more steel should be used to produce refrigerators rather than be used to produce cars will depend on whether or not those desiring more refrigerators are willing to pay a higher price for those refrigerators than others will be willing to pay for cars.

For the pricing mechanism of the market place to achieve this goal of the "best" allocation of the community's total limited resources, a supplier of goods or services must accurately reflect in the prices he seeks for his goods or services the "true" costs of making them available. If, for example, a druggist consistently sells his aspirin below his costs because of inaccurate cost accounting, but he nonetheless is able to stay in business because he more than offsets his aspirin-sales losses from the total profit he makes on his sales of other articles, the "best" allocation of the community's limited resources has not occurred. Ideally, the druggist should raise his price for aspirin. The labor and other resources allocated to the production of aspirin will be reduced because of a decrease in demand for the higher-priced aspirin. These resources will in turn become available for use in the production of other goods for which, at a lower price, there would be a greater demand. With the increased production of these other goods, the price at which they are sold should decline. As a consequence of all this, the community ends up with a better allocation of its limited resources (available labor, materials, etc.) than it had before, that is, one which does more to maximize the total individual desires of the society's members at less expense to them.

The distortions which can occur in this ideal pricing, resource allocation process are numerous and varied. Government tax policies and subsidies (whether to suppliers or purchasers) as well as its borrowing and expenditure practices and other monetary policies have the potential for distorting the process. Unrealistic cost accounting by suppliers and irrational considerations influencing purchasers, whether induced by fair or unfair advertising or other similar causes, will result in a distortion. Monopolistic business practices, control over large

---

26. Calabresi, [*Some Thoughts on Risk Distribution and the Law of Torts,* 70 Yale L.J. 499, 500–06 (1961)]. *See also* James, [*An Evolution of the Fault Concept,* 32 Tenn.L.Rev. 394, 400–01 (1965)].

amounts of investment capital, and the existence of corporate conglomerates (where the losses of an unprofitable division are in part written off against the more profitable operations of another division), likewise have the potential for distorting the process.

The relevance of these considerations to tort law is that virtually every kind of loss which tort law has historically considered compensable is a loss of part of the community's total, though limited, available resources. Whether the law shifts the loss to the defendant or leaves it on the plaintiff, the loss will (1) not be eliminated and (2) will not remain entirely on whichever party the law chooses to place the loss on, or leave it on, initially. Today, especially through one or more of the diverse public and private insurance systems available, the initial loss-bearer, whether it be the plaintiff or the defendant, will be able in most cases to pass on all or a significant part of the loss to other persons in society.

In short, the theories of liability which the tort law uses for the purpose of deciding whether the loss should be left on the plaintiff or reallocated to the defendant will also determine how such losses, or costs, are to be distributed among various segments of the society. In almost all instances these losses will be reflected as costs in the pricing mechanism of the market place and ultimately in the allocation of the community's resources and in the distribution of its wealth among its members.

III.   The Theory of Enterprise Liability Stated Generally and the Rule of Actual Cause

The rules of liability and nonliability of the tort law therefore function in most instances as cost accounting, i.e., cost distribution rules. In large measure they determine who will ultimately, through the pricing mechanism of the market place, bear the costs of the tort losses generated by the numerous activities people carry on in society.

Looking at the tort liability rules as cost accounting rules and then trying to fit this idea into the theory of enterprise liability as one which says the costs of an activity ought to be borne by the activity which creates or causes them immediately presents a problem. The problem is: no compensable tort loss is ever the "but for" result of only one enterprise or activity. It is always the result of an infinite number of "but for" causes or activities. But for the plaintiff's grandparents immigrating to this country; but for his parents meeting, marrying and conceiving him; but for the plaintiff's decision to get out of bed in the morning; but for his decision to walk to the post box to mail a letter, etc., the plaintiff would not have been struck and injured by the defendant's car, regardless of whether the defendant's driving is characterized as good or bad. To which, if any, of the plaintiff's "but for" activities, or to which one of the comparable universe of "but for" activities of the defendant, should the plaintiff's losses (as well as those of the defendant) be assigned? All these infinite "but for" activities "created" the loss in the sense that "but for" any one of them the losses would probably not have occurred. How should the tort law through its rules of liability and nonliability "cost account" for these losses? On what rational basis should the law decide which particular enterprise the loss should be treated as a cost of having engaged in?

One thing is clear. The theory of enterprise liability as it is usually put does not provide a rational answer to this basic question. An infinite number of enterprises created the loss, and the general statement of the enterprise liability theory alone provides no rational criteria for making an intelligent selection among them.

The general statement of the theory that the costs of an activity or enterprise ought to be borne by the activity or enterprise which created them should not, however, be rejected as devoid of analytic value. It has at least two uses. First, the underlying economic assumptions and values of the general statement of the theory also underlie the specific criteria of the theory, which will be considered later. Second, these assumptions and values also provide an explanation for why, as long as the tort law has been around and regardless of the changing theories of liability upon which the courts have shifted losses from plaintiffs to defendants, it has been "elementary policy that a defendant should not be held liable for the harm the plaintiff complains of unless the plaintiff can at least show that the defendant in fact caused the harm." [37]

Why should this "elementary policy" of the tort law—the "but for" rule of actual cause—have been so constant? Throughout the development of tort law, theories and rules for labeling conduct tortious have changed. So, too, the law governing the kinds of losses the courts have been willing to consider compensable, that is, worthy of being shifted, has changed. With but a few recently developed and very limited exceptions,[38] however, the rule has been: no matter how tortious the defendant's conduct may have been and no matter how long or how strongly a given loss has been considered compensable, unless the plaintiff is able to persuade the fact finder by a preponderance of the evidence that the defendant's activity was at least *one* of the infinite "but for" causes of his losses, the plaintiff cannot recover.

This requirement of "but for" cause cannot be explained on the ground that it is essential to having a tort judgment provide a deterrent effect on the defendant's future conduct. On the contrary, exactly the opposite seems true. A more valid explanation of the rule lies in the theory of enterprise liability and its rationale of using the market place

---

37. C. Gregory & H. Kalven, Cases and Materials on Torts 5 (2d ed. 1969).

38. *See, e.g.,* the rule of Summers v. Tice, 33 Cal.2d 80, 199 P.2d 1 (1948), stated and more fully explained in Haft v. Lone Palm Hotel, 3 Cal.3d 756, 478 P.2d 465, 91 Cal.Rptr. 745 (1970). Where the plaintiff has established a prima facie case of (1) tortious conduct on the defendant's part toward the plaintiff and (2) that the conduct might *possibly* have caused plaintiff's loss, but (3) the plaintiff has not been able to establish a prima facie case of probable cause because the very nature of defendant's tortious conduct has made it extremely difficult, if not impossible, for the plaintiff to do so, and (4) the plaintiff has otherwise done all that could reasonably be expected to establish such a case, then the burden of proof shifts to the defendant to prove that his conduct was not in fact an actual cause of the plaintiff's loss. * * *

as a tool for "best" allocating the community's limited resources. A case illustrating this point is *New York Central Railroad v. Grimstad*.[39] In that case the court held, notwithstanding the probable negligence of the railroad in not providing adequate life saving equipment on one of its barges, the trial court should have granted what today would be a motion for a directed verdict against the plaintiff, because the plaintiff, as the widow of a deceased employee who had drowned, had not offered sufficient evidence from which a jury could reasonably have found that "but for" the defendant's negligent omission the deceased would not have died.

Now if deterrence is the rationale behind the "but for" rule, the *Grimstad* result is wrong because, whether or not the defendant's conduct caused the loss, had liability been imposed the defendant would have understood it was being imposed because of his doing a tortious act, that is, because of his having engaged in a socially undesirable, risk creating act. That would have provided the deterrence, except for the possible dysfunctional effect which might have arisen because the defendant might have felt it "unjust" to hold him liable without adequate proof of actual cause. Aside from this consideration, however, the objective of deterrence would seem to have little to do with "but for" cause.

Consider though what might have happened in *Grimstad* if the law had not required proof of actual cause, but only proof of tortious conduct by the defendant (towards anyone) and proof of compensable loss by the plaintiff (loss of her husband's financial support). Mrs. Grimstad could then have sued, say a negligent cab driver (and his employer), and recovered simply upon proof of his negligence and her loss. Having been negligent, the cab driver is fairly in need of deterrence; having him understand he was being required to pay Mrs. Grimstad because of that negligence would provide the deterrence. I have little doubt that if the tort law were to abandon the "but for" rule, the risks of tort liability would become so much greater that the tort law would have a far greater, rather than lesser, deterrent effect on human behavior.

The theory of enterprise liability suggests a more plausible explanation for the "but for" rule. Suppose, not being burdened by a "but for" rule, Mrs. Grimstad was allowed to shift her loss to the negligent cab driver who in no way was a "but for" cause of her otherwise compensable loss. Who, ultimately, would pay for the loss? The likely answer is the cab owners (through smaller profits), the cab drivers (through lower wages), or the cab users (through higher fares). In any event, a significant distortion would occur in the pricing mechanism of the market place as it relates to cab services, with a consequent distortion in the "best" allocation of the community's total, limited resources.

While the general statement of the theory of enterprise liability does not tell us from among all the infinite "but for" causes which may have brought about the plaintiff's loss *which particular* "but for" activity or

39. 264 F. 334 (2d Cir.1920).

enterprise the loss should be assigned to, it does tell us we ought not assign it to an activity which had no "but for" causal relationship with that particular loss at all.[40]

POSNER, STRICT LIABILITY: A COMMENT
2 J.Legal Studies 205–212 (1973).

Within the last year there have appeared several major articles[1] that, while otherwise extremely diverse, share a strong preference (in one case implicit) for using the principle of "strict liability" to resolve legal conflicts over resource use.[2] I shall argue in this comment that the authors of these articles fail to make a convincing case for strict liability, primarily because they do not analyze the economic consequences of the principle correctly.

I

To explicate these consequences I shall use the now familiar example of the railroad engine that emits sparks which damage crops along the railroad's right of way. I shall assume that the costs of transactions between the railroad and the farmers are so high that the liability imposed by the law will not be shifted by negotiations between the parties.

40. For one court's recognition of the proposition that rules of "but for" cause do have an impact on the allocation of resources and the distribution of wealth, and that therefore such matters should be taken into account, particularly the "fairness" question of who ultimately should bear the costs of tort-like losses, see Haft v. Lone Palm Hotel, 3 Cal.3d 756, 478 P.2d 465, 91 Cal.Rptr. 745 (1970). In justification of the exception to the normal rules of "but for" cause which the court was articulating (see note 38 *supra* for the rule), the court observed:

> This result is also consistent with the emerging tort policy of assigning liability to a party who is in the best position to distribute losses over a group which should reasonably bear them. See generally Calabresi, *Some Thoughts on Risk Distribution and the Law of Torts* (1961) 70 Yale L.J. 499. In the instant case the defendant motel owner, and more generally the entire class of those who frequent defendants' motel, were, in an economic view, the beneficiaries of the "cost savings" accompanying the non-employment of a lifeguard. It is better that this entire group bear the burden of the loss resulting from the "economy," rather than to require one particular guest to absorb the entire loss. By assigning liability to the motel in those cases in which

no direct evidence establishes causation, we make sure that all motel guests bear their fair share of these damages, since the motel owner is likely to treat either the costs of liability insurance, or the actual costs of litigation, as a direct expense of its business and establish its fees accordingly.

Id. at 775 n. 20, 478 P.2d at 477 n. 20, 91 Cal.Rptr. at 757 n. 20.

1. William F. Baxter & Lillian R. Altree, Legal Aspects of Airport Noise, 15 J.Law & Econ. 1 (1972); Guido Calabresi & Jon T. Hirschoff, Toward a Test for Strict Liability in Torts, 81 Yale L.J. 1055 (1972); George P. Fletcher, Fairness and Utility in Tort Theory, 85 Harv.L.Rev. 537 (1972); Richard A. Epstein, A Theory of Strict Liability, 2 J.Leg. Studies 151 (1973). My analysis is also an implicit criticism of Marc A. Franklin, Tort Liability for Hepatitis: An Analysis and Appraisal, 24 Stan.L.Rev. 439 (1972), especially *id.* at 462–64, and of much judicial writing on the subject; see, *e.g.*, Escola v. Coca–Cola Bottling Co., 24 Cal.2d 453, 462, 150 P.2d 436, 440–41 (1944) (Traynor, J., concurring).

2. The concept of strict liability is a various one, but at its core is the notion that one who injures another should be held liable whether or not the injurer was negligent or otherwise at fault.

The economic goal of liability rules in such a case is to maximize the joint value of the interfering activities, railroading and farming.[3]   To identify the value-maximizing solution requires a comparison of the costs to the railroad of taking steps to reduce spark emissions to various levels, including zero, and the costs to farmers of either tolerating or themselves taking steps to reduce the damage to their property from the sparks.   The value-maximizing solution may turn out to involve changes by both parties in their present behavior; for example, the railroad may have to install a good but not perfect spark arrester and the farmer may have to leave an unplanted buffer space between the railroad right of way and his tilled fields.   Or, the value-maximizing solution may involve changes by the railroad only, by the farmer only, or by neither party.

Let us consider what, if any, different effects negligence and strict liability—competing approaches to the design of liability rules—might have in nudging railroad and farmer toward the value-maximizing (efficient) solution, under various assumptions as to what that solution is.

The railroad will be adjudged negligent if the crop damage exceeds the cost to the railroad of avoiding that damage.[4]   But the farmer will still not prevail if the cost of the measures *he* might have taken to avoid the damage to his crops is less than the crop damage; this is the rule of contributory negligence.

If the efficient solution requires only that the railroad take some measure to reduce the farmer's crop damage, then the negligence approach leads us toward the efficient solution.   Since the railroad is liable for the damage and the damage is greater than the cost to the railroad of preventing it,[5] the railroad will adopt the preventive measure in order to avoid a larger damage judgment.   If the efficient solution is either that the railroad do nothing or that both parties do nothing, the negligence standard will again lead to the efficient solution.   Not being liable, the railroad will have no incentive to adopt preventive measures; the farmer will have no incentive to take precautions either, since by hypothesis the cost of doing so would exceed the crop damage that he suffers.   If the efficient solution requires only the farmer to take precautions, the negligence approach again points in the right direction.   The railroad is not liable and does not take precautions.   The farmer takes precautions, as we want him to do, because they cost less than the crop damage they prevent.

That leaves only the case where the efficient solution involves avoidance by both parties.   Again the negligence standard should lead

---

3.   Or, stated otherwise, to maximize the joint value of the railroad's right of way and the farmer's land.

4.   The meaning of negligence is explored in Richard A. Posner, A Theory of Negligence, 1 J.Leg. Studies 29 (1972). The example in text assumes that the probability of the damage occurring is one; the assumption is not essential to the analysis. It also assumes that the only possibilities are no crops or no sparks; this assumption, which is again not essential to the analysis, will be relaxed.

5.   If the cost of prevention exceeded the damage cost, prevention would not be the efficient solution.   The efficient solution would be to permit the damage to take place.

toward an efficient solution. The farmer will adopt his cost-justified avoidance measure so as not to be barred by the contributory negligence rule and once he has done so the railroad will adopt its cost-justified avoidance measure to avoid liability for the accidents that the farmer's measure does not prevent.

The foregoing discussion must be qualified in one important respect. If the efficient solution requires only the railroad to take precautions but the farmer could take a precaution that, although more costly than the railroad's (otherwise *it* would be the optimum solution), would be less costly than the crop damage, the farmer's failure to adopt the measure will, nonetheless, be deemed contributory negligence. He will therefore adopt it and the railroad will have no incentive to adopt what is in fact the cheaper method of damage prevention.

A principle of strict liability, with no defense of contributory negligence, would produce an efficient solution where that solution was either for the railroad alone to take precautions or for neither party to do so,[6] but not in the other two cases. In the case where the efficient solution is for the farmer alone to take avoidance measures, strict liability would not encourage efficiency, for with the railroad liable for all crop damage the farmer would have no incentive to avoid such damage even if it was cheaper for him to do so; he would be indifferent between the crops and compensation for their destruction. Similarly, in the case where the efficient solution consists of precautions by both railroad and farmer, strict liability would give the farmer no incentive to shoulder his share of the responsibility. But we need only add a defense of contributory negligence in strict liability cases in order to give the farmer an incentive to take precautions where appropriate. There would still be the problem of inefficient solutions where the farmer's precaution, although less costly than his crop damage, was more costly than the railroad's precaution; but this could be remedied by redefining the contributory negligence defense—a step that should be taken in any event.

At least as a first approximation, then, a strict liability standard with a defense of contributory negligence is as efficient as the conventional negligence standard, but not more efficient. This conclusion would appear to hold with even greater force where, as in a products liability case, there is (or can readily be created) a seller-buyer relationship between injurer and victim. Indeed, it can be shown that in that situation an efficient solution is likely to be reached not only under either strict liability (plus contributory negligence) or negligence, but equally with no tort liability at all.

The cost of a possibly dangerous product to the consumer has two elements: the price of the product and an expected accident cost (for a risk-neutral purchaser, the cost of an accident if it occurs multiplied by

6. In the first case, the railroad would be liable and would have an incentive to adopt the precaution. In the second case, the railroad would still be liable but it would have no incentive to adopt precautions; it would prefer to pay a judgment cost that by hypothesis would be lower than the cost of the precautions.

the probability of occurrence). Regardless of liability, the seller will have an incentive to adopt any cost-justified precaution, because, by lowering the total cost of the product to the buyer, it will enable the seller to increase his profit.[7] Where, however, the buyer can prevent the accident at lower cost than the seller, the buyer can be counted on to take the precaution rather than the seller, for by doing so the buyer will minimize the sum of the price of the product (which will include the cost of any precautions taken by the seller) and the expected accident cost.[8]

Although both strict liability and negligence appear to provide efficient solutions to problems of conflicting resource uses, they do not have identical economic effects. The difference comes in cases where the efficient solution is for neither party to the interference to do anything. This is the category of interferences known in negligence law as "unavoidable accidents." They are rarely unavoidable in the literal sense. But frequently the cost either to injurer or to victim of taking measures to prevent an accident exceeds the expected accident cost and in such a case efficiency requires that the accident be permitted to occur. Under a negligence standard, the injurer is not liable; under strict liability, he is. What if any economic difference does this make?

It can be argued that unless an industry is liable for its unavoidable accidents, consumers may be led to substitute the product of the industry for the safer product of another industry. Suppose the only difference between railroads and canals as methods of transportation were that railroads had more unavoidable accidents. If the railroad industry were not liable for those accidents, the price of railroad transportation would be the same as the price of transportation by canal, yet we would want people to use canals rather than railroads because the former were superior in the one respect—safety—in which the two methods differed. In principle, a negligence standard would require the railroad to bear the cost of those accidents. They are not unavoidable. In fact, they could be avoided at zero cost by the substitution of canal for railroad transportation. But perhaps courts are incapable of making inter-industry comparisons in applying the negligence standard. Nonetheless the argument affords no basis for preferring strict liability to negligence, since an identical but opposite distortion is created by strict liability. Compare two different tracts of land that are identical in every respect except that one is immediately adjacent to a railroad line and one is well back from any railroad line. If the railroad is strictly liable for crop damage inflicted by engine sparks there will be no incentive to use the tract near

---

7. Suppose the price of a product is $10 and the expected accident cost 10¢; then the total cost to the (risk-neutral) consumer is $10.10. If the producer can reduce the expected accident cost to 5¢—say at a cost of 3¢ to himself—then he can increase the price of the product to $10.05, since the cost to the (risk-neutral) consumer remains the same. Thus his profit per unit is increased by 2¢. (In fact, he will be able to increase his total profits even more by raising price

less.) The extra profit will eventually be bid away by competition from producers but that is in the nature of competitive advantages.

8. This is actually a more efficient solution than either negligence or strict liability, since it avoids the problem we noted earlier of the law's economically incorrect definition of contributory negligence.
* * *

the railroad line for fire-insensitive uses and to shift the growing of flammable crops to the tract that is remote from a railroad line, even though such a rearrangement may eliminate all crop damage at zero cost.

A related misconception involves the question of the comparative safety level in the long run under strict liability versus negligence liability. The level of safety is unaffected in the short run by which liability rule is chosen. Even if the injurer is strictly liable, he will not try to prevent an accident where the cost of prevention exceeds the accident cost; he will prefer to pay the victim's smaller damages. However, he will have an incentive to invest in research and development efforts designed to develop a cost-justified method of accident prevention, for such a method would lower the cost of complying with a rule of strict liability. It is tempting to conclude that strict liability encourages higher, and in the long run more efficient, levels of safety, but this is incorrect. Rather than creating an incentive to engage in research on safety, a rule of strict liability merely shifts that incentive. Under the negligence standard the cost of unavoidable accidents is borne by the victims of accidents. They can reduce this cost in the long run by financing research into and development of cost-justified measures by which to protect themselves. The victims will not themselves organize for research, but they will provide the market for firms specializing in the development of new safety appliances.[9]

Let us consider some other possible differences, in economic effect, between strict liability and negligence. It might appear that strict liability would reduce the costs of tort litigation, both by simplifying the issues in a trial and thereby reducing its costs and by removing an element of uncertainty and thereby facilitating settlements, which are cheaper than trials. But the matter is more complex than this. By increasing the scope of liability, strict liability enlarges the universe of claims, so even if the fraction of cases that go to trial is smaller the absolute number may be larger. And, by increasing the certainty that the plaintiff will prevail, strict liability encourages him to spend more money on the litigation; conceivably, therefore, the costs of trials might actually increase.[10]

Under strict liability, in effect the railroad (in our example) insures the farmer against the loss of his crops; under negligence liability, the farmer must obtain and pay for insurance himself (or self-insure). Thus, although strict liability, under the name "enterprise liability," has long been defended on the ground [11] that it permits accident losses to be

---

9. In principle, the costs of research should be included in the basic negligence calculus; in practice, we may assume they are not.

10. On the determinants of the choice to litigate rather than to settle and of expenditures on litigation see Richard A. Posner, The Behavior of Administrative Agen-

cies, 1 J.Leg. Studies 305–23 (1972); see also William M. Landes, An Economic Analysis of the Courts, 14 J. Law & Econ. 61 (1971).

11. Not an economic ground. See Richard A. Posner, Book Review, 37 U.Chi. L.Rev. 643 (1970).

spread more widely, there is little to this argument: the farmer can avoid a concentrated loss by insuring. However, if we were confident that the cost of insuring was lower for the railroad than for the farmer, we might on this ground prefer strict liability.[12]

Strict liability increases the costs of railroading, in our example, and negligence the costs of farming. But the implications for the overall distribution of income and wealth are uncertain, at least in the example, so intertwined were the economic interests of railroads and farmers during the period when the modern system of negligence liability was taking shape. Any increase in the cost of railroading would be borne in significant part by farmers since they were the railroads' principal customers. The intertwining of economic interests is characteristic of many modern tort contexts as well, such as automobile and product accidents. Most victims of automobile accidents are owners of automobiles; victims of defective products are also consumers.

Additional considerations come into play where there is a buyer-seller relationship between victim and injurer; but they relate primarily to the question whether sellers' liability (either strict liability or negligence) has different consequences from no liability (*i.e.*, buyers' liability). There are two reasons for believing that there might be different safety consequences. First, if the buyers of a product are risk preferring, they may be unwilling to pay for a safety improvement even if the cost is less than the expected accident cost that the improvement would eliminate. Under a rule of no liability, the improvement will not be made; under a rule either of strict liability or of negligence liability, the improvement will be made.[13] But the higher level of safety is not optimum in the economic sense, since it is higher than consumers want.

Second, consumers may lack knowledge of product safety. Criticisms of market processes based on the consumer's lack of information are often superficial, because they ignore the fact that competition among sellers generates information about the products sold. There is however a special consideration in the case of safety information: the firm that advertises that its product is safer than a competitor's may plant fears in the minds of potential consumers where none existed before. If a product hazard is small, or perhaps great but for some reason not widely known (*e.g.*, cigarettes, for a long time), consumers may not be aware of it. In these circumstances a seller may be reluctant to advertise a safety improvement, because the advertisement will contain an implicit representation that the product is hazardous (otherwise,

12. The farmer may not want to insure; he may be a risk preferrer. A risk preferrer is someone who likes to take chances. He will pay $1 for a lottery ticket although the prize is $1000 and his chances of winning only one in 2000. And he may prefer to accept a one one-thousandth chance of a $1000 loss rather than pay $1 to insure against the loss. He will be especially hostile to the idea of paying $1.10 for that insurance, a more realistic example since insurance involves administrative expenses that consume a part of the premium. Hence, if many farmers are risk preferring and do not want insurance, the benefits of strict liability, as perceived by them, may be slight.

13. This assumes that the producer cannot disclaim liability; the effect of a disclaimer is to shift liability to the consumer.

the improvement would be without value). He must balance the additional sales that he may gain from his rivals by convincing consumers that his product is safer than theirs against the sales that he may lose by disclosing to consumers that the product contains hazards of which they may not have been aware, or may have been only dimly aware. If advertising and marketing a safety improvement are thus discouraged, the incentive to adopt such improvements is reduced. But make the producer liable for the consequences of a hazardous product, and no question of advertising safety improvements to consumers will arise. He will adopt cost-justified precautions not to divert sales from competitors but to minimize liability to injured consumers.

In principle, we need not assume that the only possible sources of information about product safety are the manufacturers of the product. Producers in other industries would stand to gain from exposing an unsafe product, but if their products are not close substitutes for the unsafe product, as is implicit in our designation of them as members of other industries, the gain will be small and the incentive to invest money in investigating the safety of the product and disseminating the results of the investigation slight. Firms could of course try to sell product information directly to consumers; the problem is that because property rights in information are relatively undeveloped, the supplier of information is frequently unable to recover his investment in obtaining and communicating it.

The information problem just discussed provides an arguable basis for rejecting *caveat emptor* in hazardous-products cases, but not for replacing negligence with strict liability in such cases, which is the trend of the law. The traditional pockets of strict liability, such as respondeat superior and the liability of blasters and of keepers of vicious animals, can be viewed as special applications of negligence theory.[14] The question whether a general substitution of strict for negligence liability would improve efficiency seems at this stage hopelessly conjectural; the question is at bottom empirical and the empirical work has not been done.

R. POSNER, ECONOMIC ANALYSIS OF LAW
161 (3d Ed. 1986).

There are, however, significant economic differences between negligence and strict liability. Think back to our distinction between more care and less activity as methods of reducing the probability of an accident. One way to avoid an auto accident is to drive more slowly; another is to drive less. In general, however, courts do not try to determine the optimal level of the activity that gives rise to an accident; they do not ask, when a driver is in an accident, whether the benefit of the particular trip (maybe he was driving to the grocery store to get some gourmet food for his pet iguana) was equal to or greater than the

---

14. See * * * Richard A. Posner, *supra* note 4, at 42–44, 76.

costs, including the expected accident cost to other users of the road, or whether driving was really cheaper than walking or taking the train when all social costs are reckoned in. Such a judgment is too difficult for a court to make in an ordinary tort case. Only if the benefits of the activity are obviously very slight, as where a man runs into a burning building to retrieve an old hat and does so as carefully as he can in the circumstances but is seriously burned nonetheless, will the court find that engaging in the activity was itself negligence, even though once the decision to engage in the activity was made, the actor (plaintiff or defendant) conducted himself with all possible skill and circumspection.

SHAVELL, STRICT LIABILITY VERSUS NEGLIGENCE
9 J.Legal Studies 1, 2–9 (1980).

UNILATERAL CASE

This case (as well as the bilateral case) will be considered in each of several situations distinguished by the nature of the relationship between injurers and victims.

Accidents between strangers * * *: In this subcase it is supposed that injurers and victims are strangers, that neither are sellers of a product, and that injurers may choose to engage in an activity which puts victims at risk.

By definition, under the negligence rule all that an injurer needs to do to avoid the possibility of liability is to make sure to exercise due care if he engages in his activity.[2] Consequently *he will not be motivated to consider the effect on accident losses of his choice of whether to engage in his activity or, more generally, of the level at which to engage in his activity;* he will choose his level of activity in accordance only with the personal benefits so derived. But surely any increase in his level of activity will typically raise expected accident losses (holding constant the level of care). Thus he will be led to choose too high a level of activity;[3] the negligence rule is not "efficient."

Consider by way of illustration the problem of pedestrian-automobile accidents (and, as we are now discussing the unilateral case, let us imagine the behavior of pedestrians to be fixed). Suppose that drivers of automobiles find it in their interest to adhere to the standard of due care but that the possibility of accidents is not thereby eliminated. Then, in deciding how much to drive, they will contemplate only the enjoyment they get from doing so. Because (as they exercise due care) they will not be liable for harm suffered by pedestrians, drivers will not take into

2. It is assumed for ease of exposition that courts have no difficulty in determining if a party did in fact exercise due care; the reader will have no trouble in appropriately modifying the arguments to be made so as to take into account relaxation of such simplifications as this.

3. Specifically, while he will choose to engage in the activity just up to the level at which the personal benefit from a marginal increase would equal zero, it would be best from society's viewpoint for him to engage in the activity only up to the level at which his benefit from a marginal increase would equal the (positive) social marginal cost in terms of accident losses.

account that going more miles will mean a higher expected number of accidents. Hence, there will be too much driving; an individual will, for example, decide to go for a drive on a mere whim despite the imposition of a positive expected cost to pedestrians.

However, under a rule of strict liability, the situation is different. Because an injurer must pay for losses whenever he is involved in an accident,[4] he will be induced to consider the effect on accident losses of both his level of care *and* his level of activity. His decisions will therefore be efficient. Because drivers will be liable for losses sustained by pedestrians, they will decide not only to exercise due care in driving but also to drive only when the utility gained from it outweighs expected liability payments to pedestrians.

*Accidents between sellers and strangers * * *:* In this subcase it is assumed that injurers are sellers of a product or service and that they conduct their business in a competitive market. (The assumption of competition allows us to ignore monopoly power, which is for the purposes of this article a logically tangential issue). Moreover, it is assumed that victims are strangers; they have no market relationship with sellers either as their customers or as their employees.

Under the negligence rule the outcome is inefficient, but the reasoning is slightly different from that of the last subcase. While it is still true that all a seller must do to avoid liability is to take due care, why this results in too high a level of activity has to do with market forces. Because the seller will choose to avoid liability, the price of his product will not reflect the accident losses associated with production. This means that buyers of the product will face too low a price and will purchase too much, which is to say that the seller's level of activity will be too high. Imagine that the drivers are engaged in some business activity—let us say that they are taxi drivers. Then, given that they take due care, the taxi drivers will not have liability expenses, will set rates equal to "production" cost (competition among taxi drivers is assumed), will experience a greater demand than if rates were appropriately higher, and will therefore carry too many fares and cause too many accidents.

Under strict liability, the outcome is efficient, and again the reasoning is a little different from that in the last subcase. Since sellers have to pay for accident losses, they will be led to take the right level of care. And since the product price will reflect accident losses, customers will face the "socially correct" price for the product; purchases will therefore be appropriately lower than what they would be if the product price did not reflect accident losses. Taxi drivers will now increase rates by an amount equal to expected accident losses suffered by pedestrians, and the demand for rides in taxis will fall.

*Accidents between sellers and customers—or employees * * *:* It is presumed here that victims have a market relationship with sellers as

---

4. Causal or other reasons for limiting the scope of liability are ignored.

either their customers or their employees; and since both situations are essentially the same, it will suffice to discuss only that when victims are customers. In order to understand the role (which is important) of customers' knowledge of risk, three alternative assumptions will be considered: customers know the risk presented by each seller; they do not know the risk presented by each seller but they do know the average seller's risk;[5] they misperceive even this average risk.

Under the negligence rule, the outcome is efficient only if customers correctly perceive risks. As before, when the victims were strangers, sellers will take due care in order to avoid liability, so that the product price will not reflect accident losses. However, now the accident losses are borne by the customers. Thus, the "full" price in the eyes of customers is the market price plus imputed perceived accident losses. Therefore, if risks are correctly perceived, the full price equals the socially correct price, and the quantity purchased will be appropriate. But if risks are not correctly perceived, the quantity purchased will be inappropriate; if customers underestimate risks, what they regard as the full price is less than the true full price and they will buy too much of the product, and conversely if they overestimate risks.[6]

Think, for example, of the risk of food poisoning from eating at restaurants. Under the negligence rule, restaurants will decide to avoid liability by taking appropriate precautions to prepare meals under sanitary conditions. Therefore, the price of meals will not reflect the expected losses due to the (remaining) risk of food poisoning. If customers know this risk, they will correctly consider it in their decisions over the purchase of meals. But if they underestimate the risk, they will purchase too many meals; and if they overestimate it, too few.

Under strict liability, the outcome is efficient regardless of whether customers misperceive risks. As in the last subcase, because sellers have to pay for accident losses, they will decide to take appropriate care and will sell the product at a price reflecting accident losses. Thus customers will face the socially correct price and will purchase the correct amount. Their perception of the risk is irrelevant since it will not influence their purchases; as they will be compensated under strict liability for any losses, the likelihood of losses will not matter to them. Restaurant-goers will face a price that reflects expected losses due to food poisoning when meals are prepared under sanitary conditions; they will buy the same—and appropriate—number of meals whether they

---

5. If sellers are assumed to be identical (as they are in the formal model) and therefore to act identically, the average risk will in fact be the risk presented by each seller. But it will be seen from the discussion of the situation when sellers are not liable that the first and second assumptions are nevertheless different.

6. It may be instructive to mention the parallel situation in regard to employee vic-

tims. If employees correctly perceive risks at the workplace, then they will (appropriately) choose to work for a firm only if the "net" wage—the market wage less the expected accident losses they bear—is at least equal to their opportunity elsewhere. But if, say, they underestimate risks, they might choose to work for a firm when the net wage is in fact below their opportunity elsewhere.

think the probability of food poisoning is low or high, for they will be compensated for any losses suffered.[7]

When sellers are simply not liable for accident losses, then the outcome is efficient only if customers know the risk presented by each seller. For, given this assumption, because customers will seek to buy products with the lowest full price (market price plus expected accident losses), sellers will be induced to take appropriate care (since this will lower the accident-loss component of the full price). While it is true that if a restaurant took inadequate precautions to prevent food poisoning, it could offer lower-priced meals, it is also true that customers would respond not just to the market price of meals but also to the likelihood of food poisoning—which they are presumed to know. Therefore customers would decide against giving the restaurant their business. Consequently, restaurants will be led to take adequate precautions and to charge accordingly. Moreover, because customers will base purchases on the correctly perceived full price, they will buy the correct amount.

If, however, customers do not know the risk presented by individual sellers, there are two sources of inefficiency when sellers are not liable. The first is that, given the risk of loss, the quantity purchased by customers may not be correct; of course, this will be true if customers misperceive the risk. The second source of inefficiency is that sellers will not be motivated by market forces to appropriately reduce risks. To understand why, consider the situation when customers do correctly perceive the average risk (when they do not correctly perceive this risk, an explanation similar to the one given here could be supplied). That is, assume that customers know the risk presented by sellers as a group but do not have the ability to "observe" the risk presented by sellers on an individual basis. Then sellers would have no inducement to exercise adequate care. Suppose that restaurant-goers know the risk of food poisoning at restaurants in general and it is, say, inappropriately high. Then if a *particular* restaurant were to take sufficient precautions to lower the risk, customers would not recognize this (except insofar as it eventually affected the average risk—but under the assumption that there are many competing restaurants, this effect would be negligible). Thus the restaurant could not charge a higher price for its meals— customers would have no reason not to go to the cheaper restaurants. In consequence, a situation in which sellers take inadequate care to reduce risks would persist; and similar reasoning shows that a situation in which they take adequate care would not persist. (Notice, however, that since customers are assumed to correctly perceive the average risk, at least they will purchase the correct number of meals—correct, given the high risk.)

---

7. However, it is worthwhile noticing that if they could not possibly be compensated for a kind of loss from food poisoning, then misperception of risk certainly would matter. For instance, if there were a risk of death from food poisoning and if restaurant-goers underestimated it, then they would expose themselves to a higher risk of death by eating restaurant meals than they would truly want to bear. Thus, the conclusion of this paragraph that misperception of risk does not matter under strict liability holds only in respect to risks compensable by payment of money damages.

Finally, it should be observed that the discussion of liability in the present subcase bears on the role of tort law in a contractual setting. When customers make purchases, they are willingly entering into a kind of contract—in which they agree to a price and pay it, receive goods, and expose themselves to a risk (in the absence of liability).[8] Therefore, our conclusions may be generally expressed by the statement that, when customers' knowledge of risks is perfect, the rule of liability does not matter; the "contractual" arrangement arrived at in the market is appropriate. But when the knowledge is not perfect, there is generally scope for the use of liability, and the relative performance of liability rules depends on the precise nature of the imperfection in knowledge. The force of this point, and the fact that it is not always an obvious one, is perhaps well illustrated by the situation described in the previous paragraph. In that situation, customers did correctly perceive average risk, so that there was "assumption of risk," but this did not lead to a desirable result. The situation was one therefore in which, under our assumptions, courts ought not to allow the defense of assumption of risk to be successfully asserted.

Bilateral Case

In this case, account is taken of the possibility that potential victims as well as injurers may influence the probability or magnitude of accident losses by their choice of both level of care and of level of activity.

Accidents between strangers * * *:[9] Under the negligence rule,[10] the outcome is not efficient. As was true in the unilateral case, since all that an injurer needs to do to avoid liability is to exercise due care, he will choose too high a level of activity. In regard to victims, however, the situation is different. Since a victim bears his accident losses, he will choose an appropriate level of care *and* an appropriate level of his

---

8. It should be remarked that the possibility of contractual arrangements that go beyond mere agreement on price is not considered here; for example, the possibility that sellers might give customers some form of guarantee is not allowed for in the discussion or in the analysis. However, our conclusions do have some relevance to what contractual arrangements might be made. This is because what is "efficient" is, by definition, what maximizes benefits minus costs, which is in turn what is in the mutual interest of the sellers and customers to do. (To illustrate, if customers *realize* that they do not know the risk of loss, then they might wish for, and insist on, a blanket guarantee, in effect making the seller strictly liable, and thereby giving him an incentive to reduce the risk of loss.) Of course, the reason this is not considered here is that a satisfactory treatment would require us to study at the least the value of explicit arrangements over the arrangements that

inhere in the applicable tort and contract law, the costs of making explicit arrangements as opposed to the expected costs of reliance on the applicable law, and the willingness of courts to enforce what is at variance with the applicable law.

9. The explanation given in this and in the next subcase for why neither strict liability with a defense of contributory negligence nor the negligence rule results in an efficient outcome is in its essence that given by Richard Posner, Economic Analysis of Law 139–40 (2d ed. 1977). See also Duncan Kennedy, A History of Law and Economics or the Fetishism of Commodities (1979) (unpublished mimeographed paper at Harvard University) which makes related points at 54–63.

10. In the present discussion, it will make no difference whether or not the reader thinks of this rule as incorporating the defense of contributory negligence.

activity, given the (inefficient) behavior of injurers. The drivers will exercise due care but will go too many miles. And the pedestrians, knowing that they must bear accident losses, will exercise due care (in crossing streets and so forth) and they will also reduce the number of miles they walk in accordance with expected accident losses per mile.

Under strict liability with a defense of contributory negligence, the outcome is symmetrical to the last—and again inefficient.[11] Because all that a victim needs to do to avoid bearing accident losses is to take due care, he will have no motive to appropriately reduce *his* level of activity; this is the inefficiency. However, because injurers now bear accident losses, they will take the appropriate amount of care and choose the right level of activity, given the inefficient behavior of victims. Drivers will exercise due care and go the correct number of miles. Pedestrians will also exercise due care but will walk too many miles.

From this discussion it is apparent that the choice between strict liability with a defense of contributory negligence and the negligence rule is a choice between the lesser of two evils. Strict liability with the defense will be superior to the negligence rule when it is more important that injurers be given an incentive through a liability rule to reduce their activity level than that victims be given a similar incentive; that is to say, when it is more important that drivers go fewer miles than that pedestrians walk fewer miles.

Because neither of the familiar liability rules induces efficient behavior, the question arises, *"Is there any conceivable liability rule depending on parties' levels of care and harm done that induces efficient behavior?"* * * * The answer is *"No."* The problem in essence is that for injurers to be induced to choose the correct level of activity, they must bear all accident losses; and for victims to choose the correct level of their activity, they also must bear all accident losses. Yet it is in the nature of a liability rule that both conditions cannot hold simultaneously; clearly, injurers and victims cannot each bear all accident losses.[12]

Accidents between sellers and strangers * * *: Because the reader will be able to appeal to arguments analogous to those already made and in order to avoid tedious repetition, explanation of the results stated in this and the next subcase will be abbreviated or will be omitted.

Under both the negligence rule and strict liability with a defense of contributory negligence, the outcome is inefficient, as was true in the last subcase. Under the negligence rule, sellers will take appropriate care, but since the product price will not reflect accident losses, too much will be purchased by customers. Also, since victims bear accident losses, they will take appropriate care and choose the right level of activity.

---

11. It is of course clear that under strict liability without the defense the outcome is inefficient, for victims would have no motive to take care.

12. However, when other means of social control are also employed, it is possible to achieve an efficient outcome. For example, if use of the negligence rule were supplemented by imposition of a tax on the level of injurer activity, an efficient outcome could be achieved.

Under strict liability with the defense, sellers will take appropriate care and the product price will reflect accident losses, so the right amount will be purchased. Victims will exercise due care but will choose too high a level of activity. In addition, as in the last subcase, there does not exist any liability rule that induces efficient behavior.

*Accidents between sellers and customers—or employees * * *:* As before it will be enough to discuss here only the situation when victims are customers. If customers have perfect knowledge of the risk present- ed by each seller, then the outcome is efficient under strict liability with a defense of contributory negligence or the negligence rule or if sellers are not subject to liability at all. For instance, in the latter situation, since customers wish to buy at the lowest full price, sellers will be led to take appropriate care; and since customers will make their purchases with the full price in mind, the quantity they buy will be correct; and since they bear their losses, they will take appropriate care.

There is, however, a qualification that needs to be made concerning the way in which it is imagined that customers influence accident losses. If one assumes that customers influence losses only by their choice of level of care and of the amount purchased, then what was stated in the previous paragraph is correct; and in regard to services and nondurables (such as meals at restaurants) this assumption seems entirely natural. But in regard to durable goods, it might well be thought that customers influence accident losses not only by their choice of level of care and of purchases, but also by their decision as to frequency of use per unit purchased. The expected number of accidents that a man will have when using a power lawn mower would seem to be influenced not only by whether he in fact purchases one (rather than, say, a hand mower) and by how carefully he mows his lawn with it, but also by how frequently he chooses to mow his lawn. In order for customers to be led to efficiently decide the frequency of use, they must bear their own accident losses. Thus, in regard to durables, the outcome is efficient under the negligence rule or if sellers are not liable, but the outcome is inefficient under strict liability with a defense of contributory negli- gence; for then if the man buys a power lawn mower, he will have no motive to appropriately reduce the number of times he mows his lawn.

Now suppose that customers correctly perceive only average risks. Then, subject again to a qualification concerning durables, the results are as follows. The outcome is efficient under strict liability with a defense of contributory negligence or under the negligence rule, but the outcome is not efficient if sellers are not liable, for then they will not take sufficient care. The qualification is that if the sellers produce durables, strict liability with the defense is inefficient, leaving the negligence rule as the only efficient rule.

Last, suppose that customers misperceive risks. Then the outcome is efficient only under strict liability with a defense of contributory negligence; and the qualification to this is that, if sellers produce durables, even strict liability with the defense is inefficient, so that there does not exist a liability rule which is efficient.

POWERS, A MODEST PROPOSAL TO ABANDON STRICT PRODUCTS LIABILITY
1991 U.Ill.L.Rev. 639, 644–651.

Courts have relied on various rationales to support strict products liability. One rationale for strict products liability is that it promotes product safety by requiring manufacturers to bear accident costs, thus giving manufacturers an incentive to produce safer products. This argument is controversial even on its own terms. It is debatable, both analytically and empirically, whether strict liability increases product safety, much less whether it tends to *optimize* product safety. More important for the present inquiry, however, is that this argument fails to distinguish between product injuries and other personal injuries. Strict liability also could be used to transform the cost of automobile accidents into a cost of driving, thereby providing an incentive for safety.[1] Incentives for safety might support strict liability generally (depending on the empirical evidence), but they do not explain the *selective* application of strict liability to product injuries.

A second common rationale for strict products liability is that it. helps internalize accident costs into the price of products, thereby spreading a victim's loss among an entire group of consumers. Even if this is a desirable goal, which is itself controversial, it is not a goal that is specific to product injuries. Strict liability could also spread losses from nonproduct accidents. For example, losses from automobile accidents that are not currently covered by negligence could be spread through strict liability and nearly universal liability insurance.[2] Indeed,

---

1. We might distinguish product cases from nonproduct cases on the basis that a liability rule has *less* impact on product manufacturers than on nonproduct tort-feasors. In transactions that are subject to market forces, we might be less concerned with an allocative inefficiency created by a liability rule because the parties can bargain their way back to an efficient result. For example, entitlements given to real property owners permit them to use their land frivolously, but they "pay" the price of foregoing a sale or rental at a value reflecting the more efficient use.

To the extent that strict liability is theoretically inefficient, it might be more tolerable in product cases in which a market can mitigate the inefficiency. The absence of a market among strangers prevents a similar mitigation of inefficiency in automobile accidents. Consequently, we might insist on a theoretically more efficient liability rule, such as negligence. *See generally* R. H. Coase, *The Problem of Social Cost*, 3 J.L. &

Econ. 1 (1960); William C. Powers, Jr., *A Methodological Perspective on the Duty to Act*, 57 Tex. L. Rev. 523, 529 & n.21 (1979) (reviewing Marshall S. Shapo, The Duty to Act: Tort Law, Power, & Public Policy (1977)). No court has relied on this distinction, possibly because the *actual* impact of liability rules and markets on behavior is too uncertain, regardless of the theoretical models.

2. Strict liability for product injuries spreads losses by raising a product's price. Strict liability for automobile accidents would spread losses by raising liability insurance rates. The current system of automobile insurance spreads losses only if they are caused by negligent drivers, except for the meager level of first-party coverage.

Another argument for giving product injuries special treatment is that, unlike victims of automobile injuries, victims of product injuries do not have insurance. Consequently, they need another mechanism for

losses from disease and natural disaster seem to be as worthy of spreading as losses from product injuries, solely from the perspective of spreading risks.

Equally telling in the present context is that, although the argument for spreading risks is as powerful for injuries caused by nondefective products, courts uniformly deny recovery in these cases. Although the rhetoric of risk spreading is often used to support strict products liability for victims of defective products, it does not actually justify the selective use of strict liability for victims of defective products in the context of a system that declines to use strict liability for other injuries, including injuries from nondefective products.

A third rationale for strict products liability reflects strict products liability's warranty heritage: defective products frustrate consumer expectations. Especially in early cases, courts relied on consumer expectations created by general assurances of safety and quality that were found in advertising or that were inherent in the mere fact that a product was placed on the market. The emphasis on consumer expectations has waned, however, both as a test of defectiveness and as a reason for liability. One problem with this rationale is that it is difficult to ascertain consumer expectations in all but the simplest cases. Moreover, consumer expectations fail to explain why courts should treat products differently than services. Consequently, courts have been willing to free products liability from its warranty moorings.

I will have more to say about consumer expectations when I address defectiveness in Part III. The point there will be that in most product cases—especially cases not involving manufacturing defects—consumer expectations do not provide a meaningful test of defect and therefore do not provide an adequate ground for strict products liability. In *some* cases, however, consumer expectations may be sufficiently concrete to support liability, and to the extent that the manufacturer created these expectations, they provide a reason for distinguishing product cases. Though defendants in other personal injury cases may also create expectations—such as drivers creating an expectation of following the rules of the road—expectations created in a sales situation may warrant special treatment.

Nevertheless, consumer expectations have limitations as a ground for strict products liability. In most cases, consumer expectations are too vague; in those in which they are not, strict products liability is not a necessary response. Consumer expectations are likely to be well formed only in cases involving manufacturing defects or in cases involving explicit or implicit representations by manufacturers. I already have stated that negligence law can accommodate cases involving manufacturing defects. Similarly, the law of warranty or misrepresentation adequately can address cases involving real representations, either explicit

spreading losses. One response to this argument is that people could insure against product injuries. Moreover, people typically do not insure against most types of loss through first-party automobile insurance.

or implicit. These solutions do not have as a by-product the problems inherent in maintaining strict products liability as a separate cause of action—that is, problems created by treating *all* product cases separately, simply because they involve products.

A fourth rationale for strict products liability is that it places the burden of injuries on manufacturers who are in a better position to prevent injury, "rather than [on] the injured persons who are powerless to protect themselves."[3] This rationale is itself controversial, but even more important, it does not distinguish product injuries from other types of personal injuries. Victims of automobile accidents are often "powerless" to protect themselves, and the tort-feasor is in a better position to prevent the loss. Indeed, in consumer transactions the victim often has had at least the opportunity to select the manufacturer, a choice not usually given to the victim of an automobile accident.

A fifth rationale of strict products liability is that fairness requires a manufacturer to compensate victims because the manufacturer deliberately has imposed risks on consumers for its own benefit. Similar arguments have been used to explain tort liability generally, and therein lies its weakness as a justification for special treatment of product injuries. Motorists deliberately impose risks on pedestrians for the motorists' own benefit, yet we do not impose liability on motorists absent proof of negligence.

A final rationale for strict products liability is that plaintiffs face an unduly difficult burden of proving specific acts of negligence in product cases. The "proof" rationale for strict products liability does not necessarily deny that fault is the underlying motivation for liability. Instead, it posits that negligence is a common cause of defective products and that a plaintiff's inability to *prove* negligence is more likely to be a consequence of the difficulty of proof than of the manufacturer's actual freedom from negligence.[4] Proving negligence is difficult in any person-

3. [Greenman v. Yuba Power Prods., Inc., 59 Cal.2d 57, 27 Cal.Rptr. 697, 701, 377 P.2d 897, 901 (1963)].

4. Other arguments might be constructed to support strict tort liability. For example, strict products liability might rest on an argument similar to unit pricing in supermarkets. If accident costs are reflected in a product's price, they are more visible to consumers, although the actual cost of the product (including risk) is unchanged. The increased visibility of actual product costs might help consumers shop comparatively and make better allocative decisions. The problem with this argument is that, like the risk-spreading argument, it is incompatible with the requirement of defectiveness. Of course, this could be remedied by dropping the requirement of defectiveness, but that solution is very unlikely. Moreover, no court has actually relied on this argument.

Another possible rationale is that strict tort liability avoids technical obstacles (such as timely notice) that plaintiffs face under the Uniform Commercial Code. *See* Greenman v. Yuba Power Prods., Inc., 377 P.2d 897, 899 (Cal.1963). It is difficult to take this argument seriously, however, because the obvious solution is to amend the UCC. Furthermore, this rationale does not itself explain the existence of implied warranties in the Code.

Sometimes we will find "smoke without fire," but experience and intuition might suggest that defectiveness implies negligence more often than not, even when the plaintiff cannot prove it. The plaintiff's failure might simply be due to the acute problems of proof presented by a product injury.

al injury case. Witnesses might give conflicting accounts of the events, and the mechanism of the injury might have been destroyed in the accident. The problem of proof is more acute in product cases, however, because the alleged negligence normally occurred at a place controlled by the defendant and at a time before the plaintiff had any connection with the defendant or the product. These conditions *sometimes* exist in non-product cases, such as when a motorist fails to maintain his brakes adequately, but product injuries present this problem more acutely than other types of injuries. Consequently, courts can make a principled argument for relieving plaintiffs of the burden of proving negligence in product cases while requiring proof of negligence in other types of personal injury cases.

The "proof" rationale is especially attractive because it harmonizes specific internal features of strict products liability in a way that the other rationales do not. For example, the "unavoidable danger" and "state-of-the-art" "defenses" are grounded implicitly on a judgment that we could not have expected the manufacturer to have made the product safer. (Risk spreading does not explain these defenses, because these risks are as worthy of spreading as any other risks.) Notwithstanding the normal inference of negligence from defectiveness, we are not convinced that a manufacturer was negligent in cases involving "unavoidable dangers" or "state-of-the-art" technology. The plaintiff's failure to prove negligence in these cases is not due to mere problems of proof.

Unlike some other rationales, the proof rationale is also consistent with courts' refusal to compensate victims of nondefective products. A defect raises a much stronger inference of negligence than does a mere injury. Moreover, while defectiveness is not always easy to prove, a plaintiff at least has contemporaneous access to the product itself, mitigating the special problems of proving specific acts of negligence in the manufacturing process.[5]

---

5. * * * The "proof" rationale can be generalized into an argument that includes other concerns about the litigation process. Requiring plaintiffs to prove negligence has the risk of creating too many false negatives, that is, cases in which a plaintiff is unable to prove negligence even though the defendant actually was negligent. But it also consumes resources, including the time and effort of parties and the court. The uncertainty of the outcome also diffuses the regulatory effect this body of law has on persons whose conduct we want to influence. It may be that these "administrative" considerations are more important in product cases than other personal injury cases.

Landes and Posner rely on concerns of this sort to explain strict liability for products based on long-term economic efficiency. [William M. Landes & Richard A. Pos-

ner, The Economic Structure of Tort Law 273–311 (1987)]; *see also* [William Powers, Jr., *On Positive Theories of Tort Law*, 66 Tex. L. Rev. 191, 205–11 (1987)]. Ultimately, the force of this argument depends on empirical data, but three initial observations are in order. First, courts have not, in fact, relied on an expanded "administrative" argument of this sort. Second, it is not at all clear why these "administrative" concerns (other than the fear of false negatives) should be more acute in a product case. Third, and most important, they depend mainly on differences between negligence and true strict liability, which, as a true entitlement system, would be more predictable and easier to apply. *See* Powers, [A *Methodological Perspective on the Duty to Act*, 57 Tex. L. Rev. 523, 534–36 (1979)]. But as we shall see in the next part, strict products liability is not a system

The proof rationale is important not because it necessarily represents good policy, but because it is the one rationale that offers at least a plausible reason to distinguish product injuries from other personal injuries. For this reason, I will give it close attention throughout the article. Nevertheless, it has problems of its own as a foundation for strict products liability. First, it may have been a stronger rationale when courts first adopted strict products liability than it is today. Discovery techniques have improved, the plaintiffs' bar has become more sophisticated, and trial courts may be more willing to permit juries to draw inferences of negligence from circumstantial evidence.

Second, the proof rationale applies only to manufacturing defects (flaws). It does not apply to design defects or warnings. In a case involving a manufacturing defect, the offending product is different from other products in the line. We may never know why. But a design defect or warning is common to all products in the line. They were the result of design decisions that are as susceptible to documentation and discovery as any other business decision. While the proof rationale distinguishes cases involving manufacturing defects from other personal injury cases, it also distinguishes them from other product cases. Third, to the extent the proof rationale does support special treatment of cases involving flaws, permitting the jury to draw an inference of negligence from the existence of a flaw, creating a presumption of negligence, or holding that flaws constitute negligence *per se* can all remedy proof problems. Doing so would keep product cases within the framework of negligence law and avoid certain problems that I will address below. The proof rationale does offer some support for distinguishing some product cases—cases involving manufacturing defects—from other personal injury cases. But that problem is so easily remedied within negligence law that it does not, on balance, provide an adequate basis for giving special treatment to *all* product cases under an independent cause of action.

In short, the rationales courts have offered to justify strict products liability do not adequately support a distinction between product cases and other personal injury cases. The proof rationale and consumer expectations offer some support for distinguishing *some* product cases from other personal injury cases, but they do not apply to most product cases as an integral group, and they can be satisfied by other means.[6]

of true strict liability. By depending on a jury finding of defectiveness, it lacks the formal clarity necessary to reap the administrative advantages this argument envisions.

6. A different type of argument, however, might be advanced in favor of strict products liability. Why should we make such a fuss about consistency? We would prefer, the proponent might argue, to apply strict liability (or some other version of expanded liability) to all personal injury cases. But as a political matter, we have been able to prevail only in product cases. At a deep level, law can never be perfectly rational, so we should accept this distinction as one of many inevitable, arbitrary compromises among social interests. After all, half a loaf is better than none; perfection is often an enemy of goodness. In fact, if we do not like the distinction between strict products liability and negligence, we should argue for applying strict liability to other cases, not for abandoning it in product cases.

There are several responses to this line of argument. First, it is true that my argument has attacked only the *distinction* between using strict liability in product cases and using negligence in other cases. I believe strict liability in other cases would be unworkable and pernicious; if a uniform theory is applied to all cases, it should be negligence. Moreover, applying strict liability to other cases is not politically feasible. But all of this is another matter. It is true that my real objection is the distinction between product cases and other cases.

Second, the distinction between product cases and other personal injury cases is not *merely* a failure in coherence. As I will demonstrate below, it affirmatively generates pernicious consequences. The effort to maintain the distinction has itself created serious problems, as we shall see. Sometimes half a loaf is not better than none.

Third, I agree that law cannot be perfectly rationalized. Sometimes courts (or society) must pick certain areas for reform because reform cannot take place everywhere at once. For example, advocates of universal social accident insurance may not be able to implement such a scheme every-

where, so they might try to begin with one area, such as automobile accidents, workplace accidents, or medical accidents. It is not clear, however, why pragmatic considerations such as this are applicable to strict products liability as a common law doctrine. Moreover, lack of coherence, in the sense that plausible reasons do not support important doctrinal distinctions, should at least count against a doctrinal scheme, even if it does not *ipso facto* condemn the scheme. For an interesting discussion of this issue, see [Ronald Dworkin, Law's Empire 177–90 (1986)].

At the very least, careful analysis of the reasons usually given to support strict products liability reveals that they are not as powerful as they seem. In fact, some courts have held that it is an unconstitutional violation of equal protection to distinguish between product cases and other personal injury cases when giving defendants relief through tort reform legislation. [Citation] While I do not endorse this conclusion as a matter of constitutional mandate, it does reflect the theme of this part: It is difficult to justify a distinction between product cases and other personal injury cases. * * *

Chapter 6

FUNDAMENTAL PRINCIPLES OF STRICT LIABILITY: BASIC TESTS OF DEFECT

A product can be defective in one of three ways. First, it can have a manufacturing defect. This is an unintended flaw in the product. Usually, only a small percentage of a manufacturer's products contain manufacturing defects. Such defects are easy to identify because the product differs from other similar products in the line.

Second, a product can be defective because it was improperly designed. The theory is that the manufacturer should have adopted a different design—perhaps an additional safety feature—that would have reduced the risk of accidental injury.

Third, a product can be defective because it is not accompanied by an adequate warning. Many products present risks even when properly designed. The dangers can often be minimized, however, if such products are accompanied by adequate warnings and instructions for use. Without such warnings and instructions, these products are defective.

Design and warning defects present more difficult problems than manufacturing defects. For one thing, it is harder to identify when such products are defective. Some external standard is needed because these products cannot be identified as being defective by simply comparing them to the manufacturer's other products. In addition, the repercussions of declaring that a product is defective because of design or a failure to warn are more serious for the manufacturer. The determination condemns all products in the line rather than an isolated few.

Courts have developed several tests for determining when products are defective. This chapter examines the nature of those tests and the burden of proving them. Chapter 9 examines the way the tests are applied with respect to the different types of defects. Chapter 10 covers the kinds of evidence that may be used to prove that products are defective under the tests.

As you read these cases keep in mind that the determination of defectiveness is very complex. There is no single rule that applies in all cases. Jurisdictions vary widely as to the approach used. Furthermore, even within a given jurisdiction, the approach used often varies over time. Some jurisdictions even apply different tests to different types of defects.

SECTION A. CONSUMER EXPECTATIONS

GRAY v. MANITOWOC CO., INC.
United States Court of Appeals, Fifth Circuit, 1985.
771 F.2d 866.

W. Eugene Davis, Circuit Judge:

Earnest M. Gray brought this action for injuries which he sustained when he was struck by the boom of a construction crane manufactured by defendant, The Manitowoc Company, Inc. (Manitowoc). Gray's wife, Hughlene Gray, joined in this action seeking damages for loss of consortium and companionship. The Grays sought recovery under Mississippi law on theories of strict liability, implied warranty and negligence asserting that Gray's injuries were caused by a defect in the design of the crane and that Manitowoc had provided inadequate warnings of this defect. After the jury returned a verdict for the Grays, Manitowoc moved for judgment notwithstanding the verdict and for a new trial, asserting that the Grays failed to establish either the existence of a defect or a breach of a duty to warn. The district court denied Manitowoc's motion and entered judgment for the Grays. We conclude that the evidence was insufficient to establish that the crane possessed a latent hazard, as required by Mississippi law, for recovery on any of the theories of liability presented by the Grays and, therefore, reverse.

I.

Gray was struck in two separate incidents by the butt end of the boom of a Manitowoc 4100W crane while working as an ironworker foreman on a construction project near Port Gibson, Mississippi. These incidents occurred while Gray's crew was changing sections of the crane's boom and had placed the boom in a plane roughly parallel to the ground (the "boom down" position). Gray was standing on the left side of the crane, supervising this operation, as the crane operator swung the lowered boom in Gray's direction, striking Gray in the back.

Testimony at trial established that the operator's vision to the left side of the Manitowoc crane is obscured by the boom when the crane is operated in the "boom down" position. To compensate for the operator's incomplete field of vision, users of cranes such as the 4100W place a signal-man at various locations on the ground to guide the operator. This procedure was followed by Gray's employer during both incidents in which Gray alleged that he was struck. Gray contends, however, that Manitowoc should have provided mirrors, closed circuit television cameras or other devices to enable the operator to see to the left side of the crane when the crane is operated in the "boom down" position. Gray asserts that had these safety devices been placed on the crane, the crane operator would have seen Gray standing on the left side of the boom and would have avoided hitting him with the boom.

Manitowoc responds that even if mirrors or other devices would have permitted the operator to observe the area on the left side of the crane, the omission of these devices did not render the crane defective. Manitowoc argues that the hazards of operating the crane in the boom down position were open and obvious to ordinary users of the crane and that Mississippi law does not permit recovery under any theory of products liability for a manufacturer's failure to correct such patent dangers.

* * *

III.

Under Mississippi's version of strict liability for hazardous products, manufacturers are not insurers of the products they produce; the existence of a product defect must be established before recovery may be obtained for a resulting injury. * * * Mississippi has adopted the following formulation of the doctrine of strict liability for product defects (as it applies to manufacturers) from *The Restatement (Second) of the Law of Torts*, § 402A(1) (1965): "One who sells any product in a defective condition unreasonably dangerous to the consumer or to his property is subject to liability for physical harm thereby caused to the ultimate user or consumer, or to his property. * * *" *Jackson v. Johns–Manville Sales Corp.*, 727 F.2d 506, 511 (5th Cir.1984), *reinstated en banc in relevant respects*, 750 F.2d 1314, 1317 (1985); *State Stove Manufacturing Co. v. Hodges*, 189 So.2d 113, 118 (Miss.1966), *cert. denied, sub nom. Yates v. Hodges*, 386 U.S. 912, 87 S.Ct. 860, 17 L.Ed.2d 784 (1967); *Ford Motor Co. v. Matthews*, 291 So.2d 169, 171 (Miss.1974).

Comment (g) to the Restatement § 402A defines the term "defective condition": "The rule stated in this Section applies only where the product is, at the time it leaves the seller's hands, in a condition not contemplated by the ultimate consumer, which will be unreasonably dangerous to him." Comment (i), in turn, gives substance to the phrase "unreasonably dangerous":

> The rule stated in this Section applies only where the defective condition of the product makes it unreasonably dangerous to the user or consumer. * * * The article sold must be dangerous to an extent beyond that which would be contemplated by the ordinary consumer who purchases it, with the ordinary knowledge common to the community as to its characteristics.

As these comments illustrate, the consumer expectation test of section 402A is rooted in the warranty remedies of contract law, and requires that harm and liability flow from a product characteristic that frustrates consumer expectations. *See* Keeton, *Product Liability and the Meaning of Defect*, 5 St. Mary's L.J. 30, 37 (1973).

In the seminal Mississippi case for strict liability for defective products, *State Stove*, 189 So.2d at 181, the Mississippi Supreme Court indicated that the patent danger bar adopted by the Restatement was incorporated into Mississippi's doctrine of strict liability. The court quoted the consumer expectation definition of defectiveness set forth in comment (g) to section 402A of the Restatement. In *Ford Motor Co.*, 291 So.2d 169, the Mississippi Supreme Court expounded on the concept of a product defect. The court quoted the relevant portions of comments (g) and (i) to the Restatement § 402A and also quoted the following passage from W. Prosser, *Handbook of the Law of Torts* § 99, at 659–60 (4th Ed.1971): "The prevailing interpretation of "defective' is that the product does not meet the reasonable expectations of the ordinary consumer as to its safety."[2] *Id.* The *State Stove* and *Ford* courts' commitment to the consumer contemplation test for product defects has not been undermined by any subsequent decision of the Mississippi Supreme Court, nor have we discovered any reported decisions in which Mississippi courts or we have permitted recovery in strict liability for a patently dangerous product design. *See Page v. Barko Hydraulics*, 673 F.2d 134, 137–39 (5th Cir.1982).

We recognize that excluding patent hazards from the definition of a product design defect has been subject to much scholarly criticism, and has been rejected in a number of jurisdictions. Nonetheless, the patent danger bar was, until recent years, generally thought to be the prevailing rule in the various states and, in the face of scholarly criticism, has been reaffirmed in a number of jurisdictions.[6] In the absence of any sign that this rule has been, or would be, rejected by the Mississippi Supreme Court, we are bound to apply it in this case. *See Wansor v. George Hantscho Co., Inc.*, 595 F.2d 218, 220–21 and n. 7 (5th Cir.1979). Hence, we conclude that the Gray's right to recover under the theory of strict liability depends upon whether the evidence was sufficient to permit the jury to find that the 4100W crane was "dangerous to an extent not contemplated by the ordinary consumer who purchased it, with the ordinary knowledge common to the community as to its characteristics." *See Ford Motor Co.*, 291 So.2d at 169.

IV.

We are persuaded that the record does not support a finding that the blind spot in the 4100W was a latent hazard. The evidence was overwhelming that the existence of this blind spot was common knowledge in the construction industry. Gray's supervisor, testifying as

2. Dean Prosser expanded on the language quoted above. He explained that the existence of a requirement that a hazard disappoint the expectations of the ordinary consumer "is borne out by the cases of conditions "natural' to food, such as a fish bone in a plate of chowder, or a cherry pit in cherry pie, which the ordinary consumer would expect to encounter, and against which he would normally take his own precautions." Prosser, Section 99 at 660.

Dean Prosser continued in a footnote: "It is not the fact that the defect is a natural one which is important, but the fact that the ordinary consumer would expect that he might encounter it." *Id.* at 660 n. 76.

6. *See, e.g., Delvaux v. Ford Motor Co.*, 764 F.2d 469 (7th Cir.1985) (Wisconsin law); *Young v. Tidecraft, Inc.*, 270 S.C. 453, 242 S.E.2d 671 (1978).

Gray's witness, stated that the existence of a blind spot in the crane operator's field of vision had been widely discussed at the Grand Gulf job site. The business manager of Gray's union local, again testifying as Gray's witness, indicated that the left side of the 4100W crane was referred to as the "blind side". Indeed, the photographs and physical evidence introduced at trial plainly reveal that if a workman standing in the blind spot on the left side of the 4100W had attempted to look at the crane operator, he would have been unable to see him; the record suggests no reason why, in this circumstance, the workman should expect that the crane operator would be able to see him. Finally, uncontested evidence concerning the universal industry practice of using a signalman on the ground to guide operators of cranes clearly demonstrated a common awareness in the construction industry of both the limitation on the operator's field of vision inherent in the design of such cranes and the dangers posed by this limitation. Plaintiff adduced no evidence that manufacturers of other cranes of the vintage of the 4100W equipped them with mirrors, television cameras or other similar devices. Rather, the evidence showed that there was no such industry custom of providing such devices. Industry custom therefore could not serve as a basis for a consumer to expect a crane manufacturer to furnish such devices.

Balanced against this evidence favorable to Manitowoc was Gray's testimony that he did not learn of the blind spot until after his second accident and the testimony of one inexperienced co-worker of Gray's that he also was unaware of the blindspot. Under the *Boeing* standard, we must, of course, credit this testimony. Nonetheless, both the Restatement's theory of strict liability and Mississippi's theories of negligence and implied warranty require an objective appraisal of the obviousness of a product hazard.[8] *See Restatement,* § 402A, comment (i) (the product "must be dangerous to an extent beyond that which would be contemplated by the ordinary consumer who purchases it, with the ordinary knowledge common to the community as to its characteristics"); *Harrist,* 140 So.2d at 561 (defects were "apparent and obvious to a casual observer"). Gray and his inexperienced co-worker's testimony concerning their subjective ignorance has little significance to this objective inquiry. In light of the overwhelming evidence indicating that the existence of a blind spot in the 4100W was common knowledge in the construction trade, we must conclude that the testimony of Gray and his inexperienced co-worker did not create a jury question as to the knowledge or expectations of the *ordinary* observer or consumer. We conclude that no reasonable jury could have found that the blind spot of the Manitowoc 4100W was not open and obvious, nor could any reasonable jury have concluded that the 4100W was dangerous to a degree not anticipated by the ordinary consumer of that product.

8. Gray's actual ignorance or awareness of the crane's blind spot hazard would be dispositive only if an assumption of risk issue were before us. *See Alexander v. Conveyors & Dumpers, Inc.,* 731 F.2d 1221, 1223–24 (5th Cir.1984).

Since the Grays failed to establish that the Manitowoc 4100W crane was defectively designed under any proper theory of Mississippi law,[9] the district court erred in refusing to grant defendant's motion for judgment notwithstanding the verdict. We therefore

REVERSE and RENDER the judgment.

Manitowoc 4100W cranes in "boom up" position

9. With respect to the verdict on theories of negligence and implied warranty, no serious contention is made that Manitowoc might be liable on the ground that the 4100W crane did not function properly for its intended purpose. Like the meatgrinder which adequately ground meat in *Ward,* it is not disputed that this crane adequately performed the construction tasks for which it was designed. See *Ward,* 450 F.2d at 1180.

Manitowoc 4100W crane in "boom down" position

Notes

1. This is a traditional statement of the consumer expectations test in its most conservative form. Under the test there is no liability for obvious or generally known dangers. The test is objective. The court looks to the expectations of the ordinary person who uses the product, rather than the individual plaintiff, or the public generally. Thus, if workmen who use a particular tool are generally aware of its dangers, it is not defective notwithstanding that the average member of the public would not know of them. *See* Woods v. Fruehauf Trailer Corp., 765 P.2d 770 (Okl.1988) (gasoline tanker manufacturer was not subject to strict liability for failing to equip tanker with an automatic shutoff on the nozzle because the ordinary persons who used it, experienced truck drivers, were fully aware of the risk of gasoline catching on fire).

2. Are the following products defective under the consumer expectations test?

  A. In an automobile rollover accident the driver is injured because the roof collapses.

  B. A special rotary lawn mower had a removable front blade guard so that the mower could be used to cut tall weeds along fence rows. The mower did not have a blade brake that would automatically stop the blade when the operator let go of the steering bars. While using the blade without the guard, the operator stopped cutting and walked in front of the running mower to move a barrel without first releasing the clutch controlling the blade. He slipped on freshly cut weeds and came into contact with the blade.

C. An extruding machine did not have a guard over the intake hopper. The operator's arm was amputated when material being fed into the extruder became wrapped around his arm and drew it into the moving parts of the machine.

D. A punch press did not have a safety guard. While the worker put his hand below the ram to clean out scraps of metal, without warning or activation by him, the ram suddenly descended and crushed his fingers.

E. A gas stove was equipped with one-motion burner controls rather than two-step or self-latching controls. The one-motion controls can easily be turned on by accidentally brushing against them. A very young child climbed on the stove. Her clothes caught fire when she accidentally turned on the burner.

F. A new drug which is very beneficial to a large number of people causes a serious side-effect in a small number of people. Plaintiff takes the drug and suffers the side-effect. Prior to plaintiff's illness, the risk was not known.

BRAWNER v. LIBERTY INDUSTRIES, INC.

Missouri Court of Appeals, St. Louis District, 1978.
573 S.W.2d 376.

SMITH, JUDGE.

Plaintiff appeals the order of the trial court dismissing with prejudice his suit against defendants brought under a theory of strict liability in tort. We affirm.

Plaintiff is seven years old and was burned when he and Ray Middleton, Jr., also seven years old, removed the lid from a gasoline storage container and the gasoline ignited. The gasoline container was manufactured by defendant Liberty Industries, Inc., and purchased by Ray Middleton (presumably the younger Middleton boy's father) from defendant National Food Stores, Inc. and its store manager defendant Ippellito. The allegation upon which plaintiff sought to invoke the strict liability doctrine was:

> "That the failure of said gasoline storage container to be equipped with an opening device which would render same to unable to be opened by a child of seven years constitutes a defect in design and an unreasonably dangerous condition of said gasoline storage container."

In *Keener v. Dayton Electric Mfg. Co.*, 445 S.W.2d 362 (Mo.1969), Missouri adopted the theory of strict liability in tort set forth in Restatement of Torts 2d, Sec. 402A as follows:

> "One who sells any product in a defective condition unreasonably dangerous to the user or consumer or to his property is subject to liability for physical harm thereby caused to the ultimate user or consumer or to his property, * * *."

In Missouri a defect in design can meet the requirement of "defective condition". See *Keener, supra; Higgins v. Paul Hardeman, Inc.,* 457 S.W.2d 943 (Mo.App.1970).

Under Comments to Sec. 402A para. (g), we find that a defective condition is a "condition not contemplated by the ultimate consumer which will be unreasonably dangerous to him." Paragraph (i) of the Comments states that "Unreasonably dangerous" means "The article sold must be dangerous to an extent beyond that which would be contemplated by the ordinary consumer who purchases it, with the ordinary knowledge common to the community as to its characteristics." A gasoline container which does not have a child-proof spout does not meet the definition of either defective or unreasonably dangerous. A manufacturer is not an insurer nor must he create a product which is accident proof. See *Royal v. Black and Decker Manufacturing Co.,* 205 So.2d 307 (Fla.App.1968); *Vincer v. Esther Williams All–Aluminum Swimming Pool,* 69 Wis.2d 326, 230 N.W.2d 794 (1975); *Bellotte v. Zayre Corp.,* 116 N.H. 52, 352 A.2d 723 (1976). We have found no case, nor have we been cited to one, where a product made for adult use is deemed defective and unreasonably dangerous solely because it has not been made child-proof. The trial court correctly dismissed plaintiff's petition.

Plaintiff objects to the trial court's failure to allow plaintiff an opportunity to amend. Initially, the record does not indicate plaintiff ever requested such an opportunity. Secondly, plaintiff has not indicated what amendment he would or could make to state a cause of action.

Judgment affirmed.

CLEMENS, P.J., and McMILLIAN, J., concur.

KELLER v. WELLES DEPT. STORE OF RACINE
Court of Appeals of Wisconsin, District II, 1979.
88 Wis.2d 24, 276 N.W.2d 319.

BODE, JUDGE.

This is a products liability case. On October 21, 1971, two and one-half year old Stephen Keller was playing with two year old William Sperry in the basement of the Sperry home. The boys were playing with a gasoline can which had been filled with gasoline by Wayne Sperry, William's father. The can was manufactured by Huffman Manufacturing Company, Inc. (Huffman) and was purchased by Wayne Sperry at Welles Department Store (Welles). The children were near a gas furnace and a hot water heater when gasoline, which they had poured from the can, was ignited. Stephen Keller was severely burned. Although Mrs. Sperry was home at the time of the accident, the two boys were unsupervised.

* * *

The cause of action against Huffman and Welles is pleaded both in negligence and strict liability. The defendants, Huffman and Welles, moved to dismiss the complaint for failure to state a claim upon which relief could be granted. The motion was denied and an order to that effect was entered on April 14, 1978. The defendants appeal.

The sole issue before this court is whether the complaint states a cause of action against the manufacturer and retailer of a gasoline can, * * * for injuries sustained by Stephen Keller resulting from the ignition of gasoline poured from a gasoline can without a child-proof cap.

STRICT LIABILITY

In *Dippel v. Sciano,* 37 Wis.2d 443, 155 N.W.2d 55 (1967), the Wisconsin Supreme Court adopted sec. 402A of Restatement, 2 *Torts* 2d, thereby accepting the concept of strict liability. * * *

* * *

To state a cause of action under strict liability then, the plaintiff must essentially allege that the product was defective and unreasonably dangerous. In the present case, the complaint clearly alleges that the defendants respectively manufactured or sold a gasoline can which was defective and unreasonably dangerous to children such as the plaintiff. The defect complained of was the failure to design the can with a cap sufficient to prevent children from removing it.

* * *

The defendants contend that the motion to dismiss should have been granted because, as a matter of law, no jury could have reasonably concluded that the gasoline can was either defective or unreasonably dangerous. In support of their argument, the defendants rely on *Vincer v. Esther Williams All–Aluminum Swimming Pool Co.,* 69 Wis.2d 326, 230 N.W.2d 794 (1975).

In *Vincer,* a young boy was visiting his grandparents' home. While unsupervised, he fell into a swimming pool, remained there for a prolonged period of time, and sustained severe brain damage. The allegation was that a retractable ladder to the aboveground pool had been left in the down position, thereby providing easy access to the pool. The parents brought suit against the manufacturer of the swimming pool claiming that the pool was defectively designed in that it failed to provide a self-latching and closing gate to prevent entry to the pool. The Esther Williams Company demurred to the complaint for failure to state a cause of action. The trial court sustained the demurrer and the supreme court affirmed.

In its opinion, the court determined as a matter of law that the pool did not contain an unreasonably dangerous defect. The defendants believe the principles enunciated in *Vincer* mandate a similar outcome in the instant case. We disagree.

Comment *g* to sec. 402A of Restatement, 2 *Torts* 2d, states that a product is in a defective condition when "at the time it leaves the seller's hands, [it is] in a condition not contemplated by the ultimate consumer, which will be unreasonably dangerous to him." While this comment serves as a guideline, there is no general definition for "defect," and a decision on whether a defect exists must be made on a case-by-case basis. *Jagmin v. Simonds Abrasive Co.,* 61 Wis.2d 60, 66, 211 N.W.2d 810, 813 (1973).

The *Vincer* court concluded that the swimming pool could not have been defective for failure to have the suggested gate because it had a retractable ladder which rendered the pool "as safe as it reasonably could be." *Vincer,* 69 Wis.2d at 331, 230 N.W.2d at 798. The product at issue here, a gasoline can, was not as safe as was reasonably possible since the cap was not designed in such a way as to prevent young children from removing it. Equipping the gasoline can with a child-proof cap would have rendered the can substantially safer and entailed only a nominal additional cost. The practical value of such a cap may readily be seen since gasoline cans, while not intended to be used by children unable to appreciate the attendant dangers of gasoline, are customarily stored in places accessible to children.

The second element to be considered is whether the defective product, the gasoline can, was unreasonably dangerous. Comment *i* to sec. 402A of the Restatement, in part, describes an article as unreasonably dangerous when it is "dangerous to an extent beyond that which would be contemplated by the ordinary consumer who purchases it, with the ordinary knowledge common to the community as to its characteristics." In *Arbet v. Gussarson,* 66 Wis.2d 551, 225 N.W.2d 431 (1975), the distinction between dangers which are latent or hidden and those which are obvious was explored in the context of this Restatement comment. The court observed that since an ordinary consumer would expect a Volkswagon to be less safe in an accident than a larger car, the small size would not make the Volkswagon unreasonably dangerous. *Arbet* itself dealt with a design defect in a Rambler Station Wagon which resulted in gasoline being retained in the passenger compartment. Since the danger arising from this defect was hidden rather than obvious, the supreme court reversed the trial court and upheld the complaint as against the demurrer of the car manufacturer.

Vincer noted the patent-danger rule discussed in *Arbet* and stated that the Wisconsin test of whether a product contains an unreasonably dangerous defect was as follows: "If the average consumer would reasonably anticipate the dangerous condition of the product and fully appreciate the attendant risk of injury, it would not be unreasonably dangerous and defective." *Vincer,* 69 Wis.2d at 332, 230 N.W.2d at 798. The court then concluded that the swimming pool did not contain an unreasonably dangerous defect for two reasons: first, because the absence of a self-latching gate was an obvious condition and second, because the average consumer would recognize the inherent danger of a retractable ladder in the down position when unsupervised children are about.

We think a different result is warranted in the present case. While the defect in the gasoline can was not concealed, this court is unable to conclude, as a matter of law, that the absence of a child-proof cap was an obvious as opposed to a latent condition. Nor do we believe the dangers to unsupervised children from a gasoline can without a child-proof cap are so apparent that the average consumer would be completely aware of them.

In this regard the factual circumstances in this case are clearly distinguishable from those in *Vincer*. It is common knowledge that children are attracted to swimming pools and that precautions must therefore be taken. *See McWilliams v. Guzinski,* 71 Wis.2d 57, 62, 237 N.W.2d 437, 439 (1976) (holding that an insufficiently guarded swimming pool in a residential area is an attractive nuisance to a four year old child). The danger to a young child from a swimming pool is obvious. The hazards to a child arising from a gasoline can without a child-proof cap are not so readily apparent. A child is not so clearly attracted to this product that an adult would immediately be put on guard to take precautions for the child's safety.

Based on the foregoing discussion, we conclude the complaint stated a cause of action in strict liability.

* * *

Order affirmed.

Notes

1. Some courts have broadened the scope of liability under the consumer expectations test by being very reluctant to find that a risk is generally known or obvious. Phillips, Products Liability: Obviousness of Danger Revisited, 15 Ind.L.Rev. 797 (1982). *See also,* Pardieck & Hulbert, Is the Danger Really Open and Obvious?, 19 Ind.L.Rev. 383 (1986); Note, An Analysis of *Koske v. Townsend Engineering* : The Relationship Between the Open and Obvious Danger Rule and the Consumer Expectation Test, 25 Ind.L.Rev. 235 (1991).

2. Courts accomplish this by a process of characterization. The way a court characterizes the risk that must be contemplated by the ordinary consumer will have a dramatic effect on the scope of liability. Jurisdictions requiring only that a generalized risk of injury be known or obvious will find the fewest products defective. On the other hand, jurisdictions requiring full appreciation of the details of the accident will find many more products defective. In cases where the accident is at all unusual, they can find the product defective because the average consumer would not have contemplated the exact occurrence.

3. The characterization of whose expectations are protected has the same effect. *Keller* looked to "adult" expectations. Another approach would be to look at the expectations of the child who was injured. In Williams v. Beechnut Nutrition Corp., 185 Cal.App.3d 135, 229 Cal.Rptr. 605 (1986) Daniel, a three and one-half-year-old child, fell while holding a baby bottle. It broke, and he was cut by the glass. The court held that "the inherent danger posed by a glass container, while obvious to an adult, is not cognizable by a child Daniel's age." *See* Note, Unreasonably Dangerous

Products From a Child's Perspective: A Proposal for a Reasonable Child Consumer Expectation Test, 20 Rutgers L.J. 433 (1989).

An analogous problem arises when a bystander is injured. Should the product be evaluated by looking the expectations of the product-user or the bystander? *See* Batts v. Tow–Motor Forklift Co., 978 F.2d 1386 (5th Cir.1992) (Mississippi law; forklift, without any mirror or back-up warning device, backed into a bystander. The bystander could not recover because the absence of such devices, and the danger of the operator not facing in the direction of travel, was open and obvious to the forklift operator).

4.   In a vehicle accident case, should we look to the expectations of the owner, driver, passenger, bystander, or all of them? Should infant passengers be treated differently than adult passengers?

5.   Many courts have now rejected consumer expectations as a sole test of defect. *See, e.g.,* Sperry–New Holland, a Div. of Sperry Corp. v. Prestage, 617 So.2d 248 (Miss.1993); *Micallef v. Miehle Co., Div. of Miehle–Goss Dexter, Inc., supra* p. 9, and the notes following that case. Courts have criticized the rule on the following grounds:

A.   The test may not always further the policies underlying strict liability. Rather than discouraging unreasonably dangerous designs, the rule might have the effect of encouraging them in an obvious form. Knitz v. Minster Mach. Co., 69 Ohio St.2d 460, 432 N.E.2d 814 (1982), cert. denied, 459 U.S. 857, 103 S.Ct. 127, 74 L.Ed.2d 110 (1982).

B.   The test may be unfair to third parties in some situations. For example, in some cases the user is aware of a danger that presents a risk to a third party who is ignorant of it and powerless to protect himself. The user may not be as strongly motivated to protect the third party as he would be to protect himself from a similar danger. In addition, the hazard may impair the user's ability to protect the bystander. *E.g.,* Pike v. Frank G. Hough Co., 2 Cal.3d 465, 85 Cal.Rptr. 629, 467 P.2d 229 (1970) (earthmoving machine backed over worker because of blind spot to rear of machine). Another example of unfairness are cases where a person purchases an obviously dangerous machine for use by an employee. The employee may have no real choice but to use the machine, and his knowledge of the risk may not fully protect him. *E.g.,* Brown v. Quick Mix Co., Div. of Koehring Co., 75 Wash.2d 833, 454 P.2d 205 (1969).

C.   With respect to many complex modern products the consumer has no expectations as to how safe it is. Knitz v. Minster Mach. Co., 69 Ohio St.2d 460, 432 N.E.2d 814 (1982), cert. denied, 459 U.S. 857, 103 S.Ct. 127, 74 L.Ed.2d 110 (1982). Is the consumer expectations test incapable of resolving such cases? Why not deny recovery on the basis that expectations were not frustrated? *Cf.,* Heaton v. Ford Motor Co., 248 Or. 467, 435 P.2d 806 (1967). Or should courts grant recovery on the basis that the result was unexpected? Consider the following statement from Akers v. Kelley Co., Inc., 173 Cal.App.3d 633, 651, 219 Cal.Rptr. 513, 524 (1985):

There are certain kinds of accidents—even where fairly complex machinery is involved—which are so bizarre that the average juror, upon hearing the particulars, might reasonably think: 'Whatever the user may have expected from that contraption, it certainly wasn't that.'

6. Professor Powers has criticized the consumer expectations test as follows:

> The consumer expectation test reflects the warranty heritage of strict products liability and is embodied in comment i of Restatement (Second) of Torts section 402A. It provides that a product is defective if the product is more dangerous than an ordinary consumer would contemplate. At first glance, the consumer expectation test seems clearly different from both true strict liability and negligence, and it consequently promises a stable middle ground to serve as a foundation for strict products liability. In fact, this promise is largely illusory.

> True, consumer expectations can sometimes provide an independent ground of analysis. Sometimes consumer expectations about product safety are sufficiently concrete that they can serve as a standard for evaluating a product. A manufacturer's advertising or other communications might create concrete expectations that a product can perform safely a specific task.[1] Even when a manufacturer does not affirmatively create concrete consumer expectations, the offending condition might be sufficiently simple that ordinary consumers have concrete expectations to the contrary—such as when a soft drink contains foreign material. At a more abstract level, consumers might expect at least that a product meets the manufacturer's own specifications, although even here consumers are unlikely to be aware of those specifications or even the range of details they cover.

> In most cases, however, consumer expectations do not provide an independent standard against which to judge a product. In most design cases the offending product feature is too complex to generate concrete consumer expectations. Even in simpler cases, consumers are unlikely to have thought much about the specific offending product. Actual consumer expectations about safety are likely to be vague and, more importantly, to oscillate between "it will never happen to me" and "of course, some products are poorly made." The former expectation proves too much, for it treats every offending product as defective. The latter expectation proves too little, for it treats no product as defective.

> Without actual, specific consumer expectations, courts might use the consumer expectation test as a rubric for determining what consumers have a right to expect—for example, that consumers have a right to expect that a product will have cost-effective safety features, will not be negligently manufactured, or at least will meet the manufacturer's own specifications. But this approach still would require courts to determine what consumers have a right to expect. The consumer expectation test itself would not provide the standard.

---

1. The law of express warranties could handle cases in which the manufacturer has affirmatively created a consumer's expecta- tions. *See* [Powers, The Persistence of Fault in Products Liability, 61 Tex.L.Rev. 777, 795–797 (1983)].

The consumer expectation test's inability to provide an independent standard of defectiveness for complicated products may explain why its early popularity waned as cases began to involve increasingly complex design features. Some courts have expressly abandoned the consumer expectation test;[2] others have expressly held that it is synonymous with the risk-utility test.[3]

The consumer expectation test does not provide a powerful reason for eschewing negligence as the underlying standard of liability in product cases. When a manufacturer creates concrete consumer expectations, the law of express warranties or misrepresentation can evaluate those expectations. Some people may be dissatisfied with the substantive law of express warranties and misrepresentation, but that is a different issue; such dissatisfaction provides shaky support for an independent theory of strict products liability that circumvents direct confrontation of the issues.

Powers, A Modest Proposal to Abandon Strict Products Liability, 1991 U.Ill.L.Rev. 639, 653–654. For other articles criticizing the consumer expectations test, *See* Fischer, Products Liability—The Meaning of Defect, 39 Mo.L.Rev. 339 (1974); Keeton, Products Liability—Liability Without Fault and the Requirement of Defect, 41 Tex.L.Rev. 855, 861 (1963); Marschall, An Obvious Wrong Does Not Make a Right: Manufacturers' Liability for Patently Dangerous Products, 48 N.Y.U.L.Rev. 1065 (1973); Phillips, Products Liability: Obviousness of Danger Revisited, 15 Ind.L.Rev. 797 (1982); Wade, On the Nature of Strict Tort Liability for Products, 44 Miss.L.J. 825, 829 (1973); Comment, The Consumer Expectations Test: A Critical Review of its Application in California, 17 Sw.U.L.Rev. 823 (1988).

7. In a classic article, Professor James Henderson offered the best defense of the consumer expectations test. Henderson, Judicial Review of Manufacturers' Conscious Design Choices: The Limits of Adjudication, 73 Colum.L.Rev. 1531 (1973). The test delegates to the marketplace responsibility for deciding how much safety should be designed into a product. *Id.* at 1558–1562. That is, under the test, courts do not attempt to evaluate the design itself. They merely require full disclose of risks so that buyers can make intelligent decisions about how much safety to pay for. Presumably, products with excessive safety features will be driven off the market because they do not sell. On the other hand, if the public desires that the safety of a product be improved, manufacturers will respond to that demand by marketing safer products. This approach is preferable to an attempt by courts to evaluate design through the process of adjudication. *Id.* at 1557–1558. Courts are not equipped to deal with all of the considerations that must be taken into account in making design choices about products. *Id.* at 1539–1542. Because courts would be unable to develop meaningful design standards, cases would ultimately be decided on the basis of the whim of

---

2. *See generally* Turner v. General Motors Corp., 584 S.W.2d 844 (Tex.1979). This is certainly not the only explanation. Another motivation has been substantive, that is, that the consumer expectation test deprived plaintiffs of recovery when a

"bad" product had a dangerous feature that was nevertheless obvious to ordinary consumers.

3. *See, e.g.,* Phillips v. Kimwood Mach. Co., 525 P.2d 1033, 1036–37 (Or.1974).

individual juries. *Id.* at 1558. This will ultimately cause a serious loss of confidence in the courts. *Id.*

8. The consumer expectations test remains viable. A small number of common law courts continue to use the test as the primary test of defect. *E.g.,* Lester v. Magic Chef, Inc., 230 Kan. 643, 641 P.2d 353 (1982); Woods v. Fruehauf Trailer Corp., 765 P.2d 770 (Okl.1988). Several legislatures have recently enacted statutes mandating that the consumer expectations test be used. The following notes discuss two such statutes. Note, The Consumer Expectations Test in New Jersey: What Can Consumers Expect Now?, 54 Brook.L.Rev. 1381 (1989); Note, An Analysis of *Koske v. Townsend Engineering*: The Relationship Between the Open and Obvious Danger Rule and the Consumer Expectation Test, 25 Ind.L.Rev. 235 (1991). Some jurisdictions that reject consumer expectations as the exclusive test of defect, but continue to use it as an alternative test. *See Barker v. Lull Engineering Co., infra* page 202. Other courts restrict the use of the consumer expectations test to manufacturing flaw cases. *See* Chapter 9, section A., *infra.*

SECTION B.   RISK–UTILITY

PHILLIPS v. KIMWOOD MACH. CO.

Supreme Court of Oregon, 1974.
269 Or. 485, 525 P.2d 1033.

HOLMAN, JUSTICE.

Plaintiff was injured while feeding fiberboard into a sanding machine during his employment with Pope and Talbot, a wood products manufacturer. The sanding machine had been purchased by Pope and Talbot from defendant. Plaintiff brought this action on a products liability theory, contending the sanding machine was unreasonably dangerous by virtue of defective design. At the completion of the testimony, defendant's motion for a directed verdict was granted and plaintiff appealed.

As is required in such a situation, the evidence is recounted in a manner most favorable to the plaintiff. The machine in question was a six-headed sander. Each sanding head was a rapidly moving belt which revolved in the direction opposite to that which the pieces of fiberboard moved through the machine. Three of the heads sanded the top of the fiberboard sheet and three sanded the bottom. The top half of the machine could be raised or lowered depending upon the thickness of the fiberboard to be sanded. The bottom half of the machine had powered rollers which moved the fiberboard through the machine as the fiberboard was being sanded. The top half of the machine had pinch rolls, not powered, which, when pressed down on the fiberboard by use of springs, kept the sanding heads from forcefully rejecting it from the machine.

On the day of the accident plaintiff was engaged in feeding the sheets of fiberboard into the sander. * * * During the sanding of * * * thick sheets, a thin sheet of fiberboard, which had become mixed with the lot, was inserted into the machine. The pressure exerted by the pinch rolls in the top half of the machine was insufficient to counteract the pressure which the sanding belts were exerting upon the thin sheet of fiberboard and, as a result, the machine regurgitated the piece of fiberboard back at plaintiff, hitting him in the abdomen and causing him the injuries for which he now seeks compensation.

Plaintiff asserts in his complaint that the * * * machine was defective and was unreasonably dangerous because there were no safety devices to protect the person feeding the machine from the regurgitation of sheets of fiberboard.

[T]here was evidence from which the jury could find that at a relatively small expense there could have been built into, or subsequently installed on, the machine a line of metal teeth which would point in the direction that the fiberboard progresses through the machine and which would press lightly against the sheet but which, in case of attempted regurgitation, would be jammed into it, thus stopping its backward motion. The evidence also showed that after the accident such teeth were installed upon the machine for that purpose by Pope and Talbot, whereupon subsequent regurgitations of thin fiberboard sheets were prevented while the efficiency of the machine was maintained. There was also evidence that defendant makes smaller sanders which usually are manually fed and on which there is such a safety device.

It was shown that the machine in question was built for use with an automatic feeder * * *. [A]t the time of the purchase by Pope and Talbot, defendant had automatic feeders for sale but that Pope and Talbot did not purchase or show any interest in such a feeder. Pope and Talbot furnished a feeding device of their own manufacture for the machine which was partially automatic and partially manual but which, the jury could find, at times placed an employee in the way of regurgitated sheets.

* * *

In defense of its judgment based upon a directed verdict, defendant contends there was no proof of a defect in the product, and therefore strict liability should not apply. This court and other courts continue to flounder while attempting to determine how one decides whether a product is "in a defective condition unreasonably dangerous to the user."[1] It has been recognized that unreasonably dangerous defects in products come from two principal sources: (1) mismanufacture and (2) faulty design.[2] Mismanufacture is relatively simple to identify because the item in question is capable of being compared with similar articles made by the same manufacturer. However, whether the mismanufactured article is dangerously defective because of the flaw is sometimes

1. 2 Restatement (Second) of Torts § 402A, at 347 (1965).

2. Wade, On the Nature of Strict Tort Liability for Products, 44 Miss.L.J. 825, 830

(1973) (including failure to warn as a design defect).

difficult to ascertain because not every such flaw which causes injury makes the article dangerously defective.[3]

The problem with strict liability of products has been one of limitation. No one wants absolute liability where all the article has to do is to cause injury. To impose liability there has to be something about the article which makes it dangerously defective without regard to whether the manufacturer was or was not at fault for such condition. A test for unreasonable danger is therefore vital. A dangerously defective article would be one which a reasonable person would not put into the stream of commerce *if he had knowledge of its harmful character.*[5] The test, therefore, is whether the seller would be negligent if he sold the article *knowing of the risk involved.*[6] Strict liability imposes what amounts to constructive knowledge of the condition of the product.

On the surface such a test would seem to be different than the test of 2 Restatement (Second) of Torts § 402A, Comment *i.,* of "dangerous to an extent beyond that which would be contemplated by the ordinary consumer who purchases it." This court has used this test in the past. These are not necessarily different standards, however. As stated in Welch v. Outboard Marine Corp.,[8] where the court affirmed an instruction containing both standards:

> "We see no necessary inconsistency between a seller-oriented standard and a user-oriented standard when, as here, each turns on foreseeable risks. They are two sides of the same standard. A

---

3. The California Supreme Court recognized this problem and attempted to eliminate it by requiring only a defect that causes injury, and not an unreasonably dangerous defect. In Cronin v. J.B.E. Olson Corp., 8 Cal.3d 121, 104 Cal.Rptr. 433, 501 P.2d 1153 (1972), the court felt that requiring proof of an *unreasonably dangerous* defect would put an additional burden on plaintiff which the court deemed improper.

We, however, feel that regardless of whether the term used is "defective," as in *Cronin,* or "defective condition unreasonably dangerous," as in the Restatement, or "dangerously defective," as used here, or "not duly safe," as used by Professor Wade, the same considerations will necessarily be utilized in fixing liability on sellers; and, therefore, the supposedly different standards will come ultimately to the same conclusion. *See* Wade, Strict Tort Liability of Manufacturers, 19 Sw.L.J. 5, 14–15 (1965); Wade, *supra* note 2.

5. *See* Borel v. Fibreboard Paper Products Corp., 493 F.2d 1076, 1088 (5th Cir. 1973); Welch v. Outboard Marine Corp., 481 F.2d 252, 254 (5th Cir.1973); Helene Curtis Industries, Inc. v. Pruitt, 385 F.2d 841, 850 (5th Cir.1967); cert. denied, 391 U.S. 913, 88 S.Ct. 1806, 20 L.Ed.2d 652 (1968); Olsen v. Royal Metals Corporation, 392 F.2d 116, 119 (5th Cir.1968); Dorsey v. Yoder, 331 F.Supp. 753, 759–760 (E.D.Pa. 1971), aff'd, 474 F.2d 1339 (3 Cir.1973).

See generally, P. Keeton, Manufacturer's Liability: The Meaning of "Defect" in the Manufacture and Design of Products, 20 Syracuse L.Rev. 559, 568 (1969); P. Keeton, Products Liability—Inadequacy of Information, 48 Tex.L.Rev. 398, 403–404 (1970); Wade, Strict Tort Liability of Manufacturers, 19 Sw.L.J. 5, 15–16 (1965).

6. *Cf.* Welch v. Outboard Marine Corp., 481 F.2d 252, 254 (5th Cir.1973). *See generally,* Wade, *supra* note 2, at 834–835; P. Keeton, Products Liability—Some Observations About Allocation of Risks, 64 Mich. L.Rev. 1329, 1335 (1966).

The Wade and Keeton formulations of the standard appear to be identical except that Keeton would impute the knowledge of dangers at time of trial to the manufacturer, while Wade would impute only the knowledge existing at the time the product was sold. *Compare* P. Keeton, Product Liability and the Meaning of Defect, 5 St. Mary's L.J. 30, 38 (1973), with Wade, *supra* note 3, at 15, and Wade, *supra* note 2, at 834.

8. 481 F.2d 252, 254 (5th Cir.1973).

product is defective and unreasonably dangerous when a reasonable seller would not sell the product if he knew of the risks involved or if the risks are greater than a reasonable buyer would expect.''

To elucidate this point further, we feel that the two standards are the same because a seller acting reasonably would be selling the same product which a reasonable consumer believes he is purchasing. That is to say, a manufacturer who would be negligent in marketing a given product, considering its risks, would necessarily be marketing a product which fell below the reasonable expectations of consumers who purchase it. The foreseeable uses to which a product could be put would be the same in the minds of both the seller and the buyer unless one of the parties was not acting reasonably. The advantage of describing a dangerous defect in the manner of Wade and Keeton is that it preserves the use of familiar terms and thought processes with which courts, lawyers, and jurors customarily deal.

While apparently judging the seller's conduct, the test set out above would actually be a characterization of the product by a jury. If the manufacturer was not acting reasonably in selling the product, knowing of the risks involved, then the product would be dangerously defective when sold and the manufacturer would be subject to liability.

In the case of a product which is claimed to be dangerously defective because of misdesign, the process is not so easy as in the case of mismanufacture. All the products made to that design are the same. The question of whether the design is unreasonably dangerous can be determined only by taking into consideration the surrounding circumstances and knowledge at the time the article was sold, and determining therefrom whether a reasonably prudent manufacturer would have so designed and sold the article in question had he known of the risk involved which injured plaintiff. The issue has been raised in some courts concerning whether, in this context, there is any distinction between strict liability and negligence. The evidence which proves the one will almost always, if not always, prove the other. We discussed this matter recently in the case of Roach v. Kononen, 99 Or.Adv.Sh. 1092, 525 P.2d 125 (1974), and pointed out that there is a difference between strict liability for misdesign and negligence. We said:

"However, be all this as it may, it is generally recognized that the basic difference between negligence on the one hand and strict liability for a design defect on the other is that in strict liability we are talking about the condition (dangerousness) of an article which is designed in a particular way, while in negligence we are talking about the reasonableness of the manufacturer's actions in designing and selling the article as he did. The article can have a degree of dangerousness which the law of strict liability will not tolerate even though the actions of the designer were entirely reasonable in view of what he knew at the time he planned and sold the manufactured article. As Professor Wade points out, a way of determining whether the condition of the article is of the requisite degree of dangerousness to be defective (unreasonably dangerous; greater degree of danger than a consumer has a right to expect; not duly safe) is to assume that the manufacturer knew of the product's propensity to injure as it did, and then to ask whether, with such knowledge, something should have been done about the danger before it was sold. In other words, a greater burden is placed on the manufacturer than is the case in negligence because the law assumes he has knowledge of the article's dangerous propensity which he may not reasonably be expected to have, had he been charged with negligence." 99 Or.Adv.Sh. at 1099, 525 P.2d at 129.

To some it may seem that absolute liability has been imposed upon the manufacturer since it might be argued that no manufacturer could reasonably put into the stream of commerce an article which he realized might result in injury to a user. This is not the case, however. The manner of injury may be so fortuitous and the chances of injury occurring so remote that it is reasonable to sell the product despite the danger. In design cases the utility of the article may be so great, and the change of design necessary to alleviate the danger in question may so impair such utility, that it is reasonable to market the product as it is, even though the possibility of injury exists and was realized at the time of the sale. Again, the cost of the change necessary to alleviate the danger in design may be so great that the article would be priced out of the market and no one would buy it even though it was of high utility. Such an article is not dangerously defective despite its having inflicted injury.

In this case defendant contends it was Pope and Talbot's choice to purchase and use the sander without an automatic feeder, even though it was manufactured to be used with one, and, therefore, it was Pope and Talbot's business choice which resulted in plaintiff's injury and not any misdesign by defendant. However, it is recognized that a failure to warn may make a product unreasonably dangerous.[11] Comment j, Section 402A, 2 Restatement (Second) of Torts, has the following to say:

"In order to prevent the product from being unreasonably dangerous, the seller may be required to give directions or warning, on the container, as to its use. The seller may reasonably assume that those with common allergies, as for example to eggs or strawberries, will be aware of them, and he is not required to warn against them. Where, however, the product contains an ingredient to which a substantial number of the population are allergic, and the ingredient is one whose danger is not generally known, or if known is one which the consumer would reasonably not expect to find in the product, the seller is required to give warning against it, if he had knowledge, or by the application of reasonable, developed human skill and foresight should have knowledge, of the presence of

---

11. *See* Borel v. Fibreboard Products Corp., 493 F.2d 1076, 1088–1090, (5th Cir.1973). *See generally,* P. Keeton, Products Liability—Inadequacy of Information, 48 Tex.L.Rev. 398, 403–404 (1970); P. Keeton, Product Liability and the Meaning of Defect, 5 St. Mary's L.J. 30, 33–34 (1973).

the ingredient and the danger. Likewise in the case of poisonous drugs, or those unduly dangerous for other reasons, warning as to use may be required."

Although the examples cited in the comment do not encompass machinery or such products, it has been recognized that a piece of machinery may or may not be dangerously defective, depending on the directions or warnings that may be given with it.[12]

It is our opinion that the evidence was sufficient for the jury to find that a reasonably prudent manufacturer, knowing that the machine would be fed manually and having the constructive knowledge of its propensity to regurgitate thin sheets when it was set for thick ones, which the courts via strict liability have imposed upon it, would have warned plaintiff's employer either to feed it automatically or to use some safety device, and that, in the absence of such a warning, the machine was dangerously defective. It is therefore unnecessary for us to decide the questions that would arise had adequate warnings been given.

In Anderson v. Klix Chemical, 256 Or. 199, 472 P.2d 806 (1970), we came to the conclusion that there was no difference between negligence and strict liability for a product that was unreasonably dangerous because of failure to warn of certain characteristics. We have now come to the conclusion that we were in error. The reason we believe we were in error parallels the rationale that was expressed in the previously quoted material from Roach v. Kononen, *supra,* where we discussed the difference between strict liability for misdesign and negligence. In a strict liability case we are talking about the condition (dangerousness) of an article which is sold without any warning, while in negligence we are talking about the reasonableness of the manufacturer's actions in selling the article without a warning. The article can have a degree of dangerousness because of a lack of warning which the law of strict liability will not tolerate even though the actions of the seller were entirely reasonable in selling the article without a warning considering what he knew or should have known at the time he sold it. A way to determine the dangerousness of the article, as distinguished from the seller's culpability, is to assume the seller knew of the product's propensity to injure as it did, and then to ask whether, with such knowledge, he would have been negligent in selling it without a warning.

---

12. Hursh & Bailey, 1 American Law of Products Liability 2d, § 4.13 and cases cited therein (1974); *see* Berkebile v. Brantly Helicopter Corp., 225 Pa.Super. 349, 311 A.2d 140, 143 (1973).

In fact, in the leading case in the area of strict liability, Greenman v. Yuba Power Products, 59 Cal.2d 57, 27 Cal.Rptr. 697, 377 P.2d 897, 13 A.L.R.3d 1049 (1963), the California Supreme Court stated:

"* * * To establish the manufacturer's liability it was sufficient that plaintiff

proved that he was injured while using the Shopsmith in a way it was intended to be used as a result of a defect in design and manufacture *of which plaintiff was not aware* that made the Shopsmith unsafe for its intended use." (Emphasis added.) 27 Cal.Rptr. at 701, 377 P.2d at 901.

Thus it appears that the piece of machinery might not have been "defective" had the purchaser been made aware of its propensities through proper warnings.

It is apparent that the language being used in the discussion of the above problems is largely that which is also used in *negligence* cases, *i.e.,* "unreasonably dangerous," "have reasonably anticipated," "reasonably prudent manufacturer," etc. It is necessary to remember that whether the doctrine of negligence, ultrahazardousness, or strict liability is being used to impose liability, the same process is going on in each instance, *i.e.,* weighing the utility of the article against the risk of its use. Therefore, the same language and concepts of reasonableness are used by courts for the determination of unreasonable danger in products liability cases. For example, see the criteria set out in Roach v. Kononen, *supra.*[13] The difference between the three theories of recovery is in the manner in which the decisional functions are distributed between the court and the jury. * * *

It is important to point out * * * that while the decision is made by the court whether an activity is abnormally dangerous and strict liability of the Rylands v. Fletcher[15] type is to be applied, the determination of whether a product is dangerously defective and strict liability is to be applied has been treated as one primarily for the jury, similar to the manner in which negligence is determined. Therefore, the factors set forth by Wade and used in Roach v. Kononen, *supra,* are not the bases for instructions to the jury but are for the use of the court in determining whether a case has been made out which is submissible to the jury. If such a case has been made out, then it is submitted to the jury for its determination under instructions as to what constitutes a "dangerously defective" product, much in the same manner as negligence is submitted to the jury under the "reasonable man" rule.[16]

* * *

13. (1) The usefulness and desirability of the product—its utility to the user and to the public as a whole.

(2) The safety aspects of the product—the likelihood that it will cause injury, and the probable seriousness of the injury.

(3) The availability of a substitute product which would meet the same need and not be as unsafe.

(4) The manufacturer's ability to eliminate the unsafe character of the product without impairing its usefulness or making it too expensive to maintain its utility.

(5) The user's ability to avoid danger by the exercise of care in the use of the product.

(6) The user's anticipated awareness of the dangers inherent in the product and their avoidability, because of general public knowledge of the obvious condition of the product, or of the existence of suitable warnings or instructions.

(7) The feasibility, on the part of the manufacturer, of spreading the loss by setting the price of the product or carrying liability insurance.

15. Fletcher v. Rylands, 3 H & C 774, 159 Eng.Rep. 737 (Ex.1865), *reversed in* Fletcher v. Rylands, LR 1 Ex. 265 (1866), *affirmed in* Rylands v. Fletcher, LR 3 HL 330 (1868).

16. Wade, *supra* note 2, at 834–835. Professor Wade also suggests an appropriate jury instruction which embodies the new standard. We have taken the liberty of modifying his suggestion to a form which seems to us more appropriate for use by a jury. It is as follows:

"The law imputes to a manufacturer [supplier] knowledge of the harmful character of his product whether he actually knows of it or not. He is presumed to know of the harmful characteristics of that which he makes [supplies]. Therefore, a product is dangerously defective if it is so harmful to persons [or property]

Defendant calls to our attention that one of the principal rationales behind the imposition of strict liability upon the manufacturer for injuries caused by dangerously defective products is that the manufacturer is in the position of distributing the cost of such risks among all users of the product. Defendant then argues that in the present situation Pope and Talbot would normally bear the responsibility for the injury to its employee and that because Pope and Talbot is just as capable of spreading the cost of injury by the sale of its product as is defendant, there is no logic in imposing liability without fault upon defendant for the purpose of distributing the risk.

Defendant thus confronts us with the problem we have already been faced with in Wights v. Staff Jennings,[18] where we noted the difficulty of limiting the applicability of the enterprise liability theory as a basis for recovery in tort. While the enterprise liability theory may be indifferent as to whether the defendant or plaintiff's employer should bear this loss, there are other theories which allow us to make a choice.

Where a defendant's product is adjudged by a jury to be dangerously defective, imposition of liability on the manufacturer will cause him to take some steps (or at least make calculations) to improve his product. Although such inducement may not be any greater under a system of strict liability than under a system of negligence recovery, it is certainly greater than if the liability was imposed on another party simply because that other party was a better risk distributor. We suspect that, in the final analysis, the imposition of liability has a beneficial effect on manufacturers of defective products both in the care they take and in the warning they give.

The case is reversed and remanded for a new trial.

Notes

1. Many jurisdictions have adopted a risk-utility test of defect in recent years. There has been some quibbling over terminology, such as whether to use such terms as "reasonable" or "unreasonably dangerous" in describing the way the product is evaluated. Some courts avoid using such terms because they "ring of negligence." Regardless of the terminology, the basic approach is the same.

2. *Phillips* creates a distinction between negligence and strict liability by using hindsight rather than foresight to impute knowledge of risk to the manufacturer. It does this on both the design defect claim and the failure to warn claim. We treat the use of hindsight versus foresight in more detail in Chapter 7.

3. Note the language in *Phillips* to the effect that there is no difference between the consumer expectations test and the risk-utility test. Other courts have agreed. *E.g.*, Aller v. Rodgers Mach. Mfg. Co., 268 N.W.2d 830 (Iowa 1978). In essence, they have converted the consumer expectations

that a reasonable prudent manufacturer [supplier] with this knowledge would not have placed it on the market."

18. 241 Or. 301, 405 P.2d 624 (1965).

test into a risk-utility test by stating that consumers expect products to be reasonably safe. How would such courts deal with cases where a product contains an obvious danger (such as a punch press without a point of operation guard) that could easily be corrected?

FALLON v. CLIFFORD B. HANNAY & SON, INC.

Supreme Court of New York, Appellate Division,
Third Department, 1989.
153 A.D.2d 95, 550 N.Y.S.2d 135.

Before MAHONEY, P.J., and CASEY, YESAWICH, LEVINE and HARVEY, JJ.

LEVINE, JUSTICE.

Plaintiff brought this action for products liability * * * against defendant, the manufacturer of the "Hannay Reel", a power reel installed in propane gas delivery trucks upon which the hose used to convey the propane gas from the truck to the tank of the customer is wound, stored and unwound. The facts upon which plaintiff based his causes of action can be garnered from the allegations of the complaint, bill of particulars and the transcript of plaintiff's examination before trial. Briefly summarized, plaintiff claims that, at the time when he sustained the injuries for which he sues, he was employed as a propane gas delivery person for Agway Petroleum Corporation and had been so employed for several years. When the injury-producing incident happened, he was delivering gas to a residence in the Town of Otsego, Otsego County, and in the process of bringing the hose line from the truck to the customer's tank. He was " 'running' with [the] hose", i.e., accelerating his forward movement to overcome the inert weight of the hose as it unrolled from the vehicle, when an entanglement of the hose on the reel caused it to lock abruptly, which in turn caused plaintiff to fall and sustain serious injuries to his back.

According to plaintiff, the Hannay Reel was defective in not being equipped with a "guide master", a piece of optional equipment manufactured and offered for sale by defendant with the power reel. The function of a guide master is to mechanically direct the laying of the hose back and forth on the reel when the hose is being automatically rewound and thereby prevent the snarling of the hose on the reel, which plaintiff claims ultimately caused his injuries. In his bill of particulars, plaintiff further explained the entanglement problem of the reel without a guide master as being one wherein, upon rewinding, "the hose occasionally, depending on the angle of the hose to the revolving reel, overlaps at various angles, which occasionally results in an overlapping entanglement". * * *

After joinder of issue and pretrial discovery, defendant moved for summary judgment. The moving papers consisted of affidavits of defendant's vice-president of manufacturing and a manager of plaintiff's employer, the pleadings, a bill of particulars and the transcript of plaintiff's examination before trial. The evidentiary facts in admissible form in those papers show that defendant had manufactured and sold the power reel and guide master, with the guide master as optional equipment, since the early 1950s and had sold reels both with and without guide masters to plaintiff's employer for several years prior to plaintiff's accident. As a matter of deliberate choice of plaintiff's employer, several of its trucks were equipped with guide masters while others were not. The purpose of the guide master device, to avoid entanglement of the hose on the reel and resultant lock of the hose upon unwinding, was well known by plaintiff's employer and by plaintiff and his coemployees. * * *

Plaintiff opposed defendant's motion by submitting the affidavits of plaintiff and of a university professor of mechanical and aerospace engineering. In his affidavit, plaintiff admitted know'.g the potential of the Hannay Reel not equipped with a guide master to entangle and suddenly lock when running with the hose to service a customer, but denied being "aware that it would knock me down". The affidavit of plaintiff's expert opined that the guide master was an "essential safety item that should, in fact, be a part of the standard equipment of the Hannay Reel and that it's [sic] purpose is to prevent the exact occurrence * * * which caused this accident". Supreme Court denied defendant's motion in its entirety on the ground that issues of fact were presented as to whether the guide master was actually a safety device and whether the absence of the device as a standard feature of defendant's reel created an unreasonable risk of harm to the user. This appeal by defendant ensued.

In our view, defendant was entitled to summary judgment * * *. * * * [P]laintiff's * * * claim in strict products liability [is] for a design defect and a failure to warn. The design defect claim refers to defendant's duty not to market the Hannay Reel without the guide master. Thus, it was plaintiff's burden to make out a prima facie case that, *inter alia*, absent the guide master, defendant's power reel was "not reasonably safe" (*Voss v. Black & Decker Mfg. Co.*, 59 N.Y.2d 102, 108, 463 N.Y.S.2d 398, 450 N.E.2d 204). A defectively designed product "is one which, at the time it leaves the seller's hands, is in a condition not reasonably contemplated by the ultimate consumer and is unreasonably dangerous for its intended use; that is one whose utility does not outweigh the danger inherent in its introduction into the stream of commerce" (*Robinson v. Reed–Prentice Div. of Package Mach. Co.*, 49 N.Y.2d 471, 479, 426 N.Y.S.2d 717, 403 N.E.2d 440). In applying the risk-utility facet of the definition of an unreasonably unsafe product, the Court of Appeals has identified seven factors to be considered (*Voss v. Black & Decker Mfg. Co.*, *supra*, 59 N.Y.2d at 109, 463 N.Y.S.2d 398, 450 N.E.2d 204). Basically, and as relevant here, these factors refer to the magnitude and seriousness of the danger in using the product, the product's utility to the public and the individual user, the technological and economic feasibility of a safer design and the plaintiff's awareness of the danger and ability to have avoided injury by careful use of the product. These risk-utility factors are to be considered in the first instance by the court to determine whether a plaintiff has made out a prima facie case and, if so, then submitted in some reasonably simple fashion to the jury [citations].

Here, the facts and reasonable inferences to be drawn from the evidence submitted in support of defendant's motion negated plaintiff's claim that the Hannay Reel without a guide master was not reasonably safe. The reel, sans guide master, was exactly in the condition contemplated by the consumer at the time of purchase, i.e., a useful device whose mechanical efficiency was less than if it had been equipped with a guide master, a quality common to reels of all varieties. Plaintiff himself recognized that entanglement would only occur "occasionally". Even more remote was the likelihood that the sudden locking upon unwinding of a twisted hose would result in a gas deliverer losing balance and then falling with sufficient force to sustain any significant injury. Thus, defendant also successfully demonstrated in its moving papers that the magnitude of danger factor in the risk-utility test was insubstantial. While the existence of the guide master itself established the technical feasibility of a safer reel, the economic feasibility of marketing defendant's product only with the guide master was cast in doubt by the invoices submitted by defendant on the motion, tending to show that inclusion of the guide master substantially increases the cost of the product sold by defendant. Finally, as to the factors to be considered in the risk-utility test, plaintiff's awareness of the possibility of the hose locking and the simple precautions which could have been taken to avoid the disastrous fall also militated against a finding that the reel without a guide master was unreasonably dangerous [citation].

Moreover, it is readily inferrable that the risks both of an entangled hose locking and then causing any significant injury to a delivery person will vary from one job site to another, depending upon such factors as the distance from the delivery truck to the customer's tank and the conditions of the terrain traversed. Purchasers of the reels, knowing their clientele and the conditions under which deliveries to them would be made, were in a better position than defendant, as the manufacturer, to assess the necessity of the protection against snarling and locking afforded by a guide master, even if it were to be considered a safety device. For these reasons also, defendant's proof supported the conclusion that the reel alone was reasonably safe and that defendant satisfied its duty not to market a defective product by giving purchasers the option to buy its reel with or without the guide master [citations].

What has previously been discussed also largely disposes of the failure to warn claim in plaintiff's first cause of action. On defendant's proof, the danger of injury was insubstantial and, to whatever degree there was such a risk, it was an obvious one, likely to be appreciated by the user to the same extent as any warning of it would have provided [citations].

* * *

Thus, defendant submitted evidence in admissible form establishing a prima facie defense to each of the causes of action alleged in the complaint. Therefore, the burden shifted to plaintiff to submit contradictory proof to withstand defendant's motion by creating one or more issues of fact. * * * As to plaintiff's cause of action for products liability in tort, the opposing affidavits were insufficient to create a question of fact as to whether the Hannay Reel was not reasonably safe. Since plaintiff's personal affidavit conceded prior awareness of the property of the reel without a guide master of which he complains, it failed to controvert defendant's proof on this issue. The affidavit of plaintiff's expert contained only a bare, conclusory statement that the reel was unsafe without a guide master. No foundational facts, such as a deviation from industry standards, or statistics showing some frequent incidence of injuries in using this type of reel, are averred in support of this conclusion. No inference that the conclusion of plaintiff's expert was based upon his own personal knowledge can be drawn from the summary of his qualifications attached to his affidavit, which disclosed at most a general expertise in mechanical design for heating and other energy systems not vaguely related to the manufacturer of the product which is the subject of plaintiff's action. Without even the semblance of a foundation based upon facts in the record or personal knowledge, the opinion of plaintiff's expert was purely speculative and, thus, lacked sufficient probative force to constitute prima facie evidence that the Hannay Reel was not reasonably safe for its intended use [citations]. In the absence of such a prima facie showing that defendant's reel was not reasonably safe, plaintiff failed to create an issue of fact precluding summary judgment.

Order reversed, on the law, with costs, motion granted, summary judgment awarded to defendant and complaint dismissed.

MAHONEY, P.J., and CASEY, YESAWICH, and HARVEY, JJ., concur.

Hannay Reel without guide master

Hannay Reel with guide master

Notes

1. **Product Cost.** Courts consider the cost of making the product safer as part of the risk-utility balance. In Rix v. General Motors Corp., 222 Mont. 318, 723 P.2d 195 (1986), the braking system on a truck failed because of a hydraulic brake fluid leak. Plaintiff argued that the truck was defective because it was not equipped with a dual braking system so that the truck would have a back-up braking system in the event of such a failure. The technology for such a system was available and known to General Motors at the time of manufacture. The court stated:

A jury should be instructed to weigh various factors according to the facts of each case and their own judgment. We conclude that the following elements should be considered for instructional purposes in an alternative design products liability case, recognizing that not all factors may be appropriate in every case, and also recognizing that additional factors should be considered where appropriate:

(1) A manufacturer who sells a product in a defective condition unreasonably dangerous because of a design defect is subject to liability for harm thereby caused to the ultimate user.

(2) A product may be in a defective condition unreasonably dangerous if the manufacturer should have used an alternative design.

(3) In determining whether an alternative design should have been used, the jury should balance so many of the following factors as it finds to be pertinent at the time of manufacture:

(a) The reasonable probability that the product as originally designed would cause serious harm to the claimant.

(b) Consideration of the reasonable probability of harm from the use of the original product as compared to the reasonable probability of harm from the use of the product with the alternative design.

(c) The technological feasibility of an alternative design that would have prevented claimant's harm.

(d) The relative costs both to the manufacturer and the consumer of producing, distributing and selling the original product as compared to the product with the alternative design.

(e) The time reasonably required to implement the alternative design.

2. **Product Performance.** Courts also consider the way performance is affected by suggested design changes. Cars, for example, would be much safer if they had a top speed of five miles per hour. Yet, they are not defective because they are capable of going faster. Likewise, coffee is not defective simply because it is hot and capable of causing a burn. Huppe v. Twenty–First Century Restaurants of Am., Inc., 130 Misc.2d 736, 497 N.Y.S.2d 306 (1985).

3. **Time of Ascertaining Costs and Benefits.** The costs and benefits of products can vary over time. The utility of a vaccine against a disease is much higher during an epidemic than when the disease is under control.

The relevant time for evaluating a product's utility is the time of marketing. Likewise the costs of producing a safe product can either increase or decrease. These costs should be considered as they existed at the time the product was marketed. That is, courts consider how costly it would have been initially to build the product safely. They do not consider either the cost of building it safely today or the present cost of going back and making the product safe.

4. **Benefits to the Economy.** In evaluating the utility of the product may the jury consider the economic benefits to society created in the course of producing the product? In Cipollone v. Liggett Group, Inc., 644 F.Supp. 283 (D.N.J.1986) plaintiffs claimed that defendant's cigarettes were defective, under the New Jersey risk-utility test, because the risks of smoking outweighed the utility of cigarettes. On the question of the utility of cigarettes, defendants planned to introduce evidence of the economic benefits of the cigarette industry including "consideration of profits made, employees hired, benefits to suppliers of goods and services, taxes generated and even charitable activities or contributions made by the defendant manufacturer." Plaintiffs made a motion in limine to bar such evidence. The trial court granted the motion, saying:

> Defendants' proposed evidence, when distilled to its essence, aims to establish that their product is profitable, that some of those profits are disseminated to others in society, and that such benefits would be reduced or eliminated if liability were imposed. But strict liability law is, if anything, intended to temper the profit motive by making a manufacturer or marketer aware that it may be less costly in the long run to market a product more safely, or not to market it at all. See Holford, The Limits of Strict Liability for Product Design and Manufacture, 52 Tex.L.Rev. 81, 86 (1973). As noted by Dean Wade, "Manufacturers are frankly in the business of making and selling products for the profit involved." Wade, On Product Design Defects and their Actionability, 33 Vand.L.Rev. 551, 569 (1980). To permit defendants to introduce the evidence that they here propose would undercut the very goals of strict liability law insofar as it suggests that defendants' interest in making a profit could transform an otherwise insufficient evaluation of their product's safety into a reasonable one.

> Secondly, a fundamental purpose behind the imposition of strict liability is to require that a product "pay its way" by compensating for the harms it causes. * * * For this purpose to be furthered it is of course necessary to accept that a product's profitability will be reduced as it bears the costs attendant to its use, and indeed that its true costs to society may so outweigh its usefulness that those costs, when reflected in the product's price, will ultimately lead to that product's withdrawal from the market. That some economic dislocation may thereby result in the short run is, in turn, an accepted fact of life in the operation of a free market system in which those entities who profit from the marketing of a product—rather than its individual victims, or the government, or society—are the ones who are expected to bear the risks that such products are not economically viable. Indeed, any avoidance of product liability for reasons unrelated to the inherent value of the product itself would permit the continued marketing of products

that do not truly pay their way, thus discouraging the profiting entities from devoting their energies to making their product safer, or to producing products that are more socially beneficial in the long term. To permit a manufacturer or marketer to introduce evidence of a product's profitability, and to suggest that such profitability will be endangered if legal liability is found, would thus undermine these goals of greater overall economic efficiency and product safety. * * *

The analysis was never meant to balance the risk to the consumer against the general benefit to society. Rather, the sole question presented is whether the risk to the consumers exceeds the utility to those consumers. * * *

644 F.Supp. at 288–90. This issue is discussed in Note, The Smoldering Issue in *Cipollone v. Liggett Group, Inc.*: Process Concerns in Determining Whether Cigarettes are a Defectively Designed Product, 73 Cornell Law Review 606, 615–619 (1988).

5. Are the following products defective under the risk-utility test of defect?

A. A flaw in a tire causes a blowout. The driver is injured in the resulting accident.

B. A gasoline can that does not have a child-proof top. A four-year-old child opened the can and was burned when the gasoline vapors accidentally caught fire.

C. A press without a point of operation safety guard. The worker was required to put a piece of metal stock between two halves of a die with her hand, and then activate the machine with a foot pedal. This would cause the two halves of the die to close with great force and shape the metal stock. The worker lost two fingers when she accidentally activated the foot pedal control while her hand was below the ram.

D. A riding lawn mower that does not have a dead man switch. The operator was thrown from the mower. His thumb and two fingers of his left hand were severed when he attempted to stop his fall.

E. A gas stove equipped with one-motion burner controls rather than two-step or self-latching controls. The one-motion controls can easily be turned on by accidentally brushing against them. A young child climbed on a chair in front of the stove and leaned over to get a spoon out of a fudge pan. The front burner ignited, and her clothes caught fire.

F. A beer bottle that is not strong enough to withstand the force of being thrown against a telephone pole.

G. A new drug which is very beneficial to a large number of people causes a serious side-effect in a small number of people. Plaintiff takes the drug and suffers the side-effect. Prior to plaintiff's illness, the risk was not known. The manufacturer did not warn about the risk of the side-effect.

6. Characterization can play an important role in the way the test is applied. The adoption of a global versus a narrow characterization of the factor to be evaluated can influence the result. In note 5.B., *supra,* for

example, the question of defect could be analyzed in terms of the usefulness of gasoline containers, or in terms of the availability and cost of child-proof tops.

7. For an economic appraisal of the risk-utility test of defect, consider the excerpt from the following article.

LANDES AND POSNER, A POSITIVE ECONOMIC ANALYSIS OF PRODUCTS LIABILITY
14 J. Legal Stud. 535, 553-54 (1985).

1. *Defective Design.* Here rather little need be said because the courts follow an explicit Hand formula approach.[1] This may surprise the reader, since the Hand formula is designed for negligence, and defective design cases are decided under the standard of strict liability. But it must be understood, first, that liability is strict in products cases only if a "defect" is shown (or, as we shall see, if the product, though not defective in the sense of improvable at a cost lower than the reduction in accident costs that the improvement would bring about, if "unreasonably [though unavoidably] dangerous"), and, second, that "defect" is determined in cost-benefit terms: a product is defective if it could have been made safer at a lower cost than the benefit in reducing expected accident costs.

Recall from Section II that negligence tends to be the preferred liability rule in joint care situations (that is, when it is efficient for both the consumer and manufacturer to take some care). It might seem paradoxical, therefore, that negligence rather than strict liability would be (in effect) the applicable rule for design defects, for the consumer would appear to be quite helpless to prevent accidents arising from such defects. The explanation lies in the fact that design defects typically involve durable goods, where the likelihood of an accident depends both on the product's design and on the method and intensity of consumer use. For example, a person who drives too fast and is injured when his car runs off the road could argue that his injury would have been avoided if the car had been designed differently (say, more like a tank). No doubt he is right. It is always possible to alter a product's design to make it safer. Yet in this example it is more efficient for the driver to avoid speeding than for the manufacturer to turn the car into a tank. If the manufacturer were liable for any and every injury that could have been avoided by a different design, consumers would have less incentive either to take care or to alter their activity level, for they would know they would be compensated for their injury. That is, if we are right that many product accidents that could be avoided by a different design are joint care situations, then negligence is the more efficient rule than strict liability for design defects.

1. See, for example, * * * Phillips v.   525 P.2d 1033, 1038 (1974) * * *.
Kimwood Mach. Co., 269 Ore. 485, 495–96,

O'BRIEN v. MUSKIN CORP.

Supreme Court of New Jersey, 1983.
94 N.J. 169, 463 A.2d 298.

The opinion of the Court was delivered by

POLLOCK, J.

[Plaintiff dove into an above-ground swimming pool with a vinyl liner. His outstretched hands hit the pool bottom, slid apart, and he struck his head on the bottom of the pool, sustaining injuries. He claimed that the pool was defective in design because the pool liner was slippery. Evidence indicated that there was no alternative lining material available for above-ground pools. The trial judge ruled that plaintiff had failed to prove a design defect in the pool, and refused to charge the jury on design defect. Instead, the court submitted the case to the jury solely on the adequacy of the warning. The jury found that the warning was inadequate, but that plaintiff was more at fault than defendant. Thus, because of the New Jersey modified comparative negligence rule, a judgement was entered for defendant.]

On appeal, the Appellate Division found that the trial court erred in removing from the jury the issue of design defect. Consequently, that court reversed the judgment against Muskin and remanded the matter for a new trial. * * *

* * *

The assessment of the utility of a design involves the consideration of available alternatives. If no alternatives are available, recourse to a unique design is more defensible. The existence of a safer and equally efficacious design, however, diminishes the justification for using a challenged design.

The evaluation of the utility of a product also involves the relative need for that product; some products are essentials, while others are luxuries. A product that fills a critical need and can be designed in only one way should be viewed differently from a luxury item. Still other products, including some for which no alternative exists, are so dangerous and of such little use that under the risk-utility analysis, a manufacturer would bear the cost of liability of harm to others. That cost might dissuade a manufacturer from placing the product on the market, even if the product has been made as safely as possible. Indeed, plaintiff contends that above-ground pools with vinyl liners are such products and that manufacturers who market those pools should bear the cost of injuries they cause to foreseeable users.

A critical issue at trial was whether the design of the pool, calling for a vinyl bottom in a pool four feet deep, was defective. The trial court should have permitted the jury to consider whether, because of the dimensions of the pool and slipperiness of the bottom, the risks of injury so outweighed the utility of the product as to constitute a defect. In removing that issue from consideration by the jury, the trial court erred. To establish sufficient proof to compel submission of the issue to the jury for appropriate fact-finding under risk-utility analysis, it was not necessary for plaintiff to prove the existence of alternative, safer designs. Viewing the evidence in the light most favorable to plaintiff, even if there are no alternative methods of making bottoms for above-ground pools, the jury might have found that the risk posed by the pool outweighed its utility.

In a design-defect case, the plaintiff bears the burden of both going forward with the evidence and of persuasion that the product contained a defect. To establish a prima facie case, the plaintiff should adduce sufficient evidence on the risk-utility factors to establish a defect. With respect to above-ground swimming pools, for example, the plaintiff might seek to establish that pools are marketed primarily for recreational, not therapeutic purposes; that because of their design, including their configuration, inadequate warnings, and the use of vinyl liners, injury is likely; that, without impairing the usefulness of the pool or pricing it out of the market, warnings against diving could be made more prominent and a liner less dangerous. It may not be necessary for the plaintiff to introduce evidence on all those alternatives. Conversely, the plaintiff may wish to offer proof on other matters relevant to the risk-utility analysis. It is not a foregone conclusion that plaintiff ultimately will prevail on a risk-utility analysis, but he should have an opportunity to prove his case.

* * *

In concluding, we find that, although the jury allocated fault between the parties, the allocation was based upon the consideration of the fault of Muskin without reference to the design defect. Perhaps the jury would have made a different allocation if, in addition to the inadequacy of the warning, it had considered also the alleged defect in the design of the pool.

* * *

We modify and affirm the judgment of the Appellate Division reversing and remanding the matter for a new trial.

[The opinion of CLIFFORD, J., concurring in result, is omitted.]

SCHREIBER, J., concurring and dissenting.

Until today, the existence of a defect was an essential element in strict product liability. This no longer is so. Indeed, the majority has transformed strict product liability into absolute liability and delegated the function of making that determination to a jury. I must dissent from that conclusion because the jury will not be cognizant of all the elements that should be considered in formulating a policy supporting absolute liability, because it is not satisfactory to have a jury make a value judgment with respect to a type or class of product, and because its judgment will not have precedential effect.

* * *

My research has disclosed no case where liability was imposed, utilizing the risk-utility analysis, as a matter of law for an accident ascribable to a product in the absence of a defect (manufacturing flaw, available alternative, or inadequate warning) other than in the absolute liability context.   * * *

* * *

There are occasions where the court has determined as a matter of law because of policy reasons that liability should be imposed even though there is no defect in the product. This is the absolute liability model. The typical example is fixing absolute liability when an ultrahazardous activity causes injury or damage. Liability is imposed irrespective of any wrongdoing by the defendant. [Citation] In this situation the ultimate determination is that the industry should bear such costs, provided the jury has made the requisite findings on causation and damages.

Factors similar to those used in the risk-utility analysis for products liability are applied in the ultrahazardous activity case. The Restatement (Second) of Torts lists these elements:

§ 520. *Abnormally Dangerous Activities*

In determining whether an activity is abnormally dangerous, the following factors are to be considered:

(a) existence of a high degree of risk of some harm to the person, land or chattels of others;

(b) likelihood that the harm that results from it will be great;

(c) inability to eliminate the risk by the exercise of reasonable care;

(d) extent to which the activity is not a matter of common usage;

(e) inappropriateness of the activity to the place where it is carried on; and

(f) extent to which its value to the community is outweighed by its dangerous attributes.

It is conceivable that a court could decide that a manufacturer should have absolute liability for a defect-free product where as a matter of policy liability should be imposed. Suppose a manufacturer produced toy guns for children that emitted hard rubber pellets—an obviously dangerous situation. A court could reasonably conclude that the risks (despite warnings) outweighed the recreational value of the toy, that the manufacturer should bear the costs and that there should be absolute liability to a child injured by the toy.

The *Restatement* also cautions that whether an activity is an abnormally dangerous one so that it should be placed in the ultrahazardous category is to be settled by the court, not the jury. In its comment it states:

> The imposition of [absolute] liability, on the other hand, involves a characterization of the defendant's activity or enterprise itself, and a decision as to whether he is free to conduct it at all without becoming subject to liability for the harm that ensues even though he has used all reasonable care. This calls for a decision of the court; and it is no part of the province of the jury to decide whether an industrial enterprise upon which the community's prosperity might depend is located in the wrong place or whether such an activity as blasting is to be permitted without liability in the center of a large city. [3 *Restatement (Second) of Torts* § 520 comment l, at 43 (1965)]

* * *

[Today] * * * the Court * * * decides that a jury may speculate that, though there is no manufacturing flaw, the duty to warn has been satisfied and the manufacturer could not possibly have designed the item in a safer manner, the manufacturer can be absolutely liable because the jury finds that the risk outweighs the product's usefulness. It is not appropriate to forsake uniformity of treatment of a class or type of product by permitting juries to decide these questions. Nor is it appropriate for a jury to make this value judgment in addition to resolving factual issues. Unless the jury is to consider the feasibility of spreading the loss and the intricacies of cost avoidance, *see* Calabresi & Hirschoff, "Toward a Test for Strict Liability in Torts," 81 *Yale L.J.* 1055 (1972), the jury will conduct its inquiry in the absence of evidence of all the elements that should properly be considered in adopting a policy of having the manufacturer spread the loss by setting the price to cover the costs of claims or insurance premiums.

The majority holds that the jury should have been permitted to decide whether the risks of above-ground swimming pools with vinyl bottoms exceed their usefulness despite adequate warnings and despite unavailability of any other design. The plaintiff had the burden of proving this proposition. Yet he adduced no evidence on many of the factors bearing on the risk-utility analysis. There was no evidence on the extent that these pools are used and enjoyed throughout the country; how many families obtain the recreational benefits of swimming and play during a summer; how many accidents occur in the same period of time; the nature of the injuries and how many result from diving. There was no evidence of the feasibility of risk spreading or of the availability of liability insurance or its cost. There was no evidence introduced to enable one to gauge the effect on the price of the product, with or without insurance. The liability exposures, particularly if today's decision is given retroactive effect, could be financially devastating.

These factors should be given some consideration when deciding the policy question of whether pool manufacturers and, in the final analysis, consumers should bear the costs of accidents arising out of the use of pools when no fault can be attributed to the manufacturer because of a flaw in the pool, unavailability of a better design, or inadequate warning. If this Court wishes to make absolute liability available in product cases and not leave such decisions to the Legislature, it should require that trial courts determine in the first instance as a matter of law what products should be subject to absolute liability. In that event the court would consider all relevant factors including those utilized in the risk-utility analysis.

* * *

I join in the result, however. There was proof that the pool liner was slippery and that the vinyl bottom could have been thicker and the embossing deeper. As the majority states, a "fair inference could be drawn that deeper embossing would have rendered the pool bottom less slippery." * * * The plaintiff's theory was that the dangerous condition was the extreme slipperiness of the bottom. Viewing the facts favorably from the plaintiff's frame of reference, I would agree that he had some proof that the pool was incorrectly designed and therefore was defective. This issue, together with causation, should have been submitted to the jury.

Other than as stated herein, I join in the majority's opinion and concur in the judgment reversing and remanding the matter for a new trial.

CLIFFORD, J., concurring in the result.

For affirmance as modified—CHIEF JUSTICE WILENTZ, and JUSTICES CLIFFORD, HANDLER, POLLOCK and O'HERN—5.

Concurring and dissenting—JUSTICE SCHREIBER—1.

Notes

1. In 1987 the New Jersey Legislature passed a statute that severely restricts the *O'Brien v. Muskin* theory of recovery. The statute reads in pertinent part as follows:

a. In any product liability action against a manufacturer or seller for harm allegedly caused by a product that was designed in a defective manner, the manufacturer or seller shall not be liable if:

(1) At the time the product left the control of the manufacturer, there was not a practical and technically feasible alternative design that would have prevented the harm without substantially impairing the reasonably anticipated or intended function of the product * * *

* * *

b. The provisions of paragraph (1) of subsection a. of this section shall not apply if the court, on the basis of clear and convincing evidence, makes all of the following determinations:

(1) The product is egregiously unsafe or ultra-hazardous;

(2) The ordinary user or consumer of the product cannot reasonably be expected to have knowledge of the product's risks, or the product poses a risk of serious injury to persons other than the user or consumer; and

(3) The product has little or no usefulness.

N.J. Stat. Ann. 2A:58C–3

2. Halphen v. Johns–Manville Sales Corp., 484 So.2d 110 (La.1986) ruled that a product could be defective in design even though there was not a safer alternative available. In 1988 the Louisiana legislature abolished this basis of liability. *See* Louisiana Revised Statutes Annotated Title 9, § 2800.-51, et seq. In addition to *O'Brien* and *Halphen*, several other courts have indicated, at least in dictum, that a properly designed product can be defective because its risk outweighs its utility. *See* Carter v. Johns–Manville Sales Corp., 557 F.Supp. 1317, 1320 (E.D.Tex.1983); Wilson v. Piper Aircraft Corp., 282 Or. 61, 71 n.5, 577 P.2d 1322, 1328, n.5 (1978).

3. For the most part, courts have rejected the *O'Brien v. Muskin* theory. The question of whether to adopt the theory frequently arises in cases involving properly designed handguns. The issue is whether such weapons are defective because they create a risk of harm through foreseeable criminal misuse. No court has found such guns to be defective. *See* Lapp, The Application of Strict Liability to Manufacturers and Sellers of Handguns: A Call for More Focused Debate, 10 J.Prod.Liab. 179 (1987); Note, Handgun Manufacturers' Tort Liability to Victims of Criminal Shootings: A Summary of Recent Developments in the Push for a Judicial Ban of the "Saturday Night Special", 31 Vill.L.Rev. 1577 (1986); Comment, Handguns and Products Liability, 97 Harv.L.Rev. 1912 (1984); Note, Manufacturers' Liability to Victims of Handgun Crime: A Common–Law Approach, 51 Fordham L.Rev. 771 (1983). Attempts to impose liability on an abnormally dangerous activity theory have also been unsuccessful. *See* Note, The Manufacture and Distribution of Handguns as an Abnormally Dangerous Activity, 54 U.Chi.L.Rev. 369 (1987).

4. In Kelley v. R.G. Indus., Inc., 304 Md. 124, 497 A.2d 1143 (1985) plaintiff was shot by a robber armed with a "Saturday Night Special" manufactured by defendant. According to the court:

Saturday Night Specials are generally characterized by short barrels, light weight, easy concealability, low cost, use of cheap quality materials, poor manufacture, inaccuracy and unreliability. These characteristics render the Saturday Night Special particularly attractive for criminal use and virtually useless for the legitimate purposes of law enforcement, sport, and protection of persons, property and businesses.

304 Md. at 145–46, 497 A.2d at 1153–54. The court dismissed plaintiff's product liability design defect count, ruling that the handgun is not defective:

[It is not defective under the consumer expectations test of defect because a] consumer would expect a handgun to be dangerous, by its very nature, and to have the capacity to fire a bullet with deadly force. Kelley confuses a product's *normal function,* which may very well be dangerous, with a defect in a product's design or construction. * * * For the handgun to be defective, there would have to be a problem in its manufacture or design, such as a weak or improperly placed part, that would cause it to fire unexpectedly or otherwise malfunction. * * * [Likewise, it is not defective under the risk/utility test because this] standard is only applied when something goes wrong with a product. * * * [I]n the case of a handgun which injured a person in whose direction it was fired, the product worked precisely as intended. Therefore, the risk/utility test cannot be extended to impose liability on the maker or marketer of a handgun which has not malfunctioned.

304 Md. at 136–37, 497 A.2d at 1148–49. The court's reasoning for finding no product defect is typical of the product liability cases exonerating manufacturers of properly designed handguns. Another feature of the *Kelley* opinion, however, is atypical. The court created a special cause of action, imposing strict liability on "manufacturers, as well as all in the marketing chain, of Saturday Night Specials." The court said:

There is no clear-cut, established definition of a Saturday Night Special, although there are various characteristics which are considered in placing a handgun into that category. Relevant factors include the gun's barrel length, concealability, cost, quality of materials, quality of manufacture, accuracy, reliability, whether it has been banned from import by the Bureau of Alcohol, Tobacco and Firearms, and other related characteristics. Additionally, the industry standards, and the understanding among law enforcement personnel, legislators and the public, at the time the weapon was manufactured and/or marketed by a particular defendant, must be considered. Because many of these factors are relative, in a tort suit a handgun should rarely, if ever, be deemed a Saturday Night Special as a matter of law. Instead, it is a finding to be made by the trier of facts.

On the other hand, before the question of liability may go to the trier of facts, a threshold question must be decided as a matter of law. Since both state and federal statutes reflect a policy that there are legitimate uses for handguns, the trial court must first find that the plaintiff has made a showing that the handgun in question possesses sufficient characteristics of a Saturday Night Special. Moreover, merely because a handgun is small and short barrelled is not itself sufficient for the issue to be submitted to the trier of facts. As stated earlier, the General Assembly of Maryland has recognized the need for certain persons to carry guns, for example, law enforcement personnel and persons with special permits. Non-uniformed law enforcement personnel and certain permit holders will of necessity be required to carry small, short barrelled handguns. A high-quality, small, short barrelled handgun, designed for such legitimate use, is not a Saturday Night Special, and the trier of facts should not be permitted to speculate otherwise. While the determination by the trial court that the plaintiff has passed the initial hurdle cannot be based on size and barrel length alone, these factors, coupled with evidence of low cost, poor quality of materials or workmanship, unreliability, or other identifying characteristics, may be sufficient for the trial court to allow the issue to go to the trier of facts.

Finally, once the trier of facts determines that a handgun is a Saturday Night Special, then liability may be imposed against a manufacturer or anyone else in the marketing chain, including the retailer. Liability may only be imposed, however, when the plaintiff or plaintiff's decedent suffers injury or death because he is shot with the Saturday Night Special. In addition, the shooting must be a criminal act. The shooting itself may be the sole criminal act, or it may occur in the course of another crime where the person firing the Saturday Night Special is one of the perpetrators of the crime. Although neither contributory negligence nor assumption of the risk will be recognized as defenses, nevertheless the plaintiff must not be a participant in the criminal activity. If the foregoing elements are satisfied, then the defendant shall be liable for all resulting damages suffered by the gunshot victim, consistent with the established law concerning tort damages.

304 Md. at 157–59, 497 A.2d at 1159–60. *Kelley* is noted in 16 Cumb.L.Rev. 593 (1985/86); 1986 Det.C.L.Rev. 565; 13 N.Ky.L.Rev. 519 (1987); 61 Notre Dame L.Rev. 478 (1986); 46 Md.L.Rev. 486 (1987); 60 St.John's L.Rev. 555 (1986); 21 Tort & Ins.L.J. 493 (1986); 43 Wash. & Lee L.Rev. 1315 (1986).

5. Does the result reached in *Kelley* represent good policy?

6. The cause of action created by *Kelley* was abolished by the Maryland General Assembly and the citizens of Maryland by the passage of Chapter 533 of the Acts of 1988 and its ratification in a public referendum. *See* Md.Code of 1957, Art. 27, § 36–I(h).

7. In a 1991 referendum the citizens of the District of Columbia passed the following statute:

Any manufacturer, importer, or dealer of an assault weapon shall be held strictly liable in tort, without regard to fault or proof of defect, for all direct and consequential damages that arise from bodily injury or death if the bodily injury or death proximately results from the discharge of the assault weapon in the District of Columbia.

D.C. Code Ann. § 6–2392. For a discussion of the moral basis of liability of gun manufacturers, *see* Note, Corrective Justice and the D.C. Assault Weapon Liability Act, 19 J. Legis. 287 (1993).

8. Could a court that adopts the analysis of *O'Brien* reach the same result as *Kelley?* Both cases impose strict liability for marketing products whose designs cannot be improved, but they use different approaches in reaching the decision to impose strict liability. Which approach is preferable?

9. Under the *O'Brien v. Muskin Corp.* theory, are the following products defective, even if they are carefully made, because their risk outweighs their utility: tobacco; whiskey; roller skates; hair dryers?

10. Why have attempts to impose liability for marketing products whose design cannot be improved met with so little success both in courts

and legislatures? Are these attempts misguided efforts to regulate activity level rather than the level of care? *See* Posner, *supra* page 148; Note, The Smoldering Issue in *Cipollone v. Liggett Group, Inc.*: Process Concerns in Determining Whether Cigarettes are a Defectively Designed Product, 73 Cornell L.Rev. 606, 619–622 (1988). Is the use of political power by potential defendants the explanation? *See* Folio, The Politics of Strict Liability: Holding Manufacturers of Nondefective Saturday Night Special Handguns Strictly Liable After *Kelley v. R.G. Industries, Inc.*, 16 Hamline L.Rev. 147 (1992). Is there some other explanation?

SECTION C. OTHER APPROACHES

BARKER v. LULL ENGINEERING CO.
Supreme Court of California, 1978.
20 Cal.3d 413, 143 Cal.Rptr. 225, 573 P.2d 443.

TOBRINER, ACTING CHIEF JUSTICE.

[Plaintiff was injured at a construction site while operating a high-lift loader manufactured by defendant. The loader tipped partially over, and plaintiff jumped off the loader and attempted to scramble away. He was injured when some lumber on the lift fell and hit him. Plaintiff claimed that the loader was defectively designed in several respects, including that it should have been equipped with "outriggers," a roll bar, and seat belts. Plaintiff] instituted the present tort action seeking to recover damages for his injuries. The jury returned a verdict in favor of defendants, and plaintiff appeals from the judgment entered upon that verdict, contending primarily that in view of this court's decision in *Cronin v. J.B.E. Olson Corp.* (1972) 8 Cal.3d 121, 104 Cal.Rptr. 433, 501 P.2d 1153, the trial court erred in instructing the jury "that strict liability for a defect in design of a product is based on a finding that the product was unreasonably dangerous for its intended use * * *."

* * *

As we noted in *Cronin*, the Restatement draftsmen adopted the "unreasonably dangerous" language primarily as a means of confining the application of strict tort liability to an article which is "dangerous to an extent beyond that which would be contemplated by the ordinary consumer who purchases it, with the ordinary knowledge common to the community as to its characteristics." (Rest.2d Torts, § 402A, com. i.) In *Cronin*, however, we flatly rejected the suggestion that recovery in a products liability action should be permitted *only* if a product is more dangerous than contemplated by the average consumer, refusing to permit the low esteem in which the public might hold a dangerous product to diminish the manufacturer's responsibility for injuries caused by that product. As we pointedly noted in *Cronin*, even if the "ordinary consumer" may have contemplated that Shopsmith lathes posed a risk of loosening their grip and letting a piece of wood strike the operator, "another Greenman" should not be denied recovery. (8 Cal.3d at p. 133, 104 Cal.Rptr. 433, 501 P.2d 1153.) Indeed, our decision in *Luque v.*

McLean (1972) 8 Cal.3d 136, 104 Cal.Rptr. 443, 501 P.2d 1163—decided the same day as *Cronin*—aptly reflects our disagreement with the restrictive implications of the Restatement formulation, for in *Luque* we held that a power rotary lawn mower with an unguarded hole could properly be found defective, in spite of the fact that the defect in the product was patent and hence in all probability within the reasonable contemplation of the ordinary consumer.

Thus, our rejection of the use of the "unreasonably dangerous" terminology in *Cronin* rested in part on a concern that a jury might interpret such an instruction, as the Restatement draftsman had indeed intended, as shielding a defendant from liability so long as the product did not fall below the ordinary consumer's expectations as to the product's safety.[7] As *Luque* demonstrates, the dangers posed by such a misconception by the jury extend to cases involving design defects as well as to actions involving manufacturing defects: indeed, the danger of confusion is perhaps more pronounced in design cases in which the manufacturer could frequently argue that its product satisfied ordinary consumer expectations since it was identical to other items of the same product line with which the consumer may well have been familiar.

Accordingly, contrary to defendants' contention, the reasoning of *Cronin* does not dictate that that decision be confined to the manufacturing defect context. Indeed, in *Cronin* itself we expressly stated that our holding applied to design defects as well as to manufacturing defects (8 Cal.3d at pp. 134–135, 104 Cal.Rptr. 433, 501 P.2d 1153), and in *Henderson v. Harnischfeger Corp.* (1974) 12 Cal.3d 663, 670, 117 Cal. Rptr. 1, 527 P.2d 353, we subsequently confirmed the impropriety of instructing a jury in the language of the "unreasonably dangerous" standard in a design defect case. (See also *Foglio v. Western Auto Supply* (1976) 56 Cal.App.3d 470, 475, 128 Cal.Rptr. 545.) Consequently, we conclude that the design defect instruction given in the instant case was erroneous.

* * *

Defendants contend, however, that if *Cronin* is interpreted as precluding the use of the "unreasonably dangerous" language in defining a design defect, the jury in all such cases will inevitably be left without any guidance whatsoever in determining whether a product is defective in design or not. * * * Amicus California Trial Lawyer Association (CTLA) on behalf of the plaintiff responds by suggesting that the precise intent of our *Cronin* decision was to preclude a trial court from formulating any definition of "defect" in a product liability case, thus always

---

7. This is not to say that the expectations of the ordinary consumer are irrelevant to the determination of whether a product is defective, for as we point out below we believe that ordinary consumer expectations are frequently of direct significance to the defectiveness issue. The flaw in the Restatement's analysis, in our view, is that it treats such consumer expectations as a "ceiling" on a manufacturer's responsibility under strict liability principles, rather than as a "floor." As we shall explain, past California decisions establish that *at a minimum* a product must meet ordinary consumer expectations as to safety to avoid being found defective.

leaving the definition of defect, as well as the application of such definition, to the jury. As we explain, neither of these contentions represents an accurate portrayal of the intent or effect of our *Cronin* decision.

*   *   *

Our decision in *Cronin* did not mandate such confusion. Instead, by observing that the problem in defining defect might be alleviated by reference to the "cluster of useful precedents," we intended to suggest that in drafting and evaluating instructions on this issue in a particular case, trial and appellate courts would be well advised to consider prior authorities involving similar defective product claims.

*   *   *

In general, a manufacturing or production defect is readily identifiable because a defective product is one that differs from the manufacturer's intended result or from other ostensibly identical units of the same product line. For example, when a product comes off the assembly line in a substandard condition it has incurred a manufacturing defect. * * * A design defect, by contrast, cannot be identified simply by comparing the injury-producing product with the manufacturer's plans or with other units of the same product line, since by definition the plans and all such units will reflect the same design. Rather than applying any sort of deviation-from-the-norm test in determining whether a product is defective in design for strict liability purposes, our cases have employed two alternative criteria in ascertaining, in Justice Traynor's words, whether there is something "wrong, if not in the manufacturer's manner of production, at least in his product." (Traynor, *The Ways and Meanings of Defective Products and Strict Liability, supra,* 32 Tenn. L.Rev. 363, 366.)

First, our cases establish that a product may be found defective in design if the plaintiff demonstrates that the product failed to perform as safely as an ordinary consumer would expect when used in an intended or reasonably foreseeable manner. This initial standard, somewhat analogous to the Uniform Commercial Code's warranty of fitness and merchantability (Cal.U.Com.Code, § 2314), reflects the warranty heritage upon which California product liability doctrine in part rests. As we noted in *Greenman,* "implicit in [a product's] presence on the market * * * [is] a representation that it [will] safely do the jobs for which it was built." (59 Cal.2d at p. 64, 27 Cal.Rptr. at p. 701, 377 P.2d at p. 901.) When a product fails to satisfy such ordinary consumer expectations as to safety in its intended or reasonably foreseeable operation, a manufacturer is strictly liable for resulting injuries. * * * Under this standard, an injured plaintiff will frequently be able to demonstrate the defectiveness of a product by resort to circumstantial evidence, even when the accident itself precludes identification of the specific defect at fault. * * *

As Professor Wade has pointed out, however, the expectations of the ordinary consumer cannot be viewed as the exclusive yardstick for evaluating design defectiveness because "[i]n many situations * * * the consumer would not know what to expect, because he would have no idea how safe the product could be made." (Wade, *On the Nature of Strict Tort Liability for Products, supra,* 44 Miss.L.J. 825, 829.) Numerous California decisions have implicitly recognized this fact and have made clear, through varying linguistic formulations, that a product may be found defective in design, even if it satisfies ordinary consumer expectations, if through hindsight the jury determines that the product's design embodies "excessive preventable danger," or, in other words, if the jury finds that the risk of danger inherent in the challenged design outweighs the benefits of such design. * * *

A review of past cases indicates that in evaluating the adequacy of a product's design pursuant to this latter standard, a jury may consider, among other relevant factors, the gravity of the danger posed by the challenged design, the likelihood that such danger would occur, the mechanical feasibility of a safer alternative design, the financial cost of an improved design, and the adverse consequences to the product and to the consumer that would result from an alternative design. * * *

Although our cases have thus recognized a variety of considerations that may be relevant to the determination of the adequacy of a product's design, past authorities have generally not devoted much attention to the appropriate allocation of the burden of proof with respect to these matters. * * * The allocation of such burden is particularly significant in this context inasmuch as this court's product liability decisions, from *Greenman* to *Cronin,* have repeatedly emphasized that one of the principal purposes behind the strict product liability doctrine is to relieve an injured plaintiff of many of the onerous evidentiary burdens inherent in a negligence cause of action. Because most of the evidentiary matters which may be relevant to the determination of the adequacy of a product's design under the "risk-benefit" standard—e.g., the feasibility and cost of alternative designs—are similar to issues typically presented in a negligent design case and involve technical matters peculiarly within the knowledge of the manufacturer, we conclude that once the plaintiff makes a prima facie showing that the injury was proximately caused by the product's design, the burden should appropriately shift to the defendant to prove, in light of the relevant factors, that the product is not defective. Moreover, inasmuch as this conclusion flows from our determination that the fundamental public policies embraced in *Greenman* dictate that a manufacturer who seeks to escape liability for an injury proximately caused by its product's design on a risk-benefit theory should bear the burden of persuading the trier of fact that its product should not be judged defective, the defendant's burden is one affecting the burden of proof, rather than simply the burden of producing evidence. * * *

Thus, to reiterate, a product may be found defective in design, so as to subject a manufacturer to strict liability for resulting injuries, under either of two alternative tests. First, a product may be found defective in design if the plaintiff establishes that the product failed to perform as safely as an ordinary consumer would expect when used in an intended or reasonably foreseeable manner. Second, a product may alternatively be found defective in design if the plaintiff demonstrates that the product's design proximately caused his injury and the defendant fails to establish, in light of the relevant factors, that, on balance, the benefits of the challenged design outweigh the risk of danger inherent in such design.

* * *

Finally, contrary to the suggestion of amicus CTLA, an instruction which advises the jury that it may evaluate the adequacy of a product's design by weighing the benefits of the challenged design against the risk of danger inherent in such design is not simply the equivalent of an instruction which requires the jury to determine whether the manufacturer was negligent in designing the product. (See, e.g., Wade, *On the Nature of Strict Tort Liability for Products, supra,* 44 Miss.L.J. 825, 835.) It is true, of course, that in many cases proof that a product is defective in design may also demonstrate that the manufacturer was negligent in choosing such a design. As we have indicated, however, in a strict liability case, as contrasted with a negligent design action, the jury's focus is properly directed to the condition of the product itself, and not to the reasonableness of the manufacturer's conduct. * * *

Thus, the fact that the manufacturer took reasonable precautions in an attempt to design a safe product or otherwise acted as a reasonably prudent manufacturer would have under the circumstances, while perhaps absolving the manufacturer of liability under a negligence theory, will not preclude the imposition of liability under strict liability principles if, upon hindsight, the trier of fact concludes that the product's design is unsafe to consumers, users, or bystanders. * * *

* * *

The judgment in favor of defendants is reversed.

Mosk, Clark, Richardson, Wright (Retired Chief Justice of California assigned by the Acting Chairperson of the Judicial Council), and Sullivan (Retired Associate Justice of the Supreme Court sitting under assignment by the Chairperson of the Judicial Council), JJ., concur.

Notes

1. A number of other jurisdictions have adopted the *Barker v. Lull* test of defect. Caterpillar Tractor Co. v. Beck, 593 P.2d 871 (Alaska 1979); Dart v. Wiebe Mfg., Inc., 147 Ariz. 242, 709 P.2d 876 (1985); Knitz v. Minster Mach. Co., 69 Ohio St.2d 460, 432 N.E.2d 814 (1982), cert. denied, 459 U.S. 857, 103 S.Ct. 127, 74 L.Ed.2d 110 (1982).

2. California has approved the following jury instruction for design defect cases:

The _____ of a product is liable for injuries caused by a defect in its design which existed when it left the possession of the _____ provided that they resulted from a use of the product that was reasonably foreseeable by the _____

A product is defective in design:

[if it fails to perform as safely as an ordinary consumer would expect when used in an intended or reasonably foreseeable manner]. [or]

[if there is a risk of danger inherent in the design which outweighs the benefits of that design].

[In determining whether the benefits of the design outweigh such risks you may consider, among other things, the gravity of the danger posed by the design, the likelihood that such danger would cause damage, the mechanical feasibility of a safer alternate design at the time of manufacture, the financial cost of an improved design, and the adverse consequences to the product and the consumer that would result from an alternate design.]

BAJI 9.00.5 (1992 Revision)

3. How would a court using the *Barker v. Lull* test of defect decide the following cases?

A. A punch press without a point of operation safety guard. The worker lost two fingers when she accidentally activated the foot pedal control while her hand was below the ram.

B. A new drug that is very beneficial to a large number of people causes a serious side-effect in a small number of people. Plaintiff takes the drug and suffers the side-effect. Prior to plaintiff's illness, the risk was not known.

C. A beer bottle that is not strong enough to withstand the force of being thrown against a telephone pole.

4. The *Barker v. Lull* test significantly expands the scope of liability in two ways. First, by using the two tests of defect in the disjunctive, it insures that plaintiff will recover if the product fails either test. Some products are defective under risk-utility but not under consumer expectations, and some products are defective under consumer expectations but not risk-utility. By declaring that a product is defective if it violates either test, *Barker* carries liability further than courts that use either test singly.

5. The second way that *Barker* expands the scope of liability is by shifting the burden of proof on the question of whether the utility outweighs the risk. In analyzing this aspect of the *Barker v. Lull* test, Professor Epstein states:

The careful division of burdens in the second portion of the test says that plaintiff need only show design *features* that might be implicated in the accident, leaving it to the defendant, at great expense, *routinely* to justify each feature as best he can. With this distribution of burden, the plaintiff can always show some way in which the product might have been changed in order to avert the accident, as it is always possible to generate some improvement at some price. * * * All product related accidents have become presumptively actionable.

Epstein, Products Liability: The Search for the Middle Ground, 56 N.C.L.Rev. 643, 651 (1978). *See also,* Henderson, Renewed Judicial Controversy Over Defective Product Design: Toward the Preservation of an Emerging Consensus, 63 Minn.L.Rev. 773 (1979); Schwartz, Foreword: Understanding Products Liability, 67 Calif.L.Rev. 439 (1979).

6. Are there any cases that will not go to the jury under the *Barker v. Lull* test? Suppose plaintiff drops a typewriter on his toe, and he sues the manufacturer of the typewriter for the resulting damage. Would the case go to the jury? If not, why not?

7. Another possible approach is to submit the question of defect to the jury without defining the term. Consider Nesselrode v. Executive Beechcraft, Inc., 707 S.W.2d 371, 377–78 (Mo.1986) in which the court stated:

Under Missouri's rule of strict tort liability, a product's design is deemed defective, for purposes of imposing liability, when it is shown by a preponderance of evidence that the design renders the product unreasonably dangerous. * * *

Though Missouri has adopted the rule of strict tort liability as set forth in the *Restatement,* we have not yet formally incorporated, in any meaningful way, the *Restatement's* consumer expectation test into the lexicon of our products liability law. * * * Nor have we yet decided to travel or require plaintiffs to travel the path of risks and utilities. * * *

Under our model of strict tort liability the concept of unreasonable danger, which is determinative of whether a product is defective in a design case, is presented to the jury as an ultimate issue without further definition. See Aronson's Men's Stores v. Potter Electric Signal Company, Inc., 632 S.W.2d at 472. Accordingly, our approved jury instruction which governs in a design defect case, MAI 25.04 (3rd) does not contain as one of its component elements a definitional paragraph which gives independent content to the concept of unreasonable danger.

Notwithstanding the minority character of this approach, Professor Leon Green, in his 1976 Texas Law Review article, *Strict Liability Under Sections 402A and 402B: A Decade of Litigation,* explains why an approach that avoids the use of an external standard by which to determine unreasonable danger—*i.e.,* defectiveness—is preferable to one which does use an external standard. He points out first that juries do not have "a fictitious standard by which to determine assault, battery, false imprisonment, nuisance, entry upon land, or the taking of a chattel" and then he suggests that "[n]or do juries need an external standard by which to determine the danger of a product in an unreasonably dangerous defective condition." Green, Strict Liability Under Sections 402A and 402B: A Decade of Litigation, 54 Tex.L.Rev. 1185, 1206 (1976). He concludes his discussion with the judgment that "the ritual indulged in by the giving of abstract, abstruse standards, impossible to comply with, only perpetuates the mystical trial by ordeal and *may conceal a hook in a transcendental lure that will snag an appellate court." Id.* at 1206. (emphasis added)

As we noted previously, at the trial of a design defect case, the concept of unreasonable danger is treated as an ultimate issue. The jury gives this concept content by applying their collective intelligence and experience to the broad evidentiary spectrum of facts and circumstances presented by the parties.

LOBIANCO v. PROPERTY PROTECTION, INC.

Superior Court of Pennsylvania, 1981.
292 Pa.Super. 346, 437 A.2d 417.

SPAETH, JUDGE:

Appellant seeks to recover $35,815 as the value of jewelry stolen from her home when a burglar alarm system installed by appellee failed to work. The action is in two counts. The first count is in assumpsit for breach of warranty. The second count is in trespass and alleges strict liability under the Restatement (Second) of Torts § 402A. The lower court heard the case without a jury. On the first count the court held that by the terms of the contract for the installation of the burglar alarm system, damages for breach of warranty were limited to the cost of repairs. On the second count the court held that "[Section 402A] does not apply in the present case. [The alarm system] was not dangerous and did not cause any physical harm to [appellant] or her property." * * * Appellant filed exceptions. The court dismissed the exceptions and entered judgment in favor of appellee. Appellant's appeal from this judgment was argued before a panel of this court, and was re-argued before the court *en banc*. We affirm, although on the trespass count alleging strict liability under Section 402A our reasoning is somewhat different from the lower court's.

* * *

II

In Webb v. Zern, 422 Pa. 424, 220 A.2d 853 (1966), our Supreme Court expressly adopted the Restatement (Second) of Torts § 402A. * * *

[T]he expression "physical harm" as used in Section 402A should not be construed as requiring that the plaintiff * * * prove damage to the property. * * *

Having said this much, we nevertheless agree with the lower court's conclusion that Section 402A "does not apply in the present case." Opinion of lower court, R. 62a. It is unimportant that we have reached that conclusion by reasoning different from the lower court's, for we may affirm on reasoning different from the lower court's. * * *

In *Ray v. Alad Corp.,* 19 Cal.3d 22, 136 Cal.Rptr. 574, 560 P.2d 3 (1977), the court said:

The purpose of the rule of strict tort liability "is to insure that the costs of injuries resulting from defective products are borne by the manufacturers that put such products on the market rather

than by the injured persons who are powerless to protect themselves." (*Greenman v. Yuba Power Products, Inc.* (1963) 59 Cal.2d
57, 63, 27 Cal.Rptr. 697, 701, 377 P.2d 897, 901.) However, the rule
"does not rest on the analysis of the financial strength or bargaining
power of the parties to the particular action. It rests, rather, on the
proposition that '[t]he cost of an injury and the loss of time or
health may be an overwhelming misfortune to the person injured,
and a needless one, for the risk of injury can be insured by the
manufacturer and distributed among the public as a cost of doing
business.' (*Escola v. Coca Cola Bottling Co.*, 24 Cal.2d 453, 462, 150
P.2d 436 [concurring opinion].)" (*Seely v. White Motor Co.* (1965)
63 Cal.2d 9, 18–19, 45 Cal.Rptr. 17, 23, 403 P.2d 145, 151.) Thus,
"the paramount policy to be promoted by the rule is the protection
of otherwise defenseless victims of manufacturing defects and the
spreading throughout society of the cost of compensating them."
(Italics added.) *Price v. Shell Oil Co.* (1970) 2 Cal.3d 245, 251, 85
Cal.Rptr. 178, 181, 466 P.2d 722, 725.

19 Cal.3d at 30–31, 136 Cal.Rptr. at 579, 560 P.2d at 8–9.

And see Miller v. Preitz, 422 Pa. 383, 221 A.2d 320 (1966) (concurring
and dissenting opinions, discussing with a full collection of authority the
development of the rule of strict liability; these opinions were cited with
approval in *Webb v. Zern, supra,* 422 Pa. at 427, 220 A.2d at 854);
Dawejko v. Jorgensen Steel Co., ___ Pa.Superior Ct. ___, 434 A.2d 106
(1981).

The purposes thus stated would not be served by applying Section
402A to the present case. Homeowners are not "otherwise defenseless
victims" of burglar alarm manufacturers in the same sense that a buyer
of an automobile, for example, may be the victim of the automobile
manufacturer. If the property is valuable, the homeowner may insure
it. To apply Section 402A to the present case would in practical effect
excuse the homeowner from having to insure the property and would
shift the risk of its loss to the burglar alarm manufacturer. This would
represent a less, not more, equitable allocation of the risk. The homeowner, not the manufacturer, knows what property is in the home, and
its value; the manufacturer does not. Even if the manufacturer were to
find out what property was in the home before installing the burglar
alarm system, the homeowner could, and probably would, add other
property, without notice to the manufacturer. As between the homeowner and the manufacturer, the manufacturer is more "defenseless"
than the homeowner. If the homeowner buys a silver service or a stereo
system, at least he can get insurance against its loss; but the manufacturer cannot, for it will not know that the service or stereo has been put
in the home. Thus it may not be said that " 'the risk of injury can be
insured by the manufacturer and distributed among the public as a cost
of doing business.' " *Ray v. Alad Corp., supra.* Nor may it be said that
the manufacturer ought to protect itself by increasing its charge, in that
way distributing the risk. That would mean that a homeowner with
personal property of only modest value would be required to pay for his

burglar alarm system a price high enough to protect the manufacturer against the loss it might incur if a homeowner with personal property of great value were burglarized. Those of modest means would be subsidizing the rich.

Summarizing the cases on strict liability, Prosser has said:

> The courts have tended to lay stress upon the fact that the defendant is acting for his own purposes, and is seeking a benefit or a profit of his own for such activities, and that he is in a better position to administer the uninsured risk by passing it on to the public than is the innocent victim. The problem is dealt with as one of allocating a more or less inevitable loss to be charged against a complex and dangerous civilization, and liability is imposed on the party best able to shoulder it. The defendant is held liable merely because, as a matter of social adjustment, the conclusion is that the responsibility should be his.

Prosser on Torts 495 (4th ed. 1971).

This is well said, for it recognizes—indeed, emphasizes—that whether a case is one appropriate for the imposition of strict liability is a decision that the court must make according to what "social adjustment" it believes just.

Our own Supreme Court has arrived at the same conclusion, in *Azzarello v. Black Bros. Co., Inc.*, 480 Pa. 547, 391 A.2d 1020 (1978). There the issue was whether the trial judge should have instructed the jury that it could find strict liability only if it found the product in question "unreasonably dangerous." The Court held that the judge should not have, and it approved the Proposed Standard Jury Instructions, which make no reference to "unreasonably dangerous," instead directing the jury's attention to whether the product had a "defect." "It must be understood," said the Court, "that the words, 'unreasonably dangerous' have no independent significance and merely represent a label to be used where it is determined that the risk of loss should be placed upon the supplier." 480 Pa. at 556, 391 A.2d at 1025. The Court continued:

> [T]he phrases "defective condition" and "unreasonably dangerous" as used in the Restatement formulation [Section 402A] are terms of art invoked where *strict liability* is appropriate. It is a judicial function to decide whether under plaintiff's averment of the facts, recovery would be justified; and only after this judicial determination is made is the cause submitted to the jury to determine whether the facts of the case support the averments of the complaint.

480 Pa. at 558, 391 A.2d at 1026.

And see Dawejko v. Jorgensen Steel Co., supra (deciding when it is just to impose strict liability on corporation that is successor to corporation that manufactured the product).

Here, we hold that for appellant to be permitted to recover on a theory of strict liability would not be justified. "[A]s a matter of social adjustment," Prosser, *supra,* the responsibility for protecting against the loss of her jewelry should, so far as the imposition of strict liability is concerned, be appellant's, not appellee's. Again, to avoid misunderstanding, we add that we have confined ourselves to the issue of strict liability for physical harm to property. If harm to a person were involved, as for example which might occur if a homeowner were injured by a burglar who had entered the home undetected because the burglar alarm system failed, a different case would be presented. As to what should be the disposition of such a case, we express no opinion.

AFFIRMED.

CERCONE, PRESIDENT JUDGE, files a concurring statement.

BROSKY, J., files a concurring opinion, in which CAVANAUGH, J., joins.

MONTGOMERY, J., files a dissenting opinion, in which HESTER, J., joins.

[Concurring and dissenting opinions are omitted.]

Notes

1. In Azzarello v. Black Bros. Co., 480 Pa. 547, 391 A.2d 1020 (1978) the Pennsylvania court adopted a unique approach to strict liability. The court ruled that the fundamental question as to whether to impose strict liability in a given case is to be made by the judge rather than the jury. The court stated:

While a lay finder of fact is obviously competent in resolving a dispute as to the condition of a product, an entirely different question is presented where a decision as to whether that condition justifies placing liability upon the supplier must be made. * * * Thus the mere fact that we have approved Section 402A, and even if we agree that the phrase "unreasonably dangerous" serves a useful purpose in predicting liability in this area, it does not follow that this language should be used in framing the issues for the jury's consideration. Should an ill-conceived design which exposes the user to the risk of harm entitle one injured by the product to recover? Should adequate warnings of the dangerous propensities of an article insulate one who suffers injuries from those propensities? When does the utility of a product outweigh the unavoidable danger it may pose? These are questions of law and their resolution depends upon social policy. It is a judicial function to decide whether, under plaintiff's averment of the facts, recovery would be justified; and only after this judicial determination is made is the cause submitted to the jury to determine whether the facts of the case support the averments of the complaint. They do not fall within the orbit of a factual dispute which is properly assigned to the jury for resolution. A standard suggesting the existence of a "defect" if the article is unreasonably dangerous or not duly safe is inadequate to guide a lay jury in resolving these questions.

Id. at 1025–27. The court approved the following jury instruction:

"The [supplier] of a product is the guarantor of its safety. The product must, therefore, be provided with every element necessary to make it safe for [its intended] use, and without any condition that makes it unsafe for [its intended] use. If you find that the product, at the time it left the defendant's control, lacked any element necessary to make it safe for [its intended] use or contained any condition that made it unsafe for [its intended] use, then the product was defective, and the defendant is liable for all harm caused by such defect."

Id. at 1027 n. 12.

2. *Azzarello v. Black Bros. Co.* created considerable confusion as to exactly what the judge was to decide and what the jury was to decide. *See* Henderson, Renewed Judicial Controversy Over Defective Product Design: Toward the Preservation of an Emerging Consensus, 63 Minn.L.Rev. 773, 797–801 (1979); Wade, On Product "Design Defects" and Their Actionability, 33 Vand.L.Rev. 551, 560–561 (1980). Not all of the subsequent cases clearly articulate the reasons for deciding the strict liability issue as they did. *Lobianco* decides the issue by directly considering the policies underlying strict liability. *See also* Dambacher by Dambacher v. Mallis, 336 Pa.Super. 22, 485 A.2d 408 (1984), appeal dismissed, 508 Pa. 643, 500 A.2d 428 (1985). Other courts have more narrowly restricted themselves to applying the accepted tests for determining defect. *See, e.g.*, Jordon by Jordon v. K–Mart Corp., 417 Pa.Super. 186, 611 A.2d 1328 (1992) where a ten-year-old boy lost control of his plastic sled and hit a tree. He claimed that the sled was defective in design because it lacked any independent steering or braking mechanisms. The court upheld the trial court's determination that the sled was not defective. The court said:

> The trial court, citing social policy, meticulously weighed the relative risks and utility of the sled in question and the type of sled, a toboggan, to determine whether liability should be imposed. The Court found that like most recreational activities, sledding involves a degree of risk and even changing the design to require brakes or steering would not remove the inherent risk in the activity. We agree with the trial court's analysis of social policy and hold that the trial court correctly applied the Azzarello threshold in determining the strict liability claim based on product design.

3. Two writers argue that judges should exercise greater control over the determination of defectiveness than they now do in most jurisdictions. *See* Fischer, Products Liability—Functionally Imposed Strict Liability, 32 Okla.L.Rev. 93 (1979); Twerski, Seizing the Middle Ground Between Rules and Standards in Design Defect Litigation: Advancing Directed Verdict Practice in the Law of Torts, 57 N.Y.U.L.Rev. 521 (1982); Twerski, From Risk–Utility to Consumer Expectations: Enhancing the Role of Judicial Screening in Product Liability Litigation, 11 Hofstra L.Rev. 861 (1983).

ELGIN AIRPORT INN, INC. v. COMMONWEALTH EDISON CO.

Supreme Court of Illinois, 1982.
89 Ill.2d 138, 59 Ill.Dec. 675, 432 N.E.2d 259.

SIMON, JUSTICE:

The defendant, Commonwealth Edison, a regulated utility, supplied electricity to the plaintiff, Elgin Airport Inn, a motel. In particular, it supplied "three-phase" current, which the Inn needed for certain air-conditioning motors designed to run on that type of current. On November 3, 1976, a casting in a switching mechanism in Edison's line broke, and one of the phases was cut off, a mishap known as "single phasing." The resulting abnormal current is unsuitable for three-phase motors. After about five minutes on the abnormal current, the Inn's motors overheated and burned. The smoke drove everyone out of the Inn; no one, however, was injured, and the damage to the motors amounted to less than $5,000. The Inn sued, under theories of negligence, *res ipsa loquitur,* strict tort liability, and violation of the Public Utilities Act (Ill.Rev.Stat.1977, ch. 111⅔, par. 32). The circuit court of Kane County, after trial, ruled for the defendant on all counts. The appellate court affirmed on the negligence, *res ipsa,* and statutory counts, but reversed on the issue of strict product liability in tort, holding that Edison was liable as a matter of law, and remanding for ascertainment of damages. (88 Ill.App.3d 477, 43 Ill.Dec. 620, 410 N.E.2d 620.) We granted Edison leave to appeal, and, adopting the circuit court's conclusion that the electricity, even if dangerous, was not unreasonably so, we now reverse the appellate court on the strict liability count.

The evidence supports the circuit court's finding that Edison did nothing wrong. Unlike an ordinary product, which can be made and inspected at the maker's convenience, electricity must be always ready, at the flip of the user's switch. The supplier cannot possibly inspect all its miles of wire constantly to be sure that every ampere is perfect; the casting that failed here was not visible to the naked eye, and any defect in it could not be discovered unless the switching mechanism was disassembled and examined. Edison followed its normal inspection procedures, and the Inn does not suggest how those procedures could have been improved. Single phasing seems to be simply one of those things that happen occasionally; there is nothing Edison or anyone else could have done to prevent it or detect it immediately, and nothing Edison could have done to reduce the danger the abnormal current would pose to the Inn's motors should it occur. The judgments for Edison on the negligence and *res ipsa* counts must therefore be affirmed. We also agree with the lower court's conclusion that the Inn's claim under the Public Utilities Act is meritless. That brings us to the main issue of this appeal, strict liability.

The lack of any feasible way for Edison to prevent occasional intervals of defective current or reduce the danger of such current would not by itself insulate Edison from strict tort liability for a defective product. (*Cunningham v. MacNeal Memorial Hospital* (1970), 47 Ill.2d 443, 266 N.E.2d 897.) This case, however, goes a step further. The danger of abnormal current *can* be reduced, by the user. Single phasing is a common enough phenomenon that the national electrical code, which Edison's tariffs required the Inn to comply with, provides that appliances are to be equipped with suitable protective devices. The Inn's air-conditioning units included a device supposedly designed to protect the motors in case of power failure or abnormality, such as single phasing. The device, however, failed to prevent the damage. The reason for the failure is not clear, because the record is incompletely developed on this point, as it is on many technical facets of this case. As the plaintiff had the burden of proof and lost in the circuit court, we shall assume that the failure was attributable to some defect in the protective device; there is evidence to support that hypothesis. At any rate, there is no evidence that Edison knew or should have anticipated that the device would fail.

In these circumstances, even if Edison knew that its current had single phased, to cut off that current entirely might not be the appropriate response. The defective current, while harmful to certain peculiarly sensitive appliances, namely three-phase motors—which are equipped with devices to protect against that harm—would not necessarily be unsafe or unsuitable for all other utilizations. Cutting it off in Edison's main line would protect the Inn's motors, but it could also indiscriminately black out other utilizations (and other customers along the line) for which the abnormal current supply might be, if not ideal, at least usable. The system of cutting off the abnormal current only in the sensitive appliances themselves, by means of a protective device incorporated in the appliance, seems eminently reasonable. Thus, even if Edison had known its current was abnormal, continuing to supply it (until normal current could be substituted) would not necessarily have been improper. Edison might reasonably have chosen simply to warn the Inn of the situation so that the Inn could check on its motors or take other appropriate action. Indeed, the main thrust of the Inn's argument that Edison was negligent is not that the abnormality occurred but that Edison failed to warn the Inn for over five minutes. (The danger to the motors increases as they continue to draw the abnormal current.) And because Edison did not know and could not sooner discover that its current was abnormal, it is not strictly liable for a failure to warn of the danger. *Woodill v. Parke Davis & Co.* (1980), 79 Ill.2d 26, 37 Ill.Dec. 304, 402 N.E.2d 194.

The contract between Edison and the Inn provided:

"Continuous service. The company shall not be responsible in damages for any failure to supply electricity or for interruption or reversal of the supply, if such failure, interruption, or reversal is without wilful [sic] default or negligence on its part."

Whether this provision directly exculpates Edison from liability for single phasing is not entirely clear, but it does allow Edison to cut off the current entirely with impunity. As we have explained, the Inn has not proved, and we cannot say as a matter of law, that single phasing is, on the whole, inferior to no current at all. Since Edison could do nothing to avoid being forced to the choice, it seems unfair to hold Edison strictly liable for adopting the superior alternative while absolving it from liability had it followed the inferior course of completely shutting off electricity. And Edison should not be strictly liable for unknowingly and unavoidably transmitting current that it could properly have transmitted knowingly and intentionally, under the circumstances.

It appears that, for the foreseeable future, the technological possibilities for keeping appliances from being ruined by single phasing will lie with the appliances rather than with the current. Moreover, Edison cannot, either practically or legally, control the details of what appliances with what protective devices its customers are plugging in, or vary its rates accordingly; it can only insist on compliance with general standards like the national electrical code, which will inevitably lag behind the state of the art. Only the Inn here could, by selection of a less fragile motor or a more dependable protective device, have prevented the loss; Edison could do nothing. Legally transferring losses from those who could prevent them to those who cannot will not improve safety. In *Peterson v. Lou Bachrodt Chevrolet Co.* (1975), 61 Ill.2d 17, 329 N.E.2d 785, this court held that the seller of a used car was not strictly liable for its defects, partially because liability would not serve the policy of inducing manufacturers to make safer cars. That reasoning seems far stronger here, where the effects of liability might be not merely nonexistent but perverse.

Neither is the policy of spreading losses particularly compelling here. The loss is not purely a feature of Edison's business of making electricity; it is at least as plausibly a problem of the motors. Edison did not create the risk single-handed; the danger here varies immensely from one user to another and is largely under the users' control. Product liability as a type of built-in insurance, with the premiums incorporated into the price of the electricity, seems both unfair to those users who do not have valuable, fragile, inadequately protected appliances, but must pay for the dangers of those who do, and unnecessarily expensive in the long run if more motors burn out because those who can protect and save them have no financial incentive to do so. If the Inn wanted insurance, it could have bought its own, probably at lower and more accurate rates than Edison could provide.

We conclude that while the current was defective, in the sense that it was not as Edison designed it, and was no doubt dangerous (beyond the ordinary dangers of electricity) to certain appliances, the circuit court's finding that it was not *unreasonably* dangerous is not against the manifest weight of the evidence. Edison could do nothing to prevent occasional single phasing of its current; the risk of single phasing and the danger single phasing would present to three-phase motors were well known in the electrical trade; the danger could best be minimized by the user, and the Inn, as required, had taken precautions, which proved, unfortunately, not to be infallible; given those precautions, the danger was not great; Edison, trying to provide continuous electricity at the user's whim, could reasonably suppose that, for a short while at least, even abnormal current was better than none.

Because Edison would be strictly liable in tort for a defective product only if the defect made the product unreasonably dangerous

(*Dubin v. Michael Reese Hospital & Medical Center* (1980), 83 Ill.2d 277, 47 Ill.Dec. 345, 415 N.E.2d 350; *Suvada v. White Motor Co.* (1965), 32 Ill.2d 612, 210 N.E.2d 182; Restatement (Second) of Torts sec. 402A (1965)), there is no need to consider the more fundamental questions Edison raises, such as whether electricity is a product at all, and whether a regulated utility can be strictly liable in tort.

The circuit court was correct to enter judgment for Edison on all four counts; the appellate court erred in reversing as to the strict liability count.

> *Appellate court affirmed in part and reversed in part; circuit court affirmed.*

THOMAS J. MORAN, J., concurs in the judgment.

Note

Elgin provides useful contrast with cases that apply the traditional tests of defect, such as *Barker v. Lull Engineering Co., supra* p. 202, and with *Lobianco v. Property Protection, Inc., supra* p. 209, a case where the judge determined defectiveness as a matter of policy. When *Elgin* was decided, the Illinois court was closely identified with the consumer expectations test of defect. *See* Hunt v. Blasius, 74 Ill.2d 203, 23 Ill.Dec. 574, 384 N.E.2d 368 (1978); Dunham v. Vaughan & Bushnell Mfg. Co., 42 Ill.2d 339, 247 N.E.2d 401 (1969). Illinois continues to use consumer expectations, but has also adopted risk-utility as an alternative test of defect in design cases. Lamkin v. Towner, 138 Ill.2d 510, 150 Ill.Dec. 562, 563 N.E.2d 449 (1990). Yet, the Illinois court decided *Elgin* on the basis of a sophisticated policy analysis rather than a mechanical application of a test for determining defect. This demonstrates that there is no bright line distinction between a rule oriented approach and a policy oriented approach. Few courts are as clear as the court in *Elgin* in articulating the underlying policies that influence the way they apply the applicable rules in a given case. *Elgin*, however, is an important reminder that a court's perception of the policies underlying strict liability can strongly influence its decisions. Good advocates will often pay as much attention to policy arguments as to arguments about doctrine, even in jurisdictions that have explicitly adopted rule oriented approaches.

Chapter 7

FUNDAMENTAL PRINCIPLES OF STRICT LIABILITY: CHANGES IN TECHNOLOGY AND KNOWLEDGE OF RISK

This chapter deals with the limits of knowledge and technology on the liability of manufacturers. The question is whether products will be judged in light of the knowledge and technology available at the time of distribution or at the time of trial. The issue arises in three ways. First, the manufacturer may fail to anticipate an accident caused by unforeseeable misuse of the product. Second, the manufacturer of a relatively new product may be unaware of a generic risk associated with the product, *e.g.,* that exposure to a chemical causes cancer. Third, the manufacturer may know of the risk, but not have technology available to reduce the risk, *e.g.,* sale of a car equipped with mechanical brakes before hydraulic brakes were invented. *See generally* Wade, On the Effect in Product Liability of Knowledge Unavailable Prior to Marketing, 58 N.Y.U.L.Rev. 734 (1983); Birnbaum and Wrubel, "State of the Art" and Strict Products Liability, 21 Tort & Ins. L.J. 30 (1985); Robb, A Practical Approach to Use of State of the Art Evidence in Strict Products Liability Cases, 77 Nw.U.L.Rev. 1 (1982); Spradley, Defensive Use of State of the Art Evidence in Strict Products Liability, 67 Minn.L.Rev. 343 (1982); Wertheimer, Unknowable Dangers and the Death of Strict Products Liability: The Empire Strikes Back, U.Cin.L.Rev. 1183 (1992).

There are a number of important issues. Should justifiable ignorance excuse the manufacturer with respect to any or all of the three ways the question arises? Should the resolution of these issues apply across the board to all products, or should certain products—such as drugs or asbestos—be dealt with differently?

Some courts use "state of the art" to refer to the second and third issues. The phrase has an imprecise meaning, however, because other courts often use it to refer to other concepts, such as industry custom and compliance with governmental standards.

SECTION A.   IGNORANCE OF GENERIC RISK

HABECKER v. CLARK EQUIPMENT CO.

United States Court of Appeals, Third Circuit, 1991.
942 F.2d 210.

STAPLETON, CIRCUIT JUDGE:

* * *

I.

John Habecker was killed while attempting to back a forklift down a ramp. The forklift went off the side of the ramp; Habecker was thrown out and crushed beneath the forklift. The forklift, manufactured by Clark Equipment Company ("Clark") and leased by Forklifts, Inc., ("Forklifts") was not equipped with operator restraints, such as a seat belt or harness. The accident happened during the course of Habecker's employment as a civilian employee of the New Cumberland Army Depot.

* * *

II.

In a motion in limine and throughout the trial, the Habeckers consistently objected to evidence concerning what the industry knew about the efficacy of operator restraint systems in 1977. In particular, they objected unsuccessfully to evidence offered by Clark tending to show that the industry had been unable to determine whether operator restraint systems reduced the risk of serious injury to the operator and that it was only later, after the development of more sophisticated computer modeling, that the industry decided it was desirable to equip forklifts with such systems. As of 1977, Clark's evidence suggested, a manufacturer simply could not have known whether operator restraint systems created more risks than they eliminated.

The Habeckers claim that this evidence was inadmissible and, combined with the defendant's closing argument, improperly focused the jury's attention on Clark's conduct, rather than on the forklift itself. Because Clark conceded that operator restraint systems were feasible at the time the forklift was manufactured, the Habeckers argue that the only question for the jury was whether—seen in light of all the evidence available today—a forklift without an operator restraint system is "defective." While they acknowledge that evidence of whether a restraint system results in a net reduction in the risk of serious injury is relevant to that issue, the Habeckers insist that evidence of whether one could have known of that net reduction in 1977, including evidence of computer modeling capability at that time, is irrelevant to that issue. For the reasons that follow, we agree.

A.

Section 402A of the Restatement (Second) of Torts, adopted in Pennsylvania, states in relevant part,

> (1) One who sells any product in a defective condition unreasonably dangerous to the user or consumer or to his property is subject to liability for physical harm thereby caused. * * * (2) The rule stated in Subsection (1) applies although (a) the seller has exercised all possible care in the preparation and sale of his product. * * *

Pennsylvania law recognizes that a product may be "defective" not only because of an error in manufacturing, but also because of its design:

> the jury may find a defect where the product left the supplier's control lacking any element necessary to make it safe for its intended use or possessing any feature that renders it unsafe for the intended use.

Azzarello v. Black Brothers Co., 480 Pa. 547, 391 A.2d 1020, 1027 (1978). Under the doctrine of crashworthiness, the manufacturer's liability for producing defectively designed products includes liability for failing to provide safety features and liability for providing inadequate safety features. As this court has noted,

> crashworthiness * * * is a variation of strict liability theory. * * * [It] extends the manufacturer's liability to situations in which the defect did not cause the accident or initial impact, but rather increased the severity of the injury over that which would have occurred absent the defective design.

Barris v. Bob's Drag Chutes & Equipment, 685 F.2d 94, 99 (3d Cir.1982). Thus, crashworthiness imposes liability on the manufacturer for enhancing or failing to minimize injuries suffered in an accident, rather than for causing the accident.

* * *

> * * * Unlike orthodox products liability or negligence litigation, crashworthy or second collision cases impugning the design of an automobile require a highly refined and almost invariably difficult presentation of proof in three aspects. First, in establishing that the design in question was defective, the plaintiff must offer proof of an alternative, safer design, practicable under the circumstances. * * * Second, the plaintiff must offer proof of what injuries, if any, would have resulted had the alternative, safer design been used.... Third, as a corollary to the second aspect of proof, the plaintiff must offer some method of establishing the extent of enhanced injuries attributable to the defective design.

Huddell v. Levin, 537 F.2d 726, 737–38 (3d Cir.1976).

* * *

B.

Having predicted that the Pennsylvania Supreme Court would adopt the crashworthiness doctrine, we are required by this case to predict what definition that court would give that doctrine and, specifically, what evidence it would find relevant in determining liability. The

Habeckers argue that it was error for the district court to admit evidence concerning computer modeling capabilities in 1977, because that evidence shifted the focus from the defectiveness of the product to the knowledge and conduct of the manufacturer. Clark responds that the Supreme Court of Pennsylvania would admit such evidence because excluding it would impose strict liability bounded only by the ability of "the fruitful imagination of expert witnesses" to describe safer alternative designs. In essence, Clark argues that a product is not "defective" because of its design if no one could know at the time of manufacture that an alternative design would be safer.

It is important to distinguish evidence of what safety features were *feasible* at the time a product was designed, from evidence of what safety features were *known to be desirable* at that time. Evidence of the first must be admissible in a crashworthiness case. Liability is imposed on a manufacturer in a crashworthiness case for a design defect because an alternative, *feasible*, safer design would have lessened or eliminated the injury plaintiff suffered. If no such alternative feasible design existed when the product was manufactured, then the design cannot be said to be "defective", even if more recent technology has rendered a safer design feasible. Therefore, the fact finder can only determine whether a particular design was defective after hearing evidence about what designs were feasible at the time the product was manufactured and whether they were in fact safer. *Roe*, 855 F.2d at 155 (exclusion of testimony on effectiveness of safety device was error); *see also Huddell*, 537 F.2d at 737; *Craigie v. General Motors Corporation*, 740 F.Supp. 353, 357 n. 8 (E.D.Pa.1990).

While evidence of a safety feature's feasibility is relevant to whether the product was defective under Pennsylvania law, evidence of what was known about the desirability of a safety feature is not. One commentator has explained that exclusion of evidence of foreseeability is, indeed, *the* distinction between strict liability for design defects and liability for negligence in designing products. Strict liability for design defect is distinguishable from liability for negligence only if the *actual* risks and benefits of the design are evaluated in a strict liability case without any reference to the *foreseeable* risks and benefits:

> The fact that a risk or hazard related to the use of a product was not discoverable under existing technology and in the exercise of utmost care ... [is] irrelevant if the product itself and not defendant's conduct is being evaluated.

Prosser & Keeton, *Torts* § 99 at 700 (5th ed. 1984 & Supp.1988); *see also* Note, *Perpetuating Negligence Principles in Strict Products Liability: The Use of State of the Art Concepts in Design Cases*, 36 Syracuse L.Rev. 759, 804 (1985) ("Strict products liability differs from negligence in design cases in that a manufacturer is assumed to have knowledge of all hazards [however unforeseeable] posed by its product.").

Excluding evidence of what was or was not known about the desirability of operator restraint systems in 1977 is consistent with

Pennsylvania law's general exclusion of such evidence in strict liability cases:

> Having reached the conclusion that evidence of industry standards relating to the design of the [product], and evidence of its widespread use in the industry, go to the reasonableness of [defendants'] conduct in making its design choice, we further conclude that such evidence would have improperly brought into the case concepts of negligence law. We also conclude that such evidence would have created a strong likelihood of [improperly] diverting the jury's attention from the [product] to the reasonableness of the [manufacturer's] conduct in choosing its design.

Lewis v. Coffing Hoist Division, Duff–Norton Co., 515 Pa. 334, 528 A.2d 590, 594 (1987); *see also Majdic v. Cincinnati Machine Co.*, 370 Pa.Super. 611, 537 A.2d 334, 338–39 (1988); *Santiago v. Johnson Machine and Press Corp.*, 834 F.2d 84, 85 (3d Cir.1987) (applying Pennsylvania law).

In sum, while we predict that the Pennsylvania Supreme Court would hold manufacturers liable only for choosing between the safety features feasible at the time the product was manufactured, we predict it would hold them strictly liable for that choice. Thus, the manufacturer is liable even if it must choose blindly, with no information about the relative merits of safety features, and even if it exercises all possible care in making that choice. This rule can be justified because it provides manufacturers with an incentive to invest, not only in proven safety features, but also in the testing and development of any new feature that may prove superior. "A strict standard of liability offers the strongest possible incentive, an economic one, for the production of safer products." J. Beasley, *Product Liability and the Unreasonably Dangerous Requirement* 61 (1981).

* * *

* * * Without further instruction on what "defective" or "practicable" mean, the jury could easily believe that operator restraints were not "practicable" until the industry knew that they prevented more injuries than they caused. In fact, the district court appears to have relied on that theory in admitting the evidence of computer modeling. Thus, a substantial possibility exists that the jury ruled for Clark in the mistaken belief that the forklift was not defective so long as Clark could not have known that an operator restraint system would make it safer. Accordingly, the judgment for defendants must be reversed.

* * *

IV.

Evidence of computer modeling capabilities in 1977 should not have been admitted into evidence and its admission may have affected the outcome of the proceedings. Accordingly, we will reverse the judgment for the defendants and remand for a new trial.

Notes

1. Courts are split on the question of whether inability to discover a generic risk associated with a product at the time of sale or distribution will excuse the manufacturer from liability. Courts commonly begin with the proposition that strict liability differs from negligence in that hindsight rather than foresight is used. If this were carried to its logical conclusion, justifiable ignorance of a risk would never excuse a manufacturer. Most courts, however, make exceptions in one or more types of cases.

2. Most jurisdictions have not created an exception to the hindsight rule for design defect cases. These courts hold in such cases that justifiable ignorance of generic risk does not excuse the manufacturer. *E.g.*, Robertson v. General Tire & Rubber Co., 123 Ill.App.3d 11, 78 Ill.Dec. 587, 462 N.E.2d 706 (1984) (design defect; wheel rim separation; noting that Illinois law requires that the risk be knowable in warning cases but not in design cases); Elmore v. Owens–Illinois, Inc., 673 S.W.2d 434 (Mo.1984) (asbestos); Carter v. Johns–Manville Sales Corp., 557 F.Supp. 1317 (E.D.Tex.1983) (asbestos; knowledge requirement in warning cases but not in design cases). A minority of courts disagree. *E.g.*, Heritage v. Pioneer Brokerage & Sales, Inc., 604 P.2d 1059, 1063–64 (Alaska 1979) (design defect theory; formaldehyde fumes in mobile home).

OWENS–ILLINOIS, INC. v. ZENOBIA

Court of Appeals of Maryland, 1992.
325 Md. 420, 601 A.2d 633.

Argued before MURPHY, C.J., ELDRIDGE, RODOWSKY, McAULIFFE, CHASANOW, KARWACKI and ROBERT M. BELL, JJ.

ELDRIDGE, JUDGE.   * * *

The plaintiffs Louis L. Dickerson and William L. Zenobia filed in the Circuit Court for Baltimore City separate complaints seeking damages for injuries resulting from exposure to asbestos, and the complaints were consolidated for purposes of trial and appeal. Both plaintiffs have pleural and parenchymal asbestosis. At the time of the trial, the plaintiffs abandoned all theories of liability except for strict liability under § 402A of the Restatement (Second) of Torts.

The plaintiff Dickerson sought damages from Owens–Illinois, Inc., Eagle–Picher Industries, Inc., and Celotex Corp., all of which manufactured products containing asbestos, and from MCIC, Inc., and Porter Hayden Company, both of which supplied and installed products containing asbestos. Dickerson claimed that he was exposed to asbestos from 1953 to 1963 when he worked as a laborer both at the shipyard and at the steel mill owned and operated by the Bethlehem Steel Corporation at Sparrows Point, Maryland.

The plaintiff Zenobia sought damages from the manufacturer Owens–Illinois, Inc., and the suppliers/installers MCIC, Inc., Porter Hayden Co. and Anchor Packing Co. Zenobia alleged that he was exposed to asbestos while working as a painter for four months at the Bethlehem Steel Sparrows Point shipyard in 1948, while working as a pipe fitter for eighteen months at the Maryland Shipbuilding and Drydock shipyard in 1951 and 1952, and while employed as a cleanup man at the Carling Brewery for three months in 1968.

The jury awarded compensatory [and punitive] damages to [both plaintiffs. The Court of Special Appeals affirmed all aspects of the awards for compensatory damages. It affirmed one punitive damage award and reversed another].

* * * The only manufacturer which filed a certiorari petition was Owens–Illinois. * * * MCIC, Inc., and Porter Hayden Co., which supplied and installed products containing asbestos, also filed certiorari petitions * * *.

I.

The defendants' initial argument is that certain deposition evidence should not have been admitted because it was irrelevant and because these defendants were not present at the depositions and thus were unable to cross examine the deponents. The depositions were admitted into evidence for the limited purpose of proving what the defendants should have known concerning the dangers of asbestos. Such knowledge is often referred to as "state of the art." The defendants do not argue that "state of the art" or an element of knowledge is not relevant in this strict liability case; rather they insist that these depositions, because they pertain to what other companies knew about asbestos, are not proper "state of the art" evidence. In order to resolve these arguments, it is necessary to discuss briefly why any element of knowledge is relevant in this strict liability case.

A.

Section 402A of the Restatement (Second) of Torts, adopted by this Court in *Phipps v. General Motors Corp.*, 278 Md. 337, 344, 363 A.2d 955, 958 (1976), requires that, in order to recover under a theory of strict liability, a plaintiff must show:

> "(1) [that] the product was in a defective condition at the time it left the possession or control of the seller, (2) that it was unreasonably dangerous to the user or consumer, (3) that the defect was a cause of the injuries, and (4) that the product was expected to and did reach the consumer without substantial change in its condition."

Thus, on its face, § 402A subjects a seller of a defective product to strict liability without regard to the knowledge of the defect and "even though [the seller] has exercised all possible care in the preparation and sale of the product." Restatement (Second) of Torts § 402A, Comment a (1965).

When a product is alleged to be defective because of a failure to give an adequate warning, however, many courts have relied on Comment j of § 402A. Comment j explains that "the seller is required to give warning against [the danger], if he has knowledge, or by the application of reasonable, developed human skill and foresight should have knowledge, of the * * * danger." The comment goes on to distinguish a product containing an adequate warning from a defective product, stating: "a product bearing such a warning, which is safe for use if it is followed, is not in defective condition, nor is it unreasonably dangerous." [1]

Several courts have acknowledged that the language in Comment j appears to contradict or create an exception to the basic rule set out in § 402A. [Citations] Nevertheless, the majority of courts which have considered a failure to warn case in the context of strict liability have either expressly or implicitly held that a manufacturer of a product, which is defective only because of the lack of an adequate warning, is not liable when the failure to warn resulted from an absence of knowledge of the dangerous quality of that product.

Moreover, the courts reason, the presence of the required knowledge can be established by evidence that the dangerous quality of the product should have been known by a manufacturer because it was known in the scientific or expert community. As Judge John Minor Wisdom stated for the court in another case involving a claimed injury from asbestos, *Borel v. Fibreboard Paper Products Corporation*, 493 F.2d 1076, 1089 (5th Cir.1973), *cert. denied*, 419 U.S. 869, 95 S.Ct. 127, 42 L.Ed.2d 107 (1974),

> "in cases such as the instant case, the manufacturer is held to the knowledge and skill of an expert. This is relevant in determining (1) whether the manufacturer knew or should have known the danger * * *. The manufacturer's status as expert means that at a minimum he must keep abreast of scientific knowledge, discoveries, and advances and is presumed to know what is imparted thereby."

The same point was made by the United States Court of Appeals for the Fourth Circuit in Lohrmann v. Pittsburgh Corning Corp., 782 F.2d 1156, 1164 (4th Cir.1986):

> "Industry standards and state of the art are not synonymous. State of the art includes all of the available knowledge on a subject at a given time, and this includes scientific, medical, engineering, and any other knowledge that may be available. State of the art includes the element of time: What is known and when was this knowledge available." [2] [citations].

As previously indicated, this evidence concerning the presence or absence of knowledge in the expert community is called "state of the art" evidence.

---

1. Those jurisdictions which hold that evidence of knowledge of dangerous quality is relevant in a failure to warn case, do not regard lack of knowledge as a factor in a strict liability design defect case. See C. Marvel, Annotation, *Strict Products Liability: Liability for Failure to Warn as Dependent on Defendant's Knowledge of Danger*, 33 A.L.R. 4th 368, 378 n. 14 (1984).

2. For two competing views on the desirability of allowing a knowledge compo-nent in a strict liability case, *see* W. Murray, Jr., *Requiring Omniscience: The Duty to Warn of Scientifically Undiscoverable Product Defects*, 71 Geo.L.J. 1635, 1638 n. 21 (1983); J. Martineau, *The Duty to Warn Under Strict Products Liability as Limited by the Knowledge Requirement: A Regretful Retention of Negligence Concepts*, 26 St. Louis U.L.J. 125 (1981).

Consequently, in a failure to warn case governed by the Restatement § 402A and Comment j, negligence concepts to some extent have been grafted onto strict liability. In such cases, a majority of courts hold that an element of knowledge or "state of the art" evidence is directly pertinent to a cause of action under § 402A of the Restatement (Second) of Torts, and liability is no longer entirely "strict." [3]

On the other hand, a few courts have held that neither the defendant's actual knowledge nor evidence of scientific knowledge about the dangerous characteristics of the product is relevant in a strict liability failure to warn case. [Citations]

Before the trial in the present cases the plaintiffs asserted that evidence of knowledge should not be relevant with regard to their strict liability claims. The defendants, however, argued that the plaintiffs were required to produce "state of the art" evidence as part of their case. The trial judge, apparently relying on a prior ruling in another case by Judge Levin for the Circuit Court for Baltimore City, agreed with the defendants and required that the plaintiffs introduce "state of the art" evidence. Consequently, at trial the plaintiffs introduced evidence designed to show the requisite knowledge or "state of the art." Moreover, neither side in the Court of Special Appeals or before this Court challenged the trial court's ruling that a knowledge component or "state of the art" is pertinent in a strict liability failure to warn case.

The United States Court of Appeals for the Fourth Circuit, applying Maryland law, has held that in a strict liability failure to warn case, "state of the art" is relevant with regard to the defendant's liability. See *Lohrmann v. Pittsburgh Corning Corp., supra*, 782 F.2d at 1164 ("in Maryland, state of the art can be considered in a strict liability tort case where the claimed defect is a failure to warn"). The federal Court of Appeals reasoned that in *Phipps v. General Motors Corp., supra*, this Court "adopted strict liability in tort as expressed in § 402A of the Restatement (Second) of Torts," that Comment j is part of § 402A, and that

> "[t]he language of Comment (j) is state-of-the-art language because it requires the seller to give a warning if he has knowledge, 'or by the application of reasonable, developed human skill and foresight should have knowledge' of the danger."

---

3. Professors Henderson and Twerski argue that the difference between strict liability and negligence in a failure to warn case is entirely semantic and unnecessarily confusing. They suggest that since courts apply negligence concepts in all failure to warn cases, all such cases sound in negligence. J. Henderson and A. Twerski, Doctrinal Collapse in Products Liability: The Empty Shell of Failure to Warn, 65 N.Y.U.L.Rev. 265 (1990). We note that despite the overlap of negligence principles in a strict liability failure to warn case, strict liability differs from a negligence cause of action in that contributory negligence is not a defense to a strict liability claim. Ellsworth v. Sherne Lingerie, Inc., 303 Md. 581, 597–598, 495 A.2d 348, 356–357 (1985). In addition, in light of the other comments to § 402A of the Restatement (Second) of Torts, which apply in defective design, defective construction, and failure to warn cases, there are some differences between a negligent failure to warn case and a failure to warn based upon § 402A and Comment j.

Lohrmann v. Pittsburgh Corning Corp., supra, 782 F.2d at 1164–1165.

While this Court has not previously dealt with this issue, we agree that our adoption of § 402A in the *Phipps* case included Comment j and the knowledge component provided for in Comment j. The *Phipps* opinion expressly indicated that our adoption of § 402A included the official comments (278 Md. at 346, 363 A.2d at 959–960):

> "Under § 402A, various defenses are still available to the seller in an action based on strict liability in tort. These defenses are set forth and explained in the official comments following § 402A."

Moreover, in *Phipps* we discussed with approval several of the official comments, including Comment j. *Ibid.* In addition, as pointed out by the court in *Lohrmann,* 782 F.2d at 1164, the *Phipps* opinion went on to state that "[d]espite the use of the term 'strict liability' the seller is not an insurer, as absolute liability is not imposed on the seller for any injury resulting from the use of his product." 278 Md. at 351–352, 363 A.2d at 963. [Citations]

We hold that Comment j of § 402A is applicable to a strict liability cause of action where the alleged defect is a failure to give adequate warnings. Therefore, the seller is not strictly liable for failure to warn unless the seller has "knowledge, or by the application of reasonable, developed human skill and foresight should have knowledge, of the presence of the * * * danger." Restatement (Second) of Torts § 402A, Comment j. Moreover, we agree with the numerous cases holding that, for purposes of the "should have knowledge" component of comment j, a manufacturer of a product is held to the knowledge of an expert in the field. *See Babylon v. Scruton,* 215 Md. 299, 304, 138 A.2d 375, 378 (1958), quoting 2 Harper & James, *The Law of Torts* § 28.4 (negligence case pointing out that " 'a person who undertakes such manufacturing will be held to the skill of an expert in that business and to an expert's knowledge of the arts, materials, and processes. Thus he must keep reasonably abreast of scientific knowledge and discoveries touching his product * * * ' ").[4]

---

4. It is not entirely clear whether the knowledge or state of the art component in a strict liability failure to warn case is an element to be proven by the plaintiff or is an affirmative defense. *Cf. Ellsworth v. Sherne Lingerie, Inc.,* [303 Md. 581, 592–596, 495 A.2d 348, 353–356 (1985)] (discussing whether "misuse" of a product is a part of the plaintiff's case or an affirmative defense).

Prosser and Keeton take the position that a plaintiff who seeks to recover in a strict liability failure to warn case must show that the defendant knew or should have known of the hazard about which he failed to warn. Prosser and Keeton, *Torts* § 99, at 697 (5th ed. 1984). See also M. Madden, *Products Liability* § 10.3, at 377–378 (2d

ed. 1988). On the other hand, an American Law Reports Annotation collecting cases concerning strict liability for failure to warn seems to assert that the absence of knowledge of the danger is an affirmative defense which must be proven by the defendant. C. Marvel, Annotation, *Strict Products Liability: Liability For Failure to Warn as Dependent on Defendant's Knowledge of Danger, supra,* 33 A.L.R. 4th 368, and cases cited therein. Many cases also refer to the knowledge component in a strict liability failure to warn case as a "defense."

It is not necessary for us to decide in this case whether the knowledge component is an element of the plaintiff's case or an affirmative defense because neither the plaintiffs nor the defendants have raised

B.

* * *

1.

The defendants argue that the deposition testimony should not have been admitted because they were not present at the depositions and did not have an opportunity to cross examine the witnesses. The defendant suppliers/installers Anchor Packing Co., Porter Hayden and MCIC, Inc., were not present at the deposition of Dr. Mancuso, nor were any other non-manufacturing suppliers/installers of asbestos. Several manufacturers, however, were present at this deposition, including Owens–Illinois. Similarly, although Owens–Illinois was not present, several defendant manufacturers attended the depositions of Dr. Smith, Mr. Pechstein and Mr. Humphrey.

* * *

* * * Deposition testimony is admissible if some other party, present at the deposition, had the same opportunity and similar motive to develop the testimony as the party against whom the deposition is offered. * * *

* * *

In deciding whether the deposition testimony was properly admitted in these cases, we shall first address the principal argument of the defendant suppliers/installers as to why the deposition of Dr. Mancuso was improperly admitted against them. They argue that their interests were not adequately protected by the presence of the manufacturers at the Dr. Mancuso deposition because manufacturers of asbestos would not have the same motive to develop certain testimony as a supplier/installer would. Therefore, the argument continues, the manufacturers were not the predecessors in interest of suppliers/installers. In fact, the suppliers/installers argue, their interests conflict with the interests of the manufacturers in this litigation.

The depositions were admitted for the limited purpose of proving "state of the art." As earlier explained, state of the art evidence is directly relevant to whether a product was defective when it was sold by a manufacturer. In a strict liability action, if a product is defective when it was sold by a manufacturer because it lacked a warning of its dangerous characteristics, although it should have had such a warning in light of the state of the art, and if the defective and dangerous product

any issue in this regard. Nevertheless, we agree with those authorities, and with the Circuit Court for Baltimore City, that the knowledge or state of the art component is an element to be proven by the plaintiff. In a strict liability failure to warn case, the alleged defect is the failure of the seller to give an adequate warning. The seller, however, need not give any warning if the requisite state of the art or knowledge does not require it. Thus, where a product lacks a warning because of insufficient knowledge on the part of the manufacturer or in the scientific field involved, the product is not defective. As defectiveness is an element to be proven by the plaintiff, the knowledge or state of the art component is not an affirmative defense. See *Ellsworth v. Sherne Lingerie, Inc., supra*, 303 Md. at 597, 495 A.2d at 356.

reaches the user plaintiff without substantial change, middlemen or intermediate sellers of the defective product are strictly liable to the plaintiff user just as the manufacturer is liable to the plaintiff. Restatement (Second) of Torts § 402A, Comment f; *Eaton Corp. v. Wright*, 281 Md. 80, 88–90, 375 A.2d 1122, 1126–1127 (1977). This principle, at least at the present stage of the law's development, is fully applicable in a strict liability failure to warn case. Prosser and Keeton explain as follows (Prosser and Keeton, *Torts* § 99, at 697 (5th ed. 1984), emphasis added):

> "It is commonly said that a product can be defective in the kind of way that makes it unreasonably dangerous by failing to warn or failing adequately to warn about a risk or hazard related to the way a product is designed. But notwithstanding what a few courts have said, a claimant who seeks recovery on this basis must, according to the generally accepted view, prove that the manufacturer-designer was negligent. There will be no liability without a showing that the defendant designer knew or should have known in the exercise of ordinary care of the risk or hazard about which he failed to warn.
> * * *
> "There is one aspect of this so-called strict liability in addition to the matter of defenses and limitations on liability that distinguish it from negligence liability. *When a manufacturer or assembler markets without adequate warnings, a reseller is subject to liability without negligence in reselling the product without adequate warning. Thus, all those in the marketing chain subsequent to a sale by the manufacturer are liable without negligence for the negligence of the manufacturer in failing to warn or adequately to warn.*"

See also Nissen Corp. v. Miller, 323 Md. 613, 624, 594 A.2d 564, 569 (1991) ("It is clear that Maryland espoused the doctrine of strict liability in tort in order to relieve plaintiffs of the burden of proving specific acts of negligence * * * where plaintiffs can prove a product is defective and unreasonably dangerous *when placed in the stream of commerce* ") (emphasis added). Consequently, with respect to the strict liability claim of a plaintiff, intermediate sellers such as the suppliers/installers in the present case have the same interest as the manufacturers in attempting to show that the state of the art did not require a warning and that, therefore, the product was not defective under the principles of § 402A, Comment j, of the Restatement (Second) of Torts.[5]

---

5. The supplier/installers in the present case disagree that, with respect to the strict liability claims of the plaintiffs, the suppliers/installers and the manufacturers have the same interests concerning a deposition on state of the art. The supplier/installers argue that, whereas a manufacturer may be strictly liable to the plaintiffs if the product failed to contain warnings which were dictated by the state of the art, an intermediate supplier of the same product is not strictly liable to the plaintiffs unless he knew or, based on information actually given to him, should have known that a warning was required. While there might be merit in this argument if the plaintiffs' cause of action were based on negligence, as pointed out above the argument is inconsistent with the principles of strict liability under § 402A of the Restatement even as modified by Comment j. Furthermore, the defendants cite no cases, and we are aware of none, supporting the defendants' view of

The defendant Owens–Illinois has even less cause to complain about the admission of depositions under Maryland Rule 2–419(c). A defendant manufacturer was present at each of the depositions admitted against Owens–Illinois. Owens–Illinois clearly is held to the same "state of the art" standard as those defendants present at the depositions. The defendants at the depositions are predecessors in interest to Owens–Illinois because they had the same opportunity to develop the testimony. Therefore, these depositions fall within the former testimony exception to the rule against hearsay and are admissible against Owens–Illinois under Rule 2–419(c).

2.

We now turn to the defendants' argument that these depositions should not have been admitted because they do not address what was known to the expert, medical or scientific community but, rather, address what other asbestos manufacturing companies knew. As previously stated, all manufacturers are held to the knowledge and skill of an expert. *Borel v. Fibreboard Paper Products Corporation, supra*, 493 F.2d at 1089. The defendants' argument that this expert testimony is irrelevant because it relates only to what individual companies discovered, "reflects a misunderstanding of a critical issue in any product liability action: the state of the art pertaining to any possible risks associated with the product." *Dartez v. Fibreboard Corp.*, [765 F.2d 456, 461 (5th Cir.1985)].

The United States Court of Appeals for the Fifth Circuit considered this argument in an identical context in *Dartez v. Fibreboard Corp., supra.* That court determined that similar deposition evidence was relevant to the state of the art element of a products liability case, explaining (*Ibid.*) (emphasis added):

> "Dartez was required to establish that the dangers of asbestos were reasonably foreseeable or scientifically discoverable at the time of his exposure before these defendants could be found liable * * *. *Borel* holds all manufacturers to the knowledge and skill of an expert. They are obliged to keep abreast of any scientific discoveries and are presumed to know the results of all such advances. Moreover, they each bear the duty to fully test their products to uncover all scientifically discoverable dangers before the products

an intermediate seller's liability to a plaintiff in a strict liability cause of action.

We would agree that there is a circumstance when the interests of a supplier/installer and a manufacturer would not be the same in examining a deponent such as Dr. Mancuso. To the extent that the deposition might relate to an indemnity claim by the supplier/installer against the manufacturer, it would be to the supplier/installer's benefit to elicit testimony that, whereas expert medical and scientific information existed so as to warrant a warning by manufacturers, such information was not generally known outside the scientific community and would not have been readily available to non-manufacturing suppliers/installers. In the instant cases, however, the defendant suppliers/installers complain solely about the admission of the Dr. Mancuso deposition at the trial of the plaintiffs' claims. They have made no complaint about the evidence at the separate cross-claims trial.

are sold * * *. The actual knowledge of an individual manufacturer is not the issue."

Accord Clay v. Johns–Manville Sales Corp., [722 F.2d 1289, 1294–1295 (6th Cir.1983), *cert. denied,* 467 U.S. 1253, 104 S.Ct. 3537, 82 L.Ed.2d 842 (1984)].

We agree with the United States Courts of Appeal for the Fifth and Sixth Circuits that deposition evidence concerning what scientific and medical experts in the field knew about the dangers of asbestos is relevant to the plaintiff's attempt to prove state of the art. Such expert evidence is not irrelevant merely because these experts were employed by private companies. Because manufacturers are held to the standards and knowledge of an expert, this evidence is relevant to show what was scientifically and medically available and discoverable by other experts in the field.

* * *

* * * [T]he defendants have not shown that the admission of these depositions constituted reversible error.

[The court reversed and remanded the cases on other grounds].

Notes

1.   In failure to warn cases a majority of courts recognize an exception to the rule that ignorance of generic risk is no excuse. They hold that there is no liability for failing to warn about undiscoverable risks. *E.g.,* Payne v. Soft Sheen Prod., Inc., 486 A.2d 712 (D.C.App.1985). This is the Restatement position in failure to warn cases. Restatement of Torts (Second) § 402A, comment j (1965).

2.   *Habecker v. Clark Equipment Co., supra,* and the notes following it, demonstrate that most courts do not excuse product manufacturers who are justifiably ignorant of generic risks in design defect cases. Is there any logical justification for treating design and warning cases differently in this respect? Usually courts impose the duty to warn to promote safety, but some courts impose the duty to promote individual autonomy. *See* note 10 *infra* page 353. Should the answer vary depending on whether the warning case is based on safety or autonomy?

3.   **Burden of proof.** Most courts adhering to the majority rule require plaintiff to prove that the manufacturer either knew or could have known about the risk to be warned about at the time of distribution. A small number of courts place the burden on the defendant to prove justifiable ignorance of risk. *E.g.,* Shanks v. Upjohn Co., 835 P.2d 1189 (Alaska 1992); Feldman v. Lederle Laboratories, 97 N.J. 429, 479 A.2d 374 (1984). In *Feldman* plaintiff developed gray teeth as a result of taking a tetracycline drug as an infant. She brought a strict liability case against the manufacturer for failure to warn physicians of the drug's side effect, tooth discoloration. *Feldman* gives the following reasons for shifting the burden of proof:

[A]s to warnings, generally conduct should be measured by knowledge at the time the manufacturer distributed the product. Did the defendant know, or should he have known, of the danger, given the scientific, technological, and other information available when the product was distributed; or, in other words, did he have actual or constructive knowledge of the danger? * * * Under this standard negligence and strict liability in warning cases may be deemed to be functional equivalents.

* * *

In strict liability warning cases, unlike negligence cases, however, the defendant should properly bear the burden of proving that the information was not reasonably available or obtainable and that it therefore lacked actual or constructive knowledge of the defect. Wade ["On the Effect in Product Liability of Knowledge Unavailable Prior to Marketing," 58 N.Y.U.L.Rev. 734, 76–61] (1983); see Pollock, "Liability of a Blood Bank or Hospital for a Hepatitis Associated Blood Transfusion in New Jersey," 2 Seton Hall L.Rev. 47, 60 (1970) ("burden of proof that hepatitis is not detectable and unremovable should rest on the defendant" blood bank or hospital). The defendant is in a superior position to know the technological material or data in the particular field or specialty. The defendant is the expert, often performing self-testing. It is the defendant that injected the product in the stream of commerce for its economic gain. As a matter of policy the burden of proving the status of knowledge in the field at the time of distribution is properly placed on the defendant.

4. In Beshada v. Johns–Manville Prods. Corp., 90 N.J. 191, 447 A.2d 539 (1982) plaintiffs sued asbestos manufacturers in strict liability for failure to warn about the risks of exposure to asbestos. Some of the plaintiffs were exposed as early as the 1930's. Defendants claimed that the duty to warn arose only after the risks became scientifically knowable. The court rejected the argument, and held that defendants could be liable for failure to warn about significant risks without regard to whether they could have known about them. *Feldman* adopts the opposite approach with respect to the duty to warn about unknowable risks. *Feldman*, however, does not overrule *Beshada*. How can the cases be reconciled? Does *Feldman* apply to all products except asbestos? Or does *Beshada* apply to all products except drugs?

5. A minority of courts hold defendants strictly liable for a failure to warn of risks that were scientifically unknowable at the time the product was marketed. *E.g., Phillips v. Kimwood Machine Co., supra* p. 177; Little v. PPG Indus., Inc., 19 Wash.App. 812, 579 P.2d 940 (1978), modified, 92 Wash.2d 118, 594 P.2d 911 (1979) (chemical). For citations to cases following the majority rule and the minority rule, *see* Annotation, 33 A.L.R.4th 368 (1984).

6. A second category of cases that excuse justifiable ignorance of generic risk are those involving such products as drugs, vaccines, blood, and medical devices. Most courts recognize justifiable ignorance as an excuse in such cases. Many of these cases rely on Comment k to the Restatement (Second) of Torts § 402A. *See, e.g.,* Davis v. Wyeth Laboratories, Inc., 399 F.2d 121 (9th Cir.1968). Because comment k is a specialized exception to

strict liability, the cases applying it are treated separately in Section C of this chapter.

SECTION B.   CHANGES IN TECHNOLOGY

BOATLAND OF HOUSTON, INC. v. BAILEY
Supreme Court of Texas, 1980.
609 S.W.2d 743.

McGEE, JUSTICE.

This is a product defect case involving an alleged defect in the design of a 16–foot bass boat.   The plaintiffs were the widow and adult children of Samuel Bailey, who was killed in a boating accident in May of 1973. They sued under the wrongful death statute, alleging that Samuel Bailey's death occurred because the boat he was operating was defectively designed.   The boat had struck a partially submerged tree stump, and Bailey was thrown into the water.   With its motor still running, the boat turned sharply and circled back toward the stump.   Bailey was killed by the propeller, but it is unclear whether he was struck when first thrown out or after the boat circled back toward him.

Bailey's wife and children sought damages under a strict liability theory from the boat's seller, Boatland of Houston, Inc.   At trial, they urged several reasons why the boat was defectively designed, including * * * the failure of the motor to automatically turn off when Bailey was thrown from the boat.

The trial court rendered a take-nothing judgment based on the jury's failure to find that the boat was defective and findings favorable to Boatland on several defensive issues.   The court of civil appeals, with one justice dissenting, reversed and remanded the cause for a new trial because of errors in the admission of evidence and the submission of the defensive issues.   585 S.W.2d 805.   We reverse the judgment of the court of civil appeals and affirm that of the trial court.

EVIDENCE OF DESIGN DEFECT

* * *

In *Turner v. General Motors Corp.,* [584 S.W.2d 844 (Tex.1979),] this court discussed the strict liability standard of "defectiveness" as applied in design defect cases.   Whether a product was defectively designed requires a balancing by the jury of its utility against the likelihood of and gravity of injury from its use.   The jury may consider many factors before deciding whether a product's usefulness or desirability are outweighed by its risks.   Their finding on defectiveness may be influenced by evidence of a safer design that would have prevented the injury.[2]

2. In *Turner,* this court stated that a number of evidentiary factors may be considered in determining whether a product's design is defective.   The product's usefulness and desirability, the likelihood and gravity of injury from its use, the ability to eliminate the risk without seriously increasing the product's usefulness or cost, and the

Turner v. General Motors Corp., supra at 849. See Keeton, *Product Liability and the Meaning of Defect,* 5 St. Mary's L.J. 30, 38 (1973); Wade, *Strict Tort Liability of Manufacturers,* 19 Sw.L.J. 5, 17 (1965). Because defectiveness of the product in question is determined in relation to safer alternatives, the fact that its risks could be diminished easily or cheaply may greatly influence the outcome of the case.

Whether a product was defectively designed must be judged against the technological context existing at the time of its manufacture. Thus, when the plaintiff alleges that a product was defectively designed because it lacked a specific feature, attention may become focused on the feasibility of that feature—the capacity to provide the feature without greatly increasing the product's cost or impairing usefulness. This feasibility is a relative, not an absolute, concept; the more scientifically and economically feasible the alternative was, the more likely that a jury may find that the product was defectively designed. A plaintiff may advance the argument that a safer alternative was feasible with evidence that it was in actual use or was available at the time of manufacture. Feasibility may also be shown with evidence of the scientific and economic capacity to develop the safer alternative. Thus, evidence of the actual use of, or capacity to use, safer alternatives is relevant insofar as it depicts the available scientific knowledge and the practicalities of applying that knowledge to a product's design. * * *

As part of their case-in-chief, the Baileys produced evidence of the scientific and economic feasibility of a design that would have caused the boat's motor to automatically shut off when Bailey fell out. According to the Baileys, the boat's design should have incorporated an automatic cut-off system or the boat should have been equipped with a safety device known as a "kill switch."

* * *

The deposition testimony of George Horton, the inventor of a kill switch designed for open-top carriers, was also introduced. Horton began developing his "Quick Kill" in November of 1972 and applied for a patent in January of 1973. According to Horton, his invention required no breakthroughs in the state of the art of manufacturing or production. He stated that his invention was simple: a lanyard connects the operator's body to a device that fits over the ignition key. If the operator moves, the lanyard is pulled, the device rotates, and the ignition switch turns off. When he began to market his "Quick Kill," the response by boat dealers was very positive, which Horton perceived to be due to the filling of a recognized need. He considered the kill switch to be a necessary safety device for a bass boat with stick steering. If the kill switch were hooked up and the operator thrown out, the killing of the motor would prevent the boat from circling back where it came from. Horton also testified that for 30 years racing boats had been using

expectations of the ordinary consumer are some of these factors. *Turner v. General* *Motors Corp.,* 584 S.W.2d 844, 849 (Tex. 1979).

various types of kill switches. Thus, the concept of kill switches was not new.

* * *

Boatland elicited evidence to rebut the Baileys' evidence of the feasibility of equipping boats with kill switches or similar devices in March of 1973, when the boat was assembled and sold. * * *

In response to the Baileys' evidence that the "Quick Kill" was readily available at the time of trial, Horton stated on cross-examination that until he obtained the patent for his "Quick Kill" in 1974 he kept the idea to himself. Before he began to manufacture them, he investigated the market for competitive devices and found none. The only applications of the automatic engine shut-off concept in use at the time were homemade, such as on racing boats. He first became aware of competitive devices in August of 1974.

Boatland introduced other evidence to show that kill switches were not available when Bailey's boat was sold. * * * Willis Hudson, who manufactured the boat operated by Bailey, testified that he first became aware of kill switches in 1974 or 1975 and to his knowledge no such thing was available before then. Ralph Cornelius, the vice-president of a marine appliance dealership, testified that kill switches were not available in 1973. The first kill switch he saw to be sold was in 1974, although homemade "crash throttles" or foot buttons had long been in use.

* * * After considering the feasibility and effectiveness of an alternative design and other factors such as the utility and risk, the jury found that the boat was not defective. The trial court rendered judgment for Boatland. The Baileys complained on appeal that the trial court erred in admitting Boatland's evidence that kill switches were unavailable when Bailey's boat was assembled and sold. The court of civil appeals agreed, holding that the evidence was material only to the care exercised by Boatland and thus irrelevant in a strict liability case.

In its appeal to this court, Boatland contends that the court of civil appeals misconstrued the nature and purpose of its evidence. According to Boatland, when the Baileys introduced evidence that kill switches were a feasible safety alternative, Boatland was entitled to introduce evidence that kill switches were not yet available when Bailey's boat was sold and thus were not a feasible design alternative at that time.

The primary dispute concerning the feasibility of an alternative design for Bailey's boat was the "state of the art" when the boat was sold. The admissibility and effect of "state of the art" evidence has been a subject of controversy in both negligence and strict product liability cases. In negligence cases, the reasonableness of the defendant's conduct in placing the product on the market is in issue. Evidence of industry customs at the time of manufacture may be offered by either party for the purpose of comparing the defendant's conduct with industry customs. An offer of evidence of the defendant's compliance with custom to rebut evidence of its negligence has been described as the "state of the art defense." *See generally* 2 L. Frumer & M. Friedman, Products Liability § 16A[4][i] (1980). In this connection, it is argued that the state of the art is equivalent to industry custom and is relevant only to the issue of the defendant's negligence and irrelevant to a strict liability theory of recovery.

In our view, "custom" is distinguishable from "state of the art." The state of the art with respect to a particular product refers to the technological environment at the time of its manufacture. This technological environment includes the scientific knowledge, economic feasibility, and the practicalities of implementation when the product was manufactured. Evidence of this nature is important in determining whether a safer design was feasible. The limitations imposed by the state of the art at the time of manufacture may affect the feasibility of a safer design. Evidence of the state of the art in design defect cases has been discussed and held admissible in other jurisdictions. *See, e.g., Raney v. Honeywell, Inc.,* 540 F.2d 932 (8th Cir.1976); *Caterpillar Tractor Co. v. Beck,* 593 P.2d 871 (Alaska 1979); *Barker v. Lull Engineering Co.,* 20 Cal.3d 413, 573 P.2d 443, 143 Cal.Rptr. 225 (1978); *Kerns v. Engelke,* 76 Ill.2d 154, 28 Ill.Dec. 500, 390 N.E.2d 859 (1979); *Cepeda v. Cumberland Engineering Co., Inc.,* 76 N.J. 152, 386 A.2d 816 (1978). *See generally* J. Sales & J. Perdue, The Law of Strict Tort Liability in Texas 41 (1977). Note, *The State of the Art Defense in Strict Products Liability,* 57 Marq.L.Rev. 491 (1974). Note, *Product Liability Reform Proposals: The State of the Art Defense,* 43 Albany L.Rev. 944, 944–45 (1979). In this case, the evidence advanced by both parties was relevant to the feasibility of designing bass boats to shut off automatically if the operator fell out, or more specifically, the feasibility of equipping bass boats with safety switches.

The Baileys offered state of the art evidence to establish the feasibility of a more safely designed boat: They established that when Bailey's boat was sold in 1973, the general concept of a boat designed so that its motor would automatically cut off had been applied for years on racing boats. One kill switch, the "Quick Kill," was invented at that time and required no mechanical breakthrough. The Baileys were also allowed to show that other kill switches were presently in use and that the defendant itself presently installed them.

Logically, the plaintiff's strongest evidence of feasibility of an alternative design is its actual use by the defendant or others at the time of manufacture. Even if a safer alternative was not being used, evidence that it was available, known about, or capable of being developed is relevant in determining its feasibility. In contrast, the defendant's strongest rebuttal evidence is that a particular design alternative was impossible due to the state of the art. Yet the defendant's ability to rebut the plaintiff's evidence is not limited to showing that a particular alternative was impossible; it is entitled to rebut the plaintiff's evidence of feasibility with evidence of limitations on feasibility. A suggested alternative may be invented or discovered but not be feasible for use because of the time necessary for its application and implementation. Also, a suggested alternative may be available, but impractical for reasons such as greatly increased cost or impairment of the product's usefulness. When the plaintiff has introduced evidence that a safer alternative was feasible because it was used, the defendant may then introduce contradictory evidence that it was not used.

Thus in response to the Baileys' evidence of kill switch use in 1978, the time of trial, Boatland was properly allowed to show that they were not used when the boat was sold in 1973. To rebut proof that safety switches were possible and feasible when Bailey's boat was sold because the underlying concept was known and the "Quick Kill," a simple, inexpensive device had been invented, Boatland was properly allowed to show that neither the "Quick Kill" nor any other kill switch was available at that time.

It could reasonably be inferred from this evidence that although the underlying concept of automatic motor cut-off devices was not new, kill switches were not as feasible an alternative as the Baileys' evidence implied. Boatland did not offer evidence of technological impossibility or absolute nonfeasibility; its evidence was offered to show limited availability when the boat was sold. Once the jury was informed of the state of the art, it was able to consider the extent to which it was feasible to incorporate an automatic cut-off device or similar design characteristic into Bailey's boat. The feasibility and effectiveness of a safer design and other factors such as utility and risk, were properly considered by the jury before it ultimately concluded that the boat sold to Bailey was not defectively designed.

In cases involving strict liability for defective design, liability is determined by the product's defective condition; there is no need to prove that the defendant's conduct was negligent. Considerations such as the utility and risk of the product in question and the feasibility of safer alternatives are presented according to the facts as they are proved to be, not according to the defendant's perceptions. Thus, even though the defendant has exercised due care his product may be found defective. When the Baileys introduced evidence of the use of kill switches, Boatland was entitled to introduce rebuttal evidence of non-use at the time of manufacture due to limitations imposed by the state of the art. Evidence offered under these circumstances is offered to rebut plaintiff's evidence that a safer alternative was feasible and is relevant to defectiveness. It was not offered to show that a custom existed or to infer the defendant's compliance therewith. We would be presented with a different question if the state of the art in 1973 with respect to kill switches had not been disputed and Boatland had attempted to avoid liability by offering proof that Bailey's boat complied with industry custom.

* * *

CONCLUSION

For the reasons stated above the judgment of the court of civil appeals is reversed. The judgment rendered by the trial court, that the Baileys take nothing against Boatland, is affirmed.

Pope, J., concurring, in which Barrow, J., joins.

[The concurring opinion of Pope, J. is omitted.]

On Rehearing

Campbell, Justice, dissenting.

I dissent.

"State of the art" does not mean "the state of industry practice." "State of the art" means "state of industry knowledge." At the time of the manufacture of the boat in question, the device and concept of a circuit breaker, as is at issue in this case, was simple, mechanical, cheap, practical, possible, economically feasible and a concept seventy years old, which required no engineering or technical breakthrough. The concept was known by the industry. This fact removes it from "state of the art."

* * *

The manufacturer of the boat, Mr. Hudson, testified as follows as concerns the concept of a "kill switch." It is practically without dispute that this is one of the simplest mechanical devices and concepts known to man. Its function is, can be, and was performed by many and varied simple constructions. It is more a concept than an invention. The concept has been around most of this century. It is admittedly an easily incorporated concept. Was an invention required in order to incorporate a circuit breaker on a bass boat? Absolutely not! Did the manufacturer have to wait until George Horton invented his specific "Quick Kill" switch before it could incorporate a kill switch of some sort on its bass boats? Absolutely not! Mr. Hudson uses an even simpler electrical circuit breaker on his boats.

Mr. Hudson testified he could have made a kill switch himself, of his own, and of many possible designs, but simply did not do it. Why didn't he do it? He didn't think about it. He never had any safety engineer examine his boats. He hadn't heard of such, he puts them on now, but still thinks people won't use them.

* * *

What is this Court faced with in this case? Nothing more than a defendant seller attempting to avoid liability by offering proof that Bailey's boat complied with industry practice (which it did at that time) but not because of any limitations on manufacturing feasibility at that time. This is an industry practice case. The evidence does not involve "technological feasibility." * * *

* * * The important point is that there is no dispute that at the time of the manufacture of Mr. Bailey's boat, a circuit breaker, whether electrical or mechanical could have easily and cheaply been incorporated into the boat.

* * *

I would hold that the trial court erred in permitting such evidence by Boatland to go to the jury, and would affirm the judgment of the Court of Civil Appeals.

* * *

RAY, J., joins in this dissent.

Notes

1. Justice McGee asserts that the law is concerned with the condition of the product and not "defendant's perceptions." Therefore, there is no need to show that the defendant was negligent in order to prove that the product is defective. Is this true? Recall *Garnes v. Gulf & Western Mfg. Co.,* *supra* p. 20, holding that the manufacturer is held to the standard of an expert, and is required to keep abreast of all scientific advances.

2. Most courts agree with *Boatland,* and hold that the product must be evaluated in light of the technology available at the time of distribution. *E.g.,* Maxted v. Pacific Car & Foundry Co., 527 P.2d 832 (Wyo.1974). A few courts disagree. *E.g.,* Stanfield v. Medalist Indus., Inc., 34 Ill.App.3d 635, 340 N.E.2d 276 (1975) (unavailability of safety devices is no defense to a strict liability action). As we saw in section A., however, justifiable ignorance of the harmful quality of the product (generic risk) frequently does not excuse the manufacturer from liability in design defect cases. Is there a logical justification for a court to use hindsight for generic risks and foresight for technology in design cases?

APPEL v. STANDEX INTERN. CORP.

Court of Appeals of Oregon, 1983.
62 Or.App. 208, 660 P.2d 686, review denied, 295 Or. 446, 668 P.2d 382.

BUTTLER, PRESIDING JUDGE.

Plaintiff appeals from a judgment entered on a jury verdict for defendant on plaintiff's claim for damages for personal injuries caused by an allegedly defective product. Plaintiff assigns error to a number of the court's evidentiary rulings and to the court's failure to give one of her requested jury instructions. We affirm.

Plaintiff is a registered nurse who injured her back at the nursing home where she worked while turning a patient in bed. The bed was on wheels, and there were brakes on two diagonally opposed wheels. Although the wheel brakes were locked, the bed slipped, causing plaintiff to twist and injure her back. She brought this action against the bed's manufacturer for compensatory and punitive damages, alleging that the bed's wheel brakes were defective in design and were unreasonably dangerous. The jury found for defendant, and plaintiff appeals.

Plaintiff's first two assignments of error relate to the court's refusal to admit two of her exhibits, which she argues would have established that an alternative wheel brake design could have prevented her injury. She offered two videotaped "reenactments" of the incident that caused the injury, one of which depicted the type of wheel brakes used on the bed when she was injured and one of which depicted wheel brakes of a different design. The court admitted the videotape featuring the allegedly defective wheel brakes, but excluded the one depicting the alternative design. The court found that, although evidence of a safer, technically feasible and practicable alternative design is part of plaintiff's *prima facie* case in many design defect cases, *see Wilson v. Piper Aircraft Corporation,* 282 Or. 61, 577 P.2d 1322 (1978),[1] plaintiff had not established the relevance of the allegedly safer design here, because she had introduced no evidence that wheel brakes of that design were commercially available when the bed was manufactured. Plaintiff's expert, a physicist, testified only that the scientific principles involved in the alternative brake mechanism were known when the bed was manufactured, *i.e.,* that the design was technically feasible at that time. There was no evidence that the alternative design was practicable in the sense that wheel brakes of that design were commercially available when the bed was manufactured. For the same reason, the court refused to admit a sample of the alternative braking mechanism.

Plaintiff contends that *Wilson* does not require a plaintiff to adduce evidence that an alternative, safer design was commercially available at the time the product was manufactured in order to make a *prima facie* case. In *Wilson,* the plaintiffs alleged design defects in a light airplane that had crashed as a result of engine failure allegedly caused by carburetor icing. They claimed that the plane was defective, because it was provided with a carbureted engine rather than an engine with a fuel injection system, which was less susceptible to icing. There was evidence that, at the time the plane was manufactured, fuel-injected engines of the appropriate horsepower were commercially available. The court held, however, that the plaintiffs had not made a *prima facie* case, because there was no evidence of the effect that substitution of a fuel-injected engine in the airplane would have on its "cost, economy of operation, maintenance requirements, over-all performance, or safety in respects other than susceptibility to icing." 282 Or. at 70, 577 P.2d 1322.

The plaintiffs in *Wilson* also alleged that the plane was defective because it was not equipped with crashworthy shoulder harnesses and seat belt brackets and attachments. There was evidence that workable shoulder harnesses and safer seat belt attachment designs were available when the plane was manufactured. The court held that that evidence was sufficient to raise a jury question, because the fact finder could infer, on the basis of common knowledge, that, unlike the substitution of a different engine, addition of the safer seat belt design would not "significantly affect the over-all engineering of the airplane and would not be unduly expensive." As to both design defect allegations, however, the court assured that evidence of commercial availability was required in

---

1. The *Wilson* court observed that in some cases, *e.g.,* where the danger is relatively severe and the product has limited utility, the jury may be able to find defendant liable, even though no safer design was feasible. 282 Or. at 71 n. 5, 577 P.2d 1322. No party argues that that is the case here.

order for plaintiffs to make out a *prima facie* case sufficient to submit the case to the jury.

In *Wilson,* as in this case, the defendant did not manufacture the allegedly defective component part, but rather incorporated it in the assembly of another product.[2] It is implicit in *Wilson* that in this type of case the plaintiff must adduce evidence that the alternative safer design was commercially available at the time the offending product was manufactured. Use of the alternative design cannot be said to be "practicable" if the defendant is not in the business of manufacturing the component part, and if a part incorporating the allegedly safer design is not available for purchase. As the court said in *Wilson,* a "plaintiffs' prima facie case of a defect must show more than the technical possibility of a safer design." 282 Or. at 68, 577 P.2d 1322. The court did not err in excluding plaintiff's two exhibits.

* * *

Affirmed.

Notes

1. How would the *Appel v. Standex Intern. Corp.* court have decided *Boatland v. Bailey?*

2. Why should commercial availability be an absolute requirement? What if defendant manufactured the whole bed, including the wheels?

3. Suppose the alternative design was technologically impossible at the time of manufacture. Should this be an absolute bar to liability, or merely a factor to be considered in the risk-utility analysis?

4. Recall *Barker v. Lull Engineering Co., supra* p. 202. How would a court applying the *Barker* test of defect have decided *Appel v. Standex Intern. Corp.?*

KALLIO v. FORD MOTOR CO.
Supreme Court of Minnesota, 1987.
407 N.W.2d 92.

While driving his 1977 Ford F–150 pickup truck home from work, Robert Kallio pulled over to the side of the road, shifted the automatic transmission lever into the "park" position, and left the cab to cover some tools in the open truck bed that had become exposed to the rain. He neither shut off the engine nor set the parking brake. As he jumped on the bumper to cover the tools, he suddenly realized the truck was moving in reverse. He leaped to the ground and ran to the truck's cab, but before he was able to re-enter the truck, he slipped on the pavement, fell, and the truck ran over both of his legs and one of his hands before a passenger sitting in the cab succeeded in stopping it. His subsequent

---

2. The manufacturer of the wheels was a third-party defendant below, but it is not a party to this appeal.

action against Ford was bottomed on allegations of defective design of the truck's shifting mechanism and on Ford's failure to warn of the propensity of the truck not to go completely into the "park" position. The jury concluded both that the truck was defective and that Kallio was negligent.

1.   Because it claims that Kallio failed to demonstrate the existence of a feasible, practicable, and safer alternative automatic transmission shift design, Ford asserts the trial court erred in denying Ford's motion for a directed verdict.   Alternatively, Ford argues the trial court errone-ously refused to give Ford's requested Instruction No. 11 relating to the issue.[4]

Whether the trial court erred in either case depends upon whether in a products liability alleged design defect case a plaintiff must establish as an element of his case that at the time of manufacture a safer, practicable, and technologically feasible alternative design existed—an issue of first impression for this court.   Other courts of last resort, however, have addressed the issue.   Ford buttresses its contention by reliance upon decisions from New York, Oregon, and Nebraska—all of which hold that in an alleged defective product design case, an element of plaintiff's case includes proof of the existence of a feasible, safer alternative design.   These jurisdictions hold that initially the plaintiff has the onus of presenting evidence of the existence of substantial likelihood of harm and that when the product was manufactured, it was feasible to employ an alternative safer design.   *Voss v. Black & Decker Mfg. Co.,* 59 N.Y.2d 102, 463 N.Y.S.2d 398, 450 N.E.2d 204 (1983); *Wilson v. Piper Aircraft Corp.,* 282 Or. 61, 577 P.2d 1322 (1978) *rehearing denied,* 282 Or. 411, 579 P.2d 1287 (1978); *Nerud v. Haybus-ter Mfg., Inc.,* 215 Neb. 604, 340 N.W.2d 369 (1983).   This showing must be more than a "technical possibility [of the existence] of a safer design." *Piper Aircraft,* 282 Or. at 67–68, 577 P.2d at 1326.

The rule of strict liability in tort found in *Restatement (Second) of Torts* § 402(A) (1965) had its genesis more than 20 years ago.   Almost since the rule's inception, courts have tended to borrow common law concepts of negligence in determining whether a manufactured product, as designed, is unreasonably dangerous.   *See, e.g.,* Wade, *Strict Tort*

---

4. Defendant's requested Instruction No. 11 reads:

PLAINTIFF REQUIRED TO ESTABLISH THE AVAILABILITY OF A FEASIBLE, PRACTICABLE ALTERNATIVE

For you to conclude that the design of the park system in the subject Ford vehi-cle was defective and unreasonably dan-gerous at the time of sale by Ford Motor Company, the plaintiff must establish by a preponderance of the evidence that, at the time the vehicle was designed, there was available to the defendant a feasible practicable alternative design and that that design, if it had been chosen by Ford, would have avoided or materially reduced the plaintiff's injury.   If the plaintiffs fail to prove the existence of such a feasible, practicable alternative de-sign, they will be unable to prove that Ford's choice of design was unreasonable. The plaintiff cannot carry his burden in this regard merely by showing that an alternative design was possible.   To suc-ceed in this case the plaintiffs must estab-lish that such a design would have been feasible and practicable, and that it would have avoided or materially reduced the plaintiff's injury.

Liability of Manufacturers, 19 Sw.L.J. 5, 17 (1965); *see also* Keeton, *Product Liability and the Meaning of Defect*, 5 St. Mary's L.J. 30 (1973); Steenson, *The Anatomy of Products Liability in Minnesota*, 6 Wm. Mitchell L.Rev. 1, 23–25 (1980); Wade, *On the Nature of Strict Tort Liability for Products*, 44 Miss.L.J. 825 (1973).

The design defect products liability cases arising in the three jurisdictions relied upon by Ford employ the negligence reasonable care test which requires the trier of fact to balance the product's risks against its utility and cost in determining whether it has been defectively designed. *See, e.g., Micallef v. Miehle Co.*, 39 N.Y.2d 376, 386, 384 N.Y.S.2d 115, 121, 348 N.E.2d 571, 577–78 (1976); *Wilson v. Piper Aircraft Corp.*, 282 Or. 61, 66, 577 P.2d 1322, 1325–26 (1978); *Nerud v. Haybuster Mfg., Inc.*, 215 Neb. at 614, 340 N.W.2d at 375. We have likewise adopted a similar approach citing with approval *Micallef v. Miehle Co.* in *Holm v. Sponco Manufacturing, Inc.*, 324 N.W.2d 207, 212 (Minn.1982). Later, in *Bilotta v. Kelley Co.*, 346 N.W.2d 616 (Minn.1984), we reaffirmed our *Holm* holding that we had adopted the reasonable care balancing test. *Id.* at 622. Because this court in *Holm v. Sponco Manufacturing, Inc.* and in *Bilotta v. Kelley Co.* specifically adopted the reasonable care balancing test in design cases in reliance upon the analysis of the New York Court of Appeals in *Micallef v. Miehle Co.*, Ford here argues that we should likewise extend the reasonable care balancing test reasoning, as New York has done, to require preliminarily that a plaintiff must present evidence of the existence of a safer, feasible alternative design. On the other hand, Kallio urges that we should follow *Barker v. Lull Engineering Co.*, 20 Cal.3d 413, 143 Cal.Rptr. 225, 573 P.2d 443 (1978), which held that the burden of proving the nonexistence of a safer design should rest with the manufacturer.

We decline respondent's invitation to follow *Barker*. Instead, we concur in the observation made by the Oregon Supreme Court when, in the course of denying a petition for rehearing in *Wilson v. Piper Aircraft Corp.*, urging it to adopt the *Barker* rationale, it stated:

> Under that decision [*Barker*] it appears that a design defect case will always go to the jury if only the plaintiff can show that the product caused the injury. In this jurisdiction, however, it is part of plaintiff's case to show that a product which caused an injury was dangerously defective.

282 Or. at 413, 579 P.2d at 1287–88.

Unlike California, which in *Barker* specifically removed "unreasonable" as a limitation of the compensable dangerousness of a product, *see* 20 Cal.3d at 417, 573 P.2d at 446, 143 Cal.Rptr. at 228, Minnesota, like Oregon, maintains the requirement in a strict liability products case that a plaintiff must establish not only that the product was in a defective condition, but also that it was *unreasonably dangerous*. *O'Laughlin v. Minnesota Natural Gas Co.*, 253 N.W.2d 826, 832 (1977), *Bilotta v. Kelley Co.*, 346 N.W.2d at 622. Obviously, a factor bearing upon the latter requirement will be the existence or nonexistence of a feasible alternative design. To satisfy that requirement, the plaintiff ordinarily has the burden of showing the existence of an alternative design that was safer. If the manufacturer presents evidence disputing the contention, the trier of fact will resolve the "unreasonably dangerous" issue. As in other tort cases, plaintiffs asserting a strict liability tort claim based upon alleged defective design of a product ultimately have the burden to prove the elements of the asserted claim. Generally in a case based upon alleged improper design, one of those elements requires production of evidence that the design employed was unreasonably dangerous. To establish a prima facie case that it was unreasonably dangerous normally requires production of evidence of the existence of a feasible, alternative safer design.

In this case the trial court instructed the jury using JIG 117, 4 Minn.Dist. Judges Ass'n, *Minnesota Practice,* JIG III CIVIL (3d ed. 1986).[7] Additionally the court's instructions elaborated on other factors the jury could consider in deciding whether Ford's automatic transmission as designed was unreasonably dangerous. Included among those additional factors, the jury was informed it could consider the "state of the art" and the "practices of the automotive industry" at the time of the truck's sale. The tenor, if not the literal wording, of the instructions permitted the jury to consider availability of, and failure to use, an alternative, safer design as a factor. However, Ford complains the instructions didn't go far enough; that they should have informed the jury that plaintiff had the burden to prove the existence of a safer, feasible alternative design as an element of an alleged defective product design case. We disagree. The court's instruction correctly stated the law. *See, e.g., Bilotta v. Kelley Co.,* 346 N.W.2d at 621–22. Although normally evidence of a safer alternative design will be presented initially by the plaintiff, it is not necessarily required in all cases.[8] Such evidence is relevant to, and certainly may be an important factor in, the determination of whether the product was unreasonably defective. However,

---

7. JIG 117 reads:

STRICT LIABILITY—DESIGN DEFECT

A manufacturer has a duty to use reasonable care when designing a product, so as to avoid any unreasonable risk of harm to (anyone who) (property that) is likely to be exposed to harm when the product is put to its intended use or to any use that is unintended but is reasonably foreseeable.

What constitutes reasonable care will vary with the surrounding circumstances. Reasonable care is the care that a reasonably prudent person would exercise under the same or similar circumstances.

The reasonable care to be exercised by a manufacturer when designing a product will depend on all the facts and circumstances, including, among others, the likelihood and seriousness of harm against the feasibility and burden of any precautions which would be effective to avoid the harm. You are instructed that the manufacturer is obligated to keep informed of scientific knowledge and discoveries in its field.

If the manufacturer did not use reasonable care when designing the product in question, then the product is in a defective condition unreasonably dangerous to the (user or consumer) (user's or consumer's property).

8. Conceivably, rare cases may exist where the product may be judged unreasonably dangerous because it should be removed from the market rather than be redesigned. *See, e.g., Wilson v. Piper Aircraft Corp.,* 282 Or. 61, 71 n. 5, 577 P.2d 1322, 1328 n. 5 (1978); *O'Brien v. Muskin Corp.,* 94 N.J. 169, 185, 463 A.2d 298, 306 (1983).

existence of a safer, practical alternative design is not an element of an alleged defective product design prima facie case.

Defendant's requested Instruction No. 11 is overly broad, not only because, in essence, it tends to elevate proof of the existence of a feasible alternative safer design from a factor properly for jury consideration to an element of the plaintiff's claim, but also because it tended to overemphasize that factor. As we have stated, such emphasis "is properly the function of counsel in closing argument, not by the court in its instructions." *Alholm v. Wilt,* 394 N.W.2d 488, 491 (Minn.1986). We note that counsel, indeed, made a vigorous final summation arguing Ford's position.

Finally, respondent did present some evidence, albeit weak, that a practical safer design was feasible through the testimony of William Barr and Michael Inden. Ford offered considerable evidence that, if believed, would permit the jury to conclude that, indeed, Ford had employed the state of the art in designing the transmission and that no safer practical design existed in 1977. Had we been jurors, we might have accepted Ford's position. However, the resolution of this disputed fact issue was for the trier of fact—here the jury. Sufficient evidence existed to support the conclusion it reached.

* * *

Accordingly, we affirm the court of appeals.

SIMONETT, J., specially concurs.

SIMONETT, JUSTICE (concurring specially).

* * *

My only reason for writing is to comment on further evidence offered by plaintiff on alternative design. In 1979, in a different trial, plaintiff's expert, William Barr, had testified that Ford's system was not unreasonably dangerous. In this case, however, Barr testified that he had now invented a device, as yet untested, never yet installed in any vehicle, containing some "bugs," but which he thought with "a good deal of work" might fix the problem. The majority opinion says this testimony of alternative design was "weak." In my view, Barr did not show his device was practical, and his testimony would not have withstood a motion to strike if one had been made. (Ford's expert, it might be added, thought Barr's device could not be made to work satisfactorily; that even if it could, it would not significantly reduce the problem; and that the device might make shifting more difficult.)

Conscious design defects present difficult problems of proof for both plaintiffs and manufacturers. There is much room for second guessing, and courts are being asked to establish standards of reasonableness for manufacturers (whether it be Ford or a fledgling family operation). Establishing standards entails a weighing of engineering, marketing, and financing factors, which, at times, may be a difficult task for courts to perform. *See* Henderson, *Judicial Review of Manufacturers' Conscious*

Design Choices: The Limits of Adjudication, 73 Colum.L.Rev. 1531 (1973). On the other hand, the establishment of standards cannot always be avoided by passing the problem off to the jury under a general reasonable care instruction.

In any event, the limited issue before us is whether the trial court erred in refusing to give defendant's requested instruction that plaintiff was required to prove the existence of a feasible, practical alternative design. I agree with the majority opinion that the trial court's instructions on burden of proof were adequate and that it was unnecessary to give the requested instruction which would have unduly singled out one aspect of the proof. I also agree with the court's disposition of the other issues.

Sometimes where proof is lacking for a conscious design defect, plaintiff may still be able to show breach of a duty to warn. Henderson, *supra,* at 1562–63. Here, plaintiff knew his pickup might move if the shift lever was not completely in the park position, and there was no need to warn on this elementary, obvious fact. But what plaintiff did not know was that the shift lever would feel like it was in park when it was not. The jury could have found there should have been a warning placed in the owner's manual about this illusory effect.

Notes

1. Should plaintiff have the burden of proving the existence of a feasible alternative design at the time of manufacture, or should the absence of such an alternative be a defensive issue?

2. As the main case indicates, the courts are split on the question of who has the burden of proof. The cases are collected in Annotation, 78 A.L.R.4th 154 (1990).

3. In light of the three preceding cases, and of the materials you have studied concerning the definition of defect, consider the following problem:

Philip, an eleven-year-old child, was severely injured when his left foot got caught in the agitator mechanism of a bulk fertilizer spreader manufactured by the DDD Manufacturing Co. The spreader was designed for one-person operation, and was towed by a tractor. It was 7 feet long, 8 feet wide and more than 6 feet high. The agitator, at the bottom of the spreader, broke up fertilizer lumps into granules. It ran the length of the spreader, had sharp teeth, and rotated when the spreader was pulled forward. The sides of the spreader were V-shaped, so that gravity forced the fertilizer toward the agitator in the bottom. An augur below the agitator fed the granules into a spinner which distributed the fertilizer. A baffle formed a V-shaped roof several inches above the agitator to protect it from the weight of the fertilizer when the spreader was full. It was made of two pieces of metal, 4 inches wide and 85 inches long. They were joined lengthwise at a 90–degree angle. A metal bar designed to hold a canvas top ran above the hopper.

Philip's father was using the spreader to apply fertilizer to one of his fields. Philip was riding in the spreader, using his feet to break up lumps of fertilizer that were too large to go into the agitator. At the time of the accident, Philip was standing on the baffle and holding on to the metal bar above the hopper. His left foot slipped off of the baffle and was caught in the agitator.

The agitator was clearly visible below the baffle when the spreader was empty. Philip had not seen it and did not know of its existence. Philip's father knew about it, but did not warn him. A sign on the spreader stated that people should keep off the implement while it was in use. It also warned against getting near the moving parts without first disengaging the power.

Philip is represented by an attorney who plans to bring a strict products liability suit against DDD on the theory that the spreader was defectively designed. She has an expert witness who is a retired professor of agricultural engineering safety at a state university. The witness is willing to testify that, based on his inspection, the fertilizer spreader was unreasonably dangerous. His opinion is based upon (1) the known propensity of fertilizer to clog, interfering with the flow of fertilizer to the spinner (insofar as the lumps were too large to pass under the baffle to the agitator), and (2) insufficient guarding of the agitator to prevent one inside the spreader from getting hands or feet caught in the agitator. In his opinion, unless farmers carried a club-like instrument to break up fertilizer clumps, they would have to climb inside the spreader and crush them with their feet. If another person were assisting, he naturally would remain inside the spreader as they were fertilizing to avoid having to stop the tractor each time lumps interfered with the flow of fertilizer.

This witness believes that the spreader would have been reasonably safe if grids, grillwork, bars or the equivalent had been installed at some point at the top of or inside the spreader. Further testing, however, would be necessary to determine the ultimate form and feasibility of such devices. He nevertheless believes that, based on prior experience with similar problems, some such device was workable.

Philip's attorney also has, as witnesses, three farmers who will testify that farm personnel, household members and children frequently ride in fertilizer spreaders. They do this sometimes to break up lumps of fertilizer, and sometimes to obtain transportation around the farm.

DDD has an expert engineer who will testify that the spreader was safe because it was designed for operation by one person. The operator would have to stop the tractor when it was necessary to break up lumps, and this would automatically terminate the agitator's rotation. The positioning of the agitator at the bottom of the spreader, and the warning sign on the machine are adequate safeguards. No bars or grillwork could be placed inside the machine without interfering with the flow of fertilizer. If asked on cross-examination, this expert will admit that he has never tested any of the devices suggested by plaintiff's expert.

Does Philip have sufficient evidence to get to a jury on his theory of liability in a jurisdiction that uses the consumer expectations test of defect? The risk-utility test? The *Barker v. Lull* test?

SECTION C. UNAVOIDABLY UNSAFE PRODUCTS

GRUNDBERG v. UPJOHN CO.

Supreme Court of Utah, 1991.
813 P.2d 89.

DURHAM, JUSTICE:

This case comes to us pursuant to rule 41 of the Utah Rules of Appellate Procedure as a question certified from the United States District Court for the District of Utah. The issue before us is whether Utah adopts the "unavoidably unsafe products" exception to strict products liability as set forth in comment k to section 402A of the Restatement (Second) of Torts (1965) ("comment k"). This question presents an unanswered issue of law for original disposition by this court.

We hold that a drug approved by the United States Food and Drug Administration ("FDA"), properly prepared, compounded, packaged, and distributed, cannot as a matter of law be "defective" in the absence of proof of inaccurate, incomplete, misleading, or fraudulent information furnished by the manufacturer in connection with FDA approval. We acknowledge that by characterizing all FDA-approved prescription medications as "unavoidably unsafe," we are expanding the literal interpretation of comment k.

The following facts are taken from the federal district court's certification order. Mildred Lucille Coats died at age 83 from gunshot wounds inflicted by her daughter, Ilo Grundberg, on June 19, 1988. Grundberg and Janice Gray, the personal representative of Coat's estate, brought this action, alleging that Grundberg shot her mother as a result of ingesting the drug Halcion, a prescription drug manufactured by defendant Upjohn to treat insomnia.

Plaintiffs allege that Grundberg took a .5 milligram dose of Halcion the day she shot her mother. They allege that this dose was recommended by her physician and was consistent with Upjohn's recommended dosage. Plaintiffs assert that Grundberg shot her mother while in a state of Halcion-induced intoxication, which allegedly included side effects such as depression, psychosis, depersonalization, aggressive assaultive behavior, and homicidal compulsion.

Plaintiffs' complaint states several causes of action, including common law negligence and strict liability. Plaintiffs claim that Upjohn failed to adequately warn about certain adverse side effects of Halcion and that Halcion was defectively designed. The failure-to-warn claim is scheduled for trial. The strict liability claim based on design defect is the subject of Upjohn's pending summary judgment motion, the outcome of which depends on this court's resolution of the certified question.

The parties agree that the Restatement (Second) of Torts section 402A, comment k (1965) and the principles it embodies provide an exemption from strict liability for a claimed design defect in the case of products that are "unavoidably unsafe." In moving for partial summary judgment, Upjohn argued that public policy supporting the research and development of new drugs requires a holding that *all* FDA-approved prescription medications are "unavoidably unsafe products" under comment k and, as such, manufacturers of those drugs would not be liable for a claim based on defective design. Plaintiffs argue that whether a drug is "unavoidably unsafe" must be determined on a case-by-case basis, with a determination in each case of whether the specific drug's benefit exceeded its risk at the time it was distributed. The district court found this to be a controlling question of law and certified it to this court.

* * *

I. UTAH LAW ON STRICT LIABILITY

Section 402A of the Restatement (Second) of Torts (1965) addresses the strict liability of sellers of products. This court adopted section 402A, of which comment k is one provision, in *Ernest W. Hahn, Inc. v. Armco Steel Co.*, 601 P.2d 152, 158 (Utah 1979). Since then, we have adhered to section 402A and to at least one of its accompanying comments. [Citations] We have not addressed the application of comment k in the context of prescription drugs or otherwise. * * *

In its entirety, comment k reads:

k. *Unavoidably unsafe products.* There are some products which, in the present state of human knowledge, are quite incapable of being made safe for their intended and ordinary use. These are especially common in the field of drugs. An outstanding example is the vaccine for the Pasteur treatment of rabies, which not uncommonly leads to very serious and damaging consequences when it is injected. Since the disease itself invariably leads to a dreadful death, both the marketing and the use of the vaccine are fully justified, notwithstanding the unavoidable high degree of risk which they involve. Such a product, properly prepared, and accompanied by proper directions and warning, is not defective, nor is it *unreasonably* dangerous. The same is true of many other drugs, vaccines, and the like, many of which for this very reason cannot legally be sold except to physicians, or under the prescription of a physician. It is also true in particular of many new or experimental drugs as to which, because of lack of time and opportunity for sufficient medical experience, there can be no assurance of safety, or perhaps even of purity of ingredients, but such experience as there is justifies the marketing and use of the drug notwithstanding a medically recognizable risk. The seller of such products, again with the qualification that they are properly prepared and marketed, and proper warning is given, where the situation calls for it, is not to be held to strict liability for unfortunate consequences attending their use, merely because he has undertaken to supply the public with an apparently useful and desirable product, attended with a known but apparently reasonable risk.

Comment k establishes an exception to the strict products liability section 402A imposes on "[o]ne who sells any product in a defective condition unreasonably dangerous to the user or consumer or to his [or her] property. * * *" § 402A(1). This liability applies whether or not "the seller has exercised all possible care in the preparation and sale of his product. * * *" § 402A(2)(a). Comment g defines a "defective condition" as a condition "not contemplated by the ultimate consumer which will be unreasonably dangerous to [that consumer]." Comment k, however, defines a category of "unavoidably unsafe" products that "when properly prepared, and accompanied by proper directions and warning, [are] not defective, nor * * * *unreasonably* dangerous." (Emphasis in original.)

We agree with comment k's basic proposition—that there are some products that have dangers associated with their use even though they are used as intended. We also agree that the seller of such products, when the products are properly prepared and marketed and distributed with appropriate warnings, should not be held strictly liable for the "unfortunate consequences" attending their use. Thus, we adopt comment k's basic policy as the law to be applied in this state and must now turn to the issue of how to apply that policy.

II. APPLICATION OF COMMENT K

As a condition to its application, comment k requires that the product be "properly prepared, and accompanied by proper directions and warning. * * *" There are three types of product defects: manufacturing flaws, design defects, and inadequate warnings regarding use. [Citations] By its terms, comment k excepts unavoidably unsafe products from strict liability only to the extent that the plaintiff alleges a design defect; comment k's immunity from strict liability does not extend to strict liability claims based on a manufacturing flaw or an inadequate warning. The purpose of comment k is to protect from strict liability products that cannot be designed more safely. If, however, such products are mismanufactured or unaccompanied by adequate warnings, the seller may be liable even if the plaintiff cannot establish the seller's negligence. [Citation] Both parties agree in this case that the prerequisite to a comment k exemption—that the drug "was properly prepared and accompanied by warnings of its dangerous propensities"—must be established on a case-by-case basis. This limitation on the scope of comment k immunity is universally recognized.

Even in the case of a clearly alleged design defect, however, comment k is unclear on the scope of its protection. Until recently, most courts refrained from applying a design defect theory to products liability cases involving prescription drugs. Beginning with *Brochu v. Ortho Pharmaceutical Corp.*, 642 F.2d 652 (1st Cir.1981), however, and more recently in *Savina v. Sterling Drug, Inc.*, 247 Kan. 105, 795 P.2d 915

(1990), some states have permitted recovery for a strict liability claim based on the theory that the drug was defectively designed.

Some courts have applied comment k on a case-by-case basis, conditioning application of the exemption on a finding that the drug is in fact "unavoidably unsafe." *See Savina*, 795 P.2d 915; *Toner [v. Lederle Laboratories*, 112 Idaho 328, 732 P.2d 297 (1987)]; *see also Feldman v. Lederle Laboratories*, 97 N.J. 429, 479 A.2d 374, 382–83 (1984) (involving allegations of failure to warn, but stating, "Whether a drug is unavoidably unsafe should be decided on a case-by-case basis. * * *"); *Collins v. Eli Lilly Co.*, 116 Wis.2d 166, 342 N.W.2d 37, 52 (1984) (comment k applicable only if drug in question was placed on market without adequate testing because of exigent circumstances); *Patten v. Lederle Laboratories*, 676 F.Supp. 233 (D.Utah 1987) (federal district court predicting that Utah would adopt comment k).

California was the first state to fashion a risk/benefit test to determine which drugs are entitled to comment k protection. In *Kearl v. Lederle Laboratories*, 172 Cal.App.3d 812, 218 Cal.Rptr. 453 (1985),[1] the California Court of Appeal specifically discussed the problems society would face by subjecting drugs to the same accountability as other products, allowing unlimited redress for plaintiffs injured by pharmaceutical products. Such problems, the court noted, include delayed availability of needed drugs and imposition of the costs of research, development, and marketing of new products beyond that which manufacturers, especially small manufacturers, might be willing to risk. 218 Cal.Rptr. at 459 (quoting *Feldman*, 460 A.2d at 209).

The *Kearl* court expressed discomfort, however, with the "mechanical" method by which many appellate courts had concluded that drugs are entitled to special treatment. 218 Cal.Rptr. at 463. Thus, *Kearl* set forth a risk/benefit analysis to be carried out by the trial court on a case-by-case basis. *Id.* at 463–64. Under this approach, a product may be deemed unavoidably unsafe and thus exempt from a strict liability design defect cause of action only if the court concludes that (1) the product was intended to provide an exceptionally important benefit, and (2) the risk posed was substantial and unavoidable when distributed. *Id.* at 464.[2]

Idaho adopted and to some extent refined the *Kearl* approach in *Toner v. Lederle Laboratories*, 112 Idaho 328, 732 P.2d 297 (1987), a case addressing a suit against the manufacturer of a vaccine to immunize

---

1. *Kearl* was overturned by the California Supreme Court in *Brown*, 751 P.2d at 470. Since *Brown*, the rule in California is that all prescription drugs are entitled as a matter of law to an exemption from strict liability claims based upon design defects.

2. The trial court would decide whether to exempt a product only after first taking evidence out of the jury's presence, considering: (1) whether, when distributed, the product was intended to confer an exceptionally important benefit that made its availability highly desirable; (2) whether the then-existing risk posed by the product both was "substantial" and "unavoidable;" and (3) whether the interest in availability (again measured as of the time of distribution) outweighs the interest in promoting enhanced accountability through strict liability design defect review. *Kearl*, 218 Cal. Rptr. at 464.

against diphtheria, pertussis, and tetanus ("DPT"). *Toner* required the drug manufacturer to prove at trial, on a case-by-case basis, that the benefits of the drug outweighed the risks at the time of marketing. 732 P.2d at 305–09. To qualify as an "unavoidably unsafe product" under this approach, "there must be, at the time of the subject products' distribution, no feasible alternative design which on balance accomplishes the subject product's purpose with a lesser risk." *Id.* at 306 (citing *Belle Bonfils Memorial Blood Bank v. Hansen*, 665 P.2d 118, 123 (Colo.1983)); *Kearl*, 218 Cal.Rptr. at 464. If there were alternative drug product designs that could have effectively achieved the same purpose, the court reasoned, the risk would not be "unavoidable" or "apparently reasonable" and the marketing and use of the product would not be justified. *Toner*, 732 P.2d at 306.

In direct contrast to those courts applying comment k's immunity on a case-by-case basis are courts holding that all prescription drugs are entitled as a matter of law to the exemption from strict liability claims based on design defect. In *Brown v. Superior Court*, 44 Cal.3d 1049, 245 Cal.Rptr. 412, 751 P.2d 470 (1988), the court addressed claims brought by plaintiffs who sued drug companies for injuries allegedly arising from their mothers' in utero exposure to diethystilbestrol, a synthetic hormone marketed for use during pregnancy. The court weighed the problem of whether imposing strict liability on drug manufacturers comports with the traditional goals of tort law, namely, deterrence and cost distribution. 751 P.2d at 478. The court acknowledged that a drug might be safer if pharmaceutical companies withheld it from the market until scientific skill and knowledge advanced to the point where all dangerous side effects could be discovered. *Id.* at 479. There was concern, however, that this delay, when added to the delay normally required for the FDA to approve a new drug, would not serve the public welfare. The court cited examples of several potentially useful drugs being withdrawn from the market or their availability seriously curtailed because of the liability crisis. *Id.* at 479–80.

The *Brown* court acknowledged the appeal of the *Kearl* cost/benefit approach, yet found the "mini-trial" procedure unworkable because of its negative impact on the development and marketing of new drugs. *Brown*, 751 P.2d at 481. Another of the *Brown* court's objections to *Kearl* was that it left the trial court to hear and resolve mixed questions of law and fact, placing the trial court in the role of fact finder. *Brown*, 751 P.2d at 481–82. The court found the cost/benefit test too open-ended and predicted that it would lead to disparate treatment of the same drug by different judges. *Id.* at 482.

The *Brown* court stressed three public policies mitigating against imposing strict liability for prescription drugs. First, drug manufacturers might stop producing valuable drugs because of lost profits resulting from lawsuits or the inability to secure adequate insurance. *Id.* at 479–80. Second, consumers have a vested interest in prompt availability of new pharmaceutical products. Imposing strict liability for design defects might cause manufacturers to delay placing new products on the market, even after those products receive FDA approval. *Id.* at 479. Finally, the added expense of insuring against strict liability and additional research programs might cause the cost of medication to increase to the extent that it would no longer be affordable to consumers. *Id.*

The plaintiffs and amici curiae in *Brown* asserted that the language of comment k cannot be interpreted to grant blanket immunity from strict liability to all prescription drugs. Rather, they asserted that only those drugs that are "unavoidably dangerous" are eligible for such protection. *Id.* at 482 n. 11. The court, although conceding that the comment is not entirely clear on this point, noted that "the comment was *intended* to and should apply to all prescription drugs." *Id.* (emphasis added). *Brown* concluded that "because of the public interest in the development, availability, and reasonable price of drugs, the appropriate test for determining responsibility is the test stated in comment k. * * *" *Id.* at 477.

In *Castrignano v. E.R. Squibb & Sons, Inc.*, 546 A.2d 775 (R.I.1988), the Rhode Island Supreme Court had the opportunity to review *Toner's* case-by-case risk/benefit analysis and *Brown's* broad exemption approach when formulating its own approach to drug products liability. The Rhode Island court opted for the more restrictive case-by-case approach, *id.* at 781, and developed a directed verdict standard to balance the roles of the judge and the jury in applying comment k. *Id.* at 781–82. Under the *Castrignano* test, if at the time of marketing the apparent benefit outweighed the apparent risk, comment k applies and recovery for design defect is precluded. *Id.* If a trial judge concludes that reasonable minds could not differ in deciding that a drug's benefit exceeds its risk, then as a matter of law, the trial judge can extend comment k protection. *Id.* at 782. If the judge feels that reasonable minds could differ on the question, the judge must submit the issue to the jury. *Id.*

In reviewing the approaches of other jurisdictions toward strict products liability for design defects in drug products, we are troubled by the lack of uniformity and certainty inherent in the case-by-case approach and fear the resulting disincentive for pharmaceutical manufacturers to develop new products. *Toner's* attempt to clarify the "unreasonably dangerous" standard seriously curtails the defendants' chances of success in establishing comment k immunity as a matter of law. One commentator notes that a defendant would have an easier time rebutting a plaintiff's prima facie case of design defect under the traditional standard than meeting the tough burden of "earning" the comment k exemption. *See* Reilly, *The Erosion of Comment k*, 14 U. Dayton L.Rev. 255, 266 (1989).

Toner applied a very literal and restrictive interpretation of comment k. For example, the comment cites examples of *certain* drugs and vaccines as products that "supply the public with an apparently useful and desirable product, attended with a known but apparently reasonable risk." Based on this language, *Toner* opined that (1) comment k "[c]learly * * * contemplates a weighing of the benefit of the product against its risk" and (2) was never intended to exempt *all* drugs from strict liability. *Toner*, 732 P.2d 297, 306. Even if we agree with the court in *Toner* that the comment contemplates a "weighing" of the drug's risks and benefits, we find it unnecessary to conclude that a *court* is the proper body to engage in that weighing process. Furthermore, we need not be bound by the specific language of comment k and may adopt and apply its fundamental policy without restricting ourselves to what we perceive to be its literal interpretation.

Castrignano's somewhat nebulous standard, designed to control when the question of comment k's application reaches the jury, leaves a great deal of room for plaintiffs to maneuver cases to the jury. Additionally, like the traditional case-by-case approach, this standard ignores the effectiveness of the FDA's regulatory process.

We agree with *Brown* that the case-by-case method first articulated in *Kearl* is unworkable, even in light of *Toner's* refinement of the test. We find the *Brown* result more in line with the public policy considerations in the important area of pharmaceutical product design. We do not agree, however, with the *Brown* court's apparent attempt to use the plain language of comment k as the vehicle for exempting all prescription drugs from strict liability rather than relying on the policies underlying that comment.

The American Law Institute's restatements are drafted by legal scholars who attempt to summarize the state of the law in a given area, predict how the law is changing, and suggest the direction the law should take. The restatement serves an appropriate advisory role to courts in approaching unsettled areas of law. We emphasize, however, that section 402A of the Restatement (Second) of Torts, as drafted in 1965, is not binding on our decision in this case except insofar as we explicitly adopt its various doctrinal principles. We agree with the principle comment k embodies, that manufacturers of unavoidably dangerous products should not be liable for a claim of design defect. We are persuaded that all prescription drugs should be classified as unavoidably dangerous in design because of their unique nature and value, the elaborate regulatory system overseen by the FDA, the difficulties of relying on individual lawsuits as a forum in which to review a prescription drug's design, and the significant public policy considerations noted in *Brown*. We therefore reach the same conclusion as did the California Supreme Court in *Brown*, albeit pursuant to a slightly different rationale.

III. Unique Characteristics of Drugs

Because prescription drugs are chemical compounds designed to interact with the chemical and physiological processes of the human body, they will almost always pose some risk of side effects in certain individuals. Despite these risks, new drugs are continually approved by the FDA because of their social benefit in saving lives and alleviating human suffering. The health care system and general standard of living in this country, for example, would be seriously impaired without such essential drug products as antibiotics that allow quick recovery from ailments that were once debilitating or even fatal. *See* 37 Food, Drug & Cosmetic L.J. 15 (1982).

In addition, because the expansion of tort liability is justified primarily on the basis of deterring or transferring the cost of injuries, it is appropriate to consider the increased costs that could result from the curtailment of the production of prescription drugs. One commentator notes:

> [D]rugs are our most cost-effective input in supplying the demand for health. *A ten-dollar prescription is frequently a substitute for $2,000 worth of hospital services*—a substitute that produces a positive outcome with much higher frequency than hospital care. * * * *If we are serious about minimizing costs, our best bet is to increase the number of drug innovations.*

Brozen, *Statements, Drugs & Health: Economic Issues and Policy Objectives*, 305 (Helms ed. 1981) (emphasis added).

Despite inherent risks, *and in contrast to any other product*, society has determined that prescription medications provide a unique benefit and so should be available to physicians with appropriate warnings and guidance as to use. The federal government has established an elaborate regulatory system, overseen by the FDA, to control the approval and distribution of these drugs. *See* 21 U.S.C. §§ 301–393. No other class of products is subject to such special restrictions or protections in our society.

IV. FDA REGULATION

Congress created the FDA to "protect consumers from dangerous products." *United States v. Sullivan*, 332 U.S. 689, 696, 68 S.Ct. 331, 335, 92 L.Ed. 297 (1948). In its role as "both a health promoter * * * and * * * a public protector," the FDA employs a comprehensive scheme of premarket screening and post-market surveillance to ensure the safety and efficacy of all licensed medications. 50 Fed.Reg. 7452 (1985).

Before licensing a new medication, the FDA employs an extensive screening mechanism to ensure that the potential benefits of the product outweigh any associated risks. The manufacturer initiates the review by submitting an Investigational New Drug Application ("IND"), containing information about the drug's chemistry, manufacturing, pharmacology, and toxicology. *See* 21 U.S.C. § 355(b)(1) (Supp.1991); 21 C.F.R. § 312.21 (1990). If the FDA approves the IND, the drug's sponsor may gather data on clinical safety and efficacy needed for a New Drug Application ("NDA"), the formal license application. The NDA must include very detailed reports of all animal studies and clinical testing performed with the drug, reports of any adverse reactions, and any other pertinent information from world-wide scientific literature. 21 U.S.C. § 355(b) (Supp.1991); 21 C.F.R. § 314.50 (1990).

The new drug approval process can require years of testing and review. By the time an NDA is submitted, it often consists of thousands of pages of material describing studies of the drug in several hundred to several thousand patients. *See* 47 Fed.Reg. 46626 (Oct. 19, 1982). The FDA carefully scrutinizes the data supporting the NDA, requiring "substantial evidence" consisting of adequate and well-controlled investigations. 21 U.S.C. § 355(d) (Supp.1991). The application is reviewed by physicians, pharmacologists, chemists, microbiologists, statisticians, and other professionals within the FDA's National Center for Drugs and Biologics who are experienced in evaluating new drugs. 47 Fed.Reg. 46626 (Oct. 19, 1982). Recommendations by those professionals are then reviewed by management personnel within the National Center for Drugs and Biologics before the FDA makes a final determination to approve or reject the new drug application. *Id.*

Elaborate premarket screening, however, does not ensure review of approved prescription medications where adverse reactions may appear after extensive preapproval testing. For this reason, the FDA also conducts extensive post-market surveillance. *All* reports of adverse drug reactions ("ADRs") must be reported to the FDA, regardless of whether the physician, the manufacturer, or others believe the reaction to be drug-related. 21 C.F.R. § 314.80(b). The manufacturer must also periodically submit reports as to what actions it took in response to ADRs and must submit data from any post-marketing studies, reports in the scientific literature, and foreign marketing experience. 21 C.F.R. §§ 314.80(b), .80(c). The FDA has authority to enforce these reporting requirements; any failure to comply may subject a manufacturer to civil and criminal penalties. 21 U.S.C. §§ 332–34 (1972 & Supp.1991). In response to its surveillance findings, the FDA may require labeling changes or if necessary withdraw NDA approval and thereby revoke the license to market the medication. *Id.* at § 355(e).

We find this extensive regulatory scheme capable of and appropriate for making the preliminary determination regarding whether a prescription drug's benefits outweigh its risks. The structured follow-up program imposed by law ensures that drugs are not placed on the market without continued monitoring for adverse consequences that would render the FDA's initial risk/benefit analysis invalid. Allowing individual courts and/or juries to continually reevaluate a drug's risks and benefits ignores the processes of this expert regulatory body and the other avenues of recovery available to plaintiffs.

We note that the Utah Legislature has recognized the value of the FDA approval process and the public interest in the availability and affordability of prescription drugs by restricting the extent of liability for injuries resulting from the use of those drugs. Utah Code Ann. § 78–18–2(1) (Supp.1990) states that "punitive damages may not be awarded if a drug causing the claimant's harm: (a) received premarket approval or licensure by the Federal Food, Drug, and Cosmetic Act, 21 U.S.C. Section 301 et seq. * * *" This policy, designed to avoid discouraging manufacturers from marketing FDA-approved drugs, applies even to drugs marketed with inadequate warnings.

The legislature has also acknowledged the important role of governmental standards in Utah Code Ann. section 78–15–6(3). In that section, the legislature declared that there is a rebuttable presumption that a product which fully complies with the applicable government standards at the time of marketing is not defective.[3]

Our prior case law supports this approach as well. In *Barson v. E.R. Squibb & Sons, Inc.*, 682 P.2d 832 (Utah 1984), we addressed the sufficiency of evidence for a claim that a drug manufacturer negligently failed to warn of risks associated with its product. We held that even after meeting governmental requirements, if there are dangers about which the drug manufacturer knew or should have known, the manufacturer may be subject to liability. *Id.* at 836. Thus, consistent with our holding in this case, if a manufacturer knows or should know of a risk associated with its product, it is directly liable to the patient if it fails to adequately warn the medical profession of that danger. *Id.* at 835.

Moreover, the standard in Utah to which drug manufacturers must adhere to establish an adequate warning is very strict. In *Barson*, we stated:

> In determining whether a manufacturer has breached that duty [to adequately warn] and the extent to which a manufacturer is required to know of dangers inherent in its drug, it is important to point out that *the drug manufacturer is held to be an expert in its particular field and is under a "continuous duty * * * to keep abreast of scientific developments touching upon the manufacturer's product* and notify the medical profession of any additional side effects discovered from its use." *The drug manufacturer is responsible* therefore for not only "actual knowledge gained from research and adverse reaction reports," but also *for constructive knowledge as measured by scientific literature and other available means of communication.*

Barson, 682 P.2d at 835–36 (emphasis added).

V. PROPER FORUM FOR RISK/BENEFIT ANALYSIS

Finally, we do not believe that a trial court in the context of a products liability action is the proper forum to determine whether, as a whole, a particular prescription drug's benefits outweighed its risks at the time of distribution. In a case-by-case analysis, one court or jury's determination that a particular drug is or is not "defectively designed" has no bearing on any future case. As a result, differences of opinion among courts in differing jurisdictions leaves unsettled a drug manufacturer's liability for any given drug. Although the FDA may have

---

3. Plaintiffs argue that immunizing drug manufacturers from strict liability for design defects is contrary to this statute, because that conclusion would establish an "irrebuttable presumption" that the drug was not defective or unreasonably dangerous. We disagree. Plaintiffs may still recover under a strict liability claim by demonstrating that the product was unreasonably dangerous due to an inadequate warning, a manufacturing flaw, mismarketing, or misrepresenting information to the FDA. We cite these statutes only to demonstrate the legislature's similar deference to the expertise of certain governmental agencies, particularly that of the FDA.

internal differences of opinion regarding whether a particular new drug application should be approved, the individuals making the ultimate judgment will have the benefit of years of experience in reviewing such products, scientific expertise in the area, and access to the volumes of data they can compel manufacturers to produce. Nor is the FDA subject to the inherent limitations of the trial process, such as the rules of evidence, restrictions on expert testimony, and scheduling demands.[4]

One commentator has argued that courts as a whole are unsuited to render responsible judgments in the design defect area generally. *See* Henderson, *Judicial Review of Manufacturers' Conscious Design Choices: The Limits of Adjudication*, 73 Colum.L.Rev. 1531 (1973). He argues that decisions in this area are arbitrary due to their "polycentric" nature in which "each point for decision is related to all the others as are the strands of a spider web." *Id.* at 1536. These issues are difficult to litigate because

> [i]f one strand is pulled, a complex pattern of readjustments will occur throughout the entire web. If another strand is pulled, the relationships among all the strands will again be readjusted. A lawyer seeking to base [an] argument upon established principle and required to address himself in discourse to each of a dozen strands, or issues, would find [the] task frustratingly impossible.

Id.

Although we do not accept the notion that courts are unsuited to address design defect claims in any products liability action, we do agree that prescription drug design presents precisely this type of "polycentric" problem. A drug is designed to be effectively administered to specific individuals for one or a number of indications. To determine whether a drug's benefit outweighs its risk is inherently complex because of the manufacturer's conscious design choices regarding the numerous chemical properties of the product and their relationship to the vast physiologic idiosyncrasies of each consumer for whom the drug is designed. Society has recognized this complexity and in response has reposed regulatory authority in the FDA. Relying on the FDA's screening and surveillance standards enables courts to find liability under circumstances of inadequate warning, mismanufacture, improper marketing, or misinforming the FDA—avenues for which courts are better suited. Although this approach denies plaintiffs one potential theory on which to rely in a drug products liability action, the benefits to society in

---

4. There is also a certain moral question to be addressed when determining whether a product's benefit outweighs its risk when faced with the reality of an injured plaintiff. For example, in the case of a vaccine, certain benefits of the drug's availability will accrue to group A, the individuals who are prevented from contracting the disease. A smaller number of individuals, however, may contract the disease and react violently to a component of the drug or, as some other result of the drug's properties, suffer terribly. Under a case-by-case approach, courts or juries must ask which is a more significant interest: efficacy with respect to group A versus harm to group B? The FDA must ask the same question: Does the benefit of this product outweigh its risk? The distinction is that the FDA is in a more objective and informed posture to make that determination. *See Toner*, 732 P.2d at 325–26 * * *.

promoting the development, availability, and reasonable price of drugs justifies this conclusion.

In light of the strong public interest in the availability and affordability of prescription medications, the extensive regulatory system of the FDA, and the avenues of recovery still available to plaintiffs by claiming inadequate warning, mismanufacture, improper marketing, or misrepresenting information to the FDA, we conclude that a broad grant of immunity from strict liability claims based on design defects should be extended to FDA-approved prescription drugs in Utah.

HALL, C.J., and ZIMMERMAN, J., concur.

[JUSTICE HOWE's dissent is omitted.]

STEWART, JUSTICE (dissenting):

I dissent. The majority holds that a drug that is *avoidably* unsafe to human life or health is exempt from strict liability for design defects if approved by the FDA, even though alternative drugs can provide the same, or even better, therapy, with less risk to life or health. Thus, such FDA-approved drugs as various decongestants, expectorants, deodorants, hair growth stimulants, skin moisturizers, and cough and cold remedies, for example, have the same immunity as rabies or polio vaccines or medications essential in the treatment of cancer, heart disease, or AIDS. I see no basis for according drugs used to treat comparatively minor ailments a blanket immunity from strict liability for design defects if they are unreasonably dangerous to those who use them.

The limited immunity conferred by comment k on a few drugs was given only after thorough consideration by the American Law Institute. However, this Court gives blanket immunity for design defects to all FDA-approved drugs on the basis of blind reliance upon the efficacy and integrity of FDA procedures, about which the majority knows almost nothing. I agree with Justice Huntley of the Idaho Supreme Court, who stated:

> [N]o state supreme court has yet become convinced that the FDA has either adequate staffing, expertise, or data base to warrant its being substituted for the judicial system. * * * I fear the day when any supreme court can be convinced that an agency such as the FDA, no matter how well-intentioned, can supplant the American judicial system.

Toner v. Lederle Laboratories, 112 Idaho 328, 732 P.2d 297, 313 (1987) (Huntley, J., concurring specially). Indeed, in relying on FDA approval, the majority wholly ignores our statement in *Barson v. E.R. Squibb & Sons, Inc.*, 682 P.2d 832, 836 (Utah 1984), that FDA regulations for prescription drugs "are merely minimum standards."

In truth, FDA safety procedures do not justify abdication of judicial responsibility. For example, the FDA does not require existing drugs to undergo newly developed tests which would increase the likelihood that a product is in fact safe. * * *

Numerous congressional investigations have demonstrated that the FDA has often approved drugs in complete ignorance of critical information relating to the hazards of such drugs which was contained either in its own files or in the published medical literature, or both. For example, the FDA approved Oraflex on April 19, 1982, for the treatment of arthritis. The manufacturer withdrew the drug from the market on August 4, 1982, because eleven deaths were reported to be associated with the drug's use in the United States and sixty-one deaths were reported in the United Kingdom. Of principal concern were reports of serious and sometimes fatal Oraflex-associated liver and kidney disease. In *Deficiencies in FDA's Regulation of the New Drug "Oraflex"*, H.R.Rep. No. 511, 98th Cong., 1st Sess. (1983), the House Committee on Government Operations (hereinafter "H.C.G.O."), a congressional committee overseeing the FDA, found that the FDA was unaware that during the Oraflex clinical trials it had received four reports of serious concomitant liver and kidney disease and two reports of kidney disease unaccompanied by liver injury. At the time the FDA approved Oraflex for marketing, and for several months thereafter, it was unaware of the number of reports of Oraflex-associated adverse reactions it had received prior to its approval of the drug. *Id.* at 11–12. Prior to approving Oraflex, the FDA made no effort to obtain information on its safety from foreign countries in which the drug had already been marketed and was, therefore, unaware of a large number of reports of serious and sometimes fatal reactions to the drug submitted to the British and Danish regulatory authorities. *Id.* at 13. The FDA failed to enforce the legal requirement that drug manufacturers report all adverse reactions to a drug under clinical investigation, information essential to weigh the drug's risks against its potential benefits. *Id.* at 22.

[The discussion of similar experiences with three other FDA approved drugs, Merital, Versed, and Zomax, is omitted.]

Although the FDA has a mechanism for the withdrawal of pharmaceutical agents which are found to be dangerous, 21 U.S.C. § 355(e) (1988), the mechanism is slow and sometimes unreliable. For example, several studies were published in the early 1950s which should have put diethylstilbestrol (DES) manufacturers on notice that DES injured the reproductive systems of female fetuses whose mothers were exposed to the drug. However, it was not until 1971, nearly twenty years later, that the FDA finally banned the use of DES to prevent miscarriages, the most common use of the drug. *See Castrignano v. E.R. Squibb & Sons, Inc.*, 546 A.2d 775, 777 (R.I.1988). The lengthy wait by the FDA resulted in endangering a generation of women because their mothers had used DES during pregnancy.

In relying on the efficacy of FDA approval procedures as the basis for dispensing with the judicial remedy of product liability, the majority simply ignores FDA failures to protect the public against unnecessary and unacceptable risks. * * *

Proposals before Congress and rules promulgated by the FDA to make it easier for pharmaceutical companies to obtain FDA approval for new drugs would dilute even further the safety and efficacy standards for FDA approval of drugs. *See* Note, *Regulation of Investigational New Drugs: "Giant Step for the Sick and Dying?"*, 77 Georgetown L.J. 463 (1988). Perhaps truly unavoidably unsafe drugs intended to treat life-threatening ailments should be more easily available to the public, but a lessening of safety standards is an argument for strict liability, not against. Profit motivation is likely to lead to many more unnecessarily dangerous drugs.

Furthermore, not a shred of evidence has been presented to this Court that indicates that liability under the tort system has deterred pharmaceutical companies from introducing new drugs. Even if that were the case, the question that must be answered, given the majority's holding, is why comment k does not provide a proper accommodation of all the competing policy interests involved in the issue before the Court. Why should those who are seriously injured or suffer because of the death of another have to stand the expense of such losses to support the high profit margins in the drug industry?

In my view, the Rhode Island Supreme Court adopted a better approach in *Castrignano v. E.R. Squibb & Sons, Inc.*, 546 A.2d 775 (R.I.1988). The Rhode Island court held that only products that are truly unavoidably unsafe qualify for comment k protection. The court stated:

> This comment provides a risk-benefit test for products that, given the present state of human knowledge, are incapable of being made safe for their intended use. Products that satisfy the risk-benefit test are deemed unavoidably unsafe. These products, especially drugs, will not be considered defective and unreasonably dangerous under § 402A because their known or perceived benefits exceed their known or perceived risks. Therefore, the availability and marketing of these products is justified, not withstanding the risk.
> * * *

546 A.2d at 781.

Certain drugs clearly qualify for comment k exemption, even though the drugs' risk may be comparatively great. A drug's social utility may be so great, for example, a chemotherapeutic agent used for treatment of cancer, that it would obviously qualify for comment k exemption. Other drugs, such as sleeping compounds or dandruff cures, whose social utility may not be of such a high order, would not automatically qualify. The Rhode Island court stated that for a prescription drug to qualify for comment k exemption,

> the apparent benefits of the drug must exceed the apparent risks, given the scientific knowledge available when the drug was market-ed. If the benefits outweigh the risks, then recovery for design-defect liability is precluded. If, however, the apparent risks exceed the apparent benefits, then the product is not exempt from design-

defect liability and will be subject to the traditional design-defect analysis set forth in § 402A.

546 A.2d at 782.

Furthermore, Congress has never given broad immunity, as this Court does, to all prescription drugs, notwithstanding FDA approval. *See* Note, *A Prescription for Applying Strict Liability: Not all Drugs Deserve Comment k Immunization, Brown v. Superior Court,* 44 Cal.3d 1049, 751 P.2d 470, 245 Cal.Rptr. 412 (1988), 21 Ariz.St.L.J. 809, 830 (1989). Congress has, however, provided some immunity from tort law for some vaccines when the public interest required their widespread use. For example, Congress enacted the National Childhood Vaccine Injury Act, 42 U.S.C. §§ 300aa–1 to –34 (1988), which establishes a compensation scheme for children injured by vaccines as an alternative to pursuing tort claims against the manufacturers. However, even that Act does not completely foreclose strict liability for plaintiffs injured by vaccines; instead, it only establishes presumptions to aid the trier of fact. 42 U.S.C. §§ 300aa–22(b)(2), –23(d)(2).

The majority opinion states that a case-by-case analysis would leave drug companies uncertain regarding questions of immunity and would result in patchwork verdicts when a drug may be found to be subject to comment k exemption in one case but not subject to the exemption in another case. That consideration has little merit, in my view. We tolerate nonuniformity of result in negligence cases all the time. Nothing this Court does can bring about uniformity of result with respect to drugs. The states are already divided on the issue of whether FDA approval of a drug should confer immunity from design defects, although it appears that no state has gone as far as Utah now does. Suffice to say, a number of courts apply comment k on a case-by-case basis—a task that cannot be avoided even under the majority's position if a strict liability claim is coupled with a negligence claim, as is usually the case.

* * *

If Halcion was a causative agent, it is significant that *The Physicians' Desk Reference* (1990 ed.) lists nine other hypnotic agents available for use. At least two of the other hypnotics and one other medication listed as a sleeping aid are benzodiazepines and are, therefore, of the same general type as Halcion. In addition, the same reference lists thirteen sedatives that are on the market. The majority ignores the fact that the FDA found Halcion to be neither unique nor particularly essential and presented no advancement over existing therapeutic alternatives. Perhaps not all would have been appropriate medications, but with so many possible alternatives, it is doubtful that Halcion should be immune from strict liability.

Notes

1. *Grundberg* is noted in 7 St.John's J.Legal Comment 475 (1991); 26 Suffolk U.L.Rev. 321 (1992); and 1992 Utah L.Rev. 101 and 284.

2. Comment k to the Restatement (Second) of Torts § 402A creates an exception to strict liability for "unavoidably unsafe" products. Most courts evaluate each product on its own merits to determine whether it is unavoidably unsafe. *E.g.,* Adams v. G.D. Searle & Co., Inc., 576 So.2d 728 (Fla.App. 1991); Toner v. Lederle Laboratories, 112 Idaho 328, 336, 732 P.2d 297 (1987); Feldman v. Lederle Laboratories, 97 N.J. 429, 479 A.2d 374 (1984); Castrignano v. E.R. Squibb & Sons, Inc., 546 A.2d 775 (R.I.1988). Other courts, like *Grundberg*, declare that all products within broad categories are unavoidably unsafe. *E.g.,* Brown v. Superior Court, 44 Cal.3d 1049, 245 Cal.Rptr. 412, 751 P.2d 470 (1988) (all prescription drugs if they are properly prepared and accompanied by adequate warnings).

3. In a jurisdiction that uses the risk-utility test of defect, is there any advantage to adopting comment k and applying it on a case by case basis? In Shanks v. Upjohn Co., 835 P.2d 1189 (Alaska 1992) a person committed suicide shortly after taking a prescription drug. Plaintiff sued the prescription drug manufacturer for defective design and failure to warn. In design cases, the Alaska court normally uses the test of defect announced in *Barker v. Lull Eng'g Co.,* supra p. 202, *i.e.,* consumer expectations and risk-utility in the disjunctive. In *Shanks* the Alaska court declined to adopt comment k, stating:

> In deciding whether a defendant has met the burden of proving that the benefits of the design outweigh the risk, we stated in [*Caterpillar Tractor Co. v. Beck*, 593 P.2d 871 (Alaska 1979)] that the fact finder must consider competing factors, including but not limited to
>
>> the gravity of the danger posed by the challenged design, the likelihood that such danger would occur, the mechanical feasibility of a safer alternative design, the financial cost of an improved design, and the adverse consequences to the product and to the consumer that would result from an alternative design.

593 P.2d at 886 (quoting *Barker*, 573 P.2d at 455). We believe these factors, with some modification and additions, should be considered in making the same determination in cases involving prescription drugs. Rephrasing these factors in language more appropriate to prescription drug products, the fact finder should consider the seriousness of the side effects or reactions posed by the drug, the likelihood that such side effects or reactions would occur, the feasibility of an alternative design which would eliminate or reduce the side effects or reactions without affecting the efficacy of the drug, and the harm to the consumer in terms of reduced efficacy and any new side effects or reactions that would result from an alternative design. In evaluating the benefits, the fact finder should be permitted to consider the seriousness of the condition for which the drug is indicated. In summary, what the trier of fact should determine in balancing these factors is whether the drug confers an important benefit and whether the interest in its availability outweighs the interest in promoting the enhanced accountability which strict products liability design defect review provides. See *Kearl v. Lederle Laboratories*, 172 Cal.App.3d 812, 218 Cal.Rptr. 453, 464 (1985).

* * *

While we accept the soundness of the policy underlying comment k that manufacturers of certain highly beneficial products which have inherent unavoidable risks of which the user is adequately warned should not be held strictly liable for injuries resulting from their products, we decline to formally adopt comment k * * *.

* * *

[W]e believe that the risk/benefit prong of the *Barker* test offers the manufacturers of those products intended to be protected by comment k an opportunity to avoid liability for strict liability claims based on a design defect theory. For these reasons, we find it undesirable and unnecessary to impose the additional layer of comment k on an area of law which is already strained under its own doctrinal weight. We recognize that by holding that the liability of drug manufacturers should be measured by the second prong of the *Barker* test, we are taking a position similar to those jurisdictions which apply comment k to prescription drugs on a case-by-case basis. However, we arrive at this result without specifically relying on comment k.

835 P.2d 1189, 1196–98. On the possible difference between risk-utility analysis and comment k analysis, *see* Ausness, Unavoidably Unsafe Products and Strict Products Liability: What Liability Rule Should be Applied to the Sellers of Pharmaceutical Products?, 78 Ky.L.J. 705, 738–740 (1990); Reilly, The Erosion of Comment K, 14 U.Dayton L.Rev. 255 (1989).

4. The vast majority of cases that apply comment k have involved drugs, vaccines, blood, and medical devices. *See* Wilkinson v. Bay Shore Lumber Co., 182 Cal.App.3d 594, 227 Cal.Rptr. 327 (1986) (citing numerous cases). Many people believe that the comment only applies to such products. *E.g.,* Schwartz, Unavoidably Unsafe Products: Clarifying the Meaning and Policy Behind Comment k, 42 Wash. & Lee L.Rev. 1139, 1141 (1985).

5. Not everyone agrees. The language of comment k is broad enough to apply to all types of products, not just drugs. A knife with a sharp blade, for example, could be regarded as unavoidably unsafe because it presents a risk that cannot be eliminated in the present state of human knowledge, and yet the risk is reasonable because knives are useful and desirable products. Courts have occasionally applied the doctrine to other products. Borel v. Fibreboard Paper Prod. Corp., 493 F.2d 1076, 1088–89 (5th Cir.1973), cert. denied, 419 U.S. 869, 95 S.Ct. 127, 42 L.Ed.2d 107 (1974) (asbestos); Walker v. Stauffer Chem. Corp., 19 Cal.App.3d 669, 674, 96 Cal.Rptr. 803, 806 (1971) (bulk sulfuric acid); Gross v. Nashville Gas Co., 608 S.W.2d 860 (Tenn.App.1980) (natural gas). For a comprehensive listing of products that have been held to be unavoidably unsafe, *see* Annotation, 70 A.L.R.4th 16 (1989).

6. In a jurisdiction that applies comment k only to drugs, how would the court deal with a strict liability claim against a knife manufacturer seeking damages for harm caused when a user accidentally cut himself on the sharp blade?

7. Should comment k to the Restatement (Second) of Torts § 402A exempt from strict liability products with manufacturing flaws? The excerpt from the following law review article discusses this issue.

AUSNESS, UNAVOIDABLY UNSAFE PRODUCTS AND STRICT PRODUCTS LIABILITY: WHAT LIABILITY RULE SHOULD BE APPLIED TO THE SELLERS OF PHARMACEUTICAL PRODUCTS?

78 Ky.L.J. 705, 720–23, 745, 747–48, 749–51 (1989/1990).

Ordinarily, product sellers are strictly liable for harm caused by mishaps in the production process even though they could not have discovered the condition or eliminated defective products by the exercise of due care. Strict liability is imposed on product sellers, particularly manufacturers, because they are in a good position to control production flaws. Additionally, because claims arising from manufacturing defects are relatively small in relation to the number of units produced, product sellers can usually obtain insurance at a reasonable cost.

Production flaws also occur in the pharmaceutical industry. One class of production flaw involves drugs that deviate from their accepted chemical formula. Since comment k requires that products be "properly prepared," it usually does not immunize against liability in such cases.[1] Product contamination is another type of production flaw. Although quality control standards are high in the pharmaceutical industry, impure or contaminated drugs sometimes enter the market. Although comment k shields sellers of "new and experimental drugs" from liability even when "purity of ingredients" cannot be assured,[2] it does not protect the purveyors of ordinary pharmaceutical products against liability when their products are contaminated.[3]

A more common risk arises from the failure to remove harmful byproducts from the finished product. This problem sometimes occurs in the manufacture of vaccines and other biologics.[4] For example, injuries can occur when substances used to culture vaccines are not completely removed from the finished product. This condition is associated with the Pasteur vaccine, which is cultured in the brains of small laboratory animals such as rats, mice, and rabbits.[5] Serious harm to the recipient can occur if small particles of animal brain material are left in

---

1. See Morris v. Parke–Davis & Co., 667 F.Supp. 1332, 1336 (C.D.Cal.1987); Toner v. Lederle Laboratories, 732 P.2d 297, 305 (Idaho 1987).

2. See Restatement (Second) of Torts § 402A comment k * * *.

3. See Abbott Laboratories v. Lapp, 78 F.2d 170, 174 (7th Cir.1935) (manufacturer held liable in negligence for allowing virulent bacteria to contaminate sterilized milk formula); David v. McKesson & Robbins, 253 A.D. 728, 300 N.Y.S. 635, 636 (1937) (manufacturer held liable in negligence for sodium fluoride in bicarbonate of soda), aff'd, 278 N.Y.S. 622, 16 N.E.2d 127 (1938);

see also Note, [Comment K Immunity to Strict Liability: Should All Prescription Drugs Be Protected?, 26 Hous.L.Rev. 707, 736 (1989)] (plaintiff can recover in strict liability if drug is adulterated).

4. Biologics are products that are cultured from living organisms. See Note, [Note, Mass Immunization Cases: Drug Manufacturers' Liability for Failure to Warn, 29 Vand.L.Rev. 235, n.2.245 (1976)].

5. See Comment, [Torts—Strict Liability—A Hospital is Strictly Liable for Transfusions of Hepatitis, 69 Mich.L.Rev. 1172, 1182 (1971)].

the vaccine.[6] In such cases, however, the courts have found the Pasteur vaccine to be unavoidably unsafe.[7]

Virulent organisms in vaccines also can cause serious injuries. Vaccines typically use killed or weakened disease-producing organisms to create a natural immunity in the recipient's body.[8] A vaccine, however, can cause the very disease it is supposed to prevent if these harmful organisms are not neutralized. This problem has arisen in connection with the production of both Sabin and Salk polio vaccines.[9]

The Salk vaccine uses dead polio virus organisms to induce the formation of antibodies in the recipient's body. Killed polio virus is incapable of causing disease, but can act as an antigen to stimulate the production of antibodies that will attack any live polio viruses entering the body.[10] However, in *Gottsdanker v. Cutter Laboratories,*[11] Cutter Laboratories, a manufacturer of Salk vaccine, failed to exclude live polio virus from some of its vaccine even though it relied on government approved safety tests to prevent this from happening. As a result, a number of vaccine recipients contracted polio from the vaccine.[12] The defendant contended that liability should not be imposed because the vaccine was a "new" drug, and thus not subject to a strict liability rule. The court, however, rejected this argument and held in favor of the plaintiffs.

The Sabin vaccine uses a weakened live virus that causes the recipient's immune system to produce antibodies that are effective against ordinary polio virus.[13] As the weakened strain reproduces itself in the intestinal tract of the recipient, however, it occasionally produces a form of virulent strain instead.[14] This can cause the recipient, or those who come into close contact with the recipient, to contract polio.[15] Perhaps because the dangerous condition arises after the vaccine leaves the manufacturer's control, the courts generally have refused to impose strict liability in such cases.[16]

---

6. *Id.*

7. *See* Calabrese v. Trenton State College, 162 N.J.Super. 145, 392 A.2d 600, 604 (1978), *aff'd*, 82 N.J. 321, 413 A.2d 315 (1980).

8. *See* Note, *Vaccine Related Injuries: Alternatives to the Tort Compensation System,* 30 St.Louis U.L.J. 919, 920–21 (1986); *see also* Parke–Davis & Co. v. Stromsodt, 411 F.2d 1390, 1392–93 (8th Cir.1969).

9. *See* Franklin & Mais, *Tort Law and Mass Immunization Programs: Lessons from the Polio and Flu Episodes,* 65 Calif.L.Rev. 754, 765–66 (1977).

10. *See* Note, *supra* note [4], at 237.

11. 6 Cal.Rptr. 320 (Ct.App.1960).

12. *See* Note, *supra* note [4], at 238.

13. *See* Schwartz & Mahshigian, *National Childhood Vaccine Injury Act of 1986: An Ad Hoc Remedy or a Window for*

the Future?, 48 Ohio St. L.J. 387, 388 (1987).

14. *Id.*

15. Plummer v. Lederle Laboratories, 819 F.2d 349, 351 (2d Cir.1987).

16. *See* Plummer, 819 F.2d at 356; Givens v. Lederle Laboratories, 556 F.2d 1341, 1345 (5th Cir.1977); Reyes v. Wyeth Laboratories, 498 F.2d 1264, 1274 (5th Cir. 1974), cert. denied, 418 U.S. 1096 (1974); Davis v. Wyeth Laboratories, 399 F.2d 121, 128–29 (9th Cir.1968); Williams v. Lederle Laboratories, 591 F.Supp. 381, 384 (S.D.Ohio 1984); Sheehan v. Pima County, 660 P.2d 486, 487 (Ariz. Ct.App.1982); Johnson v. American Cyanamid Co., 718 P.2d 1318, 1323 (Kan.1986); Dunn v. Lederle Laboratories, 328 N.W.2d 576, 579 (Mich.1982); Cunningham v. Charles Pfizer & Co., 532 P.2d 1377, 1380 (Okla.1975).

Another type of production flaw involves failure to detect and remove serum hepatitis from blood.[17] Only one case, *Cunningham v. MacNeal Memorial*,[18] has refused to apply comment k to serum hepatitis contamination. The Illinois Supreme Court declared in *Cunningham* that blood contaminated with serum hepatitis could not be treated as an unavoidably unsafe product because it was impure.[19] However, the *Cunningham* court's interpretation of comment k was widely criticized because comment k expressly mentioned impure drugs as one class of potentially unavoidably unsafe product.[20] For this reason, most courts apply comment k to cases involving blood impurities.[21]

* * *

3. THE ALLOCATIVE EFFICIENCY RATIONALE

The goal of allocative efficiency is to distribute society's economic resources in a way that maximizes social welfare.[22] Strict liability promotes allocative efficiency by encouraging product sellers to invest in product safety and thereby reduce the number of product-related injuries.[23] Additionally, strict liability causes product prices to reflect the true costs of production, including the cost of unavoidable product injuries, and thus ensures that members of the public will not "overconsume" dangerous products.[24]

* * *

The allocative efficiency rationale seems particularly applicable to production flaws in pharmaceutical products. Presently, suppliers of blood and vaccines often escape liability for production-related injuries

Grinnell v. Charles Pfizer & Co., 79 Cal. Rptr. 369 (1969), represents an exception to this approach. The plaintiff contracted polio from the defendant's vaccine. The court held that the vaccine was defective because it contained virulent polio virus instead of the harmless variety, apparently assuming that the virulent strain was introduced into the vaccine during the production process rather than afterwards. *Id.* at 374.

17. Blood may be contaminated by serum hepatitis, a virus that cannot be detected in the blood under present medical technology. *See* Comment, *Blood Transfusions and the Transmission of Serum Hepatitis: The Need for Statutory Reform,* 24 Am. U. L. Rev. 367, 368 (1976). This condition differs from the vaccine cases because the contaminant exists in the donor's blood before the blood comes within the producer's control.

18. 266 N.E.2d 897 (Ill.1970).

19. *Id.* at 904; *see also* McDaniel v. Baptist Memorial Hospital, 352 F.Supp. 690 (W.D.Tenn.1971), *aff'd,* 469 F.2d 230 (6th Cir.1972). The McDaniel court questioned the application of comment k to contaminated blood. Apparently, the court felt

that comment k should cover only characteristics that are common or indigenous to the product. *Id.* at 695.

20. *See* Hines v. St. Joseph's Hosp., 527 P.2d 1075, 1077 (N.M.1974); Comment, *supra* note [17], at 403.

21. *See* Belle Bonfils Memorial Blood Bank v. Hansen, 665 P.2d 118, 125–26 (Colo.1983); McMichael v. American Red Cross, 532 S.W.2d 7, 9 (Ky. 1975); Moore v. Underwood Memorial Hosp., 371 A.2d 105, 107 (N.J.Super. Ct. 1977).

22. *See* R. Posner, Economic Analysis of Law 4 (1972).

23. *See* Owen, [*Rethinking the Policies of Strict Products Liability,* 33 Vand.L.Rev. 681, 711–13 (1980)]; Note, *Prescription Drugs and Strict Liability: The Flaw in the Ointment,* 19 Pac.L.J. 193, 198 (1987).

24. *See* Ausness, *Cigarette Company Liability: Preemption, Public Policy and Alternative Compensation Systems,* 39 Syracuse L.Rev. 897, 946–47 (1988); Henderson, [*Coping with the Time Dimension in Products Liability,* 69 Calif.L.Rev. 919, 933 (1981)].

because such injuries are considered unavoidable. However, if strict liability were imposed on product sellers, they would attempt to improve current production and detection technology in order to reduce or eliminate the risk of injury from harmful byproducts.

The contamination of transfused blood by serum hepatitis virus is an example of a risk that comment k treats as unavoidable. At the present time, serum hepatitis virus cannot be physically removed from the blood. Although tests can detect the presence of serum hepatitis in the blood, these tests are not completely accurate. Arguably, strict liability would encourage blood banks and hospitals to support the development of better detection methods. Strict liability also would provide an incentive for blood suppliers to implement better donor screening procedures. It is universally acknowledged that volunteer donors are much less likely to transmit hepatitis virus than paid donors. Strict liability would encourage blood suppliers to search for new sources of volunteer donors and thereby reduce the risk of injury from impure blood.

* * *

4. THE LOSS-SPREADING RATIONALE

Loss-spreading provides yet another rationale for strict products liability. A large number of courts endorse strict liability because it shifts the costs of injuries from accident victims to product sellers, who can spread these costs among product buyers. Loss-spreading is based partly on the notion that those who benefit from an injury-producing activity should compensate those who suffer harm.[25] Loss-spreading also may be justified on secondary accident cost-avoidance grounds. According to this theory, the "secondary" or dislocation costs of injuries are reduced when they are spread among a large group of people instead of borne entirely by individual victims.[26]

Loss-spreading generally is most effective if liability for injuries is placed on the party who can best absorb and spread the cost of compensation. In the case of product-related injuries, product sellers are usually the best loss-spreaders because they can insure against such losses and treat them as a cost of production. Moreover, since product sellers typically sell to a mass market, the incremental cost to each consumer from such price increases is likely to be small.

Sellers of pharmaceutical products appear to be good loss-spreaders. The pharmaceutical industry is profitable, and the demand for its products is relatively inelastic. In theory, sellers of pharmaceutical products, like other product sellers, can obtain liability insurance and spread the cost of premiums through the pricing mechanism.

---

25. * * * James, *General Products— Should Manufacturers Be Liable Without Negligence?*, 24 Tenn.L.Rev. 923, 924 (1956–57). * * *

26. *See* Calabresi, *Some Thoughts on Risk Distribution and the Law of Torts*, 70 Yale L.J. 499, 517–18 (1960–61); Kidwell, [*The Duty to Warn: A Description of the Model of Decision*, 53 Tex.L.Rev. 1375, 1386 (1974–75)].

This reasoning seems especially applicable to risks associated with the production process. Production flaws in the manufacturing process are relatively rare and can be accurately predicted by statistical methods.[27] Arguably, production flaws in pharmaceutical products are similar to manufacturing defects. Consequently, the loss-spreading arguments that are made with respect to manufacturing defects in ordinary products also can be applied to production flaws in pharmaceutical products.[28]

Notes

1. The following articles analyze comment k. Ausness, Unavoidably Unsafe Products and Strict Products Liability: What Liability Rule Should be Applied to the Sellers of Pharmaceutical Products?, 78 Ky.L.J. 705 (1990); Landes and Posner, A Positive Economic Analysis of Products Liability, 14 J.Legal Stud. 535, 556–560 (1985); Page, Generic Product Risks: The Case Against Comment K and For Strict Tort Liability, 58 N.Y.U. L.Rev. 853 (1983); Schwartz, Unavoidably Unsafe Products: Clarifying the Meaning and Policy Behind Comment k, 42 Wash. & Lee L.Rev. 1139 (1985); Comment, Comment K Immunity to Strict Liability: Should All Prescription Drugs be Protected? 26 Hous.L.Rev. 707 (1989).

2. In light of the materials you have studied concerning the definition of defect, and the materials in this section, consider the following problem:

Mrs. Paterson, an elderly woman, became extremely ill as a result of contracting Influenza Type Z induced by a vaccine designed to immunize her from the disease. This occurred because the dose of vaccine she was given contained some live virus. The vaccine was supposed to be comprised of killed virus. She desires to pursue a products liability claim against the manufacturer of the vaccine.

The vaccine is prepared by cultivating Influenza Type Z virus on a protein-free semisynthetic medium. Formaldehyde is then used to kill the virus. The formaldehyde and unwanted debris are removed, and the only thing left is the vaccine medium and the killed virus. For some unknown reason, in an extremely small number of cases, the formaldehyde fails to kill all the influenza virus. When this occurs, live virus will remain in the vaccine, and will occasionally infect recipients of the vaccine.

Prior to marketing the vaccine, the manufacturer knew about this risk. It nevertheless marketed the vaccine because there is no other known killing agent that will work to produce a vaccine against this particular strain of influenza. Furthermore, there is no way of telling

27. See McClellan, Strict Liability for Drug Induced Injuries: An Excursion Through the Maze of Products Liability, Negligence and Absolute Liability, 25 Wayne L. Rev. 1, 30 (1978–79).

28. Contamination of blood by serum hepatitis virus may constitute an exception to this generalization because the incidence of hepatitis injuries is relatively high. Cf. Note, [Liability for Serum Hepatitis in Blood Transfusions, 32 Ohio St. L.J. 585 (1971).] (2% of blood transfusion recipients contract hepatitis); R. Titmuss, The Gift Relationship: From Human Blood to Social Policy 146 (1971) (3.5% of blood transfusion recipients contract hepatitis). According to one estimate, the cost of blood would double if blood suppliers were held strictly liable for injuries caused by contaminated blood. Note, [Liability for Serum Hepatitis in Blood Transfusions, 32 Ohio St. L.J. 585, 597 (1971)].

which doses of the vaccine contain live virus. The vaccine is otherwise effective in preventing influenza. It is particularly important for elderly people because many of them become gravely ill when infected with this strain of influenza virus.

At the manufacturer's insistence, each person who received the vaccine was informed that a small percentage of doses contain live virus which can infect the recipient, but that it is not known which doses are contaminated.

Is the manufacturer liable for Mrs. Paterson's injuries?

SECTION D. IGNORANCE OF RISK CAUSED BY MISUSE

JURADO v. WESTERN GEAR WORKS

Supreme Court of New Jersey, 1993.
131 N.J. 375, 619 A.2d 1312.

POLLOCK, J. * * *

Jurado, an employee of N & W Printing, injured his right hand when it became caught in an "in-running nip point" located between a rotating cylinder and a support bar underneath a collating machine. The machine, which was designed to collate and assemble business forms, was manufactured and distributed by defendants.

During the collating process, excess paper salvage would enter a vacuum tube beneath the machine. Frequently, the paper would build up at the mouth of the tube, forcing the operator to clear it by hand. The tube was located near the rotating cylinder underneath the collator.

On the date of the accident, Jurado reduced the speed of the machine and tried to clear salvage that was blocking the vacuum tube. As he crouched and reached under the collator with his left hand, he lost his balance and tried with his right hand to prevent himself from falling. Jurado's right hand was injured when it was drawn into the in-running nip point. He claimed that he had not turned off the collator before attempting to unclog the vacuum tube because his employer had warned that the interruption would confuse the collating sequence. N & W Printing disputes this claim. * * *.

Jurado's expert witness, Gerald Weiner, a mechanical engineer, testified that the collator did not conform to proper design standards because of the absence of a guard on the in-running nip point. Weiner stated that at the time the collator was manufactured, defendants easily and inexpensively could have installed a sheet-metal fixed-barrier guard around the nip point. According to Weiner, the guard would not have affected the function of the machine and could have been installed for as little as $40 to $50 per unit.

He testified that since 1948 design engineers have recognized the potential danger posed by nip points. Defendants should have known, according to Weiner, that salvage would obstruct the mouth of the vacuum, and that an operator of the machine ultimately would have to clear the vacuum manually. In addition, he claimed that production engineers know that employees will typically take "shortcuts" to increase their productivity. Thus, according to Weiner, a machine designer should have taken precautionary steps to prevent accidents that may result from such foreseeable shortcuts by employees.

* * *

Defendants' expert, Edward Schwalje, a mechanical engineer, asserted that the existence of the nip point did not require the installation of a sheet-metal guard. In his opinion, the nip point was already guarded by its location. Schwalje said that the location served as a guard because Jurado would not have placed his hands in the nip point during the normal course of operating the machine. He pointed out that Jurado had to squat and reach under the machine to touch the nip point, which was twenty-eight inches off the ground. * * * [T]he collator was not designed to be adjusted or repaired while in operation. Further, in the case of "salvage jams," the machine was designed to be stopped and cleaned while in "static condition." He concluded that the machine was "safe for use as intended" and met the design standards for safety when it was manufactured and distributed by defendants in the early–to–mid–1960s.

* * *

At the close of the entire case, Jurado moved for a directed verdict. * * * After reserving decision, the court charged the jury, instructing it to reach a verdict on damages even if it found for defendants on liability. Relying on Model Civil Jury Charge 5.34I, the court instructed the jury to answer four special interrogatories. The interrogatories and the jury's answers are:

1. Was the product as designed, manufactured or sold defective, in that it was not reasonably safe for its intended or reasonably foreseeable uses? No. 2. Did the defect exist when the product left the hands and control of the defendant? No. 3. At the time of the accident was the product being used for an intended or reasonably foreseeable purpose, that is, that it was not being misused or had not been substantially altered in a way that was not reasonably foreseeable? Yes. 4. Was the defect in the product a proximate cause of the accident? No.

The jury returned a verdict in favor of defendants * * *.

In his motion for a judgment notwithstanding the verdict, Jurado argued that the jury's answers to the special interrogatories were inconsistent with the evidence presented at trial. The court granted that motion * * *. It then entered a verdict in favor of Jurado * * *.

The Appellate Division affirmed the judgment on liability *n.o.v.* * * *. It found that the affirmative answer to interrogatory three constituted a rejection of the defense expert's testimony and therefore left the opinion of Jurado's expert uncontradicted. 253 *N.J.Super.* at 271–72, 601 A.2d 748. The court interpreted the jury's response to the third interrogatory as a finding that "plaintiff's use of the machine was reasonably foreseeable, and it was not being misused at the time of the accident." *Id.* at 271, 601 A.2d 748. This, according to the court, constituted a denial of the plausibility of the defense expert's theory that the nip point was guarded by its location. *Ibid.* Thus, the court found that the judgment notwithstanding the verdict was warranted. We have a different view.

-II-

We cannot tell whether the jury simply concluded that Jurado was using the collator for its intended purpose, as the trial court apparently believed, or that Jurado was not misusing the machine, as the Appellate Division believed. See *ibid.* * * *

* * *

As read by the Appellate Division, the answer to the third interrogatory * * * confuses the purpose for which a product is used with the manner in which it is used. If the jury found in answering interrogatory three that Jurado was using the collator for its intended purpose, that finding would constitute only a partial resolution of the issue of misuse. The Appellate Division assumed that the jury's response necessarily found not only that the product was being used for a reasonably foreseeable purpose, but also that Jurado's manner of use was reasonably foreseeable.

* * *

Generally, to succeed under a strict-liability design-defect theory, a plaintiff must prove that (1) the product was defective; (2) the defect existed when the product left the hands of the defendant; and (3) the defect caused the injury to a reasonably foreseeable user. *O'Brien v. Muskin Corp.*, 94 N.J. 169, 179, 463 A.2d 298 (1983). Because this case involves a design defect, as distinguished from a manufacturing defect, plaintiff must show specifically that the product " 'is not reasonably fit, suitable and safe for its intended or reasonably foreseeable purposes. * * *' " *Michalko v. Cooke Color & Chem. Corp.*, 91 N.J. 386, 394, 451 A.2d 179 (1982) (quoting *Suter v. San Angelo Foundry & Mach. Co.*, 81 N.J. 150, 169, 406 A.2d 140 (1979)).

The decision whether a product is defective because it is "not reasonably fit, suitable and safe" for its intended purposes reflects a policy judgment under a risk-utility analysis. *O'Brien*, *supra*, 94 N.J. at 181, 463 A.2d 298. That analysis seeks to determine whether a particular product creates a risk of harm that outweighs its usefulness. *Ibid.* Risk-utility analysis is especially appropriate when a product may function satisfactorily under one set of circumstances and yet, because of a possible design defect, present an unreasonable risk of injury to the user in other situations. *Id.* at 181–82, 463 A.2d 298.

Under a risk-utility analysis, a defendant may still be liable when a plaintiff misused the product, if the misuse was objectively foreseeable. [Citations] The concept of foreseeable misuse extends to cases in which a product has been substantially altered from its original design. [Citations] Hence, the plaintiff in a design-defect products-liability suit may succeed even if the product was misused, as long as the misuse or alteration was objectively foreseeable. [Citations]

The absence of misuse is part of the plaintiff's case. Misuse is not an affirmative defense. [Citation] Thus, the plaintiff has the burden of showing that there was no misuse or that the misuse was objectively foreseeable. [Citations] So, for example, when a derrick operator injured his thumb while grabbing an overhead chain, he bore the burden of proving the foreseeability of his misuse. *Beatty v. Schramm, Inc.*, 188 *N.J.Super.* 587, 591, 458 A.2d 127 (App.Div.1983).

Essentially, product misuse contemplates two kinds of conduct. One is the use of a product for an improper purpose. "If, for instance, a plaintiff undertakes to use his power saw as a nail clipper and thereby snips his digits, he will not be heard to complain. * * *" *Suter, supra,* 81 N.J. at 194, 406 A.2d 140 (Clifford, J., concurring). For a plaintiff to recover, the purpose for which the product is used at the time of the accident must be objectively foreseeable. When a plaintiff is injured while using the product for a purpose that is not objectively foreseeable, the injury does not establish that the product is defective.

The other kind of misuse concerns the manner in which the plaintiff used the product. When, for example, the operator of a high-lift forklift is injured while using the forklift on steep, instead of level, terrain, the emphasis should be on the manner, not the purpose, of the misuse. *Barker v. Lull Eng'g Co.*, 20 Cal.3d 413, 143 Cal.Rptr. 225, 573 P.2d 443 (1978). As comment h of *Restatement (Second) of Torts* § 402A states: "A product is not in a defective condition when it is safe for normal handling or consumption."

Commentators have accepted the definition of misuse in terms of purpose and manner. [Citations] So have courts in other states. [Citations] We, too, find the definition to be helpful.

Product misuse theoretically could relate to the existence of a defect, the issue of causation, or that of comparative fault. [Citation] In a work-place setting, when, because of a design defect, an employee is injured while using a machine in a reasonably foreseeable manner, the employee's comparative fault is irrelevant. [Citations]

To the extent that misuse relates to the duty to design a safe product, "a manufacturer has a duty to make sure that its manufactured products placed into the stream of commerce are suitably safe when properly used for their intended or reasonably foreseeable purposes." *Brown [v. United States Stove Co.*, 98 N.J. 155, 165, 484 A.2d 1234 (1984)] (citing *Soler, supra,* 98 N.J. at 144–45, 484 A.2d 1225; *Suter, supra,* 81 N.J. at 169, 406 A.2d 140); see also Victor E. Schwartz, *Strict Liability and Comparative Negligence,* 42 *Tenn.L.Rev.* 171, 172 (1974) ("[when] a user makes an unforeseeable misuse of a product, the supplier has breached no duty to the user."). When someone is injured while using a product for an unforeseeable purpose or in an unforeseeable manner, the misuse sheds no light on whether the product is defective, because a manufacturer is not under a duty to protect against unforeseeable misuses. [Citation] A manufacturer, however, has a duty to prevent an injury caused by the foreseeable misuse of its product.

If the jury concludes that the product is defective, it must then determine whether the misuse proximately caused the injury. [Citation] Even if a defect is a contributing or concurring cause, but not the sole cause, of an accident, the manufacturer will be liable. [Citation] For example, if, in the present case, the accident had happened when a co-employee negligently or playfully bumped plaintiff while he crouched in front of the collator, the manufacturer could be found liable notwithstanding the untoward conduct of the co-employee. In that situation, the jury should consider whether the absence of the guard was the proximate, contributing, or concurring cause of the injury.

In some situations, however, the issue of proximate cause is predetermined by the finding that the product is defective solely because of the manufacturer's failure to protect against a foreseeable misuse. As Professor Aaron D. Twerski explains:

> If a court determines that a design defect exists [solely] because the manufacturer has failed to include [ ] safety devices, there is no proximate cause question of any moment left to consider. The very reason for declaring the design defective was to prevent this kind of foreseeable misuse. Proximate cause could not, in such a case, present an obstacle on the grounds of misuse. To do so would negate the very reason for declaring the design defective in the first instance. [*The Many Faces of Misuse: An Inquiry Into the Emerging Doctrine of Comparative Causation*, 29 Mercer L.Rev. 403, 421 (1978).]

In sum, when misuse is an issue in a design-defect case, the jury should first determine whether the plaintiff used the product for an objectively foreseeable purpose. If the jury finds that the plaintiff's purpose was not foreseeable, the defendant did not breach any duty owed to the plaintiff. If, however, the jury finds that the plaintiff's purpose was foreseeable, it must then decide whether the product was defective.

Under the risk-utility analysis, the jury must then determine whether the plaintiff used the product in an objectively foreseeable manner. The effect of a finding that the plaintiff did not so use the product, like a determination that the product was not used for a foreseeable purpose, is that the jury will have found that the defendant did not breach any duty owed to the plaintiff. If, however, the jury finds that the plaintiff used the product in an objectively foreseeable manner, it should then evaluate the product's utility. [Citation] That evaluation entails the determination whether the defendant feasibly could have modified the product's design to prevent the injury or whether that modification would have either unreasonably impaired the utility of the product or excessively increased its cost. [Citation]

If the jury finds that the product is defective, it must then decide whether the misuse proximately caused the injury. In cases in which the product is defective solely because of a foreseeable misuse, the determination of defect predetermines the issue of proximate cause. In other cases, however, where a product is defective for reasons other than the particular misuse, the jury must separately determine proximate cause.

Here, the jury found that the product was not defective as designed, that it was reasonably safe for its intended or reasonably foreseeable uses, that it was not defective when it left defendants' hands, and that it was not a proximate cause of the accident. It also found that at the time of the accident, the product was being used for an intended or reasonably foreseeable purpose in that "it was not being misused or had not been substantially altered in any way that was not reasonably foreseeable." The Appellate Division concluded that the jury had found that Jurado had used the machine in a foreseeable manner and that the jury's finding was a rejection of the defense expert's theory that "the in-running nip point was guarded by reason of its location. * * *" 253 N.J.Super. at 271, 601 A.2d 748. Special interrogatory number three, the jury's answer to which was the predicate for that conclusion, however, does not mention the word "manner." Instead, the interrogatory focuses on the purpose for which the product was being used at the time of the accident.

Consequently, the Appellate Division should not have assumed that the jury had decided the issue of misuse based on the manner in which Jurado had used the collator. In particular, the Appellate Division states: "The jury found that plaintiff had to put his hand into the nip point area during foreseeable operation." Ibid. In effect, the Appellate Division defined away the alternative that the jury found only that the machine had been used for its intended purpose. The inconsistency in the jury's findings requires a retrial on liability as well as damages.

The record suggests that if on retrial the jury determines that plaintiff's misuse was objectively foreseeable, that determination will predetermine that the defect was the proximate cause of the accident. If so, the trial court should instruct the jury that its determination of the existence of a defect will have that further effect.

The Appellate Division, after concluding that the jury must have determined that Jurado had not used the collator in an improper manner, implicitly concluded further that the jury must have determined that the defect was the proximate cause of the accident. As previously stated, however, we cannot ascertain whether the jury found that plaintiff had used the collator in an improper manner or for an improper purpose. Contrary to the Appellate Division's implicit conclusion, moreover, the jury explicitly found that the defect was not the proximate cause of the accident. Given our concern about the possible inconsistency of the jury's finding on the existence of a defect and the implications of that finding for the issue of proximate cause, we believe that the interests of justice are better served by a retrial.

The judgment of the Appellate Division on liability is reversed, and the matter is remanded to the Law Division for a trial on both liability and damages.

CLIFFORD, J., dissenting.

When in a querulous mood, our colleagues at the trial bench sometimes grumble that while trial judges devote their energies to the pursuit of justice, appellate judges spend their time hunched over the record, pawing through it in an unrelenting search for error. One might find support for that dyspeptic observation in today's decision to remand this case for a new trial, given the fact that the jurors rendered a verdict after a charge that, although not squeaky clean, nevertheless fairly put the single critical issue to them in simple, comprehensible terms: was defendants' product as designed, manufactured, or sold defective in that it was not reasonably safe for its intended or reasonably foreseeable uses? Answer: No.

That question and answer should have been the end of the case. In theory, there was no need for the jury to address questions two, three, and four. * * *

Whatever shortcomings infect the current Model Civil Jury Charge, no one can be confused by the charge's definition of "defective" as "not reasonably safe for its intended or reasonably foreseeable uses." That is plain English, and I am willing to assume that the jury understood it, understood the evidence, understood what the plaintiff had done with the machine, and understood how plaintiff had been injured. To my way of thinking we go at the problem backwards if we surmise that the jury's answer to interrogatory number three informed, and rendered unacceptable, its answer to interrogatory number one.

* * *

I would reverse and remand to the Law Division for entry there of a judgment based on the jury's verdict.

For reversal and remandment—CHIEF JUSTICE WILENTZ and JUSTICES HANDLER, POLLOCK, O'HERN, GARIBALDI and STEIN—6.

Dissenting—JUSTICE CLIFFORD—1.

Notes

1. *Jurado* is typical of many design defect cases decided under the risk-utility test of defect. The defectiveness of the product often turns on the question of whether the misuse is foreseeable. This is because manufacturers must design products to be reasonably safe in light of anticipated misuse. *See, e.g.,* Self v. General Motors Corp., 42 Cal.App.3d 1, 116 Cal.Rptr. 575 (1974) (automobiles must be designed to be reasonably safe when involved in collisions); Bexiga v. Havir Mfg. Corp., 60 N.J. 402, 290 A.2d 281 (1972)

(dangerous machinery must have adequate safety guards); LaGorga v. Kroger Co., 275 F.Supp. 373 (W.D.Pa.1967), affirmed, 407 F.2d 671 (3d Cir.1969) (child's jacket must be treated with flame retardant).

2. This same issue is sometimes dealt with as a question of proximate cause. Courts can characterize the act of misuse as an intervening cause, and hold that defendant is liable only if the act is foreseeable. Only then does the defendant have a duty to protect against the intervening cause. The result, of course, is the same whether the question is dealt with as an issue of defect or of proximate cause. There is no obligation to protect against risks created by unforeseeable misuse.

3. There is also a proximate cause issue that is unrelated to defect. This is where a clearly defective product produces an unexpected type of harm because it is misused in an unforeseeable way. Proximate cause issues arising out of misuse are dealt with in Chapter 12 section A. 3., *infra.*

4. Is misuse an affirmative defense? Most courts say no, and place the burden of proving proper use on the plaintiff. *E.g.,* Rogers v. Toro Mfg. Co., 522 S.W.2d 632 (Mo.App.1975). This is sensible in cases where the use is relevant to questions of defectiveness and proximate cause, both of which are elements of plaintiff's case. Should the answer be different in cases where misuse is solely relevant to the question of contributory fault because defect and proximate cause are present? *See* Chapter 15 section B., *infra.*

5. Foreseeability is not always controlling. Manufacturers are not required to make products that are incapable of causing harm. Recall the language in *Phillips v. Kimwood Mach. Co., supra* p. 177, that the design only has to be reasonably safe, not completely safe. Certain products may not be defective in design, or because of a failure to warn, even though it is foreseeable that they can be used in such a way as to cause harm. *Cf.,* Mendez v. Honda Motor Co., 738 F.Supp. 481 (S.D.Fla.1990) (no duty to make it impossible for an inexperienced person, who failed to read owner's manual, to mount motorcycle shock absorbers upside down); Killeen v. Harmon Grain Prod., Inc., 11 Mass.App.Ct. 20, 413 N.E.2d 767 (1980) (toothpick not defective because it has a sharp point).

6. **Misuse.** *Jurado* deals with ignorance of risk because of a failure to anticipate the use to which the product is put. In cases of this kind virtually all courts use foresight rather than hindsight to determine whether there is a duty to guard against misuse. The materials in section A. demonstrate that justifiable ignorance of the harmful quality of the product (generic risk) sometimes does not excuse the manufacturer from liability. Is there a logical justification for a court to use hindsight for generic risks and foresight for misuse?

DOSIER v. WILCOX & CRITTENDON CO.

Court of Appeals of California, First District, 1975.
45 Cal.App.3d 74, 119 Cal.Rptr. 135.

ARATA, ASSOCIATE JUSTICE.

Plaintiff-appellant Edward Dosier takes this appeal from a judgment for defendants Wilcox–Crittendon Company and North and Judd Manufacturing Company in a personal injury action based on strict liability. Plaintiff's complaint against these defendants as manufacturers of an alleged "hook" is framed in two causes of action; the first is based upon a claimed defect and the second is based upon a failure to warn. The evidence reveals that North and Judd are engaged principally in the manufacture of harness and saddlery hardware, belt buckles, shoe buckles, dog leads, handbag hardware, hooks and eyes for men's trousers and a line of plastics used for electrical fittings. Wilcox–Crittendon is a wholly-owned subsidiary of North and Judd. ⌐ "hook" involved in this case was manufactured by North and Judd, and bears the company's trademark. It is described in its catalog as a No. 333 snap. The snap, hereinafter referred to as "hook" is made of cast malleable iron * * *. It is manufactured principally to be used as a bull tie, stallion chain or cattle tie; it is distributed or marketed through wholesale hardware houses, and houses that sell harness and saddlery wares. The particular "hook" at issue in this case was purchased by a buyer for United Air Lines for its plant maintenance shop at San Francisco Airport for use in connection with a "safety rope around a workstand." It was bought from Keystone Brothers, a harness and saddlery wares outlet in San Francisco in 1964. At the time of the purchase the "hook" was selected by the buyer from a display board featuring harness equipment such as bridles, spurs and bits; there was no discussion as to intended use when the purchase was made. The buyer was familiar with this type of "hook" as a result of his earlier experience on a farm.

On March 28, 1968, the plaintiff, as an employee of United Air Lines, was working with a crew installing a grinding machine at its maintenance plant. As part of the rigging process, he attached the "hook" to a 1700 pound counterweight and lifted it to a point where it was suspended in the air. At this point plaintiff reached under the suspended counterweight in search of a missing bolt when suddenly the "hook" gave way and the counterweight fell on his arm causing the injuries for which he seeks damages. The "hook" was supplied to plaintiff by a plant foreman as part of a sling; there was no marking on the "hook" as to its content or lifting capacity.

Plaintiff-appellant states the issues on appeal as follows: "1. Whether the hook was defective because defendants failed to provide warnings of its proper use and capacity; and 2. Whether plaintiff's use of the hook for lifting was reasonably foreseeable by the manufacturer." An analysis of these two issues as stated reveals that there is one common element in both; *i.e., whether the "hook" was being used in a way intended by the manufacturer.* In order to invoke the doctrine of strict liability, the plaintiff must prove that the product was being used, at the time of injury, in a way the manufacturer intended it to be used. [Citations] In applying this rule our courts have held that it should not be narrowly applied and that even an "unusual use" which the manufacturer *is required to anticipate* should not relieve the manufacturer of liability in the absence of warnings against such use. [Citations] Just what a manufacturer is "required to anticipate" in connection with the use of a product is a question of reasonable foreseeability: [Citations] It has been repeatedly held that the foreseeability of the misuse of a product is a question for the trier of fact. [Citations]

One of plaintiff-appellant's main complaints on appeal is that the trial judge committed prejudicial error by receiving evidence concerning the circumstances surrounding the purchase of the "hook" and its use by United. We cannot agree. In deciding whether or not a product is being used in a way the manufacturer intended it to be used, the market for which it is produced is a most important consideration. This bears directly upon the issue of foreseeability. In commenting on this point in Helene Curtis Industries v. Pruitt (1967) 5 Cir., 385 F.2d 841, 860, the court said: "The intended marketing scheme is one basis for deciding which users can be foreseen." The importance and relevancy of the "marketing scheme" is recognized in Johnson v. Standard Brands Paint Co., *supra,* 274 Cal.App.2d 331 at p. 338, 79 Cal.Rptr. 194 at p. 198, where the court said: " * * * there was substantial evidence to support the jury's implied finding that the decedent was *within the ambit of those entitled to protection from the risk created by the distribution and sale of the defective ladder * * *.*" [Emphasis added.]

The logic of the conclusion that the marketing scheme of the manufacturer is relevant in cases involving strict liability was demonstrated at the time of the enunciation of the rule in Greenman v. Yuba Products, *supra,* 59 Cal.2d 57 at p. 63, 27 Cal.Rptr. 697, at p. 701, 377 P.2d 897, at p. 901: "The purpose of such liability is to insure that the costs of injuries resulting from defective products are borne by manufacturers that put such products on the market rather than by injured persons who are powerless to protect themselves." And, again, in Vandermark v. Ford Motor Co. (1964) 61 Cal.2d 256, 262, 37 Cal.Rptr. 896, 899, 391 P.2d 168, 171: "Retailers like manufacturers are engaged in the business of distributing goods to the public. They are an integral part of the overall producing and marketing enterprise that should bear the cost of injuries resulting from defective products." From the foregoing it should be evident that in order to distribute the cost, the manufacturer must be able to identify and anticipate the particular market. Therefore evidence of the method of distribution of the product is relevant.

* * *

In concluding, we analyze this case upon the issues as stated in plaintiff-appellant's opening brief: " * * * the main issues to be determined by the jury were: 1. Whether the hook was defective because defendants failed to provide warnings of its proper use and capacity; 2. Whether plaintiff's use of the hook for lifting was reasonably foreseeable to the manufacturer." It should be obvious that the second issue, foreseeability of the use, is the main issue in this case, because there is no duty to warn against a use that is not reasonably foreseeable. * * * Since the issue of foreseeability was a question of fact submitted to the jury on evidence * * * sufficient to support a finding of nonforeseeability, the general verdict in favor of defendants is conclusive against plaintiffs * * *.

For the foregoing reasons the judgment is affirmed.

DRAPER, P.J., and HAROLD C. BROWN, J., concur.

Notes

1. In risk-utility jurisdictions, misuse is relevant in failure to warn cases in the same way as in design cases. Where it is not practical to design the product in such a way as to eliminate the risk created by foreseeable misuse and intervening causes, the manufacturer may still have to warn about the dangers. *E.g.,* Anderson v. Klix Chemical Co., 256 Or. 199, 472 P.2d 806 (1970) (manufacturer must warn that cleaning product should not be applied with a sprayer). As *Dosier* illustrates, if the misuse or intervening cause is unforeseeable, the product may not be defective at all.

2. What if the hook in *Dosier* had been sold in a hardware store?

3. **The consumer expectations test of defect.** Under this test of defect manufacturers are not always liable for harm caused by foreseeable misuse. There is no duty to guard against the foreseeable misuse of products whose dangers are generally known because such products are not defective.

In Venezia v. Miller Brewing Co., 626 F.2d 188 (1st Cir.1980) an eight-year-old child brought a negligence and breach of warranty action against the manufacturer of a glass bottle. Plaintiff claimed that the bottle was defective because it shattered when he threw it against a telephone pole. Particles of glass entered plaintiff's eye causing severe injury. Plaintiff's theory was that the bottle manufacturer should have been aware of the dangers inherent in their "thin walled" "non-returnable" bottles and should have designed a bottle better able to safely withstand such foreseeable misuse as breakage in the course of improper handling by children. The court held that plaintiff failed to state a cause of action. The court stated:

> [W]e can see no possible implied fitness warranty that an empty glass bottle discarded by unknown persons would more safely withstand being intentionally smashed against a solid stationary object. Under Massachusetts law the question of fitness for ordinary purposes is largely one centering around reasonable consumer expectations. [Citations] "The propensity of glass to break under pressure is common knowledge," *Vincent [v. Nicholas E. Tsiknas Co.,* 337 Mass. 726, 151 N.E.2d 263, 265 (Mass.1958)]. No reasonable consumer would expect anything but that a glass beer bottle, apparently well suited for its immediate intended use, would fail to safely withstand the type of purposeful abuse involved here. * * *

> * * *

> * * * We see no evidence that the Massachusetts courts have abandoned their previously expressed view that "a common cr straightforward product, if safe for normal uses reasonably to be anticipated at the time of manufacture, is not defective [i.e., unfit for its intended use]

simply because it is foreseeable that it may cause injury to someone using it improperly." *Tibbets v. Ford Motor Co.,* 4 Mass.App. 738, 358 N.E.2d 460, 462 (Appeals Ct.1976).

Massachusetts has not adopted § 402A of the Restatement. It imposes strict liability, however, under an implied warranty theory that is essentially the same.

Chapter 8

FUNDAMENTAL PRINCIPLES OF STRICT LIABILITY: EFFECTS OF STATUTES AND REGULATIONS

SECTION A.   RELEVANCE OF STATUTE

LORENZ v. CELOTEX CORP.
United States Court of Appeals, Fifth Circuit, 1990.
896 F.2d 148.

On Appeal from the United States District Court for the Northern District of Texas.

Before GEE, JONES, and SMITH, CIRCUIT JUDGES:

EDITH H. JONES, CIRCUIT JUDGE:

Plaintiff Janice Grafton Lorenz brought this products liability action, alleging that her husband died of lung cancer as a result of his exposure to asbestos products manufactured by defendant, the Celotex Corporation.   After a jury trial, the jury returned a verdict in favor of Celotex.   Lorenz appeals, claiming that the district court erroneously instructed the jury that compliance with government safety standards constitutes strong and substantial evidence that a product is not defective.   We affirm.

BACKGROUND

Paul Lorenz died of lung cancer in 1981.   His widow, Janice Grafton Lorenz, alleges that his illness was the result of his exposure to asbestos insulation products while he served as a boiler technician aboard a United States Navy vessel from 1966 to 1968.   As a boiler technician, Lorenz periodically removed and replaced the asbestos insulation on the pipes and valves in the boiler room.   He also occasionally installed asbestos millboard around the boilers.   At least some of the insulation and millboard used was manufactured by the Philip Carey Company, predecessor-in-interest of defendant Celotex.

Seeking to recover damages for her husband's wrongful death, Mrs. Lorenz filed this action against thirteen different asbestos manufacturers. Mrs. Lorenz sought recovery on both negligence and strict liability grounds based on the manufacturers' failure to warn of the hazards of working with asbestos. All the defendants except Celotex settled or were dismissed prior to trial.

On January 9, 1989 the case proceeded to trial, with Celotex as the sole defendant. Plaintiff offered the testimony of expert witnesses who indicated that asbestos was a substantial factor in her husband's illness, and presented evidence that Celotex had failed to warn of any such danger. Celotex attempted to establish that its products were not defective or unreasonably dangerous by presenting evidence that use of its insulation products produced asbestos dust counts below the maximum level established by the official and unofficial safety standards in place at the time of Lorenz's exposure. At the close of the evidence, the district court, upon Celotex's request, instructed the jury that:

> Compliance with government safety standards constitutes strong and substantial evidence that a product is not defective.

The jury returned a verdict in favor of Celotex on both the strict liability and negligence claims, and the district court entered judgment for Celotex. Lorenz appeals, contending that the district court erred by giving the instruction on compliance with government standards because (1) the instruction was substantively incorrect, and (2) there was no evidence to support the instruction.

DISCUSSION

A. *Substantive Correctness*

The language of the challenged instruction comes directly from this court's opinions in *Gideon v. Johns–Manville Sales Corp.*, 761 F.2d 1129, 1144 (5th Cir.1985), and *Dartez v. Fibreboard Corp.*, 765 F.2d 456, 471 (5th Cir.1985) (quoting *Gideon*). In *Gideon*, a plaintiff who had contracted asbestosis sought to recover damages from several asbestos manufacturers, including Raymark Industries, Inc. The jury determined that Raymark's asbestos textile products were defective and held the company liable for the plaintiff's injuries. On appeal, the court reversed the judgment against Raymark because there was insufficient evidence to support the findings against it. *Gideon*, 761 F.2d at 1143–45. In reaching its decision, the court placed great weight on the fact that Raymark's products complied with the applicable government safety standards. *Id.* at 1144. The court noted that "[c]ompliance with such government safety standards constitutes strong and substantial evidence that a product is not defective." *Id.* Similarly, in *Dartez* the court reversed another judgment against Raymark Industries on insufficiency of evidence grounds. *Dartez*, 765 F.2d at 470–71. Once again the court relied heavily on the fact that Raymark's products complied with applicable government standards, quoting *Gideon* for the proposition that such compliance is strong and substantial evidence that a product is not defective. *Id.* at 471.

Despite the fact that the district court took its instruction from *Gideon* and *Dartez*, Lorenz contends that the instruction was substantively incorrect for several reasons. First, she argues that the language in those opinions was intended merely as a comment on the weight of the particular evidence in those cases, not as a general rule of law. Even a casual reading of *Gideon* and *Dartez* belies Lorenz's interpretation. In each case the court states the rule as a general proposition, without qualifying the statement to the particular facts of the case. *Gideon*, 761 F.2d at 1144; *Dartez*, 765 F.2d at 471. In addition, each opinion cites authority to support the proposition.[1] We cannot agree with Lorenz that the language in *Gideon* and *Dartez* was not intended to state a general rule of law.

Lorenz next argues that the instruction is substantively incorrect because it is unsupported by Texas law. Lorenz correctly points out that in diversity cases, jury instructions must accurately describe the applicable state substantive law. *Turlington v. Phillips Petroleum Co.*, 795 F.2d 434, 441 (5th Cir.1986). It appears that no Texas case has expressly stated that compliance with government standards constitutes strong and substantial evidence that a product is not defective. However, * * * Lorenz has not cited, and the court has not found, any Texas cases establishing a rule that compliance with government standards is less than strong and substantial evidence.[2] See 59 TEX.JUR.3d *Products Liability* § 67 (1988) (reporting that the rule in Texas is that "[e]vidence of compliance with government safety standards does constitute strong and substantial evidence that a product is not defective * * *"). In the absence of controverting Texas authority, the district court and this court are bound by the interpretation of Texas law expressed in *Gideon* and *Dartez*. [Citation] Accordingly, we conclude that the district court's instruction was substantively correct.

B. No Evidence

Lorenz also contends that the district court erred by giving the instruction because Celotex did not present any evidence that its products complied with an applicable government standard. A district court may not instruct a jury on a legal theory on which no evidence is

---

1. *Gideon* relies on *Simien v. S.S. Kresge Co.*, 566 F.2d 551, 557 (5th Cir. 1978). In *Simien*, the defendant argued that a jacket it manufactured was not defective because it complied with government flammability standards. The court noted that such testimony was "evidence, indeed substantial evidence, that the jacket was not unreasonably dangerous." *Simien*, 566 F.2d at 557.

2. Lorenz relies on *Bristol–Meyers Co. v. Gonzales*, 561 S.W.2d 801 (Tex.1978); *Golden Villa Nursing Home, Inc. v. Smith*, 674 S.W.2d 343 (Tex.App.—Houston [14th Dist.] 1984, writ ref'd n.r.e.); and *Rumsey v. Freeway Manor Minimax*, 423 S.W.2d 387 (Tex.Civ.App.—Houston [1st Dist.] 1968, no

writ), but none of those cases supports Lorenz's argument that compliance with government safety standards is less than strong and substantial evidence. Rather, those cases stand for the general proposition that compliance with government standards usually does not insulate a defendant or automatically preclude a finding of liability. *E.g., Bristol–Meyers Co. v. Gonzales*, 561 S.W.2d at 804 (compliance with F.D.A. warning requirements did not preclude liability for inadequate warning); *see also Simien v. S.S. Kresge Co.*, 566 F.2d 551, 557 (5th Cir.1978) (while evidence of compliance with government standards was strong and substantial evidence, it was not conclusive on the issue of liability).

presented. [Citation] However, in this case, Celotex introduced sufficient evidence to permit the court to instruct the jury that compliance with government safety standards constitutes strong and substantial evidence that a product is not defective.

Lorenz first argues that Celotex failed to present evidence of a government standard applicable to this case. We disagree. At trial, Celotex presented evidence that until the end of the 1960's, exposure to asbestos dust counts below five million particles per cubic foot was generally considered safe. This standard was first proposed in a 1938 Surgeon General's Report, known as the Dressen Report after its principal author. The American Conference of Governmental Industrial Hygienists, a "quasi-official body responsible for making recommendations concerning industrial hygiene," *Borel v. Fibreboard Paper Products Corp.*, 493 F.2d 1076, 1084 (5th Cir.1973), cert. denied, 419 U.S. 869, 95 S.Ct. 127, 42 L.Ed.2d 107 (1974), adopted the five million particle per cubic foot standard as the threshold limit for safe exposure to asbestos in 1946, and reaffirmed the standard in 1961 and 1964. State governments also adopted the five million particle per cubic foot standard. In 1945, the state of New York, where Lorenz resided at the time of his death, adopted the five million standard. Ohio, where Philip Carey had its headquarters and principal insulation plant, adopted the standard in 1947. Most importantly, the state of Texas, whose law governs this case, adopted the five million particles per cubic foot standard in 1958. It was not until after the period of Paul Lorenz's exposure that governments began to reduce the acceptable asbestos dust count.

Lorenz contends that none of the government standards offered by Celotex should apply in this case because none of those standards applies to the *labeling* of asbestos products. This argument cannot withstand analysis. To establish Celotex's liability for failure to warn of the dangers of using its products, Lorenz had to prove that Celotex "knew or should have known of such dangers at the time the products were marketed." *Gideon v. Johns–Manville Sales Corp.*, 761 F.2d 1129, 1145 (5th Cir.1985). Evidence of compliance with government safety standards (here, evidence that use of Celotex's insulation products produced dust counts below the threshold limit) constitutes strong and substantial evidence that a product is not defective. *See Id.* at 1144. Thus, evidence that use of Celotex's products produced dust counts below the threshold limit is, logically, strong and substantial evidence that Celotex did not know or should not have known that its products were so dangerous or defective that they required a warning. Accordingly, we conclude that Celotex presented evidence of an applicable government standard.

Likewise, Celotex presented sufficient evidence that it complied with the applicable standards. First, Celotex introduced the results of several studies of asbestos exposure among insulation workers. In each case, the study concluded that exposure levels were below the five million particles per cubic foot threshold. Second, Celotex offered uncontroverted evidence that to the extent that its products differed from those being used in the studies it introduced, Celotex's insulation was less *dusty*. Arthur Mueller, a former research and development worker at Philip Carey, testified that Philip Carey's products contained a smaller percentage of asbestos than the competition's. He also testified that Philip Carey's insulation was designed to be cut with a knife rather than a saw, came with preformed fittings, and used an asbestos-free cement. Taken together, the evidence that asbestos counts for insulation workers in general were below the safety standard and that Celotex's products were less dusty than the typical insulation product constitutes evidence that Celotex's products complied with the five million particles per cubic foot standard.

CONCLUSION

The trial court did not err by instructing the jury that compliance with government safety standards constitutes strong and substantial evidence that a product is not defective. The instruction was substantively correct and was supported by the evidence. Therefore, the judgment of the district court is AFFIRMED.

Notes

1. **Compliance with statute, ordinance or regulation.** In negligence cases, compliance is relevant to the question of reasonableness, but it is not controlling. The theory is that the jury should be free to conclude that reasonable care under the circumstances required more than the statutory minimum. This rule is embodied in the Restatement of Torts (Second) § 288C, which provides:

> Compliance with a legislative enactment or an administrative regulation does not prevent a finding of negligence where a reasonable man would take additional precautions.

2. What effect should such compliance have in a strict liability case? Most courts have adopted the negligence rule, holding that the evidence is admissible but not conclusive. *E.g.,* Brech v. J.C. Penney Co., Inc., 698 F.2d 332 (8th Cir.1983); Wilson v. Piper Aircraft Corp., 282 Or. 61, 577 P.2d 1322 (1978). *Lorenz v. Celotex Corp.* takes a somewhat stronger position by ruling that compliance with statute or regulation is strong and substantial evidence that a product is not defective.

3. Few decisions explain in detail how the evidence of compliance with statute or regulation is relevant to the question of defect in strict liability actions. In a concurring opinion in Wilson v. Piper Aircraft Corp., 282 Or. 61, 79, 577 P.2d 1322, 1332 (1978), Justice Linde offered the following views as to both the relevancy and the effect of FAA approval of an aircraft design:

> It is true that compliance with government safety standards will generally not be held to negate a claim of "dangerously defective" design, but it would equally be an oversimplification to say that it can never do so. The role of such compliance should logically depend on whether the goal to be achieved by the particular government standards, the balance struck between safety and its costs, has been set higher or lower than that set by the rules governing the producer's civil liability. It may well be that when government intervenes in the product market

to set safety standards, it often confines itself to demanding only minimum safeguards against the most flagrant hazards, well below the contemporary standards for civil liability. But that was not necessarily the case when the first safety standards were legislated, and it is not necessarily so for all products today.

In the design of aircraft, government regulation obviously places a much greater weight on the side of safety than it does for most products. The FAA not only sets detailed performance standards for the operational aspects of the design, it also requires that the design be tested for compliance with these standards by the producer and ultimately by the agency itself before a certificate is issued. This does not mean that an aircraft design, to be certified, must be the safest that could be built at any cost in money, speed, or carrying capacity. No doubt the FAA does not demand for small, single-engined recreational aircraft the redundant circuits and fail-safe systems expected in commercial airliners, not to mention the space program. It does mean, however, that FAA certification of a design represents a more deliberate, technically intensive program to set and control a given level of safety in priority to competing considerations than is true of many run-of-the-mill safety regulations.

The question remains how this policy assigned to the FAA compares with Oregon's standards of products liability for design defects. In two decisions in 1974, this court quoted a series of factors suggested by Professor Wade as posing the preliminary issue for a court whether a claim of "defect" crosses the legal threshold for submission to the jury. The difficulty in the present case springs from the fact that most of these factors—briefly summarized, the safety risks, the availability of safer design, the financial and other costs of the safer alternative, and the user's awareness of and ability to avoid the risks—are at least very similar to the factors that are presumably meant to enter into the FAA's judgment whether an aircraft design is safe enough.

It must be kept in mind that this aircraft is alleged to be defective not because it fell short of the safety standards set for its type, but on the ground that these standards provide insufficient safety for the whole series. But once the common-law premise of liability is expressed as a balance of social utility so closely the same as the judgment made in administering safety legislation, it becomes very problematic to assume that one or a sequence of law courts and juries are to repeat that underlying social judgment de novo as each sees fit. Rather, when the design of a product is subject not only to prescribed performance standards but to government supervised testing and specific approval or disapproval on safety grounds, no further balance whether the product design is "unreasonably dangerous" for its intended or foreseeable use under the conditions for which it is approved needs to be struck by a court or a jury *unless* one of two things can be shown: either that the standards of safety and utility assigned to the regulatory scheme are less inclusive or demanding than the premises of the law of products liability, or that the regulatory agency did not address the allegedly defective element of the design or in some way fell short of its assigned task.

It is these two questions, rather than a de novo evaluation of the safety of a design and the technological feasibility and costs of an even safer alternative, that properly become the issues for preliminary determination by a trial court in deciding whether a "design defect" claim against a product specifically tested and approved under government safety regulations should nevertheless go to a jury. In other words, it should be defendant's burden to show that a governmental agency has undertaken the responsibility of making substantially the same judgment that the court would otherwise be called on to make; and if so, it should then be plaintiff's burden to show that the responsible agency has not in fact made that judgment with respect to the particular "defect" at issue. When the product has been tested and approved by a federal agency, these issues can normally be decided simply by examining the statutory assignment of the agency (including relevant legislative history), the further standards adopted by the agency itself, and the records and reports underlying its approval of the product. In the case of a state agency, the documentation may be less extensive but other evidence of the actual process may be more accessible to a state court.

With respect to the present case, the cited sources seem likely to show that the FAA's goals and standards match this court's criteria for a "duly safe" design, at least as far as an aircraft's airworthiness is concerned. * * * It is not inconceivable that the answers might prove to come out one way with respect to FAA criteria and tests for aircraft engines and differently with respect to seat belts, or instrument knobs, or entry and exit steps, or other features whose risks are less central to airworthiness. Of course we do not know all that the parties might be able to show in this regard.

I repeat that this need to examine the precise standards and findings of the governing safety program results not from legislative preemption of common-law standards of liability, absent indications to that effect, but rather from these standards themselves when they are identical with those underlying the regulatory scheme. It may be that the tension between the policies embodied in intensive safety regulation and licensing and in case-by-case civil liability premised on "dangerously defective" design cannot remain unresolved, especially with respect to goods federally approved for a national market. A choice may have to be made between a theory of recovery premised on the need to compensate victims of product-caused injuries and one premised on liability for "faulty" products, no matter how attenuated the "fault" has become.

282 Or. at 81–86, 577 P.2d at 1333–35.

4. Should compliance with government mandates be given greater effect than courts presently give? If so, should the effect be conclusive, or should an intermediate position be adopted? Should the answer depend on the type of defect alleged and the type of regulation involved? The various possibilities are analyzed in Schwartz, The Role of Federal Safety Regulations in Products Liability Actions, 41 Vand.L.Rev. 1121 (1988); Note, The Role of Regulatory Compliance in Tort Actions, 26 Harv.J. on Legis. 175 (1989); Comment, The Relationship Between Federal Standards and Litigation in the Control of Automobile Design, 57 N.Y.U.L.Rev. 804 (1982).

5. Some state legislatures have adopted an intermediate position. Colo.Rev.Stat. § 13–21–403 provides:

Presumptions. (1) In any product liability action, it shall be rebuttably presumed that the product which caused the injury, death, or property damage was not defective and that the manufacturer or seller thereof was not negligent if the product:

(a) Prior to sale by the manufacturer, conformed to the state of the art, as distinguished from industry standards, applicable to such product in existence at the time of sale; or

(b) Complied with, at the time of sale by the manufacturer, any applicable code, standard, or regulation adopted or promulgated by the United States or by this state, or by any agency of the United States or of this state.

(2) In like manner, noncompliance with a government code, standard, or regulation existing and in effect at the time of sale of the product by the manufacturer which contributed to the claim or injury shall create a rebuttable presumption that the product was defective or negligently manufactured.

6. **Violation of Statute.** The majority of courts agree that violation of safety statutes, ordinances, and regulations designed to protect plaintiff from the type of harm plaintiff suffered is negligence *per se*. For example, in Stanton v. Astra Pharmaceutical Prod., Inc., 718 F.2d 553 (3d Cir.1983) an eight-month old child suffered an adverse reaction to Xylocaine, a local anesthetic, and experienced cardiac and respiratory arrest, resulting in severe and irreversible brain damage. The drug manufacturer was held liable on a negligence per se theory because it failed to file annual reports and unexpected-adverse-reaction reports with the FDA, as required by 21 C.F.R. § 130.35(e) and (f) (1972).

7. For a recent general treatment of negligence *per se*, *see* Seidelson, The Appropriate Judicial Response to Evidence of the Violation of a Criminal Statute in a Negligence Action, 30 Duq.L.Rev. 1 (1991). The Restatement of the Law (Second), Torts (1965) gives the following statement of the general rules pertaining to negligence *per se* :

§ 286. When Standard of Conduct Defined by Legislation or Regulation Will Be Adopted

The court may adopt as the standard of conduct of a reasonable man the requirements of a legislative enactment or an administrative regulation whose purpose is found to be exclusively or in part

(a) to protect a class of persons which includes the one whose interest is invaded, and

(b) to protect the particular interest which is invaded, and

(c) to protect that interest against the kind of harm which has resulted, and

(d) to protect that interest against the particular hazard from which the harm results.

§ 288A. Excused Violations

(1) An excused violation of a legislative enactment or an administrative regulation is not negligence.

(2) Unless the enactment or regulation is construed not to permit such excuse, its violation is excused when

(a) the violation is reasonable because of the actor's incapacity;

(b) he neither knows nor should know of the occasion for compliance;

(c) he is unable after reasonable diligence or care to comply;

(d) he is confronted by an emergency not due to his own misconduct;

(e) compliance would involve a greater risk of harm to the actor or to others.

§ 288B. Effect of Violation

(1) The unexcused violation of a legislative enactment or an administrative regulation which is adopted by the court as defining the standard of conduct of a reasonable man, is negligence in itself.

(2) The unexcused violation of an enactment or regulation which is not so adopted may be relevant evidence bearing on the issue of negligent conduct.

8. A minority of courts treat violation of statute, ordinances, and regulations as evidence of negligence, which is relevant, but not conclusive. MacDonald v. Ortho Pharmaceutical Corp., 394 Mass. 131, 475 N.E.2d 65 (1985), cert. denied, 474 U.S. 920, 106 S.Ct. 250, 88 L.Ed.2d 258 (1985) (FDA mandated warning on birth control pills).

9. Should government standards promulgated after the product was marketed be considered?

10. A theory related to negligence *per se* is the creation by implication of statutory causes of action. Professor Sherman analyzes implied actions under federal statutes in Sherman, Use of Federal Statutes in State Negligence Per Se Actions, 13 Whittier L.Rev. 831 (1992). In the article he also analyzes the relationship between negligence *per se*, federal preemption, and the creation by implication of federal statutory causes of action.

SECTION B. PREEMPTION

CIPOLLONE v. LIGGETT GROUP, INC.
Supreme Court of the United States, 1992.
__ U.S. __, 112 S.Ct. 2608, 120 L.Ed.2d 407.

JUSTICE STEVENS delivered the opinion of the Court, except as to Parts V and VI.

I

[Plaintiff brought a diversity jurisdiction action alleging that Rose Cipollone developed lung cancer because she smoked cigarettes manufactured and sold by the three respondents. The complaint alleged several theories of recovery based on New Jersey law. After a trial in the District Court, and two appeals in the Court of Appeals, the Supreme court granted the petition for certiorari to determine the pre-emptive effect of federal statutes on plaintiff's theories alleging failure to warn, breach of express warranty, fraudulent misrepresentation, and conspiracy.]

II

Although physicians had suspected a link between smoking and illness for centuries, the first medical studies of that connection did not appear until the 1920s. [Citations] The ensuing decades saw a wide range of epidemiologic and laboratory studies on the health hazards of smoking. Thus, by the time the Surgeon General convened an advisory committee to examine the issue in 1962, there were more than 7,000 publications examining the relationship between smoking and health. [Citation]

In 1964, the advisory committee issued its report, which stated as its central conclusion: "Cigarette smoking is a health hazard of sufficient importance in the United States to warrant appropriate remedial action." U.S. Dept. of Health, Education, and Welfare, U.S. Surgeon General's Advisory Committee, Smoking and Health 33 (1964). Relying in part on that report, the Federal Trade Commission (FTC), which had long regulated unfair and deceptive advertising practices in the cigarette industry, promulgated a new trade regulation rule. That rule, which was to take effect January 1, 1965, established that it would be a violation of the Federal Trade Commission Act "to fail to disclose, clearly and prominently, in all advertising and on every pack, box, carton, or container [of cigarettes] that cigarette smoking is dangerous to health and may cause death from cancer and other diseases." 29 Fed.Reg. 8325 (1964). Several States also moved to regulate the advertising and labeling of cigarettes. See, *e.g.*, 1965 N.Y.Laws, ch. 470; see also 111 Cong.Rec. 13900–13902 (1965) (statement of Sen. Moss). Upon a congressional request, the FTC postponed enforcement of its new regulation for six months. In July 1965, Congress enacted the Federal Cigarette Labeling and Advertising Act. The 1965 Act effectively adopted half of the FTC's regulation: the Act mandated warnings on cigarette packages (§ 5(a)), but barred the requirement of such warnings in cigarette advertising (§ 5(b)).

Section 2 of the Act declares the statute's two purposes: (1) adequately informing the public that cigarette smoking may be hazardous to health, and (2) protecting the national economy from the burden imposed by diverse, nonuniform and confusing cigarette labeling and advertising regulations. In furtherance of the first purpose, § 4 of the Act made it unlawful to sell or distribute any cigarettes in the United States unless the package bore a conspicuous label stating: "CAUTION: CIGARETTE SMOKING MAY BE HAZARDOUS TO YOUR HEALTH." In furtherance of the second purpose, § 5, captioned "Preemption," provided in part:

"(a) No statement relating to smoking and health, other than the statement required by section 4 of this Act, shall be required on any cigarette package.

"(b) No statement relating to smoking and health shall be required in the advertising of any cigarettes the packages of which are labeled in conformity with the provisions of this Act."

Although the Act took effect January 1, 1966, § 10 of the Act provided that its provisions affecting the regulation of advertising would terminate on July 1, 1969.

As that termination date approached, federal authorities prepared to issue further regulations on cigarette advertising. The FTC announced the reinstitution of its 1964 proceedings concerning a warning requirement for cigarette advertisements. 34 Fed.Reg. 7917 (1969). The Federal Communications Commission (FCC) announced that it would consider "a proposed rule which would ban the broadcast of cigarette commercials by radio and television stations." 34 Fed.Reg. 1959 (1969). State authorities also prepared to take actions regulating cigarette advertisements.[1]

It was in this context that Congress enacted the Public Health Cigarette Smoking Act of 1969, which amended the 1965 Act in several ways. First, the 1969 Act strengthened the warning label, in part by requiring a statement that cigarette smoking "is dangerous" rather than that it "may be hazardous." Second, the 1969 Act banned cigarette advertising in "any medium of electronic communication subject to [FCC] jurisdiction." Third, and related, the 1969 Act modified the pre-emption provision by replacing the original § 5(b) with a provision that reads:

"(b) No requirement or prohibition based on smoking and health shall be imposed under State law with respect to the advertising or promotion of any cigarettes the packages of which are labeled in conformity with the provisions of this Act."

Although the Act also directed the FTC not to "take any action before July 1, 1971, with respect to its pending trade regulation rule proceeding relating to cigarette advertising," the narrowing of the pre-emption provision to prohibit only restrictions "imposed under State law" cleared the way for the FTC to extend the warning-label requirement to print advertisements for cigarettes. The FTC did so in 1972. See *In re Lorillard*, 80 F.T.C. 455 (1972).

III

Article VI of the Constitution provides that the laws of the United States "shall be the supreme Law of the Land; * * * any Thing in the Constitution or Laws of any state to the Contrary notwithstanding." Art. VI, cl. 2. Thus, since our decision in *M'Culloch v. Maryland*, 17

---

1. For example, the California State Senate passed a total ban on both print and electronic cigarette advertisements. "California Senate Votes Ban On Cigarette Advertising," Washington Post, June 26, 1969, p. A9.

U.S. (4 Wheat.) 316, 427, 4 L.Ed. 579 (1819), it has been settled that state law that conflicts with federal law is "without effect." *Maryland v. Louisiana*, 451 U.S. 725, 746, 101 S.Ct. 2114, 2128, 68 L.Ed.2d 576 (1981). Consideration of issues arising under the Supremacy Clause "start[s] with the assumption that the historic police powers of the States [are] not to be superseded by * * * Federal Act unless that [is] the clear and manifest purpose of Congress." *Rice v. Santa Fe Elevator Corp.*, 331 U.S. 218, 230, 67 S.Ct. 1146, 1152, 91 L.Ed. 1447 (1947). Accordingly, " '[t]he purpose of Congress is the ultimate touchstone' " of pre-emption analysis. *Malone v. White Motor Corp.*, 435 U.S. 497, 504, 98 S.Ct. 1185, 1189, 55 L.Ed.2d 443 (1978) (quoting *Retail Clerks v. Schermerhorn*, 375 U.S. 96, 103, 84 S.Ct. 219, 222, 11 L.Ed.2d 179 (1963)).

Congress' intent may be "explicitly stated in the statute's language or implicitly contained in its structure and purpose." *Jones v. Rath Packing Co.*, 430 U.S. 519, 525, 97 S.Ct. 1305, 1309, 51 L.Ed.2d 604 (1977). In the absence of an express congressional command, state law is pre-empted if that law actually conflicts with federal law, see *Pacific Gas & Elec. Co. v. Energy Resources Conservation and Development Comm'n*, 461 U.S. 190, 204, 103 S.Ct. 1713, 1722, 75 L.Ed.2d 752 (1983), or if federal law so thoroughly occupies a legislative field " 'as to make reasonable the inference that Congress left no room for the States to supplement it.' " *Fidelity Federal Savings & Loan Assn. v. De la Cuesta*, 458 U.S. 141, 153, 102 S.Ct. 3014, 3022, 73 L.Ed.2d 664 (1982) (quoting *Rice v. Santa Fe Elevator Corp.*, 331 U.S., at 230, 67 S.Ct., at 1152).

* * *

In our opinion, the pre-emptive scope of the 1965 Act and the 1969 Act is governed entirely by the express language in § 5 of each Act. When Congress has considered the issue of pre-emption and has included in the enacted legislation a provision explicitly addressing that issue, and when that provision provides a "reliable indicium of congressional intent with respect to state authority," *Malone v. White Motor Corp.*, 435 U.S., at 505, 98 S.Ct., at 1190, "there is no need to infer congressional intent to pre-empt state laws from the substantive provisions" of the legislation. *California Federal Savings & Loan Assn. v. Guerra*, 479 U.S. 272, 282, 107 S.Ct. 683, 690, 93 L.Ed.2d 613 (1987) (opinion of Marshall, J.). Such reasoning is a variant of the familiar principle of *expression unius est exclusio alterius* : Congress' enactment of a provision defining the pre-emptive reach of a statute implies that matters beyond that reach are not pre-empted. In this case, the other provisions of the 1965 and 1969 Acts offer no cause to look beyond § 5 of each Act. Therefore, we need only identify the domain expressly pre-empted by each of those sections. As the 1965 and 1969 provisions differ substantially, we consider each in turn.

IV

In the 1965 pre-emption provision regarding advertising (§ 5(b)), Congress spoke precisely and narrowly: "No *statement* relating to smoking and health shall be required *in the advertising* of [properly labeled] cigarettes." Section 5(a) used the same phrase ("No *statement* relating to smoking and health") with regard to cigarette labeling. As § 5(a) made clear, that phrase referred to the sort of warning provided for in § 4, which set forth verbatim the warning Congress determined to be appropriate. Thus, on their face, these provisions merely prohibited state and federal rule-making bodies from mandating particular cautionary statements on cigarette labels (§ 5(a)) or in cigarette advertisements (§ 5(b)).

Beyond the precise words of these provisions, this reading is appropriate for several reasons. First, as discussed above, we must construe these provisions in light of the presumption against the pre-emption of state police power regulations. This presumption reinforces the appropriateness of a narrow reading of § 5. Second, the warning required in § 4 does not by its own effect foreclose additional obligations imposed under state law. That Congress requires a particular warning label does not automatically pre-empt a regulatory field. [Citation] Third, there is no general, inherent conflict between federal pre-emption of state warning requirements and the continued vitality of state common law damages actions. For example, in the Comprehensive Smokeless Tobacco Health Education Act of 1986, Congress expressly pre-empted State or local imposition of a "statement relating to the use of smokeless tobacco products and health" but, at the same time, preserved state law damages actions based on those products. See 15 U.S.C. § 4406. All of these considerations indicate that § 5 is best read as having superseded only positive enactments by legislatures or administrative agencies that mandate particular warning labels.

This reading comports with the 1965 Act's statement of purpose, which expressed an intent to avoid "diverse, nonuniform, and confusing labeling and advertising *regulations* with respect to any relationship between smoking and health." Read against the backdrop of regulatory activity undertaken by state legislatures and federal agencies in response to the Surgeon General's report, the term "regulation" most naturally refers to positive enactments by those bodies, not to common law damages actions.

The regulatory context of the 1965 Act also supports such a reading. As noted above, a warning requirement promulgated by the FTC and other requirements under consideration by the States were the catalyst for passage of the 1965 Act. These regulatory actions animated the passage of § 5, which reflected Congress' efforts to prevent "a multiplicity of State and local regulations pertaining to labeling of cigarette packages," H.R.Rep. No. 89–449, 89th Cong., 1st Sess., 4 (1965), and to "pre-empt [all] Federal, State, and local authorit[ies] from requiring *any statement * * * relating to smoking and health in the advertising of cigarettes." *Id.*, at 5 (emphasis supplied).

For these reasons, we conclude that § 5 of the 1965 Act only pre-empted state and federal rulemaking bodies from mandating particular cautionary statements and did not pre-empt state law damages actions.

V

Compared to its predecessor in the 1965 Act, the plain language of the pre-emption provision in the 1969 Act is much broader. First, the later Act bars not simply "statements" but rather "requirement[s] or prohibition[s] * * * imposed under State law." Second, the later Act reaches beyond statements "in the advertising" to obligations "with respect to the advertising or promotion" of cigarettes.

Notwithstanding these substantial differences in language, both petitioner and respondents contend that the 1969 Act did not materially alter the pre-emptive scope of federal law. Their primary support for this contention is a sentence in a Committee Report which states that the 1969 amendment "clarified" the 1965 version of § 5(b). S.Rep. No. 91–566, p. 12 (1969). We reject the parties' reading as incompatible with the language and origins of the amendments. As we noted in another context, "[i]nferences from legislative history cannot rest on so slender a reed. Moreover, the views of a subsequent Congress form a hazardous basis for inferring the intent of an earlier one." *United States v. Price*, 361 U.S. 304, 313, 80 S.Ct. 326, 332, 4 L.Ed.2d 334 (1960). The 1969 Act worked substantial changes in the law: rewriting the label warning, banning broadcast advertising, and allowing the FTC to regulate print advertising. In the context of such revisions and in light of the substantial changes in wording, we cannot accept the parties' claim that the 1969 Act did not alter the reach of § 5(b).[2]

Petitioner next contends that § 5(b), however broadened by the 1969 Act, does not pre-empt *common law* actions. He offers two theories for limiting the reach of the amended § 5(b). First, he argues that common law damages actions do not impose "requirement[s] or prohibition[s]" and that Congress intended only to trump "state statute[s], injunction[s], or executive pronouncement[s]." We disagree; such an analysis is at odds both with the plain words of the 1969 Act and with the general understanding of common law damages actions. The phrase "[n]o requirement or prohibition" sweeps broadly and suggests no distinction between positive enactments and common law; to the contrary, those words easily encompass obligations that take the form of common law rules. As we noted in another context, "[state] regulation can be as effectively exerted through an award of damages as through some form of preventive relief. The obligation to pay compensation can be, indeed is designed to be, a potent method of governing conduct and controlling policy." *San Diego Building Trades Council v. Garmon*, 359 U.S. 236, 247, 79 S.Ct. 773, 780, 3 L.Ed.2d 775 (1959).

Although portions of the legislative history of the 1969 Act suggest that Congress was primarily concerned with positive enactments by States and localities, see S.Rep. No. 91–566, p. 12, the language of the

2. As noted above, the 1965 Act's statement of purpose (§ 2) suggested that Congress was concerned primarily with "regulations"—positive enactments, rather than common law damages actions. Although the 1969 Act did not amend § 2, we are not persuaded that the retention of that portion of the 1965 Act is a sufficient basis for rejecting the plain meaning of the broad language that Congress added to § 5(b).

Act plainly reaches beyond such enactments. "We must give effect to this plain language unless there is good reason to believe Congress intended the language to have some more restrictive meaning." *Shaw v. Delta Air Lines, Inc.*, 463 U.S. 85, 97, 103 S.Ct. 2890, 2900, 77 L.Ed.2d 490 (1983). In this case there is no "good reason to believe" that Congress meant less than what it said; indeed, in light of the narrowness of the 1965 Act, there is "good reason to believe" that Congress meant precisely what it said in amending that Act.

Moreover, common law damages actions of the sort raised by petitioner are premised on the existence of a legal duty and it is difficult to say that such actions do not impose "requirements or prohibitions." See W. Prosser, Law of Torts 4 (4th ed. 1971); Black's Law Dictionary 1489 (6th ed. 1990) (defining "tort" as "always [involving] a violation of some duty owing to plaintiff"). It is in this way that the 1969 version of § 5(b) differs from its predecessor: Whereas the common law would not normally require a vendor to use any specific *statement* on its packages or in its advertisements, it is the essence of the common law to enforce duties that are either affirmative *requirements* or negative *prohibitions*. We therefore reject petitioner's argument that the phrase "requirement or prohibition" limits the 1969 Act's pre-emptive scope to positive enactments by legislatures and agencies.

Petitioner's second argument for excluding common law rules from the reach of § 5(b) hinges on the phrase "imposed under State law." This argument fails as well. At least since *Erie R. v. Tompkins*, 304 U.S. 64, 58 S.Ct. 817, 82 L.Ed. 1188 (1938), we have recognized the phrase "state law" to include common law as well as statutes and regulations. Indeed just last Term, the Court stated that the phrase "all other law, including State and municipal law" "does not admit of [a] distinction * * * between positive enactments and common-law rules of liability." *Norfolk & Western R. Co. v. Train Dispatchers*, 499 U.S. ___, ___, 111 S.Ct. 1156, 1163, 113 L.Ed.2d 95 (1991). Although the presumption against pre-emption might give good reason to construe the phrase "state law" in a pre-emption provision more narrowly than an identical phrase in another context, in this case such a construction is not appropriate. As explained above, the 1965 version of § 5 was precise and narrow on its face; the obviously broader language of the 1969 version extended that section's pre-emptive reach. Moreover, while the version of the 1969 Act passed by the Senate pre-empted "any State *statute or regulation* with respect to * * * advertising or promotion," S.Rep. No. 91–566, p. 16, the Conference Committee replaced this language with "State *law* with respect to advertising or promotion." In such a situation, § 5(b)'s pre-emption of "state law" cannot fairly be limited to positive enactments.

That the pre-emptive scope of § 5(b) cannot be limited to positive enactments does not mean that that section pre-empts all common law claims. For example, as respondents concede, § 5(b) does not generally pre-empt "state-law obligations to avoid marketing cigarettes with manufacturing defects or to use a demonstrably safer alternative design for cigarettes." For purposes of § 5(b), the common law is not of a piece.

Nor does the statute indicate that any familiar subdivision of common law claims is or is not pre-empted. We therefore cannot follow petitioner's passing suggestion that § 5(b) pre-empts liability for omissions but not for acts, or that § 5(b) pre-empts liability for unintentional torts but not for intentional torts. Instead we must fairly but—in light of the strong presumption against pre-emption—narrowly construe the precise language of § 5(b) and we must look to each of petitioner's common law claims to determine whether it is in fact pre-empted.[3] The central inquiry in each case is straightforward: we ask whether the legal duty that is the predicate of the common law damages action constitutes a "requirement or prohibition based on smoking and health * * * imposed under State law with respect to * * * advertising or promotion," giving that clause a fair but narrow reading. As discussed below, each phrase within that clause limits the universe of common law claims pre-empted by the statute.

We consider each category of damages actions in turn. In doing so, we express no opinion on whether these actions are viable claims as a matter of state law; we assume *arguendo* that they are.

FAILURE TO WARN

To establish liability for a failure to warn, petitioner must show that "a warning is necessary to make a product * * * reasonably safe, suitable and fit for its intended use," that respondents failed to provide such a warning, and that that failure was a proximate cause of petitioner's injury. Tr. 12738. In this case, petitioner offered two closely related theories concerning the failure to warn: first, that respondents "were negligent in the manner [that] they tested, researched, sold, promoted, and advertised" their cigarettes; and second, that respondents failed to provide "adequate warnings of the health consequences of cigarette smoking." App. 85–86.

Petitioner's claims are pre-empted to the extent that they rely on a state law "requirement or prohibition * * * with respect to * * * advertising or promotion." Thus, insofar as claims under either failure to warn theory require a showing that respondents' post–1969 advertising or promotions should have included additional, or more clearly stated, warnings, those claims are pre-empted. The Act does not, however, pre-empt petitioner's claims that rely solely on respondents' testing or research practices or other actions unrelated to advertising or promotion.

---

3. Petitioner makes much of the fact that Congress did not expressly include common law within § 5's pre-emptive reach, as it has in other statutes. See, *e.g.*, 29 U.S.C. § 1144(c)(1); 12 U.S.C. § 1715z-17(d). Respondents make much of the fact that Congress did not include a savings clause preserving common law claims, again, as it has in other statutes. See, *e.g.*, 17 U.S.C. § 301. Under our analysis of § 5, these omissions make perfect sense: Congress was neither pre-empting nor saving common law as a whole—it was simply pre-empting particular common law claims, while saving others.

BREACH OF EXPRESS WARRANTY

Petitioner's claim for breach of an express warranty arises under N.J.Stat.Ann. § 12A:2–313(1)(a) (West 1991), which provides:

> "Any affirmation of fact or promise made by the seller to the buyer which relates to the goods and becomes part of the basis of the bargain creates an express warranty that the goods shall conform to the affirmation or promise."

Petitioner's evidence of an express warranty consists largely of statements made in respondents' advertising. See 893 F.2d, at 574, 576; 683 F.Supp. 1487, 1497 (N.J.1988). Applying the Court of Appeals' ruling that Congress pre-empted "damage[s] actions * * * that challenge * * * the propriety of a party's actions with respect to the advertising and promotion of cigarettes," 789 F.2d, at 187, the District Court ruled that this claim "inevitably brings into question [respondents'] advertising and promotional activities, and is therefore pre-empted" after 1965. 649 F.Supp., at 675. As demonstrated above, however, the 1969 Act does not sweep so broadly: the appropriate inquiry is not whether a claim challenges the "propriety" of advertising and promotion, but whether the claim would require the imposition under state law of a requirement or prohibition based on smoking and health with respect to advertising or promotion.

A manufacturer's liability for breach of an express warranty derives from, and is measured by, the terms of that warranty. Accordingly, the "requirements" imposed by an express warranty claim are not "imposed under State law," but rather imposed *by the warrantor*.[4] If, for example, a manufacturer expressly promised to pay a smoker's medical bills if she contracted emphysema, the duty to honor that promise could not fairly be said to be "imposed under state law," but rather is best understood as undertaken by the manufacturer itself. While the general duty not to breach warranties arises under state law, the particular "requirement * * * based on smoking and health * * * with respect to the advertising or promotion [of] cigarettes" in an express warranty claim arises from the manufacturer's statements in its advertisements. In short, a common law remedy for a contractual commitment voluntarily undertaken should not be regarded as a "requirement * * * *imposed under State law*" within the meaning of § 5(b).[5]

---

4. Thus it is that express warranty claims are said to sound in contract rather than in tort. Compare Black's Law Dictionary 1489 (6th ed. 1990) (defining "tort": "There must always be a violation of some duty * * * and generally such duty must arise by operation of law and not by mere agreement of the parties") with *id.*, at 322 (defining "contract": "An agreement between two * * * persons which creates an obligation").

5. Justice SCALIA contends that because the general duty to honor express warranties arises under state law, every express warranty obligation is a "requirement * * * imposed under State law," and that, therefore, the Act pre-empts petitioner's express warranty claim. Justice SCALIA might be correct if the Act pre-empted *"liability"* imposed under state law (as he suggests, *post*, at 298); but instead the Act expressly pre-empts only a *"requirement or prohibition"* imposed under state law. That a "contract has no legal force apart from the [state] law that acknowledges its binding character," *Norfolk & Western Railway Co. v. American Train Dispatchers*

That the terms of the warranty may have been set forth in advertisements rather than in separate documents is irrelevant to the preemption issue (though possibly not to the state law issue of whether the alleged warranty is valid and enforceable) because although the breach of warranty claim is made "with respect to advertising" it does not rest on a duty imposed under state law. Accordingly, to the extent that petitioner has a viable claim for breach of express warranties made by respondents, that claim is not pre-empted by the 1969 Act.

FRAUDULENT MISREPRESENTATION

Petitioner alleges two theories of fraudulent misrepresentation. First, petitioner alleges that respondents, through their advertising, neutralized the effect of federally mandated warning labels. Such a claim is predicated on a state-law prohibition against statements in advertising and promotional materials that tend to minimize the health hazards associated with smoking. Such a *prohibition*, however, is merely the converse of a state law *requirement* that warnings be included in advertising and promotional materials. Section 5(b) of the 1969 Act pre-empts both requirements and prohibitions; it therefore supersedes petitioner's first fraudulent misrepresentation theory.

* * *

Petitioner's second theory, as construed by the District Court, alleges intentional fraud and misrepresentation both by "false representation of a material fact [and by] conceal[ment of] a material fact." Tr. 12727. The predicate of this claim is a state law duty not to make false statements of material fact or to conceal such facts. Our pre-emption analysis requires us to determine whether such a duty is the sort of requirement or prohibition proscribed by § 5(b).

Section 5(b) pre-empts only the imposition of state law obligations "with respect to the advertising or promotion" of cigarettes. Petitioner's claims that respondents concealed material facts are therefore not pre-empted insofar as those claims rely on a state law duty to disclose such facts through channels of communication other than advertising or promotion. Thus, for example, if state law obliged respondents to disclose material facts about smoking and health to an administrative agency, § 5(b) would not pre-empt a state law claim based on a failure to fulfill that obligation.

Moreover, petitioner's fraudulent misrepresentation claims that do arise with respect to advertising and promotions (most notably claims based on allegedly false statements of material fact made in advertisements) are not pre-empted by § 5(b). Such claims are not predicated on a duty "based on smoking and health" but rather on a more general obligation—the duty not to deceive. This understanding of fraud by

Assn., 499 U.S. ___, ___, 111 S.Ct. 1156, 1164, 113 L.Ed.2d 95 (1991), does not mean that every contractual provision is "imposed under State law." To the contrary, common understanding dictates that a contractual requirement, although only enforceable under state law, is not "imposed" by the state, but rather is "imposed" by the contracting party upon itself.

intentional misstatement is appropriate for several reasons. First, in the 1969 Act, Congress offered no sign that it wished to insulate cigarette manufacturers from longstanding rules governing fraud. To the contrary, both the 1965 and the 1969 Acts explicitly reserved the FTC's authority to identify and punish deceptive advertising practices—an authority that the FTC had long exercised and continues to exercise. See § 5(c) of the 1965 Act; § 7(b) of the 1969 Act; see also nn. 7, 9, *supra*. This indicates that Congress intended the phrase "relating to smoking and health" (which was essentially unchanged by the 1969 Act) to be construed narrowly, so as not to proscribe the regulation of deceptive advertising.

Moreover, this reading of "based on smoking and health" is wholly consistent with the purposes of the 1969 Act. State law prohibitions on false statements of material fact do not create "diverse, nonuniform, and confusing" standards. Unlike state law obligations concerning the warning necessary to render a product "reasonably safe," state law proscriptions on intentional fraud rely only on a single, uniform standard: falsity. Thus, we conclude that the phrase "based on smoking and health" fairly but narrowly construed does not encompass the more general duty not to make fraudulent statements. Accordingly, petitioner's claim based on allegedly fraudulent statements made in respondents' advertisements are not pre-empted by § 5(b) of the 1969 Act.[6]

CONSPIRACY TO MISREPRESENT OR CONCEAL MATERIAL FACTS

Petitioner's final claim alleges a conspiracy among respondents to misrepresent or conceal material facts concerning the health hazards of smoking. The predicate duty underlying this claim is a duty not to conspire to commit fraud. For the reasons stated in our analysis of petitioner's intentional fraud claim, this duty is not pre-empted by § 5(b) for it is not a prohibition "based on smoking and health" as that phrase is properly construed. Accordingly, we conclude that the 1969 Act does not pre-empt petitioner's conspiracy claim.

VI

To summarize our holding: The 1965 Act did not pre-empt state law damages actions; the 1969 Act pre-empts petitioner's claims based on a

---

6. Both Justice Blackmun and Justice Scalia challenge the level of generality employed in our analysis. Justice Blackmun contends that, as a matter of consistency, we should construe failure-to-warn claims *not* as based on smoking and health, but rather as based on the broader duty "to inform consumers of known risks." *Post*, at 2631. Justice SCALIA contends that, again as a matter of consistency, we should construe fraudulent misrepresentation claims *not* as based on a general duty not to deceive but rather as "based on smoking and health." Admittedly, each of these positions has some conceptual attraction. However, our ambition here is not theoretical elegance, but rather a fair understanding of congressional purpose.

To analyze failure to warn claims at the highest level of generality (as Justice Blackmun would have us do) would render the 1969 amendments almost meaningless and would pay too little respect to Congress' substantial reworking of the Act. On the other hand, to analyze fraud claims at the lowest level of generality (as Justice Scalia would have us do) would conflict both with the background presumption against pre-emption and with legislative history that plainly expresses an intent to preserve the "police regulations" of the States. [Citation] failure to warn and the neutralization of federally mandated warnings to the extent that those claims rely on omissions or inclusions in respondents' advertising or promotions; the 1969 Act does not pre-empt petitioner's claims based on express warranty, intentional fraud and misrepresentation, or conspiracy.

The judgment of the Court of Appeals is accordingly reversed in part and affirmed in part, and the case is remanded for further proceedings consistent with this opinion.

It is so ordered.

JUSTICE BLACKMUN, with whom JUSTICE KENNEDY and JUSTICE SOUTER join, concurring in part, concurring in the judgment in part, and dissenting in part.

I

* * * Our precedents do not allow us to infer a scope of pre-emption beyond that which clearly is mandated by Congress' language. In my view, *neither* version of the federal legislation at issue here provides the kind of unambiguous evidence of congressional intent necessary to displace state common-law damages claims. I therefore join parts I, II, III, and IV of the Court's opinion, but dissent from parts V and VI.

* * *

I * * * agree with the Court's application of the foregoing principles in part IV of its opinion, where it concludes that none of petitioner's common-law damages claims are pre-empted by the 1965 Act. * * *.

II

* * * Given the Court's proper analytical focus on the scope of the express pre-emption provisions at issue here and its acknowledgement that the 1965 Act does not pre-empt state common-law damages claims, I find the Court's conclusion that the 1969 Act pre-empts at least some common-law damages claims little short of baffling. In my view, the modified language of § 5(b), 15 U.S.C. § 1334(b) ("No requirement or prohibition based on smoking and health shall be imposed under State law with respect to the advertising or promotion of any cigarettes the packages of which are labeled in conformity with the provisions of this Act"), no more "clearly" or "manifestly" exhibits an intent to pre-empt state common-law damages actions than did the language of its predecessor in the 1965 Act. * * *.

* * *

More important, the question whether common-law damages actions exert a regulatory effect on manufacturers analogous to that of positive enactments—an assumption crucial to the Court's conclusion that the phrase "requirement or prohibition" encompasses common-law actions—is significantly more complicated than the Court's brief quotation from *San Diego Building Trades Council v. Garmon*, 359 U.S. 236, 247, 79 S.Ct. 773, 780, 3 L.Ed.2d 775 (1959), see *ante*, at 2620, would suggest.

The effect of tort law on a manufacturer's behavior is necessarily indirect. Although an award of damages by its very nature attaches additional consequences to the manufacturer's continued unlawful conduct, no particular course of action (*e.g.*, the adoption of a new warning label) is required. A manufacturer found liable on, for example, a failure-to-warn claim may respond in a number of ways. It may decide to accept damages awards as a cost of doing business and not alter its behavior in any way. See *Goodyear Atomic Corp. v. Miller*, 486 U.S. 174, 185–186, 108 S.Ct. 1704, 1712–1713, 100 L.Ed.2d 158 (1988) (corporation "may choose to disregard [state] safety regulations and simply pay an additional" damages award if an employee is injured as a result of a safety violation). Or, by contrast, it may choose to avoid future awards by dispensing warnings through a variety of alternative mechanisms, such as package inserts, public service advertisements, or general educational programs. The level of choice that a defendant retains in shaping its own behavior distinguishes the indirect regulatory effect of the common law from positive enactments such as statutes and administrative regulations. See *Dewey v. R. J. Reynolds Tobacco Co.*, 121 N.J. 69, 90, 577 A.2d 1239, 1249 (1990); Garner, Cigarette Dependency and Civil Liability: A Modest Proposal, 53 S.Cal.L.Rev. 1423, 1454 (1980). Moreover, tort law has an entirely separate function—compensating victims—that sets it apart from direct forms of regulation. See *Ferebee v. Chevron Chemical Co.*, 237 U.S.App.D.C. 164, 175, 736 F.2d 1529, 1540, cert. denied, 469 U.S. 1062, 105 S.Ct. 545, 83 L.Ed.2d 432 (1984).

* * *

In light of the recognized distinction in this Court's jurisprudence between direct state regulation and the indirect regulatory effects of common-law damages actions, it cannot be said that damages claims are clearly or unambiguously "requirements" or "prohibitions" imposed under state law. The plain language of the 1969 Act's modified preemption provision simply cannot bear the broad interpretation the Court would impart to it.

* * *

III

Stepping back from the specifics of the Court's pre-emption analysis to view the result the Court ultimately reaches, I am further disturbed. Notwithstanding the Court's ready acknowledgement that " '[t]he purpose of Congress is the ultimate touchstone' of pre-emption analysis," *ante*, at 2617 (quoting *Malone v. White Motor Corp.*, 435 U.S. 497, 504, 98 S.Ct. 1185, 1190, 55 L.Ed.2d 443 (1978)), the Court proceeds to create a crazy quilt of pre-emption from among the common-law claims implicated in this case, and in so doing reaches a result that Congress surely could not have intended.

The most obvious problem with the Court's analysis is its frequent shift in the level of generality at which it examines the individual claims. For example, the Court states that fraudulent misrepresentation claims

(at least those involving false statements of material fact in advertisements) are "not predicated on a duty 'based on smoking and health' but
rather on a more general obligation—the duty not to deceive," and
therefore are not pre-empted by § 5(b) of the 1969 Act. *Ante*, at 2623–
2624. Yet failure to warn claims—which could just as easily be described as based on a "more general obligation" to inform consumers of
known risks— * * * implicitly are found to be "based on smoking and
health" and are declared pre-empted. See *ante*, at 2621. The Court
goes on to hold that express warranty claims are not pre-empted because
the duty at issue is undertaken by the manufacturer and is not "imposed
under State law." *Ante*, at 2622. Yet, as the Court itself must acknowledge, "the *general duty* not to breach warranties arises under state law,"
ibid. (emphasis added); absent the State's decision to penalize such
behavior through the creation of a common-law damages action, no
warranty claim would exist.

In short, I can perceive no principled basis for many of the Court's
asserted distinctions among the common-law claims, and I cannot believe
that Congress intended to create such a hodge-podge of allowed and
disallowed claims when it amended the pre-emption provision in 1970.
Although the Court acknowledges that § 5(b) fails to "indicate that any
familiar subdivision of common law claims is or is not pre-empted," *ante*,
at 2621, it ignores the simplest and most obvious explanation for the
statutory silence: that Congress never intended to displace state common-law damages claims, much less to cull through them in the manner
the Court does today. I can only specul te as to the difficulty lower
courts will encounter in attempting to implement the Court's decision.

* * *

JUSTICE SCALIA, with whom JUSTICE THOMAS joins, concurring in the
judgment in part and dissenting in part.

Today's decision announces what, on its face, is an extraordinary
and unprecedented principle of federal statutory construction: that
express pre-emption provisions must be construed narrowly, "in light of
the presumption against the pre-emption of state police power regulations." *Ante*, at 2618. The life-span of this new rule may have been
blessedly brief, inasmuch as the opinion that gives it birth in Part I
proceeds to ignore it in Part V, by adjudging at least some of the
common-law tort claims at issue here pre-empted. In my view, there is
no merit to this newly crafted doctrine of narrow construction. Under
the Supremacy Clause, U.S. Const., Art. VI, cl. 2, our job is to interpret
Congress's decrees of pre-emption neither narrowly nor broadly, but in
accordance with their apparent meaning. If we did that job in the
present case, we would find, under the 1965 Act, pre-emption of the
petitioner's failure-to-warn claims; and under the 1969 Act, we would
find pre-emption of the petitioner's claims complete.

I

The Court's threshold description of the law of pre-emption is
accurate enough: Though we generally " 'assum[e] that the historic

police powers of the States [are] not to be superseded by * * * Federal Act unless that [is] the clear and manifest purpose of Congress,' " *ante*, at 2617 (quoting *Rice v. Santa Fe Elevator Corp.*, 331 U.S. 218, 230, 67 S.Ct. 1146, 1152, 91 L.Ed. 1447 (1947), we have traditionally not thought that to require express statutory text. Where state law is in actual conflict with federal law, see, *e.g., Pacific Gas & Elec. Co. v. Energy Resources Conservation and Development Comm'n*, 461 U.S. 190, 204, 103 S.Ct. 1713, 1722, 75 L.Ed.2d 752 (1983), or where it "stands as an obstacle to the accomplishment and execution of the full purposes and objectives of Congress," *Hines v. Davidowitz*, 312 U.S. 52, 67, 61 S.Ct. 399, 404, 85 L.Ed. 581 (1941), or even where the nature of Congress's regulation, or its scope, convinces us that "Congress left no room for the States to supplement it," *Rice, supra*, 331 U.S., at 230, 67 S.Ct., at 1152, we have had no difficulty declaring that state law must yield. The ultimate question in each case, as we have framed the inquiry, is one of Congress's intent, as revealed by the text, structure, purposes, and subject matter of the statutes involved. [Citations]

The Court goes beyond these traditional principles, however, to announce two new ones. First, it says that express pre-emption provisions must be given the narrowest possible construction. This is in its view the consequence of our oft-repeated assumption that, absent convincing evidence of statutory intent to pre-empt, " 'the historic police powers of the States [are] not to be superseded,' " see *ante*, at 2618–2619. But it seems to me that assumption dissolves once there is conclusive evidence of intent to pre-empt in the express words of the statute itself, and the only remaining question is what the *scope* of that pre-emption is meant to be. Thereupon, I think, our responsibility is to apply to the text ordinary principles of statutory construction.

That is precisely what our express pre-emption cases have done. [discussing cases]

In light of our willingness to find pre-emption in the absence of *any* explicit statement of pre-emptive intent, the notion that such explicit statements, where they exist, are subject to a "plain-statement" rule is more than somewhat odd. * * *.

The results seem odder still when one takes into account the second new rule that the Court announces: "When Congress has considered the issue of pre-emption and has included in the enacted legislation a provision explicitly addressing that issue, * * * we need only identify the domain expressly pre-empted by [that provision]." *Ante*, at 2618. Once there is an express pre-emption provision, in other words, all doctrines of implied pre-emption are eliminated. This proposition may be correct insofar as implied "field" pre-emption is concerned: The existence of an express pre-emption provision tends to contradict any inference that Congress intended to occupy a field broader than the statute's express language defines. However, with regard to implied "conflict" pre-emption—*i.e.*, where state regulation actually conflicts with federal law, or where state regulation "stands as an obstacle to the accomplishment and execution" of Congress's purposes, *Hines, supra*, 312 U.S., at 67, 61 S.Ct., at 404—the Court's second new rule works mischief. If taken seriously, it would mean, for example, that if a federal consumer protection law provided that no state agency or court shall assert jurisdiction under state law over any workplace safety issue with respect to which a federal standard is in effect, then a state agency operating under a law dealing with a subject other than workplace safety (*e.g.*, consumer protection) could impose requirements entirely contrary to federal law—forbidding, for example, the use of certain safety equipment that federal law requires. To my knowledge, we have never expressed such a rule before, and our prior cases are inconsistent with it, [citation]. When this second novelty is combined with the first, the result is extraordinary: The statute that says *anything* about pre-emption must say *everything* ; and it must do so with great exactitude, as any ambiguity concerning its scope will be read in favor of preserving state power. If this is to be the law, surely only the most sporting of congresses will dare to say anything about pre-emption.

The proper rule of construction for express pre-emption provisions is, it seems to me, the one that is customary for statutory provisions in general: Their language should be given its ordinary meaning. [Citations] When this suggests that the pre-emption provision was intended to sweep broadly, our construction must sweep broadly as well. [Citation] And when it bespeaks a narrow scope of pre-emption, so must our judgment. [Citation] Applying its niggardly rule of construction, the Court finds (not surprisingly) that none of petitioner's claims—common-law failure to warn, breach of express warranty, and intentional fraud and misrepresentation—is pre-empted under § 5(b) of the 1965 Act. And save for the failure-to-warn claims, the Court reaches the same result under § 5(b) of the 1969 Act. I think most of that is error. Applying ordinary principles of statutory construction, I believe petitioner's failure-to-warn claims are pre-empted by the 1965 Act, and all his common-law claims by the 1969 Act.

* * *

To the extent petitioner's claims are premised specifically on respondents' failure (during the period in which the 1965 Act was in force) to include in their *advertising* any statement relating to smoking and health, I would find those claims, no less than the similar post–1969 claims, pre-empted. * * * However, since § 5(b) of the 1965 Act enjoins only those laws that *require* "statement[s]" in cigarette advertising, those of petitioner's claims that, if accepted, would penalize statements *voluntarily* made by the cigarette companies must be deemed to survive. As these would appear to include petitioner's breach-of-express-warranty and intentional fraud and misrepresentation claims, I concur in the Court's judgment in this respect.

* * *

Like Justice Blackmun, "I can only speculate as to the difficulty lower courts will encounter in attempting to implement [today's] decision." *Ante*, at 2631 (opinion concurring in part and dissenting in part). Must express pre-emption provisions really be given their narrowest reasonable construction (as the Court says in Part III), or need they not (as the plurality does in Part V)? Are courts to ignore all doctrines of implied pre-emption whenever the statute at issue contains an express pre-emption provision, as the Court says today, or are they to continue to apply them, as we have in the past? For pre-emption purposes, does "state law" include legal duties imposed on voluntary acts (as we held last Term in *Norfolk & Western R. Co.*), or does it not (as the plurality says today)? These and other questions raised by today's decision will fill the law-books for years to come. A disposition that raises more questions than it answers does not serve the country well.

Notes

1. *Cipollone v. Liggett Group, Inc.* is noted in 16 Am.J. Trial Advoc. 477 (1992); 27 Ga.L.Rev. 253 (1992); 106 Harv.L.Rev. 347 (1992); 60 Tenn.L.Rev. 243 (1992); 24 Tex.Tech L.Rev. 223 (1993); 67 Tul.L.Rev. 787 (1993); and 70 U.Det.Mercy L.Rev. 487 (1993).

2. For an analysis of how *Cipollone v. Liggett Group, Inc.* has affected the law of preemption, *see* Ausness, Federal Preemption of State Products Liability Doctrines, 44 S.C.L.Rev. 187 (1993); Galligan, Product Liability— Cigarettes and *Cipollone* : What's Left? What's Gone? 53 La.L.Rev. 713 (1993).

3. Other federal statutes that arguably preempt common law actions include the following: the National Traffic and Motor Vehicle Safety Act, 15 U.S.C. §§ 1381–1420 (1988 & Supp. III 1992), the Federal Insecticide, Fungicide and Rodenticide Act, 7 U.S.C. §§ 136–136y (1988 & Supp. III 1991), and the Food, Drug and Cosmetic Act, 21 U.S.C. §§ 301–394 (1988 & Supp. III 1991). Numerous cases prior to *Cipollone* have decided preemption questions arising under these statutes. For an analysis of how *Cipollone* might have changed the law of preemption under these statutes, *see* Ausness, The Impact of the *Cipollone* Case on Federal Preemption Law, 15 J.Prod. & Toxics Liab. 1 (1993); Note, Preemption Doctrine After *Cipollone*—Nevada Supreme Court Holds that the Federal Insecticide, Fungicide, and Rodenticide Act Impliedly Preempts State Common-law Actions Based on Inadequate Labelling, 106 Harv.L.Rev. 963 (1993); Note, One Step Closer to Exterminating the FIFRA Preemption Controversy, 81 Ky.L.J. 749 (1993). Useful articles pre-dating *Cipollone* include the following: Miller, Deflating the Airbag Pre–Emption Controversy, 37 Emory L.J. 897 (1988); Scarlett, The Relationship Among Adverse Drug Reaction Reporting, Drug Labeling, Product Liability, and Federal Preemption, 46 Food Drug Cosm.L.J. 31 (1991); Wilton, Federalism Issues in "No Airbag" Tort Claims: Preemption and Reciprocal Comity, 61 Notre Dame L.Rev. 1 (1986).

4. In Elsworth v. Beech Aircraft Corp., 37 Cal.3d 540, 208 Cal.Rptr. 874, 691 P.2d 630 (1984) (en banc), cert. denied, 471 U.S. 1110, 105 S.Ct. 2345, 85 L.Ed.2d 861 (1985), the court stated:

[W]e begin with the observation that there is nothing inherently inconsistent in the proposition that even if the federal government has entirely occupied the field of regulating an activity a state may simultaneously grant damages for violation of such regulations.

This precept was recognized in the recent decision in *Silkwood v. Kerr–McGee Corp.* (1984) 464 U.S. 238, 104 S.Ct. 615, 78 L.Ed.2d 443. The court there acknowledged the "tension between the conclusion that safety regulation is the exclusive concern of the federal law and the conclusion that a state may nevertheless award damages based on its own law of liability," but held that in the field of nuclear safety regulation "Congress intended to stand by both concepts and to tolerate whatever tension there was between them." (Id. at p. 256, 104 S.Ct. at p. 625.)

In *Silkwood* the federal government had enacted regulations concerning the safety of nuclear power plants and the licensing of such plants. These regulations occupied the field of safety to the exclusion of state enactments on the subject. Nevertheless, the high court ruled that common law tort principles of Oklahoma law were applicable to hold the defendant employer liable to an employee for compensatory and punitive damages as the result of radiation at the defendant's plant. After a close analysis of the legislative background of federal laws relating to nuclear power, the court concluded that Congress had assumed persons injured by nuclear accidents were free to utilize state court remedies, and that "traditional principles of state tort law would apply with full force unless they were expressly supplanted." (Id. at p. 255, 104 S.Ct. at p. 625.)

37 Cal.3d at 549–550, 208 Cal.Rptr. at 879, 691 P.2d at 634–635.

Chapter 9

APPLICATION OF PRINCIPLES

SECTION A. MANUFACTURING FLAWS

LEE v. ELECTRIC MOTOR DIV.
Court of Appeal, Second District, 1985.
169 Cal.App.3d 375, 215 Cal.Rptr. 195.

THOMPSON, ASSOCIATE JUSTICE.

Plaintiffs Yong Lee and In Hak Lee appeal the adverse summary judgment granted on their consolidated actions seeking to impose liability for personal injury and loss of consortium against defendant component part manufacturer, Electric Motor Division, an unincorporated division of Gould, Inc., who manufactured and supplied the motor installed in the machine that injured Yong Lee.

* * *

Plaintiff Yong Lee was injured on January 15, 1979, while using the machine to grind meat. Her right hand was caught and crushed in the grinding mechanism, resulting in the amputation of her right hand and part of her forearm.

Plaintiffs filed their respective consolidated complaints for personal injury and loss of consortium based on theories of negligent design, manufacture and failure to warn, strict liability, and breach of warranty, against several parties, including defendant and Lasar.

Defendant's motion for summary judgment was granted on August 30, 1983. Summary judgment was filed on September 16, 1983, and notice was duly served and filed. Plaintiffs appeal from the summary judgment.

We will conclude that no triable issue of fact exists, and affirm the summary judgment.

* * *

DISCUSSION

Plaintiffs contend that the defective design and manufacture of the motor and the lack of a warning proximately caused Yong Lee's injury because had the motor stopped immediately when turned off, her injuries would have been less severe.

* * *

Although plaintiffs have phrased their complaints in terms of both defective manufacture and design, they have not properly alleged a cause of action based on a manufacturing defect. A manufacturing defect is readily identifiable in general, because the defective product is one that "comes off the assembly line in a substandard condition" in comparison with the other identical units. (*Barker, supra,* 20 Cal.3d at p. 429, 143 Cal.Rptr. 225, 573 P.2d 443.) Plaintiffs do not contend that the motor, as compared to the other identically manufactured motors, came off the assembly line in a substandard condition. Hence, we find that defendant is entitled to summary judgment as a matter of law on the causes of action based on the allegation of defective manufacture.

* * *

The summary judgment is affirmed.

LILLIE, P.J., and JOHNSON, J., concur.

Notes

1. California has approved the following jury instruction for manufacturing defect cases:

The _____ of a product is liable for injuries a cause of which was a defect in its manufacture which existed when it left possession of defendant[s], provided that the injury resulted from a use of the product that was reasonably foreseeable by the defendant[s].

A defect in the manufacture of a product exists if the product differs from the manufacturer's intended result or if the product differs from apparently identical products from the same manufacturer.

BAJI 9.00.3 (1992 Revision).

2. Some jurisdictions apply the consumer expectations test of defect in manufacturing defect cases and the risk-utility test in design defect cases. *See* Ford Motor Co. v. Pool, 688 S.W.2d 879 (Tex.App.—Texarkana 1985), affirmed in part and reversed in part on other grounds, 715 S.W.2d 629 (1986). The court stated:

There are two different definitions of defectiveness for use in products liability cases in Texas. In cases involving manufacturing defects, defectiveness is defined according to a consumer expectancy test * * *. In design defect cases, defective design must be defined according to the risk-utility test * * *.

* * *

The two definitions reflect the differences between the theories of recovery underlying manufacturing and design defect cases. The application of Section 402A of the Restatement (Second) of Torts (1965) to cases involving not only flawed products, but also to perfectly made but ill-designed products, has necessarily divided what was ostensibly a single theory of liability into two distinct theories. The distinction arises partly because of the inherent difference between the analysis centered on a flawed product and a product defectively designed.

Manufacturing defect cases involve products which are flawed, i.e., which do not conform to the manufacturer's own specifications, and are not identical to their mass-produced siblings. The flaw theory is based upon a fundamental consumer expectancy: that a mass-produced product will not differ from its siblings in a manner that makes it more dangerous than the others. Defective design cases, however, are not based on consumer expectancy, but on the manufacturer's design of a product which makes it unreasonably dangerous, even though not flawed in its manufacture. See Powers, The Persistence of Fault in Products Liability, 61 Texas L.Rev. 777 (1983); Keeton, Product Liability and the Meaning of Defect, 5 St. Mary's L.J. 30 (1973). * * *

688 S.W.2d at 881. *See also* Dart v. Wiebe Mfg., Inc., 147 Ariz. 242, 709 P.2d 876 (1985); Bilotta v. Kelley Co., Inc., 346 N.W.2d 616 (Minn.1984).

3. In Wiseman v. Goodyear Tire & Rubber Co., 29 Wash.App. 883, 631 P.2d 976 (1981) plaintiff was injured in an motor vehicle accident involving a blowout. He sued the tire manufacturer claiming that a flaw in the tire caused the blowout. The jury found for defendant after being instructed that they must find that the tire was both 1) defective and 2) unreasonably dangerous. Plaintiff appealed, claiming that the judge erred by requiring the jury to find both elements. He should, instead, have required the jury to find only that the tire was defective. Plaintiff relied on Seattle–First National Bank v. Tabert, 86 Wash.2d 145, 542 P.2d 774 (1975) (en banc), holding that in a design defect case plaintiff need not prove both defect and unreasonable danger because a product that is "unreasonably dangerous" is "necessarily defective." The court ruled against plaintiff, stating:

In effect, [Plaintiff] urges us to state the converse of *Tabert* as the law, namely, that if a product has a manufacturing defect, it must necessarily be unreasonably dangerous. We decline to do so. Although there is some validity in equating the two concepts in a design defect case, *see Seattle–First Nat'l Bank v. Tabert, supra* at 151, the connection between defect in a product and unreasonable danger from the product assumes a different meaning in a manufacturing defect case. * * * Some products defectively manufactured are still reasonably safe for the consumer. A car with an inadequate heater is defective but not unreasonably dangerous; a defective toaster which always chars bread is not unreasonably dangerous; a defective television set which receives only half the channels because of frequency limitations is not unreasonably unsafe. Thus, in order for a product to be defective in a manufacturing sense, it must be " 'in a condition not contemplated by the ultimate consumer, [and] which [is] unreasonably dangerous to him.' " Bombardi v. Pochel's Appliance & TV Co., 10 Wash.App. 243, 246, 518 P.2d 202 (1973), citing Restatement (Second) of Torts § 402A, comment g at 351 (1965); *see* Curtiss v. YMCA, 82 Wash.2d 455, 511 P.2d 991 (1973). * * *

29 Wash.App. at 887–88, 631 P.2d at 979–80.

4. In manufacturing flaw cases, liability is truly strict. The seller is liable even if it has "exercised all possible care in the preparation" of its product. Restatement of Torts (Second) § 402A(2)(a) (1965). The economic justification for strict liability in such cases is set out in the following article.

LANDES AND POSNER, A POSITIVE ECONOMIC ANALYSIS OF PRODUCTS LIABILITY
14 J. Legal Stud. 535, 555–56 (1985).

* * *

2. *Process Failure.* Here the concept of strict liability has bite, as it does not in the defective design setting. Take the case where the cost-justified level of hygiene in a soft-drink plant allows mouse parts to get into one in every million bottles. By assumption there is no negligence; yet the bottle that contains the mouse parts is "defective" as a matter of products liability law, and if the consumer is made ill, the manufacturer will be liable. This result makes economic sense, however, because of the asymmetrical position of the manufacturer and the consumer with regard to avoiding this type of accident. The consumer can do nothing at reasonable cost, in the short or long run, to prevent the accident. It is out of the question that he should minutely inspect each soda bottle on the one in a million chance that it contains mouse parts. (Of course, if he does notice the mouse parts and drinks the soda anyway, he would be barred by assumption of risk from obtaining damages.) But while by assumption there is nothing cost justified the manufacturer can do *at present* to reduce the probability of the accident (otherwise he would be negligent), advances in technology may someday enable him to reduce it at a lower cost than the benefit in reducing expected accident costs. Under a negligence standard the manufacturer will simply wait till the technology is developed; strict liability will give him an incentive to foster its development. True, it will simultaneously reduce the incentive of the consumer (or of businesses that might sell to the consumer) to develop better inspection methods, but it is a reasonable guess that preserving such an incentive would lead nowhere. In addition, strict liability will result in a small price increase (to cover the cost of the occasional tort judgment), which will in turn result in a small reduction in output and in a substitution by consumers of other, safer products.

It is true that, to a perfectly informed consumer, the price increase resulting from strict liability would not be a net cost. It would just offset the benefit he would be receiving from shifting to the manufacturer the cost of injuries caused by the product; the full cost of the product to the consumer (the price adjusted for any expected accident cost he bears) would be unchanged. But now the point recurs that it does not pay consumers to obtain information about small product risks. Suppose that in making his purchasing decisions the consumer will treat minute risks as zero risks; that is, they will not affect his decisions. This is not because of any psychological peculiarity but simply because it does not pay to figure out and possibly take measures against extremely remote contingencies. Then in a world of no liability output will exceed the optimal output (see equation (5)), and the manufacturer will not have an incentive to take due care. Shifting to strict liability will result in a price increase to cover the manufacturer's expected products liability costs, and the higher price will be perceived by the consumer as an increase in the full cost of the product (because he does not realize that the price increase is compensating him for an expected accident cost), and there will be some substitution away from the product. Thus, as noted earlier, the information about risk is impounded in the higher price and "communicated" to the consumer in a form that he can understand without investing in costly information. Finally, because the manufacturer aggregates the expected accident costs of all his present and future customers, an imperceptible cost to the individual consumer becomes a noticeable cost to the manufacturer, inducing him to look for ways of making long-run improvements in safety.

The process just described illustrates our earlier point that strict liability is a sensible rule when one wants to influence the level of the potential injurer's activity. Assuming that the costs of information are much higher to the buyer than to the seller, a negligence rule would not give the buyer the correct incentive to substitute away from the product. A rule of strict liability, by inducing the seller to sell less, automatically reduces the buyer's purchases. The only way to induce a change in the mutual activity of seller and buyer is to give the seller an incentive to change the activity level, and strict liability does that.

3. *Component Defect or Failure.* The analysis here is similar to that of process failure. The consumer can do little to detect a failure in a component of the product he buys. The manufacturer of the final product, though by definition not negligent in failing to detect the defect in the component (if he were, again there would be no need to invoke a distinctive body of products liability law), is less helpless than the consumer. The manufacturer can identify the component that failed more easily than the consumer can, and can take appropriate action, legal or business, against the supplier of the component. He can also raise his price to cover potential liability costs and so induce substitution by the consumer away from products that have this hazard. And he has an incentive to explore long-run improvements in inspecting for component defects.

HUNT v. FERGUSON–PAULUS ENTERPRISES

Supreme Court of Oregon, Department 2, 1966.
243 Or. 546, 415 P.2d 13.

Lusk, J.

The plaintiff bought a cherry pie from the defendant through a vending machine owned and maintained by the defendant. On biting into the pie one of plaintiff's teeth was broken when it encountered a cherry pit. He brought this action to recover damages for the injury, alleging breach of warranty of fitness of the pie for human consumption. In a trial to the court without a jury the court found for the defendant and plaintiff has appealed.

Plaintiff assigns error to the court's failure to sustain his objection to a general finding entered in favor of the defendant and to the court's refusal to enter special findings requested by the plaintiff [that plaintiff did not and a reasonable consumer would not] expect to find a pit in the cherry pie.

* * *

Under ORS 72.3150 if the cherry pie purchased by the plaintiff from the defendant was not reasonably fit for human consumption because of the presence of the cherry pit there was a breach of warranty and plaintiff was entitled to recover his damages thereby caused.

In the consideration of similar cases some of the courts have drawn a distinction between injury caused by spoiled, impure, or contaminated food or food containing a foreign substance, and injury caused by a substance natural to the product sold. In the latter class of cases, these courts hold there is no liability on the part of the dispenser of the food. Thus in the leading case of Mix v. Ingersoll Candy Co., 6 Cal.2d 674, 59 P.2d 144, the court held that a patron of a restaurant who ordered and paid for chicken pie, which contained a sharp sliver or fragment of chicken bone, and was injured as a result of swallowing the bone, had no cause of action against the restaurateur either for breach of warranty or negligence. Referring to cases in which recovery had been allowed the court said:

"All of the cases are instances in which the food was found not to be reasonably fit for human consumption, either by reason of the presence of a foreign substance, or an impure and noxious condition of the food itself, such as for example, glass, stones, wires or nails in the food served, or tainted, decayed, diseased, or infected meats or vegetables."

The court went on to say that:

" * * * despite the fact that a chicken bone may occasionally be encountered in a chicken pie, such chicken pie, in the absence of some further defect, is reasonably fit for human consumption. Bones which are natural to the type of meat served cannot legitimately be called a foreign substance, and a consumer who eats meat dishes ought to anticipate and be on his guard against the presence of such bones."

* * *

The so-called "foreign-natural" test of the *Mix* case has been applied in the following cases: Silva v. F.W. Woolworth Co., 28 Cal.App.2d 649, 83 P.2d 76 (turkey bone in "special plate" of roast turkey); Musso v. Picadilly Cafeterias, Inc. (La.App.), 178 So.2d 421 (cherry pit in a cherry pie); Courter v. Dilbert Bros., Inc., 19 Misc.2d 935, 186 N.Y.S.2d 334 (prune pit in prune butter); Adams v. Great Atlantic & Pacific Tea Co., 251 N.C. 565, 112 S.E.2d 92 (crystalized [sic] grain of corn in cornflakes); Webster v. Blue Ship Tea Room, Inc., 347 Mass. 421, 198 N.E.2d 309 (fish bone in a fish chowder).

Other courts have rejected the so-called foreign-natural test in favor of what is known as the "reasonable expectation" test, among them the Supreme Court of Wisconsin, which, in Betehia v. Cape Cod Corp., 10 Wis.2d 323, 103 N.W.2d 64, held that a person who was injured by a chicken bone in a chicken sandwich served to him in a restaurant, could recover for his injury either for breach of an implied warranty or for negligence. "There is a distinction," the court said, "between what a consumer expects to find in a fish stick and in a baked or fried fish, or in a chicken sandwich made from sliced white meat and in roast chicken. The test should be what is reasonably expected by the consumer in the food as served, not what might be natural to the ingredients of that food prior to preparation. What is to be reasonably expected by the consumer is a jury question in most cases; at least, we cannot say as a matter of law that a patron of a restaurant must expect a bone in a chicken sandwich either because chicken bones are occasionally found there or are natural to chicken." 10 Wis.2d at 331–332.

Among other decisions adopting the reasonable expectation test are: Bonenberger v. Pittsburgh Mercantile Co., 345 Pa. 559, 28 A.2d 913, 143 A.L.R. 1417, Annotation at page 1421 (oyster shell in canned oysters used in making oyster stew); Bryer v. Rath Packing Co., 221 Md. 105, 156 A.2d 442, 77 A.L.R.2d 1 (chicken bone in chow mein); Varone v. Calarco, 22 Misc.2d 1085, 199 N.Y.S.2d 755 (struvite in canned tuna).

* * *

The foreign-natural test is criticized in Dickerson, Products Liability and the Food Consumer 184–189, and in an article by Mitchel J. Ezer, "The Impact of the Uniform Commercial Code on the California Law of Sales Warranties," 8 UCLA California Law Review 281.

In view of the judgment for the defendant, we are not required in this case to make a choice between the two rules. Under the foreign-natural test the plaintiff would be barred from recovery as a matter of law. The reasonable expectation test calls for determination of a question of fact * * *. The court has found the fact in favor of the defendant and this court has no power to disturb the finding.

Plaintiff argues that the court based its decision on the foreign-natural rule. The court did so indicate in a letter to counsel announcing its decision, but in the same letter the court also spoke of what can be "reasonably anticipated and guarded against by the consumer" and said that the question was a "mixed question of law and facts." Further, the court, as above stated, refused to make a finding of fact requested by the plaintiff that the plaintiff "did not reasonably expect to find a pit in the cherry pie." The general finding entered by the court covered all the issues of fact in the case.

* * *

There are no other assignments of error and the judgment is affirmed.

Note

1. The courts remain split over whether to apply the consumer expectations test or the foreign-natural test in impure food cases. The cases are collected in, Annotation, 2 A.L.R.5th 189 (1992). Most courts that decline to impose liability for natural substances found in food apply the rule regardless of whether the action is based on breach of warranty, negligence, or strict tort liability.

2. The argument for the consumer expectations test is presented in Jackson v. Nestle–Beich, Inc., 212 Ill.App.3d 296, 155 Ill.Dec. 508, 569 N.E.2d 1119 (1991), affirmed, 147 Ill.2d 408, 168 Ill.Dec. 147, 589 N.E.2d 547 (1992):

The position of the courts which reject the doctrine is stated in *Betehia v. Cape Cod Corp.*[, 10 Wis.2d 323, 103 N.W.2d 64 (1960)]:

"The 'foreign-natural' test applied as a matter of law does not recommend itself to us as being logical or desirable. It is true one can expect a T-bone in T-bone steak, chicken bones in roast chicken, pork bone in a pork chop, pork bone in spare ribs, a rib bone in short ribs of beef, and fish bones in a whole baked or fried fish, but the expectation is based not on the naturalness of the particular bone to the meat, fowl, or fish, but on the type of dish served containing the meat, fowl, or fish. There is a distinction between what a consumer expects to find in a fish stick and in a baked or fried fish, or in a chicken sandwich made from sliced white meat and in roast chicken. The test should be what is reasonably expected by the consumer in the food as served, not what might be natural to the ingredients of that food prior to preparation. What is to be reasonably expected is a jury question in most cases; at least, we cannot say as a matter of law that a patron of a restaurant must expect a bone in a chicken sandwich either because chicken bones are occasionally found there or are natural to chicken." (*Betehia*, 10 Wis.2d 323, 331–32, 103 N.W.2d 64, 68–69.)

The Betehia comments are amplified in O'Dell v. DeJean's Packing Co., Inc. (Okla.Ct.App.1978), 585 P.2d 399:

* * *

"If one 'reasonably expects' to find an item in his or her food then he guards against being injured by watching for that item. When one eats a hamburger he does not nibble his way along hunting for bones because he is not 'reasonably expecting' one in the food. Likewise, when one eats processed oysters, normally one does not gingerly graze through each oyster hunting for a pearl because he is not 'reasonably expecting' one in the food. It seems logical some consideration should be given to the manner in which the food is normally eaten in determining if a person can be said to 'reasonably expect' an item in processed food. In the present case we think the average, ordinary, reasonably prudent person eating processed oysters would eat same by way of bites and would not nibble her way through each oyster because of the possibility of finding a pearl." *O'Dell*, 585 P.2d at 402.

* * *

A more pointed criticism is found in a note by Charles Janes entitled *Products Liability—The Test of Consumer Expectation for "Natural" Defects in Food Products* :

"With the prevalence of processed foods on the market today and the development of technology in the food industry, consumers increasingly rely upon food processors to inspect and purify the foods they consume. Many products today are even packaged in such a manner that inspection by the consumer is difficult if not impossible. One might imagine a consumer in a jurisdiction that applies the foreign-natural test tearing away the crust from a beef pot pie to search for tiny bones, or picking apart a cherry-nut ice cream cone to remove stray shells or pits.

In an era of consumerism, the foreign-natural standard is an anachronism. It flatly and unjustifiably protects food processors and sellers from liability even when the technology may be readily available to remove injurious natural objects from foods. The consumer expectation test, on the other hand, imposes no greater burden upon processors or sellers than to guarantee that their food products meet the standards of safety that consumers customarily and reasonably have come to expect from the food industry." 37 Ohio St.L.J. 634, 651–52 (1976).

115 Ill.Dec. at 511–12, 569 N.E.2d at 1123–24.

3. Jackson v. Nestle–Beich, Inc., 147 Ill.2d 408, 168 Ill.Dec. 147, 589 N.E.2d 547 (1992), affirming, 212 Ill.App.3d 296, 155 Ill.Dec. 508, 569 N.E.2d 1119 (1991) rejected the foreign-natural test in favor of the consumer expectations test. Justice Heiple dissented. He offered the following defense of the foreign-natural test:

The majority opinion in the instant case discards the foreign-natural doctrine and substitutes the reasonable expectation test. * * *

In truth, the reasonable expectation test is what gave rise to the foreign-natural doctrine. That is to say, since it would be reasonable to expect to find a nut shell in a product containing nuts, there would be no liability. Rather than approach each broken tooth or other injury on a case-by-case basis, it was deemed more expeditious and efficient to crystallize the matter into the foreign-natural doctrine. That doctrine both did justice and promoted judicial economy.

A reversion to the reasonable expectation test simply means that each food-related injury in this State will be subject to a lawsuit to determine whether the consumer's reasonable expectation was violated.

The costs will be significant, first to the manufacturers and second to the consuming public. It is axiomatic that all production costs eventually end up in the price of the product. Additionally, if the costs exceed profitability, the product leaves the market place altogether and the consumers lose choice, selection and availability of products.

The effects of this decision will go far beyond the defendant Nestle–Beich Company, whose candy caused a broken tooth. It extends to all manufacturers and purveyors of food products including the neighborhood baker, the hot dog vendor and the popcorn man. Watch out Orville Redenbacher!

The continued march towards strict and absolute liability for others (others meaning anyone not injured who has assets) and the absence of any responsibility by the injured for their own welfare takes yet another step with this majority ruling.

115 Ill.Dec. at 152–53, 589 N.E.2d at 552–53.

4. California originated the foreign-natural test in *Mix v. Ingersoll Candy Co.* It modified the test in Mexicali Rose v. Superior Court (Clark), 1 Cal.4th 617, 4 Cal.Rptr.2d 145, 822 P.2d 1292 (1992), and adopted the following test:

The strict foreign-natural test of *Mix, supra,* 6 Cal.2d 674, 59 P.2d 144, should be rejected as the exclusive test for determining liability when a substance natural to food injures a restaurant patron. We conclude instead that in deciding the liability of a restaurateur for injuries caused by harmful substances in food, the proper tests to be used by the trier of fact are as follows:

If the injury-producing substance is natural to the preparation of the food served, it can be said that it was reasonably expected by its very nature and the food cannot be determined unfit or defective. A plaintiff in such a case has no cause of action in strict liability or implied warranty. If, however, the presence of the natural substance is due to a restaurateur's failure to exercise due care in food preparation, the injured patron may sue under a negligence theory.

If the injury-causing substance is foreign to the food served, then the injured patron may also state a cause of action in implied warranty and strict liability, and the trier of fact will determine whether the substance (i) could be reasonably expected by the average consumer and (ii) rendered the food unfit or defective. * * *

Thus, we conclude that to the extent *Mix* precludes a cause of action in negligence when injuries are caused by substances natural to the preparation of the food served, it is overruled.

4 Cal.Rptr. at 157–58, 822 P.2d at 1303–04.

5. California normally uses the "deviation from the norm" test of defect in manufacturing flaw cases. *See Lee v. Electric Motor Div., supra,* at 308. This test could be applied in food cases. Instead, the California court applies a specialized combination of the "foreign-natural" test and "consumer expectations" test in food cases. Why?

SECTION B.   DESIGN DEFECTS

1. DELEGABILITY OF THE DESIGN PROCESS

BILOTTA v. KELLEY CO.

Supreme Court of Minnesota, 1984.
346 N.W.2d 616.

Heard, considered and decided by the court en banc.

WAHL, JUSTICE.

Albert J. Bilotta, Jr., suffered severe and permanent brain damage as the result of an industrial accident on December 5, 1977. He was pinned at the neck against a doorjamb when a forklift truck tipped over onto him at a warehouse loading dock. He filed this lawsuit through his special guardian, alleging strict liability, negligence and breach of warranty against [several defendants, including] Kelley Company (Kelley), the manufacturer of the dockboard.

* * *

The jury returned a verdict finding Kelley strictly liable * * * and assessed $2,300,000 in damages.

Kelley appeals from the trial court's denial of its post-trial motions for a JNOV or a new trial * * *.

A. THE PRODUCT

Dockboards are used to bridge the gap between a loading dock and a carrier bed. Personnel and various types of forklift trucks then maneuver across the board to load or unload the carrier. Ninety percent of all dockboards are portable plates that are manually placed over the gap. The other ten percent are either mechanical or hydraulic operations.

Mechanical dockboards are operated by raising the ramp component and extending a hinged lip onto the carrier bed. They are installed over a recessed pit, giving the dockboard a capability of accommodating carrier beds either above or below the dock level. When not in use, the lip returns to a pendant position and the ramp is supported at dock level by steel legs underneath the ramp at each side.

When in use, a dockboard is supported on one side solely by the carrier bed. Thus, a major hazard at loading docks is that the carrier may become separated from the lip extension, leaving the dockboard without support on one side, perhaps with equipment and/or personnel on the dockboard at the time. This can occur either (1) if the semi truck pulls or rolls away with a load on the ramp or (2) if the angle of the lip is too steep for a forklift truck to ascend, in which case the forklift's drive wheels, upon hitting the lip, effectively push the carrier away from the dock.

In addressing the first hazard, Kelley's competitors universally employ a fixed safety leg, which prevents the dockboard from falling below dock level should the semi truck pull away. Kelley claims, however, that such a system in itself exacerbates the second hazard of the forklift pushing away the carrier. It claims that truck deflection from the weight of the load and forklift may cause the lip to drop below ramp level, while the fixed leg prevents the ramp from following the lip. The forklift driver either will not notice the deflection and resultant steep lip angle or will not bother to stop and manually adjust the legs.

Kelley addressed the hazard associated with truck deflection by its patented "cross-traffic legs." Upon raising the ramp, the lip automatically flips up. The lip flip in turn cams the safety leg into a retracted position. In this way the ramp and lip can "float" together up and down with the deflection of the carrier bed, thus preventing the creation of an angle dangerous to forklift operation. Without a load on the dock, the ramp would raise by its own upward bias, the lip would drop, and the cam would return the legs to their fixed position for support at dock level.

The cross-traffic leg, however, left the first hazard unaddressed. If the carrier pulled or rolled away while a heavy load was on the dock, there would not be time for the lip to drop and cam the safety legs into position, and thus the dockboard would fall to its lowest position. To prevent this occurrence, Kelley's engineers developed a "panic stop." This patented device is a notched post which "senses" the ramp's speed of descent and can catch a fall within 3 inches. Thus, Kelley's two patented devices corrected both hazards when used in combination, while its competitors addressed only one hazard.

Kelley's dockboards are priced above its competitors' models. In order to compete, Kelley offered both the fixed-leg safety system and the cross-traffic leg system, for which it offered a panic stop as a $200 option.

In 1970, Kelley developed Model 6280, which is a contractors' dockboard. It was "self-forming" in that it came equipped with a steel pan around which concrete for the dock was poured, thereby saving time and installation costs. It had a smaller recessed pit than the other mechanical model, Model 6081. Because of this, use of the panic stop in Model 6280 would require additional installation steps and would increase the per-unit price by several hundred dollars, to almost equal the prices of the 6081, a larger and higher-capacity board. Thus the 6280 was not marketed with a panic stop, but it did have retractable cross-traffic legs.

In 1971, the contractor for Safelite's Eagan warehouse * * * specified the Model 6081 with panic stops for its loading docks. To meet anticipated competitive bids * * * Kelley's distributor * * * requested and received permission to submit alternative bids. [The distributor's] * * * submitted bid on the 6280 contractors' boards, without panic stops, was eventually accepted to save time and costs in construction.

B. THE ACCIDENT

On December 5, 1977, Albert Bilotta, age 20, * * * was sent to the Safelite warehouse * * * [and was] assigned general clean-up chores near the loading dock. * * * [Another worker] was unloading pallets from a semitrailer with a forklift truck. He was using the Kelley dockboard a few inches above dock level. * * * [T]he forklift became stuck somehow, its right wheels on the dock and its left wheels on the raised ramp, and * * * [the operator] could not move it.[2]

* * *

[In an attempt to free the forklift] the semi driver * * * pulled [the truck] out about 15–20 feet. This removed the dockboard's support, and the ramp fell to its lowest position under the weight of the forklift truck. Somehow, Bilotta became backed up against the warehouse doorjamb and was pinned there at the neck when the forklift truck tipped over onto him.

* * *

Kelley's appeal raises the following issues:

1. In a conscious design-defect case, are instructions adequate when they fail to direct the jury to consider the factors which a manufacturer must consider in producing its product?

[The court found prejudicial error in the jury instructions because the trial court used the "consumer expectation" test of defect. The court held that the risk-utility test must be used because this is a design defect case.]

* * *

3. Does the offer of an optional safety device, without which the product is unreasonably dangerous, relieve the manufacturer from liability as a matter of law?

* * *

3. Appellant next urges this court to adopt a rule whereby the offer of safety devices to knowledgeable purchasers passes to the purchaser the risk of loss from use of that product without the device. We reject this proposal, for the reasons developed below, as inconsistent with the manufacturer's duty to produce a reasonably safe product.

Appellant argues that passing the liability on to the purchaser will encourage the development and purchase of safety options. Appellant would limit this defense to situations where (1) the purchaser is aware of both the hazard and the available option, (2) the operator could have avoided the accident through use of the due care, (3) the possibility of the accident is statistically minimal, and (4) the option was a feature beyond that normally provided by the industry. Appellant cites *Wagner*

---

2. There was testimony that this happens occasionally due to the difficulty in removing pallets from the inside corners of the carrier nearest the dock.

v. International Harvester Co., 611 F.2d 224, 231 (8th Cir.1979), in support of its argument. In *Wagner,* the manufacturer argued that it had satisfied its duty of reasonable care by making available a rollover protection device for a crawler. The court stated the option theory in this way: "[A] purchaser of multi-use equipment knows best the dangers associated with its particular use, and so it should determine the degree of safety provided." *Id.* The court stated that it accepted the theory as "basically sound" but found it inapplicable to the facts before it, where the device had been marketed as an overhead protection, rather than a rollover, device. *Id.*

The rule cited in *Wagner* and adopted by the court in *Biss v. Tenneco, Inc.,* 409 N.Y.S.2d 874, 64 A.D.2d 204 (1978), can be justified only where multi-use equipment is involved and the optional device would impair the equipment's utility in the uses for which the device is unnecessary.

The better rule, which we hereby adopt, is that a manufacturer may not delegate its duty to design a reasonably safe product. *Turney v. Ford Motor Co.,* 94 Ill.App.3d 678, 50 Ill.Dec. 85, 418 N.E.2d 1079 (1981); *Shawver v. Roberts Corp.,* 90 Wis.2d 672, 280 N.W.2d 226 (1979). The policy behind this rule is stated in *Bexiga v. Havir Manufacturing Corp.,* 60 N.J. 402, 290 A.2d 281 (1972). In *Bexiga,* safety devices for both small and large punch presses were available but were sold as standard equipment only on the large presses. One available safety device would not impair the utility of the smaller press, and the court, on appeal, held that the jury could decide whether failure to incorporate that device rendered the smaller press unreasonably dangerous. *Id.,* 60 N.J. at 410–11, 290 A.2d at 285. The court stated that, where a manufacturer introduces a finished product into the marketplace without a feasible safety device, the fact that it expects the purchaser to install that device cannot immunize it from liability. It concluded that the manufacturer should not "leave safety to the haphazard conduct of the ultimate purchaser" and that the only way to ensure use of a needed safety device is to place the duty to install that device upon the manufacturer. *Id.,* 60 N.J. at 410, 290 A.2d at 285.

The suggested option offer defense thus would not apply to dockboards which are not multi-use and whose functioning is never impaired by the installation of the panic stop device. The fact that installation or standardization of a safety device will cost more money and take more time, thus decreasing sales, should be a factor considered within the balancing approach given to the jury but should not provide an absolute defense for the manufacturer. As respondent notes, such a defense would permit an entire industry to market unreasonably dangerous "stripped down" devices and offer as optional all safety devices. Liability for improper choice of a safety device or failure to purchase a particular safety device would then fall on the purchaser. This result would circumvent the general duty of the manufacturer to provide a reasonably safe design for its products.

(F. & P.) Prod.Liab. 2d Ed. ACB—12 * * *

Reversed and remanded.

[The concurring opinion of SIMONETT, JUSTICE is omitted.]

Notes

1.   Bexiga v. Havir Mfg. Corp., 60 N.J. 402, 290 A.2d 281 (1972), is the leading case holding that a manufacturer has a non-delegable duty to install necessary safety devices. This means that the manufacturer is liable if it sells the product without a necessary device even if it reasonably believes that some subsequent owner will install the device. A majority of courts are in accord with *Bexiga.*

2.   Of course the manufacturer is still free to argue that the product without the safety feature is not unreasonably dangerous. In the new trial in *Bilotta v. Kelley Co.,* for example, Kelley would be permitted to argue that a dockboard without a panic stop was not unreasonably dangerous because the utility of its design outweighed the risk. *See Fallon v. Clifford B. Hannay & Son, Inc., supra* page 185. Stated differently, the manufacturer can delegate design responsibility to the consumer by offering optional designs, some of which are safer than others, but only if all the models are reasonably safe. In this connection, consider the following cases. Can they be reconciled?

A.   In Hammond v. International Harvester Co., 691 F.2d 646 (3rd Cir.1982) defendant manufactured a tractor with a rollover protective structure (ROPS) as a standard feature. The buyer insisted that the ROPS be removed so that the tractor could move through a low barn door. The manufacturer complied with the request, and an employee of the purchaser was fatally injured in a subsequent accident. A ROPS would have averted the fatal injury. The court held the manufacturer liable for selling the tractor without the ROPS. The court stated:

> [T]he ROPS is standard equipment on the International Harvester Series 3300 loader tractor. This reflects the manufacturer's judgment that a [tractor] with a ROPS will not be unduly expensive or inconvenient to use, and that for safety's sake a loader tractor should come equipped with a ROPS. Without a ROPS, a loader tractor falls short of the optimal design; its design is legally defective and the defect is not cured because the removal of the safety device is specifically requested by the purchaser.

691 F.2d at 651.

B.   In Linegar v. Armour of America, Inc., 909 F.2d 1150 (8th Cir.1990) defendant manufactured several styles of bullet-resistant vests. The contour style had a front and back panel held together with Velcro closures under the arms. It did not meet at the sides of the wearer's body, leaving an area along the sides of the body under the arms exposed when the vest was worn. The wrap-around style vest style provides greater coverage for the sides, but still must have an armhole that will be open four-inches below the armpit to allow freedom of movement. A State Highway Patrol trooper, who was wearing a contour style vest, was killed by a bullet that hit him in the side, an area that was unprotected by the vest. Plaintiff brought an action against the manufacturer, claiming that the contour style vest was defective because it did not cover the wearer's sides. The court held that the vest was not defective as a matter of law. The court stated:

> Trooper Linegar's protective vest performed precisely as expected and stopped all of the bullets that hit it. No part of the vest nor any malfunction of the vest caused Linegar's injuries. * * * The vest was designed to prevent the penetration of bullets where there was coverage, and it did so; the amount of coverage was the buyer's choice. The Missouri Highway Patrol could have chosen to buy, and Armour could have sold the Patrol, a vest with more coverage; no one contests that. But it is not the place of courts or juries to set specifications as to the parts of the body a bullet-resistant garment must cover. A manufacturer is not obliged to market only one version of a product, that being the very safest design possible. If that were so, automobile manufacturers could not offer consumers sports cars, convertibles, jeeps, or compact cars. All boaters would have to buy full life vests instead of choosing a ski belt or even a flotation cushion. Personal safety devices, in particular, require personal choices, and it is beyond the province of courts and juries to act as legislators and preordain those choices.
>
> In this case, there obviously were trade-offs to be made. A contour vest like the one here in question permits the wearer more flexibility and mobility and allows better heat dissipation and sweat evaporation, and thus is more likely to be worn than a more confining vest. It is less expensive than styles of vests providing more complete coverage. If manufacturers like Armour are threatened with economically devastating litigation if they market any vest style except that offering maximum coverage, they may decide, since one can always argue that more coverage is possible, to get out of the business altogether. Or they may continue to market the vest style that, according to the latest lawsuit, affords the "best" coverage. Officers who find the "safest" style confining or uncomfortable will either wear it at risk to their mobility or opt not to wear it at all. * * * Law enforcement agencies trying to work within the confines of a budget may be forced to purchase fewer vests or none at all. * * * We are firmly convinced that to allow this verdict to stand would run counter to the law's purpose of promoting the development of safe and useful products, and would have an especially pernicious effect on the development and marketing of equipment designed to make the always-dangerous work of law enforcement officers a little safer.

909 F.2d at 1154–55.

3. A similar issue arises when a manufacturer sells a product with a removable guard. In Hagans v. Oliver Mach. Co., 576 F.2d 97 (5th Cir.1978) plaintiff was cut by the blade of a table saw because the blade guard had been removed. Plaintiff claimed that the saw was defective because the guard should have been permanently attached to the saw. The jury found for plaintiff, and defendant appealed. The appellate court reversed, holding that the saw was not defective as a matter of law. The evidence showed that

the saw could not perform certain important operations with the guard in place. The court found that the removable guard represented a reasonable compromise between safety and utility.

4. Suppose Kelley continues to offer both a fixed leg dockboard and a model with both "cross-traffic legs" and a "panic stop." A company buys the fixed leg model and a worker is injured in an accident caused by the forklift pushing away the carrier. Can the worker get to the jury on the theory that the dockboard was defective in design because it did not have "cross-traffic legs" and a "panic stop?" Are other dockboard manufacturers subject to liability for not equipping their dockboards with cross-traffic legs and panic stops?

5. **Multi–Functional Machines**. Some multi-functional machinery cannot be equipped with a single guard or safety system that will work effectively with all functions. Therefore, different types of safeguards must be installed, depending on how the machine is to be used. May the manufacturer sell the machine without a guard, leaving it to the purchaser to install a guard that is appropriate for his use? Courts have dealt with this problem in a variety of ways. Wagner v. International Harvester Co., 611 F.2d 224 (8th Cir.1979), discussed in *Bilotta v. Kelley Co.*, offers one approach. Other courts have found different solutions. *See, e.g.,* Rios v. Niagara Mach. & Tool Works, 12 Ill.App.3d 739, 299 N.E.2d 86 (1973), affirmed, 59 Ill.2d 79, 319 N.E.2d 232 (1974) (no duty as a matter of law to put a guard on a multi-functional machine if one guard cannot serve all uses); Jiminez v. Dreis & Krump Mfg. Co., Inc., 736 F.2d 51 (2d Cir.1984) (even where a safety guard limits the utility of a machine with multi-functional capabilities, the jury must decide whether the machine without a guard is reasonably safe. That the guard impairs the utility of the machine is relevant but not controlling because utility is only one factor to used in determining defectiveness).

6. **Custom Made Products**. Defendant manufactures a product according to plans and specifications supplied by its customer. The product as designed lacks a necessary safety feature. Is the manufacturer liable to a user who is injured by the product? There is general agreement that it is not liable on a negligence theory unless the plans create an obvious danger. *E.g.,* Hunt v. Blasius, 74 Ill.2d 203, 23 Ill.Dec. 574, 384 N.E.2d 368 (1978); Restatement of Torts (Second) § 404, comment a. (1965). This is because the contractor is justified in relying on the adequacy of the plans and specifications.

7. Is a contractor who follows its customer's plans and specifications exempt from strict liability by analogy to the above rule? The courts have disagreed. *See, e.g.,* Garrison v. Rohm & Haas Co., 492 F.2d 346 (6th Cir.1974) (no liability); Lesnefsky v. Fischer & Porter Co., Inc., 527 F.Supp. 951 (E.D.Pa.1981) (manufacturer of component part not liable under section 402A unless it knows or should know that the part is unsafe for the intended use); Lenherr v. NRM Corp., 504 F.Supp. 165 (D.Kan.1980) (liability under section 402A because the product is defective at the time it leaves the hands of the manufacturer); Michalko v. Cooke Color and Chem. Corp., 91 N.J. 386, 451 A.2d 179 (1982) (contractor who rebuilt part of a machine according to owner's specifications strictly liable).

MOTT v. CALLAHAN AMS MACH. CO.

Superior Court of New Jersey, Appellate Division, 1980.
174 N.J.Super. 202, 416 A.2d 57.

The opinion of the court was delivered by LORA, P.J.A.D.

On March 22, 1974, plaintiff Shirley Mott was injured in the course of her employment for Clevepak Corporation as a "packer" on or near a punch press machine. At the time of her accident steel coil was being fed from a stock reel to the punch press at which she was working. Plaintiff turned and stepped between the reel and the roll feed at a point where the steel coil was running approximately ½ inch above the ground from the stock reel to the punch press to which the roll feed was affixed, and the tendon and nerves in her ankle and foot were severed by the sharp stock material.

Plaintiff brought suit against Callahan AMS Machinery Company (Callahan), Cooper Weymouth Company, Cooper Weymouth Maine, Inc., Cooper Weymouth Peterson Inc., Carl G. Peterson Co., Sterling Radiator Company Inc. and Reed National Corporation—all of which, except for Callahan, are related corporations through merger and consolidation. The machinery consisted of a punch press, a double roll feed and a double-motorized stock reel which were ordered by plaintiff's employer Clevepak from defendant Callahan and delivered on November 4, 1970. The punch press was manufactured by defendant Callahan, the roll feed by Cooper Weymouth Company and the stock reel by Cooper Weymouth Maine, Inc. When the roll feed was delivered to Callahan it was attached by bolts to the punch press by Callahan.

Callahan denies that it advised Clevepak how to install this equipment and, more particularly, the distance to be maintained between the stock reel and the punch press. The roll feed and the stock reel could be utilized with machines other than a punch press.

Plaintiff's products liability action is bottomed on alleged defective design in that it failed to provide safety guards between the stock reel and punch press, thereby exposing the steel coil notwithstanding it not only permitted but contemplated that they be far enough apart so as to permit someone to walk between them. The instruction sheet for the motorized stock reel, issued by its manufacturer, Cooper Weymouth Maine, Inc., specified that when its stock reel is used there should be a distance of six to ten feet between the reel and the other machine to which material is being fed.

Callahan, by way of cross-claim, contends Cooper Weymouth was negligent in specifying the distance between the stock reel and punch press without providing a guard or barrier since it knew and should have foreseen that there would be a zone of danger created by the unguarded space. Callahan further asserts that it "simply supplied" both parts to Clevepak and did not inform Clevepak as to how far apart the machines should be when in operation.

Sterling Radiator, Reed National and Carl G. Peterson argued that it was Callahan's responsibility to place safety devices between the reel and the press machine since the reel is designed to feed different kinds of machines and a uniform guard rail would be inappropriate because some materials such as cloth that are fed with the Cooper Weymouth reel are not dangerous.

Summary judgments in favor of the Cooper Weymouth companies were granted below on the grounds that they had furnished only a component part rather than a separate machine and that Callahan sold the punch press, motorized reel and roll feed as a package and therefore was the only defendant responsible for installing safety devices. The remaining controversy between plaintiffs and Callahan was settled. Both plaintiffs and Callahan contend that the dismissal of the complaint as against all other defendants was error since there was a genuine issue of material fact as to the liability of the Cooper–Weymouth defendants precluding summary judgment. Defendants counter that as manufacturers of a component part, they may not be held liable for injuries proximately resulting from a design defect in a final assembled product.

Aside from the question of whether the stock reel and roll-feed furnished by the Cooper Weymouth defendants are component parts of the drill press rather than a separate machine used in tandem as a unit to perform the function of manufacturing the bottoms of chocolate cans, under the circumstances of this case there is a proper jury question as to the strict liability of the manufacturers of the stock reel and roll feed for their alleged defective design in failing to provide for a safety device between the motorized reel and the roll feed which was bolted to the punch press. *See, Prosser, Law of Torts* (4 ed. 1971), § 101 at 664; 2 *Frumer & Friedman, Products Liability*, § 16A[4][b][i] at 3B–38.2 (1979).

In *Roy v. Star Chopper Co., Inc.,* 584 *F.*2d 1124, 1134 (1 Cir.1978), *cert.* den. 440 *U.S.* 916, 99 *S.Ct.* 1234, 59 *L.Ed.*2d 466 (1979), the court, in ruling on Star Chopper's objection to the District Court's failure to instruct the jury that, as a manufacturer of a component part, it could not be held liable, held that the law was clear that a manufacturer of a component part could be held liable under strict liability. In that case plaintiff was injured by a motorized "take up" unit (two motor-driven pinch rolls and a spool) manufactured by Star Chopper and which had no safety guards. The *Roy* court noted that there was "considerable uncertainty" as to whether the "take up" unit was self-contained or a component. 584 *F.*2d at 1134, n. 12. The same uncertainty is present in the case at bar.

In *Verge v. Ford Motor Co.,* 581 *F.*2d 384 (3 Cir.1978), plaintiff had been pinned under a garbage truck that had been put into reverse gear. Ford had supplied the cab and chassis to a corporation (Leach) which then manufactured the garbage truck. Plaintiff had settled with that manufacturer. Ford appealed the trial court's denial of entry of a judgment *n.o.v.* in its favor. Plaintiff's central allegation was that

Ford's cab and chassis was defective when it left Ford's hands because it did not contain a warning buzzer that would sound when the truck was put into reverse gear. Plaintiff's expert witness testified that a garbage truck without such a device is unreasonably dangerous.

The court stated the issue on appeal to be whether the responsibility for installing such a safety device should be placed solely upon the company that manufactured the cab and chassis, or solely upon the company that modified the chassis by adding the compactor unit or both. It went on to state

* * * Where, as here, the finished product is the result of substantial work by more than one party, we must determine responsibility for the absence of a safety device by looking primarily to at least three factors:

1.   Trade Custom—at what stage is that device generally installed. See *State Stove Mfg. Co. v. Hodges,* 189 *So.*2d 113 (Miss.1966), *cert. denied, sub nom. Yates v. Hodges,* 386 *U.S.* 912, 87 *S.Ct.* 860, 17 *L.Ed.*2d 784 (1967); *Schipper v. Levitt and Sons, Inc.,* 44 *N.J.* 70, 207 *A.*2d 314 (1965).

2.   Relative expertise—which party is best acquainted with the design problems and safety techniques in question. *Cf. Schell v. AMF, Inc.,* 567 *F.*2d 1259, 1263 (3d Cir.1977) ("The expected expertise of the manufacturer in a highly specialized field" is a factor in determining whether the manufacturer is liable for failure to install a safety device.)

3.   Practicality—at what stage is installation of device most feasible. *See Taylor, supra; Bexiga v. Havir Mfg. Co.,* 60 *N.J.* 402, 290 *A.*2d 281 (1972); *State Stove Mfg. Co., supra.*

As we analyze these factors, we will remain mindful of the words of New Jersey Supreme Court Justice Nathan L. Jacobs, in *Schipper v. Levitt, supra,* 44 *N.J.* at 99, 207 *A.*2d at 330: "In developing steps toward higher consumer and user protection through higher trade morality and responsibility, the law should view trade relations realistically rather than mythically." [at 386–87]

In reviewing the evidence and entering judgment *n.o.v.* in favor of Ford, the court found that there was not an adequate basis for determining the trade custom; that the garbage truck manufacturer had more expertise than Ford in the design of refuse collection vehicles and installation of warning devices, and that it was much more practical for warning devices to be installed by the garbage truck manufacturer than by Ford.

The *Verge* court, in discussing the "practicality" prong of the three-part test, relied on the reasoning of *Bexiga v. Havir Mfg. Corp.,* 60 *N.J.* 402, 290 *A.*2d 281 (1972), but distinguished *Bexiga* on the facts. In *Bexiga* the trial court and the Appellate Division had held that the manufacturer of a punch press machine could not be strictly liable for failure to install a safety device because the machine could be used to perform various tasks and it would be impractical for the punch press manufacturer to install different safety devices for each separate use, 60 *N.J.* at 408–409, 290 *A*.2d 281. The Supreme Court, however, concluded that there was evidence from which a jury could have found that one safety device (a two-hand push button) could be installed for all uses of the machine. The court stated:

> Where a manufacturer places into the channels of trade a finished product which can be put to use and which should be provided with safety devices because without such it creates an unreasonable risk of harm, and where such safety devices can feasibly be installed by the manufacturer, the fact that he expects that someone else will install such devices should not immunize him. [at 410, 290 *A*.2d at 285].

Thus, the court stated, the trial judge had erred in granting defendant's motion for an involuntary dismissal at the close of plaintiff's case.

The *Verge* court noted, however, that the evidence in the case before it was that it would not be feasible to install the safety devices in question on all F–700 trucks and that there was no evidence that it would be feasible for Ford to determine which trucks were to be converted for refuse collection use; hence it was more practical for Leach to install the warning devices.

It should be noted that Cooper Weymouth Maine has taken the position that the "finished product" language in *Bexiga* limits the liability to Callahan. But we are of the view, as was the *Verge* court, that *Bexiga* should not be read so narrowly.

Our review of the record discloses that there are factual issues to be determined in applying the three-part test of *Verge*. As to trade custom, the report by plaintiff's expert stated:

> As a general rule of good safety practice, wherever there is a situation that is a continuous source of danger, one does not depend on the employee to exercise undue continuous caution. It behooved the manufacturers to safeguard the danger zone in order to eliminate, or at least, to minimize the hazard. This procedure is standard practice, and many of the components of the press and take-off reel are so guarded.

> Both manufacturers are obviously aware of the necessary physical separation and the creation of the expanse of slack stock. Both are also aware of the burrs and sharp edges that are prevalent on thin steel stock since Cooper Weymouth manufactures equipment that eliminates these sharp edges, and it is highly probable that Callahan has sold such equipment as part of a package. These sharp edges are common knowledge in the metal working industry.

The vice-president of Cooper Weymouth stated in his deposition, however, that he had never seen or heard of a safety device or guard of the material or stock that would go between the motorized reel and punch press. Then too, it is noted that the *Bexiga* court stated that the fact that it was a custom of the trade that the purchaser and not the manufacturer installed safety devices was only evidential and not conclusive. *Id.* at 411. As to expertise and practicality, the record is devoid of anything to support a finding therein.

In this respect, the report of plaintiff's expert stated:

> In regard to Cooper Weymouth, it is, of course, very evident that their equipment must be operated utilizing a separation. In regard to Callahan AMS, they sold a "package", and thus were certainly aware of the conditions. Furthermore, the press, as factory fitted, was designed to be used in an automatic feed mode which made them as aware as Cooper Weymouth of the operative conditions.

It is our considered opinion that a plenary trial must be held to determine whether the facts to be developed at that trial will support the imposition of a duty on the Cooper Weymouth companies to install a safety device or to exercise a standard of conduct commensurate with a reasonably foreseeable hazard. * * *

Although the parts in question were manufactured by Cooper Weymouth Maine and Cooper Weymouth Company, the other named defendants are all related by merger or consolidation. As successor corporations they are responsible for the product liability claims against their predecessor. * * *

Reversed and remanded to the Law Division for trial and further proceedings consistent with this opinion. Jurisdiction is not retained.

Notes

1. Plaintiff was injured when a ram on a punch press descended, causing the die (which was attached thereto) to crush his hand. He claimed that the manufacturer of the press was liable because it sold the press to plaintiff's employer without a point of operation guard. The manufacturer claimed that it was not responsible for equipping the press with a guard because it was a general purpose, multifunctional unit, having no point of operation because it was unequipped with dies. The manufacturer's evidence showed that the press was capable of performing thousands of functions. Until it was equipped with a die, and put to a specific use, its work area could not be adequately safeguarded. Each safety device had to be tailored to the manner in which the machine was used. How should the case be resolved?

2. **Duty to warn about another manufacturer's product**. Does a manufacturer have a duty to warn about another manufacturer's product? The courts have generally said no. Consider the following cases:

A. In Walton v. Harnischfeger, 796 S.W.2d 225 (Tex.App.—San Antonio 1990) plaintiff was injured when a nylon strap rigged to a load of tin and attached to a crane broke, and the load of tin dropped on him. Plaintiff alleged that the manufacturer of the crane was liable for failure to warn or to provide instructions regarding rigging of the crane. The court held that the crane manufacturer had no duty as a matter of law to warn or instruct concerning the nylon strap, a product manufactured by someone else.

B. In Crossfield v. Quality Control Equipment Company, Inc., 1 F.3d 701 (8th Cir.1993) plaintiff was injured by the chain/sprocket mechanism of a chitterling cleaning machine. The machine lacked a guard and an interlock that would have prevented the accident. The manufacturer of the machine was no longer in business. Plaintiff sued the supplier of the replacement chain that was on the machine at the time of the accident. The chain was specifically manufactured to fit the machine. Plaintiff alleged that the chain was defective because it lacked a warning stating that it could be hazardous when used on the machine. The court held that there was no duty to warn as a matter of law. The court stated:

> To impose responsibility on the supplier of the chain in the context of the larger defectively designed machine system would simply extend liability too far. This would mean that suppliers would be required to hire machine design experts to scrutinize machine systems that the supplier had no role in developing. Suppliers would be forced to provide modifications and attach warnings on machines which they never designed nor manufactured. Mere suppliers cannot be expected to guarantee the safety of other manufacturers' machinery.

1 F.3d at 704.

C. In Clarke Industries, Inc. v. Home Indem. Co., 591 So.2d 458 (Ala.1991) plaintiff rented a floor sanding machine manufactured by defendant and did not empty the dust collection bag after use. A fire started by the spontaneous combustion of sawdust in the dust collection bag, and plaintiff's property was damaged. The dust collection bags manufactured by defendant for use with the sander contained a fire hazard warning. The bag that was on the machine was another brand that contained no warnings. There was testimony that the defendant was aware that the bags that came with the sander would routinely wear out and that replacement bags would be required. Further, there was testimony that defendant was aware that rental companies did not use its bags as replacements because they were too expensive. Plaintiff alleged that the sander was defective because a warning about the risk of spontaneous combustion should have been on the machine itself, rather than on the bag. The court upheld a jury verdict for plaintiff on this theory.

Can the holding in *Clarke Industries, Inc. v. Home Indem. Co.* be reconciled with the holdings in *Walton v. Harnischfeger* and *Crossfield v. Quality Control Equipment Company*?

3. **Substantial Change.** *Mott v. Callahan* offers one approach to the question of whether a manufacturer of a component part is required to provide the needed safety device. Another line of cases analyze the liability of a component part manufacturer in terms of whether its product has undergone a substantial change by virtue of having been incorporated into a final product. Under this approach, the component part manufacturer escapes liability if its product has undergone a substantial change.

Section 402A of the Restatement (Second) of Torts states that a seller of a defective product is liable if the product "is expected to and does reach the consumer without substantial change in the condition in which it is sold." Caveats (2) and (3) to section 402A state:

The Institute expresses no opinion as to whether the rules stated in this Section may not apply

* * *

(2) to the seller of a product expected to be processed or otherwise substantially changed before it reaches the user or consumer; or

(3) to the seller of a component part of a product to be assembled.

Comments p and q to section 402A elaborate:

p. Further processing or substantial change. Thus far the decisions applying the rule stated have not gone beyond products which are sold in the condition, or in substantially the same condition, in which they are expected to reach the hands of the ultimate user or consumer. In the absence of decisions providing a clue to the rules which are likely to develop, the Institute has refrained from taking any position as to the possible liability of the seller where the product is expected to, and does, undergo further processing or other substantial change after it leaves his hands and before it reaches those of the ultimate user or consumer.

It seems reasonably clear that the mere fact that the product is to undergo processing, or other substantial change, will not in all cases relieve the seller of liability under the rule stated in this Section. If, for example, raw coffee beans are sold to a buyer who roasts and packs them for sale to the ultimate consumer, it cannot be supposed that the seller will be relieved of all liability when the raw beans are contaminated with arsenic, or some other poison. Likewise the seller of an automobile with a defective steering gear which breaks and injures the driver, can scarcely expect to be relieved of the responsibility by reason of the fact that the car is sold to a dealer who is expected to "service" it, adjust the brakes, mount and inflate the tires, and the like, before it is ready for use. On the other hand, the manufacturer of pigiron, which is capable of a wide variety of uses, is not so likely to be held to strict liability when it turns out to be unsuitable for the child's tricycle into which it is finally made by a remote buyer. The question is essentially one of whether the responsibility for discovery and prevention of the dangerous defect is shifted to the intermediate party who is to make the changes. No doubt there will be some situations, and some defects, as to which the responsibility will be shifted, and others in which it will not. The existing decisions as yet throw no light upon the questions, and the Institute therefore expresses neither approval nor disapproval of the seller's strict liability in such a case.

q. Component parts. The same problem arises in cases of the sale of a component part of a product to be assembled by another, as for example a tire to be placed on a new automobile, a brake cylinder for the same purpose, or an instrument for the panel of an airplane. Again the question arises, whether the responsibility is not shifted to the assembler. It is no doubt to be expected that where there is no change in the component part itself, but it is merely incorporated into something larger, the strict liability will be found to carry through to the ultimate user or consumer. But in the absence of a sufficient number of decisions on the matter to justify a conclusion, the Institute expresses no opinion on the matter.

Union Supply Co. v. Pust, 196 Colo. 162, 583 P.2d 276 (1978) is a leading case using the substantial change analysis. In that case plaintiff was cleaning pulp off of a conveyor, and he was injured when his arm was caught in an unguarded "nip point" of the conveyor. Defendant sold many of the components of the conveyor system. The purchaser assembled them at its plant. The purchaser also added the parts necessary to complete the conveyor system, including the motor, conveyor belt, support legs, walkways and stairs, a counterweight, and the electrical controls. The conveyor was allegedly defective because it lacked an automatic cleaning device, a safety guard, and a warning at the "nip point." The court ruled that the defendant's liability was a question for the jury. Among the fact issues for the jury to resolve in deciding the case was whether defendant's product had undergone substantial change before it reached the plaintiff.

4. How do you think a jury would resolve the "substantial change" question in *Union Supply Co. v. Pust*? On what basis would they decide whether a substantial change had taken place in the components supplied by defendant? How would *Mott v. Callahan* have decided the *Union Supply Co. v. Pust* case? Which approach is superior?

5. **Raw Materials.** Comment, Substantial Change: Alteration of a Product as a Bar to a Manufacturer's Strict Liability, 80 Dick.L.Rev. 245, 257–258 (1976) discusses the liability of a supplier of raw materials which are incorporated into a finished product:

> Determining responsibility for a defect is especially difficult when raw materials require processing to become usable products. Because of the great change from raw material to final product, the defect that actually caused an injury is often impossible to pinpoint. In these cases the liability of the seller of the raw material turns on "whether the responsibility for discovery and prevention of the dangerous defect is shifted to the intermediate party who is to make the change." [90]

> The two cases that have faced the question of change in raw material are excellent examples of how the burden of defect discovery and prevention can shift. In *Walker v. Stauffer Chemical Corp.*[91] the court held that a manufacturer of bulk sulfuric acid was not strictly liable for injury caused by an explosion of drain cleaner produced from the acid.

> > We do not believe it realistically feasible or necessary to the protection of the public to require the manufacturer and supplier of a standard chemical ingredient such as bulk sulfuric acid, not having control over the subsequent compounding, packaging or marketing

90. Restatement § 402A, comment *p* at 357.

91. 19 Cal.App.3d 669, 96 Cal.Rptr. 803 (1971).

of an item eventually causing injury to the ultimate consumer, to bear the responsibility for that injury.[92]

Responsibility for prevention of the defect clearly lay with the processor, thus relieving the acid manufacturer of liability. *States Steamship Co. v. Stone Manganese Marine Ltd.*[93] provides a contrast to *Walker.* Defendant was a manufacturer of an alloy used in the production of ship propellers. Certain propellers were found defective and a ship owner brought suit for property damage. Noting that "a change in the shape of the product, however noticeable, is not dispositive of the change issue," the court denied defendant's motion for summary judgment and left the substantial change issue to the jury.[94]

In *States Steamship* the alloy was specifically produced for propellers. The manufacturer was aware of the minimum qualities necessary for adequate propeller strength. On the other hand, the acid in *Walker* was not solely for drain cleaners. The acid manufacturer was unable to determine the eventual characteristics of his product after its combination with other elements. Thus, in *States Steamship* the manufacturer had the best opportunity to prevent propeller defects, but in *Walker* that responsibility shifted to an intermediate party, the drain cleaner producer.

2. ENHANCED INJURIES

GENERAL MOTORS CORP. v. EDWARDS

Supreme Court of Alabama, 1985.
482 So.2d 1176.

MADDOX, JUSTICE.

These appeals arise from an automobile accident resulting in the tragic deaths of two boys and severe burns to their parents. Most of the facts in this case were disputed at trial; from those not in dispute, we have distilled the following: On the night of April 18, 1981, Robert and Marion Edwards and their two sons, Kelvin, age seven, and Reginald, age six, were en route from Marion to Montgomery in a 1980 Chevrolet Chevette automobile, which Mr. Edwards had borrowed from his brother. Mr. Edwards drove; Mrs. Edwards rode in the right front passenger seat; Reginald lay on the rear seat, and Kelvin lay in the hatch-back or trunk area immediately behind the rear seat. As the Chevette travelled through Lowndes County along U.S. Highway 80 approaching Montgomery, it was struck from behind by an Oldsmobile driven by Dan Jerome Jarrett. Although Jarrett's speed was hotly disputed at trial, it is undisputed that he was exceeding the fifty-five mile per hour speed limit by at least twenty miles per hour, and that he had been drinking.

Upon impact, the Chevette burst into flames and spun to the right shoulder of the road. Mr. Edwards, after finding the front driver's-side door jammed, managed to kick open the front passenger-side door, crawl

92. *Id.* at 674, 96 Cal.Rptr. at 806.   94. *Id.* at 505.
93. 371 F.Supp. 500 (D.N.J.1973).

over his wife, through that door, and pull her from the flames after him. He then attempted to rescue his sons from the rear of the car, but was unable to do so because of the intense heat. Both children perished in the flames.

The Edwardses brought suit against General Motors (G.M.), the manufacturer of the Chevette, and Jarrett, asserting, *inter alia*, that Jarrett was negligent in the operation of his vehicle, and that G.M. sold the Chevette in a defective and unreasonably dangerous condition, within the meaning of the Alabama Extended Manufacturer's Liability Doctrine (A.E.M.L.D.), as first set forth in *Casrell v. Altec Industries, Inc.*, 335 So.2d 128 (Ala.1976), and *Atkins v. American Motors Corp.*, 335 So.2d 134 (Ala.1976). In particular, they alleged that the design of the gas tank, which was placed in the "crush zone" (between the rear bumper and axle of the Chevette), the fuel filler neck, which was rigidly connected to the left rear quarter panel, and the doors, were defective.

[The jury verdict exonerated Jarrett but held General Motors liable. The trial court remitted some of the damages in both wrongful death actions. General Motors appealed, and plaintiff cross-appealed from the remittitur].

I

The "crashworthiness doctrine," which is also referred to as the "second collision doctrine" or the "enhanced injury doctrine," is a recent development in the area of products liability law, so recent, in fact, that prior to 1968 a case of this nature would likely have been subject to dismissal for failure to state a claim upon which relief could be granted. While all jurisdictions which have adopted one of the various forms of liability applicable to manufacturers, such as our Alabama Extended Manufacturer's Liability Doctrine (A.E.M.L.D.), have always recognized that a cause of action exists where a defect in an automobile causes an accident which injures the ultimate consumer or one within the foreseeable scope of the automobile's use, until the landmark decision of *Larsen v. General Motors Corp.*, 391 F.2d 495 (8th Cir.1968), many jurisdictions, following the reasoning expressed in *Evans v. General Motors Corp.*, 359 F.2d 822 (7th Cir.1968), *cert. denied*, 385 U.S. 836, 87 S.Ct. 83, 17 L.Ed.2d 70 (1966), *overruled, Huff v. White Motor Corp.*, 609 F.2d 286 (7th Cir.1979), held that, where there was no allegation that the defect in the automobile caused the accident to happen, no cause of action arose against the vehicle's manufacturer. Ropiequet, *Current Issues Under the "Second Collision" Doctrine*, For the Defense, Oct. 1983, at 12–17.

The decisions in *Evans* and its progeny were based upon the reasoning that, although an automobile manufacturer has a duty to design vehicles which are reasonably safe for their intended use, the intended use of an automobile does not include participation in collisions, regardless of the fact that such collisions are foreseeable. *Id.; Evans, supra*, at 825. Therefore, *Evans* held, no manufacturer has a duty to design an accident-proof vehicle nor a vehicle that is safer from the obvious danger of collision than any other vehicle.

Although a few jurisdictions have continued to follow *Evans* and others have used the reasoning expressed therein to limit the scope of the "crashworthiness doctrine," Foland, *Enhanced Injury: Problems of Proof in "Second Collision" and "Crashworthy" Cases,* 16 Washburn L.J. 601 (1977), the majority of jurisdictions have adopted the *Larsen* view, i.e., that an automobile manufacturer may be held liable where its design enhances the injuries sustained in a collision. *Larsen, supra,* at 503; *Ropiequet, supra,* at 14; Note, *Apportionment of Damages in the "Second Collision" Case,* 63 Va.L.Rev. 475 (1977).

In *Larsen,* the plaintiff was severely injured when the 1963 Chevrolet Corvair he was driving was involved in a head-on collision that caused the car's steering mechanism to be thrust into his head. G.M., the manufacturer, successfully moved for summary judgment in federal district court, and the plaintiff appealed to the Eighth Circuit Court of Appeals, which reversed, holding that, while a manufacturer is under no duty to design an accident-proof vehicle, the manufacturer of a vehicle does have a duty to design its product so as to avoid subjecting its user to an unreasonable risk of injury in the event of a collision. *Larsen, supra,* at 502. The court's reasoning was that collisions are a statistically foreseeable and inevitable risk within the intended use of an automobile, which is to travel on the streets, highways, and other thoroughfares, and that, while the user must accept the normal risk of driving, he should not be subjected to an unreasonable risk of injury due to a defective design. *Larsen, supra,* at 502–05.

Neither *Evans* nor *Larsen* has ever been cited in Alabama and no Alabama court has dealt, per se, with the issue of "crashworthiness." Although *Evans* and *Larsen* are not binding upon this Court, they may, of course, be considered as persuasive authority. Having studied both opinions and the cases following them, we find that the rule stated in *Larsen* is more in keeping with the purpose of the A.E.M.L.D., which is to protect consumers against injuries caused by defective products. * * *

We must now consider how a "crashworthiness" cause of action may arise against a manufacturer. Generally, in cases where a defect in a vehicle is alleged to have caused an injury-producing accident, manufacturers have been sued on one or more of three legal theories: implied warranty, under Alabama's implied warranty of merchantability statute, Code 1975, § 7–2–314; common law negligence; and liability under the A.E.M.L.D. C. Gamble & D. Corley, *Alabama Law of Damages,* § 30–10 (1982). Presumably, all three theories would also apply in cases like the present one, where the defect is not alleged to have caused the collision but only to have caused the injuries suffered therein. However, since breach of warranty was never raised, and since the Edwardses' negligence claim against G.M. was dropped, we will not address the applicability of those two theories. Instead, we will limit our discussion to the theory considered by the jury, the A.E.M.L.D.

As previously stated, the A.E.M.L.D. was first announced in *Casrell, supra,* and *Atkins, supra,* and, since that time, it has been applied against manufacturers of machinery, *Andrews v. John E. Smith's Sons Co.,* 369 So.2d 781 (Ala.1979); airplanes, *First National Bank of Mobile v. Cessna Aircraft Co.,* 365 So.2d 966 (Ala.1978); and automobiles, *Jett v. Honda Motor Co., Ltd.,* 339 So.2d 66 (Ala.1976), and *Joe Sartain Ford, Inc. v. American Indemnity Co.,* 399 So.2d 281 (Ala.1981). We see no reason why the A.E.M.L.D. should not be applied, so long as all the elements thereof are present.

The elements of an A.E.M.L.D. cause of action are as follows:

"To establish liability, a plaintiff must show:

"(1) he suffered injury or damages to himself or his property by one who sells a product in a defective condition unreasonably dangerous to the plaintiff as the ultimate user or consumer, if

"(a) the seller is engaged in the business of selling such a product, and

"(b) it is expected to and does reach the user or consumer without substantial change in the condition in which it is sold.

"(2) Showing these elements, the plaintiff has proved a prima facie case although

"(a) the seller has exercised all possible care in the preparation and sale of his product, and

"(b) the user or consumer has not bought the product from, or entered into any contractual relation with, the seller." (Footnote omitted.) *Casrell, supra,* at 132–33; *Atkins, supra,* at 141."

The term "injury or damages" has been held to include death. *Caterpillar Tractor Co. v. Ford,* 406 So.2d 854 (Ala.1981).

* * *

Affirmed as to both appeal and cross-appeal.

[The dissenting opinion of ALMON, JUSTICE is omitted].

Notes

1. The question of whether a manufacturer has a duty to make an automobile or airplane crashworthy was not addressed in the Restatement (Second) of Torts § 402A (1965). The issue was much debated for several years, but is now largely resolved. A great majority of courts impose the duty.

2. In design defect cases some jurisdictions shift the burden of proving that the design is unreasonable to the defendant. Should these jurisdictions treat second collision design defect cases the same way? Consider Comment, Aircraft Crashworthiness: A Return To a Negligence Standard?, 1980 U.Ill. L.F. 1103, 1120–1122:

This shift makes the defendant's burden in crashworthiness cases almost unsurmountable. The plaintiff can nearly always provide expert testimony that the injuries would have been less severe, or would not have occurred, had the aircraft been designed differently. The defendant, therefore, is in the unenviable position of having to convince a jury that among all the possible design choices, his was "right."

The difficulty of justifying a particular aircraft design is complicated by the various compromises which are an inevitable part of the design process. Enlarging cockpit windows to create better outside visibility, for example, may weaken the cabin shell or impair instrument visibility. Strengthening the cabin shell adds weight, and the resulting decreased load capacity or instrument inaccessibility may make the aircraft dangerous or unmarketable. Thousands of these potential trade-offs complicate design decisions. Aided by hindsight, jurors usually will not accept trading-off some safety to minimize cost or increase load capacity, especially if the jury is faced with a sympathetic plaintiff. Thus, permitting a jury to "reverse" aircraft design decisions years after manufacture without requiring a finding of manufacturer negligence may result in an unwise expansion of a manufacturer's liability.

The dangers of dealing with conscious design decisions under strict liability theory are especially acute in the crashworthiness area. The usual strict liability case centers on the manufacturer's duty to design an aircraft "reasonably fit for its intended purpose," the transportation of persons and property. In these cases, the jury can objectively ascertain whether the aircraft performed this function properly. Crashworthiness, conversely, is difficult to define, inviting jury speculation about what constitutes a "reasonably safe" design from the perspective of years of hindsight. Because a manufacturer cannot predict how a jury several years hence will react to design decisions made today, the manufacturer is left without any objective standard to guide his conduct. By the time a jury does decide the crashworthiness issue, moreover, a new design may have superseded the one at issue in the litigation. The jury's decision on the proper standard of conduct therefore comes too late for the manufacturer to act. Hence, the strict liability approach to crashworthiness fails to promote a primary goal of product liability law—encouraging the design, manufacture, and sale of products that society wants available. In addition, the uncertainty generated by strict liability theory is a disincentive to innovation and to developing high-risk but potentially beneficial products.

Are these problems really greater in second collision cases than they are in other design defect litigation?

3. Should courts hold manufacturers liable for enhanced injuries that do not result from second collisions? Consider, Harris, Enhanced Injury Theory: An Analytic Framework, 62 N.C.L.Rev. 640, 649–650 (1984):

The terms "crashworthiness" and "second collision" are not descriptive of many nonvehicular accidents. Enhanced injuries can result when a defective window or a pair of sunglasses shatters, rather than fractures, upon impact, when a beverage bottle shatters into particles, some of which enter and damage the eye of the person who threw the bottle, when dangerously combustible wall insulation or other material allows a fire to spread more extensively or to give off noxious fumes, when clothing or other fabrics burn rapidly rather than slowly, when a rigid utility pole or an exposed electrical wire causes more extensive damages to a person or property than if the pole had been flexible or the wire had been concealed, or when a physician's negligent treatment increases the extent of the injuries suffered in an earlier accident.

4. *See generally* Drago, Crashworthiness on Land and in the Air: A Historical Overview with an Analysis of Proposed Legislation, 19 Forum 435 (1984); Harris, Enhanced Injury Theory: An Analytic Framework, 62 N.C.L.Rev. 643 (1984); Comment, Limitations on Manufacturer Liability in Second Collision Actions, 43 Mont.L.Rev. 109 (1982); Editorial Note, Litigating Enhanced Injury Cases: Complex Issues, Empty Precedents, and Unpredictable Results, 54 U.Cin.L.Rev. 1257 (1986).

5. Enhanced injury cases often raise extremely difficult problems of proof. Plaintiff's ability to recover often turns on determination of the quantum of proof required and allocation of the burden of proof. These issues are dealt with in Chapter 11 B. 2., *infra.*

6. It is also possible for plaintiff's conduct to enhance his injuries. An example is when a victim of an automobile accident is injured more severely than he otherwise would have been because he was not wearing a seat belt. The effect of such conduct is treated in Chapter 15.

3. GOVERNMENT CONTRACTOR DEFENSE

BOYLE v. UNITED TECHNOLOGIES CORP.

Supreme Court of the United States, 1988.
487 U.S. 500, 108 S.Ct. 2510, 101 L.Ed.2d 442.

SCALIA, J., delivered the opinion of the Court, in which REHNQUIST, C.J., and WHITE, O'CONNOR, and KENNEDY, JJ., joined. BRENNAN, J., filed a dissenting opinion, in which MARSHALL and BLACKMUN, JJ., joined. STEVENS, J., filed a dissenting opinion.

JUSTICE SCALIA delivered the opinion of the Court.

This case requires us to decide when a contractor providing military equipment to the Federal Government can be held liable under state tort law for injury caused by a design defect.

I

On April 27, 1983, David A. Boyle, a United States Marine helicopter copilot, was killed when the CH–53d helicopter in which he was flying crashed off the coast of Virginia Beach, Virginia, during a training exercise. Although Boyle survived the impact of the crash, he was unable to escape from the helicopter and drowned. Boyle's father, petitioner here, brought this diversity action in Federal District Court against the Sikorsky Division of United Technologies Corporation (Sikorsky), which built the helicopter for the United States.

At trial, * * * petitioner alleged [under Virginia tort law] that Sikorsky had defectively designed the copilot's emergency escape system: the escape hatch opened out instead of in (and was therefore ineffective in a submerged craft because of water pressure), and access to the escape hatch handle was obstructed by other equipment. The jury returned a general verdict in favor of petitioner and awarded him $725,000. The District Court denied Sikorsky's motion for judgment notwithstanding the verdict.

The Court of Appeals reversed and remanded with directions that judgment be entered for Sikorsky. 792 F.2d 413 (CA4 1986). It found, * * * as a matter of federal law, that Sikorsky could not be held liable for the allegedly defective design of the escape hatch because, on the evidence presented, it satisfied the requirements of the "military contractor defense," which the court had recognized the same day in *Tozer v. LTV Corp.*, 792 F.2d 403 (CA4 1986). 792 F.2d, at 414–415.

Petitioner sought review here, challenging the Court of Appeals' decision on three levels: First, petitioner contends that there is no justification in federal law for shielding government contractors from liability for design defects in military equipment. Second, he argues in the alternative that even if such a defense should exist, the Court of Appeals' formulation of the conditions for its application is inappropriate. Finally, petitioner contends that the Court of Appeals erred in not remanding for a jury determination of whether the elements of the defense were met in this case. We granted certiorari, 479 U.S. 1029, 107 S.Ct. 872, 93 L.Ed.2d 827 (1986).

II

Petitioner's broadest contention is that, in the absence of legislation specifically immunizing Government contractors from liability for design defects, there is no basis for judicial recognition of such a defense. We disagree. In most fields of activity, to be sure, this Court has refused to find federal pre-emption of state law in the absence of either a clear statutory prescription, [Citations], or a direct conflict between federal and state law, [Citations]. But we have held that a few areas, involving "uniquely federal interests," *Texas Industries, Inc. v. Radcliff Materials, Inc.*, 451 U.S. 630, 640, 101 S.Ct. 2061, 2067, 68 L.Ed.2d 500 (1981), are so committed by the Constitution and laws of the United States to federal control that state law is pre-empted and replaced, where necessary, by federal law of a content prescribed (absent explicit statutory directive) by the courts—so-called "federal common law." [Citations]

The dispute in the present case borders upon two areas that we have found to involve such "uniquely federal interests." We have held that obligations to and rights of the United States under its contracts are governed exclusively by federal law. [Citations] The present case does not involve an obligation to the United States under its contract, but rather liability to third persons. That liability may be styled one in tort, but it arises out of performance of the contract—and traditionally has been regarded as sufficiently related to the contract that until 1962

Virginia would generally allow design defect suits only by the purchaser and those in privity with the seller. [Citations]

Another area that we have found to be of peculiarly federal concern, warranting the displacement of state law, is the civil liability of federal officials for actions taken in the course of their duty. We have held in many contexts that the scope of that liability is controlled by federal law. [Citations] The present case involves an independent contractor performing its obligation under a procurement contract, rather than an official performing his duty as a federal employee, but there is obviously implicated the same interest in getting the Government's work done.[1]

We think the reasons for considering these closely related areas to be of "uniquely federal" interest apply as well to the civil liabilities arising out of the performance of federal procurement contracts. We have come close to holding as much. In *Yearsley v. W.A. Ross Construction Co.*, 309 U.S. 18, 60 S.Ct. 413, 84 L.Ed. 554 (1940), we rejected an attempt by a landowner to hold a construction contractor liable under state law for the erosion of 95 acres caused by the contractor's work in constructing dikes for the Government. We said that "if (the) authority to carry out the project was validly conferred, that is, if what was done was within the constitutional power of Congress, there is no liability on the part of the contractor for executing its will." *Id.*, at 20–21, [60 S.Ct., at 414.] The federal interest justifying this holding surely exists as much in procurement contracts as in performance contracts; we see no basis for a distinction.

Moreover, it is plain that the Federal Government's interest in the procurement of equipment is implicated by suits such as the present one—even though the dispute is one between private parties. It is true that where "litigation is purely between private parties and does not touch the rights and duties of the United States," *Bank of American Nat. Trust & Sav. Assn. v. Parnell*, 352 U.S. 29, 33, 77 S.Ct. 119, 121, 1 L.Ed.2d 93 (1956), federal law does not govern. Thus, for example, in *Miree v. DeKalb County*, 433 U.S. 25, 30, 97 S.Ct. 2490, 2494, 53 L.Ed.2d 557 (1977), which involved the question whether certain private parties could sue as third-party beneficiaries to an agreement between a municipality and the Federal Aviation Administration, we found that state law was not displaced because "the operations of the United States in connection with FAA grants such as these * * * would (not) be burdened" by allowing state law to determine whether third-party beneficiaries could sue, *id.*, at 30[, 97 S.Ct., at 2494], and because "any federal interest in the outcome of the [dispute] before us '[was] far too speculative, far too remote a possibility to justify the application of federal law to transactions essentially of local concern.'" *Id.*, at 32–33, 97 S.Ct., at

1. [The] dissent misreads our discussion here to "intimat(e) that the immunity (of federal officials) * * * might extend * * * to nongovernment employees" such as a government contractor. * * * But we do not address this issue, as it is not before us. We cite these cases merely to demonstrate that the liability of independent contractors performing work for the Federal Government, like the liability of federal officials, is an area of uniquely federal interest.

2495, quoting *Parnell, supra*, 352 U.S., at 33–34, 77 S.Ct., at 121; see also *Wallis v. Pan American Petroleum Corp.*, 384 U.S. 63, 69, 86 S.Ct. 1301, 1304, 16 L.Ed.2d 369 (1966). But the same is not true here. The imposition of liability on Government contractors will directly affect the terms of Government contracts: either the contractor will decline to manufacture the design specified by the Government, or it will raise its price. Either way, the interests of the United States will be directly affected.

That the procurement of equipment by the United States is an area of uniquely federal interest does not, however, end the inquiry. That merely establishes a necessary, not a sufficient, condition for the displacement of state law. Displacement will occur only where, as we have variously described, a "significant conflict" exists between an identifiable "federal policy or interest and the (operation) of state law," *Wallis, supra*, at 68, [86 S.Ct., at 1304,] or the application of state law would "frustrate specific objectives" of federal legislation, [United States v. Kimbell Foods, Inc., 440 U.S. 715, 728, 99 S.Ct. 1448, 1458, 59 L.Ed.2d 711 (1979)]. The conflict with federal policy need not be as sharp as that which must exist for ordinary pre-emption when Congress legislates "in a field which the States have traditionally occupied." *Rice v. Santa Fe Elevator Corp.*, [331 U.S. 218, 231, 67 S.Ct. 1146, 1152, 91 L.Ed 1447 (1947)]. Or to put the point differently, the fact that the area in question is one of unique federal concern changes what would otherwise be a conflict that cannot produce pre-emption into one that can. But conflict there must be. In some cases, for example where the federal interest requires a uniform rule, the entire body of state law applicable to the area conflicts and is replaced by federal rules. *See, e.g., Clearfield Trust* [Co. v. United States, 318 U.S. 363, 366–67, 63 S.Ct. 573, 574–75, 87 L.Ed. 838 (1943)], (rights and obligations of United States with respect to commercial paper must be governed by uniform federal rule). In others, the conflict is more narrow, and only particular elements of state law are superseded. See, *e.g.*, [United States v. Little Lake Misere Land Co., 412 U.S. 580, 595, 93 S.Ct. 2389, 2398, 37 L.Ed.2d 187 (1973)] (even assuming state law should generally govern federal land acquisitions, particular state law at issue may not); *Howard v. Lyons*, [360 U.S. 593, 597, 79 S.Ct. 1331, 1333, 3 L.Ed.2d 1454 (1959)] (state defamation law generally applicable to federal official, but federal privilege governs for statements made in the course of federal official's duties).

In *Miree, supra*, the suit was not seeking to impose upon the person contracting with the Government a duty contrary to the duty imposed by the Government contract. Rather, it was the contractual duty *itself* that the private plaintiff (as third party beneficiary) sought to enforce. Between *Miree* and the present case, it is easy to conceive of an intermediate situation, in which the duty sought to be imposed on the contractor is not identical to one assumed under the contract, but is also not contrary to any assumed. If, for example, the United States contracts for the purchase and installation of an air conditioning unit, specifying the cooling capacity but not the precise manner of construction, a state law imposing upon the manufacturer of such units a duty of care to include a certain safety feature would not be a duty identical to anything promised the Government, but neither would it be contrary. The contractor could comply with both its contractual obligations and the state-prescribed duty of care. No one suggests that state law would generally be pre-empted in this context.

The present case, however, is at the opposite extreme from *Miree*. Here the state-imposed duty of care that is the asserted basis of the contractor's liability (specifically, the duty to equip helicopters with the sort of escape-hatch mechanism petitioner claims was necessary) is precisely contrary to the duty imposed by the Government contract (the duty to manufacture and deliver helicopters with the sort of escape-hatch mechanism shown by the specifications). Even in this sort of situation, it would be unreasonable to say that there is always a "significant conflict" between the state law and a federal policy or interest. If, for example, a federal procurement officer orders, by model number, a quantity of stock helicopters that happen to be equipped with escape hatches opening outward, it is impossible to say that the Government has a significant interest in that particular feature. That would be scarcely more reasonable than saying that a private individual who orders such a craft by model number cannot sue for the manufacturer's negligence because he got precisely what he ordered.

In its search for the limiting principle to identify those situations in which a "significant conflict" with federal policy or interests does arise, the Court of Appeals, in the lead case upon which its opinion here relied, identified as the source of the conflict the *Feres* doctrine, under which the Federal Tort Claims Act does not cover injuries to armed service personnel in the course of military service. See *Feres v. United States*, 340 U.S. 135, 71 S.Ct. 153, 95 L.Ed. 152 (1950). Military contractor liability would conflict with this doctrine, the Fourth Circuit reasoned, since the increased cost of the contractor's tort liability would be added to the price of the contract, and "(s)uch pass-through costs would * * * defeat the purpose of the immunity for military accidents conferred upon the government itself." *Tozer*, 792 F.2d, at 408. Other courts upholding the defense have embraced similar reasoning. See, *e.g., Bynum v. FMC Corp.*, 770 F.2d 556, 565–566 (CA5 1985); *Tillett v. J.I. Case Co.*, 756 F.2d 591, 596–597 (CA7 1985); *McKay v. Rockwell Int'l Corp.*, 704 F.2d 444, 449 (CA9 1983), cert. denied, 464 U.S. 1043, 104 S.Ct. 711, 79 L.Ed.2d 175 (1984). We do not adopt this analysis because it seems to us that the *Feres* doctrine, in its application to the present problem, logically produces results that are in some respects too broad and in some respects too narrow. Too broad, because if the Government contractor defense is to prohibit suit against the manufacturer whenever *Feres* would prevent suit against the Government, then even injuries caused to military personnel by a helicopter purchased from stock (in our example above), or by any standard equipment purchased by the Government, would be covered. Since *Feres* prohibits all service-related tort claims against the Government, a contractor defense that rests upon it should prohibit all service-related tort claims against the manufacturer—making inexplicable the three limiting criteria for contractor immunity (which we will discuss presently) that the Court of Appeals adopted. On the other hand, reliance on *Feres* produces (or logically should produce) results that are in another respect too narrow. Since that doctrine covers only service-related injuries, and not injuries caused by the military to civilians, it could not be invoked to prevent, for example, a civilian's suit against the manufacturer of fighter planes, based on a state tort theory, claiming harm from what is alleged to be needlessly high levels of noise produced by the jet engines. Yet we think that the character of the jet engines the Government orders for its fighter planes cannot be regulated by state tort law, no more in suits by civilians than in suits by members of the Armed Services.

There is, however, a statutory provision that demonstrates the potential for, and suggests the outlines of, "significant conflict" between federal interests and state law in the context of government procurement. In the [Federal Tort Claims Act] FTCA, Congress authorized damages to be recovered against the United States for harm caused by the negligent or wrongful conduct of Government employees, to the extent that a private person would be liable under the law of the place where the conduct occurred. 28 U.S.C. § 1346(b). It excepted from this consent to suit, however,

> "(a)ny claim * * * based upon the exercise or performance or the failure to exercise or perform a discretionary function or duty on the part of a federal agency or an employee of the Government, whether or not the discretion involved be abused." 28 U.S.C. § 2680(a).

We think that the selection of the appropriate design for military equipment to be used by our Armed Forces is assuredly a discretionary function within the meaning of this provision. It often involves not merely engineering analysis but judgment as to the balancing of many technical, military, and even social considerations, including specifically the trade-off between greater safety and greater combat effectiveness. And we are further of the view that permitting "second-guessing" of these judgments, see *United States v. Varig Airlines*, 467 U.S. 797, 814, 104 S.Ct. 2755, 2765, 81 L.Ed.2d 660 (1984), through state tort suits against contractors would produce the same effect sought to be avoided by the FTCA exemption. The financial burden of judgments against the contractors would ultimately be passed through, substantially if not totally, to the United States itself, since defense contractors will predictably raise their prices to cover, or to insure against, contingent liability for the Government-ordered designs. To put the point differently: It makes little sense to insulate the Government against financial liability for the judgment that a particular feature of military equipment is necessary when the Government produces the equipment itself, but not when it contracts for the production. In sum, we are of the view that state law which holds Government contractors liable for design defects in military equipment does in some circumstances present a "significant conflict" with federal policy and must be displaced.

We agree with the scope of displacement adopted by the Fourth Circuit here, which is also that adopted by the Ninth Circuit, see *McKay v. Rockwell Int'l Corp., supra,* at 451. Liability for design defects in military equipment cannot be imposed, pursuant to state law, when (1) the United States approved reasonably precise specifications; (2) the equipment conformed to those specifications; and (3) the supplier warned the United States about the dangers in the use of the equipment that were known to the supplier but not to the United States. The first two of these conditions assure that the suit is within the area where the policy of the "discretionary function" would be frustrated—*i.e.,* they assure that the design feature in question was considered by a Government officer, and not merely by the contractor itself. The third condition is necessary because, in its absence, the displacement of state tort law would create some incentive for the manufacturer to withhold knowledge of risks, since conveying that knowledge might disrupt the contract but withholding it would produce no liability. We adopt this provision lest our effort to protect discretionary functions perversely impede them by cutting off information highly relevant to the discretionary decision.

We have considered the alternative formulation of the Government contractor defense, urged upon us by petitioner, which was adopted by the Eleventh Circuit in *Shaw v. Grumman Aerospace Corp.,* 778 F.2d 736, 746 (1985), cert. pending, No. 85–1529. That would preclude suit only if (1) the contractor did not participate, or participated only minimally, in the design of the defective equipment; *or* (2) the contractor timely warned the Government of the risks of the design and notified it of alternative designs reasonably known by it, *and* the Government, although forewarned, clearly authorized the contractor to proceed with the dangerous design. While this formulation may represent a perfectly reasonable tort rule, it is not a rule designed to protect the federal interest embodied in the "discretionary function" exemption. The design ultimately selected may well reflect a significant policy judgment by Government officials whether or not the contractor rather than those officials developed the design. In addition, it does not seem to us sound policy to penalize, and thus deter, active contractor participation in the design process, placing the contractor at risk unless it identifies all design defects.

III

Petitioner raises two arguments regarding the Court of Appeals' application of the Government contractor defense to the facts of this case. First, he argues that since the formulation of the defense adopted by the Court of Appeals differed from the instructions given by the District Court to the jury, the Seventh Amendment guarantee of jury trial required a remand for trial on the new theory. We disagree. If the evidence presented in the first trial would not suffice, as a matter of law, to support a jury verdict under the properly formulated defense, judgment could properly be entered for the respondent at once, without a new trial. And that is so even though (as petitioner claims) respondent

failed to object to jury instructions that expressed the defense differently, and in a fashion that would support a verdict. [Citations]

It is somewhat unclear from the Court of Appeals' opinion, however,
whether it was in fact deciding that no reasonable jury could, under the
properly formulated defense, have found for the petitioner on the facts
presented, or rather was assessing on its own whether the defense had
been established. The latter, which is what petitioner asserts occurred,
would be error, since whether the facts establish the conditions for the
defense is a question for the jury. The critical language in the Court of
Appeals' opinion was that "(b)ecause Sikorsky has satisfied the requirements of the military contractor defense, it can incur no liability for
* * * the allegedly defective design of the escape hatch." 792 F.2d, at
415. Although it seems to us doubtful that the Court of Appeals was
conducting the factual evaluation that petitioner suggests, we cannot be
certain from this language, and so we remand for clarification of this
point. If the Court of Appeals was saying that no reasonable jury could
find, under the principles it had announced and on the basis of the
evidence presented, that the Government contractor defense was inapplicable, its judgment shall stand, since petitioner did not seek from us, nor
did we grant, review of the sufficiency-of-the-evidence determination. If
the Court of Appeals was not saying that, it should now undertake the
proper sufficiency inquiry.

Accordingly, the judgment is vacated and the case is remanded. *So
ordered.*

[The dissenting opinions of BRENNAN, J., and STEVENS, J., are omitted.]

Notes

1. *Boyle v. United Technologies Corp.* is noted in 39 Am.U.L.Rev. 391
(1990); 70 B.U.L.Rev. 691 (1990); 22 Conn.L.Rev. 239 (1989); 39 DePaul
L.Rev. 825 (1990)77; 40 Mercer L.Rev. 753 (1989); 67 N.C.L.Rev. 1172
(1989); 42 Okla.L.Rev. 359 (1989); 20 St.Mary's L.J. 993 (1989); 57 UMKC
L.Rev. 655 (1989); and 24 Wake Forest L.Rev. 745 (1989).

2. Does the government contractor defense apply to manufacturing
defects? *See* McGonigal v. Gearhart Industries, Inc., 851 F.2d 774 (5th
Cir.1988) (defective fuse in grenade; defense does not apply); Mitchell v.
Lone Star Ammunition, Inc., 913 F.2d 242 (5th Cir.1990) (cracked mortar
shell and voids in explosive filler; defense does not apply); Bailey v.
McDonnell Douglas Corp., 989 F.2d 794 (5th Cir.1993) (flaw in the metallurgic content of bellows canister; the defense applies if the three *Boyle*
conditions are satisfied with respect to the metallurgic content of the bellows
canister, i.e., defendant must satisfy the second condition by showing that
the canister conforms with government specifications despite the flaw because those specifications are silent about the type or quality of metal to be
used). *See also,* Harduvel v. General Dynamics Corp., 878 F.2d 1311, 1317
(11th Cir.1989) (presumption under state law that "where a product is
destroyed in an accident, and the plaintiff presents evidence to negate
possible causes other than a product defect, an inference of manufacturing

defect arises"; held: federal rather than state law determines whether the product was defective in manufacture or design) cert. denied, 494 U.S. 1030, 110 S.Ct. 1479, 108 L.Ed.2d 615 (1990).

3. Should the government contractor defense apply to civilian products manufactured for the government? The courts are split on this issue. *Compare* Nielsen v. George Diamond Vogel Paint Co., 892 F.2d 1450 (9th Cir.1990) (paint for dam; the defense does not apply to civilian products) *with* Carley v. Wheeled Coach, 991 F.2d 1117 (3rd Cir.1993) (ambulance; the defense applies to nonmilitary contractors) cert. denied, ___ U.S. ___, 114 S.Ct. 191, 126 L.Ed.2d 150 (1993). *See* Ausness, Surrogate Immunity: The Government Contract Defense and Products Liability, 47 Ohio St.L.J. 985, 1014–1018 (1986).

4. In addition to the articles and notes previously cited, *see* Cass and Gillette, The Government Contractor Defense: Contractual Allocation of Public Risk, 77 Va.L.Rev. 257 (1991); Green and Matasar, The Supreme Court and the Products Liability Crisis: Lessons From *Boyle's* Government Contractor Defense, 63 S.Cal.L.Rev. 637 (1990).

SECTION C. FAILURE TO WARN

1. DUTY TO WARN

CAVERS v. CUSHMAN MOTOR SALES, INC.

Court of Appeals of California, First District, 1979.
95 Cal.App.3d 338, 157 Cal.Rptr. 142.

SABRAW, ASSOCIATE JUSTICE.

[Plaintiff was injured while riding on a motorized golf cart. While the evidence was disputed, plaintiff claimed that the cart tipped over while the driver was making a turn. He brought a strict liability action against the manufacturer and lessor of the cart. The jury found in favor of defendants, and plaintiff appeals.]

Appellant's sole theory of recovery was strict liability in tort for failure to warn of the golf cart's propensity to tip while turning. He presented no evidence that the golf cart was defective in either its design or its manufacture.

Appellant claims the trial court committed error in the following instruction which it gave to the jury: "An article otherwise appropriately made and maintained is defective within the meaning of the instruction which I have just given if the manufacturer and/or lessor fails to adequately warn of dangerous propensities of such article which in the absence of an adequate warning renders the article *substantially dangerous* to the user." (Emphasis added)

The appellant contends that the trial court's use of the adverb "substantially" to modify the term "dangerous" is contrary to California law and prejudicially increased the appellant's burden of proof.

Prior to the California Supreme Court decision in *Cronin v. J.B.E. Olson Corp.* (1972) 8 Cal.3d 121, 104 Cal.Rptr. 433, 501 P.2d 1153, the cases involving products liability actions required that a two-pronged test be met to establish liability. The claimant was required to prove (1) "a defective condition" and also that the defect was (2) "unreasonably dangerous". In 1972, in a case involving a products liability action based on "manufacturing defects," the Supreme Court in *Cronin* eliminated the plaintiff's burden of having to establish that a proven defect was also "unreasonably dangerous."

The appellant argues in the instant case that the prohibition of *Cronin* against the use of the term "unreasonably dangerous" applies with equal force to the failure to warn cases and that the term "substantially dangerous" is the equivalent term and is equally defective.

We conclude that the *Cronin* decision, while eliminating in the manufacturing defect cases the previous dual burden of proving both the existence of a defect and an unreasonable degree of danger resulting therefrom, nevertheless did not preclude weighing the degree of dangerousness in the failure to warn cases.

* * *

Fortunately, the Supreme Court has provided us with further guidance through its recent decision in *Barker v. Lull Engineering Co.* (1978) 20 Cal.3d 413, 143 Cal.Rptr. 225, 573 P.2d 443. In *Barker,* * * * the court noted that numerous California decisions have implicitly held that a defect in design may exist where, despite meeting ordinary consumer expectations, the product's design is found by the jury to have embodied "excessive preventable danger," "or in other words * * * the jury finds that the risk of danger inherent in the challenged design outweighs the benefits of such design." Pursuant to this standard, " * * * a jury may consider, among other relevant factors, the gravity of the danger posed by the challenged design, the likelihood that such danger would occur, the mechanical feasibility of a safer alternative design, the financial cost of an improved design, and the adverse consequences to the product and to the consumer that would result from an alternative design. [Citations.]" (*Barker,* supra, 20 Cal.3d at 431, 143 Cal.Rptr. at 237, 573 P.2d at 455.)

We believe the foregoing principles to be adaptable to a failure to warn case. In assisting the jury's determination of whether the absence of a warning makes a product defective, the trial court should focus their attention on such relevant considerations as the normal expectations of the consumer as to how the product will perform, degrees of simplicity or complication in the operation or use of the product, the nature and magnitude of the danger to which the user is exposed, the likelihood of injury, and the feasibility and beneficial effect of including a warning. [Citations]

We disagree with appellant's assertion that he was entitled to an instruction which eliminated from jury consideration all references to degrees of danger.[2] First of all, the Supreme Court in *Cronin* recognized that the words "*unreasonably* dangerous" were inserted by the Restatement in order to prevent the seller "from being treated as an insurer of its products," in manufacturing and design defect cases; the court determined that these words could nevertheless be eliminated because "such protective end is attained by the necessity of proving that there was a defect in the manufacture or design of the product and that such defect was a proximate cause of the injuries." Where, as here, plaintiff is relieved of the burden of proving either a defect in manufacture *or* design, permitting recovery upon proof that the product was merely "dangerous" would in fact turn every manufacturer into an insurer as long as plaintiff could show (a) that the product contained no warning and (b) that he was injured while using it. Why else was the plaintiff injured, a jury would reasonably ask itself, unless the product was "dangerous"? Thus, as one commentator has aptly observed, "Since the use of almost any product involves some degree of danger, the duty of a manufacturer to warn of danger must be related, or made dependent upon, the degree of danger involved in the use of the product." (Korpela, A., "Failure to Warn as Basis of Liability Under Doctrine of Strict Liability in Tort" (1973) 53 A.L.R.3d 239, 251)

Elimination of any consideration of degrees of danger is also contrary to the principles articulated by the Supreme Court in *Barker,* i.e. that the concept of "*excessive* preventable danger" and the balancing of risks must be employed where the term "defect" does not easily lend itself to definition. Just as the Supreme Court has concluded that "an instruction [on design defect] which appears to preclude such a weighing process under all circumstances may mislead the jury" (*Barker,* supra, 20 Cal.3d at 434, 143 Cal.Rptr. at 239, 573 P.2d at 457), we too recognize that a failure to warn instruction which predicates liability on a finding of "danger," without regard for degree or without consideration of the relevant factors mentioned previously, does not accurately reflect existing case precedent.

We now turn to the instructions on defect for failure to warn given by the trial court. We feel that the court wisely chose to omit the word "unreasonably" from the original *Canifax* formulation, since the Supreme Court has indicated that the word improperly "introduces an element which 'rings of negligence' " in a strict liability case (*Barker,* supra, 20 Cal.3d at 433, 143 Cal.Rptr. 225, 573 P.2d 443, citing *Cronin,* supra, 8 Cal.3d at 132, 104 Cal.Rptr. 443, 501 P.2d 1153) and may tend to divert the jury's attention from the condition of the product to the conduct of the seller. Instead, the trial court told the jurors that an

2. Appellant offered the following two instructions, which he claims were improperly rejected by the trial court: " * * * [A] product, though faultlessly made, may nevertheless be deemed 'defective' * * * (in terms of strict liability) and subject the supplier thereof to strict liability if it is dangerous to place the product in the hands of the user without a suitable warning and the product is supplied and no warning is given."

"A product is also defective if the supplier fails to adequately warn of dangerous conditions or propensities which in the absence of an adequate warning make the product dangerous to the user."

otherwise faultlessly made article may be deemed defective if the manufacturer/lessor fails to warn of dangerous propensities " * * * which in the absence of an adequate warning render the article *substantially* dangerous to the user." (Emphasis added) By using the modifying adverb "substantially," the court appropriately indicated that a weighing of degrees of danger was necessarily involved in determining the existence of a defect. But the court did not end its instruction here. It went on to give the jury detailed guidance on what was meant by a "substantial danger": "The term substantial danger as used in these instructions does not mean any danger, however remote, or a trivial danger nor conversely is the term synonymous with great or extreme danger. A substantial danger does not fall precisely in any specific area in the spectrum of danger. The term substantial danger means danger which is real and not insignificant. The word danger is to some extent self defining when one considers its antonym insubstantial. Whether a danger is substantial or insubstantial must be determined from the evidence and measured in the light of several criteria none of which is totally controlling including the potential injurious consequences of such danger, the likelihood that injury might result, the quality and extent of danger to which the user is exposed, and whether a danger is latent or patent (patent means apparent and latent is its antonym)."

Thus, when the instructions on the definition of "defect" are viewed as a whole, it is evident that they adequately focused the jury's attention upon the relevant factors which must be considered in determining whether the magnitude of the danger inherent in the use of a product was sufficiently great as to require a warning. We therefore cannot conclude that the jury were misled or confused as a result of the instructions given. (See 4 Witkin, Cal.Procedure (2d ed.) Trial § 193, p. 3013; *Chandler v. Benafel* (1934) 3 Cal.App.2d 368, 371, 39 P.2d 890) Prejudice has not been shown. * * *

Judgment is affirmed.

TAYLOR, P.J., and ROUSE, J., concur.

Notes

1. **Negligence.** Under the law of negligence the supplier of a product must use reasonable care to warn product users of risks that they are unlikely to fully appreciate. Restatement of Torts (Second) § 388 (1965). Suppliers need only warn against significant risks, and not every conceivable accident that might occur. Madden, The Duty to Warn in Products Liability: Contours and Criticism, 89 W.Va.L.Rev. 221, 235 (1987); Noel, Products Defective Because of Inadequate Directions or Warnings, 23 Sw.L.J. 256, 264–265 (1969). In determining what warnings are necessary, courts balance the gravity and probability of the harm against the burden and feasibility of giving an effective warning. *Id.*

2. **Strict Liability.** The duty to warn arises under the law of strict liability because of the recognition that many useful products cannot be made completely safe. Yet it is often reasonable to market such products. Restatement of Torts (Second) § 402A, comment i (1965). In order to

prevent such products from being unreasonably dangerous, however, the seller must give appropriate directions and warnings with respect to risks that are not generally known and recognized. Restatement of Torts (Second) § 402A, comment j (1965).

3. **Breach of Warranty.** Failure to warn can also give rise to a breach of implied warranty. This is because products unaccompanied by adequate instructions and warnings are not reasonably fit for the ordinary purposes for which such products are used. *See, e.g.,* Wolfe v. Ford Motor Co., 6 Mass.App.Ct. 346, 376 N.E.2d 143 (1978) (inadequate warnings concerning the effect of overloading a camper).

4. When the only alleged defect in the product is a failure to warn adequately, is there a difference among the three theories? Many courts hold that there is no difference because liability under all three theories turns on the question of whether the warning is reasonable. *E.g.,* Smith v. E.R. Squibb & Sons, Inc., 405 Mich. 79, 273 N.W.2d 476 (1979) (warning about the side-effects of a drug). In Russell v. G.A.F. Corp., 422 A.2d 989, 991 (D.C.App.1980) the court stated:

> A plaintiff may limit the claim to negligence in failing to warn about foreseeable harm from a product, *see* Burch v. Amsterdam Corporation, D.C.App., 366 A.2d 1079, 1086 (1976), or claim strict liability for injury derived from the same failure. *See* Restatement (Second) of Torts § 402A, Comment j (1965). In either case, however, the duty is the same: ordinary care. *See* Basko v. Sterling Drug, Inc., 416 F.2d 417, 426 (2d Cir.1969) (Restatement, *supra* § 402A, Comment k, adopting the ordinary negligence standard of duty to warn). More specifically, whether a manufacturer can be held strictly liable for failure to warn, or held liable only for negligence, the threshold question whether there has been a "failure to warn" (triggering potential liability) is judged by the following standard of care:

>> The seller or manufacturer of a product whose use could result in foreseeable harm has a duty to give a warning which adequately advises the user of attendant risks and which provides *specific* directions for safe use. [*Burch v. Amsterdam Corp., supra* at 1086 (emphasis in original).]

> The trial court did not follow this standard but mistakenly added an element of "defectiveness" to the *Burch* test. One of the grounds for granting the directed verdict was the absence of evidence that the sheet was *defective* when it left G.A.F.'s hands. Of course, there must be a *danger* to warn about. *See* Beier v. International Harvester Co., 287 Minn. 400, 402, 178 N.W.2d 618, 620 (1970) (insufficient evidence to show danger of which defendant had a duty to warn in that it was impossible for bolts to become loose while outer nuts were tight). Evidence of a defect is unnecessary, however. A product can be perfectly made and still require directions or warnings on proper use in order to be safe. *See* Biller v. Allis Chalmers Manufacturing Co., 34 Ill.App.2d 47, 180 N.E.2d 46 (1962) (manufacturer owed duty to warn of latent limitations of even a perfectly made tractor).

5. **Risk–Utility Balancing.** Several courts have indicated that risk-utility balancing should not play an important role in strict liability warning

cases. Consider Dambacher by Dambacher v. Mallis, 336 Pa.Super. 22, 485 A.2d 408 (1984), appeal dismissed, 508 Pa. 643, 500 A.2d 428 (1985):

> As has been said, "In the case of an inadequate warning, * * * imposing the requirements of a proper warning will seldom detract from the utility of the product." Freund v. Cellofilm Properties, Inc., 87 N.J. 229, 238 n. 1, 432 A.2d 925, 930 n. 1 (1981). At the same time, the cost of adding a warning, or of making an inadequate warning adequate, will at least in most cases be outweighed by the risk of harm if there is no adequate warning.

In states that follow this view, must manufacturers warn against all conceivable product hazards, no matter how remote? If so this would represent a significant difference between negligence and strict liability.

6. Is this difference desirable? Consider Twerski, Weinstein, Donaher, Piehler, The Use and Abuse of Warnings in Products Liability—Design Defect Litigation Comes of Age, 61 Cornell L.Rev. 495, 513–517 (1976). The authors argue that warnings cannot be effective unless they selectively focus on the most significant hazards. Therefore, courts should not induce manufacturers routinely to "overwarn" about trivial risks. If this should happen warnings would lose their credibility, and users will no longer pay attention to them. Keep this question in mind as you read the cases in the next section.

7. **Foresight/Hindsight.** Under the law of negligence, manufacturers must only warn about foreseeable risks. One potential difference between negligence and strict liability turns on whether, under the law of strict liability, manufacturers must warn about unknowable risks. Courts are split on the question of whether to use foresight or hindsight in strict liability failure to warn cases. This issue is dealt with in Section A. 4 of this chapter.

8. California has approved the following jury instruction for failure to warn cases:

> A product is defective if the use of the product in a manner that is reasonably foreseeable by the defendant involves a substantial danger that would not be readily recognized by the ordinary user of the product and the manufacturer fails to give adequate warning of such danger.

> [A manufacturer has a duty to provide an adequate warning to the user on how to use the product if a reasonably foreseeable use of the product involves a substantial danger that would not be readily recognized by the ordinary user.]

> [A manufacturer has a duty to provide an adequate warning to the consumer of a product of potential risks or side effects which may follow the foreseeable use of the product, and which are known or knowable in light of the generally recognized and prevailing best scientific and medical knowledge at the time of manufacture and distribution.]

> [In the case of prescription drugs, such warning must be given to the physician.]

BAJI 9.00.7 (1991 Revision).

Does California law create a distinction between negligence and strict liability in failure to warn cases? Anderson v. Owens–Corning Fiberglas Corporation, 53 Cal.3d 987, 281 Cal.Rptr. 528, 810 P.2d 549 (1991) involved a strict liability failure to warn claim against an asbestos manufacturer. The court held that defendant had a duty to warn only about risks that were scientifically knowable at the time of manufacture. In comparing strict liability and negligence, the court stated:

> [D]espite its roots in negligence, failure to warn in strict liability differs markedly from failure to warn in the negligence context. Negligence law in a failure-to-warn case requires a plaintiff to prove that a manufacturer or distributor did not warn of a particular risk for reasons which fell below the acceptable standard of care, i.e., what a reasonably prudent manufacturer would have known and warned about. Strict liability is not concerned with the standard of due care or the reasonableness of a manufacturer's conduct. The rules of strict liability require a plaintiff to prove only that the defendant did not adequately warn of a particular risk that was known or knowable in light of the generally recognized and prevailing best scientific and medical knowledge available at the time of manufacture and distribution. Thus, in strict liability, as opposed to negligence, the reasonableness of the defendant's failure to warn is immaterial.
>
> Stated another way, a reasonably prudent manufacturer might reasonably decide that the risk of harm was such as not to require a warning as, for example, if the manufacturer's own testing showed a result contrary to that of others in the scientific community. Such a manufacturer might escape liability under negligence principles. In contrast, under strict liability principles the manufacturer has no such leeway; the manufacturer is liable if it failed to give warning of dangers that were known to the scientific community at the time it manufactured or distributed the product. Whatever may be reasonable from the point of view of the manufacturer, the user of the product must be given the option either to refrain from using the product at all or to use it in such a way as to minimize the degree of danger. *Davis v. Wyeth Laboratories, Inc.* (9th Cir.1968) 399 F.2d 121, 129–130, described the need to warn in order to provide "true choice": "When, in a particular case, the risk qualitatively (e.g., of death or major disability) as well as quantitatively, on balance with the end sought to be achieved, is such as to call for a true choice judgment, medical or personal, the warning must be given. [Fn. omitted.]" (See also *Finn, supra,* 35 Cal.3d at pp. 699–700, 200 Cal.Rptr. 870, 677 P.2d 1147, on the kinds of warnings and their implications.) Thus, the fact that a manufacturer acted as a reasonably prudent manufacturer in deciding not to warn, while perhaps absolving the manufacturer of liability under the negligence theory, will not preclude liability under strict liability principles if the trier of fact concludes that, based on the information scientifically available to the manufacturer, the manufacturer's failure to warn rendered the product unsafe to its users.

53 Cal.3d at 1002–03, 281 Cal.Rptr. at 537–38, 810 P.2d at 558–59. Suppose a manufacturer has superior knowledge of a risk that the scientific commu-

nity has not yet discovered. Under the rationale of *Anderson*, does it have a duty to warn?

9. In those jurisdictions that treat negligence, strict liability, and breach of warranty as imposing the same standard of liability for failure to warn, what purpose is served by recognizing more than one theory of recovery? In other words, why should such jurisdictions not impose liability for failure to warn on a negligence theory only?

10. **Autonomy vs. Safety.** In most cases the duty to warn is based on the notion that adequate warnings are necessary because they enhance the safety of the product. They do this by providing information which enables the user to minimize or avoid the risks associated with the product. When viewed in this sense, a warning is no different than any other proposed safety feature of a product. It is required only if necessary to make the product reasonably safe.

Should there be a duty to provide warnings which cannot materially enhance safety? Some authors argue that there should be if a reasonable person would want to have the information before choosing to use the product. Twerski, Weinstein, Donaher, Piehler, The Use and Abuse of Warnings in Products Liability—Design Defect Litigation Comes of Age, 61 Corn.L.Rev. 495, 519 (1976). The obligation to warn under such circumstances is based on notions of individual autonomy rather than on accident reduction. The authors cite Davis v. Wyeth Laboratories, Inc., 399 F.2d 121 (9th Cir.1968) as an example. There, an adult contracted polio from a dose of polio vaccine. The chances of this occurring were about one in one million. The risk of contracting polio from a wild strain if the vaccine were not taken was approximately the same for adults. The court found that the vaccine was unavoidably unsafe, and that there was no way to identify which users would contract the disease. In deciding to impose a duty to warn of the risk, the court stated:

> In such cases, then, the drug is fit and its danger is reasonable only if the balance is struck in favor of its use. Where the risk is otherwise known to the consumer, no problem is presented, since choice is available. Where not known, however, the drug can properly be marketed only in such fashion as to permit the striking of the balance; that is, by full disclosure of the existence and extent of the risk involved.

> As comment k recognizes, human experimentation is essential with new drugs if essential knowledge ever is to be gained. No person, however, should be obliged to submit himself to such experimentation. If he is to submit it must be by his voluntary and informed choice or a choice made on his behalf by his physician.

> In such cases, then, the drug is fit and its danger is reasonable only if the balance is struck in favor of its use. It can properly be marketed only in such fashion as to permit the striking of that balance; that is, by full disclosure of the existence and extent of the risk involved.

* * *

There will, of course, be cases where the personal risk, although existent and known, is so trifling in comparison with the advantage to be gained as to be de minimis. Appellee so characterizes this case. It would approach the problem from a purely statistical point of view: less than one out [of] a million is just not unreasonable. This approach we reject. When, in a particular case, the risk qualitatively (e.g., of death or major disability) as well as quantitatively, on balance with the end sought to be achieved, is such as to call for a true choice judgment, medical or personal, the warning must be given.

Appellee contends that even under such a test no true choice situation is presented here. It asserts that "common sense and knowledge of the mainstreams of human conduct would unavoidably bring one to the conclusion" that appellant would have chosen to take the risk. It says, "Simply stated that proposition is this: A man has less than one in a million chance of contracting the dreaded disease of polio if he takes the vaccine. If he does not take the vaccine his chances of contracting polio are abundantly increased."

We do not so read the record. The Surgeon General's report of September, 1962, as we have quoted it, predicted that for the 1962 season only .9 persons over 20 years of age out of a million would contract polio from natural sources. While appellant was the father of two young children, he resided in an area that not only was not epidemic but whose immediate past history of incidence was extremely low. We have no way of knowing the extent to which either factor would affect the critical statistics. Thus appellant's risk of contracting the disease without immunization was about as great (or small) as his risk of contracting it from the vaccine. Under these circumstances we cannot agree with appellee that the choice to take the vaccine was clear.

We may note further that where the end sought is prevention of disease (and the likelihood of contracting the disease from natural sources is a relevant factor) the situation is a different one from that in which the disease has already struck and the end sought is relief or cure. Risks are far more readily taken in the latter case.

We conclude that the facts of this case imposed on the manufacturer a duty to warn the consumer (or make adequate provision for his being warned) as to the risks involved, and that failure to meet this duty rendered the drug unfit in the sense that it was thereby rendered unreasonably dangerous. Strict liability, then, attached to its sale in absence of warning.

399 F.2d at 129–30.

11. For general treatments of liability for failure to warn, see Gershonowitz, The Strict Liability Duty To Warn, 44 Wash. & Lee L.Rev. 71 (1987); Henderson and Twerski, Doctrinal Collapse in Products Liability: The Empty Shell of Failure to Warn, 65 N.Y.U.L.Rev. 265 (1990); Madden, The Duty to Warn in Products Liability: Contours and Criticism, 89 W.Va.L.Rev. 221 (1987); Noel, Products Defective Because of Inadequate Directions or Warnings, 23 Sw.L.J. 256 (1969); Twerski, Weinstein, Donaher, Piehler, The Use and Abuse of Warnings in Products Liability—Design Defect Litigation Comes of Age, 61 Cornell L.Rev. 495 (1976); Sales, The Duty To Warn And Instruct For Safe Use In Strict Tort Liability, 13 St. Mary's L.J. 521 (1982).

2. ADEQUACY OF WARNING

In order for a warning to be adequate it must make the product safe for both its intended and its foreseeable uses. A warning achieves this objective if it has the following characteristics. First, it must be displayed in such a way as to reasonably catch the attention of the persons expected to use the product. Second, it must fairly apprise a reasonable user of the nature and extent of the danger. Third, it must instruct the user as to how to use the product in such a way as to avoid the danger. *See* Madden, The Duty to Warn in Products Liability: Contours and Criticism, 89 W.Va.L.Rev. 221, 310–320 (1987); Noel, Products Defective Because of Inadequate Directions or Warnings, 23 Sw.L.J. 256, 283–288 (1969).

The following cases illustrate the way courts apply these principles.

SPRUILL v. BOYLE–MIDWAY, INC.
United States Court of Appeals, Fourth Circuit, 1962.
308 F.2d 79.

J. SPENCER BELL, CIRCUIT JUDGE.

This is an appeal by the defendants, Boyle–Midway, Incorporated, and American Home Products Corporation, from a judgment of the District Court for the Eastern District of Virginia entered upon a jury verdict for the plaintiffs in a wrongful death action. The defendants having preserved their rights by proper motions throughout the trial now ask us to set aside the judgment and rule that the case ought properly not to have gone to the jury; or that if it was properly submitted to the jury that the evidence in the case does not support the verdict.

The defendants are manufacturers and distributors of a product identified as "Old English Red Oil Furniture Polish". The plaintiffs in the court below were the parents and siblings of a fourteen months old infant who died as a result of chemical pneumonia caused by the ingestion of a small quantity of the defendants' product.

The mother of the deceased stated that she had purchased the polish on the morning of November 13, 1959, and later in the day was using it in her home to polish furniture. While using it in the deceased's bedroom she noticed a catalog which her mother had asked to see. While still in the course of polishing the furniture, she left the room and took the catalog next door to her mother's home. She testified that she was out of the room for four or five minutes.

At the time she left the room the deceased was in his crib in one corner of the room which was near one end of a bureau. The child could reach the end of the bureau nearest the crib but could not reach articles beyond the very edge of the bureau. The mother placed the polish, prior to leaving the room, upon the end of the bureau that was out of the child's reach. When she returned she found that the child had pulled a cover-cloth which was on the bureau into the crib, and the bottles and other articles sitting on the cloth came into the crib with it.   The child had removed the cap of the bottle and had consumed a small portion of the polish.

The child was admitted to a hospital that same day, and according to the testimony of Dr. Barclay ultimately died on November 15th from hydrocarbon pneumonia.   This particular type of pneumonia is a form of chemical pneumonia which usually results from the ingestion or inhalation of a petroleum distillate.

Old English Red Oil Furniture Polish is a liquid of a bright cherry red color contained in a clear glass bottle which is about 6¾″ tall and 2¼″ in diameter.   The bottle has a red metal cap. The evidence shows that there are one and one-half to two threads upon the neck of the bottle and the cap.

The ingredients of Old English Red Oil Furniture Polish are 98.2% mineral seal oil, 1.8% cedar oil, a trace of turpentine, and oil soluble red dye.   Chemical analysis of the product states: "This preparation consists almost entirely of [a] petroleum distillate which is somewhat heavier than kerosene and commonly designated as Mineral Seal Oil, or 300 degree oil, as it distills near 300 degrees C."

The label consists of a piece of paper of deep red hue which passes completely around the bottle at its center.   On the front part of the label appear the words "Old English Brand Red Oil Furniture Polish" in large letters; beneath this in small letters "An all purpose polish for furniture, woodwork, pianos, floors".   The reverse side of the label, the background of which is white, contains the following printed matter: at the top in red letters about ⅛th of an inch in height, all in capitals, "CAUTION COMBUSTIBLE MIXTURE".   Immediately beneath this in red letters ¹⁄₁₆th of an inch high "Do not use near fire or flame"; several lines down, again in letters ¹⁄₁₆th of an inch in height, in brown ink, all in capitals, the word "DIRECTIONS"; then follow seven lines of directions printed in brown ink in letters about ¹⁄₃₂nd of an inch in height.   On the eighth line in letters ¹⁄₁₆th of an inch high in brown ink appear the words "Safety Note"; following this in letters approximately ¹⁄₃₂nd of an inch in height:

> "Contains refined petroleum distillates.   May be harmful if swallowed, especially by children."

Following this is the name of the manufacturer and various other information with which we are not here concerned.

There was testimony that mineral seal oil is a toxic substance, and that it is a petroleum distillate.   The defendants' expert chemists testified that one teaspoonful of this product would kill a small child.   There was uncontroverted evidence of several doctors that the child died of hydrocarbon pneumonia resulting from the ingestion of the defendants' polish.   Dr. Julius Caplan, one of the doctors treating the deceased, attributed death to the nature of the polish, and stated that because of its toxic quality it was capable of penetrating the intestinal tract, thus getting into the blood stream and thereby setting up fatal lung damage. Dr. James Morgan, another treating physician, testified that this polish contained a hydrocarbon that was toxic and that such resulted in the death of the child.

The mother testified that she had no knowledge that the defendants' product would have caused injury or death to her child. She stated that she had read the statement at the top of the label in large colored letters "Caution Combustible", but did not read the directions because she knew how to use furniture polish.

At the trial the plaintiffs were allowed to put into evidence certain interrogatories they had served upon the defendants together with the defendants' answers and admissions which showed that the defendants had knowledge or notice of at least thirty-two cases of chemical pneumonia since 1953 resulting from the ingestion of this product. Ten of these thirty-two cases resulted in death. At least seven of these thirty-two cases were infants; four of these infants died as a result of chemical pneumonia. The defendants vigorously objected to the admission of this testimony, and on this appeal assigned its admission as error.

The jury in returning its verdict excluded the mother from sharing in any part of the judgment. The defendants made no request for a special verdict; therefore, the jury returned a general verdict. It was in favor of the plaintiffs other than the child's mother.

* * *

The defendants here have at no time raised the issue of lack of privity between themselves and the deceased and it appears that the point is conceded. In any event it is apparent that this case comes within the exception to the doctrine of Winterbottom v. Wright, 10 Mees & W. 109, 152 Eng.Reprint 402 (1842) which is made for inherently dangerous products. There can be no doubt but that this exception to that doctrine is well established in Virginia. General Bronze Corp. v. Kostopulos, 203 Va. 66, 122 S.E.2d 548 (1961); Norfolk Coca–Cola Bottling Works v. Krausse, 162 Va. 107, 173 S.E. 497 (1934); Robey v. Richmond Coca–Cola Bottling Works, 192 Va. 192, 64 S.E.2d 723 (1951). Indeed it is significant to note that the product involved in the leading case of Thomas v. Winchester, 6 N.Y. 397, 57 Am.Dec. 455 (1852), which firmly established the exception made for inherently dangerous products, was a poison.

Within the last year the courts of Virginia held that the test of whether a product is inherently dangerous is whether, "the danger of injury stems from the product itself, and not from any defect in it." General Bronze Corp. v. Kostopulos, supra. We hold that the danger of injury from the product stems from the product itself and not from any defect arising out of, or resulting from, negligence in the course of manufacture. It is therefore, an inherently dangerous product.

The defendants have contended throughout that they are liable only for injuries caused in the course of the intended use of their product.

Since their product was not intended to be consumed, they say, there is no liability for death or injury resulting from consumption of it. We agree with the general principle but the application the defendants would have us make of it here is much too narrow. "Intended use" is but a convenient adaptation of the basic test of "reasonable foreseeability" framed to more specifically fit the factual situations out of which arise questions of a manufacturer's liability for negligence. "Intended use" is not an inflexible formula to be apodictically applied to every case. Normally a seller or manufacturer is entitled to anticipate that the product he deals in will be used only for the purposes for which it is manufactured and sold; thus he is expected to reasonably foresee only injuries arising in the course of such use.

However, he must also be expected to anticipate the environment which is normal for the use of his product and where, as here, that environment is the home, he must anticipate the reasonably foreseeable risks of the use of his product in such an environment. These are risks which are inherent in the proper use for which his product is manufactured. Thus where such a product is an inherently dangerous one, and its danger is not obvious to the average housewife from the appearance of the product itself, the manufacturer has an obligation to anticipate reasonably foreseeable risks and to warn of them, though such risks may be incidental to the actual use for which the product was intended. As the courts of Virginia have stated it,

> "The common law requires a higher degree of care and vigilance in dealing with a dangerous agency than is required in the ordinary affairs of life and business which involve small risk of injury." American Oil Co. v. Nicholas, 156 Va. 1, 157 S.E. 754, 757 (1931). See also Standard Oil Co. v. Wakefield, 102 Va. 824, 47 S.E. 830, 66 L.R.A. 792 (1904).

We have no doubt but that under the circumstances of its use the courts of Virginia would regard Old English Red Oil Furniture Polish as a dangerous agency. A very small quantity of it is lethal to children and extremely dangerous to adults, yet the product gives no indication by its appearance of its life endangering capacity. It appears as harmless as a bottle of soft drink, yet this product is sent daily into thousands of homes in which dwell persons incompetent to safely judge its capacity for harm. It goes there without any reasonable indication from its natural character of its death dealing power if improperly used. It would be quite reasonable to anticipate that in the process of using it for its intended purpose it would be placed in close proximity to children. *They* certainly cannot be expected to recognize it as a lethal poison. Under these circumstances we think that a reasonable jury could properly find that it was foreseeable that sooner or later some child would draw the fatal draught.

* * *

However, even though a reasonable manufacturer should have foreseen that the product would have been consumed by humans, that manufacturer may not be liable if it has adequately warned of the danger to be reasonably foreseen. But a mere indication of danger, in and of itself, does not accomplish an inevitable tergiversation of liability. If warning of the danger is given and this warning is of a character reasonably calculated to bring home to the reasonably prudent person the nature and extent of the danger, it is sufficient to shift the risk of harm from the manufacturer to the user. To be of such character the warning must embody two characteristics: first, it must be in such form that it could reasonably be expected to catch the attention of the reasonably prudent man in the circumstances of its use; secondly, the content of the warning must be of such a nature as to be comprehensible to the average user and to convey a fair indication of the nature and extent of the danger to the mind of a reasonably prudent person.

The only protection available to children living in homes where this product is used is the caution of their parents, who are incapable of recognizing this harmless looking product for the dangerous agency it is. Without additional warning these adults have not the knowledge to invoke their caution on behalf of their young.

Under such circumstances as these the Virginia Courts have imposed upon the manufacturer or seller of the product a duty to warn of the danger.

"A person who knowingly sells or furnishes an article which, by reason of defective construction *or otherwise,* is eminently dangerous to life or property, *without notice or warning of the defect or danger,* is liable to third persons who suffer therefrom." (Emphasis added). McClanahan v. California Spray–Chemical Corp., [194 Va. 842, 75 S.E.2d 712 (1953)]; quoting with approval, 3 Cooley, Torts, § 498 at 467 (4th ed., 1932).

Where one is under a duty to warn another of danger and he fails to perform this duty by giving adequate warning, he is liable to the person to whom the duty is owed for injuries he suffers due to ignorance of the danger. Low Moore Iron Co. v. La Bianca, 106 Va. 83, 55 S.E. 532 (1906). The sufficiency of the warning is to be judged on the basis of the nature of the danger, and the degree of care required is "commensurate with the risk therefrom reasonably to be foreseen". Sadler v. Lynch, 192 Va. 344, 64 S.E.2d 664 (1951).

The duty to call attention to the danger is properly on defendant under the Virginia law. Moreover the question of the sufficiency of the warning is normally for the jury. McClanahan v. California Spray–Chemical Corp., supra; American Oil Co. v. Nicholas, supra; C.F. Maize v. Atlantic Refining Co., 352 Pa. 51, 41 A.2d 850, 160 A.L.R. 449 (1945) quoted with approval in McClanahan, supra. See generally Dillard and Hart, "Product Liability: Directions For Use And The Duty To Warn", 41 Va.L.Rev. 145, 177–78 (1955).

* * *

Keeping in mind the nature of the danger as described above we think reasonable men could properly differ as to the sufficiency of the notice here given, and that the finding of insufficiency of notice made by the jury in this case is amply supported by the evidence. The notice here given was not printed on the label in such a manner as to assure that a user's attention would be attracted thereto. Indeed, we think one might reasonably conclude that it was placed so as to conceal it from all but the most cautious users. It is located in the midst of a body of print of the same size and color, with nothing to attract special attention to it except the words "Safety Note".

Further, even if the user should happen to discover the warning it states only "contains refined petroleum distillates. May be harmful if swallowed especially by children". The first sentence could hardly be taken to convey any conception of the dangerous character of this product to the average user. The second sentence could be taken to indicate to the average person that harm is not certain but merely possible. The expert medical evidence in this case shows that "harm" will not be contingent but rather inevitable, to young and old alike. Moreover, the last phrase of the sentence hardly conveys the thought that a very small quantity of the polish is lethal to children.

There were two elements of danger inherent in this product, first, its character as a lethal poison, and second, its combustibility. We think that a reasonable jury could conclude that the greater danger in the environment of the modern home, and therefore the danger which due caution would require to be given the greater prominence on the label, was its poisonous character. Certainly a reasonable jury could conclude that this danger was required to be given a prominence at least *equal* to that arising from its combustible nature. A jury convinced that the poisonous character of this polish poses the greater danger could reasonably conclude that a manufacturer which hides its warning of the greater danger within its warning of the lesser is indulging its mercantile interests at the expense of the duty of due care it owes to the purchasing public.

The defendants contend, however, that,

"The question of the sufficiency of the warning is alleviated by the mother's admission that she never read the label. Not having availed herself of the information contained on the bottle she cannot be permitted to ask for a more explanatory label."

The short answer to this is that where the manufacturer is obligated to give an adequate warning of danger the giving of an inadequate warning is as complete a violation of its duty as would be the failure to give any warning. In this case had the warning been in a form calculated to attract the user's attention, due to its position, size, and the coloring of its lettering, and had the words used therein been reasonably calculated to convey a conception of the true nature of the danger, this mother might not have left the product in the presence of her child. Indeed, she might not have purchased the product at all, a fact of which the manufacturer appears to be aware. Having deprived the mother of an adequate warning which might have prevented the injury, it cannot be permitted to rely upon a warning which was insufficient to prevent the injury. This is the reasoning behind the rule laid down by the courts of Virginia that, " * * * [A]n insufficient warning is in legal effect no warning". Sadler v. Lynch, 192 Va. 344, 347, 64 S.E.2d 664, 666 (1951); McClanahan v. California Spray–Chemical Corp., supra. The jury in this case could reasonably find that the warning given was insufficient both in form and in content, and did, in fact, so find. The warning being insufficient, defendants cannot be permitted to take aid and comfort from it to any extent.

* * *

Perceiving no error by the court below, we
Affirm.

Notes

1. *Spruill's* treatment of the adequacy of the warning is excellent and up to date. The requirement in *Spruill* that the product be "inherently dangerous" in order for there to be a duty to warn is a vestige of the past. This characterization is no longer necessary to avoid the rule that the parties be in privity of contract. Gardner v. Q.H.S., Inc., 448 F.2d 238, 242 (4th Cir.1971).

2. In some jurisdictions the "inherent danger" requirement produced an attempt to make a sharp distinction between negligent manufacturing of a flawed product and negligent failure to warn. A product was "inherently dangerous" if it was dangerous even though properly made. Liability arose for failure to warn about such dangers rather than for improper manufacture. If a product was not dangerous unless defectively manufactured, liability was for negligence in causing the defect, not for failure to warn. *See* Dillard and Hart, Product Liability: Directions for Use and the Duty to Warn, 41 Va.L.Rev. 145, 153 (1955).

3. Most courts no longer make this distinction. They recognize that even a defective product may sometimes safely be used for some purposes, but not for others. Such a product may often reasonably be marketed if it is accompanied by warnings against unsafe uses. *See* Restatement of Torts (Second) § 388 (1965). The modern statement of the rule is that there is a duty to warn against significant risks if the absence of the warning is likely to make the product unduly dangerous. Madden, The Duty to Warn in Products Liability: Contours and Criticism, 89 W.Va.L.Rev. 221, 234–235 (1987).

4. **Relationship Between Design and Warning Theories.** In many cases there is a very close relationship between product defect because of a failure to warn and product defect because of design. *See* Twerski, Weinstein, Donaher, Piehler, The Use and Abuse of Warnings in Products Liability—Design Defect Litigation Comes of Age, 61 Cornell L.Rev. 495, 500–505 (1976). In *Spruill*, for example, the warning was inadequate in large part because of the way the product was designed. Its red color made it more appealing to children than other polishes, and its formula made it

much more poisonous to children than one would expect. The warning might have been sufficient if the polish had been far less toxic and a different color. One might even argue that the polish was defective and unreasonably dangerous because of its color and toxicity. If the jury found this to be true, then the product would be defective both in design and for a failure to warn. Another possibility is a finding that the design is reasonable, but only if an adequate warning is given. In this event, the polish would be defective because of a failure to warn only.

It is because of this close relationship between the two theories that plaintiffs frequently sue in the alternative, claiming that the product is defective both because of the way it is designed and because of a failure to warn. The warning theory is particularly appealing in such cases because it may be easier to persuade a jury that the manufacturer should change his warning than that he should change his design.

5. There are some products where the design is clearly unreasonable regardless of what warning is given. Should manufacturers of such products be able to escape liability by giving a sufficient warning? *See* Brownlee v. Louisville Varnish Co., 641 F.2d 397 (5th Cir.1981) (Alabama law; aerosol spray paint can without a relief valve to protect against explosion in the event that it is subjected to excessive heat); Heckman v. Federal Press Co., 587 F.2d 612 (3d Cir.1978) (Pennsylvania law; power press without a guard to protect the worker's hand from the ram); Note, The Interrelationship Between Design Defects and Warnings in Products Liability Law: *Abbot v. American Cyanamid Co.*, 11 Geo.Mason U.L.Rev. 171 (1989). Should the answer depend on whether the court uses consumer expectations or risk-utility as the test of defect?

6. As *Spruill* indicates, manufacturers have a duty to warn against foreseeable misuse. This is now generally accepted. *See, e.g.,* Knowles v. Harnischfeger Corp., 36 Wash.App. 317, 674 P.2d 200 (1983) (using a crane to lift a person). Manufacturers also, of course, must warn against generic risks associated with the proper use of their products. *See, e.g.,* Borel v. Fibreboard Paper Prod. Corp., 493 F.2d 1076 (5th Cir.1973), cert. denied, 419 U.S. 869, 95 S.Ct. 127, 42 L.Ed.2d 107 (1974) (risk that inhaling asbestos can cause asbestosis and cancer).

EDWARDS v. CALIFORNIA CHEMICAL CO.

District Court of Appeal of Florida, Fourth District, 1971.
245 So.2d 259, cert. denied, 247 So.2d 440 (1971).

WALDEN, JUDGE.

This negligence case was terminated in the trial court by entry of summary judgment against the plaintiff. He appeals. We reverse because of the existence of genuine issues of material fact that preclude summary disposition.

A summary judgment review of the record reveals that plaintiff, an illiterate, labored at the Boca Raton Hotel and Country Club taking care of the golf course grounds. He became ill from arsenic poisoning following use of Ortho Standard Lead Arsenate. This product was manufactured by the defendant, California Chemical Co., and was sold and distributed by the defendant, Hector Supply Co.

Lead arsenate is highly toxic. It can be absorbed into the body by inhalation, contact with unbroken skin and digestion. To safely use the product the user must wear protective clothing and employ a respirator.

The gravamen of plaintiff's complaint and the crux of this appeal centers upon the defendant's failure to warn the plaintiff of the necessity for a user to employ a respirator and protective rubber or neoprene clothing. More particularly, we must decide if the warning contained upon the product's label was a sufficient warning as a matter of law so as to entitle defendants to summary judgment.

On one side of the bag containing the lead arsenate were printed lengthy and specific instructions for use as an insecticide as concerns its application to various agricultural crops including that of lawns and golf greens, as follows:

"ORTHO® STANDARD LEAD ARSENATE
READ ENTIRE LABEL. USE STRICTLY IN ACCORDANCE WITH CAUTIONS, WARNINGS AND DIRECTIONS, AND WITH APPLICABLE STATE AND FEDERAL REGULATIONS. USES, TIMING AND DOSAGE MAY VARY AS A CONSEQUENCE OF LOCAL WEATHER OR CONDITIONS; WE RECOMMEND REFERENCE TO LOCAL AGRICULTURAL AUTHORITIES CONCERNING SPECIFIC USAGE.

DIRECTIONS

Official recommendations for the use and dosage of Lead Arsenate vary in different sections. Use ORTHO Standard Lead Arsenate according to the standard practices in your locality for the control of those insects against which Lead Arsenate is effective. The following general directions are suggested as a guide for the use of this material.

APPLES, PEARS, QUINCES: Codling Moth, Leafrollers, Plum Curculio, Tent Caterpillars--Use 3 lbs. to 100 gals. water for Calyx and cover sprays. For Apple Maggot-Use 2 lbs. per 100 gals. Consult your ORTHO Fieldman or your local Agricultural Authority in regard to the number and dates of applications. Californis Oak Moth, Red Humped Caterpillar and Tent Caterpillar-Use 3 to 4 lbs. to 100 gals. water when insects first attack foliage.

CHERRIES (Eastern States): Cherry Maggot--2 1/2 lbs. to 100 gals. water. Apply according to local recommendations.

GRAPES: Achemon Sphinx Moth, Grape Root Worm, Grape Leaf Folder--Use 3 to 4 lbs. to 100 gals. water. (400 gals. diluted spray per acre) when insects first attack foliage. Do not apply after edible parts start to form.

WALNUTS: Codling Moth (California)--2 to 3 lbs. in 100 gals. water. (1500 gals. diluted spray per acre). Combine with 1/2 lb. safener, DELMO-Z Spray or ORTHO Spray Lime and 1/3 gal. ORTHOL-K Light Medium Flowable Emulsion plus 1/2 lb. ORTHO DDT 50 Wettable for first bloom spray usually early May. Under severe conditions a second application may be needed during late June. Do not apply to walnuts after the husks open.

POTATOES, TOMATOES: Colorado Potato Beetle, Armyworms, Tomato Fruitworm, Sphinx Moth--Use 4 to 6 lbs. either alone or with about 3 lbs. of ORTHO Spray Lime in 100 gals. water. Use no more than 200 gals. diluted spray per acre. For Small Quantity Dosage-Use 2 level teaspoonfuls to 1 qt. water (8 level teaspoonfuls (3 1/3 tablespoonfuls) to 1 gal. water). Tomato Fruitworm-Treat up to harvesting. For dusting Potatoes for above pests: Use this material as it comes from the package at the rate of 5 to 7 lbs. per acre, or mixed with from 3 to 5 times as much ORTHO Spray Lime.

LAWNS AND GOLF GREENS: Sod Webworm, Lawn Moth, Cutworms, White Grubs, Earthworms (Night Crawlers)-Use in accordance with the recommendations of local Agricultural Authorities. 5 lbs. per 1000 sq. ft. of turf is the usual rate of application. Japanese Beetle Larvae (Eastern States)--Use 10 lbs. per 1000 sq. ft. Keep children and pets off treated areas until this material has been washed into the soil.

TO MIX: Put water in spray tank slightly above agitator. Start the agitator. Slowly shake the required quantity of ORTHO Standard Lead Arsenate into the water, agitate until a uniform mixture is made, then fill tank with water. Keep the solution constantly agitated while spraying. When combining with ORTHO oil sprays, follow mixing directions on labels.

NOTE: When using on plants having tender foliage, always add from 8 to 10 lbs. ORTHO Spray Lime to each 100 gals. diluted spray. When used alone on plants with hardy, or reasonably hardy, foliage, the addition of Chemically Hydrated Lime in this way is a good practice also.

2. Because critical, unforeseeable factors beyond the manufacturer's control prevent it from eliminating all risks in connection with the use of chemicals even though reasonably fit for such use, buyer and user acknowledge and assume all risks and liability (except those assumed by the manufacturer under 1 above) resulting from handling, storage, and use of this material. These risks include, but are not limited to, damage to plants, crops and animals to which the material is applied, failure to control pests, damage caused by drift to other plants or crops, and personal injury. Buyer and user accept and use this material on these conditions, whether or not such use is in accordance with directions. FORM 6158-D"
[A3841]

The product was labeled on the other side, as concerns its warning of danger, as follows:

COLORED

SOLD AS AN INSECTICIDE

Active Ingredient	By Wt.
Standard Lead Arsenate ($PbHAsO_4$	95%
Inert Ingredients	5%
Lead expressed as Metallic	56.7%
Arsenic expressed as Metallic	20.5%
Water soluble Arsenic expressed as Metallic, not more than	0.5%

[A3635]

POISON

ANTIDOTE: For Arsenic--Give a tablespoonful of salt in a glass of warm water and repeat until vomit fluid is clear. Then give two tablespoonfuls of Epsom Salt or Milk of Magnesia in water and plenty of milk and water. Have victim lie down and keep quiet. CALL A PHYSICIAN IMMEDIATELY.
DANGER:
KEEP OUT OF REACH OF CHILDREN
DO NOT INHALE
DO NOT GET ON SKIN
DO NOT TAKE INTERNALLY

WARNING: Poisonous if swallowed. Avoid breathing dust or spray mist. Avoid contact with skin, eyes, or clothing. Wash thoroughly after using. Do not apply to fruits and vegetables except Tomatoes within 30 days of harvest unless otherwise specified. Wash sprayed fruit and vegetables at harvest. Avoid contamination of forage crops and pasture. Do not apply under conditions involving possible drift to food, forage or other plantings that might be damaged or the crops thereof rendered unfit for sale, use or consumption.

- -

DIRECTIONS ON BACK

NET WEIGHT 4 POUNDS	Completely empty bag and dispose of waste pesticide by burying. Burn bag immediately and stay out of smoke. Residue and ashes from burned bags must also be buried.

[A3636]

—————◆—————

As can be seen—this without dispute—there was no warning or indication upon the label that a respirator and protective clothing were required for safe use.

It is clear that manufacturers and sellers of inherently dangerous products have a duty to give users a fair and adequate warning of its dangerous potentialities. And clearly plaintiff was within a class who would foreseeably use the product and be harmed in the absence of adequate warning.

Turning to the warning label and the question of its adequacy, we believe that * * * [the adequacy of the warning label is] a question of fact properly to be decided by the jury.

* * *

In the instant case the labelings present an anomalous situation when viewed by a potential user. He is told how to use it as an insecticide but he is not told how to use it with safety.

On one side of the container the label tells him that the product may be used as an insecticide. He is furnished with a careful catalog of twenty-three insects that are controllable by the product. Ten crops are itemized as being amenable to treatment. He is given the exact proportion of arsenate and water that must be blended depending upon the particular insect to be eradicated. He is told with exactness at what stage of growth applications are to be made, depending upon the crop. Additives are prescribed in certain circumstances. He is told the amount of the product to be applied to a given area. He is given the amount of arsenate to be employed per 1000 square feet to be used for certain insects. He is instructed in detail as to how to mix, maintain in suspension, and spray the mixture. In sum, he is told with extreme particularity *how, where, when* and *for what purpose* to use the product as an insecticide.

On the other hand and side, we have the label warning of danger. It is red, and reflects a skull and cross-bones together with a large word,

"Poison." The exact label is set forth above. Primarily it admonishes that the product is not to be inhaled, touched to the skin or taken internally. There is a total failure or omission of the defendants to tell or instruct the user as to *how* the product may be safely used. It does not prescribe, as earlier noted, that a respirator and protective clothing must be used.

As a matter of reason and everyday common sense the jury would be authorized, in light of these two labels, to believe that it would be difficult if not impossible, for a user to use the product in the fashions detailed by defendants without in some measure inhaling, touching or ingesting some of the product.

In light of the specific instructions in one area and the failure in the other and more important area to prescribe protective clothing and a respirator and to tell the user *how to safely use the product,* the jury would be warranted in believing that the label warning was inadequate. It could be inferred from the omission that the product was not sufficiently dangerous and virulent to require protective devices or else the label would have so stated and warned. In other words, the jury could determine that the duty to warn under these circumstances could only be fulfilled by putting the user on specific notice as to how the product might be safely used, in addition to its advices as to how it might be efficiently used.

From our survey we feel that only a jury could determine if plaintiff had been fairly and adequately warned. It would have to decide in the language of the Wait case, supra, if the defendants here fulfilled their duty to warn " * * * with a degree of intensity that would cause a reasonable man to exercise for his own safety the caution commensurate with the potential danger." And in the language of the Williams case, supra, " * * * was the degree of warning commensurately proportionate to the potential danger * * *?"

Having considered the complete appellate treatment and discussed the matters that we deem deserving, we reverse and remand for further proceedings consistent herewith.

Reversed and remanded.

REED, J., and WILLIAMS, ROBERT L., ASSOCIATE JUDGE, concur.

Notes

1. There is a distinction between instructions and warnings. A warning apprises the user of the risks associated with the product. Instructions explain how to use the product. As *Edwards* indicates, there is a duty to instruct in addition to a duty to warn when this is reasonably necessary.

Midgley v. S.S. Kresge Co., 55 Cal.App.3d 67, 127 Cal.Rptr. 217 (1976) provides another example. The manufacturer of a child's telescope provided a special filter to be attached to the eyepiece for viewing the sun. The instructions warned against looking at the sun without the filter, but they did not clearly show the proper method of attaching the filter. A 13 year old child bought the telescope. He understood from the warning that he had to use the filter when looking at the sun, but he did not understand how to attach it. He received eye damage because he viewed the sun with the filter improperly attached. The manufacturer was held liable for failing to provide adequate instructions for installation of the sun filter.

2. It is also true that instructions unaccompanied by a warning of the consequences of failing to follow the instructions will result in liability. This is true even if following the instructions would have prevented the accident. This is because the user may fail to understand the significance of failing to follow the instructions. He may, for example, regard the instructions as being concerned with the efficient use of the product, and having nothing to do with safety. Under these circumstances, he may not realize that failing to follow the instructions could lead to an accident. *See* Dillard & Hart, Product Liability: Directions for Use and the Duty to Warn, 41 Va.L.Rev. 145, 147–152 (1955); Noel, Products Defective Because of Inadequate Directions or Warnings, 23 Sw.L.J. 256, 263 (1969). This is illustrated by the following cases.

A. In Hiigel v. General Motors Corp., 190 Colo. 57, 544 P.2d 983 (1975), the rear wheels came off of plaintiff's motor home while it was being driven because the wheel studs sheared. This occurred because the wheel stud bolts were not tightened to the proper torque. The owner's manual stated the proper torque, and prescribed intervals when the torque should be checked. The manual did not explain the risks resulting from a failure to meet the torque requirements. Because of this deficiency, the duty to warn was not satisfied.

B. In McLaughlin v. Mine Safety Appliances Co., 11 N.Y.2d 62, 226 N.Y.S.2d 407, 181 N.E.2d 430 (1962) defendant manufactured heat blocks designed to revive injured persons. The instructions said to wrap the blocks in insulating material before use. These instructions were inadequate because they did not say that serious burns could result if the insulation was not used.

3. Suppose a manufacturer equips its product with a safety device that adequately protects users from injury. Must it warn against the consequences of circumventing the device? *See* Miller v. Anetsberger Bros., 124 A.D.2d 1057, 508 N.Y.S.2d 954 (1986).

RHODES v. INTERSTATE BATTERY SYS. OF AM., INC.

United States Court of Appeals, Eleventh Circuit, 1984.
722 F.2d 1517.

KRAVITCH, CIRCUIT JUDGE:

In this Georgia diversity action plaintiff-appellant Rhodes seeks damages for personal injuries suffered in an explosion occurring when he struck a match and loosened the vent caps on an automobile battery manufactured and distributed by defendant-appellees. Rhodes appeals an order of the district court dismissing his claim on summary judgment. We reverse and remand.

The battery was manufactured by Johnson Controls, Inc. ("Johnson") for distribution by Interstate Battery System of America, Inc.

("Interstate"), which sold the product under its own name. The plastic top of the battery contained two vent caps designed to cover six cell holes leading to the acid below. Permanently embossed into the vent caps is the following warning:

DANGER–EXPLOSIVE GASES

BATTERIES PRODUCE EXPLOSIVE GASES. KEEP SPARKS FLAME, CIGARETTES AWAY. VENTILATE WHEN CHARGING OR USING IN ENCLOSED SPACE. ALWAYS SHIELD EYES WHEN WORKING NEAR BATTERIES.

POISON—CAUSES SEVERE BURNS

CONTAINS SULFURIC ACID. AVOID CONTACT WITH SKIN, EYES OR CLOTHING. ANTIDOTE EXTERNAL—FLUSH WITH WATER. EYES—FLUSH WITH WATER FOR 15 MINUTES AND GET PROMPT MEDICAL ATTENTION. INTERNAL—DRINK LARGE AMOUNTS OF WATER OR MILK, FOLLOW WITH MILK OF MAGNESIA, BEATEN EGG OR VEG. OIL. CALL PHYSICIAN IMMEDIATELY. KEEP OUT OF REACH OF CHILDREN.

The first line in each paragraph of the warning appears in letters approximately twice as large as the remaining text.

Fifteen months prior to the date of Rhodes' injury, his wife purchased the battery and had it installed at a local service station. On the night of the accident, Rhodes stopped after work for two to three hours at a tavern, and when he emerged he discovered the battery was dead. To ascertain whether the battery was low on water, he struck a match to check the fluid level. When the flame was about twelve to fifteen inches from the battery, the battery exploded, covering Rhodes' face and eyes with sulfuric acid.

In his deposition, Rhodes admitted he had not read the warning label. In fact, although he had owned several cars over the years, he stated that he had never seen or read a warning label on an automobile battery.

Rhodes sought recovery in negligence and strict liability against both Johnson and Interstate for their failure to provide an adequate warning of the dangers associated with their product. The defendants maintained Rhodes was precluded from recovery as a matter of law because he failed to read the warning label, which fully and adequately described the inherent dangers of the battery. The district court agreed with the defendants and granted summary judgment on both the negligence and strict liability claims. Concluding that Rhodes' claims present genuine issues of fact as to the adequacy of the warning, we reverse the order of the district court.

I. NEGLIGENCE

Rhodes' negligence theory is predicated on the principle that a manufacturer or supplier is under a duty to inform potential users of the product of any facts making it dangerous. *Kicklighter v. Nails by*

Jannee, Inc., 616 F.2d 734, 740 n. 4 (5th Cir.1980);[1] *Reddick v. White Consolidated Indus., Inc.,* 295 F.Supp. 243, 245 (S.D.Ga.1969). This duty may be breached in either of two ways: (1) failure to take adequate measures to communicate the warning to the ultimate user, or (2) failure to provide a warning that, if communicated, was adequate to apprise the user of the product's potential risks. *Stapleton v. Kawasaki Heavy Indus., Ltd.,* 608 F.2d 571, 573 (1979), *modified on other grounds,* 612 F.2d 905 (5th Cir.1980). Both of these issues are uniformly held to be questions for the jury. *Id.* Nevertheless, the district court ordered summary judgment because under Georgia law Rhodes' failure to read the warning label constituted contributory negligence, thus barring plaintiff's recovery as a matter of law.

The district court relied upon three decisions of the Georgia Court of Appeals holding that any insufficiency in the adequacy of the warning label of a product cannot be the proximate cause of the injury when the plaintiff is contributorily negligent by failing to read the warning. *See Cobb Heating & Air Conditioning Co. v. Hertron Chemical Co.,* 139 Ga.App. 803, 229 S.E.2d 681 (1976); *Parzini v. Center Chemical Co.,* 129 Ga.App. 868, 201 S.E.2d 808 (1973), *rev'd on other grounds,* 234 Ga. 868, 218 S.E.2d 580 (1975); *McCleskey v. Olin Mathieson Chemical Corp.,* 127 Ga.App. 178, 193 S.E.2d 16 (1972). Although these cases do stand for the general proposition that failure to read a warning is contributory negligence, they do not necessarily preclude recovery in this case. The plaintiffs in *Cobb, Parzini* and *McCleskey* did not assert, as Rhodes does here, that the warning was not adequately communicated to the user. Rhodes does not maintain that the warning itself, if communicated, was inadequate to apprise him of the danger. He claims his failure to read the label resulted from the defendants' negligence in communicating the warning, i.e., that other, more effective ways of communicating the battery's dangers were available and should have been employed.[2] If the defendants did not take reasonable steps to communicate the warning to Rhodes, his failure to read it would not constitute contributory negligence. *See Stapleton,* 608 F.2d at 573.

* * *

Cobb, Parzini and *McCleskey* * * * hold only that an injured party cannot claim inadequacy of the contents of a warning if he never bothered to read the warning. They do not bar a claim, such as Rhodes', that an injury was caused by the manufacturer's failure to take appropriate measures to communicate the potential risks to the ultimate user. Unlike the plaintiffs in those three cases, Rhodes alleges he was not accustomed to handling this product and did not have the opportunity to view the battery and its accompanying warning under sufficient lighting.

---

1. The Eleventh Circuit in *Bonner v. City of Prichard,* 661 F.2d 1206, 1209 (11th Cir.1981) (en banc), adopted as binding precedent decisions of the Fifth Circuit rendered prior to October 1, 1981.

2. Rhodes suggests alternative means of communication such as phosphorus paint that would be visible at night, advertising through the media, and verbal or written warnings issued by the seller.

His claim is that an embossed warning on the top of the battery is not likely to warn a consumer in his position of the potential dangers and that the defendants were negligent in not attempting to convey the risks in a more effective manner.

Summary judgment is not appropriate unless the moving party demonstrates that there was no genuine issue of any material fact and that he is entitled to judgment as a matter of law. Fed.R.Civ.P. 56(c). Since we have determined that Rhodes is not prevented from asserting a claim based upon the defendants' negligent failure to provide a warning reasonably likely to apprise him of a battery's dangerous qualities, he should be allowed to attempt to persuade a jury to so find. A factual issue exists as to the adequacy of the defendants' adopted means of conveying the warning. It is for the jury to decide whether or not their chosen method was negligent. We therefore reverse the order of summary judgment on plaintiff's negligence claim.

II.   STRICT LIABILITY

The district court dismissed Rhodes' strict liability claim against Interstate * * *.

The court * * * held "as a matter of law" that the language embossed on the vent caps was an adequate warning of the potential danger to the plaintiff and that the battery was therefore not defective. Its decision apparently was premised upon a number of factual determinations leading to a conclusion that the appropriate place for a warning on an automobile battery is on its cell cover.

It generally has been held that a jury is to determine whether a product is defective, whether the user was aware of the danger, and whether his use of the product in view of this knowledge was unreasonable. *Parzini v. Center Chemical Co.,* 136 Ga.App. 396, 221 S.E.2d 475 (1975). The doctrine of strict liability requires a manufacturer of a dangerous product to use reasonable efforts to bring the warning to the attention of the potential user. A product without such a warning is defective. *Chemical Center Co. v. Parzini,* 234 Ga. 868, 870, 218 S.E.2d 580, 582 (1975). Whether the warning in this case was adequate to apprise an automobile owner of the battery's inherent dangers is a question of fact. A jury could conclude that the danger posed by the emission of flammable gases was sufficiently great that the warning should have been presented in a more effective manner. *See Stapleton,* 608 F.2d at 573. The district court erred in deciding the issue as a matter of law, and its order of summary judgment on plaintiff's strict liability claim must be reversed.

Reversed and Remanded.

JAMES C. HILL, CIRCUIT JUDGE, dissenting:

* * *

The warning embossed on the battery involved in this case is set out in the majority opinion. It not only warned of danger; it cautioned users of the exact danger from which Rhodes' injuries flowed—*i.e.,* the warning importuned users that the battery contained explosive gases which would ignite if exposed to flame.

In order to submit himself to this danger, Rhodes had to remove the battery's vent caps, on which were embossed the explicit warnings. Rhodes admitted that he did not read the warning. Furthermore, in response to questions by the defendants, Rhodes testified:

Q. Have you ever looked at a car battery?

A. I don't mess with batteries.

Q. Well, you've looked at a battery before, haven't you?

A. I've looked at them, but even if there was a warning on it, I wouldn't have paid attention to it.

Q. You wouldn't have paid attention to it?

A. Well, it would have to be a big warning.

Q. What form would the warning have to take for you to pay attention to it?

A. I would say if it said "Warning" and it was in big enough letters, something that I could see, I may pay attention to it, I don't know if I would pay attention to it then.

(R. 21–22) It thus appears that any product manufacturer would have been hard pressed to bring its warning message home to Rhodes.

The law to be applied to these facts is clear. Without exception, the Georgia courts hold that, as a matter of law, a plaintiff's failure to read a warning printed on an injury-producing product constitutes contributory negligence and precludes plaintiff from recovering against the product manufacturer and distributor. *Cobb Heating and Air Conditioning Co. v. Hertron Chemical Co.,* 139 Ga.App. 803, 229 S.E.2d 681 (1976); *Parzini v. Center Chemical Co.,* 129 Ga.App. 868, 201 S.E.2d 808, *rev'd on other grounds,* 234 Ga. 868, 218 S.E.2d 580 (1975); *McCleskey v. Olin Mathieson Chemical Corp.,* 127 Ga.App. 178, 193 S.E.2d 16 (1972). Rhodes, having failed to read the warning embossed on the battery vent caps, is thus barred from recovering against the battery manufacturer and distributor.

In spite of the fact that Rhodes suggests some exotic methods whereby the warning might have been better forced upon him—*e.g.,* using letters printed with phosphorescent paint, etc.—the Georgia cases cited above do not require more of defendants than was done here.[1] Simply stated, the extent of a product manufacturer's exposure to strict

---

1. We need not decide whether phosphorescent paint on the vent caps of a battery confined in darkness beneath the closed hood of an automobile would absorb enough radiated light to return it visibly in the dark of night. Rhodes probably does not suggest that battery manufacturers employ paint containing radium or other sources of self-illumination said to be carcinogenic.

liability is not, and can not be, limited only by the scope of a litigant's imagination.

For this very reason, the rule must be that product manufacturers are required to employ warnings that are "reasonably calculated" to reach potential users. *West v. Broderick & Bascom Rope Co.,* 197 N.W.2d 202, 212 (Iowa 1972); Noel, Products Defective Because of Inadequate Directions or Warnings, 23 Sw.L.J. 256, 281–85 (1969); Restatement (Second) of Torts § 388(c) (1965). In most cases, whether a warning is "reasonably calculated" to reach the product's users will present a factual issue precluding summary judgment. For such a determination "depends on the language used and the impression that it is calculated to make upon the mind of the average user of the product and involves questions of display, syntax and emphasis." *Stapleton v. Kawasaki Heavy Industries, Ltd.,* 608 F.2d 571, 573 n. 4 (5th Cir.1979), *modified on other grounds,* 612 F.2d 905 (1980), *quoting, D'Arienzo v. Clairol, Inc.,* 125 N.J.Super. 224, 230–31, 310 A.2d 106, 112 (1973).

However, summary judgment may be entered in any negligence action where the uncontested facts demonstrate that only one result could be supported and that one party is entitled to judgment as a matter of law. *Gross v. Southern Railway Co.,* 414 F.2d 292 (5th Cir.1969); *Atlantic Coast Line Rwy. v. Key,* 196 F.2d 64 (5th Cir.1952). Here, the undisputed facts establish that the battery carried a warning of its dangers, that the warning clearly appeared on the top of the battery (the portion exposed to anyone attempting to service the battery), and that the warning in no uncertain terms cautioned users to keep flame away from the battery. The district court, on these facts, was entitled to hold that, as a matter of law, this warning was "reasonably calculated" to reach potential users.

Under established Georgia law, this action should have ended with the district court granting summary judgment to defendants. * * *

If courts are to continue to function efficiently and to consider and resolve those serious disputes that are presented, they must be allowed to dispose of cases without substantial dispute by summary judgment. Certainly, courts should not be put to the task of conducting a trial each time a litigant suggests that, under some remotely conceivable set of facts, he could recover on his claim or maintain a satisfactory defense to the action. For if left to the fertile imaginations of those scrambling to avoid summary judgment, the standard governing a Rule 56 motion would soon prove to be insurmountable. Fearing that we are fast approaching that standard, I

Dissent.

Notes

1. How should a court decide the following case?

Plaintiff stopped to help a stranded motorist. It was evening and the visibility was poor. After discovering that the battery was dead plaintiff looked under the hood. He located the battery and observed the name of the manufacturer. He found the battery caps and removed one or two of them. He went to his car to look for a flashlight, but was unable to find one. He returned, leaned over the battery, lit a cigarette lighter, and the battery exploded. Plaintiff sued the battery manufacturer for failing to provide an adequate warning. A warning label was attached to the top of the battery at the time of the accident. Below is a photograph of the battery and label viewed from the front of the car:

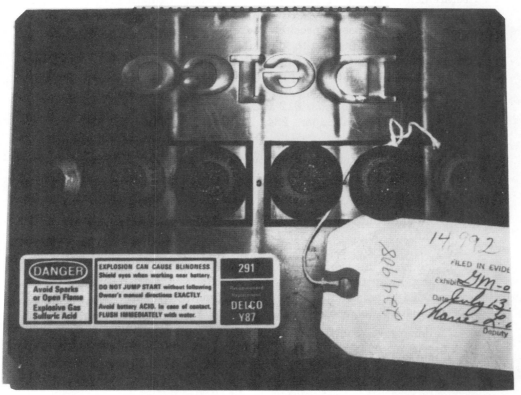

Plaintiff claimed that he did not see the label. The jury found for defendant on the basis that the warning was adequate. Plaintiff appeals, claiming that the finding was against the weight of the evidence. Decide the case.

2. Mr. Rhodes apparently did not pay much attention to warnings. Is he atypical? Empirical research on this question is not conclusive, but it indicates that many people often fail to read warnings. *See* Dorris & Purswell, Warnings and Human Behavior: Implications for the Design of Product Warnings, 1 J.Prod.Liab. 254 (1977). What implications does this have for the law of products liability?

3. In cases where plaintiff did not read the warning, defendants frequently argue that the alleged inadequacy of the warning did not cause the injury. This causation issue is treated in Chapter 11, section B.1. Does *Rhodes* present a causation problem?

HAHN v. STERLING DRUG, INC.

United States Court of Appeals, Eleventh Circuit, 1986.
805 F.2d 1480.

PER CURIAM:

This is an appeal from the district court order directing the verdict in favor of the defendant-appellee, Sterling Drug Company, Inc. Plaintiffs Stanley and Vicki Hahn sought a recovery on behalf of their daughter, Valerie Anne Hahn, for the injuries sustained by her when she swallowed one and one-half ounces of Campho–Phenique, an over-the-counter topical analgesic sold by the defendant. * * * We * * * reverse the district court's grant of a directed verdict and remand for a new trial.

On December 19, 1982, four year old Valerie Anne Hahn swallowed one and one-half ounces of Campho–Phenique, an over-the-counter topical analgesic. One half hour later, she was convulsing, vomiting, and for a time she stopped breathing. After treatment at the Rockdale County Hospital, she was transferred to the intensive care unit at the Henrietta Eggleston Children's Hospital. After an approximate 24–hour stay in the intensive care unit, Valerie was released and has suffered no permanent disability from the incident.

Earlier in the evening of the 19th, the Hahns allowed their seven year old child to use Campho–Phenique to treat a cold sore. This child evidently misplaced the lid to the container. There was some speculation that the seven year old administered the medicine to Valerie.

Valerie's parents sued Sterling Drug, alleging that Campho–Phenique was a defective product because the warning on the container was inadequate and for the further reason that the product did not have a child-proof cap. The complaint sounds in tort and strict liability. The district court directed a verdict for the defendant, holding that the warning on the package was adequate and that reasonable men could not arrive at a contrary verdict. The warning label on the defendant's product contains the following:

> WARNING: Keep this and all medicines out of children's reach. In case of accidental ingestion, seek professional assistance or contact a poison control center immediately. DIRECTIONS: For external use: apply with cotton three or four times daily.

Appellants contend that they produced evidence from which a jury could conclude that the danger posed by the product when ingested by small children was great enough to require a more stringent warning. The Hahns rely principally on the testimony of their toxicology expert, Dr. Albert P. Rauber, Professor of Pediatrics at Emory University and also Medical Director of the Georgia Poison Center. Dr. Rauber testified that the warning was very general and that its effect is "watered down" by the fact that the same warning appears on numerous products that are not harmful (i.e., Flintstone Vitamins and Hydrocortisone Cream). Rauber said he was not "satisfied" with the Campho–Phenique label.

The Hahns point to several other facts which could have led a jury to believe that the warning was inadequate. First, the Hahns themselves testified that they had read the label in its entirety and were still unaware that the product could harm their child if ingested. Second, Sterling was aware that many children had been injured after ingesting the product, yet the product continued to use the same warning. Third, the product was known to be quite toxic, and as such it required a more dramatic warning. Fourth, the warning was in a smaller print than other messages on the label. The Hahns say that this was confusing even though the warning was in bold-face type. Fifth, the direction "for external use" was not followed by the word "only." Sixth, the label stated that the product may be used on the gums, possibly indicating to a reasonable person that internal use might be acceptable. Seventh, the label was silent as to the possibility of seizures and respiratory failure if taken internally. Eighth, the warning to contact the poison control center was insufficient since it would have been just as easy to put the word "poison" on the label. Also, the warning is said to be more like a "helpful hint meant merely to please and placate a concerned parent and not a clue that the contents of the bottle are poisonous."

Appellee, of course, argues that no reasonable person could find that the warning on the Campho–Phenique label was inadequate. Sterling relies on Dr. Rauber's admission during cross examination that the warning advised a reasonable person that the product was potentially toxic and that ingestion might create "grave danger." The district court agreed. The court below held that both the references to external use and to the poison control center in combination with the reference to keep this and all medicines out of the reach of children were sufficient to convey the message to an average adult that there is a risk of serious harm if the child swallows the medicine.

At oral argument, Sterling's attorneys conceded that they could not refer to the court any case decided in the Eleventh Circuit or in the Georgia courts which held that the adequacy of a product manufacturer's warning is a proper subject for a directed verdict. There are, however, three products liability cases decided in recent years that present the issue of the adequacy of warnings to Georgia consumers. In *Stapleton v. Kawasaki Heavy Indus., Ltd.*, 608 F.2d 571 (5th Cir.1979), *modified on other grounds*, 612 F.2d 905 (5th Cir.1980), we held that "whether adequate efforts were made to communicate a warning to the ultimate user and whether the warning if communicated was adequate are uniformly held questions for the jury." 608 F.2d at 573.[1] *Stapleton v. Kawasaki Heavy Indus., Ltd.*, *supra* was followed by another Georgia case *Rhodes v. Interstate Battery System of America, Inc.*, 722 F.2d 1517

1. In *Bonner v. City of Prichard*, 661 F.2d 1206 (11th Cir.1981) (en banc), this court adopted as binding precedent all of the decisions of the former Fifth Circuit handed down prior to the close of business on September 30, 1981. *Id.* at 1209.

(11th Cir.1984), and still another case, *Watson v. Uniden Corp. of America,* 775 F.2d 1514 (11th Cir.1985).

We see no reason to elaborate on this principle of law. Appellee in its argument sought to make a distinction in this case because the Hahns were well-educated, had read the label, undoubtedly understood the meaning of "ingestion," and, according to their testimony, knew of the necessity of keeping medicines away from children. As we understand the decided cases in this area of law, the simple question is whether the warning is adequate, given the unsafe nature of the product. It is appropriate for a jury to determine that adequacy. While the jury may or may not consider the intelligence and experience of the consumer-plaintiff, that does not play a part in our rationale in determining whether or not the question should or should not be presented to a jury. Since our authorities are clear and unanimous, we reverse and remand on the basis of these authorities.

* * *

The district court's grant of directed verdict is REVERSED and the matter is REMANDED for retrial.

Notes

1. A warning is not adequate if it minimizes the danger associated with the product. In Gardner v. Q.H.S., Inc., 448 F.2d 238 (4th Cir.1971), defendant manufactured plastic hair rollers filled with paraffin. They were designed to be boiled in water for fifteen minutes before use. The user put them in a pot of water on an electric stove which she set on high. She forgot about them and the water boiled away. The melted paraffin caught on fire and produced an intense flame that billowed four or five feet above the pan. This caused extensive property damage. The rollers came with the following warning:

> Use plenty of water. Do not let water boil away. Cautionary note: Rollers may be inflammable only if left over flame in pan without water. Otherwise Q.H.S. Setting/Rollers are perfectly safe.

The court held that a jury could conclude that the warning was inadequate. The court said:

> [T]he jury could * * * conclude that the "cautionary note" was inadequate to inform the user to use the extraordinary degree of caution necessary to avoid the dangerous consequences of improper or extraordinary use of the product. It is true that the user was instructed to use plenty of water and not to let the water boil away. But if the user disobeyed these instructions, he was told only that the product *"may"* be inflammable if left over *"flame"* in pan without water; otherwise, the product was *"perfectly* safe." The user was not told that the rollers contained paraffin. Some users would certainly conclude that "flame" did not include electrical heat. The user was not told that there was a strong possibility that the paraffin would ignite if the water boiled away and that flames of a considerable height could erupt if the paraffin ignited. And what cautionary notice was given was in printing of the

same size as the general instructions and unobtrusively made part of them.

448 F.2d at 243 (4th Cir.1971).

See also, Borel v. Fibreboard Paper Prod. Corp., 493 F.2d 1076 (5th Cir.1973), cert. denied, 419 U.S. 869, 95 S.Ct. 127, 42 L.Ed.2d 107 (1974). The manufacturer of an insulation product containing asbestos warned that "Inhalation of asbestos in excessive quantities over long periods of time may be harmful." The court held that this was not adequate to inform insulation workers of the substantial risk of contracting asbestosis and cancer.

2. A warning that is otherwise adequate will not exonerate the manufacturer if he undermines its effectiveness. For example, in Maize v. Atlantic Ref. Co., 352 Pa. 51, 41 A.2d 850 (1945) plaintiff's decedent died as a result of inhaling the fumes of a poisonous cleaning fluid named "Safety–Kleen." The name of the product was printed on four sides of the container in large letters. The following warning was printed on the can in much smaller letters:

Caution

Do not inhale fumes.
Use only in well ventilated place.

The court held that a jury could find that the warning was inadequate. The prominent display of the word "safety" could well make the cautionary note seem unimportant. It could even prevent the user from reading the entire label. *See also,* Incollingo v. Ewing, 444 Pa. 263, 444 Pa. 299, 282 A.2d 206 (1971) (a proper warning concerning a dangerous prescription drug can be nullified by overpromotion by the drug company's detail men).

BROUSSARD v. CONTINENTAL OIL CO.

Court of Appeal of Louisiana, Third Circuit, 1983.
433 So.2d 354, writ denied, 440 So.2d 726 (1983).

STOKER, JUDGE.

This is a personal injury suit by Mildredge T. Broussard against Black & Decker (U.S.), Inc. and The Home Insurance Company. Plaintiff-appellant (Broussard) was badly burned in an explosion of natural gas sparked by a Black & Decker hand drill. Broussard was using the drill while working at a Continental Oil Company (Conoco) plant at Grand Chenier, Louisiana. Plaintiff also sued Conoco and its plant supervisor but reached a settlement agreement with those defendants before trial. * * *

The verdict of the jury at trial was that Black & Decker was not at fault for failure to adequately warn in connection with the accident. Judgment was for the defendants and against plaintiff. * * * [Plaintiff appealed, claiming that the jury committed manifest error in finding that defendant was not at fault for failing to warn adequately.]

We find no error in the jury's verdict * * *. We affirm.

BACKGROUND FACTS

Plaintiff was directly employed by Crain Brothers Construction Company, and the trial court found he was the statutory employee of

Conoco. On the day of the accident, plaintiff and four other men, including Sanders Miller, were in the process of building a sump box enclosure at the end of a natural gas vent line (pipe) at the Grand Chenier plant. Plaintiff was a carpenter's helper and Miller was a carpenter. Upon arriving at the site, both men noticed that natural gas could be heard and smelled coming from the vent line. Miller immediately notified Conoco's relief plant foreman about the escaping gas and asked if it could be shut off. The foreman refused to do so because the whole plant would have had to be shut down to prevent the gas from being vented at the location of the sump box. After Miller requested a shut down a second time, the foreman talked to Mr. Leeman, another Conoco employee and the plant supervisor. Miller was again told nothing could be done.

Miller testified that he recognized the danger of working around the flammable natural gas. The workers took what precautions they could to minimize the risk of igniting the natural gas fumes. Cigarettes, cigarette lighters and matches were left in the work vehicles. The vehicles were parked some distance away from the site. A gasoline powered electricity generator was placed at the end of two 50-foot extension cords. Miller warned the plaintiff to be careful not to cause a spark while hammering, especially when the fumes were heavy.

The explosion occurred as plaintiff was standing inside a plywood box loosely held together and being constructed as a concrete form. He was positioned inside the form to drill holes in its sides through which rods were to be inserted. It is not seriously contested that sparks from the drill plaintiff was using ignited the natural gas fumes coming from the vent line. Such sparks are normally emitted from this and similar type drills when the "brushes" inside the armature of the drill contact and slide along the inside surface of the rapidly spinning cylinder in which the brushes sit. There is no evidence, nor is the issue before this Court, that the design which allows the creation and emission of these sparks constitutes a design defect. Rather, the issues relate to the failure to warn on the part of the defendant manufacturer of the hazard of explosion.

Both the plaintiff Broussard and Sanders Miller testified that they were unaware at the time of the accident that sparks from electrical power drills could ignite gaseous atmospheres. Allen Nunez, the relief foreman, likewise testified that neither he nor anyone at the Conoco plant knew of the potential of explosion in a like situation before the accident occurred. However, a warning that would have informed the users of the drill of the precise cause and effect encountered appears in the owner's manual. Black & Decker claim that a copy of this manual is placed in every box containing one of their drills as it leaves the manufacturer's control. See Appendix, Item No. 18.

The owner's manual is not attached to the drill but is loosely placed in the box. Thus, unless the box with the owner's manual inside (or the owner's manual itself, with the safety warnings inside its folded pamphlet form) is kept with the drill, the warning is not available to users other than the buyer. In addition to the owner's manual warning, there is a small notice on the side of the drill which simply reads, "CAUTION: For Safe Operation See Owner's Manual." This notice is approximately one-eighth inch high and one inch long.

Sanders Miller received the drill at the office of the Crain Brothers Construction Company from the secretary who worked in the office. The secretary asked Miller if he wanted the box the drill came in. Miller replied he had no use for it, and the box was thrown away. Neither Miller nor the plaintiff saw the owner's manual.

DID BLACK & DECKER FAIL TO PROVIDE ADEQUATE WARNING?

With reference to adequacy of warning of the danger from the emission of sparks, Black & Decker contends item eighteen in the owner's manual was sufficient. Plaintiff Broussard contends that it was not. Broussard contends that Black & Decker was guilty of fault in not putting the warning on the drill itself. Item eighteen reads as follows:

> "18. DO NOT OPERATE portable electric tools in gaseous or explosive atmospheres. Motors in these tools normally spark, and the sparks might ignite fumes."

The warning set forth in these words is adequate; the question is whether it was sufficient to put it in the owner's manual or whether it was unreasonable under the circumstances not to put this warning on the drill itself. As noted above there was a warning on the drill which read, "CAUTION: For Safe Operation See Owner's Manual."

We are confronted here with the application of absolute liability of a manufacturer. The product, the drill, does not contain a defect in the ordinary sense of design or manufacturing defect, but ordinary use of the drill is dangerous under the factual circumstances which were present in this case, i.e., use in the presence of natural gas fumes. Unreasonable risk is a requirement of strict liability just as it is in negligence. *Entrevia v. Hood,* 427 So.2d 1146 (La.1983); *DeBattista v. Argonaut–Southwest Ins. Co.,* 403 So.2d 26 (La.1981); *Cobb v. Insured Lloyds,* 387 So.2d 13 (La.1980); *Hunt v. City Stores, Inc.,* 387 So.2d 585 (La.1980); *Chappuis v. Sears Roebuck & Company,* 358 So.2d 926 (La.1978); *Olsen v. Shell Oil Company,* 365 So.2d 1285 (La.1978) and *Loescher v. Parr,* 324 So.2d 441 (La.1976).

The judicial process involved in deciding whether a risk is unreasonable in strict liability is similar to that employed in determining whether a risk is unreasonable in a traditional negligence problem and in deciding the scope of duty or legal cause under the duty risk analysis. *Entrevia v. Hood,* supra, and *Hunt v. City Stores, Inc.,* supra. Strict liability and negligence are not identical in all respects. A major distinction between the two theories is that the inability of a defendant to know or prevent the risk is not a defense in a strict liability case but precludes a finding of negligence. *Entrevia v. Hood,* supra, and the cases cited therein. Knowledge of the risk is not a problem here for Black & Decker knew of the risk. The question is what was adequate warning.

In *Entrevia v. Hood,* the Supreme Court said:

"The unreasonable risk of harm criterion, however, is not a simple rule of law which may be applied mechanically to the facts of a case. [It is] to be determined after a study of the law and customs, a balancing of claims and interests, a weighing of the risk and the gravity of harm, and a consideration of individual and societal rights and obligations. * * *

In approaching our decision in this case we accept at face value the assertions of Broussard and Sanders Miller that they were unaware that the drill in question would emit sparks when in operation. Building upon this assertion plaintiff relies heavily on the case of *Chappuis v. Sears Roebuck & Company,* supra, and especially the following pronouncement from that case:

"Absolute liability upon a manufacturer whose product is useful, traditional, but which might become dangerous in some circumstances must be distinguished from the obligation here involved. There may be many tools or other products which become dangerous for normal use in certain conditions. But when the danger is known to the manufacturer and cannot justifiably be expected to be within the knowledge of users generally, the manufacturer must take reasonable steps to warn the user."

In *Chappuis* the ordinary claw hammer, the subject of that case, did have a warning label on the handle. The Louisiana Supreme Court held that the warning was not adequate to put the user on notice of the particular risk involved. The particular risk was that once the steel hammer face became chipped, it is liable to chip again when used and a flying chip might physically injure someone.

The questions before us are:

1. Was adequate warning given through the general caution on Black & Decker's drill directing users to consult the owner's manual for safe operation?

2. If the general warning was not adequate, was it unreasonable for Black & Decker not to place on the drill itself the warning contained in item 18 of its safety rules contained in the owner's manual?

These questions must be tested together as they rest on the same practical considerations.

Plaintiff's own expert witness unwittingly pointed up the difficulty in putting warnings on the drill itself. This expert demonstrated the use of warnings through symbols as opposed to words. The expert devised a series of symbols of his own creation based on international symbols which he suggested could have been placed on the drill itself. The symbols purportedly represent ten of the eighteen warnings Black &

Decker set forth in the owner's manual. Plaintiff relies on *Chappuis v. Sears Roebuck & Company,* supra, as support of his contention that such warnings should have been placed on the drill itself.

While we think the use of symbols as suggested by plaintiff's expert merits no consideration, we note that the expert deemed at least ten of the warnings represented by the symbols were worthy of being noted on the drill. The fact that numerous risks other than sparking explosions or fires merit notice is a significant factor. The suggested use of symbols is also significant because the reason for it is the recognition that the space on the drill is not large enough to contain extensive warnings and cautions in words. This factor will be discussed later, but at this point we will state our opinion relative to the efficacy symbols in lieu of words.

Plaintiff's expert testified that the symbols he proposed are neither standard nor easily recognizable by the general public. Further, the testimony indicates that the symbols are unclear and subject to different interpretations. The symbols fail in one aspect of sufficiency according to expert (as distinguished from legal) standards in that they do not inform why the activities are dangerous, just that they are dangerous. Above all, however, we are convinced that the use of symbols would require users of the drill to refer to an owner's manual or other written material to discover what the symbols meant. This would be no more efficacious than what Black & Decker did when it put a caution on the drill directing users to consult the owner's manual for safe operation.

We think counsel for plaintiff recognized lack of merit in the suggested use of symbols. On plaintiff's behalf Exhibit P–17 was introduced in evidence. On the side of this exhibit a label measuring approximately 2⅝ inches by 1¾ inches was affixed on which the following words were typed:

"SAFETY RULES

"• Don't abuse cord
• Wear proper apparel
• Don't use in damp areas
• Use proper extension cords outdoors
• Don't touch metal parts when drilling near any electrical wiring
• Remove tightening key
• Unplug to change bits
• Use safety glasses
• Avoid gaseous areas
• Secure work

SEE MANUAL FOR COMPLETE TEXTS"

The whole of the above quoted material is typed in small letter characters in a slant-wise or diagonal fashion on the label in order to fit.

It will be noted that the only reference to the risk of igniting gas from emission of sparks is contained in the three words, "Avoid gaseous areas."

We are not impressed with plaintiff's Exhibit P–17. The most important failing of the exhibit is that the mere words, "Avoid gaseous areas" does not meet the test of the *Chappuis* case because it does not explain or point out the precise risk of injury posed by use in gaseous areas. Moreover, this exhibit graphically illustrates the problem of attempting to put multiple warnings on a hand drill of the size and nature involved.

Defendant considers that more than ten warnings should be given. Nevertheless, if only ten are selected, deficiencies in any scheme for putting them all on the drill become apparent. As a practical matter, the effect of putting at least ten warnings on the drill would decrease the effectiveness of all of the warnings. A consumer would have a tendency to read none of the warnings if the surface of the drill became cluttered with the warnings. Unless we should elevate the one hazard of sparking to premier importance above all others, we fear that an effort to tell all about each hazard is not practical either from the point of view of availability of space or of effectiveness. We decline to say that one risk is more worthy of warning than another.

With the merits and demerits of the arguments urged by the parties in mind, we now decide whether Black & Decker exposed plaintiff to unreasonable risk. We follow the interest balancing procedure discussed in the jurisprudence and most recently in *Entrevia v. Hood,* supra. We conclude that defendant acted reasonably toward plaintiff and all persons who might use its hand drill. In view of the numerous risks which a manufacturer of a hand drill must explicitly describe in *Chappuis* terms, the most practical and effective thing which the manufacturer could do is to direct the user to the owner's manual as Black & Decker did.

For the reasons we have given we hold that the jury's finding of no fault on the part of Black & Decker was correct.

* * *

Decree

For the reasons assigned, the judgment of the trial court is affirmed. All costs of this appeal are to be paid by plaintiff.

Affirmed.

Notes

1. Decide the following case:

Plaintiff, age 14, was injured while riding as a passenger on a small motorcycle. He rode with his feet extending out away from the motorcycle because it had no rear foot rests. The motorcycle hit a bump and his leg bounced backward and was caught between the rear tire and the fender/muffler assembly. As a result his foot suffered burns and abrasions. The driver, also age 14, bought the motorcycle two weeks prior to the accident. Plaintiff sued the manufacturer of the motorcycle claiming that it failed to warn him adequately of the dangers of riding as a passenger on the motorcycle. The gas tank had two decals which read as follows:

WARNING—OPERATOR ONLY—NO PASSENGERS

Remember: Preserve Nature/Always Wear Helmet/Ride Safely/Read Owner's Manual Carefully Before Riding.

The following warning appeared on the inside front cover of the owner's manual:

Important Notice.

OPERATOR ONLY.

NO PASSENGERS.

This motorcycle is designed and constructed as an operator-only model. The seating configuration does not safely permit the carrying of a passenger.

Plaintiff understood that the motorcycle was built for only one rider. Neither he nor the owner read the owner's manual. Defendant moves for a summary judgment. How should the court rule?

2. Suppose the jury in *Broussard* had found in favor of the plaintiff, and defendant appealed on the basis that the warning was sufficient as a matter of law. How should the appellate court rule?

3. Is it ever proper for a court to grant a summary judgment or directed verdict in a case involving an issue of the adequacy of a warning? The Eleventh Circuit apparently thinks not. Does this promote the policies underlying strict liability?

3. OBVIOUS OR KNOWN DANGERS

GRAHAM v. JOSEPH T. RYERSON & SONS

Court of Appeals of Michigan, 1980.
96 Mich.App. 480, 292 N.W.2d 704.

KELLY, PRESIDING JUDGE.

Plaintiff David Graham claims damages resulting from injuries sustained when the side ring of a truck wheel blew off and struck him while he was inflating a flat tire. The side ring was part of an "RH5" multi-piece wheel assembly manufactured by defendant Firestone Tire and Rubber Company (Firestone). Graham was a diesel mechanic in the employ of Kinnie Annex Cartage Company (Kinnie) which leased and serviced trucks. On May 1, 1973, Kinnie received a call from one of its customers, defendant Joseph T. Ryerson & Sons, a/k/a Ryerson Steel Company (Ryerson), concerning a flat tire on one of its leased trucks. The Ryerson driver was directed by Kinnie to complete his deliveries and then park the truck at the Ryerson garage. During the early morning hours of May 2, 1973, Kinnie dispatched Graham to replace the flat tire.

In order to properly place the jack under the truck, Graham attempted to elevate the vehicle about ⅜″ by inflating the flat tire. In response to the inflation pressure the side ring explosively disengaged from the rim base and struck plaintiff, causing severe injuries to his arms and legs.

Graham filed his complaint in February, 1974, the final amended complaint being filed in November, 1977. * * * Count II sounded in negligence against Firestone. It charged breach of a duty to warn of the hazards of the RH5° wheel and negligence in the design of that wheel. * * *

The jury found no cause of action against Firestone. The plaintiffs moved for a new trial, which the court denied in a written opinion dated October 5, 1978. The plaintiffs appeal by right.

The trial court ruled as a matter of law that defendant Firestone, manufacturer of the side ring, had no duty to warn plaintiff of the danger involved in inflating a tire that had been run while flat because of Graham's status as an "expert" in changing truck tires. Plaintiffs claim error in the trial court's refusal to submit to the jury the question of Firestone's duty to warn. An examination of the cases cited by defendant Firestone and relied upon by the trial court does not support the proposition that there is no duty to warn experts.

The trial court's reliance on *Parsonson v. Construction Equipment Co.*, 386 Mich. 61, 191 N.W.2d 465 (1971) and its progeny is misplaced. Based upon a latent/patent defect analysis, the *Parsonson* Court found that a gasoline engine need not be designed to safeguard against the possibility that someone might fill the gas tank of the engine without first stopping the heater blower or engine, both obvious heat sources in very close proximity to the tank. "Here the danger of fire or explosion by the careless use of gasoline was visible and patent rather than concealed or latent". 386 Mich. at 76, 191 N.W.2d at 471. The Court concluded that plaintiff's own conduct, in the face of an obvious danger known to all adults of reasonable intelligence, was the proximate cause of injury. The duty to warn issue was not raised or discussed; however, the reasoning of the *Parsonson* Court was adopted in *Crews v. General Motors Corp.*, 400 Mich. 208, 253 N.W.2d 617 (1977), and *Holbrook v. Koehring Co.*, 75 Mich.App. 592, 255 N.W.2d 698 (1977), both of which deal, at least tangentially, with the warning question.

The evenly divided *Crews* Court upheld this Court's decision affirming a directed verdict for the defendant on the grounds that " 'even if the evidence sufficed to show a defect in the engine, there was absolutely no showing that this defect caused the fire' ". 400 Mich. at 214, 253 N.W.2d at 618. Plaintiff in *Crews* did not plead failure to warn. Justice Coleman opined that this was most likely due to his full awareness of the specific danger that could, and, in fact, did result from his conduct. Plaintiff's trial testimony, included within Justice Coleman's opinion, indicated that Mr. Crews, an experienced mechanic, knew that turning the ignition key without first disconnecting the ignition from the wires in the coil might produce sparks. Mr. Crews was working with a fuel line at the time; a spark ignited the gasoline and he was severely burned.

This Court reached a similar conclusion in *Holbrook, supra,* where plaintiff was an experienced crane operator who was injured when lifting an object 19,000 pounds heavier than the crane's maximum capacity. In response to plaintiff's failure to warn argument the Court stated:

> "We find plaintiffs' argument on defendants' failure to warn irrelevant because plaintiff was an experienced operator of this crane *and had experienced difficulties with it similar to those here complained of."* 75 Mich.App. at 595, 255 N.W.2d at 700. (Emphasis added.)

We do not find the above cases supportive of the "expert" rule advanced by defendant and adopted by the trial court. Rather, these cases stand for the proposition that there is no duty to warn of dangers obvious to all users of the product or of specific dangers fully known to the complainant at the time the injury occurred.

The strongest support for defendant's position concerning the duty to warn "experts" is found in those cases which hold that the duty does not extend to members of a particular trade or profession where the danger involved is a matter of common knowledge. *Eyster v. Borg–Warner Corp.,* 131 Ga.App. 702, 206 S.E.2d 668 (1974); *Parker v. State,* 201 Misc. 416, 105 N.Y.S.2d 735 (1951), *aff'd* 280 App.Div. 157, 112 N.Y.S.2d 695 (1952); *Lockett v. General Electric Co.,* 376 F.Supp. 1201 (E.D.Pa.1974). These cases, however, do not establish an across-the-board rule eliminating the duty to warn tradespeople and professionals. The *Eyster* Court noted:

> "[P]laintiff's evidence demonstrated that those who are franchised to install this Borg–Warner product should, in the ordinary course of events, have been aware of the danger of the questionable connection, since such peril was a matter of common knowledge to those in the trade. More importantly, plaintiffs' evidence showed that *it was contrary to the generally accepted practice* to connect aluminum and copper wiring." 131 Ga.App. 704, 206 S.E.2d 670. (Emphasis added.)

If members of the particular trade or profession commonly engage in a dangerous practice, the manufacturer's knowledge of this conduct may give rise to a duty to warn. In *Casetta v. United States Rubber Co.,* 260 Cal.App.2d 792, 67 Cal.Rptr. 645 (1968), the Court held that the issue of failure to warn was erroneously withdrawn from the jury. Plaintiff, a tire repairman, was injured when a tire he was mounting for a customer exploded. In performing this task plaintiff used a "safety" or "hump-type" rim which called for the use of a lubricant during mounting to lessen or eliminate the danger of explosion. The defendant manufacturer provided mounting instructions, including a direction to use a lubricant, but failed to warn of the danger presented by failure to follow this direction. The Court stated:

"Questions of fact were presented with respect to the issue of whether the manufacturer should have known that the general instructions to use a lubricant were more respected in the breach than by observance, and, if so, whether special warning should have been given of the particular hazard from safety rims." 260 Cal.App. 817, 67 Cal.Rptr. 661.

In the instant case there was ample testimony that it was the common practice of diesel mechanics, Graham and others, to inflate tires in order to elevate the vehicle. We must assume that defendant was aware of this practice since it had been informed of about 40 similar blowout incidents. In light of this knowledge in particular, as well as common knowledge that vehicles with flat tires are likely to be run in that condition for varying distances and causes, we find a question exists as to the duty to warn even tire repairmen of the special danger involved. In the absence of any general rule eliminating the duty to warn "experts" we find that the trial court erred in excluding this issue from jury consideration on that basis. Although Michigan Courts have found no duty or have excused failure to warn when the danger involved is obvious or specifically known to the user of the product, the extent of the risk and the appreciation of the danger are more subtle factors. Since we are not presented with the question of obvious danger, we proceed to consider whether the trial court could properly have removed the issue of duty to warn from the jury on the basis of plaintiff's knowledge of the particular risk. Although the question of duty is generally for determination by the trial court as a matter of law, the jury should examine the issue pursuant to proper instructions, when the facts adduced at trial are in dispute, giving rise to a reasonable difference of opinion as to the foreseeability of the particular risk and the reasonableness of defendant's conduct in that regard. *Robertson v. Swindell–Dressler Co.*, 82 Mich.App. 382, 267 N.W.2d 131 (1978), *lv. den.* 403 Mich. 812 (1978), relying on Prosser, Torts (4th ed.), § 37, p. 206 and § 45, p. 290.

Plaintiff herein testified that, though he had never been warned, he knew that it was dangerous to inflate a tire that had been run while flat because the wheel or rim could be damaged. He further testified that he did not know if this tire had been run flat, but that, as far as he could tell, the rim appeared concentric. The record is devoid of evidence of his awareness of the nature or degree if the risk. Even if he was aware that the side ring might disengage in response to inflation pressure, did he realize that the amount of pressure he exerted would result in such explosive thrust and consequential life threatening hazard? Consciousness of a vague danger, without appreciation of the seriousness of the consequences may require the manufacturer to provide warning; presentation of credible evidence results in a jury question. *Hardy v. Proctor & Gamble Manufacturing Co.*, 209 F.2d 124 (CA 5, 1954); *Hopkins v. E.I. du Pont De Nemours & Co.*, 199 F.2d 930 (CA 3, 1952); *West v. Broderick & Bascom Rope Co.*, 197 N.W.2d 202 (Iowa, 1972); *Cf. Coger v. Mackinaw Products Co.*, 48 Mich.App. 113, 210 N.W.2d 124 (1973);

Simonetti v. Rinshed–Mason Co., 41 Mich.App. 446, 200 N.W.2d 354 (1972), *lv. den.* 388 Mich. 784 (1972).

In addition, evidence was presented that the rim base and side ring were affected by varying degrees of rust corrosion and that this condition deteriorated the bonding of the rim and ring. This defective condition was not readily observable and there was no evidence that defendant was aware of internal rust in the wheel or the implications of this condition. Firestone blamed any accident related fault for this condition on Titan Tire Company which was responsible for maintenance. Titan Tire Company is not a party to this suit. Even accepting defendant's position on this matter does not eliminate the possible need to warn of the dangers involved.

We conclude that plaintiff raised a jury submissible issue which the trial court improperly removed from its consideration.

* * *

The jury verdict of no cause of action is challenged as being against the great weight of the evidence. Once the warning issue was excluded, plaintiffs were left to proceed on a design defect theory. Firestone presented reliable evidence that the product conformed with industry design standards and that it was fit for its intended use. See *Owens v. Allis–Chalmers Corp.,* 83 Mich.App. 74, 268 N.W.2d 291 (1978), *lv. gtd.,* 405 Mich. 827 (1979); *Piercefield v. Remington Arms Co.,* 375 Mich. 85, 96, 133 N.W.2d 129 (1965). Firestone argued that the real cause of the injury was plaintiff's improper use of the wheel. Manufacturers are duty bound to design products that are safe for their intended or reasonably anticipated use, which may include reasonably anticipated misuse. *Byrnes v. Economic Machinery Co.,* 41 Mich.App. 192, 200 N.W.2d 104 (1972). This is true under both implied warranty and negligence theories. *Elsasser v. American Motors Corp.,* 81 Mich.App. 379, 385, 265 N.W.2d 339 (1978). We cannot conclude that, limited to the question of design defect, the jury returned a verdict against the great weight of the evidence.

* * *

Affirmed in part; reversed in part and remanded for proceedings consistent with this opinion.

Notes

1. **Professional Users.** In deciding what kind of a warning to give, the manufacturer can take into consideration the knowledge and expertise of those who may reasonably be expected to use the product. If the product is marketed only to professionals, who are aware of its dangers and how to deal with them, it may reasonably give a much less detailed warning than it would have to give to members of the general public. *See, e.g.,* Martinez v. Dixie Carriers, Inc., 529 F.2d 457 (5th Cir.1976). A worker was overcome by dripolene fumes while cleaning out a barge. He was a member of a professional crew which was aware of the nature of the liquid and the

dangers associated with handling it. The manufacturer of the dripolene gave a warning, but not a detailed one. It was held not liable for failure to give a more adequate warning. *See also,* Loughan v. Firestone Tire & Rubber Co., 749 F.2d 1519 (11th Cir.1985) (Florida law; no duty to warn experienced mechanic about the risk of mismatching the component parts of a multi-piece rim-wheel assembly).

2. **Obvious Dangers.** A majority of courts adhere to the rule that there is no duty to warn about obvious or generally known dangers. The rule applies regardless of whether plaintiff seeks recovery on a negligence, strict liability, or breach of warranty theory. The Restatement of Torts (Second) § 402A comment j (1965) states:

> [A] seller is not required to warn with respect to products, or ingredients in them, which are only dangerous, or potentially so, * * * when the danger, or potentiality of danger, is generally known and recognized.

Where the risk is obvious or generally known, there is no duty to warn even if a given plaintiff lacks subjective knowledge of the danger. Pemberton v. American Distilled Spirits Co., 664 S.W.2d 690 (Tenn.1984).

3. The statement of this rule is reminiscent of the consumer expectations test of defect, *i.e.,* that there is no liability for marketing dangerous products as long as the dangers are open and obvious or generally known. The rationale underlying the rule, however, is very different. The consumer expectations test of defect is based on the notion that the manufacturer's obligation is merely to make the dangers associated with its products known so that consumers can choose intelligently whether to purchase them. It does not matter whether the dangers are reasonable or unreasonable. The basis of the rule against warning about obvious or known dangers is that such a warning would serve no purpose because it would tell the user nothing that she does not already know. It follows that a court could quite logically reject the consumer expectations test of defect and yet continue to require warnings only with respect to unknown risks.

4. Must a manufacturer warn about the following dangers?

A. That diving into a four-foot, above-ground swimming pool can cause a serious spinal cord injury?

B. That a child under four years of age can choke on peanut butter?

C. That drinking an excessive quantity of alcohol can result in death from alcohol poisoning; that prolonged and excessive consumption of alcohol can produce alcoholism; or that drinking moderate amounts of alcohol for a prolonged period can cause fatal pancreatic disease. *See* Note, Warning Labels May be Hazardous to Your Health: Common–Law and Statutory Responses to Alcoholic Beverage Manufacturer's Duty to Warn, 75 Cornell L.Rev. 158 (1989).

5. The obviousness of the danger has traditionally been decided by the judge as question of law. In recent years this has changed in many jurisdictions. In cases where the obviousness of the specific danger involved in the case is at all debatable, many courts tend to submit the question of obviousness to the jury. *See* Pardieck & Hulbert, Is the Danger Really Open and Obvious?, 19 Ind.L.Rev. 383 (1986).

Consider, for example, Laaperi v. Sears, Roebuck & Co., Inc., 787 F.2d 726 (1st Cir.1986). Defendant sold a smoke detector powered by house current. It failed to function in an electrical fire caused by a short circuit. The smoke detector was hooked up to the circuit that shorted out, and it could not function because it received no electricity after the circuit cut off. Plaintiff sued for negligent failure to warn that a short circuit that starts a fire could also incapacitate the smoke detector. Defendant argued that no warning was necessary because the risk was obvious to the average consumer. The court stated:

> Defendants ask us to declare that the risk that an electrical fire could incapacitate an AC-powered smoke detector is so obvious that the average consumer would not benefit from a warning. This is not a trivial argument; in earlier—some might say sounder—days, we might have accepted it. *Compare* Jamieson v. Woodward & Lothrop, 247 F.2d 23 (D.C.Cir.1957). Our sense of the current state of the tort law in Massachusetts and most other jurisdictions, however, leads us to conclude that, today, the matter before us poses a jury question; that "obviousness" in a situation such as this would be treated by the Massachusetts courts as presenting a question of fact, not of law. To be sure, it would be obvious to anyone that an electrical outage would cause this smoke detector to fail. But the average purchaser might not comprehend the specific danger that a fire-causing electrical problem can simultaneously knock out the circuit into which a smoke detector is wired, causing the detector to fail at the very moment it is needed. Thus, while the failure of a detector to function as the result of an electrical malfunction due, say, to a broken power line or a neighborhood power outage would, we think, be obvious as a matter of law, the failure that occurred here, being associated with the very risk—fire—for which the device was purchased, was not, or so a jury could find.

787 F.2d at 731.

6. **Known Dangers.** Most courts agree that there is also no liability for failing to warn where plaintiff knows of the risk, even though it is not generally known or obvious. *E.g.,* Lister v. Bill Kelley Athletic, Inc., 137 Ill.App.3d 829, 92 Ill.Dec. 672, 485 N.E.2d 483 (1985) (football helmet manufacturer not liable for failure to warn that helmet would not protect against spine injury where player had repeatedly been warned by his coach).

7. For a discussion of liability for failure to warn about known and obvious dangers, *see* Madden, The Duty to Warn in Products Liability: Contours and Criticism, 89 W.Va.L.Rev. 221, 253–259 (1987); Noel, Products Defective Because of Inadequate Directions or Warnings, 23 Sw.L.J. 256, 272–274 (1969).

CAMPOS v. FIRESTONE TIRE & RUBBER CO.
Supreme Court of New Jersey, 1984.
98 N.J. 198, 485 A.2d 305.

The opinion of the Court was delivered by

SCHREIBER, J.

This failure-to-warn product liability case presents for consideration the effect of a foreseeable user's knowledge of a danger on a manufacturer's responsibility to distribute a product free from defect. Does that knowledge eliminate any duty to warn? Or is it a link to be considered on whether the failure to warn was a substantial factor in causing the accident and injuries?

Plaintiff Armando Campos was born and raised in Portugal. He emigrated to this country in 1971. Shortly after his arrival in the United States he obtained a job with Theurer Atlantic, Inc. (Theurer), a manufacturer of truck trailers.

In connection with its trailer operation Theurer placed new truck tires on rims before their installation on the trailers. Plaintiff's work was to assemble the tires. This involved placing a tire containing an inner tube on a three-piece rim assembly, putting the assembled tire into a steel safety cage designed to prevent injuries in case the assembled parts separated under pressure, and then inserting air into the tire by inflating the tube inside it. He generally worked a five-day, forty-hour week, and assembled about eight tires an hour. Plaintiff's employment continued in this manner until the accident on November 1, 1978.

About 9:30 a.m. on that day, plaintiff was readying a new Dunlop tire to be mounted on a trailer. He assembled the three-piece rim and tire, placed the tire in the cage, and clamped the air pressure hose into place so that air was being forced into the tire. He then noticed that a locking element on the rim components was opening. Fearing that there would "be a very big accident" if the pieces separated under pressure, he immediately tried to disengage the hose. He explained, "Because if I didn't, it could kill me and kill everybody that was around there." As he reached into the cage, the assembly exploded and plaintiff was severely injured.

Defendant, Firestone Tire & Rubber Company, had manufactured the rim assembly. We were advised at oral argument that Theurer, not defendant, had made the protective cage. Defendant had delivered manuals describing the proper method of preparing the tire to its customers, including Theurer. Defendant had also given Theurer a large chart prepared by the National Highway Traffic Safety Administration of the United States Department of Transportation. That chart was kept on the wall at the Theurer shop and contained instructions on safety precautions, including the following advice: "ALWAYS INFLATE TIRE IN SAFETY CAGE OR USE A PORTABLE LOCK RING GUARD. USE A CLIP–ON TYPE AIR CHUCK[2] WITH REMOTE VALVE SO THAT OPERATOR CAN STAND CLEAR DURING TIRE INFLATION." However, Campos could not read or write Portuguese or English and these written warnings were therefore ineffective.

In addition to the written instructions, plaintiff had received some oral instructions from his supervisor. He had been told that a truck tire was to be placed in the cage before inflating it. Further, he had had a

---

2. This is a device that clamps on the air hose so as to hold the air hose and valve in place when air is being injected into the tube within the tire. The worker is then free to stand clear while the tire is being inflated.

similar accident in July, 1972, when, to prevent a mishap, he had inserted his hand into the protective cage while air was being blown into the tire. The injuries that he received then were less severe than in this accident.

Plaintiff proceeded against defendant, Firestone Tire & Rubber Company, on two strict liability theories, improper design and failure to warn. His contention that the rim had been improperly designed because it should have consisted of one rather than three pieces was rejected by the jury. His second claim, which was accepted by the jury, was that defendant had not adequately warned him of the danger and that that failure to warn was a proximate cause of his injury. The jury returned a verdict of $255,000.

Defendant appealed. A divided Appellate Division reversed and entered judgment for the defendant. *See* 192 *N.J.Super.* 251, 469 *A.*2d 943 (1983). This Court granted plaintiff's petition for certification. 96 *N.J.* 310, 475 *A.*2d 600 (1984).

I

* * *

Plaintiff's expert suggested that defendant should have produced a graphic or symbolic warning against inserting one's hand in the protective cage during the inflation process. He thought that it would have been appropriate to have prepared a sign containing a symbol similar to the picture of a cigarette with a diagonal red line across that informs one not to smoke. He testified that the manufacturer should have anticipated that illiterate people would be exposed to these dangers and added, "we have to do things which will protect them as well."

Although plaintiff's similar accident six years earlier may have served as some warning against reaching into the cage while the tire was being inflated, plaintiff's expert stated that plaintiff's "instinctive" reaction was to try to stop the accident by inserting his hand into the cage. Plaintiff's expert responded as follows to a question regarding how symbols would have helped the plaintiff avoid the accident:

A. Not very much. A little perhaps. That is, if there was a reminder in graphical form against putting his hands in telling him that explosive separations can take place, and he's instructed verbally by somebody in his own native tongue as to what that symbol means. Then at least that amount of information has been provided to him.

I don't think it's going to be very effective beyond a certain point because this particular incident situationally starts before the tire even gets into the cage. It starts either on the assembly line or it starts when the man is assembling it and doesn't assemble it correctly. I certainly agree that the warning graphical which the man let's say understands is not—it's better than nothing, but not very much better.

Q. Is it better than the pain caused by a prior injury in terms of suppressing his instincts for putting his hands in the cage?

A. No.

The Appellate Division majority and dissenting opinions viewed the effect of this evidence differently. The majority relied on the proposition that "there is no duty to warn where the danger is obvious and the user knowledgeable." 192 *N.J.Super.* at 267, 469 A.2d 943. It concluded that this was such a case and held that there being no duty to warn this plaintiff, plaintiff's case necessarily failed. The dissent, acknowledging that the "fact that the danger may have been [objectively] obvious [could] affect the [manufacturer's] duty," *id.,* 192 *N.J.Super.* at 267, 469 A.2d 943, contended that the particular plaintiff's subjective knowledge is relevant on the issue of proximate cause rather than duty, *id.,* 192 *N.J.Super.* at 269, 469 A.2d 943. The dissent concluded that since the trial court's charge on proximate cause had consisted only of general principles without relating them to the factual circumstances, the cause should be remanded for a new trial. *Id.,* 192 *N.J.Super.* at 270–71, 469 A.2d 943.

The duty to warn in the strict liability cause of action is based on the notion that absent a warning or adequate warning, a product is defective, in that it is not reasonably fit, suitable, or safe for its intended purposes. *Freund v. Cellofilm Properties, Inc.,* 87 *N.J.* 229, 242, 432 A.2d 925 (1981). * * *

A manufacturer has a duty to warn * * * foreseeable users of all hidden or latent dangers that would arise out of a reasonably anticipated use of its product. As we have heretofore stated, the duty to warn embodies "the notion that the warning be sufficient to adequately protect any and all foreseeable users from hidden dangers presented by the product." *Freund, supra,* 87 *N.J.* at 243, 432 A.2d 925. That accords with the general view. * * *

We turn next to consider whether a duty to warn exists when the danger is obvious. Although some jurisdictions have adopted an "obvious danger rule" that would absolve a manufacturer of a duty to warn of dangers that are objectively apparent, *see* 2 *R. Hursch & H. Bailey, American Law of Products Liability* 2d § 8:15, at 181–84 (1974) (summarizing case law on the subject), in our state the obviousness of a danger, as distinguished from a plaintiff's subjective knowledge of a danger, is merely one element to be factored into the analysis to determine whether a duty to warn exists. A manufacturer is not automatically relieved of his duty to warn merely because the danger is patent. *See Schipper v. Levitt & Sons,* 44 *N.J.* 70, 81, 87, 207 A.2d 314 (1965) (suggesting that obviousness of danger should not necessarily preclude recovery in negligence against mass developer of homes); Marshall, "An Obvious Wrong Does Not Make a Right: Manufacturers' Liability for Patently Dangerous Product," 48 *N.Y.U.L.Rev.* 1065 (1973); Darling, "The Patent Danger Rule: An Analysis and a Survey of its Vitality," 29 *Mercer L.Rev.* 583 (1978). Rather, the general proposition is as stated in *Michalko v. Cooke Color & Chem. Corp.*, 91 *N.J.* 386, 403, 451 *A.*2d 179 (1982):

> [A] manufacturer is under a duty to warn owners and foreseeable users of the dangers of using a particular machine if, without such a warning, the machine is not reasonably safe. A manufacturer which does not caution against the dangers inherent in the use of its product should be held strictly liable for injuries resulting from the absence of such warnings. [*Id.*, 91 *N.J.* at 403, 451 *A.*2d 179 (footnote omitted).]

Whether a duty exists "involves a weighing of the relationship of the parties, the nature of the risk, and the public interest in the proposed solution." *Goldberg v. Housing Auth.*, 38 *N.J.* 578, 583, 186 *A.*2d 291 (1962). The additional cost of a warning will in most cases have but a slight impact on the risk-utility analysis, since such cost would generally have little, if any, effect on a product's utility. *Freund, supra*, 87 *N.J.* at 238 n. 1, 242, 432 *A.*2d 925; *see also Cepeda v. Cumberland Eng'g Co.*, 76 *N.J.* 152, 174, 386 *A.*2d 816 (1978) (listing risk-utility factors). More relevant questions in the warning context include the following. Is the lack of the warning consonant with the duty to place in the stream of commerce only products that are reasonably safe, suitable, and fit? Will the absence of a duty encourage manufacturers to eliminate warnings or to produce inadequate warnings? Is the danger so basic to the functioning or purpose of the product—for example, the fact that a match will burn—that a warning would serve no useful purpose?

We have no difficulty in holding that under the facts and circumstances of this case defendant had a duty to warn plaintiff of the danger of inserting his hand into the cage. Defendant has consistently argued that "[t]his case is not about objective knowledge" and that the "obvious danger rule," even if it were the law in New Jersey, is inapplicable. * * * Moreover, there was evidence that written warnings were insufficient and that pictorial warnings should have been used. *See Hubbard–Hall Chem. Co. v. Silverman*, 340 *F.*2d 402, 405 (1st Cir.1965). In view of the unskilled or semi-skilled nature of the work and the existence of many in the work force who do not read English, warnings in the form of symbols might have been appropriate, since the employee's "ability to take care of himself" was limited. *See Cepeda v. Cumberland Eng'g Co., supra*, 76 *N.J.* at 199, 386 *A.*2d 816 (Schreiber, J., concurring and dissenting).

II

Defendant has strongly urged that it should be exonerated as a matter of law, not because the danger was objectively obvious, but because plaintiff had actual knowledge of the danger. Because of that subjective knowledge, the defendant argued, a warning requirement was irrelevant.

A duty to warn is not automatically extinguished because the injured user or consumer perceived the danger. That preexisting knowledge, however, might negate a claim that the absence of a warning was a cause in fact of plaintiff's injury. We thus agree with the dissenting Appellate Division opinion that viewing the plaintiff's conduct subjectively, the fact finder might properly assess plaintiff's awareness of the danger in terms of causation rather than duty. As the dissent has commented:

> Since the duty is to place on the market a product free of defects, and this duty attaches at the time the product is introduced into the stream of commerce, a particular user's subjective knowledge of a danger does not and cannot modify the manufacturer's duty. Such subjective knowledge may be either relevant or decisive in determining whether, when the proximate cause of this defect is assessed, the manufacturer will be held liable, but it does not limit the manufacturer's duty to distribute only defect-free products into the market place. [192 *N.J.Super.* at 266–67, 469 A.2d 943.]

See also Michalko, supra, 91 *N.J.* at 402, 451 A.2d 179 ("The question whether the failure to warn proximately caused plaintiff's injury is a factual dispute that the jury should decide."); *accord Whitehead v. St. Joe Lead Co.,* 729 F.2d 238, 249 (3d Cir.1984).

We continue to adhere to the principle that "the defect [must have] *caused injury* to a reasonably foreseeable user." *Michalko, supra,* 91 *N.J.* at 394, 451 A.2d 179 (emphasis supplied). Professor, now United States District Court Judge, Dean Keeton stated the proposition in this manner:

> If the basis for recovery under strict liability is inadequacy of warnings or instruction about dangers, then plaintiff would be required to show that an adequate warning or instruction would have prevented the harm. [Keeton, "Products Liability—Inadequacy of Information," 48 *Tex.L.Rev.* 398, 414 (1970).]

Here the issue of causation was vigorously contested. Defendant claimed that a prior accident in which plaintiff had been injured by inserting his hand into the cage while a tire was being inflated had served as a dramatic warning and yet was of no avail. In addition, there was evidence that plaintiff's conduct in putting his hand into the cage was an instinctive reaction and that a pictorial warning therefore would not have prevented the accident. *See G. Calabresi, The Costs of Accidents: A Legal and Economic Analysis* 109 (1972) (noting that specific deterrence is not served in circumstances when individuals cannot control their acts). Indeed, plaintiff's own expert stated that a pictorial warning might have been of little help in preventing the accident. In view of the crucial role that causation played in the case, it was essential that an appropriate charge on that issue be given to the jury.

A strict liability charge to a jury "should be tailored to the factual situation to assist the jury in performing its fact finding responsibility." *Suter, supra,* 81 *N.J.* at 176, 406 A.2d 140, quoted in *Freund, supra,* 87 *N.J.* at 242, 432 A.2d 925. The instructions should set forth an understandable and clear exposition of the issues, and should cover all essential matters. These include proximate cause and its place in the liability scheme. * * * A proper jury charge is essential for a fair trial. * * *

The trial court charged only generally that plaintiff had the burden of proving that the failure to give adequate warnings was a proximate cause of the accident and injuries and that the failure was a substantial factor in bringing about the happening of the accident. No attempt was made to place this issue before the jury in the factual context of the case. * * * Indeed, plaintiff made little, if any, showing that with a proper warning the accident would not have occurred. Although there may be some question whether plaintiff sustained his burden of proving causation, *see Brown v. United States Stove Co., supra, 98 N.J.* 155, 484 A.2d 1234, we are of the opinion that the matter should be remanded for a new trial. *See also* Twerski, "Seizing the Middle Ground Between Rules and Standards in Design Defect Litigation: Advancing Directed Verdict Practice in the Law of Torts," 57 *N.Y.U.L.Rev.* 521, 562 (1982) (noting that in failure to warn products liability cases some courts have helped plaintiffs overcome the burden of proof by positing a rebuttable presumption that the warning would have been heeded if given).

CONCLUSION

The judgment of the Appellate Division entering a judgment in favor of the defendant is reversed; the plaintiff's cause of action predicated upon a failure to provide an adequate warning is remanded for a new trial. Costs to abide the event.

For reversal and remandment—CHIEF JUSTICE WILENTZ and JUSTICES CLIFFORD, SCHREIBER, HANDLER, POLLOCK, O'HERN and GARIBALDI—7.

For affirmance—None.

Notes

1. In similar cases, a number of other courts have held that there is no duty to warn as a matter of law because the risk of separation was common knowledge and known to the plaintiff. Bishop v. Firestone Tire & Rubber Co., 814 F.2d 437 (7th Cir.1987) (Indiana law); Tri–State Ins. Co. of Tulsa, Okl. v. Fidelity & Cas. Ins. Co. of N.Y., 364 So.2d 657 (La.App.1978), writ denied, 365 So.2d 248 (1978).

2. **Obvious Dangers.** A minority of courts agree with *Campos* that a defendant must sometimes warn about obvious dangers. In Olson v. A.W. Chesterton Co., 256 N.W.2d 530 (N.D.1977), an employee was injured while applying belt dressing with a pour on applicator to the unguarded pinch point of a conveyor belt. Plaintiff's expert testified that the label on the belt dressing container should have warned of the dangers inherent in running conveyor belts, and should have advised the use of a product with an aerosol applicator with top-drive, power pulley systems. The manufacturer of the belt dressing was held liable for failure to warn. The court stated:

There is no valid reason for automatic preclusion of liability based solely upon "obviousness" of danger in an action founded upon the risk-spreading concept of strict liability in tort which is intended to burden the manufacturers of defectively dangerous products with special responsibilities and potential financial liabilities for accidental injuries. 256 N.W.2d at 537.

3. **Known Dangers.** *Campos* treats knowledge of danger as relating to the question of causation. A number of courts agree. *E.g.,* Laaperi v. Sears, Roebuck & Co., Inc., 787 F.2d 726 (1st Cir.1986). Other courts, such as *Graham v. Joseph T. Ryerson & Sons, supra,* treat it as relevant to the question of duty to warn. Which view is correct? Does it make any real difference whether courts treat this as a question of duty or causation?

4. In Vallillo v. Muskin Corp., 212 N.J.Super. 155, 514 A.2d 528 (1986), a very experienced adult swimmer was injured when he dove into a four and one-half foot, above-ground swimming pool while unsuccessfully attempting to make a shallow dive. He sued the manufacturer of the pool for failing to provide better warnings against this practice. The court held that the failure to warn was not a cause of the injury as a matter of law because the danger of diving into a shallow pool was in plaintiff's mind at the time he executed the dive. The court distinguished *Campos* as requiring warnings against known dangers only when necessary to jog a plaintiff's memory of the danger or to guard against instinctive actions. Is this distinction valid?

4. WHO TO WARN

(a) Users, Consumers, and Bystanders

GOODBAR v. WHITEHEAD BROS.

United States District Court, Western District Virginia, 1984.
591 F.Supp. 552.

MEMORANDUM OPINION

KISER, DISTRICT JUDGE.

[Plaintiffs, 132 present and former employees of the Lynchburg Foundry, sued twelve manufacturers who supplied the foundry with silica sand and related products used in the casting process. Plaintiffs have each contracted silicosis. They claim that the defendants breached a duty to warn them directly of the risks of contracting silicosis by working with their products. Defendants have moved for summary judgment.

In its molding process the foundry used huge quantities of silica sand which defendants delivered to the foundry in bulk in railroad cars. In the manufacturing process] the silica is fractured and respirable free-floating dust * * * is produced. * * * The [smallest of these dust particles] escape the natural barriers of the body, enter the lungs, and cause the formation of scar tissue or nodules which inhibits breathing. If inhaled in sufficient quantities over extended periods of time ranging from 5 to 20 years, the respiratory disease of silicosis results.

* * *

Essentially, Defendants have made a two-pronged argument on the duty to warn issue. They contend that there was no obligation on their part to warn the Foundry's employees of the risks of silicosis because: (1) silicosis is an occupational respiratory disease about which the foundry industry and, more importantly the Lynchburg Foundry, has been knowledgeable since at least the 1930's; and (2) only the Plaintiff's employer, the Lynchburg Foundry, can communicate any type of effective warnings.

In response, Plaintiffs principally argue that Defendant suppliers owed a non-delegable duty to warn about the dangers associated with the use of silica products not only to the Lynchburg Foundry, but more importantly its employees; and that these hazards are latent.

* * *

Both parties agree that Restatement (Second) of Torts § 388 (1965) [4] controls.

* * *

I.

In the negligent failure to warn claim, the analysis under § 388 is that the supplier of the chattel (i.e. Defendants) is liable when he: (a) supplies a defective or dangerous product; (b) has no reason to believe that the user (i.e. the Plaintiff foundry employees) lacks [sic; has?] knowledge of this defect or dangerous condition; and (c) cannot reasonably rely upon the purchaser/employer (i.e. the Foundry) to supply necessary warnings to Plaintiffs, the ultimate users of the product. Defendants have conceded, for argument purposes, that the products they supplied contain a dangerous substance and that the Plaintiff users were not aware of these dangers. Thus, in view of these concessions on the first two prongs of § 388 and since all three provisions of § 388 must be satisfied before liability attaches, *see McKay v. Rockwell Intern. Corp.,* 704 F.2d 444 (9th Cir.1983), *cert. denied,* ___ U.S. ___, 104 S.Ct. 711, 79 L.Ed.2d 175 (1984), this matter turns upon whether the requirements of clause (c) have been met, namely whether the Defendants failed to exercise reasonable care in relying upon the Foundry to supply its employees with the necessary information to satisfy the duty to warn. For the reasons explained below, I find as a matter of law that there was a reasonable basis for Defendants in this litigation to rely upon the Foundry to give appropriate information of all the hazards of working with silica sand and related products to its employees.

4. "§ 388. *Chattel Known to be Dangerous for Intended Use.* One who supplies directly or through a third person a chattel for another to use is subject to liability to those whom the supplier should expect to use the chattel with the consent of the other or to be endangered by its probable use, for physical harm caused by the use of the chattel in the manner for which and by a person for whose use it is supplied, if the supplier (a) knows or has reason to know that the chattel is or is likely to be dangerous for the use for which it is supplied, and (b) has no reason to believe that those for whose use the chattel is supplied will realize its dangerous condition, and (c) fails to exercise reasonable care to inform them of its dangerous condition or of the facts which make it likely to be dangerous."

A.

I begin my analysis of clause (c) of § 388 by turning to comment n of the official comments entitled "[w]arnings given to third person", which provides an explanation of this third element of the Restatement (Second) of Torts § 388 (1965). Comment n, which has been determined to be included in the law of Virginia, *see Barnes v. Litton Indus. Products, Inc.*, 555 F.2d 1184, 1188 (4th Cir.1977), delineates various factors that must be balanced in determining what precautions the supplier of the product must take to satisfy the clause (c) requirement of reasonable care. These include: (1) the dangerous condition of the product; (2) the purpose for which the product is used; (3) the form of any warnings given; (4) the reliability of the third party as a conduit of necessary information about the product; (5) the magnitude of the risk involved; and (6) the burdens imposed on the supplier by requiring that he directly warn all users. This comment recognizes that a balancing of these considerations is necessary in light of the fact that no single set of rules could possibly be advanced that would automatically cover all situations. Critical in my view is the recognition that "[m]odern life would be intolerable unless one were permitted to rely to a certain extent on others doing what they normally do, particularly if it is their duty to do so." *Id.* at 308.

Next, I address the case law cited by Plaintiffs, all of which I find to be distinguishable from the case before the Court. Their principal authority, *Dougherty v. Hooker Chemical Corp.*, 540 F.2d 174 (3rd Cir.1976), a diversity case applying Pennsylvania law, did not even deal with the issue presented here, namely whether the supplier had a duty to warn the users in the first place. Instead, it was tried solely on the issue of the adequacy of the warnings which were given by the supplier.

There, the widow of a helicopter transmission builder sued the Hooker Chemical Corporation ("Hooker") which supplied to the deceased's employer, Boeing Vertol Company ("Boeing"), the chemical solvent trichloroethylene ("TRI"). The employee's cause of death was believed to be TRI poisoning, a possibility that was not mentioned in either the warnings given by Hooker on the 55 gallon drums of TRI or in its safety data sheets supplied to Boeing. Boeing, however, possessed additional information not obtained from Hooker that discussed possible death from TRI poisoning.

At the close of the plaintiff's evidence, the district court granted a directed verdict in Hooker's favor, holding as a matter of law that its warnings were adequate and that in any event Boeing possessed independent knowledge of the possible dangers of prolonged TRI inhalation. In reversing, the divided panel of the Third Circuit held that there was sufficient evidence to create a triable jury issue on the adequacy of warnings. Especially significant in majority's reasoning is its conclusion that on the evidence presented "a jury could reasonably find * * * that there was no reasonable basis for Hooker to rely on Boeing's independent knowledge of the fatal properties of TRI * * * [or] * * * upon

Boeing giving appropriate information to its employees of all the hazards of working with TRI." 540 F.2d at 181–182. In contrast, I find that in the instant controversy reasonable men could not differ on whether the Lynchburg Foundry: (1) was a knowledgeable industrial purchaser of silica sand and related products; (2) had intimate knowledge of the dangerous properties of silica products since at least the 1950s; and (3) had every reason to try to protect its employees from these hazards by communicating to them information on harmful properties of silica.

* * *

Turning to Defendants' authority, they maintain that in Virginia there is no duty on product suppliers to warn employees of knowledgeable industrial purchasers as to product-related hazards. I agree.

In *Marker v. Universal Oil Products Company,* 250 F.2d 603 (10th Cir.1957), an oil company employee was asphyxiated by carbon monoxide gas when he was lowered into a petroleum refining vessel constructed by his employer pursuant to a design furnished by Universal Oil Products Company ("Universal"), who had also supplied the catalyst used in the vessel. The employee's beneficiary sued Universal, alleging that it was negligent in failing to warn the decedent of the danger of entering the vessel in which the chemical had been placed.

The Tenth Circuit affirmed the lower court's directed verdict for Universal, holding that since this danger was equally within the technical knowledge of decedent's employer and Universal, no duty existed upon Universal to warn. *Id.* at 606. Instructive in this regard is court's conclusion that Universal had a right to rely upon the employer to protect his employees from harm and that Universal should not be liable under § 388 even though employer never conveyed to its employees vital information about the product in question. *Id.* at 607.

[Discussion of the other authorities relied on by Defendants is omitted.]

Plaintiffs try to distinguish [Defendant's authorities] from this litigation by directing my attention to three other Fourth Circuit decisions, *Barnes v. Litton Indus. Products, Inc., supra, Gardner v. Q.H.S., Inc.,* 448 F.2d 238 (4th Cir.1971), and *Spruill v. Boyle–Midway, Inc.,* 308 F.2d 79 (4th Cir.1962). Each of these cases involved *consumer* products, i.e. burning alcohol, hair rollers, and furniture polish respectively, that were determined to be inherently dangerous and the dangers there were neither obvious nor known to the user.

I find this argument, as well as Plaintiffs' contention that the silica-related hazards are latent, to be without merit for two reasons. First, as contrasted with these three consumer product cases, here we have an industrial product and, more importantly, a knowledgeable, sophisticated employer who supplies it for use to its employees. Second, the latent/patent distinction has no place in this litigation in light of Defendants' concession for argument purposes that Plaintiffs did not know of the dangers of silicosis and the evidence clearly shows that the inherent dangers of silica [were] not latent insofar as the Foundry is concerned.

* * *

B.

From my review of the various appendices, affidavits, depositions, and exhibits submitted by the parties, I find that a plethora of material exists on the Lynchburg Foundry's extensive knowledge of the hazards of inhaling silica dust, the disease of silicosis, and proper dust control methods. It clearly shows that the Foundry is a knowledgeable employer within a knowledgeable industry.

[The court's summary of this evidence is omitted.]

Thus, in light of the above, it is well-established that the Lynchburg Foundry was cognizant of the problems of silica dust and silicosis since at least the 1930s. More importantly, from the late 1950s and early 1960s onward, the Foundry's knowledge was nothing less than extensive.

C.

Touching briefly on another point raised by Defendants, I agree that a sand supplier to a large, knowledgeable foundry like the Lynchburg Foundry has no duty to warn the foundry employees about the occupational disease of silicosis and its causes when only the Foundry is in a position to communicate effective warning and accordingly should be the one to shoulder any burden of effective warning. The difficulties that the sand suppliers face in attempting to warn the Foundry's employees of the hazards inherent in the use of sand in a foundry setting are numerous. These include (1) the identification of the users or those exposed to its products would require a constant monitoring by the suppliers in view of the constant turnover of the Foundry's large work force; (2) the manner in which the sand products are delivered in bulk (i.e. unpackaged railroad car lots or truck); (3) no written product warnings placed on the railroad cars would ever reach the workers involved in casting or those in the immediate vicinity due to the way the loose sand is unloaded, conveyed, and kept in storage bins until needed; (4) only the Foundry itself would be in a position to provide the good housekeeping measures, training and warnings to its workers on a continuous and systematic basis necessary to reduce the risk of silicosis; (5) the sand suppliers must rely on the Foundry to convey any safety information to its employees; (6) the confusion arising when twelve different suppliers and the Foundry each try to cope with the awesome task of instructing the Foundry workers; and (7) in a commercial setting, it would be totally unrealistic to assume that the suppliers would be able to exert pressure on a large, industrial customer such as the Foundry to allow the suppliers to come in and educate its workers about the hazards of silicosis. *See e.g. Reed v. Pennwalt Corp.*, 22 Wash.App. 718, 591 P.2d 478 (Wash.Ct.App.1979); Schwartz and Driver, *Warnings In The Workplace: The Need For A Synthesis Of Law And Communication Theory*, 52 U.Cin.L.Rev. 38 (1983).

In addition, the responsibility of providing a safe workplace and giving warnings of employment-related dangers should be borne by the Foundry for still another reason:

> The extension of workplace warnings liability unguided by practical consideration has the unreasonable potential to impose absolute liability in those situations where it is impossible for the manufacturer to warn the product user directly. In the workplace setting, the product manufacturer often cannot communicate the necessary safety information to product users in a manner that will result in reduction of risk. Only the employer is in a position to ensure workplace safety by training, supervision and use of proper safety equipment. Designating the manufacturer an absolute insurer of its product removes the economic incentives that encourage employers to protect the safety of their employees.

Schwartz and Driver, *supra,* at 43. (Footnotes omitted.)

* * *

In conclusion, having determined that there remains no genuine issue of material fact and that Defendants are clearly entitled to judgment as a matter of law on Plaintiffs' remaining * * * claims, summary judgment will be entered in Defendants' favor.

An appropriate order will issue.

ORDER

For the reasons set forth in the accompanying Memorandum Opinion, it is ADJUDGED and ORDERED as follows:

1. The Joint Motions for Summary Judgment on the duty to warn issue * * * shall be, and they hereby are, GRANTED.

Notes

1. The manufacturer's obligation is to use reasonable care to protect the people who are likely to be injured by his goods. Manufacturers of consumer goods, which are individually packaged and sold, usually must warn the user or consumer. A warning given to a non-consuming purchaser, such as a retailer or wholesaler, will not satisfy the manufacturer's obligation. Thus, to be effective, the warning must often accompany the product. *E.g.,* Chappuis v. Sears Roebuck & Co., 358 So.2d 926 (La.1978), writ denied, 366 So.2d 576 (1979) (warning not to use a chipped hammer must be on hammer).

2. In Sills v. Massey–Ferguson, Inc., 296 F.Supp. 776 (N.D.Ind.1969), a bystander was injured when he was hit by an object thrown by the blade of a rotary-type lawnmower 150 feet away. He sued the manufacturer on negligence and strict liability theories, claiming that defendant should have warned the general public to stay a safe distance from the mower. The court recognized that the manufacturer might be acting reasonably in warning the user only. This is because the user is in a position to protect bystanders, and warning the general public would be difficult. The court

held that whether there is a duty to warn the general public is a jury question.

3. **Sophisticated Purchasers.** When products are sold in bulk to sophisticated industrial users for use in the manufacturing process, many courts have held that the supplier is not required to warn the purchaser's employees. The supplier can escape liability by adequately warning and training the purchaser. Rusin v. Glendale Optical Co., Inc., 805 F.2d 650 (6th Cir.1986) (Michigan law; protective glasses; warning required); Alm v. Aluminum Co. of America, 717 S.W.2d 588 (Tex.1986) (bottle capping machine; training the purchaser may be necessary). This is because of the difficulty of warning the individual employees, and because of the reasonableness of relying on the purchaser to protect his employees.

4. Is the sophisticated user defense determined as a question of fact or a question of law? The courts are split on this question. For an excellent analysis of the cases, *see* Note, Failures to Warn and the Sophisticated User Defense, 74 Va.L.Rev. 579 (1988).

5. Consider Oman v. Johns–Manville Corp., 764 F.2d 224 (4th Cir. 1985), cert. denied, 474 U.S. 970, 106 S.Ct. 351, 88 L.Ed.2d 319 (1985). Four shipyard workers were required to use products containing asbestos. They contracted asbestosis because of exposure to air-borne asbestos fibers which came from the products. They sued the manufacturers for failure to warn them about the risks associated with the products. The court discussed the duty to warn issue as follows:

> The third and final issue presented for review concerns the sufficiency of the district court's charge to the jury regarding the defendants' duty to warn. The defendants argue that the district court should have charged the jury that the manufacturer's duty to warn the ultimate users, the employees, is satisfied if a sophisticated employer is aware of the dangers involved in the use of the product.

> In Featherall v. Firestone Tire and Rubber Co., 219 Va. 949, 252 S.E.2d 358 (1979), the Supreme Court of Virginia adopted *Restatement (Second) of Torts* § 388 (1965) to govern a manufacturer's duty to warn about dangers associated with a product's use. *Featherall,* 219 Va. at 962, 252 S.E.2d at 366. Virginia law includes comment n of § 388, "Warnings given to third person." Jones v. Meat Packers Equipment Co., 723 F.2d 370, 373 (4th Cir.1983); Barnes v. Litton Indus. Products, Inc., 555 F.2d 1184, 1188 (4th Cir.1977); Goodbar v. Whitehead Bros., 591 F.Supp. 552, 557 (W.D.Va.1984).

> Comment n discusses the various factors a court must balance to determine what precautions the manufacturer or supplier of a product must take to satisfy the requirement of reasonable care found in § 388(c). These factors include: (1) the dangerous condition of the product; (2) the purpose for which the product is used; (3) the form of any warnings given; (4) the reliability of the third party as a conduit of necessary information about the product; (5) the magnitude of the risk involved; and (6) the burdens imposed upon the supplier by requiring that he directly warn all users. These considerations must be balanced to determine if the manufacturer owes a duty to place a warning on his product.

In this case the product, because it contained asbestos fibers, was very dangerous. The burden on the manufacturers in placing a warning on the product was not great. The employer was unaware of the danger until 1964. Finally, once the employer became aware of the potential danger it failed to convey its knowledge to its employees. We cannot say that the district court erred in refusing to give the charge requested by the manufacturers under the set of facts involved in this case.

764 F.2d at 232–33. Note that the court which decided *Oman* also affirmed *Goodbar v. Whitehead Bros.* on appeal in a decision which adopted Judge Kiser's opinion as the opinion of the court. Beale v. Hardy, 769 F.2d 213 (4th Cir.1985). Both decisions were governed by the substantive law of the same state, and both opinions were written by the same judge. Can the two opinions be reconciled?

6. Some courts reject the sophisticated user doctrine. *See, e.g.,* Whitehead v. St. Joe Lead Co., 729 F.2d 238 (3d Cir.1984). An employee in a solder manufacturing plant suffered lead poisoning as a result of long term exposure to minute particles of airborne lead released by the manufacturing process. She sued the companies that supplied lead ingot to her employer on both strict liability and negligence theories. She claimed that they should have warned her of the dangers associated with the use of lead. The court rejected defendants' argument that they had no duty to warn plaintiff because her employer (the purchaser) knew of the danger. The court concluded that under New Jersey law the sophisticated user doctrine did not apply to strict liability actions. This is because the defendants had a nondelegable duty to make the product safe, and hindsight is used to impute knowledge to defendants that the employer would not adequately protect plaintiff. On the negligence theory, the court ruled that it was for the jury to determine whether defendants reasonably relied on the employer to protect plaintiff.

7. The sophisticated user doctrine is discussed in Madden, The Duty to Warn in Products Liability: Contours and Criticism, 89 W.Va.L.Rev. 221, 285–298 (1987); Goggin & Brophy, Toxic Torts: Workable Defenses Available to the Corporate Defendant, 28 Vill.L.Rev. 1208, 1268–1276 (1983); Comment, Duty to Warn and the Sophisticated User Defense in Products Liability Cases, 15 U.Balt.L.Rev. 276 (1986); Note, Failures to Warn and the Sophisticated User Defense, 74 Va.L.Rev. 579 (1988).

(b) Learned Intermediaries

BACARDI v. HOLZMAN

Superior Court of New Jersey, Appellate Division, 1981.
182 N.J.Super. 422, 442 A.2d 617.

BISCHOFF, P.J.A.D.

In this pharmaceutical products liability case the chief issue presented is whether the manufacturer of a drug which is dispensed only on a physician's renewable prescription has a duty to warn the consumer of potential adverse effects which may occur from extended use of the drug. We hold no such duty exists.

Plaintiff Antone Bacardi suffered from glaucoma since 1969. For a significant portion of those years he had been taking the drug Diamox to control that condition. This drug had been prescribed for him by a series of doctors and the prescriptions were renewable, one being renewed by plaintiff 13 times over a period of 17 months. In October 1975 plaintiff developed a pain in his right flank and was hospitalized for diagnosis and treatment. After examination it was determined plaintiff had developed kidney stones. The stones were passed spontaneously. In 1977 plaintiff developed additional urinary tract problems. He was again hospitalized and again kidney stones were diagnosed as the source of his trouble. They were surgically removed. At this time the doctors suspected Diamox as a cause of the recurring kidney stones and recommended the use of the drug Neptazane in place of Diamox. Plaintiff discontinued the use of Diamox and has ever since been symptom-free insofar as his urinary tract is concerned. The drug Diamox is manufactured by defendant Lederle Laboratories, Inc. That company recognized the occurrence of "renal calculus" as a common adverse reaction to the use of the drug, and this information was published in the *Physician's Desk Reference* and provided in package circulars. Lederle further provided brochures to physicians to supplement the package circulars upon request.

Plaintiff instituted this action against the doctor who prescribed Diamox and also Lederle. Plaintiff thereafter settled with the doctor. In the action against Lederle plaintiff alleged that (1) Lederle had a duty to warn all users of Diamox of its potential adverse effects, which duty it negligently breached, and (2) Lederle was strictly liable in tort.

Plaintiff contended that despite the printed material available, he had never been furnished with a package insert or with information concerning possible adverse consequences following his use of Diamox.

Defendant's motion for summary judgment was granted, the judge holding that while it is the general rule that an ethical drug manufacturer has "a duty to warn the intended or foreseeable consumer of a product of its dangerous aspects," this duty does not exist where there is an intermediary who "is not a mere conduit of the product, but rather administers it on an individual basis or recommends it in some way implying an independent duty to evaluate the risk and transmit relevant warnings to the user."

Plaintiff appeals and argues that (1) defendant is strictly liable to plaintiff in tort and (2) his injuries were proximately caused by defendant's defective product.

Plaintiff explains that in the context of this case the alleged defect upon which his allegation of strict liability is predicated consists of the failure of the manufacturer to warn plaintiff of potential adverse consequences following the use of the drug, and also that the "renal and uretal calculi" which he developed was the result of "the very condition that the defendant failed to warn him about." *See Torsiello v. Whitehall*

Laboratories, 165 *N.J.Super.* 311, 320, n. 2, 398 *A.*2d 132 (App.Div.1979), certif. den. 81 *N.J.* 50, 404 *A.*2d 1150 (1979).

It is the general rule that in the case of prescription drugs warnings of potential adverse effects to the prescribing physician is sufficient. *Torsiello, supra,* 165 *N.J.Super.* at 322–323, 398 *A.*2d 132; *Davis v. Wyeth Laboratories, Inc.,* 399 *F.*2d 121, 130 (9 Cir.1968); *Reyes v. Wyeth Laboratories,* 498 *F.*2d 1264 (5 Cir.1974), *cert.* den. 419 *U.S.* 1096, 95 *S.Ct.* 687, 42 *L.Ed.*2d 688 (1974); Products Liability, "The Ethical Drug Manufacturer's Liability," 18 *Rutg.L.Rev.* 947, 985–986 (1964), 3 *Frumer and Friedman, Products Liability,* § 33.01[3] at 2412 *et seq.* The reason for the rule is explained in the *Davis* case in the following terms:

> Ordinarily in the case of prescription drugs warning to the prescribing physician is sufficient. In such cases the choice involved is essentially a medical one involving an assessment of medical risks in the light of the physician's knowledge of this patient's needs and susceptibilities. Further it is difficult under such circumstances for the manufacturer, by label or direct communication, to reach the consumer with a warning. A warning to the medical profession is in such cases the only effective means by which a warning could help the patient. [at 130]

Plaintiff argues that the duty to warn should be extended to the consumer in this case because of the circumstances under which the drug was administered. In an attempt to bring his case within the holdings of the *Davis* and *Reyes* cases, plaintiff points to the fact that over the years he was treated by several doctors; that he had gone to clinics and hospitals and was an outpatient at a large hospital, and that he did not even know the names of some of the physicians who had treated him.

Davis and *Reyes* are clearly distinguishable. Both of those cases involve polio vaccine administered in mass public immunization projects. The drug was administered by a registered nurse or other intermediary who was a mere conduit for the drug. There was no "individualized balancing by a physician of the risks involved." *Davis,* 399 *F.*2d at 131; in accord *Reyes,* 498 *F.*2d at 1276. Here, on the other hand the Diamox was prescribed to treat an existing condition rather than to prevent a disease. Diagnosis and treatment removes this case from the "mere conduit" category.

Plaintiff also claims that since this is the type of a drug that is normally taken for an extended period of time and can be prescribed by renewable prescriptions, the drug manufacturer should have foreseen that the physician is not continuously monitoring the patient and should have warned the consumer of the dangers of long use of the drug. We disagree. The manufacturer has no duty to prepare a warning for the consumer when, under all circumstances, the product only comes into the consumer's hands after it is prescribed by the physician. There is no basis for concluding that the manufacturer should have foreseen that the ultimate consumer would be in the position to make a layman's judgment in terms of whether to continue with the use of the drug or not.

Plaintiff finally contends that it was improper for the trial judge to grant summary judgment because there was a "genuine issue as to a material fact." *R.* 4:46–2, *Judson v. Peoples Bank and Trust Co. of Westfield,* 17 *N.J.* 67, 75, 110 *A.*2d 24 (1954).

Plaintiff concedes that Diamox can only be obtained by means of a physician's prescriptions but argues that it is a factual issue whether the manner in which he gained access to the drug made it a nonprescription drug, thus imposing on defendant the obligation of warning the consumer directly of potential adverse consequences following the use of the drug. This issue, he argues, results from the renewable nature of the prescriptions written by the doctors for the drug. Plaintiff refers to the fact that one prescription alone was renewed 13 times in 17 months. Again, plaintiff relies upon the cases of *Davis* and *Reyes,* both *supra,* and *Givens v. Lederle,* 556 *F.*2d 1341 (5 Cir.1977). As we pointed out above, while the drug (vaccine) was acknowledged to be a prescription drug in those cases, it was not dispensed as such. "It was dispensed to all comers at mass clinics without an individualized balancing by a physician of the risks involved." *Davis,* 399 *F.*2d at 131. Moreover, in those cases the drug company had taken an active part in setting up the immunization programs and knew the program did not make provisions for advertising or consultation, for advising the public of potential side effects. The courts in those cases did not hold that the vaccine, by its method of use, became a nonprescription drug. They held that the unique method of administration of the prescription drug extended the duty to warn beyond the physician. No such unique circumstances exist here. Diamox is conceded to be a prescription drug and was administered to plaintiff as such. We hold no genuine issue of a material fact was presented and the trial judge properly considered and ruled upon defendant's motion for summary judgment.

Affirmed.

Notes

1. Reyes v. Wyeth Laboratories, 498 F.2d 1264 (5th Cir.1974), cert. denied, 419 U.S. 1096, 95 S.Ct. 687, 42 L.Ed.2d 688 (1974), gives the most frequently cited rationale for the learned intermediary doctrine:

[W]here *prescription* drugs are concerned, the manufacturer's duty to warn is limited to an obligation to advise the prescribing physician of any potential dangers that may result from the drug's use. This special standard for prescription drugs is an understandable exception to the Restatement's general rule that one who markets goods must warn foreseeable ultimate users of dangers inherent in his products. See Restatement (Second) of Torts, Section 388 (1965). Prescription drugs are likely to be complex medicines, esoteric in formula and varied in effect. As a medical expert, the prescribing physician can take into account the propensities of the drug, as well as the susceptibilities of his patient. His is the task of weighing the benefits of any medication against its potential dangers. The choice he makes is an informed one, an individualized medical judgment bottomed on a knowledge of both patient and palliative. Pharmaceutical companies then, who must warn ultimate purchasers of dangers inherent in patent drugs sold over the counter, in selling prescription drugs are required to warn only the prescribing physician, who acts as a "learned intermediary" between manufacturer and consumer.

498 F.2d at 1276. The history of the doctrine is traced in Comment, Pharmaceutical Manufacturers and Consumer–Directed Information—Enhancing the Safety of Prescription Drug Use, 34 Cath.U.L.Rev. 117, 122–29 (1984).

2. Under the doctrine the manufacturer has no duty to warn the patient directly. Whether or not the intermediary must warn the patient is governed by the law of informed consent. Under that rule, the doctor may sometimes be required to pass on some or all of the warnings to the patient. At other times, he may weigh the risks and benefits and make the decision to prescribe the drug without informing the patient. *See* Comment, Pharmaceutical Manufacturers and Consumer–Directed Information—Enhancing the Safety of Prescription Drug Use, 34 Cath.U.L.Rev. 117, 129 (1984).

3. The learned intermediary doctrine has been generally accepted. Some courts apply it to professional nurses as well as physicians. Walker v. Merck & Co., Inc., 648 F.Supp. 931 (M.D.Ga.1986). It has also been applied to warnings about the risks of treatment with potentially dangerous medical equipment. Kirsch v. Picker Intern., Inc., 753 F.2d 670 (8th Cir.1985) (X-ray machine); Terhune v. A.H. Robins Co., 90 Wash.2d 9, 577 P.2d 975 (1978) (intrauterine device).

4. The doctrine does not apply to non-prescription drugs. Here the manufacturer must warn the consumer directly. Torsiello v. Whitehall Laboratories, Div. of Home Products Corp., 165 N.J.Super. 311, 398 A.2d 132 (1979), certification denied, 81 N.J. 50, 404 A.2d 1150 (1979); Michael v. Warner/Chilcott, 91 N.M. 651, 579 P.2d 183 (1978), cert. denied, 91 N.M. 610, 577 P.2d 1256 (1978). May the manufacturer avoid liability by advising the consumer to see a doctor before using the product for more than ten days?

5. **Immunization Clinics.** In Davis v. Wyeth Laboratories, Inc., 399 F.2d 121 (9th Cir.1968), polio vaccine was distributed in a mass immunization program in which the drug manufacturer participated. The court required that warnings be given directly to the consumers because the drug "was dispensed to all comers at mass clinics without an individualized balancing by a physician of the risks involved." *Id.* at 131.

6. The courts are split over the question of how far to expand the exception to the learned intermediary doctrine. In Reyes v. Wyeth Laboratories, 498 F.2d 1264 (5th Cir.1974), cert. denied, 419 U.S. 1096, 95 S.Ct. 687, 42 L.Ed.2d 688 (1974), the court required that the consumer be warned directly even though she did not receive the vaccine as part in a mass immunization clinic. There, the polio vaccine was given to plaintiff at her parents request by a nurse at a public health clinic. The clinic dispensed the vaccine as a part of an ongoing program, and no doctor was present to make an individualized determination for plaintiff of the risks and benefits. The

court held that the learned intermediary exception did not apply because the manufacturer could foresee that the vaccine would be routinely administered in this fashion.

7. Other courts disagree. *See* Walker v. Merck & Co., Inc., 648 F.Supp. 931 (M.D.Ga.1986), refusing to apply the exception where a mass immunization program was not involved. In Walker, a practical nurse administered measles vaccine to plaintiff in a local program designed to inoculate certain high school students. The court held that the manufacturer did not have to warn the students directly. It distinguished this program from those involving mass immunization clinics because of the difficulty involved in identifying and warning individual recipients.

8. **Individually Prescribed Drugs.** In Givens v. Lederle, 556 F.2d 1341 (5th Cir.1977), the Fifth Circuit expanded the exception to the learned intermediary doctrine to apply it in certain cases where the drug is prescribed by the patient's doctor. These are cases where the doctor prescribes the drug without having made an individualized determination of the risks and benefits of the drug on plaintiff's behalf. In *Givens*, polio vaccine was administered by the patient's doctor in his office. The doctor testified that the administration did not differ from that of a public health center. The court ruled that the rationale of *Reyes* applied because "the vaccine was administered here in a manner more like that at a small county health clinic, as in *Reyes*, than by prescription." *Accord,* Samuels v. American Cyanamid Co., 130 Misc.2d 175, 495 N.Y.S.2d 1006 (1985) (vaccine routinely administered in company clinic to employee prior to overseas travel).

9. Most courts have refused to expand the exception this far. *See, e.g.,* Plummer v. Lederle Laboratories, Div. of Am. Cyanamid Co., 819 F.2d 349 (2d Cir.1987) (the manufacturer of polio vaccine has no duty to warn the patient when the drug is prescribed by his physician).

10. **Birth Control Pills.** The courts are also split on the question of whether manufacturers of birth control pills must directly warn the consumer. The majority of courts hold that the duty is to warn the prescribing physician only. *E.g.,* Brochu v. Ortho Pharmaceutical Corp., 642 F.2d 652 (1st Cir.1981). *But see* MacDonald v. Ortho Pharmaceutical Corp., 394 Mass. 131, 475 N.E.2d 65 (1985), cert. denied, 474 U.S. 920, 106 S.Ct. 250, 88 L.Ed.2d 258 (1985) imposing a duty. *MacDonald* based its conclusion on the following reasoning:

> The rule in jurisdictions that have addressed the question of the extent of a manufacturer's duty to warn in cases involving prescription drugs is that the prescribing physician acts as a "learned intermediary" between the manufacturer and the patient, and "the duty of the ethical drug manufacturer is to warn the doctor, rather than the patient, [although] the manufacturer is directly liable to the patient for a breach of such duty." *McEwen v. Ortho Pharmaceutical Corp.,* 270 Or. 375, 386–387, 528 P.2d 522 (1974). Oral contraceptives, however, bear peculiar characteristics which warrant the imposition of a common law duty on the manufacturer to warn users directly of associated risks. Whereas a patient's involvement in decision-making concerning use of a prescription drug necessary to treat a malady is typically minimal or nonexistent, the healthy, young consumer of oral contraceptives is

usually actively involved in the decision to use "the pill," as opposed to other available birth control products, and the prescribing physician is relegated to a relatively passive role.

Furthermore, the physician prescribing "the pill," as a matter of course, examines the patient once before prescribing an oral contraceptive and only annually thereafter. J. Willson, E. Carrington, & W. Ledger, Obstetrics and Gynecology 184 (7th ed. 1983). D. Danforth, Obstetrics and Gynecology 267 (4th ed. 1982). T. Green, Gynecology: Essentials of Clinical Practice 593 (3d ed. 1977). At her annual check-up, the patient receives a renewal prescription for a full year's supply of the pill. Thus, the patient may only seldom have the opportunity to explore her questions and concerns about the medication with the prescribing physician. Even if the physician, on those occasions, were scrupulously to remind the patient of the risks attendant on continuation of the oral contraceptive, "the patient cannot be expected to remember all of the details for a protracted period of time." 35 Fed.Reg. 9002 (1970).

Last, the birth control pill is specifically subject to extensive Federal regulation. The FDA has promulgated regulations designed to ensure that the choice of "the pill" as a contraceptive method is informed by comprehensible warnings of potential side effects. * * * These regulations, and subsequent amendments, have their basis in the FDA commissioner's finding, after hearings, that "[b]ecause oral contraceptives are ordinarily taken electively by healthy women who have available to them alternative methods of treatment, and because of the relatively high incidence of serious illnesses associated with their use, * * * users of these drugs should, without exception, be furnished with written information telling them of the drug's benefits and risks." 43 Fed.Reg. 4215 (1978). The FDA also found that the facts necessary to informed decisions by women as to use of oral contraceptives are "too complex to expect the patient to remember everything told her by the physician," and that, in the absence of direct written warnings, many potential users of "the pill" do not receive the needed information "in an organized, comprehensive, understandable, and handy-for-future-reference form." 35 Fed.Reg. 9002 (1970).

The oral contraceptive thus stands apart from other prescription drugs in light of the heightened participation of patients in decisions relating to use of "the pill"; the substantial risks affiliated with the product's use; the feasibility of direct warnings by the manufacturer to the user; the limited participation of the physician (annual prescriptions); and the possibility that oral communications between physicians and consumers may be insufficient or too scanty standing alone fully to apprise consumers of the product's dangers at the time the initial selection of a contraceptive method is made as well as at subsequent points when alternative methods may be considered. We conclude that the manufacturer of oral contraceptives is not justified in relying on warnings to the medical profession to satisfy its common law duty to warn, and that the manufacturer's obligation encompasses a duty to warn the ultimate user. Thus, the manufacturer's duty is to provide to the consumer written warnings conveying reasonable notice of the nature, gravity, and likelihood of known or knowable side effects, and advising the consumer to seek fuller explanation from the prescribing physician or other doctor of any such information of concern to the consumer.

394 Mass. at 136–38, 475 N.E.2d at 69–70. The *MacDonald* case is noted in 20 Suffolk U.L.Rev. 155 (1986). Two Federal District courts have reached a similar conclusion on the basis of their prediction of state law. Odgers v. Ortho Pharmaceutical Corp., 609 F.Supp. 867 (E.D.Mich.1985); Stephens v. G.D. Searle & Co., 602 F.Supp. 379 (E.D.Mich.1985).

11. As the excerpt from *MacDonald* indicates, a Food and Drug Administration regulation requires that a warning directly to the consumer accompany birth control pills. One court has held that violation of this regulation constitutes negligence *per se*. Lukaszewicz v. Ortho Pharmaceutical Corp., 510 F.Supp. 961 (E.D.Wis.1981), amended, 532 F.Supp. 211 (E.D.Wis.1981). On the other hand, MacDonald v. Ortho Pharmaceutical Corp., 394 Mass. 131, 475 N.E.2d 65 (1985), cert. denied, 474 U.S. 920, 106 S.Ct. 250, 88 L.Ed.2d 258 (1985), held that the regulation did not have conclusive effect. Either compliance or noncompliance with the regulation was admissible as evidence of the adequacy of the warning that was given, but was not controlling.

12. For discussions of the learned intermediary doctrine, see Thompson, The Drug Manufacturer's Duty to Warn—To Whom Does it Extend? 13 Fla.St.U.L.Rev. 135 (1985); Comment, Pharmaceutical Manufacturers and Consumer–Directed Information—Enhancing The Safety of Prescription Drug Use, 34 Cath.U.L.Rev. 117 (1984); Comment, Products Liability: The Continued Viability of the Learned Intermediary Rule as it Applies to Product Warnings for Prescription Drugs, 20 Univ.Rich.L.Rev. 405 (1986).

(c) Allergies and Idiosyncratic Reactions

KAEMPFE v. LEHN & FINK PRODS. CORP.

Supreme Court of New York, Appellate Division, First Department, 1964.
21 A.D.2d 197, 249 N.Y.S.2d 840.

EAGER, JUSTICE.

The plaintiff, in a suit against the manufacturer of the spray deodorant "Etiquet", has recovered judgment for a severe case of dermatitis resulting from an allergic reaction in the use of the product. The action was tried and submitted to the jury on the theory that the defendant-manufacturer was negligent in its alleged failure to give adequate warning to the very few persons who might possibly suffer some allergic reaction in the use of the product.

The plaintiff, a 19 year old woman, had purchased at a local drug store two containers of the product labeled "Etiquet Spray–On Deodorant", which was prepared, sold and used for the purpose of preventing body perspiration and odor. The label on the container read as follows: "Easy to use A quick squeeze—it sprays Stops underarm odor Checks perspiration Safe for normal skin Harmless to clothes." The container also was marked with the statement, "Contains Aluminum Sulphate".

Aluminum sulphate, the essential ingredient in the preparation, when applied to the skin, has the effect of closing the pores, stopping perspiration and eliminating odor. According to the testimony, practically all of the deodorants on the market contain aluminum sulphate.

After her purchase of the product, the plaintiff, following the directions thereon, applied the spray in the area of both armpits. Thereafter, during that day, she detected an itching sensation and observed an inflammation where the spray had been applied. Subsequently, a rash or dermatitis developed which spread to adjacent parts of her body. It was accompanied by burning, blistering and itching. Although permanent injury was not claimed, the sequelae persisted for sometime until it was fully healed. This was plaintiff's first allergic reaction to this or any other product.

The plaintiff's medical expert testified that the aluminum sulphate in the product was the cause of plaintiff's dermatitis. By his testimony, it was established that a few persons may be sensitive to products containing this particular ingredient. The doctor stated, however, that the chemical agent aluminum sulphate, which is used in almost all deodorants, is not normally harmful to skin; that it is in fact safe for "normal skin" as claimed.

This is the typical case where a peculiar reaction to a product in common use was due solely to an allergy possessed by the user. Plaintiff's medical expert testified that her rash was due to an allergy, and, in this connection, he described an allergy as "the reaction of the skin to a substance which, as a rule, does not bother normal people but which in people who are susceptible, sensitized, makes them react differently from normal people." The plaintiff is apparently one in a multitude of persons who has an allergy to the ingredient aluminum sulphate. Here, as measured by defendant's sales figures for this product for the year 1956 (the year in which plaintiff used this preparation) and the number of complaints it received therefrom, it appears that some sensitivity was experienced in the ratio of about one to 150,000 customers.

* * *

In the case of the non-poisonous and reasonably safe product in general use, the duty to warn depends upon whether or not it was reasonably foreseeable by the supplier that a substantial number of the population may be so allergic to the product as to sustain an injury of consequence from its use. (See Tentative Draft No. 7, Restatement of the Law of Torts, Second (April 16, 1963), § 402A, subd. (j), p. 5.) "If the danger of such an allergy is known or should be known to the maker, and if the consequences of the idiosyncrasy are serious enough, reasonable care may well require the taking of some precaution such as warning and instructions for making tests." (Harper and James, The Law of Torts, § 28.8, p. 1551.)

The fundamental test of negligence—reasonable foreseeability of harm and reasonable care to guard against same—is applicable in these cases. The manufacturer or seller may be held liable where he knows or with reasonable diligence should anticipate that the normal use of his product may result in substantial harm and where he fails to exercise reasonable care to warn of such danger. On the other hand, it is clear that the manufacturer or seller should not be held bound to anticipate and warn against a remote possibility of injury in an isolated and unusual case. The law requires a person to exercise reasonable care to guard against probabilities, not mere remote possibilities. A supplier of a product in daily use ought not to be placed in the position of an insurer. We have not yet reached the point where the manufacturer is under the absolute duty of making a product, useful to many, free from all possible harm to each and every individual; nor the point where the manufacturer is to be held under an absolute duty of giving special warning against a remote possibility of harm due to an unusual allergic reaction from use by a minuscule percentage of the potential customers. "Every substance, including food which is daily consumed by the public, occasionally becomes anathema to him peculiarly allergic to it. To require insurability against such an unforeseeable happenstance would weaken the structure of common sense, as well as present an unreasonable burden on the channels of trade." (Bennett v. Pilot Products Co., 120 Utah 474, 478, 235 P.2d 525, 527, 26 A.L.R.2d 958, 961; Gerkin v. Brown & Sehler Co., 177 Mich. 45, 143 N.W. 48.)

So, according to the prevailing authority, the existence of a duty on the part of a manufacturer to warn depends upon whether or not, to his actual or constructive knowledge, the product contains an ingredient "to which a substantial number of the population are allergic" (see Tentative Draft No. 7, Restatement of the Law, Torts, Second, supra), or an ingredient potentially dangerous to an identifiable class of an appreciable number of prospective customers. (See Merrill v. Beaute Vues Corporation, 235 F.2d 893 (Murrah, J., concurring at 898). See, also, Note, 46 Cornell L.Q. 465 (1961).) "If the allergy is one common to any substantial number of possible users, the seller may be required at least to give warning of the danger." (Prosser, Torts (2d ed.), § 84, p. 503.) On the other hand, "in the ordinary case, the maker may also assume a normal user; and he is not liable where the injury is due to some allergy or other personal idiosyncrasy of the consumer, found only in an insignificant percentage of the population." (Prosser, idem.)

Knowledge or constructive notice of an unreasonable danger to users of a particular product may impose upon the manufacturer a duty of warning. But, in the case of a useful and reasonably safe product, in general use, the supplier owes no special duty of warning to the unknown few who constitute a mere microscopic fraction of potential users who may suffer some allergic reaction not common to the ordinary or normal person. (See, further, Bish v. Employers Liability Insurance Co., 5 Cir., 236 F.2d 62; Merrill v. Beaute Vues Corporation, supra; Bennett v. Pilot Products Co., supra; Casagrande v. F.W. Woolworth Co., 340 Mass. 552, 556, 165 N.E.2d 109, 112; Crotty v. Shartenberg's–New

Haven, Inc., 147 Conn. 460, 162 A.2d 513, 516; Levi v. Colgate–Palmolive Proprietary Ltd., 41 New So W St 48, 58 New So W W N 63.)

In light of the foregoing, the plaintiff, as the basis for imposing upon defendant a special duty of warning, was bound at the very least to show (1) that she was one of a substantial number or of an identifiable class of persons who were allergic to the defendant's product, and (2) that defendant knew, or with reasonable diligence should have known of the existence of such number or class of persons. There was, however, a failure of proof as to both of these requirements. Furthermore, it does not appear that a special warning here would have been effective for any purpose.

Without question, aluminum sulphate is an ingredient generally used in all deodorant and anti-perspirants. These products, containing this particular sulphate, are considered safe for normal skin and are universally used without harm. The plaintiff was one of an unknown and very insignificant few, who, because of a state of hypersensitiveness to the sulphate, unknown even to herself, would acquire dermatitis on the application of the product to her skin. There was no proof of the precise nature of or the exact cause for her allergy. There was no showing that she was one of any identifiable class of an appreciable number of persons with a similar allergy. Her medical expert did say that there was a class or group of persons who are sensitive to aluminum sulphate but did not elaborate. It does not appear, however, that the members of such class or group were of consequential numbers or exposed to serious and unreasonable danger. The only evidence in this connection was that, in one year, the defendant, in connection with 600,000 sales of its products, had but four complaints of a sensitive reaction in the use of the same; and, for all that appears, the affliction in each case may have been differently caused or comparatively minor. Such evidence establishes no more than a remote possibility of allergic sensitivity in isolated cases to the defendant's product.

Furthermore, the defendant did give notice, by statement on the container, of the presence of aluminum sulphate in the deodorant. If, as further stated on the container, the product was "safe for normal skin"—and there was no credible evidence to the contrary—what special warning would the defendant, acting reasonably, be expected to give to the very exceptional few who, unknown even to themselves, might have an allergy to the aluminum sulphate expressly stated to be contained in the product. This is left solely to a matter of speculation because there is not one iota of evidence in the record as to any customary or adequate mode of warning or as to known or proper tests to be suggested for use by the unknown few who might possibly suffer an allergic reaction.

Of course, the statement that the product contained a particular sulphate was adequate to warn any and all persons who knew that they had an allergy with respect to the same. As to those persons, an additional express warning not to use the product would serve no purpose. Specific words of caution would be meaningless as to those, such as the plaintiff, who did not know of their allergy to the particular sulphate. The plaintiff's prior use of deodorants containing the particular ingredient did not yield any manifestations of sensitivity and she expected none when she applied the defendant's product. So, it is difficult to see that a special warning in general terms of danger to the infinitesimal few with an allergy would be of any help or have persuaded plaintiff here from the purchase and use of defendant's merchandise. Under the circumstances, the special warning would have been wholly ineffective. (See Merrill v. Beaute Vues Corporation, supra, 235 F.2d at 897.) And the defendant should not be held negligent in failing to give a warning which would have served no purpose.

The conclusion we reach is that the plaintiff failed as a matter of law to establish that the defendant was derelict in any duty of warning to plaintiff. This conclusion is supported by the reasoning underlying the decisions which have denied recovery in these cases on theory of breach of implied warranty. It has been universally held that a person, who sustains harm due solely to an unusual hypersensitiveness to a reasonably safe product, may not recover against the seller or manufacturer on such theory.

* * *

Since the plaintiff failed as a matter of law to establish negligence of the defendant, the defendant's motion to dismiss, made at the close of the case, should have been granted. Consequently, the order of the Appellate Term, affirming the judgment for plaintiff entered upon the verdict of the jury rendered in City Court, should be reversed on the law, with costs, the judgment for plaintiff vacated and the complaint dismissed, with costs, to defendant.

Determination unanimously reversed, on the law, with costs to the appellant in this Court and in the Appellate Term, the judgment for plaintiff vacated and the complaint dismissed.

All concur.

Notes

1. The rule stated in the main case has been adopted by a substantial number of courts. *E.g.,* Presbrey v. Gillette Co., 105 Ill.App.3d 1082, 61 Ill.Dec. 816, 435 N.E.2d 513 (1982) (deodorant; reaction extremely rare); Booker v. Revlon Realistic Professional Prods., Inc., 433 So.2d 407 (La.App. 1983) (hair care product; four of seven million users complained). The Restatement of Torts (Second) § 402A (1965) takes a similar approach. Comment j states:

j. Directions or warning. In order to prevent the product from being unreasonably dangerous, the seller may be required to give directions or warning, on the container, as to its use. The seller may reasonably assume that those with common allergies, as for example to eggs or strawberries, will be aware of them, and he is not required to warn against them. Where, however, the product contains an ingredient to which a substantial number of the population are allergic, and the ingredient is one whose danger is not generally known, or if known is one which the consumer would reasonably not expect to find in the product, the seller is required to give warning against it, if he has knowledge, or by the application of reasonable, developed human skill and foresight should have knowledge, of the presence of the ingredient and the danger. Likewise in the case of poisonous drugs, or those unduly dangerous for other reasons, warning as to use may be required.

2. **Nature of Allergies.** Professor Noel gives the following description of the nature of allergic reactions:

> Medical descriptions of how allergic reactions occur are complicated and still developing. From a legal standpoint, the established and significant factor is that an allergic reaction is one suffered by only a minority of the persons exposed to a particular substance. In this connection, a "sensitizer" is to be distinguished from a "primary irritant," which is something that produces irritation on the skin of the majority of normal persons.

> The sensitizing capacity of various substances differs enormously. Sometimes many exposures are necessary to develop allergic reactions, and these reactions may be confined to a very few people. Where a "strong sensitizer" is involved, the allergic reaction develops within a very limited time of exposure in much larger numbers of people.

Noel, Products Defective Because of Inadequate Directions or Warnings, 23 Sw.L.J. 256, 289 (1969). *See also,* Schattman, A Cause of Action for the Allergic Consumer, 8 Hous.L.Rev. 827, 829–833 (1971). Virtually every chemical ingredient in every product can cause an allergic reaction in some persons. Mobilia, Allergic Reactions to Prescription Drugs: A Proposal for Compensation, 48 Alb.L.Rev. 343, 345 (1984).

3. Courts adhering to the requirement that a substantial class of persons be affected by the allergy before there is a duty to warn generally impose this requirement regardless of whether suit is brought on the theory of negligence, strict liability, or breach of implied warranty. Noel, Products Defective Because of Inadequate Directions or Warnings, 23 Sw.L.J. 256, 289–298 (1969).

4. The special rule imposing a duty to warn only if a substantial number of people are likely to be harmed by the ingredient only applies to true allergic reactions. In cases where plaintiff is harmed by a "primary irritant" in a product, the duty to warn is based on general principles of foresight and reasonableness, with no absolute requirement that a "substantial" group of potential victims be involved. This is true even though a given plaintiff may suffer an unusually severe reaction to a primary irritant because of a peculiar susceptibility. *See, e.g.,* Advance Chem. Co. v. Harter, 478 So.2d 444 (Fla.App.1985), review denied, 488 So.2d 829 (Fla.1986) (ammonia).

5. The cases vary considerably on the question of how big the class must be in order to be considered substantial. Both the severity of the injury and its prevalence are factors. Comment, Strict Liability and Allergic Drug Reactions, 47 Miss.L.J. 526, 531 (1976). Courts are more willing to find a small group "substantial" if the harm is severe. For an excellent

analysis of this issue, *see* Noel, Products Defective Because of Inadequate Directions or Warnings, 23 Sw.L.J. 256, 289–298 (1969).

6. **Express Warranty.** Many courts do not impose a "substantial" number requirement in express warranty cases involving allergic reactions. A manufacturer, for example, who warrants that the product is "absolutely safe!" will be liable to an allergic user even if the allergy is rare. Spiegel v. Saks 34th Street, 43 Misc.2d 1065, 252 N.Y.S.2d 852 (1964), affirmed, 26 A.D.2d 660, 272 N.Y.S.2d 972 (1966).

7. An important line of authority rejects the requirement that the allergy affect a substantial group of people. These cases permit a jury to find that a warning was reasonably necessary even if a substantial group were not affected. The leading case is Wright v. Carter Prods., Inc., 244 F.2d 53 (2d Cir.1957), also involving an allergic reaction to aluminum sulfate in a deodorant. The evidence showed that the manufacturer received one complaint for approximately every 220,000 jars of deodorant sold. Defendant argued that it had no duty to warn because only a "minuscule" percentage of users were adversely affected. The court rejected a "quantitative standard," holding that foreseeability is the determinative factor.

8. Courts appear particularly apt to reject the substantial group requirement in cases involving prescription drugs. *See* Basko v. Sterling Drug, Inc., 416 F.2d 417 (2d Cir.1969); Crocker v. Winthrop Lab., Div. of Sterling Drug, Inc., 514 S.W.2d 429 (Tex.1974).

9. Which line of authority states the better rule?

10. Why not apply "true" strict liability in allergy cases, and hold manufacturers liable for all harm caused by all allergic reactions regardless of foreseeability? *See* Henderson, Process Norms in Products Litigation: Liability for Allergic Reactions, 51 U.Pitt.L.Rev. 761 (1990).

5. THE CONTINUING DUTY TO WARN

COVER v. COHEN

Court of Appeals of New York, 1984.
61 N.Y.2d 261, 473 N.Y.S.2d 378, 461 N.E.2d 864.

[Plaintiff, a pedestrian, was seriously injured when he was hit by a runaway 1973 Chevrolet Malibu. The driver of the car was attempting to parallel park on a city street. He put the car in reverse, and started to back up. The accelerator spring caused the throttle to stick in the full open position, and the car shot backward at high speed, hitting plaintiff and crushing him against a wall. Plaintiff sued the driver, manufacturer, and dealer who sold the car. The jury found in plaintiff's favor against all three defendants. The manufacturer appealed.

Beginning with 1974 models the federal government required a "redundant and failsafe" accelerator control system which presumably would have prevented this accident. The trial judge admitted evidence of this subsequent design change on the question of whether the car was defective in design and for a failure to warn at the time of manufacture.

The court reversed and remanded for retrial because such evidence was not admissible in strict liability actions in New York to prove defect.

The manufacturer also argued that the trial court improperly admitted a 1974 technical service bulletin issued by the manufacturer with respect to the carburetor spring of the 1973 Chevrolet Malibu.]

For the same reasons that govern the Federal standard, the technical service bulletin issued by General Motors some 13 months after delivery of the Cohen Chevrolet was not admissible on the design defect cause of action or the failure to warn cause of action insofar as it turned on the design and risk status of the vehicle at the time of delivery. A manufacturer or retailer may, however, incur liability for failing to warn concerning dangers in the use of a product which come to his attention after manufacture or sale, through advancements in the state of the art, with which he is expected to stay abreast, or through being made aware of later accidents involving dangers in the product of which warning should be given to users (see *Schumacher v. Richards Shear Co.,* 59 N.Y.2d 239, 247, 464 N.Y.S.2d 437, 451 N.E.2d 195; 1 N.Y.P.J.I.2d 364–365; 1A Frumer & Friedman, Products Liability, § 8.02). Because liability on the theory of negligent failure to warn was presented during trial of the instant action and can be expected to arise again during retrial and because it is a necessary predicate for determining admissibility of the technical service bulletin, we outline the governing law.

Although a product be reasonably safe when manufactured and sold and involve no then known risks of which warning need be given, risks thereafter revealed by user operation and brought to the attention of the manufacturer or vendor may impose upon one or both a duty to warn (*Rekab, Inc. v. Hrubetz & Co.,* 261 Md. 141, 274 A.2d 107; *doCanto v. Ametek, Inc.,* 367 Mass. 776, 328 N.E.2d 873; *Comstock v. General Motors Corp.,* 358 Mich. 163, 99 N.W.2d 627; *Bottazzi v. Petroleum Helicopters,* 664 F.2d 49; *Rozier v. Ford Motor Co.,* 573 F.2d 1332 reh. en banc, den. 578 F.2d 871; *Schenebeck v. Sterling Drug,* 423 F.2d 919; *Braniff Airways v. Curtiss–Wright Corp.,* 411 F.2d 451; see *Jackson v. New Jersey Mfrs. Ins. Co.,* 166 N.J.Super. 448, 400 A.2d 81, cert. den. 81 N.J. 330, 407 A.2d 1204; Prosser, Torts [4th ed.], p. 647; Restatement, Torts 2d, § 388). Not entirely clear from the cases, however, is what constitutes sufficient notice to the manufacturer or vendor to require its issuance of a warning, whether the manufacturer satisfies its obligation by notifying the vendor or must notify the user as well, or what the obligation of the vendor who receives such notice is to the user.

What notice to a manufacturer or vendor of problems revealed by use of the product will trigger his postdelivery duty to warn appears to be a function of the degree of danger which the problem involves and the number of instances reported (*Comstock,* 358 Mich., at p. 176, 99 N.W.2d 627 [thousands of defective power brakes]; *Bottazzi,* 664 F.2d, at p. 52 [several instances of corrosion of propeller shaft of a helicopter]; *Braniff Airways,* 411 F.2d, at p. 453, cert. den. 396 U.S. 959, 90 S.Ct. 431, 24 L.Ed.2d 423 [instances of cylinder barrel separation in an aircraft engine]; Restatement, Torts 2d, § 388, Comment *i* ["part of a lot, some of which he has discovered to be so imperfect as to be dangerous"]). When a prima facie case on that issue has been made will, of course, depend upon the facts of each case. Where, as here, however, the manufacturer has issued and sent to the vendor a technical service bulletin acknowledging that "[s]ome 1973 passenger cars * * * may exhibit an erratic idle speed and slow return to idle", that acknowledgment, * * * together with testimony that erratic idle speed or slow return to idle or both may seriously impair control of the vehicle presents a question of fact (*General Motors Corp. v. Dodson,* 47 Tenn. App. 438, 338 S.W.2d 655; see *Rozier v. Ford Motor Co.,* 573 F.2d 1332, *supra; Bowman v. General Motors Corp.,* 64 F.R.D. 62).

The nature of the warning to be given and to whom it should be given likewise turn upon a number of factors, including the harm that may result from use of the product without notice, the reliability and any possible adverse interest of the person, if other than the user, to whom notice is given, the burden on the manufacturer or vendor involved in locating the persons to whom notice is required to be given, the attention which it can be expected a notice in the form given will receive from the recipient, the kind of product involved and the number manufactured or sold, and the steps taken, other than the giving of notice, to correct the problem (*McLaughlin v. Mine Safety Appliances Co.,* 11 N.Y.2d 62, 226 N.Y.S.2d 407, 181 N.E.2d 430; *Rosebrock v. General Elec. Co.,* 236 N.Y. 227, 140 N.E. 571; *Petzold v. Roux Labs.,* 256 App.Div. 1096, 11 N.Y.S.2d 565; *Rekab, Inc. v. Hrubetz & Co.,* 261 Md. 141, 274 A.2d 107, *supra; Comstock v. General Motors Corp.,* 358 Mich. 163, 99 N.W.2d 627, *supra; Kozlowski v. Smith's Sons Co.,* 87 Wis.2d 882, 275 N.W.2d 915; *LaBelle v. McCauley Ind. Corp.,* 649 F.2d 46; *Jones v. Bender Welding & Mach. Works,* 581 F.2d 1331; *Pan-Alaska Fisheries v. Marine Constr. & Design Co.,* 565 F.2d 1129; *Noto v. Pico Peak Corp.,* 469 F.2d 358; see Restatement, Torts 2d, § 388, Comment *n;* Prosser, *loc. cit.*). Germane also will be any governmental regulation dealing with notice (*Clement v. Rousselle Corp.,* 372 So.2d 1156, cert. den. 383 So.2d 1191 [Fla.]). Generally, the issue will be one of fact for the jury (*Rekab, Inc.,* 261 Md., at p. 150, 274 A.2d 107) whose function will be to assess the reasonableness of the steps taken by the manufacturer or vendor in light of the evidence concerning the factors listed above presented in the particular case, as well as any expert testimony adduced on the question. The manufacturer and the vendor do not necessarily have the same obligation to warn concerning dangers learned of after delivery of the product, as the Trial Judge recognized by dismissing for insufficiency of evidence the cause of action against Kinney for negligent failure to warn. On trial of the case, therefore, the technical service bulletin will be admissible, * * * but the instructions to the jury on the duty to warn should outline the factors for them to consider under the evidence presented.

* * *

For the foregoing reasons, the order of the Appellate Division should be reversed, with costs, and a new trial granted * * *.

COOKE, C.J., and JASEN, JONES, WACHTLER and KAYE, JJ., concur.

SIMONS, J., taking no part.

Order reversed, with costs to defendant General Motors against plaintiffs, and a new trial granted * * *.

Notes

1. **Defective Products.** Where the product was defective at the time of sale because the manufacturer failed to guard against or warn about known or knowable risks, the question is whether a post-sale warning will cut off the liability that otherwise would result. Should such a warning ever absolve the manufacturer? In some cases the courts have held that it will. This is particularly likely to be true where, in addition to warning, the manufacturer offers to repair or replace the product at no charge, and the owner disregards the offer. *See, e.g.,* Balido v. Improved Mach., Inc., 29 Cal.App.3d 633, 105 Cal.Rptr. 890 (1972).

2. **Dangers Not Discoverable at the Time of Sale.** If a product contains a scientifically unknowable generic risk at the time it is sold, a majority of courts hold that there is no liability for a failure to warn at the time of sale. These cases are discussed in Chapter 2 Section A.4. Once the risk is subsequently discovered, a number of courts impose a duty to warn at that time. This duty is less onerous than the duty arising at the time of sale because it is often harder to warn when the product is out of the manufacturer's control. *Cover v. Cohen* contains a good statement of the considerations pertinent to the question of whether reasonable care requires a post-sale warning.

3. Courts have shown a particular willingness to require post-sale warnings in the case of prescription drugs. *E.g.,* Davis v. Wyeth Laboratories, Inc., 399 F.2d 121 (9th Cir.1968); Wooderson v. Ortho Pharmaceutical Corp., 235 Kan. 387, 681 P.2d 1038 (1984), cert. denied, 469 U.S. 965, 105 S.Ct. 365, 83 L.Ed.2d 301 (1984). What explains this?

4. A minority of courts use a hindsight standard for determining what warnings are required. In such jurisdictions a product can be defective because of a failure to warn about risks that were scientifically unknowable at the time of manufacture. In such a jurisdiction, should a manufacturer who discovers a previously unknown risk associated with a product already on the market be able to escape liability by giving a post-sale warning? Suppose it issues an adequate post-sale warning, and plaintiff receives it prior to his injury? What if plaintiff does not receive it? What effect would all this have on the manufacturer's willingness to discover and warn about unknown risks?

5. **Changes in Technology.** Suppose a change in technology takes place that makes it possible to improve the safety of a product already in use. Does the manufacturer have a duty to inform the owner of the change? Some courts have flatly said no, as long as the product was not defective at the time it was marketed. Jackson v. New Jersey Mfrs. Ins. Co., 166 N.J.Super. 448, 400 A.2d 81 (1979), certification denied, 81 N.J. 330, 407

A.2d 1204 (1979). Other courts have held that a warning is sometimes required. In Kozlowski v. John E. Smith's Sons Co., 87 Wis.2d 882, 275 N.W.2d 915 (1979) a worker was killed when a sausage stuffing machine's 500 pound piston burst through the machine's safety ring. The machine was first marketed in 1938. In 1946 the manufacturer developed a by-pass safety valve that would have prevented the accident. The valve was first marketed as optional equipment. Later, in 1971, it was made a standard feature of new sausage stuffing machines. In discussing the post-sale duty to warn about the necessity for the by-pass valve, the court said:

> We do not in this decision hold that there is an absolute continuing duty, year after year, for all manufacturers to warn of a new safety device which eliminates potential hazards. A sausage stuffer and the nature of that industry bears no similarity to the realities of manufacturing and marketing household goods such as fans, snowblowers or lawn mowers which have become increasingly hazard proof with each succeeding model. It is beyond reason and good judgment to hold a manufacturer responsible for a duty of annually warning of safety hazards on household items, mass produced and used in every American home, when the product is 6 to 35 years old and outdated by some 20 newer models equipped with every imaginable safety innovation known in the state of the art. It would place an unreasonable duty upon these manufacturers if they were required to trace the ownership of each unit sold and warn annually of new safety improvements over a 35 year period.

> As noted, the sausage stuffer machine industry is far more limited in scope. Consequently, a jury in determining a manufacturer's duty in this restricted area must look to the nature of the industry, warnings given, the intended life of the machine, safety improvements, the number of units sold and reasonable marketing practices, combined with the consumer expectations inherent therein.

275 N.W.2d at 923–24.

6. Is there a justification for requiring a post-sale warning about generic risks but not requiring one for improvements in technology?

7. **Misuse.** Should the manufacturer be required to give post-sale warnings against subsequently discovered misuse that was unforeseeable at the time of sale? There are very few cases. Rodriguez v. Besser Co., 115 Ariz. 454, 565 P.2d 1315 (App.1977) held that there was no duty to warn about the risks of a dangerous product modification that the manufacturer learned about after the sale. Should dangers from misuse be treated differently from generic risks with respect to imposing a post-sale obligation to warn?

In Bell Helicopter Co. v. Bradshaw, 594 S.W.2d 519 (Tex.Civ.App.—Corpus Christi 1979), the defendant manufactured a 1961 helicopter with a tail rotor that could be used for only 600 hours, and that required detailed maintenance and inspection. At the time of manufacture, this rotor represented the most advanced technology available. Bell became aware of accidents caused by widespread disregard of its recommended maintenance and inspection procedures. In 1970 it developed an improved rotor that could be used for 2500 hours and that required much less maintenance and inspection. Between 1969 and 1973 the helicopter in question was owned by a Bell service station. Because of its relationship with the service station, Bell could have required it to replace the old rotor system with the new one. It did not require replacement, and the service station sold the helicopter in 1973 with the old rotor system. An accident occurred because it was not equipped with the new system. The court upheld a jury verdict for plaintiff. It held that Bell was required either to mandate replacement of the old system or to recommend to users in very strong language that the system be replaced.

8. *See generally* Allee, Post–Sale Obligations of Product Manufacturers, 12 Fordham Urban L.J. 625 (1983–84); Schwartz, The Post–Sale Duty to Warn: Two Unfortunate Forks in the Road to a Reasonable Doctrine, 58 N.Y.U.L.Rev. 892 (1983); Comment, Post–Sale Warnings: Products That Go "Bump" in the Night, 1984 Ariz.St.L.J. 719; Comment, Products Liability: Post–Sale Warnings, 1978 Ariz.St.L.J. 49; Note, Efficient Accident Prevention as a Continuing Obligation: The Duty to Recall Defective Products, 42 Stan.L.Rev. 103 (1989); Note, The Manufacturer's Duty to Notify of Subsequent Safety Improvements, 33 Stan.L.Rev. 1087 (1981); Note, Manufacturers of Inherently Dangerous Products: Should They Have a Continuing Duty to Make Their Previously Sold Products Conform to State of the Art Safety Features? 92 W.Va.L.Rev. 153 (1989). For a discussion of federally mandated recalls, *see* Adler and Schwartz, Product Recalls: A Remedy in Need of Repair, 34 Case W.Res.L.Rev. 401 (1984).

Chapter 10

PROOF OF DEFECT

SECTION A. INDUSTRY STANDARDS AND CUSTOM

BRUCE v. MARTIN–MARIETTA CORP.

United States Court of Appeals, Tenth Circuit, 1976.
544 F.2d 442.

BREITENSTEIN, CIRCUIT JUDGE.

These consolidated appeals relate to a product liability case arising out of an airplane crash. Plaintiffs-appellants are persons injured, and representatives of persons killed, in the crash. Defendant-appellee Martin–Marietta Corporation manufactured the plane. Defendant-appellee Ozark Airlines was an intermediate owner and seller of the plane. Jurisdiction is based on diversity. The district court gave summary judgment for the defendants. We affirm.

The airplane, a Martin 404, was chartered to carry the Wichita State University team and some of its supporters to a football game in Logan, Utah. On October 2, 1970, the plane crashed into a mountain west of Silver Plume, Colorado. The plane first struck trees at an altitude of approximately 10,800 ft. and then travelled 425 ft. before coming to rest. Seats in the passenger cabin broke loose from their floor attachments, were thrown forward against the bulkhead of the plane, and blocked exit. A fire then developed. Of the 40 persons on the plane, 32 died in the crash.

Martin manufactured the plane and sold it to Eastern Airlines in March, 1952. Eastern used the plane about ten years and in 1962 sold it to Mohawk Airlines which used it about three years and sold it to Ozark Airlines in 1965.

In 1967, Ozark sold the plane to Fairchild–Hiller Corporation, a manufacturer of aircraft. The plane was in storage until sometime in 1970 when it was sold to Jack Richards Aircraft Company. Golden Eagle Aviation contracted with Wichita State University to provide transportation for its football games away from home. Golden Eagle supplied the crew and used the Richards aircraft. Eastern, Mohawk and

Ozark are all carriers providing scheduled services under pertinent federal aviation regulations. The defendants in the instant suit are Martin and Ozark.

On these appeals the plaintiffs do not contend that any action of either defendant caused the plane to crash. Their claims are that the defendants' failures to design, manufacture, or maintain the plane in crashworthy condition caused the deaths, or enhanced the injuries, of the passengers. The alleged defects are the inadequacy of the seat fastenings and the lack of protection against fire. Plaintiffs seek recovery on theories of negligence, implied warranty, and strict liability in tort.

* * *

I.

LIABILITY OF MARTIN

Martin was the manufacturer and original seller of the plane. Martin does not claim any change in the condition of the plane. As to strict liability, the question is whether the plane was sold "in a defective condition unreasonably dangerous to the user." The negligence question is whether Martin exercised reasonable care. See *Volkswagen of America, Inc. v. Young,* 272 Md. 201, 321 A.2d 737.

* * *

The question is whether there is any genuine issue as to any material fact. Plaintiffs claim that the plane was not equipped with crashworthy design characteristics in two particulars: (1) the seats and seat fastenings were not designed or manufactured to withstand a crash and, (2) the aircraft was not designed so as to minimize the possibility of fire occurring after a crash.

* * *

[P]laintiffs presented the affidavit of an aircraft accident investigator whose qualifications are not questioned. He said:

> "My studies thus far indicate that there were airline passenger seats in common use on October 2, 1970, which, if installed in the subject Martin 404 aircraft, would have remained in place throughout this otherwise survivable accident and would not have trapped the occupants in the burning aircraft. An occupant in this crash should not have had his escape from the burning aircraft impeded by seat failures. In the crash in question the seat failures constituted an unreasonable dangerous condition to the passengers because the seat failures prevented them from exiting the burning aircraft."

* * *

The plaintiffs' specific allegations relate to the fire hazard and the adequacy of the seat fastenings. * * * The only fact shown by plaintiffs with regard to the seats is that in 1970, 18 years after Martin made and sold the plane, airplane passenger seats, which would have withstood the crash, were in use. The record establishes that when the plane was made and first sold, its design was within the state of the art. The plaintiffs' affidavit that 18 years after the manufacture and sale of the plane safer passenger seats were in use is not relevant to the determination of whether Martin, by satisfying the 1952 state-of-art requirements, exercised reasonable care and, hence, was not negligent.

Plaintiffs say that state-of-art evidence is not material when the claim is based on strict liability. They argue that a showing of a design defective in 1970 establishes that the plane was defective in 1952, the time of the original sale, absent a subsequent alteration of the plane. For support of their position, plaintiffs rely on *Pryor v. Lee C. Moore Corp.*, 10 Cir., 262 F.2d 673, and *Mickle v. Blackmon*, 252 S.C. 202, 166 S.E.2d 173. These cases hold that prolonged safe use of a product is evidence of lack of defect but is not conclusive. We have no quarrel with the rule but have no need to apply it here.

There is authority that state-of-art evidence is not relevant to a strict liability claim. *Cunningham v. MacNeal Memorial Hospital*, 47 Ill.2d 443, 226 N.E.2d 897, 902, 904; and *Gelsumino v. E.W. Bliss Co.*, 10 Ill.App.3d 604, 295 N.E.2d 110, 113. The basic reasoning is that the principles noted in § 402A(1) are, by subsection (a), made applicable although "the seller has exercised all possible care in the preparation and sale of his product." To our knowledge, none of the states whose laws might apply to the instant case have adopted the Illinois rule. We respectfully reject it.

The crucial words in § 402A are "defective condition" and "unreasonably dangerous." A majority of the courts have required a plaintiff to prove both. See e.g. *Kleve v. General Motors Corp.*, Iowa, 210 N.W.2d 568; *Brown v. Western Farmers Ass'n*, Or., 521 P.2d 537; and *Jagmin v. Simonds Abrasive Co.*, 61 Wis.2d 60, 211 N.W.2d 810. Some courts have eliminated the "unreasonably dangerous" requirement. See *Anderson v. Fairchild Hiller Corp.*, D.Alas., 358 F.Supp. 976; *Cronin v. J.B.E. Olson Corp.*, 8 Cal.3d 121, 104 Cal.Rptr. 433, 501 P.2d 1153; and *Glass v. Ford Motor Co.*, 123 N.J.Super. 599, 304 A.2d 562. Other courts have eliminated the "defective condition" requirement. See *Ross v. Up Right, Inc.*, 5 Cir., 402 F.2d 943; and *Seattle–First National Bank v. Tabert*, 86 Wash.2d 145, 542 P.2d 774. We proceed on the basis that both requirements must be satisfied.

With regard to "defective condition" Comment g to § 402A Restatement of Torts 2d at 351, says:

"The rule stated in this Section applies only where the product is, at the time it leaves the seller's hands, in a condition not contemplated by the ultimate consumer, which will be unreasonably dangerous to him."

With regard to "unreasonably dangerous" Comment i says, Ibid. at 352:

"The article sold must be dangerous to an extent beyond that which would be contemplated by the ordinary consumer who purchases it, with the ordinary knowledge common in the community as to its characteristics."

Whether concern is with one or both of the requirements, there is "general" agreement that to prove liability under § 402A the plaintiff must show that the product was dangerous beyond the expectation of the ordinary customer. A consumer would not expect a Model T to have the safety features which are incorporated in automobiles made today. The same expectation applies to airplanes. Plaintiffs have not shown that the ordinary consumer would expect a plane made in 1952 to have the safety features of one made in 1970. State-of-art evidence was properly received and considered by the trial court.

* * *

[The court's discussion of liability of defendant Ozark is omitted].

The judgments in favor of Martin and Ozark are severally affirmed.

Notes

1. Other courts have disagreed, and held that industry custom and standards are not admissible on the question of consumer expectations. *See* Lenhardt v. Ford Motor Co., 102 Wash.2d 208, 683 P.2d 1097 (1984), noted in 60 Wash.L.Rev. 195 (1984).

2. What other evidence is admissible to prove that the expectations of the ordinary consumer were frustrated? Is expert testimony admissible? May plaintiff testify that he did not realize that the product was dangerous?

3. Some courts refer to industry custom and standards as "state of the art" evidence. Other courts use "state of the art" to refer to evidence of what is scientifically knowable or technologically feasible. This latter type of evidence addressed in Chapter 7, *supra*.

UNION SUPPLY CO. v. PUST
Supreme Court of Colorado, En Banc, 1978.
196 Colo. 162, 583 P.2d 276.

[Plaintiff was a sugar beet refinery worker whose arm was caught in an unguarded "nip point" of a conveyor as he was cleaning pulp off of the conveyor. As a result of the accident his arm and part of his shoulder were amputated. He brought an action based on strict liability and breach of implied warranty against the manufacturer of the conveyor. He alleged that the conveyor was defective in design because it should have had safety guards and an automatic cleaning device. He also alleged that the product was defective because of a failure to warn of the hazards of working at the "nip point."]

At the close of all the evidence, the district court granted Union Supply's motion to dismiss the complaint. On appeal, the court of appeals reversed the judgment dismissing Pust's complaint, and held that jury questions had been presented on the issues of strict liability and implied warranty. * * *

B. INDUSTRY SAFETY STANDARDS

Union Supply argues that the trial court erred in permitting Pust to introduce parts of two sets of nongovernmental conveyor safety codes. Safety Code B20.1 of the American Standards Association has been approved by the Conveyor Equipment Manufacturer's Association (CEMA) and the American Society of Mechanical Engineers (ASME). The National Safety Council Data Sheets 569 and 570 were drafted by an engineering committee of the National Safety Council, and have been approved by many groups, including CEMA and ASME. Thus, they are consensus standards of safety for conveyor systems, approved by the conveyor manufacturers. They were in effect at the time of Pust's injury.

The trial court ruled that these standards were admissible on the issue of whether the conveyor was in a "defective condition unreasonably dangerous." The court specified that they were to be introduced by an expert witness and must be shown to be recognized standards of safety in the conveyor manufacturing field.

The principal objections raised by Union Supply to the use of the safety standards in this case are that they are irrelevant and that they are inadmissible hearsay. We note initially that the parts introduced from Safety Code B20.1 and Data Sheets 569 and 570 do *not* presume to assess who has the duty to provide safety features. Thus, they do not raise extraneous issues of negligence. *Cf. Murphy v. L & J Press Corp.,* 558 F.2d 407 (8th Cir.).

In our view, these safety standards are relevant, especially in design defect cases. In cases of defects in manufacture, the jury is frequently able to judge the defective item by comparing it to others similarly produced by the manufacturer. However, as the California Supreme Court has noted: " * * * A design defect, by contrast, cannot be identified simply by comparing the injury-producing product with the manufacturer's plans or with other units of the same product line, since by definition the plans and all such units will reflect the same design." *Barker v. Lull Engineering Co., Inc.,* 20 Cal.3d 413, 143 Cal.Rptr. 225, 573 P.2d 443. By reason of the nature of the case, the trier of fact is greatly dependent on expert evidence and industry standards in deciding whether a defect is present.

In the case of *Wallner v. Kitchens of Sara Lee, Inc.,* 419 F.2d 1028 (7th Cir.), an employee's hand was injured when it was caught in the unguarded moving parts of a conveyor. The trial court admitted a conveyor industry safety code into evidence on the strict liability cause of action because it was: "sufficiently relevant to the questions of the dangerousness of the conveyor when it left Thiele's manufacturing plant to make its admission proper."

Union Supply appropriately points out that these safety codes fit within the classical definition of hearsay as out-of-court statements being offered into evidence to prove the truth of the matter asserted therein. However, since these industry safety standards contain sufficient indicia of reliability, we hold that they may be introduced as substantive evidence.

These codes were formulated by groups of experts in the conveyor designing and manufacturing field, and were approved by many organizations. They are likely to be more probative than a single learned treatise or an expert opinion, as they represent the consensus of an entire industry. There is no motive for the formulators to falsify, and there is no danger that the standards will be subsequently altered or incorrectly remembered by a witness. Finally, since we require that the safety standards be introduced through an expert witness, the adverse party will have a fair opportunity to cross-examine the expert on any inconsistencies, misrepresentations or other limitations of the standards. Given these guarantees of trustworthiness, we approve the admission of industry safety codes as substantive evidence on the strict liability issue of whether a product is in a "defective condition unreasonably dangerous." *Accord, Murphy v. L & J Press Corp.*, 558 F.2d 407 (8th Cir.); *Dorsey v. Yoder Co.*, 331 F.Supp. 753 (E.D.Pa.); *Price v. Buckingham Manufacturing Co., Inc.*, 110 N.J.Super. 462, 266 A.2d 140.

The trial court correctly ruled that these standards must be introduced through an expert and must be authenticated as reliable and bona fide industry-wide safety codes. This was carefully done here by the expert testimony of Dr. Youngdahl, who participated in the formulation of each of the standards. Finally, we require that sufficient advance notice of the intended use of such standards be given to the adverse party so that he will have sufficient time to prepare to meet the evidence.

* * *

IV. Conclusion

In sum, we hold that this case should have been submitted to the jury on the strict liability and implied warranty causes of action. We affirm the judgment of the court of appeals.

ERICKSON and CARRIGAN, JJ., do not participate.

Notes

1. Industry custom and standards has always been admissible in negligence cases. The Restatement (Second) of Torts § 295A comments b and c explain how the evidence is relevant:

   b. Relevance of custom. Any such custom of the community in general, or of other persons under like circumstances, is always a factor to be taken into account in determining whether the actor has been negligent. Evidence of the custom is admissible, and is relevant, as indicating a composite judgment as to the risks of the situation and the precautions required to meet them, as well as the feasibility of such precautions, the difficulty of any change in accepted methods, the actor's opportunity to learn what is called for, and the justifiable expectation of others that he will do what is usual, as well as the justifiable expectation of the actor that others will do the same. If the actor does what others do under like circumstances, there is at least a possible inference that he is conforming to the community standard of reasonable conduct; and if he does not do what others do, there is a possible inference that he is not so conforming. In particular instances, where there is nothing in the situation or in common experience to lead to the contrary conclusion, this inference may be so strong as to call for a directed verdict, one way or the other, on the issue of negligence. Thus, even in the absence of any applicable traffic statute, one who drives on the right side of a private way is under ordinary circumstances clearly not negligent in doing so, and one who drives on the left side is under ordinary circumstances clearly negligent.

On the same basis, evidence of the past practices of the parties to the action in dealing with each other is admissible, and relevant, as indicating an understood standard of conduct, or the reasonable expectation of each party as to what the other will do.

c. When custom not controlling. Any such custom is, however, not necessarily conclusive as to whether the actor, by conforming to it, has exercised the care of a reasonable man under the circumstances, or by departing from it has failed to exercise such care. Customs which are entirely reasonable under the ordinary circumstances which give rise to them may become quite unreasonable in the light of a single fact in the particular case. It may be negligence to drive on the right side of the road, and it may not be negligence to drive on the left side when the right side is blocked by a dangerous ditch. Beyond this, customs and usages themselves are many and various. Some of them are the result of careful thought and decision, while others arise from the kind of inadvertence, neglect, or deliberate disregard of a known risk which is associated with negligence. No group of individuals and no industry or trade can be permitted, by adopting careless and slipshod methods to save time, effort, or money, to set its own uncontrolled standard at the expense of the rest of the community. If the only test is to be what has always been done, no one will ever have any great incentive to make any progress in the direction of safety. It follows, therefore, that whenever the particular circumstances, the risk, or other elements in the case are such that a reasonable man would not conform to the custom, the actor may be found negligent in conforming to it; and whenever a reasonable man would depart from the custom, the actor may be found not to be negligent in so departing.

2. In strict liability cases there is a split of authority. Some courts are in accord with the principal case, and admit the evidence. *E.g.,* Thibault v. Sears, Roebuck & Co., 118 N.H. 802, 395 A.2d 843 (1978) (the evidence is admissible and relevant to the question of whether the design is reasonable, but it is not binding on the jury). Other courts disagree, and hold that the evidence is not admissible. *E.g.,* Matthews v. Stewart Warner Corp., 20 Ill.App.3d 470, 314 N.E.2d 683 (1974). They reason that the evidence is

irrelevant because it establishes due care, which is not an issue in strict liability cases. *Compare,* Rexrode v. American Laundry Press Co., 674 F.2d 826, 831 (10th Cir.1982), cert. denied, 459 U.S. 862, 103 S.Ct. 137, 74 L.Ed.2d 117 (1982) (plaintiff may introduce evidence of violation of safety standards to show defect, but defendant may not introduce evidence of compliance with safety standards to show no defect).

3. Plaintiff is burned by hot coffee and claims that it is defective because it was too hot. May defendant introduce evidence of the temperature at which coffee is usually served by restaurants? *See* Huppe v. Twenty–First Century Restaurants of Am., Inc., 130 Misc.2d 736, 497 N.Y.S.2d 306 (1985).

4. *See generally,* Spradley, Defensive Use of State of the Art Evidence in Strict Products Liability, 67 Minn.L.Rev. 343, 350–367 (1982); Comment, Custom's Proper Role in Strict Product Liability Actions Band on Design Defect, 38 U.C.L.A. Rev. 439 (1990).

ALEVROMAGIROS v. HECHINGER COMPANY
United States Court of Appeals, Fourth Circuit, 1993.
993 F.2d 417.

RESTANI, JUDGE:

This is a products liability case, brought by an injured individual against the manufacturer and seller of a ladder allegedly containing a design defect. At trial, the expert witness for plaintiff testified that the ladder did not conform to advisory industry standards, although he had never tested or examined an undamaged model of the ladder. At the close of plaintiff's case, the court granted defendants' motion for a directed verdict on the ground that plaintiff had not established the violation of any standard. We affirm the district court's decision, holding that a directed verdict in a products liability case is appropriate where an expert witness fails to prove that advisory industry standards have been violated or that those standards fall below an acceptable level.

I

Plaintiff-appellant Theodore Alevromagiros is the owner of a chain of eating establishments called Fantastic Family Restaurants, which offer Greek and American cuisine. In the summer of 1989, while conducting repairs on his restaurant in Herndon, Virginia, Alevromagiros directed a contractor to buy a ladder from defendant-appellee Hechinger Company ("Hechinger"). On behalf of Alevromagiros, the contractor purchased a six-foot high stepladder manufactured by defendant-appellee White Metal Rolling and Stamping Corporation of Atlanta, Georgia ("White Metal"). No accident occurred when the ladder was used at that time.

Several months later in December 1989, Alevromagiros climbed on the ladder to reset some ceiling tiles. While resetting the tiles, Alevromagiros felt "some bending or something" in the ladder. He then fell to the floor, severely fracturing his arm. Two eye-witnesses to the incident confirmed that the ladder twisted, causing Alevromagiros to fall backwards.

The only expert witness to testify at trial was Stanley Kalin, called to the stand by plaintiff-appellant Alevromagiros. The district court found that Kalin, who received a bachelor's degree in industrial engineering from Johns Hopkins University, was qualified to be an expert witness. On direct examination, Kalin drew the judge's and jury's attention to the bent and twisted appearance of the ladder from which Alevromagiros fell. In particular, he noted the buckling of the spreader bars, which connected the front and rear portions of the ladder. The front part of the ladder was also not aligned with the rear part. Kalin continued on to point out the absence of safety features such as triangular bracing, better designed spreaders, and stiffeners.

Alevromagiros did not seek to introduce into evidence an undamaged ladder otherwise exactly like the one involved in the accident. After discovering that local Hechinger stores no longer carried that particular model, Alevromagiros stopped searching. Therefore, Kalin never conducted a physical examination of an identical but undamaged ladder to determine its safe or unsafe design. During Kalin's testimony, Alevromagiros sought to introduce a competitor's ladder containing safety features not present in the ladder sold by Hechinger to Alevromagiros. The district judge refused to admit the competitor's ladder on the grounds that "I don't believe that the expert can bring in one ladder from a competitor and attempt to make a standard out of that." The judge also sustained an objection to Kalin's testimony about the safety features of other ladders because "[t]he question is not what other ladders have."

On cross-examination, Kalin acknowledged that there were advisory industry standards promulgated by the American National Standards Institute (ANSI) and Underwriters Laboratories (UL). Kalin also admitted the existence of a UL acceptance file, indicating that the ladder at issue in the case complied with UL standards. He did not agree that the ladder conformed to ANSI standard 14.2, which requires a metal spreader or locking device of sufficient size and strength to securely hold the front and back sections of a ladder in the open position. Although Kalin failed to perform the recommended ANSI tests on an identical but undamaged ladder, he maintained that the construction of the ladder was not in accordance with the literal wording of the standard. He also stated that, "tragically," the ANSI and UL standards did not require triangular braces on the rear portion of a ladder.

After Alevromagiros had presented all of his evidence, Hechinger and White Metal moved for a directed verdict. In discussing the motion, the district judge note that Kalin "didn't testify to any standards" and "no tests * * * Have been performed." The judge inquired of the parties,

> Don't we have to have more than just somebody saying, I am an
> industrial engineer and I have looked at this ladder, it is the only

one I have really looked at for this purpose, but I don't like it, there ought to be something else done to it? Doesn't there have to be more than that to make out a case of defective design?

The district judge ultimately granted defendants' motion for directed verdict, from which plaintiff Alevromagiros now appeals.

II

* * *

There are two issues presented by this appeal: 1) whether plaintiff introduced sufficient evidence to withstand a motion for directed verdict; and 2) whether the judge erred in refusing to admit physical or testimonial evidence regarding a competing product.

A

To prevail in a products liability case under Virginia law, the plaintiff must prove that the product contained a defect which rendered it unreasonably dangerous for ordinary or foreseeable use. In addition, the plaintiff must establish that the defect existed when it left the defendant's hands and that the defect actually caused the plaintiff's injury. * * * The product need not incorporate the best or most highly-advanced safety devices. * * *

In determining what constitutes an unreasonably dangerous defect, a court will consider safety standards promulgated by the government or the relevant industry, as well as the reasonable expectations of consumers. Consumer expectations, which may differ from government or industry standards, can be established through "evidence of actual industry practices, * * * published literature, and from direct evidence of what reasonable purchasers considered defective." *Id.*[6]

"Absent an established norm in the industry," a court is constrained to rely on the opinion testimony of experts to ascertain the applicable safety standard. * * * The credibility of competing experts is a question for the jury only if the party with the burden of proof has offered enough evidence to sustain a verdict in its favor. * * *

The cases that plaintiff-appellant cites are distinguishable either on the law or on the facts. In Carney v. Sears, Roebuck & Co., the Fourth Circuit reversed a decision made in favor of a store that sold a ladder which subsequently broke, thereby injuring plaintiff. 309 F.2d 300, 306 (4th Cir.1962). The legal significance of *Carney*, which has no application here, is that a judge may not release a defendant from liability for a manufacturing defect solely because the product has been in the possession of plaintiff for fifteen months. *Id.* at 305.

Bartholomew, relied upon heavily by Alevromagiros, presents a markedly different factual situation. *Bartholomew* involved the design

---

6. We recognize that conformity with industry custom does not automatically absolve a manufacturer or seller of a product from liability. Nevertheless, a product's compliance with industry custom "may be conclusive when there is no evidence to show that it was not reasonably safe." *Turner v. Manning, Maxwell & Moore, Inc.,* 216 Va. 245, 251, 217 S.E.2d 863, 868 (1975).

of a car whose dashboard instruments indicated the car was in park when the gear shift lever was not fully in the park position. 224 Va. at 427, 297 S.E.2d at 678. The court found that the automobile industry had not yet promulgated safety standards relating to this particular problem. Consequently, the court admitted the opinion of plaintiff's expert that the car's design was unreasonably dangerous, based on information published by the National Highway Traffic Safety Administration, consultation with other experts, and experiments with transmission systems in at least three types of cars. *Id.* at 430, 297 S.E.2d at 679. In the case at bar, there is neither an absence of industry standards, nor an expert opinion based on extensive testing and published reports.

In the case before us, Kalin concededly never performed the recommended physical tests to determine whether the ladder sold by Hechinger to Alevromagiros conformed to the published industry standards. He testified to no customs of the trade, referred to no literature in the field, and did not identify the reasonable expectations of consumers. His comment that the advisory industry standards "tragically" did not require the use of triangular braces does not constitute proof that industry standards are inadequate. It is merely another example of his own subjective opinion. Like the Fifth Circuit, we are unprepared to agree that "it is so if an expert says it is so." Viterbo v. Dow Chemical Co., 826 F.2d 420, 421 (5th Cir.1987).

Viewing the evidence in the light most favorable to the non-movant, this court finds that Alevromagiros had not proven that the ladder was unreasonably dangerous and therefore no reasonable jury could have concluded that he was entitled to judgment. The district judge's grant of a directed verdict for the defendants-appellees Hechinger and White Metal is affirmed.

B

Alevromagiros argues that his case was stymied by his inability to introduce into evidence a competing ladder with more safety features than the ladder he purchased from Hechinger. The district judge refused to admit the competing ladder or any testimony about it, saying "[s]imply because certain manufacturers put certain features on ladders, that is not the test." The judge later remarked, "bringing in one particular competitor's ladder * * * and making that an industry standard, that is terribly misleading."

Both parties rely on Eighth Circuit cases which have directly addressed the issue of admitting samples of competitive merchandise in a products liability case. Hoppe v. Midwest Conveyor Co. found that the comparative design of a competing product was relevant in a case concerning a "highly complicated piece of machinery." 485 F.2d 1196, 1202 (8th Cir.1973). The later case of Kontz v. K–Mart Corp. refused to apply Hoppe to a fact situation involving a simple folding lawn chair. 712 F.2d 1302, 1304 (8th Cir.1983). As in *Kontz*, the jury in the case currently being appealed did not need to see examples of competing products in order to understand the nature of the product at issue. The jurors easily could have been misled or confused by the assumption that one competing product represented the relevant industry-wide standard. Therefore, the judge did not abuse his discretion in refusing to admit the competing product into evidence.

III

In conclusion, a plaintiff may not prevail in a products liability case by relying on the opinion of an expert unsupported by any evidence such as test data or relevant literature in the field. Such a plaintiff may not introduce a single example of a competing product and purport to make it a standard for the industry. He or she must establish the violation of industry or government standards, or prove that consumer expectations have risen above such standards. Because we find insufficient evidence to withstand a motion for directed verdict, the judgment of the district court is therefore

AFFIRMED.

Notes

1. *Accord*, Owens v. Allis–Chalmers Corp., 414 Mich. 413, 326 N.W.2d 372 (1982); Sexton v. Bell Helmuts, Inc., 926 F.2d 331 (4th Cir.1991).

2. Should compliance with design standards such as those promulgated by ANSI or ASME protect a defendant from liability, irrespective of other evidence? Does it matter in this regard whether the plaintiff's claim was that a different design would be safer without creating new, competing risks (such as a stronger axle on a tractor) or that a different design would represent a better trade-off between competing risks (such as a door on a tractor that might prevent intrusions in some situations but might trap the occupant in other situations)? In the latter case, would a defendant's failure to follow standards such as those promulgated by ASME not be powerful evidence of defect? Does this put the manufacturer in an untenable position?

SECTION B.   TRACING A DEFECT
TO THE DEFENDANT

PITTSBURG COCA-COLA BOTTLING
WORKS v. PONDER

Supreme Court of Texas, 1969.
443 S.W.2d 546.

CALVERT, CHIEF JUSTICE.

Mrs. Cuma Ponder, respondent, brought suit against petitioner, Pittsburg Coca–Cola Bottling Works of Pittsburg, Texas, for personal injuries sustained as a result of an alleged explosion of a "coke" bottle distributed by petitioner. Based upon answers by the jury to special issues, the trial court entered judgment for Mrs. Ponder in the amount of $11,500.

* * *

Respondent operated a cafe in Omaha, Texas. She received her supply of Coca Cola directly from petitioner. She kept the wooden cases in a small storeroom along with five other brands of soft drinks. She testified that on September 27, 1965, she was carrying three "king size cokes" from the storeroom to the cooler behind the counter and, as she prepared to put them in the cooler, one of them exploded, injuring her left knee, leg, and ankle.

Respondent pleaded two distinct grounds of recovery, negligence under the doctrine of res ipsa loquitur, and strict liability. * * * Petitioner's first two points of error assert that there is in the record no evidence of probative value to support a recovery by respondent on either of her two theories. More specifically, petitioner argues that there is no evidence that the explosion was caused by a defect which existed in the bottle when it left the care, custody and control of petitioner.

* * *

The prime requirement for imposing liability on a seller under the rule of strict liability is proof by the plaintiff that he was injured because of a defective condition in the product when it left the hands of the particular seller. Jack Roach–Bissonet, Inc. v. Puskar, 417 S.W.2d 262, at 278 (Tex.Sup.1967). This is not to say that proof of the defect must be made by direct or opinion evidence; it usually can only be made by circumstantial evidence.

* * *

While the theories of liability predicated upon res ipsa loquitur and strict liability are different, the problems of making proof confronting plaintiffs who seek to impose liability under the differing theories are quite similar. In an article in 23 Sw.L.J. 1, Dean Page Keeton, University of Texas School of Law, states:

"When seeking a recovery on a theory that a product was defective when sold by the defendant, plaintiff has substantially the same proof problems for recovering on a theory of strict liability as he does on a theory of negligence. Under both theories plaintiff must establish to the satisfaction of a jury a defect at the time of sale. Once the proof is sufficient to get to the jury on the existence of a defect, there is generally a basis for an inference of negligence."

Dean Keeton, in writing on exploding bottle cases, recognizes that two factors of importance in determining whether a plaintiff in a particular case has established a prima facie case are "the length of time between surrender of possession by defendant and the breakage" and "the number of persons who could have had access to the bottle during that time." Keeton, Products Liability–Problems Pertaining to Proof of Negligence, 19 Sw.L.J. 26 [, 39 (1965)]. The evidence on these two factors was obviously controlling in Honea v. Coca Cola Bottling Co., 143 Tex. 272, 183 S.W.2d 968 (1944), in which we held that the plaintiff's evidence made a prima facie case, and in Hankins v. Coca Cola Bottling

Co., 151 Tex. 303, 249 S.W.2d 1008 (1952), in which we held that the plaintiff's evidence did not make a prima facie case. In the first case, there was evidence that the bottle which exploded had been out of the hands of the bottler for only some five or ten minutes, that it had undergone no change during the interval, and that the plaintiff was exercising some care in handling it. In the latter case, the bottle which exploded had been out of the hands of the bottler for at least twenty-four hours during which time it had been in a retail store where it was subject to almost constant handling by customers before being sold to the injured plaintiff. We held that the plaintiff's evidence "did not satisfy the controlling requirement that he negative the possibility of an intermediate actor on the agency causing the injury, by a preponderance of the evidence, so as to allow the jury to decide whether negligence on the part of the Coca Cola Company might be inferred."

We turn now to an examination of the evidence in this case.

* * * The * * * evidence will support a reasonable inference that the bottle was defective when respondent removed it from the case in the storeroom to carry it to the cooler. The question remaining is whether the evidence will support a reasonable inference that the bottle did not sustain damage while in the storeroom, and thus that it must have contained the defect causing the explosion when it was placed in the storeroom by petitioner's deliveryman. Respondent relies entirely upon her own testimony to raise this inference.

It is undisputed that the bottle had been in the storeroom for at least four days before the day of its explosion. However, according to the testimony of respondent, the only persons, other than herself, who ever entered the storeroom were five other deliverymen of bottled drinks and her two employees. She testified further that all of the six delivery-men had separate areas in the storeroom in which to stack their cases of bottled drinks, and none ever placed his cases on the wrong stack; that if any cases were ever found in the wrong stack, it was because she put them there, and, in so doing, she handled them with care; that she alone transferred bottled drinks from the storeroom to the cooler, which she did with care, and her employees did not go into the storeroom except to take the empties and that they had no occasion to touch the full cases.

We hold that the respondent's testimony will support a reasonable inference that the exploded Coca Cola bottle was not mishandled or damaged after it had been delivered to her by petitioner, and thus that the bottle was defective when delivered. To hold otherwise would be to invade the province of the jury and determine the credibility of respondent as a witness.

[The court then held that certain special issues submitted to the jury were erroneous.]

The judgments of the court of civil appeals and trial court are reversed and the cause is remanded to the trial court.

Notes

1. The plaintiff must prove that the defect existed when the product left the defendant's control irrespective of the type of defect. This burden is not difficult to meet in most cases involving design defects and warnings. In cases involving alleged manufacturing defects (flaws), however, defendants commonly claim that the product became flawed after it left the defendant's control.

2. A common situation is a product sold in a sealed container. As the court said in McKisson v. Sales Affiliates, Inc., 416 S.W.2d 787 (Tex.1967), "[w]hen it is shown that the product involved comes in a sealed container, it is inferrable that the product reached the consumer without substantial changes in the conditions in which it was sold." If other evidence proves that the sealed container was invaded or that the product became flawed after it left the defendant's control, however, the inference breaks down. *See, e.g.,* Carroll v. Ford Motor Co., 462 S.W.2d 57 (Tex.Civ.App.-Houston [14th Dist.] 1970, no writ); Klein v. Continental–Emsco, 445 F.2d 629 (5th Cir.1971).

3. A product's failure caused merely by normal wear is not sufficient to establish that it was defective when it was sold. The plaintiff need not, however, prove that the product failed immediately upon delivery. If the product is designed or manufactured to have a propensity to deteriorate more quickly than normal, it might be defective when it is delivered, even though the danger is not manifested until later. In such cases, the defect is the propensity to deteriorate too quickly, which defect was present when the product was delivered.

SECTION C. POST–ACCIDENT REMEDIAL MEASURES

GRENADA STEEL INDUS., INC. v. ALABAMA OXYGEN CO., INC.

United States Court of Appeals, Fifth Circuit, 1983.
695 F.2d 883.

[Grenada Steel and its insurer sued in United States District Court for the Northern District of Mississippi to recover damages caused by a fire in Grenada Steel's factory. They alleged that the fire was caused by a leaky valve on an acetylene tank sold to Grenada Steel by Alabama Oxygen. The valve itself had been manufactured by Sherwood–Selpac Corporation (SSC). Alabama Oxygen and SSC were both named as defendants. The jury found for the defendants, and Grenada Steel appealed.]

ALVIN B. RUBIN, CIRCUIT JUDGE:

* * *

We start with an elementary proposition: in diversity cases, state substantive law applies. *Erie Railroad v. Tompkins,* 304 U.S. 64, 58 S.Ct. 817, 82 L.Ed. 1188 (1938). * * * In matters of procedure, however, such as the admissibility of evidence, federal rules apply. Fed.R.Evid. 1101(b); *Rabon v. Automatic Fasteners, Inc.,* 672 F.2d 1231, 1238 n. 14 (5th Cir.1982); *Johnson v. C. Ellis & Sons Iron Works, Inc.,* 604 F.2d 950, 957 (5th Cir.1979).

The district court relied on Rule 407 of the Federal Rules of Evidence to exclude evidence that, after the accident, SSC and Rego [a competitor of SSC] marketed valves that were designed differently from the one patented in 1965. That rule provides:

> When, after an event, measures are taken which, if taken previously, would have made the event less likely to occur, evidence of the subsequent measures is not admissible to prove negligence or culpable conduct in connection with the event. This rule does not require the exclusion of evidence of subsequent measures when offered for another purpose, such as proving [ownership, control, or] feasibility of precautionary measures, if controverted [, or impeachment].

In excluding the testimony, the district judge held that the rule applies not only to claims of negligence but also to those based on strict liability. He also found that the feasibility of a different design had not been challenged by SSC, and, therefore, ruled that evidence of the new design was inadmissible on that issue.

The initial question is whether Rule 407 applies to product liability cases. * * * We examine first its applicability to the evidence concerning changes by SSC because the rule on its face, as discussed more fully below, does not deal with alternative designs or products introduced by third parties.

The Eighth Circuit has held repeatedly that Rule 407 is simply inapplicable to products liability cases. *Unterburger v. Snow Co.,* 630 F.2d 599, 603 (8th Cir.1980); *Farner v. Paccar, Inc.,* 562 F.2d 518, 528 n. 20 (8th Cir.1977); *Robbins v. Farmer's Union Grain Terminal Ass'n,* 552 F.2d 788, 793 (8th Cir.1977); *Abel v. J.C. Penney Co.,* 488 F.Supp. 891 (D.Minn.1980), *aff'd,* 660 F.2d 720 (8th Cir.1981). This view rests on two arguments. First, the rule is limited by its terms to efforts to prove negligence or culpable conduct. Yet in strict liability cases, the Eighth Circuit reasons, the focus is not on negligence or culpable conduct. Instead, liability stems from the unreasonably dangerous nature of the product. Second, its decisions rely heavily upon the policy considerations set forth in *Ault v. International Harvester Co.,* 13 Cal.3d 113, 117 Cal.Rptr. 812, 528 P.2d 1148 (1974).

In *Ault,* decided before the adoption of the Federal Rules of Evidence, the court concluded that the blanket exclusionary rule was inapplicable to strict liability cases for economic reasons. The court asserted that it is "manifestly unrealistic to suggest that * * * a producer will forego making improvements in its product, and risk innumerable additional lawsuits and the attendant adverse effect upon its public image, simply because evidence of the adoption may be admitted in an action founded on strict liability." *Id.* at 121, 117 Cal.Rptr. at 815, 528 P.2d at 1151.[2]

Other circuits have taken a different path and held that Rule 407 applies with equal force in strict liability cases. *Hall v. American Steamship Co.,* 688 F.2d 1062 (6th Cir.1982); *Josephs v. Harris Corp.,* 677 F.2d 985, 990–91 (3d Cir.1982); *Cann v. Ford Motor Co.,* 658 F.2d 54 (2d Cir.1981), *cert. denied,* 456 U.S. 960, 102 S.Ct. 2036, 72 L.Ed.2d 484 (1982); *Werner v. Upjohn Co.,* 628 F.2d 848 (4th Cir.1980); *cert. denied,* 449 U.S. 1080, 101 S.Ct. 862, 66 L.Ed.2d 804 (1981). In *Bauman v. Volkswagenwerk Aktiengesellschaft,* 621 F.2d 230 (6th Cir. 1980), and *Roy v. Star Chopper Co.,* 584 F.2d 1124, 1134 (1st Cir.1978), the courts applied Rule 407 in product liability cases without discussing the issue. In *Oberst v. International Harvester Co.,* 640 F.2d 863 (7th Cir.1980), the court held evidence of subsequent repairs inadmissible. It is not clear, however, whether this decision was based on Rule 407 or on Illinois law.[3]

In *Werner* the Fourth Circuit noted that one of the basic concerns underlying Rule 407 was the encouragement of voluntary repairs by manufacturers. The court questioned "why this policy should apply any differently where the complaint is based on strict liability as well as negligence." 628 F.2d at 848. The *Werner* opinion further notes that the *Ault* approach would admit subsequent repairs as evidence that the product was defective even in cases where the manufacturer was simply

2. The *Ault* decision has been followed in other states both by decision and by legislative action or court rule. *See Caterpillar Tractor Co. v. Beck,* 624 P.2d 790, 793–94 (Alaska 1981); *Good v. A.B. Chance Co.,* 39 Colo.App. 70, 78–80, 565 P.2d 217, 224 (1977); *Caprara v. Chrysler Corp.,* 52 N.Y.2d 114, 124–25, 436 N.Y.S.2d 251, 256, 417 N.E.2d 545, 550 (1981); *Ginnis v. Mapes Hotel Corp.,* 86 Nev. 408, 416–17, 470 P.2d 135, 140 (1970); *Shaffer v. Honeywell, Inc.,* 249 N.W.2d 251 (S.D.1976); *Chart v. General Motors Corp.,* 80 Wis.2d 91, 258 N.W.2d 680 (1977).

Maine admits evidence of subsequent repairs even if they are offered to show negligence. Me.R.Evid. 407(a). There is thus no need for a strict liability exception in that state. The text of Committee Comments to Wyo.R.Evid. 407 and Colo.R.Evid. 407 indicate that, while those states adopted the language of the federal rule, they also incorporated the *Ault* decision. Hawaii R.Evid. 407 is also identical in wording to the federal rule, except that it adds to the list of exceptions: "proving dangerous defect in products liability cases." Alaska R.Evid. 407 contains a similar proviso.

3. Several states have also continued to follow the traditional rule excluding evidence of subsequent repair even in strict liability cases. *See Hallmark v. Allied*

Prods. Corp., 132 Ariz. 434, 440–41, 646 P.2d 319, 325–26 (1982); *Moldovan v. Allis Chalmers Mfg. Co.,* 83 Mich.App. 373, 268 N.W.2d 656 (Mich.Ct.App.1978); *Price v. Buckingham Mfg. Co.,* 110 N.J.Super. 462, 266 A.2d 140, 141 (1970) (per curiam); *Lamonica v. Outboard Marine Corp.,* 48 Ohio App.2d 43, 355 N.E.2d 533, 535 (Ohio Ct. App.1976); *Haysom v. Coleman Lantern Co.,* 89 Wash.2d 474, 573 P.2d 785 (1978) (en banc).

Ariz.Rev.Stat.Ann. § 12–686(a) expressly excludes evidence of subsequent repair to prove evidence of a defect in products liability actions. Neb.Rev.Stat. § 27–407 is identical to the federal rule, but adds at the end: "Negligence or culpable conduct, as used in this rule, shall include, but not be limited to, the manufacture and sale of a defective product."

Other cases continue to apply the traditional rule in products liability actions based upon a failure to warn. In those cases, however, the basis for liability more closely resembles negligence than strict liability. *See Ortho Pharmaceutical Corp. v. Chapman,* 388 N.E.2d 541, 561–63 (Ind. App.1979); *Smith v. E.R. Squibb & Sons, Inc.,* 405 Mich. 79, 273 N.W.2d 476 (Mich. 1979).

making further improvements to an already safe product. *Id. See also Hall v. American Steamship Co.,* 688 F.2d at 1067 (following *Werner*).

Voluntary change to improve a product and reduce the possible hazard to a user should be encouraged. While there is no evidence concerning whether admission of evidence of change would deter such action by manufacturers, the assumption in the rule that it might have a deterrent effect is not demonstrably inapplicable to manufacturers upon whom strict liability is imposed. But our decision does not rest only on theses about the influence of possible tort liability on human conduct. It rests more firmly on the proposition that evidence of subsequent repair or change has little relevance to whether the product in question was defective at some previous time.

* * *

We cannot really know why changes are made by industry generally or why a change was made in a particular product in the absence of evidence on the question. Instead, we ought to consider the probative value of such evidence on the point at issue. The real question is whether the product or its design was defective at the time the product was sold. *See* S. Saltzburg & K. Redden, Federal Rules of Evidence Manual 181 (3d ed. 1982). The jury's attention should be directed to whether the product was reasonably safe at the time it was manufactured. In this case, for example, there was ample expert testimony concerning that very point. The introduction of evidence about subsequent changes in the product or its design threatens to confuse the jury by diverting its attention from whether the product was defective at the relevant time to what was done later. *Id.* at 182 (addressing only product design). Interpreted to require the evidence to focus on the time when the product was sold, Rule 407 would conform to the policy expressed in Rule 403, the exclusion of relevant information if its probative value is substantially outweighed by the danger of confusion. *See* 23 C. Wright & K. Graham, *supra,* § 5288, at 144.

For these reasons, we follow the path taken by the First, Second, Third, Fourth and Sixth Circuits and hold Rule 407 applicable to strict liability cases.

Grenada Steel argues that, even if Rule 407 applies, the evidence was admissible under the exception to that rule for evidence offered to show feasibility of precautionary measures. But this exception pertains if the issue of feasibility is contested. Grenada Steel argues that, in design defect cases, feasibility is "inherently" an issue and an integral element of its proof. This, however, assumes that their claim that another design was feasible makes a contest. It takes two to tango, in court as well as on the ballroom floor, and the mere assertion that the manufacturer did not make a change does not controvert the feasibility of change. The manufacturer raised no issue that the alternative design suggested by Grenada Steel's experts was not feasible. Its defense was only that the design it used was not defective.

Feasibility may "almost always" be in question in design defect cases, as suggested by Professors S. Saltzburg and K. Redden, in their excellent Federal Rules of Evidence Manual 180 (3d ed. 1982). But "almost always" like "hardly ever" admits of the unusual case that prompts the qualifying adverb. Sometimes, as here, the manufacturer does not suggest that another design was impractical but only that it adopted an acceptable one. It is not obliged to prove perfection but only that the product "meets the reasonable expectations of the ordinary consumer as to its safety." *Page v. Barko Hydraulics,* 673 F.2d [134, 138 (5th Cir.1982)].

The Fourth Circuit has ruled that "it is clear from the fact of * * * rule [407] that an affirmative concession is not required. Rather, feasibility is not in issue unless controverted by the defendant." *Werner v. Upjohn Co.,* 628 F.2d at 855. Two commentators suggest a uniform rule:

> The administration of Rule 407 would be greatly simplified if the appellate courts were to hold that in all of these [negligence and product liability] situations, feasibility of precautionary measures will be deemed "controverted" unless the defendant is prepared to make an unequivocal admission of feasibility.

23 C. Wright & K. Graham, Federal Practice & Procedure § 5288, at 144 (1980). The defendant manufacturer was not put to that alternative. We need not, therefore, determine whether denial of a request for an admission of feasibility would *per se* create a contest. In this case, however, the defendant clearly stated that feasibility was not controverted. No request for an admission to that effect was made. Therefore, the evidence was properly excluded under rule 407.

The district court also excluded evidence that Rego, another manufacturer, later offered an alternatively designed valve. Grenada Steel argues that the admission of evidence showing that someone other than the defendant made a design change cannot discourage voluntary repairs. The party making the repair is not penalized by the admission of the evidence. Therefore, neither the text of rule 407 nor the policy underlying it excludes evidence of subsequent repairs made by someone other than the defendant. *See Louisville & Nashville Railroad Co. v. Williams,* 370 F.2d 839, 843–44 (5th Cir.1966); *Farner v. Paccar, Inc.,* 562 F.2d 518, 520 n. 20 (8th Cir.1977); *Lolie v. Ohio Brass Co.,* 502 F.2d 741 (7th Cir.1974) (per curiam); *Wallner v. Kitchens of Sara Lee, Inc.,* 419 F.2d 1028, 1032 (7th Cir.1970); *Steele v. Wiedemann Co.,* 280 F.2d 380 (3d Cir.1960); 10 J. Moore & H. Bendix, Moore's Federal Practice § 407.05 (1982); 23 C. Wright & K. Graham, Federal Practice & Procedure § 5284, at 113 (1980); McCormick on Evidence § 275, at 667 (E. Cleary 2d ed. 1972).

Nevertheless, we think the district court's exclusion of this evidence was proper because it lacked sufficient probative value and injected the dangers of confusion and misleading the jury. In *Ward v. Hobart Manufacturing Co.,* 450 F.2d 1176 (5th Cir.1971), a Mississippi diversity-based negligent design case, we held that it was error for a district court to consider design changes developed after the manufacture of the product in question. Such repairs were simply irrelevant to the reasonableness of the design at the time of manufacture. Alternative designs may indicate that the product was unreasonably dangerous, *see* Wade, *On the Nature of Strict Tort Liability For Products,* 44 Miss.L.J. 825, 837 (1973), but only if they were available at the time of manufacture. We fail to see how an alternative design, developed by another person years after the product in question was manufactured, is relevant to whether the product was reasonably safe at the time it was made. Therefore, the district court properly excluded evidence of Rego's alternative design in the absence of an issue on which that evidence would have had sufficient probative value to outweigh its unfair prejudicial effect.

* * *

Notes

1. As the court states in *Grenada Steel, Ault* was the seminal case holding that, whereas evidence of subsequent remedial measures is inadmissible in negligence cases, it is admissible in strict liability cases. In addition to relying on the assertion that the policy of not discouraging post-accident safety measures is not as strong in strict liability cases (discussed in *Grenada Steel*), the *Ault* court also reasoned that negligence cases differ from strict liability cases in that only *foreseeable* risks count against a defendant in negligence cases. Presumably, the court was suggesting that a post-accident recognition of danger does not necessarily prove that the risk was foreseeable. Since foreseeability is usually not an aspect of defectiveness, this rationale would not be applicable to cases based on strict liability.

2. Should evidence in a negligence case be excluded merely because it does not necessarily prove *all* the elements of negligence? Might it still be relevant on one element—the dangerousness of the behavior—even if it is not relevant on another element—foreseeability? Does this suggest that a concern about deterring safety improvements rather than lack of relevance is the primary rationale underlying the exclusionary rule in negligence cases?

3. A third rationale for Rule 407 is suggested by *Grenada Steel:* Although a post-accident remedial measure is relevant circumstantial evidence of risk, it is likely to be overvalued by a juror who could view it as being tantamount to an admission, forgetting that foreseeability is also an issue. Note that the court in *Grenada Steel* cites Rule 403, dealing with evidence whose probative value is substantially outweighed by a danger of confusion or prejudice. If this is a rationale underlying Rule 407, does the court in *Grenada Steel* take sufficient account of the difference between negligence and defectiveness? Does the requirement that the plaintiff must prove that the product was defective *at the time of sale* help?

4. Under the various possible rationales underlying Rule 407, should evidence of post-accident remedial measures be admissible in a product case based on negligence? Texas Rule of Evidence 407 expressly provides that post-accident remedial measures are admissible in products liability cases based on "strict liability."

5. Under the various possible rationales underlying Rule 407, should evidence of post-accident remedial measures be admissible in a product case based on an alleged failure to warn? *Compare* DeLuryea v. Winthrop Laboratories, Div. of Sterling Drugs, Inc., 697 F.2d 222, 228–29 (8th Cir. 1983) *with* Unterburger v. Snow Co., 630 F.2d 599, 603 (8th Cir.1980).

6. Should post-accident changes in warnings, notifications of defect to consumers, and recall letters be admissible to prove defectiveness? Do any of the possible underlying rationales of Rule 407 apply differently to this type of evidence?

7. The court in *Grenada Steel* also held that the trial court properly excluded evidence of a post-accident design change by another manufacturer (unrelated to the valve that allegedly caused the fire). Do the various rationales underlying Rule 407 support this conclusion? Is this type of evidence just a form of industry custom?

8. As the court in *Grenada Steel* points out, Federal Rule of Evidence 407 rather than the corresponding state rule applies to diversity cases in federal courts. For an especially good analysis of this issue, see Wellborn, The Federal Rules of Evidence and the Application of State Law in Federal Courts, 55 Tex.L.Rev. 371 (1977). In states that follow *Ault,* defendants in state court have an incentive to remove the case to federal court. Plaintiffs can prevent removal by joining a local retailer, thereby defeating diversity.

9. *See generally,* Powers, Torts–Personal, 38 Sw.L.J. 1 (1984); 23 C. Wright & K. Graham, Federal Practice and Procedure § 5285 (1980); Davis, Evidence of Post–Accident Failures, Modifications and Design Changes in Products Liability Litigation, 6 St. Mary's L.J. 792 (1975); Note, Products Liability and Evidence of Subsequent Repairs, 1972 Duke L.J. 837.

SECTION D. EXPERT WITNESSES

FORD MOTOR CO. v. BLAND
Court of Civil Appeals of Texas, Waco, 1974.
517 S.W.2d 641.

HALL, JUSTICE.

This is a products liability suit. It stems from a single-car accident in which the plaintiff sustained personal injuries when a Mercury Capri automobile he owned and was driving overturned. Plaintiff alleged, inter alia, that the accident and his injuries were caused by a defective left-front shock tower on the Capri automobile; and that this defect existed when the car left the possession of Ford Motor Company, the defendant-manufacturer, and when it was sold to him by Marstaller Motors, Inc., the defendant-retailer. Following a jury trial, judgment was rendered on the verdict that plaintiff recover damages totaling $358,180 from the defendants, jointly and severally, and that Marstaller Motors have full indemnity from Ford Motor Company. We affirm.

* * *

One theory upon which plaintiff prosecuted this case is that the left-front shock tower broke while he was in the skid, that the car was thereby caused to roll, and that the shock tower was structurally defective when placed on the car by Ford Motor Company. This was defended on assertions that the left-front shock tower was not defective when the car left the factory, and that both shock towers were broken after the car began to roll. The jury made findings in favor of plaintiff's theory which support the judgment.

Defendants contend that the evidence is legally and factually insufficient to establish (a) that the left shock tower broke *before* the car began to roll, and (b) that it was defective when it left Ford Motor Company's possession.

Plaintiff does not remember the circumstances surrounding the accident. He employed Dr. William H. Tonn, Jr., a consulting engineer who specializes in reconstructing accidents and determining their causes, to evaluate this one. Dr. Tonn began his investigation 25 days after the accident. It included, among other things, a view of the site, using photographs taken immediately after the accident which show skid marks and gouges on the roadway; the making of measurements; a determination of the friction coefficient of the road surface; the taking of photographs; and a detailed inspection of the automobile, especially of the damaged and broken parts. Based upon the results of this investigation, which we need not detail, Dr. Tonn concluded that just prior to the rolling of plaintiff's car, it went into a broadside skid, skidded out of the lane of travel onto the median-shoulder, then partially back onto plaintiff's lane of travel; that during the early stages of the skid plaintiff's vehicle was rotating clockwise out of control, and at one stage the front of the car was pointed "at about 3:00 o'clock," but as it began its return to the traveled lane plaintiff was regaining control and the car had begun rotating counter-clockwise; that soon after the car partially returned to the lane of travel, and while plaintiff was still in the skid, the left-front shock tower broke; that the left-front wheel and tire then turned under with the bottom of the wheel and tire turning to the inside; that this resulted in the car literally vaulting into the air and then, after landing, rolling down the highway; and that but for the breaking of the shock tower, plaintiff would have recovered control of the vehicle. These conclusions are supported by highway skid marks and gouge marks made by plaintiff's car; by the condition of the car body; by the damaged condition of the left-front tire and wheel rim, the left-front shock tower, and the arm of the left tie rod, after the accident.

* * *

Dr. Tonn's testimony shows that the left shock tower broke before the car began to roll. And the other testimony we have recited is circumstantial proof that the defect existed when Ford Motor Company relinquished possession of the car. Direct proof of this fact is not required. Darryl v. Ford Motor Company (Tex.Sup., 1969) 440 S.W.2d 630, 632. Moreover, a review of all of the evidence convinces us that the evidence is factually sufficient to establish these two facts.

Defendants argue that Dr. Tonn was not qualified to express an opinion as to whether a crack existed in the tube of the left-front shock tower prior to the accident, and that this testimony by him was therefore erroneously admitted by the trial court. Similarly, defendants assert error in the trial court's refusal to permit Charlie Marstaller, Jr., to express his opinion as an expert witness that the left-front wheel of plaintiff's car was broken loose in the roll, and not before.

The question of whether a witness is qualified by experience, training and observation to express an opinion as an expert on a particular subject is addressed to the sound discretion of the trial court; and the court's ruling in this regard will not be disturbed on appeal without a clear showing of abuse.

* * *

Dr. Tonn received his doctorate in engineering in 1942. He is a member of National and State Societies of Professional Engineers, The Society of Automotive Engineers, The American Institute of Chemical Engineers, The American Society of Mechanical Engineers, The American Society For Testing Materials, The American Society of Metals, and a number of other academic and industrial associations related to his specialty. These organizations aid him to stay abreast of day-to-day and year-to-year developments in his field. Since 1949, he has handled about 3,500 problems dealing with analysis and reconstruction of accidents. In the light of Dr. Tonn's expertise and his investigation in this case, the court did not abuse its discretion in permitting him to give the questioned testimony.

Mr. Marstaller testified that he began as a mechanic in 1933 and for 15 or 20 years thereafter reconstructed "total loss" cars, doing both body work and mechanical work; that since 1953 he has been an automobile dealer selling Lincoln and Mercury automobiles, but still, from time to time, works on cars; that he is thoroughly familiar with automobile bodies and motors, and the body and the mechanical workings of the car in question; that his background has not provided him any formal training or experience in accident reconstruction; and that he has been "strictly involved in trying to repair and fix cars that have been in accidents." His investigation of this accident consisted only of what the court could properly have considered as a rather cursory view of plaintiff's car one week before trial, almost two years after the occurrence. There is no abuse of discretion in the court's holding that this witness was not qualified to express the opinion in question.

* * *

The judgment is affirmed.

GRENADA STEEL INDUS., INC.
v. ALABAMA OXYGEN CO.

United States Court of Appeals, Fifth Circuit, 1983.
695 F.2d 883.

[Grenada Steel and its insurer sued to recover damages caused by a fire in Grenada Steel's factory. They alleged that the fire was caused by a leaky valve on an acetylene tank. The jury found for the defendants. Grenada Steel moved for judgment notwithstanding the verdict on the ground, *inter alia,* that the defendants' evidence concerning the origin of the fire was insufficient to support the verdict. A portion of the court's opinion addressing the admissibility of post accident design changes is reproduced on p. 437, *supra.*]

ALVIN B. RUBIN, CIRCUIT JUDGE:

* * *

As Grenada Steel observes, the trial was fought in a classic battle of the experts. The defendants' experts testified, based largely on their interpretation of post-fire photographs, that the fire started in another part of the plant than the room where the acetylene cylinder was used. Grenada Steel argues that this testimony "was general, self-serving, and based on secondhand data and information, whereas [Grenada Steel's] proof of the defective and unreasonably dangerous condition of the subject valve was firmly supported by firsthand observations, tests, and examinations of the subject valve and its interior as well as the fire-damaged premises shortly after the fire." These orotund arguments were addressed to the jury and that was the proper audience. It was for the jury to decide which of the experts was more credible, which used the more reliable data, and whose opinion—if any—the jury would accept. The jury might credit one or more of the expert opinions or it might reject them all. Post-*Boeing,* the argument that, when the jury accepts one expert rather than another, we substitute our appraisal for theirs will not fly, for the standard is fastly placed: after reviewing *all* of the evidence "in the light and with all reasonable inferences most favorable to the party opposed to the motion," we must be persuaded that "the facts and inferences point so strongly and overwhelmingly in favor of one party that * * * reasonable [jurors] could not arrive at a contrary verdict." *Boeing Co. v. Shipman,* 411 F.2d 365, 374 (5th Cir.1969) (en banc). Neither the trial court nor this one decides "by which side has the better of the case, nor * * * [on the basis of] a complete absence of probative facts to support a jury verdict." Judges decide only whether there is "a conflict in substantial evidence" that creates a jury question. *Id.* at 375. The district court acted well within its discretion in denying Grenada Steel's motion for judgment notwithstanding the verdict.

For these reasons, the judgment is Affirmed.

Notes

1. If the trial court in *Bland* had permitted Marstaller to testify as an expert, would the Court of Appeals have reversed?

2. Courts have permitted highway patrolmen, mechanics, and wrecker drivers to express opinions as to the cause of automobile accidents. *See, e.g.,* Pool v. Ford Motor Co., 715 S.W.2d 629 (Tex.1986).

3. Does the approach to expert testimony in *Bland* and *Grenada Steel* actually reflect a substantive judgment about allocating losses from accidents in situations in which we will never really know what happened?

DAUBERT v. MERRELL DOW PHARMACEUTICALS, INC.

United States Supreme Court, 1993.
—— U.S. ——, 113 S.Ct. 2786, 125 L.Ed.2d 469.

JUSTICE BLACKMUN delivered the opinion of the Court.

In this case we are called upon to determine the standard for admitting expert scientific testimony in a federal trial.

I

Petitioners Jason Daubert and Eric Schuller are minor children born with serious birth defects. They and their parents sued respondent in California state court, alleging that the birth defects had been caused by the mothers' ingestion of Bendectin, a prescription anti-nausea drug marketed by respondent. Respondent removed the suits to federal court on diversity grounds.

After extensive discovery, respondent moved for summary judgment, contending that Bendectin does not cause birth defects in humans and that petitioners would be unable to come forward with any admissible evidence that it does. In support of its motion, respondent submitted an affidavit of Steven H. Lamm, physician and epidemiologist, who is a well-credentialed expert on the risks from exposure to various chemical substances. Doctor Lamm stated that he had reviewed all the literature on Bendectin and human birth defects—more than 30 published studies involving over 130,000 patients. No study had found Bendectin to be a human teratogen (i.e., a substance capable of causing malformations in fetuses). On the basis of this review, Doctor Lamm concluded that maternal use of Bendectin during the first trimester of pregnancy has not been shown to be a risk factor for human birth defects.

Petitioners did not (and do not) contest this characterization of the published record regarding Bendectin. Instead, they responded to respondent's motion with the testimony of eight experts of their own, each of whom also possessed impressive credentials. These experts had concluded that Bendectin can cause birth defects. Their conclusions were based upon "in vitro" (test tube) and "in vivo" (live) animal studies that found a link between Bendectin and malformations; pharmacological studies of the chemical structure of Bendectin that purported to show similarities between the structure of the drug and that of other substances known to cause birth defects; and the "reanalysis" of previously published epidemiological (human statistical) studies.

The District Court granted respondent's motion for summary judgment. The court stated that scientific evidence is admissible only if the principle upon which it is based is " 'sufficiently established to have general acceptance in the field to which it belongs.' " * * * quoting *United States v. Kilgus*, 571 F.2d 508, 510 (CA9 1978). The court concluded that petitioners' evidence did not meet this standard. Given the vast body of epidemiological data concerning Bendectin, the court held, expert opinion which is not based on epidemiological evidence is not admissible to establish causation. * * * Thus, the animal-cell studies, live-animal studies, and chemical-structure analyses on which petitioners had relied could not raise by themselves a reasonably disputable jury issue regarding causation. * * * Petitioners' epidemiological analyses, based as they were on recalculations of data in previously published studies that had found no causal link between the drug and birth defects, were ruled to be inadmissible because they had not been published or subjected to peer review. * * *

The United States Court of Appeals for the Ninth Circuit affirmed. * * * Citing *Frye v. United States*, 54 App.D.C. 46, 47, 293 F. 1013, 1014 (1923), the court stated that expert opinion based on a scientific technique is inadmissible unless the technique is "generally accepted" as reliable in the relevant scientific community. * * * The court declared that expert opinion based on a methodology that diverges "significantly from the procedures accepted by recognized authorities in the field * * * cannot be shown to be 'generally accepted as a reliable technique.' " * * * quoting United States v. Solomon, 753 F.2d 1522, 1526 (CA9 1985).

We granted certiorari * * * in light of sharp divisions among the courts regarding the proper standard for the admission of expert testimony. Compare, *e.g., United States v. Shorter*, 257 U.S.App.D.C. 358, 363–364, 809 F.2d 54, 59–60 (applying the "general acceptance" standard), cert. denied, 484 U.S. 817, 108 S.Ct. 71, 98 L.Ed.2d 35 (1987), with *DeLuca v. Merrell Dow Pharmaceuticals, Inc.*, 911 F.2d 941, 955 (CA3 1990) (rejecting the "general acceptance" standard).

II

A

In the 70 years since its formulation in the *Frye* case, the "general acceptance" test has been the dominant standard for determining the admissibility of novel scientific evidence at trial. See E. Green & C. Nesson, Problems, Cases, and Materials on Evidence 649 (1983). Although under increasing attack of late, the rule continues to be followed by a majority of courts, including the Ninth Circuit.

The *Frye* test has its origin in a short and citation-free 1923 decision concerning the admissibility of evidence derived from a systolic blood pressure deception test, a crude precursor to the polygraph machine. In what has become a famous (perhaps infamous) passage, the then Court of Appeals for the District of Columbia described the device and its operation and declared:

> "Just when a scientific principle or discovery crosses the line between the experimental and demonstrable stages is difficult to define. Somewhere in this twilight zone the evidential force of the principle must be recognized, and while courts will go a long way in admitting expert testimony deduced from a well-recognized scientific principle or discovery, *the thing from which the deduction is made must be sufficiently established to have gained general acceptance in the particular field in which it belongs.*" * * *

Because the deception test had "not yet gained such standing and scientific recognition among physiological and psychological authorities as would justify the courts in admitting expert testimony deduced from the discovery, development, and experiments thus far made," evidence of its results was ruled inadmissible. * * *

The merits of the *Frye* test have been much debated, and scholarship on its proper scope and application is legion. Petitioners' primary attack, however, is not on the content but on the continuing authority of the rule. They contend that the *Frye* test was superseded by the adoption of the Federal Rules of Evidence. We agree.

We interpret the legislatively-enacted Federal Rules of Evidence as we would any statute. *Beech Aircraft Corp. v. Rainey*, 488 U.S. 153, 163, 109 S.Ct. 439, 446, 102 L.Ed.2d 445 (1988). Rule 402 provides the baseline:

> "All relevant evidence is admissible, except as otherwise provided by the Constitution of the United States, by Act of Congress, by these rules, or by other rules prescribed by the Supreme Court pursuant to statutory authority. Evidence which is not relevant is not admissible."

"Relevant evidence" is defined as that which has "any tendency to make the existence of any fact that is of consequence to the determination of the action more probable or less probable than it would be without the evidence." Rule 401. The Rule's basic standard of relevance thus is a liberal one.

Frye, of course, predated the Rules by half a century. In *United States v. Abel*, 469 U.S. 45, 105 S.Ct. 465, 83 L.Ed.2d 450 (1984), we considered the pertinence of background common law in interpreting the Rules of Evidence. We noted that the Rules occupy the field, * * * but, quoting Professor Cleary, the Reporter, explained that the common law nevertheless could serve as an aid to their application:

> "In principle, under the Federal Rules no common law of evidence remains. 'All relevant evidence is admissible, except as otherwise provided. * * *'" In reality, of course, the body of common law knowledge continues to exist, though in the somewhat altered form of a source of guidance in the exercise of delegated powers." * * *

We found the common-law precept at issue in the *Abel* case entirely consistent with Rule 402's general requirement of admissibility, and considered it unlikely that the drafters had intended to change the rule. In *Bourjaily v. United States*, 483 U.S. 171, 107 S.Ct. 2775, 97 L.Ed.2d 144 (1987), on the other hand, the Court was unable to find a particular common-law doctrine in the Rules, and so held it superseded.

Here there is a specific Rule that speaks to the contested issue. Rule 702, governing expert testimony, provides:

> "If scientific, technical, or other specialized knowledge will assist the trier of fact to understand the evidence or to determine a fact in issue, a witness qualified as an expert by knowledge, skill, experience, training, or education, may testify thereto in the form of an opinion or otherwise."

Nothing in the text of this Rule establishes "general acceptance" as an absolute prerequisite to admissibility. Nor does respondent present any clear indication that Rule 702 or the Rules as a whole were intended to incorporate a "general acceptance" standard. The drafting history makes no mention of Frye, and a rigid "general acceptance" requirement would be at odds with the "liberal thrust" of the Federal Rules and their "general approach of relaxing the traditional barriers to 'opinion' testimony." *Beech Aircraft Corp. v. Rainey*, 488 U.S., at 169, 109 S.Ct., at 450 (citing Rules 701 to 705). * * * Given the Rules' permissive backdrop and their inclusion of a specific rule on expert testimony that does not mention "general acceptance," the assertion that the Rules somehow assimilated Frye is unconvincing. Frye made "general acceptance" the exclusive test for admitting expert scientific testimony. That austere standard, absent from and incompatible with the Federal Rules of Evidence, should not be applied in federal trials.

B

That the *Frye* test was displaced by the Rules of Evidence does not mean, however, that the Rules themselves place no limits on the admissibility of purportedly scientific evidence. Nor is the trial judge disabled from screening such evidence. To the contrary, under the Rules the trial judge must ensure that any and all scientific testimony or evidence admitted is not only relevant, but reliable.

The primary locus of this obligation is Rule 702, which clearly contemplates some degree of regulation of the subjects and theories about which an expert may testify. "If scientific, technical, or other specialized knowledge will assist the trier of fact to understand the evidence or to determine a fact in issue" an expert "may testify thereto." The subject of an expert's testimony must be "scientific * * * knowledge." The adjective "scientific" implies a grounding in the methods and procedures of science. Similarly, the word "knowledge" connotes more than subjective belief or unsupported speculation. The term "applies to any body of known facts or to any body of ideas inferred from such facts or accepted as truths on good grounds." Webster's Third New International Dictionary 1252 (1986). Of course, it would be unreasonable to conclude that the subject of scientific testimony must be "known" to a certainty; arguably, there are no certainties in science.

See, *e.g.*, Brief for Nicolaas Bloembergen et al. as *Amici Curiae* 9 ("Indeed, scientists do not assert that they know what is immutably 'true'—they are committed to searching for new, temporary theories to explain, as best they can, phenomena"); Brief for American Association for the Advancement of Science and the National Academy of Sciences as Amici Curiae 7–8 ("Science is not an encyclopedic body of knowledge about the universe. Instead, it represents a process for proposing and refining theoretical explanations about the world that are subject to further testing and refinement") (emphasis in original). But, in order to qualify as "scientific knowledge," an inference or assertion must be derived by the scientific method. Proposed testimony must be supported by appropriate validation—i.e., "good grounds," based on what is known. In short, the requirement that an expert's testimony pertain to "scientific knowledge" establishes a standard of evidentiary reliability.

Rule 702 further requires that the evidence or testimony "assist the trier of fact to understand the evidence or to determine a fact in issue." This condition goes primarily to relevance. "Expert testimony which does not relate to any issue in the case is not relevant and, ergo, non-helpful." 3 Weinstein & Berger P 702[02], p. 702–18. * * * The consideration has been aptly described by Judge Becker as one of "fit." * * * "Fit" is not always obvious, and scientific validity for one purpose is not necessarily scientific validity for other, unrelated purposes. * * * The study of the phases of the moon, for example, may provide valid scientific "knowledge" about whether a certain night was dark, and if darkness is a fact in issue, the knowledge will assist the trier of fact. However (absent creditable grounds supporting such a link), evidence that the moon was full on a certain night will not assist the trier of fact in determining whether an individual was unusually likely to have behaved irrationally on that night. Rule 702's "helpfulness" standard requires a valid scientific connection to the pertinent inquiry as a precondition to admissibility.

That these requirements are embodied in Rule 702 is not surprising. Unlike an ordinary witness, see Rule 701, an expert is permitted wide latitude to offer opinions, including those that are not based on first-hand knowledge or observation. See Rules 702 and 703. Presumably, this relaxation of the usual requirement of first-hand knowledge—a rule which represents "a 'most pervasive manifestation' of the common law insistence upon 'the most reliable sources of information,'" Advisory Committee's Notes on Fed.Rule Evid. 602 (citation omitted)—is premised on an assumption that the expert's opinion will have a reliable basis in the knowledge and experience of his discipline.

C

Faced with a proffer of expert scientific testimony, then, the trial judge must determine at the outset, pursuant to Rule 104(a), whether the expert is proposing to testify to (1) scientific knowledge that (2) will assist the trier of fact to understand or determine a fact in issue.[11] This

11. Although the *Frye* decision itself focused exclusively on "novel" scientific techniques, we do not read the requirements of Rule 702 to apply especially or exclusively

entails a preliminary assessment of whether the reasoning or methodology underlying the testimony is scientifically valid and of whether that reasoning or methodology properly can be applied to the facts in issue. We are confident that federal judges possess the capacity to undertake this review. Many factors will bear on the inquiry, and we do not presume to set out a definitive checklist or test. But some general observations are appropriate.

Ordinarily, a key question to be answered in determining whether a theory or technique is scientific knowledge that will assist the trier of fact will be whether it can be (and has been) tested. "Scientific methodology today is based on generating hypotheses and testing them to see if they can be falsified; indeed, this methodology is what distinguishes science from other fields of human inquiry." Green [Expert Witnesses and Sufficiency of Evidence in Toxic Substance Litigation: The Legacy of *Agent Orange* and Bendectin Litigation, 86 N.W. L. Rev. 643, 645 (1992).]. See also C. Hempel, Philosophy of Natural Science 49 (1966) ("[T]he statements constituting a scientific explanation must be capable of empirical test"); K. Popper, Conjectures and Refutations: The Growth of Scientific Knowledge 37 (5th ed. 1989) ("[T]he criterion of the scientific status of a theory is its falsifiability, or refutability, or testability").

Another pertinent consideration is whether the theory or technique has been subjected to peer review and publication. Publication (which is but one element of peer review) is not a *sine qua non* of admissibility; it does not necessarily correlate with reliability, and in some instances well-grounded but innovative theories will not have been published. * * * Some propositions, moreover, are too particular, too new, or of too limited interest to be published. But submission to the scrutiny of the scientific community is a component of "good science," in part because it increases the likelihood that substantive flaws in methodology will be detected. * * * The fact of publication (or lack thereof) in a peer-reviewed journal thus will be a relevant, though not dispositive, consideration in assessing the scientific validity of a particular technique or methodology on which an opinion is premised.

Additionally, in the case of a particular scientific technique, the court ordinarily should consider the known or potential rate of error, * * * and the existence and maintenance of standards controlling the technique's operation. * * *

Finally, "general acceptance" can yet have a bearing on the inquiry. A "reliability assessment does not require, although it does permit, explicit identification of a relevant scientific community and an express determination of a particular degree of acceptance within that communi-

to unconventional evidence. Of course, well-established propositions are less likely to be challenged than those that are novel, and they are more handily defended. Indeed, theories that are so firmly established

as to have attained the status of scientific law, such as the laws of thermodynamics, properly are subject to judicial notice under Fed. Rule Evid. 201.

ty." *United States v. Downing*, 753 F.2d, at 1238. Widespread acceptance can be an important factor in ruling particular evidence admissible, and "a known technique that has been able to attract only minimal support within the community," Downing, supra, at 1238, may properly be viewed with skepticism.

The inquiry envisioned by Rule 702 is, we emphasize, a flexible one. Its overarching subject is the scientific validity—and thus the evidentiary relevance and reliability—of the principles that underlie a proposed submission. The focus, of course, must be solely on principles and methodology, not on the conclusions that they generate.

Throughout, a judge assessing a proffer of expert scientific testimony under Rule 702 should also be mindful of other applicable rules. Rule 703 provides that expert opinions based on otherwise inadmissible hearsay are to be admitted only if the facts or data are "of a type reasonably relied upon by experts in the particular field in forming opinions or inferences upon the subject." Rule 706 allows the court at its discretion to procure the assistance of an expert of its own choosing. Finally, Rule 403 permits the exclusion of relevant evidence "if its probative value is substantially outweighed by the danger of unfair prejudice, confusion of the issues, or misleading the jury. * * *" Judge Weinstein has explained: "Expert evidence can be both powerful and quite misleading because of the difficulty in evaluating it. Because of this risk, the judge in weighing possible prejudice against probative force under Rule 403 of the present rules exercises more control over experts than over lay witnesses." Weinstein, 138 F.R.D., at 632.

III

We conclude by briefly addressing what appear to be two underlying concerns of the parties and amici in this case. Respondent expresses apprehension that abandonment of "general acceptance" as the exclusive requirement for admission will result in a "free-for-all" in which befuddled juries are confounded by absurd and irrational pseudoscientific assertions. In this regard respondent seems to us to be overly pessimistic about the capabilities of the jury, and of the adversary system generally. Vigorous cross-examination, presentation of contrary evidence, and careful instruction on the burden of proof are the traditional and appropriate means of attacking shaky but admissible evidence. * * * Additionally, in the event the trial court concludes that the scintilla of evidence presented supporting a position is insufficient to allow a reasonable juror to conclude that the position more likely than not is true, the court remains free to direct a judgment, Fed.Rule Civ.Proc. 50(a), and likewise to grant summary judgment, Fed.Rule Civ.Proc. 56. * * * These conventional devices, rather than wholesale exclusion under an uncompromising "general acceptance" test, are the appropriate safeguards where the basis of scientific testimony meets the standards of Rule 702.

Petitioners and, to a greater extent, their amici exhibit a different concern. They suggest that recognition of a screening role for the judge that allows for the exclusion of "invalid" evidence will sanction a stifling and repressive scientific orthodoxy and will be inimical to the search for truth. * * * It is true that open debate is an essential part of both legal and scientific analyses. Yet there are important differences between the quest for truth in the courtroom and the quest for truth in the laboratory. Scientific conclusions are subject to perpetual revision. Law, on the other hand, must resolve disputes finally and quickly. The scientific project is advanced by broad and wide-ranging consideration of a multitude of hypotheses, for those that are incorrect will eventually be shown to be so, and that in itself is an advance. Conjectures that are probably wrong are of little use, however, in the project of reaching a quick, final, and binding legal judgment—often of great consequence—about a particular set of events in the past. We recognize that in practice, a gatekeeping role for the judge, no matter how flexible, inevitably on occasion will prevent the jury from learning of authentic insights and innovations. That, nevertheless, is the balance that is struck by Rules of Evidence designed not for the exhaustive search for cosmic understanding but for the particularized resolution of legal disputes.

IV

To summarize: "general acceptance" is not a necessary precondition to the admissibility of scientific evidence under the Federal Rules of Evidence, but the Rules of Evidence—especially Rule 702—do assign to the trial judge the task of ensuring that an expert's testimony both rests on a reliable foundation and is relevant to the task at hand. Pertinent evidence based on scientifically valid principles will satisfy those demands.

The inquiries of the District Court and the Court of Appeals focused almost exclusively on "general acceptance," as gauged by publication and the decisions of other courts. Accordingly, the judgment of the Court of Appeals is vacated and the case is remanded for further proceedings consistent with this opinion.

It is so ordered.

CHIEF JUSTICE REHNQUIST, with whom JUSTICE STEVENS joins, concurring in part and dissenting in part.

The petition for certiorari in this case presents two questions: first, whether the rule of *Frye v. United States*, 54 App.D.C. 46, 293 F. 1013 (1923), remains good law after the enactment of the Federal Rules of Evidence; and second, if *Frye* remains valid, whether it requires expert scientific testimony to have been subjected to a peer-review process in order to be admissible. The Court concludes, correctly in my view, that the *Frye* rule did not survive the enactment of the Federal Rules of Evidence, and I therefore join Parts I and II–A of its opinion. The second question presented in the petition for certiorari necessarily is mooted by this holding, but the Court nonetheless proceeds to construe Rules 702 and 703 very much in the abstract, and then offers some "general observations." * * *

"General observations" by this Court customarily carry great weight with lower federal courts, but the ones offered here suffer from the flaw common to most such observations—they are not applied to deciding whether or not particular testimony was or was not admissible, and therefore they tend to be not only general, but vague and abstract. This is particularly unfortunate in a case such as this, where the ultimate legal question depends on an appreciation of one or more bodies of knowledge not judicially noticeable, and subject to different interpretations in the briefs of the parties and their amici. Twenty-two amicus briefs have been filed in the case, and indeed the Court's opinion contains no less than 37 citations to amicus briefs and other secondary sources.

The various briefs filed in this case are markedly different from typical briefs, in that large parts of them do not deal with decided cases or statutory language—the sort of material we customarily interpret. Instead, they deal with definitions of scientific knowledge, scientific method, scientific validity, and peer review—in short, matters far afield from the expertise of judges. This is not to say that such materials are not useful or even necessary in deciding how Rule 703 should be applied; but it is to say that the unusual subject matter should cause us to proceed with great caution in deciding more than we have to, because our reach can so easily exceed our grasp.

But even if it were desirable to make "general observations" not necessary to decide the questions presented, I cannot subscribe to some of the observations made by the Court. In Part II–B, the Court concludes that reliability and relevancy are the touchstones of the admissibility of expert testimony. * * * Federal Rule of Evidence 402 provides, as the Court points out, that "[e]vidence which is not relevant is not admissible." But there is no similar reference in the Rule to "reliability." The Court constructs its argument by parsing the language "[i]f scientific, technical, or other specialized knowledge will assist the trier of fact to understand the evidence or to determine a fact in issue * * * an expert * * * may testify thereto. * * *" Fed.Rule Evid. 702. It stresses that the subject of the expert's testimony must be "scientific * * * knowledge," and points out that "scientific" "implies a grounding in the methods and procedures of science," and that the word "knowledge" "connotes more than subjective belief or unsupported speculation." * * * From this it concludes that "scientific knowledge" must be "derived by the scientific method." * * * Proposed testimony, we are told, must be supported by "appropriate validation." * * *

Questions arise simply from reading this part of the Court's opinion, and countless more questions will surely arise when hundreds of district judges try to apply its teaching to particular offers of expert testimony. Does all of this dicta apply to an expert seeking to testify on the basis of "technical or other specialized knowledge"—the other types of expert knowledge to which Rule 702 applies—or are the "general observations" limited only to "scientific knowledge"? What is the difference between scientific knowledge and technical knowledge; does Rule 702 actually contemplate that the phrase "scientific, technical, or other specialized knowledge" be broken down into numerous subspecies of expertise, or did its authors simply pick general descriptive language covering the sort of expert testimony which courts have customarily received? The Court speaks of its confidence that federal judges can make a "preliminary assessment of whether the reasoning or methodology underlying the testimony is scientifically valid and of whether that reasoning or methodology properly can be applied to the facts in issue." * * * The Court then states that a "key question" to be answered in deciding whether something is "scientific knowledge" "will be whether it can be (and has been) tested." * * * Following this sentence are three quotations from treatises, which speak not only of empirical testing, but one of which states that "the criterion of the scientific status of a theory is its falsifiability, or refutability, or testability." * * *

I defer to no one in my confidence in federal judges; but I am at a loss to know what is meant when it is said that the scientific status of a theory depends on its "falsifiability," and I suspect some of them will be, too.

I do not doubt that Rule 702 confides to the judge some gatekeeping responsibility in deciding questions of the admissibility of proffered expert testimony. But I do not think it imposes on them either the obligation or the authority to become amateur scientists in order to perform that role. I think the Court would be far better advised in this case to decide only the questions presented, and to leave the further development of this important area of the law to future cases.

Notes

1. Note that *Daubert* addressed the admissibility of expert testimony on the issue of causation. Of course, whether Bendectin causes injury is also relevant to the issue of defect. There is no suggestion in *Daubert* that the appropriate test under Federal Rule of Evidence 702 differs for the issues of defect and causation.

2. The use of "junk" science or "innovative" science (depending on one's point of view) has sparked a heated debate in the academic and popular presses. An excellent article describing and analyzing this issue is Green, Expert Witnesses and Sufficiency of Evidence in Toxic Substances Litigation: The Legacy of *Agent Orange* and Bendectin Litigation, 86 Nw. L.Rev. 643 (1992). Professor Green's overall conclusion is that courts should be flexible in evaluating scientific evidence and expert witnesses rather than apply an absolute, threshold test. Notice that the Supreme Court relied on Professor Green in *Daubert*. His description of the debate on this issue provides useful background:

> The expansion of liability theories over the past twenty-five years, especially in the products liability and environmental tort areas, raises increasingly frequent and complex scientific questions. The tort crisis of the mid–1980s contributed to the perception that the courts had gone too far in advantaging plaintiffs. Procedurally, case management and docket control have become the buzzwords for a judiciary that finds

itself chronically overwhelmed with its caseload. The Supreme Court, in a trilogy of recent decisions, has revived and encouraged employment of summary judgment to truncate cases without the time-consuming need for jury trial. Summary judgment has proved a potent weapon to combat the perceived abuse of science in the courts.

By the mid–1980s, the courts also were confronting the impact of the liberalization of expert witness testimony reflected in the Federal Rules of Evidence. This liberalization, in conjunction with the expansion of liability, brought more experts into court with more marginal credentials and more tenuous theories and opinions. The liberalization of expert witness testimony inevitably created its own backlash. The perception that the expert witness business has simply gone too far—in misleading juries rather than assisting them in resolving a broad range of cases—has become quite prevalent.

Judge Weinstein has contributed to this perception, writing extensively and repeatedly about expert witness abuse:

> [A]n expert can be found to testify to the truth of almost any factual theory, no matter how frivolous, thus validating the case sufficiently to avoid summary judgment and forcing the matter to trial. At the trial itself, an expert's testimony can be used to obfuscate what would otherwise be a simple case. The most tenuous factual bases are sufficient to produce firm opinions to a high degree of "medical (or other expert) probability" or even of "certainty." Juries and judges can be, and sometimes are, misled by the expert-for-hire.

[Weinstein, Improving Expert Testimony, 20 U. Rich. L. Rev. 473, 482 (1986).] Other commentators vividly joined in the criticism of expert witness testimony. For example, the federal government's investigation of the tort crisis yielded the following view of expert testimony in toxic substances cases:

> It has become all too common for "experts" or "studies" on the fringes of or even well beyond the outer parameters [sic] of mainstream scientific or medical views to be presented to juries as valid evidence from which conclusions may be drawn. The use of such invalid scientific evidence (commonly referred to as "junk science") has resulted in findings of causation which simply cannot be justified or understood from the standpoint of the current state of credible scientific and medical knowledge.

Perhaps most saliently, even members of the plaintiffs' bar have added their concurrence. Paul Rheingold, one of the best respected plaintiffs' attorneys and the organizer of the successful mass litigation over MER/29 in the 1960s, has written of the abuse of expert witnesses and singled out his colleagues in Bendectin litigation for using questionable experts who are long on speculation and short on substance.

Id. at 668–71 (footnotes omitted).

3. To what extent is this really a debate about the jury system? Again, Professor Green provides a helpful context:

> Professor Rosenberg has described the paradox that the jury's virtues of injecting community values and knocking the harsh edges off

the law often form the basis of the criticism that the jury engages in unbridled and unprincipled lawmaking. Maurice Rosenberg, Contemporary Litigation in the United States, *in* Legal Institutions Today: English and American Approaches Compared 176–77 (H. Jones ed. 1977). *Compare* Patrick Devlin, Trial by Jury (1956); Charles W. Joiner, Civil Justice and the Jury (1962); Alexis de Tocqueville, Democracy in America 248–54 (J. Mayer & M. Lerner eds. 1966); Harry Kalven, The Dignity of the Civil Jury, 50 Va. L. Rev. 1055 (1964) *with* Jerome Frank, Courts on Trial 108–45 (1949); Dale W. Broeder, The Functions of the Jury—Fact or Fiction?, 21 U. Chi. L. Rev. 386 (1954); Milton D. Green, Juries and Justice—The Jury's Role in Personal Injury Cases, 1962 U. Ill. L. Forum 152; Leon Sarpy, Civil Juries, Their Decline and Eventual Fall, 11 Loy. L. Rev. 243 (1962).

The debate over juries has raged for centuries. *Compare* Parsons v. Bedford, 28 U.S. (3 Pet.) 433, 446–48 (1830) (detailing importance of right to jury trial) *with* Charles W. Wolfram, The Constitutional History of the Seventh Amendment, 57 Minn. L. Rev. 639 (1973) (detailing federalists' opposition to jury trials).

Even Mark Twain expressed his views on the jury: "The jury system puts a ban upon intelligence and honesty, and a premium upon ignorance, stupidity and perjury. It is a shame that we must continue to use a worthless system because it *was* good a thousand years ago." Mark Twain, Roughing It 247 (Am. Pub. & F.G. Gilman & Co. 1872) (emphasis in original).

Green, *supra*, note 2, at 674 n. 143.

4. The most outspoken critique of "junk" science has been Peter Huber. *See* P. Huber, Liability: The Legal Resolution and its Consequences (1988); Huber, Safety and the Best: The Hazards of Public Risk Management and the Courts, 85 Colum. L. Rev. 227 (1985); Huber, Junk Science and the Jury, 1990 U. Chi. Legal F. 273. There is a vast literature on both sides of the debate. In addition to Professor Green's excellent article, *see, e.g.* Becker & Orenstein, The Federal Rules of Evidence After Sixteen Years—The Effect of "Plain Meaning" Jurisprudence, the Need for an Advisory Committee on the Rules of Evidence, and Suggestions for Selective Revision of the Rules, 60 Geo. Wash.L.Rev. 857, 867–885 (1992); Hanson, James Alphonso Frye is Sixty–Five Years Old; Should He Retire?, 16 W. St. U. L. Rev. 357 (1989); Black, A Unified Theory of Scientific Evidence, 56 Ford. L. Rev. 595 (1988); Imwinkelried, The "Bases" of Expert Testimony: The Syllogistic Structure of Scientific Testimony, 67 N.C. L. Rev. 1 (1988); Proposals for a Model Rule on the Admissibility of Scientific Evidence, 26 Jurimetrics J. 235 (1986); Gianelli, The Admissibility of Novel Scientific Evidence: Frye v. United States, A Half–Century Later, 80 Colum. L. Rev. 1197 (1980); The Supreme Court, 1986 Term, 101 Harv. L. Rev. 7, 119, 125–127 (1987).

5. In cases involving design defects, a plaintiff can use an expert to opine that a design feature has risks that outweigh its utility. *See, e.g.*, Caterpillar Tractor Co. v. Boyett, 674 S.W.2d 782, 788 (Tex.App.—Corpus Christi 1984, no writ). Some courts have held that the expert must explain

or have a basis for his opinion. *See* Ingram v. Caterpillar Mach. Corp., 535 So.2d 723 (La.1988).

6. For an analysis of the interaction between expert testimony and industry standards, *see Alevromagiros v. Hechinger Co., supra* p. 430.

SECTION E. OTHER METHODS OF PROOF

A plaintiff can use direct evidence or circumstantial evidence (or either or both in combination with expert testimony) to establish that a product was flawed. If the product is available after the accident, the plaintiff may perform out-of-court scientific tests on the product to determine whether it has impurities or defects and introduce the results of these tests into evidence. The plaintiff may also perform out-of-court experiments on the product that are designed to recreate some aspect of the accident, as long as the experiments are conducted under conditions that are substantially similar to the conditions existing at the time of the accident. A plaintiff must often accompany scientific tests with expert testimony to explain them. A plaintiff can also prove a manufacturing flaw with lay testimony about the condition of the product.

Under some circumstances, the mere occurrence of a product malfunction is circumstantial evidence that the product was flawed, but it is not conclusive. A plaintiff can attempt to negate other possible causes of an accident, which provides circumstantial evidence that the product was defective. A plaintiff can use these two types of circumstantial evidence together, and several cases recognizing a product malfunction as evidence of defectiveness have done so only when that evidence was buttressed with evidence tending to negate other causes. Evidence that several other users were injured by a product can also support a finding of defectiveness.

Because the legal standard for design defects is complex, many types of evidence are relevant to prove the existence of a design defect. As a general rule, a party can introduce any evidence that is related to the risk or utility of a design feature, such as the existence of a safer alternative design.

A plaintiff can use an admission of the defendant or the defendant's witnesses to demonstrate that a different design would have been safer. Alternative designs actually used by the defendant or other manufacturers at the time the product was sold are relevant to show that a safer alternative design was available. (Post-accident design changes are addressed in section C, *supra*.) A plaintiff can also rely on evidence that other products with the same or similar design have failed.

To prove a marketing defect, a plaintiff must prove that the manufacturer imposed an inappropriate risk on the consumer either by failing to give an adequate warning or by failing to give adequate instructions for using the product. To prove the existence of an inappropriate risk, the plaintiff can use the same methods that are available to prove the existence of such risks in cases involving design defects. The plaintiff must also prove that the manufacturer knew or should have known about the product's risks at the time the product was sold. A plaintiff can use expert testimony, lay testimony, or documentary evidence to show that information about the risks was available to the defendant. Recall letters warning earlier consumers of the risk also tend to establish knowledge by the manufacturer, but the admissibility of recall letters raises special issues that are discussed in section C in connection with post-accident remedial measures. The plaintiff may also use other warnings made by the defendant or warnings made by other manufacturers of similar products to show that the manufacturer knew or should have known about the risks imposed by the product in question.

If the manufacturer gave a warning or instruction for use, the plaintiff can attempt to prove that it was inadequate to apprise the ordinary consumer of the product's risks or of the steps that he should take to avoid or counteract them. The adequacy or inadequacy of a particular warning is a fact question for the jury that is heavily dependent on circumstances. In Kritser v. Beech Aircraft Corp., 479 F.2d 1089 (5th Cir.1973), the court held that the plaintiff's proof that he was injured after carefully following the manufacturer's instructions was sufficient to support a finding that the instructions were inadequate.

Chapter 11

CAUSATION IN FACT

SECTION A. TESTS FOR DETERMINING CAUSATION [1]

To recover under strict tort liability, a plaintiff must prove that the product's defect was a cause-in-fact of his injury. The plaintiff need not prove that the defect was the sole cause of his injury; injuries can have multiple causes. The plaintiff's burden is merely to prove that the product defect was *a* cause-in-fact of his injury.

Courts usually define cause-in-fact by the "but for" or "sine qua non" test, which requires the plaintiff to prove that his injury would not have occurred if the product defect had not existed. This test is sometimes difficult to apply because a court cannot be certain what would have happened had events been different than they actually were. Moreover, proof of causation under the "but for" test can be problematic because the fact-finder has difficulty determining what actually happened. For example, in a case involving an automobile accident, a court may have difficulty determining whether a broken axle caused the accident or vice versa. In most cases, however, the "but for" test is not difficult to apply. For example, a court can be relatively certain that a plaintiff who was cut by glass in a soft drink would not have been injured if there had been no glass. Problems of proving causation through the use of circumstantial evidence are addressed in Chapter 2, Section D. Aside from these issues of proof, the "but for" test is straightforward, easy to apply, and provides the basic framework for analyzing cause-in-fact.

The "but for" test of causation is inadequate in cases in which each of two or more independently sufficient causes produces an injury. If a victim ingests two drugs, either of which would have caused an injury, neither is a "but for" cause, because even without the ingestion of one

---

1. This note is adapted from W. Powers, (1986). Texas Products Liability Law, pp. 6–3—6–7.

drug, the victim would still have been injured.[2] In these cases, courts use the "substantial factor" test to conclude that each of the independently sufficient causes is a cause-in-fact. The "substantial factor" test does not apply to all cases that involve multiple causes. It applies only to cases that involve multiple, *independently sufficient* causes.[3] Multiple, *jointly necessary* causes satisfy the "but for" test because the absence of any one of these causes would have prevented the injury.[4]

The "substantial factor" test is extremely difficult to apply. In *Saunders System Birmingham Co. v. Adams,*[5] for example, a driver rented an automobile with defective brakes. The court held that the defective brakes were not a cause of an ensuing accident because the driver failed to apply the brakes soon enough. Neither the defective brakes nor the driver's failure to apply them was a "but for" cause of the accident because the accident would have occurred in the absence of either one of them. Both seem to be independently sufficient causes, however, since either alone would have sufficed to cause the accident. Nevertheless, the court held that the defect in the brakes was not a cause of the accident. Although the court did not explain this distinction, the relative temporal proximity to the accident of each potential cause may explain it. Despite the difficulties in applying the "substantial factor" test, it at least provides a potential basis for a finding of cause-in-fact in cases involving independently sufficient causes that fail to meet the "but for" test.

Some courts have held that an independently sufficient cause subjects a defendant to liability under the "substantial factor" test only if the other independently sufficient cause was of human or culpable origin.[6] Under this approach, a fire that was caused independently by a railroad's defective spark arrester and by lightning would not establish liability for the manufacturer of the spark arrester. This distinction has been rejected by the Restatement (Second) of Torts.[7] Even courts that draw the distinction between natural and human causes usually place the burden of proving the natural origin of the second cause on the defendant seeking to escape liability.[8] Nevertheless, some courts draw the distinction in negligence cases, suggesting that they might also do so in strict tort liability.

In *Basko v. Sterling Drug, Inc.,*[9] the Second Circuit held a drug manufacturer liable even though its defective drug was one of two

---

2. See Restatement (Second) of Torts § 432(2) (1965); Basko v. Sterling Drug, Inc., 416 F.2d 417 (2d Cir.1969).

3. See Kingston v. Chicago & N.W. Ry. Co., 191 Wis. 610, 211 N.W. 913 (1927).

4. See, e.g., Dover Corp. v. Perez, 587 S.W.2d 761 (Tex.Civ.App.—Corpus Christi 1979, writ refused no reversible error 1979) (combination of defective heater and improper venting caused plaintiff's injuries).

5. 217 Ala. 621, 117 So. 72 (1928).

6. See, e.g., Cook v. Minneapolis, St. P. & S.S.M. Ry., 98 Wis. 624, 74 N.W. 561 (1898).

7. Restatement (Second) of Torts § 432, comment d (1965). See also Anderson v. Minneapolis, St. P. & S.S.M. Ry. Co., 146 Minn. 430, 440, 179 N.W. 45, 49 (1920).

8. See, e.g., Kingston v. Chicago & N.W. Ry. Co., 191 Wis. 610, 211 N.W. 913 (1927).

9. 416 F.2d 417 (2d Cir.1969).

independently sufficient causes of the plaintiff's injury. The other independently sufficient cause was another of the manufacturer's drugs. This other drug was not defective only because the risk of injury was not foreseeable when it was sold. Both independently sufficient causes were of human origin in the sense that each drug was manufactured. One cause, however, was legally innocent. Nevertheless, the court had no difficulty holding the manufacturer of the defective drug liable.

The following materials deal with some special problems of proof of causation-in-fact in products liability cases.

SECTION B.   PROOF OF CAUSATION

1. RELIANCE ON WARNINGS

DeLURYEA v. WINTHROP LABORATORIES, A DIV. OF STERLING DRUG, INC.

United States Court of Appeals, Eighth Circuit, 1983.
697 F.2d 222.

JOHN R. GIBSON, CIRCUIT JUDGE.

Sterling Drug, Inc. and its division, Winthrop Laboratories, appeal from a judgment in favor of plaintiff Leota A. DeLuryea in the amount of $80,000. Mrs. DeLuryea brought suit against defendants (Sterling) for damages suffered as a result of drug dependence and tissue damage caused by the drug Talwin manufactured by Sterling. The case was submitted to the jury on theories of strict liability, negligence, and breach of express warranty.

* * *

DeLuryea's ponytail was caught in the shaft of some machinery in the shoe factory in which she was working on January 3, 1959, and her scalp, forehead, upper eyelids and the area around her ears were torn off completely. She had surgery on several occasions and the use of painkilling medication was required. In the summer of 1968, DeLuryea's treating physician, Dr. McCarthy DeMere, became concerned that she had become dependent upon her principal painkilling medication, Demerol. DeLuryea was hospitalized on August 28, 1968 and Dr. Charles Cooke was called in for consultation. Dr. Clarke prescribed Talwin in lieu of Demerol. After the initial prescription by Dr. Clarke, DeLuryea obtained prescriptions for Talwin from Drs. Clopton and Futrell, two general practitioners in northeast Arkansas, and self-administered the drug in [injectable] form until June 3, 1974.

* * *

DeLuryea developed severe ulcerations on her left thigh with necrotic tissue caused by injections of Talwin over a period of time. Later she developed tissue necrosis of her other thigh and her hips, shoulders, and upper arms. Sterling stipulated that DeLuryea's tissue problems were caused by her use of Talwin.

Insofar as the evidence bears upon the issues raised on appeal, it will be discussed with reference to each such issue.

I.

Sterling claims that DeLuryea failed to make a submissible case because no doctor who prescribed Talwin for DeLuryea testified that the warnings were inadequate or that he would have acted differently if different warnings had been given. Thus, Sterling argues there was a complete absence of proof of causal connection between the warnings and the damage suffered by DeLuryea.

None of the doctors prescribing Talwin testified. One was deceased at the time of trial.

DeLuryea produced testimony from Dr. McCarthy DeMere that the warnings given prior to May 1974 regarding tissue damage at injection sites were inadequate to warn the medical profession of the danger involved. He stated that the manufacturer knew in 1967, prior to marketing, that Talwin would cause tissue damage after prolonged use. An adequate warning could have been given at that time. Dr. Richard McShane testified that Sterling's premarketing animal studies revealed tissue damage similar to that found in humans. This, however, was not publicized until May 1974. He agreed with Dr. DeMere that the warnings prior to May 1974 were inadequate to warn of damage at injection sites.

Information concerning not only Talwin but other prescription drugs is contained in a package insert accompanying each drug. The package insert is updated as further information on the drug becomes available. The Physicians' Desk Reference, which in the case of Talwin contained the same information as the package insert, is furnished to all physicians without charge by its publisher, Medical Economics.

Under these circumstances, with evidence of inadequate warnings, and that the warnings were placed in the hands of all physicians, which would include the three prescribing physicians, we conclude that DeLuryea's evidence established a submissible issue on negligence and proximate cause. We must, of course, consider the evidence in the light most favorable to DeLuryea. *De Witt v. Brown*, 669 F.2d 516, [523] (8th Cir.1982); *Garoogian v. Medlock*, 592 F.2d 997, 999 n. 3 (8th Cir.1979).

This court in *Sterling Drug, Inc. v. Cornish*, 370 F.2d 82 (8th Cir.1966), discussed the importance of warning prescribing physicians as follows:

> (T)he purchaser's doctor is a learned intermediary between the purchaser and the manufacturer. If the doctor is properly warned of the possibility of a side effect in some patients, and is advised of the symptoms normally accompanying the side effect, there is an excellent chance that injury to the patient can be avoided. This is

particularly true if the injury takes place slowly, as is the case with the injury in question here.

370 F.2d at 85.

* * *

Under *Cornish* we conclude that failure to produce testimony of the prescribing doctors was not fatal to DeLuryea's case on the issue of proximate cause. In *Schenebeck v. Sterling Drug, Inc.*, 423 F.2d 919, 923 (8th Cir.1970), we held that one of several permissible inferences was that the doctors would have heeded the warning and altered the course of treatment had an adequate warning been given. Here there was evidence that the warnings were inadequate, that DeLuryea continued using the medication, and that the usage produced the tissue damage, all subjects of the court's reasoning in *Schenebeck*. As in *Schenebeck*:

> (W)e think the plaintiff presented sufficient evidence for the jury to find that Sterling's failure to timely warn constituted an omission on its part which operated through a natural sequence of events to proximately cause or contribute to plaintiff's harm. See *Parke–Davis and Co. v. Stromsodt*, 411 F.2d 1390 (8th Cir.1969).

423 F.2d at 923.

> Sterling relies upon *Douglas v. Bussabarger*, 73 Wash.2d 476, 438 P.2d 829 (Wash.1968) (en banc); *Oppenheimer v. Sterling Drug, Inc.*, 7 Ohio App.2d 103, 219 N.E.2d 54 (1964); *Chambers v. G.D. Searle & Co.*, 441 F.Supp. 377 (D.Md.1975), aff'd, 567 F.2d 269 (4th Cir.1977) (per curiam); and *Brochu v. Ortho Pharmaceutical Corp.*, 642 F.2d 652 (1st Cir.1981).

The prescribing physician in *Douglas* specifically stated that he did not read the allegedly inadequate warnings, rather he relied on his own medical knowledge. The court concluded that any negligence in failing to warn was not the proximate cause of plaintiff's disability. In *Oppenheimer* the prescribing physician did not specifically recall reading the precautions in question. The doctor stated that he relied on his own experience in prescribing the drug. The court held that the doctor's failure to rely on the warnings was sufficient to defeat plaintiff's claim. In *Chambers* the prescribing physician testified that he had no knowledge of plaintiff's predisposition toward stroke and therefore would not have altered his prescription had there been an adequate warning about use of the drug in question by those predisposed to stroke. The court concluded that plaintiff had not furnished sufficient proof of causation.

Sterling argues that plaintiff was obligated to put on evidence similar to that in *Brochu* in which the court upheld a jury verdict for plaintiff. We do not read *Brochu* as creating a pattern of evidence that is necessary for plaintiff to make a submissible case.

The specific testimony of the doctors in each of the cases relied upon by Sterling distinguishes those cases from this case in which the prescribing physicians did not testify. *Chambers,* 441 F.Supp. at 385; *McEwen v. Ortho Pharmaceutical Corp.,* 270 Or. 375, 528 P.2d 522, 526 (Or.1974). The issue of proximate cause was properly submitted to the jury. While we have discussed the question in light of negligence cases, proximate cause in the strict liability submission in this case involves similar considerations.

* * *

[The court reversed and remanded the case for a new trial because the trial judge erroneously excluded certain evidence offered by defendant.]

Note

A failure to warn is not a cause of the harm if the person to be warned is already fully aware of the dangers that should have been warned against. *See, e.g.,* Stanback v. Parke, Davis & Co., 657 F.2d 642 (4th Cir.1981) (drug company's failure to warn about a risk associated with a vaccine did not cause the harm because the physician who administered it was fully aware of the risk).

MENARD v. NEWHALL
Supreme Court of Vermont, 1977.
135 Vt. 53, 373 A.2d 505.

BILLINGS, JUSTICE.

On August 24, 1972, four grade school aged children engaged in a BB gun fight. As a result of the altercation, plaintiff-appellant Menard was struck in the eye and injured. The BB gun was owned and fired by defendant Newhall; it was manufactured and sold by defendant Daisy.

* * *

Trial was commenced against defendant Daisy and, on the second day, the trial court granted defendant Daisy's motion for summary judgment. V.R.C.P. 56. The plaintiff appeals from that summary judgment.

Prior to the entry of summary judgment for defendant Daisy, the plaintiff stipulated as follows:

　　1. The plaintiff's claim was based solely upon the theory of strict liability as set forth in the Restatement (Second) of Torts § 402A (1965).

　　2. Mr. Newhall testified in a pretrial deposition that he had instructed his son in the use of the BB gun referred to in the complaint.

　　3. The only evidence the [plaintiff] would introduce at trial on the issue of whether or not Daisy's alleged failure to warn was a proximate cause of the plaintiff's injury was contained in Mr. Newhall's deposition testimony.

Upon consideration of the stipulation, the trial court denied Daisy's Rule 12(b)(6) motion based upon no duty to warn of obvious danger, but the trial court did grant the summary judgment on the ground that Mr. Newhall's deposition testimony established as a matter of law that Daisy's alleged failure to warn was not a proximate cause of plaintiff's injury. Mr. Newhall had testified that when he gave his son the Daisy BB gun that fired the shot, he instructed him "how to fire, and what to shoot at, and things like that".

This Court adopted Restatement (Second) of Torts, § 402A (1965) in *Zaleskie v. Joyce,* 133 Vt. 150, 333 A.2d 110 (1975). Assuming that the seller or manufacturer had a duty to warn under the facts in the case at bar, * * * § 402A requires that the plaintiff must prove not only that the lack of a warning made the product unreasonably dangerous and hence defective, but the plaintiff also has the burden of showing that the lack of a warning was a proximate cause of the injury. *Technical Chemical Co. v. Jacobs,* 480 S.W.2d 602 (Tex.1972). If the defendant Daisy had a duty to warn of the dangers associated with the use of the BB gun and failed to do so, a presumption is created that the defendant would have read the warning and heeded it. In effect, a presumption of causation is created in failure-to-warn cases. This does not impose absolute liability on the manufacturer, but merely shifts the burden to the manufacturer to go forward with the evidence. *Nissen Trampoline Co. v. Terre Haute First National Bank,* Ind.App., 332 N.E.2d 820 (1975). Under such circumstances, as far as the case at bar is concerned, Daisy was obligated to go forward with evidence that the defendant Newhall would have ignored any warning given and, after introduction of that evidence, the presumption disappears. As Chief Justice Powers stated in *Tyrrell v. Prudential Insurance Co. of America,* 109 Vt. 6, 23–24, 192 A. 184, 192 (1937):

> A presumption, of itself alone, contributes no evidence and has no probative quality. It takes the place of evidence, temporarily, at least, but if and when enough rebutting evidence is admitted to make a question for the jury on the fact involved, the presumption disappears and goes for naught. In such a case, the presumption does not have to be overcome by evidence; once it is confronted by evidence of the character referred to, it immediately quits the arena.

Once the plaintiff stipulated that the only evidence of causation was that Newhall's father instructed him in the use of the BB gun, the defendant Daisy's burden of going forward was sustained. Once the defendant Newhall ignored his father's instructions, no warning Daisy could have given would have prevented the accident; thus the presumption disappeared and there was no genuine issue of fact as to causation. The trial court did not err when it granted defendant Daisy's motion for summary judgment.

* * *

Affirmed.

BARNEY, C.J., did not sit.

Notes

1. In failure to warn cases, a number of courts use a presumption that a proper warning would have been followed. The leading case is Technical Chem. Co. v. Jacobs, 480 S.W.2d 602 (Tex.1972). That court found the origin of the presumption in comment j to the Restatement of Torts (Second) § 402A which states that "Where warning is given, the seller may reasonably assume that it will be read and heeded." The court stated:

> Such a presumption works in favor of the manufacturer when an adequate warning is present. Where there is no warning, as in this case, however, the presumption that the user would have read an adequate warning works in favor of the plaintiff user. In other words, the presumption is that Jacobs would have read an adequate warning. The presumption, may, however, be rebutted if the manufacturer comes forward with contrary evidence that the presumed fact did not exist. [Citations] Depending upon the individual facts, this may be accomplished by the manufacturer's producing evidence that the user was blind, illiterate, intoxicated at the time of the use, irresponsible or lax in judgment or by some other circumstance tending to show that the improper use was or would have been made regardless of the warning.

480 S.W.2d at 606.

2. Plaintiff's husband died from a case of contact polio that he contracted from his two-month-old daughter after she had been given Sabin Polio Vaccine. This vaccine contained a live attenuated virus, and was the only polio vaccine on the market at the time of the inoculation. The chance of getting contact polio from this vaccine was 1 in 5,000,000. The vaccine was approved and recommended by the federal government and the National Academy of Pediatricians. Plaintiff brought an action for the wrongful death of her husband against the manufacturer of the vaccine. The action was based on a strict liability theory for failure to warn about the risk of contact polio. Plaintiff testified that if she had been warned, she would have deferred action and discussed the matter with other people. She would have either not permitted the use of the vaccine at all, or she would have permitted its use at a later time. May plaintiff rely on the presumption that she would have followed a proper warning?

3. Defendant manufacturer fails to put an important warning on its product label. The buyer uses the product without reading the label, and a bystander is injured by the hazard that was not warned against. The bystander sues defendant for failure to warn. What result? *See* Fischer, Causation in Fact in Omission Cases, 1992 Utah L.Rev. 1335.

2. ENHANCED INJURIES

LEE v. VOLKSWAGEN OF AMERICA, INC.

Supreme Court of Oklahoma, 1984.
688 P.2d 1283.

PER CURIAM:

I.

This suit arises from a collision between the station wagon driven by Marilyn Guffey and the 1964 Volkswagen "Beetle" driven by the plaintiff, Tom Lee.

Plaintiff's car was traveling north at approximately 15 miles per hour when it was struck on the right front side by Guffey's station wagon traveling west at a speed of approximately 35 miles per hour. Immediately prior to the impact, Guffey applied her brakes, causing the front of the station wagon to dip and strike plaintiff's car below its center of gravity, causing it to roll or tip to its right side. The much greater speed and weight of Guffey's car drove the plaintiff's car into a counter-clockwise rotation which resulted in the vehicles "side-slapping." At the end of the side-slap, the vehicles parted, with the Volkswagen being knocked forty feet west.

At a point somewhere between the first impact of the vehicles and the Volkswagen's final resting place, the right door came open and plaintiff and his brother, who was a passenger in the car, were ejected onto the street. As a result of the accident, the plaintiff sustained a cervical fracture, rendering him quadriplegic.

Plaintiff brought suit against Guffey on the basis of a traditional negligence theory. Plaintiff brought suit against Volkswagen on the basis of "manufacturers' products liability." The application of the latter theory was based on the contention that a defective door latch caused plaintiff's cervical fracture by allowing the door to come open, thus causing plaintiff to be thrown from the car.

The jury, in trial at the district court level, found in favor of plaintiff and awarded a judgment of 1.8 million dollars, plus interest and costs against both defendants.

Defendants Volkswagen of America, Inc. and Volkswagen Werk, Inc., GMBH (collectively referred to as Volkswagen) appeal.

II.

A.

The theory of manufacturers' products liability, as adopted in *Kirkland v. General Motors*, Okl., 521 P.2d 1353 (1974), provides the framework for this case.

Benita Kirkland brought action against the manufacturer of the automobile which she had been driving for injuries sustained in a collision which allegedly occurred when the driver's seat collapsed and she fell backwards. The district court ruled in favor of the defendant. This Court, while affirming the trial court's decision, also outlined the conceptual guides that govern a case when manufacturers' products liability is at issue.

Kirkland held that one who sells any product in a defective condition, that is unreasonably dangerous to the user or consumer, is strictly liable for the physical harm to person or property caused by the defect. This liability is not predicated on either a negligence or warranty basis. Plaintiffs utilizing this theory must prove that the product was the cause of the injury, that the defect existed in the product at the time it left the control of the defendant and that the defect made the product unreasonably dangerous as defined by ordinary consumer expectations.

In *Kirkland* we also addressed the level of proof necessary to fulfill plaintiff's burdens. Circumstantial evidence, coupled with the proper inferences drawn from it, is clearly an acceptable minimal basis. Actual or absolute proof is not required because this type of proof may be within the possession or peculiar knowledge of the defendant.

B.

Our first task is to determine if the *Kirkland* mode of analysis can be applied to the facts of the immediate case. The factual difference between the two cases is commonly referred to by drawing a distinction between injuries received in the "first collision or impact" and "injuries received in the second collision or impact." Products are said to be involved in "first impact injuries" when the product causes the impact to occur. Products are involved in "second impact injuries" when they operate as a causative agent after the original impact. For instance, Ms. Kirkland argued that the defective seat caused the accident and resultant injuries, while in this case Mr. Lee contends that the door latch caused the contact with the street and the resultant cervical fracture. The contact with the street could not have occurred without the initial impact between Ms. Guffey's station wagon and Mr. Lee's Volkswagen. This distinction is important because we have not previously decided a case involving "injuries from second impact."

Early in the development of the "second impact injury" doctrine, there was considerable discussion as to whether manufacturers had a duty to consider "collision impact" when designing an automobile. *Larsen v. General Motors*, 391 F.2d 495 (8th Cir.1968), involved this issue, holding that manufacturers have a duty to consider the environment in which the product will be used. We agree with the *Larsen* holding that the manufacturer's liability for injuries proximately caused by latent defects should not be limited to collisions in which the defect caused the accident, but should extend to situations in which the defect caused injuries over and above that which would have occurred from the accident, but for the defective design.

"Second impact" cases present no unique problems in reference to the actual defect. Plaintiff has the same burden as in other products cases as to whether the product was in a defective condition that was unreasonably dangerous as defined by ordinary consumer expectations when it left the control of the manufacturer.

"Second impact" cases do require a slightly different perspective when discussing the plaintiff's causation burden. A review of the case law of other jurisdictions reveals that courts speak of the manufacturer's liability in second impact cases in terms of "enhancement" or "aggravation" of injuries. In other words, the manufacturer is liable for damages only if the plaintiff can prove that he suffered injuries as a result of the latent defect or "second impact" in addition to those suffered as a result of the accident or "first impact." Further, the manufacturer is liable for damages only for enhanced injuries attributable to the second impact, i.e., only for injuries resulting from the latent defect.

This "aggravation" or "enhancement" can occur in two ways: A plaintiff might suffer an increase in the severity of the injury as a result of the "second impact," e.g., a worsening of a back injury suffered in the first collision, or a plaintiff might suffer an entirely new injury as a result of the "second impact," e.g., a broken leg in addition to a broken arm. In either situation, the causation burden is the same as in all products cases. Plaintiff must offer sufficient proof to convince the jury that the defect was responsible for a new injury or enhancement of an injury sustained as a result of the first impact. Thus "aggravation" or "enhancement" are labels applied to second impact injuries to avoid confusion with injuries caused by the "first impact." However, the problem is that, except for the instance in which the injuries caused by the design defect are clearly distinguishable from those caused by the initial collision (e.g., burn injuries from the explosion of a defectively designed gas tank, as in *Turcotte v. Ford Motor Co.,* 494 F.2d 173 (1st Cir.1974)), the evidence will necessarily include a determination of what injuries might have happened in the collision absent the defect. Not only must the jury attempt to determine what injuries plaintiff would have suffered absent the design defect, i.e., in this case, if the door had not opened, but it must also determine what enhanced injuries plaintiff suffered by reason of the door opening. In this case, plaintiff claimed damages for one indivisible injury, a cervical fracture rendering him quadriplegic.

C.

We now turn to an evaluation of defendants' specific claim. Volkswagen contends that this case should not have been presented to the jury because there was insufficient evidence to meet the plaintiff's burden of proof in terms of causation. The trial court denied the motion for a directed verdict, and it is that decision we now consider.

The necessary assessment requires a standard to determine the sufficiency of the evidence. It is this standard-making process that has provided a point of controversy in the reported cases involving "second impact injuries."

One group of decisions requires the plaintiff to precisely and exactly prove those injuries that are attributable to the accident and those that are attributable to the alleged design defect. The case of *Huddell v. Levin,* 537 F.2d 726 (3rd Cir.1976) is representative of this approach. In *Huddell,* plaintiff's decedent's head struck the head restraint after his car was hit in the rear. Plaintiff claimed that the head restraint had an unusually sharp edge, which caused decedent's death when it struck him on the rear of the head. At trial, plaintiff offered proof that the head restraint was defective and that the defect was a proximate cause of death. The court ruled that this proof was insufficient to make out a prima facie claim under the "second impact" theory. The court indicated that its test would require plaintiff to prove that the design was defective, the existence of a practical alternative design, what injuries would have resulted with the alternative design, and a method to evaluate the extent of the enhanced injury.

Other cases have ruled that a plaintiff only has to offer "some evidence of enhancement" to frame a jury issue. In case of *Lahocki v. Contee Sand & Gravel Co.,* 41 Md.App. 579, 398 A.2d 490 (1979), plaintiff Lahocki was a passenger in a General Motors van. The van was proceeding between 40 and 55 miles per hour when it struck heavy timber barricades placed there by Contee. The van went up into the air and flipped. It came to rest upside down, separated from its roof panel which lay nearby. Although the driver was still inside and relatively uninjured, passenger Lahocki lay with his back broken on the road some distance from both van and roof panel. Based upon expert evidence, Mr. Lahocki claimed that the roof panel came off because it was inadequately welded, and that his broken back was the direct result of having been thrown out of the vehicle through the open roof. The Maryland Court of Appeals, when discussing the sufficiency of plaintiff's proof regarding possible injuries in the absence of the defect, ruled that "some" evidence of a causal connection was necessary and if that evidence was provided it would be sufficient to present the case to a jury.

These decisions are not as conflicting as they appear to be at first glance. Both decisions agree that the manufacturer is liable only for the enhanced injuries, and the plaintiff must prove causation between the alleged defect and the injuries. The difference is the degree of proof that is required. The standard represented by *Huddell* requires a precise, certain, almost mathematical, level of proof, while the "some evidence" standard of Lahocki presents disturbing visions of unreasonable jury speculation.

We expressly reject the *Huddell* standard for several reasons. To require that exacting level of proof would make reasoning impossible. The goal of limiting a manufacturer's liability to a manageable burden can be accomplished without mandating an almost rigid level of proof. There are other standards that can be used without making insurers out of the manufacturers. There is no justifiable reason for placing this type of burden on one area of products liability and not on the other.

In addition, application of the *Huddell* standard might impair the promotion of "safer products" design by manufacturers, which this Court expressly recognized as desirable in *Kirkland,* by weakening the deterrent value of products action.

In rejecting the stricter standard of proof, we do not intend to travel to the other extreme. We find that the proof standards outlined in *Kirkland* constitute a reasonable compromise. Plaintiffs in first impact cases under the manufacturers' products liability theory must prove their case by a preponderance of evidence on the prima facie issues to avoid a directed verdict. We therefore hold that there is nothing about "second impact cases" that would justify changing that standard. Thus in "second impact cases" the plaintiff must prove by a preponderance of the evidence that the product was in a defective condition that was unreasonably dangerous as defined by ordinary consumer expectations when it left the control of the manufacturer and must prove after the original impact such defect caused or enhanced his injuries. Further, while we reject the exact levels of harm approach as espoused in the *Huddell* case, the plaintiff should be required to prove by a preponderance of the evidence the extent of the enhanced injuries resulting from the defect. The manufacturer of course will only be liable for the injuries resulting from the latent defect which was caused or enhanced by such defect.

III.

What we have heretofore said applies to "second impact" cases where the injuries sustained are separate and divisible. In such cases, the burden of proof remains solely upon the plaintiff, including the burden of proving "enhancement," i.e., the plaintiff must prove which of the several injuries are attributable to the manufacturer's defective product and the degree of "enhancement" occasioned by the product as distinguished from the injuries flowing from the third party's acts of negligence.

But a different rule applies where the principal injury complained of is single and indivisible (such as death or, as here, quadriplegia) and therefore are incapable of apportionment. In other words, there can be no "enhancement" in single indivisible injury cases.

Having established the overall burden of proof imposed upon the plaintiff in "second impact" cases, we therefore next address the succeeding consequential problem of who has the burden of going forward with the evidence where the principal injury complained of is single and indivisible such as in the case before us. Here again we reject the repressive rule of *Huddell* which requires a plaintiff to prove with specificity that the single injury was caused by the specific defects in the product to make a submissible case. The *Huddell* rule too readily permits the manufacturer to escape what otherwise would be its liability by the fortuitous commingling of a third party's negligence into the causal chain. The relation of the manufacturer and the third party is not that of concurrent joint tort-feasors in the strict sense (manufacturer is still liable only for the "enhancement" of the injuries flowing from the defect in the product if established by proof). But they are concurrent tortfeasors in the sense that their independent acts combine to cause a single injury.

In the case of *Richardson v. [Volkswagenwerk]*, A.G., 552 F.Supp. 73 (D.C., W.D.Mo.1982), the Court observed:

> "Other jurisdictions have followed orthodox tort principles set forth in *Restatement (Second) of Torts* §§ 433, 433A and 433B (1965) and hold that a plaintiff need not prove the nature and extent of the enhanced injuries but makes a submissible case by offering enough evidence of enhancement to present a jury issue. Defendants are deemed concurrent tortfeasors because their independent acts combined to cause a single injury. Under this theory, plaintiff has the burden of presenting sufficient evidence to prove to the jury that each defendant's act (the original tort-feasor's negligence and the manufacturer's defective product) was a *substantial* factor in producing the plaintiff's injuries. Should the plaintiff's injuries be indivisible, the defendants are held jointly and severally liable as concurrent tort-feasors for plaintiff's total damage. If reasonable minds could differ on whether the plaintiff's injuries are divisible, the trier of fact determines whether the injury can be reasonably apportioned among the defendants and the extent of each defendant's liability. *Mitchell v. Volkswagenwerk, A.G.*[,] 669 F.2d 1199 (8th Cir. Feb. 8, 1982); *Fietzer v. Ford Motor Co.*, 590 F.2d 215, 218 (7th Cir.1978); *Fox v. Ford Motor Co.*, 575 F.2d 774, 787–788 (10th Cir.1978); *Lahocki v. Contee Sand & Gravel Co., Inc.*, 41 Md.App. 579, 398 A.2d 490, 501 (1979)." (Emphasis added.)

We subscribe to the above-quoted language, except that we are of the opinion that the following language more correctly reflects our determination of the law: Under this theory, plaintiff has the burden of presenting sufficient evidence to prove to the jury that each defendant's act was a *contributing* (not *substantial*) factor in producing the plaintiff's injuries.

In our opinion, Lee did offer sufficient evidence to meet his general burden of proof and to withstand a motion for directed verdict. Plaintiff offered testimony that his cervical fracture was caused by the defective door latch's failure to operate and his subsequent contact with the road. The plaintiff offered medical testimony that showed that the plaintiff's injuries more likely than not occurred as a result of the collision with the ground. Testimony also included expert witnesses who testified there were other door latches available that operated in a safer manner.

Volkswagen, of course, offered testimony to dispute these conclusions, but it is that very dispute that required such factual issues to be submitted to the jury; and the weight to be accorded testimony was within the province of the jury to decide.

Having thus met the overall burden of proof imposed upon him, and the principal injury complained of being single and indivisible, the burden of proving that plaintiff's single injury was solely the result of Guffey's negligence and not attributable to the manufacturer's defective product then shifted to Volkswagen. * * *

[The court discussed the jury instructions given by the trial judge. It concluded that they were not prejudicially erroneous.]

* * *

Having found no reversible error, the judgment of the trial court is affirmed.

AFFIRMED.

LAVENDER, DOOLIN, HARGRAVE and OPALA, JJ., and WILSON, (CHAS.), SP.J., concur.

SIMMS, V.C.J., concurs in result.

* * *

Restatement of The Law (Second), Torts (1965)

§ 433A. Apportionment of Harm to Causes

(1) Damages for harm are to be apportioned among two or more causes where

(a) there are distinct harms, or

(b) there is a reasonable basis for determining the contribution of each cause to a single harm.

(2) Damages for any other harm cannot be apportioned among two or more causes.

See Reporter's Notes

Comment:

a. The rules stated in this Section apply whenever two or more causes have combined to bring about harm to the plaintiff, and each has been a substantial factor in producing the harm, as stated in §§ 431 and 433. They apply where each of the causes in question consists of the tortious conduct of a person; and it is immaterial whether all or any of such persons are joined as defendants in the particular action. The rules stated apply also where one or more of the contributing causes is an innocent one, as where the negligence of a defendant combines with the innocent conduct of another person, or with the operation of a force of nature, or with a pre-existing condition which the defendant has not caused, to bring about the harm to the plaintiff. The rules stated apply also where one of the causes in question is the conduct of the plaintiff himself, whether it be negligent or innocent.

Comment on Subsection (1):

b. Distinct harms. There are other results which, by their nature, are more capable of apportionment. If two defendants independently shoot the plaintiff at the same time, and one wounds him in the arm and the other in the leg, the ultimate result may be a badly damaged plaintiff in the hospital, but it is still possible, as a logical, reasonable, and practical matter, to regard the two wounds as separate injuries, and as distinct wrongs. The mere coincidence in time does not make the two wounds a single harm, or the conduct of the two defendants one tort. There may be difficulty in the apportionment of some elements of damages, such as the pain and suffering resulting from the two wounds, or the medical expenses, but this does not mean that one defendant must be liable for the distinct harm inflicted by the other. It is possible to make a rough estimate which will fairly apportion such subsidiary elements of damages.

c. *Successive injuries.* The harm inflicted may be conveniently severable in point of time. Thus if two defendants, independently operating the same plant, pollute a stream over successive periods, it is clear that each has caused a separate amount of harm, limited in time, and that neither has any responsibility for the harm caused by the other.

It should be noted that there are situations in which the earlier wrongdoer may be liable for the entire damage, while the later one will not. Thus an original tortfeasor may be liable not only for the harm which he has himself inflicted, but also for the additional damages resulting from the negligent treatment of the injury by a physician. (See § 457.) The physician, on the other hand, has played no part in causing the original injury, and will be liable only for the additional harm caused by his own negligence in treatment. There may be many other cases in which the original wrongdoer is liable for the additional harm caused by the intervening negligence of the later one, while the latter is liable only for what he has himself caused.

* * *

§ 433B. Burden of Proof

(1) Except as stated in Subsections (2) and (3), the burden of proof that the tortious conduct of the defendant has caused the harm to the plaintiff is upon the plaintiff.

(2) Where the tortious conduct of two or more actors has combined to bring about harm to the plaintiff, and one or more of the actors seeks to limit his liability on the ground that the harm is capable of apportionment among them, the burden of proof as to the apportionment is upon each such actor.

(3) Where the conduct of two or more actors is tortious, and it is proved that harm has been caused to the plaintiff by only one of them, but there is uncertainty as to which one has caused it, the burden is upon each such actor to prove that he has not caused the harm.

Notes

1. The question of proof of causation in enhanced injury cases has perplexed the courts. A majority of recent cases have treated the issue as being analogous to the problem of apportioning damages among joint tortfeasors. They generally have placed the burden of proof of apportionment on

the defendant. *E.g.,* Mitchell v. Volkswagenwerk, A.G., 669 F.2d 1199 (8th Cir.1982). A smaller number of courts follow *Huddell v. Levin,* discussed in the main case, and place of burden of proof on plaintiff. *E.g.,* Caiazzo v. Volkswagenwerk, A.G., 647 F.2d 241 (2d Cir.1981) noted in 47 Alb.L.Rev. 560 (1983) and 48 Brooklyn L.Rev. 177 (1981).

2. One of the reasons that this presents such a difficult problem is because of the close relationship between proof of defect and proof of causation in many of these cases. Manufacturers must design products in such a way as to avoid the risk of unreasonably enhancing injuries in the event of an accident. In some cases it may not be possible to prove that the product's design creates an unreasonable risk of enhancing injuries without proving that it enhanced plaintiff's injuries. *Huddell v. Levin* raises this problem. It is difficult to determine whether the design of a head restraint is unreasonable without knowing how much harm the design caused, and comparing this to the amount of harm that would have been caused by an alternative design. In such cases, shifting the burden of proof on the question of enhancement of injury may also have the practical effect of shifting the burden of proof on the question of defect. *Lee v. Volkswagen of America, Inc.* is an example of an enhanced injury case that does not present this problem. Presumably, one could determine whether the door latch was defective independently of whether plaintiff suffered enhanced injuries. *See* Note, Second Collision Liability: A Critique of Two Approaches to Plaintiff's Burden of Proof, 68 Iowa L.Rev. 811 (1983).

3. In addition to the note cited above, *see* Harris, Enhanced Injury Theory: An Analytic Framework, 62 N.C.L.Rev. 643 (1984); Hoenig, Resolution of "Crashworthiness" Design Claims, 55 St. John's L.Rev. 633 (1981); Levenstam and Lapp, Plaintiff's Burden of Proving Enhanced Injury in Crashworthiness Cases: A Clash Worthy of Analysis, 38 DePaul L.Rev. 55 (1988); Tietz, Bushman, and Podraza, Crashworthiness and *Erie* : Determining State Law Regarding the Burden of Proving and Apportioning Damages, 62 Temp.L.Rev. 587 (1989); Editorial Note, Litigating Enhanced Injury Cases: Complex Issues, Empty Precedents, and Unpredictable Results, 54 U.Cin.L.Rev. 1257 (1986); Note, Apportionment of Damages in the "Second Collision" Case, 63 Va.L.Rev. 475 (1977).

3. LINKING THE DEFENDANT TO THE PRODUCT

MULCAHY v. ELI LILLY & CO.

Supreme Court of Iowa, 1986.
386 N.W.2d 67.

SCHULTZ, JUSTICE.

* * *

The plaintiffs Linda Mulcahy and Michael Mulcahy seek damages personally and as natural guardians for their two children. In 1949 Cleo Rorman was prescribed and ingested DES during her pregnancy with Linda Mulcahy. Plaintiffs allege Linda sustained injury by *in utero* exposure to DES. Further, they claim such exposure caused Linda to give birth prematurely to her two children in 1973 and 1976 and that they sustained injury as a result.

Plaintiffs commenced their action in the United States District Court for the Northern District of Iowa. They filed suit against 25 companies alleged to have manufactured and marketed DES at the time of the ingestion. Plaintiffs have set forth theories of recovery against the defendants based upon strict liability, negligence, misrepresentation, breach of warranties, alternate liability, enterprise liability, market share liability, and concert of action. The record reflects that only three defendants sold DES in Ames, Iowa, in 1949; however, plaintiffs request we assess industry-wide liability against all defendants.

All defendants filed motions for summary judgment in federal district court arguing that there was no evidence as to which defendant marketed or manufactured the DES which Mrs. Rorman ingested. The federal district court reserved ruling on the motions of the three companies that had sales in Ames, Iowa, but held that summary judgment in favor of the remaining defendants would be appropriate "unless Iowa law permits imposition of liability on a defendant without evidence that the defendant manufactured or marketed the particular product that is alleged to have caused the injury." Pursuant to Iowa Code chapter 684A and Iowa Rules of Appellate Procedure 451–61, the federal district court certified [the following] questions of law to us * * *.

a. In a DES product liability case when a product has been ingested by a user and when, after exhaustive discovery, and through no fault of any party, the manufacturer or seller of the ingested product cannot be positively identified, will Iowa law recognize any of the following theories of liability:

(1) Market share liability;

(2) Alternative liability; and

(3) Enterprise liability?

b. If Iowa law will recognize any of these theories of recovery when the product ingested and its manufacturer or seller cannot be positively identified,

(1) What must the plaintiff prove before the burden of proof and/or production shifts to the defendant manufacturers or sellers; and

(2) What must a manufacturer or seller demonstrate to exculpate itself from liability?

We note preliminarily that a plaintiff in a products liability action must ordinarily prove that a manufacturer or supplier produced, provided or was in some way responsible for the particular product that caused the injury. *See Osborn v. Massey–Ferguson, Inc.*, 290 N.W.2d 893, 901 (Iowa 1980); *see also* Restatement (Second) of Torts §§ 402A, 433B (1965); W. Prosser, *The Law of Torts* § 98 (4th ed. 1971). In the present action plaintiffs rely on theories which would be exceptions to the rule that a plaintiff must show a causal connection between the defendant's product and plaintiff's injury. Such theories advanced by plaintiffs would allow recovery without proof of which drug company actually manufactured or supplied the DES ingested by Mrs. Rorman.

We proceed to the federal court's question "a" and to the three theories specified there, considering them in reverse order. In addressing the questions posed, we restrict our answers to the facts provided with the certified questions or referred to in our answers. We neither suggest nor foreclose adoption of any of these theories under other circumstances.

I. *Enterprise liability.* Enterprise liability, also termed "industry-wide liability," *see, e.g., Starling v. Seaboard Coast Line Railroad,* 533 F.Supp. 183, 187 (S.D.Ga.1982); *Zafft v. Eli Lilly & Co.,* 676 S.W.2d 241, 245 (Mo.1984), was first advanced in *Hall v. E.I. Du Pont De Nemours & Co.,* 345 F.Supp. 353 (E.D.N.Y.1972). *Hall* was summarized as follows in *Morton v. Abbott Laboratories,* 538 F.Supp. 593, 598 (M.D.Fla.1982):

> Like concert of action, plaintiff's second theory—enterprise liability—would impose liability on each DES manufacturer on the basis of their group conduct. The concept of enterprise, or industry-wide, liability derives from Judge Weinstein's opinion in *Hall v. Du Pont De Nemours & Co.,* 345 F.Supp. 353 (E.D.N.Y.1972). In that case, 13 children sued six blasting cap manufacturers alleging that they had been injured in explosions of the caps. Although the six defendants were not the only possible sources of blasting caps, they did comprise virtually the entire blasting cap industry in this country. Plaintiffs based their claim on the practices of that industry in failing to take reasonable safety precautions and make reasonable warnings. They alleged that members of the industry had adhered to industry-wide safety standards and had delegated substantial safety investigation and design functions to their trade association.

> The *Hall* court focused on the joint conduct of the defendants, finding that their joint control of the risk presented by their industry warranted the imposition of joint liability. *Id.* at 371–76. The facts in this DES case in no way suggest application of *Hall's* theory of joint liability. In *Hall* there were six manufacturers in the industry; here there were 149. Judge Weinstein limited his holding in *Hall* by warning against its application to a "decentralized" industry with many individual members. There was no industry-wide delegation of safety functions to a drug manufacturers' trade association; indeed, if there was any body responsible for safety in the drug industry it was the Food and Drug Administration.

A Pennsylvania court recently summarized the criteria necessary to establish enterprise liability in *Burnside v. Abbott Laboratories,* [351] Pa.Super. [264], [285], 505 A.2d 973, 984 (1985):

> (1) The injury-causing product was manufactured by one of a small number of defendants in an industry; (2) the defendants had

joint knowledge of the risks inherent in the product and possessed a joint capacity to reduce those risks; and (3) each of them failed to take steps to reduce the risk but, rather, delegated this responsibility to a trade association.

Were we to accept an enterprise theory of liability, the theory would not apply here. The first criteria in *Burnside,* that the product was manufactured by a small number of defendants in the industry, is not satisfied. Plaintiffs' petition names 25 companies as defendants because they allegedly manufactured and sold DES in 1949. We believe this is not a small number. The number of manufacturers and sellers named, however, may be conservative as revealed by the case law which refers to the DES industry between 1947 and 1971. *See Martin v. Abbott Laboratories,* 102 Wash.2d 581, 589, 689 P.2d 368, 374 (1984) ("The number of firms marketing DES has fluctuated considerably over the years. Estimates are that up to 200 or 300 companies manufactured and marketed DES between 1947 and 1971."); *see also Sindell v. Abbott Laboratories,* 26 Cal.3d 588, 609, 607 P.2d 924, 935, 163 Cal.Rptr. 132, 143 (1980) ("at least 200 manufacturers produced DES"); *Zafft,* 676 S.W.2d at 245 ("reject industry-wide liability in DES cases because of the large number of drug manufacturers involved"); *Collins v. Eli Lilly Company,* 116 Wis.2d 166, 186, 342 N.W.2d 37, 47 (1984) ("involves perhaps hundreds of potential defendant drug companies"). Based on the large number of manufacturers, the assumption underlying the enterprise concept—that defendants jointly control the risk—becomes "necessarily weak." *Collins,* 116 Wis.2d at 186, 342 N.W.2d at 47. The overall number of DES manufacturers mitigates against group conduct requiring imposition of liability on all for the acts of the unidentified wrongdoer.

Under the statement of facts provided us in this case, we are unable to decide whether the other criteria enumerated in *Burnside* have been satisfied. We note, however, that other courts have rejected enterprise liability in DES cases because these other criteria were not met. Unlike the blasting cap industry, DES manufacturers did not control their conduct by jointly imposed safety standards. *Burnside,* [351] Pa.Super. at [286], 505 A.2d at 985. Members of the DES industry did not delegate control or responsibility for safety functions to a trade association. *Id.* at [286], 505 A.2d at 985; *Morton,* 538 F.Supp. at 598; *Zafft,* 676 S.W.2d at 245. Instead, the Food and Drug Administration exercised pervasive regulation and control. *Sindell,* 26 Cal.3d at 609, 607 P.2d at 935, 163 Cal.Rptr. at 143; *Morton,* 538 F.Supp. at 598; *Zafft,* 676 S.W.2d at 245.

The enterprise liability theory avoids the legal causation problem that arises from an inability to identify the manufacturer of the specific injury-causing product. It does so by shifting responsibility to the industry for causing the injury because of the concert of action by manufacturers of such products through their trade associations or their collective action.

We agree with the court in *Martin* that "enterprise liability as described in *Hall* is predicated upon industry-wide cooperation of a much greater degree than occurred among DES manufacturers." 102 Wash.2d at 599, 689 P.2d at 380. We also agree with the following statement in *Morton*, 538 F.Supp. at 598:

> Accordingly, like the many other courts that have considered the question, this Court finds that the enterprise liability theory espoused in *Hall* cannot support liability in this DES case. *See, e.g., Ryan, supra* at 1017; *Namm v. Charles E. Frosst & Co.*, 178 N.J.Super. 19, 427 A.2d 1121, 1129 (N.J.App.Div.1981); *Sindell, supra*, 26 Cal.3d 588, 163 Cal.Rptr. at 141–42, 607 P.2d at 633–35.

We hold that the facts certified by the federal court in this proceeding are inappropriate for application of enterprise liability in any event.

II. *Alternative liability*. In contrast to the enterprise theory, "alternative liability" does address the problem of causation with respect to the making or the providing of the DES which brought about the injury. Although "alternate liability" also involves wrongful conduct by more than one party, the conduct of one of the parties must have caused the injury to plaintiff. Under this theory the burden of proof as to which actor caused the harm shifts to the defendants because there is uncertainty as to which of them caused the injury. *Morton*, 538 F.Supp. at 598 (citing Restatement (Second) of Torts § 433B(3) (1965)).

The general rule in Iowa, as elsewhere, is that a plaintiff has the burden of proving by a preponderance of the evidence that the defendant caused the complained of harm or injury. Iowa R.App.P. 14(f)(8); Restatement (Second) of Torts § 433B(1) (1965). Causation is an essential element in a tort action. *Iowa Electric Light & Power Co. v. General Electric Co.*, 352 N.W.2d 231, 234 (Iowa 1984). In a negligence action the causation requirement entails proof of a "causal connection between the defendant's alleged negligence and the injury." *Sponsler v. Clarke Electric Cooperative, Inc.*, 329 N.W.2d 663, 665 (Iowa 1983). In strict liability, plaintiff must establish inter alia "(1) manufacture of a product by defendant * * * [and] (6) said defect was the proximate cause of personal injuries." *Osborn*, 290 N.W.2d at 901.

The causation requirement necessarily involves two links in a case of this kind: first, that the defendant manufactured the DES ingested by the mother in question, and second, that the DES brought about injuries. *See* Prosser, *The Fall of the Citadel (Strict Liability to the Consumer)*, 50 Minn.L.Rev. 791, 840 (1966). We are only concerned here with the first link, the "identification" requirement. *Payton v. Abbott Labs*, 386 Mass. 540, 571, 437 N.E.2d 171, 188 (1982); *cf. McElhaney v. Eli Lilly & Co.*, 564 F.Supp. 265, 268 (D.S.D.1983) (In distinguishing the two elements: "Causation goes to the question of what instrumentality or mechanism caused the plaintiff's injury * * * whereas the issue here is the identity of the source of that instrumentality.").

The identification requirement is summarized thus in an annotation in 51 A.L.R.3d 1344, 1349 (1973):

> Regardless of the theory which liability is predicated upon * * * it is obvious that to hold a producer, manufacturer, or seller liable for injury caused by a particular product, there must first be proof that the defendant produced, manufactured, sold or was in some way responsible for the product. * * *

The "alternative liability" theory has been frequently proposed as a means of avoiding the identification problem. *E.g., Morton,* 538 F.Supp. at 595; *Ryan v. Eli Lilly & Co.,* 514 F.Supp. 1004, 1016 (D.S.C.1981); *Sindell,* 26 Cal.3d at 598, 607 P.2d at 928, 163 Cal.Rptr. at 136; *Abel v. Eli Lilly & Co.,* 418 Mich. 311, 325, 343 N.W.2d 164, 170 (1984); *Zafft,* 676 S.W.2d at 244. The American Law Institute succinctly states the theory in section 433B(3) of the Restatement (Second) of Torts (1965):

> Where the conduct of two or more actors is tortious, and it is proved that harm has been caused to the plaintiff by only one of them, but there is uncertainty as to which one has caused it, the burden is upon each such actor to prove that he has not caused the harm.

The basis for this exception is said to be

> the injustice of permitting proved wrongdoers, who among them have inflicted an injury upon the entirely innocent plaintiff, to escape liability merely because the nature of their conduct and the resulting harm has made it difficult or impossible to prove which of them has caused the harm.

Restatement (Second) of Torts § 433B(3) comment f. The theory has its roots in *Summers v. Tice,* 33 Cal.2d 80, 199 P.2d 1 (1948). The facts of *Summers* were summarized as follows in *Namm v. Charles E. Frosst & Co.,* 178 N.J.Super. 19, 32, 427 A.2d 1121, 1127–28 (App.Div.1981):

> [P]laintiff went hunting with the two defendants and specifically cautioned them to stay in line and be careful. However, when a bird was flushed, both defendants fired at it even though plaintiff Summers was directly in the line of fire and clearly visible. Summers was hit once in the eye and once in the lip. It was determined that both defendant hunters were negligent in firing their guns in the direction of plaintiff and that plaintiff could not identify which of the negligent defendants' shots hit him. The court shifted the burden of proof as to whose shot actually hit plaintiff to the two admittedly negligent hunters, the only possible tortfeasors.

See also Restatement (Second) of Torts § 433B(3) illustration 9.

Summers has generally been distinguished from the DES cases. *See, e.g., Sindell,* 26 Cal.3d at 602–03, 607 P.2d at 931, 163 Cal.Rptr. at 139; *Payton,* 386 Mass. at 572, 437 N.E.2d at 189; *Zafft,* 676 P.2d at 244; *Collins,* 116 Wis.2d at 183, 342 N.W.2d at 46. We agree with the majority of courts holding the "pure" alternative liability theory embodied in section 433B(3) "does not present a viable theory for DES cases."

Collins, 116 Wis.2d at 183, 342 N.W.2d at 46; *accord, Martin,* 102 Wash. at 595, 689 P.2d at 377. *See also Morton,* 538 F.Supp. at 598–99; *Ryan,* 514 F.Supp. at 1016; *Namm,* 178 N.J.Super. at 34, 427 A.2d at 1128; *Zafft,* 676 S.W.2d at 244. (We note that a contrary result was reached in *Ferrigno v. Eli Lilly & Co.,* 175 N.J.Super. 551, 420 A.2d 1305 (Law Div.1980). *Namm* expressly disagrees with *Ferrigno. Namm,* 178 N.J.Super. at 32, 427 A.2d at 1127 n. 3.)

An element of the alternative liability theory, the conduct of one of the parties caused the injury, is absent in the facts given to us. In the parent case of *Summers,* two defendants were in fact present and both discharged their guns in the plaintiff's direction. An analogous DES case might exist—a question we do not decide—if a plaintiff established that only two manufacturers' DES products were sold at a certain pharmacy, and the mother bought her DES only at that pharmacy but cannot identify which brand she purchased.

Plaintiffs argue that alternative liability is applicable here because they have limited the field to three defendants—Eli Lilly, Abbott, and Upjohn. They rely on "evidence that DES manufactured by Eli Lilly & Co. was available in at least one pharmacy in Ames, Iowa in 1949" and on their assertion that DES manufactured by Abbott and Upjohn "may have been available in one Ames, Iowa pharmacy in 1949." Assuming arguendo that plaintiffs have substantial evidence that DES from Lilly, Abbott, and Upjohn was marketed in Ames, Iowa, plaintiffs' *Summers* problem is that they do not possess evidence to negate marketing of DES in Ames by other manufacturers. To say that the three named companies constitute the only possible manufacturers of the DES Mrs. Rorman ingested is sheer speculation; any number of other manufacturers may have supplied DES to the Ames market. As stated in *Namm,* 178 N.J.Super. at 33, 427 A.2d at 1128:

> The application of the principle of alternative liability to any one or all of the [named] defendants herein would impose liability without fault upon any one who manufactured a product manufactured by others as well. It would result in the taking of the property of all the named defendants in order to pay for harm which may have been caused by only one of the defendants, or even by one who is not a party to the lawsuit, who is unknown to the defendants, over whom they have no control or even any meaningful contact.

A decision frequently cited as applying the alternative liability theory in the DES context is *Abel v. Eli Lilly & Co.,* 418 Mich. 311, 343 N.W.2d 164 (1984). On a motion to dismiss, the Michigan Supreme Court held that the plaintiffs stated a cause of action based on the theory of alternative liability. *Id.* at 339, 343 N.W.2d at 177. The court noted several significant differences between *Summers* and the factual situation involving DES. Despite these differences, the court fashioned a "DES-modified alternative liability" theory "to accommodate the unique facts of this unusual litigation." *Id.* at 329, 343 N.W.2d at 172. The *Abel* court's version still requires plaintiffs to prove they have been harmed by the conduct of one of the defendants—requiring plaintiffs to "bring before the court all the actors who may have caused the injury in fact." *Id.* at 331, 343 N.W.2d at 173. Plaintiffs also have the burden of showing that all the defendants have acted tortiously, and that plaintiffs, through no fault of their own, are unable to identify which actor caused the injury. *Id.* For the reasons we have stated regarding the inapplicability of the alternative liability theory to this case, we decline to follow *Abel.*

We hold that alternative liability is inapplicable under the facts presented to us.

III. *Market share liability.* Some courts have structured new theories to overcome one of the problems encountered in applying alternative liability in DES cases—failure to have all possible producers before the court. *See, e.g., Sindell v. Abbott Laboratories,* 26 Cal.3d 588, 607 P.2d 924, 163 Cal.Rptr. 132 (1980); *Martin v. Abbott Laboratories,* 102 Wash.2d 581, 689 P.2d 368 (1984); *Collins v. Eli Lilly Co.,* 116 Wis.2d 166, 342 N.W.2d 37 (1984).

The California Supreme Court in *Sindell* discussed the need for a cause of action for injured plaintiffs:

> In our contemporary complex industrialized society, advances in science and technology create fungible goods which may harm consumers and which cannot be traced to any specific producer. The response of the courts can be either to adhere rigidly to prior doctrine, denying recovery to those injured by such products, or to fashion remedies to meet these changing needs.

26 Cal.3d at 610, 607 P.2d at 936, 163 Cal.Rptr. at 144.

The court cited the "most persuasive" policy reason supporting a remedy was that "as between an innocent plaintiff and negligent defendants, the latter should bear the cost of the injury." *Id.* at 610–11, 607 P.2d at 936, 163 Cal.Rptr. at 144. Further, the court relied on a "broader policy standpoint" that "defendants are better able to bear the cost of injury resulting from the manufacture of a defective product." *Id.* at 611, 607 P.2d at 936, 163 Cal.Rptr. at 144.

The "market share" theory, fashioned in *Sindell,* apportions liability among defendants based on their respective shares of the "relevant" market. The plaintiff must first join "the manufacturers of a substantial share of the DES which her mother might have taken," and also meet her burden as to all other elements. *Id.* at 612, 607 P.2d at 937, 163 Cal.Rptr. at 145. The burden of proof then shifts to the defendants to demonstrate they could not have manufactured the DES that caused the plaintiff's injuries. *Id.* If a defendant fails to meet this burden, the court fashions a "market share" theory to apportion damages according to the likelihood that any of defendants supplied the product by holding each defendant liable "for the proportion of the judgment represented by its share of that market." *Id.* The intended result under this approach is that "each manufacturer's liability for an injury would be approximately equivalent to the damage caused by the DES it manufactured." *Id.* at 613, 607 P.2d at 938, 163 Cal.Rptr. at 146. The market share theory was approved by a federal district court as expressing South Dakota law, in *McElhaney v. Eli Lilly & Co.*, 564 F.Supp. 265, 271 (D.S.D.1983). *See also Zafft*, 676 S.W.2d at 247 (Gunn, J., dissenting).

The Washington and Wisconsin Supreme Courts also advocate a modification of alternative liability based on substantially the same policy considerations. *Martin*, 102 Wash.2d at 603, 689 P.2d at 381; *Collins*, 116 Wis.2d at 189, 342 N.W.2d at 48. They add that all manufacturers and distributors of DES "contributed to the *risk* of injury to the public and, consequently the risk of injury to individual plaintiffs," and therefore share a degree of culpability. *Collins*, 116 Wis.2d at 191, 342 N.W.2d at 49; *accord Martin*, 102 Wash.2d 604, 689 P.2d 382. The approaches of these two jurisdictions differ from the *Sindell* market share theory only in the apportionment of damages.

The Washington court, finding the *Sindell* theory distorts liability because only a substantial share of likely defendants share all of the damages, developed an approach termed the "market-share alternate liability." *Martin*, 102 Wash.2d at 602, 689 P.2d at 381. Application of this theory permits a plaintiff to commence an action against only one defendant and requires the plaintiff to establish by a preponderance of the evidence that the defendant produced or marketed the type of DES ingested by the plaintiff's mother. *Id.* at 604, 689 P.2d at 382. A defendant may bring in other defendants. Damages are allocated initially by presuming that each defendant has an equal share. Defendants are entitled to rebut this presumption by establishing their respective market share in plaintiff's geographic area, thus reducing their potential liability. *Id.* at 605–06, 689 P.2d at 383. If the defendants are able to establish their market share, they are only liable for that percentage of the total judgment. Other defendants who fail to establish their relevant market share are liable for a readjusted, equal share of the remaining damages. *Id.* at 606, 689 P.2d at 383. *See also McCormack v. Abbott*, 617 F.Supp. 1521 (D.Mass.1985) (adopting *Martin* approach which the federal court held was consistent with Massachusetts court's guidelines in *Payton v. Abbott*, 386 Mass. 540, 437 N.E.2d 171 (1982)).

The Wisconsin court, finding that "unalloyed market share theory does not constitute the most desirable course to follow in DES cases because the theory, while conceptually attractive, is limited in practical applicability," fashioned what is frequently termed the "risk contribution theory." *Collins*, 116 Wis.2d at 189, 342 N.W.2d at 48. Under this theory, as in *Martin*, the plaintiff is only required to sue one defendant and to allege the defendant produced or marketed the type of DES taken by the plaintiff's mother. If only one defendant is sued and no others are impleaded by the defendant, that defendant is liable for all of the damages. *Id.* at 193, 342 N.W.2d at 50. If more than one defendant is joined or impleaded, damages are determined according to the jury's assignment of liability under Wisconsin's comparative negligence statute. *Id.* at 199, 342 N.W.2d at 52–53. The court lists several factors that the jury should consider in apportioning damages among the defendants. *Id.* at 200, 342 N.W.2d at 53.

We reject the market share liability theory on a broad policy basis. We acknowledge that plaintiff in a DES case with an unidentified product manufacturer presents an appealing claim for relief. Endeavoring to provide relief, courts have developed theories which in one way or another provided plaintiffs recovery of loss by a kind of court-constructed insurance plan. The result is that manufacturers are required to pay or contribute to payment for injuries which their product may not have caused.

This may or may not be a desirable result. We believe, however, that awarding damages to an admitted innocent party by means of a court-constructed device that places liability on manufacturers who were not proved to have caused the injury involves social engineering more appropriately within the legislative domain. In order to reach such a determination, three broad policy questions must be answered. One is whether the burden of damages for these injuries should be transferred in a constitutional manner to the industry irrespective of an individual manufacturer's connection with the particular injury. If so, the second question relates to the principles and procedures by which the burden would be transferred. Finally, how do we ascertain the extent of damages to be assessed against each manufacturer? As to the latter, we note a wide divergency of solutions advanced by courts in fashioning relief without the benefit of legislation.

Our General Assembly has not entered this field, and we in the judicial branch adhere to our established principles of legal cause. *Starling v. Seaboard Coast Line Railroad,* 533 F.Supp. 183, 190 (S.D.Ga. 1982); *Zafft v. Eli Lilly & Co.,* 676 S.W.2d 241, 247 (Mo.1984). *Cf. Mizell v. Eli Lilly & Co.,* 526 F.Supp. 589 (D.S.C.1981) (relying on *Ryan,* 514 F.Supp. 1004, court rejects *Sindell* market share theory as choice of law because it violates public policy of the forum). A commentator in the field of negligence has stated, "Proof of negligence in the air, so to speak, will not do." F. Pollock, *The Law of Torts* 455 (11th ed. 1920). Plaintiffs request that we make a substantial departure from our fundamental negligence requirement of proving causation, without previous warning or guidelines. The imposition of liability upon a manufacturer for harm that it may not have caused is the very legal legerdemain, at least by our long held traditional standards, that we believe the courts should avoid unless prior warnings remain unheeded. It is an act more closely identified as a function assigned to the legislature under its power to enact laws.

We hold correspondingly that under Iowa common law a plaintiff in a products liability case must prove that the injury-causing product was a product manufactured or supplied by the defendant. We reserve for later consideration the case which involves actual concert of action by the defendants and the case which is genuinely factually analogous to

Summers v. Tice, 33 Cal.2d 80, 199 P.2d 1 (1948). This proceeding does not present such facts.

We thus answer certified question "a" in the negative. Certified question "b" requires no answer.

CERTIFIED QUESTION ANSWERED.

All Justices concur except LAVORATO, J., who takes no part.

Note

McCormack v. Abbott Laboratories, 617 F.Supp. 1521 (D.Mass.1985), predicted that Massachusetts would adopt the form of market share liability fashioned in Martin v. Abbott Laboratories, 102 Wash.2d 581, 689 P.2d 368 (1984). The court offered the following justification for the doctrine:

> The emergence of a market-share theory of liability in American jurisprudence stems from the recognition by several courts that the field of products liability has been changed drastically with the advent of mass production of fungible goods and complex marketing methods. Consumers may be harmed by a product not traceable to a specific producer. Clearly, the traditional tests of liability are insufficient to govern the obligations of manufacturer to consumer in such situations, and some adaptation of the rules of causation and liability seems appropriate.

> Lack of identification evidence in DES cases is rarely attributable to any fault on the part of the plaintiff. Rather, it results from the fact that DES was, for the most part, produced in a "generic" form which lacked any identifying markings. DES was a fungible drug produced by as many as 300 drug companies from a chemically identical formula. Secondly, courts have suggested that pharmacies and drug companies have contributed to the dearth of identification evidence by not keeping or not being able to locate pertinent records. Lastly, the very fact that DES is a drug whose effects are delayed for many years has played a significant role in the unavailability of proof. See, e.g., Sindell v. Abbott Laboratories, 1980, 26 Cal.3d 588, 163 Cal.Rptr. 132, 607 P.2d 924; Martin v. Abbott Laboratories, 1984, 102 Wash.2d 581, 689 P.2d 368.

> Additionally, one of the functions of the identification requirement—separating wrongdoers from innocent actors—is of minor importance in the situation before this court. By producing and marketing an allegedly defective drug, all the defendants contributed to the risk of injury to the public and consequently, the risk of injury to individual plaintiffs. Under the market-share theory, a plaintiff must still prove that the defendants were negligent before the court may proceed to apportion damages on the basis of market share. Thus, none of the defendants can be considered truly innocent actors. Although the defendants may not have caused the actual injury of a given plaintiff, each may be shown to share, in some measure, a degree of culpability in producing and marketing DES. Furthermore, the court, while recognizing that the identification requirement also serves to protect defendants from being held liable for more harm than they have caused, believes that a market-share theory of liability, if properly fashioned, will not

subject a particular defendant to liability for more harm than it statistically could have caused in the relevant market.

Finally, the magnitude of the physical and psychological injuries which are at issue in DES cases counsels toward permitting a remedy under some form of a market-share theory of liability. As between the injured plaintiff and the possibly responsible drug company, the latter is in a better position to absorb the cost of the injury. The company can insure itself against liability, absorb the damage award, or distribute it among the public as a cost of doing business, thereby spreading the cost over all consumers. In many cases, the only alternative will be to place the burden solely on the injured plaintiff. Comment, "Market Share Liability: An Answer to the DES Causation Problem," 94 Harv.L.Rev. 668 (1981).

617 F.Supp. at 1525–26.

GEORGE v. PARKE–DAVIS
Supreme Court of Washington, En Banc, 1987.
107 Wash.2d 584, 733 P.2d 507.

DORE, JUSTICE.

The federal district court in Spokane certified seven questions to this court regarding a tort claim filed by Kathleen George against the defendant DES manufacturers and distributors. These questions focus on how liability should be apportioned among the defendants, and ask for explanation and clarification of this court's decision in *Martin v. Abbott Labs.*, 102 Wash.2d 581, 689 P.2d 368 (1984).

In *Martin,* we developed the theory of market share alternate liability. Under this theory, a plaintiff can state a cause of action for injuries associated with her mother's ingestion of DES by suing one or more DES manufacturers and alleging the following: (1) her mother took DES, (2) the DES caused her subsequent injuries, (3) the defendant or defendants produced or marketed the type of DES taken by her mother, and (4) this production or marketing of DES constituted the breach of a recognized legal duty to the plaintiff. *Martin,* at 604, 689 P.2d 368. Individual defendants can exculpate themselves if they can establish that for whatever reason they did not market the DES which could have caused the plaintiff's injuries. If the defendants cannot exculpate themselves from liability then they are presumed to have equal market shares unless they can establish their actual market share in the relevant geographic market. *Martin,* at 605–06, 689 P.2d 368. If any defendant can establish its actual market share, then this figure, rather than the presumptive share, controls.

George contends she was injured because of DES ingested by her mother. The federal court has certified seven questions to discuss liability apportionment among defendants in light of *Martin.*

* * *

QUESTION THREE

In defining the geographic market for the purposes of establishing actual market shares of the defendants, should a nationwide market be used, and market share be calculated on the basis of nationwide data regarding product distribution, or should the market share of the defendants be determined based upon sales only in the local market, *e.g.,* the particular pharmacy or pharmacies or city in which plaintiff's mother allegedly bought her DES (depending on the specificity of her proof), with actual market share calculated on the basis of evidence of distribution to that particular local market? Does the result change if data is unavailable to establish the extent of defendants' participation in a local market?

In *Martin,* we held that drug companies producing DES would not be liable if

> they did not produce or market the particular type DES taken by the plaintiff's mother; that they did not market the DES in the geographic market area of plaintiff mother's obtaining the drug; or that they did not distribute DES in the [proper] time period * * *.

Martin, 102 Wash.2d at 605, 689 P.2d 368. This statement requires that the relevant market for determining liability be as narrow as possible. Thus, in this case, in which the plaintiff's mother allegedly purchased the DES in one pharmacy in Idaho, that particular pharmacy should be the relevant market. This definition is in keeping with the overall purpose of "market-share alternate liability": the imposition of liability only on those companies who potentially could have manufactured the drug which caused the injuries.

We recognize, however, that our adoption of a very small market for determining liability makes the determination of defendants' actual market shares in some cases very difficult if not impossible. We are dealing with events which occurred decades ago, and the relevant records may have been lost, the pharmacies may have gone out of business, and the witnesses may have forgotten which brand of DES was used. This, of course, will not always be the case. If there does exist evidence which with sufficient probability yields accurate market share figures in the plaintiff's particular geographic market, these figures should be used to the exclusion of any other data. If these figures do not exist, however, then other figures, such as distribution figures within the county, state, or even in the country may in certain circumstances be introduced.

We are cognizant that even the national set of figures for DES may not reliably reflect the true distribution of that drug to the relevant geographic market. We are not in a position to decide in this case, or in any case because of the varying geographic markets and local data available, whether the national figures are sufficiently accurate to justify their use. This is not a novel situation. Judges are often required to determine if the evidence presented is sufficiently representative and material to meet the relevancy thresholds of Rules of Evidence 401 and 402. This determination of whether the evidence is relevant will be left to the trial court's discretion as it is in the best position to decide in each case whether the national or regional figures are a good approximation for the relevant geographic market. *Ladley v. St. Paul Fire & Marine Ins. Co.,* 73 Wash.2d 928, 442 P.2d 983 (1968).

National figures should therefore be admitted when the trial court determines that they tend to establish an accurate approximation of the drug companies' local market shares. We note, however, that the finder of fact may discount the value of these figures, especially if a combination of local, regional and national data is available. The fact finder must decide what the defendants' market shares are and if the drug companies' admissible evidence does not satisfactorily establish what their market shares are, then the pro rata presumptions described in *Martin* will apply. *See Martin,* 102 Wash.2d at 605–06, 689 P.2d 368.

QUESTION FOUR

Should the market shares of the respective defendants be calculated by comparing the number of DES pills of the pertinent dosage and type sold during the period of ingestion in the relevant market, or by comparing the total milligrams of DES sold during that time in that market, or revenue from the sale of said DES, or some other standard of measurement?

The purpose of the market share alternate liability is to hold liable only those drug companies which potentially could have manufactured the DES taken by the plaintiff's mother, and only in the proportion in which it manufactured the DES that could have caused the injury. In a case such as this one, in which the defendant only took 25 milligram tablets, the best measure of market share would therefore be based on a comparison of the number of pills of that dosage and type sold by the drug manufacturers during the relevant time period. Any other basis of measurement would tend to distort the amount of DES manufactured by the drug companies which actually could have caused the plaintiff's injuries.

Nevertheless, not all cases will have such simple facts. A plaintiff's mother could have taken a variety of dosages or a combination of different pills to arrive at the same dosage. Furthermore, some drug companies may not have accurate records for the number of pills manufactured, but do have reliable figures on the total number of milligrams produced or revenue generated from their DES production. In these cases, if the trial judge determines that those figures are sufficiently reliable to meet the evidence rule relevancy threshold for admissibility, then that information may also be used to calculate market share. Again, however, the drug companies have the burden of establishing their market shares, and if the figures they present are viewed as too speculative by either the judge in a relevancy determination or are discounted as inaccurate or unrepresentative by the fact finder at trial, then the pro rata formula in *Martin* applies. *See Martin,* at 605–06, 689 P.2d 368.

QUESTION FIVE

For the purposes of calculating actual and presumptive market share of a defendant DES manufacturer, should consideration be made of the shares of DES manufacturers who could not have been exculpated from the lawsuit under *Martin,* but have been dismissed on the basis of successor nonliability, or are defunct, or otherwise unavailable as defendants for reasons of bankruptcy, receivership and/or insolvency, or otherwise?

The plaintiff in this case urges us to reconsider the part of our holding in *Martin,* in which liability is held to be several, rather than joint and several. Thus, in a case in which the only two defendants can establish that they each had 30 percent of market share, the plaintiff would recover 60 percent from those two defendants and have the remaining 40 percent uncompensated. This, the plaintiff argues is unfair, and would be avoided if the court would adopt joint and several liability.

This result was specifically considered and rejected by *Martin,* at 600–02, 689 P.2d 368. The result, which may have been countenanced by the California Supreme Court in *Sindell v. Abbott Labs.,* 26 Cal.3d 588, 607 P.2d 924, 163 Cal.Rptr. 132, *cert. denied,* 449 U.S. 912, 101 S.Ct. 285, 66 L.Ed.2d 140 (1980) was rejected because it distorts liability in favor of the plaintiff. We believe that our prior reasoning was correct and see no reason to modify that part of the decision in *Martin.*

Furthermore, we believe that the fact that a corporation is bankrupt, defunct or otherwise unamenable to suit should have no impact in determining actual market shares. Under traditional rules of tort recovery, the mere lack of amenability to suit did not relieve a company from liability. The plaintiff who could not recover from a tortfeasor could not obtain compensation from another tortfeasor unless liability was joint and several. Thus, applying these rules to this case, an insolvent drug company which distributed DES to the relevant market should be calculated in the market share analysis. That the plaintiff will not receive damages because the judgment will be unsatisfied is a problem facing all plaintiffs.

The previous analysis covers those cases in which all defendant drug manufacturers establish their actual market share. The cornerstone of market share alternate liability is that if a defendant can establish its actual market share, it will not be liable under any circumstances for more than that percentage of the plaintiff's total injuries. If a defendant establishes that its actual market share was 5 percent, and the plaintiff's injuries were $100,000, then the defendant would always be liable for $5,000, irrespective of other defendant's actual or presumptive shares.

However, if the defendants cannot establish their actual market share, then the presumptive pro rata liability formula announced in *Martin* is used. A problem unfortunately develops when we consider the effect defunct corporations would have when liability is calculated by presumptive shares. If defendant drug corporations could file third party complaints against defunct corporations, then the viable drug corporations would reduce their pro rata share as more defendants would be proportionally responsible for the plaintiff's damage award. The additional shares would not be recovered by the plaintiff, as the new defendants would be judgment proof. Thus, presumptive liability under the *Martin* approach would be a vehicle by which the defendants could reduce their own liability while at the same time requiring the plaintiff to absorb the presumptive liability of these newly added defunct corporations. This is neither fair nor equitable.

We therefore order the application of the following method to reduce the likelihood that this sort of abuse will occur. If the defendants implead a third party defendant who for whatever reason is not amenable to suit, then the impleading defendants have the burden of establishing the actual market share of the impleaded defendant. If this actual damage can be calculated, then it should be included in the market share calculations. Because we have rejected joint and several liability, the other viable drug companies do not have to pay for its damages. The plaintiff simply will not recover those damages. However, a defendant should not be able to use the presumptions of liability as a sword to reduce its liability by impleading third party defendants who are not amenable to suit, and whose market shares cannot be calculated. Otherwise, a potential for abuse is possible, and the viable defendants would be more interested in joining insolvent corporations to lower their share of presumptive liability than establishing their actual market shares.

The preceding rules can best be illustrated by an example. Assume a plaintiff, who has suffered $100,000 worth of damages, sues two viable drug companies, A and B. A can establish its actual market share was 20 percent, while B cannot establish its actual market share and must rely on the pro rata presumptions established in *Martin*. In order to reduce its liability, B impleads third party drug manufacturers C, D and E. C is a viable company which cannot establish its actual market share and which must rely on the pro rata presumption of *Martin*. D is not amenable to suit, but it is established that its actual market share is 10 percent. E is not amenable to suit and its actual market share *cannot* be calculated. The following chart represents the liabilities of the various parties:

Drug Company	Percent Liable	Total Liability	Plaintiff's Recovery
A	20	$20,000	$20,000
B	35	35,000	35,000
C	35	35,000	35,000
D	10	10,000	0
E	0	(not a proper defendant)	

TOTAL PLAINTIFF RECOVERY $90,000

A is liable for 20 percent on the basis of its actual market share. D is liable for 10 percent on the basis of its actual market share, but because it is judgment proof, the plaintiff cannot collect the $10,000. B and C are presumptively liable for the remaining $70,000, and must split this liability pro rata so that they are each liable for $35,000. E is not a proper defendant, both because it is unamenable to suit and because its actual market share cannot be calculated. The plaintiff will recover only $90,000 of her damages, because she cannot recover the $10,000 judgment against drug company D.

QUESTION SIX

Under *Martin* and the Washington Tort Reform Act, RCW 4.22, is a bulk supplier of raw diethylstilbestrol liable in a product liability action for indemnification and/or contribution to a tableter of DES, *i.e.,* a pharmaceutical company which processes the raw DES by adding various binders and other inert ingredients, makes tablets of various dosages, and packages the DES with its own directions and warnings, assuming that said tableter is found liable to a plaintiff for injuries sustained *in utero* by a fetus whose mother ingested the DES sold to the tableter by the bulk supplier? Does the result differ if the bulk supplier also distributed its own DES at retail, with its own directions and warnings?

The factual background to this question is as follows. Stanley Drug Company has asserted that Eli Lilly Drug Company supplied it with the DES it used to make 25 mg tablets. Eli Lilly apparently also made 25 mg tablets, but sold them for a greater wholesale price than the plaintiff's mother had paid for the pills. Thus, Eli Lilly had exculpated itself from liability. The plaintiff has requested this court to allow her to sue Eli Lilly as manufacturer and Stanley has submitted a claim against Eli Lilly for contribution and indemnity. Stanley and the plaintiff, in essence, ask this court to create *vertical* liability between the manufacturer of DES and the distributor, in addition to the horizontal liability which *Martin* established among the various distributors of DES.

In Washington, products liability claims are governed by statute. RCW 7.72.010(2) defines a manufacturer as a party who "designs, produces, makes, fabricates, constructs, or remanufactures *the relevant product or component part of a product * * *"* (Italics ours.) Stanley argues that, following the rationale of *Martin,* each defendant who "contributed to the risk of injury" bears some culpability to the plaintiff. A bulk supplier of DES, who manufactured the drug knowing it would be used for pregnant women's disorders, did contribute to the risk of injury and should be jointly and severally responsible for the plaintiff's injuries pursuant to RCW 4.22. Furthermore, since Eli Lilly also manufactured and sold DES tablets, then at least in this case it had an affirmative duty to prevent such distribution, both at the retail and wholesale level. Breach of this duty also creates joint and several liability between the manufacturer and distributor and pursuant to RCW 4.22.050, a right of contribution would exist between them.

Eli Lilly counters, however, with the assertion that the decision in *Martin* as well as other jurisdictions mandates the opposite result. Eli Lilly was dismissed in *Martin* after it showed it did not manufacture the "type of DES" taken in that case. *Martin,* 102 Wash.2d at 590, 689 P.2d 368. DES is an unpatented chemical, easy to manufacture, and therefore, Lilly infers that this court meant the type of tablet when it referred to the type of DES.

We agree with Lilly that there should be no vertical liability in DES cases. DES is not inherently harmful, and still is prescribed today for ailments not associated with pregnant women. Thus, it is the way in which DES is used, and not DES per se, which is harmful. Furthermore, the United States Federal Drug Administration requires the tablet manufacturers, and not the bulk manufacturers, to account for and warn of a drug's properties. 21 U.S.C. § 355. It would therefore be anomalous to require the raw manufacturer to conduct separate tests to determine the adverse effects of the drug when by federal statute, the tablet manufacturer bears this responsibility. Finally, allowing an action for contribution would put a potentially abusive weapon into the plaintiff's hands. A plaintiff could sue defunct corporations who received the drug from solvent bulk suppliers on the grounds that recovery could be obtained from this source.

QUESTION SEVEN

Under *Martin* and the Washington Tort Reform Act, RCW 4.22, if plaintiff settles with a defendant DES manufacturer, to what extent and in what manner, if any, will a remaining defendant be able to reduce its presumptive and actual market share with reference to the settling defendant? What, if any, effect does the trial court's determination that the settlement was reasonable in amount have on nonsettling defendants' reduction of presumptive or actual market share?

The plaintiff and the drug companies propose different ways in which a settlement should be factored into market share liability calculations. These are best demonstrated by the following example. Assuming there were three defendants, and plaintiff's injuries were $100,000. The plaintiff settled with one defendant for $20,000 and the other two could not establish their proportionate liabilities and those were therefore governed by presumption. (If the drug companies can establish their actual market shares, then their shares of liability would be this percent of market shares multiplied by the plaintiff's proven damages irrespective of the settlement.)

The drug companies propose that the fact that a settlement occurred be ignored except that the settling defendant would only pay the amount of the settlement regardless of the outcome of the case. Thus, if the settling defendant's market share could not be established, (by either the plaintiff or any defendant) then all three defendants would be responsible for one-third the plaintiff's injuries, or $33,333. The settling defendant, by virtue of the settlement, would only pay $20,000, and the difference between the settlement and the "deserved" recovery, $13,333 ($33,333 − 20,000) would be uncompensated.

The plaintiff proposes an alternate procedure in which the settling defendant is simply removed from the picture as if it had never existed.

Thus, there would be only two defendants, and $80,000 worth of damages ($100,000 − 20,000 received as a settlement). This would be split evenly between the two remaining defendants, $40,000 each, as the presumption of equal liability would control. Thus, the plaintiff would receive the full $100,000: $20,000 from the settling defendant and $40,000 from each of the remaining two defendants.

The drug companies argue the plaintiff's option leaves room for flagrant abuse. If the plaintiff settles for nominal amounts with all but one defendant, the last defendant would be required to pay the lion's share of the damages. Furthermore, RCW 4.22.050, which gives the defendant the right of contribution, would not apply because the statute requires joint and several liability, and that is not present here. While we believe a settlement hearing procedure like that set down in RCW 4.22.060 should be used to determine if the settlement is reasonable, we believe the plaintiff's proposed option has the inherent problem that neither the plaintiff nor the settling defendant has any incentive to make a reasonable settlement.

No such difficulty exists with the drug companies' option. Although the plaintiff is concerned that an unreasonable market share may be assigned to the settling defendant, this does not seem likely. Market share will be determined by fact or presumption as usual, and it makes sense that a settlement should not alter this historically established figure. There is no reason why the plaintiff should be able to profit from a settlement that is too low, and no reason why both the plaintiff and the drug companies should not be able to determine approximately what figure represents a reasonable settlement in light of the liability rules established by *Martin*.

* * *

PEARSON, C.J., and UTTER, BRACHTENBACH, DOLLIVER, ANDERSEN, GOODLOE and DURHAM, JJ., concur.

Notes

1. *See* Murphy v. E.R. Squibb & Sons, Inc., 40 Cal.3d 672, 221 Cal.Rptr. 447, 710 P.2d 247 (1985) (ten percent of the nationwide market of DES sold is not a substantial share); Brown v. Superior Court (Abbott Laboratories), 44 Cal.3d 1049, 245 Cal.Rptr. 412, 751 P.2d 470 (1988) (rejecting joint liability in market share liability cases; each defendant is severally liable for the proportion of the judgment represented by its market share).

2. Hymowitz v. Eli Lilly and Co., 73 N.Y.2d 487, 541 N.Y.S.2d 941, 539 N.E.2d 1069 (1989), cert. denied, 493 U.S. 944, 110 S.Ct. 350, 107 L.Ed.2d 338 (1989) adopted a version of market share liability that holds defendants severally liable; mandates use of a national market in all cases; and holds defendants, who could not have sold the DES that plaintiff's mother ingested, liable as long as they participated in the marketing of DES for pregnancy use. Is this version of market share liability superior to the

California approach? *See* Fischer, Products Liability—An Analysis of Market Share Liability, 34 Vand.L.Rev. 1623, 1642–1650 (1981).

3. Should courts that accept market share liability apply the theory in the following cases?

A. Plaintiff's decedent died from cancer caused by exposure to asbestos used in various products. Plaintiff brings suit against all manufacturers who could have supplied the products to which he was exposed. The products had widely divergent toxicities, some creating a much higher risk of harm than others.

B. A bystander in a service garage was injured when a multi-piece tire and rim assembly exploded while being inflated. After the accident, the service garage operator remounted the assembly and placed it in the stream of commerce without observing the brand name on the assembly. The manufacturer cannot now be identified. Plaintiff sues twelve manufacturers of truck wheels and rims.

C. Plaintiff contracted encephalitis as a result of being inoculated with a defective dose of Salk anti-polio vaccine. Being unable to identify the manufacturer of the vaccine, plaintiff brought an action against all the drug companies that manufactured the vaccine at the time of her inoculation.

4. LINKING THE PRODUCT TO THE HARM

BLOOMQUIST v. WAPELLO COUNTY

Supreme Court of Iowa, 1993.
500 N.W.2d 1.

Considered by LARSON, P.J., and CARTER, LAVORATO, NEUMAN, and ANDREASEN, JJ.

LARSON, JUSTICE.

Five workers in a Department of Human Services (DHS) office building in Ottumwa became ill, allegedly the result of a contaminated atmosphere in the building. A combination of factors, including the use of an insecticide, sewer gas, and poor ventilation were to blame, according to their claims. Following a ten-week trial, the jury returned substantial verdicts for the plaintiffs. On the defendants' posttrial motions to dismiss and for judgment notwithstanding the verdict, the court vacated its earlier judgments for the plaintiffs. The plaintiffs appealed, and two of the defendants cross-appealed. We affirm in part and reverse in part on the appeal and affirm on the cross-appeals.

* * * For purposes of ruling on the motion for judgment notwithstanding the verdict, we view the evidence in the light most favorable to the plaintiffs.

Prior to 1980, DHS and the county employees working with them were located in the Wapello County Courthouse. When these offices became crowded, the county purchased a 100–year–old building and remodeled it. The workers moved in in 1980. A serious infestation of fleas moved in at the same time.

Soon after the employees moved in, they began to complain about the quality of the air and the fleas. A spraying program was commenced by defendant Atomic Termite & Pest Control. The spray, an organo-phosphate called Dursban, was applied in a "crack and crevice" method, on a monthly basis. However, in 1984, more fleas moved in. Atomic Termite began to broadcast spray in the building and continued to apply the spray to the cracks and crevices. According to the plaintiffs' evidence, the spray was broadcast over the carpet, in violation of established standards of care, while workers were still in the building. In addition, the offices were sprayed without removing papers being used by the employees, and the workers who were gone during the spraying were allowed to return to the building while the carpet was still wet.

In 1986, an inspection revealed that there were additional problems in the building. The inspectors found an open sewer line in the basement, a leak in a sewer line, floor drains with no traps, floor drains with no clean-out plugs, floor drains that open to the sewer line, a two-inch opening in the stack open to the sewer line, and a lack of combustion air to the boiler in the hot water heater.

It was eventually discovered that the fresh air intake on one of the air handling units on the roof had never been connected, seriously reducing the amount of fresh air taken into the building. In addition, while the rooftop ventilating units were designed to provide intake of fresh air, controls on them were set to reduce the intake of fresh air below acceptable standards; the reason was to reduce the cost of heating and cooling outside air.

On repeated occasions, workers in the building complained to the state and to the county, asking them to inspect the building and determine the cause of the workers' problems. According to the plaintiffs, these complaints went largely unheeded. Too costly, according to the responses.

Tests done on the carpet in the building several months after the carpet was sprayed revealed that there were still residues of pesticide. It was recommended by Dr. Nyle Kauffman, an internist from Iowa City, that the carpet be removed. The county refused, but it did have the carpet shampooed. The residue from the pesticide remained.

The plaintiffs sought medical assistance. All of the workers were initially treated by Dr. Kauffman, who observed several similarities of the plaintiffs' symptoms. Their problems basically consisted of respiratory problems, immune problems, brain damage, urinary incontinence, and fecal incontinence.

Other doctors, including Dr. Frank Gersh, a neuropsychologist, and Dr. Vernon Varner, a psychiatrist, concurred in Dr. Kauffman's diagnoses. Two of the plaintiffs, Miller and Owens, were treated by Dr.

Marc Hines, a certified neurologist in Ottumwa. Dr. Hines diagnosed them as suffering from chronic organophosphate poisoning.

The plaintiffs' experts concurred in their opinions that medical problems experienced by the plaintiffs were permanent and were caused by the conditions present in the DHS building, primarily the flea spray.

In sustaining the defendants' motions for judgment notwithstanding the verdict, the district court ruled as a matter of law that the plaintiffs had failed to establish proximate cause, failed to establish a duty running from the state to the respective plaintiffs, and failed to establish subject matter jurisdiction in the loss-of-consortium claims by plaintiff Owens' children.

I. THE PROXIMATE CAUSE ISSUE.

The most difficult issue in this case, and one that is common to all of the plaintiffs' claims, is whether the plaintiffs sufficiently established a proximate cause between the conditions in the DHS building and the resulting injuries. Most of the plaintiffs' evidence of causation, produced through their experts' testimony, was admitted without objection. The defendants argue, nevertheless, that this case, which is commonly referred to as a "toxic tort" case, requires more than conventional evidence of causation. The health effects of Dursban, the chief problem in the DHS office, are not fully understood, and the plaintiffs' evidence of proximate cause was merely speculative. In such a case, "epidemiological" evidence is required, according to the defendants. The district court agreed, observing that the plaintiffs' evidence of causation was nothing "other than unproven medical speculation, which is not accepted by mainstream medicine." The court noted that, in any event, any probative value in the plaintiffs' evidence was outweighed by its prejudicial effect. *See* Iowa R.Evid. 403.

The key issue is whether we will recognize as sufficient, in toxic tort cases, proof of causation based on traditional cause-and-effect testimony, such as by treating doctors, or whether we will require epidemiological evidence as suggested by the defendants and required by the district court.

One of the best known fields of toxic tort litigation involves a drug called Bendectin, an antinausea drug taken by pregnant women. Bendectin has been alleged in many suits to have caused severe birth defects in children. The federal circuits have split on the question of whether causation may be established without epidemiological evidence. *See Turpin v. Merrell Dow Pharmaceuticals, Inc.*, 959 F.2d 1349, 1351–53 (6th Cir.), *cert. denied*, ___ U.S.___, 113 S.Ct. 84, 121 L.Ed.2d 47 (1992) (discusses divergent views, among federal circuits, on toxic tort cases and epidemiological evidence).

The district court, in finding no proximate cause as a matter of law, relied on *Brock v. Merrell Dow Pharmaceuticals, Inc.*, 884 F.2d 167 (5th Cir.1989) (second opinion, en banc). *Brock* was a Bendectin case, and the court ruled that, in the present state of knowledge about Bendectin, the conventional proof of causation presented by the plaintiffs was insufficient. The *Brock* court, in its earlier opinion, had suggested that, as more is known about Bendectin, the rule might be relaxed:

> Assuredly, one day in the future, medical science may have a clearer understanding of the mechanics of tissue development in the fetus. However, that is not the case today, and speculation unconfirmed by epidemiologic proof cannot form the basis for causation in a court of law.

Brock v. Merrell Dow Pharmaceuticals, Inc., 874 F.2d 307, 315 (5th Cir.1989) (panel opinion).

Epidemiology is an accepted scientific discipline dealing with the integrated use of statistics and biological/medical science to identify and establish the causes of human disease. Through epidemiology it is possible to assess a percentage of the risk of a disease that is properly attributable to a given factor such as exposure to an allegedly harmful substance. Through the use of epidemiologic standards, courts are provided with a rational and consistent means for evaluating evidence of a causal relationship between exposure to a particular factor and the incidence of a disease. B. Black & D. Lilienfeld, *Epidemiologic Proof in Toxic Tort Litigation*, 52 Fordham L.Rev. 732, 736 (1984).

An epidemiological study attempts to determine the incidence of certain problems with the exposure of the patient to certain alleged causes. Epidemiological studies do not provide direct evidence that a particular victim was injured by exposure to a substance. They have the potential, however, of generating circumstantial evidence of cause and effect. *DeLuca v. Merrell Dow Pharmaceuticals, Inc.*, 911 F.2d 941, 945 (3d Cir.1990). Epidemiological studies involve

> a process which "amounts to an attempt to falsify the null hypothesis and by exclusion accept the alternative." The null hypothesis is the hypothesis that there is no association between two studied variables; in this case the key null hypothesis would be that there is no association between [the suspected] exposure and [the alleged effects]. The important alternative hypothesis in this case is that [the suspected agent's] use is associated with [the plaintiff's problem].

Id. (citations omitted).

According to one authority, the most important generalized evidence of causation of illnesses whose cause is incompletely understood is epidemiology. Michael Dore, *A Commentary on the Use of Epidemiological Evidence in Demonstrating Cause–in–Fact*, 7 Harv.Envtl.L.Rev. 429, 430–31 (1983) [hereinafter Dore]. One example of such studies involve the effect of cigarette smoking in causing lung cancer. *Id.* However, as Dore notes, epidemiological evidence is often inaccurate. For example, if the normal incidence of leukemia of 107 per 100,000 population is doubled, by radiation on the job, to an additional 107 per 100,000 population, the question in a particular case would still be whether the plaintiff contracted leukemia from the radiation on the job or from some other source. Dore, at 436–37. Another problem is that it tends to be too complex for juries to understand. *Id.* at 437.

This potential for confusing a jury is evident in this discussion of the complex study of epidemiology:

> Significance testing has a "P value" focus; the P value "indicates the probability, assuming the null hypothesis is true, that the observed data will depart from the absence of association to the extent that they actually do, or to a greater extent, by actual chance." If P is less than .05 (or 5%) a study's finding of a relationship supportive of the alternative hypothesis is considered statistically significant, if P is greater than 5% the relationship is rejected as insignificant. Accordingly, the results of a particular study are reported as simply "significant" or "not significant" or as P<.05 or P>.05.

DeLuca, 911 F.2d at 947 (citation omitted).

There is a risk that the difference between epidemiologist testimony and the testimony of treating doctors might be confused by the jury, Dore, at 437, and experts must make numerous subjective decisions in choosing the control population, evaluating the underlying data, and interpreting the results. The best that can be said for epidemiology is that it can prove the risk but cannot prove individual causation. Dore, at 440.

The *DeLuca* court discussed this problem in the context of Bendectin exposure. As it noted,

> a showing of increased risk for birth defects among women using Bendectin in a particular study does not automatically prove that Bendectin use creates a higher risk of having a child with birth defects because the discrepancy between the exposed and unexposed groups could be the product of chance resulting from the use of only a small sample of the relevant populations.

Id. at 946 (footnote omitted).

Another problem in epidemiological studies is that they require large numbers of patients whose backgrounds are similar in every respect except their exposure to the suspected substance. When studies are made of only a small sample of the relevant population, a so-called "sampling error," the validity of the epidemiological study is brought into question. *Id.* at 946–47.

To be effective, an epidemiological study requires a large number of cases. For example, in one epidemiological study involving Bendectin, 2218 "pairs" of women were studied. *Oxendine v. Merrell Dow Pharmaceuticals, Inc.,* 506 A.2d 1100, 1107 (D.C.App.1986). If we were to require epidemiological evidence in all cases of toxic tort injury, we would automatically deny recovery to all claimants who are injured by a toxic substance that is relatively new and as to which a statistical track record has not yet been fully established. We decline to apply a per se requirement of epidemiological evidence simply because of a lack of substantial numbers of cases. The lack of similar cases, of course, would affect the weight of the plaintiffs' evidence of proximate cause.

In our view, while epidemiological evidence is helpful, it should not be held to be an absolute requirement in establishing causation. *See Ferebee v. Chevron Chem. Co.*, 736 F.2d 1529, 1535–36 (D.C.Cir.1984), *cert. denied*, 469 U.S. 1062, 105 S.Ct. 545, 83 L.Ed.2d 432 (claim for wrongful death allegedly caused by Paraquat; court held that neither epidemiologic or animal study evidence required if proper methodology is implemented), *but see Christophersen v. Allied–Signal Corp.*, 939 F.2d 1106, 1115 (5th Cir.1991) (en banc), *cert. denied*, ___ U.S.___, 112 S.Ct. 1280, 117 L.Ed.2d 506 (1992) (overruled earlier division case; applied restrictive rule on acceptance of scientific evidence). As the court in Oxendine noted, epidemiological evidence is not necessarily persuasive on either side of an issue; different experts looking at the same studies may come to different conclusions. *See Oxendine*, 506 A.2d at 1110.

We reject the reasoning of *Brock*, and therefore the reasoning of the district court in its posttrial ruling, for several reasons: We have long been committed to the principle that issues of proximate cause are only rarely decided as a matter of law. Further, the alleged harmful substances in the Bendectin cases and the present case are substantially different. The amount of knowledge available as to Bendectin, the drug in question in *Brock*, is relatively limited when compared to the body of knowledge available regarding Dursban. Ancestors of Dursban have long been known and were in fact used to exterminate prisoners in Nazi Germany.

In *State v. Hall*, 297 N.W.2d 80 (Iowa 1980), this court rejected the *"Frye"* requirement of "general scientific acceptance" as a prerequisite for introduction of scientific evidence if the reliability could otherwise be established. *Id.* at 85. *See Frye v. United States*, 293 F. 1013, 1014 (D.C.Cir.1923). [Scientific evidence is now admissible in Iowa if it "will assist the trier of fact".]

* * * In light of our liberal rules regarding admission of expert testimony and our view that such evidence would assist the trier of fact, the evidence presented by the plaintiffs in support of their proximate cause claim was properly admitted. The jury found that the evidence was sufficient on causation, and the court erred in deciding otherwise, as a matter of law, simply on the ground that no epidemiological evidence was presented.

* * *

We hold there was sufficient evidence of causation to generate a jury issue, and the court erred as a matter of law in concluding otherwise simply on the basis that epidemiological evidence was not a part of the record. We therefore reverse on the judgment notwithstanding the verdict as to all of the plaintiffs, except the Owens' children, whose claims are discussed in Division V.

[The court's discussion of the duty issue and the loss-of-consortium claims is omitted.]

VII. DISPOSITION.

On the plaintiffs' appeal, we affirm that part of the district court judgment that dismissed the loss-of-consortium claims on behalf of Linda Owens' children. We reverse as to the balance of the posttrial order and remand for reinstatement of the remaining verdicts other than those originally entered on behalf of the Owens children. * * *

Costs are taxed to the appellees.

AFFIRMED IN PART, REVERSED IN PART, AND REMANDED ON APPEAL; AFFIRMED ON CROSS–APPEAL.

Notes

1. On the standards for admission of expert testimony, and the "junk science" debate, *see Daubert v. Merrell Dow Pharmaceuticals, Inc.*, *supra* p. 447 and the notes following.

2. On the admissibility of statistical evidence, and the way its use has altered the burden of proof in civil cases, *see* Note, Causation in Toxic Torts: Burdens of Proof, Standards of Persuasion, and Statistical Evidence, 96 Yale L.J. 376 (1986).

3. In many toxic tort cases plaintiff is unable to prove causation. These are cases where particularistic evidence of causation is unavailable, and the statistical evidence (e.g., epidemiological studies) shows that the risk that the toxic substance caused plaintiff's harm is less than fifty-one percent. Numerous writers have advocated the use of proportional liability in such cases. *See* 2 American Law Institute, Reporter's Study, Enterprise Responsibility for Personal Injury, Approaches to Legal and Institutional Change, 369–75 (1991); Estep, Radiation Injuries and Statistics: The Need for a New Approach to Injury Litigation, 59 Mich.L.Rev. 259 (1960); Farber, Toxic Causation, 71 Minn.L.Rev. 1219 (1987); Makdisi, Proportional Liability: A Comprehensive Rule to Apportion Tort Damages Based on Probability, 67 N.C.L.Rev. 1063 (1989); Landes and Posner, Tort Law as a Regulatory Regime for Catastrophic Personal Injuries, 13 J.Legal Stud. 417 (1984); Robinson, Probabilistic Causation and Compensation for Tortious Risk, 14 J.Legal Stud. 779 (1985); Rosenberg, The Causal Connection in Mass Exposure Cases: A "Public Law" Vision of the Tort System, 97 Harv.L.Rev. 849 (1984); Comment, Toxic Torts & Latent Diseases: The Case for an Increased Risk Cause of Action, 38 Kan.L.Rev. 1087 (1984); Comment, Decreasing the Risks Inherent in Claims for Increased Risk of Future Disease, 43 U.Miami L.Rev. 1081 (1989); Comment, Increased Risk of Disease From Hazardous Waste: A Proposal for Judicial Relief, 60 Wash. L.Rev. 635 (1985); Note, Causation in Toxic Torts: Burdens of Proof, Standards of Persuasion, and Statistical Evidence, 96 Yale L.J. 376 (1986); Harvey, Comment, Epidemiologic Proof of Probability: Implementing the Proportional Recovery Approach in Toxic Exposure Torts, 89 Dickinson L.Rev. 233 (1984); Note, Increased Risk of Cancer as an Actionable Injury, 18 Ga.L.Rev. 563 (1984); Note, An Analysis of the Enhanced Risk Cause of Action (or How I Learned to Stop Worrying and Love Toxic Waste), 33

Vill.L.Rev. 437 (1988). While these proposals for proportional liability take many forms, they may be divided into three major categories:

> The [first] category would permit plaintiff to recover a portion of her damages only after she has suffered the injury or acquired the disease. Thus, if defendant created a twenty percent probability of having caused the harm, an injured plaintiff would recover twenty percent of her damages. If defendant created a sixty percent probability of having caused the harm, plaintiff would recover sixty percent of her damages. [Under this category plaintiffs would sue after the harm manifests itself.]

> [The second] category would permit plaintiff to recover a portion of her prospective damages before she has been injured or made ill. Thus, if defendant exposed ten persons to a toxin that created a ten percent risk of causing a certain disease in the future, each exposed person would recover ten percent of her prospective damages in advance.

> Under the third category * * * plaintiffs also would sue before injury. A judgment for plaintiff would require the tortfeasor either to set aside an amount equal to the exposure victims' prospective damages in an insurance fund or to buy insurance. Money from the fund, or proceeds from the insurance policy, would later go to those exposed persons who actually contracted the illness or injury.

Fischer, Proportional Liability: Statistical Evidence and the Probability Paradox, 46 Vand.L.Rev. 1201, 1202 (1993).

4. The courts have yet to adopt proportional liability in such cases. Should they? For a criticism of the theory, *see* Fischer, Proportional Liability: Statistical Evidence and the Probability Paradox, 46 Vand.L.Rev. 1201 (1993).

5. Is the tort system capable of dealing with the complex evidentiary and causation issues that arise in toxic tort cases? For the view that it is not, *see* Harris, Complex Product Design Litigation: A Need for More Capable Fact–Finders, 79 Ky.L.J. 477 (1991); Harris, Toxic Tort Litigation and the Causation Element: Is There any Hope of Reconciliation? 40 Sw.L.J. 909 (1986).

Chapter 12

SCOPE OF LIABILITY

SECTION A. PROXIMATE CAUSE [1]

In negligence cases, courts recognized the necessity of restricting liability for harm caused by careless acts in order to avoid unduly discouraging socially useful conduct. They devised rules concerning proximate cause, intervening cause, and duty as tools for limiting liability. These rules will collectively be referred to as "proximate cause doctrines." The policy behind these doctrines is also important in strict product liability cases.[2] Regardless of whether the primary justification for strict liability is loss spreading, deterrence, or easing the plaintiff's burden of proof, no one seriously contends that absolute liability for all harm caused by all products is desirable. Many courts have borrowed these proximate cause doctrines from the law of negligence and apply them in strict liability cases in order to keep the scope of liability within proper bounds.

The proximate cause doctrines impose three basic types of policy limits which restrict the scope of liability.[3] One restriction requires that the tortious conduct produce a foreseeable type of harm. Another requires that the harm come about in a foreseeable manner. The third limits recovery to a foreseeable class of persons. Not all courts use all three, but many commonly employ more than one of these limits.

These policy limitations are not always three mutually exclusive and distinct categories, but can be related to one another. That is, there are some situations where one type of policy limit yields the same result as another; they just amount to different ways of saying the same thing. In other cases the different approaches yield distinctly different results.

1. This note is adapted from Fischer, Products Liability—Proximate Cause, Intervening Cause, and Duty, 52 Mo.L.Rev. 547, 547–50 (1987).

2. Helene Curtis Industries, Inc. v. Pruitt, 385 F.2d 841, 862–64 (5th Cir.1967), cert. denied, 391 U.S. 913, 88 S.Ct. 1806, 20 L.Ed.2d 652 (1968); W. Prosser, Handbook of the Law of Torts 22 (4th ed. 1971); Epstein, Products Liability: The Search for the Middle Ground, 56 N.C.L.Rev. 643, 644–45, 659 (1978); Henderson, Products Liability, DES Litigation: The Tidal Wave Approaches Shore, 3 Corporation L.Rev. 143 (1980); Wade, A Conspectus of Manufacturers' Liability for Products, 10 Ind. L.Rev. 755, 767, 784 (1977).

3. Harper, Liability Without Fault and Proximate Cause, 30 Mich.L.Rev. 1001, 1001–1004 (1932).

To add to the confusion, the terminology that courts use can be confusing because courts use a variety of labels to implement these three restrictions. Some courts, for example, might impose one of these limitations as an aspect of duty while others might treat it as a question of proximate cause. Likewise, proximate cause and intervening cause are sometimes interchangeable.

For general discussions of the topic, see H. Hart and A. Honore, Causation in the Law (1959); R. Keeton, Legal Cause in the Law of Torts (1963); Fischer, Products Liability—Proximate Cause, Intervening Cause, and Duty, 52 Mo.L.Rev. 547 (1987); Harper, Liability Without Fault and Proximate Cause, 30 Mich.L.Rev. 1001 (1932); Polelle, The Foreseeability Concept and Strict Products Liability: The Odd Couple of Tort Law, 8 Rut.-Cam.L.J. 101 (1976); Twerski, The Many Faces of Misuse: An Inquiry into the Emerging Doctrine of Comparative Causation, 29 Mercer L.Rev. 403 (1978); Note, Torts—Proximate Cause in Strict Liability Cases, 50 N.C.L.Rev. 714 (1972).

1. CLASS OF PERSONS

ELMORE v. AMERICAN MOTORS CORP.

Supreme Court of California, 1969.
70 Cal.2d 578, 75 Cal.Rptr. 652, 451 P.2d 84.

[Plaintiff Anna Waters was injured and her husband was killed when the car her husband was driving and in which she was riding was struck by a car driven by plaintiff Sandra Elmore. Waters and Elmore sued American Motors under strict tort liability, claiming that the accident was caused by a defect in Elmore's car. After holding that the plaintiffs could rely on circumstantial evidence to support a finding that Elmore's car was defective, the court addressed a finding that Ms. Waters could recover against American Motors for her injuries and the wrongful death of her husband.]

PETERS, J.

* * *

The authors of the restatement have refrained from expressing a view as to whether the doctrine of strict liability of the manufacturer and retailer for defects is applicable to third parties who are bystanders and who are not purchasers or users of the defective chattel. (Rest.2d Torts, § 402A, com. *o.*) The authors pointed out that as yet (1965) no case had applied strict liability to a person who was not a user or consumer. Two recent cases, however, have held manufacturers of defective goods strictly liable in tort for injuries caused to persons who were mere bystanders and were not users or consumers. (Piercefield v. Remington Arms Company, 375 Mich. 85, 133 N.W.2d 129, 134–136; Mitchell v. Miller, 26 Conn.Sup. 142, 214 A.2d 694, 697–699.) There are also several cases which have permitted recovery in strict liability by persons who were not purchasers or users, although possibly they should not be categorized as bystanders. (Connolly v. Hagi, 24 Conn.Sup. 198, 188 A.2d 884, 887–888; Toombs v. Fort Pierce Gas Company (Fla.) 208 So.2d 615, 617; Ford Motor Company v. Cockrell (Miss.) 211 So.2d 833, 834; Lonzrick v. Republic Steel Corp., 6 Ohio St.2d 227, 218 N.E.2d 185, 188 et seq.; Webb v. Zern, 422 Pa. 424, 220 A.2d 853, 854.) Several cases, most of them earlier, have refused to extend the doctrine in favor of the bystander. (See Prosser, The Fall of the Citadel, 50 Minn.L.Rev. 791, 820, fn. 154.) In Vandermark v. Ford Motor Co., [61 Cal.2d 256, 37 Cal.Rptr. 896, 391 P.2d 168 (1964)], one of the plaintiffs was a passenger in the car, but we did not discuss the issue of liability to her separately from the issue of liability to the owner-driver.

In Greenman v. Yuba Power Products, Inc., [59 Cal.2d 57, 63, 27 Cal.Rptr. 697, 701, 377 P.2d 897, 901 (1962)], we pointed out that the purpose of strict liability upon the manufacturer in tort is to insure that "the costs of injuries resulting from defective products are borne by the manufacturers that put such products on the market rather than by the injured persons who are powerless to protect themselves." We further pointed out that the rejection of the view that such liability was governed by contract warranties rather than tort rules was shown by cases which had recognized that the liability is not assumed by agreement but imposed by law and which had refused to permit the manufacturer to define its own responsibility for defective products (59 Cal.2d at p. 63, 27 Cal.Rptr. 697, 377 P.2d 897.) Similarly, in Vandermark v. Ford Motor Co., *supra,* 61 Cal.2d 256, 263, 37 Cal.Rptr. 896, 391 P.2d 168, we held that, since the retailer is strictly liable in tort, the fact that it restricted its contractual liability was immaterial.

These cases make it clear that the doctrine of strict liability may not be restricted on a theory of privity of contract. Since the doctrine applies even where the manufacturer has attempted to limit liability, they further make it clear that the doctrine may not be limited on the theory that no representation of safety is made to the bystander.

The liability has been based upon the existence of a defective product which caused injury to a human being, and in both *Greenman* and *Vandermark* we did not limit the rules stated to consumers and users but instead used language applicable to human beings generally.

It has been pointed out that an injury to a bystander "is often a perfectly foreseeable risk of the maker's enterprise, and the considerations for imposing such risks on the maker without regard to his fault do not stop with those who undertake to use the chattel. [A restriction on the recovery by bystanders] is only the distorted shadow of a vanishing privity which is itself a reflection of the habit of viewing the problem as a commercial one between traders, rather than as part of the accident problem." (2 Harper and James, The Law of Torts (1956) p. 1572, fn. 6.)

If anything, bystanders should be entitled to greater protection than the consumer or user where injury to bystanders from the defect is reasonably foreseeable. Consumers and users, at least, have the opportunity to inspect for defects and to limit their purchases to articles manufactured by reputable manufacturers and sold by reputable retailers, whereas the bystander ordinarily has no such opportunities. In short, the bystander is in greater need of protection from defective products which are dangerous, and if any distinction should be made between bystanders and users, it should be made, contrary to the position of defendants, to extend greater liability in favor of the bystanders.

An automobile with a defectively connected drive shaft constitutes a substantial hazard on the highway not only to the driver and passenger of the car but also to pedestrians and other drivers. The public policy which protects the driver and passenger of the car should also protect the bystander, and where a driver or passenger of another car is injured due to defects in the manufacture of an automobile and without any fault of their own, they may recover from the manufacturer of the defective automobile.

It is urged that even assuming that the doctrine of strict liability in tort is available to an injured bystander in an action against the manufacturer, the doctrine should not be available against the retailer. In *Vandermark,* we considered the related question of the liability of the retailer to the purchaser and user, and we stated: "Retailers like manufacturers are engaged in the business of distributing goods to the public. They are an integral part of the overall producing and marketing enterprise that should bear the cost of injuries resulting from defective products. (See Greenman v. Yuba Power Products, Inc., 59 Cal.2d 57, 63, 27 Cal.Rptr. 697, 377 P.2d 897.) In some cases the retailer may be the only member of that enterprise reasonably available to the injured plaintiff. In other cases the retailer himself may play a substantial part in insuring that the product is safe or may be in a position to exert pressure on the manufacturer to that end; the retailer's strict liability thus serves as an added incentive to safety. Strict liability on the manufacturer and retailer alike affords maximum protection to the injured plaintiff and works no injustice to the defendants, for they can adjust the costs of such protection between them in the course of their continuing business relationship. Accordingly, as a retailer engaged in the business of distributing goods to the public, Maywood Bell is strictly liable in tort for personal injuries caused by defects in cars sold by it." (61 Cal.2d at pp. 262–263, 37 Cal.Rptr. 896, 899–890, 391 P.2d 168, 171–172.)

All of the foregoing considerations are as applicable to the bystander's action as that of the purchaser or user, and we are satisfied that the doctrine of strict liability in tort is available in an action for personal injuries by a bystander against the manufacturer and the retailer.

The judgments are reversed.

TRAYNOR, C.J., and McCOMB, TOBRINER, MOSK, BURKE and SULLIVAN, JJ., concur.

Notes

1. Section 402A provides that a seller of a defective product is liable to "the ultimate user or consumer." As the court in *Elmore* noted, caveat 1 to section 402A provides that "[t]he Institute expressed no opinion as to whether the rules stated in this Section may not apply * * * to harm to persons other than users or consumers." No doubt, the early concern over the extent of liability reflected the warranty heritage of strict products liability: since privity of contract was a central issue in cases involving breach of warranty, it was possible that remote plaintiffs would also have difficulty recovering under strict products liability. *Elmore* made clear that since strict tort liability was not based on contract principles, it should not be affected by notions of privity of contract.

Section 402A(2)(b) states that strict tort liability is not defeated by the fact that "the user or consumer has not bought the product from or entered into any contractual relation with the seller."

2. After *Elmore,* other courts followed suit to permit bystanders to recover under strict tort liability. *See, e.g.,* Haumersen v. Ford Motor Co., 257 N.W.2d 7 (Iowa 1977); Giberson v. Ford Motor Co., 504 S.W.2d 8 (Mo.1974); Howes v. Hansen, 56 Wis.2d 247, 201 N.W.2d 825 (1972); Passwaters v. General Motors Corp., 454 F.2d 1270 (8th Cir.1972); Darryl v. Ford Motor Co., 440 S.W.2d 630 (Tex.1969).

3. The fact that bystanders can recover under strict tort liability does not mean that anyone whose injury is caused by a defective product, no matter how attenuated the causal connection, can recover from the manufacturer. For example, if Mr. Waters' children had been injured on a trip to visit their father's grave, the causal connection between the defect in Ms. Elmore's car and the injury would undoubtedly have been too attenuated to support recovery against American Motors. *Elmore* merely stands for the proposition that bystanders are not, *ipso facto,* precluded from recovering under strict tort liability. Injuries that have attenuated causal nexes with the defective product raise issues of legal causation that are addressed in the following materials.

4. By its own terms, section 402A applies to a product's users and consumers. Because courts have uniformly also permitted bystanders to recover under strict tort liability, it has not been necessary to determine precisely who qualifies as a user or consumer. Nevertheless, some courts have done so, usually using a fairly liberal definition. For example, in Ethicon, Inc. v. Parten, 520 S.W.2d 527 (Tex.Civ.App.—Houston [14th Dist.] 1975, no writ), the Texas Court of Civil Appeals held that a patient whose doctor uses a defective surgical needle is a "consumer" of the needle.

5. Comment *l* to section 402A provides that a victim of a product injury can recover if he is

> a member of the family of the final purchaser, or his employee, or a guest at his table, or a mere donee from the purchaser. The liability stated is one in tort, and does not require any contractual relation, or privity of contract, between the plaintiff and the defendant.

Comment *l* also provides for recovery by persons who prepare food for the consumption of others.

WINNETT v. WINNETT

Supreme Court of Illinois, 1974.

57 Ill.2d 7, 310 N.E.2d 1.

UNDERWOOD, CHIEF JUSTICE:

Four-year-old Teresa Kay Winnett was injured when she placed her hand on a moving conveyor belt or screen on a forage wagon then being operated on her grandfather's farm. An amended two-count complaint on her behalf sought recovery in count I from her grandfather predicated upon his negligence. Count II is a strict-tort-liability action against defendant Helix Corporation, manufacturer of the forage wagon. The defendant corporation filed a motion to dismiss count II for failure to state a cause of action, and the circuit court of Coles County allowed that motion. The count I cause of action was apparently settled, and it was dismissed without prejudice. The Appellate Court for the Fourth District held count II stated a cause of action and reversed its dismissal by the trial court. (9 Ill.App.3d 644, 292 N.E.2d 524.) We allowed leave to appeal.

Count II of the amended complaint alleged in substance that plaintiff was visiting her grandfather by invitation at his farm home, that he was operating a forage wagon in the barnyard * * *. [The forage wagon had two exposed conveyor belts with numerous holes of sufficient size to admit the fingers of small children. When in operation the belts moved slowly and carried bits of vegetation under the steel end of the forage wagon. The steel end would shear off any objects in or on the belts. Plaintiff was attracted to the forage wagon while it was operating, and placed her fingers in or on the belts. Her fingers were pulled into or beneath the steel end of the forage wagon.] * * * Among other allegations, including the absence of rear-view mirrors and warning signs, it is charged that the conveyor belts on the wagon were exposed with no shield or guard affixed to prevent persons from coming into contact with the belts and the steel end of the wagon, and no bolts, latches or holes were present to allow for the attachment of a shield or guard. These and other conditions were alleged to render the wagon unreasonably dangerous, and it is alleged that they existed at the time the forage wagon left defendant's control and that plaintiff's injuries resulted from one or more of these conditions. * * *

The arguments of the parties here have focused largely upon whether "use" of this forage wagon by a four-year-old child was "foreseeable" by the manufacturer. Plaintiff urges that foreseeability has no place in strict-tort-liability doctrine but that, in any event, the likelihood of small children being in the vicinity of operating farm equipment is not so unforeseeable as to warrant taking the case from the jury; defendant contends that the product was being "used" by a child for whose use it was not intended and whose use of it was not foreseeable. Consequently, argues defendant, no liability for the injury may be imposed upon the manufacturer.

Our earlier decisions establish the duty of the manufacturer to make a product reasonably fit for its intended use. [Citations] That the scope of a forage wagon's "intended use" does not embrace its use by a four-year-old child seems obvious, as does the conclusion that such child is neither a "user" nor a "consumer" of this product as those terms are spoken of in products-liability law. [Citations] Whether this forage wagon was unreasonably dangerous when operated for its intended purpose by one for whose use it was intended is simply not a relevant consideration unless plaintiff is a person entitled to the protections afforded by the concepts of strict-tort-liability actions against manufacturers.

The large majority of courts which have considered the question of recovery in a strict-tort-liability action by persons other than those for whose use the product was intended have found the terms "bystander" or "innocent bystander" a convenient means of categorizing an additional group of persons for whose injuries courts have allowed recovery. [Citations] We also note that the Supreme Court of California has suggested that bystanders should be entitled to even greater protection than consumers or users where injury to bystanders from the defect is reasonably foreseeable, since bystanders do not have the opportunity, prior to purchase or use, to inspect products for defects as do users and consumers. Elmore v. American Motors Corp. (1969), 70 Cal.2d 578, 586, 75 Cal.Rptr. 652, 657, 451 P.2d 84, 89.

We, however, find this categorization of plaintiffs as users, consumers or innocent bystanders helpful only in a general sense. In the unusual case the application of these labels does not assist resolution of the issues. In our judgment the liability of a manufacturer properly encompasses only those individuals to whom injury from a defective product may reasonably be foreseen and only those situations where the product is being used for the purpose for which it was intended or for which it is reasonably foreseeable that it may be used. Any other approach to the problem results in making the manufacturer and those in the chain of product distribution virtual insurers of the product, a position rejected by this court in *Suvada* [*v. White Motor Co.*, 32 Ill.2d 612, 210 N.E.2d 182 (1965)].

It is apparent from the majority of cases in which recovery was allowed for injuries to persons for whose use the product was not intended that the injuries were reasonably foreseeable, and that such foreseeability was recognized by the courts as a factor in deciding the cases. Thus, it is held that injury to other vehicles, their occupants and pedestrians is the foreseeable result of defective steering mechanisms, transmissions, *etc*. [Citations]

Likewise, it is foreseeable that a defective shell will cause a shotgun barrel to explode and injure persons standing nearby, and recovery against the manufacturer of the shell should accordingly be allowed. [Citation]

* * *

Whether the plaintiff here is an individual who is entitled to the protections afforded by the concepts of strict tort liability depends upon whether it can be fairly said that her conduct in placing her fingers in the moving screen or belt of the forage wagon was reasonably foreseeable. A foreseeability test, however, is not intended to bring within the scope of the defendant's liability every injury that might possibly occur. "In a sense, in retrospect almost nothing is entirely unforeseeable." (Mieher v. Brown, 54 Ill.2d 539, 544, 301 N.E.2d 307, 309.) Foreseeability means that which it is *objectively reasonable* to expect, not merely what might conceivably occur. *Cf.* Williams v. Brown Mfg. Co., 45 Ill.2d 418, 425, 261 N.E.2d 305.

Questions of foreseeability, we believe, are ordinarily for a jury to resolve, as is the question whether a product is defective or unreasonably dangerous. (Dunham v. Vaughan & Bushnell Mfg. Co., 42 Ill.2d 339, 247 N.E.2d 401.) But where the facts alleged in a complaint on their face demonstrate that the plaintiff would never be entitled to recover, that complaint is properly dismissed. [Citations] Such is the case before us. While in retrospect it can be asserted that the manufacturer of the forage wagon should have foreseen that the unfortunate event in this case might conceivably occur, we do not believe its occurrence was objectively reasonable to expect. It cannot, in our judgment, fairly be said that a manufacturer should reasonably foresee that a four-year-old child will be permitted to approach an operating farm forage wagon or that the child will be permitted to place her fingers in or on the holes in its moving screen. We believe the trial court properly dismissed plaintiff's amended complaint.

The judgment of the Appellate Court for the Fourth Judicial District is accordingly reversed and the judgment of the circuit court of Coles County is affirmed.

Appellate court reversed; circuit court affirmed.

[The dissenting opinion of GOLDENHERSH, J., is omitted]

PIERCE v. HOBART CORP.

Appellate Court of Illinois, First District, 1987.
159 Ill.App.3d 31, 111 Ill.Dec. 110, 512 N.E.2d 14.

JUSTICE LINN delivered the opinion of the court:

On behalf of the minor plaintiff, Morrell Pierce, an action was brought against Hobart Corporation (sued as Hobart Manufacturing Company) on a theory of strict product liability to recover for permanent injuries that he suffered when his hand was caught in a food grinding machine manufactured by Hobart.

* * *

Hobart successfully moved for summary judgment * * * on the ground that Hobart could not "reasonably foresee" that a ten-year-old child would operate the commercial food grinding machine and that

Hobart could not therefore be held liable for the child's injuries. * * *
[Plaintiff appealed.]

[The central question is] whether there is a genuine issue of material fact concerning the foreseeability of Pierce's injury from operation of the food grinder. Pierce contends that summary judgment was inappropriate because of the following disputed factual matters: (1) it was reasonably foreseeable that a ten-year-old could have access to and use of the commercial grinding machine, particularly in light of Hobart's patent application of 1923, which recognized that hands of minors had been injured in the use of food grinding machines similar to Hobart's; (2) Hobart could reasonably have foreseen that any person, child or adult, whose hands were of a certain size could be injured while using the machine because the intake [aperture] was large enough to permit entry by small hands; and (3) Hobart's machine was unreasonably dangerous in its design and lack of safety guards.

For the reasons that follow, we reverse the motion court's [order] granting summary judgment in favor of Hobart and remand * * * for trial.

BACKGROUND

[Pierce was injured while operating the food grinder in Tony & Frank's Restaurant.]

According to the deposition testimony of Pierce and one of Tony & Frank's employees, Rey Poindexter, Pierce and his brother often performed odd jobs and errands for the restaurant after school. In return, they were paid in cash or food.

On October 29, 1981, Poindexter asked Pierce to help him grind cheese for pizzas. He took him to a work area in the basement to demonstrate how to operate the commercial meat grinder. Although the grinder was equipped with a metal stomper, Poindexter did not use the stomper or mention its use to Pierce. Instead, he put the cheese into the grinder with his hand. Poindexter then left the area to answer the telephone, admonishing Pierce to be careful. He left the machine on.

Pierce, then ten years old, had never operated a meat grinding machine. He placed a piece of cheese into the grinder and pressed it down with the palm of his hand. The second time that Pierce put cheese into the machine it "jumped" and his fingers were caught inside. He lost part of his thumb and part or all of each finger of his right hand except for the small finger.

* * *

The court granted Hobart's motion for summary judgment against Pierce, finding that "it is not foreseeable that a ten-year-old child would be operating a grinding machine such as the grinding machine involved."

During the hearing on Pierce's motion for reconsideration Pierce's attorney tendered an affidavit of David P. Litchtenstein, M.D. The affidavit, which the court struck on Hobart's motion, offered the doctor's opinion that "it is reasonably common for a 10–year–old male to have a hand size similar or greater than the hand size of a 16–year–old male and/or female child." The court denied Pierce's motion to reconsider.

* * *

OPINION

* * *

In the pending case, the trial court held that Pierce's use of the commercial meat grinder was not reasonably foreseeable by Hobart as a matter of law; accordingly, the product was not unreasonably dangerous. Hobart argued, and the court found persuasive, that commercial food grinders are not intended to be operated by children rather than adults. According to Hobart, the effect of allowing [Pierce's suit] against it would be to require that commercial machinery be "child-proofed."

Pierce and Tony & Frank's, on the other hand, assert that the key consideration regarding foreseeability is not Pierce's age but rather his physical characteristics and those of the machine. There was evidence offered to the effect that the opening of the meat grinder was slightly greater than 2½ inches in diameter and thereby exceeded certain recommended safety standards of Underwriters' Laboratories, Inc.; that the hands of ten-year-old children could be the same size as those of some females and adult males; and that a 1923 patent application for a meat grinder indicated Hobart's awareness of the potential danger to users of grinders. The application noted that "many injuries" had occurred to operators of meat grinders and that it was "not an uncommon occurrence in stores [and] restaurants * * * for operators to have one or more fingers cut off during operation through accidentally getting the fingers into the worm as the meat is being fed into the device for grinding. And a number of very deplorable accidents have happened in which children, whose hands are naturally small, have lost a whole hand * * *."

The sole question that we must resolve on this appeal is whether or not the foreseeability question poses a *bona fide* issue of material fact sufficient to survive the motion for summary judgment. All pleadings, depositions, and affidavits must be construed most strictly against the moving party and it is only when the undisputed facts are susceptible of but one inference that the issue becomes one of law. *Stanfield v. Medalist Industries, Inc.* (1975), 34 Ill.App.3d 635, 340 N.E.2d 276.

* * *

In *Winnett v. Winnett* (1974), 57 Ill.2d 7, 310 N.E.2d 1, a four-year-old child was injured when she put her fingers in the small holes of a conveyor belt on a forage wagon. The Illinois Supreme Court held that the child was neither a user nor a consumer of the product as those terms are used in products liability law and that her injury on the machine did not render it unreasonably dangerous because she was not "objectively foreseeable" as a user. The court ruled that "liability of a manufacturer properly encompasses only those individuals to whom injury from a defective product may reasonably be foreseen and only those situations where the product is being used for the purpose for which it was intended or for which it is reasonably foreseeable that it may be used." 57 Ill.2d 7, 11, 310 N.E.2d 1, 4.

In *Richelman v. Kewanee Machinery & Conveyor Co.* (1978), 59 Ill.App.3d 578, 16 Ill.Dec. 778, 375 N.E.2d 885, a child of fewer than three years entangled his foot and leg in a grain auger. Affirming a verdict for the plaintiff, the appellate court ruled that in determining whether the injury to the child was "objectively foreseeable," the issue was whether any person with a similar shoe size, whether adult or minor, could sustain a similar injury. Testimony adduced at trial included that of the designer of the safety guards, who used his own shoe width to determine the spacing of gaps between the guards. The court reasoned that any one with a shoe width of less than 4⅝ inch could have tripped near the auger, commenting, "The fact that the individual injured is a child should not preclude recovery where an adult, albeit one with a narrower foot than that of the design engineer, could likewise have sustained injury." 59 Ill.App.3d 578, 582–83, 16 Ill.Dec. 778, 781, 375 N.E.2d 885, 888.

None of the above * * * cases found the plaintiff's age to be determinative of the foreseeability issue. In *Winnett* and *Richelman*, rather, the courts looked to the physical characteristics of the plaintiffs and the physical characteristics of the machine in question.

* * *

In the instant case, Hobart conceded at oral argument that Pierce's age is not the controlling factor. Nevertheless, Hobart argues that it did not design the machine for use by a ten-year-old child and that this plaintiff lacked the necessary maturity to operate the machine according to its intended use.

One of the cases that Hobart relies on is *Yassin v. Certified Grocers of Illinois, Inc.* (1986), 150 Ill.App.3d 1052, 104 Ill.Dec. 52, 502 N.E.2d 315. In that case a three-year-old girl was injured when she put her hand in a commercial meat tenderizer. The machine was located in a separate work area in the rear of a grocery store, but the door to the area had been left open and the machine left running. The child had wandered away from her mother and subsequently entangled her hand in the meat tenderizer. The appellate court affirmed the jury's verdict in favor of the defendant, which found the meat tenderizer not to be unreasonably dangerous. The court cited the Winnett test of "objective reasonableness" and concluded that the machine was not intended for home use and that small children would not be expected to use the machine.

We find *Yassin* to be distinguishable on at least two counts. First, the jury determined foreseeability as a matter of fact. The court did not enter judgment against plaintiff as a matter of law, as in the present case. Second, the toddler was not attempting to operate the machine but simply approached it out of curiosity and apparently was able to get close enough to injure herself. In contrast, Pierce was operating the machine as he had been shown and for the purpose intended: to grind food. He was not a toddler who stumbled into trouble because he was left unattended.

Other cases are consistent with the rationale that a very small child may not be a foreseeable user or may be injured, not because of an unreasonably dangerous condition, but because of misuse of the product. For example, in *Schierer v. Sears Roebuck & Co.* (1980), 81 Ill.App.3d 90, 36 Ill.Dec. 492, 400 N.E.2d 1072, a three-year-old wearing a floor-length nightgown pulled up a chair to a gas stove and was injured when her highly flammable gown ignited. The court affirmed summary judgment in favor of the defendant, noting that there was no evidence of any type, including expert opinion, that the stove was unreasonably dangerous simply because it had knobs that could turn easily. The court further concluded that it was not foreseeable that a three-year-old wearing a flammable gown would climb on top of the stove. Hence, there was no indication of potential harm to one who might reasonably be foreseen to use the stove.

In contrast, in the pending case Pierce * * * presented evidence of foreseeable harm to all persons with small enough hands to fit through the 2½ inch diameter aperature of the meat grinder.

In *Wenzell v. MTD Products, Inc.* (1975), 32 Ill.App.3d 279, 336 N.E.2d 125, a four-year-old child was injured by a riding lawn mower operated by a seven-year-old who was driving the mower in reverse at the time of the occurrence. The court held that it was not reasonably foreseeable that the owner or user of the lawn mower would permit a seven-year-old to operate the machine in the presence of other small children and use it "virtually as a toy." (32 Ill.App.3d 279, 336 N.E.2d 125, 134.) Therefore, the court affirmed the jury's verdict in favor of the manufacturer.

In *Richelman* the court analyzed the rationale of *Winnett* and *Wenzell* and stated, "In our opinion, these cases indicate nothing more than a reluctance by the judiciary to hold a manufacturer liable when children are allowed to play with dangerous objects." 59 Ill.App.3d 578, 582, 16 Ill.Dec. 778, 781, 375 N.E.2d 885, 888.

To reiterate: Pierce was operating the machine to grind food. He was not playing with the machine, nor did he just happen upon it and decide to stick his fingers inside. There is some indication, moreover, that the cutting element or "worm" is not visible from the aperature, and, while Pierce admitted knowing that he could be injured by the machine, he was simply feeding in the cheese in the manner that Poindexter had done, by hand. We believe that the jury should hear all relevant evidence to determine the foreseeability issue. To aid in that determination, proper evidence regarding hand size is relevant. We need not reach any other evidentiary matters at this point, since it will be up to the trial court to consider and admit or exclude the evidence presented at trial.

For the foregoing reasons, we reverse [the order] appealed from, which granted summary judgment in favor of Hobart, and remand this cause for further proceedings.

Reversed and remanded.

McMorrow, P.J., and Jiganti, J., concur.

Notes

1. Virtually all courts restrict liability to foreseeable victims of the defective product. One exception is Howes v. Hansen, 56 Wis.2d 247, 201 N.W.2d 825 (1972). A two-year-old plaintiff "somehow" came into contact with a power riding mower operated by a twelve year old boy and suffered serious injuries. The court rejected the argument that liability depended on whether plaintiff was foreseeable, stating that "the doctrine of foreseeability, although a recognized doctrine where ordinary negligence in tort is involved, has no part in the concept of strict liability in tort." Is *Howes v. Hansen* correct? Foreseeability is a negligence concept. Why should it play any role in a strict liability case?

2. Given that foreseeability is the test of liability, was *Winnett* properly decided? Just what was unforeseeable in that case? That children will follow their parents and grandparents around on the farm? That children will be attracted to moving machinery? That the parents or grandparents will inadvertently fail to protect them from the risk?

3. Compare the results in the following cases.

A. Palmer v. Avco Distrib. Corp., 82 Ill.2d 211, 45 Ill.Dec. 377, 412 N.E.2d 959 (1980). An eleven-year-old child rode in a fertilizer spreader, and got his foot caught in the agitator mechanism at the bottom of the spreader. The baffle covering the agitator created a deceptive appearance of safety, but gave less protection than similar devices on other spreaders. Plaintiff was foreseeable.

B. Mohrdieck v. Morton Grove, 94 Ill.App.3d 1021, 50 Ill.Dec. 409, 419 N.E.2d 517 (1981). A metal bristle dislodged from the brush of street sweeper. Plaintiff's brother found it in the street and threw it at a tree. Part of it broke off and hit Plaintiff in the eye. Plaintiff was unforeseeable.

C. Barr v. Rivinius, Inc., 58 Ill.App.3d 121, 15 Ill.Dec. 591, 373 N.E.2d 1063 (1978). A road grader was pushing a shoulder spreader at a speed of one mile per hour toward Plaintiff, who was walking in front of it. The operator had an unobstructed view, but was not looking, and ran into Plaintiff with the front wheel. The alleged defect was a failure to guard the front wheels of the spreader. Plaintiff was unforeseeable.

4. *Compare* Gilbert v. Stone City Const. Co., 171 Ind.App. 418, 357 N.E.2d 738 (1976), *with Barr v. Rivinius, supra* note 3.C. In *Gilbert* a road roller struck Plaintiff because the operator, whose view was obstructed by the design of the machine, did not see him. The court held that a jury could

find that plaintiff was foreseeable and that a defective condition of the roller caused his harm. Would an Illinois court have decided *Gilbert* differently?

5. *Passwaters v. General Motors Corp.*, 454 F.2d 1270 (8th Cir.1972), is an early case extending liability to foreseeable bystanders. In his opinion, Judge Lay made the following observations about foreseeability:

> The difficulty is that "foreseeability" is a hazardous term to define in the abstract and, like so many other doctrines, must turn on the judgmental process. [Noting that judges sometimes differ about which risks are foreseeable.] Such an outcome could be explained by the telling exposure of the judicial mind expressed by Professor Gregory in the University of Chicago Law Review over thirty years ago:
>
> "It all depends upon what factors in the evidence a court is willing to isolate and emphasize for the purpose of making this decision, which process in turn depends pretty much on what outcome the court wishes to achieve or thinks to be politic. This factor in the judgment process, in turn, is not usually a matter of conscious choice but may be a function of the judge's accumulated experience in and observations of the world he lives in." Gregory, Proximate Cause in Negligence—A Retreat from "Rationalization." 6 U.Chi. L.Rev. 36, 50 (1938).

2. TYPE OF HARM

BIGBEE v. PACIFIC TEL. & TEL. CO.

Supreme Court of California, En Banc, 1983.
34 Cal.3d 49, 192 Cal.Rptr. 857, 665 P.2d 947.

BIRD, CHIEF JUSTICE.

This appeal questions the correctness of a summary judgment entered in favor of four defendants in this personal injury action. The determinative issue is whether, under the evidence presented on the motion, foreseeability remains a question of fact for the jury. (See *Weirum v. RKO General, Inc.* (1975) 15 Cal.3d 40, 46, 123 Cal.Rptr. 468, 539 P.2d 36.)

I.

On November 2, 1974, plaintiff, Charles Bigbee, was severely injured when an automobile driven by Leona North Roberts struck the telephone booth in which he was standing. Plaintiff thereafter brought an action for damages against Roberts and the companies allegedly responsible for serving her alcoholic beverages. A settlement was reached as to these defendants. In addition, plaintiff sued the companies allegedly responsible for the design, location, installation, and maintenance of the telephone booth, including Pacific Telephone and Telegraph Company (Pacific Telephone), the owner of the booth, Western Electric Company, Inc. (Western Electric), Western Industrial Services, Inc. (Western Industrial), and D.C. Decker Company (Decker).

Plaintiff sought recovery against the latter defendants[1] on theories of negligence and strict liability in tort. A second amended complaint (hereafter, the complaint), filed in 1978, alleged in substance that on the night of the accident, at approximately 12:20 a.m., plaintiff was standing in a public telephone booth located in the parking lot of a liquor store on Century Boulevard in Inglewood, California. Roberts, who was intoxicated, was driving east along Century Boulevard. She lost control of her car and veered off the street into the parking lot, crashing into the booth in which plaintiff was standing.

Plaintiff saw Roberts' car coming toward him and realized that it would hit the telephone booth. He attempted to flee but was unable to do so. According to the allegations of the complaint, the telephone booth was so defective in design and/or manufacture, or so negligently installed or maintained that the door to the booth "jammed and stuck, trapping" plaintiff inside. Had the door operated freely, he averred, he would have been able to escape and would not have suffered injury.

Additionally, plaintiff alleged that the telephone booth was negligently located in that it was placed too close to Century Boulevard * * *.

* * * [A]ll four defendants filed answers generally denying the material allegations of the complaint. Discovery was conducted and on July 29, 1980, defendants filed a joint motion for summary judgment, arguing that the undisputed facts demonstrated the absence of two elements essential to plaintiff's case. (See Code Civ.Proc., § 437c; *Frazier, Dame, Doherty, Parrish & Hanawalt v. Boccardo, Blum, Lull, Niland, Teerlink & Bell* (1977) 70 Cal.App.3d 331, 338, 339, 138 Cal. Rptr. 670.) More specifically, defendants argued that they had no duty to protect phone booth users from the risk encountered by plaintiff—a car veering off the street and crashing into the phone booth—since that risk was unforeseeable as a matter of law.[3] For the same reason, they maintained that Roberts' intervening negligent driving constituted a "superseding cause" of plaintiff's injuries. Therefore, no act or omission of theirs could be found to be a proximate cause of those injuries.[4]

* * * At the close of argument, the court granted the motion and entered a judgment of dismissal.

This appeal by the plaintiff followed.

II.

Defendants contend that their duty to use due care in the location, installation, and maintenance of telephone booths does not extend to the

---

1. As used hereafter, the term defendants refers only to these four companies who are the only other parties to this appeal.

3. A legal duty to use due care is a necessary element of a negligence action. (*United States Liab. Ins. Co. v. Haidinger-Hayes, Inc.* (1970) 1 Cal.3d 586, 594, 83 Cal.Rptr. 418, 463 P.2d 770.)

4. Proximate cause is a necessary element of both negligence and strict products liability actions. (*United States Liab. Ins. Co. v. Haidinger-Hayes, Inc., supra,* 1 Cal.3d at p. 594, 83 Cal.Rptr. 418, 463 P.2d 770; *Greenman v. Yuba Power Products, Inc.,* (1963) 59 Cal.2d 57, 62, 27 Cal.Rptr. 697, 337 P.2d 897.).

risk encountered by plaintiff and that neither their alleged negligence in carrying out these activities nor any defect in the booth was a proximate cause of plaintiff's injuries. These contentions present the same issue in different guises. Each involves this question—was the risk that a car might crash into the phone booth and injure plaintiff reasonably foreseeable in this case? (See, e.g., *Weirum v. RKO General, Inc., supra,* 15 Cal.3d 40, 45–46, 123 Cal.Rptr. 468, 539 P.2d 36; *Akins v. County of Sonoma* (1967) 67 Cal.2d 185, 198–199, 60 Cal.Rptr. 499, 430 P.2d 57; see generally, 2 Harper & James, Law of Torts (1956) §§ 18.2, 20.5, at pp. 1022, 1141–1143; Rest.2d Torts, § 281, coms. e, f and h; see also *Cronin v. J.B.E. Olson Corp.* (1972) 8 Cal.3d 121, 127, 104 Cal.Rptr. 433, 501 P.2d 1153.)

Ordinarily, foreseeability is a question of fact for the jury. (*Weirum v. RKO General, Inc., supra,* 15 Cal.3d 40, 46, 123 Cal.Rptr. 468, 539 P.2d 36.) It may be decided as a question of law only if, "under the undisputed facts there is no room for a reasonable difference of opinion." (*Schrimscher v. Bryson* (1976) 58 Cal.App.3d 660, 664, 130 Cal.Rptr. 125; accord *Richards v. Stanley* (1954) 43 Cal.2d 60, 66, 271 P.2d 23; see generally, Rest.2d Torts, § 453, com. b.) Accordingly, this court must decide whether foreseeability remains a triable issue in this case. If any triable issue of fact exists, it is error for a trial court to grant a party's motion for summary judgment. (Code Civ.Proc., § 437c: see generally, *Stationers Corp. v. Dun & Bradstreet, Inc.* (1965) 62 Cal.2d 412, 417, 42 Cal.Rptr. 449, 398 P.2d 785.)

* * *

Turning to the merits of this case, the question presented is a relatively simple one. Is there room for a reasonable difference of opinion as to whether the risk that a car might crash into the phone booth and injure an individual inside was reasonably foreseeable under the circumstances set forth above?

In pursuing this inquiry, it is well to remember that "foreseeability is not to be measured by what is more probable than not, but includes whatever is likely enough in the setting of modern life that a reasonably thoughtful [person] would take account of it in guiding practical conduct." (2 Harper & James, Law of Torts, *supra,* § 18.2, at p. 1020.) One may be held accountable for creating even " 'the risk of a slight possibility of injury if a reasonably prudent [person] would not do so.' " (*Ewart v. Southern Cal. Gas Co.* (1965) 237 Cal.App.2d 163, 172, 46 Cal.Rptr. 631, quoting from *Vasquez v. Alameda* (1958) 49 Cal.2d 674, 684, 321 P.2d 1 (dis. opn. of Traynor, J.); see also *Crane v. Smith* (1943) 23 Cal.2d 288, 299, 144 P.2d 356; see generally, Rest.2d Torts, § 291.) Moreover, it is settled that what is required to be foreseeable is the general character of the event or harm—e.g., being struck by a car while standing in a phone booth—not its precise nature or manner of occurrence. (*Taylor v. Oakland Scavenger Co.* (1941) 17 Cal.2d 594, 600, 110 P.2d 1044; *Gibson v. Garcia* (1950) 96 Cal.App.2d 681, 684, 216 P.2d 119; see generally, Rest.2d Torts, § 435, subd. 1, com. a.)

Here, defendants placed a telephone booth, which was difficult to exit, in a parking lot 15 feet from the side of a major thoroughfare and near a driveway. Under these circumstances, this court cannot conclude as a matter of law that it was unforeseeable that the booth might be struck by a car and cause serious injury to a person trapped within. A jury could reasonably conclude that this risk was foreseeable. (Cf. *Barker v. Wah Low* (1971) 19 Cal.App.3d 710, 723, 97 Cal.Rptr. 85 [reasonable jurors could find that the chance that a car in the parking lot of a drive-in restaurant might strike a patron at the adjacent service counter was foreseeable].) This is particularly true where, as here, there is evidence that a booth at this same location had previously been struck. (See, *ante,* p. 859 of 192 Cal.Rptr., pp. 949–950 of 665 P.2d and fn. 6.)

Indeed, in light of the circumstances of modern life, it seems evident that a jury could reasonably find that defendants should have foreseen the possibility of the very accident which actually occurred here. Swift traffic on a major thoroughfare late at night is to be expected. Regrettably, so too are intoxicated drivers. (See *Coulter v. Superior Court, supra,* 21 Cal.3d 144, 154, 145 Cal.Rptr. 534, 577 P.2d 669.) Moreover, it is not uncommon for speeding and/or intoxicated drivers to lose control of their cars and crash into poles, buildings or whatever else may be standing alongside the road they travel—no matter how straight and level that road may be.

Where a telephone booth, which is difficult to exit, is placed 15 feet from such a thoroughfare, the risk that it might be struck by a car veering off the street, thereby causing injury to a person trapped within, cannot be said to be unforeseeable as a matter of law.

It is of no consequence that the harm to plaintiff came about through the negligent or reckless acts of Roberts.[13] "If the likelihood that a third person may act in a particular manner is the hazard or one of the hazards which makes the actor negligent, such an act whether innocent, negligent, intentionally tortious, or criminal does not prevent the actor from being liable for harm caused thereby." (Rest.2d Torts, § 449; accord *Weirum v. RKO General, Inc., supra,* 15 Cal.3d 40, 46, 123 Cal.Rptr. 468, 539 P.2d 36; *Vesely v. Sager* (1971) 5 Cal.3d 153, 164, 95 Cal.Rptr. 623, 486 P.2d 151; *Richardson v. Ham* (1955) 44 Cal.2d 772, 777, 285 P.2d 269; see also *Cronin v. J.B.E. Olson Corp., supra,* 8 Cal.3d 121, 126–127, 104 Cal.Rptr. 433, 501 P.2d 1153.) Here, the risk that a car might hit the telephone booth could be found to constitute one of the hazards to which plaintiff was exposed.

* * *

Considering the case law and the circumstances of this case, this court cannot conclude as a matter of law that injury to plaintiff, inflicted by negligent or reckless third party drivers, was unforeseeable. "[J]ust

---

13. The police officer who investigated this accident was of the opinion that Roberts' blood alcohol was above 0.10, the legal limit. However, no blood alcohol or other chemical sobriety test was done.

as we may not rely upon our private judgment on this issue, so the trial court may not impose its private judgment upon a situation, such as this, in which reasonable minds may differ." (*Schwartz v. Helms Bakery Limited, supra,* 67 Cal.2d 232, 244, 60 Cal.Rptr. 510, 430 P.2d 68.)

Since the foreseeability of harm to plaintiff remains a triable issue of fact, the judgment is reversed and the case is remanded to the trial court for further proceedings consistent with the views expressed in this opinion.

MOSK, KAUS, BROUSSARD, REYNOSO and BANCROFT, JJ., concur.

[The concurring and dissenting opinion of KRONINGER, J., is omitted.]

Notes

1. Several other courts have also used foreseeability of harm as the test of proximate cause. *See, e.g.,* Helene Curtis Indus., Inc. v. Pruitt, 385 F.2d 841, 859–64 (5th Cir.1967), cert. denied, 391 U.S. 913, 88 S.Ct. 1806, 20 L.Ed.2d 652 (1968); Payne v. Soft Sheen Prod., Inc., 486 A.2d 712 (D.C.App. 1985); Robinson v. Williamsen Idaho Equip. Co., 94 Idaho 819, 498 P.2d 1292 (1972); Back v. Wickes Corp., 375 Mass. 633, 378 N.E.2d 964 (1978).

2. *Compare* Oehler v. Davis, 223 Pa.Super. 333, 298 A.2d 895 (1972). Defendant sold a dog collar ring that was defective because of improper casting and improper composition. A dog escaped when the ring broke because of the defect. The dog later injured the plaintiff through excessive playfulness. The court exonerated defendant because the risk of harm through playfulness was unforeseeable. If plaintiff had been injured by a foreseeable risk, such as by attack by a vicious dog, the court would have held defendant liable.

3. How would the court have decided *Oehler v. Davis* if the attack had been by a vicious dog, but the harm was unforeseeable to the defendant because it could not reasonably have discovered the flaw in the ring?

4. Courts borrowed the "foreseeability-of-risk" test from the law of negligence. They apply it somewhat differently, however, in strict liability cases. Under the law of negligence, inability of a reasonable person to foresee a risk will always exonerate the defendant. Thus, a manufacturer who cannot foresee a risk of harm because the defect in its product is undiscoverable will not be negligent. That manufacturer may, however, be subject to strict liability because knowledge of defect is often imputed to the manufacturer even where a reasonable person could not have discovered it. This is especially true in the case of manufacturing flaws. *See* Lartigue v. R.J. Reynolds Tobacco Co., 317 F.2d 19, 36–37 (5th Cir.1963), cert. denied, 375 U.S. 865, 84 S.Ct. 137, 11 L.Ed.2d 92 (1963); Feldman v. Lederle Laboratories, 97 N.J. 429, 450, 479 A.2d 374, 385 (1984); Restatement (Second) of Torts § 402A(2) comment a (1966). In such cases courts necessarily determine "foreseeability" of harm by imputing knowledge of the defect to the hypothetical reasonable manufacturer and asking what kinds of accidents the defect is likely to cause. Thus, in strict liability cases, courts use an element of "hindsight" to determine which risks are "foreseeable." This creates a broader scope of liability in strict liability cases than in negligence cases.

BAKER v. INTERNATIONAL HARVESTER CO.
Missouri Court of Appeals, Eastern District, Division Two, 1983.
660 S.W.2d 21.

SIMON, JUDGE.

Products liability case.

Appeal by plaintiffs (widow and two children of deceased) from a directed verdict for defendant International Harvester Company (manufacturer) on the ground plaintiffs failed to present a submissible case of strict liability in tort. Plaintiffs alleged (a) defective design, and (b) inadequate warning of a danger alleged to exist in the use of an International Harvester Model 815 Combine. We affirm.

* * *

[The combine had a ladder that "could be pulled up by the operator to an unboardable position so as to prevent anyone using the ladder to board the combine." Earl Dell was using the combine to harvest beans with the ladder in the down position. Without Earl Dell's knowledge, decedent boarded the combine with his gun for the purpose of hunting from the combine. "The combine was operating at about 3 to 4 miles per hour." Earl Dell was] setting the header while looking out the right side of the machine to see the height at which the beans were being cut when he saw a movement out of the corner of his left eye. Turning, he saw the decedent who appeared to be standing on the combine ladder. Decedent's gun was pointed at the cab. Earl was afraid the gun would go off and "blow" him out of the combine, so he prepared to stop the machine by letting up on the throttle. He intended to ask decedent to please get off. When Earl turned back to his instruments to prepare to stop, he felt a bump. Decedent had fallen from the combine and was killed by the combine wheel which ran over him. * * *

["A product safety engineer employed by manufacturer admitted from his experience as a hunter, people illegally hunted from combines."]

In *Keener v. Dayton Electric Mfg. Co.*, 445 S.W.2d 362 (Mo.1969) our Supreme Court adopted the rule of strict liability in tort as stated in Restatement of Torts (Second) § 402A.

The issue to be resolved is whether plaintiffs' evidence showed the combine contained a design defect which made the combine unreasonably dangerous when put to a use reasonably anticipated, and proximately caused decedent's death. The primary use to which a combine is put is harvesting grain or beans in a field in a rural area. Combines are infrequently operated on public roadways or in populated areas. It has a complicated control panel. The combine ladder must at all times be kept a certain, good harvesting distance above the ground.

Plaintiffs claim the omission of four safety items constituted a design defect in the combine. The absence of a safety factor may constitute a dangerous condition and therefore be defective. Strict liability in tort applies to defective design cases. *Blevins v. Cushman Motors*, 551 S.W.2d 602, 606–607 (Mo.Banc 1977); *Higgins v. Paul Hardeman, Inc.*, 457 S.W.2d 943, 947 (Mo.App.1970). But the manufacturer does not have a duty to design an accident proof product. *Brawner v. Liberty Industries, Inc.*, 573 S.W.2d 376, 377 (Mo.App.1978).

Plaintiffs presented evidence by expert opinion that International Harvester should have:

(1) Installed a guard to protect the decedent from falling under the combine; and

(2) Installed adequate right-hand and bubble mirrors to give the combine operator complete awareness of the activity of decedent in the vicinity of the combine; and

(3) Placed a more adequate warning of the danger to decedent about riding on the combine; and

(4) Provided an interlock to prevent the operation of the combine while the ladder was in a down position, or otherwise design the ladder so as to prevent decedent from riding on the combine while it was moving.

Without finding there was substantial evidence of a design defect in the combine, we do find any such design defect did not make the combine unreasonably dangerous when put to its anticipated use of harvesting grain or beans. Strict liability focuses on foreseeable or reasonably anticipated use of the combine, rather than on the reasonably anticipated harm the combine may cause. *Blevins v. Cushman Motors*, 551 S.W.2d 602, 607–608 (Mo.Banc 1977).

The use of the ladder by decedent while holding onto a gun, without knowledge of such use by the combine operator, and at a time when the combine was being used to harvest beans in a rural area, was a use by decedent not intended nor anticipated by the manufacturer. Decedent was a user, and not a bystander, of the combine. *Mead v. Corbin Equipment, Inc.*, 586 S.W.2d 388, 392 (Mo.App.1979). The unannounced and unexpected boarding of the combine ladder by decedent while holding a gun was a species of abnormal use which bars recovery under the doctrine of strict liability. *Coulter v. Michelin Tire Corp.*, 622 S.W.2d 421, 430–431 (Mo.App.1981). And, the manufacturer has no duty to warn of an unintended use.

Judgment affirmed.

GEORGE F. GUNN, SPECIAL JUDGE and CRIST, P.J., concur.

Notes

1. Several other courts also reject the requirement that harm be foreseeable in strict liability cases. They focus instead on foreseeability of use. *See, e.g.,* Eshbach v. W.T. Grant's & Co., 481 F.2d 940 (3d Cir.1973); Brown v. United States Stove Co., 98 N.J. 155, 166, 484 A.2d 1234, 1240 (1984); Newman v. Utility Trailer & Equip. Co., 278 Or. 395, 564 P.2d 674

(1977). These courts do not necessarily impose a broader scope of liability than courts that require foreseeability of harm. In addition to requiring foreseeability of use, they may also require foreseeability of the plaintiff and of any intervening causes. The scope of liability depends on how narrowly or broadly these restrictions are applied.

2. How would a court following the *Baker* approach decide *Oehler v. Davis, supra* note 2, page 521?

3. In *Baker,* how could the use be unforeseeable if the manufacturer's product safety engineer knew that people hunted from combines?

4. Suppose that in *Baker* the operator backed the combine over a farm worker who was standing in the field behind the combine. The operator did not see the co-worker because his visibility was obstructed, but adequate "right-hand and bubble mirrors" would have made it possible for the operator to see the worker. Would the court have decided the case differently? *Cf.,* Pike v. Frank G. Hough Co., 2 Cal.3d 465, 85 Cal.Rptr. 629, 467 P.2d 229 (1970) (paydozer backed over worker because of blind spot to rear which could have been corrected with mirrors; manufacturer held strictly liable).

5. If the answer to the question in the preceding note is yes, why would the court not impose liability under the facts of *Baker?* A person was run over because of a defective design that created a risk of being run over. Why should it matter whether he was illegally hunting at the time?

3. INTERVENING CAUSE AND MISUSE [1]

The distinction between misuse and intervening cause is merely a matter of terminology. An intervening cause is an actively operating force that comes on the scene after the defendant's tortious conduct has taken place. If the relevant intervening act is done by the user of the product, courts often label the conduct as misuse rather than as an intervening cause, but the effect is clearly the same regardless of the label. Kuisis v. Baldwin–Lima–Hamilton Corp., 457 Pa. 321, 331 n. 13, 319 A.2d 914, 920 n. 13 (1974) (intervening cause and abnormal use are equivalent); Pegg v. General Motors Corp., 258 Pa.Super. 59, 78, 391 A.2d 1074, 1083 (1978). Both intervening causes and acts of misuse are judged by the same foreseeability standard. *E.g.,* Pegg v. General Motors Corp., 258 Pa.Super. 59, 78, 391 A.2d 1074, 1083 (1978); Keeton, Products Liability and Defenses—Intervening Misconduct, 15 Forum 109, 112–113 (1978).

A great many products liability cases involve either misuse or intervening causes. Leistra v. Bucyrus–Erie Co., 443 F.2d 157 (8th Cir.1971). Defendant's tortious conduct must be complete when the product leaves its hands because the law requires the product to be defective at that time. Restatement (Second) of Torts § 402A(1), comment g (1966). Accidents cannot happen unless someone subsequently acts, and these acts are intervening causes. Liability frequently turns

---

1. This note is adapted from Fischer, Products Liability—Proximate Cause, In- tervening Cause, and Duty, 52 Mo.L.Rev. 547, 557–58 (1987).

on a determination of whether these acts cut off the manufacturer's liability.

VENTRICELLI v. KINNEY SYS. RENT A CAR, INC.

Court of Appeals of New York, 1978.
45 N.Y.2d 950, 411 N.Y.S.2d 555, 383 N.E.2d 1149.

[Plaintiff leased a car with a defective trunk lid from defendant Kinney System Rent A Car. The trunk lid flew open while the car was moving and blocked his view. Plaintiff parked the car in a parking place on the side of the road, went behind the car, and attempted to close the truck lid. A car parked behind him, operated by defendant Maldonado, lurched forward and severely injured plaintiff. The trial court granted an award against defendant Kinney and others. The Supreme Court, Appellate Division affirmed after modification to dismiss the complaint as against defendant Kinney.]

OPINION OF THE COURT

Memorandum.

Order of the Appellate Division affirmed, with costs. Proximate cause and foreseeability are relative terms, "nothing more than a convenient formula for disposing of the case" (Prosser, Law of Torts [4th ed.], § 43, p. 267). In writing of the "orbit of the duty", Chief Judge Cardozo said "[t]he range of reasonable apprehension is at times a question for the court, and at times, if varying inferences are possible, a question for the jury" (*Palsgraf v. Long Is. R.R. Co.,* 248 N.Y. 339, 345, 162 N.E. 99, 101). So it is with proximate cause and foreseeability (compare *Sheehan v. City of New York,* 40 N.Y.2d 496, 502–503, 387 N.Y.S.2d 92, 95–96, 354 N.E.2d 832, 834–835, and *Rivera v. City of New York,* 11 N.Y.2d 856, 227 N.Y.S.2d 676, 182 N.E.2d 284, with *Pagan v. Goldberger,* 51 A.D.2d 508, 511–512, 382 N.Y.S.2d 549, 551–552).

Although the negligence of the automobile renter, defendant Kinney, is manifest, and was, of course, a "cause" of the accident, it was not the proximate cause. "What we do mean by the word 'proximate' is, that because of convenience, of public policy, of a rough sense of justice, the law arbitrarily declines to trace a series of events beyond a certain point" (*Palsgraf v. Long Is. R.R. Co.,* 248 N.Y. 339, 352, 162 N.E. 99, 103, *supra* [Andrews, J., dissenting]). The immediately effective cause of plaintiff's injuries was the negligence of Maldonado, the driver of the second car, in striking plaintiff while he was standing behind his parked automobile. That Kinney's negligence in providing an automobile with a defective trunk lid would result in plaintiff's repeated attempts to close the lid was reasonably foreseeable. Not "foreseeable", however, was the collision between vehicles both parked a brief interval before the accident. Plaintiff was standing in a relatively "safe" place, a parking space, not in an actively traveled lane. He might well have been there independent of any negligence of Kinney, as, for example, if he were loading or unloading the trunk. Under these circumstances, to hold the accident a foreseeable consequence of Kinney's negligence is to stretch the concept of foreseeability beyond acceptable limits (see Prosser, Law of Torts [4th ed.], pp. 267–270; Restatement, Torts 2d, § 435, subd. 2).

FUCHSBERG, JUDGE (dissenting).

When Dean Prosser suggested that proximate cause may at times seem to be "nothing more than a convenient formula for disposing of the case", he also observed that the existence of proximate cause must " 'be determined on the facts of each case upon mixed considerations of logic, common sense, justice, policy and precedent' " (Prosser, Law of Torts [4th ed.], § 42, pp. 267, 249).

The generality of both these statements recognizes that torts is a branch of the law in which the decisional process is usually so dependent on the vagaries of particular facts in individual cases that it calls for a high degree of flexibility in judgment (see Pound, Introduction to the Philosophy of Law, 139). Thus, disputes as to whether conduct is negligent, contributorily negligent or the proximate cause of an injury are usually best left to the fact finder. Since the record here convinces me that this case [falls] well within the range of these cautions, I believe the Trial Judge did not err as a matter of law in leaving the issue of proximate cause to the jury.

Ample was the proof that, to the knowledge of the rental company, the trunk door on the automobile it furnished to the plaintiff had a penchant for flying open so as to obstruct the operator's view while the vehicle was moving. Given those facts, it was not only foreseeable, but a most reasonable rather than a remote expectation, that a driver confronted by such an emergency would alight and promptly proceed to the rear of the car to attempt to secure the lid manually so that he might continue on his way without further danger to others and himself. The seemingly ineluctable consequence was to expose the driver to the danger of being struck by another vehicle while he was positioned behind the trunk. On these facts, it could readily be found, as the jury apparently did here, that the choice between the alternatives—the danger from the obstruction of the driver's view from the vehicle and the danger of being struck while engaged in the act of removing the danger—was thrust on the plaintiff by Kinney's negligence. Of course, whether in making the choice he did plaintiff himself was negligent similarly raised a factual issue within the province of the jury.

To be sure, at other times and for other reasons, the plaintiff may have had occasion to undergo similar risks while in a roadway on foot, but the fact remains that defendant's conduct increased the occasions for such risks: specifically, the one on which plaintiff was injured would not have transpired. To paraphrase what Judge (later Chief Judge) Crane said for a unanimous court in *O'Neill v. City of Port Jervis*, 253 N.Y. 423, 431–432, 171 N.E. 694, 697 [the defendant's obstruction of a sidewalk had led a pedestrian to enter the roadway], if the defendant "had been there and forced [Ventricelli] into the wheels of traffic, no doubt would exist in the minds of any one as to liability for consequences. Is the conclusion any different because necessity, and not force, is the moving cause? [Kinney] created the necessity which led to danger. * * * The accident would not have happened but for the [defective trunk lid]."

Moreover, I perceive no sufficient reason to depart from these principles because the plaintiff, before exiting from the car to make the trunk adjustment, thought it preferable to park the car at an available spot in the curb lane instead of the middle lane of the block of New York City's busy and narrow Pell Street, where he found himself when the trunk suddenly sprung open. In either case, he was where he could be expected to be—in the roadway with his attention diverted by the trunk on which he was working. Those who drive along a curb lane or pull in or out of one for the purpose of parking are not necessarily more careful or more observant than those to be found in an inner lane. In any event, being at most but a quantitative factor which did not detract from the qualitative risk, it was peculiarly one for consideration by the jury under all the circumstances and not a basis for determination as a matter of law.

All this is not to say that the jury had to find that there was a reasonable likelihood of danger resulting from the act of which plaintiff complains. It could have found that there was not. But, by its verdict it did in effect find that the accident that caused the plaintiff to lose his leg was at least in part the "ordinary and natural result" of the defendant's negligent act. And that it also had a right to do. (*O'Neill v. City of Port Jervis, supra*, p. 432, 171 N.E. p. 697.)

I therefore would vote to reverse the order of the Appellate Division and remit the case to it for the determination of any remaining questions.

BREITEL, C.J., and JASEN, GABRIELLI, JONES, WACHTLER and COOKE, JJ., concur.

FUCHSBERG, J., dissents and votes to reverse in a separate opinion.

Order affirmed in a memorandum, with costs to respondents-appellants Kinney against appellant-respondent Ventricelli and third-party respondents American.

Notes

1. In a great many product liability cases the defectiveness of the product turns on the question of whether the intervening cause or misuse is foreseeable. This is because manufacturers must design products to be reasonably safe in light of anticipated misuse and intervening causes. Cases of this sort are treated in Chapter 7, Section D. This Section focuses on cases where the product is clearly defective, but the intervening cause or misuse may nevertheless cut off liability.

2. In determining whether an intervening cause is "foreseeable," some courts use hindsight rather than foresight. That is, they look back on the whole sequence of events and rule that the intervening cause is unforeseeable if the sequence of events appears extraordinary. *See* Griggs v. Firestone Tire & Rubber Co., 513 F.2d 851, 861 (8th Cir.1975), cert. denied, 423

U.S. 865, 96 S.Ct. 124, 46 L.Ed.2d 93 (1975); Eshbach v. W.T. Grant's & Co., 481 F.2d 940, 945 (3d Cir.1973); Young v. Tide Craft, Inc., 270 S.C. 453, 465–66, 242 S.E.2d 671, 677 (1978).

TUCCI v. BOSSERT
Supreme Court, Appellate Division, Second Department, 1976.
53 A.D.2d 291, 385 N.Y.S.2d 328.

Before GULOTTA, P.J., and HOPKINS, LATHAM, MARGETT and SHAPIRO, JJ.

HOPKINS, JUSTICE.

Essentially, the question before us is whether the complaint states a cause of action against the defendant Drackett Products Company (Drackett). We hold that it does and, accordingly, modify the order of Special Term which dismissed the complaint against Drackett by reinstating the complaint. * * *

The complaint pleads six causes of action, each of which is directed toward certain of the defendants, but we deal here only with the sufficiency of the causes of action naming Drackett as defendant. Besides the formal pleading, the allegations are amplified by affidavits submitted on behalf of the parties. The core of the plaintiffs' claim against Drackett may be summarized thus:

The defendants Durr purchased a can of Drano in April, 1974. Drano, a product manufactured by Drackett, is designed and sold for the purpose of unclogging drains. The Durrs discarded the can by placing it within a trash bag in front of their house, although only a part of the contents of the can had been used. Drano is designed and intended to be used by the consumer through pouring one tablespoon of the product down a drain, followed by one cup of cold water. The infant plaintiff was injured when the infant defendant Bossert, together with the infant plaintiff, removed the can from the bag in which it had been discarded and poured water into the can, whereupon it exploded. This action by the infant plaintiff and his parents was then instituted.

The causes of action against Drackett assert that Drano is a dangerous, volatile and explosive product, which was inadequately and unsafely packaged, that the product and package had latent defects which rendered them unreasonably dangerous and that Drackett warranted, both expressly and impliedly, that the product was merchantable and without great danger in its use and that it was fit for the purpose to which it was intended to be put. The question is, consequently, whether the complaint, liberally viewed as a pleading, states valid causes of action on the theories of strict liability and warranty.

Drackett's ground for dismissal is that, under any theory of product liability, no recovery may be allowed when it appears that the infant plaintiff was injured as a result of the misuse and mishandling of the can of Drano. Drackett points out that the infant plaintiff was neither a buyer nor a third-party beneficiary of the buyer and, therefore, derived no rights under the law of warranty. We cannot say, however, at this pleading stage in the litigation, that the plaintiffs may not ultimately be entitled to recovery.

The allegations in the complaint that Drackett manufactured and marketed a dangerous product, defectively and unsafely packaged, liberally construed (see *Condon v. Associated Hosp. Service,* 287 N.Y. 411, 414, 40 N.E.2d 230, 231), are fairly susceptible of the claim that inadequate or no warning was given by Drackett of the latent dangers reasonably to be foreseen which might result from the use or misuse of the product. The manufacturer of a dangerous product under such circumstances is under a duty to exercise reasonable care to provide proper warnings (*McLaughlin v. Mine Safety Appliances Co.,* 11 N.Y.2d 62, 68–69, 226 N.Y.S.2d 407, 411–412, 181 N.E.2d 430, 433; *Howard Stores Corp. v. Pope,* 1 N.Y.2d 110, 115, 150 N.Y.S.2d 792, 796, 134 N.E.2d 63, 66; *Carey v. Hercules Chem. Corp.,* 51 A.D.2d 697, 379 N.Y.S.2d 407; Restatement, Torts 2d, § 402A; 1 N.Y. Pattern Jury Instructions [2d ed.], 2:135). No longer is it a barrier to recovery that the loss suffered came about as the result of the use of the product by one not the purchaser, or an employee or relative of the purchaser (cf. *Codling v. Paglia,* 32 N.Y.2d 330, 338–341, 345 N.Y.S.2d 461, 465–468, 298 N.E.2d 622, 625–627). In *Howard Stores Corp. v. Pope (supra),* for example, the plaintiffs alleged that a destructive fire occurred when an unknown person ignited lacquer inadequately labelled or unlabelled and that the plaintiffs' building was thereby damaged; the complaint was held to state a cause of action because the cans of lacquer were alleged to be improperly labelled or not labelled at all by the manufacturer and distributor.

Indeed, the true test of liability is not the identity or character of the user who is injured; it is, rather, whether the risks reasonably to be foreseen would arise from a misuse reasonably to be foreseen (*Suchomajcz v. Hummel Chem. Co.,* 3 Cir., 524 F.2d 19, 28; *Mazzi v. Greenlee Tool Co.,* 2 Cir., 320 F.2d 821, 823; *Kuisis v. Baldwin–Lima–Hamilton Corp.,* 457 Pa. 321, 319 A.2d 914). That test is derived from the principle that foreseeability includes the probability of the occurrence of a general type of risk involving the loss, rather than the probability of the occurrence of the precise chain of events preceding the loss (2 Harper & James, Law of Torts, § 18.2, p. 1026; § 20.5[6], pp. 1147–1149; and see the particularly perceptive and thorough discussion by Weinstein, J., in *Hall v. E.I. Du Pont De Nemours & Co.,* D.C., 345 F.Supp. 353, 362–363, dealing with the question of the liability of the manufacturers of blasting caps which exploded and injured children who found them after the caps had been lost or discarded by the purchasers).[1] Thus, a casual bystander or an aimless interloper may not be excluded from recovery for an injury resulting from a dangerous product, if the injury arose from a reasonably foreseeable risk which might befall a

---

1. Other cases which treat the issue of liability where an injury occurs after an unusual but reasonably foreseen use are *Moran v. Faberge,* 273 Md. 538, 332 A.2d 11; *Jonescue v. Jewel Home Shopping Serv.,* 16 Ill.App.3d 339, 306 N.E.2d 312 and *Anderson v. Klix Chem. Co.,* 256 Or. 199, 472 P.2d 806.

consumer. In this case, given the existence of a dangerous product without proper labelling to warn against the use of excessive water, the fact that Drackett might not foresee the exact series of events (that is, the discarding of the material by the purchaser in the manner described) does not in itself prevent recovery.[2]

An indication that Drano's chemical content might reasonably be foreseen to be dangerous if mixed with water is the statement in the affidavit submitted by Drackett's officer, on its motion to dismiss the complaint, that only one tablespoon of Drano, followed by one cup of water, should be used to clear a drain. Moreover, other instances of the explosive character of Drano appear in the books (*Blue v. Drackett Prods. Co.*, 143 So.2d 897 [Fla.App.]; *Moore v. Jewel Tea Co.*, 116 Ill.App.2d 109, 253 N.E.2d 636). In any event, the issues of the knowledge of the dangers to be encountered in the use of Drano, the use or misuse by the infant plaintiff of the product, the kind and quality of the warning given by Drackett accompanying the product, the general question of proximate cause under the circumstances and the conduct of the infant plaintiff at the time of the incident, are all matters within the domain of the jury, to be decided upon the proof presented.

We thus uphold the sufficiency of the complaint. * * *

The order appealed from, accordingly, should be modified by reinstating the complaint, and otherwise affirmed.

GULOTTA, P.J., and LATHAM, MARGETT and SHAPIRO, JJ., concur.

SHAPIRO, J., with a separate concurring opinion, in which GULOTTA, P.J., and LATHAM, J., join.

[The concurring opinion of SHAPIRO, J., is omitted.]

Notes

1. There is a split of authority on the question of whether the seller is liable in cases where the type of harm is foreseeable but the manner of harm is not. In addition to the main case, a number of other cases have not required that the manner of harm be foreseeable. Pust v. Union Supply Co., 38 Colo.App. 435, 561 P.2d 355 (1976), affirmed, 196 Colo. 162, 583 P.2d 276 (1978) (strict liability); Noonan v. Buick Co., 211 So.2d 54 (Fla.App.1968), cert. denied, 219 So.2d 698 (1968) (negligence); Moran v. Faberge, Inc., 273 Md. 538, 332 A.2d 11 (1975) (negligence); American Laundry Mach. Indus. v. Horan, 45 Md.App. 97, 412 A.2d 407 (1980) (negligence); Haberly v. Reardon Co., 319 S.W.2d 859 (Mo.1958) (negligence); Libbey–Owens Ford Glass Co. v. L & M Paper Co., 189 Neb. 792, 205 N.W.2d 523 (1973) (negligence). Other cases have required foreseeability of manner of harm. Dyer v. Best Pharmacal, 118 Ariz. 465, 577 P.2d 1084 (App.1978) (strict liability; negligence); Mohrdieck v. Morton Grove, 94 Ill.App.3d 1021, 50

2. It is a jury question, for example, whether the manufacturer might reasonably foresee that the product, without container or proper label giving warning, might come into the hands of an ultimate user (*McLaughlin v. Mine Safety Appliances Co.*, 11 N.Y.2d 62, 69, 226 N.Y.S.2d 407, 411, 181 N.E.2d 430, 433, *supra*).

Ill.Dec. 409, 419 N.E.2d 517 (1981) (negligence); Ritter v. Narragansett Elec. Co., 109 R.I. 176, 283 A.2d 255 (1971) (negligence, strict liability).

2. In one particular type of case most courts require foreseeability of the manner of harm. Where a third party discovers the defect and either continues to use it himself or fails to warn others who will use it, courts generally impose liability only where the third person's conduct was foreseeable. Consider the following cases:

A. Peck v. Ford Motor Co., 603 F.2d 1240 (7th Cir.1979) (Strict liability; a Ford truck stalled in the middle of a heavily traveled lane of traffic due to a defect. The driver put out inadequate warning markers and left the scene without notifying the police. Three hours later Plaintiff's vehicle crashed into the truck. The court held that Ford's duty terminated shortly after the truck stalled because the driver's negligence was unforeseeable).

B. Mull v. Ford Motor Co., 368 F.2d 713 (2d Cir.1966) (Negligence, implied warranty; a taxicab stalled in a busy street because of a defect. The driver attempted to "buck" it to the curb by using the starter. The hood popped up and completely obscured the driver's vision. He, nevertheless, continued to "buck" the cab, and ran into plaintiff, severely injuring him. The court held that it was unforeseeable as a matter of law that the driver would proceed after the hood flew up).

C. Conder v. Hull Lift Truck, Inc., 435 N.E.2d 10 (Ind.1982) (Negligence; strict liability; Employer's use of forklift truck with knowledge of carburetor linkage problem; upholding jury finding that the use was unforeseeable).

3. How would a New York court have decided *Baker v. International Harvester Co., supra* page 522?

4. Consider the following problem:

Paul, a nine year old child, was severely injured when he fell into the exposed auger blades of a Dover Feed–O–Matic Cattle Feeder. The feeder was purchased by Paul's father, and was located in his barn. The feeder transported grain from the barn to the feed yard. The system was comprised, in part, of augers that moved the grain. The augers were located in the bottoms of uncovered troughs. The troughs met at right angles at various places in the barn. At these locations, the grain from one trough/auger would spill into another trough/auger. At the time of the accident, Paul was playing a game involving squirt guns with his younger brothers. The boys turned on the cattle feeder by reaching the on/off switch with a pitchfork. Paul fell into one of the troughs when he attempted to climb over it. He failed to step widely enough because he misjudged his distance.

Dover manufactured a trough/auger cover for the feeder that could be purchased separately by special order. It did not warn purchasers of the necessity of purchasing such covers. It also did not warn purchasers of the dangers associated with the cattle feeder. All of its literature depicted the feeder without covers. Dover's advertising stated that "Even a child can do your feeding." Paul's father did not order trough/auger covers when he purchased the cattle feeder.

The feeder is allegedly defective in two ways. First, it was improperly designed because it did not come equipped with trough/auger covers. Dover has some evidence that it was reasonable to sell the covers separately because in many instances it was impractical to use covers. Second, the feeder was defective because Dover failed to warn about the dangers associated with the unguarded augers. Paul has some evidence that the feeder was more dangerous than most people would expect, especially because the auger blades sharpened themselves as the feeder was used, and became more sharp over time.

Will Paul recover against Dover on a strict liability theory? You need not address the question of whether the feeder is defective. You may assume that Paul has sufficient evidence to make a jury question on that issue. Focus your attention instead on the other issues raised by the facts.

HOLLENBECK v. SELECTONE CORP.

Appellate Court of Illinois, Third District, 1985.
131 Ill.App.3d 969, 87 Ill.Dec. 44, 476 N.E.2d 746.

SCOTT, JUSTICE.

The plaintiff, James Hollenbeck, brings the instant interlocutory appeal from an order dismissing those counts of his complaint which stated causes of action against the defendant, Selectone Corporation.

The plaintiff was a police officer for the city of Marseilles. As part of his equipment, he was issued a mobile pager manufactured by Selectone. On February 28, 1982, the plaintiff activated the pager in an effort to obtain assistance in effectuating an arrest. The pager unit failed to operate. During the course of the arrest, the plaintiff was assaulted by several individuals and was severely injured.

The plaintiff brought suit against his assailants and the defendant Selectone. The plaintiff asserted three grounds for recovery against Selectone. Count IX of the complaint set forth a cause of action based upon breach of an implied warranty. Count X set forth a claim under the theory of strict liability. The cause of action stated in Count XI was based upon negligence. On the defendant's motion, the trial court dismissed Counts IX, X and XI. This appeal followed.

The trial court based its dismissal on the holding in *Williams v. RCA Corp.* (1st Dist., 1978), 59 Ill.App.3d 229, 17 Ill.Dec. 144, 376 N.E.2d 37. The plaintiff in *Williams* was employed as a private security guard. The plaintiff's employer supplied him with a two-way portable receiver manufactured by RCA. A robbery occurred while the plaintiff was on duty. The plaintiff activated the receiver to request assistance. Believing that additional officers would be arriving, Williams attempted to arrest the robber. However, the receiver had malfunctioned. While acting alone in attempting the arrest, Williams was severely injured.

Williams filed suit against RCA under a products liability theory. The trial court dismissed Williams' complaint for failure to state a cause of action. The trial court ruled that the complaint failed to establish the element of proximate cause because the robber's action in wounding Williams was, as a matter of law, an independent intervening cause.

The *Williams* court affirmed the decision of the trial court. The court began its review with the legal principle that an intervening criminal act does not break the causal connection between the product and the injury if that criminal act is probable and foreseeable. The *Williams* court construed probable and foreseeable to mean "objectively reasonable to expect." The injury to Williams was not objectively reasonable to expect, according to the court, because a manufacturer may assume that no one will violate the law; the receiver was not designed to prevent criminal attack; and the manufacturer could not have foreseen that Williams would act before determining whether he had support.

We consider first the dismissal of Count [X], which alleged strict liability by misrepresentation. The cause of action in *Williams* was based upon strict liability for an unreasonably dangerous product. Williams was therefore required to prove that the defective, dangerous product was the proximate cause of his injury. (Restatement (Second) of Torts § 402A (1965).) In the instant case, the plaintiff based the cause of action in Count X on strict liability based upon misrepresentation. (Restatement (Second) of Torts § 402B (1965).) Thus, the plaintiff was required to allege that his injury was proximately caused by the failure of the [pager] to conform to the defendant's representations. *Klages v. General Ordinance Equipment Corp.* (1976), 240 Pa.Super. 356, 367 A.2d 304.

The issue before this court, then, is whether the plaintiff properly set forth the element of proximate cause so as to defeat a motion to dismiss. Specifically, we must determine whether the intervening criminal acts of the arrestee's family were probable and foreseeable so that the causal connection between the plaintiff's injury and the pager's failure to conform to the defendant's representations remained unbroken.

We find that the intervening criminal acts were not so improbable and unforeseeable as to break the causal connection. As the *Williams* court stated, probable and foreseeable means "objectively reasonable to expect." In the instant case, the plaintiff has alleged that the defendant represented that its product was suitable for use by police agencies and that it marketed its product specifically for use by such agencies. It was, therefore, objectively reasonable to expect that [pagers] would be used by police officers in emergency situations where communication by pager was necessary. Given the undisputable fact that one of the critical functions of a police officer is to deal with persons violating the law, it was objectively reasonable to expect that the pager would be utilized in a situation involving a criminal offense. In short, we cannot say, as the court in *Williams* did, that the defendant manufacturer could assume that no one will violate the law.

It was also objectively reasonable to expect that the plaintiff, after activating the pager, would proceed to make the arrest. It is a police officer's duty to apprehend and arrest those violating the law. The defendant knew or should have known of this duty when it marketed its product to police departments. Thus, the instant case is distinguishable from *Williams* in that the defendant manufacturer should have foreseen that the plaintiff would act after activating his pager.

We, therefore, find that the intervening criminal acts did not break the causal connection because the acts were probable and foreseeable. The plaintiff has alleged the requisite element of proximate cause so as to defeat the defendant's motion to dismiss Count X.

The plaintiff asserts that Counts IX and X are based upon strict liability. However, a reading of Count IX clearly shows that it states a theory of breach of the implied warranty of merchantability. Because no issue has been raised concerning this theory of liability, we decline to review the merits of the dismissal as to Count IX.

Similarly, the plaintiff has not argued on appeal that the acts of the defendant which he alleges were negligently performed were the proximate cause of his injury. Because the plaintiff has not raised the merits of the dismissal of Count XI, which sounds in simple negligence, we decline to review the merits as to the dismissals of Count XI.

Accordingly, the judgment of the circuit court of LaSalle County is affirmed as to Counts IX and XI and reversed as to Count X; the cause is remanded for further proceedings consistent with this decision.

Affirmed in part, reversed in part, and remanded.

BARRY, J., concurs.

HEIPLE, J., specially concurring.

HEIPLE, PRESIDING JUSTICE, specially concurring.

I agree with the result reached. The attempt to distinguish *Williams v. RCA Corp.,* however, is not convincing. The effect of the instant decision is to overrule *Williams.*

It is significant in this case that the pager was allegedly marketed specifically for use by police agencies. As the majority opinion correctly points out, it is a police officer's duty to apprehend and arrest lawbreakers. The defendant should be charged with the knowledge that the pager would be used by a police officer to summon help in dangerous situations and that the officer's safety would be seriously compromised if the device failed to work. That is the theory. The case should not have been dismissed on the pleadings. The plaintiff was entitled to a trial.

Notes

1. Would the court have decided the case differently if plaintiff sued under § 402A of the Restatement (Second) of Torts (1965) rather than under § 402B?

2. Courts have generally been reluctant to find that intervening criminal misconduct is foreseeable. For example, Bennet v. Cincinnati Checker Cab Co., 353 F.Supp. 1206 (E.D.Ky.1973), dealt with whether the importer of a handgun was strictly liable for intentional harm caused by criminal misuse of the gun. In addition to finding that the gun was not defective, the court held that the criminal act was not foreseeable. The court stated:

> The rule concerning foreseeability of a subsequent criminal act is stated in Prosser, [Torts], 3d Edition, page 176:

> There is normally much less reason to anticipate acts on the part of others which are malicious and intentionally damaging than those which are merely negligent; and this is all the more true where, as is usually the case, such acts are criminal. Under all ordinary and normal circumstances, in the absence of any reason to expect the contrary, the actor may reasonably proceed upon the assumption that others will obey the criminal law.

> * * * It is clear that the above authority erects no duty upon a manufacturer of a nondefective product to anticipate the various unlawful acts possible through the misuse of that item.

Most other courts that have decided this issue are in agreement. *See, e.g.,* Martin v. Harrington and Richardson, Inc., 743 F.2d 1200 (7th Cir.1984) (applying Illinois law). *But see* Kelley v. R.G. Indus., Inc., 304 Md. 124, 497 A.2d 1143 (1985), *supra,* note 4, page 199, (manufacturer of "Saturday Night Special" is strictly liable for criminal misuse).

3. In Crowther v. Ross Chem. & Mfg. Co., 42 Mich.App. 426, 202 N.W.2d 577 (1972), two young children were murdered by a man who had been sniffing glue. The parent of the children brought a wrongful death action against the glue manufacturer for negligence and breach of warranty. Plaintiff alleged that sniffing the glue caused "hallucination, depression, loss of self-control and insanity," that defendant knew of the widespread practice of glue sniffing, and that it failed to warn about the effects of the practice. The court held that the pleadings stated a cause of action. Is *Crowther* distinguishable from the handgun cases?

4. In cases like *Hollenbeck*, where the product is designed to protect the user from criminal attack, courts are much more likely to find that the criminal misconduct is foreseeable. In Klages v. General Ordnance Equip. Corp., 240 Pa.Super. 356, 367 A.2d 304 (1976), cited in *Hollenbeck*, plaintiff attempted to subdue a robber with a mace pen. The robber shot plaintiff in the head because the pen failed to instantly subdue the robber as represented. The manufacturer was held strictly liable for plaintiff's injury on a misrepresentation theory. The court held that criminal attack was clearly foreseeable in the event that the pen failed to perform as represented.

5. A rug burns when a hotel is deliberately set on fire by an arsonist. Is the manufacturer of the rug liable for harm to the guests? Delk v. Holiday Inns, Inc., 545 F.Supp. 969 (S.D.Ohio 1982) (no; rug allegedly gave off excessive smoke and hazardous gases when burned); d'Hedouville v. Pioneer Hotel Co., 552 F.2d 886 (9th Cir.1977) (yes; rug excessively flammable).

6. A car is equipped with tires that are not safe at speeds in excess of 85 miles per hour, and the manufacturer fails to warn against exceeding this speed. A tire blows out because the car is being driven in excess of 100 miles per hour. Is the manufacturer of the car liable? *See* LeBouef v. Goodyear Tire & Rubber Co., 623 F.2d 985 (5th Cir.1980) (yes); Hegwood v. General Motors Corp., 286 N.W.2d 29 (Iowa 1979) (no).

WHEELER v. ANDREW JERGENS CO.
Court of Appeals of Kentucky, 1985.
696 S.W.2d 326.

[Plaintiff lost 80% of her hair as a result of using shampoo manufactured by defendant. She brought an action against defendant on strict liability, negligence, and breach of warranty theories. The trial court directed a verdict in favor of the defendant, ruling that there was no liability under Ky.Rev.Stat.Ann.§ 411.320 because the shampoo had been modified by a third person. Plaintiff appealed.]

In the case before us, appellant's evidence shows that she bought a bottle of "Gee Your Hair Smells Terrific" shampoo from a Taylor drug store. Appellant testified that she opened the new bottle of shampoo and poured the product on her hair, experienced an immediate burning sensation, and subsequently lost nearly all her hair. We think that reasonable minds could easily conclude from the evidence that appellee's shampoo caused appellant's hair loss. Whether or not the product was subsequently modified by a third person is a question of fact for the jury. The trial court clearly erred by settling that issue in favor of appellee at the close of appellant's case.

Even if the evidence establishes that appellee's shampoo was tampered with by a third person, we do not think a directed verdict is appropriate in this case. If appellant convinces a jury that a reasonably prudent manufacturer would have sealed its product before placing it on the market, appellant can recover for appellee's negligence in failing to do so. In the alternative, appellant could establish that the shampoo bottle was defectively designed and recover from appellee under Kentucky's Products Liability Act.

In cases of this nature, we prefer to place the risk of personal injury and property damage with the manufacturer rather than the consumer. In *Embs v. Pepsi Cola Bottling Company of Lexington,* Ky. 528 S.W.2d 703 (1975), our Supreme Court expressed the public policy in the state as follows:

> Our expressed public policy will be furthered if we minimize the risk of personal injury and property damage by charging the cost of injuries against the manufacturer who can procure liability insurance and distribute its expense among the public as a cost of doing business[.] * * * The imposition of strict liability places no unreasonable burden upon sellers because they can adjust the cost of insurance protection among themselves in the course of their continuing business relationship. [Citations omitted]. *Id.* at 705.

We conclude that the motion for a directed verdict should have been denied and appellee should have been required to come forward with its evidence.

The judgment of the Bullitt Circuit Court is reversed and the case is remanded for further proceedings consistent with this opinion.

All concur.

Note

Ky.Rev.Stat.Ann. § 411.320 (Michie Supp.1986) provides:

(1) In any product liability action, a manufacturer shall be liable only for the personal injury, death or property damage that would have occurred if the product had been used in its original, unaltered and unmodified condition. For the purpose of this section, product alteration or modification shall include failure to observe routine care and maintenance, but shall not include ordinary wear and tear. This section shall apply to alterations or modifications made by any person or entity, except those made in accordance with specifications or instructions furnished by the manufacturer.

* * *

GUARINO v. MINE SAFETY APPLIANCE CO.

Court of Appeals of New York, 1969.
25 N.Y.2d 460, 306 N.Y.S.2d 942, 255 N.E.2d 173.

JASEN, JUDGE.

These consolidated actions arose out of an accident wherein three men died and five others were injured.

On October 2, 1957, one John J. Rooney, an engineer employed by the Bureau of Sewage Disposal of the City of New York, died of gas asphyxiation after descending into an interceptor sewer located 30 or 40 feet below the ground in the Borough of Queens to ascertain the source of water in the bulkhead. At the time of the accident, he was wearing an oxygen-type protective mask manufactured by the defendant herein. The estate of John J. Rooney recovered a judgment against the defendant on a theory of breach of implied warranty of merchantability, in "that the mask did not work because the plunger was defective." (Rooney v. Healy Co., 20 N.Y.2d 42, 46, 281 N.Y.S.2d 321, 324–325, 228 N.E.2d 383, 385–386 [1967].)

The two other decedents, and the surviving plaintiffs, were all sewage treatment workers and members of Rooney's work team at the time of the accident. Plaintiff Fattore entered the sewer tunnel with Rooney after testing for gas and finding none. Decedent Guarino was stationed at the bottom level of the shaft, decedent Messina was at the next level, and a survivor, Mirabile, was at the upper level. After correcting the water leakage problem, Rooney and Fattore began to recross the tunnel and return to the shaft, at which time Fattore felt Rooney slump behind him. He attempted to drag Rooney from the sewer tunnel, but finding himself having difficulty breathing, he released Rooney, ripped off his own mask, and hollered for help. Guarino and Messina were fatally stricken by the lethal gas present in the sewer when they left their posts in the sewer shaft and entered the sewer tunnel without masks in answer to Fattore's call for help. The other surviving plaintiffs were injured as they also descended into the sewer in response to Rooney's plight.

This appeal presents for our review the "danger invites rescue" doctrine.

In New York the rescue doctrine had its historical genesis in Eckert v. Long Is. R.R. Co. (43 N.Y. 502 [1871]), which stated that the plaintiff's intestate, who was killed while attempting to rescue a child on the railroad tracks, was not to be found contributorily negligent unless acting rashly or recklessly. The purpose of the doctrine, we said, was to prevent a plaintiff from being found contributorily negligent, as a matter of law, when he voluntarily placed himself in a perilous situation to prevent another from suffering serious injury.

The doctrine has been most frequently applied when a defendant through his negligence either injured or imperilled another and a third person was injured in attempting to rescue the person in jeopardy. (Wagner v. International Ry. Co., 232 N.Y. 176, 133 N.E. 437, 19 A.L.R. 1 [1921]; Paul v. Flag Fish Co., 7 A.D.2d 656, 180 N.Y.S.2d 73 [2d Dept., 1958].) However, the doctrine has also been applied when a person negligently places himself in danger (Carney v. Buyea, 271 App.Div. 338, 65 N.Y.S.2d 902 [4th Dept., 1946]) or attempts suicide (Talbert v. Talbert, 22 Misc.2d 782, 199 N.Y.S.2d 212 [Sup.Ct., Schenectady County, 1960]) so as to invite rescue.

In these actions plaintiffs seek application of the "danger invites rescue" doctrine to a situation where a breach of warranty endangers a person so as to invite rescue by a third party. It is significant to note that all of the cases that have invoked the rescue doctrine since it was first promulgated by this court have been negligence actions. This is, we believe, the first instance in which the doctrine has been invoked in an action where the gravamen of the wrong complained of has been breach of warranty.

We do not believe that the theory of the action, whether it be negligence or breach of warranty, is significant where the doctrine of "danger invites rescue" applies. A breach of warranty and an act of negligence are each clearly wrongful acts. Both terms are synonymous as regards fixation of liability, differing primarily in their requirements of proof.

As we recently held in Provenzo v. Sam (23 N.Y.2d 256, 260, 296 N.Y.S.2d 322, 325, 244 N.E.2d 26, 28 [(1968)]), the rescue doctrine should be applied when "one party *by his culpable act* has placed another person in a position of imminent peril which invites a third person, the rescuing plaintiff, to come to his aid." (Emphasis supplied.)

Moreover, we have held that "[a] breach of warranty * * * is not only a violation of the sales contract out of which the warranty arises but is a tortious wrong" (Goldberg v. Kollsman Instrument Corp., 12 N.Y.2d 432, 436, 240 N.Y.S.2d 592, 594–595, 191 N.E.2d 82–83 [1963]; see Greco v. Kresge Co., 277 N.Y. 26, 35, 12 N.E.2d 557, 561–562 [1938] for similar language).

Here the defendant committed a culpable act against the decedent Rooney, by manufacturing and distributing a defective oxygen-producing mask, for which it has been held accountable in damages. (Rooney v. Healy Co., *supra.*) By virtue of this defendant's culpable act, Rooney was placed in peril, thus inviting his rescue by the plaintiffs who were all members of Rooney's sewage treatment crew. There was no time for reflection when it became known that Rooney was in need of immediate assistance in the dark tunnel some 30 to 40 feet below the street level. These plaintiffs responded to the cries for help in a manner which was reasonable and consistent with their concern for each other as members of a crew. To require that a rescuer answering the cry for help make inquiry as to the nature of the culpable act that imperils someone's life would defy all logic.

As Judge Cardozo so eloquently stated in Wagner v. International Ry. Co. (*supra*): "Danger invites rescue. The cry of distress is the summons to relief. * * * The *wrong* that imperils life is a wrong to the imperilled victim; it is a wrong also to his rescuer." (232 N.Y. 176, 180, 133 N.E. 437 [emphasis added].)

"[T]hese judgments," the Appellate Division correctly held, "while nominally premised on a breach of warranty theory as applied to a user, rest fundamentally on the rescue doctrine, a concept unaffected by the exact label put upon the wrong which created the danger to the imperiled victim. For the same reason, the rescuer's status as a user or non-user of the defective instrumentality is not directly relevant to our analysis. It is enough that the plaintiffs attempted to rescue a user with respect to whom a breach of warranty or 'tortious wrong' had been committed." (31 A.D.2d 261, 297 N.Y.S.2d 644.)

We conclude that a person who by his culpable act, whether it stems from negligence or breach of warranty, places another person in a position of imminent peril, may be held liable for any damages sustained by a rescuer in his attempt to aid the imperilled victim.

Defendant raises several objections to the trial court's charge to the jury which we do not sustain. * * *

Similarly as to proximate cause, we find no prejudicial error.[2] The jury was instructed that if they find that the defective mask "brought the chain of events into being * * * then the plaintiffs are entitled to verdicts." Additionally, they were charged that plaintiffs could not have

---

2. Although the Judge specifically refused to charge the jury as to whether or not the defect in the mask was the proximate cause of the injuries to plaintiffs, he did state that "[t]he fact is that it [the mask] was defective and if that brought the chain of events into being, if you so find, then the plaintiffs are entitled to verdicts."

acted in a reckless or improvident manner in attempting rescue. Although the precise phraseology requested was absent, the essence of defendant's request was adequately conveyed to the jury.

Accordingly, the order and judgment appealed from should be affirmed.

[The concurring opinion of SCILEPPI, J., is omitted]

FULD, C.J., and BERGAN, BREITEL and GIBSON, JJ., concur with JASEN, J.

SCILEPPI, J., concurs in result only in an opinion in which BURKE, J., concurs.

Order and judgment affirmed, with costs.

Notes

1. *Guarino* is noted in 46 Notre Dame L.Rev. 228 (1970). Other courts have also permitted rescuers to recover in strict liability actions. Fedorchick v. Massey–Ferguson, Inc., 438 F.Supp. 60 (E.D.Pa.1977) (worker injured while attempting to stop runaway crawler loader which was about to run over co-worker); Court v. Grzelinski, 72 Ill.2d 141, 19 Ill.Dec. 617, 379 N.E.2d 281 (1978) (firefighter attempting to extinguish fire in car was severely burned when the gas tank exploded). *But see* Welch v. Hesston Corp., 540 S.W.2d 127 (Mo.App.1976) (firefighter injured while attempting to extinguish fire in haystacker; rescue doctrine applies only to rescuers of persons, not property).

2. In Caldwell v. Ford Motor Co., 619 S.W.2d 534 (Tenn.App.1981), a pickup truck caught on fire because of a defect. The driver injured his back while hurriedly unloading the cargo. The court applied the rescue doctrine and permitted him to recover in strict liability against the manufacturer of the truck. The court stated:

> Prosser describes activities such as plaintiff undertook as a "normal intervening cause" and considered foreseeable by the courts. He concludes that reasonable attempts by the actor to defend his property or his rights or privileges do not supersede defendant's liability and the rule is not limited to spontaneous or instinctive actions but applies though there is time for thought. Prosser, *The Law of Torts*: ch. 7, *Proximate Cause,* § 44 *Intervening Causes* (4th ed., 1971).

> A normal intervening cause is described by Prosser as (1) an event which may reasonably be expected to occur now and then; (2) an event not unlikely if it did suggest itself to the actor's mind; (3) the event is closely and reasonably associated with the immediate consequences of the defendant's act and form a normal part of its aftermath; and (4) * * * to that extent the act is not foreign to the scope or risk created by the original negligence. *Id.,* at 276–7.

* * *

The foregoing language presents the rescue doctrine as one of foreseeability, *i.e.,* if the attempt at rescue is a rational one in the light of facts and circumstances existing at the time, it is a foreseeable risk of one's culpable act or omission. This is clearly the majority view.

3. The Restatement of Torts (Second) § 444 (1965) defines a normal intervening cause as "a normal consequence of a situation created by the actor's negligent conduct." Examples, in addition to rescue cases, include subsequent accidents caused by the first accident (*Id.* at Illus. 3), subsequent illness caused by plaintiff's weakened condition due to the injury inflicted by defendant (*Id.* at Illus. 1), efforts by plaintiff to avert harm threatened by defendant (*Id.* at § 445), and acts done in response to fear or emotional disturbance caused by defendant (*Id.* at § 444). Another example that commonly arises in negligence cases involves subsequent negligent medical treatment of an injury inflicted by defendant.

4. The significance of characterizing an intervening cause as "normal" is that the actor may be liable even if the intervening cause is unforeseeable. In Wagner v. International Ry. Co., 232 N.Y. 176, 133 N.E. 437 (1921), cited in the main case, Judge Cardozo stated, "The wrongdoer may not have foreseen the coming of a deliverer. He is accountable as if he had." 232 N.Y. at 180, 133 N.E. at 438. The Restatement of Torts (Second) § 443 (1965) uses a hindsight test. The actor is liable for unforeseeable normal intervening causes as long as they do not appear extraordinary in retrospect. *Id.* at comment b. Some courts, however, state that the rescuer must be foreseeable. *See* Court v. Grzelinski, 72 Ill.2d 141, 19 Ill.Dec. 617, 379 N.E.2d 281 (1978). Aside from the rescue doctrine, it is not clear to what extent the rules regarding normal intervening causes will be applied in strict product liability cases.

5. Plaintiff's brother, a fireman, was severely burned in the line of duty because the protective fire clothing he was wearing was defective. Plaintiff submitted to skin graft surgery in order to donate skin to her brother. This type of surgery usually results in permanent scarring and discoloration even if it is properly performed. Plaintiff's operation was negligently performed. Is the manufacturer of the protective clothing strictly liable to plaintiff for her injuries? *See* Bobka v. Cook County Hospital, 97 Ill.App.3d 351, 52 Ill.Dec. 790, 422 N.E.2d 999 (1981).

6. Plaintiff consumes contaminated food or drink without noticing anything unusual. Later Plaintiff observes contamination in the unconsumed portion, and becomes extremely upset upon realizing that he consumed some of the product. Is the manufacturer of the product strictly liable for physical harm to plaintiff resulting from his emotional reaction? *See* Wisniewski v. Great Atlantic & Pacific Tea Co., 226 Pa.Super. 574, 323 A.2d 744 (1974) (yes); Caputzal v. Lindsay Co., 48 N.J. 69, 222 A.2d 513 (1966) (no). Which court was right?

4. PRODUCT ALTERATION

ROBINSON v. REED–PRENTICE DIV. OF PACKAGE MACH. CO.

Court of Appeals of New York, 1980.
49 N.Y.2d 471, 426 N.Y.S.2d 717 403 N.E.2d 440.

OPINION OF THE COURT

COOKE, CHIEF JUDGE.

We hold that a manufacturer of a product may not be cast in damages, either on a strict products liability or negligence cause of action, where, after the product leaves the possession and control of the manufacturer, there is a subsequent modification which substantially alters the product and is the proximate cause of plaintiff's injuries.

Plaintiff Gerald Robinson, then 17, was employed as a plastic molding machine operator by third-party defendant Plastic Jewel Parts Co. A recent arrival to New York from South Carolina where he had been an itinerant farm worker, Robinson had been employed by Plastic Jewel for approximately three weeks. On October 15, 1971, plaintiff suffered severe injuries when his hand was caught between the molds of a plastic molding machine manufactured by defendant Reed–Prentice and sold to Plastic Jewel in 1965, some six and one-half years prior to the accident.

Plaintiff commenced this action against Reed–Prentice which impleaded third-party defendant Plastic Jewel. At the close of proof, causes of action in strict products liability and negligence in the design and manufacture of the machine were submitted to the jury. A sizeable general verdict was returned in favor of plaintiff, the jury apportioning 40% of the liability against Reed–Prentice, the remainder against Plastic Jewel. On appeal, the Appellate Division reversed and ordered a new trial limited to the issue of damages unless plaintiff stipulated to a reduced verdict. Plaintiff so stipulated and the judgment, as amended and reduced, was affirmed. This court then granted Reed–Prentice and Plastic Jewel leave to appeal (CPLR 5602, subd. [a], par. 1, cl. [ii]). We now reverse.

The plastic injection molding machine is designed to melt pelletized plastic inside a heating chamber. From the heating chamber, the liquefied plastic is forced into the mold area by means of a plunger. The mold area itself is composed of two rectangular platens on which the plastic molds are attached. One of the platens moves horizontally to open and close the mold; the other remains stationary. When the operating cycle is begun, hydraulic pressure causes the movable platen to be brought up against the stationary platen, thus forming a completed mold into which the heated plastic is pumped. After the plastic is cured, the movable platen returns to its original position, thereby permitting the operator to manually remove the finished product from its mold.

To protect the operator from the mold area, Reed–Prentice equipped the machine with a safety gate mounted on rollers and connecting interlocks in conformity with the State Industrial Code (12 N.Y.C.R.R. 19.34). Completely covering the mold area, the metal safety gate contained a Plexiglas window allowing the operator to monitor the molding process. Since the gate shielded the mold area, access to the platens was impossible while the machine was operating. Only when the molding sequence was completed could the operator roll the safety gate to the open position, allowing him to reach into the mold area to remove the finished product. The interlocks were connected to electrical switches which activated the hydraulic pump. When the safety gate was closed, the interlocks complete a circuit that activates the hydraulic pump, thereby causing the movable platen to close upon its stationary counterpart. When the safety gate was opened, however, this essential circuit would not be completed and hence the machine would not be activated.

After the machine was delivered by Reed–Prentice, Plastic Jewel discovered that its design did not comport with its production requirements. Plastic Jewel purchased the machine in order to mold beads directly onto a nylon cord. The cord was stored in spools at the back of the machine and fed through the mold where the beads were molded around it. After each molding cycle, the beads were pulled out of the mold and the nylon cord was reset in the mold for the next cycle. To allow the beads to be molded on a continuous line, Plastic Jewel determined that it was necessary to cut a hole of approximately 6 by 14 inches in the Plexiglas portion of the safety gate. The machine, as designed, contracted for and delivered, made no provision for such an aperture. At the end of each cycle, the now corded beads would be pulled through the opening in the gate, the nylon cord would be restrung, and the next cycle would be started by opening and then closing the safety gate without breaking the continuous line of beads. While modification of the safety gate served Plastic Jewel's production needs, it also destroyed the practical utility of the safety features incorporated into the design of the machine for it permitted access into the molding area while the interlocking circuits were completed. Although the record is unclear on this point, plaintiff's hand somehow went through the opening cut into the safety gate and was drawn into the molding area while the interlocks were engaged. The machine went through the molding cycle, causing plaintiff serious injury.

The record contains evidence that Reed–Prentice knew, or should have known, the particular safety gate designed for the machine made it impossible to manufacture beads on strings. During the period immediately prior to the purchase of the machine, Reed–Prentice representatives visited the Plastic Jewel plant and observed two identical machines with holes cut in the Plexiglas portion of their safety gates. At that meeting, Plastic Jewel's plant manager discussed the problem with a Reed–Prentice salesman and asked whether a safety gate compatible with its product needs could be designed. Moreover, a letter sent by Reed–Prentice to Plastic Jewel establishes that the manufacturer knew precisely what its customer was doing to the safety gate and refused to modify its design. However, the letter pointed out that the purchaser had "completely flaunted the safeties built into this machine by removing part of the safety window", and that it had not "held up your end of the purchase when you use the machine differently from its design" and the manufacturer stated "[a]s concerns changes, we will make none in our safety setup or design of safety gates". At trial, plaintiff's expert indicated that there were two modifications to the safety gate which could have been made that would have made it possible to mold beads on a string without rendering the machine unreasonably dangerous. Neither of these modifications were made, or even contemplated, by Reed–Prentice.

Defendants maintain that a manufacturer may not be held to answer in damages where the purchaser of its product deliberately destroys the functional utility of that product's safety features and, as a result of that intentional act, a third party is injured. Once a product which is not defective is injected into the stream of commerce, they argue, the responsibility of the manufacturer is at an end. Thus, having delivered to Plastic Jewel a plastic injection molding machine which was free from defect and in conformity with State promulgated safety regulations, Reed–Prentice fully discharged any legal duty it may have owed to Plastic Jewel and its employees. Plaintiff asserts that a manufacturer's duty is tempered by principles of foreseeability. Thus, if a manufacturer knows or has reason to know that its product would be used in an unreasonably dangerous manner, for example by cutting a hole in a legally required safety guard, it may not evade responsibility by simply maintaining that the product was safe at the time of sale.

A cause of action in strict products liability lies where a manufacturer places on the market a product which has a defect that causes injury (*Codling v. Paglia*, 32 N.Y.2d 330, 342, 345 N.Y.S.2d 461, 469, 298 N.E.2d 622, 628). As the law has developed thus far, a defect in a product may consist of one of three elements: mistake in manufacturing (*Victorson v. Bock Laundry Mach. Co.*, 37 N.Y.2d 395, 373 N.Y.S.2d 39, 335 N.E.2d 275; *Codling v. Paglia, supra*), improper design (*Micallef v. Miehle Co., Div. of Miehle–Goss Dexter*, 39 N.Y.2d 376, 384 N.Y.S.2d 115, 348 N.E.2d 571; *Bolm v. Triumph Corp.*, 33 N.Y.2d 151, 350 N.Y.S.2d 644, 305 N.E.2d 769), or by the inadequacy or absence of warnings for the use of the product (*Torrogrossa v. Towmotor Co.*, 44 N.Y.2d 709, 405 N.Y.S.2d 448, 376 N.E.2d 920). Plaintiff maintains that the safety gate of the molding machine was improperly designed for its intended purpose.

Where a product presents an unreasonable risk of harm, notwithstanding that it was meticulously made according to detailed plans and specifications, it is said to be defectively designed. This rule, however, is tempered by the realization that some products, for example knives, must by their very nature be dangerous in order to be functional. Thus, a defectively designed product is one which, at the time it leaves the seller's hands, is in a condition not reasonably contemplated by the ultimate consumer and is unreasonably dangerous for its intended use; that is one whose utility does not outweigh the danger inherent in its introduction into the stream of commerce (Restatement, Torts 2d, § 402A). Design defects, then, unlike manufacturing defects, involve products made in the precise manner intended by the manufacturer (2 Frumer & Friedman, Products Liability, § 16A[4][f][iv]). Since no product may be completely accident proof, the ultimate question in determining whether an article is defectively designed involves a balancing of the likelihood of harm against the burden of taking precaution against that harm (*Micallef v. Miehle Co., supra,* 39 N.Y.2d p. 386, 384 N.Y.S.2d p. 121, 348 N.E.2d p. 577; 2 Harper and James, Torts, § 28.4).

But no manufacturer may be automatically held liable for all accidents caused or occasioned by the use of its product (see Wade, A Conspectus of Manufacturers' Liability for Products, 10 Ind.L.Rev. 755, 768). While the manufacturer is under a nondelegable duty to design and produce a product that is not defective, that responsibility is gauged as of the time the product leaves the manufacturer's hands (Restatement, Torts 2d, § 402A, Comments *g, p; Hanlon v. Cyril Bath Co.,* 541 F.2d 343, 345 (3rd Cir.); *Santiago v. Package Mach. Co.,* 123 Ill.App.2d 305, 312, 260 N.E.2d 89; *Temple v. Wean United,* 50 Ohio St.2d 317, 322–323, 364 N.E.2d 267). Substantial modifications of a product from its original condition by a third party which render a safe product defective are not the responsibility of the manufacturer (*Keet v. Service Mach. Co.,* 472 F.2d 138, 140; *Hardy v. Hull Corp.,* 446 F.2d 34, 35–36 (9th Cir.); *Coleman v. Verson Allsteel Press Co.,* 64 Ill.App.3d 974, 21 Ill.Dec. 742, 382 N.E.2d 36; Ariz.Rev.Stat.Ann., § 12–683, subd. 2; R.I.Gen.Laws, § 9–1–32; Proposed Uniform Product Liability Act, § 112, subd. [D], 44 Fed.Reg. 62737).

At the time Reed–Prentice sold the molding machine, it was not defective. Had the machine been left intact, the safety gate and connecting interlocks would have rendered this tragic industrial accident an impossibility. On closer analysis, then, plaintiff does not seek to premise liability on any defect in the design or manufacture of the machine but on the independent, and presumably foreseeable, act of Plastic Jewel in destroying the functional utility of the safety gate. Principles of foreseeability, however, are inapposite where a third party affirmatively abuses a product by consciously bypassing built-in safety features. While it may be foreseeable that an employer will abuse a product to meet its own self-imposed production needs, responsibility for that willful choice may not fall on the manufacturer. Absent any showing that there was some defect in the design of the safety gate at the time the machine left the practical control of Reed–Prentice (and there has been none here), Reed–Prentice may r be cast in damages for strict products liability.

Nor does the record disclose any basis for a finding of negligence on the part of Reed–Prentice in the design of the machine. Well settled it is that a manufacturer is under a duty to use reasonable care in designing his product when "used in the manner for which the product was intended * * * as well as an unintended yet reasonably foreseeable use" (*Micallef v. Miehle, supra,* 39 N.Y.2d pp. 385–386, 384 N.Y.S.2d p. 121, 348 N.E.2d p. 577). Many products may safely and reasonably be used for purposes other than the one for which they were specifically designed. For example, the manufacturer of a screwdriver must foresee that a consumer will use his product to pry open the lid of a can and is thus under a corresponding duty to design the shank of the product with sufficient strength to accomplish that task. In such a situation, the manufacturer is in a superior position to anticipate the reasonable use to which his product may be put and is obliged to assure that no harm will befall those who use the product in such a manner. It is the manufacturer who must bear the responsibility if its purposeful design choice presents an unreasonable danger to users. A cause of action in negligence will lie where it can be shown that a manufacturer was responsible for a defect that caused injury, and that the manufacturer could have foreseen the injury. Control of the instrumentality at the time of the accident in such a case is irrelevant since the defect arose while the product was in the possession of the manufacturer.

The manufacturer's duty, however, does not extend to designing a product that is impossible to abuse or one whose safety features may not be circumvented. A manufacturer need not incorporate safety features into its product so as to guarantee that no harm will come to every user no matter how careless or even reckless (cf. *Aetna Ins. Co. v. Loveland Gas & Elec. Co.*, 369 F.2d 648 (6th Cir.); *Drazen v. Otis Elevator Co.*, 96 R.I. 114, 189 A.2d 693). Nor must he trace his product through every link in the chain of distribution to insure that users will not adapt the product to suit their own unique purposes. The duty of a manufacturer, therefore, is not an open-ended one. It extends to the design and manufacture of a finished product which is safe at the time of sale. Material alterations at the hands of a third party which work a substantial change in the condition in which the product was sold by destroying the functional utility of a key safety feature, however foreseeable that modification may have been, are not within the ambit of a manufacturer's responsibility. Acceptance of plaintiff's concept of duty would expand the scope of a manufacturer's duty beyond all reasonable bounds and would be tantamount to imposing absolute liability on manufacturers for all product-related injuries (see Henderson, Judicial Review of Manufacturers' Conscious Design Choices: The Limits of Adjudication, 73 Col.L.Rev. 1531).

Unfortunately, as this case bears out, it may often be that an injured party, because of the exclusivity of workers' compensation, is barred from commencing an action against the one who exposes him to unreasonable peril by affirmatively rendering a safe product dangerous. However, that an employee may have no remedy in tort against his employer gives the courts no license to thrust upon a third-party manufacturer a duty to insure that its product will not be abused or that its safety features will be callously altered by a purchaser (cf. *McLaughlin v. Mine Safety Appliances Co.*, 11 N.Y.2d 62, 71–72, 226 N.Y.S.2d 407, 413–414, 181 N.E.2d 430, 435). Where the product is marketed in a condition safe for the purposes for which it is intended or could reasonably be intended, the manufacturer has satisfied its duty.

Accordingly, the judgment appealed from and the order of the Appellate Division brought up for review should be reversed, with costs, and the complaint and third-party complaint dismissed.

[The dissenting opinion of FUSCHBERG, J., is omitted]

JASEN, GABRIELLI, JONES, WACHTLER and MEYER, JJ., concur with COOKE, C.J.

FUCHSBERG, J., dissents and votes to affirm in a separate opinion.

Judgment appealed from and order of the Appellate Division brought up for review reversed, etc.

Notes

1.   The Restatement of Torts (Second) § 402A(1)(b) (1965) states that the seller of a defective product that causes physical harm is liable if the product is "expected to and does reach the user or consumer without substantial change in the condition in which it is sold." The Institute took no position on whether the seller is liable if he does expect his product to undergo a substantial change. *Id.* at Caveat (2); comment p. It also took no position on the liability of a seller of component parts. *Id.* at Caveat (3); comment q. The Restatement terms provide a basis for exonerating the manufacturer only if a substantial change occurs *before* the product reaches the consumer. This clearly includes raw materials and components that are incorporated into a final product. The liability of manufacturers of such products is discussed in Chapter 9 section B.1., *supra* pages 330–32.

2.   *Robinson v. Reed–Prentice* involves the situation where the change occurs *after* the product reaches the consumer. Some courts hold that the "substantial change" language in the Restatement does not apply in this situation. They resolve the issue by other doctrines, such as the law of causation. *See* Dennis v. Ford Motor Co., 471 F.2d 733 (3d Cir.1973). Other courts interpret the Restatement as applying to modifications made after purchase. *See, e.g.,* Saupitty v. Yazoo Mfg. Co., 726 F.2d 657 (10th Cir.1984). A majority of these courts hold that subsequent changes exonerate the manufacturer only if they are unforeseeable. *See, e.g.,* Sheldon v. West Bend Equip. Corp., 718 F.2d 603 (3d Cir.1983) (a modification is not "substantial" if it is foreseeable).

3.   While some courts talk in terms of intervening cause or misuse and others talk in terms of substantial change, a majority of courts hold the seller liable if the alteration was foreseeable. *E.g.,* Thompson v. Package Mach. Co., 22 Cal.App.3d 188, 99 Cal.Rptr. 281 (1971) (strict liability, design; alteration of safety gate on plastic molding machine); Soler v. Castmaster, Div. of H.P.M. Corp., 98 N.J. 137, 484 A.2d 1225 (1984) (strict liability; die-casting machine defective because it did not contain an interlock; subsequent conversion of machine from manual operation to continuous operation made the machine more dangerous; the combination of both defects caused the accident); D'Antona v. Hampton Grinding Wheel Co., 225 Pa.Super. 120, 310 A.2d 307 (1973) (strict liability, warranty, negligence; substitution of different grinding wheel on a grinding machine; alleged defect in machine caused wheel to explode). There are some limitations on this doctrine. Even an unforeseeable alteration will not cut off the manufacturer's liability if it is not a cause in fact of the harm. Saupitty v. Yazoo Mfg. Co., 726 F.2d 657 (10th Cir.1984) (strict liability; design defect; removal of brakes and belt guard from lawn mower; absence of these safety features played no role in the accident).

4.   One common type of case involves the removal of a safety device. The utility or necessity of removing the device has a bearing on whether its removal is foreseeable. *E.g.,* Kuziw v. Lake Eng'g Co., 586 F.2d 33 (7th

Cir.1978) (Illinois law; foreseeable that safety guard would be removed because this was the only way to clean the machine).

5. While *Robinson v. Reed–Prentice* represents a minority view, there are a significant number of other cases in which courts have refused to impose liability even though the modification was foreseeable. *E.g.,* Latimer v. General Motors Corp., 535 F.2d 1020 (7th Cir.1976) (strict liability, implied warranty, negligence; removal of cotter key permitted drive shaft to come loose and tear brake lines; manufacturer had no duty to install a guard to protect the brake lines even if removal of cotter key was foreseeable); Union Carbide Corp. v. Holton, 136 Ga.App. 726, 222 S.E.2d 105 (1975) (negligence; plaintiff was injured when a disposable cylinder originally containing pressurized gas exploded because it was refilled; manufacturer of the cylinder was not liable for failure to make it impossible to refill or for failure to warn against refilling even if refilling was foreseeable).

6. In Hill v. General Motors Corp., 637 S.W.2d 382 (Mo.App.1982), the owners of a Chevrolet Blazer installed oversize wheels and tires, and modified its suspension system by installing lifts. The vehicle overturned because these changes altered its center of gravity. A passenger, injured in the accident, brought an action against Chevrolet for negligent failure to warn of the risk of making such modifications. Relying on *Robinson v. Reed–Prentice,* the court dismissed the claim. It held that there was no "duty to warn in anticipation that a user will alter its product so as to make it dangerous" even if the modification is foreseeable. *Compare* Griggs v. Firestone Tire & Rubber Co., 513 F.2d 851 (8th Cir.1975), cert. denied, 423 U.S. 865, 96 S.Ct. 124, 46 L.Ed.2d 93 (1975). A truck tire mounted on a multi-piece rim exploded and injured plaintiff. The explosion occurred because the components of the rim assembly were mismatched by a prior owner of the truck. One component was manufactured in 1945 and the other in 1957. Both components were manufactured by Firestone, but they were not compatible. Applying Missouri law, the court held Firestone liable for failure to give an adequate warning against mismatching the components. Is the case consistent with *Hill v. General Motors Corp?* Would the result have been different if only one of the rim components had been manufactured by Firestone?

7. In Lopez v. Precision Papers, Inc., 107 A.D.2d 667, 484 N.Y.S.2d 585 (1985), affirmed, 67 N.Y.2d 871, 501 N.Y.S.2d 798, 492 N.E.2d 1214 (1986), plaintiff was using a forklift in a warehouse to unload a wooden pallet of paper rolls stacked on top of other merchandise. He had to lift the fork blades over his head in order to insert them into the pallet. After the pallet was raised, a roll of paper fell off and injured plaintiff. The forklift was originally equipped with an overhead guard that would have protected Plaintiff. The guard was removable so that it could be driven into low clearance areas, such as trucks, to unload merchandise. The guard was unnecessary when the forklift was being used in confined spaces because the operator could not lift the load above his head in such places. Plaintiff's employer removed the guard so that it could be used to unload trucks. At the time of the accident plaintiff was violating a company policy that prohibited use of forklifts without overhead guards in the warehouse. Plaintiff alleged that the manufacturer could foresee that the forklift would sometimes be used in open spaces without the guard; therefore, it was

defective because it was not equipped with a safety interlock mechanism that would have prevented the lift from being raised above the operator's head if the guard was not in place. The court held that plaintiff stated a cause of action against the manufacturer. Is this holding consistent with *Robinson v. Reed–Prentice?*

SOUTHWIRE CO. v. BELOIT EASTERN CORP.

United States District Court, E.D. Pennsylvania, 1974.
370 F.Supp. 842.

[The court noted the paucity of cases concerning the burden of proof on the issue of whether a product has undergone substantial change. It stated:]

* * *

In view of the plethora of cases which have been brought under § 402A, it is surprising that so little has been written on the subject of § 402A(1)(b), which deals with substantial changes in the condition of the product. It seems to us that one essential element of a plaintiff's case under § 402A is proof that the product is expected to and does reach the user and consumer without substantial change in the condition in which it is sold. While no reported case that we can find contains any discussion of the point of burden of proof (or, more precisely, risk of non-persuasion), there are several cases which mention it in passing. Judge Spaulding, in dissent in the case of Kuisis v. Baldwin–Lima Hamilton Co., 224 Pa.Super. 65, 301 A.2d 911 (1973), wrote that it is the plaintiff's burden to show that there was no substantial change in the defective part of the product between the time it was sold and the time of the accident.[20] Assuming that plaintiff had the burden of negating all reasonable causes for the malfunction except for the manufacturing defect relied on in a § 402A suit, Judge Staley, in Greco v. Bucciconi Engineering Co., 407 F.2d 87 (3d Cir.1969), spoke of the substantial change concept in terms of intervening superseding cause.[21] And, in an opinion just filed, Judge Weis wrote:

20. Judge Spaulding cited Burbage v. Boiler Engineering & Supply Co., *supra*, as authority. While we agree with Judge Spaulding's statement of the law, we note that in *Burbage* the Pennsylvania Supreme Court merely upheld the jury's finding that the changes in question did not cause the defect; the court did not confront the burden of proof question.

21. Intervening superseding cause is a concept used in negligence cases and may be defined as an act of another person or force which by its intervention prevents the defendant from being liable for harm to another which his antecedent negligence is a substantial factor in bringing about. Restatement (Second) of Torts §§ 440–53

(1965). *See also* 27 P.L.E. § 80 at pp. 152–53 (1960).

We are not unmindful of the fact that the notion of "substantial change" is difficult to define, except perhaps on an *ad hoc* basis. A substantial change which negates § 402A liability may well be posited as something less significant than an intervening superseding ca[u]se. The rationale behind this argument is as follows. Since a defendant in a § 402A action can be held liable without proof of any fault on his part, this broad liability should not be imposed on a faultless defendant unless the plaintiff can prove a chain of causation linking the defendant's defective product to plaintiff's injury without substantial changes that

Thus the plaintiff failed to prove a critical prerequisite that the product was in the same condition, so far as was relevant, on the day of the accident as it was at the time Bethlehem acquired possession.

Schreffler v. Birdsboro Corporation, 490 F.2d 1148, at 1153 (3d Cir.1974) (footnotes omitted). In effect, these cases imply that plaintiffs' failure to negate substantial changes is the same as saying that they failed to prove proximate cause, since they failed to negate the break in the causal connection between the original defect and the ultimate injury.

Rarely do judges comment, except in charges to the jury, on who has the burden of proving proximate cause, since it is such a fundamental element of plaintiff's case that it is assumed *sub silentio* to be within plaintiff's burden of proof. *See* Restatement of Torts (Second) § 433B (1965). Similarly, we believe that plaintiffs have the burden of proving no substantial change in order to prevail under § 402A(1)(b), although, as indicated above, we can find no case that directly reaches this holding. The plaintiffs' brief suggests that the question of proving substantial changes is an affirmative defense. They cite no case or commentator to support their proposition, and we have not found any authority or persuasive reason for their conclusion. To be sure, there are reasons for requiring the defendant to carry the burden of coming forward and alleging a substantial change. In many cases, the alleged substantial change is perceived only by the defendant who should, therefore, have to allege it and maintain the burden of going forward with the evidence on the point. The plaintiff is accordingly put on notice to try to prove no substantial changes were made. And as a general rule, rather than requiring a plaintiff to negate an infinite number of possible changes, it seems more reasonable and in keeping with our adversary process to expect the defendant to allege the substantial changes he expects a plaintiff to try to disprove. But once the defendant has come forward, we believe that the burden of proof (or again, more precisely, the risk of non-persuasion) must remain with the plaintiff; if the scales remain in equilibrium on the point, plaintiff is the loser.

To impose on the plaintiff the burden of proving both proximate cause and no substantial change is consistent with the underlying concept of § 402A. In the seminal case of Greenman v. Yuba Power

may be less significant than intervening superseding causes needed to negate the liability of a negligent defendant. On the other hand, since § 402A liability is designed to be broader than negligence liability, it would be consistent with the intent of § 402A to require that, for a substantial change to negate § 402A liability, it must be at least as significant a break in the chain of causation as an intervening superseding cause is in negligence law. One could even argue that substantial change should be defined as the sole proximate cause before negating the § 402A liability of a defendant with a defective and unreasonably dangerous product. In the case at

bar, we do not need to adopt any of these approaches, since we have found: (1) that plaintiffs failed to prove that the casting was a defective and unreasonably dangerous product which would have broken had there been no welding or undue stress; and (2) that the defendant has proved, although it did not have to, that a substantial change (i.e., the counterweight welding) was a cause of the accident. In this case then, plaintiffs failed to prove both causation in fact and proximate cause, since they failed to establish an unbroken chain of causation (or repair a broken one) between an originally defective casting and the ultimate injury.

Products, 59 Cal.2d 57, 27 Cal.Rptr. 697, 377 P.2d 897 (1963), Chief Justice Traynor articulated the rationale behind § 402A as follows:

> The purpose of [strict] liability is to insure that the costs of injuries resulting from defective products are borne by the manufacturers who put them on the market rather than by the injured persons who are powerless to protect themselves.[22]

While § 402A is meant to require manufacturers and sellers to bear much of the responsibility and cost of injuries to consumers resulting from their defective products, it is not meant to impose upon each manufacturer and seller an absolute liability as insurer for all injuries to consumers, regardless of the relation of plaintiff's injuries to the particular defendant's product.

In the instant case, we have found that plaintiffs failed to negate the substantial change alleged by Beloit and similarly failed to demonstrate the proximate cause element necessary for recovery. Indeed, we have found that Beloit proved (although it had no such burden) that the casting failed, not as a self-contained component part with a defect unreasonably dangerous at the time it left Beloit, but due to the changes that were made in it by the counterweight welding. Accordingly, plaintiffs cannot recover.

* * *

Note

On the subject of substantial change, see Comment, Substantial Change: Alteration of a Product as a Bar to a Manufacturer's Strict Liability, 80 Dick.L.Rev. 245 (1976); Note, Product Modification: The Effect of Foreseeability, 42 U.Pitt.L.Rev. 431 (1981); Products Liability: Alteration of Product After it Leaves Hands of Manufacturer or Seller as Affecting Liability for Product–Caused Harm, 41 A.L.R.3d 1251 (1972).

5. SHIFTING RESPONSIBILITY

MEULLER v. JEFFREY MFG. CO.

United States District Court, Eastern District of Pennsylvania, 1980.
494 F.Supp. 275.

MEMORANDUM AND ORDER

TROUTMAN, DISTRICT JUDGE.

Early in 1976 plaintiff, a maintenance man employed by Hofmann Industries, Inc. (Hofmann) of Sinking Spring, Pennsylvania, fell through a three-foot square opening in the concrete slab floor of a foundry building owned by his employer. Plaintiff seeks to recover for his injuries under theories of simple negligence and strict liability. Restate-

---

22. In addition to Judge Traynor's reason, Dean Prosser notes that permitting a plaintiff to sue the manufacturer directly on a theory of strict liability avoids a series of actions which would accomplish the same result, after an otherwise time-consuming and wasteful process. *See* Prosser, Law of Torts 674 (3d ed. 1964).

ment (Second) of Torts § 402A. Defendant, which manufactured and designed the sand handling system involved in plaintiff's accident, now moves for summary judgment [2] on the grounds that it did not design, manufacture or sell any product which caused injury to plaintiff and that his injury resulted from an alleged defect in the construction and maintenance of a building, not a "product" within the meaning of § 402A.[3]

The sand handling system at issue actually consisted of a collection of conveyors, elevators, hopper and other devices arranged in a fashion to remove sand from an automatic gray iron molding machine (known as a spomatic), to recycle and return the sand to the molding machine for further use. One component of the sand handling equipment, a magnetic belt, extracted small pieces of scrap metal from the sand prior to reuse and collected these tailings in metal boxes. To enable Hofmann employees to lift these boxes out of the pit, where the magnetic belt is located, required making the opening through which plaintiff fell. A steel plate, set into angle irons built into the concrete sides of the opening, covered it when not in use. Hofmann purchased the automatic molding machine from a third party in 1960. The size and complexity of the system made it necessary for Hofmann to build a substantial addition to its then-existing foundry to house the equipment. Hofmann constructed the addition, including the concrete slab floor, openings and protection therefor. Hofmann purchased the mold conveyor and sand handling equipment in 1961 from defendant, which assumed no responsibility for installation. Hofmann furnished not only the one-quarter inch plate to cover the opening for the tailings boxes but also all concrete work, anchor bolts and curb angles. The importance of this information lies in the fact that Hofmann designed and installed the opening where plaintiff fell. Indisputably, defendant designed and supplied only certain components for the automatic molding system, none of which it installed in the foundry. Hofmann or others designed and furnished the building, cupola, monorail and spomatic molding system. Defendant only indicated the size and location of openings necessary for the operation of the system and the location of anchor bolts necessary to support and secure the equipment. The manner in which employees removed tailings boxes from the pit remained strictly a matter for the purchaser, Hofmann, to determine.

2. "[S]ummary judgment * * * may be granted when no genuine issues of material fact exist * * *."

In the case at bar plaintiff argues that several genuine issues of material fact exist: whether defendant designed the sand handling equipment negligently, whether defendant advised Hofmann of proper safety devices to be used in conjunction with the system and whether defendant warned Hofmann of dangers [attendant] to use thereof. However, these issues presuppose a duty and its breach on the part of defendant.

We have assumed for present purposes that defendant *did* owe Hofmann a duty and breached it. Therefore, no genuine issues of material fact obstruct the resolution of defendant's motion.

3. Resolving the issue of whether a building is a product within the meaning of § 402A is superfluous in light of our conclusion, *but see Lowrie v. City of Evanston,* 50 Ill.App.3d 376, 8 Ill.Dec. 537, 365 N.E.2d 923 (1977) and *Cox v. Shaffer,* 223 Pa.Super. 429, 302 A.2d 456 (1973).

To recover under theories of either simple negligence or strict liability, plaintiff must establish that defendant manufactured a product which was defective at the time of sale in 1961 or failed in a duty to provide adequately for the guarding of that product. *See Vizzini v. Ford Motor Co.*, 569 F.2d 754 (3d Cir.1977). Even assuming that defendant had a legal duty to warn plaintiff or Hofmann of any dangers connected with the operation of the sand handling system and that defendant breached that duty, the apparent negligence of Hofmann and/or its employees constituted a superseding cause of plaintiff's injury. True, a jury ordinarily determines proximate cause, but where the parties do not dispute the critical facts and only their legal effect remains in issue the court properly should rule on the question. *Schreffler v. Birdsboro Corp.*, 490 F.2d 1148 (3d Cir.1974). A third person's failure to prevent harm may become a superseding cause

> where, because of lapse of time or otherwise, the duty to prevent harm to another threatened by the actor's negligent conduct is found to have shifted from the actor to a third person * * *

Restatement (Second) of Torts § 452(2). *See Griffith v. Wheeling–Pittsburgh Steel Corp.*, 610 F.2d 116 (3d Cir.1979). Identifying what circumstances will shift the duty requires reference to the

> degree of danger and magnitude of the risk of harm, the character and position of the third person who is to take the responsibility, his knowledge of the danger and the likelihood that he will or will not exercise proper care, his relation to the plaintiff or to the defendant [and] the lapse of time * * *

Restatement (Second) of Torts § 452(2), comment f. Particularly where a substantial amount of time intervenes, the overtness of the danger, the nature of the product sold, the identity of the consumer, the relative abilities of the manufacturer and the employer to remedy the alleged defect and the nature and availability of the remedy should be considered as well as any other consideration which comports with the universally accepted policy of assigning and imposing ultimate liability for negligence upon the person primarily responsible therefor. *See Roe v. Bryant & Johnston Co.*, 193 F.Supp. 804 (E.D.Mich.1961). *Cf. Vizzini v. Ford Motor Co.*, 569 F.2d at 767 (" 'proximate cause' * * * is a flexible concept designed to effectuate varied policies that determine whom the law holds liable for harm suffered by the plaintiff").

In the case at bar fifteen years elapsed between the sale of the sand handling machine and the date of plaintiff's injury. Hofmann was plaintiff's employer and as such had a duty to keep the workplace safe and free from unreasonable danger and unnecessary risk. *See Industrial Union Department v. American Petroleum Institute*, [448] U.S. [607], 100 S.Ct. 2844, 65 L.Ed.2d 1010 (1980), *Kimbler v. Pittsburgh & Lake Erie Railroad*, 331 F.2d 383 (3d Cir.1964), *Emig v. Erie Lackawanna Railway*, 350 F.Supp. 986 (E.D.Pa.1972), *aff'd*, 485 F.2d 679 (3d Cir. 1973). *See also* Occupational Safety & Health Act, 29 U.S.C. § 651 *et seq.*, and Federal Employers' Liability Act, 45 U.S.C. § 51 *et seq.* Certainly an open hole would alert the prudent employer to the need to prescribe, implement and follow sound safety regulations. In fact, Hofmann had issued regulations which its employees apparently failed to obey on the day plaintiff fell. Hofmann guarded the opening with a four-sided railing designed to fit over the opening when the steel cover was removed. This "cage" had no bottom or top so that employees could lift the tailings boxes out of the pit by means of an overhead hoist and chain arrangement. Hofmann instructed employees to protect the opening when in use. At least one of plaintiff's co-workers observed the cage in the vicinity of the accident but recalled that it was not then in use.

Moreover, Hofmann was not an unsophisticated "consumer" in the usual sense of the word. Rather, it was a large corporation engaged in the production and fabrication of steel and iron products. Hofmann employed a safety director and safety committee. Thus, the present circumstances differed from the usual § 402A case with a "standard production item sold to the general public which malfunctioned or otherwise evidenced a manufacturing defect". *Schreffler v. Birdsboro Corp.*, 490 F.2d at 1152. Clearly, Hofmann was or should have been aware of the manifest danger of an unprotected opening. *Cf. Gordon v. Niagara Machine & Tool Works*, 574 F.2d 1182 (5th Cir.1978) (the danger zone of a manually operated press machine). Hofmann, plaintiff's employer and owner of the machine for fifteen years, stood in a position to remedy or at a minimum cope effectively with the problem. *See* W. Prosser, *Handbook on the Law of Torts*, 273 (4th ed. 1971). In other words,

> the practical means to protect the working men at the plant * * * was capable of implementation by [the employer] without any advice, knowledge or assistance from [the manufacturer]. * * * [L]ending strength to the superseding cause theory is the evidence that there was [a long] interval between the date of sale and the accident, during which time [the employer] was in sole possession and control of the equipment and, in view of its obligations as an employer, justifiably would be expected to take necessary steps for the safety of its employees.

Schreffler v. Birdsboro Corp., 490 F.2d at 1154. In the case at bar the intervention of fifteen years between the date of sale and injury, the atypical nature of the § 402A product and sale, the obvious nature of the danger, the ready ability of the employer to remedy the danger without technical assistance or advice from the manufacturer, the indisputable duty of the employer to keep the workplace safe and the employer's sole possession and control of the equipment for fifteen years created circumstances which shifted the duty from the manufacturer to the employer. As a matter of law, defendant's conduct cannot be said to be the proximate cause of plaintiff's injury. Therefore, defendant's motion for summary judgment will be granted.

HYMON v. BLAW KNOX CO.

United States District Court, Eastern District of Pennsylvania, 1981.
511 F.Supp. 646.

MEMORANDUM AND ORDER

TROUTMAN, DISTRICT JUDGE.

Employed by American Color and Chemical Corporation, a dye manufacturer in Reading, Pennsylvania, plaintiff operated a drum dryer made by defendant. While cleaning this machine, plaintiff slipped on a wet floor and fell into one of the conveyors which carried dried dye from and through the unit to another phase of production. Plaintiff instituted this action, based on theories of simple negligence and strict liability, Restatement of Torts (Second) § 402A, to recover for injuries which she suffered in this accident. Defendant, now moving for summary judgment, argues that the employer's intervening negligence constituted a superseding cause of plaintiff's injuries.

The employer's predecessor in interest purchased the drum dryer from the defendant in 1964, thirteen years before the accident. Defendant equipped the machine with safety shields which covered the dryer conveyors. During normal operation employees kept the shields in place but during cleaning removed them. In 1968 the employer added safety gratings over the conveyors but eliminated them three years later because a dust shield added to the drum dryer at that time would not fit over them. Following plaintiff's accident the employer reinstalled safety gratings which did not interfere with the use of the dust shields. Plaintiff testified at depositions that she would not have gotten her arm caught in the conveyor if these shields had been in place when she fell and that her employer had instructed her to remove the shields and to keep the conveyors running during the cleaning process. Defendant contends that consideration of the factors articulated in *Meuller v. Jeffrey Manufacturing Co.,* 494 F.Supp. 275 (E.D.Pa.1980), indisputably leads to the conclusion that the company's intervening failure to prevent harm to plaintiff superseded defendant's conduct as the proximate cause of plaintiff's injuries.

* * *

In the case at bar defendant admitted that cleaning the machine required use of water, operation of the conveyor belts and removal of the safety shields. Defendant knew at the time of sale that any person who cleaned the machine would not be protected by any safety device, even though the conveyor belts would be running and the floor would be wet, and nonetheless failed to recommend a safe cleaning procedure. Clearly, the manufacturer had the ability and opportunity to remedy this omission but failed to do so. The fact that the employer experimented with the use of safety gratings as an additional precaution will not relieve the manufacturer from the duty to make a safe machine, particularly since plaintiff alleged that the absence of the safety shields, not gratings, caused her injuries. In *Meuller,* the plaintiff's injuries resulted not from defective design but rather improper installation, the responsibility for which the employer voluntarily assumed. Therefore, defendant's motion for summary judgment will be denied.

Notes

1. Is *Hymon* really so easily distinguishable from *Meuller?* Did not the employer in *Hymon* also assume responsibility for safety? In *Meuller,* should not the manufacturer also have recommended safe procedures?

2. Older cases often ruled as a matter of law that responsibility shifted from the manufacturer when a subsequent purchaser or user continued to use, or permitted others to use, a product after discovery of the defect. *E.g.,* Stultz v. Benson Lumber Co., 6 Cal.2d 688, 59 P.2d 100 (1936) (sale of defective plank with knowledge that it would be used to build a scaffold); Ford Motor Co. v. Atcher, 310 S.W.2d 510 (Ky.1957) (use of car with knowledge that doors tended to fly open). Courts often did not shift responsibility, however, in the case of extremely dangerous products. *E.g.,* Clement v. Crosby & Co., 148 Mich. 293, 111 N.W. 745 (1907) (flammable stove polish).

3. In recent years courts have been less inclined to shift responsibility as a matter of law. In the following cases, for example, the court did not shift responsibility from a defendant who sold a defectively designed product and subsequently informed its buyer of the defect and offered to fix it for a fee. Balido v. Improved Mach., Inc., 29 Cal.App.3d 633, 105 Cal.Rptr. 890 (1972) (inadequate safety devices on molding press; distinguishing *Stultz v. Benson Lumber Co., supra* note 2, as being based on "highly extraordinary facts."); Montgomery Elevator Co. v. McCullough, 676 S.W.2d 776 (Ky.1984) (inadequately guarded escalator; disapproving *Ford Motor Co. v. Atcher, supra* note 2; where a user or bystander without notice of the defect is injured, the intermediate purchaser's failure to remedy the defect is no defense. Responsibility will not shift in the absence of special circumstances such as where the purchaser agrees to correct the defect). *Montgomery Elevator Co. v. McCullough* is noted in 12 N.Ky.L.Rev. 347 (1985).

4. Rather than shift responsibility as a matter of law, many recent cases rule that liability depends on whether the conscious failure of the intermediate purchaser to correct the defect or to warn is foreseeable, and foreseeability is a jury question. *E.g.,* Cropper v. Rego Dist. Center, Inc., 542 F.Supp. 1142 (D.Del.1982) (dangerous release of chemical because of absence of guard on release valve to prevent tampering). See also note 2 following *Tucci v. Bossert, supra* page 531. Courts, however, occasionally dismiss such cases without submission to the jury on the basis that the conscious intervening agency is unforeseeable as a matter of law. *See, e.g.,* Peck v. Ford Motor Co., 603 F.2d 1240 (7th Cir.1979) and Mull v. Ford Motor Co., 368 F.2d 713 (2d Cir.1966) discussed in note 2 following *Tucci v. Bossert, supra* page 531.

5. Courts are still inclined to shift responsibility as a matter of law in certain kinds of cases. *Meuller v. Jeffrey Mfg. Co.* is an example of one such situation. This is where the intermediate owner is a sophisticated industrial or professional user. *See, e.g.,* Helene Curtis Indus., Inc. v. Pruitt, 385 F.2d

841 (5th Cir.1967), cert. denied, 391 U.S. 913, 88 S.Ct. 1806, 20 L.Ed.2d 652 (1968); Schreffler v. Birdsboro Corp., 490 F.2d 1148 (3d Cir.1974). A related type of case where courts sometimes shift responsibility is where a bulk supplier of a caustic chemical sells the product to a commercial user and relies on the user to inform its employees of the proper use of the chemical. *E.g.,* Reed v. Pennwalt Corp., 22 Wash.App. 718, 591 P.2d 478 (1979), appeal dismissed, 93 Wash.2d 5, 604 P.2d 164 (1979).

6. Where the product is defective solely because of a failure to warn, intervening discovery of the danger is also likely to shift responsibility as a matter of law. Are these decisions based on principles of proximate cause or causation in fact? Compare the following cases:

A. McLaughlin v. Mine Safety Appliances Co., 11 N.Y.2d 62, 226 N.Y.S.2d 407, 181 N.E.2d 430 (1962). A drowning victim was burned by "heat blocks" placed next to her body. She sued the manufacturer of the heat blocks for negligently failing to put an adequate warning on the blocks stating that they had to be wrapped in insulation prior to being a applied to the skin. A firefighter, who knew of the need for insulation, activated the blocks and gave them to a nurse who used them on the plaintiff without insulation. The firefighter did not tell the nurse of the need for insulation when he gave them to her, and he said nothing after observing her put the blocks next to the victim's skin. Held: the firefighter's conduct insulated the manufacturer from liability as a matter of law.

B. Sherk v. Daisy–Heddon, Div. of Victor Comptometer Corp., 498 Pa. 594, 450 A.2d 615 (1982). The manufacturer of an unusually powerful type of BB gun was sued in strict liability for failure to warn of the gun's lethal propensities. A fourteen year old boy was using the gun without his parents permission. He was aware that the gun was very powerful. As a joke, he pointed the gun at the head of another boy and pulled the trigger. He mistakenly thought that the safety was on, but did not check to verify this. The gun fired and the BB penetrated the boy's head and killed him. Held: the user is exclusively responsible for the consequences of his misuse in view of his knowledge of the danger.

C. Rost v. C.F. & I. Steel Corp., 189 Mont. 485, 616 P.2d 383 (1980). A passenger on an elevator in a store was injured when the elevator fell because a worn out cable broke. He sued the cable manufacturer for failure to warn adequately of the necessity for inspecting the cable. The store owner inspected the cable shortly before the accident and failed to observe that it was very badly frayed and torn. The appellate court upheld a jury verdict for defendant manufacturer even though the trial court gave erroneous instructions concerning the duty to warn. The court reasoned that based on the factors in § 452(2) of the Restatement (Second) of Torts (the owner's knowledge and ability to prevent the danger, the relative safety of the product at the time it was sold, and lapse of time), the jury had ample basis for finding that responsibility shifted to the store owner.

Courts do not always shift responsibility in failure to warn cases where an intermediary discovers the danger. *See* Minert v. Harsco Corp., 26 Wash.

App. 867, 614 P.2d 686 (1980) (Plaintiff was injured when scaffolding fell. Lessor of scaffolding gave safety instructions to plaintiff's employer, but the employer failed to pass them on to its employees. Held: lessor had a non-delegable duty to warn the ultimate user by attaching the instructions to the scaffolding itself. The lessor is liable unless it is unforeseeable that the employer would fail to pass on the instructions to the employees.). Is *Minert* distinguishable from the cases described above?

7. Note that defendant in *Meuller v. Jeffrey Mfg. Co.* argued that it was not the manufacturer of a product. That issue is addressed in Chapter 17.

SECTION B. CATEGORICAL RULES RESTRICTING RECOVERY

This section deals with scope of liability problems. The question is whether to permit recovery for either pure economic loss or pure mental distress without accompanying personal injury or harm to property. These issues raise important policy questions. Some courts deal with these issues as questions of duty, and some deal with them as questions of proximate cause. The basic analysis used, however, appears to be much the same regardless of which rubric is used.

1. PECUNIARY LOSS AND HARM TO PROPERTY

MORROW v. NEW MOON HOMES, INC.
Supreme Court of Alaska, 1976.
548 P.2d 279.

[In 1969 plaintiffs purchased a mobile home from Golden Heart Mobile Homes, a retail dealer. The home was manufactured by New Moon. Plaintiffs experienced numerous problems with the trailer. The doors would not close all the way; the windows were cracked; water leaked from the bathtub; the roof leaked; the electrical system developed a short circuit; the interior walls did not fit together properly; paneling came off the walls; the bathroom door frames fell off; and the finish came off the kitchen cabinet doors.

Plaintiffs were unable to get the problems with the trailer corrected. Golden Heart went out of business. Plaintiffs filed an action against New Moon alleging breach of "implied warranties of merchantability and fitness for particular purpose in manufacturing and selling an improperly constructed mobile home." The court dismissed the claim against New Moon because there was no privity of contract between plaintiffs and New Moon.]

RABINOWITZ, CHIEF JUSTICE.

* * *

The heart of this appeal concerns the remedies which are available to a remote purchaser against the manufacturer of defective goods for direct economic loss. The superior court held that the Morrows had no legal claim against New Moon because they were not in privity of contract with New Moon. The first argument advanced here by the Morrows amounts to an end run around the requirement of privity. The Morrows contend that their complaint asserted a theory of strict liability in tort. They further argue that they should have prevailed irrespective of any lack of privity of contract between New Moon and themselves, because lack of privity of contract is not a defense to a strict tort liability claim. It is true that in *Bachner v. Pearson*, 479 P.2d 319 (Alaska 1970), we held:

> that implied warranty and strict products liability are sufficiently similar to require that a complaint worded in terms of the former theory should be deemed to raise a claim under the latter theory.[3]

Thus, although the Morrows' complaint sounded in breach of implied warranties, it also raised a strict liability claim if such a claim is legally cognizable against New Moon.

In *Clary v. Fifth Avenue Chrysler Center, Inc.*, 454 P.2d 244 (Alaska 1969), Alaska adopted the *Greenman v. Yuba Power Products, Inc.*,[4] rule of strict products liability, which provides that

> [a] manufacturer is strictly liable in tort when an article he places on the market, knowing that it is to be used without inspection for defects, proves to have a defect that causes injury to a human being.[5]

By its terms the *Greenman* formulation applies only when the defective product causes personal injury. Since the Morrows did not sustain any personal injuries which were caused by the defects in their mobile home, strict liability is seemingly unavailable to them in the instant case. However, the Morrows argue that strict liability should nonetheless apply in the situation where a consumer sues a manufacturer solely for economic loss attributable to the manufacturer's defective product. This precise contention presents a question of first impression in Alaska.

The issue whether strict liability in tort should extend to economic loss has prompted no small amount of discussion in legal journals.[6] The

3. 479 P.2d at 326–27 n. 15; *cf.* Annot., Necessity and Propriety of Instructing on Alternative Theories of Negligence or Breach of Warranty, Where Instruction on Strict Liability in Tort is Given in Products Liability Case, 52 A.L.R.3d 101 (1973).

4. 59 Cal.2d 57, 27 Cal.Rptr. 697, 377 P.2d 897 (1962).

5. 454 P.2d at 247, quoting *Greenman v. Yuba Power Products, Inc.*, 59 Cal.2d 57, 27 Cal.Rptr. 697, 700, 377 P.2d 897, 900 (1962).

6. Among the better articles are: Speidel, *Products Liability, Economic Loss and the UCC*, 40 Tenn.L.Rev. 309 (1973); Prosser, *The Fall of the Citadel (Strict Liability to the Consumer)*, 50 Minn.L.Rev. 791 (1966); Comment, *The Vexing Problem of Purely Economic Loss in Products Liability:*

An Injury in Search of a Remedy, 4 Seton Hall L.Rev. 145 (1972); Note, *Economic Loss in Products Liability Jurisprudence*, 66 Colum.L.Rev. 917 (1966); Comment, *Manufacturers' Liability to Remote Purchasers for 'Economic Loss' Damages—Tort or Contract?*, 114 U.Pa.L.Rev. 539 (1966).

Other articles on the subject include: Note, *Products Liability in Oregon: Present and Future*, 8 Willamette L.J. 410 (1972); Comment, 7 Creighton L.Rev. 396 (1974); Note, *Economic Loss from Defective Products*, 4 Willamette L.J. 402 (1967); Note, *The Demise of Vertical Privity: Economic Loss Under the Uniform Commercial Code*, 2 Hofstra L.Rev. 749 (1974). *See also* W. Prosser, Law of Torts 664–67 (4th ed. 1971).

two leading judicial opinions are probably *Santor v. A. and M. Karagheu-sian, Inc.*, 44 N.J. 52, 207 A.2d 305 (1965), and *Seely v. White Motor Co.*, 63 Cal.2d 9, 45 Cal.Rptr. 17, 403 P.2d 145 (1965). In the former case, Santor purchased from a retailer certain carpeting manufactured and advertised by Karagheusian. Almost immediately after the carpet was laid, Santor noticed an unusual line in it. As the pile wore down, the line became worse and two additional lines appeared. Since the retailer had gone out of business, Santor sued the manufacturer for damages for breach of the implied warranty of merchantability. In a unanimous decision, the Supreme Court of New Jersey held that the plaintiff, as the ultimate purchaser of defective carpeting, could maintain an action against the manufacturer on either of two theories, breach of implied warranty of reasonable fitness or strict liability in tort. Privity of contract was not necessary in order to pursue either theory, although damages were limited to loss of value of the carpeting. Although the opinion emphasized the widespread advertising carried on by Karagheusian, the *Santor* court made clear that "strict liability in tort is not conditioned upon advertising to promote sales." [7]

> [W]hen the manufacturer presents his goods to the public for sale he accompanies them with a representation that they are suitable and safe for the intended use. * * * [S]uch a representation must be regarded as implicit in their presence on the market. * * * The obligation of the manufacturer thus becomes what in justice it ought to be—an enterprise liability, and one which should not depend on the intricacies of the law of sales. The purpose of such liability is to insure that the cost of injuries or damage, either to the goods sold or to other property, resulting from defective products, is borne by the makers of the products who put them in the channels of trade, rather than by the injured or damaged persons who ordinarily are powerless to protect themselves. [8]

Barely four months after *Santor* came down, its strict liability holding was rejected by the Supreme Court of California in *Seely v. White Motor Co., supra.* Seely purchased a truck manufactured by White Motor Co. for use in his heavy duty hauling business. Upon taking possession of the truck, Seely found that it bounced violently. This "galloping" continued for 11 months until the truck's brakes failed and the truck overturned, sustaining in excess of $5,000 in damages. Seely was not injured in the incident.

Seely sued White Motor Co. seeking damages for the cost of repairing the truck and for both the money paid on the purchase price and the profits lost in his business because he was unable to make normal use of the truck. The Supreme Court of California affirmed the trial court's award of damages in the amount of the payments made plus lost profits, on the grounds that White Motor Co. had breached an express warranty to Seely, the ultimate purchaser. The majority opinion, written by Chief

---

7. 207 A.2d at 312.

8. 207 A.2d at 311–12 (citation omitted).

Justice Traynor, condemned in broad *dicta Santor's* application of strict liability principles to a case involving only economic loss:

> The distinction that the law has drawn between tort recovery for physical injuries and warranty recovery for economic loss is not arbitrary and does not rest on the 'luck' of one plaintiff in having an accident causing physical injury. The distinction rests, rather, on an understanding of the nature of the responsibility a manufacturer must undertake in distributing his products. He can appropriately be held liable for physical injuries caused by defects by requiring his goods to match a standard of safety defined in terms of conditions that create unreasonable risks of harm. He cannot be held for the level of performance of his products in the consumer's business unless he agrees that the product was designed to meet the consumer's demands. A consumer should not be charged at the will of the manufacturer with bearing the risk of physical injury when he buys a product on the market. He can, however, be fairly charged with the risk that the product will not match his economic expectations unless the manufacturer agrees that it will.[9]

Seely appears to enjoy the support of the vast majority of the other courts which have considered the question whether strict liability in tort should extend to instances of economic loss.[10] We also prefer the result in *Seely,* although our reasoning differs slightly in emphasis from that of the *Seely* court. Under the Uniform Commercial Code the manufacturer is given the right to avail himself of certain affirmative defenses which can minimize his liability for a purely economic loss. Specifically, the manufacturer has the opportunity, pursuant to AS 45.05.100, to disclaim liability and under AS 45.05.230 to limit the consumer's remedies, although the Code further provides that such disclaimers and limitations cannot be so oppressive as to be unconscionable and thus violate AS 45.05.072. In addition, the manufacturer is entitled to reasonably prompt notice from the consumer of the claimed breach of warranties, pursuant to AS 45.05.174(c)(1).[11]

In our view, recognition of a doctrine of strict liability in tort for economic loss would seriously jeopardize the continued viability of these

---

9. 45 Cal.Rptr. at 23, 403 P.2d at 151.

10. * * * Only one case follows the *Santor* decision, *Cova v. Harley Davidson Motor Co.,* 26 Mich.App. 602, 182 N.W.2d 800 (1970). Notwithstanding lack of privity, other courts have permitted suits against the manufacturer of a product, based on a misrepresentation theory, where the product has been widely advertised and the buyer relied on the advertising. *See, e.g., Ford Motor Co. v. Lonon,* 217 Tenn. 400, 398 S.W.2d 240 (1966); *Randy Knitwear, Inc. v. American Cyanamid Co.,* 11 N.Y.2d 5, 226 N.Y.S.2d 363, 181 N.E.2d 399 (1962). The misrepresentation theory has no application here because the Morrows have made no showing that they were

aware of, or relied on, advertising by New Moon.

11. These disclaimer, liability limitation and notice rights of the manufacturer are not abrogated by a relaxation of the privity requirement in the realm of warranty liability, and might, within the confines of the doctrine of unconscionability, be available to the manufacturer against the remote purchaser suing on a theory of implied warranties. We will treat this matter in more detail subsequently. *See* Comment, *The Vexing Problem of the Purely Economic Loss In Products Liability: An Injury in Search of a Remedy,* 4 Seton Hall L.Rev. 145, 173–74 (1972).

rights. The economically injured consumer would have a theory of redress not envisioned by our legislature when it enacted the U.C.C., since this strict liability remedy would be completely unrestrained by disclaimer, liability limitation and notice provisions. Further, manufacturers could no longer look to the Uniform Commercial Code provisions to provide a predictable definition of potential liability for direct economic loss. In short, adoption of the doctrine of strict liability for economic loss would be contrary to the legislature's intent when it authorized the aforementioned remedy limitations and risk allocation provisions of Article II of the Code. To extend strict tort liability to reach the Morrows' case would in effect be an assumption of legislative prerogative on our part and would vitiate clearly articulated statutory rights.[12] This we decline to do. Thus, we hold that the theory of strict liability in tort which we recognized in *Clary* does not extend to the consumer who suffers only economic loss because of defective goods.

* * *

[The court held that vertical privity was not required in a warranty action for direct economic loss brought by the purchaser against the manufacturer.]

Reversed and remanded for a new trial in accordance with this opinion.

Notes

1. The court concluded that it would not undermine the policy underlying the Uniform Commercial Code to permit recovery for personal injury in strict liability cases. Is this true? The code imposes many restrictions on recovery that are circumvented by the strict liability doctrine. *See* note 1, *supra* p. 131.

2. A clear majority of courts follow *Morrow v. New Moon Homes, Inc.* and deny recovery for pure economic loss. If, however, the plaintiff establishes a strict liability cause of action (as by showing physical harm to person or property), a majority of these courts permit him to recover compensation for economic losses that flow from the physical harm. *See, e.g.,* Hales v. Green Colonial, Inc., 490 F.2d 1015 (8th Cir.1974). In that case a defective heater caused a fire in a commercial building. The fire destroyed the building and its contents, and disrupted the business for eight months. The court granted recovery for the profits that were lost during this eight month period because they resulted directly from the destruction of the business,

---

12. Our decision in *Clary v. Fifth Avenue Chrysler Center, Inc.,* 454 P.2d 244 (Alaska 1969), in which we approved strict liability in tort for personal injuries, was not in derogation of these rights, for the reason that a manufacturer has no right to disclaim or limit the liability for personal injury. The Code provides that such restrictions are prima facie unconscionable, AS 45.05.230(c), and they are rarely upheld by the courts. *See generally,* Braucher, *The Unconscionable Contract or Terms,* 31 U.Pitt.L.Rev. 337 (1970); Lauer, *Sales Warranties Under the Uniform Commercial Code,* 30 Mo.L.Rev. 236 (1965); Leff, *Unconscionability and the Code—The Emperor's New Clause,* 115 U.Pa.L.Rev. 485 (1967); Murray, *Unconscionability, Unconscionability,* 31 U.Pitt.L.Rev. 1 (1968); Spanogle, *Analyzing Unconscionability Problems,* 117 U.Pa.L.Rev. 931 (1969).

and they were foreseeable. Lost profits are compensable only if they are established with reasonable certainty. Recovery is not permissible if the proof is speculative. *Id.*

A minority of these courts deny compensation for economic loss even if it flows from physical harm to person or property. Plaintiff must bring a warranty action to recover such losses. *See, e.g.,* Star Furniture Co. v. Pulaski Furniture Co., 171 W.Va. 79, 297 S.E.2d 854 (1982) (a defective clock caused a fire in a commercial enterprise; the court granted recovery for harm to the building, but denied recovery for lost profits resulting from disruption of the business).

SPRING MOTORS DISTRIBUTORS, INC. v. FORD MOTOR CO.

Supreme Court of New Jersey, 1985.
98 N.J. 555, 489 A.2d 660.

[An action was brought against the manufacturer and supplier of defective transmissions installed in commercial trucks. The buyer sought damages for repair expenses, lost profits, and diminution in value of the trucks.

The court limited its decision in Santor v. A & M Karagheusian, Inc., 44 N.J. 52, 207 A.2d 305 (1965), ruling that commercial buyers seeking damages for economic loss caused by defective products cannot recover either in strict tort liability or in negligence. The court stated:]

In the present case, which involves an action between commercial parties, we need not reconsider the *Santor* rule that an ultimate consumer may recover in strict liability for direct economic loss. To determine whether a commercial buyer may recover economic loss, however, we must reconsider the policies underlying the doctrine of strict liability and those underlying the U.C.C. Those policy considerations include, among others, the relative bargaining power of the parties and the allocation of the loss to the better risk-bearer in a modern marketing system. As a general rule, the rights and duties of a buyer and seller are determined by the law of sales, which throughout this century has been expressed first in the Uniform Sales Act and more recently in the U.C.C. As indicated, however, strict liability evolved as a judicial response to inadequacies in sales law with respect to consumers who sustained physical injuries from defective goods made or distributed by remote parties in the marketing chain.

The considerations that give rise to strict liability do not obtain between commercial parties with comparable bargaining power. *Iowa Elec. Light & Power Co. v. Allis–Chalmers Mfg. Co.,* [360 F.Supp. 25, 32 (S.D.Iowa 1973)] (stating doctrine of strict liability loses all meaning when plaintiff is a large company suing for commercial loss). Furthermore, perfect parity is not necessary to a determination that parties have substantially equal bargaining positions. *Cf. Moreira Constr. Co., Inc. v. Moretrench Corp.,* 97 N.J.Super. 391, 394–95, 235 A.2d 211 (App.Div. 1967), *aff'd o.b.,* 51 N.J. 405, 241 A.2d 236 (1968) (refusing to apply rule of *Santor* to suit between corporations even though plaintiff was a small company and defendant was the world's largest well point company). Suffice it to state that Spring Motors had sufficient bargaining power to persuade Ford to install Clark transmissions in the trucks that were the subject of the contract.

Insofar as risk allocation and distribution are concerned, Spring Motors is at least as well situated as the defendants to assess the impact of economic loss. Indeed, a commercial buyer, such as Spring Motors, may be better situated than the manufacturer to factor into its price the risk of economic loss caused by the purchase of a defective product. *See* Note, "Economic Loss in Products Liability Jurisprudence," [66 Colum.L.Rev. 917, 952–58 (1966)].

Presumably the price paid by Spring Motors for the trucks reflected the fact that Ford was liable for repair or replacement of parts only. By seeking to impose the risk of loss on Ford, Spring Motors seeks, in effect, to obtain a better bargain than it made. In such a context, the imposition of the risk of loss on the manufacturer might lead to price increases for all of its customers, including individual consumers. *Id.* at 956–57. As between commercial parties, then, the allocation of risks in accordance with their agreement better serves the public interest than an allocation achieved as a matter of policy without reference to that agreement.

Delineation of the boundary between strict liability and the U.C.C. requires appreciation not only of the policy considerations underlying both sets of principles, but also of the role of the Legislature as a coordinate branch of government. By enacting the U.C.C., the Legislature adopted a carefully-conceived system of rights and remedies to govern commercial transactions. Allowing Spring Motors to recover from Ford under tort principles would dislocate major provisions of the Code. For example, application of tort principles would obviate the statutory requirement that a buyer give notice of a breach of warranty, *N.J.S.A.* 12A:2–607, and would deprive the seller of the ability to exclude or limit its liability, *N.J.S.A.* 12A:2–316. In sum, the U.C.C. represents a comprehensive statutory scheme that satisfies the needs of the world of commerce, and courts should pause before extending judicial doctrines that might dislocate the legislative structure.

* * *

Insofar as a commercial buyer is concerned, strict liability is not an appropriate basis of a claim for economic loss. The policy considerations underlying both strict liability and the U.C.C. favor restricting a commercial buyer to an action for breach of warranty when seeking economic damages.

Plaintiff also misplaces its reliance on *Monsanto Co. v. Alden Leeds, Inc.,* 130 *N.J.Super.* 245, 326 A.2d 90 (Law Div.1974), to support the availability of tort theories for recovery of purely economic loss in a commercial setting. In *Monsanto,* a corporate plaintiff sued the seller of allegedly defective chemicals for damages resulting from a fire caused by the chemicals, which had been sold to a related corporation and stored in the plaintiff's building. *Id.* at 249, 326 A.2d 90. One of the issues was whether strict liability in tort would apply to a commercial plaintiff in a suit for property damage and consequential economic loss. *Id.* at 250, 256, 326 A.2d 90. *Monsanto* is distinguishable because it involved property damage, which is recoverable under strict liability. The case of *ICI Australia Ltd. v. Elliott Overseas Co.,* 551 F.Supp. 265 (D.N.J.1982), on which plaintiff likewise relies, also involved negligence and strict liability claims by a commercial buyer against an immediate seller for property damage caused by an accident. *Id.* at 268–69. *ICI Australia Ltd.* is distinguishable because it involved both an accident and property damage, neither of which is present in the instant case. Also distinguishable are cases involving claims for actual or potential personal injuries, claims that Spring Motors does not assert. See *Kodiak Electric Ass'n v. DeLaval Turbine, Inc.,* 694 P.2d 150, 153–54 (Alaska 1984) (denying summary judgment seeking dismissal of strict liability claim arising out of failure of electrical generator where there was "serious danger to persons.").

For the preceding reasons, we hold that a commercial buyer seeking damages for economic loss only should proceed under the U.C.C. against parties in the chain of distribution. * * *

III

What we have said about Spring Motors' strict liability claim applies substantially to its negligence claim. Underlying that conclusion is the principle that a seller's duty of care generally stops short of creating a right in a commercial buyer to recover a purely economic loss. Thus viewed, the definition of the seller's duty reflects a policy choice that economic losses inflicted by a seller of goods are better resolved under principles of contract law. In that context, economic interests traditionally have not been entitled to protection against mere negligence. *See, e.g., Wyatt v. Cadillac Motor Car Div.,* 145 Cal.App.2d 423, 302 P.2d 665, 667 (1956) (no recovery in negligence against manufacturer for loss of value of automobile); *Trans World Airlines, Inc. v. Curtiss–Wright Corp.,* 1 Misc.2d 477, 148 N.Y.S.2d 284, 290 (Sup.Ct.1955) (absent an accident, airplane purchaser may not recover in negligence against manufacturer for repair costs of malfunctioning engines); *Inglis v. American Motors Corp.,* 3 Ohio St.2d 132, 209 N.E.2d 583, 588 (1965) (purchaser of automobile could not recover in negligence from manufacturer for difference between purchase price and market value); [W. Prosser & W. Keeton Handbook of the Law of Torts (5th ed. 1984)] § 92 at 657; § 101 at 708 (recovery of intangible economic loss is normally determined by contract law).

The demarcation of duties arising in tort and those arising in contract is often indistinct, but one difference appears in the interest protected under each set of principles. Prosser & Keeton, *supra,* § 92 at 655–56. The purpose of a tort duty of care is to protect society's interest in freedom from harm, *i.e.*, the duty arises from policy considerations formed without reference to any agreement between the parties. A contractual duty, by comparison, arises from society's interest in the performance of promises. Generally speaking, tort principles, such as negligence, are better suited for resolving claims involving unanticipated physical injury, particularly those arising out of an accident. Contract principles, on the other hand, are generally more appropriate for determining claims for consequential damage that the parties have, or could have, addressed in their agreement.

Although the nature of the damage may be a useful point of distinction, it also signals more subtle differences in the roles that tort and contract play in our legal system. The differences include judicial evaluation of the status, relationship, and expectations of the parties; the ability of the parties to protect themselves against the risk of loss either by contractual provision or by insurance; and the manner in which the loss occurred. *See Pennsylvania Glass Sand Corp. v. Caterpillar Tractor Co.*, 652 *F.*2d 1165, 1173 (3rd Cir.1981) (allowing recovery for damage to defective machinery resulting from fire caused by defect). This evaluation reflects, among other things, policy choices about the relative roles of contracts and tort law as sources of legal obligations. As among commercial parties in a direct chain of distribution, contract law, expressed here through the U.C.C., provides the more appropriate system for adjudicating disputes arising from frustrated economic expectations.

Some courts, however, have rejected the distinction between physical harm and economic loss as arbitrary, thereby allowing recovery in tort for repair costs and lost profits. *See, e.g., Berg v. General Motors Corp.*, 87 *Wash.*2d 584, 555 *P.*2d 818, 822–23 (1976) (purely economic loss, including lost fishing profits, recoverable in negligence against remote manufacturer of diesel engine); *cf. Emerson G.M. Diesel, Inc. v. Alaskan Enterprise*, 732 *F.*2d 1468, 1474 (9th Cir.1984) (recovery under strict liability for economic loss available in admiralty against manufacturer of diesel engine parts). Other courts have rejected the requirement of an accident as a prerequisite to recovery in negligence. *See, e.g., State ex rel. Western Seed Prod. Corp. v. J.R. Campbell*, 250 *Or.* 262, 442 *P.*2d 215, 218 (1968) (recovery in negligence allowed against remote supplier for crop losses caused by defective seed); *see also, Nobility Homes of Texas v. Shivers, supra*, 557 *S.W.*2d at 78, 83 (purchaser of defectively designed and constructed mobile homes may recover in negligence and for breach of implied warranties under U.C.C., but not in strict liability).

Nonetheless, the weight of authority supports the proposition that economic expectations that are protected by the U.C.C. are not entitled to supplemental protection by negligence principles. * * *Clark v. International Harvester Co., supra*, 99 *Idaho* 326, 581 *P.*2d 784, 794 (1978) (the law of negligence does not impose a duty to "build a tractor that plows fast enough and breaks down infrequently enough" for plaintiff to make a profit); *Moorman Mfg. Co. v. National Tank Co., supra*, 91 *Ill.*2d at 86, 61 *Ill.Dec.* at 754, 435 *N.E.*2d at 451 (purchaser may not recover in strict liability or negligence against manufacturer of defective grain storage tank); *Superwood Corp. v. Siempelkamp Corp.*, 311 *N.W.*2d 159, 162 (Minn.1981) (no recovery in strict liability or negligence for lost profits or damage to hot plate press); Wade, "Tort Liability for Products Causing Physical Injury and Article 2 of the U.C.C.," *supra,* 48 *Mo. L.Rev.* at 26 n. 87 (substantial majority rule has come to be that economic losses are not actionable in negligence); Note, "Manufacturers' Liability for Economic Loss," *supra,* 66 *Colum.L.Rev.* at 929–31 (negligence is one of the least fruitful avenues of recovery for economic loss). Stated otherwise, the U.C.C. "is generally regarded as the *exclusive source* for ascertaining when a seller is subject to liability for damages if the claim is based on intangible economic loss not attributable to physical injury to person or harm to a tangible thing other than the defective product itself." Prosser & Keeton, *supra,* § 95A at 680. In the present case, the commercial buyer understandably was disappointed in its purchase. The point remains, however, that the U.C.C. provides an adequate set of rights and remedies to resolve the differences between Spring Motors and the Ford defendants.

* * *

Notes

1. *Spring Motors* is noted in 17 Rutgers L.J. 381 (1986) and 17 Seton Hall L.Rev. 330 (1987).

2. The majority of courts permit commercial parties to sue in strict liability if a defective product causes physical harm to property. New Jersey also permits such actions. *See* Consumers Power Co. v. Curtiss–Wright Corp., 780 F.2d 1093 (3d Cir.1986). Consider the approach taken by Salt River Project Agr. Imp. and Power Dist. v. Westinghouse Elec. Corp., 143 Ariz. 368, 694 P.2d 198 (1984), noted in 27 Ariz.L.Rev. 777 (1985). The case recognizes a tort cause of action for harm to property, but it permits commercial parties with equal bargaining power to disclaim tort liability.

3. Should contract law control when commercial parties are involved, and have dealt with each other directly? *See* Note, Privity Revisited: Tort Recovery by a Commercial Buyer for a Defective Product's Self–Inflicted Damage, 84 Mich.L.Rev. 517 (1985).

4. **Negligence.** In negligence cases the majority of courts do not allow recovery for economic loss unaccompanied by physical harm to person or property. This rule applies to both commercial and non-commercial parties. *See generally,* Gaebler, Negligence, Economic Loss, and the U.C.C., 61 Ind.L.J. 593 (1986).

5. A minority of courts grant a negligence cause of action for pure economic harm caused by defective products. *E.g.,* Berg v. General Motors Corporation, 87 Wash.2d 584, 555 P.2d 818 (1976) (lost profits). Some of these courts deny a strict liability cause of action for such damages. *See, e.g.,* Ales–Peratis Foods Intern., Inc. v. American Can Co., 164 Cal.App.3d 277, 209 Cal.Rptr. 917 (1985) (negligence action lies against can manufacturer who supplied defective cans to seafood company, causing company to lose

a contract to sell canned abalone). What basis is there for treating negligence and strict liability actions differently in this respect?

6. *See generally,* Rabin, Tort Recovery for Negligently Inflicted Economic Loss: A Reassessment, 37 Stan.L.Rev. 1513 (1985); Ribstein, Guidelines for Deciding Product Economic Loss Cases, 29 Mercer L.Rev. 493 (1978); Solimine, Recovery of Economic Damages in Products Liability Actions and the Reemergence of Contractual Remedies, 51 Mo.L.Rev. 977 (1986); Schwartz, Economic Loss in American Tort Law: The Examples of *J'Aire* and of Products Liability, 23 San Diego L.Rev. 37 (1986).

BAGEL v. AMERICAN HONDA MOTOR CO., INC.

Appellate Court of Illinois, First District, Third Division, 1985.
132 Ill.App.3d 82, 87 Ill.Dec. 453, 477 N.E.2d 54.

McNAMARA, JUSTICE.

Plaintiff purchased a used Honda CX500 motorcycle from Fred Humphreys, the original purchaser, in 1979. * * *

In November 1978, American Honda undertook a recall campaign of its CX500 motorcycles to correct a possible cam chain defect, which would cause breakage and engine lock-up. Pursuant to the recall directive, Carr's Honda modified and repaired Humphreys' motorcycle. On April 19, 1981, while plaintiff's motorcycle was idling in his garage, the engine seized and the motorcycle ceased operating. Plaintiff did not sustain personal injury and there was no property damage other than to the motorcycle.

In 1983, plaintiff filed a three-count complaint against American Honda and Carr's Honda. Plaintiff alleged that the engine seizure was a direct result of cam chain breakage, causing a complete mechanical failure of the motorcycle. Count I alleged that American Honda negligently designed and manufactured the motorcycle and that its defective condition was unreasonably dangerous to plaintiff and his property. Count II alleged that Carr's Honda negligently repaired the cam shaft mechanism prior to the engine seizure. Count III alleged that American Honda breached an implied warranty of merchantability pursuant to the Uniform Commercial Code. Finally, plaintiff alleged that he sustained damages, including cost of repair, loss of use, of profits, and of value of the motorcycle, due to its mechanical failure.

American Honda filed its motion to dismiss, contending that count I of plaintiff's complaint failed to state a cause of action allowing tort recovery for negligence or strict products liability according to the economic loss doctrine set out in *Moorman Manufacturing Co. v. National Tank Co.* (1982), 91 Ill.2d 69, 61 Ill.Dec. 746, 435 N.E.2d 443. American Honda also contended that count III failed to state a cause of action for breach of implied warranty pursuant to the terms of the express limited warranty which limited the duration of the implied warranty and type of damage recoverable. The trial court granted American Honda's motion to dismiss both counts of the complaint directed against it. Count II of plaintiff's complaint remains pending in the trial court against Carr's Honda.

* * *

Plaintiff initially contends that the complaint, which alleges only damage to a defective product and resulting losses, states a cause of action allowing tort recovery. Both parties agree that *Moorman* and *Vaughn v. General Motors Corp.* (1984), 102 Ill.2d 431, 80 Ill.Dec. 743, 466 N.E.2d 195, are controlling. Plaintiff contends that damages to a motorcycle caused by a defective cam chain in the engine which posed a risk of harm to plaintiff and his property are the type of loss for which tort recovery is allowed. Defendant counters that the present allegations preclude recovery under *Moorman* and *Vaughn*.

In *Moorman,* the court delineated the scope of tort and contract actions for economic losses caused by defective products. The court held that physical injury to a person or his property was compensable under tort theories of strict products liability or negligence where plaintiff has been exposed to unreasonable risk of injury. On the other hand, economic loss resulting from a qualitative defect in a product was within the realm of contract law which protected a consumer's expectation interests. In a situation where the harm alleged is damage to a product itself, the court distinguished between physical property damage (tort remedy) and economic loss (contract remedy). Quoting with approval the reasoning of *Pennsylvania Glass Sand Corp. v. Caterpillar Tractor Co.* (3rd Cir.1981), 652 F.2d 1165, the court stated:

> " 'In drawing this distinction (between physical damage and economic loss) the items for which damages are sought, such as repair costs, are not determinative. Rather, the line between tort and contract must be drawn by analyzing interrelated factors such as the nature of the defect, the type of risk, and the manner in which the injury arose. These factors bear directly on whether the safety-insurance policy of tort law or the expectation-bargain protection policy of warranty law is most applicable to a particular claim.' (citation.)"   91 Ill.2d 69, 85, 61 Ill.Dec. 746, 435 N.E.2d 443.

The court further explained the distinction by focusing on the element of causation to determine the type of loss involved:

> "When the defect causes an accident 'involving some violence or collision with external objects,' the resulting loss is treated as property damage. On the other hand, when the damage to the product results from deterioration, internal breakage, or other non-accidental causes, it is treated as economic loss * * *."   (citation). 91 Ill.2d 69, 83, 61 Ill.Dec. 746, 435 N.E.2d 443.

See also *Vaughn v. General Motors Corp.* (1983), 118 Ill.App.3d 201, 73 Ill.Dec. 643, 454 N.E.2d 740, *aff'd* 102 Ill.2d 431, 80 Ill.Dec. 743, 466 N.E.2d 195.

In *Moorman,* the supreme court found that the type of loss resulting from a crack in a grain storage tank was economic loss for which there was no recovery in tort. Although plaintiff had alleged a "sudden and violent" occurrence, the court concluded that since the crack had developed over a period of time the harm resulted from a qualitative defect. In *Vaughn*, the court held that plaintiff had stated a cause of action based on strict products liability where plaintiff's truck sustained damage due to an accident involving defective brakes. Plaintiff was driving the truck when the brakes locked, causing the truck to overturn. The court reiterated the distinction announced in *Moorman* between physical harm or property damage and economic loss with respect to damage to the product itself. The court concluded that the complaint alleged a "sudden and calamitous occurrence" caused by a defect in the product.

Therefore, *Moorman* and *Vaughn* require an inquiry into the type of damage alleged, the nature of the defect and the manner in which the damage occurred. If property damage results from a sudden or dangerous occurrence, then tort theory may provide recovery. If the loss relates to a purchaser's disappointed expectations due to deterioration, internal breakdown or non-accidental cause, then the remedy lies in contract. See *Bi–Petro Refining Co. v. Hartness Painting, Inc.* (1983), 120 Ill.App.3d 556, 76 Ill.Dec. 70, 458 N.E.2d 209.

Here, plaintiff alleged damages as follows: cost of repair, lost profits, and loss of use and loss of value of the motorcycle. Plaintiff clearly alleged damage to the product itself and resulting losses, falling within the *Moorman* definition of economic loss. The nature of the alleged defect was a breakage of the engine's cam chain. The damage allegedly occurred when the "engine suddenly stopped and seized" while the motorcycle was idling in plaintiff's garage. Although plaintiff alleges that this was a sudden occurrence, we find that the loss resulted from a qualitative defect in the motorcycle like the crack in the grain storage tank in *Moorman*. Here, as in *Moorman,* the defect developed over a period of time. The engine ceased operating over two years and several thousand miles after the cam chain was repaired pursuant to American Honda's recall directive. Whether the damage to the engine resulted from gradual deterioration or internal breakage, it did not occur in a dangerous manner that posed an unreasonable risk of injury to plaintiff or his property. The loss related to plaintiff's disappointed commercial expectations.

This occurrence is clearly different from the truck accident in *Vaughn*. In that case, the brakes locked, causing the truck to overturn while plaintiff was driving the vehicle. The damage to the product in *Vaughn* resulted from a dangerous and calamitous event which threatened plaintiff with physical injury and property damage. The defect itself actually caused a risk of injury. Here, the damage to the product occurred while the engine was idling, not while the motorcycle was in use or motion. There was no sudden and calamitous event; there was no actual threat of injury to plaintiff or to his property. The supposition that plaintiff could have been injured had he been riding on the motorcycle is merely a possibility that did not occur. In Illinois, a motor vehicle is not a dangerous instrumentality per se. See *Brill v. Davajon* (1964), 51 Ill.App.2d 445, 201 N.E.2d 253.

In a similar situation where the engine of an electrical generator failed, the Supreme Court of Alaska held that the plaintiff's loss was economic and nonrecoverable under a strict products liability theory. (*Northern Power & Engineering Corp. of Alaska v. Caterpillar Tractor Co.* (1981), 623 P.2d 324.) There, plaintiff alleged that the engine sustained damage as a result of a defective oil pressure mechanism which failed to operate and caused the engine to seize. In finding that this was not a dangerous occurrence, the court found that there was no showing that the defect presented a danger to persons or other property and no showing of violence, fire, collision with external objects, or other calamity as a result of this failure. "The engine apparently just stopped operating." (623 P.2d 324, 329.) Likewise in *Gibson v. Reliable Chevrolet, Inc.* (Mo.App.1980), 608 S.W.2d 471, the court denied recovery in strict liability in tort where plaintiff was driving her automobile and the engine ceased to function. The court concluded that plaintiff's pecuniary loss did not result from a violent occurrence or imminently dangerous product, but rather from internal breakage.

* * *

[W]e hold as a matter of law, that plaintiff's complaint does not state a cause of action for negligence or strict products liability. Therefore, the trial court correctly dismissed count I of plaintiff's complaint.

[The court also held that the trial court properly dismissed court III of the complaint against American Honda. Plaintiff could not maintain a claim for breach of implied warranty of merchantability because he "was not in privity of contract with American Honda" and because he "purchased the used motorcycle from a seller who was not a merchant. * * * "]

For the foregoing reasons, the judgment of the circuit court of Cook County dismissing counts I and III of plaintiff's complaint directed against American Honda is affirmed.

Judgment affirmed.

McGILLICUDDY and RIZZI, JJ., concur.

Notes

1. Does a strict liability action lie against the product manufacturer in the following cases?

A. A grain storage silo is destroyed by a tornado. Plaintiff claims it is defective because it was not "tornado-proof."

B. A defective burglar alarm malfunctions, and property is stolen by a burglar.

C. A defective burglar alarm malfunctions, and the homeowner is attacked by a burglar.

D. A defective smoke detector fails to sound an alarm in a fire. The resulting delay in calling the fire department enhances the fire damage to plaintiff's home.

E. A defective humidifier system in a home puts excessive amounts of moisture into the air. This causes wet carpets, sticking doors, squeaking steps, warped studs, cracked sheetrock, swelled paneling, rusted fixtures, and furniture damage.

2. *See* Comment, Recovery for Economic Loss Under a Products Liability Theory: From the Beginning Through the Current Trend, 70 Marq. L.Rev. 320 (1987).

EAST RIVER S.S. CORP. v. TRANSAMERICA DELAVAL, INC.

Supreme Court of the United States, 1986.
476 U.S. 858, 106 S.Ct. 2295, 90 L.Ed.2d 865.

JUSTICE BLACKMUN delivered the opinion of the Court.

In this admiralty case, we must decide whether a cause of action in tort is stated when a defective product purchased in a commercial transaction malfunctions, injuring only the product itself and causing purely economic loss.

[Several ships were equipped with turbines manufactured by defendant. The turbines malfunctioned and caused harm only to themselves. The charterers sued for repair costs and lost profits. The case arose under admiralty law. The District Court granted summary judgment for defendant, and plaintiffs appealed. The Court of Appeals affirmed, and the Supreme Court granted certiorari. It held that principles of common law products liability applied in admiralty cases. It ruled, however, that the plaintiffs could not recover in tort for the kind of damage that occurred here.]

[The court rejected the approach to economic loss cases taken in Santor v. A & M Karagheusian, Inc., 44 N.J. 52, 207 A.2d 305 (1965) because it "fails to account for the need to keep products liability and contract law in separate spheres and to maintain a realistic limitation on damages."]

[The court also rejected the line of cases, such as Pennsylvania Glass Sand Corp. v. Caterpillar Tractor Co., 652 F.2d 1165, 1173 (3d Cir.1981), which attempt to differentiate physical harm from economic loss in cases where the product injures only itself.]

We find [this approach] * * * unsatisfactory. [P]ositions, which essentially turn on the degree of risk, are too indeterminate to enable manufacturers easily to structure their business behavior. Nor do we find persuasive a distinction that rests on the manner in which the product is injured. We realize that the damage may be qualitative, occurring through gradual deterioration or internal breakage. Or it may be calamitous. Compare *Morrow* v. *New Moon Homes, Inc.*, 548 P.2d 279 (Alaska 1976), with *Cloud* v. *Kit Mfg. Co.*, 563 P.2d 248, 251 (Alaska

1977). But either way, since by definition no person or other property is damaged, the resulting loss is purely economic. Even when the harm to the product itself occurs through an abrupt, accident-like event, the resulting loss due to repair costs, decreased value, and lost profits is essentially the failure of the purchaser to receive the benefit of its bargain—traditionally the core concern of contract law. See E. Farnsworth, Contracts § 12.8, pp. 839–840 (1982).

* * *

Exercising traditional discretion in admiralty, see *Pope & Talbot, Inc. v. Hawn,* 346 U.S. 406, 409, 74 S.Ct. 202, 204, 98 L.Ed. 143 (1953), we * * * hold that a manufacturer in a commercial relationship has no duty under either a negligence or strict products-liability theory to prevent a product from injuring itself.[6]

"The distinction that the law has drawn between tort recovery for physical injuries and warranty recovery for economic loss is not arbitrary and does not rest on the 'luck' of one plaintiff in having an accident causing physical injury. The distinction rests, rather, on an understanding of the nature of the responsibility a manufacturer must undertake in distributing his products." *Seely v. White Motor Co.,* 63 Cal.2d, at 18, 45 Cal.Rptr., at 23, 403 P.2d, at 151. When a product injures only itself the reasons for imposing a tort duty are weak and those for leaving the party to its contractual remedies are strong.

The tort concern with safety is reduced when an injury is only to the product itself. When a person is injured, the "cost of an injury and the loss of time or health may be an overwhelming misfortune," and one the person is not prepared to meet. *Escola v. Coca Cola Bottling Co.,* 24 Cal.2d, at 462, 150 P.2d, at 441 (concurring opinion). In contrast, when a product injures itself, the commercial user stands to lose the value of the product, risks the displeasure of its customers who find that the product does not meet their needs, or, as in this case, experiences increased costs in performing a service. Losses like these can be insured. See 10A Couch on Insurance §§ 42:385–42:401, 42:414–417 (2nd ed. 1982); 7 Benedict on Admiralty, Form No. 1.16–7 (7th ed. 1985); 5A Appleman, Insurance Law and Practice § 3252 (1970). Society need not presume that a customer needs special protection. The increased cost to the public that would result from holding a manufacturer liable in tort for injury to the product itself is not justified. Cf. *United States v. Carroll Towing Co.,* 159 F.2d 169, 173 (CA2 1947).

Damage to a product itself is most naturally understood as a warranty claim. Such damage means simply that the product has not met the customer's expectations, or, in other words, that the customer has received "insufficient product value." See J. White and R. Summers, Uniform Commercial Code 406 (2d ed. 1980). The maintenance of

---

6. We do not reach the issue whether a tort cause of action can ever be stated in admiralty when the only damages sought are economic. Cf. *Ultramares Corp. v. Touche,* 255 N.Y. 170, 174 N.E. 441 (1931). But see *Robins Dry Dock & Repair Co. v. Flint,* 275 U.S. 303, 48 S.Ct. 134, 72 L.Ed. 290 (1927).

product value and quality is precisely the purpose of express and implied warranties.[7] See UCC § 2–313 (express warranty), § 2–314 (implied warranty of merchantability), and § 2–315 (warranty of fitness for a particular purpose). Therefore, a claim of a nonworking product can be brought as a breach-of-warranty action. Or, if the customer prefers, it can reject the product or revoke its acceptance and sue for breach of contract. See UCC §§ 2–601, 2–608, 2–612.

Contract law, and the law of warranty in particular, is well suited to commercial controversies of the sort involved in this case because the parties may set the terms of their own agreements. The manufacturer can restrict its liability, within limits, by disclaiming warranties or limiting remedies. See UCC §§ 2–316, 2–719. In exchange, the purchaser pays less for the product. Since a commercial situation generally does not involve large disparities in bargaining power, cf. *Henningsen v. Bloomfield Motors, Inc.,* 32 N.J. 358, 161 A.2d 69 (1960), we see no reason to intrude into the parties' allocation of the risk.

While giving recognition to the manufacturer's bargain, warranty law sufficiently protects the purchaser by allowing it to obtain the benefit of its bargain. See White and Summers, *supra,* ch. 10. The expectation damages available in warranty for purely economic loss give a plaintiff the full benefit of its bargain by compensating for forgone business opportunities. See Fuller and Perdue, *The Reliance Interest in Contract Damages: 1,* 46 Yale L.J. 52, 60–63 (1936); R. Posner, Economic Analysis of Law § 4.8 (3d ed. 1986). Recovery on a warranty theory would give the charterers their repair costs and lost profits, and would place them in the position they would have been in had the turbines functioned properly.[9] See *Hawkins v. McGee,* 84 N.H. 114, 146 A. 641 (1929). Thus, both the nature of the injury and the resulting damages indicate it is more natural to think of injury to a product itself in terms of warranty.

A warranty action also has a built-in limitation on liability, whereas a tort action could subject the manufacturer to damages of an indefinite amount. The limitation in a contract action comes from the agreement

7. If the charterers' claims were brought as breach-of-warranty actions, they would not be within the admiralty jurisdiction. Since contracts relating to the construction of or supply of materials to a ship are not within the admiralty jurisdiction, see *Thames Towboat Co. v. The Schooner "Francis McDonald",* 254 U.S. 242, 243, 41 S.Ct. 65, 66, 65 L.Ed. 245 (1920); *Kossick v. United Fruit Co.,* 365 U.S. 731, 735, 81 S.Ct. 886, 889, 6 L.Ed.2d 56 (1961), neither are warranty claims grounded in such contracts. See 1 Benedict, Admiralty § 188, p. 11–36 (7th ed. 1985). State law would govern the actions. See *North Pacific S.S. Co. v. Hall Brothers Marine Railway & Shipbuilding Co.,* 249 U.S. 119, 127, 39 S.Ct. 221, 223, 63 L.Ed. 510 (1919). In particu-

lar the Uniform Commercial Code, which has been adopted by 49 States, would apply.

9. In contrast, tort damages generally compensate the plaintiff for loss and return him to the position he occupied before the injury. Cf. *Sullivan v. O'Connor,* 363 Mass. 579, 584–586, 588, n. 6, 296 N.E.2d 183, 187–188, 189, n. 6 (1973); Prosser, The Borderland of Tort and Contract, in Selected Topics on the Law of Torts 380, 424–427 (Thomas M. Cooley Lectures, Fourth Series 1953). Tort damages are analogous to reliance damages, which are awarded in contract when there is particular difficulty in measuring the expectation interest. See, *e.g., Security Store & Mfg. Co. v. American Railways Express Co.,* 227 Mo.App. 175, 51 S.W.2d 572 (1932).

of the parties and the requirement that consequential damages, such as lost profits, be a foreseeable result of the breach. See *Hadley v. Baxendale,* 9 Ex. 341, 156 Eng.Rep. 145 (1854). In a warranty action where the loss is purely economic, the limitation derives from the requirements of foreseeability and of privity, which is still generally enforced for such claims in a commercial setting. See UCC § 2–715; White and Summers, [Uniform Commercial Code] at 389, 396, 406–410 [(2d ed. 1980)].

In products-liability law, where there is a duty to the public generally, foreseeability is an inadequate brake. Cf. *Petitions of Kinsman Transit Co.,* 388 F.2d 821 (CA2 1968). See also Perlman, Interference with Contract and Other Economic Expectancies: A Clash of Tort and Contract Doctrine, 49 U.Chi.L.Rev. 61, 71–72 (1982). Permitting recovery for all foreseeable claims for purely economic loss could make a manufacturer liable for vast sums. It would be difficult for a manufacturer to take into account the expectations of persons downstream who may encounter its product. In this case, for example, if the charterers—already one step removed from the transaction—were permitted to recover their economic losses, then the companies that subchartered the ships might claim their economic losses from the delays, and the charterers' customers also might claim their economic losses, and so on. "The law does not spread its protection so far." *Robins Dry Dock & Repair Co. v. Flint,* 275 U.S. 303, 309, 48 S.Ct. 134, 135, 72 L.Ed. 290 (1927).

And to the extent that courts try to limit purely economic damages in tort, they do so by relying on a far murkier line, one that negates the charterers' contention that permitting such recovery under a products-liability theory enables admiralty courts to avoid difficult linedrawing. Cf. *Ultramares Corp. v. Touche,* 255 N.Y. 170, 174 N.E. 441 (1931); *State ex rel. Guste v. M/V Testbank,* 752 F.2d 1019, 1046–1052 (CA5 1985) (en banc) (dissenting opinion), cert. pending, No. 84–1808.

* * *

[W]hether stated in negligence or strict liability, no products-liability claim lies in admiralty when the only injury claimed is economic loss.

* * *

[W]e affirm the entry of judgment for Delaval.

It is so ordered.

Notes

1.   *East River S.S. Corp. v. Transamerica Delaval, Inc.* is noted in 32 Loy.L.Rev. 1007 (1987); 18 Rutgers L.J. 375 (1987); 11 Suffolk Transnat'l L.J. 137 (1987); and 61 Tul.L.Rev. 1229 (1987).

2.   Many courts deny recovery in strict liability for harm to the product itself. *E.g.,* Mid Continent Aircraft Corp. v. Curry County Spraying Service, Inc., 572 S.W.2d 308 (Tex.1978). Should this rule apply to non-commercial plaintiffs? In jurisdictions that apply this rule, should recovery for harm to

the product itself be permitted where the accident also causes harm to other property?

3. Defective bull semen causes genetic problems in calves of artificially inseminated cattle. Does a strict liability action lie against the seller of the bull semen?

2. MENTAL DISTRESS

GNIRK v. FORD MOTOR CO.

United States District Court, District of South Dakota, 1983.
572 F.Supp. 1201.

MEMORANDUM OPINION

DONALD J. PORTER, DISTRICT JUDGE.

I

Plaintiff Wilma Gnirk seeks compensatory damages against The Ford Motor Company (Ford) for emotional distress inflicted upon her while witnessing the death of her child, a passenger in a Ford car. Ford moves for summary judgment, contending that plaintiff, as a "bystander" cannot recover for emotional distress because (1) it was not intentionally inflicted upon her by Ford; and (2) since she sustained no "accompanying physical injury, i.e., a physical impact and attendant, contemporaneous physical injury", even if Ford's legal liability for her child's death were assumed, she may not recover. Ford further contends that all damages incident to the child's death must be sought under the South Dakota wrongful death act, SDCL 21–5–7 which act does not allow recovery for emotional distress. For the reasons following, Ford's motion for summary judgment is denied.

II

Plaintiff alleges that on November 20, 1980 she and her thirteen month old son were traveling in a 1976 Ford L.T.D. car. She co-owned and was then driving the car. In order to open a fence gate she stopped the car, shifted the gear selector into park, and left the engine running. She got out on the driver's side, leaving her son in the front seat with a seat belt fastened around him. While she was opening the gate the car gear shifted from park to reverse and the car backed up, struck a post, and then went forward a distance into a stock dam. From the time the car first moved, plaintiff chased it and tried unsuccessfully several times to get into the moving car to stop it. When it finally stopped, the car was completely submerged in the stock dam. The child was in the car alone. Plaintiff, a non-swimmer, entered the water but could not locate the car. She then walked a mile and a half to the nearest farmhouse for help.

The event above described, plaintiff alleges, caused her great depression, insomnia, permanent psychological injury, and physical illness.

Plaintiff's claim is analyzed under 402A. This is not to say it is the only theory which will survive defendant's motion. Essentially the same principles apply to an action under 402A as to an action for breach of implied warranty. *Pearson v. Franklin Laboratories, Inc.*, 254 N.W.2d 133, 138–39 (S.D.1977).

III

Upon the facts here, it is appropriate to view plaintiff in the role of a user of Ford's product, rather than as a "bystander".[2] Bystander cases are typically void of any product liability implications running from the defendant tort-feasor to the bystander-plaintiff.[3] Having no connection with the tort-feasor, or his negligent tort, the only part played by the bystander is to serve as the unwilling eyewitness to the death or injury of the victim by the tort-feasor. Thus, the bystander has nowhere to look but to the common law rules of negligence, if she [he] is to find a legal duty upon the tort-feasor not to inflict emotional distress upon her by negligently killing or injuring the victim in her presence.

Plaintiff here has a legal connection with Ford which goes to the heart of the case, making it unnecessary for her, or for this court, to look beyond the Restatement (Second) of Torts § 402A (1965) [hereinafter

2. *See* Note, *Emotional Distress In Products Liability: Distinguishing Users from Bystanders,* 50 Fordham L.Rev. 291 (1981); Note, *The Negligent Infliction of Mental Distress: The Scope of Duty and Foreseeability of Injury,* 57 N.D.L.Rev. 577, 599–602 (1981).

3. *See generally* Annot., 29 A.L.R.3d 1337 (1970). A minority of courts adhere to the "impact rule" which precludes recovery unless the plaintiff-bystander suffered some contemporaneous physical injury or impact from the tortious acts of defendant committed against a third party. *See, e.g., Champion v. Gray,* 420 So.2d 348 (Fla.Dist. Ct.App.1982); *Little v. Williamson,* 441 N.E.2d 974 (Ind.Ct.App.1982). A second level of courts, following the lead of New York's highest court in *Tobin v. Grossman,* 24 N.Y.2d 609, 249 N.E.2d 419, 301 N.Y.S.2d 554 (1969), deny recovery unless the plaintiff-bystander was in the "zone of danger"—meaning that in order to recover, plaintiff must have actually feared for her own safety as a result of the defendant's acts. *See, e.g. Rickey v. Chicago Transit Authority,* 98 Ill.2d 546, 75 Ill.Dec. 211, 457 N.E.2d 1 (Ill.1983) (available on Westlaw, All States library); *Stadler v. Cross,* 295 N.W.2d 552 (Minn.1980); *Keck v. Jackson,* 122 Ariz. 114, 593 P.2d 668 (1979); *Shelton v. Russell Pipe & Foundry Co.,* 570 S.W.2d 861 (Tenn.1978); *Towns v. Anderson,* 195 Colo. 517, 579 P.2d 1163 (1978); *Whetham v. Bismarck Hospital,* 197 N.W.2d 678 (N.D. 1972); *Guilmette v. Alexander,* 128 Vt. 116,

259 A.2d 12 (1969); *Klassa v. Milwaukee Gas Light Co.,* 273 Wis. 176, 77 N.W.2d 397 (1956). *See also* Restatement (Second) of Torts § 313(2) comment d. (1965) (adopting zone of danger rule); Still, an approximately equal number of courts have abolished the impact rule and the zone of danger rule in favor of a broader "foreseeability test." Under this test, if the plaintiff-bystander's emotional distress is reasonably foreseeable to the defendant-tort-feasor—considering on a case by case basis such factors as the relationship between the plaintiff and the third party-victim, the proximity of the plaintiff to the scene of the accident, and the method by which the plaintiff is made aware of the accident—then recovery is allowed. *See, e.g., Dillon v. Legg,* 68 Cal.2d 728, 441 P.2d 912, 69 Cal.Rptr. 72 (1968) (landmark); *Haught v. Maceluch,* 681 F.2d 291 (5th Cir.1982) (applying Texas law); *Paugh v. Hanks,* 6 Ohio St.3d 72, 451 N.E.2d 759 (1983); *Culbert v. Sampson's Supermarkets, Inc.,* 444 A.2d 433 (Me. 1982); *Barnhill v. Davis,* 300 N.W.2d 104 (Iowa 1981); *Walker v. Clark Equipment,* 320 N.W.2d 561 (Iowa 1982); *Portee v. Jaffee,* 84 N.J. 88, 417 A.2d 521 (1980); *Corso v. Merrill,* 119 N.H. 647, 406 A.2d 300 (1979); *Sinn v. Burd,* 486 Pa. 146, 404 A.2d 672 (1979); *Dziokonski v. Babineau,* 375 Mass. 555, 380 N.E.2d 1295 (1978); *D'Ambra v. United States,* 114 R.I. 643, 338 A.2d 524 (1975); *Leong v. Takasaki,* 55 Hawaii 398, 520 P.2d 758 (1974); *Hughes v. Moore,* 214 Va. 27, 197 S.E.2d 214 (1973).

cited as 402A]. By virtue of her status as the user of the Ford car involved, at the time involved, Ford under 402A owed to plaintiff an independent legal duty not to harm her. *Engberg v. Ford Motor Co.,* 87 S.D. 196, 205 N.W.2d 104 (1973); *Shaffer v. Honeywell, Inc.,* 249 N.W.2d 251 (S.D.1976). Moreover, Ford's duty to plaintiff under *Engberg* stems not from the South Dakota wrongful death act but rather from 402A. Ford's legal duty to plaintiff under 402A endures even if the victim does not survive.

IV

In 1918 the South Dakota Supreme Court considered an issue pertinent to the damage issue here. In *Sternhagen v. Kozel,* 40 S.D. 396, 167 N.W. 398 (1918) it was plaintiff's claim that, owing to an alleged tort "she suffered a severe fright and through such fright received a severe mental and physical shock." The Court saw the question presented as whether or not "one, who, through a tort committed against him, suffers a fright—which fright is not the result of an accompanying physical injury, but is itself the proximate cause of a physical injury—can recover damages for such fright and the resulting physical injury." The Court answered as follows:

> "Without determining whether one could recover for fright alone, such fright not accompanying physical injury either as its result or cause we are of the opinion that: When physical injury accompanies a fright as its effect, the injured party may recover for the fright, for the physical injury, and for any mental injury accompanying such fright and physical injury, exactly as one can recover where the fright is the result of a physical injury."

* * *

The *Sternhagen* court did not indicate what physical phenomena or manifestation is sufficient to constitute the "physical injury" referred to in the quotation from the case, *supra* [167 N.W. at 399]. That issue has not yet been addressed by the state Supreme Court. In the absence of a controlling statute or decision of the highest court of the state, this court, exercising diversity jurisdiction, 28 U.S.C. § 1332, must apply the rule it believes the Supreme Court of South Dakota would adopt. *McElhaney v. Eli Lilly & Co.,* 564 F.Supp. 265, 268 (D.S.D.1983).

In recent years, [due to increased understanding of the relationship between physical and psychic injury] courts have realistically construed the term "physical injury". *See, e.g., Haught v. Maceluch,* 681 F.2d 291, 299 n. 9 (5th Cir.1982) (applying Texas law; depression, nervousness, weight gain, and nightmares are equivalent to physical injury); *D'Ambra v. United States,* 396 F.Supp. 1180, 1183–84 (D.R.I.1973) ("psychoneurosis" or acute depression constitutes physical injury); *Corso v. Merrill,* 119 N.H. 647, 658, 406 A.2d 300, 307 (1979) (depression constitutes a physical injury); *Mobaldi v. Board of Regents,* 55 Cal.App.3d 573, 578, 127 Cal.Rptr. 720, 723 (1976) (depression and weight loss constitute physical injury), *overruled on other grounds, Baxter v. Superior Court,* 19

Cal.3d 461, 466 n. 4, 563 P.2d 871, 874 n. 4, 138 Cal.Rptr. 315, 318 n. 4 (1977); *Hughes v. Moore,* 214 Va. 27, 29, 35, 197 S.E.2d 214, 216, 220 (1973) (anxiety reaction, phobia and hysteria constitute physical injury); *Daley v. LaCroix,* 384 Mich. 4, 15–16, 179 N.W.2d 390, 396 (1970) (weight loss and nervousness constitute physical injury); *Toms v. McConnell,* 45 Mich.App. 647, 657, 207 N.W.2d 140, 145 (1973) (depression constitutes physical injury).[6]

There is no fine line distinguishing physical from emotional injury. *D'Ambra v. United States,* 396 F.Supp. 1180, 1184 (D.R.I.1973) (quoting from *Sloane v. Southern Cal. Ry. Co.,* 111 Cal. 668, 680, 44 P. 320, 322 (1896)); *Molien,* 27 Cal.3d at 929, 616 P.2d at 820–21, 167 Cal.Rptr. at 838–39. The Restatement acknowledges this much:

> [Emotional distress] accompanied by transitory, non-recurring physical phenomena, harmless in themselves, such as dizziness, vomiting, and the like, does not make the actor liable where such phenomena are in themselves inconsequential and do not amount to any substantial bodily harm. On the other hand, long continued nausea or headaches may amount to physical illness, which is bodily harm; and even long continued mental disturbance, as for example in the case of repeated hysterical attacks, or mental aberration, may be classified by the courts as illness, notwithstanding their mental character.

Restatement (Second) of Torts, § 436A comment c (1965).

Comment c, above quoted, is a reasonable rule or guide for trial of the issue of whether plaintiff sustained bodily injury proximately caused by alleged emotional disturbance inflicted by Ford. If plaintiff makes out a case for the jury on the issue, and if the jury find for her on the issue she is entitled to recover damages for emotional distress suffered during the event in which her son drowned, for physical injury proximately caused, and for any mental injury accompanying such emotional distress and physical injury, *Sternhagen, supra,* 167 N.W. 398.

* * *

The court concludes that a genuine issue of fact exists concerning whether the event in which her son lost his life inflicted great depression, insomnia, and permanent psychological injury upon plaintiff, which injury proximately caused bodily injury to plaintiff. * * * [T]he Ford motion must be overruled * * *.

Notes

1. Courts traditionally refused to allow recovery for mental distress unaccompanied by physical harm. *E.g.,* Ellington v. Coca Cola Bottling Co.,

---

6. An increasing number of courts have dispensed with the requirement that plaintiff's emotional distress must have manifested itself in some form of physical injury in order to be recoverable. *See Paugh v. Hanks,* 6 Ohio St.3d 72, 451 N.E.2d 759 (1983); *Culbert v. Sampson's Supermar-* *kets, Inc.,* 444 A.2d 433, (Me.1982); *Barnhill v. Davis,* 300 N.W.2d 104, (Iowa 1981); *Molien v. Kaiser Foundation Hospitals,* 27 Cal.3d 916, 616 P.2d 813, 167 Cal.Rptr. 831 (1980); *Sinn v. Burd,* 486 Pa. 146, 404 A.2d 672 (1979); *Leong v. Takasaki,* 55 Hawaii 398, 520 P.2d 758 (1974).

717 P.2d 109 (Okl.1986). As *Gnirk v. Ford Motor Co.* indicates, many courts have liberalized this rule by adopting a very broad definition of physical harm. Other courts have rejected the rule outright, and grant recovery for serious mental distress without physical harm. *E.g.*, Jeannelle v. Thompson Medical Co., 613 F.Supp. 346 (E.D.Mo.1985); Kately v. Wilkinson, 148 Cal.App.3d 576, 195 Cal.Rptr. 902 (5th Dist.1983).

2. **Bystanders.** Most courts apply hard and fast rules to limit liability where third parties suffer mental distress resulting from concern about another person injured by a defective product. A few courts deny recovery in all such cases. *See* Mead, Recovery for Psychic Harm in Strict Products Liability: Has the Interest in Psychic Equilibrium Come the Final Mile?, 59 St. John's L.Rev. 457, 510–517 (1985). Other courts permit recovery, but impose special restrictions in such actions. One approach requires plaintiff to have been in the "zone of danger." *See* Rickey v. Chicago Transit Authority, 98 Ill.2d 546, 75 Ill.Dec. 211, 457 N.E.2d 1 (1983), noted in 60 Chi.-Kent L.Rev. 735; 17 J.Mar.L.Rev. 563; 15 Loy.U.Chi.L.J. 453; 1984 S.Ill.U.L.J. 497.

3. Another approach applies the factors in Dillon v. Legg, 68 Cal.2d 728, 69 Cal.Rptr. 72, 441 P.2d 912 (1968), a negligence case. The factors require that 1) the parties be closely related, 2) the plaintiff be sufficiently near the scene of the accident, and 3) the plaintiff contemporaneously observe the accident. *See* Shepard v. Superior Court, 76 Cal.App.3d 16, 142 Cal.Rptr. 612 (1977) (strict liability, warranty); Walker v. Clark Equipment Co., 320 N.W.2d 561 (Iowa 1982), noted in 68 Iowa L.Rev. 853 (strict liability, warranty); Culbert v. Sampson's Supermarkets, Inc., 444 A.2d 433 (Me.1982), noted in 21 Duq.L.Rev. 797 (negligence).

4. *Gnirk v. Ford Motor Co.* avoids the application of these hard and fast rules by characterizing plaintiff as a product user rather than a bystander. One other court has followed this approach. Kately v. Wilkinson, 148 Cal.App.3d 576, 195 Cal.Rptr. 902 (5th Dist.1983). *See* Silverman, Recovery for Emotional Distress in Strict Products Liability, 61 Chi.-Kent L.Rev. 545 (1985).

5. In addition to the articles previously cited, *see* Note, The Merger of Emotional Distress and Strict Liability in Tort, 19 New England L.Rev. 403 (1983–1984).

6. Consider the following problem:

Mr. Phillips is one of two operators of a garnett, a large machine which converts clumped fibers into matting. The garnett has a succession of large chains and pulleys that operate the gears and rollers that align the fibers. The Dandy Machine Company manufactured the garnett and sold it to Phillips' employer, the Big Material Company. The garnett was not equipped with any safety devices to protect employees from moving parts. The sales contract required the buyer to supply all necessary guards and disconnect switches. The only safety device installed by Big Material was a mesh fence around the gear and pulley area. The fence had several wide doors. When these doors were opened, all the pulleys, chains, and gears were exposed. The doors were kept closed with an ordinary hook and eye latch. There was no interlock, or other device to cut off the power to the garnett when the doors were opened. Thus, the garnett was fully operative when the doors were open.

At certain times workers operated the garnett with the doors open. This occurred once each day, for example, when the debris produced by the machine was raked up. An operator performed this task by entering the fenced area, kneeling next to the machine, and using a rake to pull the debris from the floor below the garnett. The two operators customarily alternated this task.

One afternoon, when it was Mr. Phillips' turn to rake the debris, he was unable to do so because of severe back pain. He asked his co-worker to do it for him. The co-worker agreed to do it, and was seriously injured as a result. While raking the floor, the co-worker was startled by a very loud noise, and he instinctively tried to stand up and move away from the garnett. As he did this, he hit his back on the fence and rebounded toward the garnett. His right hand came into contact with an exposed chain and gear that severed his thumb and several fingers.

Mr. Phillips was standing near his co-worker and saw the accident happen. He was horrified by it, and has suffered severe mental anguish ever since. He feels bad because he knows that his co-worker's injury is disabling, and will affect him for the rest of his life. In addition, he feels very guilty because it was his turn to rake the debris that day. Most of all, Mr. Phillips has become extremely fearful of working with any type of machinery. Even though his employer equipped the garnett with proper safety devices after the accident, Mr. Phillips is unable to do his old job. He is plagued by a constant fear that he will somehow be injured in a freak accident. He quit his job because of this fear, and he is now working as a janitor for considerably less pay.

In a strict product liability action against the Dandy Machine Company, would the harm suffered by Mr. Phillips be compensable? You need not address the other questions in the problem such as defect, misuse, contributory fault, etc. For purposes of this question you may assume that the machine was defective and the use was foreseeable.

BURNS v. JAQUAYS MINING CORP.

Court of Appeals of Arizona, 1987.
156 Ariz. 375, 752 P.2d 28.

HOWARD, PRESIDING JUDGE.

This is an appeal from the granting of a summary judgment.[1] The main issue in this case is whether subclinical asbestos-related injury is sufficient to constitute the actual loss or damage required to support a cause of action. We hold that it is not.

Jaquays owned land in Gila County upon which it operated an asbestos mill and had a tailings pile. In 1973, the City of Globe

1. The defendants who were awarded the summary judgment are Jaquays Mining Corporation, D.W. Jaquays Mining and Contractors Equipment Co., D.W. Jaquays and Ethelyn (sic) Jaquays (hereinafter referred to collectively as "Jaquays"), Mr. and Mrs. Larry M. Schwartz, Gila County, Pinal–Gila Counties Air Quality Control District, City of Globe, State of Arizona, Mr. and Mrs. Rex Town and Neal Beaver.

approved the creation of a mobile home subdivision, Mountain View Mobile Home Estates, on adjacent land. The plaintiffs were all at one time residents of the trailer park. Asbestos fiber was blown from the mill and tailings pile into the trailer park. In 1979, the plaintiffs learned the asbestos was dangerous and life threatening. In December 1979, the governor declared the trailer park a disaster area. Steps were taken to clean up the contamination and, in 1983, the state began to relocate the residents who stayed on the premises. It was not until September 16, 1985, that the asbestos hazard was finally contained.

The first lawsuits were filed in 1980 and 1981. Other suits were filed in 1982 and 1983.[2] Plaintiffs seek damages for personal injuries and property damage based on negligence, gross negligence, strict liability and nuisance. They also claim damages for the increased risk of developing cancer or other asbestos-related diseases, the need for life-long medical surveillance to monitor the development of those diseases and emotional distress caused by the knowledge and fear of these impending developments. The trial court granted summary judgment on all counts except the count for damages to property.

We view the facts in the light most favorable to the plaintiffs. [Citation] According to the plaintiffs' expert witnesses, the residents of the trailer park were exposed to substantial and cumulative quantities of asbestos fiber. Their cumulative exposure was comparable to and greater than the exposure experienced by workers in asbestos mines, milling and manufacturing industries. They all have asbestos fibers in their lungs which are causing changes in the lung tissue. Sooner or later some of the residents, if they live long enough, will suffer from asbestosis and other asbestos-related diseases. Some of the children who have been exposed will die of asbestos-related diseases and some will become seriously handicapped.

It is clear from the record that none of the plaintiffs has been diagnosed as having asbestosis. Some of the plaintiffs claim to be suffering from mental anguish as a result of their exposure to asbestos, but there is no competent evidence of any physical impairment or harm caused by this exposure. "The threat of future harm, not yet realized, is not enough." Prosser and Keeton on the Law of Torts § 30 at 165 (5th ed. 1984). [Citations] We believe the following quote from *Schweitzer v. Consolidated Rail Corp. (Conrail)*, 758 F.2d 936, 942 (3rd Cir.1985), cert. denied, 474 U.S. 864, 106 S.Ct. 183, 88 L.Ed.2d 152, is applicable here:

> "It is true that the possible existence of subclinical asbestos-related injury prior to manifestation may be of interest to a histologist. [citations omitted.] Likewise, the existence of such injury may be of vital concern to insurers and their insureds who have bargained for liability coverage triggered by 'bodily injury.' [citation omitted.] We believe, however, that subclinical injury resulting from exposure to asbestos is insufficient to constitute the actual loss or damage to a

2. Fifty-six plaintiffs remain in this case.

plaintiff's interest required to sustain a cause of action under generally applicable principles of tort law.

Moreover, we are persuaded that a contrary rule would be undesirable as applied in the asbestos-related tort context. If mere exposure to asbestos were sufficient to give rise to a F.E.L.A. cause of action, countless seemingly healthy railroad workers, workers who might never manifest injury, would have tort claims cognizable in federal court. It is obvious that proof of damages in such cases would be highly speculative, likely resulting in windfalls for those who never take ill and insufficient compensation for those who do. Requiring manifest injury as a necessary element of an asbestos-related tort action avoids these problems and best serves the underlying purpose of tort law: the compensation of victims who have suffered. Therefore we hold that, as a matter of federal law, F.E.L.A. actions for asbestos-related injury do not exist before manifestation of injury."

The reasoning in *Schweitzer* was approved in *Jackson v. Johns–Manville Sales Corp. (Jackson III)*, 781 F.2d 394, 412 n. 22 (5th Cir.1986), cert. denied, ___ U.S. ___, 106 S.Ct. 3339, 92 L.Ed.2d 743. See also *Urie v. Thompson*, 337 U.S. 163, 69 S.Ct. 1018, 93 L.Ed. 1282 (1949) (cause of action for silicosis accrues when the disease manifests itself); *Clutter v. Johns–Manville Sales Corp.*, 646 F.2d 1151 (6th Cir.1981) (a cause of action under Ohio law for asbestosis accrues when the disease manifests itself); *Bendix Corp. v. Stagg*, 486 A.2d 1150 (Del.1984) (statute of limitations for injuries arising from inhalation of asbestos fiber began to run when harmful effect of asbestosis first manifested itself and became physically ascertainable, and not at time of exposure or time scar tissue began to form).

Arizona follows the "discovery rule" as far as the statute of limitations for personal injuries is concerned. [Citations] The statute of limitations does not begin to run until there is a manifestation of disease or physical injury. The purpose of the discovery rule, in the context of a latent disease, is to protect a plaintiff who, through no fault of his own, discovers only belatedly that he has the disease. Allowing plaintiffs to sue for injuries when the disease is still subclinical would be an abrogation of the discovery rule in asbestos cases and mandate the commencement of a suit as soon as the contact with the asbestos fiber occurs, hardly a desirable result.

We agree with the observations made by the court in *Schweitzer v. Consolidated Rail Corp. (Conrail)*, supra. Justice would not be done either to the plaintiffs or the defendants by allowing a suit prior to manifestation of any physical injuries or disease. In addition to the reasons given by the federal court, we also note that until the asbestosis manifests itself one can only speculate as to the debilitating effects the plaintiff will suffer. Not all asbestosis is one hundred percent debilitating. We see no reason to depart from traditional tort concepts and allow recovery for injuries before any disease becomes manifest. The statute of limitations does not begin to run until there is a manifestation of physical injuries or disease.

In order to overcome the lack of manifestation of any asbestos-related diseases and to supply the necessary physical harm required for a claim of damages for enhanced risk of cancer and emotional distress, the plaintiffs point to the affidavit of one of their experts, Dr. Michael Gray, who did not conduct a physical examination of all the residents. He states that many of the residents have suffered severe and clinically significant mental distress as a consequence of the asbestos situation. He did not specifically identify any of the plaintiffs as being in this class. He also stated that the emotional distress manifested itself "in a variety of disorders affecting normal sleep patterns, normal gastrointestinal functions, alterations in the ability to cope with other life stress, manifestations of anger, headaches, personality disorders, sexual dysfunction, and other adverse health effects which in no fashion could be termed trivial, insignificant, or of only minor or temporary inconvenience for these people." In addition to the fact that the affidavit fails to link any of the plaintiffs with these so-called physical manifestations, there is another reason why plaintiffs' claims for enhanced risk of cancer and for emotional distress are insufficient. There can be no claim for damages for the fear of contracting asbestos-related diseases in the future without the manifestation of a bodily injury. [Citations] We agree with the New Jersey Supreme Court in *Ayers v. Township of Jackson*, 106 N.J. 557, 525 A.2d 287 (1987), that neither the single controversy rule, nor the statute of limitations will preclude a timely filed cause of action for damages prompted by the future discovery of a disease or injury related to the exposure to a toxic substance, even though there has been prior litigation between the parties on different claims based on the same tortious conduct.

The psychosomatic injuries diagnosed by Dr. Gray consist of headaches, acid indigestion, weeping, muscle spasms, depression and insomnia. There is no evidence that these were other than transitory physical phenomena. They were not linked to any specific plaintiff, and they are not the type of bodily harm which would sustain a cause of action for emotional distress. Comment c to the Restatement (Second) of Torts § 436(A) (1965) is applicable here:

> "The rule [preventing recovery for emotional disturbance alone] applies to all forms of emotional disturbance, including temporary fright, nervous shock, nausea, grief, rage, and humiliation. The fact that these are accompanied by transitory, non-recurring physical phenomena, harmless in themselves, such as dizziness, vomiting, and the like, does not make the actor liable where such phenomena are in themselves inconsequential and do not amount to any substantial bodily harm. On the other hand, long continued nausea or headaches may amount to physical illness, which is bodily harm; and even long continued mental disturbance, as for example in the case of repeated hysterical attacks, or mental aberration, may be

classified by the courts as illness, notwithstanding their mental character. * * *"

The complaints in this case also alleged a private and public nuisance as follows:

"As a direct and proximate result of the continued maintenance of a nuisance on said property Plaintiffs were caused to become sick, ill and disabled and were prevented from attending to their usual duties and occupation and were compelled to secure medical care and attention in an effort to heal and/or alleviate said injuries and illnesses and will, in the future, be continuously exposed to risk of grave illnesses and harm and may be compelled to secure additional medical care and attention in an effort to heal their said injuries, to their damage. As a further direct and proximate result of the exposure to carcinogenic asbestos the plaintiffs have incurred psychological and emotional trauma and distress."

Restatement (Second) of Torts § 929 sets forth the damages one can recover as a result of a nuisance:

"(1) If one is entitled to a judgment for harm to land resulting from a past invasion and not amounting to a total destruction of value, the damages include compensation for (a) the difference between the value of the land before the harm and the value after the harm, or at his election in an appropriate case, the cost of restoration that has been or may be reasonably incurred, (b) the loss of use of the land, and (c) discomfort and annoyance to him as an occupant."

The Comment on Subsection (1), Clause (c) states:

"(e) *Discomfort and other bodily and mental harms.* Discomfort and annoyance to an occupant of the land and to the members of the household are distinct grounds of compensation for which in ordinary cases the person in possession is allowed to recover in addition to the harm to his proprietary interests. He is also allowed to recover for his own serious sickness or other substantial bodily harm but is not allowed to recover for serious harm to other members of the household, except so far as he maintains an action as a spouse or parent, under the rules stated in §§ 693 and 703. The owner of land who is not an occupant is not entitled to recover for these harms except as they may have affected the rental value of his land."

Those damages that are recoverable are those for the disruption and inconvenience resulting from, in this case, the contamination by asbestos. See *Ayers v. Township of Jackson*, supra. While some of the damages prayed for in plaintiffs' nuisance counts are not recoverable, the counts do set forth a claim for damages for inconvenience, discomfort and annoyance and for property damage, all of which is within the permissible ambit of § 929 of the Restatement. We conclude that the trial court erred in dismissing the nuisance counts.

The last issue is the plaintiffs' claim for recovery of damages to institute a medical surveillance. Dr. Gray testified that as of 1981, all of the adults of ages 65 or under are at greatly advanced risk of asbestos-related lung cancers, mesothelioma, gastrointestinal cancers and asbestosis. Some of the children will die from these diseases and some will become severely handicapped. Dr. Gray also testified that because of the risk, all of the residents should be provided with present and future medical surveillance in order to minimize, detect and treat the diseases as they arise. He described the type of surveillance that should be available, which included physical exams, blood and urine laboratory work-up, electro-cardiograms, periodic chest x-rays, CT scanning techniques and/or magnetic resonance imaging and pulmonary function testing. For individuals over 40 years of age and/or individuals who are 20 years from their initial exposures to asbestos, periodic rectal examinations and gastrointestinal consultation was required as well as additional testing when respiratory disease was apparent. He believed that the frequency of the medical surveillance would, in substantial measure, be influenced by the nature and prevalence of various asbestos-related abnormalities detected on the population as a whole and in each individual. He recommended that the testing be conducted approximately every other year, with the frequency increased as time progresses because the probability of asbestos-related disease increases directly as a latency period increases. He suggested that radiologic chest assessments, if utilized, should occur approximately every five years.

We believe, under the facts of this case and despite the absence of physical manifestation of any asbestos-related diseases, that the plaintiffs should be entitled to such regular medical testing and evaluation as is reasonably necessary and consistent with contemporary scientific principles applied by physicians experienced in the diagnosis and treatment of these types of injuries. We agree with the court in *Ayers v. Township of Jackson*, supra 525 A.2d at 312, that when the evidence shows "through reliable expert testimony predicated on the significance and extent of exposure * * * the toxicity of [the contaminant], the seriousness of the diseases for which the individuals are at risk, the relative increase in the chance of onset of the disease in those exposed and the value of early diagnosis, * * * surveillance to monitor the effects of exposure to toxic chemicals is reasonable and necessary," and its cost is a compensable item of damages. As the New Jersey Supreme Court said at 525 A.2d 311:

> "Compensation for reasonable and necessary medical expenses is consistent with well accepted legal principles. [citation omitted.] It is also consistent with the important public health interest in fostering access to medical testing for individuals whose exposure to toxic chemicals creates an enhanced risk of disease. The value of early diagnosis and treatment for cancer patients is well documented. [citation omitted.]"

The New Jersey court gave another cogent reason for its ruling:

"Recognition of pre-symptom claims for medical surveillance serves other important public interests. The difficulty of proving causation, where the disease is manifested years after exposure, has caused many commentators to suggest that tort law has no capacity to deter polluters, because the costs of proper disposal are often viewed by polluters as exceeding the risk of tort liability. [citations omitted.] However, permitting recovery for reasonable pre-symptom, medical-surveillance expenses subjects polluters to significant liability when proof of the causal connection between the tortious conduct and the plaintiffs' exposure to chemicals is likely to be most readily available. The availability of a substantial remedy before the consequences of the plaintiffs' exposure are manifest may also have the beneficial effect of preventing or mitigating serious future illnesses and thus reduce the overall costs of the responsible parties. Other considerations compel recognition of a pre-symptom medical surveillance claim. It is inequitable for any individual, wrongfully exposed to dangerous toxic chemicals but unable to prove that disease is likely, to have to pay his own expenses when medical intervention is clearly reasonable and necessary."

The next question is whether the plaintiffs are entitled to a lump sum award for this medical surveillance or whether a court-supervised fund should be utilized. We believe that the latter approach is proper. As the court said in *Ayers*, 525 A.2d at 314:

"In our view, the use of a court-supervised fund to administer medical-surveillance payments in mass exposure cases, * * * is a highly appropriate exercise of the Court's equitable powers. [citation omitted.] * * * Such a mechanism offers significant advantages over a lump-sum verdict * * *. In addition, a fund would serve to limit the liability of defendants to the amount of expenses actually incurred. A lump-sum verdict attempts to estimate future expenses, but cannot predict the amounts that actually will be expended for medical purposes. Although conventional damage awards do not restrict plaintiffs in the use of money paid as compensatory damages, mass-exposure toxic-tort cases involve public interests not present in conventional tort litigation. The public health interest is served by a fund mechanism that encourages regular medical monitoring for victims of toxic exposure. Where public entities are defendants, a limitation of liability to amounts actually expended for medical surveillance tends to reduce insurance costs and taxes, * * *. Although there may be administrative and procedural questions in the establishment and operation of such a fund, we encourage its use by trial courts in managing mass-exposure cases. In litigation involving public-entity defendants, we conclude that the use of a fund to administer medical-surveillance payments should be the general rule, in the absence of factors that render it impractical or inappropriate. [footnote omitted.] This will insure that in future mass-exposure litigation against public entities, medical-surveillance damages will be paid only to compensate for medical examinations and tests actually administered, and will encourage plaintiffs to safeguard their health by not allowing them the option of spending the money for other purposes. * * *"

The judgment below is reversed as to plaintiffs' claims for damages based on nuisance and for medical surveillance, and it is affirmed in all other respects.

Note

When a plaintiff is exposed to a toxic substance that increases his risk of contracting cancer, but he shows no signs of illness, can he recover for the mental distress resulting from his fear of getting the disease? Most courts have said no. *See* Mead, Recovery for Psychic Harm in Strict Products Liability: Has the Interest in Psychic Equilibrium Come the Final Mile?, 59 St.John's L.Rev. 457, 520–526 (1985); Reina, Recovery for Fear of Cancer and Increased Risk of Cancer: Problems With *Gideon* and a Proposed Solution, 7 Rev.Litig. 39 (1987); Note, Predicting the Future: Present Mental Anguish for Fear of Developing Cancer in the Future as a Result of Past Asbestos Exposure, 23 Mem.St.U.L.Rev. 337 (1993). *See also* Edwards & Ringleb, Exposure to Hazardous Substances and the Mental Distress Tort: Trends, Applications, and a Proposed Reform, 11 Colum.J.Envtl.L. 119 (1986); Note, 6 W.New Eng.L.Rev. 1037 (1984). A number of courts have begun to recognize a cause of action for medical monitoring expenses in such cases. The parameters of this cause of action are still uncertain. *See* McCarter, Medical Sue–Veillance: A History and Critique of the Medical Monitoring Remedy in Toxic Tort Litigation, 45 Rutgers L.Rev. 227 (1993); Note, Medical Surveillance Damages: Using Common Sense and the Common Law to Mitigate the Dangers Posed by Environmental Hazards, 12 Harv.Envtl.L.Rev. 265 (1988).

Chapter 13

PUNITIVE DAMAGES

ACOSTA v. HONDA MOTOR CO., LTD.

United States Court of Appeals, Third Circuit, 1983.
717 F.2d 828.

BECKER, CIRCUIT JUDGE.

[Plaintiff was injured in an accident which occurred when the rear wheel of his motorcycle collapsed. He sued the manufacturer of the motorcycle (Honda Motor Co., Ltd., "Honda"), the company responsible for manufacturing and assembling the rear wheel of the motorcycle (Daido Kogyo, Co., Ltd.), and the motorcycle's distributor (American Honda Motor Co., Inc., "American Honda"). The jury found the defendants strictly liable and assessed plaintiff $175,000 in compensatory damages. It also awarded punitive damages of $210,000 against each defendant. Defendants subsequently moved for judgment n.o.v. The trial judge granted American Honda's motion and denied the motions of the other defendants. Plaintiff appealed from the grant of judgment n.o.v. for American Honda, and defendants Honda and Daido Kogyo cross-appealed from the denial of their motions.]

* * *

III.

Defendants' principal contention on appeal is that the evidence was insufficient as a matter of law to sustain the award of punitive damages and that the district court erred in submitting the issue to the jury in the first place. Before turning to that question, however, we first must address their argument that punitive damages are unavailable in this case because, no matter what the evidence, punitive damages are fundamentally inconsistent with a regime of strict products liability in general, and with section 402A in particular.

A. THE AVAILABILITY OF PUNITIVE DAMAGES IN THE STRICT LIABILITY CONTEXT

Although this question is one of first impression in the Virgin Islands, we do not lack guidance. Many courts, both state and federal, have already considered the issue, and the overwhelming majority have concluded that there is no theoretical problem in a jury finding that a defendant is liable because of the defectiveness of a product and then judging the conduct of the defendant in order to determine whether punitive damages should be awarded on the basis of 'outrageous conduct' in light of the injuries sustained by the plaintiff. *Hoffman v. Sterling Drug, Inc.,* 485 F.2d 132, 144–47 (3d Cir.1973); *Thomas v. American Cystoscope Makers, Inc.,* 414 F.Supp. 255, 263–267 (E.D.Pa.1976). Punitive damage awards provide a useful function in punishing the wrongdoer and deterring product suppliers from making economic decisions not to remedy the defects of the product.

Neal v. Carey Canadian Mines, Ltd., 548 F.Supp. 357 (E.D.Pa.1982) (Bechtle, J.) (construing Pennsylvania law).

* * *

[A]s long as a plaintiff can carry his burden of proof under section 402A, there is no inconsistency in his also being permitted to offer proof regarding the nature of the manufacturer's conduct.

The Restatement (Second) of Torts does include a generally applicable provision regarding punitive damages. Section 908(2) declares:

> Punitive damages may be awarded for conduct that is outrageous, because of the defendant's evil motive or his reckless indifference to the rights of others. In assessing punitive damages, the trier of fact can properly consider the character of the defendant's act, the nature and extent of the harm to the plaintiff that the defendant caused or intended to cause and the wealth of the defendant.

Nowhere in that section or the comments did the drafters suggest that these principles should not apply to strict products liability, and we concur with the considered opinion of the Court of Appeals for the Fifth Circuit that "[p]unishment and deterrence, the basis for punitive damages * * *, are no less appropriate with respect to a product manufacturer who knowingly ignores safety deficiencies in its product that may endanger human life" than in other cases in which "the defendant's conduct shows wantonness or recklessness or reckless indifference to the rights of others." *Dorsey v. Honda Motor Co.,* 655 F.2d 650, 658 (5th Cir.1981) (construing Florida law), *opinion modified on rehearing,* 670 F.2d 21 (5th Cir.), *cert. denied,* [459] U.S. [880], 103 S.Ct. 177, 74 L.Ed.2d 145 (1982).

* * *

B. STANDARD OF PROOF

Although we reject each of the various arguments against awarding punitive damages in the strict liability context, we agree with Judge Friendly's observation in [*Roginsky v. Richardson–Merrell, Inc.,* 378 F.2d 832 (2d Cir.1967)], that "the consequences of imposing punitive damages in a case like the present are so serious" that "particularly careful scrutiny" is warranted. 378 F.2d at 852 (denying petition for rehearing); cf. Comment, *Criminal Safeguards and the Punitive Dam-*

ages Defendant, 34 U.Chi.L.Rev. 408, 417 (1967) ("If one accepts the proposition that the consequences of punitive damages can be 'momentous and serious,' then justice requires increasing the burden of persuasion of the plaintiff in a punitive damages action.") We therefore hold under Virgin Islands law that a plaintiff seeking punitive damages, at least in an action in which liability is predicated on section 402A, must prove the requisite "outrageous" conduct by clear and convincing proof.[1] Accord Wangen v. Ford Motor Co., [97 Wis.2d 260, 294 N.W.2d 437, 446 (1980)]; Model Uniform Product Liability Act § 120(A), 44 Fed.Reg. 62748 (1979).[2]

C. THE STANDARD APPLIED

Applying the "clear and convincing" standard to the facts of this case, we conclude that the district court should have entered judgments n.o.v. on the punitive damages issue for all three defendants, and not just for American Honda. We recognize, of course, that we are bound to "view all the evidence and the inferences reasonably drawn therefrom" in plaintiff's favor, see *Chuy v. Philadelphia Eagles Football Club,* 595 F.2d 1265, 1273 (3d Cir.1979) (in banc), and that "[o]ur limited function at this point is to ascertain from a review of the record whether there is sufficient evidence to sustain the verdict of the jury on this issue," *id.* It nevertheless appears to us that the record "is critically deficient of that minimum quantum of evidence from which a jury might reasonably afford relief." *Denneny v. Siegel,* 407 F.2d 433, 439 (3d Cir.1969).

Plaintiff's evidence allegedly supporting his claim for punitive damages essentially consisted of the following:

　　1. The rear wheel of his motorcycle collapsed from a thirty-five mile per hour impact with a ditch four inches deep;

　　2. The particular wheel of plaintiff's motorcycle suffered from an inherent lack of strength as evidenced by the fact that it weighed sixteen percent less than several other randomly sampled rear wheels of motorcycles of the same model;

　　3. The owner's manual represented the CB750 as a high-speed touring motorcycle but provided no warning that the rear wheel might collapse upon the type of impact that occurred in this case;

　　4. Although the owner's manual instructed users to set and maintain the tension of the motorcycle's shock absorbers and wheel spokes, the manual did not warn that the failure to do so might result in the collapse of the wheel;

　　5. Defendants merely spot-checked rear wheels during the assembly process and did not crush test or weigh each wheel;

---

1. Even with such proof, however, a plaintiff is not entitled to recover such damages as a matter of right. Rather the Restatement is quite clear that the award is discretionary with the trier of fact. See § 908 comment d.

2. Section 120(A) provides:

Punitive damages may be awarded to the claimant if the claimant proves by clear and convincing evidence that the harm suffered was the result of the product seller's reckless disregard for the safety of product users, consumers, or others who might be harmed by the product.

6. Plaintiff's expert witness testified that the above evidence constituted defective manufacture and a failure adequately to inspect or to warn; and

7. Plaintiff's expert concluded that defendant's conduct manifested a "colossal disregard for the safety of the users of the motor vehicle," App. II at 125–26.

Plaintiff contends that the jury was entitled to infer from this evidence that defendants recklessly disregarded his rights and safety as a user of the motorcycle. We cannot agree. As we have suggested above, section 908 of the *Restatement* declares that reckless or outrageous conduct on the part of the defendant is the touchstone of punitive damages. See *Berroyer v. Hertz,* 672 F.2d 334 (3d Cir.1982); *Chuy v. Philadelphia Eagles, supra,* 595 F.2d at 1277. Although section 908 does not elaborate on the kind of conduct for which punitive damages are appropriate, comment b refers to section 500, which in turn provides:

> The actor's conduct is in reckless disregard of the safety of another if he does an act or intentionally fails to do an act which it is his duty to the other to do, knowing or having reason to know of facts which would lead a reasonable man to realize, not only that his conduct creates an unreasonable risk of physical harm to another but also that such risk is substantially greater than that which is necessary to make his conduct negligent.

The commentary accompanying section 500 explains further:

> Recklessness may consist of either of two different types of conduct. In one the actor knows, or has reason to know * * * of facts which create a high degree of risk of physical harm to another, and deliberately proceeds to act, or to fail to act, in conscious disregard of, or indifference to, that risk. In the other the actor has such knowledge, or reason to know, of the facts, but does not realize or appreciate the high degree of risk involved, although a reasonable man in his position would do so. An objective standard is applied to him and he is held to the realization of the aggravated risk which a reasonable man in his place would have, although he does not himself have it.

> * * *

> For either type of conduct, to be reckless it must be unreasonable; but to be reckless, it must be something more than negligent. It must not only be unreasonable, but it must involve a risk of harm to others substantially in excess of that necessary to make the conduct negligent. It must involve an easily perceptible danger of death or substantial physical harm, and the probability that it will so result must be substantially greater than is required for ordinary negligence.

We have examined the evidence; viewed in the light most favorable to plaintiff, it does not show that the conduct of any defendant was outrageous or reckless. Indeed we discern no basis upon which the jury could have concluded that defendants knew or had reason to know that the rear wheel of Acosta's motorcycle was defective in design or manufacture and that they decided not to remedy the defect in conscious disregard of or indifference to the risk thereby created. Although the wheel had been used in over 275,000 motorcycles, and the model first offered in 1970 (six years before plaintiff's accident), there was no evidence of previous consumer complaints or lawsuits that might have called to defendants' attention that there might be a problem. Moreover, plaintiff offered no proof that defendants developed or failed to modify the engineering designs for the rear wheel of the CB750 with any knowledge or reason to know of its alleged lack of safety.[21] Such matters would have been admissible on the punitive damages issues.

In short, a jury could not have reasonably concluded that the evidence by the clear and convincing standard showed defendants to have acted with reckless disregard for the safety of users of the CB750.[22] Accordingly, we hold that the district court should have granted defendants' motions for directed verdicts on the punitive damage claim and that it was error to deny the subsequent motions for judgment n.o.v. on behalf of Honda and Daido Kogyo.

VI. Conclusion

For the foregoing reasons, we will reverse the judgment of the district court denying Honda's and Daido Kogyo's motions for judgment n.o.v. on the award of punitive damages and the district court will be directed to enter judgment for Honda and Daido Kogyo on that claim. [The court also vacated an award of attorney's fees under a Virgin Island's statute and remanded the case to the district court for reconsideration of that award in light of its disposition of the punitive damages issue.] In all other respects, the judgment of the district court will be affirmed.

OWEN, PROBLEMS IN ASSESSING PUNITIVE DAMAGES AGAINST MANUFACTURERS OF DEFECTIVE PRODUCTS
49 U.Chi.L.Rev. 1, 15–25 (1982).

C. PROBLEMS WITH PUNISHING A MANUFACTURING ENTITY

Punitive damages were developed largely as a punishment and deterrent for trespassers, oxen thieves and other such human male-

---

21. In fact, defendants adduced evidence, which was not contradicted, that pre-production testing followed standard procedures, including on-the-road testing and laboratory testing (including wheel crushing to determine durability), and that samples from each production run of completed motorcycles were subjected to final dynamometer tests before shipping.

22. The clear and convincing standard of proof we announce today pertains to the degree of proof needed to be found by the trier of fact before it assesses punitive dam-

ages. The standard is not applicable to an appellate court in reviewing the determination of the trier of fact that there was or was not clear and convincing evidence of outrageous conduct. Rather the applicable standard of review on appeal is whether the record "is critically deficient of that minimum quantum of evidence from which a jury might reasonably afford relief." *Denneny v. Siegel*, 407 F.2d 433, 439 (3d Cir. 1969).

factors. When the device is transferred to the complex bureaucracy of a modern manufacturing concern, the fit is awkward in many respects. Final "decisions" concerning a complex product are often the result of a splintered, bureaucratic process involving a complicated combination of human judgments made by scores of persons at different levels in the hierarchy who pass on different aspects of the problem at different times. Various engineers may have to rely upon the work of research chemists, physicists, and other scientists; input from the financial and marketing arms of the enterprise must be factored in along the way. The entire process may take years. Each of these human actors makes decisions based on his own motives and on different types and amounts of information, and even the responsible executive at the end of the decisional line can possess only a small bit of the total information involved. Moreover, the corporate owners of the enterprise are usually far removed from most decisions of even the top executives.

This is not to say that institutional safety procedures cannot be put in place and monitored to ensure that safety gets its day in the manufacturer's decisional court, and the modern company without procedures of this type should be held to some account. Yet we must remember that the concepts of moral responsibility, punishment, and deterrence can mean vastly different things when judging the "conduct" of an institution rather than of a human being.

The serious difficulty of attempting to apply human standards of culpability to manufacturers in this context is highlighted by the problem of defining the proscribed misconduct * * *. The problem in capsule form is simply this: humans are clearly culpable when they act to gain a minor advantage in a way they know will be likely to kill or injure others. Thus, we usually punish a person who deliberately or recklessly kills or maims another without good reason. Yet manufacturers of hazardous products such as automobiles (which kill and maim thousands every year) must design them in many different ways they know with virtual certainty will result in harm or death at some time to a certain number of unfortunate, statistical persons. In a sense, then, such manufacturers always act "intentionally" in derogation of human life, yet surely punishment is inappropriate for simply being in the business of making high speed machines.

* * *

Virtually all important actions involve some risks to some people, and responsible individuals and institutions give careful consideration to such risks before they act. It is fundamental to life in a dynamic world with an unpredictable future that one must proceed to act, notwithstanding the presence of some foreseeable risks, provided that the benefits of the contemplated action (or inaction) appear at the time to exceed the risks. If this basic tenet of risk-benefit analysis were not virtually the universal rule, life would grind nearly to a halt. Everyone employs this process hundreds of times each day, ticking off the balance of advantages versus disadvantages (which may affect other persons adversely) of one choice after another, often in only fractions of a second. The rules of negligence law provide that an actor generally will not be liable even for compensatory damages unless the balance of trade-offs was a bad one—that is, one in which the costs exceeded the benefits, thus making the action on balance cost-*in*effective. Punishment for such decisions usually can be justified only when the actor not only made the wrong decision but also made a deliberate choice to advance his good over what he knew to be the greater good of others.

* * *

Cost-benefit analysis is fundamental to the design engineer's trade. The depth of the rubber on an automobile's bumper forever may be increased by another one-tenth inch. One more crossbeam always may be added to protect the occupants in certain types of collisions. The configuration of crossbeams may be changed to increase their strength; thicker or harder steel may be used in the beams; perhaps they may be made of another metal, or perhaps even of a form of plastic. Many hundreds of such choices are made by design engineers in the production of a single complex product, and each such decision involves a range of trade-offs between cost, weight, appearance, performance capabilities (for separate functions in varying environments), and safety in one type of accident versus another. A steel beam that protects an occupant in one type of accident may endanger him in another, as by rendering that portion of the vehicle less energy absorbent, and may endanger pedestrians and the occupants of other vehicles as well. Although much of this decision making involves the application of proven scientific principles, much is art, and some by its nature can be little more than trial and error.

Notes

1. **Standard of Liability.** Courts generally agree that a showing of simple negligence is not enough to justify an award of punitive damages. One basis for imposing punitive damages is intentional or malicious desire to harm the plaintiff. Most courts also authorize punitive damages upon a showing of such states of mind as "recklessness" or "conscious disregard" of plaintiff's rights. E.g., Wangen v. Ford Motor Co., 97 Wis.2d 260, 275, 294 N.W.2d 437, 446 (1980) (malice, vindictiveness, ill-will, or wanton, willful or reckless disregard of plaintiff's rights). Most punitive damage claims in products liability cases involve allegations of "recklessness" or "conscious disregard" because intent to harm is almost never present in such cases.

2. Courts vary considerably in the definition of the kind of conduct that qualifies as "recklessness" or "conscious disregard." A good many courts have adopted the Restatement of Torts (Second) § 500 definition of recklessness. Consider some of the other formulations courts have used:

A. Reckless disregard is "conscious indifference to the safety of persons or entities that might be harmed by a product." Model Uniform Product Liability Act, § 102(J).

B. A manufacturer must act in:

reckless disregard for the public safety. To meet this standard the manufacturer must either be aware of, or culpably indifferent to, an unnecessary risk of injury. Awareness should be imputed to a company to the extent that its employee(s) possess such information. Knowing of this risk, the manufacturer must also fail to determine the gravity of the danger or fail to reduce the risk to an acceptable minimal level. 'Disregard for the public safety' reflects a basic disrespect for the interests of others.

Thiry v. Armstrong World Indus., 661 P.2d 515, 518 (Okl.1983).

C. Malice is conduct done in conscious disregard of the probability of injury to members of the consuming public. Grimshaw v. Ford Motor Co., 119 Cal.App.3d 757, 174 Cal.Rptr. 348 (1981).

D. Fischer v. Johns–Manville Corp., 103 N.J. 643, 512 A.2d 466 (1986) adopted the following standard:

> [P]unitive damages are available in failure-to-warn, strict products liability actions when a manufacturer is (1) aware of or culpably indifferent to an unnecessary risk of injury, and (2) refuses to take steps to reduce that danger to an acceptable level. This standard can be met by a showing of "a deliberate act or omission with knowledge of a high degree of probability of harm and reckless indifference to consequences."

Do each of these word formulas adequately identify the kind of behavior that is deserving of punishment? *See* Owen, Problems in Assessing Punitive Damages Against Manufacturers of Defective Products, 49 U.Chi.L.Rev. 1, 20–28 (1982).

3. Several courts have adopted as the standard of liability the requirement that defendant's conduct reflect flagrant indifference to public safety. Moore v. Remington Arms Co., Inc., 100 Ill.App.3d 1102, 1115, 56 Ill.Dec. 413, 422, 427 N.E.2d 608, 617 (1981); Leichtamer v. American Motors Corp., 67 Ohio St.2d 456, 472, 424 N.E.2d 568, 580 (1981), noted in 11 Cap. U.L.Rev. 363 (1981). This standard was suggested by Professor Owen. *See* Owen, Punitive Damages in Products Liability Litigation, 74 Mich.L.Rev. 1257, 1366–1371 (1976).

4. A five year old child put a cotton swab inside his ear canal in an attempt to clean his ear. The swab tore his tympanic membrane (ear drum) and dislocated the bones of his inner ear causing tinnitus and dysequilibrium. In the ten years prior to the injury, the manufacturer received approximately forty complaints regarding ear injuries from using its cotton swabs. Over this same ten year period it sold 36 billion cotton swabs. The manufacturer sold the swabs without an adequate warning. Plaintiff sues the manufacturer, seeking actual and punitive damages. State law permits the imposition of punitive damages where defendant "intentionally acts knowing that its conduct involves a high degree of probability that substantial harm will result." Is defendant liable to plaintiff for punitive damages?

5. Should compliance with government regulations be a defense to punitive damage claims? *See* Schwartz, Punitive Damages and Regulated Products, 42 Am.U.L.Rev. 1335 (1993).

6. *See generally,* Ausness, Retribution and Deterrence: The Role of Punitive Damages in Products Liability Litigation, 74 Ky.L.J. 1 (1985/1986); Ghiardi & Kircher, Punitive Damages Recovery in Products Liability Cases, 65 Marq.L.Rev. 1 (1981); Owen, Punitive Damages in Products Liability Litigation, 74 Mich.L.Rev. 1257 (1976); Owen, Problems in Assessing Punitive Damages Against Manufacturers of Defective Products, 49 U.Chi.L.Rev. 1 (1982); Rustad, In Defense of Punitive Damages in Products Liability: Testing Tort Anecdotes With Empirical Data, 78 Iowa L.Rev. 1 (1992); Note, An Economic Analysis of the Plaintiff's Windfall From Punitive Damage Litigation, 105 Harv.L.Rev. 1900 (1992).

FISCHER v. JOHNS–MANVILLE CORP.

Supreme Court of New Jersey, 1986.
103 N.J. 643, 512 A.2d 466.

[The court authorized punitive damages in a case involving harm caused by exposure to asbestos. It addressed the difficult problems caused by the likelihood of multiple recoveries in such cases.]

[T]he massive amount of litigation generated by exposure to asbestos [is startling]. Although we are mindful of the fact that the case before us involves one worker, whose exposure to asbestos caused legally compensable injury to him and his wife—it is not a class action, not a "mass" case—nevertheless we would be remiss were we to ignore the society-wide nature of the asbestos problem. Recognizing the mass-tort nature of asbestos litigation, we address the concerns that that characteristic of the litigation brings to a decision to allow punitive damages.

Studies show that between eleven million and thirteen million workers have been exposed to asbestos. Special Project, "An Analysis of the Legal, Social, and Political Issues Raised by Asbestos Litigation," 36 *Vand.L.Rev.* 573, 580 (1983). More than 30,000 lawsuits have been filed already for damages caused by that exposure, with no indication that there are no more victims who will seek redress. Of the multitude of lawsuits that are faced by asbestos defendants as a group, Johns–Manville alone has been named in more than 11,000 cases. New claims are stayed because Johns–Manville is attempting reorganization under federal bankruptcy law. *In re Johns–Manville Corp.,* 26 B.R. 420 (Bankr.S.D.N.Y.1983).

Defendant argues that the amount of compensatory damages assessed and to be assessed is so great that it will effectively serve the functions of punitive damages—that is, defendants are more than sufficiently punished and deterred. We are not at all satisfied, however, that compensatory damages effectively serve the same functions as punitive damages, even when they amount to staggering sums. Compensatory damages are often foreseeable as to amount, within certain limits difficult to reduce to a formula but nonetheless familiar to the liability insurance industry. Anticipation of these damages will allow potential defendants, aware of dangers of a product, to factor those anticipated damages into a cost-benefit analysis and to decide whether to market a particular product. The risk and amount of such damages can, and in some cases will, be reflected in the cost of a product, in which event the product will be marketed in its dangerous condition.

Without punitive damages a manufacturer who is aware of a dangerous feature of its product but nevertheless knowingly chooses to market it in that condition, willfully concealing from the public information regarding the dangers of the product, would be far better off than an innocent manufacturer who markets a product later discovered to be dangerous—this, because both will be subjected to the same compensatory damages, but the innocent manufacturer, unable to anticipate those damages, will not have incorporated the cost of those damages into the cost of the product. All else being equal, the law should not place the innocent manufacturer in a worse position than that of a knowing wrongdoer. Punitive damages tend to meet this need.[4]

Defendant argues further that the cumulative effect of punitive damages in mass-tort litigation is "potentially catastrophic." The Johns–Manville bankruptcy is offered as proof of this effect. We fail to see the distinction, in the case of Johns–Manville, between the effect of compensatory damages and that of punitive damages. The amount of punitive damages and the determination that they would cause insolvency that could be avoided in their absence are so speculative as to foreclose any sound basis for judicial decision. *See also Jackson v. Johns–Manville, supra,* 781 F.2d at 403 n. 11 ("defendants * * * do not indicate why their ability to pay future damage awards will be more affected by punitive damage awards than by the multiplicity of compensatory damage awards.").

Heretofore the typical setting for punitive damage claims has been the two-party lawsuit in which, more often than not, a punitive damages award was supported by a showing of some element of malice or intentional wrongdoing, directed by a defendant to the specific plaintiff. Even if the actual object of the malicious conduct was unknown to defendant, the conduct nevertheless was directed at a single person or a very limited group of potential plaintiffs.

Punishable conduct in a products liability action, on the other hand, will often affect countless potential plaintiffs whose identities are unknown to defendant at the time of the culpable conduct. We agree with the Illinois court that the mere fact that a defendant, "through outrageous misconduct, * * * manage(s) to seriously injure a large number of persons" should not relieve it of liability for punitive damages. *Froud v. Celotex Corp.,* 107 Ill.App.3d 654, 658, 63 Ill.Dec. 261, 264, 437 N.E.2d 910, 913 (1982), rev'd on other grounds, 98 Ill.2d 324, 74 Ill.Dec. 629, 456 N.E.2d 131 (1983).

---

4. In addition, it is questionable how much punishment is effected by compensatory damages alone, which are generally covered by liability insurance. We consider our observation in that regard to be valid despite a restricted insurance market and increasing insurance costs.

Of greater concern to us is the possibility that asbestos defendants' assets may become so depleted by early awards that the defendants will no longer be in existence and able to pay compensatory damages to later plaintiffs. Again, it is difficult if not impossible to ascertain the additional impact of punitive damages as compared to the impact of mass compensatory damages alone.

Many of the policy arguments against punitive damages in mass tort litigation cases can be traced to *Roginsky v. Richardson–Merrell, Inc.,* 378 F.2d 832 (2d Cir.1967). The *Roginsky* court denied punitive damages to a plaintiff who suffered cataracts caused by MER/29, an anti-cholesterol drug. Although the denial of punitive damages rested on a determination that the evidence was insufficient to send the matter to the jury, the court expressed several concerns over allowing punitive damages for injuries to multiple plaintiffs. The fear that punitive damages would lead to "overkill" turned out to be unfounded in the MER/29 litigation. Approximately 1500 claims were made, of which only eleven were tried to a jury verdict. Punitive damages were awarded in only three of those cases, one of which was reversed on appeal. (*Roginsky, supra,* 378 F.2d 832.) [Owen, Punitive Damages in Products Liability Litigation 74 Mich.L.Rev. 1257, 1324, 1330 n. 339 (1976).] While we do not discount entirely the possibility of punitive damage "overkill" in asbestos litigation, we do recognize that the vast majority of cases settle without trial.

Accepting the possibility of punitive damage "overkill," we turn to means of addressing that problem. Because the problem is nationwide, several possible remedial steps can be effective only on a nationwide basis, and hence are beyond our reach. One such solution is the setting of a cap on total punitive damages against each defendant. *E.g.,* [Owen, Problems in Assessing Punitive Damages Against Manufacturers of Defective Products, 49 U.Chi.L.Rev. 1, 48–49 & n. 227 (1982)]. Such a cap would be ineffective unless applied uniformly. To adopt such a cap in New Jersey would be to deprive our citizens of punitive damages without the concomitant benefit of assuring the availability of compensatory damages for later plaintiffs. This we decline to do.

Perhaps the most likely solution to the problem of cumulative punitive damages lies in the use of a class action for those damages. *Froud v. Celotex Corp., supra,* 107 Ill.App.3d at 657–60, 63 Ill.Dec. at 264–65, 437 N.E.2d at 913–14. Several courts have recognized the need to streamline and consolidate issues that come up repeatedly in asbestos litigation. For instance, the non-availability of the state-of-the-art defense was decided in a consolidated case governing all asbestos cases in the federal district of New Jersey. *In re Asbestos Litigation,* 628 F.Supp. 774 (D.N.J.1986).

* * *

For a thoughtful analysis of the advantages and problems of resolving mass tort punitive damage claims through the class-action technique, see Seltzer, "Punitive Damages in Mass Tort Litigation," 52 *Fordham L.Rev.* 37, 61–92 (1983).

Defendants as well as plaintiffs can seek class certification. * * *
In addition, the asbestos industry itself is free to—and has begun to—
develop alternatives and supplements to federal class action. A step in
this direction is the establishment of the Asbestos Claims Facility
pursuant to the Wellington Agreement, an organization whose purpose is
to establish expeditious and uniform settlement, payment, or defense of
asbestos-related claims.[5]

At the state court level we are powerless to implement solutions to
the nationwide problems created by asbestos exposure and litigation
arising from that exposure. That does not mean, however, that we
cannot institute some controls over runaway punitive damages. When a
defendant manufacturer engages in conduct warranting the imposition
of punitive damages, the harm caused may run to countless plaintiffs.
Each individual plaintiff can fairly charge that the manufacturer's
conduct was egregious as to him and that punitive damages should be
assessed in his lawsuit. "Each tort committed by the defendant is
individual and peculiar to that particular plaintiff who has brought
suit." *Neal v. Carey Canadian Mines,* 548 F.Supp. 357, 377 (E.D.Pa.
1982), aff'd *sub nom. Van Buskirk v. Carey Canadian Mines, Ltd.,* 760
F.2d 481 (3d Cir.1985). Nonetheless, there should be some limits placed
on the total punishment exacted from a culpable defendant. We conclude that a reasonable imposition of those limits would permit a
defendant to introduce evidence of other punitive damage awards already assessed against and paid by it, as well as evidence of its own
financial status and the effect a punitive award would have. We note
with approval that this approach has already been looked on with favor
by our trial courts. See *Brotherton v. Celotex Corp.,* 202 N.J.Super. 148,
163, 493 A.2d 1337 (Law Div.1985).

We realize that defendants may be reluctant to alert juries to the
fact that other courts or juries have assessed punitive damages for
conduct similar to that being considered by the jury in a given case.
Although the evidence may convince a jury that a defendant has been
sufficiently punished, the same evidence could nudge a jury closer to a
determination that punishment is warranted. That is a risk of jury
trial. The willingness to accept that risk is a matter of strategy for
defendant and its counsel, no different from other strategy choices facing
trial lawyers every day.

When evidence of other punitive awards is introduced, trial courts
should instruct juries to consider whether the defendant has been
sufficiently punished, keeping in mind that punitive damages are meant

---

5. It is also possible that the needs of
future plaintiffs will be attended to, as to
defendants in bankruptcy, by innovative
procedures in the federal Bankruptcy
Courts, such as reduced priority for punitive damages claims as a condition of a
reorganization plan.

to punish and deter defendants for the benefit of society, not to compensate individual plaintiffs.

A further protection may be afforded defendants by the judicious exercise of remittitur. Should a trial court determine that an award is "manifestly outrageous" or "grossly excessive," *Cabakov v. Thatcher, supra,* 37 N.J.Super. at 260, 117 A.2d 298, it may reduce that award or order a new trial on punitive damages. In evaluating the excessiveness of challenged punitive damage awards, trial courts are expressly authorized to consider prior punitive damage awards.

* * *

Notes

1. Most courts have permitted recovery of punitive damages in such mass-tort cases notwithstanding the problem of multiple recoveries.

2. With respect to the problems of punitive damages in mass tort cases, see Forde, Punitive Damages in Mass Tort Cases: Recovery on Behalf of a Class, 15 Loy.U.Chi.L.J. 397 (1984); Seltzer, Punitive Damages in Mass Tort Litigation: Addressing the Problems of Fairness, Efficiency and Control, 52 Fordham L.Rev. 37 (1983).

3. **Constitutionality of punitive damages.** In two cases, the Supreme Court has recently addressed the constitutionality of punitive damages in a non-product liability context. In the first case, Pacific Mut. Life Ins. Co. v. Haslip, 499 U.S. 1, 111 S.Ct. 1032, 113 L.Ed.2d 1 (1991) several insureds sued a life insurer because its agent fraudulently continued to accept premium payments even though the policy had been cancelled without notice to them. Mrs. Haslip was awarded $200,000 in actual damages and $840,000 in punitive damages. The insurer appealed, claiming that the award of punitive damages violated due process. In rejecting the argument the court stated:

> One must concede that unlimited jury discretion—or unlimited judicial discretion for that matter—in the fixing of punitive damages may invite extreme results that jar one's constitutional sensibilities. [Citation] We need not, and indeed we cannot, draw a mathematical bright line between the constitutionally acceptable and the constitutionally unacceptable that would fit every case. We can say, however, that general concerns of reasonableness and adequate guidance from the court when the case is tried to a jury properly enter into the constitutional calculus. With these concerns in mind, we review the constitutionality of the punitive damages awarded in this case.

> We conclude that the punitive damages assessed by the jury against Pacific Mutual were not violative of the Due Process Clause of the Fourteenth Amendment. It is true, of course, that under Alabama law, as under the law of most States, punitive damages are imposed for purposes of retribution and deterrence. [Citation] They have been described as quasi-criminal. [Citation] But this in itself does not provide the answer. We move, then, to the points of specific attack.

1. We have carefully reviewed the instructions to the jury. By these instructions * * * the trial court expressly described for the jury the purpose of punitive damages, namely, "not to compensate the plaintiff for any injury" but "to punish the defendant" and "for the added purpose of protecting the public by [deterring] the defendant and others from doing such wrong in the future." App. 105–106. Any evidence of Pacific Mutual's wealth was excluded from the trial in accord with Alabama law. [Citation]

To be sure, the instructions gave the jury significant discretion in its determination of punitive damages. But that discretion was not unlimited. It was confined to deterrence and retribution, the state policy concerns sought to be advanced. And if punitive damages were to be awarded, the jury "must take into consideration the character and the degree of the wrong as shown by the evidence and necessity of preventing similar wrong." App. 106. The instructions thus enlightened the jury as to the punitive damages' nature and purpose, identified the damages as punishment for civil wrongdoing of the kind involved, and explained that their imposition was not compulsory.

These instructions, we believe, reasonably accommodated Pacific Mutual's interest in rational decisionmaking and Alabama's interest in meaningful individualized assessment of appropriate deterrence and retribution. The discretion allowed under Alabama law in determining punitive damages is no greater than that pursued in many familiar areas of the law as, for example, deciding "the best interests of the child," or "reasonable care," or "due diligence," or appropriate compensation for pain and suffering or mental anguish. As long as the discretion is exercised within reasonable constraints, due process is satisfied. [Citations]

2. Before the trial in this case took place, the Supreme Court of Alabama had established post-trial procedures for scrutinizing punitive awards. In *Hammond v. City of Gadsden*, 493 So.2d 1374 (1986), it stated that trial courts are "to reflect in the record the reasons for interfering with a jury verdict, or refusing to do so, on grounds of excessiveness of the damages." *Id.*, at 1379. [In a subsequent decision the Supreme Court of Alabama elaborated and refined the *Hammond* criteria such that the following could be taken into consideration in determining whether the award was excessive or inadequate: (a) whether there is a reasonable relationship between the punitive damages award and the harm likely to result from the defendant's conduct as well as the harm that actually has occurred; (b) the degree of reprehensibility of the defendant's conduct, the duration of that conduct, the defendant's awareness, any concealment, and the existence and frequency of similar past conduct; (c) the profitability to the defendant of the wrongful conduct and the desirability of removing that profit and of having the defendant also sustain a loss; (d) the "financial position" of the defendant; (e) all the costs of litigation; (f) the imposition of criminal sanctions on the defendant for its conduct, these to be taken in mitigation; and (g) the existence of other civil awards against the defendant for the same conduct, these also to be taken in mitigation.]

3. By its review of punitive awards, the Alabama Supreme Court provides an additional check on the jury's or trial court's discretion. It first undertakes a comparative analysis. [Citation] It then applies the detailed substantive standards it has developed for evaluating punitive awards. In particular, it makes its review to ensure that the award does "not exceed an amount that will accomplish society's goals of punishment and deterrence." *Green Oil Co. v. Hornsby*, 539 So.2d 218, 222 (1989) * * *. This appellate review makes certain that the punitive damages are reasonable in their amount and rational in light of their purpose to punish what has occurred and to deter its repetition.

* * *

The application of these standards, we conclude, imposes a sufficiently definite and meaningful constraint on the discretion of Alabama fact finders in awarding punitive damages. The Alabama Supreme Court's post-verdict review ensures that punitive damages awards are not grossly out of proportion to the severity of the offense and have some understandable relationship to compensatory damages. While punitive damages in Alabama may embrace such factors as the heinousness of the civil wrong, its effect upon the victim, the likelihood of its recurrence, and the extent of defendant's wrongful gain, the fact finder must be guided by more than the defendant's net worth. Alabama plaintiffs do not enjoy a windfall because they have the good fortune to have a defendant with a deep pocket.

* * *

Pacific Mutual thus had the benefit of the full panoply of Alabama's procedural protections. The jury was adequately instructed. The trial court conducted a post-verdict hearing that conformed with Hammond.
* * *

We are aware that the punitive damages award in this case is more than 4 times the amount of compensatory damages, is more than 200 times the out-of-pocket expenses of respondent Haslip, * * * and, of course, is much in excess of the fine that could be imposed for insurance fraud under Ala.Code §§ 13A–5–11 and 13A–5–12(a) (1982), and §§ 27–1–12, 27–12–17, and 27–12–23 (1986). Imprisonment, however, could also be required of an individual in the criminal context. While the monetary comparisons are wide and, indeed, may be close to the line, the award here did not lack objective criteria. We conclude, after careful consideration, that in this case it does not cross the line into the area of constitutional impropriety. Accordingly, Pacific Mutual's due process challenge must be, and is, rejected.

499 U.S. at 17–23, 111 S.Ct. at 1043–46, 113 L.Ed.2d at 20–23.

The second Supreme Court case to analyze the constitutionality of punitive damages, TXO Production Corp. v. Alliance Resources Corp., ___ U.S. ___, 113 S.Ct. 2711, 125 L.Ed.2d 366 (1993), raised a question concerning the ratio between actual and punitive damages. The jury awarded $19,000 in actual damages and $10,000,000 in punitive damages based on defendant's fraudulent conduct. The court upheld the verdict against defendant's claim of a due process violation, with six judges voting to affirm. Those judges wrote three opinions giving their reasons, but no opinion was joined by a majority of judges.

4.   Neither *Haslip* nor *TXO* produced a "bright line" rule for analyzing the constitutionality of punitive damages. It appears from the cases, however, that defendants will have a difficult time overturning punitive damages on constitutional grounds if courts impose them pursuant to fair procedures. For a discussion of the constitutionality of punitive damages, *see* Ellis, Punitive Damages, Due Process, and the Jury, 40 Ala.L.Rev. 975 (1989); Jeffries, A Comment on the Constitutionality of Punitive Damages, 72 Va.L.Rev. 139 (1986); Jones, Sutton and Greenwald, Multiple Punitive Damages Awards for a Single Course of Wrongful Conduct: The Need for a National Policy to Protect Due Process, 43 Ala.L.Rev. 1 (1991); Riggs, Constitutionalizing Punitive Damages: The Limits of Due Process, 52 Ohio St.L.J. 859 (1991); Note, Judicial Assessment of Punitive Damages, the Seventh Amendment, and the Politics of Jury Power, 91 Colum.L.Rev. 142 (1991).

Chapter 14

CONTRIBUTION AND INDEMNITY

In many situations a plaintiff has the option of suing one of several tortfeasors to recover the entire amount of his damages. Sometimes this is because various sellers in the chain of a product's distribution are each liable. Sometimes it is because joint tortfeasors are independently liable to the plaintiff under the doctrine of joint and several liability. If one of several tortfeasors is required to pay the plaintiff's entire damages, that tortfeasor may be able to recover contribution or indemnity from one or more of the other tortfeasors. If one tortfeasor settles with the plaintiff, the settlement may affect the liability of other tortfeasors.

The basic rules of joint and several liability, contribution, indemnity, and settlement were developed primarily in cases involving ordinary negligence. You should be familiar with these basic doctrines from your first-year torts class. Consequently, this chapter does not contain a comprehensive treatment of contribution and indemnity. Instead, it focuses primarily on special problems that arise in the context of product cases.

The doctrine of joint and several liability provides that when a plaintiff's injury has been caused jointly by two or more tortfeasors, the plaintiff can recover for the injury in its entirety from any of the joint tortfeasors. The plaintiff can actually collect only once; if he collects an entire judgment or settlement from one joint tortfeasor, the judgment is "satisfied," and he cannot thereafter collect or obtain a judgment against the other joint tortfeasors. But until the claim is satisfied, the plaintiff can obtain judgments against all jointly and severally liable tortfeasors for the entire harm.

Joint and several liability is not necessarily applicable to every situation in which a plaintiff's injuries are caused by multiple tortfeasors. If different tortfeasors cause distinguishable injuries, each tortfeasor is normally liable only for the harm that that tortfeasor in fact caused. Only tortfeasors who have jointly caused an indivisible injury are jointly and severally liable.* In cases involving divisible injuries, the

* Multiple tortfeasors who cause separate injuries can be liable for each other's separate injuries under vicarious liability.

plaintiff normally has the burden to prove which defendant caused which harm. In cases involving injuries that are theoretically divisible but practicably indivisible, several courts shift the burden to the defendants to sort out who caused what portion of the injury. Otherwise these courts treat the injury as though it were indivisible, holding each tortfeasor jointly and severally liable. *See, e.g.,* Landers v. East Texas Salt Water Disposal Co., 151 Tex. 251, 248 S.W.2d 731 (1952). Other courts have developed special doctrines—such as the market share theory adopted in Sindell v. Abbott Laboratories, 26 Cal.3d 588, 163 Cal.Rptr. 132, 607 P.2d 924 (1980), cert. denied, 449 U.S. 912, 101 S.Ct. 285, 66 L.Ed.2d 140 (1980)—to help plaintiffs meet their burden when they cannot reasonably be expected to sort out ambiguous or confusing causal connections.

Divisible and indivisible injuries can occur in the same accident. For example, a plaintiff might suffer two separate injuries, one of which was caused jointly by two tortfeasors and the other of which was caused solely by one of the tortfeasors. Problems concerning divisible and indivisible injuries can be complicated, due to the fact that it is often difficult to sort out who caused what portion of an injury. Problems involving causation are addressed in detail in Chapter 11. The point here is that you should be very careful to sort out who caused what portions of an injury before applying the rules of joint and several liability.

In some states, most notably California, Florida and Texas, "tort reform" legislation or constitutional amendment has limited the application of joint and several liability, even in cases involving an indivisible injury caused by two or more tortfeasors. Some reform measures preclude joint and several liability for noneconomic damages, such as pain and suffering. Others preclude joint and several liability for any defendant whose percentage of responsibility in a comparative fault scheme is less than that of the plaintiff or less than a fixed percentage. Thus, it has become increasingly important to refer to possible legislation in a particular state before reaching conclusions concerning joint and several liability. As with many other features of joint and several liability, contribution, and indemnity, these statutory and constitutional limitations on joint and several liability often apply to tort law generally, not just products liability.

A tortfeasor who is jointly and severally liable for an entire injury can recover *contribution* (a portion of the damages) or sometimes can recover *indemnity* (the entire damages) from the other tortfeasor or tortfeasors. Before the advent of comparative negligence, contribution shares were determined on a *pro rata* basis, but in jurisdictions that use comparative negligence schemes, contribution shares are now typically determined according to the percentages assigned by the jury to each defendant. A few jurisdictions adopted comparative contribution even before they adopted comparative negligence. *See, e.g.,* Dole v. Dow Chemical Co., 30 N.Y.2d 143, 331 N.Y.S.2d 382, 282 N.E.2d 288 (1972). Regardless of which method is used, in many states a tortfeasor is not required to pay contribution beyond its own *pro rata* or percentage share. Thus, if one of the tortfeasors is insolvent, the tortfeasor who originally paid the plaintiff is left holding the bag.

A major issue concerning contribution and indemnity is determining when indemnity rather than mere contribution is appropriate. Courts have taken a variety of approaches to this distinction, but all agree that indemnity rather than contribution is appropriate (1) if the parties have entered into an express contract for indemnity, (2) if the party seeking indemnity is liable solely on the basis of vicarious liability for a tort actually committed by the party from whom indemnity is sought, and (3) when an innocent product seller (such as a retailer) is held liable for a defective product that was supplied to it by a seller higher in the chain of distribution (such as a manufacturer). Some courts also allow indemnity rather than contribution when the party seeking indemnity is qualitatively less culpable than the party from whom indemnity is sought.

TROMZA v. TECUMSEH PRODUCTS COMPANY

United States Court of Appeals, Third Circuit, 1967.
378 F.2d 601.

KALODNER, CIRCUIT JUDGE.

* * *

Tecumseh manufactured and sold to Marquette a sealed compressor refrigeration unit which Marquette incorporated in a refrigerator which it manufactured. The compressor unit was enclosed in a steel casing or shell, whose two halves were welded by Tecumseh. The refrigerator manufactured by Marquette carried a plate which stated that the factory test pressure of the refrigeration unit was 195 pounds.

The casing or shell of the compressor unit exploded when the plaintiff, a repair man, submitted the refrigerator to a pressure of 170 pounds in proceeding to repair a gas leak in its refrigeration system. The plaintiff was seriously injured by the explosion.

* * *

The case was submitted to the jury on the plaintiff's theory that Tecumseh was negligent both in its manufacture of the compressor unit and in failing to discover the defect by a proper inspection, and that Marquette was negligent in failing to make a proper test or inspection of the unit. * * *

Coming now to Marquette's contention that the District Court erred in entering judgment in favor of Tecumseh on Marquette's cross-claim for indemnity:

The sum of Marquette's contentions on this score is (1) it was only "secondarily liable" and Tecumseh was "primarily liable", and therefore it is entitled to recover indemnity from Tecumseh; and (2) it is entitled to recovery for breach of an implied warranty by Tecumseh.

In reply, Tecumseh contends that the principle of primary-secondary liability in tort does not apply generally to an indemnity claim between manufacturers.

It must here be noted that the District Court, in its opinion reported at 253 F.Supp. 26, 27 (E.D.Pa.1966), premised its ruling in favor of Tecumseh on the cross-claim on its following stated reasoning:

"Since the identical negligence (failure to make proper inspection) was charged against each defendant, in the light of the jury's verdict the defendants must be found to be joint or concurrent tort-feasors rather than as occupying a relationship of primary and secondary liability. There was no legal relationship between them, such as master and servant, which is ordinarily the basis for distinction of primary and secondary liability * * * "

* * *

The District Court's determination, in its opinion, that Marquette and Tecumseh were charged with "identical negligence (failure to make proper inspection)" thereby making them "joint or concurrent tort-feasors rather than as occupying a relationship of primary and secondary liability", is at variance with its own prior statement that "the only negligence alleged against defendant Marquette was failure to make a proper test or inspection at the time of assembly; whereas defendant Tecumseh was charged with a two-pronged negligence, both in the welding process and in failure to find the defect by a proper inspection", and its further statement that "The Court remains of opinion that the evidence and the jury's verdict, on the two-fold grounds above stated, clearly support plaintiff's verdict against defendant Tecumseh." 253 F.Supp. 26, 27.

Since the District Court premised its determination that Marquette and Tecumseh "must be found to be joint or concurrent tort-feasors rather than as occupying a relationship of primary and secondary liability" on its view that they were both charged with "identical negligence (failure to make proper inspection)", the circumstance that the negligence charged against the defendants was not "identical", renders the categorization of the defendants as "joint or concurrent tort-feasors" clear error.

Further, the District Court erred in its view that under Pennsylvania law, applicable here, a "legal relationship * * * such as master and servant * * * is ordinarily the basis for distinction of primary and secondary liability." *Pittsburgh Steel Company* [404 Pa. 53, 171 A.2d 185 (1961)] and *Builders Supply Co.* [366 Pa. 322, 77 A.2d 368 (1951)] which it cites, afford no nourishment to its view, since they specifically do not limit application of the primary-secondary liability doctrine to cases where a legal relationship exists between the party primarily liable and the party secondarily liable.

That that is so is clearly evident from the following quotation from the Pennsylvania Supreme Court's opinion in Builders Supply Co. at 366 Pa. 327–328, 77 A.2d 371:

"Without multiplying instances, it is clear that the right of a person vicariously or secondarily liable for a tort to recover from one primarily liable has been universally recognized. But the important point to be noted in all the cases is that secondary as distinguished from primary liability rests upon a fault that is imputed or constructive only, being based on some legal relation between the parties, *or* arising from some positive rule of common or statutory law *or* because of a failure to discover or correct a defect or remedy a dangerous condition caused by the act of the one primarily responsible." (emphasis supplied)

The foregoing quotation was preceded by this statement at 366 Pa. 325–326, 77 A.2d 370:

"The right of *indemnity* rests upon a difference between the primary and the secondary liability of two persons each of whom is made responsible by the law to an injured party. It is a right which enures to a person who, without active fault on his own part, has been compelled, by reason of some legal obligation, to pay damages occasioned by the initial negligence of another, and for which he himself is only secondarily liable. The difference between primary and secondary liability is not based on a difference in *degrees* of negligence or on any doctrine of *comparative* negligence, a doctrine which, indeed, is not recognized by the common law. See Fidelity & Casualty Co. of New York v. Federal Express, Inc., 6 Cir., 136 F.2d 35, 40. It depends on a difference in the *character* or *kind* of the wrongs which cause the injury and in the nature of the legal obligation owed by each of the wrongdoers to the injured person."

The principles stated in *Builders Supply Co.* were succinctly epitomized in the leading case of Union Stock Yards Co. of Omaha v. Chicago B. & Q.R.R. Co., 196 U.S. 217, 228, 25 S.Ct. 226, 229, 49 L.Ed. 453 (1905), as follows:

"In all these cases [where indemnity was sought] the wrongful act of the one held finally liable created the unsafe or dangerous condition from which the injury resulted. The principal and moving cause, resulting in the injury sustained, was the act of the first wrongdoer, and the other has been held liable to third persons for failing to discover or correct the defect caused by the positive act of the other."

* * *

Applying the principles stated to Marquette's cross-claim against Tecumseh, we are of the opinion that Marquette was entitled to judgment against Tecumseh. The latter was primarily responsible for manufacturing a defective compressor unit and failing to detect the defect by a proper inspection. Since Marquette's liability arose "because of a failure to discover or correct a defect or remedy a dangerous condition caused by the act of the one [Tecumseh] primarily responsible", its liability is secondary.

For the reasons stated the judgment entered pursuant to the jury's verdict in favor of Tromza against Tecumseh and Marquette will be affirmed, and the judgment entered in favor of Tecumseh against Marquette on Marquette's cross-claim will be vacated with directions to the District Court to enter judgment on the cross-claim in favor of Marquette and against Tecumseh.

Notes

1. Jurisdictions that have adopted comparative negligence schemes have typically abandoned the distinction between primary and secondary culpability, holding that indemnity is appropriate only (1) when the parties have a contract for indemnity, (2) when the party seeking indemnity is merely vicariously liable, and (3) when an "innocent" product seller seeks indemnity from a seller higher in the chain of distribution. In other situations, different degrees of culpability merely affect the percentages assigned to each defendant by the jury, and thereby affect the contribution shares of each defendant. *See* Duncan v. Cessna Aircraft Co., 665 S.W.2d 414 (Tex.1984).

2. At early common law, contribution was not permitted at all, on the ground that the law should not aid a wrongdoer, who, after all, had paid for no more than the damages he had caused. Many courts still deny contribution to intentional tortfeasors, but most have abrogated the no-contribution rule for non-intentional tortfeasors, either by statute or judicial decision.

3. You should pay special attention to a specific jurisdiction's rules about contribution and indemnity and the impact of comparative negligence. The history of these issues in California is more complex than usual, but it illustrates the types of issues that can arise. It was described in a non-products context by Justice Tobriner in American Motorcycle Ass'n v. Superior Court, 20 Cal.3d 578, 146 Cal.Rptr. 182, 578 P.2d 899 (1978). The plaintiff was seriously injured in a motorcycle race. He alleged that the American Motorcycle Association [AMA] and a local motorcycle club were negligent in designing the course and running the race. AMA filed a cross-complaint against the plaintiff's parents seeking indemnity. AMA argued that its negligence, if any, was passive, whereas the parents' negligence was active in that they helped their child enter the race and negligently failed to supervise him. Tracing the convoluted history of indemnity and contribution in California, Justice Tobriner wrote:

> Three years ago, in Li v. Yellow Cab Co. (1975) 13 Cal.3d 804, 119 Cal.Rptr. 858, 532 P.2d 1226, we concluded that the harsh and much criticized contributory negligence doctrine, which totally barred an injured person from recovering damages whenever his own negligence had contributed in any degree to the injury, should be replaced in this state by a rule of comparative negligence, under which an injured

individual's recovery is simply proportionately diminished, rather than completely eliminated, when he is partially responsible for the injury.

* * *

In California, as in most other American jurisdictions, the allocation of damages among multiple tortfeasors has historically been analyzed in terms of two, ostensibly mutually exclusive, doctrines: contribution and indemnification. In traditional terms, the apportionment of loss between multiple tortfeasors has been thought to present a question of contribution; indemnity, by contrast, has traditionally been viewed as concerned solely with whether a loss should be entirely shifted from one tortfeasor to another, rather than whether the loss should be shared between the two.

* * *

Although early common law decisions established the broad rule that a tortfeasor was never entitled to contribution, it was not long before situations arose in which the obvious injustice of requiring one tortfeasor to bear an entire loss while another more culpable tortfeasor escaped with impunity led common law courts to develop an equitable exception to the no contribution rule. (See generally Leflar, Contribution and Indemnity Between Tortfeasors (1932) 81 U.Pa.L.Rev. 140, 146–158.) As Chief Justice Gibson observed in Peters v. City & County of San Francisco (1953) 41 Cal.2d 419, 431, 260 P.2d 55, 62: "[T]he rule against contribution between joint tort-feasors admits of some exceptions, and a right of indemnification may arise as a result of contract *or equitable considerations* and is not restricted to situations involving a wholly vicarious liability, such as where a master has paid a judgment for damages resulting from the voluntary act of his servant." (Emphasis added.)

* * *

[T]he equitable indemnity doctrine originated in the common sense proposition that when two individuals are responsible for a loss, but one of the two is more culpable than the other, it is only fair that the more culpable party should bear a greater share of the loss. Of course, at the time the doctrine developed, common law precepts precluded any attempt to ascertain comparative fault; as a consequence, equitable indemnity, like the contributory negligence doctrine, developed as an all-or-nothing proposition.

Because of the all-or-nothing nature of the equitable indemnity rule, courts were, from the beginning, understandably reluctant to shift the entire loss to a party who was simply slightly more culpable than another. As a consequence, throughout the long history of the equitable indemnity doctrine courts have struggled to find some linguistic formulation that would provide an appropriate test for determining when the relative culpability of the parties is sufficiently disparate to warrant placing the entire loss on one party and completely absolving the other.

* * *

As one Court of Appeal has charitably stated: "The cases are not always helpful in determining whether equitable indemnity lies. The test[s] utilized in applying the doctrine are vague. Some authorities characterize the negligence of the indemnitor as 'active,' 'primary,' or 'positive,' and the negligence of the indemnitee as 'passive,' 'secondary,' or 'negative.' [Citations.] Other authorities indicate that the application of the doctrine depends on whether the claimant's liability is 'primary,' 'secondary,' 'constructive,' or 'derivative.' [Citations.] These formulations have been criticized as being artificial and as lacking the objective criteria desirable for predictability in the law. [Citations.]" (*Atchison, T. & S.F. Ry. Co. v. Franco, supra,* 267 Cal.App.2d 881, 886, 73 Cal.Rptr. 660, 664.)

* * *

If the fundamental problem with the equitable indemnity doctrine as it has developed in this state were simply a matter of an unduly vague or imprecise linguistic standard, the remedy would be simply to attempt to devise a more definite verbal formulation. In our view, however, the principal difficulty with the current equitable indemnity doctrine rests not simply on a question of terminology, but lies instead in the all-or-nothing nature of the doctrine itself.

* * *

[T]he New York Court of Appeals, in the celebrated decision of *Dole v. Dow Chemical Co., supra,* 30 N.Y.2d 143, 331 N.Y.S.2d 382, 282 N.E.2d 288, modified that state's traditional all-or-nothing indemnity doctrine to permit a tortfeasor to obtain "partial indemnification" from another tortfeasor on the basis of comparative fault. The *Dole* court, after noting that the previously existing "active-passive" indemnification test "has in practice proven elusive and difficult of fair application," went on to observe: "But the policy problem involves more than terminology. If indemnification is allowed at all among joint-tortfeasors, the important resulting question is how ultimate responsibility should be distributed. There are situations when the facts would in fairness warrant what [the named defendant] here seeks—passing on to [a concurrent tortfeasor] all responsibility that may be imposed on [the named defendant] for negligence, a traditional full indemnification. There are circumstances where the facts would not, by the same test of fairness, warrant passing on to a third party any of the liability imposed. There are circumstances which would justify apportionment of responsibility between third-party plaintiff and third-party defendant, in effect a partial indemnification." (331 N.Y.S.2d at p. 386, 282 N.E.2d at p. 291.)

Concluding that the all-or-nothing common law indemnity doctrine did not, in many situations, produce the equitable allocation of loss to which it aimed, the *Dole* court proceeded to modify the doctrine, holding that the "[r]ight to apportionment of liability or to full indemnity, * * * as among parties involved together in causing damage by negligence, should rest on relative responsibility * * *." (331 N.Y.S.2d at pp. 391–392, 282 N.E.2d at p. 295.) The *Dole* court was undeterred from undertaking this modification of the prior common law indemnity doctrine either by the existence of a contribution statute which, like that currently in force in California, provided joint tortfeasors with a right of pro rata contribution in limited circumstances, or by the fact that at that time New York still adhered to the all-or-nothing contributory negligence doctrine.

* * *

None of the parties to the instant proceeding, and none of the numerous amici who have filed briefs, seriously takes issue with our conclusion that a rule of comparative partial indemnity is more consistent with the principles underlying *Li* than the prior "all-or-nothing" indemnity doctrine. The principal argument raised in opposition to the recognition of a common law comparative indemnity rule is the claim that California's existing contribution statutes, section 875 et seq. of the Code of Civil Procedure, * preclude such a judicial development. As we explain, we reject the contention on a number of grounds.

First, as we have already noted, the New York Court of Appeals adopted a similar partial indemnity rule in *Dole v. Dow Chemical Co., supra,* 331 N.Y.S.2d 382, 282 N.E.2d 288, despite the existence of a closely comparable statutory contribution scheme.

* * *

We believe that a similar conclusion must be reached with respect to the pertinent California legislation. The legislative history of the 1957 contribution statute quite clearly demonstrates that the purpose of the legislation was simply "to lessen the harshness" of the then prevailing common law no contribution rule. Nothing in the legislative history suggests that the Legislature intended by the enactment to preempt the field or to foreclose future judicial developments which further the act's principal purpose of ameliorating the harshness and inequity of the old no contribution rule. Under these circumstances, we see no reason to interpret the legislation as establishing a bar to judicial innovation.

* * *

Several amici argue alternatively that even if the contribution statute was not intended to preclude the development of a common law comparative indemnity doctrine, our court should decline to adopt such a doctrine because it would assertedly undermine the strong public policy in favor of encouraging settlement of litigation embodied in section 877 of the Code of Civil Procedure, one of the provisions of the current, statutory contribution scheme.

* * *

Although section 877 reflects a strong public policy in favor of settlement, this statutory policy does not in any way conflict with the recognition of a common law partial indemnity doctrine but rather can,

* [Editor's note: § 875 provides in pertinent part: "Where a money judgment has been rendered jointly against two or more defendants in a tort action there shall be a right of contribution among them as hereinafter provided."]

and should, be preserved as an integral part of the partial indemnity doctrine that we adopt today. Thus, while we recognize that section 877, by its terms, releases a settling tortfeasor only from liability for contribution and not partial indemnity, we conclude that from a realistic perspective the legislative policy underlying the provision dictates that a tortfeasor who has entered into a "good faith" settlement (see *River Garden Farms, Inc. v. Superior Court, supra,* 26 Cal.App.3d 986, 103 Cal.Rptr. 498) with the plaintiff must also be discharged from any claim for partial or comparative indemnity that may be pressed by a concurrent tortfeasor.

* * *

Accordingly, we conclude that Code of Civil Procedure section 875 et seq. do not preclude the development of new common law principles in this area, and we hold that under the common law of this state a concurrent tortfeasor may seek partial indemnity from another concurrent tortfeasor on a comparative fault basis.

4. A few courts have thought that a retailer cannot obtain indemnity from a seller higher in the chain of distribution on the ground that pure economic loss (without personal injury or property damage) is not recoverable under section 402A. *See* Chapter 12, section B1, *supra.* For example, in United Tractor, Inc. v. Chrysler Corp., 563 S.W.2d 850 (Tex.Civ.App.1978), the plaintiff was injured when a tractor struck him. The tractor was manufactured by United Tractor, from whom the plaintiff recovered damages in a suit based on negligence. The tractor contained an engine manufactured by Chrysler, from whom United Tractor sought indemnity under section 402A for the damages paid to the plaintiff. The court denied indemnity to United Tractor on the ground, *inter alia,* that United Tractor's damages were purely economic and, therefore, not recoverable under section 402A. The court relied on General Motors Corp. v. Simmons, 558 S.W.2d 855 (Tex.1977).

In *Simmons* the plaintiff was injured when a defective piece of glass in his automobile shattered during a collision and injured his eyes. He sued General Motors, as manufacturer of the automobile, for strict tort liability. He also sued the driver of the vehicle for negligence and that driver's employer under respondeat superior. The court held that the other driver and his employer were not entitled to indemnity from General Motors. The court relied on the fact that a claim of indemnity by the driver and his employer was for mere economic damages, whereas strict tort liability can be used only to recover for physical injury or property damage. The court also relied on the fact that the other driver (and vicariously his employer) was independently negligent, and therefore was *in pari delicto* with General Motors.

Note that, in both *Simmons* and *United Tractor,* the party seeking indemnity was culpable and could have been denied indemnity (but not contribution) on that ground alone. The courts, however, at least *stated* that indemnity was improper because the party seeking indemnity had not itself suffered personal injury or property damage, as is required under section 402A.

The rationale that pure economic harm is not recoverable under section 402A would, on its face, seem to be just as applicable to contribution as to indemnity. Suppose driver 1 is injured when his defective brakes fail and he collides with driver 2, who negligently fails to avoid the collision. Would the rationale of *United Tractor* preclude driver 2 from obtaining contribution from the automobile manufacturer? Courts have not held that *contribution* would be precluded in this situation, casting doubt on the "pure economic loss" rationale as an impediment to *indemnity*.

Moreover, in most states, pure economic loss is not recoverable even for negligence, but this does not preclude a joint tortfeasor from recovering contribution or indemnity. Again, the "pure economic loss rationale" as an impediment to indemnity, whether in negligence or strict tort liability, is dubious. The "real" rule is that, under section 402A, *innocent* retailers can obtain indemnity and *culpable* retailers can obtain contribution from sellers further up in chain of distribution, notwithstanding the fact that the retailer has not suffered personal injury or property damage. Most courts expressly recognize this rule, *see, e.g.,* Duncan v. Cessna Aircraft Co., 665 S.W.2d 414 (Tex.1984); Thiele v. Chick, 631 S.W.2d 526 (Tex.App.1982), and the *facts* of cases such as *United Tractor* and *Simmons* are consistent with it. Nevertheless, you may occasionally confront the "pure economic loss" rationale in the context of indemnity, so you need to be able to recognize it and deal with it.

5. A party seeking either contribution or indemnity must prove that the party from whom contribution or indemnity is sought would be liable to the original plaintiff. A common issue in strict tort liability cases is whether the product was defective when it left the control of the party from whom indemnity is sought, usually the manufacturer. It is not enough that a retailer show that the product was defective when it left the retailer's own control.

6. Another common problem involves on-the-job injuries caused jointly by a defective product and the employer's negligence. The employer is usually immune from common law liability, being liable instead under the state's worker's compensation statute. In Lambertson v. Cincinnati Corp., 312 Minn. 114, 257 N.W.2d 679 (1977), the court held that a joint tortfeasor can recover contribution from the plaintiff's negligent employer, even though the plaintiff himself would be barred from recovering common law damages from his employer. Most courts, however, have held that the employer's immunity from common law tort actions brought by the employee extends to contribution actions brought by a joint tortfeasor from whom the employee has recovered. *See, e.g.,* Outboard Marine Corp. v. Schupbach, 93 Nev. 158, 561 P.2d 450 (1977). Indeed, in most states the employer can recoup its entire worker's compensation payment from the joint tortfeasor or out of the plaintiff's recovery from the joint tortfeasor, although here some courts permit the joint tortfeasor to raise the employer's own negligence as a defense. The effect of the employer's negligence on the plaintiff's own recovery from the other joint tortfeasor is addressed in note 9, *infra*, in conjunction with settlements.

7. How should courts treat other forms of immunity? Should the manufacturer of a defective automobile be able to obtain contribution from the victim's negligent spouse in a jurisdiction that still recognizes spousal

immunity? Should a manufacturer be able to obtain contribution from a negligent but immune governmental unit?

8. Procedurally, an action for indemnity or contribution can be brought in the principal action—by impleading the party from whom contribution or indemnity is sought as a third party defendant—or, in most states, it can be brought as an independent action, at least if the other tortfeasor is not already a party to the principal lawsuit.

9. If one joint tortfeasor enters into a partial settlement with the plaintiff, the other joint tortfeasors cannot obtain contribution from the settlor. Otherwise, there would be little incentive to settle. But the non-settling tortfeasors may still benefit from the settlement by having their own liability to the plaintiff reduced. Courts have used two approaches. Some courts reduce the plaintiff's claim against the other joint tortfeasors *pro tanto,* that is, dollar for dollar by the amount of the settlement. Other courts reduce the plaintiff's claim against the other joint tortfeasors *pro rata,* for example, by one-third if there are three tortfeasors.

In some states that use comparative negligence, a settlement reduces the plaintiff's claim against the other tortfeasors by the percentage of negligence attributed by the jury to the settling tortfeasor, or, if the jury does not make such a finding, it reduces the plaintiff's recovery as a *pro tanto* credit. This type of approach can raise difficult procedural issues. For example, which, if any, of the non-settling parties has a right to submit a settling party's percentage of negligence to the jury? Moreover, will a court abide by the percentage finding even when it constitutes a smaller reduction than would a *pro tanto* credit? For an extensive examination of these issues in the context of negligence, see Cypress Creek Utility Service Co. v. Muller, 640 S.W.2d 860 (Tex.1982).

These issues can also arise under a comparative allocation scheme for products liability, and they are addressed in more detail in connection with the material on comparative fault schemes in Chapter 15.

10. Should other "tortfeasors" who are immune from contribution be treated like settlors by causing a reduction of the plaintiff's recovery against the remaining defendants? For example, recall from note 6, *supra,* that most courts do not permit a tortfeasor to obtain contribution from the original plaintiff's negligent employer. Should the plaintiff's recovery nevertheless be reduced by the percentage of negligence or fault attributed to the employer? For a negative but unpersuasive answer, see Magro v. Ragsdale Brothers, Inc., 721 S.W.2d 832 (Tex.1986); Varela v. American Petrofina Co., 658 S.W.2d 561 (Tex.1983).

What about other types of immune tortfeasors?

11. Sometimes a settlement entitles the settling tortfeasor to share in the plaintiff's recovery from the other tortfeasors. For example, the settling tortfeasor might be paid a percentage of the plaintiff's recovery in excess of a specific amount. This type of settlement is called a "Mary Carter" agreement, after the case of Booth v. Mary Carter Paint Co., 202 So.2d 8 (Fla.App.1967). Typically, the settling defendant in such a case testifies for the plaintiff at trial.

Some courts have held that such agreements are void. *See, e.g.,* Lum v. Stinnett, 87 Nev. 402, 488 P.2d 347 (1971); Trampe v. Wisconsin Telephone Co., 214 Wis. 210, 252 N.W. 675 (1934). Other courts have permitted "Mary Carter" agreements but have permitted the non-settling defendants to discover the terms of the settlement and disclose its existence to the jury. *See, e.g.,* General Motors Corp. v. Simmons, 558 S.W.2d 855 (Tex.1977); Hemet Dodge v. Gryder, 23 Ariz.App. 523, 534 P.2d 454 (1975); Ward v. Ochoa, 284 So.2d 385 (Fla.1973); Gatto v. Walgreen Drug Co., 61 Ill.2d 513, 337 N.E.2d 23 (1975); Grillo v. Burke's Paint Co., Inc., 275 Or. 421, 551 P.2d 449 (1976). *But see* Klotz v. Lee, 36 N.J.Super. 6, 114 A.2d 746 (1955), appeal dismissed, 21 N.J. 148, 121 A.2d 369 (1956).

In a jurisdiction that gives remaining defendants a dollar for dollar credit for a settlement, what should be the dollar amount attributed to a "Mary Carter" settlement?

MORRISSETTE v. SEARS, ROEBUCK & CO.

Supreme Court of New Hampshire, 1974.
114 N.H. 384, 322 A.2d 7.

DUNCAN, JUSTICE.

In 1963 Doris Morrissette Przybyla was a tenant of her sister-in-law, Lucienne Morrissette, plaintiff in the present third-party action, in premises in Nashua owned and partly occupied by Lucienne. Allegedly one of the terms of the tenancy was that the tenants should mow the lawn. On June 22, 1963, Doris Przybyla was injured while operating a rotary lawn mower furnished by Lucienne on the leased premises. The mower had been purchased from defendant Sears, Roebuck & Company by Lucienne's husband in 1961. On May 15, 1969, Doris Przybyla brought a negligence action against Lucienne Morrissette. Lucienne Morrissette, in turn, brought the present third-party action over against Sears with counts in negligence, warranty, and strict liability.

* * *

[During the trial] the action of Przybyla against Morrissette was settled by a covenant not to sue. The Court, *Loughlin, J.,* declined to proceed with trial of this third-party action by Morrissette against Sears, and reserved and transferred to this court five questions of law considered below.

"1. Where a defendant settles a claim with a plaintiff on the basis of only a negligence count in the plaintiff's writ (being the only count brought by the plaintiff against the defendant) is the defendant in a third-party action limited in such action to a count of negligence against the third-party defendant; or can the third-party plaintiff expand his action against the third-party defendant by including counts in strict liability, implied warranty and express warranty?"

Sears concedes that the concept of third-party practice requires that the third-party plaintiff be permitted to expand her pleadings beyond the single count contained in the original complaint against her. This view is consistent with the purpose of the rule to consolidate as many claims as possible in one proceeding, and the answer is that the third-party plaintiff may include additional counts in the action over.

* * *

"3. In the third-party action, can the third-party defendant attempt to show contributory negligence on the part of the original plaintiff?"

"4. In the third-party action, what is the burden of proof of the third-party plaintiff? Must the third-party plaintiff prove the amount of the original settlement; that he was liable and had a duty to settle the original claim and that such settlement was reasonable?"

Questions three and four are interrelated and may be considered together. Question four outlines a third-party plaintiff's burden of proof in an action for indemnity where the original action has been settled. A right to "[i]ndemnity arises where one is legally required to pay an obligation for which another is primarily liable. In actions of tort it can arise only where one who, without [active] fault on his part, has been compelled by a legal obligation to pay an injured party for injuries caused by active fault of another." Merck & Co. v. Knox Glass, Inc., 328 F.Supp. 374, 376–377 (E.D.Pa.1971). * * * While a prejudgment payment in settlement does not extinguish a right of indemnity * * * the third-party plaintiff must show that the settlement was made under legal compulsion, rather than as a mere volunteer, for indemnity is not available for payment voluntarily made.

* * *

The parties agree that third-party plaintiff, Morrissette, must make some showing that she settled under a legal compulsion. The conflict surrounds the scope of her burden in this area. Sears argues that she must prove *"actual* liability" on her part to Pryzbyla, in effect forcing her to try out the case of the original plaintiff. As plaintiff herein, Morrissette argues that she need only show *"probable* liability". The problem has been considered with varying results. Some courts support Sears' view. "While the fact of voluntary payment does not negative the right to indemnity, legal liability, *i.e.,* proof by a preponderance of the evidence of the obligation * * * that cannot be legally resisted is a fundamental prerequisite to recovery by an indemnitee who has made a voluntary payment." Cason v. Geis Irrigation Co., 211 Kan. 406, 413, 507 P.2d 295, 300 (1973). * * * Some cases adopt a less precise statement that one voluntarily paying a claim "should be required to show that he was legally liable for it." Ashland Oil & Refining Co. v. General Tel. Co., 462 S.W.2d 190 (Ky.1970) * * *.

Other cases say that the third-party plaintiff must "establish potential liability" but need not prove the case against himself. St. Paul Fire & Marine Ins. Co. v. Michelin Tire Corp., 12 Ill.App.3d 165, 298 N.E.2d 289 (1973).

If a third-party plaintiff is not to be discouraged from making a settlement his burden in an action for indemnity must not be too great. He would in effect be forced to proceed to trial against the original plaintiff in order to achieve the burden imposed by the court in Cason v. Geis Irrigation Co., 211 Kan. 406, 413, 507 P.2d 295, 300 (1973), and would find settlement to little advantage. On the other hand, equitable considerations require that the third-party defendant have a reasonable opportunity to show that the third-party plaintiff was not liable to the original plaintiff but paid the claim as a volunteer.

In the case before us, it appears that Morrissette's tender to Sears of the defense of the original action by Przybyla was declined, and that consolidation for trial of the third-party action with the original tort suit was subsequently ordered by denial of Sears' motion for separate trial. Morrissette asserts in her brief that Sears was also afforded an opportunity to participate in the proposed settlement, but chose to leave the matter to Morrissette and therefore should be bound by her action. * * * While Sears concedes that having declined to participate in the original action it would be bound by any judgment rendered * * * it asserts that in fact it participated in the partial trial of that action, and now seeks only to preserve its right to a hearing on relevant issues, including that of the contributory negligence of the plaintiff Przybyla which was foreshortened by the compromise settlement. Whether Sears was tendered an opportunity to approve of the proposed settlement, or in the alternative to assume defense of the action, does not appear.

The solution of the "actual-versus-potential problem" advanced by the court in Parfait v. Jahncke Service, Inc., 484 F.2d 296 (5th Cir.1973) strikes us as logical, equitable, and worthy of adoption here. The court there quoted from Jennings v. United States, 374 F.2d 983, 986 (4th Cir.1967) as follows: "The indemnitee's unilateral acts, albeit reasonable and undertaken in good faith, cannot bind the indemnitor; notice and an opportunity to defend are the indispensable due process satisfying elements." The court in Parfait then continued: "If the indemnitor approves the settlement or defends unsuccessfully against the original claim, he cannot later question the indemnitee's liability to the original claimant. If the indemnitor declines to take either course, then the indemnitee will only be required to show potential liability to the original plaintiff in order to support his claim over against the indemnitor." 484 F.2d at 305. In the event that no offer is made to the indemnitor to either approve or defend, then the indemnitee should have the burden of showing actual liability to the original plaintiff.

* * *

Accordingly the answer to question 4 is that if it appears that Sears was not afforded the alternative of participating in the settlement or conducting the defense, then Morrissette will have the burden of establishing her actual liability to Przybyla rather than the lesser burden of showing potential liability. In either event, the reasonableness of the amount of the settlement must be established by Morrissette.

Question three is whether Sears "can * * * attempt to show contributory negligence on the part of [Przybyla]". It is settled that contributory negligence was a defense to the original action. * * * We consider that it is likewise a defense available to Sears in this third-party action and answer the third question, "Yes". The question whether the burden of showing Przybyla's contributory negligence should fall upon Sears or the burden of showing the absence of it should fall upon Morrissette may be more difficult. The latter's burden of proving either actual or potential liability in order to justify the settlement would encompass the burden of showing the absence or weakness of any defense of Przybyla's contributory negligence. Hence in the indemnification action before us the burden of proving contributory negligence on the part of either Przybyla, or of Morrissette personally * * * ought to rest upon Sears; and we so hold.

* * *

"5. Where the Statute of Limitations on warranty has run as against the original plaintiff, has it also expired as to the third-party plaintiff?"

Since the third-party action for indemnity was brought on May 1, 1970 it is obvious that the statute of limitations has not run against the third-party plaintiff's claim for indemnification against loss by reason of the compromise settlement of her liability made on May 22, 1972. The liability originally alleged by Przybyla and later compromised was a liability for negligent conduct in supplying a defective mower. If however Morrissette had then been subject to potential liability by reason of Sears' breach of warranty, even though not then the subject of suit, that liability could have constituted a consideration entering into the reasonableness of the settlement.

The plaintiff Morrissette suggests that since the original action was brought on May 15, 1969 and within six years of the date of injury which was June 22, 1963, it was brought within the limitation of six years imposed by RSA 508:4. It is her position that this statute rather than the four-year limitation of the Uniform Commercial Code (RSA 382–A:2–725) applied * * *.

* * *

[T]he Uniform Commercial Code provides that a cause of action for breach of warranty accrues at the time of delivery regardless of the time when the breach is discovered. RSA 382–A:2–725(2). Hence by the time Przybyla brought her negligence action in 1969, any action for breach of warranty was barred by the statute RSA 382–A:2–725(1).

It follows that since no claim based upon warranty was enforceable when the Przybyla suit was compromised, any claim for indemnification by the plaintiff Morrissette sounding in warranty, whether in her own right, or because of her settlement with Przybyla, was unenforceable * * * because under the Uniform Commercial Code any such cause of action was barred by the statute of limitations. As applied to this case, the fifth question is answered in the affirmative.

Insofar as the plaintiff Morrissette claims indemnification arising out of her liability to Przybyla in tort or in strict liability, her claim is not barred by limitation. Such a right of action cannot be barred before it comes into existence and her right to indemnity did not accrue until the settlement was made. * * * "[T]he statute of limitations cannot possibly start to run on an indemnity claim until the party seeking indemnification suffers a loss." United States v. Farr & Co., 342 F.2d 383, 387 (2d Cir.1965) * * *.

Remanded.

All concurred.

Notes

1. One court has held that a plaintiff must be a judgment debtor to recover contribution. Thus, a party who has merely settled with the injured plaintiff cannot recover contribution. *See* Beech Aircraft Corp. v. Jinkins, 739 S.W.2d 19 (Tex.1987); Bonniwell v. Beech Aircraft Corp., 663 S.W.2d 816 (Tex.1984). Should the same result hold for indemnity? Consider the different consequences of denying contribution and denying indemnity to a settling tortfeasor.

2. The procedure whereby Morrissette tendered the defense of the lawsuit to Sears is called "vouching in." Section 2–607(5) of the Uniform Commercial Code codifies this practice for cases arising under Article 2:

> Where the buyer is sued for breach of a warranty or other obligation for which his seller is answerable over
>
> (a) he may give his seller written notice of the litigation. If the notice states that the seller may come in and defend and that if the seller does not do so he will be bound in any action against him by his buyer by any determination of fact common to the two litigations, then unless the seller after seasonable receipt of the notice does come in and defend he is so bound.

Comment 7 to section 2–607 states simply that "[s]ubsection (5)(a) codifies for all warranties the practice of voucher to defend."

3. In warranty cases involving contribution and indemnity, many courts apply the same rules about active and passive tortfeasors as they apply in negligence or strict tort liability cases. *See, e.g.,* Digregorio v. Champlain Valley Fruit Co., 127 Vt. 562, 255 A.2d 183 (1969).

Chapter 15

CONSUMER CONDUCT DEFENSES AND COMPARATIVE FAULT

―――――

You should already be familiar with two defenses that are based on the plaintiff's own conduct—contributory negligence and assumption of risk-as these defenses are applicable to negligence actions and were addressed in your first—year torts course. A third defense—product misuse—is new.

The application of these defenses to products liability litigation raises two sets of issues. First, courts must determine whether a specific defense is applicable to the various theories of products liability and whether the contours of the defense are the same in the context of products liability as in the context of negligence. For example, some courts do not apply contributory negligence to strict tort liability, and even those that do often use a different version of contributory negligence in strict tort liability than they use in negligence.

Second, courts must determine the effect of the defenses that are applicable to a particular theory of recovery. Specifically, courts must determine whether the defense totally bars recovery or merely reduces the plaintiff's recovery under a comparative scheme. If a court adopts a comparative scheme, it must also determine the specific contours of the scheme, such as whether a plaintiff who is more than 50% at fault can still recover. As a general proposition, a court must determine whether its comparative scheme for product cases is the same as its comparative scheme for negligence.

SECTION A.   ASSUMPTION OF RISK

You should recall the basic defense of assumption of risk from your study of negligence. Assumption of risk has two distinct versions: express or contractual assumption of risk and implied assumption of risk. Express or contractual assumption of risk involves an actual agreement between the parties that one party rather than the other will bear the risk of injury, even if it is caused by the other party's negligence. A limit on liability—such as a shipping company limiting its liability for damage to a specific dollar amount—is a version of express assumption of risk for damages above the limit.

As long as a contractual assumption of risk is not unconscionable, it will be honored as a defense to an action for negligence. In actions for breach of warranty, express assumptions of risk are usually in the form of warranty disclaimers or limitations on damages. Disclaimers are governed by section 2–316 of the Uniform Commercial Code, and limitations on damages are governed by section 2–719. Both forms are permitted, but they are subject to important exceptions and formal requirements that are addressed in Chapter 4.

Express assumption of risk can affect a cause of action for misrepresentation under the rubric of justifiable reliance. A consumer who has expressly agreed to assume a risk might not have justifiably relied on a representation that the product would not impose the risk. Conversely, the representation and the express assumption of risk, being contrary to each other, might be interpreted in a way that negates the express assumption of risk.

Express, contractual assumption of risk as a defense to strict tort liability is more complex. As in the case of breach of warranty, a general express assumption of risk as a defense to strict tort liability, is, in effect, a disclaimer. Since a disclaimer is not valid as a defense to strict tort liability, a general express assumption of risk is likewise invalid. As we shall see in the material on implied assumption of risk that follows, however, an express assumption of risk that demonstrates the plaintiff was actually aware of a specific risk imposed by the product might be a defense in strict tort liability.

Implied assumption of risk is a more common topic of litigation than is express assumption of risk. In its basic form, implied assumption of risk involves a plaintiff who voluntarily encounters a risk that he subjectively knows and appreciates, even though the parties have not expressly allocated the risk by oral or written agreement. It is not sufficient that the plaintiff should have known about the risk; he must actually be aware of and appreciate the nature of the risk, and he must voluntarily subject himself to it. Much litigation about assumption of risk as a defense in negligence cases addresses the questions of whether the plaintiff was actually aware of the risk and whether he voluntarily encountered it.

Under the traditional form of implied assumption of risk, the defendant is not required to prove that the plaintiff acted unreasonably by subjecting himself to the risk. Several courts, especially after the advent of comparative negligence schemes, have altered the traditional rule, holding that assumption of risk is applicable only when the plaintiff voluntarily encounters a known and appreciated risk that, under the circumstances, is an unreasonable risk to encounter. This change renders the defense of assumption of risk nothing more than a specific type of contributory negligence. Thus, some courts have appropriately characterized this change as an abandonment of assumption of risk as an independent defense in negligence actions. Regardless of the nomenclature, jurisdictions that use comparative negligence schemes typically include assumption of risk along with contributory negligence in a single percentage finding by the jury. Even in these jurisdictions, however, an express, contractual assumption of risk continues to be an absolute bar, according to its terms.

Courts often use the nomenclature "*volenti non fit injuria*" to refer to the defense of assumption of risk. Some courts distinguish in their nomenclature between parties who have a contractual relationship (such as an employment relationship) and parties who are strangers, using the term "assumption of risk" in the former situation and "*volenti non fit injuria*" in the latter. Even if different nomenclature is used, however, the contours of the defense remain the same.

The effect of implied assumption of risk is somewhat unclear in actions for breach of warranty. Some courts have held that implied assumption of risk is a separate defense, just as it is in a negligence action. *See, e.g.,* Phillips v. Allen, 427 F.Supp. 876 (W.D.Pa.1977); Pritchard v. Liggett & Myers Tobacco Co., 350 F.2d 479 (3d Cir.1965); Duncan v. Cessna Aircraft Co., 665 S.W.2d 414 (Tex.1984). But the Uniform Commercial Code does not itself establish such a defense.

Language in the Uniform Commercial Code and its comments suggests that a plaintiff's actual knowledge of a risk might negate the warranty itself or affect a determination of whether breach of the warranty was a proximate cause of the plaintiff's injuries. Comment 13 to section 2–314 (which deals with implied warranties of merchantability) provides that "[a]ction by the buyer following an examination of the goods which ought to have indicated the defect complained of can be shown as a matter bearing on whether the breach itself was the cause of the injury." Presumably, action after an inspection that actually reveals a defect will have the same effect.

Comment 8 to section 2–316 (which deals with disclaimers) states that "if the buyer discovers the defect and uses the goods anyway, * * * the resulting injuries may be found to result from his own action rather than proximately from a breach of warranty."

Several courts have used the rubric of proximate causation suggested by the comments to the Code rather than hold that implied assumption of risk is an independent defense. *See, e.g.,* Hensley v. Sherman Car Wash Equipment Co., 33 Colo.App. 279, 520 P.2d 146 (1974). In jurisdictions that have adopted comparative schemes for breach of warranty cases, the difference in approach might determine whether conduct that amounts to an assumption of risk is an absolute bar to recovery or merely a percentage reduction. The difference in approach might also affect a decision whether an assumption of risk by one person affects recovery by another person who is injured. If such conduct affects the scope of the warranty or proximate causation, it is difficult to limit the effect of the conduct to the person who engaged in it, or to use it merely to reduce the plaintiff's recovery under a comparative scheme.

In actions for misrepresentation, conduct that would constitute assumption of risk undermines the plaintiff's claim that he justifiably relied on the representation. *See, e.g.,* Klages v. General Ordnance Equipment Corp., 240 Pa.Super. 356, 367 A.2d 304 (1976). *Cf.* Kolb v. Texas Employers' Ins. Ass'n, 585 S.W.2d 870, 872–73 (Tex.Civ.App.— Texarkana 1979, writ refused n.r.e.).

Comment n to section 402A clearly states that implied voluntary assumption of risk is a defense to an action for strict tort liability. From the beginning of strict tort liability, courts have uniformly recognized implied assumption of risk as a defense to strict tort liability, either as an absolute bar or as a percentage reduction under a comparative scheme. The main issues have been whether the details of the defense are the same for strict tort liability as for negligence—for example, whether the defense applies only to unreasonable risks—and whether special issues arise in the context of products liability litigation concerning the plaintiff's actual awareness of the risk.

HEIL CO. v. GRANT
Court of Civil Appeals of Texas, 1976.
534 S.W.2d 916.

DUNAGAN, CHIEF JUSTICE.

This is a products liability case which involves the doctrines of assumption of risk and misuse. * * * Valmarie Grant and her children sued for the death of James Grant (hereinafter referred to as Decedent), their husband and father respectively. The defendant-appellant is the Heil Company, a major manufacturer of hydraulic hoists.

* * *

Decedent and Vernon [Grant] were working beneath the raised bed [of a dump truck] when it somehow descended. Vernon jumped away but Decedent did not. Heil Company's engineer found no malfunction in the hoist mechanism and concluded that the pullout cable had been tripped. Immediately before the accident, Vernon told Decedent that if he hit the pullout cable, the bed would come down.

* * *

Plaintiffs sued the Heil Company under a theory of strict liability for defective design of the hoist mechanism and for failure to warn of the hazard.

* * *

The Heil Company pleaded, offered evidence of and requested Special Issues on the defenses of assumption of risk and misuse. The trial court, applying the Dead Man's Statute, excluded that portion of Vernon Grant's testimony which related to those defenses and refused to submit Special Issues thereon since there was no other evidence to support such issues. Heil Company's primary contention before this court is that the exclusion of Vernon Grant's testimony was harmful error because that testimony was admissible and established or raised fact issues of those defenses. ·

* * *

Plaintiffs contend that Vernon Grant's warning to Decedent ("I stated * * * that if he hit the cable, the bed would come down") did not constitute evidence that Decedent "knew" of the risk. Plaintiffs argue that Decedent might not have heard, understood or remembered the warning and that Vernon Grant's testimony was merely evidence that Decedent *could* have known of the risk.

An injured person's knowledge of a dangerous condition or defect is measured subjectively; i.e., by that person's actual, conscious knowledge. *Massman–Johnson v. Gundolf,* 484 S.W.2d 555, 557 (Tex.1972). The fact that the injured person *should have known* of the danger will not support the assumption of risk defense. *Halepeska v. Callihan Interests, Inc.,* [371 S.W.2d 368 (Tex.1963)]. Sometimes, however, that person may know such facts as to be charged with knowledge of the danger. *Halepeska v. Callihan Interests, Inc.,* supra. This standard would be applied when it was difficult or impossible to determine the state of the injured person's mind; as it was in the instant case of a fatal injury. The "actual knowledge or charged knowledge" test has been applied in determining the strict liability of a supplier of defective products. See *Rourke v. Garza,* 530 S.W.2d 794 (Tex.1975).

* * *

Whether an injured person actually knew of the danger is peculiarly within the province of the jury. *Hillman–Kelley v. Pittman,* 489 S.W.2d 689, 692 (Tex.Civ.App.—El Paso 1972, n.w.h.). Here, there was some evidence from which the jury could have found that Decedent "knew" of the danger, to-wit: the fact that he had been told of the effect of hitting the pullout cable. Although the jury could also have found that Decedent did not know of the danger because he did not hear, understand or remember the warning, we are not able to say, as a matter of law, that he did not know of that danger.

Plaintiffs argue that even if Decedent had knowledge of some danger, there is no evidence that he knew of the specific defect involved. Knowledge of the general hazard involved in operating a punch-press machine will not support the assumption of risk defense. *Rhoads v. Service Machine Co.,* 329 F.Supp. 367 (E.D.Ark.1971). The general hazard in the instant case was working beneath the raised bed of the dump truck. Vernon Grant and Heil Company's engineer both concluded that the bed descended because the pullout cable was tripped. This evidence indicates that the specific danger was that striking the pullout cable would cause the bed to descend. The jury, upon consideration of Vernon Grant's testimony, could have found that Decedent knew of this specific hazard. Plaintiffs also contend that the requisite knowledge must be of a "defect" and that "knowledge that a phenomenon will occur in a product * * * is not knowledge that the product is dangerously defective." [Henderson v. Ford Motor Co., 519 S.W.2d 87, 89 (Tex. 1974)] * * * It is clear, however, that the assumption of risk defense is premised upon knowledge of the dangerous condition of a product rather than recognition of its defectiveness.

* * *

Plaintiffs argue that even if Decedent knew of the danger of the pullout cable, there is no evidence that he knew of the other dangerous defects, to-wit: the defectively designed control valve; the failure to supply a support brace; and the failure to instruct as to proper bracing procedures. These defects may well have been producing or proximate causes of the death in that (1) but for the defects, the death might not have occurred, and (2) the death was a foreseeable result of the defects. * * * In our opinion, however, all of the above producing causes were part of the same danger. The assumption of risk defense is based upon the injured person's awareness of the danger of injury rather than an awareness of the producing causes of the injury. Since there was some evidence that Decedent knew of the specific danger in hitting the pullout cable, plaintiffs' argument is without merit.

The danger encountered must be both known and appreciated to raise the assumption of risk defense. * * * Again, the test is subjective. * * * We look for some evidence that Decedent actually appreciated the risk or was in possession of facts from which he would be legally charged with appreciation of the danger. *Halepeska v. Callihan Interests, Inc.,* supra, 371 S.W.2d at 379. If by reason of age, or lack of information, experience, intelligence or judgment, Decedent did not understand the risk involved, he will not be taken to have assumed that risk. Restatement (Second) of Torts, Section 496D, comment c.

* * *

There is some evidence that Decedent might not have appreciated the danger of hitting the pullout cable. However, by reason of Decedent's information, age and experience, we conclude that there was some evidence of probative force that he did appreciate that danger. Thus, an issue for the jury exists.

Plaintiffs' final point in support of their contention of no evidence of the necessary elements of the assumption of risk defense is that Decedent's encounter of the risk was not shown to have been voluntary. A voluntary encounter means by free and intelligent choice. * * * We have thoroughly considered each of these arguments and find them to be without merit. We conclude that there was some evidence that would support a jury finding that Decedent's encounter with the risk was by free and intelligent choice.

Plaintiffs' second contention under * * * Point I is that any error in excluding the testimony of Vernon Grant which related to assumption of risk was harmless because that defense is inapplicable when strict liability is based upon a failure to warn of a dangerous condition.

Plaintiffs rely upon statements to the effect that when there is a breach of the duty to warn, there is no assumption of the risk. * * * These statements were made in situations in which no warning had been given to the injured person. The function of the warning is to give that person knowledge and an opportunity to appreciate the danger. * * * The supplier of a defective product is usually in the best position to supply this warning but there is no reason why the warning cannot come from another source. "One who voluntarily chooses to use a chattel with a complete realization, *regardless of how it was acquired,* of the risks to which he thus exposes himself voluntarily assumes such risks * * * " 1 Hursh & Bailey, *American Law of Products Liability 2d,* sec. 2:107 (Emphasis added.)

* * *

Plaintiffs' final argument * * * is that any error in excluding evidence of assumption of risk was harmless because that defense is inapplicable when strict liability is based upon the defective design of a product being used in a manner reasonably foreseeable to the supplier. Plaintiffs argue that the supplier is in the best position to discover a design defect and should not be permitted to avoid liability on the ground that the injured person made a foolish judgment to encounter the danger. The thrust of this argument is that assumption of risk *should* not be applicable in any case when strict liability is based upon the defective design of a product. The defense of assumption of risk was held available in such a case in *Rourke v. Garza,* supra, 530 S.W.2d 794. Plaintiffs' contention is overruled.

Notes

1. Do the policies underlying strict tort liability support or undermine the application of assumption of risk to strict tort liability? In this regard, does assumption of risk differ from contributory negligence?

2. Note that without Vernon Grant's testimony, assumption of risk was not an issue for the jury, which meant that the plaintiff could recover. Implicit in this aspect of the case is that the defendant has the burden of proof on assumption of risk.

SECTION B. PRODUCT MISUSE

PERFECTION PAINT & COLOR CO. v. KONDURIS
Indiana Court of Appeals, 1970.
147 Ind.App. 106, 258 N.E.2d 681.

PFAFF, JUDGE.

The plaintiff-appellee, Kosmos Alexander Konduris, instituted this action on behalf of his deceased father, Kosmos Kountouris, who died from burns inflicted in a fire in the plant of his employer, Alrimo Pizza, Inc. (Alrimo). The defendant-appellant, Perfection Paint & Color Company (Perfection), furnished Alrimo with a lacquer reducer for the purpose of removing a paint film on Alrimo's storage room floor. The lacquer reducer proved to be highly flammable and when applied to the storage room floor was ignited by an operative gas hot water heater in one corner of the storage room. This fire resulted in the death of Kosmos Kountouris.

* * *

[The plaintiff sued Perfection for strict tort liability, and Perfection claimed as a defense that the lacquer reducer had been misused.]

On the question of misuse of the lacquer reducer, the appellant contends that by virtue of the repeated oral warnings against smoking, "scuffling around", and the necessity for adequate ventilation given immediately prior to the time the lacquer reducer was applied to the storage room floor and, further, by virtue of the written warnings on the container of the lacquer reducer's high flammability, dangerous propensities, and the prohibition against using the lacquer reducer near an open flame, the use of the lacquer reducer in a room which contained an operative gas hot water heater (the storage room), constituted a misuse of appellant's product and a defense to strict liability in tort.

Misuse of a defective product is a defense to strict liability in tort. * * * Judge Sharp of this court correctly stated that the defense of misuse is available when the product is used "for a purpose not reasonably foreseeable to the manufacturer" or when the product is used "in a manner not reasonably foreseeable for a reasonably foreseeable purpose". Cornette v. Searjeant Metal Products, [147 Ind.App. 46, 258 N.E.2d 652 (1970)] (concurring opinion). * * * A consumer who incurs or assumes the risk of injury by virtue of his continuing use of a product after having discovered a defect or who uses a product in contravention of a legally sufficient warning, misuses the product and, in the context of the defenses of incurred or assumed risk, is subject to the defense of misuse.

* * *

A legal description of those acts which constitute a "misuse" of a product has proven to be difficult to achieve. The problem appears to us to be one of failing to differentiate between misuse of a product which does not exhibit any defective condition until misused, or which does not appear to be defective and unreasonably dangerous, and misuse of a product when the defective and unreasonably dangerous condition is either discovered by the consumer or brought to his attention by a legally sufficient warning. While in either situation a product is being misused, the former constitutes the true category of misuse while the latter form of misuse is tantamount to the traditional concepts of incurred or assumed risk. The former, which Judge Sharp in *Cornette,* *supra,* previously categorized as use of a product for a purpose not reasonably foreseeable to the manufacturer "or in using the product in a manner not reasonably foreseeable for a reasonably foreseeable purpose", will apply in a situation in which a product is used for a purpose which is unforeseeable with that for which it was manufactured, or when used for a foreseeable purpose, is subjected to an unforeseeable or overly harsh use. We again refer to Greeno v. Clark Equipment Company, [237 F.Supp. 427, 429 (N.D.Ind.1965)], wherein it is stated:

> "Neither would contributory negligence constitute a defense, although use different from or more strenuous than that contemplated to be safe by ordinary users/consumers, that is, 'misuse,' would either refute a defective condition or causation."

The latter form of misuse, that which is analogous to the defenses of incurred or assumed risk, occurs when a product, being used in the manner intended by the manufacturer and for the purpose intended by the manufacturer, proves to be defective and the defect is discovered, or when a defective and unreasonably dangerous product, acknowledged to be such by a manufacturer's warnings or instructions on proper use, is used in contravention of the instructions or warnings.

Appellant's lacquer reducer is admittedly a defective and unreasonably dangerous product. Because the lacquer reducer is "more dangerous than would be contemplated by the ordinary consumer/user with the ordinary knowledge of the community as to its characteristics and uses", Greeno v. Clark Equipment Company, *supra,* appellant owed a duty to consumers to warn of the product's unreasonably dangerous propensities, and did so warn of the product's defective condition on the container. Using the product, however, on a concrete floor in order to remove a paint film was not a use of the product inconsistent with the use for which the lacquer reducer was manufactured. It is undisputed that subsequent to the drying problems encountered in the application of appellant's epoxy paint on the concrete floors, appellant, after declaring that it would remedy the drying problem, provided paint remover, lacquer reducer, instructions, and on the scene supervision of the paint removing operation. Not only was the use of appellant's lacquer reducer a foreseeable use of the product, appellant furnished and expressly directed the use of its product in order to remove the paint film from the storage room floor. The use of the lacquer reducer for this purpose was unquestionably done for a reasonably foreseeable purpose inasmuch as the record establishes that the manufacturer provided the product for the express purpose of removing the paint film, gave directions as to its use, supervised the operation and, additionally, the manufacturer, by its representative, applied the product to the storage room floor immediately prior to the fire.

The question of misuse in this case is not, therefore, one of using a product for an unforeseeable purpose or overly harsh or unforeseeable user for a foreseeable purpose; rather, the question is whether or not the defective and unreasonably dangerous lacquer reducer was used in contravention of warnings and instructions on the correct use of said product.

* * *

The jury must make the determination of whether or not a defective product was misused. In this case there is evidence from which the jury could have determined that either the appellant's representative, Mr. Francis, or Alrimo misused the product. * * * The defense of misuse will defeat strict liability in tort when a jury determines that the consumer misused the product. If the evidence is conflicting on this point, as it is in this instance, we are not at liberty to invade the province of the jury on this question, and its determination that the lacquer reducer was not misused must stand.

For the foregoing reasons, the trial court was correct in refusing to direct a verdict in favor of the defendant-appellant and in overruling its motion for a new trial.

Judgment affirmed. Costs are to be taxed against the appellant.

HOFFMAN, P.J., and SHARP and WHITE, JJ., concur.

Notes

1. Comment g to section 402A provides:

* * * The rule stated in this Section applies only where the product is, at the time it leaves the seller's hands, in a condition not contemplated by the ultimate consumer, which will be unreasonably dangerous to him. The seller is not liable when he delivers the product in a safe condition, and subsequent mishandling or other causes make it harmful by the time it is consumed. The burden of proof that the product was in a defective condition at the time that it left the hands of the particular seller is upon the injured plaintiff; and unless evidence can be produced which will support the conclusion that it was then defective, the burden is not sustained.

Safe condition at the time of delivery by the seller will, however, include proper packaging, necessary sterilization, and other precautions required to permit the product to remain safe for a normal length of time when handled in a normal manner.

2. Comment h to section 402A provides:

A product is not in a defective condition when it is safe for normal handling and consumption. If the injury results from abnormal handling, as where a bottled beverage is knocked against a radiator to remove the cap, or from abnormal preparation for use, as where too much salt is added to food, or from abnormal consumption, as where a child eats too much candy and is made ill, the seller is not liable. Where, however, he has reason to anticipate that danger may result from a particular use, as where a drug is sold which is safe only in limited doses, he may be required to give adequate warning of the danger (see Comment j), and a product sold without such warning is in a defective condition.

The defective condition may arise not only from harmful ingredients, not characteristic of the product itself either as to presence or quantity, but also from foreign objects contained in the product, from decay or deterioration before sale, or from the way in which the product is prepared or packed. No reason is apparent for distinguishing between the product itself and the container in which it is supplied; and the two are purchased by the user or consumer as an integrated whole. Where the container is itself dangerous, the product is sold in a defective condition. Thus a carbonated beverage in a bottle which is so weak, or cracked, or jagged at the edges, or bottled under such excessive pressure that it may explode or otherwise cause harm to the person who handles it, is in a defective and dangerous condition. The container cannot logically be separated from the contents when the two are sold as a unit, and the liability stated in this Section arises not only when the consumer drinks the beverage and is poisoned by it, but also when he is injured by the bottle while he is handling it preparatory to consumption.

3. Courts have had a difficult time determining precisely how to account in strict tort liability for an unforeseeable product use. Comment h addresses misuse in terms of product defectiveness. The language in *Konduris* suggests that unforeseeable use is a defense, similar to contributory negligence and assumption of risk. Unforeseeability of a product's use might also be considered under the rubric of proximate causation.

The difference in these approaches can have a substantial effect on a case. One effect is that, if a plaintiff's unforeseeable use of a product negates a claim of defectiveness or proximate causation, the plaintiff would presumably be barred from any recovery. If, on the other hand, unforeseeable misuse is treated as a defense, a court that otherwise uses a comparative scheme might merely reduce the plaintiff's recovery.

A second effect is that the rubric a court uses might affect the burden of proof. The plaintiff has the burden of proof on defectiveness and causation. *See, e.g.,* Rogers v. Toro Mfg. Co., 522 S.W.2d 632 (Mo.App.1975) (plaintiff has burden to prove proper use). The defendant has the burden on "defenses."

A third effect is that, as a defense similar to contributory negligence or assumption of risk, unforeseeable misuse might bar or reduce the plaintiff's recovery only if the plaintiff was the one who misused the product. If the unusual use negates defectiveness or proximate causation, it would presumably affect recovery by third persons as well.

Consider a plaintiff who is injured by a windshield that shatters when he drives a car through a closed gate to escape attackers. Should the plaintiff's unusual use of the car affect the plaintiff's recovery as a (possibly comparative) defense, as a matter of proximate causation, or as a matter of the car's defectiveness? Should the defendant be permitted to use this aspect of the case in all three ways? Should it have no affect on the plaintiff's recovery?

4. In Colvin v. Red Steel Co., 682 S.W.2d 243 (Tex.1984), the plaintiff was injured when he lost his balance and fell at a construction site. As he was falling, he grabbed a loose I-beam to stabilize himself. The I-beam was shorter than prescribed by the specifications. Consequently, it was lighter than it should have been, and it failed to support him.

The court held that the I-beam was not defective. Since it was shorter than prescribed by the specifications, however, it might be argued that it was "flawed." Should the court have held that the product was misused? Should it have held that the flaw, if any, was not a proximate cause of the injury? What difference does the choice make to this case or other cases involving these I-beams? What if the building collapsed because the I-beams were too short?

A similar problem arose in Fitzgerald Marine Sales v. LeUnes, 659 S.W.2d 917 (Tex.App.—Fort Worth 1983, writ dismissed). The plaintiff claimed that the steering wheel of a power boat he was driving broke due to voids in the plastic, causing him to be thrown from the boat. The court held that the purpose of the steering wheel was to steer the boat, not to restrain the driver, and that the plaintiff therefore could not recover under strict tort liability. The court did not make clear whether the product was not defective, the defect did not proximately cause the injury, or the plaintiff misused the steering wheel.

Given the test of misuse announced in *Konduris,* did the plaintiff's conduct in *LeUnes* constitute a misuse? If voids existed in the plastic as alleged, wasn't the product flawed? Suppose the plaintiff cut himself because the steering wheel broke as he was making a sharp turn? Should the problem be treated as an issue of legal or proximate causation?

5. If a product's only risks are manifested when it is used in an unusual manner, it might not be defective at all. Unusual injuries that are caused by a product that is defective because it also imposes risks in non-unusual situations could be analyzed as an issue of proximate or legal causation. If so, is there any reason to have an independent "defense" of misuse?

6. For further discussion of the relationship between misuse and defectiveness, see Jurado v. Western Gear Works, p. 270 *supra,* and Dosier v. Wilcox & Crittendon Co., p. 277 *supra,* and the ensuing notes. For a discussion of the relationship between misuse and proximate or legal causation see Chapter 12.

7. As the opinion in *Konduris* indicates, part of the confusion about misuse as a defense stems from the fact that misuse is sometimes used to refer to an unforeseeable use and sometimes used to refer to a plaintiff's use of a product after discovering the defect. The latter type of "misuse" is clearly a true defense, although it is properly labeled assumption of risk. In jurisdictions that use a comparative scheme for consumer conduct defenses, the assumption of risk version of misuse reduces the plaintiff's recovery according to the percentage allocated by the jury. Should an unforeseeable use cause a percentage reduction, or should it be an absolute bar?

8. As the opinion in *Konduris* indicates, the test for the unforeseeable use version of misuse is not whether the plaintiff used the product for the purpose intended by the manufacturer. Rather, it is whether the plaintiff's use was unforeseeable. Thus, using a screwdriver to open a can of paint is not a misuse.

9. In General Motors Corp. v. Hopkins, 548 S.W.2d 344 (Tex.1977), the court held that misuse *by the plaintiff* is a defense that reduces the plaintiff's recovery by the percentage "causation" assigned to the plaintiff by the jury if the misuse was a proximate cause of the plaintiff's injury. In addition to

applying comparative principles to misuse, *Hopkins* presents an interesting application of the misuse defense itself.

The plaintiff was injured when the carburetor on his car stuck in the open position, causing the car to go out of control. Prior to the accident, the plaintiff noticed a problem with the carburetor and replaced it with one of his own. Later, he reinstalled the original carburetor, which caused the accident. The court stated that plaintiff's conduct constituted a misuse, and that the "misuse may bear upon the issue of whether the product was defective when it left the hands of the supplier or the misuse may bear on the issue of what caused the harm."

It is unclear whether the court in *Hopkins* really thought it is unforeseeable that car owners will occasionally repair or replace the carburetor. It is also unclear whether the court thought the facts that the plaintiff noticed a problem with the carburetor, replaced it, and then reinstalled it constituted a voluntary assumption of a known and appreciated risk. Maybe the court suspected that the plaintiff botched the job. If so, maybe the carburetor was not defective at all when it left the manufacturer, but in that case, the plaintiff should have lost, not merely had his recovery reduced. Is it possible that the court was using misuse to cover conduct that was actually contributory negligence, which at the time *Hopkins* was decided was not nominally a defense to strict tort liability in Texas?

Fudging misuse to cover conduct that is actually contributory negligence is more palatable when it only reduces the plaintiff's recovery rather than bars it. As we shall see in the next section, the advent of comparative schemes in strict tort liability caused many courts explicitly to recognize some forms of contributory negligence as a defense in strict tort liability.

As *Hopkins* and *Konduris* indicate, the defense of misuse has been used to cover a variety of issues. When you encounter a case involving misuse, you should be careful to ascertain precisely how the court is using the defense.

10. Unforeseeable misuse is also a "defense" to an action for breach of warranty. *See* Singer v. Walker, 39 A.D.2d 90, 331 N.Y.S.2d 823 (1972). Again, the test is whether the manufacturer should have foreseen the use, not whether the manufacturer intended the product to be used in the manner that the plaintiff used it. Many courts analyze misuse as an issue of the scope of the warranty or an issue of proximate causation. *See, e.g.,* Hardman v. Helene Curtis Ind., Inc., 48 Ill.App.2d 42, 198 N.E.2d 681 (1964); Chisholm v. J.R. Simplot Co., 94 Idaho 628, 495 P.2d 1113 (1972). Moreover, an implied warranty of merchantability under section 2–314 applies only to products that are used for their ordinary purposes.

11. Conduct that would constitute unforeseeable product misuse would probably defeat recovery in an action for negligence under the rubric of proximate causation. *See* Restatement (Second) of Torts § 395, comments j and k.

12. Do the policies underlying strict tort liability support unforeseeable misuse as a defense to strict tort liability? Do they suggest that unforeseeable misuse should be a percentage reduction or an absolute bar?

SECTION C. CONTRIBUTORY NEGLIGENCE AND COMPARATIVE FAULT

You should recall from your first-year torts course that contributory negligence consists of a plaintiff failing to exercise reasonable care for his or her own safety. In a normal negligence case, the defense of contributory negligence can involve all of the intricate issues associated with proving the defendant's own negligence. Thus, for the plaintiff's contributory negligence to affect the plaintiff's recovery—either as a total bar or as a percentage reduction—the defendant must establish (1) that the plaintiff had a duty to use reasonable care, (2) that the plaintiff breached this duty by failing to use reasonable care, and (3) that the plaintiff's failure to use reasonable care proximately caused all or some of the plaintiff's injuries.

The basic test of contributory negligence is whether the plaintiff created a foreseeable, unreasonable risk to his own safety. Whether or not the plaintiff was a child, had a physical handicap, faced an emergency not of his own making, violated a statute, and so on, are factors that affect a determination of the plaintiff's contributory negligence in much the same way that they would affect a determination of the defendant's negligence. These issues will not be rehearsed in this chapter; the principal concern here is whether and how contributory negligence affects products liability litigation.

In a product case based on negligence, the plaintiff's contributory negligence has the same effect as it does in an ordinary action for negligence. The basic contours of the defense are not affected merely because a product was the cause of a plaintiff's injuries. Nevertheless, some issues that arise in product cases and nonproduct cases alike can be especially acute in products cases.

Even in nonproduct cases, several courts have held that a plaintiff's contributory negligence does not affect his recovery when the defendant's own negligence consisted of violating a statute that was itself designed to protect people like the plaintiff from their own carelessness. *See, e.g.,* Zerby v. Warren, 297 Minn. 134, 210 N.W.2d 58 (1973) (defendant sold glue to minor in violation of statute). Similarly, it is not unusual in a product case for a manufacturer's own negligence to be its failure to design a product that guards against the consumer's occasional carelessness. Permitting the defendant to benefit from the plaintiff's contributory negligence in such a case would frustrate the very purpose of finding the manufacturer negligent in the first place, and some courts have declined to do so. For example, in Bexiga v. Havir Mfg. Corp., 60 N.J. 402, 290 A.2d 281 (1972), the manufacturer of a punch press was negligent for not installing a safety device that would have prevented a user from putting his hand under the press. The court noted that the plaintiff's own contributory negligence in placing his hand under the press was the very danger a safety device would have prevented. Consequently, the court held that this particular version of contributory negligence did not affect the plaintiff's recovery.

The applicability of contributory negligence as a defense in breach of warranty cases is more complex. Article 2 of the Uniform Commercial Code does not expressly cover contributory negligence, but some of its provisions and official comments tangentially address the plaintiff's conduct in the guise of proximate causation. Comment 13 to section 2–314 (which deals with an implied warranty of merchantability) provides that "[a]ction by the buyer following an examination of the goods which ought to have indicated the defect complained of can be shown as a matter bearing on whether the breach itself was the cause of the injury."

Section 2–316(3)(b), which deals with disclaimers, provides that when a buyer has inspected goods or refuses to inspect them, no implied warranty exists with regard to defects that the inspection should have revealed. Comment 8 to section 2–316 elaborates: "[I]f the buyer discovers the defect and uses the goods anyway, or if he unreasonably fails to examine the goods before he uses them, resulting injuries may be found to result from his own action rather than proximately from the breach of warranty."

Section 2–715(2)(b) provides that the plaintiff can recover consequential damages for breach of warranty including "injury to person or property proximately resulting from any breach of warranty." Comment 5 to section 2–715 provides that

> [w]here the injury involved follows the use of goods without discovery of the defect causing the damage, the question of "proximate" cause turns on whether it was reasonable for the buyer to use the goods without such inspection as would have revealed the defects. If it was not reasonable for him to do so, or if he did in fact discover the defect prior to his use, the injury would not proximately result from the breach of warranty.

Often without referring to these code provisions, several courts have held that contributory negligence constitutes a defense in an action for breach of warranty. For example, in Signal Oil and Gas Co. v. Universal Oil and Gas Products, 572 S.W.2d 320 (Tex.1978), the court held that a plaintiff's contributory negligence constitutes a comparative defense (and consequently reduces rather than bars the plaintiff's recovery) in an action for breach of an implied warranty of merchantability. In Erdman v. Johnson Bros. Radio & Television Co., 260 Md. 190, 271 A.2d 744 (1970), the court held that the plaintiff's contributory negligence is a complete bar to recovery for breach of an implied warranty of merchantability. The plaintiff in *Erdman* apparently was actually aware of the defect, so the court may have been applying a more limited defense of assumption of risk. *See also,* Duncan v. Cessna Aircraft Co., 665 S.W.2d 414 (Tex.1984) (holding that certain forms of contributory negligence constitute a comparative defense in product cases for all theories not based on negligence). Other courts, however, have held that contributory negligence is not a defense to an action of breach of warranty (at least if the plaintiff was not actually aware of the defect). Many of these cases dealt with express warranties. *See, e.g.,* Holt v. Stihl, Inc., 449 F.Supp. 693 (E.D.Tenn.1977) (applying Tennessee law); Hensley v. Sherman Car Wash Equip. Co., 33 Colo.App. 279, 520 P.2d 146 (1974); Shields v. Morton Chemical Co., 95 Idaho 674, 518 P.2d 857 (1974).

In an action for fraud or for innocent misrepresentation under section 402B of the Restatement (Second) of Torts, the plaintiff's conduct may affect his or her recovery under the rationale that the plaintiff's reliance on the representation was not "justifiable." The plaintiff has no duty to investigate facts that are the subject of the misrepresentation, so a mere failure to inspect goods is unlikely to affect recovery. If the plaintiff does inspect the goods and fails to discover a defect, however, reliance on the representation might not be justifiable. But at least for an action for fraud, section 545A of the Restatement (Second) of Torts provides that the plaintiff's contributory negligence as such is not a defense.

For an action for negligent misrepresentation, section 552A of the Restatement (Second) of Torts provides that the plaintiff's contributory negligence in relying on the representation is a defense. Comment a to section 552A provides that in determining whether the plaintiff was negligent, "the plaintiff is held to the standard of care, knowledge, intelligence and judgment of a reasonable man, even though he does not possess the qualities necessary to enable him to conform to that standard." This standard differs from justifiable reliance in cases involving fraud, where a plaintiff with idiosyncratic mental characteristics might justifiably rely on a representation, even though a reasonable person would not do so.

Few courts have addressed the effect of other forms of contributory negligence, such as negligence in using the product, on an action for misrepresentation. One court has held that in product cases contributory negligence constitutes a comparative defense that reduces the plaintiff's recovery in all theories of recovery other than negligence. (Contributory negligence in its full version operates as a defense in products cases based solely on negligence). Duncan v. Cessna Aircraft Co., 665 S.W.2d 414 (Tex.1984). Presumably, this holding applies to misrepresentation.

The most common issue involving contributory negligence in the context of product liability litigation has been whether contributory negligence is a defense in an action based on strict tort liability.

RESTATEMENT (SECOND) OF TORTS

§ 402A, comment n. *Contributory negligence.* Since the liability with which this Section deals is not based upon negligence of the seller, but is strict liability, the rule applied to strict liability cases (see § 524) applies. Contributory negligence of the plaintiff is not a defense when such negligence consists merely in a failure to discover the defect in the product, or to guard against the possibility of its existence. On the other hand the form of contributory negligence which consists in voluntarily and unreasonably proceeding to encounter a known danger, and commonly passes under the name of assumption of risk, is a defense under this Section as in other cases of strict liability. If the user or consumer discovers the defect and is aware of the danger, and nevertheless proceeds unreasonably to make use of the product and is injured by it, he is barred from recovery.

McCOWN v. INTERNATIONAL HARVESTER CO.

Supreme Court of Pennsylvania, 1975.
463 Pa. 13, 342 A.2d 381.

JONES, CHIEF JUSTICE.

Appellant, manufacturer of large over-the-road tractors, was held liable under Section 402A of Restatement (Second) of Torts (1965) for the injuries sustained by the appellee in a one-vehicle accident. The Superior Court affirmed and we granted allocatur limited to the issue of the availability of contributory negligence as a defense to a 402A action.

Appellee was injured while driving a tractor manufactured by appellant. The design of the steering mechanism of the tractor made the vehicle unusually difficult to maneuver. Specifically, twelve to fifteen percent more mechanical effort than that normally expended had to be applied to the steering wheel to accomplish any given turn. Appellee, after driving the vehicle for several hours, stopped for an equipment check on the blacktopped shoulder of the Pennsylvania Turnpike. After completing the inspection the appellee proceeded to reenter the Turnpike.

Unrelated to any steering difficulty appellee struck a guardrail adjoining the shoulder with the right front tire of the tractor. This collision caused the steering wheel to spin rapidly in the direction opposite to the turn. The spokes of the spinning steering wheel struck appellee's right arm, fracturing his wrist and forearm. Evidence adduced at trial indicated that the force and speed of the steering wheel's counterrotation were directly related to the design of the steering mechanism.

For the purposes of this appeal appellant concedes the defect in the steering system's design, but argues that appellee's contributory negligence in colliding with the guardrail should at least be considered in determining appellee's recovery. We disagree and affirm.

In *Webb v. Zern*, 422 Pa. 424, 220 A.2d 853 (1966), this Court adopted Section 402A of the Restatement and in *Ferraro v. Ford Motor Co.*, 423 Pa. 324, 223 A.2d 746 (1966), permitted the assertion of assumption of the risk as a defense to a 402A action, citing with approval comment *n* to Section 402A. Today, we complete our acceptance of the principles delineated in comment *n* by rejecting contributory negligence as an available defense in 402A cases.

Appellant's position that contributory negligence should affect 402A liability could have two possible applications. Either contributory negligence should serve to diminish any recovery in an amount adjudged equal to a plaintiff's lack of care or, as in most other tort actions, contributory negligence should be available as a complete defense to liability.

Acceptance of the appellant's first alternative would create a system of comparative assessment of damages for 402A actions. Neither the General Assembly by statute nor this Court by case law has established such a scheme of comparative negligence in other areas of tort law. Without considering the relative merits of comparative negligence, we think it unwise to embrace the theory in the context of an appeal involving Section 402A.

Adoption of contributory negligence as a complete defense in 402A actions would defeat one theoretical basis for our acceptance of Section 402A. "Our courts have determined that a manufacturer by marketing and advertising his products impliedly represents that it is safe for its intended use." *Salvador v. Atlantic Steel Boiler Co.*, 457 Pa. 24, 32, 319 A.2d 903, 907 (1974). Based on that implied representation is the consumer's assumption that a manufacturer's goods are safe. Recognition of consumer negligence as a defense to a 402A action would contradict this normal expectation of product safety. One does not inspect a product for defects or guard against the possibility of product defects when one assumes the item to be safe. The law should not require such inspection or caution when it has accepted as reasonable the consumer's anticipation of safety. We reject contributory negligence as a defense to actions grounded in Section 402A.

Judgment affirmed.

MR. JUSTICE ROBERTS did not participate in the consideration or decision of this case.

MR. JUSTICE POMEROY filed a concurring opinion.

POMEROY, JUSTICE (concurring).

* * *

Contrary to what the opinion of the Court seems to suggest, the answer to the question presented by this appeal is not to be found altogether in the language of Comment [n] to Section 402A. Comment *n* provides, on the one hand, that the negligent failure to discover a defect in a product or to guard against the possibility of its existence is not defense to a strict liability action, and, on the other hand, that assumption of risk is a defense. But the conduct of John McCown, the appellee, fits into neither of the above categories. His negligence, if any, was the manner of his operation of an International Harvester tractor. Although Comment *n* is silent with regard to the consequences of negligent use of a product, it points to a resolution of the issue by referring to Section 524 of the Restatement (Second) of Torts. That section provides that in general "the contributory negligence of the plaintiff is not a defense to the strict liability of one who carries on an abnormally dangerous activity." Neither the Comments to Section 524 nor Comment *n* to Section 402A offer a rationale for the application of this rule in products liability cases, but I am satisfied that the elimination of the defense of plaintiff's negligence is in accord not only with the weight of authority in other jurisdictions but also with the policy which underlies the concept of strict liability in tort.

The strict liability of Section 402A is founded in part upon the belief that as between the sellers of products and those who use them, the former are the better able to bear the losses caused by defects in the products involved. * * * This greater loss-bearing capacity is unrelated to negligence in the manufacture or marketing of products. Indeed, retail and wholesale sellers of chattels are themselves often in no position to discover or avoid defects in their inventories, even by the exercise of a high degree of care. Thus, defendants in Section 402A actions are subjected to liability without regard to fault. It is a proper corollary to this principle that the lesser loss-bearing capacity of product users exists independently of their negligence or lack of it. It follows that such negligence should not ordinarily or necessarily operate to preclude recovery in a strict liability case. On the other hand, where assumption of risk is involved, the "loss-bearing" policy underlying Section 402A is outweighed by a countervailing policy, one which refuses recovery to persons who consciously expose themselves to known dangers. This policy is deemed stronger than the one, reflected in the normal law of contributory negligence, which denies recovery to individuals whose conduct is merely lacking in due care under the circumstances.

This is not to say, however, that evidence of ordinary negligence on the part of a plaintiff is never relevant in a Section 402A action; such evidence may bear directly upon the determination of whether the plaintiff has proved all the elements necessary to make out a cause of action. Thus, negligence in the use of a product may tend to show that the plaintiff caused a defect and therefore that the product was not defective when sold. See Comment g to Section 402A. Again, if the negligent use of a product amounts to abnormal use, it may be inferred that the product was not defective if it is safe for normal handling and use. See Comment h to Section 402A. Similarly, negligence in the use of a product may have a bearing on the question whether a defect in a product was the legal cause of the plaintiff's injury. See Restatement (Second) of Torts §§ 5 and 9 and the Comments to these sections.

What has been said is not intended as an exhaustive listing of the purposes for which evidence of the plaintiff's negligence may be relevant in Section 402A cases. It is intended merely to indicate that, although such negligence is not per se a bar to recovery, it may nevertheless have that effect in a proper case where it negates an essential element of the cause of action. I do not read the opinion of the Court as suggesting anything to the contrary.

Notes

1. As Justice Pomeroy's concurrence points out, the result in *McCown* was not compelled by the language of comment n, since the plaintiff's negligence was more than a mere failure to discover or guard against possibility of a defect. Several courts have followed the *McCown* approach. By declining to distinguish between negligent failure to discover or guard against the possibility of a defect and other forms of contributory negligence, *McCown* held that no version of contributory negligence is applicable to strict tort liability.

2. The first sentence of comment n suggests that the irrelevance of the defendant's negligence in strict tort liability implies that the plaintiff's negligence should also be irrelevant. Justice Pomeroy suggests the same point in *McCown* when he says that it is "a proper corollary" of the principle that defendants are subjected to liability without fault "that the lesser loss-bearing capacity of product users exists independently of their negligence or lack of it." Is this a sound argument? In this regard, how does contributory negligence differ from assumption of risk, which Justice Pomeroy believes is consistent with section 402A because of a "countervailing policy"?

3. Do the policies underlying strict tort liability support or undermine the application of contributory negligence to strict tort liability actions?

DALY v. GENERAL MOTORS CORP.

Supreme Court of California, 1978.
20 Cal.3d 725, 144 Cal.Rptr. 380, 575 P.2d 1162.

RICHARDSON, JUSTICE.

The most important of several problems which we consider is whether the principles of comparative negligence expressed by us in *Li v. Yellow Cab Co.* (1975) 13 Cal.3d 804, 119 Cal.Rptr. 858, 532 P.2d 1226, apply to actions founded on strict products liability. We will conclude that they do.

* * *

In the early hours of October 31, 1970, decedent Kirk Daly, a 36-year-old attorney, was driving his Opel southbound on the Harbor Freeway in Los Angeles. The vehicle, while traveling at a speed of 50–70 miles per hour, collided with and damaged 50 feet of metal divider fence. After the initial impact between the left side of the vehicle and the fence the Opel spun counterclockwise, the driver's door was thrown open, and Daly was forcibly ejected from the car and sustained fatal head injuries. It was equally undisputed that had the deceased remained in the Opel his injuries, in all probability, would have been relatively minor.

The sole theory of plaintiffs' complaint was strict liability for damages allegedly caused by a defective product, namely, an improperly designed door latch claimed to have been activated by the impact. It was further asserted that, but for the faulty latch, decedent would have been restrained in the vehicle and, although perhaps injured, would not have been killed. Thus, the case involves a so-called "second collision" in which the "defect" did not contribute to the original impact, but only to the "enhancement" of injury.

* * *

Over plaintiffs' objections, defendants were permitted to introduce evidence indicating that: (1) the Opel was equipped with a seat belt-shoulder harness system, and a door lock, either of which if used, it was contended, would have prevented Daly's ejection from the vehicle; (2) Daly used neither the harness system nor the lock; (3) the 1970 Opel owner's manual contained warnings that seat belts should be worn and doors locked when the car was in motion for "accident security"; and (4) Daly was intoxicated at the time of collision, which evidence the jury was advised was admitted for the limited purpose of determining whether decedent had used the vehicle's safety equipment. After relatively brief deliberations the jury returned a verdict favoring all defendants, and plaintiffs appeal from the ensuing adverse judgment.

STRICT PRODUCTS LIABILITY AND COMPARATIVE FAULT

In response to plaintiffs' assertion that the "intoxication-nonuse" evidence was improperly admitted, defendants contend that the deceased's own conduct contributed to his death. Because plaintiffs' case rests upon strict products liability based on improper design of the door latch and because defendants assert a failure in decedent's conduct, namely, his alleged intoxication and nonuse of safety equipment, without which the accident and ensuing death would not have occurred, there is thereby posed the overriding issue in the case, should comparative principles apply in strict products liability actions?

* * *

[In Li v. Yellow Cab Co., 13 Cal.3d 804, 119 Cal.Rptr. 858, 532 P.2d 1226 (1975), we adopted] a "pure" form of comparative negligence which, when present, reduced but did not prevent plaintiff's recovery. * * * We held that the defense of assumption of risk, insofar as it is no more than a variant of contributory negligence, was merged into the assessment of liability in proportion to fault. * * * Within the broad guidelines therein announced, we left to trial courts discretion in the particular implementation of the new doctrine.

* * *

Those counseling against the recognition of comparative fault principles in strict products liability cases vigorously stress, perhaps equally, not only the conceptual, but also the semantic difficulties incident to such a course. The task of merging the two concepts is said to be impossible, that "apples and oranges" cannot be compared, that "oil and water" do not mix, and that strict liability, which is not founded on negligence or fault, is inhospitable to comparative principles. The syllogism runs, contributory negligence was only a defense to negligence, comparative negligence only affects contributory negligence, therefore comparative negligence cannot be a defense to strict liability. * * *

While fully recognizing the theoretical and semantic distinctions between the twin principles of strict products liability and traditional negligence, we think they can be blended or accommodated.

The inherent difficulty in the "apples and oranges" argument is its insistence on fixed and precise definitional treatment of legal concepts. In the evolving areas of both products liability and tort defenses, however, there has developed much conceptual overlapping and interweaving in order to attain substantial justice. The concept of strict liability itself, as we have noted, arose from dissatisfaction with the wooden formalisms of traditional tort and contract principles in order to protect the consumer of manufactured goods. Similarly, increasing social awareness of its harsh "all or nothing" consequences led us in *Li* to moderate the impact of traditional contributory negligence in order to accomplish a fairer and more balanced result. We acknowledged an intermixing of defenses of contributory negligence and assumption of risk and formally effected a type of merger.

* * *

Furthermore, the "apples and oranges" argument may be conceptually suspect. It has been suggested that the term "contributory negligence," one of the vital building blocks upon which much of the argument is based, may indeed itself be a misnomer since it lacks the first element of the classical negligence formula, namely, a duty of care owing to another. A highly respected torts authority, Dean William Prosser, has noted this fact by observing, "It is perhaps unfortunate that contributory negligence is called negligence at all. 'Contributory fault' would be a more descriptive term. Negligence as it is commonly understood is conduct which creates an undue risk of harm to others. Contributory negligence is conduct which involves an undue risk of harm to the actor himself. Negligence requires a duty, an obligation of conduct to another person. Contributory negligence involves no duty, unless we are to be so ingenious as to say that the plaintiff is under an obligation to protect the defendant against liability for the consequences of his own negligence." (Prosser, Law of Torts, *supra*, § 65, p. 418.)

We think, accordingly, the conclusion may fairly be drawn that the terms "comparative negligence," "contributory negligence" and "assumption of risk" do not, standing alone, lend themselves to the exact measurements of a micrometer-caliper, or to such precise definition as to divert us from otherwise strong and consistent countervailing policy considerations. Fixed semantic consistency at this point is less important than the attainment of a just and equitable result. The interweaving of concept and terminology in this area suggests a judicial posture that is flexible rather than doctrinaire.

We pause at this point to observe that where, as here, a consumer or user sues the manufacturer or designer alone, technically, neither fault nor conduct is really compared functionally. The conduct of one party in combination with the product of another, or perhaps the placing of a defective article in the stream of projected and anticipated use, may produce the ultimate injury. In such a case, as in the situation before us, we think the term "equitable apportionment or allocation of loss" may be more descriptive than "comparative fault."

Given all of the foregoing, we are, in the wake of *Li*, disinclined to resolve the important issue before us by the simple expedient of matching linguistic labels which have evolved either for convenience or by custom. Rather, we consider it more useful to examine the foundational reasons underlying the creation of strict products liability in California to ascertain whether the purposes of the doctrine would be defeated or diluted by adoption of comparative principles. We imposed strict liability against the manufacturer and in favor of the user or consumer in order to relieve injured consumers "from *problems of proof* inherent in pursuing negligence * * * and warranty * * * remedies, * * *." (*Cronin v. J.B.E. Olson Corp., supra,* 8 Cal.3d at p. 133, 104 Cal.Rptr. at p. 442, 501 P.2d at p. 1162, italics added; *Greenman v. Yuba Power Products, Inc., supra,* 59 Cal.2d at p. 63, 27 Cal.Rptr. 697, 377 P.2d 897; *Escola v. Coca Cola Bottling Co.* (1944) 24 Cal.2d 453, 461–462, 150 P.2d 436 (conc. opn. by Traynor, J.).) As we have noted, we sought to place the burden of loss on manufacturers rather than " * * * injured persons *who are powerless to protect themselves* * * *." (*Greenman, supra,* 59 Cal.2d at p. 63, 27 Cal.Rptr. at p. 701, 377 P.2d at p. 901, italics added; see *Escola, supra,* 24 Cal.2d at p. 462, 150 P.2d 436; *Price v. Shell Oil Co.* (1970) 2 Cal.3d 245, 251, 85 Cal.Rptr. 178, 182, 466 P.2d 722, 726 ["*protection of otherwise defenseless victims* of manufacturing defects and the spreading throughout society of the cost of compensating them"] italics added.)

The foregoing goals, we think, will not be frustrated by the adoption of comparative principles. Plaintiffs will continue to be relieved of proving that the manufacturer or distributor was negligent in the production, design, or dissemination of the article in question. Defendant's liability for injuries caused by a defective product remains strict. The principle of protecting the defenseless is likewise preserved, for plaintiff's recovery will be reduced *only* to the extent that his own lack of reasonable care contributed to his injury. The cost of compensating the victim of a defective product, albeit proportionately reduced, remains on defendant manufacturer, and will, through him, be "spread among society." However, we do not permit plaintiff's own conduct relative to the product to escape unexamined, and as to that share of plaintiff's damages which flows from his own fault we discern no reason of policy why it should, following *Li,* be borne by others. Such a result would directly contravene the principle announced in *Li,* that loss should be assessed equitably in proportion to fault.

* * *

A second objection to the application of comparative principles in strict products liability cases is that a manufacturer's incentive to produce safe products will thereby be reduced or removed. While we fully recognize this concern we think, for several reasons, that the problem is more shadow than substance. First, of course, the manufacturer cannot avoid its continuing liability for a defective product even when the plaintiff's own conduct has contributed to his injury. The manufacturer's liability, and therefore its incentive to avoid and correct product defects, remains; its exposure will be lessened only to the extent that the trier finds that the victim's conduct contributed to his injury. Second, as a practical matter a manufacturer, in a particular case, cannot assume that the user of a defective product upon whom an injury is visited will be blameworthy. Doubtless, many users are free of fault, and a defect is at least as likely as not to be exposed by an entirely innocent plaintiff who will obtain full recovery. In such cases the manufacturer's incentive toward safety both in design and production is wholly unaffected. Finally, we must observe that under the present law, which recognizes assumption of risk as a complete defense to products liability, the curious and cynical message is that it profits the manufacturer to make his product so defective that in the event of injury he can argue that the user had to be aware of its patent defects. To that extent the incentives are inverted. We conclude, accordingly, that no substantial or significant impairment of the safety incentives of defendants will occur by the adoption of comparative principles.

In passing, we note one important and felicitous result if we apply comparative principles to strict products liability. This arises from the fact that under present law when plaintiff sues in negligence his own contributory negligence, however denominated, may diminish but cannot wholly defeat his recovery. When he sues in strict products liability, however, his "assumption of risk" *completely bars* his recovery. Under *Li*, as we have noted, "assumption of risk" is merged into comparative principles. (13 Cal.3d at p. 825, 119 Cal.Rptr. 858, 533 P.2d 1226.) The consequence is that after *Li* in a negligence action, plaintiff's conduct which amounts to "negligent" assumption of risk no longer defeats plaintiff's recovery. Identical conduct, however, in a strict liability case acts as a complete bar under rules heretofore applicable. Thus, strict products liability, which was developed to free injured consumers from the constraints imposed by traditional negligence and warranty theories, places a consumer plaintiff in a worse position than would be the case were his claim founded on simple negligence. This, in turn, rewards adroit pleading and selection of theories. The application of comparative principles to strict liability obviates this bizarre anomaly by treating alike the defenses to both negligence and strict products liability actions. In each instance the defense, if established, will reduce but not bar plaintiff's claim.

A third objection to the merger of strict liability and comparative fault focuses on the claim that, as a practical matter, triers of fact, particularly jurors, cannot assess, measure, or compare plaintiff's negligence with defendant's strict liability. We are unpersuaded by the argument and are convinced that jurors are able to undertake a fair apportionment of liability.

* * *

We note that the majority of our sister states which have addressed the problem, either by statute or judicial decree, have extended comparative principles to strict products liability.

* * *

Moreover, we are further encouraged in our decision herein by noting that the apparent majority of scholarly commentators has urged adoption of the rule which we announce herein.

* * *

Having examined the principal objections and finding them not insurmountable, and persuaded by logic, justice, and fundamental fairness, we conclude that a system of comparative fault should be and it is hereby extended to actions founded on strict products liability. In such cases the separate defense of "assumption of risk," to the extent that it is a form of contributory negligence, is abolished. While, as we have suggested, on the particular facts before us, the term "equitable apportionment of loss" is more accurately descriptive of the process, nonetheless, the term "comparative fault" has gained such wide acceptance by courts and in the literature that we adopt its use herein.

[The court then held that its decision would not be applied retroactively, not even to the case before it. Under the law existing at the time of trial, evidence of the plaintiff's intoxication and failure to use a seat belt should have been excluded.]

The judgment is reversed.

TOBRINER, CLARK and MANUEL, JJ., concur.

* * *

JEFFERSON, JUSTICE, concurring and dissenting.

* * * The majority * * * does not consider it significant that it is unable to determine what labels should be given to the new comparative principles—whether the new doctrine should be known as comparative fault, equitable apportionment of loss, or equitable allocation of loss. This inability to give the new doctrine an appropriate label is some indication of the shaky ground upon which the majority has decided to tread.

The majority rejects what I consider to be a sound criticism of its holding—that it is illogical and illusory to compare elements or factors that are not reasonably subject to comparison. The majority states that it is convinced that jurors will be able to compare the noncomparables— plaintiff's negligence with defendant's strict liability for a defective product—and still reach a fair apportionment of liability.

I consider the majority conclusion a case of wishful thinking and an application of an impractical, ivory-tower approach. The majority's assumption that a jury is capable of making a fair apportionment between a plaintiff's negligent conduct and a defendant's defective product is no more logical or convincing than if a jury were to be instructed that it should add a quart of milk (representing plaintiff's negligence) and a metal bar three feet in length (representing defendant's strict liability for a defective product), and that the two added together equal 100 percent-the total fault for plaintiff's injuries; that plaintiff's quart of milk is then to be assigned its percentage of the 100 percent * * *.

* * *

What the majority envisions as a fair apportionment of liability to be undertaken by the jury will constitute nothing more than an *unfair reduction* in the plaintiff's total damages suffered, resulting from a jury process that necessarily is predicated on speculation, conjecture and guesswork. Because the legal concept of negligence is so utterly different from the legal concept of a product defective by reason of manufacture or design, a plaintiff's negligence is no more capable of being rationally compared with a defendant's defective product to determine what percentage each contributes to plaintiff's total damages than is the quart of milk with the metal bar-posed in the above illustration.

* * *

The guessing game that will be imposed on juries by the application of comparative negligence principles to defective product liability cases will be further enhanced in those cases in which several defendants are joined in an action-some being sued on a negligence theory and others on the defective product theory and where there are several plaintiffs whose conduct may range from no negligence at all to varying degrees of negligence. The jury will be required to determine percentages of fault with respect to all the parties (and perhaps some nonparties) by seeking to compare and evaluate the *conduct* of certain parties with the *product* of other parties to produce 100 percent of fault as the necessary starting point in order to calculate a reduction in the damages suffered by each plaintiff found to be negligent. I cannot agree with the majority that such a process is reasonably workable or that it will produce an equitable result to injured plaintiffs. If a just or fair result is reached by a jury under the majority's holding, it will be strictly accidental and accomplished by pure happenstance.

* * *

There is no common denominator by which factors such as pounds, circles, quarts, triangles, inches, and squares can be added together for a total so that a determination can be made of the percentage contribution of each to the total.

* * *

BIRD, C.J., concurs.

MOSK, JUSTICE, dissenting.

I dissent.

This will be remembered as the dark day when this court, which heroically took the lead in originating the doctrine of products liability (*Greenman v. Yuba Power Products, Inc.* (1963) 59 Cal.2d 57, 27 Cal. Rptr. 697, 377 P.2d 897) and steadfastly resisted efforts to inject concepts of negligence into the newly designed tort (*Cronin v. J.B.E. Olson Corp.* (1972) 8 Cal. 121, 104 Cal.Rptr. 433, 501 P.2d 1153), inexplicably turned 180 degrees and beat a hasty retreat almost back to square one. The pure concept of products liability so pridefully fashioned and nurtured by this court for the past decade and a half is reduced to a shambles.

The majority inject a foreign object—the tort of negligence—into the tort of products liability by the simple expedient of calling negligence something else: on some pages their opinion speaks of "comparative fault," on others reference is to "comparative principles," and elsewhere the term "equitable apportionment" is employed, although this is clearly not a proceeding in equity. But a rose is a rose and negligence is negligence; thus the majority find that despite semantic camouflage they must rely on *Li v. Yellow Cab Co.* (1975) 13 Cal.3d 804, 119 Cal.Rptr. 858, 532 P.2d 1226, even though *Li* is purely and simply a negligence case which merely rejects contributory negligence and substitutes therefor comparative negligence.

* * *

The defective product is comparable to a time bomb ready to explode; it maims its victims indiscriminately, the righteous and the evil, the careful and the careless. Thus when a faulty design or otherwise defective product is involved, the litigation should not be diverted to consideration of the negligence of the plaintiff. The liability issues are simple: was the product or its design faulty, did the defendant inject the defective product into the stream of commerce, and did the defect cause the injury? The conduct of the ultimate consumer-victim who used the product in the contemplated or foreseeable manner is wholly irrelevant to those issues.

The majority devote considerable effort to rationalizing what has been described as a mixture of apples and oranges. Their point might be persuasive if there were some authority recognizing a defense of contributory products liability, for which they are now substituting comparative products liability. However, all our research to discover such apples and oranges has been fruitless. The conclusion is inescapable that the majority, in avoiding approval of comparative negligence in name as a defense to products liability, are thereby originating a new defense that can only be described as comparative products liability.

* * *

The majority deny their opinion diminishes the therapeutic effect of products liability upon producers of defective products. It seems self-evident that procedures which evaluate the injured consumer's conduct in each instance, and thus eliminate or reduce the award against the producer or distributor of a defective product, are not designed as an effective incentive to maximum responsibility to consumers. The converse is more accurate: the motivation to avoid polluting the stream of commerce with defective products increases in direct relation to the size of potential damage awards.

In sum, I am convinced that since the negligence of the defendant is irrelevant in products liability cases, the negligence—call it contributory or comparative—of the plaintiff is also irrelevant.

Notes

1. Justice Mosk's opinion in *Daly* reflects a common objection to applying comparative negligence principles to strict tort liability. In addition to applying comparative principles, the court also recognizes the plaintiff's negligence as a defense. Why is it that Mosk thinks an analysis of the plaintiff's negligence is intrinsically incompatible with the theory of strict tort liability? Does *Daly* suggest that originally the real objection to contributory negligence as a defense to strict tort liability was the draconian, all-or-nothing effect of contributory negligence? Note that the advent of comparative negligence affected the *content*, not just the *effect*, of the defenses in some jurisdictions. Courts are much more likely to recognize a defense when its effect is to reduce a plaintiff's recovery than when its effect is to bar a plaintiff's recovery.

2. Following the advent of comparative negligence, many states faced the problem of determining whether to apply their comparative negligence scheme or a similar comparative "allocation" scheme to strict tort liability and breach of warranty actions. As the opinion in *Daly* indicates, most states that have comparative negligence schemes have applied some type of comparative scheme to strict tort liability.

3. Justice Jefferson's opinion in *Daly* reflects a common objection to the application of comparative fault principles to strict tort liability: asking a jury to compare the product's defectiveness with the plaintiff's conduct is like asking it to compare apples and oranges. Is this really a problem? Don't we compare seemingly "noncomparable" items all the time, such as when we decide how much money to spend on food versus education? Is Justice Jefferson's analogy of a comparison between quarts and feet an apt one? Aren't there ways to compare apples and oranges? How might a court compare a product's defectiveness with the plaintiff's conduct?

4. What precisely should be compared in cases like *Daly,* and how should the jury be instructed to make this comparison? Courts have used different nomenclature, referring to the process as comparative fault, comparative causation, and comparative allocation. Which is a better term? Can causation really be compared?

5. In Sandford v. Chevrolet Division of General Motors, 292 Or. 590, 642 P.2d 624 (1982), the Oregon Supreme Court grappled with the problem of what is to be compared in a comparative allocation scheme applied to strict tort liability. Justice Linde's analysis of the possibilities is instructive. Notice that his analysis must account for the Oregon statute. Many states have adopted comparative negligence by statute, so their application of a

comparative scheme to strict tort liability must account for the statute's provisions.

A second problem posed by the statute is the question exactly what is to be assessed in determining the "percentage of fault attributable to the person" seeking recovery, and whether that person's fault was "greater than the combined fault of the person or persons against whom recovery is sought." The question has puzzled commentators as well as courts. At least three views are possible.

A. *Quantifying "fault."* The first is that the formula calls upon the factfinder to assess the relative magnitude of the parties' respective "fault." As stated by a leading textbook on these laws: The process is *not* allocation of physical causation, which could be scientifically apportioned, but rather of allocating *fault,* which cannot be scientifically measured." Schwartz, Comparative Negligence 276 (1974). It has been recognized that fault is an evaluation that does not lend itself to quantification, so that a comparison of fault magnifies the subjective elements already intrinsic to the ordinary judgment of negligence. This is true even in assigning proportions to two or more distinct types of negligence, but critics have found a greater theoretical obstacle when the responsibility of one party is grounded in fault other than negligence, or in no fault at all. The obstacle is greater where strict products liability is explained as a device for spreading losses from economic activity regardless of fault, but this court early disavowed that explanation, at least in the absence of legislation.

* * *

B. *"Comparative causation."* Some courts, applying comparative negligence law to products liability under statutes different from ours or under no statute, have tried to escape the difficulty by stating that the allocation of damages is to reflect relative causation, that is to say, an assessment of the proportion in which the plaintiff's injuries were caused by the product defect on the one hand and by plaintiff's own negligence on the other. * * * They have done so in the belief that this is conceptually more logical or pragmatically easier than to compare the defect of a product with the negligence of one whom it has injured.

* * * With due respect to these courts, however, we are not persuaded that the concept of "comparative causation" is more cogent or meaningful than comparative fault, if by "causation" is meant some relation of cause and effect in the physical world rather than the very attribution of responsibility for which "causation" is to serve as the premise.

Both the defect and the plaintiff's fault must in fact be causes of one injury before a question of apportionment of fault arises.

* * *

The concept of apportioning causation must be tested on the assumption that both causes had to join to produce the injury for which damages are to be allocated. There are cases in which it may be possible to segregate the harm done by one cause from different or incremental harm done by a second cause, so as to apply proportional allocation to the additional harm only. * * * Once it is assumed, however, that two or more distinct causes had to occur to produce an indivisible injury, we doubt that the purpose of the proportional fault concept is to subject the combined causation to some kind of vector analysis, even in the rare case of simultaneous, physically commensurable forces. In most cases, it would be a vain exercise to search for a common physical measure for the causative effect of a product defect and of the injured party's negligent conduct.

C. *Mixing "fault" with "proximate" causation.* A third view considers it futile to attempt to explain what is to be compared, because it is equally illogical to compare strict liability with negligence and to quantify the relative causative effect of either when it would have caused no harm in the absence of the other. Thus Dean Twerski, in the cited article, describes the technical problems of making the comparison as a "red herring": "The short answer to the dilemma of how one can compare strict liability and negligence is that one must simply close one's eyes and accomplish the task." 10 Ind.L.Rev. 796, 806–808.

* * *

In part this * * * view rests on the assumption that rational analysis in tort cases dissolves in the collegial judgment of juries. That is probably an unwarranted generalization; ability and effort to decide in accordance with law can be expected to differ from one jury to the next with such variables as the makeup of the particular jury, with the quality of evidence and advocacy, and not least with the rationality of the legal formulations in which the court explains the jury's task to it.

In any event, the assumption does not let us escape the need to state coherent rules of liability. Some tort cases are tried to the court without a jury * * *. Trial judges must know on what findings an apportionment of damages depends, whether these are to be made by the judge or by a jury. Our system of appeal as well as trial predicates that jurors will conscientiously attempt to apply the law if it is explained in comprehensible terms. * * * A juror who wants to know how to treat cause and how to treat fault is entitled to an answer, whatever comes of it in a collective decision. Counsel need to know whether to address the relative gravity of the parties' fault or to seek expert testimony on the relative impact of their respective fault in causing the asserted harm. We cannot dismiss the question as a distinction without a difference.

* * *

D. *Proportionate fault under ORS 18.470.* ORS 18.470, *supra,* by its terms applies whenever "the fault attributable to the person seeking recovery was not greater than the combined fault of the person or persons against whom recovery is sought." If there was such fault, "any damages allowed shall be diminished in the proportion to the percentage of fault attributable to the person recovering."

* * *

ORS 18.470 falls within the first of the different approaches that we have reviewed. It calls upon the factfinder to assess and quantify fault. If the plaintiff's conduct is not faultless, the assessment has two purposes: to determine whether her fault is "not greater than" that of defendants, and if it is not, then to reduce the plaintiff's recovery of damages "in the proportion to the percentage of fault attributable to" the plaintiff. The question remains against what standard this "percentage of fault" introduced by the 1975 amendment is to be measured.

The answer is implicit in the two steps found in the statute, one in the amended ORS 18.470 and the second in section 2 of the act, codified in ORS 18.480. First, if the plaintiff's behavior which was one cause of the injury is alleged to have been negligent or otherwise "fault," it is to be measured against behavior that would have been faultless under the circumstances. The factfinder is to determine the degree to which the plaintiff's behavior fell short of that norm and express this deficit as a numerical percentage, which then is applied to diminish the recoverable damages. There necessarily must be some comparable assessment of the fault attributable to defendants as a departure from the norm invoked against them (which, in products liability, will involve the magnitude of the defect rather than negligence or moral "blameworthiness") in order to determine which is greater. In this comparison, the benchmark for assessing a defendant's fault for marketing a product which is dangerously defective in design, manufacture, or warning is what the product should have been without the defect. The benchmark for the injured claimant's fault is conduct which would not be unlawful or careless in any relevant respect.

* * *

If the claimant's fault in this sense is greater than the fault of defendants, recovery is barred. Thereafter, ORS 18.470 standing alone does not seem to assign any further role to the magnitude of defendants' fault in calculating the percentage of plaintiff's damages that she may recover. Section 2 of the 1975 act, however, added directions for the second step. ORS 18.480 provides:

"(1) When requested by any party the trier of fact shall answer special questions indicating:

"(a) The amount of damages to which a party seeking recovery would be entitled, assuming that party not to be at fault;

"(b) The degree of each party's fault expressed as a percentage of the total fault attributable to all parties represented in the action.

"(2) A jury shall be informed of the legal effect of its answer to the questions listed in subsection (1) of this section."

Accordingly, after determining whether and how far each party's conduct was at fault, measured against the norm governing that party's conduct, these respective degrees of fault are to be converted into a percentage which will be applied to the plaintiff's total damages to determine his actual recovery.

To summarize: When an injured claimant's misconduct is a cause in fact of the injury, it can defeat a products liability claim if the claimant's fault is "greater than" the defendants' combined fault involved in marketing the defective product. If it is not greater, plaintiff's fault proportionately reduces her recoverable damages. "Fault" includes contributory negligence except for such unobservant, inattentive, ignorant, or awkward failure of the injured party to discover the defect or to guard against it as is taken into account in finding the particular product dangerously defective.

* * *

6. *Daly* involved the application of comparative fault to strict tort liability. What about breach of warranty and innocent representation under section 402B? Is there any reason to apply comparative fault to strict tort liability but not to these other causes of action? What should be compared if the defendant has breached an express warranty or innocently misrepresented the product?

7. For discussions of comparative fault in strict tort liability, see Fischer, Products Liability–Applicability of Comparative Negligence, 43 Mo. L.Rev. 431 (1978); Levine, Strict Products Liability and Comparative Negligence: The Collision of Fault and No Fault, 14 San Diego L.Rev. 337 (1978); Twerski, The Use and Abuse of Comparative Negligence in Products Liability, 10 Ind.L.Rev. 796 (1977).

8. The application of comparative fault to strict tort liability can become extremely complex in litigation involving multiple defendants who are sued under different theories of liability. Comparative fault schemes affect more than just defenses. They also affect contribution and indemnity, issues of multiple causation, and the effect of settlements. A recurring issue in each of these areas has been the potentially different treatment each issue might receive under negligence, strict tort liability, breach of warranty, and misrepresentation.

Before the adoption of comparative fault, these issues could usually be treated separately even if they arose in a lawsuit involving multiple parties and/or multiple causes of action. The advent of comparative schemes changed all that, however.

The essence of a comparative fault scheme is that all of the parties, and presumably all of the causes of action, are reduced to a single set of percentages that allocate the loss among the multiple parties. The scheme governs both the reduction of the plaintiffs' recovery and contribution and indemnity among the multiple defendants. Such a unified scheme is very difficult to administer, however, if different rules apply to different causes of action and/or different parties. For example, how can a court allocate damages in a single system governing negligence, strict tort liability, and breach of warranty if the rules governing what counts as the plaintiff's contributory negligence are different under these three theories of recovery? The next case and the material that follows it examine some of these issues.

DUNCAN v. CESSNA AIRCRAFT CO.

Supreme Court of Texas, 1984.

665 S.W.2d 414.

[James Parker and Benjamin Smithson were killed when a Cessna 150, in which Smithson was giving Parker a flying lesson, crashed. Duncan, Parker's wife, sued Smithson's estate and Smithson's employer for negligence, but she settled with them before trial. She and Smithson's wife then sued Cessna, alleging that "design and manufacturing defects in the legs of the cockpit seats caused the legs to break during the crash, causing the deaths of their husbands."

Cessna counterclaimed against Smithson's estate for contribution for any damages recovered from Cessna by Duncan, alleging that Smithson was negligent. Cessna also claimed that any recovery by Duncan should be reduced by one-half, based on her settlement with Smithson's estate and his employer. In response to the suit by Smithson's estate, Cessna asserted that Smithson's own contributory negligence should bar or reduce his recovery.]

Cessna argues that it is entitled to contribution from Smithson's estate for part of Duncan's damages because Smithson's pilot negligence proximately caused the fatal crash. The court of appeals agreed and remanded the cause for a partial retrial to allow Cessna to adduce proof of Smithson's negligence. In this court, Cessna claims that on remand its liability to Duncan should be reduced in accordance with principles of comparative apportionment. Because Cessna also seeks a similar reduction in its liability to Smithson's estate, we must address two distinct, but closely related questions: (1) whether a plaintiff's contributory negligence is a defense in strict products liability actions when that negligence does not rise to the level of assumed risk or unforeseeable product misuse, but is more than a mere failure to discover a product defect; and (2) whether comparative contribution among tortfeasors is possible when at least one is strictly liable.

A. APPORTIONING LIABILITY UNDER EXISTING TEXAS LAW

* * *

Under present Texas law * * * the only defenses to a strict product liability action are the absolute defense of assumption of the risk and the comparative defense of unforeseeable product misuse. By contrast, in product liability actions based on negligence and breach of warranty, these defenses are subsumed within contributory negligence, which operates as a comparative defense. *See Signal Oil & Gas Co. v. Universal Oil Products,* 572 S.W.2d 320 (Tex.1978); Tex.Rev.Civ.Stat. Ann. art. 2212a, § 1. "The procedural problems generated by this state of the substantive law are apparent." Pope & Lowerre, *The State of the Special Verdict–1979,* 11 St. Mary's L.J. 47, 48 (1979). In Texas, a plaintiff can predicate a product liability action on one or more of at least three theories of recovery: (1) strict liability under § 402A, (2) breach of warranty under the U.C.C., and (3) negligence. If either breach of warranty or negligence is alleged in addition to strict liability, the product supplier is entitled to submit three defensive issues, namely, contributory negligence, assumption of the risk, and misuse. In addition, he may also be entitled to submission of both a comparative negligence issue *and* a comparative causation (product misuse) issue.

If there were any qualitative difference between contributory negligence, on the one hand, and assumed risk and misuse, on the other, this procedural complexity might be justified. Assumed risk and unforeseeable misuse, however, are nothing more than extreme variants of contributory negligence. To varying degrees, all three defenses focus on the reasonableness of a plaintiff's conduct.

* * *

A similar problem has confronted courts attempting to apportion joint liability among negligent and strictly liable tortfeasors. Texas has two statutes that allow contribution among tortfeasors. Article 2212a provides for comparative contribution among joint tortfeasors in negligence cases according to their respective percentages of fault. Article 2212, on the other hand, mandates pro rata contribution from co-tortfeasors in other tort actions.

In *General Motors Corp. v. Simmons,* 558 S.W.2d 855 (Tex.1977), we stated that article 2212a is inapplicable to cases in which a strict liability claim is asserted against at least one defendant. We concluded that strict liability under § 402A of the *Restatement (Second) of Torts* is not based on negligence and that article 2212 governs contribution among joint tortfeasors when one of them is strictly liable. We also observed, however, that the apparent failure of articles 2212 and 2212a to fairly and sensibly compare causation in such situations promised to engender serious problems in future products liability cases. For this reason, we invited legislative study and corrective action.

* * * This court has previously attempted to ameliorate the harsh and inequitable consequences stemming from this anomalous treatment of loss allocation in products liability actions. Thus, instead of recognizing "all or nothing" issues in product misuse and breach of implied warranty cases, we created comparative apportionment schemes. *See General Motors Corp. v. Hopkins,* 548 S.W.2d at 351–52 (pure comparative causation); *Signal Oil & Gas Co. v. Universal Oil Products,* 572 S.W.2d at 329 (pure comparative negligence). Nevertheless, our limited efforts in *Hopkins* and *Signal Oil,* though positive, have not substantially alleviated the intolerable confusion, unmanageability, and inherent unfairness in this area of Texas products law.

* * *

B.   Judicial Trend Toward Comparative "Fault"

A significant majority of the numerous commentators addressing the question have strenuously urged the implementation of comparative fault, also referred to as comparative responsibility or comparative causation, as a means of distributing accident costs among negligent plaintiffs, negligent defendants, and strictly liable defendants. * * * "[A]ll or nothing" strict liability defenses are outmoded and undesirable doctrinal throwbacks resulting in unfairness to plaintiffs, to defendants, and to other product purchasers who ultimately absorb the loss through price setting. * * * In the absence of apportionment, some manufacturers bear the total expense of accidents for which others are partly to blame, while other manufacturers totally escape liability even though they have sold defective products. Either result is unacceptable.

Unfairness, however, is not the only serious flaw of virtually ignoring plaintiff and third party misconduct in strict products liability actions. The failure to allocate accident costs in proportion to the parties' relative abilities to prevent or to reduce those costs is economically inefficient. * * * An ideal tort system should impose responsibility on the parties according to their abilities to prevent the harm. Existing law, however, encourages manufacturers to make safety improvements that are not cost justified, while failing to deter the substandard conduct of other tortfeasors. * * * Thus, equitable and rational risk distribution, a fundamental policy underlying the imposition of strict products liability, logically depends on the existence of some system for comparing causation in cases involving plaintiff or third party misconduct.

For these reasons, most of the courts addressing the issue have decided to adopt some form of comparative causation for strict liability in tort.

* * *

We recognize that because strict liability is closely analogous to negligence per se, our comparative negligence statute, article 2212a, might reasonably be interpreted to include both types of actions. * * * However, article 2212a refers only to negligence actions, even though strict products liability had been judicially adopted six years earlier. * * * Consequently, we reaffirm our observation in *General Motors Corp. v. Simmons,* 558 S.W.2d 855 (Tex.1977), that article 2212a does not apply to actions in which strict liability is established.

The legislature's decision to limit Art. 2212a to negligence cases does not, however, preclude this court from fashioning a common law comparative apportionment system for strict products liability cases. * * *

The older contribution statute, Art. 2212, likewise does not preclude judicial adoption of comparative loss allocation. In *General Motors Corp. v. Simmons* we held Art. 2212 applicable to a case involving both negligent and strictly liable defendants. Article 2212 was enacted in 1917, long before any identifiable body of strict products liability law existed. It is unlikely that the legislature intended for the statute to control in cases based [on] the unforeseen theories of products liability, presenting unforeseen questions of loss allocation. It thus appears that our holding in *Simmons* was not mandated by the legislative purpose supporting Art. 2212. As a result, *Simmons* is an unjustified obstacle to the development of a rational and fair system of allocating losses among negligent plaintiffs, negligent defendants and strictly liable defendants. Therefore, we hold that Art. 2212 does not apply when strict products liability, including uncrashworthiness and breach of warranty, is established.

* * *

Many courts and commentators have labeled this type of loss allocation system comparative *fault*. We choose comparative *causation* instead because it is conceptually accurate in cases based on strict liability and breach of warranty theories in which the defendant's "fault," in the traditional sense of culpability, is not at issue. The trier of fact is to compare the harm caused by the defective product with the harm caused by the negligence of the other defendants, any settling tortfeasors and the plaintiff.[8] The fault or conduct of the products defendant is not at issue.

* * *

In cases not controlled by Art. 2212a, the system we adopt will allow comparison of plaintiff's conduct, whether it is characterized as assumption of risk, misuse, or failure to mitigate or avoid damages, with the conduct or product of a defendant, whether the suit combines crashworthiness or other theories of strict products liability, breach of warranty, or negligence. *Cf.* Uniform Comparative Fault Act § 1 (1977) (proposing similar statutory system). Assumption of risk and misuse will no longer be separate defenses, but will be subsumed under the more familiar notion of contributory negligence.

* * *

C. PURE VERSUS MODIFIED COMPARISON

We must now decide, however, whether to adopt modified or "pure" comparative apportionment. Under a modified system, as exemplified by article 2212a, a claimant's recovery is entirely barred if his share of causation is found to be greater than the total causation attributed to the defendants. Under a "pure" system, on the other hand, a claimant

---

8. We suggest that the following general form, adapted to the specific allegations of each case, provides a general idea of the submission of the comparative apportionment issue in these cases:

If, in answer to Questions _____, _____, and _____, you have found that more than one party's act(s) or product(s) contributed to cause the plaintiff's injuries, and only in that event, then answer the following question.

Find from a preponderance of the evidence the percentage of plaintiff's injuries caused by:

Product X	_____
Defendant Y	_____
Plaintiff Z	_____
Total	100%

Cf. Daly v. General Motors Corp., 20 Cal.3d 725, 575 P.2d 1162, 144 Cal.Rptr. 380 (1978) (suggesting analogous special issues from maritime seaworthiness cases).

can recover the percentage of damages caused by the defendants, regardless of the extent of his own causation.

* * *

In this case, the policies underlying strict liability in tort will be best served by pure comparison. The rule of Art. 2212a, barring recovery by a plaintiff found to be 51% or more responsible, was a legislative compromise in negligence cases, a holdover from contributory negligence. No sound reason exists for allowing a defendant to escape liability which the jury has allocated to him, irrespective of the responsibility allocated to the plaintiff. *See Murray v. Fairbanks Morse,* 610 F.2d 149, 162 (3d Cir.1979). Accordingly, we decline to judicially engraft the rule contained in Art. 2212a barring recovery by a plaintiff found to be 51% or more responsible. We therefore hold that in products liability cases in which at least one defendant is found liable on a theory other than negligence, the plaintiff's damages shall be reduced only by the percentage of causation attributed to the plaintiff, regardless of how large or small that percentage may be. A plaintiff may recover the percentage of damages caused by the defendants, even though his own share of causation is greater than that attributed to the defendants individually or combined.

Additionally, each defendant found to have been a cause of the plaintiff's injuries shall be jointly and severally liable for the entire amount that the plaintiff is entitled to recover, subject to a right of contribution for payments in excess of the defendant's percentage share. We reject any limitation on joint and several liability such as that contained in Art. 2212a § 2(c) [which provides that a defendant who is less negligent than the plaintiff is not jointly and severally liable].

* * *

Imposing the risk of an insolvent defendant on the remaining defendants is justified as a matter of policy because the defendants' conduct or products endangered another person, the plaintiff, while the plaintiff's conduct only endangered himself. *See American Motorcycle Association v. Superior Court,* 20 Cal.3d 578, 578 P.2d 899, 146 Cal.Rptr. 182 (1978). Furthermore, the plaintiff seeks recovery for physical injuries, but defendants' claims for contribution are merely economic. Finally, a solvent manufacturer is better able to spread the loss than is the plaintiff.

Article 2212a will, of course, continue to govern cases in which the plaintiff alleges only negligence or where the plaintiff fails to obtain findings of defect and producing cause, or breach of warranty, against a product supplier who has been joined with a negligent defendant.

D. THE EFFECT OF PARTIAL SETTLEMENTS

We must also address the question of how a settlement with one tortfeasor affects the remaining defendants' liability and the plaintiff's recovery. We hold that in multiple defendant cases in which grounds of recovery other than negligence are established, the non-settling defendants' liability and the plaintiff's recovery shall be reduced by the percent share of causation assigned to the settling tortfeasor by the trier of fact.

The effect of a partial settlement in cases involving negligent tortfeasors was addressed by this court in *Palestine Contractors, Inc. v. Perkins,* 386 S.W.2d 764 (Tex.1964). In *Palestine* the court was faced with a choice between allowing a dollar credit or a pro rata credit and chose the latter. This court approved a pro rata credit because the rule allowed finality of settlement without prejudicing the non-settling defendants' rights. A pro rata credit reduces the non-settling defendants' liability by an amount equal to the number of settling tortfeasors divided by the total number of tortfeasors. Allowing a pro rata credit removes the incentive for collusive settlements because the plaintiff bears the risk of accepting an inadequate settlement. The court considered it fair to impose this risk on plaintiffs inasmuch as plaintiffs may avoid the risk entirely by rejecting the settlement offers. *Id.* at 771–73.

A dollar credit reduces the liability of the non-settling defendants, pro tanto, by the dollar amount of any settlement. The defendant's liability thus may fluctuate depending on the amount of a settlement to which he was not a party. This fluctuation cannot be reconciled with the policy of apportioning liability in relation to each party's responsibility, the conceptual basis of comparative causation. A dollar credit also encourages collusion by shielding plaintiffs from the effect of bad settlements while denying them the benefit of good settlements. Allowing a dollar credit does, however, ensure one recovery. *Id.*

Even though the reasoning in *Palestine Contractors* remains sound, we do not consider pro rata credit to be suitable in a comparative causation system. Pro rata allocation merely divides the damages by the number of defendants without considering their relative roles in causing the injuries. In the twenty years since *Palestine,* the law has advanced from crude headcounting [sic] to a more refined percent allocation of liability based on the relative harm caused by each defendant. *Compare* Art. 2212, *with* Art. 2212a. Accordingly, we hold that a settlement with one tortfeasor will reduce the liability of the nonsettling defendants by the percentage of causation allocated to the settling tortfeasor rather than by a pro rata share. The term "tortfeasor" includes those whose liability is based on strict products liability, breach of warranty, and negligence.

A percent credit necessarily means that settling plaintiffs may recover more than the amount of damages ultimately determined, but they also may recover less. Plaintiffs bear the risk of poor settlements; logic and equity dictate that the benefit of good settlements should also be theirs. One objection to giving plaintiffs this benefit is that doing so would violate the one recovery rule of *Bradshaw v. Baylor University,* 126 Tex. 99, 84 S.W.2d 703 (1935). This case thus requires that we answer a question expressly left open in *Cypress Creek v. Muller,* 640

S.W.2d 860 (Tex.1982)-how does the *Bradshaw* one recovery rule apply in cases not controlled by Art. 2212a?

* * *

The reasoning behind the one recovery rule no longer applies. The system of comparative causation we adopt allows allocation of liability between the parties, even when the injury itself is indivisible. *Cf.* Art. 2212a (apportioning liability in negligence cases). Because each defendant's share can now be determined, it logically follows that each may settle just that portion of the plaintiff's suit. The settlement does not affect the amount of harm caused by the remaining defendants and likewise should not affect their liability.

An additional rationale supporting the one recovery rule was that it prevented unjust enrichment; however, any enrichment of plaintiffs under the new system of comparative causation is not unjust, for the simple reason that no one is harmed. The settling defendant cannot complain, because he agreed to pay. The non-settling defendant has no right to complain, because he was not a party to and is not affected by the settlement.

* * *

For the reasons stated, we hold that the one recovery rule does not prevent our adopting a system that reduces the plaintiff's recovery and the non-settling defendants' liability by the percentage of causation assigned to any tortfeasor with whom plaintiff has settled. We hereby adopt a percent credit rule, which will leave defendants unaffected by settlements in which they do not participate. Each party's share of liability will be that determined by the jury. Plaintiffs will benefit from good settlements and bear the risk of bad ones, just as they do in single-tortfeasor cases. Allowing plaintiffs to keep the excess from a good settlements may violate the one recovery rule, but no one is harmed. Accordingly, to the extent it conflicts with this opinion, we overrule *Bradshaw v. Baylor University.*

E.   REMAINING ISSUES

Because of the scope of this opinion, we consider it appropriate to note two important rules which remain unchanged. We reaffirm the rule in § 402A comment n of the *Restatement (Second) of Torts* that negligent failure to discover or guard against a product defect is not a defense.

* * *

Comparative causation does not affect the right of a retailer or other member of the marketing chain to receive indemnity from the manufacturer of the defective product when the retailer or other member of the marketing chain is merely a conduit for the defective product and is not independently culpable. *See General Motors Corp. v. Simmons,* 558 S.W.2d 855, 860–61 (Tex.1977); *see also* Edgar, [Products Liability in Texas, 11 Tex.Tech L.Rev. 23, 47 (1979)]. *Compare Thiele v. Chick,* 631

S.W.2d 526 (Tex.App.—Houston [1st Dist.] 1982, writ ref'd n.r.e.) (seller allowed indemnity where no independent culpability shown); *with United Tractor, Inc. v. Chrysler Corp.,* 563 S.W.2d 850 (Tex.Civ.App.—El Paso 1978, no writ) (independently negligent manufacturer-assembler denied indemnity); *and Ford Motor Co. v. Russell & Smith Ford Co.,* 474 S.W.2d 549 (Tex.Civ.App.—Houston [14th Dist.] 1971, no writ) (independently negligent retailer denied indemnity). If there is no allegation of independent liability, the liability of the members of the marketing chain should be submitted as one. The jury will determine the causation attributable to the defective product. Of course, each defendant member of the marketing chain remains liable to the plaintiff.

Notes

1. Section B of the court's opinion in *Duncan* rehearses the issue addressed in *Daly:* whether a comparative scheme should be applied to strict tort liability. Before turning to the problem of coordinating multiple causes of action and multiple parties in a single comparative finding, consider the *Duncan* court's decision to adopt a comparative scheme. The court states that "[t]he failure to allocate accident costs in proportion to the parties' relative abilities to prevent or reduce those costs is economically inefficient * * *. Thus, equitable and rational risk distribution * * * logically depends on the existence of some system for comparing causation in cases involving plaintiff or third party misconduct." Is this argument sound? Putting aside arguments about fairness, will a comparative scheme promote efficiency?

2. Section A of the opinion in *Duncan* describes the different treatment given to consumer conduct defenses under strict tort liability, negligence, and breach of warranty. The court recognized that it would be impossible to combine these different schemes into a single comparative system without applying the same rules to each theory of recovery. For example, different conduct could not be counted as contributory negligence against different defendants who were sued under different theories, or against the same defendant sued under multiple theories. Thus, the court recognized that it must adopt a single set of rules to apply to the entire case.

As the court noted, however, the *Duncan* scheme varies in a number of significant ways from Texas' comparative negligence scheme, although it is applicable to all defendants, even those who are sued only for negligence, as long as one defendant is held liable for breach of warranty or strict tort liability. Is there any justification for having a different scheme for cases involving strict tort liability or breach of warranty than for cases involving only negligence?

3. Note that the court lumped contributory negligence, assumed risk, and unforeseeable misuse into a single percentage finding. The court also claimed that all three "are nothing more than extreme versions of contributory negligence. To varying degrees, all three focus on the reasonableness of a plaintiff's conduct." Is this correct for unforeseeable misuse?

4. How is the jury supposed to compare causation? Does its comparison include considerations of causation in fact?

Consider a driver who was injured in a collision with a negligent motorist. Suppose that (1) the original impact caused injury to the plaintiff's back, (2) a defective steering wheel shattered and caused injury to his hand, and (3) a doctor then negligently administered a drug to treat the plaintiff's hand, and the drug caused a rash. The negligent motorist was a cause-in-fact of all the plaintiff's injuries. The steering wheel manufacturer was a cause-in-fact only of the injured hand and the rash. The doctor was a cause-in-fact only of the rash. (The plaintiff's driving, of course, was a cause-in-fact of all three injuries.)

Since the back injury was caused only by the negligent motorist, he alone should be liable for it. Since the hand injury was caused by both the negligent motorist and the steering wheel manufacturer, the hand injury should be allocated between them according to comparative fault. Since the rash was caused jointly by all three defendants, it should be allocated among all three of them according to comparative fault.

But how will all of this be submitted to the jury? Will the jury be asked to segregate the three separate injuries according to cause-in-fact (*i.e.*, the back, the hand, and the rash) and *then* apportion each injury, according to fault, among its causes? Doing so would require three separate strings of percentages, each totaling 100, because different sets of defendants caused each injury. This approach, however, would be very difficult to implement in most cases. Injuries are not always so easy to divide as are a back injury, a hand injury, and a rash. Maybe the doctor's malpractice aggravated the hand injury or caused more pain to the plaintiff's back. If so, the trial court could not simply ask the jury to ascertain comparative fault findings for each injury identified by the court in advance. The jury itself would have to resolve fact questions about how to divide the injuries on the basis of cause-in-fact. It would *then* somehow have to compare the fault of each defendant who caused each separate injury. This, to say the least, would be cumbersome.

All of this could be avoided by asking the jury to perform both operations—division by cause-in-fact and allocation according to fault—in one step. The jury's percentage findings could reflect, under proper instruction, a determination of each party's responsibility for the plaintiff's injuries, taking into account *both* cause-in-fact and fault. Thus, in the example above, the jury could assign percentages to the motorist, the steering wheel manufacturer, and the doctor by taking into account *both* the relative *fault* of the parties *and* the facts that the doctor had no *causal* connection with the back injury or the hand injury and that the steering wheel manufacturer had no *causal* connection with the back injury.

A difficulty arises, however, if a court takes this approach *and* retains joint and several liability. Again referring to the example, suppose the jury assigns 10% responsibility to the plaintiff, 60% responsibility to the other motorist, 20% responsibility to the steering wheel manufacturer, and 10% responsibility to the doctor. If the other motorist was insolvent, the steering wheel manufacturer and the doctor would be required to pay for the other motorist's 60% share. But this share includes liability for the back injury, which the steering wheel manufacturer and the doctor did not cause! Joint and several liability has never been used to make a defendant pay for an injury that it did not cause.

5.   The court recognized that a single set of rules must be applied to the entire case, even though it involves defendants who are sued under different causes of action.   But did the court create new problems by creating a scheme that is different from comparative negligence in cases involving only negligence?   Consider, for example, the court's decision to adopt comment n, whereby a plaintiff's contributory negligence that is no more than a mere failure to know or guard against a defect does not count in a strict products liability case, even though it would count in a pure negligence case.

Suppose Motorists 1 and 2 collide and that Motorist 1 should have known that his brakes were defective.   Motorist 1 sues Motorist 2 for negligent driving and sues the automobile manufacturer for defective brakes. Motorist 2 sues Motorist 1 for negligent driving and for negligent failure to inspect his brakes and sues the automobile manufacturer for the defective brakes.   In such a case, it would be confusing to submit the case to the jury if different parts of Motorist 1's conduct counted for some aspects of the case but not others.

Under comment n, Motorist 1's failure to inspect his brakes would be relevant in Motorist 2's negligence claim.   It would also be relevant as contributory negligence in Motorist 1's claim against Motorist 2.   It would not be relevant, however, to Motorist 1's product liability claim against the automobile manufacturer.   It would be confusing for the jury to compare all of the parties, if Motorist 1's failure to inspect his brakes counted for some purposes but not others.   The jury would hear evidence about Motorist 1's failure to inspect his brakes, but it would be told that this conduct is relevant to some comparisons between parties but not others.

The *Duncan* court solved this problem by applying one rule to the entire lawsuit, but this creates problems of its own.   The *Duncan* rule is that Motorist 1's failure to inspect his brakes does not count in the entire case. Thus, Motorist 2 is deprived of a relevant piece of evidence.   If, on the other hand, the rule had been to count this conduct for the entire lawsuit, Motorist 1 would have been deprived of the benefit of comment n on his strict products liability action against the automobile manufacturer.

Moreover, the *Duncan* solution creates some administrative problems. The parties will not know whether they have a "negligence case" or a "products liability case," and therefore will not even know the applicable rules, until after the jury comes back with its verdict.   If the jury acquits all of the parties on negligence but finds the product manufacturer liable under strict products liability, Motorist 1's failure to inspect his brakes will not count.   If the jury acquits the product manufacturer, then comment n is not applicable, and Motorist 1's failure to inspect his brakes will count, both to reduce his own recovery and to provide a basis for Motorist 2's recovery.   If the jury finds liability on the negligence claims *and* the product liability claim, Motorist 1's failure to inspect his brakes will not count.   Since the parties and the trial court will not know what the jury will do, they have to conduct the lawsuit without knowing the ground rules.   They will not know the relevancy of certain evidence or how to instruct the jury until after the verdict.

6. Consider a case that involves multiple defendants and multiple causes of action, in which the strict tort liability defendants are drug manufacturers, one of which produced a defective drug, and in which the plaintiff relies on the "market share" theory to prove causation. *See* Sindell v. Abbott Laboratories, 26 Cal.3d 588, 163 Cal.Rptr. 132, 607 P.2d 924 (1980), cert. denied, 449 U.S. 912, 101 S.Ct. 285, 66 L.Ed.2d 140 (1980). Should the court ask the jury to find market share percentages for each manufacturer, and then to find "comparative causation" percentages, or should these two inquiries be merged into a single set of percentages?

7. In ordinary negligence actions, some courts have distinguished among three types of conduct by a plaintiff. First, a plaintiff's substandard care might occur before an accident and be a proximate cause of the accident, such as when a plaintiff negligently runs a red light and hits a car passing through the intersection. This is regular contributory negligence. Second, a plaintiff's substandard care might occur after an injury and be a proximate cause of an aggravation to the injury, such as when an injured plaintiff fails to follow his doctor's orders and, in doing so, aggravates his condition. Many courts label this type of conduct as failure to mitigate damages, although section 918 of the Restatement (Second) of Torts calls this type of conduct "avoidable consequences." Third, a plaintiff's substandard conduct might occur before the injury-producing accident and be a proximate cause of a portion of the plaintiff's injuries, but not a proximate cause of the accident itself. A plaintiff's failure to wear a seat belt is an example. Some courts label this type of conduct "avoidable consequences," although, we have seen, section 918 uses this term to refer to post-accident plaintiff conduct. You must be very careful about the nomenclature in your jurisdiction.

For courts that draw these distinctions at all, mitigation of damages and avoidable consequences (as we have used the terms) are not absolute bars to recovery. Failure to mitigate damages merely reduces the plaintiff's damages by precluding recovery for the aggravated damage caused by the failure to mitigate. The same result could be reached simply by holding that such conduct is a form of contributory negligence, but that contributory negligence is an absolute bar to recovery only for the injuries it proximately causes. Nevertheless, the rubric of mitigation of damages is sometimes used rather than the rubric of contributory negligence.

The doctrine of avoidable consequences is more complex. For example, some courts have held that such conduct is not a defense at all, although it is unclear whether these holdings are limited to specific plaintiff behavior, such as failure to wear a seat belt or motorcycle helmet. *See* Dare v. Sobule, 674 P.2d 960 (Colo.1984)(helmet); Fischer v. Moore, 183 Colo. 392, 517 P.2d 458 (1973)(seatbelt); Carnation Co. v. Wong, 516 S.W.2d 116 (Tex.1974)(seat belt). If the doctrine is limited, it is effectively nothing more than a selective "no duty" rule concerning seat belts or helmets. If it is applicable to all types of "avoidable consequences" conduct, it excludes a broad range of contributory negligence from consideration.

Whatever approach a specific jurisdiction uses in ordinary negligence cases, two important issues arise in the context of products liability litigation. First, do the details developed in negligence cases apply also to strict tort liability? For example, after *McCown* should the Pennsylvania Supreme Court nevertheless consider failure to mitigate damages as a defense to strict tort liability, on the ground that it is not a form of "contributory negligence"? Or should a court that follows comment n nevertheless decline to count against a plaintiff his or her failure to wear a seatbelt?

Second, to what extent would a shift away from contributory negligence as an absolute bar in favor of comparative negligence affect these distinctions, even in ordinary negligence cases? For example, would mitigation of damages continue to be an absolute bar for the appropriate portion of the damages, or would it be part of the comparative percentages? And if such a shift affects these distinctions in negligence, does it have the same effect in strict tort liability?

Note that the court in *Duncan* collapsed all of these doctrines into one comparative finding, apparently abandoning the previously recognized consequences of these distinctions.

8. Recall the discussion in section A concerning contributory negligence as a defense in breach of warranty actions. Comment 13 to section 2-314, comment 8 to section 2-316, and comment 5 to section 2-715 suggest that negligent failure to discover a defect is a defense to an action for breach of warranty under the Uniform Commercial Code. Why do you suppose the opinion in *Duncan* does not account for this material? Can the jury charge in a case involving both an action for breach of warranty and strict tort liability be made consistent both with comment n to section 402A and with the comments to the U.C.C.?

9. Would the problems inherent in *Duncan* be eliminated if the court called its scheme "comparative fault," rather than "comparative causation"?

10. Under *Duncan* multiple defendants were jointly and severally liable regardless of their relative percentages of causation. Under Texas' then existing comparative negligence scheme, a defendant was jointly and severally liable unless it was less negligent than the plaintiff. Is there any reason to apply a different scheme to cases involving a strict tort liability claim?

Most courts have held that the adoption of comparative negligence does not abrogate joint and several liability. *See, e.g.,* American Motorcycle Ass'n v. Superior Court, 20 Cal.3d 578, 146 Cal.Rptr. 182, 578 P.2d 899 (1978). *But see* Brown v. Keill, 224 Kan. 195, 580 P.2d 867 (1978); Bartlett v. New Mexico Welding Supply, Inc., 98 N.M. 152, 646 P.2d 579 (App.1982).

11. As the court indicates, settling defendants were treated differently under *Duncan* than under Texas' comparative negligence scheme. Is there any reason for doing this?

12. How should a court treat the negligence of the plaintiff's employer, who is immune from liability to the plaintiff and also to contribution? Should the employer's negligence be submitted to the jury and reduce the plaintiff's recovery from the other defendants, as it would in the case of a settlement? Should it be treated like the negligence of an insolvent defendant? Should it be ignored? Is there any reason to have a different result in strict tort liability than in negligence? *See* Magro v. Ragsdale Brothers, Inc., 721 S.W.2d 832 (Tex.1986); Varela v. American Petrofina Co., 658

S.W.2d 561 (Tex.1983). *But see* Erickson v. Harvey Hubbell, Inc., 593 F.Supp. 1319 (N.D.Tex.1984).

13. How should other non-party tortfeasors be treated? Should their negligence or other culpability be submitted to the jury? If so, how should it affect the plaintiff's recovery?

14. There are several other features of comparative negligence that cannot be addressed here in detail, such as whether judgments on counterclaims are offset against judgments on primary claims, and whether settling defendants can obtain contribution. Are the rules that were developed for these issues in the context of negligence up for grabs under *Duncan?* *See* Beech Aircraft Corp. v. Jinkins, 739 S.W.2d 19 (Tex.1987); Bonniwell v. Beech Aircraft Corp., 663 S.W.2d 816 (Tex.1984).

15. Suppose a plaintiff settles with the product defendant and then sues the non-product defendants. Should the ensuing lawsuit be governed by *Duncan* ? Even if the settlement is for $1?

16. Do these problems suggest that courts should not distinguish between the contours of their comparative negligence scheme and their comparative allocation scheme for strict tort liability?

17. In the summer of 1987, the Texas legislature modified chapter 33 of the Civil Practice and Remedies Code (which codified article 2212a). The legislation was motivated partly by a desire to simplify the bifurcated system adopted in *Duncan*. The result was far from simple. The legislation replaced both *Duncan* and article 2212a with a system that itself distinguishes between negligence and strict liability. For example, a 51% bar rule applies to pure negligence cases, but a 60% bar rule applies to product cases decided on a ground other than negligence. The rules of joint and several liability differ under negligence and strict liability. They even differ within strict liability depending on whether the plaintiff is contributorily negligent. The percentage reduction scheme for settling tortfeasors recognized both by article 2212a and *Duncan* was replaced by a sliding scale credit, whereby the non settling defendants are given a fixed percentage credit (from 5% to 20%), depending on the size of the final damage award.

Obviously, this silliness could be avoided by adopting a single comparative scheme for all personal injury cases. But is this type of bifurcation (or trifurcation) at least invited by a system that proliferates different "theories" and "causes of action" to govern single events?

KEEN v. ASHOT ASHKELON, LTD.

Supreme Court of Texas, 1988.
748 S.W.2d 91.

OPINION

MAUZY, JUSTICE.

This is a products liability case. Daryel Keen sued to recover for personal injuries he sustained when a trailer fell over onto the hostler he was driving. The trial court disregarded the jury's answers to issues that found Keen contributorily negligent and rendered judgment in

Keen's favor for the full amount of the jury verdict. The court of appeals reversed the trial court's judgment and rendered judgment reducing Keen's damages in accordance with the contributory negligence finding. * * * Because Keen's contributory negligence constituted a failure to guard against a product defect, we reverse and affirm that of the trial court.

Daryel Keen was a hostler driver for Santa Fe Transportation Company. A "hostler" is a motorized vehicle used for pulling loaded trailers from one off-road location to another. When unattached to a truck, these trailers are supported in the front by their "dolly legs." Each "dolly leg" is afforded ground support and stability by a "sand shoe."

Keen and a co-worker, Sam Moody, were relocating two loaded trailers in the Santa Fe yard. The plan was to position the trailers, one in front of the other with Moody's in the rear. Moody settled his trailer first and began to disengage. Keen pulled his hostler alongside Moody's trailer. Shortly after Moody disengaged his hostler, the loaded trailer sitting on its dolly legs fell over on Keen's hostler and injured him.

Keen sued Ashot Ashkelon which manufactured the sand shoe and Strick Corporation which manufactured and assembled the trailer. Keen also sued the company that loaded the trailer, Arsham Metals. The case was submitted to the jury on issues of negligence and strict liability. The jury refused to find Arsham Metals negligent in the manner in which it loaded the trailer. Instead the jury found that the sand shoe was defective and found Ashot and Strick liable on the theory of products liability. The jury also answered "yes" to the following contributory negligence issue:

Special Issue No. 7

Do you find from a preponderance of the evidence that on the occasion in question Daryel Keen moved his hostling tractor beside the trailer-chassis combination when it would not have appeared to a person using ordinary care that such movement could be made with safety?

The jury then found that Keen's negligence was a proximate cause of the occurrence and contributed 50% to cause his injuries. The trial court disregarded these contributory negligence findings and rendered judgment in favor of Keen for the full amount of the jury verdict.

The question before this court is what was the nature of Keen's negligent conduct. In *Duncan v. Cesna Aircraft Co.*, 665 S.W.2d 414 (Tex.1984), this court adopted a system of comparative causation for apportioning accident costs. Although the changes wrought by *Duncan* were broad in scope, the opinion expressly noted an important rule that did *not* change. *Duncan* reaffirmed the rule of § 402A comment n of the *Restatement (Second) of Torts* that a negligent failure to discover or guard against a product defect is not a defense against strict liability. Thus, if Keen's conduct constituted a failure to discover or guard against a product defect, it is not a defense against the strict liability of Ashot and Strick.

* * *

What the evidence in this case shows is that Keen knew of the risk that trailers could sometimes fall. It was common for trailers to lean; and it was a recognized safety rule not to pull alongside a trailer in motion or one in the disengagement process. However, what Keen did not know was that this particular trailer had a defective sand shoe. As the jury found the facts, the trailer did not fall because of an unbalanced load but instead fell because the sand shoe was defective. Thus, Keen had no knowledge of the dangerous condition that caused the accident.

* * *

Keen's contributory negligence amounted to getting too close to a product which turned out to be defective. Because the nature of Keen's negligence was a failure to guard against a defective product, it cannot be used as a defense to reduce the amount of Keen's damage award. As we noted in *Duncan* when we affirmed this rule, consumers have a right to rely on product safety. We therefore hold that the trial court properly disregarded the jury's contributory negligence findings.

* * *

ON MOTION FOR REHEARING

PHILLIPS, C.J., dissenting.

By holding that Keen's admitted negligence is irrelevant merely because he "had no knowledge of the dangerous condition that caused the accident," the majority comes perilously close to requiring a defendant to prove assumption of the risk in order for plaintiff's conduct to be considered. Such an approach violates the language and spirit of *Duncan v. Cessna Aircraft Co.*, 665 S.W.2d 414 (Tex.1984). * * * Under *Duncan*, I believe that Keen's negligent conduct was more than a mere failure to discover or guard against a product defect. Therefore such conduct was properly considered by the finder of fact, and the judgment of the court of appeals should be affirmed.

Regardless of the result we reach in this case, however, I would change the law prospectively in one fundamental respect. I would abandon any further reliance on the outmoded concepts of comment n of Section 402A of the Restatement (Second) of Torts. Much confusion and uncertainty results when the fact finder is not permitted to consider a negligent plaintiff's failure to discover or guard against a product defect. I find little, if any, social utility to justify the effort. I would henceforth adopt a system of pure comparative causation, which would allow the trier of fact to consider all negligent conduct by all parties in apportioning responsibility.

FAILURE TO DISCOVER OR GUARD AGAINST PRODUCT DEFECT

Even under current law, I would hold that the harm caused by Keen's conduct was properly comparable with the harm caused by the defective product of Ashot Ashkelon. *Duncan*, 665 S.W.2d at 427. I disagree that this comparison was foreclosed by this court's reaffirmation of comment n in *Duncan*.

Comment n of Section 401A the Restatement (Second) of Torts provides:

> Contributory negligence of the plaintiff is not a defense when such negligence consists *merely* in a failure to discover the defect in a product, or to guard against the possibility of its existence. On the other hand the form of contributory negligence which consists in voluntarily and unreasonably proceeding to encounter a known danger, and commonly passes under the name of assumption of risk, is a defense under this Section as in other cases of strict liability. If the user or consumer discovers the defect and is aware of the danger, and nevertheless proceeds unreasonably to make use of the product and is injured by it, he is barred from recovery.

(Emphasis added). This comment identifies only two types of contributory negligence: (1) a mere failure to discover or guard against a product defect, and (2) assumption of the risk. Under this polarized scheme for labeling a plaintiff's negligent conduct, contributory negligence in the "mere failure" category in no way reduces recovery, while conduct in the "assumption of the risk" category operates as a total bar. Using this analysis, it is little wonder that courts labored mightily to fit an injured plaintiff's conduct within the former category. * * *

Duncan v. Cessna, however, presented a factual setting which did not fit neatly into either of the available categories of comment n. None of the parties contended that pilot Smithson was aware of the design and manufacturing defects in the legs of the cockpit seat, yet Cessna, a strictly liable manufacturer, sought contribution from Smithson's estate on the theory that his negligence as a pilot caused the fatal crash. *Duncan*, 655 S.W.2d at 418. Because those facts presented a third category of contributory negligence, we framed the question for decision as follows:

> whether a plaintiff's contributory negligence is a defense in strict liability actions when that negligence does not rise to the level of assumed risk or unforeseeable product misuse, but is more than a mere failure to discover a product defect. * * *

Id. at 422. Although this comparison was never made in a new trial because Cessna failed to preserve error, it is clear that waiver, and not the retention of comment n, was responsible for Cessna's loss. *Id.* at 434. And even though comment n was expressly reaffirmed, we held as follows:

> [T]he system we adopt will allow comparison of plaintiff's conduct, whether it is characterized as assumption of risk, misuse, or failure

to mitigate or avoid damages, with the conduct or product of a defendant. * * * Assumption of risk and misuse will no longer be separate defenses, but will be subsumed under the more familiar notion of contributory negligence.

Id. at 428.

Duncan, therefore, implicitly recognizes a middle category of plaintiff conduct not previously provided for in comment n: contributory negligence without regard to discovery of a product defect. This case fits squarely within this category.

The jury found that Keen was contributorily negligent in moving his hostling tractor beside the trailer-chassis combination. The majority concedes that Keen knew of the risk that trailers might fall and that he violated a recognized safety rule not to pull alongside a trailer in motion or one in the disengagement process. The jury was instructed to "not consider any conduct of the plaintiff which amounts only to a failure to discover or guard against a product defect, if any." As in *Duncan*, evidence of contributory negligence (here the safety rule violation) exists even though Keen had no knowledge of the product defect. But contrary to *Duncan*, comparison is not allowed. The majority has thus expanded the scope of comment n beyond that envisioned by *Duncan* and has retreated to a method of apportioning fault that predates our current comparative concepts. Under *Duncan*, the majority has erred.

PURE COMPARATIVE CAUSATION

I would, however, overrule that part of *Duncan* that reaffirms the viability of comment n. A relic from the pre-comparative fault-era, it unduly complicates our law without sufficient corresponding benefit.

Comment n was promulgated in 1965, before the advent of comparative principles in either negligence or strict products liability cases. In the emerging doctrine of strict liability, the drafters of the Restatement (Second) of Torts wisely attempted to avoid the unjust effects of the all-or-nothing concepts of contributory negligence by providing that only extreme forms of behavior would bar recovery under the new theory. The drafters thus drew a sharp distinction between aggravated behavior, i.e., assumption of the risk, which would prevent any recovery by a plaintiff, and all other unreasonable behavior, which would not. But the distinction was rooted more in fairness than in logic. As one recognized treatise states:

> Perhaps if comparative negligence had preceded the development of strict liability, contributory negligence would have been recognized as a defense that would diminish recovery in proportion to the percentage of the plaintiff's fault. But courts were operating under the all-or-nothing doctrines of common law.

W. Prosser & P. Keeton, The Law of Torts 712 (5th ed. 1984).

In *Duncan*, this court joined a growing number of states in sweeping aside generations of convoluted legal precedent and adopting a system of comparative causation for product liability cases in which at least one defendant is found liable on a theory other than negligence. The all-or-nothing concepts of contributory negligence and assumption of risk were abandoned in an effort to create a less confusing and more efficient system of loss allocation. Out of a desire to "protect consumer reliance on product safety", however, we did reaffirm the rule of comment n that "negligent failure to discover or guard against a product defect is not a defense." *Duncan v. Cessna*, 665 S.W.2d at 432. I believe that even this limited adherence to the old approach was a mistake.

The unfortunate truth is that everyday situations sometimes defy textbook classifications. This case is an excellent example of the difficulties that judges can and do encounter in deciding how to label particular conduct. Yet our choice of that label results in a substantial difference in the amount of the judgment. I suggest that finders of fact, with the best opportunity to consider all the facts and circumstances, should be allowed to analyze the relative contribution of the respective parties' conduct to the plaintiff's injuries. Under the broad form submission now mandated by our rules, the fairest results will be obtained by letting the finder of fact decide to what degree, if any, the plaintiff's own negligence has contributed to his injury. In short, I would hold that all of plaintiff's conduct which contributes to his injury should be compared to the defendant's liability, irrespective of the labels attached to that conduct. * * *

I am persuaded by the reasoning of the California Supreme Court in *Daly v. General Motors Corp.*, 20 Cal.3d 725, 144 Cal.Rptr. 380, 575 P.2d 1162 (1978). In adopting pure comparative causation, the court said:

> Plaintiffs will continue to be relieved of proving that the manufacturer or distributor was negligent in the production, design, or dissemination of the article in question. Defendant's liability for injuries caused by a defective product remains strict. The principle of protecting the defenseless is likewise preserved, for plaintiff's recovery will be reduced only to the extent that his own lack of reasonable care contributed to his injury. The cost of compensating the victim of a defective product, albeit proportionately reduced, remains on defendant manufacturer, and will, through him, be "spread among society." However, we do not permit plaintiff's own conduct relative to the product to escape unexamined, and as to that share of plaintiff's damages which flows from his own fault we discern no reason of policy why it should * * * be borne by others. Such a result would directly contravene the principle * * * that loss should be assessed equitably in proportion to fault.

20 Cal.3d at 736–37, 144 Cal.Rptr. at 386–87, 575 P.2d at 1168–69.

The "failure to discover or guard against a product defect" rule which today's dissent recognizes and today's majority expands is an anachronism. The continued retention of a rule which allows a plaintiff to recover full damages, even though concededly at fault, is inconsistent with comparative fault principles. Such a rule is unfair and inequitable in its operation because it places the entire burden of loss on one party when, in truth, two parties are at fault. As the court stated in *Pan-Alaska Fisheries, Inc. v. Marine Const. & Design Co., Inc.*, 565 F.2d 1129, 1139–40 (9th Cir.1977): "[T]here is no reason why other consumers and society in general should bear that portion of the burden attributable to the plaintiff's own blameworthy conduct." *Id.* at 1140.

* * *

WALLACE, J., joins in this dissent.

GONZALEZ, JUSTICE, dissenting.

* * *

I believe that Keen's negligence was more than a mere failure to discover or guard against a product defect. Since there is some evidence to support the jury verdict, the court of appeals correctly reduced Keen's recovery in accordance with the jury's findings on contributory negligence. I would affirm the judgment of the court of appeals.

* * *

* *ˑ* *Duncan* reaffirmed our prior adherence to that part of comment n of § 402A of the Restatement (Second) of Torts which provides that the contributory negligence of the plaintiff in failing to discover a defect, or to guard against the possibility of its existence, is not a defense. * * * Strong public policy reasons dictate that we continue to reject suggestions that we abandon comment n altogether in fashioning comparative causation schemes. As one court stated, "to penalize a consumer for failing to discover defects or to guard against them places a burden on consumers which strict liability was intended to remove." *Star Furniture Co. v. Pulaski Furniture Co.*, 297 S.E.2d 854, 862–63 (W.Va.1981). Thus, I advocate the continued adherence to comment n. However, it is unfair for the majority to ignore the jury finding that Keen's conduct fell below that of a person using ordinary care. * * *

* * *

The majority concedes two crucial pieces of undisputed testimony: Keen knew (1) it was very common for trailers to lean, and (2) it was a recognized safety rule not to pull alongside a trailer in motion or in the process of being set down because of the risk that it could fall and cause injury. In violation of this safety rule, Keen pulled his hostler alongside Moody's trailer while Moody was disengaging. Keen's co-worker, Moody, also testified that it was a recognized practice to park behind trailers which were being set down rather than alongside them.

* * *

* * * Keen himself testified he knew about a safety rule not to pull alongside a trailer because of the risk it could fall and cause injury. In disregard of this safety rule, Keen pulled alongside the trailer and was injured. From this evidence, the jury could have found that Keen moved his hostling tractor alongside the trailer-chassis combination when an ordinarily prudent person in the same circumstances would not have done so. It matters not that the cause of the accident was due to a defective sandshoe rather than an improperly balanced load, a windstorm, or some other type of occurrence which caused the trailer to fall. *The issue is not what caused the trailer to fall, but what caused the injury to Keen.*

* * *

The court in *Duncan* focused on the question of:

"whether a plaintiff's contributory negligence is a defense in strict products liability actions when that negligence *does not rise to the level of assumed risk* or unforeseeable product misuse, *but is more than a mere failure to discover a product defect.* * * *"

Duncan, 665 S.W.2d at 422 (emphasis added). Thus, it is clear that our court in *Duncan* recognized a middle category of plaintiff's conduct that is neither assumed risk nor a mere failure to guard against a product defect.

In *Duncan*, the pilot of the airplane was negligent in the manner in which he flew the plane, but he had no knowledge of the defect in the plane's construction. Yet the court plainly suggested that the pilot's contributory negligence would have been a comparative defense. Is it the majority's intent, without taking any notice of this matter, to reverse *Duncan*? Henceforth, will we require that an injured plaintiff have knowledge of the defect before his own negligent conduct will constitute a comparative defense?

Professor William Powers, Jr., in an amicus brief filed on motion for rehearing, presents the following illustration regarding *Duncan* and comment n. There are three categories of contributory negligence recognized in *Duncan*.

Category 1	Category II	Category III
Plaintiff is negligent *only* because he fails to discover or guard against the defect.	Plaintiff does not know of a defect, but is negligent without regard to the defect.	Plaintiff is actually aware of the defect (assumption of risk).

Keen's conduct falls into the second category. By failing to recognize this category of conduct, the majority has ignored *Duncan* and comment n, and has created uncertainty and confusion about the continued validity of the court's writing in *Duncan*. Furthermore, by disregarding the jury findings, the court has denied respondents their right to a trial by jury.

Notes

1. Under comparative negligence, most courts at least count a plaintiff's contributory negligence that is more than a mere failure to discover or guard against a defect. In addition to *Keen* and *Duncan*, see West v.

Caterpillar Tractor Co., 336 S.2d 80 (Fla.1976), and Busch v. Busch Construction, Inc., 262 N.E.2d 377 (Minn.1977). Some courts have abandoned the distinction in comment n and count all forms of contributory negligence. An example is Pan–Alaska Fisheries, Inc. v. Marine Construction & Design Co., 565 F.2d 1129 (9th Cir.1977), which Chief Justice Phillips discusses in his dissent in *Keen*.

2. If a court draws a line between two types of contributory negligence, it must apply the line to ambiguous cases. Was the majority in *Keen* convincing that the plaintiff's conduct was no more than a mere failure to discover or guard against the defect? What about a person who touches an overhead power line, knowing it can give a shock but not knowing it can kill a person? Does the difficulty of applying this rule argue for abandoning it?

Chapter 16

STATUTES OF LIMITATION AND REPOSE

RAYMOND v. ELI LILLY AND CO.
Supreme Court of New Hampshire, 1977.
117 N.H. 164, 371 A.2d 170.

KENISON, CHIEF JUSTICE.

The facts of this case are detailed in *Raymond v. Eli Lilly & Co.*, 412 F.Supp. 1392 (D.N.H.1976), and need not be repeated in full here. For the present purposes the relevant facts are as follows: On February 26, 1975, Patricia Raymond brought suit in Hillsborough County Superior Court alleging that C–Quens, an oral contraceptive manufactured and distributed by the defendant, caused hemorrhages in her optic nerves causing her to become legally blind. Arthur Raymond, the plaintiff's husband, sued the defendant for consequential damages resulting from his wife's blindness. The defendant removed the action to the United States District Court for the District of New Hampshire based upon diversity of citizenship of the parties and moved for summary judgment in both actions on the ground that the New Hampshire six year statute of limitations for personal actions, RSA 508:4 (Supp.1975), barred the claims.

The federal district court denied the motions for summary judgment applying principles underlying the so-called "*Shillady* rule" that "actions for malpractice based on the leaving of a foreign object in a patient's body do not accrue until the patient learns or in the exercise of reasonable care and diligence should have learned of its presence." *Shillady v. Elliot Community Hosp.*, 114 N.H. 321, 324, 320 A.2d 637, 639 (1974). Based upon Mrs. Raymond's testimony, depositions and medical records, the district court found that, although the plaintiff was injured in 1968, she did not know, nor had any reason to know of her potential claim against the defendant until "[s]ometime in 1970 or 1971," *Raymond v. Eli Lilly & Co.*, 412 F.Supp. at 1396, 1402, and held that her cause of action did not accrue until then.

[Rather than proceed to trial on the merits, the defendant made an interlocutory appeal to the United States Court of Appeals for the First

Circuit. The Court of Appeals then certified the question of interpreting New Hampshire's statute of limitations to the New Hampshire Supreme Court.]

The statute of limitations applicable in this case provides that "personal actions may be brought within six years after the cause of action accrued, and not afterwards." RSA 508:4 (Supp.1975). The statute does not define the word "accrued." In the absence of a statutory definition, the time of accrual is left to judicial determination. * * * There are at least four points at which a tort cause of action may accrue: (1) When the defendant breaches his duty; (2) when the plaintiff suffers harm; (3) when the plaintiff becomes aware of his injury; and (4) when the plaintiff discovers the causal relationship between his harm and the defendant's misconduct. *See* 3 R. Hursh & Bailey, American Law of Products Liability 2d § 17:9–10 (1975), *Developments in the Law–Statute of Limitations,* 63 Harv.L.Rev. 1177, 1200–01 (1950); Annot., 80 A.L.R.2d 368, 373 (1961). In many tort cases the above events occur simultaneously and the moment of accrual is clear. However, in some cases there may be a delay between the breach of duty and the injury, * * * or between the injury and the plaintiff's discovery of the cause of his injury, * * * or there may be a delay between each of the four events. * * * Where any such delay exists, the choice of accrual becomes complex. * * *

White v. Schnoebelen, 91 N.H. 273, 18 A.2d 185 (1941) involved a delay between the defendant's negligence and the plaintiff's injury. The defendant negligently installed a lightning rod in 1930. As a result, a lightning fire destroyed the plaintiff's house in 1937. The plaintiff filed suit in 1938. The defendant claimed that the limitations period began to run in 1930 when he allegedly breached his duty of care. The plaintiff argued that the cause of action did not accrue until 1937 when he suffered the damage to his property. We held that the suit was not barred by the six-year statute of limitations because injury is an element of a cause of action for negligence and the action could not accrue until all the elements, including injury, were present.

* * *

White did not involve, as this case does, the problem of accrual when there is a delay between the date of injury and the date upon which the plaintiff discovers the causal relationship between the injury and the wrongdoing. In fact, if anything, the *White* rule assumes that the plaintiff knows of the cause of his injury at the moment he suffers harm. With obvious reference to *White v. Schnoebelen,* we have stated that "[i]n the usual tort case some physical impact would serve to notify the plaintiff of the violation of her rights and there is no reason why the time within which her action for the resulting damages must be brought should not start to run from that date." *Shillady v. Elliot Community Hosp.,* 114 N.H. at 323, 320 A.2d at 638 * * *.

Because *White* did not address the question in this case, it is erroneous to assume that under the *White* rule Mrs. Raymond's cause of action would be barred.

On two occasions we have dealt with the problem of accrual where, as in this case, a person was harmed but did not discover that he had a claim against the tortfeasor until a later date. In a case in which the defendant fraudulently concealed facts necessary to put the injured person on notice of his claim, we held that the cause of action accrued not when the injury occurred, but rather when the plaintiff discovered or in the exercise of reasonable diligence should have discovered the concealed facts. *Lakeman v. LaFrance*, 102 N.H. 300, 303, 156 A.2d 123, 126 (1959). Similarly, in a case in which a surgeon left a foreign object in a patient's body, and the patient was ignorant of that fact, although the object did cause him pain, we held that his cause of action did not accrue until he learned or in the exercise of reasonable care and diligence should have learned of the presence of the object in his body. *Shillady v. Elliot Community Hosp.*, 114 N.H. at 324, 320 A.2d at 639. A substantial number of other states have reached the same conclusions in fraudulent concealment cases * * *.

The concept that a cause of action does not accrue until the plaintiff knows or should reasonably know of the causal connection between his injury and the defendant's wrongdoing has been called the discovery rule. *Lopez v. Swyer*, 62 N.J. at 272, 300 A.2d at 565 (1973). Those jurisdictions that have adopted the rule do not regard its application as violating the policies behind the limitations statute. *Wyler v. Tripi*, 25 Ohio St.2d 164, 170, 267 N.E.2d 419, 422–23 (1971). "A primary consideration underlying the statute of limitations is fairness to the defendant." 9 Suff.U.L.Rev. at 1455. "There comes a time when [the defendant] ought to be secure in his reasonable expectation that the slate has been wiped clean of ancient obligations, and he ought not to be called on to resist a claim when 'evidence has been lost, memories have faded, and witnesses have disappeared.'" *Developments, supra* at 1185. However, a person cannot be said to have been "sleeping on his rights" when he does not know and reasonably could not have known that he had such rights. *Wyler v. Tripi, supra* at 178, 267 N.E.2d at 427. By employing the discovery rule we avoid the harsh and illogical consequences of interpreting the statute in a manner that outlaws the plaintiff's claim before he was or should have been aware of its existence. *Shillady v. Elliot Community Hosp.*, 114 N.H. at 324, 320 A.2d at 639.

The discovery rule is based upon equitable considerations; in determining whether and how the rule should be applied we must identify, evaluate and weigh the interests of the opposing parties. *Shillady v. Elliot Community Hosp.*, 114 N.H. at 325, 320 A.2d at 639; *Lopez v. Swyer*, 62 N.J. at 274, 300 A.2d at 567. The federal district court has undertaken this task pursuant to *Shillady* and has concluded that the defendant's interests have not changed or been prejudiced in any way by the delay in this case. *Raymond v. Eli Lilly & Co.*, 412 F.Supp. at 1403. Before we independently weigh the equities, we will explain our understanding of what the rule means and then review the extent to which courts have adopted the rule in product liability cases.

One might read several discovery rule cases and conclude that the courts are applying two substantively distinct rules. In most cases the courts frame the rule in terms of the plaintiff's discovery of the causal relationship between his injury and the defendant's conduct. In some cases, including *Shillady,* a court will state simply that, under the discovery rule, a cause of action accrues when the plaintiff discovers or should have discovered his injury. Still other courts use both statements of the rule within the same case. The reason for these apparent differences is that in most cases in which the court states the rule in terms of the discovery of the injury, the injury is the kind that puts the plaintiff on notice that his rights have been violated. Thus, there is no reason for the court to express the rule in terms of the discovery of the causal connection between the harm and the defendant's conduct. In a case, such as the one before us, in which the injury and the discovery of the causal relationship do not occur simultaneously, it is important to articulate exactly what the discovery rule means. We believe that the proper formulation of the rule and the one that will cause the least confusion is the one adopted by the majority of the courts: A cause of action will not accrue under the discovery rule until the plaintiff discovers or in the exercise of reasonable diligence should have discovered not only that he has been injured but also that his injury may have been caused by the defendant's conduct.

One of the first product liability cases in which the discovery rule was applied was *R.J. Reynolds Tobacco Company v. Hudson,* 314 F.2d 776 (5th Cir.1963). Mr. Hudson smoked cigarettes from 1924 to 1957. He experienced severe trouble breathing two years before his suit. The tobacco company argued that Mr. Hudson's suit was barred by the one-year limitations statute because he knew of his injury more than one year prior to suit. The court rejected this contention holding that the cause of action accrued when Mr. Hudson learned or should have learned that his acute respiratory distress and diseased larynx were caused by smoking. 77 Harv.L.Rev. 1343 (1964). In *Breaux v. Aetna Casualty & Surety Company,* 272 F.Supp. 668 (E.D.La.1967), the plaintiff alleged that his consumption of a drug called Kantrex manufactured by Bristol Laboratories, Inc., caused him to go deaf and that the company negligently failed to warn him of the harmful propensities of the drug. The court cited *Hudson* for the proposition that the discovery rule applied in products liability cases and held that under Louisiana law the statute of limitations did not begin to run until the plaintiff knew or, as a reasonable person under the circumstances, should have known that there was a causal nexus between his deafness and the administration of the drug Kantrex.

* * *

The defendant argues that three cases in particular support its view that Mrs. Raymond's cause of action accrued when she first experienced difficulties with her vision, not when she discovered that the drugs may have caused the injury.

* * *

The second case, *Patrick v. Morin,* 115 N.H. 513, 345 A.2d 389 (1975), is clearly inapposite. In that case the question was whether the statute of limitations begins to run when the harmful effects of the defendant's discovered negligence first become manifest or when the plaintiff's ultimate damage occurs. *See Raymond v. Eli Lilly & Co.,* 412 F.Supp. at 1397.

Having reviewed the case law, we now consider whether adopting the discovery rule in a drug-products liability case would be equitable. *Shillady v. Elliot Community Hosp.,* 114 N.H. at 325, 320 A.2d at 639. We must focus on the defendant's reasonable expectation of the duration of its exposure to liability and the extent to which the defendant might be prejudiced by the loss of evidence due to the passage of time. *Developments, supra* at 1185. With respect to their expectations of repose, drug companies are unique among most potential tortfeasors. The harmful propensities of drugs are often not fully known at the time the drugs are marketed. These companies know or at least should expect that some time may pass before the harmful effects of their products manifest themselves in drug users and that there may be another lapse of time before the injured person is able to discover the causal connection between his injury and the drug he consumed. * * * Given these unique circumstances and the fact that the scope of a drug manufacturer's liability is substantial and seems to expand continually through the growth of substantive tort and warranty doctrines. * * *

[W]e do not think the drug company can reasonably expect to be immune to suit before its customer has a fair opportunity to discover the company's tortious conduct.

With respect to the problem of lost or inaccurate evidence due to the passage of time, several reasons exist why the potential for prejudice to the defendant is not significant in a drug case of this kind. Most of the evidence necessary to prove or defend against liability is likely to be documentary in nature. It is not the kind of evidence that is lost or becomes unreliable as time passes. Companies generally compile and maintain research records that document the extent of their knowledge of the harmful propensities of their drugs. Certainly, doctors and hospitals meticulously maintain and store records of patient treatments. * * * Additionally, unlike the situation in most cases, the passage of time in a drug case is likely to increase both the amount and the accuracy of the evidence—in this case the scientific community's knowledge of the causal relationship between certain drugs and injury or disease. Finally, we note that manufacturers are in a superior position to control the discovery of the hazards of their products. "Through the processes of design, testing, inspection and collection of data on product safety performance in the field, the manufacturer has virtually exclusive access to much of the information necessary for effective control of dangers facing product consumers. Indeed, the strict principles of modern products liability law evolved in part to motivate manufacturers to use this information to help combat the massive problem of product accidents." Owen, *Punitive Damages in Products Liability Litigation,* 74 Mich.L.Rev. 1258, 1258 (1976). We do not think that in suits such as the instant one "the passage of time would increase problems of proof or entail the danger of false, fraudulent, frivolous, speculative or uncertain claims." *Wigginton v. Reichold Chemicals, Inc.,* 133 Ill.App.2d 776, 779, 274 N.E.2d 118, 120 (1971). It is manifestly unrealistic and unfair to bar a tort suit before the injured party has an opportunity to discover that he has a cause of action, *Lipsey v. Michael Reese Hosp.,* 46 Ill.2d 32, 41, 262 N.E.2d 450, 455 (1970), at least in a case in which the defendant has not demonstrated that the delay itself has been prejudicial to him. In conclusion, the equities clearly support application of the discovery rule in this case.

One of the principal justifications for applying the discovery rule in medical malpractice cases is that it provides protection against substandard medical care. * * * Protection against the manufacture and distribution of harmful drugs is also desirable and necessary. The additional burdens placed upon the defendant by the discovery rule are justified if they cause the defendant to conform to a higher standard of care.

* * *

In a final attempt to prevent an affirmative answer to the certified question, the defendant argues that Mrs. Raymond's action should be barred because, even after she discovered her cause of action, she still had a reasonable amount of time within which to sue. The defendant takes the position that the discovery rule should apply only where the plaintiff discovers his claim after the statutory time has already expired or the time left within which to sue is unreasonably short. In so arguing, the defendant fundamentally misconceives the issue before us. Our task is to determine when a cause of action accrues. It is at that point that the limitation period commences. From that date the plaintiff is statutorily entitled to no less than six years within which to file his claim. If we adopted the defendant's position, Mrs. Raymond would have only three or four years from the date of accrual within which to sue, contrary to the explicit wording of the statute. A simple example further exposes the weakness of the defendant's argument. If a person injured in 1977 discovers his cause of action in 1980, he has, under the defendant's proposal, three more years or until 1983 to sue. If another person is injured on the same day in 1977 but discovers his cause of action six or more years after his injury, say in 1984, he has six more years or until 1990 to sue. This reasoning puts the late discovering plaintiff in a more favorable position than the person who discovers his claim relatively early. We cannot permit an interpretation of the word "accrual" to produce such illogical results.

Analysis of the case law and the equitable considerations cause us to answer "Yes" to the certified question.

So ordered.

DOUGLAS, J., did not sit; the others concurred.

Notes

1.   The opinion in *Raymond* examines several policies underlying statutes of limitation.   Do you agree that the discovery rule adopted by the Court in *Raymond* does not substantially undermine these policies?   In addition to evidentiary problems, does a manufacturer or its insurer also have an interest in "closing the books" after a specified period of time?   Is your answer affected by the fact that insurers must hold "reserves" to cover potential liability?

2.   Suppose Ms. Raymond knew that her blindness was caused by defendant's birth control pills, but did not know that the pills were defective (possibly because she mistakenly thought her reaction to the pills was an unforeseeable, extremely rare abreaction).   Or suppose she did not know that the law provides a remedy for injuries caused by defective products.   Would it be "fair" in either case not to toll the statute of limitation until she knew or should have known that she had a cause of action against Lilly?

3.   In a wrongful death claim based on products liability, should the statute of limitation begin to run when the decedent knew or should have known of the underlying products liability claim, or should it begin to run only when the decedent dies?   In Cowgill v. Raymark Indus., Inc., 780 F.2d 324 (3d Cir.1985), the court held that because a wrongful death claim is derivative of the decedent's underlying claim, the statute of limitation for the wrongful death claim begins to run at the time of accrual of the decedent's underlying claim, not at the time of the decedent's death.

In *Cowgill,* the plaintiff was the decedent's wife.   Suppose she tried to get her husband to sue before his death, but was not successful?   Should her rights be cut off by her husband's refusal to sue?   Should the result be the same if the plaintiff was the decedent's minor child for whom the statute of limitation would normally be tolled until majority?

4.   In a claim for contribution or indemnity, should the statute of limitations run from the time it starts to run against the original plaintiff or from the time the contribution or indemnity plaintiff's cause of action accrued.   *See* Morrissette v. Sears, Roebuck & Co., 114 N.H. 384, 322 A.2d 7 (1974).   *Morrissette* is reproduced at page 617, above, in connection with contribution and indemnity.

HEATH v. SEARS, ROEBUCK & CO.

Supreme Court of New Hampshire, 1983.
123 N.H. 512, 464 A.2d 288.

[Nine separate cases were consolidated for appeal to the New Hampshire Supreme Court.   Each case involved the application of New Hampshire's twelve-year statute of repose and two of New Hampshire's statutes of limitation to products liability claims.   The plaintiffs argued that the statutes violated the "open courts" and equal protection provisions of the New Hampshire constitution.]

DOUGLAS, JUSTICE.

* * *

The constitutional challenges in these cases focus principally upon the twelve-year "statute of repose" in RSA 507–D:2, II(a) (Supp.1979) and the three-year limitation provision of RSA 507–D:2, I (Supp.1979). Generally, both federal and State courts recognize the power of legislative bodies to enact statutes of limitations which prescribe a reasonable time within which a party is permitted to bring suit for the recovery of his rights. The United States Supreme Court has stated:

> "It may be properly conceded that all statutes of limitation[s] must proceed on the idea that the party has full opportunity afforded him to try his rights in the courts. A statute could not bar the existing rights of claimants without affording this opportunity; if it should do so, it would not be a statute of limitations, but an unlawful attempt to extinguish rights arbitrarily, whatever might be the purport of its provisions."

Wilson v. Iseminger, 185 U.S. 55, 62, 22 S.Ct. 573, 575, 46 L.Ed. 804 (1902).

The concept of allowing a reasonable period of time for suit to be brought after the cause of action arises is not new in our law, for along with "substantive rights, the first settlers brought over the incidental rights of adequate remedy and convenient procedure." *State v. Saunders,* 66 N.H. 39, 74, 25 A. 588, 589 (1889). Thus, the "right to an adequate remedy [exists] for the infringement of a right derived from the unwritten law." *Id.,* 25 A. at 589. When it came time to establish a post-revolution form of government, the first part of our Constitution was devoted to chronicling our inherent rights. Part one, article fourteen of the New Hampshire Constitution provides:

> "Every subject of this state is *entitled to a certain remedy,* by having recourse to the laws, for *all injuries he may receive* in his person, property, or character; to obtain right and justice freely, without being obliged to purchase it; completely, and without any denial; promptly, and without delay; conformably to the laws."

(Emphasis added.)

In an effort to facilitate the vindication of tort victims' rights, legislatures and courts have developed the "discovery" rule, under which a cause of action does not accrue until the plaintiff discovers or, in the exercise of reasonable diligence, should have discovered both the fact of his injury and the cause thereof. *Raymond v. Eli Lilly & Co.,* 117 N.H. 164, 171, 371 A.2d 170, 174 (1977); *see United States v. Kubrick,* 444 U.S. 111, 117–25, 100 S.Ct. 352, 356–60, 62 L.Ed.2d 259 (1979). The rule is premised on "the manifest unfairness of foreclosing an injured person's cause of action before he has had even a reasonable opportunity to discover its existence." *Brown v. Mary Hitchcock Memorial Hosp.,* 117 N.H. 739, 741–42, 378 A.2d 1138, 1139–40 (1977).

Although the legislature's power is broad in determining how long a plaintiff may have to initiate a cause of action and when that limitation period begins to run, this power may not be exercised in an unconstitutional manner. In *Carson v. Maurer,* 120 N.H. 925, 424 A.2d 825 (1980), we held that, although not a fundamental right, "the right to recover for personal injuries is * * * an important substantive right." *Id.* at 931–32, 424 A.2d at 830. Thus, the classifications there at issue were required to be "reasonable" and to "rest upon some ground of difference having a fair and substantial relation to the object of the legislation * * *." *Id.* at 932, 424 A.2d at 831.

In *Carson,* we ruled that the legislature's extension of the discovery rule to some medical injury plaintiffs, while denying its applicability to others, constituted an impermissible discrimination between classes of plaintiffs. We therefore held that RSA chapter 507–C (Supp.1979) violated the equal protection provisions of our Constitution to the extent that it limited application of the rule to only a narrow class of medical-malpractice plaintiffs. *Id.* at 936, 424 A.2d at 833.

More recently, in *Henderson Clay Products, Inc. v. Edgar Wood & Associates, Inc.,* 122 N.H. 800, 451 A.2d 174 (1982), we struck down RSA 508:4–b insofar as it precluded application of the discovery rule against architects, but allowed its application against materialmen and suppliers of labor. Relying upon *Carson,* we concluded:

"It is difficult to rationally permit a situation to exist whereby the supplier of labor and material has a liability exposure for a period of six years after the injury has been discovered or, in the exercise of due care, should have been discovered when, at the same time, the designers of the premises can be immunized from the liability before the cause of action even accrues or can be factually asserted."

Id. at 801–02, 451 A.2d at 175; *see* 26 ATLA L.Rep. 152–53 (1983).

Here, too, our standard of review is whether the statute-of-limitations provisions contained in RSA 507–D:2 (Supp.1979) are reasonable and are substantially related to the legislative objective of reducing products liability insurance rates.

RSA 507–D:2, II(a) (Supp.1979), the twelve-year "statute of repose," requires a products liability action to be brought not "later than 12 years after the manufacturer of the final product parted with its possession and control or sold it, whichever occurred last." The effect of this absolute limitation on suits against manufacturers is to nullify some causes of actions before they even arise. As compared with nonproducts liability causes of action, which generally must be brought within six years after they accrue, *whenever* that may be, *see* RSA 508:4 (Supp. 1981), we hold that the twelve-year bar imposed by RSA 507–D:2, II(a) (Supp.1979) is neither reasonable nor substantially related to the object of the legislation.

The twelve-year limit is unreasonable because the mere purchase of pills produced by a drug manufacturer in California, or of a defective automobile made in Michigan, does not place the consumer on notice of a hidden defect injurious to his health or safety. When product defects lead to injury, our law has long provided for recovery without regard to *when* the substance or object was made or placed into the national or international stream of commerce. This is particularly important in cases where the injuries may not clearly manifest themselves until years later, such as the clear-cell adenocarcinomas found in the daughters of mothers who twenty or more years previously took a female estrogen pill commonly known as DES (diethylstilbestrol). *See, e.g., Bichler v. Eli Lilly and Co.*, 55 N.Y.2d 571, 577–78, 436 N.E.2d 182, 184, 450 N.Y.S.2d 776, 778 (1982).

The unreasonableness inherent in a statute which eliminates a plaintiff's cause of action before the wrong may reasonably be discovered was noted by Judge Frank in his dissent in *Dincher v. Marlin Firearms Co.*, 198 F.2d 821, 823 (2d Cir.1952), in which he condemned the "Alice in Wonderland" effect of such a result:

> "Except in topsy-turvy land, you can't die before you are conceived, or be divorced before ever you marry, or harvest a crop never planted, or burn down a house never built, or miss a train running on a non-existent railroad. For substantially similar reasons, it has always heretofore been accepted, as a sort of logical "axiom,' that a statute of limitations does not begin to run against a cause of action before that cause of action exists, *i.e.,* before a judicial remedy is available to a plaintiff."

(Footnotes omitted.)

Nor do we think that the twelve-year "statute of repose" is substantially related to a legitimate legislative object. As previously noted, the crisis in products liability insurance had abated nationwide independent of RSA chapter 507–D (Supp.1979). Nonetheless, persons injured by defective products are deprived arbitrarily of a right to sue the manufacturers responsible for those defective products by virtue of a statute that has become entirely divorced from its underlying purpose. *Cf. Boucher v. Sayeed*, 459 A.2d 87, 92–93 (R.I.1983) (medical malpractice crisis existing at time of enactment but not at time of suit was insufficient basis to uphold statute against equal protection challenge). We do not believe that the legislature may constitutionally bar suits against manufacturers by products liability plaintiffs, as a class, twelve years after the manufacturer sold or parted with control of the product, while allowing other plaintiffs to recover for personal injuries not related to a defective product, at any time within six years after the cause of action accrues.

Our sister States of Alabama, Florida, and North Carolina have come to the same conclusion under similar provisions of their State Constitutions. [citations]

The plaintiffs also challenge the three-year statute of limitations established in RSA 507–D:2, I (Supp.1979). This three-year period begins to run from the "time the injury is, or should, in the exercise of reasonable diligence, have been discovered by the plaintiff." As previously mentioned, personal actions generally must be brought within six years of the time they accrue, with the exception of libel or slander actions, to which a three-year limit applies. RSA 508:4 (Supp.1981). We do not think that merely because a manufactured product causes the injury, or because the cause of action is legislatively defined as a "product liability action," *see* RSA 507–D:1, I (Supp.1979), a plaintiff's injury is therefore different from any other injury.

For instance, in the context of an automobile collision case, it makes no sense to say that for that part of an injury caused by another driver's alleged negligence a six-year statute applies while a product defect that may have been a factor in causing the harm to the plaintiff is subject to a three-year statute. Libel and slander were and are separate common-law torts which may reasonably be distinguished for statute of limitations purposes; however, there is no tort called "products liability."

For the reasons stated in our analysis of the twelve-year "statute of repose," we hold that RSA 507–D:2, I (Supp.1979) also denies products liability plaintiffs equal protection of the laws. This is not to say that the legislature could not constitutionally establish a statute of limitations of three years for *all* personal injury actions if it so desired. However, it may not constitutionally discriminate against one class of plaintiffs for the purpose of protecting manufacturers by means of a statute of limitations which is neither reasonable nor substantially related to a legitimate legislative object.

The last statute-of-limitations provision under attack in these cases, RSA 507–D:2, III (Supp.1979), requires third-party claims in products liability cases to be initiated within ninety days of the end of the time periods set forth in paragraphs I and II of that section. To the extent that the statute of limitations for third-party actions is dependent upon RSA 507–D:2, I and II(a) (Supp.1979), which we have already ruled invalid, we further hold that RSA 507–D:2, III (Supp.1979) is unconstitutional.

Notes

1. Several other courts have held that statutes of repose in product cases are unconstitutional, either under an "open courts" provision similar to Part 1, article 14, of the New Hampshire Constitution or under an equal protection provision of the state or federal constitution. *See, e.g.,* Perkins v. Northeastern Log Homes, 808 S.W.2d 809 (Ky. 1991)(construction)("discrimination"); Berry By and Through Berry v. Beech Aircraft Corp., 717 P.2d 670 (Utah 1985) (open courts); Lankford v. Sullivan, Long & Hagerty, 416 So.2d 996 (Ala.1982) (open courts); Diamond v. E.R. Squibb & Sons, Inc., 397 So.2d 671 (Fla.1981) (open courts); Kennedy v. Cumberland Engineering Co., Inc., 471 A.2d 195 (R.I.1984) (open courts); Nelson v. Krusen, 678 S.W.2d 918 (Tex.1984) (medical malpractice; open courts); Shibuya v. Architects Hawaii Ltd., 65 Hawaii 26, 647 P.2d 276 (1982) (architects and builders statute of repose; equal protection); Kallas Millwork Corp. v. Square D Co., 66 Wis.2d 382, 225 N.W.2d 454 (1975) (architects, engineers, and designers statute of repose; equal protection).

Not all courts have agreed, however. *See, e.g.,* Thornton v. Mono Mfg. Co., 99 Ill.App.3d 722, 54 Ill.Dec. 657, 425 N.E.2d 522 (1981) (open courts); Dague v. Piper Aircraft Corp., 275 Ind. 520, 418 N.E.2d 207 (1981) (open courts); Tetterton v. Long Mfg. Co., Inc. 314 N.C. 44, 332 S.E.2d 67 (1985) (open courts); Davis v. Whiting Corp., 66 Or.App. 541, 674 P.2d 1194 (1984) (open courts).

2. What, precisely, was wrong with the New Hampshire statute of repose? Would it have been upheld if it had applied to all personal injury causes of action, not just products liability claims?

3. Is the Court's reasoning in *Heath* consistent with the fact that special liability rules are applicable to products liability claims? In this regard, is strict tort liability itself subject to an equal protection attack?

4. Section 2–725 of the Uniform Commercial Code provides:

(1) An action for breach of any contract for sale must be commenced within four years after the cause of action has accrued. By the original agreement the parties may reduce the period of limitation to not less than one year but may not extend it.

(2) A cause of action accrues when the breach occurs, regardless of the aggrieved party's lack of knowledge of the breach. A breach of warranty occurs when tender of delivery is made, except that where a warranty explicitly extends to future performance of the goods and discovery of the breach must await the time of such performance the cause of action accrues when the breach is or should have been discovered.

(3) Where an action commenced within the time limited by subsection (1) is so terminated as to leave available a remedy by another action for the same breach such other action may be commenced after the expiration of the time limited and within six months after the termination of the first action unless the termination resulted from voluntary discontinuance or from dismissal for failure or neglect to prosecute.

(4) This section does not alter the law on tolling of the statute of limitations nor does it apply to causes of action which have accrued before this Act becomes effective.

Would this section be constitutional under the analysis in *Heath* ?

5. Shortened statutes of limitation and statutes of repose are samples of "tort reform" legislation, much of which is directed at products liability litigation. (Medical malpractice litigation is the other common target.) Common reform provisions include abrogation or reduction of joint and several liability, caps on damages generally, caps on non-economic damages (such as pain and suffering), and caps on punitive damages. Do these provisions violate an "open courts" provision such as Part 1, article 14, of the New Hampshire Constitution? If they were applied only to products liability claims, would they violate equal protection?

6. In Sax v. Votteler, 648 S.W.2d 661 (Tex.1983), a child plaintiff challenged a statute of limitation (repose) that, in medical malpractice cases, both abrogated the discovery rule and abrogated the normal rule that tolls the limitation period until a child reaches the age of majority. The Court

held that the statute violated the "open courts" provision of the Texas
Constitution. Although the case did not involve a products liability claim,
the Court's analysis of the "open courts" provision is instructive:

> Article I, section 13, provides: "Excessive bail shall not be required,
> nor excessive fines imposed, nor cruel or unusual punishment inflicted.
> All courts shall be open, and every person for an injury done him, in his
> lands, goods, person or reputation, shall have remedy by due course of
> law." While it is true that this provision is sometimes referred to as the
> "Open Courts Provision," it is, quite plainly, a due process guarantee.
> *See* Hanks v. City of Port Arthur, 121 Tex. 202, 48 S.W.2d 944, 945
> (1932).

* * *

Legislative action * * * is not without bounds. As early as 1932, this
Court recognized that article I, section 13, of the Texas Constitution
ensures that Texas citizens bringing common law causes of action will
not unreasonably be denied access to the courts. *Hanks v. City of Port
Arthur, supra.* In *Hanks,* this Court was confronted with an ordinance
that exempted Port Arthur from liability for injuries caused by defective
streets unless the city had received notice of the defect twenty-four
hours prior to the accident. The ordinance was challenged as being
violative of article I, section 13. In holding that the ordinance was
unconstitutional, this Court reasoned:

> As written * * * [the ordinance] applies to all persons who may be
> upon the streets; to children * * * [who] have the right to use the
> sidewalks. * * * Are we to say that a small child running an
> errand, or a small boy selling newspapers to help make the family
> living, who is injured by reason of a defective sidewalk, due to the
> negligence of the city, or by reason of otherwise actionable negli-
> gence of the city, cannot recover because the infant, or some one for
> him, has not notified one of the city commissioners twenty-four
> hours before the accident of the existence of the defect? Would that
> be reasonable? *Is the requirement of a thing impossible from an
> infant, or one incapacitated for any other reason, due process?* We
> think not; and yet it is a condition precedent to a recovery * * *

Id. 48 S.W.2d at 948 (emphasis added). *See* McCrary v. City of Odessa,
482 S.W.2d 151 (Tex.1972). In conclusion, the Court set out the test for
analyzing future violations of the open courts-due process provision: A
statute or ordinance that unreasonably abridges a justiciable right to
obtain redress for injuries caused by the wrongful acts of another
amounts to a denial of due process under article I, section 13, and is,
therefore, void. 48 S.W.2d at 948.

* * *

We reaffirm today the interpretation of article I, section 13, set out
in *Hanks* [and other cases]. In doing so, we note that the basis for the
Court's conclusion in these cases was that the litigant's right of redress
outweighed the legislative basis for the respective ordinances and statute. We hold, therefore, that the right to bring a well-established

common law cause of action cannot be effectively abrogated by the legislature absent a showing that the legislative basis for the statute outweighs the denial of the constitutionally-guaranteed right of redress. In applying this test, we consider both the general purpose of the statute and the extent to which the litigant's right to redress is affected.

Article 5.82 was enacted to establish standards for setting liability insurance rates for physicians and other health care providers. *See* Tex.Ins.Code Ann. art. 5.82, caption; Littlefield v. Hays, 609 S.W.2d 627 (Tex.Civ.App.—Amarillo 1980, no writ). Specifically, the legislation's proponents argued that the number and amount of health care claims had increased to the point that it was indirectly affecting the availability and quality of health care. This effect was due to the higher costs of medical malpractice insurance and its unavailability. The general purpose of the statute, therefore, was to provide an insurance rate structure that would enable health care providers to secure liability insurance and thereby provide compensation for their patients who might have legitimate malpractice claims. The specific purpose of the provision in question was to limit the length of time that the insureds would be exposed to potential liability.

In analyzing the litigant's right to redress, we first note that the litigant has two criteria to satisfy. First, it must be shown that the litigant has a cognizable common law cause of action that is being restricted. Second, the litigant must show that the restriction is unreasonable or arbitrary when balanced against the purpose and basis of the statute.

Texas courts have long recognized that a minor has a well-defined common law cause of action to sue for injuries negligently inflicted by others.

* * *

The second criterion we examine is the effect of the restriction on the child's right to bring his cause of action. A child has no right to bring a cause of action on his own unless disability has been removed.

* * *

If the parents, guardians, or next friends of the child negligently fail to take action in the child's behalf within the time provided by article 5.82, the child is precluded from asserting his cause of action under that statute. Furthermore, the child is precluded from suing his parents on account of their negligence, due to the doctrine of parent-child immunity. *See* Felderhoff v. Felderhoff, 473 S.W.2d 928 (Tex.1971). The child, therefore, is effectively barred from any remedy if his parents fail to timely file suit. Respondents argue that parents will adequately protect the rights of their children. This Court, however, cannot assume that parents will act in such a manner. It is neither reasonable nor realistic to rely upon parents, who may themselves be minors, or who may be ignorant, lethargic, or lack concern, to bring a malpractice lawsuit action within the time provided by article 5.82.

We agree with Dr. Votteler that both the purpose and basis for article 5.82 are legitimate. Additionally, we recognize that the length of time that insureds are exposed to potential liability has a bearing on the rates that insurers must charge. We cannot agree, however, that the means used by the legislature to achieve this purpose, article 5.82, section 4, are reasonable when they are weighed against the effective abrogation of a child's right to redress. Under the facts in this case, Lori Beth Sax is forever precluded from having her day in court to complain of an act of medical malpractice. Furthermore, the legislature has failed to provide her any adequate substitute to obtain redress for her injuries. *See, e.g.,* Middleton v. Texas Power & Light Co., 108 Tex. 96, 185 S.W. 556 (1916).

We conclude that as to that part of the cause of action for medical malpractice unique to the minor, article 5.82, section 4, is unreasonable. This statute effectively abolishes a minor's right to bring a well-established common law cause of action without providing a reasonable alternative. Therefore, we declare the limitations provision of article 5.82, section 4, to be in violation of article I, section 13 of the Texas Constitution.

648 S.W.2d at 664–67.

7. *See generally* McGovern, The Variety, Policy and Constitutionality of Product Liability Statutes of Repose, 30 Am.U.L.Rev. 579 (1980); Phillips, An Analysis of Proposed Reform of Products Liability Statutes of Limitations, 56 N.C.L.Rev. 663 (1978).

WILBER v. OWENS–CORNING FIBERGLASS CORPORATION

Supreme Court of Iowa, 1991.
476 N.W.2d 74.

HARRIS, JUSTICE.

An insulation worker's suit against an asbestos manufacturer for personal injuries was dismissed because of a two-year statute of limitations. The question involves the discovery rule. The worker knew for more than two years that he suffered from asbestosis, but did not know he would develop mesothelioma. The trial court determined the discovery rule did not excuse the late filing. We think it did and hence reverse and remand.

Donald Wilber, the insulation worker, brought this suit August 24, 1988. He died a month later and his widow Charlotte was substituted as plaintiff. From April 1941 to June 1976 Wilber was exposed to various asbestos products said to have been manufactured by the defendants. On January 31, 1984, Wilber was diagnosed as having asbestosis, a condition which was never the subject of claim or suit. It was not until August 1988, a month prior to bringing this suit, that Wilber learned he had developed mesothelioma.

We learned from the record made on defendant's motion for summary judgment that mesothelioma is a rare tumor arising from the mesothelial cells lining the pleural, pericardial and peritoneal cavities. The latency period of mesothelioma ranges from twenty to forty years. Unilateral chest pain and shortness of breath are the most common presenting symptoms of the tumor. Pleural mesothelioma, the type of mesothelioma that Wilber had, is a progressive malignant tumor. Most patients who are diagnosed with pleural mesothelioma die within a year of that diagnosis.

Asbestosis is a pneumoconiosis produced by inhaling asbestos fibers. It is characterized by bilateral diffuse interstitial fibrosis of the lung parenchyma. The most common symptom of asbestosis is dyspnea, which is shortness of breath.

Asbestosis and mesothelioma are separate and distinct diseases. Either disease can exist in the absence of the other. The diseases do share one common characteristic: both may be caused by exposure to asbestos.

The trial court sustained defendant's motion for summary judgment on the basis of Iowa Code section 614.1(2) (1989) (two-year statute of limitations for personal injury suits). The court determined that the claim was time barred because it was filed more than two years after the diagnosis of asbestosis. The district court reasoned that the statute of limitations began to run when Wilber became aware of an asbestos-related injury on January 31, 1984.

The trial court placed considerable reliance on our holding in LeBeau v. Dimig, 446 N.W.2d 800 (Iowa 1989). LeBeau was injured in an automobile accident. Although her injuries at first seemed minor, she was later diagnosed with epilepsy. Her suit, ascribing the epilepsy to the accident, was brought within two years of the diagnosis but more than two years after the accident. We were faced with the question whether to apply the two-year statute of limitations from (1) the accident (the first injury) or (2) discovery of epilepsy (the second injury). LeBeau, 446 N.W.2d at 801–02.

To answer the question we distinguished "pure latent" injury cases from "traumatic event/latent manifestation" injury cases. LeBeau, 446 N.W.2d at 802. Pure latent injury cases can be brought by plaintiffs who fail to discover either their injury or its cause until long after the negligence occurs. These cases, we said, arise in one of three situations: (1) actions by workers afflicted with occupational disease; (2) medical malpractice actions by patients who discover their injuries long after the treatment ends; (3) product liability actions brought by consumers of medically related products, such as drugs, who discover a side effect caused by the products. Id. The discovery rule is applied in these cases to prevent the unfairness which would result from assuming a plaintiff was aware of facts which were "unknown and inherently unknowable." Id. * * *

Wilber qualifies under the first situation as a worker afflicted with an occupational disease, and therefore can claim to have suffered a pure latent injury. But this in itself does not mean he can escape the statute of limitations because Wilber's injury also has characteristics in common with traumatic events/latent manifestation cases.

Traumatic event/latent manifestation cases are brought by plaintiffs who sustain both immediate and latent injuries from a noticeable, traumatic occurrence. * * * The plaintiff realizes that an injury has occurred and its cause, but the full extent of the harm has not become manifest.

Because we classified LeBeau's suit as a traumatic event/latent manifestation case, we refused to apply the discovery rule. * * *

Other courts have considered whether a latent manifestation of one disease, following an earlier diagnosis of another disease which stemmed from the same cause, is barred by the statute of limitations. A clear majority have allowed the subsequent action. Wilson v. Johns–Manville Sales Corp., 684 F.2d 111, 120–21 (D.C.Cir.1982) (earlier diagnosis of mild asbestosis did not cause claim for mesothelioma attributable to same asbestos exposure to be time barred). * * *

* * *

In urging us to adopt the majority view and allow the subsequent action, Charlotte [Wilber] is faced with our LeBeau holding. In LeBeau we mentioned the policy against splitting a cause of action. LeBeau had previously claimed and been paid for $200 in medical expenses which were paid without suit being filed, or even a release being given. In the present case, on the other hand, Donald made no previous claim but we think LeBeau's receipt of minimal medical expenses under the circumstances is not significantly different from Donald's election not to make a claim when he thought he had suffered only from asbestosis.

Authorities from other courts teach us that we can never know when, or how, some latent injury may manifest itself from exposure to asbestos. One study indicates that approximately fifteen percent of asbestosis sufferers will develop mesothelioma. * * * Selikoff, Churg & Hammond, Relation Between Exposure Between Asbestosis and Mesothelioma, 272 New Eng.J.Med. 560, 662 (1965)[ ]. Although we have no record on the matter, we think it is apparent that LeBeau had even less reason to fear later developing epilepsy. To some extent Wilber's higher likelihood of developing mesothelioma distinguishes this case from LeBeau especially when the focus is on the "reasonable expectations of a defendant as to when exposure to the liability will be terminated." LeBeau, 446 N.W.2d at 803.

Although it does not distinguish this case from LeBeau it must be remembered that Wilber could not have recovered for increased risk of developing cancer had he sued immediately upon learning of his asbestosis. It is well known that a showing of reasonable medical certainty is a predicate for recovery for future physical consequences.

* * *

We nevertheless think the discovery rule should be available in the present case. Statutes of limitations are designed to prevent fraudulent and stale actions, while still preserving a reasonable period of time in which to bring a claim. * * * They are statutes of repose affecting only the remedy sought, leaving the underlying cause of action intact. * * * Statutes of limitations are based more on necessity and convenience than on logic. * * * Legislation limiting the time for bringing an action has been primarily motivated by two considerations. Wilson v. Johns–Manville Sales Corp., 684 F.2d at 111. The first consideration is evidentiary in nature and involves the concern that, over time, the search for truth may be impaired by the loss of evidence. * * * The second consideration is the repose of stale claims against potential defendants who need to make plans for the future, which would be extremely difficult with the uncertainty inherent in potential liability. * * *

The Wilson court, faced with the precise issue we face, pointed out that these two considerations must sometimes yield to a more fundamental one. We quote and adopt the following:

> [I]n situations involving the risk of manifestation of a latent disease, unlike the mine run of litigation, the evidentiary consideration counsels narrower delineation of the dimensions of a claim. Key issues to be litigated in a latent disease case are the existence of the disease, its proximate cause, and the resultant damage. Evidence relating to these issues tends to develop, rather than disappear, as time passes.

Looking beyond repose and evidentiary considerations, we take into account the interests generally involved in personal injury and death cases: plaintiff's in obtaining adequate compensation, defendant's in paying no more than that. Integrating these two, the community seeks to advance, through the system of adjudication, relief that will sufficiently, but not excessively, compensate persons for injuries occasioned by the tortious acts of others. In latent disease cases, this community interest would be significantly undermined by a judge-made rule that upon manifestation of any harm, the injured party must then, if ever, sue for all harms the same exposure may (or may not) occasion sometime in the future.

* * *

Our LeBeau opinion, though cited with approval, was distinguished on the same basis in Potts v. Celotex Corp., 796 S.W.2d 678, 684 (Tenn.1990).

We conclude that our LeBeau holding should not cause us to reject the clear and proper majority view. The manifestation of asbestosis does not trigger the running of the statute of limitations on all separate, distinct, and later-manifested diseases which may have stemmed from the same asbestos exposure.

The judgment of the trial court is reversed and the case is remanded for further proceedings.

REVERSED AND REMANDED.

Notes

1. *Accord* Smith v. Bethlehem Steel Corp., 303 Md. 213, 492 A.2d 1286 (1985); Larson v. Johns–Manville Sales Corp., 427 Mich. 301, 399 N.W.2d 1 (1986). *Contra* Joyce v. A.C. & S., Inc., 785 F.2d 1200 (4th Cir.1986); Ross v. Johns–Manville Corp., 766 F.2d 823 (3d Cir.1985).

2. What, precisely, is the distinction between *Wilber* and *LeBeau*? What if a plaintiff suffered stomach pain and later discovered he had an ulcer? Had an ulcer, and later discovered he had cancer?

3. *See generally* Green, The Paradox of Statutes of Limitations in Toxic Substances Litigation, 76 Calif. L. Rev. 965 (1988).

Chapter 17

PARTIES AND TRANSACTIONS GOVERNED BY STRICT LIABILITY

This chapter addresses the problem of whether strict liability—mostly strict tort liability but also warranty—governs a particular claim. The chapter is divided into two sections, the first dealing with the types of defendants in the chain of distribution who can be held liable and the second dealing with the types of transactions that are governed by strict liability. The distinction between types of defendants and types of transactions is somewhat artificial, because defendants are often identified by the type of transaction in which they engage. For example, a case involving a chattel lease as a transaction might be analyzed as a case involving a lessor as a type of defendant. Nevertheless, some of the issues turn primarily on attributes of the party itself and its place in the chain of a product's distribution, whereas others turn primarily on attributes of the transaction in which the party has engaged.

In addition to raising an issue of practical importance—whether strict liability applies to a particular type of claim—the cases in this chapter also present a reprise of the policy considerations underlying the adoption of strict liability. A coherent theory of products liability requires more than general rationales for preferring strict liability over negligence, it requires rationales that explain the selective application of strict liability to claims involving product injuries. Because the cases in this chapter form the boundary between cases that are governed by strict liability and those that are not, they raise issues concerning the decision to treat product injury claims differently than other personal injury claims. As you read the material, you should consider whether the policy rationales underlying the adoption of strict liability apply to the case at hand with the same force as they apply to the paradigm product sale.

The cases in this chapter deal primarily with strict tort liability. Similar problems involving warranties, including Article 2 warranties, are addressed primarily in the notes. Some of them are also addressed in Chapter 4. Although a decision whether to apply an Article 2 warranty to a particular transaction might raise policy considerations similar to those raised by a decision whether to apply strict tort liability to the same transaction, the scopes of application of these two theories do not necessarily coincide. You should be cautious about extrapolating from one theory to the other. You should also look for the advantages of suing under one theory or the other that arise from the differences in their respective scopes of coverage.

SECTION A. PARTIES WHO CAN BE SUED

1. RETAILERS, WHOLESALERS, AND DISTRIBUTORS

VANDERMARK v. FORD MOTOR CO.

Supreme Court of California, 1964.
61 Cal.2d 256, 37 Cal.Rptr. 896, 391 P.2d 168.

[Plaintiff was injured when he lost control of his automobile and collided with a light post. He sued the manufacturer, Ford Motor Company, and the retailer from whom he had purchased the car, Maywood Bell Ford. After considering several issues concerning the liability of Ford, the court addressed the application of strict tort liability to Maywood Bell Ford.]

TRAYNOR, J.

* * *

Plaintiffs contend that Maywood Bell is also strictly liable in tort for the injuries caused by the defect in the car and that therefore the trial court erred in directing a verdict for Maywood Bell on the warranty causes of action. Maywood Bell contends that the rule of strict liability in the Greenman case applies only to actions against manufacturers brought by injured parties with whom the manufacturers did not deal. It contends that it validly disclaimed warranty liability for personal injuries in its contract with Vandermark[1] (see Civ.Code, § 1791; Burr v.

---

1. The warranty clause of the contract provided:

"Dealer warrants to Purchaser (except as hereinafter provided) each part of each Ford Motor Company product sold by Dealer to Purchaser to be free under normal use and service from defects in material and workmanship for a period of ninety (90) days from the date of delivery of such product to Purchaser, or until such product has been driven, used or operated for a distance of four thousand (4,000) miles, whichever event first shall occur. Dealer makes no warranty whatsoever with respect to tires or tubes. Dealer's obligation under this warranty is limited to replacement, without charge to Purchaser, of such parts as shall be re- turned to Dealer and as shall be acknowledged by Dealer to be defective. This warranty shall not apply to any Ford Motor Company product that has been subject to misuse, negligence, or accident, or in which parts not made or supplied by Ford Motor Company shall have been used if, in the determination of Dealer, such use shall have affected its performance, stability, or reliability, or which shall have been altered or repaired outside of Dealer's place of business in a manner which, in the determination of Dealer, shall have affected its performance, stability, or reliability. This warranty is expressly in lieu of all other warranties, express or implied, and of all other obligations on the part of Dealer."

Sherwin Williams Co., 42 Cal.2d 682, 693, 268 P.2d 1041), and that in any event neither plaintiff gave it timely notice of breach of warranty. (Civ.Code, § 1769.)

Retailers like manufacturers are engaged in the business of distributing goods to the public. They are an integral part of the overall producing and marketing enterprise that should bear the cost of injuries resulting from defective products. (See Greenman v. Yuba Power Products, Inc., 59 Cal.2d 57, 63, 27 Cal.Rptr. 697, 377 P.2d 897.) In some cases the retailer may be the only member of that enterprise reasonably available to the injured plaintiff. In other cases the retailer himself may play a substantial part in insuring that the product is safe or may be in a position to exert pressure on the manufacturer to that end; the retailer's strict liability thus serves as an added incentive to safety. Strict liability on the manufacturer and retailer alike affords maximum protection to the injured plaintiff and works no injustice to the defendants, for they can adjust the costs of such protection between them in the course of their continuing business relationship. Accordingly, as a retailer engaged in the business of distributing goods to the public, Maywood Bell is strictly liable in tort for personal injuries caused by defects in cars sold by it. (See Greenberg v. Lorenz, 9 N.Y.2d 195, 200, 213 N.Y.S.2d 39, 173 N.E.2d 773; McBurnette v. Playground Equipment Corp. Fla., 137 So.2d 563, 566–567; Graham v. Butterfield's Inc., 176 Kan. 68, 269 P.2d 413, 418; Henningsen v. Bloomfield Motors, Inc., 32 N.J. 358, 406, 161 A.2d 69, 75 A.L.R.2d 1; State Farm Mut. Auto. Ins. Co. v. Anderson–Weber, Inc., 252 Iowa 1289, 110 N.W.2d 449, 450, 455–456; Rest.2d Torts (Tent. Draft No. 7), § 402A, com. f.)

Since Maywood Bell is strictly liable in tort, the fact that it restricted its contractual liability to Vandermark is immaterial. Regardless of the obligations it assumed by contract, it is subject to strict liability in tort because it is in the business of selling automobiles, one of which proved to be defective and caused injury to human beings. The requirement of timely notice of breach of warranty (Civ.Code, § 1769) is not applicable to such tort liability just as it is not applicable to tort liability based on negligence (Greenman v. Yuba Power Products, Inc., 59 Cal.2d 57, 60–62, 27 Cal.Rptr. 697, 377 P.2d 897; see Rest.2d Torts (Tent.Draft No. 7), § 402A, com. m).

* * *

[T]he judgment in favor of Maywood Bell Ford is reversed.

GIBSON, C.J., and SCHAUER, McCOMB, PETERS, TOBRINER and PEEK, JJ., concur.

Notes

1. Comment f to section 402A states:

The rule stated in this Section applies to any person engaged in the business of selling products for use or consumption. It therefore applies to any manufacturer of such a product, to any wholesale or retail dealer or distributor, and to the operator of a restaurant.

2. The overwhelming majority of courts have followed the position taken in *Vandermark* and comment f by applying strict tort liability to retailers. In Sam Shainberg Co. of Jackson v. Barlow, 258 So.2d 242 (Miss.1972), however, the Mississippi Supreme Court refused to apply strict tort liability either to the retailer or the wholesaler of a pair of shoes. The court stated:

> We are unwilling to extend the rule of strict products liability in tort to the wholesaler and retailer under the undisputed facts of this case. These shoes were never out of their cardboard box, (original package) until the retailer transferred them from the box to a rack in the Jackson store. If there were a defect, as to which we express no opinion, it was a latent defect not discoverable by Shainberg–Jackson, or indeed by Mrs. Barlow herself when she looked at these shoes on the rack, tried them on, and decided to purchase them. Where the wholesaler or distributor purchases an article from a reputable and reliable manufacturer, sells it to a retailer in its original condition, and the retailer in turn sells the article—exactly as it came from the manufacturer—to a customer in the regular course of business, no duty devolves on the wholesaler or retailer to inspect and discover a latent defect.

3. Most courts have also held that strict tort liability is applicable to wholesalers and distributors. *See, e.g.*, Pittsburgh Coca–Cola Bottling Works v. Ponder, 443 S.W.2d 546 (Tex.1969); Keener v. Dayton Electric Manufacturing Co., 445 S.W.2d 362 (Mo.1969); Cooley v. Quick Supply Co., 221 N.W.2d 763 (Iowa 1974).

4. An *innocent* retailer or wholesaler who is held liable under strict tort liability can obtain indemnity from the manufacturer or other intermediate sellers in the chain of distribution. *See* Chapter 14. Consequently, the effect of applying strict tort liability to a retailer or wholesaler is to place responsibility on the retailer or wholesaler to seek recovery from the manufacturer or other sellers in the chain of distribution. This responsibility is not free of cost for the retailer or wholesaler, however. The retailer or wholesaler who is liable in the first instance faces litigation costs in seeking indemnity, and it bears the risk of the manufacturer being insolvent. To recover indemnity from a manufacturer, a retailer or wholesaler must prove that the defect existed at the time the product left the manufacturer's control. Consequently, the application of strict tort liability to a retailer or wholesaler places the burden of tracing the defect back to the manufacturer on the retailer or wholesaler rather than on the consumer.

5. Some state legislatures have enacted statutes that protect retailers from the application of strict tort liability. *See* Colo.Rev.Stat. § 13–21–402(1) (restricting the application of strict tort liability to manufacturers); Ky.Rev.Stat. 411.340 (protecting retailers from the application of strict tort liability if they sell a product in a sealed container); Tenn.Code Ann. § 23.3706 (protecting retailers from the application of strict tort liability if they sell a product in a sealed container).

Section 114 of the draft Uniform Product Liability Law provides:

(a) * * * in the absence of express warranties to the contrary, [non-manufacturer] sellers shall not be subject to liability in circumstances where they do not have a reasonable opportunity to inspect the product in a manner which would or should, in the exercise of reasonable care, reveal the existence of the defective condition.

(b) The duty limitation of subsection (a) shall not apply, however, if:

(1) the manufacturer is not subject to service of process in the claimant's own state;

(2) the manufacturer has been judicially declared insolvent;

(3) the court determines that the claimant would have appreciable difficulty enforcing a judgment against the product manufacturer.

Several versions of proposed federal products liability legislation contain similar provisions limiting the liability of retailers.

6. The applicability of the three warranties under Article 2 of the U.C.C. to various sellers in the chain of distribution depends on the type of warranty. An express warranty or an implied warranty of fitness for a particular purpose is applicable only to sellers whose words or conduct creates them. An implied warranty of merchantability is automatically applicable to all sellers in the chain of distribution who are merchants. These points are addressed in more detail in Chapter 4.

2. MERCHANTS AND PERSONS IN THE BUSINESS OF SELLING PRODUCTS

GALINDO v. PRECISION AMERICAN CORP.

United States Court of Appeals, Fifth Circuit, 1985.
754 F.2d 1212.

RANDALL, CIRCUIT JUDGE:

Georgia–Pacific Corporation operates a large number of sawmills and manufacturing plants. In 1978, Georgia–Pacific sold an obsolete sawmill trimmer from its plant in El Dorado, Arkansas, to a used equipment dealer. The trimmer was eventually sold to Moises Galindo's employer and was involved in an accident in which Galindo was severely injured. This appeal presents the question whether, by virtue of the 1978 sale and other sales of used equipment, Georgia–Pacific is "engaged in the business of selling" such equipment for purposes of the doctrine of strict liability for product defects under section 402A of the Restatement (Second) of Torts. We conclude from the record before us that unresolved questions of fact preclude an answer to that question at this point in the litigation. Accordingly, we vacate the summary judgment in favor of Georgia–Pacific.

I.

BACKGROUND

The few facts that have been developed thus far are not in dispute. Moises Galindo (Galindo) worked for Middlebrook Lumber Company

(Middlebrook) at a sawmill in Nacogdoches, Texas. On August 21, 1980, he suffered severe injuries while operating a sawmill trimmer. Galindo alleges that the defective condition of the trimmer caused his injuries. Following the accident, he filed this diversity lawsuit for damages under Texas law against several parties that he claims manufactured or marketed the allegedly defective trimmer.

Galindo's complaint alleges that Georgia–Pacific Corporation (Georgia–Pacific) once owned the trimmer that caused his injuries. According to the first amended complaint, Georgia–Pacific sold the trimmer to defendant Modern Iron Works, Inc., (Modern Iron Works) who in turn sold it to Middlebrook. It is undisputed that from 1960 to 1978 Georgia–Pacific in fact owned a trimmer similar to the one involved in Galindo's accident. Georgia–Pacific[1] purchased a new trimmer in 1960 and used it at its El Dorado, Arkansas, plant until 1978. In 1978, the trimmer was sold to Vincent Rice (Rice). If Georgia–Pacific's trimmer is the one involved in Galindo's accident, Rice must have sold it to Modern Iron Works who in turn sold it to Middlebrook.

Georgia–Pacific moved for summary judgment on the ground that, even if it sold the trimmer involved in Galindo's accident, and even if the trimmer is defective, Georgia–Pacific is not liable for Galindo's injuries because Georgia–Pacific is not engaged in the business of selling sawmill trimmers. According to the motion for summary judgment, Georgia–Pacific's sale of the trimmer was an isolated, "occasional" sale upon which strict liability may not be premised.

The district court granted summary judgment on the strength of an affidavit from Georgia–Pacific which avers that Georgia–Pacific "is not in the business of selling trimmers."

* * *

Section 402A imposes liability, without regard to privity of contract or the degree of care exercised by the defendant, on those who sell defective products that are unreasonably dangerous. Liability only attaches, however, if the seller "is engaged in the business of selling" the product that causes harm. Comment f to section 402A[7] makes clear

---

1. Actually, the trimmer was purchased by Reynolds & Draper Lumber Co., which owned the Arkansas plant in 1960. Georgia–Pacific purchased the Arkansas plant from Reynolds & Draper in 1969.

7. Comment f provides:

f. Business of selling. The rule stated in this Section applies to any person engaged in the business of selling products for use or consumption. It therefore applies to any manufacturer of such a product, to any wholesale or retail dealer or distributor, and to the operator of a restaurant. It is not necessary that the seller be engaged solely in the business of selling such products. Thus the rule ap-

plies to the owner of a motion picture theater who sells popcorn or ice cream, either for consumption on the premises or in packages to be taken home.

The rule does not, however, apply to the occasional seller of food or other such products who is not engaged in that activity as a part of his business. Thus it does not apply to the housewife who, on one occasion, sells to her neighbor a jar of jam or a pound of sugar. Nor does it apply to the owner of an automobile who, on one occasion, sells it to his neighbor, or even sells it to a dealer in used cars, and this even though he is fully aware that the dealer plans to resell it. The basis for that strict liability for product defects does not apply to "the occasional seller * * * who is not engaged in that activity as a part of his business." Comment f does not, however, create a test of easy application for distinguishing the occasional seller from one engaged in the business of selling. Our research confirms the district court's conclusion that Texas courts have yet to address this distinction in detail.

* * *

The district court determined that the Texas courts would exempt from liability, on an occasional seller rationale, those who sell "depreciated owner-user equipment * * * if the * * * equipment [was] used by the seller in its business and [is] not otherwise any part of a line of products or goods sold by the seller in its ordinary course of business." The court apparently concluded that Texas courts would reach this result regardless of the number of sales or the extent of sales efforts.[9] We cannot agree. To assess the validity of this determination, we begin with the rationale underlying strict liability for product defects. Comment c to section 402A provides the following justifications for strict liability: (1) those engaged in the business of selling products have assumed a special responsibility to the public; (2) the public is often forced to rely on commercial sellers and has a right to expect that they will stand behind their products; and (3) the commercial seller is better able to spread the loss caused by defective products. The Texas courts have not only adopted the rule of section 402A but have apparently embraced this statement of its rationale. *See Pittsburg Coca–Cola Bottling Works v. Ponder,* 443 S.W.2d 546, 548 (Tex.1969). The Texas Supreme Court has indicated that section 402A was adopted to further the goals of (1) equitable loss distribution and (2) risk minimization. *See, e.g., Duncan v. Cessna Aircraft Co.,* 665 S.W.2d 414, 425, 432 (Tex.1984) ("equitable and rational risk distribution [is] a fundamental policy underlying * * * strict products liability"; between consumer and retailer, retailer should bear the loss; between innocent retailer and manufacturer, manufacturer should indemnify); *Carryl v. Ford Motor*

the rule is the ancient one of the special responsibility for the safety of the public undertaken by one who enters into the business of supplying human beings with products which may endanger the safety of their persons and property, and the forced reliance upon that undertaking on the part of those who purchase such goods. This basis is lacking in the case of the ordinary individual who makes the isolated sale, and he is not liable to a third person, or even to his buyer, in the absence of his negligence. An analogy may be found in the provision of the Uniform Sales Act, § 15, which limits the implied warranty of merchantable quality to sellers who deal in such goods; and in the similar limitation of the Uniform Commercial Code, § 2–314, to a seller who is a merchant. This Section is also not intended to apply to sales of the stock of merchants out of the usual course of business, such as execution sales, bankruptcy sales, bulk sales, and the like.

9. Perhaps, by including the phrase "not otherwise any part of a line of products or goods sold by the seller in its ordinary course of business," the district court recognized that there may be circumstances in which the seller of retired equipment used in the seller's primary business is "engaged in the business of selling" the used equipment. If so, the district court nonetheless erred because the court did not inquire whether any of those circumstances obtain here. As we develop later, Georgia-Pacific's affidavit does not demonstrate that there are no remaining fact questions that are material to this issue.

Co., 440 S.W.2d 630, 633 (Tex.1969) (extending § 402A to bystanders "to minimize risks of personal injury and/or property damages"); *Hovenden v. Tenbush,* 529 S.W.2d 302 (Tex.Civ.App.—San Antonio 1975, no writ) (§ 402A applies to intermediate seller of used goods; rejecting representational theory of strict liability in favor of enterprise theory expressed in comments to § 402A).

It is clear that the rationale for imposition of strict liability is served only if the defendant is *in the business* of releasing products into the stream of commerce. The existence of a business justifies consumer reliance and the assumption that the seller has undertaken a special responsibility for product safety, and supplies the mechanism for loss spreading. According to comment f, "[t]he basis for the rule [that occasional sellers are not strictly liable] is the ancient one of the special responsibility for the safety of the public undertaken by one who enters into the business of supplying human beings with products which may endanger [their] safety * * *, and the forced reliance upon that undertaking on the part of those who purchase such goods." The comment provides two examples of occasional sellers: (1) "the housewife who, on one occasion, sells to her neighbor a jar of jam or a pound of sugar" and (2) "the owner of an automobile who, on one occasion, sells it to his neighbor or even sells it to a dealer in used cars." These examples involve "ordinary individual[s] who make[ ] isolated sale[s]," a category into which Georgia–Pacific obviously does not fall. The rationale expressed in comment f, however, reveals that the occasional seller category is not necessarily limited to such facts. At least on the face of comment f, the occasional seller category applies where sales are so infrequent or sales efforts are so minimal that it cannot be said that the seller has voluntarily assumed a special responsibility for product safety, that the public has the right to expect that the seller will stand behind the product, or that the seller is best able to spread the loss caused by the product's defects.

As we have already noted, there is no Texas case discussing in detail the requirement that the defendant be engaged in the business of selling the defective product. The district court based its analysis on the following prerequisites to section 402A liability which the court distilled from the Texas cases: "(1) [a] commercial or commercially based transaction is required" and "(2) * * * the source of the product must have more than a merely incidental relationship to the transaction, arising either because the product is one the source produces, distributes, or otherwise has a vested interest in placing into the stream of commerce, or because the manner in which the product is passed from the source to the user creates the comment f 'forced reliance.' " (Citations omitted.) Even if we agree that this is a fair summary of Texas law, we do not believe that it necessarily follows that "getting rid of the depreciated equipment used for production of the goods and services that constitute the business of the seller" can never constitute a business in which the seller is engaged.

The first principle upon which the district court based this conclusion—that a transaction must be commercial—simply means that the product must be made available to the consuming public. *See Armstrong Rubber*, 570 S.W.2d at 376 (stream of commerce means "release[ ] in some manner to the consuming public"); *Thate*, 595 S.W.2d at 598 ("[c]hannels of commerce implies that a product is placed for use by or sale to the consuming public"). Clearly, the sale of depreciated equipment may be commercial in this sense. The second principle—that the seller must have a vested interest in placing the product into the stream of commerce or must create forced reliance on the part of consumers—might also exist in the context of depreciated equipment sales. Suppose, for example, that Georgia–Pacific has a policy of purchasing new equipment at all of its sawmills every five years. Suppose further that Georgia–Pacific has a division or department devoted to selling the used equipment, that the department advertises the availability of equipment on a widespread basis, and that it realizes substantial revenues from this activity. Clearly, on such facts, Georgia–Pacific would not be exempted from section 402A liability simply because the equipment is used. In *Hovenden*, 529 S.W.2d at 302, the court rejected the argument that a seller of used equipment, as opposed to the manufacturer, cannot be held liable under section 402A. Significantly, the court reached its holding by specifically relying on the enterprise theory of liability expressed in the comments to section 402A. Moreover, we can discern no other reason why the rationale underlying section 402A would not apply to the hypothetical case we have described. On such facts, the consuming public might well expect Georgia–Pacific to stand behind the equipment it sells; Georgia–Pacific would have a vested interest in placing the equipment into the stream of commerce, and would be equipped to spread the loss caused by defective equipment. The rationale underlying section 402A's strict liability would apply to Georgia–Pacific to the same extent that it would to a used equipment dealer that did not happen to be the same entity that used the equipment in the first instance.

* * *

[O]ur review of the caselaw reveals that most of the decisions that have found the seller of depreciated equipment used in the seller's business to be an "occasional seller" involved a single sale or transaction in which the rationale for imposition of strict liability was lacking.[11]

* * *

11. *See, e.g., Bailey v. ITT Grinnell Corp.*, 536 F.Supp. 84 (N.D.Ohio 1982) (applying Ohio law) (summary judgment in favor of seller of single punch press used in seller's manufacturing business); *Siemen v. Alden*, 34 Ill.App.3d 961, 341 N.E.2d 713, 715 (1975) (summary judgment in favor of seller where "only sale of a saw or sawmill equipment was to plaintiff"); *McKenna v. Art Pearl Works, Inc.*, 225 Pa.Super. 362, 310 A.2d 677, 680 (1973) (summary judgment in favor of seller who, "in an effort to terminate its business operations, sold all its corporate assets"); *Daniels v. McKay Machine Co.*, 607 F.2d 771 (7th Cir.1979) (applying Illinois law) (summary judgment for lessor of entire plant which included an allegedly defective "hot shear" machine);

[W]e find no basis for the district court's conclusion that the Texas Supreme Court will ultimately determine that the seller of depreciated equipment used in his primary business will never be considered engaged in the business of selling such equipment. Rather, we believe that there may well exist circumstances in which, because of the number of sales or the extent of sales activities, a seller of depreciated equipment would fit squarely within the rationale for imposition of strict liability as it has been recently stated by the Texas courts. It would be premature on the record before us to attempt a definitive delineation of those circumstances. The relevant inquiry, however, is whether the seller's conduct would justify a conclusion that (1) he has undertaken a special responsibility for product safety; (2) the public has a right to expect that he will stand behind the product; and (3) as between the consumer and the seller, it is equitable to impose upon the seller the loss caused by the product and the burden of spreading that loss as a cost of doing business.

* * *

For the reasons set forth above, the summary judgment is vacated, and the case is remanded for proceedings consistent with this opinion. Georgia–Pacific shall bear the costs of this appeal.

VACATED and REMANDED.

Notes

1. Note that section 402A requires the seller to be in the business of selling the product that is allegedly defective. In *Galindo* the defendant was clearly in the business of selling products (lumber and paper products). The question was whether it was in the business of selling saws.

2. Section 402B applies to "[o]ne engaged in the business of selling chattels." Unlike section 402A, section 402B does not expressly refer to a person in the business of selling the chattel in question. No court has drawn upon this distinction. Is there any reason for distinguishing between section 402A and section 402B in this regard?

3. An express warranty under section 2–313 of the U.C.C. and an implied warranty of fitness for particular purpose under section 2–315 apply to any seller of goods who engages in conduct that creates the warranty. An implied warrant of merchantability under section 2–314, however, applies only to "a merchant with respect to goods of that kind." Why should the different warranties be treated differently?

4. In Sieman v. Alden, 34 Ill.App.3d 961, 341 N.E.2d 713 (1975), the court held that a sawmill operator who sold a saw was not a merchant with respect to saws. The court reasoned that even a person with skill and knowledge about the transaction is not a merchant with respect to an

Bevard v. Ajax Manufacturing Co., 473 F.Supp. 35, 39 (E.D.Mich.1979) (applying Michigan law) (summary judgment for "one shot" seller of press used in its business); *Luna v. Rossville Packing Co.,* 54 Ill.App.3d 290, 12 Ill.Dec. 115, 369 N.E.2d 612 (1977) (summary judgment for party who leased the only conveyor it owned to its own corporation); *Balido v. Improved Machinery, Inc.,* 29 Cal.App.3d 633, 639, 105 Cal.Rptr. 890, 895 (1972) ("one-time" sale of molding press). *See generally* Annot., 99 A.L.R.3d 651 (1980).

isolated sale. The court relied on comment 3 to section 2–314, which provides:

> A person making an isolated sale is not a "merchant" within the meaning and scope of this section and, thus, no warranty of merchantability would apply.

Sieman is set out at length in the material dealing with implied warranties of merchantability in Chapter 4.

3. EMPLOYERS

BELL v. INDUSTRIAL VANGAS, INC.

Supreme Court of California (In Bank), 1981.
30 Cal.3d 268, 179 Cal.Rptr. 30, 637 P.2d 266.

STANIFORTH, JUSTICE. **

Appellant William Bell was employed by respondent Industrial Vangas, Inc. (Vangas), as a route salesman. He was severely injured in a fire which occurred when he delivered a flammable gas to the premises of a customer—Long Chemical, Inc.

Bell brought suit, charging Vangas and Long Chemical, Inc., and others as joint tortfeasors with strict "manufacturer's" liability as that term has been defined in California products liability law. * * * He alleged they "were engaged in the business of designing, manufacturing, purchasing, producing, constructing, assembling, processing, preparing, testing, inspecting, maintaining, repairing, installing, endorsing, selling, leasing, bailing, licensing the use of, and otherwise marketing" defective products that proximately caused his injuries. The trial court finding no triable issue of fact, granted Vangas' motion for summary judgment on the ground Bell's exclusive remedy against Vangas, his employer, was workers' compensation. Bell appeals.

* * *

I

The finding of a triable issue of fact, however, does not ipso facto require reversal, for Vangas has a second, a legal, arrow in its quiver to support the trial court's grant of summary judgment. Vangas reasons: Bell was Vangas' employee, injured while engaged in his employer's work; he has already received a workers' compensation award and therefore is precluded from suing his employer for tort damages as a matter of law; workers' compensation is the "exclusive remedy"; "Pandora's box" will be opened, argues the employer, if Bell is permitted to sue; there is a recognized statutory "tradeoff" embodied in the workers' compensation scheme and to whittle away at one side of that equation is to upset a delicately struck balance.

To support its underlying thesis, Vangas points to judicial declarations to this effect: "In the most explicit terms, [Labor Code] section

** Assigned by the Chairperson of the Judicial Council.

3600 declares the exclusive character of the employer's workmen's compensation liability in lieu of any *other* liability to *any* person. Sections 3600 and 3601 form a complementary, unmistakable declaration of legislative policy * * * " [2] (*Dixon v. Ford Motor Co.,* 53 Cal.App.3d 499, 503, 125 Cal.Rptr. 872, quoting *Pacific Gas and Elec. Co. v. Morse,* 6 Cal.App.3d 707, 713–714, 86 Cal.Rptr. 7.)

* * *

What has come to be known as the "dual capacity" doctrine [4] was first recognized and applied in the landmark case of *Duprey v. Shane,* 39 Cal.2d 781, 249 P.2d 8, where Duprey, a nurse, sustained an industrial injury while employed by Shane, a chiropractor. Although he carried workers' compensation insurance, Shane and another chiropractor employed by him undertook personally to treat Duprey for the injury and, as it was found, did so negligently. This court upheld a recovery in an action for malpractice, reasoning that in treating Duprey, Shane was acting as an attending doctor rather than as an employer and that " 'the employer-doctor is a "person other than the employer" within the meaning of section 3852 of the Labor Code * * *.' " (*Id.,* at p. 793, 249 P.2d 8.)

* * *

Since *Duprey,* California courts have applied the dual capacity concept in a variety of factual situations.

* * *

In face of a claim of exclusivity of remedy under Labor Code section 3601, this court in *Unruh v. Truck Insurance Exchange,* 7 Cal.3d 616, 630, 102 Cal.Rptr. 815, 498 P.2d 1063, allowed an action at law against an *insurer* of the employer for assault, battery and intentional infliction of emotional distress based upon deceitful conduct in investigating the workers' compensation action. The *Unruh* holding that the insurer

---

2. Labor Code section 3600, excluding certain exceptions not relevant herein, provides: "Liability for the compensation provided by this division, *in lieu of any other liability whatsoever to any person * * * shall, without regard to negligence, exist against an employer for any injury sustained by his employees arising out of and in the course of the employment * * ** in those cases where the following conditions of compensation concur:

" * * *

"(b) Where, at the time of injury, *the employee is performing service growing out of and incidental to his employment* and is acting within the course of his employment.

"(c) *Where the injury is proximately caused by the employment, either with or without negligence.*" (Italics added.)

(F. & P.) Prod.Liab. 2d Ed. ACB—24

And Labor Code section 3601, insofar as relevant here, provides: "(a) Where the conditions of compensation exist, the right to recover such compensation, pursuant to the provisions of this division is * * * the exclusive remedy for injury or death of an employee against the employer or against any other employee of the employer acting within the scope of his employment * * *."

4. This concept assumes a logical[,] rational and legally self-evident premise. An individual can act in two or more different, distinct capacities, either simultaneously or sequentially, giving rise in law to separate and distinct sets of obligations. There is no fictional character, no need to create any "Doppelganger" to support the rule as long applied in California; only a recognition of a simple fact-one person can have separate and distinct legal personalities.

could be sued as a "person other than the employer" (§ 3852) was based upon the "dual capacity" principle enunciated in *Duprey v. Shane, supra,* 39 Cal.2d 781, 249 P.2d 8.

This court most recently in referring to the *Unruh* holding said:

"By analogy to *Duprey,* it was determined that the insurer in *Unruh* was 'invested with a dual personality' so that while it was performing its proper role within the compensation system it stood in the position of plaintiff's employer and was immune from suit, but when it stepped outside that role by committing an intentional tort, it 'became a person other than the employer' like the doctor in the *Duprey* case, and subject to liability at law * * *. *Unruh* involved the liability of the insurer as the alter ego of the employer * * *." (*Johns–Manville Products Corp. v. Superior Court,* 27 Cal.3d 465, 476, fn. 10, 165 Cal.Rptr. 858, 612 P.2d 948.)

Closest in point of factual application are the recent California appellate court cases in which the dual capacity doctrine has been applied to a defendant who occupied the dual positions of employer and manufacturer of a defective product sold to the public. In *Douglas v. E. & J. Gallo Winery,* 69 Cal.App.3d 103, 107, 137 Cal.Rptr. 797, the defendant—both an employer and a manufacturer of scaffolds sold to the general public—was held liable for damages in the latter role to an employee injured while using one of the scaffolds. And in *Moreno v. Leslie's Pool Mart* (1980) 110 Cal.App.3d 179, 167 Cal.Rptr. 747, an employer engaged in the selling of pools also was a "manufacturer"-distributor to the public of swimming pool maintenance products. The Court of Appeal reversed a summary judgment in favor of the employer where the employees' suit for damages was based on strict liability for a defective product.

Most recently, this court (*D'Angona v. County of Los Angeles,* 27 Cal.3d 661, 666–667, 166 Cal.Rptr. 177, 613 P.2d 238) applied the dual capacity concept, saying:

"Underlying *Duprey* is the rationale that if any injury arises from a relationship which is distinct from that of employer and employee and invokes a different set of obligations than the employer's duties to its employee, there is no justification for shielding the employer from liability at common law.

"*Larson* declares that the decisive test of dual capacity is whether the nonemployer aspect of the employer's activity generates a different set of obligations by the employer toward the employee."

This court then held:

"In treating plaintiff's disease the county owed her a duty separate and distinct from its duty as her employer, and this was the duty to provide medical care free of negligence—the same duty that it owes to any member of the public who becomes a patient at its hospital." (Id., at p. 669, 166 Cal.Rptr. 177, 613 P.2d 238.)

These principles parallel and support Bell's precise legal and factual claim here.

III

* * *

The purpose of the [Workers' Compensation] Act was to compensate for losses resulting from the risks to which the fact of employment in the industry exposes the employee. Liability under the Act is based, not upon any act or omission of the employer, but upon the existence of the relationship which the employee bears to the employment and because the injury arose out of and in the course of the employment. If the duty flows solely from the employment relationship and the injury "arises out of" and "during the course of" that employment, then the recited policy considerations behind the exclusive remedy in workers' compensation mandating that the employer be immune from tort liability have viability. If, however, an additional concurrent duty flows from an "extra" employer status or a relationship that is distinct from that of employer-employee and invokes a different set of obligations, then a second capacity arises and the employer status is coincidental. The employer should then be treated as any third-party tortfeasor, not immune from a common law tort action. To extend, to enlarge, the limitation on the injured employees' remedy beyond the purposes of the Act is to violate the spirit of the workers' compensation law. A failure to recognize the dual capacity doctrine in this case would accomplish such a wrong.

Workers' compensation laws were adopted long before a manufacturer's strict liability in tort—the *Greenman v. Yuba Power Products* * * * doctrine—came into vogue. Thus, there is no justification whatsoever for finding any legislative intent to adopt a scheme in 1911–1917 that would withhold from an employee the protection that *Greenman v. Yuba Power Products* now requires "manufacturers" provide every member of the using public. The "historic tradeoff" did not encompass the giving up of rights not yet in being.

Former article XX, section 21 of the California Constitution authorized the Legislature to enact laws to create and enforce liability for compensation to be paid by employers for injuries to employees. It did not, it does not now, expressly or by implication place any limitation on the amount to be recovered for injuries from parties other than the employer.

To accept Vangas' construction and application of these statutes would require this court to hold that employees are not entitled to maintain a products liability action against a manufacturer in circumstances where all other users of defective products could maintain such an action. By interpreting the workers' compensation law in harmony with product liability doctrine, a manufacturer will not escape liability to its employees for defective products where there would be liability to any other injured person.

* * *

The public policy goals underlying product liability doctrine should not be subverted by the mere fortuitous circumstance that the injured individual was an employee of the manufacturer whose product caused the injury. If the injured individual had not been an employee, he would have had a cause of action against the defendant. To deny Bell such a cause of action because he is an employee, gives the employer more protection than envisioned by the 1911 Act. In effect, the trial court rule would permit a manufacturer to test new products, utilizing his employees, and limit his liability from resulting injuries from a defective product to workers' compensation remedies. This is unsound social engineering grossly unfair to the worker.

One final thought germane to societal concerns with the rule selected: A most perceptive scholar has criticized those decisions refusing to apply the dual capacity rule, saying:

> "[This view] considers the dual capacity doctrine to be antagonistic to the perpetuation of the workmen's compensation scheme. This conclusion may not necessarily be warranted because, under both workmen's compensation or a consumer rights theory, the ultimate goal is to reduce the burden of recovery faced by the employee or consumer, and to shift any loss onto the industry that created the initial risk of injury. By rejecting the dual capacity doctrine, the employer is permitted to escape full liability for the defective manufacture of goods simply by using those goods in his own plant. * * * The employee, an intended and foreseeable user, must, therefore, bear the full loss under the consumer loss-disbursement mechanism, while a non-employee party can force that loss onto the manufacturer. Thus, a smaller loss will usually be shifted onto the industry through the worker loss-disbursement mechanism of workman's compensation than that which would be shifted if the consumer loss-disbursement mechanism were to be invoked." (Note, *Dual Capacity Doctrine: Third–Party Liability of Employer–Manufacturer in Products Liability Litigation* (1979) *supra,* 12 Ind. L.Rev. 553, 580.)

V

California's historic and current preeminence in applying the dual capacity doctrine must be contrasted with prevailing-weight of authority-views found in sister states. Without doubt, if Bell's case is to be decided by an arithmetic head count of jurisdictions that have considered the issue, the prevailing weight of authority would hold workers' compensation to be the exclusive remedy. (See *Douglas v. E. & J. Gallo Winery, supra,* 69 Cal.App.3d at p. 110, fn. 5(b), 137 Cal.Rptr. 797; 2A Larson, *supra,* § 7280, and 1979 supp.) [8]

---

8. Of greater significance than a counting of judicial noses is the trend of recent decisions from courts in jurisdictions with socio-economic-labor-demographic-historical characteristics more closely akin to California which have adopted the dual capacity doctrine. (See *Smith v. Metropolitan Sanitary Dist., etc.* (1979) 77 Ill.2d 313, 33 Ill. Dec. 135, 396 N.E.2d 524; *Goetz v. Avildsen Tool & Machines, Inc.* (1980) 82 Ill.App.3d

A close examination of decisions which refuse to apply the dual capacity doctrine demonstrates that these decisions come from jurisdictions that (1) have wide variants in statutory "exclusivity" language, (2) still adhere to our abandoned contributory negligence/assumption of risk rules, (3) stubbornly refuse to allow actions against a third party tortfeasor, and (4) flatly refuse to apply equitable indemnity or contribution principles in jobsite injuries.

Perhaps the clearest, most authoritative (outside California) exposition of the dual capacity concept is to be found in the United States Supreme Court decision of *Reed v. Steamship Yaka*, 373 U.S. 410, 83 S.Ct. 1349, 10 L.Ed.2d 448. There plaintiff's employer, a stevedoring company, leased a ship under a bareboat charter; the plaintiff, a longshoreman, was injured while loading the vessel. Although the plaintiff was entitled to his compensation benefits, he brought an action against his employer as charterer alleging unseaworthiness of the vessel. The employer defended on the basis of the exclusive remedy provision in the Longshoremen's and Harbor Workers' Compensation Act. Without using the dual-capacity terminology, the court's holding was consistent with the reasoning behind the dual-capacity theory. The employer was liable to his employee *as a bareboat charterer* for injuries arising from the unseaworthiness of the chartered vessel. The defendant had the duty as the bareboat charterer to provide the employee a seaworthy vessel. That duty was "traditional, absolute and nondelegable" (*id.*, at p. 415, 83 S.Ct., at p. 1353) and could not be avoided by the exclusive remedy provision of the Longshoremen's Act.

* * *

VI

* * *

The principle enunciated and approved by this court from *Duprey, supra,* to *D'Angona, supra,* compels the conclusion that a coincidental employment relationship will not shield an employer from a common law liability where the concurrent cause of the injury is attributable to the employer's separate and distinct relationship to the employee and which invokes a different set of obligations than the employer's duties to its employees.

A refusal to apply the "dual capacity" principles where facts fulfilling these conditions are posited by the complaint would constitute a specie of legal wrong in the form of an unjustified abandonment of long established, well reasoned precedent. Such refusal would as well inflict

1054, 38 Ill.Dec. 324, 403 N.E.2d 555, 559–560; *McCormick v. Caterpillar Tractor Co.* (1980) 82 Ill.App.3d 77, 37 Ill.Dec. 522, 402 N.E.2d 412, 414–415; *Mercer v. Uniroyal, Inc.* (1976) 49 Ohio App.2d 279, 361 N.E.2d 492); *Guy v. Arthur H. Thomas Co.* (1978) 55 Ohio St.2d 183, 378 N.E.2d 488, 490– 492; *DePaolo v. Spaulding Fiber Co., Inc.* (1979) 119 N.H. 89, 397 A.2d 1048 (a *Shook v. Jacuzzi,* 59 Cal.App.3d 978, 129 Cal.Rptr. 496, ruling [product not manufactured for sale generally to public]); *Toland v. Atlantic Gahagan Joint Venture Dredge,* # 1, 57 N.J. 205, 271 A.2d 2, 3.)

"a harsh and incongruous result" in the form of an inadequate recovery for injuries received.

* * *

Judgment reversed.

BIRD, C.J., and TOBRINER, NEWMAN and WIENER (Assigned by the Chairperson of the Judicial Council), JJ., concur.

RICHARDSON, JUSTICE, dissenting.

* * *

The so-called "dual capacity" doctrine originated in *Duprey v. Shane* (1952) 39 Cal.2d 781, 249 P.2d 8, wherein we announced a limited exception to the exclusive remedy rule. In *Duprey*, a nurse, injured in a previous work-related accident, sued her employer-physician for medical malpractice committed during the course of treating her injuries. We sustained the action, concluding that once an employer assumes the role of physician in treating the industrial injury, "the employer-doctor is a "person other than the employer' within the meaning of section 3852 of the Labor Code [authorizing tort recovery by the injured employee] * * *. In treating the injury Dr. Shane did not do so because of the employer-employee relationship, but * * * as an attending doctor, and his relationship to [plaintiff] was that of doctor and patient." (39 Cal.2d at p. 793, 249 P.2d 8 * * *.)

* * *

A substantial majority of cases which have considered the issue, including those of our California appellate courts, fully agrees with the foregoing analysis. Thus, in *Shook v. Jacuzzi* (1976) 59 Cal.App.3d 978, 129 Cal.Rptr. 496, the plaintiff-employee was injured while operating a machine used to manufacture automobile wheels. He attempted to recover tort damages from his employer based upon its allegedly separate capacity as "designer-manufacturer" of the machine. The *Shook* court observed that our *Duprey* decision was "readily distinguishable," stating that "In undertaking to treat the injured nurse [in *Duprey*], Dr. Shane assumed a role distinct in both time and nature from that of employer. Attempts to extend the rule of *Duprey* have been repeatedly rejected [citations]." (P. 980, 129 Cal.Rptr. 496.)

Similarly, in *Williams v. State Compensation Ins. Fund* (1975) 50 Cal.App.3d 116, 123 Cal.Rptr. 812, plaintiff-employee sought to impose products liability upon his employer on the theory that it designed, manufactured and supplied a defective spraying machine for use by its employees, thereby assuming a dual role as employer and manufacturer. The court properly rejected this theory, stating that "The analogy to *Duprey* is faint and unpersuasive. There the doctor-employer stepped outside his role as employer, elected to treat the injured employee as a doctor and subjected himself to malpractice liability. * * * [¶] Here there is no allegation that [employer] manufactured spraying machines

as a business enterprise separate from that employing plaintiff. * * * "
(P. 121, 123 Cal.Rptr. 812.)

* * *

I am convinced that the majority's adoption of the *Douglas* rule will
drive a substantial wedge into the exclusivity principle which has characterized the workers' compensation laws from their very inception. If an
employer is to be held civilly liable to injured workers in the employer's
capacity as a "manufacturer," what compelling reason can exist for
denying similar liability for injuries attributable to the employer's other
relationships including his status as "landowner," "motor vehicle operator," or "cafeteria proprietor"? Yet employers in our "pluralistic society" frequently assume multiple roles in the course of their ordinary
business pursuits. For over 60 years, however, so long as the injury
occurs while the employee is acting in the course of his employment, the
employer's liability properly has been statutorily limited to the payment
of workers' compensation in each of these situations.

The majority opinion, in extended fashion, emphasizes the social
policies favoring adequate recovery by injured employees such as Bell.
There is no reason to believe that the Legislature is insensitive to these
policies. Yet, the majority wholly fails to explain how we properly may
ignore the plain, specific, unambiguous language appearing in both
sections 3600 and 3601, statutorily mandating the exclusive remedy rule.
It is not our function to tinker with these laws for the purpose of
"improving" them. Moreover, if policy considerations were relevant
here, surely the exclusivity rule is founded upon a sound policy of
"reciprocal concessions," a policy which has been recognized historically
as underlying the entire workers' compensation scheme. Unlike the
ordinary consumer or user of manufactured goods, the employee-user
under the workers' compensation laws is given an assured protection
from impairment of earning capacity, and payment of medical expenses,
without regard to any principles of comparative fault (see *Daly v.
General Motors Corp.* (1978) 20 Cal.3d 725, 144 Cal.Rptr. 380, 575 P.2d
1162) or proof of defect (see *Barker v. Lull* (1978) 20 Cal.3d 413, 143
Cal.Rptr. 225, 573 P.2d 443) which are applicable in strict liability
actions.

* * *

I would affirm the judgment.

MOSK, J., concur[s].

Rehearing denied; RICHARDSON, J., dissenting.

KAUS, J., did not participate.

Notes

1. The dual capacity doctrine is an instance of a larger problem
involving suits by workers against their employers. As *Bell* indicates, the
normal rule is that an employee's *exclusive* remedy for a job-related injury is

to sue under the worker's compensation statute. Typically, a plaintiff need show only that his injury occurred in the scope of, and arising out of, his employment. He need not show that the employer was negligent. Damages under a workers' compensation scheme are often scheduled, and they are typically much lower than common law tort damages. This fact has caused injured employees to search for ways to escape the exclusive nature of the workers' compensation remedy. The dual capacity doctrine, whereby the employer-manufacturer is sued as a "manufacturer" rather than as an "employer" is one such device.

Another approach has been to sue the employer for an intentional tort, which typically is not covered by the exclusivity provision of the workers' compensation scheme. For example, would a decision by an asbestos manufacturer to subject its employees to asbestos without warning them of its dangers constitute a battery or an assault?

2.   The dual capacity doctrine has not gained wide support. *See* Atchison v. Archer–Daniels–Midland Co., 360 So.2d 599, 600 (La.App.1978), cert. denied, 362 So.2d 1389 (1978); DePaolo v. Spaulding Fibre Co., Inc., 119 N.H. 89, 397 A.2d 1048 (1979); Kottis v. United States Steel Corp., 543 F.2d 22, 24–26 (7th Cir.1976); Mapson v. Montgomery White Trucks, Inc., 357 So.2d 971, 972–73 (Ala.1978); Needham v. Fred's Frozen Foods, Inc., 171 Ind.App. 671, 359 N.E.2d 544, 545 (1977); Rosales v. Verson Allsteel Press Co., 41 Ill.App.3d 787, 354 N.E.2d 553, 556–57 (1976); Schlenk v. Aerial Contractors, Inc., 268 N.W.2d 466, 473–74 (N.D.1978); Strickland v. Textron, Inc., 433 F.Supp. 326, 328–29 (D.S.C.1977); Vaughn v. Jernigan, 144 Ga.App. 745, 242 S.E.2d 482, 483 (1978); Winkler v. Hyster Co., 54 Ill. App.3d 282, 12 Ill.Dec. 109, 111–12, 369 N.E.2d 606, 608–10 (1977).

3.   Consider an employee who is injured as a result of his employer's *negligence.* Would the employer have a dual capacity as "employer" and "negligent tortfeasor?" How does this differ from the dual capacity of "employer" and "manufacturer" in *Bell,* or the dual capacity as "employer" and "doctor" in *Duprey,* discussed in *Bell*? If a "negligent tortfeasor" and an "employer" constitute a dual capacity, what would be left of the exclusive nature of the remedy under workers' compensation?

4.   SUCCESSOR AND PREDECESSOR CORPORATIONS

BERNARD v. KEE MANUFACTURING CO., INC.

Supreme Court of Florida, 1982.
409 So.2d 1047.

SUNDBERG, CHIEF JUSTICE.

The issue we confront in this case is whether the purchaser of the assets of a manufacturing firm which continues under the same trade name the general product line of the seller can be liable for a defective product manufactured by the seller, even though the traditional corporate law rule would impose no liability. We adhere to the traditional rule.

I.

Petitioners, the Bernards, brought a products liability claim against respondent Kee Manufacturing Company, Inc. (Kee, Inc.). They claimed that a lawn mower manufactured and sold in 1967 by Kee Manufacturing Company (Kee), the predecessor business to Kee, Inc., caused an injury in 1976 to James Bernard, Jr., who with his mother sought recovery based on negligence, implied warranty and strict liability. Kee, Inc. had incorporated in 1972 when it had acquired for cash the assets of Kee from the owner, Flechas J. Kee, who did business as Kee Manufacturing Company. These assets included the manufacturing plant, inventory, good will, and the right to use the name "Kee Manufacturing Company." Kee, Inc., by the terms of this acquisition, had not assumed liabilities or obligations of its predecessor, Kee. The former owner of the business had no interest in the new company. Kee, Inc. used these assets to continue the manufacture of lawn mowers, maintaining the same factory personnel and using the trade name of Kee Mowers. The entire manufacturing process was effectively continued, but under a new owner and management. Kee, Inc. still provides replacement parts for the model of lawn mower involved here, though it has discontinued manufacturing the model. The brochure of Kee, Inc. states that it has been manufacturing lawn mowers since 1948. The Bernards have also sought separate recovery from Flechas J. Kee, individually, and from the retailer who sold the lawn mower.

The trial court granted Kee, Inc.'s motion for summary judgment, and this was affirmed by the District Court of Appeal, Second District, which refused to consider the financial responsibility of the predecessor to determine potential liability of a successor company, creating conflict with *Kinsler v. Rohm Tool Corp.*, 386 So.2d 1280 (Fla. 3d DCA 1980); Art. V, § 3(b)(3), Fla. Const. (1980).

II.

The vast majority of jurisdictions follow the traditional corporate law rule which does not impose the liabilities of the selling predecessor upon the buying successor company unless (1) the successor expressly or impliedly assumes obligations of the predecessor, (2) the transaction is a de facto merger, (3) the successor is a mere continuation of the predecessor, or (4) the transaction is a fraudulent effort to avoid liabilities of the predecessor. * * * The general corporate law rule applies to products liability. * * *

Courts in a few jurisdictions have begun to extend products liability to the successor corporation in an effort to effectuate an acknowledged purpose of strict liability for defective products, that the costs of a defective product should be included in that product. A first series of cases, led by *Cyr v. B. Offen & Co.*, 501 F.2d 1145 (1st Cir.1974), has expanded the continuity exception to the traditional rule by deleting a historical requirement of substantial identity of ownership. *Turner v. Bituminous Casualty Co.*, 397 Mich. 406, 244 N.W.2d 873 (1976), followed *Cyr* in expanding this exception. A second line of cases, begun by *Ray v. Alad Corp.*, 19 Cal.3d 22, 136 Cal.Rptr. 574, 560 P.2d 3 (1977), developed a new exception to the general rule of a corporate successor's non-liability, the product-line exception:

[A] party which acquires a manufacturing business and continues the output of its line of products * * * assumes strict tort liability for defects in units of the same product line previously manufactured and distributed by the entity from which the business was acquired.

Id. at 34, 136 Cal.Rptr. at 582, 560 P.2d at 11.

This rule has been adopted by only two other jurisdictions. *Ramirez v. Amsted Industries, Inc.,* 86 N.J. 332, 431 A.2d 811 (1981); *Dawejko v. Jorgensen Steel Co.,* 290 Pa.Super. 15, 434 A.2d 106 (1981). The courts in these cases based justification of the product-line exception on (1) the lack of remedy for the plaintiff, (2) the successor's ability to spread the risk through insurance by estimating risks in the previously manufactured product, and (3) the fairness of requiring the successor to assume the burdens as well as the benefits of the original manufacturer's good will. Though these justifications have undeniable appeal, we find countervailing considerations more convincing.

III.

We choose not to join this vanguard of courts, due in part to the threat of economic annihilation that small businesses would face under such a rule of expanded liability. Because of their limited assets, small corporations would face financial destruction from imposition of liability for their predecessor's products:

> The economy as a whole suffers when small successor corporations lose such cases since corporate acquisitions are discouraged due to business planners' fears of being held so liable. Furthermore, the marketability of on-going corporations is diminished, perhaps forcing the sellers into the undesirable process of liquidation proceedings. Currently, small manufacturing corporations comprise ninety percent of the nation's manufacturing enterprises. If small manufacturing corporations liquidate rather than transfer ownership, the chances that the corporations will be replaced by other successful small corporations are decreased. As a result, there will be fewer small manufacturers and the larger more centralized manufacturers will increase their production to meet the demands of the marketplace. Greater centralization of business is adverse to the long held American notion that the small business represents independence, freedom and perseverance.[2]

One court has dubbed these concerns "cassandrian."[3] But due to the recognized difficulty and high costs that a small business experiences in obtaining products liability insurance for defects in a predecessor's product,[4] we perceive the increased burden on small business as a very

2. Note, *Products Liability and Successor Corporations: Protecting the Product User and the Small Manufacturer Through Increased Availability of Products Liability Insurance,* 13 U.Calif. Davis L.Rev. 1000, 1002–3 (1980) (footnotes omitted).

3. *See Turner,* 397 Mich. at 428, 244 N.W.2d at 883.

4. *See Products Liability and Successor Corporations, supra* note 3, at 1024–25 & nn. 90–96.

real threat, as real a threat as the Trojan Horse.[5]

> instamus tamen inmemores caecique furore, et monstrum infelix
> sacrata sistimus arce.tunc etiam fatis aperit Cassandra futuris ora,
> dei iussu non umquam credita Teucris. [Nevertheless, we struggle
> madly, without thought or sight, to plant the ruinous monster
> within our holy citadel. Even now Cassandra reveals our overhang-
> ing doom, and as before we ignore her words by the gods' fiat.]

2 Virgil, The Aeneid 30, lines 244–47 (T. Page ed. 1967).

Although we do not consider that the legislature is alone suited to make the determination of whether successor corporate liability should be extended,[6] we do perceive other legitimate policy considerations for refusing to expand such liability. Extending liability to the corporate successor is not consistent with at least one major premise of strict liability, which is to place responsibility for a defective product on the manufacturer who placed that product into commerce. The corporate successor has not created the risk, and only remotely benefits from the product. The successor has not invited usage of the product or implied its safety. Since the successor was never in a position to eliminate the risk, a major purpose of strict liability in modifying a manufacturer's behavior is also lost. *See Domine v. Fulton Iron Works,* 76 Ill.App.3d 253, 32 Ill.Dec. 72, 395 N.E.2d 19 (1979); *see also Tucker v. Paxson Machine Co.,* 645 F.2d 620 (8th Cir.1981) (refuses to follow product-line exception because not well established); *Leannais v. Cincinnati, Inc.,* 565 F.2d at 441 n. 8 (refuses to expand corporate law rule).[7]

For these reasons we adhere to the traditional corporate law rule, and approve the decision of the District Court of Appeal, Second District, in this case, other than its deference to the legislature. *Bernard v. Kee Manufacturing Co., Inc.,* 394 So.2d 552 (Fla. 2d DCA 1981). On the other hand *Kinsler v. Rohm Tool Corp.,* 386 So.2d 1230 (Fla. 3d DCA 1980), looked at the financial responsibility of the predecessor to determine the successor's liability and thus expanded the corporate law rule.

---

5. In passing we note that Cassandra, although predicting disaster, was unerringly accurate. Her lot was to be unbelieved and to know her prophecies were ineluctable.

6. *See Leannais v. Cincinnati, Inc.,* 565 F.2d at 441; *Bernard v. Kee Mfg. Co., Inc.,* 394 So.2d 552, 555 (Fla. 2d DCA 1981).

7. Several courts have also recognized that the sale of a sole proprietorship to a successor corporation does not justify expanding successor liability since the selling entity does not disappear as could a selling corporation. Kee, the selling entity, appears to have been a sole proprietorship, based upon Flechas J. Kee's signing individually the agreement for sale and purchase of assets and not as a corporate officer. Even in Michigan, which has adopted an expanded interpretation of successor corporate liability in *Turner,* an appellate court did not find imposition of successor liability was warranted when the seller was a sole proprietorship. *Lemire v. Garrard Drugs,* 95 Mich.App. 520, 291 N.W.2d 103 (1980). A Wisconsin appellate court has similarly refused to adopt the product-line exception or expand the continuation exception where a sole proprietorship was the selling entity, because the sole proprietorship could still be liable for manufacture of the defective product. *Tift v. Forge King Indus., Inc.,* 102 Wis.2d 327, 306 N.W.2d 289 (Wis.App. 1981). *Tift* noted that no case had expanded the general rule under these circumstances, distinguishing *Cyr v. B. Offen & Co.* because their former employees of the sole proprietorship bought and continued the business. *Tift,* 102 Wis. at 330, 306 N.W.2d at 291.

We disapprove that conflicting decision insofar as it is inconsistent with our opinion.

It is so ordered.

BOYD, OVERTON, ALDERMAN and McDONALD, JJ., concur.

ADKINS, J., dissents.

Notes

1.   As *Bernard* indicates, the leading case recognizing the product line exception to the normal rule of no liability is Ray v. Alad Corp., 19 Cal.3d 22, 136 Cal.Rptr. 574, 560 P.2d 3 (1977):

* * *

Our discussion of the law starts with the rule ordinarily applied to the determination of whether a corporation purchasing the principal assets of another corporation assumes the other's liabilities.   As typically formulated the rule states that the purchaser does not assume the seller's liabilities unless (1) there is an express or implied agreement of assumption, (2) the transaction amounts to a consolidation or merger of the two corporations, (3) the purchasing corporation is a mere continuation of the seller, or (4) the transfer of assets to the purchaser is for the fraudulent purpose of escaping liability for the seller's debts.

* * *

If this rule were determinative of Alad II's liability to plaintiff it would require us to affirm the summary judgment.   None of the rule's four stated grounds for imposing liability on the purchasing corporation is present here.   There was no express or implied agreement to assume liability for injury from defective products previously manufactured by Alad I.   Nor is there any indication or contention that the transaction was prompted by any fraudulent purpose of escaping liability for Alad I's debts.

* * *

Plaintiff relies on Cyr v. B. Offen & Co., Inc. (1st Cir.1974) 501 F.2d 1145, 1152, where tort liability for injury from a defective product manufactured by an enterprise whose assets a corporation had acquired for adequate consideration in an arm's-length transaction was imposed on the corporation as a mere continuation of the enterprise.   We hereafter refer to the *Cyr* case as helpful authority on the separate issue of what if any *special* rule should be applicable to a successor corporation's *tort* liability for its predecessor's *defective products*.   We disagree, however, with any implication in *Cyr* or contention by plaintiff that the settled rule governing a corporation's succession to its predecessor's liabilities *generally* should be modified so as to require such succession merely because of the factors of continuity present in *Cyr* and in the instant case.

We therefore conclude that the general rule governing succession to liabilities does not require Alad II to respond to plaintiff's claim.   * * *

[W]e must decide whether the policies underlying strict tort liability for defective products call for a special exception to the rule that would otherwise insulate the present defendant from plaintiff's claim.

* * *

The purpose of the rule of strict tort liability "is to insure that the costs of injuries resulting from defective products are borne by the manufacturers that put such products on the market rather than by the injured persons who are powerless to protect themselves." (Greenman v. Yuba Power Products, Inc. (1963) 59 Cal.2d 57, 63, 27 Cal.Rptr. 697, 701, 377 P.2d 897, 901.) However, the rule "does not rest on the analysis of the financial strength or bargaining power of the parties to the particular action. It rests, rather, on the proposition that '[t]he cost of an injury and the loss of time or health may be an overwhelming misfortune to the person injured, and a needless one, for the risk of injury can be insured by the manufacturer and distributed among the public as a cost of doing business.' (Escola v. Coca Cola Bottling Co., 24 Cal.2d 453, 462, 150 P.2d 436 [concurring opinion].)" (Seeley v. White Motor Co. (1965) 63 Cal.2d 9, 18–19, 45 Cal.Rptr. 17, 23, 403 P.2d 145, 151.) Thus, "the paramount policy to be promoted by the rule is the protection of otherwise defenseless victims of manufacturing defects and the *spreading throughout society* of the cost of compensating them." (Italics added.) Price v. Shell Oil Co. (1970) 2 Cal.3d 245, 251, 85 Cal.Rptr. 178, 181, 466 P.2d 722, 725.) Justification for imposing strict liability upon a *successor* to a manufacturer under the circumstances here presented rests upon (1) the virtual destruction of the plaintiff's remedies against the original manufacturer caused by the successor's acquisition of the business, (2) the successor's ability to assume the original manufacturer's risk-spreading r[o]le, and (3) the fairness of requiring the successor to assume a responsibility for defective products that was a burden necessarily attached to the original manufacturer's good will being enjoyed by the successor in the continued operation of the business. We turn to a consideration of each of these aspects in the context of the present case.

We must assume for purposes of the present proceeding that plaintiff was injured as a result of defects in a ladder manufactured by Alad I and therefore could assert strict tort liability against Alad I under the rule of Greenman v. Yuba Power Products, Inc., *supra,* 59 Cal.2d 57, 27 Cal.Rptr. 697, 377 P.2d 897. However, the practical value of this right of recovery against the original manufacturer was vitiated by the purchase of Alad I's tangible assets, trade name and good will on behalf of Alad II * * * and the dissolution of Alad I within two months thereafter in accordance with the purchase agreement. The injury giving rise to plaintiff's claim against Alad I did not occur until more than six months after the filing of the dissolution certificate declaring that Alad I's "known debts and liabilities have been actually paid" and its "known assets have been distributed to its shareholders." This distribution of assets was perfectly proper as there was no requirement that provision be made for claims such as plaintiff's that had not yet come into existence.[5] Thus, even if plaintiff could obtain a judgment on his claim against the dissolved and assetless Alad I (see Corp.Code, former § 5400, now § 2010, subd. (a)) he would face formidable and probably insuperable obstacles in attempting to obtain satisfaction of the judgment from former stockholders or directors.

* * *

These barriers to plaintiff's obtaining redress from the dissolved Alad I set him and similarly situated victims of defective products apart from persons entitled to recovery against a dissolved corporation on claims that were capable of being known at the time of its dissolution. Application to such victims of the general rule that immunizes Alad I's successor from the general run of its debts would create a far greater likelihood of complete denial of redress for a legitimate claim than would the rule's application to most other types of claimants. Although the resulting hardship would be alleviated for those injured plaintiffs in a position to assert their claims against an active and solvent retail dealer who sold the defective product by which they were injured, the retailer would in turn be cut off from the benefit of rights against the manufacturer. (See Vandermark v. Ford Motor Co. (1964) 61 Cal.2d 256, 262–263, 37 Cal.Rptr. 896, 391 P.2d 168; Escola v. Coca Cola Bottling Co. (1944) 24 Cal.2d 453, 464, 150 P.2d 436 (conc. opn.).)

While depriving plaintiff of redress against the ladder's manufacturer, Alad I, the transaction by which Alad II acquired Alad I's name and operating assets had the further effect of transferring to Alad II the resources that had previously been available to Alad I for meeting its responsibilities to persons injured by defects in ladders it had produced. * * * Moreover, in a liquidation proceeding subject to court supervision "the amount of any unmatured, contingent, or disputed claim against the corporation which has been presented and has not been disallowed" must be "paid into court" and suit on rejected claims must be commenced within 30 days after notice of rejection. (Corp.Code, former § 4608, now § 1807.) No provision need be made for the satisfaction of claims that may arise in the future on account of defective products the corporation has manufactured in the past.

The acquisition of the Alad enterprise gave Alad II the opportunity formerly enjoyed by Alad I of passing on to purchasers of new "Alad" products the costs of meeting these risks. Immediately after the takeover it was Alad II, not Alad I, which was in a position to promote the "paramount policy" of the strict products liability rule by "spreading throughout society * * * the cost of compensating [otherwise defenseless victims of manufacturing defects]" (Price v. Shell Oil Co., supra, 2

---

5. Former section 5000 of the Corporations Code, which was then in effect and has since been replaced by section 2004, provided:

"After determining that all the *known debts and liabilities* of a corporation in the process of winding up have been paid or adequately provided for, the board shall distribute all the remaining corporate assets among the shareholders and owners of shares according to their respective rights and preferences. If the winding up is by court proceeding or subject to court supervision, the distribution shall not be made until after the expiration of any period for the presentation of claims which has been prescribed by order of court." (Italics added).

Cal.3d 245, 251, 85 Cal.Rptr. 178, 182, 466 P.2d 722, 726). (See Knapp v. North American Rockwell Corp. (3d Cir.1974) 506 F.2d 361, 372–373 (conc. opn.).)

Finally, the imposition upon Alad II of liability for injuries from Alad I's defective products is fair and equitable in view of Alad II's acquisition of Alad I's trade name, good will, and customer lists, its continuing to produce the same line of ladders, and its holding itself out to potential customers as the same enterprise. This deliberate albeit legitimate exploitation of Alad I's established reputation as a going concern manufacturing a specific product line gave Alad II a substantial benefit which its predecessor could not have enjoyed without the burden of potential liability for injuries from previously manufactured units. Imposing this liability upon successor manufacturers in the position of Alad II not only causes the one "who takes the benefit [to] bear the burden" (Civ.Code, § 3521) but precludes any windfall to the predecessor that might otherwise result from (1) the reflection of an absence of such successor liability in an enhanced price paid by the successor for the business assets and (2) the liquidation of the predecessor resulting in avoidance of its responsibility for subsequent injuries from its defective products.

* * *

We therefore conclude that a party which acquires a manufacturing business and continues the output of its line of products under the circumstances here presented assumes strict tort liability for defects in units of the same product line previously manufactured and distributed by the entity from which the business was acquired.

* * *

2. If the rule were clear that a successor who continues the product line is liable for the product claims against the predecessor, the successor would presumably be willing to pay less for the predecessor's assets by approximately the estimated amount of liability (or cost of insuring against liability). This would presumably place the ultimate cost of the predecessor's defective products on the predecessor.

3. Even if the injured plaintiff cannot sue the successor, he may be able to sue the predecessor who actually manufactured the product. If the predecessor goes out of business, however, it may not be available as a defendant. Most states permit a corporation to wind up its affairs and be insulated from liability after a specific period of time. This rule concerning predecessors, coupled with a rule that insulates successor corporations from liability, leaves an injured plaintiff without a remedy if the product was sold prior to liquidation but the injury occurred after liquidation.

4. As *Bernard* and *Alad* indicate, even courts that reject the product line exception to the traditional no-liability rule recognize other exceptions (a) when the successor expressly or impliedly agrees to assume the predecessor's liability, (b) when the successor corporation takes over enough of the predecessor's assets and operations that the transaction constitutes a *de facto* merger, (c) when the transfer of assets is a sham that effects a fraud on

the predecessor corporation's creditors, and (d) when the successor corporation is a mere "continuation" of the predecessor. Aside from the product line exception, the *de facto* merger exception has been the most controversial.

5. To determine whether the transfer of assets is a sham, courts have asked whether the successor corporation is substantially controlled by the same persons or entities that controlled the predecessor corporation and whether the assets were sold to the successor corporation for fair market value. If the predecessor corporation did not receive fair market value for its assets, the predecessor corporation's creditors are left without a fund from which to collect their debts.

6. Most of the cases dealing with successor corporation liability have involved obligations other than tort liability for defective products. Are there special considerations in the area of products liability that would support special rules in this area, irrespective of a state's position (either through case law or statute) on successor corporation liability outside the area of products liability? Are these special considerations limited to cases in which the successor corporation continues the predecessor corporation's product line?

SECTION B. TRANSACTIONS COVERED BY STRICT TORT LIABILITY AND WARRANTY

Section 402A of the Restatement (Second) of Torts refers to "[o]ne who *sells any product* [and who] * * * is engaged in the business of *selling such a product* * * *." Although section 402A is not a statute and should not be treated as such, it is clear that, on this issue, its language reflects a clear consensus among courts that strict tort liability applies to "product sales."

The warranties created by Article 2 of the Commercial Code are similarly limited in their application. The warranty provisions themselves (sections 2–313, 2–314, and 2–315) refer to a "seller," and section 2–102 provides that Article 2 "applies to transactions in goods."

The material in this section addresses the applicability of strict tort liability (and to a lesser extent the Article 2 warranties) to transactions that are not technically product sales but that nevertheless evoke many of the policies underlying strict liability. The first group of cases—dealing with leases and bailments—focus on the problem of whether a "sale" has taken place. The second group—dealing with franchises, used products, real estate, and services—focus on the problem of whether the subject of the transaction is sufficiently similar to a normal "product" to justify the application of strict tort liability. Cases involving services are especially difficult to analyze because they often involve products that have not technically been sold.

It is important to distinguish between cases involving the scope of strict tort liability or common law warranties on the one hand and those involving Article 2 on the other. Although some courts have analyzed the application of strict tort liability and an Article 2 warranty to a specific transaction interchangeably, other courts have used different analyses for these two theories. A court has considerably more leeway defining the scope of strict tort liability than it does interpreting the legislative mandate of the Commercial Code. Although precedents involving the scope of one theory might be useful in defining the scope of the other, you should exercise caution before crossing the boundary between these two theories.

Even if a transaction is governed by some form of strict liability, it is important to determine whether strict tort liability, breach of warranty, or both are applicable, because the details of each theory differ. For example, pure economic damages are recoverable under an Article 2 warranty but normally are not recoverable under strict tort liability. Conversely, a manufacturer can disclaim an implied warranty of merchantability but not strict tort liability.

As was indicated at the outset of this chapter, these cases involving the scope of strict tort liability have a dual importance. They have practical importance in their own right, and they again raise the issue of why product sales should be governed by special rules of tort liability. Although all boundary problems create some degree of ambiguity, a coherent theory of strict tort liability should at least identify the factors that distinguish between transactions that fall within its scope and those that do not. As you study these cases, ask yourself whether the policies courts and commentators have used to justify strict tort liability help in determining whether borderline cases fall within its scope of application.

1. LEASES

MARTIN v. RYDER TRUCK RENTAL, INC.

Supreme Court of Delaware, 1976.
353 A.2d 581.

HERRMANN, CHIEF JUSTICE.

We hold today that a bailment-lease of a motor vehicle, entered into in the regular course of a truck rental business, is subject to application of the doctrine of strict tort liability in favor of an injured bystander.

I.

According to the plaintiffs in this case:

A truck was leased by the defendant, Ryder Truck Rental, Inc., to Gagliardi Brothers, Inc., in the regular course of Ryder's truck rental business. The truck, operated by a Gagliardi employee, was involved in an intersectional collision. Due to a failure of its braking system, the truck did not stop for a traffic light and struck the rear of an automobile which had stopped for the signal, causing that automobile to collide with the vehicle driven by the plaintiff, Dorothy Martin. As a result, she was injured, her car was damaged, and this suit was brought by her and her husband against Ryder.

The plaintiffs base their cause of action solely upon the doctrine of strict tort liability, *i.e.,* tort liability without proof of negligence. The Superior Court granted summary judgment in favor of Ryder, holding that the doctrine is not applicable to the factual situation here presented. We disagree.

II.

* * *

The defendant contends that if the Legislature intended to create a strict liability for bailments for hire, it would have done so in the UCC. Thus, the threshold question in the instant case is whether, by the enactment of the UCC and the limitation of its strict warranty provisions to sales, the Legislature has preempted this field of the law of products liability; or whether, the UCC notwithstanding, the courts are free to provide for bailments and leases the alternate, but somewhat conflicting, remedy of strict tort liability.

The warranty provisions of Article 2 of the UCC, §§ 2–313 (express) and 2–315 (implied), are clearly limited to the sales of goods; the Statute is "neutral" as to other types of relationships.[6] Manifestly, the Legislature has not preempted the field as to bailments and leases by enactment of the UCC.[7] Silence on the subject may not be deemed to be such preemption.

Hence, we are free, in the common law tradition, to apply the doctrine of strict tort liability to a bailment-lease. The question is whether that course should be adopted; and for that decision, consideration of the nature and evolution of the doctrine is important:

III.

* * *

A.

In *Cintrone v. Hertz Truck Leasing, etc.,* 45 N.J. 434, 212 A.2d 769 (1965), the New Jersey Supreme Court applied strict liability in tort to a motor vehicle bailment situation because "[a] bailor for hire, such as a person in the U-drive-it business, puts motor vehicles in the stream of commerce in a fashion not unlike a manufacturer or retailer"; subjects

---

6. The A.L.I. Official Comment to § 2–313 reads:

"Although this section is limited in its scope and direct purpose to warranties made by the seller to the buyer as part of a contract for sale, the warranty sections of this Article are not designed in any way to disturb those lines of case law growth which have recognized that warranties need not be confined either to sales contracts or to the direct parties to such a contract. They may arise in other appropriate circumstances such as in the case of bailments for hire * * *. [T]he matter is left to the case law with the intention that the policies of this Act may offer useful guidance in dealing with further cases as they arise."

7. Reserved for another day is the question of whether the Legislature has preempted the field as to direct sales cases and whether the warranty provisions of the UCC are, therefore, the exclusive source of strict liability in such cases.

such a leased vehicle "to more sustained use on the highways than most ordinary car purchasers"; and by the very nature of his business, exposes "the bailee, his employees, passengers and the traveling public * * * to a greater *quantum* of potential danger of harm from defective vehicles than usually arises out of sales by the manufacturer." 212 A.2d at 777.

The California Supreme Court endorsed the *Cintrone* "step" in *Price v. Shell Oil Company,* 2 Cal.3d 245, 85 Cal.Rptr. 178, 466 P.2d 722 (1970):

> " * * * [A] broad philosophy evolves naturally from the purpose of imposing strict liability which 'is to insure that the costs of injuries resulting from defective products are borne by the manufacturers that put such products on the market rather than by the injured persons who are powerless to protect themselves.' [Citing *Yuba*]. Essentially the paramount policy to be promoted by the rule is the protection of otherwise defenseless victims of manufacturing defects and the spreading throughout society of the cost of compensating them. * * *

> " * * * [W]e can perceive no substantial difference between *sellers* of personal property and *non-sellers,* such as bailors and lessors. In each instance, the seller or non-seller 'places [an article] on the market, knowing that it is to be used without inspection for defects, * * *.' [Citing *Yuba*] In the light of the policy to be subserved, it should make no difference that the party distributing the article has retained title to it. Nor can we see how the risk of harm associated with the use of the chattel can vary with the legal form under which it is held. Having in mind the market realities and the widespread use of the lease of personalty in today's business world, we think it makes good sense to impose on the lessors of chattels the same liability for physical harm which has been imposed on the manufacturers and retailers. The former, like the latter, are able to bear the cost of compensating for injuries resulting from defects by spreading the loss through an adjustment of the rental." 85 Cal. Rptr. at 181, 466 P.2d at 725–26.

The extension of the doctrine of strict tort liability to bailors-lessors has been limited, however, to leases made in the regular course of a rental business, the doctrine being applicable only in a commercial setting by its very nature. *Price, supra,* 85 Cal.Rptr. at 183–84, 466 P.2d at 727–28; *Cintrone, supra,* 212 A.2d at 777. Strict tort liability has been found "peculiarly applicable" to the lessor of motor vehicles in "today's society with 'the growth of the business of renting motor vehicles, trucks and pleasure cars' * * * and the persistent advertising efforts to put one 'in the driver's seat.' " *Price, supra,* 85 Cal.Rptr. at 183, 466 P.2d at 727, quoting from *Cintrone, supra,* 212 A.2d at 776, 777.

For the reasons so well stated by the leading authorities in this field, we are of the opinion that, since the General Assembly has not preempted this area of the field, the common law must grow to fulfill the requirements of justice as dictated by changing times and conditions.

The present-day magnitude of the motor vehicle rental business, and the trade practices which have developed therein, require maximum protection for the victims of defective rentals. This translates into the imposition of strict tort liability upon the lessor. The public policy considerations which appeared in the development of the doctrine during the past decade, are especially relevant where, as in the instant case, the bailor-lessor retains exclusive control and supervision over the maintenance and repair of the motor vehicle it places in circulation upon the highways. All of the societal policy reasons leading to the expansion of strict tort liability in sales cases are equally applicable in this motor vehicle rental case: (1) the concept that the cost of compensating for injuries and damages arising from the use of a defective motor vehicle should be borne by the party who placed it in circulation, who is best able to prevent distribution of a defective product, and who can spread the cost as a risk and expense of the business enterprise; (2) the concept that the defective motor vehicle was placed on the highways in violation of a representation of fitness by the lessor implied by law from the circumstances and trade practices of the business; and (3) the concept that the imposition upon the lessor of liability without fault will result in general risk-reduction by arousing in the lessor an additional impetus to furnish safer vehicles.

Accordingly, we hold that the doctrine of strict tort liability is applicable to Ryder in the instant case. *Accord, Stang v. Hertz Corporation,* 83 N.M. 730, 497 P.2d 732 (1972); *Stewart v. Budget Rent–A–Car Corporation,* 52 Haw. 71, 470 P.2d 240 (1970); *Coleman v. Hertz Corporation,* Okl.App., 534 P.2d 940 (1975); *Galuccio v. Hertz Corporation,* 1 Ill.App.3d 272, 274 N.E.2d 178 (1971); *see Bachner v. Pearson,* Alaska, 479 P.2d 319 (1970); *Rourke v. Garza,* Tex.Civ.App., 511 S.W.2d 331 (1974).

* * *

IV.

Ryder contends that the imposition of any new measure of liability in this field (1) should be left to the Legislature, citing *Bona v. Graefe,* 264 Md. 69, 285 A.2d 607 (1972); or (2) should be made effective prospectively only. As to the first point: where, as here, the Legislature has not preempted the field the common law must be kept abreast of the time and must grow to fulfill the demands of justice. As to the second point: these plaintiffs may not be deprived of the benefits of the development of the law they have prompted by their perseverance in this litigation; to do so would render this opinion pure *dictum.* See *Great Northern Ry. Co. v. Sunburst Oil & Refining Co.,* 287 U.S. 358, 53 S.Ct. 145, 77 L.Ed. 360 (1932); Schaefer, *The Control of "Sunbursts"; Tech-*

niques of Prospective Overruling, 42 N.Y.U.L.Rev. 631 (1967). We decline to limit the rulings herein to prospective application.

* * *

The judgment below is reversed and the cause remanded for further proceedings consistent herewith.

[The concurring opinion of JUSTICE DUFFY is omitted.]

Notes

1. As *Martin* indicates, a lease is governed by strict tort liability only if the lessor is in the business of leasing products of that type, just as a sale is governed by strict tort liability only if the seller is in the business of selling products of that type. *See* Brescia v. Great Road Realty Trust, 117 N.H. 154, 373 A.2d 1310 (1977).

2. Is there any reason to treat product leases differently than product sales?

3. In Garcia v. Halsett, 3 Cal.App.3d 319, 82 Cal.Rptr. 420 (1970), the court held that a laundromat owner was strictly liable to a boy whose arm became entangled in a defective washing machine. The court characterized the transaction as a "license."

Suppose a child fell while riding the defendant's merry-go-round? Would it make a difference whether the accident was caused by a defect in the wooden horse or by the operator starting the merry-go-round before the patrons were ready? Do the policies underlying strict tort liability apply with equal force to these two situations?

4. By their own terms, sections 2–313, 2–314, and 2–315 of the Commercial Code apply to a "seller." Section 2–314 also refers to "a contract for * * * sale." Section 2–106(1) provides that a " '[c]ontract for sale' includes both a present sale of goods and a contract to sell goods at a future time. A 'sale' consists in the passing of title from the seller to the buyer for a price." Consequently, the Article 2 warranties seem not to apply to leases. Nevertheless, a few courts have applied an Article 2 warranty to a lease. *See, e.g.,* Owens v. Patent Scaffolding Co., 77 Misc.2d 992, 354 N.Y.S.2d 778 (1974); Hawkins Const. Co. v. Matthews Co., Inc., 190 Neb. 546, 209 N.W.2d 643 (1973). Of course, a court might also create a common law warranty to cover leases.

2. BAILMENTS

ARMSTRONG RUBBER CO. v. URQUIDEZ

Supreme Court of Texas, 1978.
570 S.W.2d 374.

McGEE, JUSTICE.

This appeal involves the question whether the doctrine of strict liability in tort applies where the product has not entered the stream of commerce and where there has been no sale of the product by the manufacturer but a bailment for mutual benefit. The widow and son of test driver Clemente Urquidez brought suit against Armstrong Rubber Company. The plaintiffs pled that Urquidez was killed as the result of a blowout of a tire alleged to be defective in design and manufacture. The trial court rendered judgment on the jury's determination that the tire was defective in its design or manufacture and that the defect was the producing cause of the accident. The widow was awarded $75,000 and the son $12,000 with the award subject to the subrogation rights of the intervening worker's compensation carrier. The Court of Civil Appeals affirmed. 560 S.W.2d 781. We reverse the judgments below and render judgment that the plaintiffs take nothing.

Automotive Proving Grounds, Inc. owns and operates a tire-testing facility near Pecos. On January 1, 1970, Automotive contracted to provide testing facilities to the defendant, Armstrong, on a part-time basis for a period of ten years. Under the contract Armstrong agreed to provide and maintain all trucks and vehicles required for its testing. It was Automotive's responsibility to maintain the track and buildings comprising the testing facility, to provide drivers, mechanics, and other personnel necessary for testing purposes and to promulgate safety rules and driver qualifications.

The deceased, Clemente Urquidez, was employed by Automotive as a test driver. At the time of the accident, he was driving a tractor/trailer rig owned by Armstrong. Urquidez was performing a standard test at 60 m.p.h. on the oval test track when the left front tire of the tractor blew out. Urquidez decelerated the truck into the infield area of the oval track where he encountered soft sand, overturned and was killed. The tire that blew out was an Allstate Express Cargo Nylon 12–ply non-interest spare manufactured by Armstrong. Both front tires on the tractor were non-interest spares. A "non-interest spare" is a term applied to a tire mounted on the test truck along with the tires being tested, but which is not itself being tested. The tire in question had never been sold by Armstrong. It was new when received at the Pecos facility. The tire was never tested at the Pecos facility but was manufactured and provided for use only as a non-interest spare on Armstrong's trucks. The tire was of the same quality as tires manufactured by Armstrong and sold across the nation.

The doctrine of strict liability as enunciated in the Restatement (Second) of Torts § 402A has been adopted as the rule in Texas. * * * Although phrased in terms of sellers, it is not necessary that the defendant actually sell the product, but only that he be engaged in the business of introducing the product into channels of commerce.

* * *

Armstrong initially questions the application of the doctrine of strict liability to the tire in question. Armstrong contends that the tire was provided for the industrial purpose of testing other tires and that the accident occurred in its "testing laboratory." Armstrong argues that the defective tire was neither manufactured for market nor placed in the stream of commerce. We agree that the tire never entered the stream of commerce.

In extending the doctrine of strict liability to the present bailment, the Court of Civil Appeals emphasized that tires of the same design and manufacture were "regularly sold by Armstrong in regular channels of commerce." We do not believe it sufficient, however, that the seller merely introduce products of similar design and manufacture into the stream of commerce. To invoke the doctrine of strict liability in tort the product producing injury or damage must enter the stream of commerce. In *General Motors Corp. v. Hopkins,* 548 S.W.2d 344, 351 (Tex.1977) we said that liability rests on the defendant "placing into the stream of commerce a product which is demonstrated at trial to have been dangerous."

The Court of Civil Appeals further emphasized that Urquidez was not employed to test non-interest spares. In that court's opinion the dual policy considerations of "loss distribution" and "injury reduction" might best be served by extending the doctrine of strict liability to the present bailment transaction. Armstrong, on the other hand, urges that the policy considerations underlying the doctrine of strict liability in tort should not be advanced as the basis for the doctrine's protection where the essential elements of the doctrine have not been satisfied. Clemente Urquidez was employed to test tires. It was in part his job to provide safe tires for the public. Armstrong therefore argues that he was not the ordinary user or consumer entitled to the protection afforded by strict liability in tort.

While we agree that Clemente Urquidez was not hired to test the non-interest spare, we would not extend the doctrine of strict liability in tort on that basis. Although the defective tire was not itself the subject of the test, it was manufactured and provided for the limited purpose of testing other tires. The non-interest spare was never sold and, more importantly, never entered the stream of commerce. We recognize that application of strict liability in tort does not depend upon a sale of the product, nevertheless the product must be released in some manner to the consuming public. *See, Rourke v. Garza, supra; McKisson v. Sales Affiliates, Inc., supra.* The Restatement does not make a manufacturer an insurer of every person who is injured by one of its products. *Martinez v. Dixie Carriers, Inc.,* 529 F.2d 457 (5th Cir.1976).

As this is a case of first impression, the plaintiffs direct our attention to several cases originating in other jurisdictions which extend the doctrine of strict liability in tort to bailment transactions. *Cf. Whitfield v. Cooper,* 30 Conn.Sup. 47, 298 A.2d 50 (1972); *Nowakowski v. Hoppe Tire Co.,* 39 Ill.App.3d 155, 349 N.E.2d 578 (5th Dist.1974); *Bainter v. Lamoine LP Gas Co.,* 24 Ill.App.3d 913, 321 N.E.2d 744 (3d Dist.1974); *Full[ ]bright v. Klamath Gas Co.,* 271 Or. 449, 533 P.2d 316 (1975). We have reviewed these authorities, but do not find them persuasive as each bailment arose in a transaction essentially commercial in character. In *Whitfield,* the defendant bailed its customer a defective car for use while defendant repaired the customer's car. In *Full Jbright,* the defendant provided a defective potato vine burner to its customer in connection with defendant's sale of gas. In *Bainter,* the defendant loaned a defective gas tank in which its customer stored gas purchased from defendant. In *Nowakowski,* the defendant substituted a defective wheel assembly from its own stock in the course of repairing its customer's truck. An employee of the customer was subsequently injured while mounting a tire on the defective wheel assembly provided by defendant. In each case cited, the bailment for mutual benefit accompanied a sale of goods or services. In each instance the manufacturer, supplier or retailer released the product to its customer. Accordingly, the product provided was in the stream of commerce. These cases are clearly distinguishable from our present facts where Armstrong pursuant to its contract with Automotive provided non-interest spares for the purpose of testing new or experimental tires.

Armstrong never released the non-interest spare to an ordinary user or consumer within the meaning of the Restatement. The defective tire, although not itself the subject of the test, always remained within the industrial, testing process. Accordingly, the tire never entered the stream of commerce. The lower courts, therefore, inappropriately applied the doctrine of strict liability to the present industrial transaction.

The judgments of the Court of Civil Appeals and the trial court are reversed and judgment is here rendered that the plaintiffs take nothing.

Notes

1. The suggestion in *Urquidez*—that a bailment is governed by strict tort liability only if the bailment is incidental to a sale of another product or service—was used to preclude the application of strict tort liability in Thate v. Texas & Pac. Ry. Co., 595 S.W.2d 591 (Tex.Civ.App.—Dallas 1980, writ dismissed). The plaintiff was injured while loading his employer's trucks onto a railroad car supplied by the defendant. The court held that the defendant had not placed the railroad car into the stream of commerce. It distinguished the stream-of-commerce test for strict tort liability from a similar test to determine whether goods are in interstate commerce. The court also interpreted *Urquidez* to exclude from strict tort liability bailments that are not incidental to a sale of a product or a service. Moreover, the court relied, as did the court in *Urquidez,* on the plaintiff's status as an employee of an industrial entity as opposed to that of an ordinary consumer.

Notwithstanding the language of *Urquidez* and *Thate,* bailment cases cannot be resolved by identifying one or two factors. Commercial consumers can recover for strict tort liability in appropriate circumstances, and the mere association of a defective product with the sale of another product or service does not necessarily trigger strict tort liability. For example, a defendant who merely uses a defective product while selling another product or service is not necessarily subject to strict tort liability. A doctor who uses a defective needle is probably not subject to strict tort liability, even though the needle is clearly a product and is used in association with the sale of service. *See* Ethicon, Inc. v. Parten, 520 S.W.2d 527 (Tex.Civ.App.—Houston [14th Dist.] 1975, no writ). In Thomas v. St. Joseph Hospital, 618

S.W.2d 791 (Tex.Civ.App.—Houston [1st Dist.] 1981, writ refused, no reversible error), however, a hospital was held strictly liable for supplying a patient with a flammable gown. The distinction between the needle and the gown cannot be explained merely on the basis of their association with another product or service. The distinction seems to rest on the extent to which the plaintiff controlled the product.

Even when the plaintiff has control of a product, the defendant has not necessarily placed it into the stream of commerce. *Thate* is one example. Keen v. Dominick's Finer Foods, Inc., 49 Ill.App.3d 480, 7 Ill.Dec. 341, 364 N.E.2d 502 (1977), an Illinois case involving a supermarket customer who was injured by a defective shopping cart, is another. The bailment of the cart was associated with the sale of other products, and the customer had temporary control of the cart, but the court held that the supermarket was not subject to strict tort liability. Although the case might have been decided differently in another state, it demonstrates the difficulty of drawing clear lines for determining whether or not a product has been placed in the stream of commerce. The difficulty is further illustrated by considering that even if a court were to hold that a shopping-cart injury is governed by strict tort liability, it might nevertheless hold that an injury caused by a drinking fountain in a defendant's store is not. A distinction between the shopping-cart and the drinking fountain does not seem to be implausible, even though the plaintiff temporarily controlled each product, and each product was associated with the sale of other products in the defendant's store. The extent of the plaintiff's control of the product, the association of the product with the sale or lease of other products or services, and the industrial or consumer aspects of the transaction all seem to be factors in determining whether a defendant has placed a product in the stream of commerce. No single factor seems to be determinative, and no clear rule has emerged to determine whether a defendant has placed a product in the stream of commerce. Courts are likely to use an *ad hoc* approach that depends heavily on the facts of each case.

2. If one defendant escapes strict tort liability because it has not placed a product in the stream of commerce, the plaintiff might still recover under strict tort liability from another seller in the chain of distribution. For example, even though a doctor using a defective needle is probably not strictly liable to the patient, the manufacturer who sold the needle to the doctor is subject to strict tort liability. The fact that the manufacturer did not sell the needle to the plaintiff is irrelevant, because bystanders can recover under strict tort liability.

3. Several courts have applied strict tort liability to product demonstrations even though a sale had not taken place. *See* First National Bank v. Cessna Aircraft Co., 365 So.2d 966 (Ala.1978) (airplane demonstration); Delaney v. Towmotor Corp., 339 F.2d 4 (2d Cir.1964) (forklift demonstration). In McKisson v. Sales Affiliates, Inc., 416 S.W.2d 787 (Tex.1967), the court applied strict tort liability to a free sample given to a prospective customer.

4. Should a grocer be strictly liable for a soft drink bottle that explodes before the customer pays for the bottle at the checkout counter? Do any of the policies underlying strict tort liability apply differently depending on

whether the customer has paid at the time of the explosion? Would it make a difference if the bottle exploded on the shelf and injured a passing customer who had no intention of buying the soft drink? If the customer slipped on the floor after the bottle exploded and spilled? If the customer slipped on the floor because a tomato had been dropped by a sales clerk?

Do the policies underlying strict tort liability help determine whether strict tort liability should be applicable in these situations?

5. Several cases involving bailments have involved reusable containers. In Bainter v. Lamoine LP Gas Co., 24 Ill.App.3d 913, 321 N.E.2d 744 (1974), discussed in *Urquidez,* the court applied strict tort liability to a gas supplier for an injury caused by a defective returnable gas container supplied to the plaintiff without charge. *See also,* Fulbright v. Klamath Gas Co., 271 Or. 449, 533 P.2d 316 (1975). Should strict tort liability apply to a defective returnable soft drink bottle?

7. As in the case of leases, the language of sections 2–313, 2–314, and 2–315 seems to preclude the application of the Article 2 warranty to bailments. Sections 2–313, 2–314, and 2–315 each refer to a "seller," and section 2–314 also refers to a "contract for * * * sale." Section 2–106(1) defines a "sale" as "the passing of title from the seller to the buyer for a price." *See e.g.,* Garfield v. Furniture Fair–Hanover, 113 N.J.Super. 509, 274 A.2d 325 (1971).

3. FRANCHISES AND TRADEMARK LICENSES

KOSTERS v. SEVEN–UP CO.

United States Court of Appeals, Sixth Circuit, 1979.
595 F.2d 347.

MERRITT, CIRCUIT JUDGE.

During the past two decades, franchising has become a common means of marketing products and services, but our legal system has not yet settled the principles that define the liabilities of franchisors for injuries sustained by customers of their franchisees. This diversity case requires us to interpret the theories of tort and contract liability which Michigan law allows a jury to consider when deciding whether an injured purchaser is entitled to recover against the franchisor of a product.

I. STATEMENT OF THE CASE

The defendant, the Seven–Up Company, appeals from a $150,000 jury verdict awarded for injuries caused by an exploding 7–Up bottle. The plaintiff removed a cardboard carton containing six bottles of 7–Up from a grocery shelf, put it under her arm and headed for the check-out counter of the grocery store. She was blinded in one eye when a bottle slipped out of the carton, fell on the floor and exploded, causing a piece of glass to strike her eye as she looked down. The 7–Up carton was a so-called "over-the-crown" or "neck-thru" carton designed to be held from the top and made without a strip on the sides of the carton which would prevent a bottle from slipping out if held underneath.

The carton was designed and manufactured by Olinkraft, Inc. Olinkraft sold it to the Brooks Bottling Company, a franchisee of the defendant, Seven–Up Company. Seven–Up retains the right to approve the design of articles used by the bottler, including cartons. The franchise agreement between Seven–Up and the Brooks Bottling Company requires that "cases, bottles, and crowns used for 7–Up will be of a type * * * and design approved by the 7–Up Company," and "any advertising * * * material * * * must be approved by the 7–Up Company before its use by the bottler."

Using an extract provided by Seven–Up, Brooks produced the beverage and poured it into bottles. After securing Seven–Up's approval of the design under the franchise agreement, Brooks packaged the bottles in cartons selected and purchased by Brooks from various carton manufacturers, including Olinkraft. Brooks then sold cartons of 7–Up to stores in some 52 Michigan counties, including Meijers Thrifty Acres Store in Holland, Michigan, where the plaintiff picked up the carton and carried it under her arm toward the checkout counter. Plaintiff settled her claims against the bottler, the carton manufacturer and the grocer for $30,000.

Seven–Up denied liability, insisting its approval of the cartons was only of the "graphics" and for the purpose of assuring that its trademark was properly displayed.

* * *

The District Judge submitted the case to the jury on five related theories of product liability—a negligence theory, three strict liability theories and one contract theory * * *.

* * * We do not know which of these theories the jury accepted because it returned a general verdict. On appeal, Seven–Up argues that all of the theories are wrong except negligence. We begin our consideration of this diversity case by acknowledging that the views of an experienced District Judge on questions concerning the law of the state in which he sits are entitled to great respect.

* * *

Michigan appellate courts have not had the occasion to consider these principles in the context of franchising. It appears to be a new question not generally considered in other jurisdictions.[11] The franchise system is a method of selling products and services identified by a particular trade name which may be associated with a patent, a trade secret, a particular product design or management expertise. The

---

11. *But see City of Hartford v. Associated Constr. Co.,* 34 Conn.Supp. 204, 384 A.2d 390 (1978) (trademark licensor held liable under principles of strict liability for property damage caused by defective roofing base product mixed, sold and applied by trademark licensee); *Kasel v. Remington Arms Co., Inc.,* 24 Cal.App.3d 711, 101 Cal. Rptr. 314 (1972) (trademark licensor held liable under principles of strict liability in tort for personal injuries caused by defective shell manufactured by its trademark licensee). *See also Carter v. Bancroft & Sons Co.,* 360 F.Supp. 1103 (E.D.Pa.1973) (trademark licensor a "seller" within meaning of Pennsylvania law).

franchisee usually purchases some products from the franchisor—in this case, the 7–Up syrup—and makes royalty payments on the basis of units sold, in exchange for the right to offer products for sale under the trademark. The franchise agreement establishes the relationship between the parties and usually regulates the quality of the product, sales territory, the advertising and other details; and it usually requires that certain supplies be purchased from the franchisor.

Seven–Up Company concedes that a franchisor, like a manufacturer or supplier, may be liable to the consumer for its own negligence, without regard to privity, under the doctrine of *MacPherson v. Buick Motor Co.* [, 217 N.Y. 382, 111 N.E. 1050 (1916)]. Seven–Up contends, however, that it does not carry the liabilities of a supplier when it did not supply the product and that other theories of strict tort liability do not apply. Liability may not be laid on the basis of implied warranty, it says, when the franchisor did not manufacture, handle, design or require the use of the particular product. The precise question before us here is whether Michigan's principles of "strict accountability" for breach of implied warranty extend to a franchisor who retains the right of control over the product (the carton) and specifically consents to its distribution in the form sold but does not actually manufacture, sell, handle, ship or require the use of the product.

Different questions may arise in other franchising contexts. In some instances, the franchisor may not retain the right of control or may not actually approve the form of the product. The franchisee may sell a product contrary to the instructions or without the knowledge of the franchisor. The consumer may attempt to hold the franchisor liable for the conduct of the franchisee under the agency doctrines of *respondeat superior* or apparent authority. We do not deal with these questions here.

In this case, the Seven–Up Company not only floated its franchisee and the bottles of its carbonated soft drink into the so-called "stream of commerce." The Company also assumed and exercised a degree of control over the "type, style, size and design" of the carton in which its product was to be marketed. The carton was submitted to Seven–Up for inspection. With knowledge of its design, Seven–Up consented to the entry in commerce of the carton from which the bottle fell, causing the injury. The franchisor's sponsorship, management and control of the system for distributing 7–Up, plus its specific consent to the use of the carton, in our view, places the franchisor in the position of a supplier of the product for purposes of tort liability.

We are not saying that the Seven–Up Company is absolutely liable as an insurer of the safety of the carton under the theory of implied warranty, simply by virtue of its status as a franchisor. In the first place, under Michigan's theory of implied warranty of fitness, the carton must be found to be "defective," or as the District Judge more accurately put it, "not reasonably safe." It must be harmful or unsafe because something is wrong with it, and the jury must so find. Moreover, here the franchisor inspected the carton and approved it. Thus, we need not reach the question whether the franchisor would carry the liabilities of a supplier if it had not been made aware of the product and given the opportunity to assess the risks.

When a franchisor consents to the distribution of a defective product bearing its name, the obligation of the franchisor to compensate the injured consumer for breach of implied warranty, we think, arises from several factors in combination: (1) the risk created by approving for distribution an unsafe product likely to cause injury, (2) the franchisor's ability and opportunity to eliminate the unsafe character of the product and prevent the loss, (3) the consumer's lack of knowledge of the danger, and (4) the consumer's reliance on the trade name which gives the intended impression that the franchisor is responsible for and stands behind the product. Liability is based on the franchisor's control and the public's assumption, induced by the franchisor's conduct, that it does in fact control and vouch for the product.

These are factors Michigan courts have relied on in the past in determining who may be held liable for breach of implied warranty of fitness in other products liability situations. We believe Michigan courts would apply these principles in the franchising situation presented by this case, and we therefore conclude that the case was correctly submitted to the jury to assess liability for breach of implied warranty.

[The court then held that three other theories upon which the case was submitted to the jury were erroneous. Because the jury returned with a general verdict for the plaintiff, the court reversed and remanded for a new trial.]

Note

As the opinion in *Kosters* indicates, only a few courts have considered the applicability of strict tort liability or breach of warranty to franchisors. In addition to the cases cited in note 11 of the opinion, *see* Connelly v. Uniroyal, Inc., 75 Ill.2d 393, 27 Ill.Dec. 343, 389 N.E.2d 155 (1979) (holding a trademark licensor subject to strict tort liability); Scheuler v. Aamco Transmissions, Inc., 1 Kan.App.2d 525, 571 P.2d 48 (1977) (holding a franchisor liable for breach of express warranty).

4. PUBLICATIONS

CARDOZO v. TRUE

District Court of Appeals of Florida, Second District, 1977.
342 So.2d 1053.

SCHEB, JUDGE.

The Circuit Court for Sarasota County certified the following questions to this court pursuant to Fla.App. Rule 4.6(a):

I. IS A RETAIL BOOK DEALER LIABLE UNDER SECTION 672.314, FLORIDA STATUTES, TO A PURCHASER OF A

COOKBOOK FOR HER INJURIES AND DAMAGES CAUSED BY IMPROPER INSTRUCTIONS OR LACK OF ADEQUATE WARNINGS AS TO POISONOUS INGREDIENTS USED IN A RECIPE?

II.   IS A RETAIL BOOK DEALER LIABLE UNDER THE COMMON LAW OF IMPLIED WARRANTIES TO A PURCHASER OF A COOKBOOK FOR HER INJURIES FOR LACK OF ADEQUATE WARNINGS AS TO POISONOUS INGREDIENTS USED IN A RECIPE?

The plaintiffs' amended complaint set forth the essential facts which the trial court has summarized as follows:

"Norma True authored a book entitled 'Trade Winds Cookery', an anthology of recipes selected and prepared by her using tropical fruits and vegetables. It was published by a Virginia corporation, which sold the book to Ellie's Book and Stationery, Inc. Ellie's was and is a retail book dealer located in Sarasota, Florida.

On September 15, 1971, Ingrid Cardozo purchased a copy of 'Trade Winds Cookery' from Ellie's. Four days later, Mrs. Cardozo was using the book and following a recipe in it for the preparation and cooking of the Dasheen plant, commonly known as 'elephant's ears'. While preparing the roots for cooking, she ate a small slice and immediately experienced a burning of the lips, mouth, throat and tongue, coughing and gasping, and intense stomach cramps. This persisted over several days, despite medical care.

Defendant True did not answer plaintiff's complaint, and is not involved in this certificate. As to defendant Ellie's Mrs. Cardozo and her husband alleged that the book did not have adequate instructions; that it failed to warn that uncooked Dasheen roots are poisonous; and that the ingredients contained in the recipes for Dasheen plant dishes were inadequately tested to insure their safety for human consumption. It was further alleged that Ellie's impliedly warranted that the book was reasonably fit for its intended use, and that it was not due to inadequate instructions and warning. Finally, it was alleged that Mrs. Cardozo's injuries and Mr. Cardozo's derivative claim were proximately caused by the breach of this warranty."

It appears to us that our answer will be dispositive of the case as to the claim against Ellie's. *See* Fla.App. Rule 4.6(a). Of course, our answers do not bear on the plaintiffs' action against the defendant, True.

Plaintiffs argue that the first question is controlled by the Uniform Commercial Code (U.C.C.), Section 672.314, Florida Statutes; that the second question is answered by the common law of implied warranties. Section 672.314, Florida Statutes provides:

(1) Unless excluded or modified (§ 672.316), a warranty that the goods shall be merchantable is implied in a contract for their sale if the seller is a merchant with respect to goods of that kind.

Under this section the serving for value of food or drink to be consumed either on the premises or elsewhere is a sale.

(2) Goods to be merchantable must be at least such as:

(a) Pass without objection in the trade under the contract description; and

(b) In the case of fungible goods, are of fair average quality within the description; and

(c) Are fit for the ordinary purposes for which such goods are used; and

(d) Run, within the variations permitted by the agreement, of even kind, quality and quantity within each unit and among all units involved; and

(e) Are adequately contained, packaged, and labeled as the agreement may require; and

(f) Conform to the promises or affirmations of fact made on the container or label if any.

(3) Unless excluded or modified (§ 672.316) other implied warranties may arise from course of dealing or usage of trade.

Plaintiffs see the quoted statute as one of general applicability to all retail dealers in consumer goods. They point out that this section of the U.C.C. creates a statutory implied warranty of merchantability imposed by law on the merchant who regularly sells goods and that defendant Ellie's falls in that category in respect to the sale of books. And, while plaintiffs find no decisional law to directly support their contention that Ellie's is liable, the applicability of the statute, they maintain, is obvious from its plain meaning.

Defendant, while recognizing that Ellie's may be subject to the doctrine of implied warranty now imposed by the U.C.C., claims such warranty is limited to the physical characteristics of the books they sell and cannot be construed to include the thought processes conveyed by the author and produced in writing by the publishers of that book. They urge the practical impossibility of book sellers testing every recipe in the books they sell. Moreover, they contend that if such a burden were to be imposed upon the book seller, then the merchant would have to be an expert or retain an expert in every field embraced by the numerous publications they offer. Ultimately, they argue, this would mean the stores which now disseminate information would be forced to close with the resultant infringement on freedom of speech and expression.

The definition of "goods" under the U.C.C. is sufficiently broad to include books. Section 672.105, Florida Statutes. *Cf. Lake Wales Publishing Co. v. Florida Visitor,* 335 So.2d 335 (Fla.App.2d DCA 1976), holding printed pamphlets as goods under U.C.C. Clearly, the defendant Ellie's qualifies as a merchant with respect to books. Section 672.-314(1), Florida Statutes.

Thus, we approach the novel question of not whether Ellie's impliedly warranted the recipe book it sold to Mrs. Cardozo, but rather, the scope of that warranty. From reading Section 672.314(2), the requirement of merchantability most relevant here is (c), which requires goods to be "fit for the ordinary purposes for which such goods are used."

As we have observed, books are goods. As such Ellie's is held to have impliedly warranted the tangible, physical properties; *i.e.*, printing and binding of books. But, at this point it becomes necessary to distinguish between the tangible properties of these goods and the thoughts and ideas conveyed thereby. The principle involved is not directly controlled by any precedent of the decisional law, either under the doctrine of implied warranty under common law or as codified under the U.C.C. It is unthinkable that standards imposed on the quality of goods sold by a merchant would require that merchant, who is a book seller, to evaluate the thought processes of the many authors and publishers of the hundreds and often thousands of books which the merchant offers for sale. One can readily imagine the extent of potential litigation. Is the newsdealer, or for that matter the neighborhood news carrier, liable if the local paper's recipes call for inedible ingredients? We think not.

While not directly in point, it is interesting to note that even publishers have not been held liable where injuries have occurred through use of products advertised in their magazines. Thus, in *Yuhas v. Mudge,* 129 N.J.Super. 207, 322 A.2d 824 (1974), the court said that Popular Mechanics Corp. could not be held liable to a plaintiff injured by fireworks resulting from an allegedly defective product advertised in the corporation's magazine. The court pointed out that the magazine had neither endorsed the product or secured any direct pecuniary benefit from the sale of the fireworks. To impose that legal duty upon the publisher, the court said, would have a staggering adverse effect upon the commercial world and our economic system. More closely in point is the pre-U.C.C. case, *Mac Kown v. Ill. Publishing & Printing Co.,* 289 Ill.App. 59, 6 N.E.2d 526 (1937), where the court refused to hold a newspaper liable for injuries to one of its readers allegedly resulting from the reader's use of a dandruff remedy recommended as one given to the writer of the article by a reputable physician. The principles of law and considerations of public policy which support denial of liability of a publisher in these instances more urgently mandates denial of liability of a newsdealer.

Closely analogous is the principle that distributors of newspapers and periodicals cannot be even held legally responsible for defamatory material contained therein where the dealer did not know and reasonably could not have known that the publication contained defamatory material.

* * *

Thus liability without fault, which may be present in an action for breach of implied warranty, has long been held inappropriate in an action against one passing on printed words without an opportunity to investigate them. The principle against imposing liability without fault on a publisher in a defamation action has recently been given constitutional status. *See Gertz v. Robert Welch, Inc.,* 418 U.S. 323, 94 S.Ct. 2997, 41 L.Ed.2d 789 (1974); *Time Inc. v. Firestone,* 424 U.S. 448, 96 S.Ct. 958, 47 L.Ed.2d 154 (1976).

The common theme running through these decisions is that ideas hold a privileged position in our society. They are not equivalent to commercial products. Those who are in the business of distributing the ideas of other people perform a unique and essential function. To hold those who perform this essential function liable, regardless of fault, when an injury results would severely restrict the flow of the ideas they distribute. We think that holding Ellie's liable under the doctrine of implied warranty would, based upon the facts as certified to us, have the effect of imposing a liability without fault not intended by the Uniform Commercial Code.

The reasoning applicable to our response to the first question must also conclude the answer to the second. The U.C.C. in codifying the law of sales did nothing to restrict the common law doctrine of implied warranty under Florida law. To the contrary, the code raised the dignity of the doctrine to statute and made it a certainty that warranties would be implied in accordance with the statutory design where the seller is a merchant with respect to goods of that particular kind being sold.

We make no statements concerning the liability of an author or publisher under the facts as certified to us. Nor do we pass upon the question of whether Ellie's could be held liable if it actually knew the book it sold contained recipes with poisonous ingredients. Rather, we hold that absent allegations that a book seller knew that there was reason to warn the public as to contents of a book, the implied warranty in respect to sale of books by a merchant who regularly sells them is limited to a warranty of the physical properties of such books and does not extend to the material communicated by the book's author or publisher.

Accordingly, we answer each of the questions certified in the negative and remand this cause for further proceedings consistent with this opinion.

BOARDMAN, C.J., and HOBSON, J., concur.

Notes

1. The court in *True* did not directly consider the applicability of strict tort liability to a publication, although it did address a common law warranty. Are any of the policies underlying strict tort liability any less applicable to the informational content of a book than to its physical characteristics?

2. Suppose Ellie's were a grocer that sold "elephant ears" to its customers along with extensive, but defective, instructions for their preparation. Would the transaction be governed by strict tort liability or an implied

warranty of merchantability? If so, is there a reason not to hold Ellie's liable in the actual case?

3. Do the policies underlying the adoption of strict tort liability help determine whether to apply the doctrine in cases of this type?

4. A few courts have addressed the issue of liability on the part of product certifiers, such as Good Housekeeping and Underwriters Laboratories. The cases have generally held that such a defendant who *negligently* makes representation about a product's quality can be held liable, but no court has applied strict tort liability or an implied warranty of merchantability to a product certifier. *See* Hempstead v. General Fire Extinguisher Corp., 269 F.Supp. 109 (D.Del.1967); Hanberry v. Hearst Corp., 276 Cal. App.2d 680, 81 Cal.Rptr. 519 (1969).

5. A few courts have applied strict tort liability or an implied warranty of merchantability to air and sea navigational charts. *See* Fluor Corp. v. Jeppesen & Co., 170 Cal.App.3d 468, 216 Cal.Rptr. 68 (1985) (strict tort liability); Saloomey v. Jeppesen & Co., 707 F.2d 671 (2d Cir.1983) (strict tort liability); Times Mirror Co. v. Sisk, 122 Ariz. 174, 593 P.2d 924 (App.1978) (jury question on strict tort liability, innocent misrepresentation under section 402B, and implied warranty). *Cf.* De Bardeleben Marine Corp. v. United States, 451 F.2d 140 (5th Cir.1971) (negligent misrepresentation; no liability for government). In In re Korean Air Lines Disaster of Sept. 1, 1983, 597 F.Supp. 619 (D.D.C.1984), the court held that a navigational chart was not defective solely for failing to warn aircraft that they might be shot if they entered Soviet airspace.

Should it matter whether the "defect" in a navigational chart is a result of faulty surveying or faulty printing?

5. USED PRODUCTS

TILLMAN v. VANCE EQUIPMENT CO.

Supreme Court of Oregon, 1979.
286 Or. 747, 596 P.2d 1299.

DENECKE, CHIEF JUSTICE.

Plaintiff brought this action based upon the theory of strict liability in tort to recover for personal injuries caused by a 24–year–old crane sold by defendant, a used equipment dealer, to plaintiff's employer, Durametal. The court tried the case without a jury and found for the defendant. The plaintiff appeals and we affirm.

Durametal asked the defendant to locate a crane for purchase by Durametal. Defendant found one that looked suitable; Durametal inspected and approved it. The defendant purchased the crane and immediately resold it to Durametal. Defendant prepared documents making the sale "as is."

Durametal assigned plaintiff to operate the crane, including greasing it. Plaintiff believed the greasing of the gears could not be done properly without removing the gear cover and applying the grease while the gears were moving. While he was so greasing the gears, plaintiff's hand was drawn into them and he was injured.

Plaintiff alleged the defendant seller was liable because the crane was defectively designed in that it could not be properly greased without removing the protective gear covering and for failing to provide warnings of the danger. The trial court found for the defendant because the crane was a used piece of equipment and sold "as is."

The parties disagree about the effect of the "as is" disclaimer in the documents of sale. The issues raised include whether that disclaimer has any effect in an action of strict liability in tort, and whether, if so, it is effective to disclaim liability for a design defect as distinguished from a defect in the condition of the individual product. We do not answer these questions because we conclude that the trial court was correct in holding that a seller of used goods is not strictly liable in tort for a defect in a used crane when that defect was created by the manufacturer.

* * *

In order to determine whether the defendant seller may be held liable we are required to re-examine why we arrived at the decision that a seller "who is free from fault in the usual legal sense" should be held strictly liable for a defective product. *Wights v. Staff Jennings,* 241 Or. 301, 306, 405 P.2d 624, 626 (1965).

"* * * Usually liability has been predicated on a breach of an implied warranty without explaining why the warranty was judicially implied. When the action was brought by the buyer against his immediate seller, it seemed enough that the plaintiff and defendant were parties to a contract, the warranty being born in some mysterious way out of the contractual relationship even in the absence of any promise express or implied in fact made by the seller. * * *." *Wights v. Staff Jennings, supra,* at 306, 405 P.2d at 626–27.

Because of the impediments accompanying a contractual remedy, including the requirement of privity, we evolved the tort of strict liability. *Redfield v. Mead, Johnson & Co.,* 266 Or. 273, 285, 512 P.2d 776 (1973) (specially concurring). Strict liability could be imposed upon a party with whom the plaintiff was not in privity. For this reason the manufacturer who created the defect could be sued directly. The injured party could usually obtain personal jurisdiction over the manufacturer by the use of the long-arm statutes. Because of the circumstances, there was no longer any urgent necessity to continue a cause of action against the seller who had not created the defect.

Nevertheless, courts did impose strict liability on the nonmanufacturer sellers of new goods * * *.

* * *

As Mr. Justice Traynor said in *Vandermark v. Ford Motor Company,* 61 Cal.2d 256, 37 Cal.Rptr. 896, 899, 391 P.2d 168, 171 (1964):

"Retailers like manufacturers are engaged in the business of distributing goods to the public. They are an integral part of the overall producing and marketing enterprise that should bear the cost of injuries resulting from defective products. (See *Greenman v. Yuba Power Products, Inc.,* 59 Cal.2d 57, 63, 27 Cal.Rptr. 697, 377 P.2d 897). In some cases the retailer may be the only member of that enterprise reasonably available to the injured plaintiff. In other cases the retailer himself may play a substantial part in insuring that the product is safe or may be in a position to exert pressure on the manufacturer to that end; the retailer's strict liability thus serves as an added incentive to safety. * * *."

Mr. Justice Schaefer stated in *Dunham v. Vaughan & Bushnell Mfg. Co.,* 42 Ill.2d 339, 247 N.E.2d 401, 404 (1969): "The strict liability of a retailer arises from his integral role in the overall producing and marketing enterprise and affords an additional incentive to safety."

Moreover, if a jurisdiction has adopted the principle of strict liability on the basis of enterprise liability, the liability of the seller of either a new or used product would logically follow.

* * *

This court has never been willing to rely on enterprise liability alone as a justification for strict liability for defective products. See *Markle v. Mulholland's, Inc., supra,* 265 Or. at 265, 509 P.2d 529. Instead, we have identified three justifications for the doctrine:

" * * * [C]ompensation (ability to spread the risk), satisfaction of the reasonable expectations of the purchaser or user (implied representational aspect), and over-all risk reduction (the impetus to manufacture a better product) * * *." *Fulbright v. Klamath Gas Co.,* 271 Or. 449, 460, 533 P.2d 316, 321 (1975).

While dealers in used goods are, as a class, capable like other businesses of providing for the compensation of injured parties and the allocation of the cost of injuries caused by the products they sell, we are not convinced that the other two considerations identified in *Fulbright* weigh sufficiently in this class of cases to justify imposing strict liability on sellers of used goods generally.

Our opinions have discussed, on other occasions, what we called in *Fulbright* the "implied representational aspect" of the justification for strict products liability. In *Heaton v. Ford Motor Co.,* 248 Or. 467, 435 P.2d 806 (1967), both the majority and the dissent indicated that at least in some cases it was for the jury to decide what degree of safety the average consumer of a product expects. However, in *Markle v. Mulholland's, Inc., supra,* 265 Or. 259, 509 P.2d 529, a majority of the court agreed that the question was not solely a factual one.

* * *

We consider, then, whether the trier of fact may infer any representation as to safety from the sale of a used product.

We conclude that holding every dealer in used goods responsible regardless of fault for injuries caused by defects in his goods would not only affect the prices of used goods; it would work a significant change in the very nature of used goods markets. Those markets, generally speaking, operate on the apparent understanding that the seller, even though he is in the business of selling such goods, makes no particular representation about their quality simply by offering them for sale. If a buyer wants some assurance of quality, he typically either bargains for it in the specific transaction or seeks out a dealer who routinely offers it (by, for example, providing a guarantee, limiting his stock of goods to those of a particular quality, advertising that his used goods are specially selected, or in some other fashion). The flexibility of this kind of market appears to serve legitimate interests of buyers as well as sellers.

We are of the opinion that the sale of a used product, without more, may not be found to generate the kind of expectations of safety that the courts have held are justifiably created by the introduction of a new product into the stream of commerce.

As to the risk-reduction aspect of strict products liability, the position of the used-goods dealer is normally entirely outside the original chain of distribution of the product. As a consequence, we conclude, any risk reduction which would be accomplished by imposing strict liability on the dealer in used goods would not be significant enough to justify our taking that step. The dealer in used goods generally has no direct relationship with either manufacturers or distributors. Thus, there is no ready channel of communication by which the dealer and the manufacturer can exchange information about possible dangerous defects in particular product lines or about actual and potential liability claims.

In theory, a dealer in used goods who is held liable for injuries caused by a design defect or manufacturing flaw could obtain indemnity from the manufacturer. This possibility supports the argument that permitting strict liability claims against dealers in used goods will add to the financial incentive for manufacturers to design and build safe products. We believe, however, that the influence of this possibility as a practical factor in risk prevention is considerably diluted where used goods are involved due to such problems as statutes of limitation and the increasing difficulty as time passes of locating a still existing and solvent manufacturer.

Both of these considerations, of course, are also obstacles to injured parties attempting to recover directly from the manufacturer. However, although the provision of an adequate remedy for persons injured by defective products has been the major impetus to the development of strict product liability, it cannot provide the sole justification for imposing liability without fault on a particular class of defendants.

For the reasons we have discussed, we have concluded that the relevant policy considerations do not justify imposing strict liability for defective products on dealers in used goods, at least in the absence of some representation of quality beyond the sale itself or of a special position vis-a-vis the original manufacturer or others in the chain of original distribution. Accord: *Rix v. Reeves,* 23 Ariz.App. 243, 532 P.2d 185 (1975).

We have suggested, although we have never had occasion to rule on the question, that those who are in the business of leasing products to others may be strictly liable for injuries caused by defective products on the same basis as sellers of new products. *Fulbright v. Klamath Gas Co., supra,* 271 Or. at 455–458, 459, 533 P.2d 316. It has been urged that recognizing such a liability on the part of lessors while refusing to hold sellers of used goods liable would be logically inconsistent, because most leased goods are used when they reach the lessee. *Hovenden v. Tenbush, supra,* 529 S.W.2d at 310. We see no such inconsistency when the focus of analysis is not on the status of the product but on that of the potential defendant. The lessor chooses the products which he offers in a significantly different way than does the typical dealer in used goods; the fact that he offers them repeatedly to different users as products he has selected may constitute a representation as to their quality; and it may well be that he has purchased them, either new or used, from a dealer who is directly related to the original distribution chain. Our rationale in the present case leaves the question of a lessor's strict liability an open one in this jurisdiction.

* * *

Affirmed.

LENT, J., did not participate in the decision in this matter.

Notes

1. Most courts have held that strict tort liability is not applicable to the sale of used products. *See* Bruce v. Martin–Marietta Corp., 544 F.2d 442 (10th Cir.1976); Sell v. Bertsch & Co., 577 F.Supp. 1393 (D.Kan.1984); Rix v. Reeves, 23 Ariz.App. 243, 532 P.2d 185 (1975); LaRosa v. Superior Ct., Santa Clara County, 122 Cal.App.3d 741, 176 Cal.Rptr. 224 (1981); Tauber–Arons Auctioneers Co. v. Superior Ct., 101 Cal.App.3d 268, 161 Cal.Rptr. 789 (1980); Peterson v. Lou Bachrodt Chevrolet Co., 61 Ill.2d 17, 329 N.E.2d 785 (1975); Pridgett v. Jackson Iron & Metal Co., 253 So.2d 837, 841, 844 (Miss.1971); Crandell v. Larkin and Jones Appliance Co., Inc., 334 N.W.2d 31 (S.D.1983).

A few courts, however, have applied strict tort liability to a sale of used products. *See* Turner v. International Harvester Co., 133 N.J.Super. 277, 336 A.2d 62 (1975); Hovenden v. Tenbush, 529 S.W.2d 302 (Tex.Civ.App.—San Antonio 1975, no writ); Galindo v. Precision American Corp., 754 F.2d 1212 (5th Cir.1985).

2. Some courts have suggested that a seller of used products should be permitted to disclaim strict tort liability in some situations, even if a seller of new products cannot. In Turner v. International Harvester Co., 133 N.J.Super. 277, 336 A.2d 62 (1975), the court declined to hold that a sale of a used product is automatically beyond the scope of strict tort liability. It then addressed the issue of whether the seller could disclaim liability:

Should a simple "as is" disclaimer effectively insulate the dealer from a claim of strict liability in tort following an accident resulting from a *safety* defect present in the vehicle when it was in the control of the dealer? When selling to the ordinary consumer, the answer must be No. Bargaining power and ability to protect one's interests are generally disproportionate as between the buyer of used goods and one in the business of selling them. While freedom to contract need not be impaired if a buyer wishes to contract away his right to protection, an unequivocal waiver of safety defects must be shown (see the discussion with respect to waiver of tort claims under section III of this opinion, infra). Otherwise, when the additional indirect costs will be borne by the public through insurance costs, a decent regard for the public safety requires the thumb of the State to be on the buyer's side of the scale. Cf. Henningsen v. Bloomfield Motors, Inc., 32 N.J. 358, 161 A.2d 69 (1960).

The third question also raises a jury issue. It may be found that the buyer in this case was (or represented himself to be) knowledgeable about this product because of his background or experience. This will not necessarily result from the transaction being denominated "commercial" [citation]. Also, the effect upon plaintiff and her family, and upon injured persons in general, is no less because the injury occurred in a nonconsumer atmosphere. In fact, the pleadings and affidavits submitted here suggest that plaintiff's decedent may have been personally familiar with the particular truck he bought. The goods should be viewed, not in the abstract, but as they affect a particular seller, purchaser or user, and the circumstances of the sale.

* * *

Looking at the used automobile situation, one can readily envision an antique car buff or "hot rod" enthusiast purchasing a car which is defective in many respects and where the relationship between the buyer and seller is such that both reasonably expect that all aspects of the automobile will be separately appraised and all defects corrected by the purchaser. In this connection see Greenman v. Yuba Power Products, Inc., 59 Cal.2d 57, 62, 27 Cal.Rptr. 697, 700, 377 P.2d 897, 900 (1963), in which Justice Traynor stated that a manufacturer "is strictly liable in tort when an article he places on the market, *knowing* that it is to be used without inspection for defects, proves to have a defect that causes injury to a human being."

Even with respect to the sale of a truck, the actual situation of the parties to the contract may present a question. A used truck purchased by a large trucking company known by both buyer and seller to have extensive repair facilities might be expected to undergo great scrutiny only by the buyer, while a similar truck purchased by a merchant to make his retail deliveries might not reasonably be expected to be so examined unless special circumstances exist. Thus, in some circumstances the relationship of the parties and apparent sophistication of the purchaser might indicate the defect did not present an unreasonable danger to the particular purchaser as user of the product. In others the purchaser's conduct in not discovering or correcting a defect which a reasonable person of his background and experience should have corrected might warrant a finding that the defect was not unreasonably dangerous. * * *

3. Note also from the language of *Turner,* a decision about defectiveness may be different when a used product is sold. Certainly consumer expectations differ concerning a used product. Does the fact that a product is used affect a risk-utility balance?

4. Would it make any difference if a seller of a used product refurbished or reconditioned it? *See* Mid Continent Aircraft Corp. v. Curry County Spraying Service, Inc., 572 S.W.2d 308 (Tex.1978). The court in *Mid Continent* held that the seller of a rebuilt engine was not liable for economic damages under strict tort liability and was not liable at all for breach of warranty because the warranty had been disclaimed. The court did not seem concerned that the engine was not new. Moreover, the Court did not hold that the disclaimer was effective as a defense in strict tort liability.

5. Distinguish an action against a seller of a used product and an action against the original manufacturer or retailer by a subsequent purchaser who bought the product used from an intermediate seller. *See* Gibbs v. General Motors Corp., 450 S.W.2d 827 (Tex.1970). What issues are likely to arise in such a case?

6. Comment 3 to section 2–314 of the Commercial Code states that an implied warranty of merchantability attaches to a sale of used goods, and most courts have held that the Article 2 warranties are applicable to a sale of used goods. *See, e.g.,* Roupp v. Acor, 253 Pa.Super. 46, 384 A.2d 968 (1978). *But see* Valley Datsun v. Martinez, 578 S.W.2d 485 (Tex.Civ.App.—Corpus Christi 1979, no writ).

6. REAL ESTATE

KRIEGLER v. EICHLER HOMES, INC.

Court of Appeals, First District, 1969.
269 Cal.App.2d 224, 74 Cal.Rptr. 749.

TAYLOR, JUSTICE.

Respondent Kriegler filed this action for physical damage sustained as the result of the failure of a radiant heating system in a home constructed by appellants, Eichler Homes, Inc. and Joseph L. Eichler (hereafter Eichler), who cross-complained against the supplier, respondent, General Motors Corporation (hereafter General Motors) and the heating contractors, respondents, Anderson and Rother, individually and doing business as Arro Company (hereafter collectively referred to as Arro). Eichler appeals from the judgment in favor of Kriegler on the complaint and in favor of General Motors and Arro on the cross-complaint.

The questions presented are: 1) whether Eichler was liable to Kriegler on the theory of strict liability * * *.

The basic facts are not in dispute. In April 1957 Kriegler purchased a home in Palo Alto that had been constructed by Eichler in the last quarter of 1951 and sold to Kriegler's predecessors, the Resings, in January 1952. Eichler employed Arro as the heating contractor. Because of a copper shortage caused by the Korean war, Arro obtained terne coated steel tubing from General Motors. In the fall of 1951, Arro installed this steel tubing in the Kriegler home and guaranteed the radiant heating system in writing. Arro installed steel tubing radiant heating systems in at least 4,000 homes for Eichler.

* * *

In November 1959, as a result of the corrosion of the steel tubing, the radiant heating system of the Kriegler home failed. The emergency and final repairs required removal and storage of furniture, as well as the temporary acquisition by Kriegler and his family of other shelter.

* * *

Eichler concedes that the doctrine of strict liability in tort applies to physical harm to property (Gherna v. Ford Motor Co., 246 Cal.App.2d 639, 649, 55 Cal.Rptr. 94) but argues that the doctrine cannot be applied to homes or builders. We do not agree. As set forth in Greenman v. Yuba Power Products, Inc., 59 Cal.2d 57, 27 Cal.Rptr. 697, 377 P.2d 897, 13 A.L.R.3d 1049, and Vandermark v. Ford Motor Co., 61 Cal.2d 256, 37 Cal.Rptr. 896, 391 P.2d 168, the strict liability doctrine applies when the plaintiff proves that he was injured while using the instrumentality in a way it was intended to be used as a result of a defect in design and manufacture of which plaintiff was not aware and which made the instrumentality unsafe for its intended use. So far, it has been applied in this state only to manufacturers, retailers and suppliers of personal property and rejected as to sales of real estate (Conolley v. Bull, 258 A.C.A. 254, 265, 65 Cal.Rptr. 689). We recently pointed out in Barth v. B.F. Goodrich Tire Co., 265 A.C.A. 253 at 278, 71 Cal.Rptr. 306, that the reasoning behind the doctrine applies to any case of injury resulting from the risk-creating conduct of a seller in any stage of the production and distribution of goods.

We think, in terms of today's society, there are no meaningful distinctions between Eichler's mass production and sale of homes and the mass production and sale of automobiles and that the pertinent overriding policy considerations are the same. Law, as an instrument of justice, has infinite capacity for growth to meet changing needs and mores. Nowhere is this better illustrated than in the recent developments in the field of products liability. The law should be based on current concepts of what is right and just and the judiciary should be alert to the never-ending need for keeping legal principles abreast of the times. Ancient distinctions that make no sense in today's society and that tend to discredit the law should be readily rejected as they were step by step in Greenman and Vandermark.

We find support in our view in the comments of our most eminent authority in the law of torts (see Prosser, Strict Liability to the Consumer in California, 18 Hastings L.J., 9, 20), and the exceptionally able and well-thought out opinion of the Supreme Court of New Jersey, in a case almost on all fours with the instant one (Schipper v. Levitt & Sons, Inc. (1965) 44 N.J. 70, 207 A.2d 314). In Schipper, the purchaser of a mass-produced home sued the builder-vendor for injuries sustained by the child of a lessee. The child was injured by excessively hot water drawn from a faucet in a hot water system that had been installed without a mixing valve, a defect as latent as the incorrect positioning of the pipes in the instant case. In reversing a judgment of nonsuit, the Supreme Court held that the builder-vendor was liable to the purchaser on the basis of strict liability. In language equally applicable here, the court said: "When a vendee buys a development house from an advertised model, as in a Levitt or in a comparable project, he clearly relies on the skill of the developer and on its implied representation that the house will be erected in reasonably workmanlike manner and will be reasonably fit for habitation. He has no architect or other professional adviser of his own, he has no real competency to inspect on his own, his actual examination is, in the nature of things, largely superficial, and his opportunity for obtaining meaningful protective changes in the conveyancing documents prepared by the builder vendor is negligible. If there is improper construction such as a defective heating system or a defective ceiling, stairway and the like, the well-being of the vendee and others is seriously endangered and serious injury is foreseeable. The public interest dictates that if such injury does result from the defective construction, its cost should be borne by the responsible developer who created the danger and who is in the better economic position to bear the loss rather than by the injured party who justifiably relied on the developer's skill and implied representation." (Pp. 325–326.)

"Buyers of mass produced development homes are not on an equal footing with the builder vendors and are no more able to protect themselves in the deed than are automobile purchasers in a position to protect themselves in the bill of sale." (P. 326.) The court then pointed out that the imposition of strict liability principles on builders and developers would not make them insurers of the safety of all who thereafter came on the premises. In determining whether the house was defective, the test would be one of reasonableness rather than perfection.

As it cannot be disputed that Kriegler here relied on the skill of Eichler in producing a home with a heating system that was reasonably fit for its intended purpose, the trial court properly concluded that Eichler was liable to Kriegler on the basis of strict liability, and the judgment in favor of Kriegler must be affirmed on that ground alone.

* * *

Affirmed.

SHOEMAKER, P.J., and AGEE, J., concur.

Hearing denied; MOSK, J., did not participate.

Notes

1. It is quite clear that the Article 2 warranties do not apply to real estate. *See, e.g.,* G–W–L, Inc., v. Robichaux, 643 S.W.2d 392 (Tex.1982). Section 2–102 states that Article 2 applies to transactions in "goods." Section 2–105 defines "goods" as "all things * * * which are *movable* at the time of identification * * *" (emphasis added). Nevertheless, several courts have adopted common law warranties to apply to real estate sales. *See, e.g.,* Humber v. Morton, 426 S.W.2d 554 (Tex.1968).

2. As the opinion in *Kriegler* indicates, the seminal case applying strict tort liability to home sales was Schipper v. Levitt & Sons, Inc., 44 N.J. 70, 207 A.2d 314 (1965). Both *Kriegler* and *Schipper* involved a builder-vendor of mass-produced houses, and some courts have limited the application of strict tort liability to such cases by declining to apply the doctrine to custom built homes. *See, e.g.,* Chapman v. Lily Cache Builders, Inc., 48 Ill.App.3d 919, 6 Ill.Dec. 176, 362 N.E.2d 811 (1977).

3. Some courts have declined to apply strict tort liability to real estate transactions but have instead applied a common law implied warranty of habitability to certain home sales. *See, e.g.,* Humber v. Morton, 426 S.W.2d 554 (Tex.1968). Other courts have applied both strict tort liability and a common law implied warranty of habitability to certain home sales. *See* Vincent v. Jim Walter Homes, Inc., 1978 CCH Prod. Liab. Rep. # 8278 (Tenn.Ct.App.). One potential difference between the two theories is that warranties normally can be disclaimed. *See* G–W–L, Inc. v. Robichaux, 643 S.W.2d 392 (Tex.1982) (holding that a common law implied warranty of habitability can be disclaimed without regard to the disclaimer requirements of Section 2–316 of the Uniform Commercial Code).

4. Courts that have applied a common law warranty of habitability to home sales have done little to define the standard of habitability. Most cases have involved clear flaws, such as a leaking roof. *See* Holifield v. Coronado Bldg., Inc., 594 S.W.2d 214 (Tex.Civ.App.—Houston [14th Dist.] 1980, no writ). *Kriegler* seems to have involved a design defect, however. It is unclear whether courts will borrow from the definition of defectiveness under strict tort liability, borrow from the standard of merchantability under section 2–314 of the Uniform Commercial Code, or develop yet a third standard to determine whether a house is uninhabitable. Presumably, courts that apply strict tort liability to home sales will apply the standard of defectiveness developed in strict tort liability cases.

5. It is still unclear in many jurisdictions whether strict tort liability or a common law implied warranty of merchantability applies to real estate transactions other than the sale of a new house by a builder-vendor. Some courts have extended coverage to sales of used houses. *See, e.g.,* Gupta v. Ritter Homes, Inc., 646 S.W.2d 168 (Tex.1983).

Sales other than those of new houses by a builder-vendor raise a variety of issues that courts have not sorted out. First, strict tort liability and breach of warranty might not apply to the sale of a used house on the ground that these theories do not cover the sale of used goods. *See* subsection 5, *supra.*

Second, a purchaser of a used home who sues the original builder-vendor might face problems of privity. Normally, privity is not required in strict tort liability, and a builder should be able to foresee future resales of its houses. Privity under the Uniform Commercial Code depends on the version of section 2–318 a state adopts. Privity under a common law implied warranty depends on a particular court's decision on the issue.

Third, a court might decide that a seller other than a builder-vendor (or even mass builder-vendor) is not the right type of defendant to be governed by strict tort liability or breach of warranty. Normally, the standard under strict tort liability would be whether the defendant is in the business of selling homes, and under the Uniform Commercial Code it is whether the defendant is a merchant. A court would have more flexibility under an implied, common-law warranty.

6. Should it make any difference whether the alleged defect is in a product installed in the home, such as a water heater, or in the house's overall design? One case suggesting such a distinction is Lowrie v. Evanston, 50 Ill.App.3d 376, 8 Ill.Dec. 537, 365 N.E.2d 923 (1977). In *Lowrie,* the plaintiff's decedent fell from a parking garage, and the plaintiff alleged that the garage was defectively designed because, *inter alia,* it "did not have guard rails and/or restraints to prevent individuals from falling from the windows and openings." 8 Ill.Dec. at 539, 365 N.E.2d at 925. The court declined to apply strict tort liability, noting that several cases applying strict tort liability to real estate transactions "do not deal with a defect in the home *per se* but with a defect in some product installed therein." 8 Ill.Dec. at 542, 365 N.E.2d at 928. *See also* Cox v. Shaffer, 223 Pa.Super. 429, 302 A.2d 456 (1973), distinguishing between defective components installed in a building and a defective design of the overall building itself. *But see* Hyman v. Gordon, 35 Cal.App.3d 769, 111 Cal.Rptr. 262 (1973) (house defectively designed because water heater placed in garage). Do the policies underlying strict tort liability apply with different force to houses that contain defective products and houses that are themselves defectively designed or constructed?

7. Some courts have refused to apply any form of strict liability to the sale of houses. In Bruce Farms, Inc. v. Coupe, 219 Va. 287, 247 S.E.2d 400 (1978), the court declined to apply strict liability to the sale of a house largely on the ground that doing so would raise questions about the types of house sales that should be covered, and that these line-drawing issues are better left to the legislature. Are these line-drawing issues intrinsically any more difficult than determining the scope of strict liability in other types of transactions? Nevertheless, can a case be made that the policies underlying strict tort liability do not apply as forcefully to real estate, even the sale of a new house by a builder-vendor?

BECKER v. IRM CORP.
Supreme Court of California, 1985.
38 Cal.3d 454, 213 Cal.Rptr. 213, 698 P.2d 116.

BROUSSARD, JUSTICE.

In this personal injury action plaintiff's complaint asserted causes of action of strict liability and negligence against defendant landlord.

Defendant moved for summary judgment urging that a landlord is not liable to a tenant for a latent defect of the rented premises absent concealment of a known danger or an expressed contractual or statutory duty to repair. The trial court granted the motion and denied a motion for reconsideration. Plaintiff appeals.

We have concluded that the trial court erred as to both causes of action.

The complaint alleged that plaintiff was injured when he slipped and fell against the frosted glass shower door in the apartment he leased from defendant. The door was made of untempered glass. It broke and severely lacerated his arm. It is undisputed that the risk of serious injury would have been substantially reduced if the shower door had been made of tempered glass rather than untempered glass.

* * *

STRICT LIABILITY

In *Greenman v. Yuba Power Products, Inc.* (1963) 59 Cal.2d 57, 62, 27 Cal.Rptr. 697, 377 P.2d 897, we established the rule: "A manufacturer is strictly liable in tort when an article he places on the market, knowing that it is to be used without inspection for defects, proves to have a defect that causes injury to a human being. Recognized first in the case of unwholesome food products, such liability has now been extended to a variety of other products that create as great or greater hazards if defective. [Citations.]" The court recognized that the cases imposing strict liability had "usually been based on the theory of an express or implied warranty running from the manufacturer to the plaintiff." (59 Cal.2d at p. 63, 27 Cal.Rptr. 697, 377 P.2d 897.) The justification for departing from warranty theory and for establishing a doctrine of strict liability in tort was the recognition that the liability was imposed by law and the refusal to permit the manufacturer to define the scope of its own liability for defective products. (*Ibid.*)

Our concern was not that warranty law failed to adequately define the manufacturer's duty but that the " 'intricacies of the law of sales' " applicable to commercial transactions might defeat the obvious representation of safety for intended use made by the manufacturer. (*Id.,* at pp. 63–64, 27 Cal.Rptr. 697, 377 P.2d 897.) In declining to discuss the basis of the strict liability, *Greenman* pointed out that the basis of it had been fully articulated, citing to the classical concurring opinion in *Escola v. Coca Cola Bottling Co.* (1944) 24 Cal.2d 453, 461, 150 P.2d 436. (*Id.,* 59 Cal.3d at p. 63, 27 Cal.Rptr. 697, 377 P.2d 897.) In the concurring opinion in *Escola,* Justice Traynor pointed out: "The retailer, even though not equipped to test a product, is under an absolute liability to his customer, for the implied warranties of fitness for proposed use and merchantable quality include a warranty of safety of the product. [Citations.]" (24 Cal.2d at p. 464, 150 P.2d 436.) It was also pointed out that the retailer should not bear the burden of his warranty alone but that he could recoup any losses by means of the warranty of safety attending the wholesaler's or manufacturer's sale to him. (*Ibid.*)

Greenman also noted that the purpose of strict liability in tort is "to insure that the costs of injuries resulting from defective products are borne by the manufacturers that put such products on the market rather than by the injured persons who are powerless to protect themselves." (59 Cal.2d at p. 63, 27 Cal.Rptr. 697, 377 P.2d 897; see *Daly v. General Motors* (1978) 20 Cal.3d 725, 732–733, 736, 144 Cal.Rptr. 380, 575 P.2d 1162.)

* * *

[A]pplication of strict liability in tort has not been limited to those engaged in commerce in personalty but has been applied where appropriate to those engaged in real estate businesses who impliedly represent the quality of their product. In *Kriegler v. Eichler Homes, Inc.* (1969) 269 Cal.App.2d 224, 74 Cal.Rptr. 749, a builder who mass-produced homes was held strictly liable when the heating system placed in a home failed. The court relied upon *Schipper v. Levitt & Sons, Inc.* (1965) 44 N.J. 70, 207 A.2d 314, 325–326, where the court pointed out that when in our modern society a person purchases a tract house from an advertised model, he relies upon the skill of the developer and the implied representation that the house will be erected in a reasonably workmanlike manner and reasonably fit for habitation, that the purchaser ordinarily does not have the means to protect himself either by hiring experts to supervise and inspect or by provision in the deed, and that the public interest dictates that the cost of injury from defects should be borne by the developer who created the danger and who is in a better economic position to bear the loss rather than the injured party who relied on the developer's skill and implied representation. In *Avner v. Longridge Estates* (1969) 272 Cal.App.2d 607, 615, 77 Cal.Rptr. 633, it was held that a manufacturer of a residential lot may be held strictly liable in tort for damages suffered by the owner as the result of defect in the manufacturing process causing subsidence.

A similar development appears with respect to the landlord-tenant relationship. The earlier legal concepts regarded the lease as an equivalent to a sale of the premises for the term and under traditional common law rules the landlord owed no duty to place leased premises in a habitable condition and no obligation to repair absent an agreement. (*Green v. Superior Court* (1974) 10 Cal.3d 616, 622, 111 Cal.Rptr. 704, 517 P.2d 1168; *McNally v. Ward* (1961) 192 Cal.App.2d 871, 878, 14 Cal.Rptr. 260.) [ ]The common law placed the risk on the tenant as to whether the condition of the leased property made it unsuitable for the use contemplated by the parties. In recent years, the definite judicial trend has been in the direction of increasing the responsibility of the landlord, in the absence of a valid contrary agreement, to provide the tenant with property in a condition suitable for the use contemplated by the parties.

* * *

Pointing out that the traditional common law rule that the landlord had no duty to make the dwelling habitable arose in the agrarianism of the Middle Ages and is incompatible with contemporary social conditions and modern legal values, California courts have recognized that a lease for a dwelling contains an implied warranty of habitability.

* * *

We are satisfied that the rationale of the foregoing cases, establishing the duties of a landlord and the doctrine of strict liability in tort, requires us to conclude that a landlord engaged in the business of leasing dwellings is strictly liable in tort for injuries resulting from a latent defect in the premises when the defect existed at the time the premises were let to the tenant. It is clear that landlords are part of the "overall producing and marketing enterprise" that makes housing accommodations available to renters. (Cf. *Vandermark v. Ford Motor Co., supra,* 61 Cal.2d at p. 262, 37 Cal.Rptr. 896, 391 P.2d 168; *Green v. Superior Court, supra,* 10 Cal.3d at pp. 623, 627, 111 Cal.Rptr. 704, 517 P.2d 1168.) A landlord, like defendant owning numerous units, is not engaged in isolated acts within the enterprise but plays a substantial role. The fact that the enterprise is one involving real estate may not immunize the landlord. Our courts have long recognized that contracts relating to realty may give rise to implied warranties. (*Aced v. Hobbs–Sesack Plumbing Co., supra,* 55 Cal.2d 573, 580–583, 12 Cal.Rptr. 257, 360 P.2d 897.)

Absent disclosure of defects, the landlord in renting the premises makes an implied representation that the premises are fit for use as a dwelling and the representation is ordinarily indispensable to the lease. (*Pollard v. Saxe & Yolles Dev. Co., supra,* 12 Cal.3d 374, 377–380, 115 Cal.Rptr. 648, 525 P.2d 88.) The tenant purchasing housing for a limited period is in no position to inspect for latent defects in the increasingly complex modern apartment buildings or to bear the expense of repair whereas the landlord is in a much better position to inspect for and repair latent defects. (*Green v. Superior Court, supra,* 10 Cal.3d at p. 626, 111 Cal.Rptr. 704, 517 P.2d 1168.) The tenant's ability to inspect is ordinarily substantially less than that of a purchaser of the property. (Cf. *Pollard v. Saxe & Yolles Dev. Co., supra,* 12 Cal.3d at p. 379, 115 Cal.Rptr. 648, 525 P.2d 88.)

The tenant renting the dwelling is compelled to rely upon the implied assurance of safety made by the landlord. It is also apparent that the landlord by adjustment of price at the time he acquires the property, by rentals or by insurance is in a better position to bear the costs of injuries due to defects in the premises than the tenants.

In these circumstances, strict liability in tort for latent defects existing at the time of renting must be applied to insure that the landlord who markets the product bears the costs of injuries resulting from the defects "rather than the injured persons who are powerless to protect themselves." (*Greenman v. Yuba Power Products, Inc., supra,* 59 Cal.2d at p. 63, 27 Cal.Rptr. 697, 377 P.2d 897.)

Defendant argues that a landlord who purchases an existing building which is not new should be exempt from strict liability in tort for latent defects because, like dealers in used personalty, he assertedly is not part of the manufacturing and marketing enterprise. Defendant relies on a statement in *Vandermark v. Ford Motor Co., supra,* 61 Cal.2d 256, 262–263, 37 Cal.Rptr. 896, 391 P.2d 168: "Strict liability on the manufacturer and retailer alike affords maximum protection to the injured plaintiff and works no injustice to defendants, for they can adjust the costs of such protection between them in the course of their continuing business relationship." Defendant states that it has never been in a business relationship with the builder and that purchasers of used rental properties do not have a continuing business relationship with builders permitting adjustments of the costs of protecting tenants.

* * *

However, a continuing business relationship is not essential to imposition of strict liability. The unavailability of the manufacturer is not a factor militating against liability of others engaged in the enterprise. The paramount policy of the strict products liability rule remains the spreading throughout society of the cost of compensating otherwise defenseless victims of manufacturing defects. (*Ray v. Alad Corp.* (1977) 19 Cal.3d 22, 33–34, 136 Cal.Rptr. 574, 560 P.2d 3; *Price v. Shell Oil Co.* (1970) 2 Cal.3d 245, 251, 85 Cal.Rptr. 178, 466 P.2d 722; *Rawlings v. D.M. Oliver, Inc* (1979) 97 Cal.App.3d 890, 899 et seq., 159 Cal.Rptr. 119.) If anything, the unavailability of the manufacturer is a factor militating in favor of liability of persons engaged in the enterprise who can spread the cost of compensation. (See *Ray v. Alad Corp., supra,* 19 Cal.3d 22, 33–34, 136 Cal.Rptr. 574, 560 P.2d 3.) Just as the unavailability of the manufacturer does not militate against liability, the absence of a continuing business relationship between builder and landlord is not a factor warranting denial of strict liability of the landlord.

* * *

The cost of protecting tenants is an appropriate cost of the enterprise. Within our marketplace economy, the cost of purchasing rental housing is obviously based on the anticipated risks and rewards of the purchase, and thus it may be expected that along with numerous other factors the price of used rental housing will depend in part on the quality of the building and reflect the anticipated costs of protecting tenants, including repairs, replacement of defects and insurance. Further, the landlord after purchase may be able to adjust rents to reflect such costs. The landlord will also often be able to seek equitable indemnity for losses.

We conclude that the absence of a continuing business relationship between builder and landlord does not preclude application of strict liability in tort for latent defects existing at the time of the lease because landlords are an integral part of the enterprise and they should bear the cost of injuries resulting from such defects rather than the injured persons who are powerless to protect themselves. (*Greenman v. Yuba Power Products, Inc., supra,* 59 Cal.2d 57, 63, 27 Cal.Rptr. 697.)

* * *

LUCAS, JUSTICE, concurring and dissenting.

I concur in that portion of the majority opinion which holds that a landlord may be held liable for dangerous conditions of which he knew or should have known. However, I cannot join in imposing upon landlords strict liability for latent defects in any component of their property no matter who built or installed the defective item.

* * *

Discounting other crucial and long-recognized justifications for imposition of strict liability, my colleagues focus primarily on the "risk-spreading" function of this form of liability. Essentially they ignore the fact that landlords of used property have no special position with regard to original manufacturers and sellers and thus have no influence to wield in order to improve product safety. Moreover, contrary to the majority's implication, the landlord, while impliedly representing that the premises are habitable, is not representing to tenants that he has expertise and guarantees the perfection of every item forming the premises. Instead of considering what role landlords of used property realistically play with regard to that property, the majority concentrates narrowly on the advancement of "The paramount policy of the strict products liability rules [namely] the spreading throughout society of the cost of compensating otherwise defenseless victims of manufacturing defects." (*Ante,* p. 220 of 213 Cal.Rptr., at p. 123 of 698 P.2d.)

* * *

* * * As the [Missouri] Court of Appeal observed, "No case has been cited, nor has one been found, imposing strict liability upon the non-builder landlord for latent defects, rendering the premises unsafe or dangerous, absent some actual or constructive notice of the defects." (*Henderson v. W.C. Haas Rlty. Management, Inc.* (Mo.App.1977) 561 S.W.2d 382, 387.) Cases rejecting application of liability without knowledge have utilized various approaches. (See, e.g., *Meyer v. Parkin* (Minn.App.1984) 350 N.W.2d 435, 438–439 [recent legislation did not eliminate requirement of scienter on part of landlord before he has duty to warn lessee of concealed defects]; *George Washington University v. Weintraub* (D.C.App.1983) 458 A.2d 43, 49 and fn. 9 [landlord exercising reasonable care may not be held liable for losses caused from defects of which he neither knew nor should have known]; *Livingston v. Begay,* supra, 652 P.2d 734 [lessor of motel room not strictly liable; theory not meant to apply to "unsafe design of a hotel room"]; *Boudreau v. General Elect. Co.* (1981) 2 Haw.App. 10, 625 P.2d 384, 389–390 [strict liability requires lessor be engaged in business of supplying goods in which defect is claimed]; *Segal v. Justice Court Mut. Housing Co-op* (N.Y.Civ.Ct.1980) 105 Misc.2d 453, 432 N.Y.S.2d 463, 467, affd. (1981)

108 Misc.2d 1074, 442 N.Y.S.2d 686 [no strict liability of landlords under public policy or legislation; they are not insurers of property]; *Kidd v. Price* (Ky.1970) 461 S.W.2d 565, 567 [liability for latent defect depends on notice or knowledge thereof].)

I would hold that a subsequent purchaser of property who has not installed, altered or created the item or condition which is claimed to be defective, and who has no actual or constructive knowledge of any defect therein, should not be held strictly liable. If the landlord knows or should know of the defect, then he has a duty to take appropriate action to correct or warn of the problem. However, where the landlord has no continuing relationship with the chain of marketing leading back to the manufacturer of the defective product, and thus has no way of influencing the production or design of the product or of adjusting potential costs of the *manufacturer's* enterprise or others in the business of marketing the item at issue, imposition of strict liability is inappropriate. The only rationales supporting such responsibility are ease of proof for the injured party and "distributing" the risk of damages to the landlord. The costs of such an extension of liability to those *without* expertise or continuing relationships for the multiple products and parts for which they may now bear responsibility will entail a significant shift in how our tort system has heretofore operated. It amounts, in effect to insurance for tenants, because it does nothing to aid in the goals of deterrence or product safety.

I would affirm the trial court's decision to the extent that it granted summary judgment to defendant on the cause of action sounding in strict liability, while joining in the majority's reversal as to the negligence cause of action.

MOSK, J., concurs.

Notes

1.   Some courts have applied a common law warranty of habitability to permit a lessee to recover for defects in the rented premises. *See, e.g.,* Pines v. Perssion, 14 Wis.2d 590, 111 N.W.2d 409 (1961); Kamarath v. Bennett, 568 S.W.2d 658 (Tex.1978) (superseded by Tex.Rev.Stat.Ann. 5236f (Vernon 1979)).

2.   In Armstrong v. Cione, 69 Hawaii 176, 738 P.2d 79 (1987), the Hawaii Supreme Court declined to apply strict tort liability to a landlord for defects in residential rental property. As in *Becker,* the court reasoned that several purposes underlying strict liability are not applicable to leased residential property. Specifically, the plaintiff has no unique problems of proof, the landlord cannot pass the cost of liability up the chain of distribution to the manufacturer, and the landlord is not in a good position to make specific products in the rental property safer. The court expressly disapproved of the holding in *Becker.*

7. SERVICES

Cases involving services raise two related but distinct issues: (1) whether to apply strict liability to pure services and (2) if pure services are not governed by strict liability, how to distinguish between products and services in hybrid transactions involving both products and services. Although these two issues are distinct, they are also related: distinguishing between products and services in hybrid cases should be resolved consistently with the reasons for treating products and services differently in the first place.

Courts have relied on various forms of analysis to determine whether individual hybrid sales-service cases are governed by strict liability, but they have failed to develop a comprehensive approach. One impediment to a comprehensive approach is that the so-called "sales-service" problem actually consists of four distinct problems that courts often conflate.

The first problem, which is the primary focus of this section, is whether pure services are governed by strict liability and, if they are not, how "products" and "services" are to be distinguished. For example, a plumber who installs a water heater might be dealing in a product (an installed water heater) or a service (installation).

A second issue is whether a transaction that involves a product involves a "sale" of the product. This issue, which was considered in the sections dealing with leases and bailments, is a common one in cases involving services because service providers often use products while rendering their services. For example, a permanent wave solution is clearly a product, but it is unclear whether a beauty salon that has applied it to a customer has sold it or merely used it while performing a service. Similarly, defective hypodermic needles and hospital gowns are clearly products, but has a doctor who has used the needles or a hospital that has issued the gowns sold them to the patients?

A third issue is whether defendants engaged in a profession merit special treatment. Many of the sales-service cases have arisen in situations involving professional services, especially health care services, and it is often unclear whether a court's analysis applies equally to nonprofessional services.

A final issue is whether the sales-service distinction in cases relying on strict tort liability is the same as the sales-service distinction in cases relying on the warranty provisions of Article 2 of the Uniform Commercial Code.

Each of these issues is important in its own right. The primary purpose of this section is to examine the first issue: whether pure services are governed by strict liability and, if they are not, the distinction between products and services. Nevertheless, the other three issues are relevant because courts have intertwined all four issues in cases involving hybrid sales-service transactions. Because most sales-service cases involve more than one of the four issues, it is often difficult to determine what a particular case holds for any one of them, especially since courts have not always distinguished carefully among them.

Courts must disentangle these related but distinct issues before progress can be made toward a comprehensive approach to the sales-service distinction. While the focus of this section is on the distinction between products and services in strict tort liability, it is important to understand that a court's apparent position on this issue may be influenced by the court's failure to disentangle it from one or more of the other three issues.

Even if courts separate the product-service distinction from these other issues, the distinction itself poses problems that have a dual significance. In addition to impeding the resolution of specific cases, the failure to develop a comprehensive approach in the product-service distinction reveals a latent general problem of strict products liability. A premise of strict products liability is that product injuries constitute a discrete, integral problem that merits special treatment. Otherwise, it would be inappropriate to distinguish product injuries from other personal injuries, liability for which is governed by negligence. But courts have not always clearly articulated the features of a product case and the policies they evoke that distinguish product injuries from other personal injuries. Without a clear understanding of *why* products cases are distinct, it has been difficult to ascertain *what* constitutes a products case in borderline situations presented by hybrid product-service transactions.

Both the proponents and opponents of strict products liability have relied on various general arguments to support their respective positions. Many of the arguments on both sides, however, do not distinguish between product injuries and other personal injuries; they apply equally to all personal injury cases. Consequently, they do not explain the selective use of strict liability in products cases, and they do not help identify "products cases" in borderline situations. The difficulty courts have encountered in defining the boundaries of strict products liability in the hybrid product-service cases reflects this underlying confusion about the values that strict products liability purports to embody. *See generally,* Powers, Distinguishing Between Products and Services in Strict Liability, 62 N.C.L.Rev. 415 (1984).

HOFFMAN v. SIMPLOT AVIATION, INC.
Supreme Court of Idaho, 1975.
97 Idaho 32, 539 P.2d 584.

Shepard, Justice.

This is an appeal from a judgment in favor of plaintiffs-respondents following trial and jury verdict in an action resulting from an airplane accident. The principal questions presented are: 1) whether the rule of strict liability in tort in the field of products liability as adopted by this Court in *Shields v. Morton Chemical Co.,* 95 Idaho 674, 518 P.2d 857 (1974) should be extended beyond sales and into the area of personal services, and, 2) the application of the doctrine of implied warranty to personal services and availability of the defenses of fault or negligence. We decline to so extend the rule of strict liability and hold that the jury was erroneously instructed as to the doctrine of implied warranty. We reverse and remand for a new trial.

The facts giving rise to this action, while lengthy in recitation, are not particularly complex or involved nor are they essentially in dispute between the parties. The case is remarkable in this respect, however, that a structural part of an early vintage single engine airplane failed during flight causing its crash and the pilot is alive to prosecute this action.

[Hoffman alleged that the accident was caused by failure of a bolt, and that after repairing the airplane due to unrelated problems, Simplot returned the airplane to Hoffman with the bolt in a rusted condition.]

It is apparently conceded by all that none of the repair work performed by the Simplot employees was a causative factor in the crash of the aircraft. Similarly no part or product placed upon the aircraft by the Simplot employees was a causative factor. While the Simplot employees were repairing the damage to the left landing gear which was occasioned by the first accident, they were working in close proximity to the clevis bolt which attached the left wing strut to the fuselage.

The principal factual dispute relates to the condition of the clevis bolt at the time that the Simplot employees had completed the repairs and made the visual inspection of the aircraft. There was testimony to the effect that the bolt showed signs of rust and therefore failure could have been anticipated. However, the Simplot employees denied that the rust was visible to them as they worked on and inspected the aircraft and that because of the age and condition of the aircraft rust had no significance.

* * *

In *Shields v. Morton Chemical Company*, 95 Idaho 674, 518 P.2d 857 (1974) this court adopted the rule of strict liability in tort as set forth in the Restatement of the Law, Torts 2nd, § 402(A) (1965). The Restatement deals specifically and only with the sale of a product. Neither this court nor, with one exception, any other court has adopted strict liability in tort absent fault in the context of personal services. We decline to extend the rule of *Shields* to cases involving personal services. We find no consideration of such extension of the rule of strict liability in either the Uniform Commercial Code or the Restatement of Torts, 2nd. Almost uniformly any such extension of the rule has been consistently and expressly rejected. *See Gagne v. Bertran*, 43 Cal.2d 481, 275 P.2d 15 (1954); *Shepard v. Alexian Bros. Hospital*, 33 Cal.App.3d 606, 109 Cal.Rptr. 132 (1973); *Hoover v. Montgomery Ward & Co., Inc.*, 528 P.2d 76 (Or.1974); *Pepsi Cola Bottling Co. v. Superior Burner Service Co.*, 427 P.2d 833 [(]Alaska 1967). We find *Broyles v. Brown Engineering Co.*, 275 Ala. 35, 151 So.2d 767 (1963) to be unpersuasive. *See also*

Prosser, Law of Torts, 679 (4th ed. 1971), 2 R. Hursh & H. Bailey, American Law Products Liability, 2nd § [§] 6–15, 6–18 (1974).

It would serve no purpose herein to extensively review the policy considerations which militate against the extension of the strict liability rule to cases involving personal service. The rationale has been thoroughly explored in the authorities and commentators set forth above and reiteration herein would serve no purpose. It is sufficient to say that as contrasted with the sales of products, personal services do not involve mass production with the difficulty, if not inability, of the obtention of proof of negligence. The consumer in the personal service context usually comes into direct contact with the one offering service and is aware or can determine what work was performed and who performed it.

* * *

It is clear that in a sales transaction an implied warranty may be imposed upon the seller to the effect that the goods are merchantable or are fit for the particular purpose for which purchased. I.C. §§ 28–2–314, 315. In circumstances involving personal services, however, the warranty is implied that the services will be performed in a workmanlike manner. The standard imposed may vary depending upon the expertise of the actor, either possessed or represented to be possessed, the nature of the services and the known resultant danger to others from the actor's negligence or failure to perform.

However, as stated in the landmark case of *Gagne v. Bertran,* 43 Cal.2d 481, 275 P.2d 15 (1954):

> "The services of experts are sought because of their special skill. They have a duty to exercise the ordinary skill and competence of members of their profession, and a failure to discharge that duty will subject them to liability for negligence. *Those who hire such persons are not justified in expecting infallibility, but can expect only reasonable care and competence. They purchase service, not insurance."* (Emphasis supplied) 275 P.2d at 21.

See American Law of Products Liability 2nd, Hursh & Bailey, § 6–15 and Restatement of Torts, 2nd § 404.

The more vexing problem of theory is the distinction, if any between the doctrines of implied warranty and negligence in circumstances involving the rendering of personal services. Although such causes of action are generally thought to be independent of each other, in the instant circumstances they merge into one cause of action. A fundamental component in a negligence action is the existence of a duty (most often to refrain) toward another and a breach thereof. In circumstances involving the rendition of personal services the duty upon the actor is to perform the services in a workmanlike manner. *Pepsi Cola Bottling Co. v. Superior Burner Service,* 427 P.2d 833 (Alaska 1967) is remarkably similar in its problems of theory and doctrine to the case at bar. Justice Rabinowitz there concluded that in the area of personal services there is a duty upon the actor to perform in a workmanlike manner and there is an implied warranty that the services will so be provided. However, it was there stated:

> "Whether the tort standard of care is considered, or the duty of care imposed by an implied warranty of workmanlike performance is taken as the applicable standard, in our view the resultant standard of care required of appellee's employees in the circumstances of this case is identical. In both instances the standard of care is imposed by law and under either theory there is no difference in the standard of care required of the party rendering the personal services.

> "Characterization of the gist, of gravamen, of appellant's cause of action in the factual context of this case is not free of difficulties. Whether an action is one in contract or tort may have significant procedural and substantive ramifications. In the case at bar appellant's central argument in support of its contention that it was entitled to go to the jury on both a tort cause of action and breach-of-an-implied-warranty-of-workmanlike-quality cause of action is that *contributory negligence would not be a bar to recovery under the latter*." (Emphasis supplied) 427 P.2d at 840–841.

* * *

* * * We hold that under the circumstances of the case at bar the implied warranty theory of plaintiffs should have been submitted to the jury with proper instructions. *Contra: Pepsi Cola Bottling Co. v. Superior Burner Service, supra*. The jury should have been instructed that plaintiffs were entitled to have defendants' services rendered in a workmanlike manner. The standard of care so imposed on the defendants should be determined in light of relevant factors such as: The inherent danger posed by an aircraft; the expertise possessed, or represented as possessed, by the defendants; the knowledge of the defendants' intended use of the aircraft, and the contributory negligence of or assumption of the risk by the plaintiffs, if any, in consideration of factors such as the age of the aircraft, its previous status and record of repair and maintenance and the previous accident.

* * *

In summary we hold that plaintiffs-respondents were entitled to have their theory of implied warranty submitted to the jury. Since the case involved the rendition of personal service, a cause of action does not exist for breach of implied warranty in the absence of fault on the part of the actor. The jury should be instructed also that the defenses of contributory negligence or assumption of the risk are available to defendants-appellants.

Appellants also assert that the special verdict forms returned by the jury were inherently contradictory to one another, therefore fatally defective and should have been rejected by the trial court. That contention does not merit discussion or treatment here since we have held *supra* that the trial court's instructions on the theory of strict liability were error and on retrial, hopefully, the possibility of contradictory special verdicts will not exist.

Reversed and remanded for a new trial consistent with this opinion. Costs to appellants.

McQUADE, C.J., and DONALDSON and BAKES, JJ., and SCOGGIN, DISTRICT JUDGE (Retired), concur.

Notes

1. The passage from *Gagne v. Bertran* quoted in *Hoffman* is quoted in nearly every opinion rejecting the application of strict liability to pure service transactions. Does it help the analysis? We could just as easily say:

> Those who hire such persons to build their *products* are not justified in expecting infallibility, but can expect only reasonable care and competence. They purchase a *product,* not insurance.

2. The opinion in *Hoffman* suggests that the standards of strict liability (at least in the warranty version) and negligence are in fact the same. In Lewis v. Big Powderhorn Mountain Ski Corp., 69 Mich.App. 437, 245 N.W.2d 81 (1976), the court made a similar argument by asserting that since a judgment about the defectiveness of a service necessarily evaluates the defendant's *conduct,* rather than a *product,* it is equivalent to a judgment about the defendant's negligence. Is this correct?

3. The opinion in *Hoffman* also relies on the argument that one of the rationales underlying strict liability—the difficulty of proving specific acts of negligence—is not as powerful in cases involving services. What of the other rationales supporting strict liability? Are they any less powerful when applied to commercial service transactions?

4. Section 2–102 of the Uniform Commercial Code provides that the Article 2 warranties apply to "transactions in goods."

5. Broyles v. Brown Eng'g Co., 275 Ala. 35, 151 So.2d 767 (1963) (per curiam), applied strict liability, under the rubric of a common law implied warranty, to a pure service transaction. Some commentators have also argued that services should be governed by strict liability. *See, e.g.,* Greenfield, Consumer Protection in Service Transactions–Implied Warranties and Strict Liability in Tort, 1974 Utah L.Rev. 661; Comment, Guidelines for Extending Implied Warranties to Service Markets, 125 U.Pa.L.Rev., 365 (1976); Note, Continuing the Common Law Response to the New Industrial State: The Extension of Enterprise Liability to Consumer Services, 22 U.C.L.A.L.Rev. 401 (1974).

HOOVER v. MONTGOMERY WARD & CO., INC.
Supreme Court of Oregon, 1974.
270 Or. 498, 528 P.2d 76.

HOWELL, JUSTICE.

* * *

[Hoover purchased tires from Montgomery Ward, who installed them. Hoover was then injured in a one-car accident and alleged that the tires were improperly installed.]

The trial court refused to submit the issue of strict liability to the jury, and the jury returned a verdict for the defendants on the issue of negligence. The plaintiff appeals.

* * * This case presents the question of whether the definition of "dangerously defective product" should be expanded to include within the scope of strict liability the negligent installation of a nondefective product. We have found no court which has stretched the doctrine of strict liability in tort to this extreme, and we decline to do so.

Plaintiff has directed the court's attention to a series of cases from other jurisdictions holding that, in a commercial transaction, the supplier of a product could be held liable under a theory of either strict liability in tort or breach of warranty, although the transaction did not fall within the traditional "sale" concept. However, these sale-service hybrid cases are inapposite to the case at hand.

In Newmark v. Gimbel's Incorporated, 54 N.J. 585, 258 A.2d 697 (1969), the New Jersey Supreme Court held a beauty shop strictly liable under an implied warranty of fitness when defective permanent wave lotion was applied to a patron's hair. The court reasoned that if the lotion had been sold over the counter there would have been strict liability. There was no logical reason to hold otherwise merely because the defective lotion was applied in a service context, especially when the cost of the service included the price of the lotion.

In *Newmark,* as in all sale-service hybrid cases, it is clear that the product, as opposed to the service, was defective. *See e.g.,* Friend v. Childs Dining Hall Co., 231 Mass. 65, 120 N.E. 407 (1918) (restaurant supplied tainted food); State Stove Manufacturing Company v. Hodges, 189 So.2d 113 (Miss.1966) cert. denied 386 U.S. 912, 87 S.Ct. 860, 17 L.Ed.2d 784 (1967) (contractor supplied defective hot water heater); Worrell v. Barnes, 87 Nev. 204, 484 P.2d 573 (1971) (redecorator of house supplied defective gas pipe fittings); and Carpenter v. Best's Apparel, Inc., 4 Wash.App. 439, 481 P.2d 924 (1971) (beauty shop supplied defective permanent wave lotion). In the case at hand, as stated above, there was no allegation that the tire was defective.

As one author notes:

> "When the contract between plaintiff and defendant is commercial in character, the courts are willing to extend liability without fault to the hybrid sale-service transaction, *provided that a defective product is supplied to the plaintiff* or used by the defendant in the course of performing the service. * * * " (Emphasis added; footnote omitted.) Note, Products and the Professional: Strict Liability in the Sale–Service Hybrid Transaction, 24 Hastings J. 111, 116 (1972).

See also, Phipps, When Does a "Service" Become a "Sale"?, 39 Ins. Counsel J. 274 (1972).

In cases other than the sale-service hybrid transaction courts have also been reluctant to extend the definition of "product" beyond the article actually manufactured or supplied. *See* Flippo v. Mode O'Day Frock Shops of Hollywood, 248 Ark. 1, 449 S.W.2d 692 (1970).

In the instant case it is obvious that the product sold to plaintiff was not dangerously defective. Even if we accepted plaintiff's version of the cause of the accident, it was not a dangerously defective tire which caused plaintiff's injuries, but rather the installation of the wheel on the hub and axle of the auto. In such case it might be said that plaintiff's auto became dangerously defective, but certainly not the tire. Plaintiff herself must have recognized this feature, because in her complaint she does not allege that the tire was an unreasonably dangerous product but that "the automobile was unreasonably dangerous for its intended use * * *."

It is clear that this was not a proper case for strict liability in tort and the trial court correctly refused to submit that issue to the jury.

We have carefully considered the plaintiff's other assignments of error and find that they are either without merit or were not properly preserved at trial. The jury obviously relied on defendants' disinterested witnesses and believed that the cause of the accident was plaintiff's manner of driving rather than negligence in the installation of the wheel on the hub and axle.

Affirmed.

Notes

1. The court in *Hoover* distinguished between the installation of a defective tire and the defective installation of a tire. What policies underlying strict tort liability support this distinction? Consider the reasoning used by the court in *Hoffman* to conclude that pure services are not governed by strict tort liability. Does this reasoning support the distinction suggested in *Hoover?*

2. Suppose the plaintiff claimed that the defendant defectively installed a defective tire. Would the first claim be governed by negligence and the second claim be governed by strict tort liability?

3. In cases involving Article 2 warranties, several courts have applied the "essence of the transaction" test to determine whether a hybrid product-service transaction is a "transaction in goods" and therefore governed by Article 2 of the Uniform Commercial Code. Under this test, the court examines the entire transaction to determine whether it *essentially* involves a service or a good. *See, e.g.,* G–W–L, Inc., v. Robichaux, 643 S.W.2d 392 (Tex.1982). This approach seems to rule out the possibility suggested by *Hoover* that part of a transaction is governed by strict tort liability while another part is not.

Some courts have used the essence of the transaction test for Article 2 warranties but a different approach for strict tort liability. *Compare* G–W–L, Inc. v. Robichaux, 643 S.W.2d 392 (Tex.1982) *with* Barbee v. Rogers, 425 S.W.2d 342 (Tex.1968).

4. In Newmark v. Gimbel's, Inc., 102 N.J.Super. 279, 246 A.2d 11 (1968), affirmed, 54 N.J. 585, 258 A.2d 697 (1969), which is discussed in

Hoover, a New Jersey court applied strict tort liability to a beauty parlor that applied a permanent wave solution to the injured plaintiff. This case is often compared to another New Jersey case, Magrine v. Krasnica, 94 N.J.Super. 228, 227 A.2d 539 (1967), affirmed *sub nom.* Magrine v. Spector, 100 N.J.Super. 223, 241 A.2d 637 (1968), affirmed 53 N.J. 259, 250 A.2d 129 (1969). In *Magrine* the plaintiff was injured when a defective needle being used by her dentist broke off in her gum. The court held that the dentist's services were not governed by strict tort liability. In addition to involving a professional, an issue which is raised in *Barbee v. Rogers* which follows, *Magrine* is an example of a common class of cases in which a service provider *uses* a defective product in rendering the service. This may distinguish the case from *Newmark,* in which the defective wave solution was "sold" to the plaintiff in the sense that it was used up. But would the result in *Magrine* have been different if the needle had been disposable? Maybe the distinction is that the defendant in *Newmark* was intended to take some of the wave solution away with her (on her hair). But would the result have been different if the case had involved shampoo, which was intended to be totally washed from the hair?

Cases involving the *use* of defective products by service providers—as distinguished from cases like *Hoover* in which the service provider also sells a product—have caused courts a great deal of difficulty. *Newmark* demonstrates the difficulty courts face in categorizing a transaction as one type or the other. Do the policies underlying strict tort liability or underlying the decision not to apply strict tort liability to pure services help sort out these types of cases?

Remember that in a case like *Magrine,* the plaintiff can sue the needle manufacturer under strict tort liability. The manufacturer clearly sold a product, and the plaintiff's status as a "bystander" (that is, she did not herself purchase the product) does not defeat liability.

5. *Hoover, Magrine,* and *Newmark* involve transactions that are truly "hybrid," that is, the transactions have a component that is clearly a service. Other cases do not involve a complex transaction of this sort but nevertheless are difficult to classify as a product or a service. For example, is the delivery of a utility, such as electricity, natural gas, or water, a product or a service?

Several courts have considered two types of cases involving the sale of electricity. One type involves a plaintiff who touches an overhead line with a ladder or antenna. Nearly all courts have held that in such a case the plaintiff must prove negligence and cannot rely on strict liability, either because electricity is not a product or because it has not yet entered the stream of commerce. *See, e.g.,* United Pacific Insurance Co. v. Southern California Edison Co., 163 Cal.App.3d 700, 209 Cal.Rptr. 819 (1985); Genaust v. Illinois Power Co., 62 Ill.2d 456, 343 N.E.2d 465 (1976); Kemp v. Wisconsin Electric Power Co., 44 Wis.2d 571, 172 N.W.2d 161 (1969); Hedges v. Public Service Co. of Indiana, Inc., 396 N.E.2d 933 (Ind.App.1979); Pilkington v. Hendricks County Rural Electric, 460 N.E.2d 1000 (Ind.App. 1984); Petroski v. Northern Indiana Public Service Co., 171 Ind.App. 14, 354 N.E.2d 736 (1976); Williams v. Detroit Edison Co., 63 Mich.App. 559, 234 N.W.2d 702 (1975) (warranty); Farina v. Niagara Mohawk Power Corp., 81

A.D.2d 700, 438 N.Y.S.2d 645 (1981); Wirth v. Mayrath Industries, Inc., 278 N.W.2d 789 (N.D.1979); Cratsley v. Commonwealth Edison Co., 38 Ill. App.3d 55, 347 N.E.2d 496 (1976); Wood v. Public Service Co. of New Hampshire, 114 N.H. 182, 317 A.2d 576 (1974); Smith v. Home Light and Power Co., 695 P.2d 788 (Colo.App.1984); Kentucky Utilities Co. v. Auto Crane Co., 674 S.W.2d 15 (Ky.App.1983).

A second type of case involves a power surge through the plaintiff's meter that causes a fire or other damage. Several courts have permitted plaintiffs to recover under strict tort liability in this type of case. *See, e.g.,* Pierce v. Pacific Gas & Electric Co., 166 Cal.App.3d 68, 212 Cal.Rptr. 283 (1985); Ransome v. Wisconsin Electric Power Co., 87 Wis.2d 605, 275 N.W.2d 641 (1979).

Pierce and *United Pacific Insurance* contain especially good analyses. In *Pierce,* a California Court of Appeals surveyed the policies underlying strict tort liability and concluded that they support the application of strict liability to a power surge caused by a faulty transformer. The surge caused a fire in plaintiff's house. In *United Pacific Insurance,* another California Court of Appeals surveyed these policies and concluded that they do not support the application of strict liability to a plaintiff who touched an overhead line. How would you analyze the difference between these two types of cases?

Elgin Airport Inn, Inc. v. Commonwealth Edison Co., 89 Ill.2d 138, 59 Ill.Dec. 675, 432 N.E.2d 259 (1982), presents an interesting variant of a "power surge" case. Power delivered at the wrong voltage burned out a piece of plaintiff's equipment. The court reasoned that unlike most "power-surge" cases, here the plaintiff could have easily protected itself by installing a protective device, and that its susceptibility to injury was greater than most consumers of electricity. Consequently, the defendant was not in a better position to prevent the injury, and spreading the loss to other rate payers would not have been fair.

Should strict tort liability or an implied warranty of merchantability apply to the delivery of gas-laden water? *See* Moody v. Galveston, 524 S.W.2d 583 (Tex.Civ.App.—Houston [1st Dist.] 1975, writ refused, n.r.e.).

6. Should strict liability apply to a map, a cookbook, a financial newsletter, or a legal brief?

7. In Chubb Group v. C.F. Murphy & Associates, Inc., 656 S.W.2d 766 (Mo.App.1983), the court held that strict tort liability was not applicable to the designer of the Kemper Arena in Kansas City, which had collapsed. Similarly, in Hunt v. Guarantee Electrical Co., 667 S.W.2d 9 (Mo.App.1984), the court declined to apply strict liability to a defendant who provided and installed an electrical timer in an industrial production process. The timer had been installed to solve a specific problem with the process, and the alleged defect was the overall design of the process and the timer's part in that design. There was no allegation that the timer itself was defective.

But in Worrell v. Barnes, 87 Nev. 204, 484 P.2d 573 (1971), the court applied strict tort liability and an implied warranty of merchantability to a defendant who installed a leaky gas fitting while remodeling the plaintiff's home. In Thomas v. Bove, 687 P.2d 534 (Colo.App.1984), the court applied an implied warranty of merchantability and an implied warranty of fitness to a defendant who installed a faulty heating system in a home. And in O'Laughlin v. Minnesota Natural Gas Co., 253 N.W.2d 826 (Minn.1977), the court applied strict tort liability and an implied warranty of merchantability to a supplier and installer of a home heating system.

Do the policies underlying strict tort liability or liability for breach of warranty support a conclusion, as in *Chubb,* that strict liability should not be applied to the designer or builder of an entire building, so long as the alleged defect is in the design, not in a faulty component? If so, should there be a different result when, as in *Thomas, O'Laughlin,* and *Worrell,* the defendant installs a defective component in a building, such as a heating system? Are the cases distinguishable even if the alleged defect in the component is a design defect?

BARBEE v. ROGERS
Supreme Court of Texas, 1968.
425 S.W.2d 342.

STEAKLEY, JUSTICE.

Petitioner sued N. Jay Rogers and S.J. Rogers, doing business as Texas State Optical, Respondents, and Texas State Optical, Inc., for damages. He alleged that he purchased contact lenses from them which were improperly fitted and that he was given improper prescriptions and instructions for their use.

* * *

Petitioner attacks the holding of the intermediate court upon three points of error * * *. These points assert in substance that the court erred in holding that Respondents were not liable upon the theory of strict liability in tort or for breach of a contractual implied warranty of fitness; and that the court erred in recognizing a professional relationship between Petitioner and Respondents. [The court held that, under the circumstances, the plaintiff had not established a claim of breach of warranty.] The question is thus narrowed to whether the doctrine of strict liability, which is tortious and not contractual, will be extended to the prescription, fitting and sale of contact lenses under the circumstances here shown.

Respondent, Dr. N. Jay Rogers, testified that he and his brother are licensed optometrists and compose a partnership operating eighty-four offices throughout Texas. They employ approximately one hundred twenty-five licensed optometrists and promote the sale of contact lenses by newspaper, television and radio advertisements. The contact lenses are sold for the same price regardless of the difficulty or the simplicity of the eye problems and the number of subsequent examinations which may be required. The charge is made for the product and not for the time of the optometrist. Respondents warrant to those responding to their advertisements of contact lenses that they will be properly cared for and fitted, subject to the qualification of care and use in accordance with specific instructions.

Petitioner's eyes were examined by a licensed optometrist in one of the offices of Respondents in May, 1959, and contact lenses were prescribed and subsequently fitted for him. They were unsatisfactory to Petitioner, and there followed a series of examinations and corrections by optometrists in the employ of Respondents at offices of Respondents in the Houston area. Petitioner testified that he suffered pain and discomfort when he wore the lenses and that he ceased using them approximately sixteen months later. He subsequently moved to California where he was examined by Dr. Robert E. Christensen, a medical doctor of Ophthalmology. Dr. Christensen testified by deposition that it was his opinion that the contact lenses worn by Petitioner were of a flatter curve than the corneal curve; that he found unusual scarring in Petitioner's eyes and that "it would be logical to relate the corneal scars to the contact lenses." A contact lens manufacturer, Jack R. Case, testified that "in checking the lenses on Mr. Barbee we found that the lenses, in our opinion, would be too large and too thick."

Article 4552 defines the practice of optometry as follows:

[The court quoted from the relevant statutes regulating optometrists.]

The licensed optometrist, such as Respondents and their employees, is thus enjoined by statute from treatment of the eyes and from the administration or prescription of drugs. The service he renders is the prescription and fitting of corrective devices for visual defects. It is shown by the evidence that the optometrist performs this service by means of mechanical instruments in the use of which he has special training. * * * It further appears from the evidence that there are two methods of fitting contact lenses, and there is no way to predetermine whether a particular contact lens curve or size will be easily adapted to the patient or can ever be adapted to him. The acts of prescription and fitting are described as an art with many variables and call for an exercise of judgment by the practitioner.

It is apparent that the activities of Respondents fall between those ordinarily associated with the practice of a profession and those characteristic of a merchandising concern. A professional relationship is present in the facts that contact lenses are prescribed and fitted by a licensed optometrist after examination of the eyes and in the exercise of his judgment. A merchandising relationship is suggested by the multiple offices of Respondents throughout the State; by their advertising and sales techniques designed to promote the sale of contact lenses at a predetermined and advertised price; and by their standardization of procedures and methods. Petitioner argues that the latter in effect destroys the statutory distinction between the professional act of fitting lenses or prisms to correct or remedy visual defects and the merchandising act of selling corrective eye devices. Respondents, on the other hand, point to this statutory distinction as making clear that the licensed optometrist is not considered a mere merchant.

In McKisson v. Sales Affiliates, Inc., [416 S.W.2d 787 (Tex.1967)], we extended the rule of strict liability applicable to foodstuffs for human consumption, Decker and Sons, Inc. v. Capps, 139 Tex. 609, 164 S.W.2d 828, 142 A.L.R. 1479 (1942), to defective products which cause physical harm to persons. In so doing, we adopted the rule of the Torts Restatement. It is to be noted that the jury findings here closely parallel those in *McKisson*. In our opinion, however, and we so hold, the rule of strict liability is inapplicable. Respondents and the licensed optometrists in their employ exercise skill and judgment in the examination, prescription and fitting process whereby it is sought to remedy visual abnormalities by the use of curved lenses or prisms. The failure here is not attributable to the product itself, i.e., the contact lenses, but to the professional and statutorily authorized act of "measuring the powers of vision" of Petitioner's eyes and "fitting lenses * * * to correct or remedy * * * [his] defect or abnormal condition of vision." This is not the act of one selling a "product in a defective condition unreasonably dangerous to the user" in the terms of the Torts Restatement. It is the act of one deemed in law to have the competence to remedy a visual defect by furnishing particularly prescribed contact lenses. Apart, then, from Respondents way of practicing optometry, the fact remains that the contact lenses sold to Petitioner were designed in the light of his particular physical requirements and to meet his particular needs. Presumably, and insofar as this record shows, they were not in existence when Petitioner sought the services of Respondents. They were not a finished product offered to the general public in regular channels of trade. The considerations supporting the rule of strict liability are not present. Petitioner cites no case authority for so extending the rule, and we have found none in our research. In addition to the disqualifying factor of the professional relationship, Petitioner's claim for application of the rule is not premised on any defect in the lenses as such, nor was it contemplated that Petitioner would use them without changes or adjustments to fit his needs. The miscarriage, if such there was, rests in the professional acts of Respondents and not in the commodity they prescribed, fitted and sold. As to this, the jury found that the negligence of Respondents in failing to properly fit the natural curvature of Petitioner's eyes was not the proximate cause of his injury.

The judgment of the Court of Civil Appeals is affirmed.

Notes

1. Do any of the policies supporting strict liability support a distinction between professional defendants and other defendants? Does it matter that a defendant is engaged in an activity that allegedly is already subject to regulation from an external source or through internal norms? Does this

rationale suggest that other "industries" that are heavily regulated, such as the drug industry, should be given special treatment?

2. Aside from defendant's status as a professional, can *Barbee* be explained solely under the rationale of *Hoover,* that is, that "[t]he miscarriage, if such there was, rests in the professional acts of respondents and not in the commodity they prescribed, fitted and sold"? Would the plaintiff have been able to recover if the lens had been made from toxic material that the optometrist bought from a supplier?

Like many cases involving services, the multiplicity of issues in *Barbee* makes it difficult to know with certainty what the court's position is with respect to any one of them.

3. Should a pharmacist be strictly liable for a drug sold pursuant to a doctor's prescription? Should it matter whether the alleged defect was (a) a failure to warn of side effects, (b) improper labeling by the pharmacist, (c) an impurity in the drug due to the pharmacist's handling, (d) an impurity inserted by the manufacturer, or (e) an unforeseen danger with the drug itself? Should it matter that the pharmacist dispensed a drug without a prescription, for example by refilling a prescription when the doctor had not authorized doing so? In addition to accounting for the professional status of a pharmacist, what issues are raised by imposing strict liability on a pharmacist?

On the liability of pharmacists in various situations, see Stafford v. Nipp, 502 So.2d 702 (Ala.1987) (possible warranty liability for unauthorized refill); Makripodis v. Merrell–Dow Pharmaceuticals, Inc., 361 Pa.Super. 589, 523 A.2d 374 (1987) (no implied warranty and no strict liability for failure to warn of risk to fetus from Bendectin when physician prescribed drug); Ramirez v. Richardson–Merrell, Inc., 628 F.Supp. 85 (E.D.Pa.1986) (no liability for failure to warn if drug prescribed by physician); Murphy v. E.R. Squibb & Sons, Inc., 40 Cal.3d 672, 221 Cal.Rptr. 447, 710 P.2d 247 (1985) (no strict liability for injuries caused by DES if drug prescribed by physician).

In cases such as *Murphy,* why should the physician's prescription shield the pharmacist, but not the drug manufacturer? Can this, in turn, be reconciled with the ordinary application of strict liability to retailers?

See generally, Vandall, Applying Strict Liability to Pharmacists, 18 Toledo L.Rev. 1 (1986).

4. In Ethicon, Inc. v. Parten, 520 S.W.2d 527 (Tex.Civ.App.—Houston [14th Dist.] 1975, no writ), the court held that a doctor was not strictly liable for an injury caused by a defective needle used during treatment. In Thomas v. St. Joseph Hospital, 618 S.W.2d 791 (Tex.Civ.App.—Houston [1st Dist.] 1981, writ refused, n.r.e.), a hospital was held strictly liable for supplying a patient with a flammable gown. In Providence Hospital v. Truly, 611 S.W.2d 127 (Tex.Civ.App.—Waco 1980, writ dismissed), a hospital was held strictly liable for providing a patient with a defective drug. Can these cases be reconciled with each other and with *Barbee*? In addition to the issue of professional services, what other issues do they raise?

Index

References are to Pages

769

†